IMMIGRATION AND CITIZENSHIP

PROCESS AND POLICY

Eighth Edition

■ ■ ■

T. Alexander Aleinikoff

Visiting Professor of Law and Huo Global Policy Initiative Research Fellow
Columbia Global Policy Initiative, Columbia University
Senior Fellow, Migration Policy Institute

David A. Martin

Warner-Booker Distinguished Professor of International Law Emeritus
University of Virginia

Hiroshi Motomura

Susan Westerberg Prager Professor of Law
University of California, Los Angeles, School of Law

Maryellen Fullerton

Professor of Law
Brooklyn Law School

Juliet P. Stumpf

Robert E. Jones Professor of Advocacy and Ethics
Lewis & Clark Law School

AMERICAN CASEBOOK SERIES®

WEST
ACADEMIC
PUBLISHING

To the Aleinikoffs, Marrows, Mays, and Wises
And for Rachel, Shoshana, Sam, and Eli

To the Martins, Meekers, Johnstons, and Bowmans
And for Cyndy; Amy, Drew, Webb, Isa, and Doran;
Jeff and Aggie

To the Motomuras, Sakumas, Kishis, and Katos
And for Linda and Amy

To the Fullertons, McDonnells, Roberts, and Ingersolls
And for Tom, Owen, Cullen, and Eleanor

To the Stumpfs, Docketts, Levys, and Castles
And for Eric, Liam, and Kai

PREFACE TO THE EIGHTH EDITION

For the past few editions of this casebook, we have been thinking that our next edition would surely contain complex and extensive changes to incorporate comprehensive immigration reform. Conditions looked especially promising for reform after President Barack Obama's reelection in 2012, in which he enjoyed strong support from Latino-American and Asian-American voters, the two fastest growing demographic sectors in the American population. Many Republican leaders expressed strong interest in passing a workable bill, both to solve a genuine and lingering public policy problem, and to take the issue out of major contention for at least a few election cycles. A bipartisan group of Senators crafted immigration reform legislation, and the Senate passed it in June 2013 by the surprisingly strong margin of 68 votes to 32. But the polarized climate in the House of Representatives blocked floor consideration in that chamber, and the legislative reform effort again lapsed.

As a result, the legislative changes that you will find reflected in this edition are more modest. The main action in our field over the past four years has come from case law and from increasingly ambitious executive-branch initiatives, as well as from state-level policies adopted to augment, to impede, or simply to influence federal enforcement.

Immigration cases continue to claim a sizable percentage of the workload shouldered by the federal courts of appeals, and the U.S. Supreme Court may have quickened its recent pace in issuing immigration precedents. For example, since our last edition, the Court has issued a string of cases interpreting the criminal-conviction-related provisions of the Immigration and Nationality Act (INA). The cases have reinforced a strong presumption that interpretation should follow the traditional "categorical approach"—which is modestly more favorable to persons facing removal charges based on criminal convictions than other approaches that had gained some administrative momentum at the time our seventh edition appeared. In 2012, the Court in *Arizona v. United States* struck down, on federal preemption grounds, major portions of Arizona's restrictive state enforcement legislation, known as SB 1070. *Kerry v. Din* produced a fractured majority, but in the end the Court reinforced strong judicial deference to executive branch decisions on visas, disappointing those who had hoped for at least some inroads into the plenary power doctrine. And two decisions in non-immigration cases, *United States v. Windsor* and *Obergefell v. Hodges,* led to significant changes in immigration admission practices; same-sex spouses of citizens and lawful permanent residents (LPRs) are now eligible for immigration benefits. All these developments claim attention in this volume.

Executive initiatives have also grown in significance as an arena for immigration changes—and for political and judicial controversy. Deferred Action for Childhood Arrivals (DACA) was implemented in 2012, providing a renewable two-year reprieve from removal, plus work authorization, for some 700,000 unauthorized residents who had arrived before age 16 and had lived in the country for five years. In November 2014, President Obama announced an expansion of the eligibility standards for DACA, as well as a new and larger deferred action program (DAPA) for unauthorized residents who are the parents of U.S. citizens or LPR children. Twenty-six states sued to block those changes. They prevailed in the lower courts, and the matter is pending before the Supreme Court (*United States v. Texas*) as this book goes to press.

As part of the broad executive reform package in November 2014, the Secretary of Homeland Security also announced a major revision in overall enforcement priorities. And he terminated the controversial Secure Communities program. Secure Communities had become, by 2013, the primary framework for cooperation between Immigration and Customs Enforcement (ICE) and state or local law enforcement agencies (LEAs)—but it had generated resistance from many LEAs. Nonetheless, the Secretary preserved some key elements of that framework (primarily the instant check against ICE databases of fingerprints of arrestees that LEAs send to the FBI), while making other changes to address LEA objections and help restore better cooperation. The new framework, known as PEP (Priority Enforcement Program), has met with mixed reactions.

In this time of intermittently ambitious proposals but modest on-the-ground results, we have retained the book's basic structure and coverage. Those who taught from the seventh edition will find the order and general coverage familiar, though we have moved the chapter on removal, detention and judicial review to precede the chapter on enforcement and proposed reforms.

At the same time, we have tried to be more selective and lean in our coverage, to improve teachability and to offer closer focus for classroom discussion. We have kept the book's coverage comprehensive—more than what a one-semester course would warrant—because we want to provide a wide range of coverage choices for teachers of immigration and citizenship law.

As in the past two editions, we give only limited treatment of refugee law and related humanitarian protection, focusing on core principles and provisions. The intense case-law growth of this subfield has led many law schools to offer a separate course on that subject. Our companion casebook, *Forced Migration: Law and Policy* (West, 2d ed. 2013), provides more extensive and detailed teaching materials for such a course, or for selective use to augment what we cover here in Chapter Eight.

We are pleased to welcome Juliet Stumpf of Lewis & Clark Law School, a leading scholar on the intersections of criminal law and immigration law (among many other topics) to our coauthor team beginning with this edition, a change that marks a continuing transition in our writing and production responsibilities. Alex Aleinikoff has not been directly involved in recent editions, though of course his contributions remain evident in many parts of this casebook. David Martin is moving to emeritus status at the University of Virginia this year and has reduced his authorship responsibility now that Juliet has joined the venture.

During some of the time covered by this casebook (in the mid-1990s), both Aleinikoff and Martin served as policy-level officials of the Immigration and Naturalization Service. Aleinikoff served as General Counsel and later as Executive Associate Commissioner for Programs. Martin was Aleinikoff's successor in the General Counsel position, and then returned to government service from January 2009 to December 2010, as Principal Deputy General Counsel for the Department of Homeland Security. He has also served since early 2015 as a member of the Homeland Security Advisory Council. Both of these coauthors took part in developing regulations and in crafting positions for the INS or DHS on many of the issues addressed in the book. Of course, none of the opinions expressed or implied in this book should be taken as representing the views of INS, DHS, or the U.S. government. Aleinikoff also served as United Nations Deputy High Commissioner for Refugees from 2010 through 2015 (and therefore has not participated directly in the preparation of this edition); nothing in this edition should be understood as necessarily reflecting the views of UNHCR or the United Nations. Hiroshi Motomura served as co-counsel or volunteer consultant on behalf of the noncitizen respondent or detainee in several principal cases or cases mentioned in the Notes, including *INS v. Aguirre-Aguirre, Zadvydas v. Davis,* and the early stages of what became *INS v. St. Cyr,* and he was part of the advocacy team for what became DACA and DAPA. Juliet Stumpf has served as a volunteer consultant on advocacy around family detention.

Acknowledgments. This book owes a great deal to the advice, reactions, and helpful suggestions received from colleagues and users— both instructors and students—as well as other knowledgeable experts who have helped to clarify our thinking on specific subjects covered here. With particular reference to this edition (and at the risk of omitting some who have contributed to the coauthors' understanding and perspectives on the field over many years), we gratefully acknowledge comments, suggestions, or stimulating conversations from Kerry Abrams, Jon Bauer, Lenni Benson, Phil Busch, Stacy Caplow, Alina Das, Doug Ford, César Cuauhtémoc García Hernández, Elizabeth Godfrey, Lucas Guttentag, Alvaro Huerta, Alan Hyde, Kit Johnson, Dan Kanstroom, Joe Landau, Kevin Lapp, Anna Law, Stephen Legomsky, Adam Loiacono, Stephen Manning, Peter Markowitz, Doug NeJaime, Michael Olivas, Juan Osuna, Nicholas Perry, Jaya Ramji-Nogales, Cristina Rodríguez, Paul Schmidt, Lori Scialabba, David Shahoulian, Margaret Taylor, Karen Tumlin, and Paul Virtue. Full responsibility for the choice of materials and for any views expressed here of course remains with the coauthors.

We have benefited greatly from excellent research assistance by Sarah Allen and Theresa Meehan at Virginia; Jeng-Ya Chen, Andrés Kwon, and Brittney Stanley at UCLA; Bradford Bray, Erin Callahan, Peter Feher, Gabriel Guimaraes, Meghan Lenahan, and Jia Shi at Brooklyn; and Sara Blankenship, Sarah Bieri, Daniel Bugni, Laney Ellisor, Michael Reyes, Jenny Linnéa Myrick, and Shane Young at Lewis & Clark. We also express our gratitude for help with proofing, copying, preparation of figures, assembling and transmission of drafts and documents, and for a range of other indispensable administrative attention, to our faculty assistants Samantha Abelove, Jenna Burt, Ronna Craig, Aileen Kim, Pennie Newell, Beth Pollastro, and Kasse Reyes.

Finally, we gratefully acknowledge research support for this edition provided by Brooklyn Law School, Lewis & Clark Law School, the UCLA School of Law, the UCLA Academic Senate, the University of Virginia School of Law, and the Virginia Law School Foundation. Responsibility for any errors rests with the authors alone. We welcome ongoing suggestions and corrections from any of the book's users.

DAVID A. MARTIN
HIROSHI MOTOMURA
MARYELLEN FULLERTON
JULIET P. STUMPF

May 2016

PREFACE TO THE FIRST EDITION

For decades, immigration and nationality law has been something of a neglected stepchild in the law schools. Most schools offer no immigration course at all. Where courses exist, they typically focus on the practical business of learning a complex statute and preparing students for careers as immigration attorneys, often finding little time to devote to larger issues of policy and principle.

Immigration law has suffered from the lack of sustained academic attention. All too often, instead of measured policy debate, one encounters in this field merely the polarized confrontation of charge and countercharge: government supporters reflexively advocating a hardline response; government opponents reflexively assuming that maximum advocacy for the particular aliens involved will bring about the best public policy. We don't deny that the issues are the kind that stir—and ought to stir—deep feelings. But we believe there is far more room for careful and balanced study of long-term policy options, even among those who care passionately about the ultimate values at stake. Law schools should serve as one important forum for such exploration.

As law students, we too enjoyed little exposure to the subject. Later, during stints in government service in Washington, each of us found himself dealing occasionally with immigration matters, but we discovered our mutual interest in the subject only when the Cuban boatlift of 1980 brought lawyers from the Departments of Justice and State together. There is nothing like a full-fledged crisis—especially one offering no satisfactory solutions—to cement an appreciation of the subject's fascinations and frustrations. We carried that interest with us when we moved into the academy, along with vague intentions to teach immigration law, but with little idea of just what was in store.

Now, after teaching and writing in the field for several years, we have come to wonder how the intrinsic attractions of the subject for classroom teaching have gone so widely unnoticed. Immigration law, we have learned, can be one of the richest and most rewarding subjects for both students and professors. It is redolent of our national history, reflecting both successes that are the legitimate source of national pride, and dispiriting failures. Major public policy issues appear repeatedly, posing deeper questions concerning national identity, membership, moral philosophy, constitutional interpretation, public law, public administration, international relations, and the limits of practical politics. Immigration law also furnishes a vital setting for studying the interaction of our three branches of government. Indeed, we have been struck by how many major Supreme Court decisions on larger questions of administrative and constitutional law have been decided in immigration cases—the legislative veto case, *INS v. Chadha*, 103 S.Ct. 2764 (1983), being only the latest example.

An immigration course, however, need not always keep the student at the heights occupied by great questions of philosophy, public policy, and constitutional interpretation. Immigration law also provides a worthy vehicle for refining basic lawyering skills, especially the capacity for close reading of an intricate statute and the discipline of mastering a specialized technical vocabulary. One judge who had just struggled through a complex interpretive task reflected on his experience:

Whatever guidance the regulations furnish to those cognoscenti familiar with [immigration] procedures, this court, despite many years of legal experience, finds that they yield up meaning only grudgingly and that morsels of comprehension must be pried from mollusks of jargon.

Dong Sik Kwon v. INS, 646 F.2d 909, 919 (5th Cir.1981). Students ought to learn how to wield their *escargot* forks expertly, and then they should be inspired to ask whether the food could not be prepared in a more sensible way.

Beyond this, the student of immigration law must develop an awareness of how legislation evolves and an ability to make use of the materials of legislative history—for today's Immigration and Nationality Act (INA) is the product of over a hundred years of congressional efforts to fashion laws that regulate immigration. There are also thousands of administrative and judicial precedents, often in remarkable conflict with one another in both holding and spirit. These provide excellent raw materials for practice in the art of advocacy, hypothetically representing either a private client or a government agency.

There may be many reasons for immigration law's historical insularity. But we wrote this book with the conviction that a lack of good teaching materials has played a role—materials with which nonspecialists might feel comfortable but which specialists might also find challenging. (In this respect, we remember well our own problems when we first taught the course.) When we began our work on this book, there was no casebook at all on the subject of immigration law. Treatises existed, and various kinds of manuals that have been used as the basis for the course by practitioners of many years' experience. But it is a daunting prospect for nonspecialists to put together workable supplemental materials on their own, especially if they aspire to teaching more than just the technical details.

We hope this book will contribute toward ending the law schools' neglect and the subject's insularity. We have consciously sought to make the reader aware of the broader dimensions of the subject, but without ignoring the nuts-and-bolts foundation that a novice practitioner in the field would find necessary. We don't spend time, for example, exploring all 19 grounds for deportation appearing in INA § 241(a). We do devote enough attention to selected grounds, however, as well as the basic structure of those provisions, so that a student would know where to turn for answers to the detailed questions that might arise in practice. We have aimed, above all, at recapturing immigration law as a worthy and exciting area for academic study, without losing sight of the basic learning a student must master if he or she chooses to open an immigration practice the following year. Whether we have succeeded in these aims remains to be seen, but we invite users of this book— instructors and students—to write us with their reactions and suggestions for expanded or reduced coverage.

We have also consciously tried to avoid the polarities that often beset the field. It is easy to develop sympathy for the individual alien involved in a particular case, and to strive to mold the legal doctrine to bring about a warm-hearted result for that person. Too many law review notes, and often judges as well, succumb to this temptation, neglecting to take adequate account of the long-term implications for an immigration system that must cope with millions of applications each year. We try to keep the reader aware of that larger systemic perspective—without suggesting that systems should always prevail over warm-heartedness, of course.

ALEX ALEINIKOFF
DAVID MARTIN

November 30, 1984

TECHNICAL MATTERS

Editing Style

In editing cases and other materials reprinted here, we have marked textual deletions with triple asterisks, but we have often omitted simple citations to cases or other authorities without any printed indication. Similarly, we have deleted footnotes from reprinted materials without signaling the omission. Where we chose to retain a footnote, however, we have maintained the original numbering. Our own footnotes appearing in the midst of reprinted materials are marked with alphabetical superscripts; they also end with the notation "—eds." When we drop footnotes to text that we wrote ourselves, we have used the ordinary numerical designations.

INA Citations

How to cite the sections of the Immigration and Nationality Act (INA) has posed an ongoing problem for teachers and writers in this field. Most court decisions refer to INA provisions by means of the numbers employed in Title 8 of the U.S. Code, where the Act is codified. This is understandable as a matter of convenience, even though technically incorrect, because Title 8 has not been codified—that is, directly enacted by Congress to serve as the official version of the legislation. Citation to the INA, not the U.S. code is the correct method. But perhaps more importantly as a practical matter, specialists in the field almost religiously employ the INA section numbers and are not always familiar with references to the U.S. Code enumeration (in part because the system used to translate Act numbers into U.S. Code numbers appears to us to be eccentric and unpredictable). Moreover, the administrative framework for regulations and certain other manuals and instructions is closely linked to the numbering scheme of the original Act. For example, the regulations of the Department of Homeland Security implementing the asylum provision, § 208 of the INA, appear in Part 208 of 8 C.F.R., while the equivalent asylum-related regulations of the Executive Office for Immigration Review (in the Department of Justice) appear in Part 1208.

For these reasons, we have decided to use the section numbers of the Act consistently throughout this book, to the exclusion of the U.S. Code numbers. This means that we have excised references to the Act using the U.S. Code numbering system from all cases and materials, and substituted direct INA section references, without expressly indicating where such substitutions have occurred. Readers who must know the corresponding U.S. Code number will find a conversion chart in the opening pages of our Statutory Supplement, *Immigration and Nationality*

Laws of the United States: Selected Statutes, Regulations, and Forms. The supplement also indicates with each section what its U.S. Code citation would be.

Citations and Abbreviations

Most citations in the book conform generally to *A Uniform System of Citation*, customarily used by law journals. For a few items that are cited frequently, however, we have abbreviated even further. Abbreviations that appear frequently, either in our material or in cases, are also set forth below.

1990 Act	Immigration Act of 1990, Pub. L. 101–649, 104 Stat. 4978.
1996 Act	Illegal Immigration Reform and Immigrant Responsibility Act of 1996, Pub. L. 104–208, Div. C., 110 Stat. 3009–546. Also sometimes referred to as IIRIRA.
AAO	Administrative Appeals Office of the U.S. Citizenship and Immigration Services, an office that handles specified types of administrative appeals. Also sometimes called the Administrative Appeals Unit (AAU).
AEDPA	Antiterrorism and Effective Death Penalty Act of 1996, Pub. L. 104–132, 110 Stat. 1214. It contained many provisions relating to immigration, particularly with respect to criminal and terrorist grounds of removal. Many of those provisions were further modified by the 1996 Act.
AG	Attorney General, the Cabinet officer who heads the U.S. Department of Justice.
Bender's Imm. Bull.	Bender's Immigration Bulletin. A leading reporting service on administrative, legislative and judicial developments in the immigration field, published twice monthly by LexisNexis.
BIA	Board of Immigration Appeals, a component of the Executive Office for Immigration Review within the U.S. Department of Justice.

CBP	U.S. Customs and Border Protection, U.S. Department of Homeland Security. Created in 2003, CBP houses border inspection functions and the Border Patrol.
DHS	U.S. Department of Homeland Security. Created by a 2003 reorganization spurred by the September 11 terrorist attacks, this department inherited most of the functions formerly carried out by the Immigration and Naturalization Service. Those functions are distributed, primarily, among three DHS components: CBP, ICE, and USCIS.
DHS Statistical Yearbook	Office of Immigration Statistics, U.S. Department of Homeland Security, Yearbook of Immigration Statistics.
EOIR	Executive Office for Immigration Review. This unit of the Department of Justice houses both the Board of Immigration Appeals and the corps of immigration judges.
EWI	Entrant without inspection.
FY	Fiscal year.
GMYW	Charles Gordon, Stanley Mailman, Stephen Yale-Loehr & Ronald Y. Wada, Immigration Law and Procedure (2016). A leading treatise in the field, now published as a multi-volume loose-leaf set, including several volumes containing primary materials (including the INA, implementing regulations, Operations Instructions, INS manuals and handbooks, and the visa-related portions of the Foreign Affairs Manual).
ICE	U.S. Immigration and Customs Enforcement, U.S. Department of Homeland Security. Created in 2003, ICE houses interior enforcement functions transferred from the former Immigration and Naturalization Service, including investigations, detention and removal, and the trial attorneys who represent

	the government in immigration court.
IIRIRA	Illegal Immigration Reform and Immigrant Responsibility Act of 1996, Pub. L. 104–208, Div.C., 110 Stat. 3009–546. We sometimes refer to it as the 1996 Act or the 1996 Immigration Act.
IJ	Immigration judge. The corps of immigration judges is a component of the Executive Office for Immigration Review within the U.S. Department of Justice.
IMFA	Immigration Marriage Fraud Amendments of 1986, Pub. L. 99–639, 100 Stat. 3537.
INA	The Immigration and Nationality Act. Pub. L. 82–414, 66 Stat. 163. Passed in 1952 as a comprehensive codification replacing earlier immigration and nationality laws, it has been frequently amended since then. The Act itself is unofficially codified, according to an idiosyncratic numbering scheme, in Title 8 of the United States Code; a conversion chart, showing corresponding section numbers, appears in our Statutory Supplement. In this book we cite by INA section number, not U.S.C. section number, to the current amended statute.
INS	Immigration and Naturalization Service. Until 2003, as a component of the Department of Justice, INS was the lead federal agency on immigration policy and operations. In 2003, INS was abolished and its functions were transferred to three separate units of the new Department of Homeland Security (see CBP, ICE, USCIS).
IRCA	Immigration Reform and Control Act of 1986, Pub. L. 99–603, 100 Stat. 3359.
Interp. Rel.	Interpreter Releases. A leading reporting service on administrative, legislative and judicial developments in the immigration field, published weekly by Thomson Reuters and

	available on Westlaw.
O.I.	Operations Instructions. The manual of detailed guidelines and policy statements issued by the Immigration and Naturalization Service and used by immigration officers in implementing the statute and the regulations. Those Instructions that have been released to the public are reprinted in an appendix volume of the GM & Y treatise. The Operations Instructions are now being phased out, as they are gradually replaced by newly issued DHS field manuals.
UNHCR	United Nations High Commissioner for Refugees.
USCIS	U.S. Citizenship and Immigration Services, Department of Homeland Security. Created in 2003, USCIS houses the principal services and adjudications functions inherited from the Immigration and Naturalization Service. Sometimes also referred to as CIS.

ACKNOWLEDGMENTS

The authors wish to express their thanks to copyright holders and authors for permission to reprint excerpts from the following materials.

Abrams, Kerry, Immigration Law and the Regulation of Marriage, 91 Minnesota Law Review 1625 (2007). Reprinted by permission.

Ackerman, Bruce, Social Justice in the Liberal State. Copyright © 1980 by the Yale University Press. Reprinted by permission of the publisher.

Aleinikoff, T. Alexander, & Klusmeyer, Douglas, eds., From Migrants to Citizens: Membership in a Changing World (2000). Copyright © 2000 by Carnegie Endowment for International Peace. Reprinted by permission of the publisher from From Migrants to Citizens: Membership in a Changing World (Washington, DC: Carnegie Endowment for International Peace, 2000), pp. 137–141.

American Bar Association, Model Rules of Professional Conduct (2016). Copyright © 2016 by the American Bar Association. Reprinted with permission. All rights reserved. This information or any or portion thereof may not be copied or disseminated in any form or by any means or stored in an electronic database or retrieval system without the express written consent of the American Bar Association.

Andreas, Peter, Border Games: Policing the U.S.-Mexico Divide (2000). Reprinted by permission from Political Science Quarterly, 113 (Winter 1998–99): 591–615.

Bipartisan Policy Center, Entry-Exit System: Progress, Challenges, and Outlook, Immigration Task Force, Bipartisan Policy Center (May 2014). Reprinted by permission.

Borjas, George J., The Labor Demand Curve *Is* Downward Sloping: Reexamining the Impact of Immigration on the Labor Market, 118 Quarterly Journal of Economics 335 (2003), copyright © 2003 by Oxford University Press, Inc. Published on behalf of the President and Fellows of Harvard University. Used by permission of Oxford University Press, Inc.

Bosniak, Linda, Being Here: Ethical Territoriality and the Rights of Immigrants, 8 Theoretical Inquiries in Law 389 (2007). Reprinted by permission. Walter De Gruyter GmbH Berlin Boston, 2007. Copyright and all rights reserved. Material from this publication has been used with the permission of Walter De Gruyter GmbH.

Bosniak, Linda S., Membership, Equality, and the Difference That Alienage Makes, 69 New York University Law Review 1047 (1994). Reprinted by permission.

Bosniak, Linda S., Opposing Prop. 187: Undocumented Immigrants and the National Imagination, 28 Connecticut Law Review 555 (1996). Reprinted by permission.

Briggs, Vernon M., Jr., Mass Immigration and the National Interest: Policy Directions for the New Century, 3d ed. (Armonk, NY: M.E. Sharpe, 2003), pp. 274–280. Copyright © 2003 M.E. Sharpe, Inc. Reproduced by permission of Taylor and Francis Group, LLC, a division of Informa plc; permission conveyed through Copyright Clearance Center, Inc.

Brown, Eleanor Marie Lawrence, Outsourcing Immigration Compliance, 77 Fordham Law Review 2475 (2009). Reprinted by permission.

Burke, Melissa Nann, To Have and Hold a Green Card, Legal Affairs, January/February, 2006, at 10. Reprinted by permission.

Bush, Jeb, McLarty, Thomas F. III, & Alden, Edward, U.S. Immigration Policy. Copyright © 2009 by the Council on Foreign Relations Press. Reproduced with permission.

Calavita, Kitty, The Immigration Policy Debate: Critical Analysis and Future Options, in Mexican Migration to the United States: Origins, Consequences, and Policy Options 151 (W. Cornelius & J. Bustamante eds. 1989). Copyright © 1989 by the Center for U.S.-Mexican Studies, University of California, San Diego. Reprinted by permission.

Camarota, Steven A., The High Cost of Cheap Labor: Illegal Immigration and the Federal Budget 37 (Center for Immigration Studies 2004). Reprinted by permission.

Card, David, The Impact of the Mariel Boatlift on the Miami Labor Market (ILRR Review 43: 2) p. 13, copyright © 1990 by Cornell University. Reprinted by Permission of SAGE Publications, Inc., http://ilr.sagepub.com.

Carens, Joseph H., The Ethics of Immigration (2013). Copyright © 2013 by Oxford University Press, Inc. Used by permission of Oxford University Press, Inc.

Cave, Damien, An American Life, Lived in Shadows, Section A, page 9. From the New York Times, June 8, 2014 © 2014 The New York Times. All rights reserved. Used by permission and protected by the Copyright Laws of the United States. The printing, copying, redistribution, or retransmission of this Content without express written permission is prohibited.

Cave, Damien, Better Lives for Mexicans Cut Allure of Going North, Section A, page 1. From The New York Times, July 6, 2011 © 2011 The New York Times. All rights reserved. Used by permission and protected by the Copyright Laws of the United States. The printing, copying, redistribution, or retransmission of this Content without express written permission is prohibited.

Chothani, Poorvi, Certain U.S. Immigrant and Nonimmigrant Visa Processes and Other Services Available at the U.S. Consulate General in Mumbai, 83 Interpreter Releases 1597 (July 31, 2006). Reprinted by permission of Thomson West.

Clark, David. "It is better to have one child only." Photo of billboard in China reprinted by permission.

De la Garza, Rodolfo O., & DeSipio, Louis, Save the Baby, Change the Bathwater, and Scrub the Tub: Latino Electoral Participation After Seventeen Years of Voting Rights Act Coverage, 71 Texas Law Review 1479 (1993). Reprinted by permission.

Dingeman, M. Kathleen, & Rumbaut, Rubén G., The Immigration-Crime Nexus and Post-Deportation Experiences: En/Countering Stereotypes in Southern California and El Salvador, 31 University of La Verne Law Review 363 (2010). Reprinted by permission.

Durand, Jorge, & Massey, Douglas S., Borderline Sanity. Reprinted with permission from The American Prospect: September 2001. Volume 12, Issue 17. http://www.prospect.org. The American Prospect, 1225 Eye Street, NW, Suite 600, Washington, DC 20005. All rights reserved.

Eagly, Ingrid V., Prosecuting Immigration, 104 Northwestern University Law Review 1281 (2009). Reprinted by permission.

Fallows, James, Immigration: How It's Affecting Us, The Atlantic Monthly, Nov. 1983, at 88. Copyright © 1983 The Atlantic Monthly. Reprinted by permission.

Fitz, Marshall, Martinez, Gebe, & Wijewardena, Madura, The Costs of Mass Deportation: Impractical, Expensive, and Ineffective. Center for American Progress (March 2010). Reprinted by permission.

Fry, Brian N., Responding to Immigration: Perceptions of Promise and Threat, in The New Americans: Recent Immigration and American Society, Carola Suarez-Orozco & Marcelo Suarez-Orozco, editors. New York: LFB Scholarly Publishing LLC, 2001. Reprinted by permission.

Gordon, Charles, Mailman, Stanley, Yale-Loehr, Stephen, & Wada, Ronald Y., Immigration Law and Procedure, §§ 17.01, 17.03, 17.05–17.06, 94.01[2] (2015, 2016). Reprinted from Immigration Law and

Procedure with permission. Copyright © 2016 by Matthew Bender & Company, Inc., a member of the LexisNexis® Group. All rights reserved.

Griswold, Daniel T., "Willing Workers: Fixing the Problem of Illegal Mexican Migration to the United States," in Trade Policy Analysis no. 19, Oct. 15, 2002. © Cato Institute. Reprinted by permission.

Gross, Samuel R., & Livingston, Debra, Racial Profiling Under Attack, 102 Columbia Law Review 1413 (2002). Reprinted by permission.

Haney López, Ian F., White by Law: The Legal Construction of Race (1996). Copyright © 1996 by the New York University Press. Reprinted by permission of the publisher.

Henkin, Louis, Foreign Affairs and the Constitution 16–18 (1972).

Henkin, Louis, The Constitution and United States Sovereignty: A Century of Chinese Exclusion and Its Progeny, 100 Harvard Law Review 853 (1987). Copyright © 1987 by the Harvard Law Review Association. Reprinted by permission; permission conveyed through Copyright Clearance Center, Inc.

Herzog, Paul, The National Interest Waiver: Understanding Its History and Navigating Its Terrain, 90 Interp. Rel. 1955, 1956 (2013). Reprinted by permission.

Higham, John, Strangers in the Land: Patterns of American Nativism. Copyright © 1955 The Trustees of Rutgers College in New Jersey. Reprinted by permission of Rutgers University Press.

Hyde, Alan, The Law and Economics of Family Unification, 28 Georgetown Immigration Law Journal, 2014, pp. 355, 362, 365–66, 369–77, 384–85, 389–90. Reprinted by permission.

Jacoby, Tamar, Immigration Nation, 85 Foreign Affairs 50 (2006). Reprinted by permission of FOREIGN AFFAIRS, Volume 85, Issue no. 6, November/December 2006. Copyright 2006 by the Council on Foreign Relations, Inc.

Kanstroom, Daniel, Deportation Nation: Outsiders in American History (2007). Reprinted by permission of the publisher from DEPORTATION NATION: OUTSIDERS IN AMERICAN HISTORY by Daniel Kanstroom, pp. 5–6, 231–232, Cambridge, Mass.: Harvard University Press, Copyright © 2007 by the President and Fellows of Harvard College.

Krikorian, Mark, Contra Nadler 2.0: On Immigration, Conservatives Advocate Attrition through Enforcement, not Mass Deportation, Reprinted with permission from Mark Krikorian, Center for Immigration Studies, Copyright 2009, Center for Immigration Studies.

LeMoyne, Roger, Kosovo Refugees Photo, March 1999, UNHCR/Roger LeMoyne. Reprinted by permission.

Martin, David A., Eight Myths about Immigration Enforcement, 10 New York University Journal of Legislation and Public Policy 525 (2006–07). Reprinted by permission.

Martin, David A., Membership and Consent: Abstract or Organic?, 11 Yale Journal of International Law 278 (1985). Reprinted by permission.

Martin, David A., Refining Immigration Law's Role in Counterterrorism, from Legislating the War on Terror: An Agenda for Reform (B. Wittes ed. 2009). Reprinted by permission.

Martin, David A., Resolute Enforcement is Not Just for Restrictionists: Building a Stable and Efficient Immigration Enforcement System, 30 Journal of Law and Politics 411 (2015). Reprinted by permission of the author.

Martin, David A., Waiting for Solutions, Legal Times, May 29, 2001, at 66. Reprinted with permission from the May 29, 2001 edition of the Legal Times. © 2011 ALM Media Properties, LLC. All rights reserved. Further duplication without permission is prohibited. For information, contact 877-257-3382 or reprints@alm.com or visit www. almreprints.com.

Martin, Philip L., & Teitelbaum, Michael S., The Mirage of Mexican Guest Workers, 80 Foreign Affairs 117 (2001). Republished by permission of FOREIGN AFFAIRS, Volume 80, Issue no. 6, November/December 2001. Copyright 2001 by the Council on Foreign Relations, Inc.: permission conveyed through Copyright Clearance Center, Inc.

Martin, Philip, & Midgley, Elizabeth, Immigration: Shaping and Reshaping America (2d edition). © 2006 by the Population Reference Bureau. Reprinted by permission.

Martin, Susan F., A Nation of Immigrants. New York, NY: Cambridge University Press, 2010. Reprinted with permission of the author.

Massey, Douglas S., "Backfire at the Border: Why Enforcement Without Legalization Cannot Stop Illegal Immigration," in Trade Policy Analysis no. 29 (June 13, 2005). © Cato Institute. Reprinted by permission.

Massey, Douglas S., Goldring, Luin, & Durand, Jorge, Continuities in Transnational Migration: An Analysis of Nineteen Mexican Communities, 99 American Journal of Sociology 1492 (1994). Copyright © 1994 by the University of Chicago Press. Reprinted by permission.

Massey, Douglas S., Durand, Jorge, & Malone, Nolan J. Republished with permission of Russell Sage Foundation, from "Principles of Operation: Theories of International Migration," in Beyond Smoke and Mirrors: Mexican Immigration in an Era of Economic Integration. © 2002 Russell Sage Foundation, 112 East 64th Street, New York, NY 10065. Permission conveyed through Copyright Clearance Center, Inc.

Matza, Michael, House of Dreams, Philadelphia Inquirer, Dec. 19, 2010, at A1. Used with permission of Philadelphia Inquirer Permissions. Copyright © 2016. All rights reserved.

McNew, David. U.S. Population Passes 300 Million. David McNew/Getty Images News/Getty Images. Photo of San Diego border station reprinted by permission.

Medige, Patricia, The Labyrinth: Pursuing a Human Trafficking Case in Middle America, 10 J. Gender Race & Just. 269, 273–78 (2007). Reprinted by permission.

Meissner, Doris, Myers, Deborah W., Papademetriou, Demetrios, & Fix, Michael, Immigration and America's Future: A New Chapter, Report of the Independent Task Force on Immigration and America's Future (2006). Copyright 2006, Migration Policy Institute. Reprinted by permission.*

Migration Policy Institute. The following figures were originally published by the Migration Policy Institute Data Hub, www.migration policy.org/programs/datahub and are reprinted by permission:*

Estimates of the Top 20 Diaspora Groups in the United States, 2011.

Legal Immigration to the United States 1820–Present.

Top 10 Largest U.S. Immigrant Groups, 2014.

U.S. Immigrant Population and Share Over Time, 1850–Present.

U.S. Refugee Admissions and Refugee Resettlement Ceilings, Fiscal Years 1980–2015.

Motomura, Hiroshi, Americans in Waiting: The Lost Story of Immigration and Citizenship in the United States, copyright © 2006 by Oxford University Press, Inc. Used by permission of Oxford University Press, Inc.

Motomura, Hiroshi, Choosing Immigrants, Making Citizens, 59 Stanford Law Review 857 (2007). Reprinted by permission.

Motomura, Hiroshi, Immigration and Alienage, Federalism and Proposition 187, 35 Virginia Journal of International Law 201 (1994). Reprinted by permission.

Motomura, Hiroshi, Immigration Outside the Law, copyright © 2014 by Oxford University Press, Inc. Used by permission of Oxford University Press, Inc.

Muller, Eric L., 12/7 and 9/11: War, Liberties, and the Lessons of History. Originally published in the West Virginia Law Review, 104 W. Va. L. Rev. 571 (2002). Reprinted by permission.

Murguia, Janet, A Change of Heart on Guest Workers, Washington Post, February 11, 2007, at B7. Reprinted by permission.

Neuman, Gerald L., Terrorism, Selective Deportation and the First Amendment after Reno v. AADC, 14 Georgetown Immigration Law Journal 313 (2000). Reprinted with permission of the publisher, Georgetown Immigration Law Journal © 2000.

Ngai, Mae, We Need a Deportation Deadline, Washington Post, June 14, 2005, at A21. Reprinted by permission.

Ottaviano, Gianmarco I.P., & Peri, Giovanni, Rethinking the Effects of Immigration on Wages, National Bureau of Economic Research Working Paper (2006). Reprinted with permission of the authors.

Papademetriou, Demetrious G., & Sumption, Madeleine, Rethinking Points Systems and Employer-Selected Immigration (June 2011), http://www.migrationpolicy.org/pubs/rethinkingpointssystem.pdf. Reprinted by permission.*

Passel, Jeffrey S., & Cohn, D'Vera, Number of Babies Born in U.S. to Unauthorized Immigrants Declines, Reprinted with permission from Pew Research Center, Washington, D.C. (September 11, 2015) http://www.pewresearch.org/fact-tank/2015/09/11/number-of-babies-born-in-u-s-to-unauthorized-immigrants-declines/.

Peri, Giovanni, Shih, Kevin, Sparber, Chad, & Marek Zeitlin, Angie, Closing Economic Windows: How H1-B Visa Denials Cost U.S.-Born Tech Workers Jobs and Wages During the Great Recession, Partnership for A New American Economy, June 2014, at 4, 8, 12, 14–16, 20, 23. Reprinted by permission.

Portes, Alejandro, & Böröscz, József, Contemporary Immigration: Theoretical Perspectives on Its Determinants and Modes of Incorporation, 23 International Migration Review 606 (1989). Copyright © 1989 by the Center for Migration Studies of New York, Inc. Reprinted by permission.

Ramadan, Tariq, Why I'm Banned in the USA, Washington Post, Oct. 1, 2006, at B1. Reprinted by permission.

Raskin, Jamin B., Legal Aliens, Local Citizens: The Historical, Constitutional, and Theoretical Meanings of Alien Suffrage, 141

University of Pennsylvania Law Review, 1391 (1993). Reprinted by permission.

Renwick, Danielle, & Lee, Brianna, The U.S Immigration Debate, 2015. Copyright © (2015) by the Council on Foreign Relations. Reprinted with permission. www. cfr.org/immigration/US-immigration-debate/p11149.

Roberts, Maurice, The Exercise of Administrative Discretion Under the Immigration Laws, 13 San Diego Law Review 144 (1975). Copyright 1975 San Diego Law Review. Reprinted with permission of the San Diego Law Review.

Rodríguez, Cristina M., Guest Workers and Integration: Toward a Theory of What Immigrants and Americans Owe One Another, 2007 University of Chicago Legal Forum 219 (2007). Reprinted by permission.

Rosberg, Gerald M., Aliens and Equal Protection: Why Not the Right to Vote?, 75 Michigan Law Review 1092 (1977). Reprinted from Michigan Law Review, April-May 1977, Vol. 75, Nos. 5 & 6. Copyright 1977 by The Michigan Law Review Association. Reprinted with permission of the author.

Ruhs, Martin, Migrants Don't Need More Rights, Section A, page 39. From The New York Times, Dec. 19, 2013 © 2013 The New York Times. All rights reserved. Used by permission and protected by the Copyright Laws of the United States. The printing, copying, redistribution, or retransmission of this Content without express written permission is prohibited.

Schuck, Peter H., & Smith, Rogers M., Citizenship Without Consent: Illegal Aliens in the American Polity (1985). Copyright © 1985 by The Yale University Press. Reprinted by permission of the publisher.

Sharpless, Rebecca, Toward a True Elements Test: Taylor and the Categorical Analysis of Crimes in Immigration Law, 62 University of Miami Law Review 979 (2008). Reprinted by permission.

TRAC Immigration Database Online 1998–2015, http://trac.syr.edy/php tools/immigration/court_backlog/. Used by permission.

Trillin, Calvin, Making Adjustments. Copyright © 1984 by Calvin Trillin. Originally appeared in The New Yorker, May 28, 1984. Reprinted by permission. All rights reserved.

Volpp, Leti, The Citizen and the Terrorist. Originally published in 49 UCLA Law Review 1575 (2002). Reprinted by permission.

* Originally published by the Migration Policy Institute (MPI). MPI is an independent, nonpartisan think tank in Washington, DC, dedicated to the study of the movement of people worldwide. (www.migrationpolicy.org).

Summary of Contents

———

TABLE OF CONTENTS

TABLE OF CASES

The principal cases are in bold type.

TABLE OF STATUTES

TABLE OF REGULATIONS

TABLE OF RULES

TABLE OF AUTHORITIES

IMMIGRATION AND CITIZENSHIP

PROCESS AND POLICY

Eighth Edition

CHAPTER ONE

IMMIGRATION AND CITIZENSHIP LAW IN HISTORICAL CONTEXT

• • •

Welcome to the study of immigration and citizenship law, an area of complex laws, fundamental humanitarian concerns, major economic importance, and passionate debate. The immigration and citizenship laws define who we are as a society: who are full members of our society; who can become members; which nonmembers can enter; and the conditions upon which nonmembers can remain. These decisions by the United States do not exist in a vacuum, but rather in a contemporary world of nation states. For the most part, each nation state's population consists of its citizens—a term generally understood to mean full members of the state, entitled to the basic rights and opportunities afforded by the state. Virtually all states have laws regulating the entry and stay of noncitizens, and these laws affect very large numbers of people. As of 2013, according to UN data, over 232 million persons reside in states of which they are not citizens. Most immigrants follow prescribed procedures in obtaining admission to state territory, but many individuals cross state borders or remain in state territory in violation of domestic law. We will refer to such persons as undocumented or unauthorized migrants or aliens.

This book concerns the law regarding citizenship, immigration, and the treatment of immigrants in the United States. The primary federal immigration statute is the Immigration and Nationality Act (INA), which is codified in Title 8 of the United States Code. The primary federal agency charged with administering and enforcing the INA is the Department of Homeland Security (DHS), with lesser roles for the Department of Justice, the Department of State, and the Department of Labor. Until 2003, the key agency was the Immigration and Naturalization Service (INS), located within the Justice Department, and many of the cases and materials here will still speak of INS. (Chapter Four explains the agency structure in more detail.) We will examine the basic categories for entry and residence of immigrants and the procedures for admission and removal; and we will identify and elaborate themes of due process, fair treatment of immigrants, and the social, economic and political implications of immigration. In so doing, we will be concerned with fundamental issues of *membership*—what it means, how it is

1

attained (and lost), and what rights and opportunities accompany it. Thus, throughout the course we will ask what particular understandings of membership inform societal decisions about immigration, immigrants, and citizens, and to what extent U.S. law—embodied in the Constitution, statutes, administrative policies and judicial decisions—establishes varying degrees of membership.

A. IMMIGRANTS IN UNITED STATES HISTORY

We think it important to provide historical and political context to your study of U.S. citizenship and immigration law. Writing in the Federalist Papers, John Jay observed: "Providence has been pleased to give this one connected country to one united people—a people descended from the same ancestors, speaking the same language, professing the same religion, attached to the same principles of government, very similar in their manners and customs." The Federalist No. 2. This statement, clearly false when written in 1787, cannot begin to describe the ethnic, racial, religious and political richness that two hundred years of immigration have brought the United States.

Our immigration history has shown America at its best and worst. Tens of millions of noncitizens have been welcomed to our shores. The United States has accepted more refugees for permanent settlement than any other country in the world. And in a time of growing restrictionism in most of the countries of the world, the United States currently admits for permanent residence roughly one million noncitizens a year. Unlike many of the Western industrialized nations, the United States makes it relatively easy for lawfully admitted immigrants to attain citizenship; and virtually any person born in the United States is an American citizen, irrespective of the nationality of her parents.

But there is also a less welcoming side to the history of American immigration policy—one that often has overshadowed the national symbol of the Statue of Liberty. Some federal laws have been blatantly racist, prohibiting immigration and naturalization of noncitizens from China and Japan and favoring northern and western Europeans over southern and eastern Europeans. Persons have been excluded or deported for their political beliefs. Enforcement of the immigration laws has, at times, violated fundamental notions of fairness and decency. Noncitizens continue to be scapegoats for some of the problems of American society.

To provide a summary of the major legal and political developments in U.S. immigration policy, we have selected two sketches of American immigration history. The first, part of a report issued by the Select Commission on Immigration and Refugee Policy, surveys the evolving U.S. immigration policy up to 1980. The second, excerpted from a new study of immigration history, takes us up to the second decade of the twenty-first century. As you read these summaries, focus not on the details but on the general trends that the various developments embody. Note particularly the role that economic, political, and international events have played in the evolution of immigration policy. Later in the course you may wish to return from time to time to these background sketches as you encounter discussions of the historical periods or successive laws mentioned here.

SELECT COMMISSION ON IMMIGRATION AND REFUGEE POLICY, U.S. IMMIGRATION POLICY AND THE NATIONAL INTEREST
Staff Report 161–216 (1981).

IMMIGRATION AND U.S. HISTORY—THE EVOLUTION OF THE OPEN SOCIETY[a]

* * * The first inhabitants to the New World, scientists believe, came when the last great Ice Age lowered the level of the Pacific Ocean sufficiently to expose a land bridge between Asia and North America, enabling people to cross the ocean from Asia. Recent evidence suggests that the ancestors of the present-day native Americans settled in North America more than 30,000 years ago and by about 10,000 B.C. had expanded their settlement as far as the tip of South America.

Some 116 centuries later, migration to America occurred again, this time coming from the opposite direction. European monarchs and merchants—whether Spanish, Portuguese, French, English or Dutch—encouraged exploration and then settlement of the newly "discovered" lands of the Americas. The descendants of the occupants of these lands, native American Indians, sometimes joke that the "Indians had bad immigration laws." In fact, there were a variety of responses. In some cases, Indian tribes welcomed the new settlers, negotiating treaties, many of which were abrogated by the colonists. In other instances, the Indians fought newcomers who encroached upon their lands. Whatever the response, though, most tribes found themselves overwhelmed by the better-armed Europeans.

The continents of the Western Hemisphere soon became a microcosm of the European continent, peopled in the north by northern and western Europeans and in the south by the Spanish and Portuguese.

Because of the diversity of national origins, it was by no means certain at the time of English settlement that those who spoke the English language would dominate the development of the area that eventually became the United States. To the south of the British-occupied territories were Spanish colonies, to the north were the French, between

---

[a] Lawrence H. Fuchs & Susan Forbes Martin, principal authors. [The footnotes have been renumbered—eds.]

were Dutch and Swedish settlements. By the second half of the eighteenth century, though, the French had been defeated and had withdrawn from Canada, a modus vivendi of sorts had been established with Spain and the small Dutch and Swedish settlements had been incorporated into the middle colonies of New York, New Jersey, Pennsylvania and Delaware. Hence, it was a certainty by the time of the Revolution that the newly formed republic would be one in which the English influence would prevail.

Despite Anglo-American dominance, however, the colonial period saw the establishment of a tendency towards ethnic pluralism that also was to become a vital part of U.S. life. At least a dozen national groups found homes in the area. Most came in search of religious toleration, political freedom and/or economic opportunity. Many, particularly some ancestors of those who later thought of themselves as "the best people," came as paupers, or as bond servants and laborers who paid for their passage by promising to serve employers, whom they could not leave for a specified number of years. Not all came of their own free will. Convicts and vagrants were shipped from English jails in the seventeenth century. Beginning in Virginia in 1619, some 350,000 slaves were brought from Africa until the end of the slave trade in 1807.

Non-English arrivals were treated with ambivalence, whether they were Dutch, German or even Scotch-Irish Presbyterians from Great Britain. The Germans who came to Pennsylvania, for example, had first learned of the colony through an advertising campaign designed by William Penn to attract their attention and migration. The earliest German settlers came in the hopes of finding liberty of conscience, and once their glowing reports were sent back to Germany, others of their nationality—seeking not only religious toleration but economic opportunity—followed. They were welcomed by many English colonists who applauded their industry and piety. Yet, they were attacked by others who questioned if they would ever assimilate.

This question asked about each successive wave of immigrants was to become a familiar refrain in U.S. history, but the ambivalence towards foreigners was by no means great enough during the colonial period to cause restrictions on immigration. In fact, the Declaration of Independence cites as one of the failings of King George III, and thus a justification for revolution, that "He has endeavored to prevent the Population of these States; for that purpose obstructing the Laws for Naturalization of Foreigners; refusing to pass others to encourage their migrations hither, and raising the conditions of new Appropriations of Lands."

After the revolution and the creation of a new government, Americans kept the gates of their new country open for several reasons.

The land was vast, relatively rich and sparsely settled. At the time of the first census, taken in 1790, America had a recorded population of 3,227,000—all immigrants or descendants of seventeenth and eighteenth century arrivals.[1] The population density at that time was about 4.5 persons per square mile. Labor was needed to build communities as well as to clear farms on the frontier and push back the Indians. People were needed to build a strong country, strong enough to avoid coming once again under the rule of a foreign power. Moreover, many U.S. citizens thought of their new nation as an experiment in freedom—to be shared by all people, regardless of former nationality, who wished to be free.

experiment in freedom

Despite all of these reasons for a liberal immigration policy, some doubts still remained about its wisdom. Although people were needed to build the new nation, some feared that the entry of too many aliens would cause disruptions and subject the United States to those foreign influences that the nation sought to escape in independence.

With the signing of the Treaty of Paris in 1783, the United States was officially recognized as an independent nation and the history of official U.S. immigration policy began. * * *

indep. nation

Beginning in 1790, Congress passed a series of acts regulating naturalization. The first act permitted the liberal granting of citizenship to immigrants. After a heated debate—in which the losing side argued not only for strict naturalization requirements but also for barriers against the admission of "the common class of vagrants, paupers and other outcasts of Europe"—Congress required a two-year period of residence and the renunciation of former allegiances before citizenship could be claimed.

Naturalization Act of 1790

citizenship reg's before

By 1795, though, the French Revolution, and the ensuing turmoil in Europe, had raised new fears about foreign political intrigue and influence. A new naturalization act, passed in 1795, imposed more stringent requirements including a five-year residency requirement for citizenship and the renunciation of not only allegiances but titles of nobility. Still, some thought U.S. standards for naturalization were too liberal, and, in 1798, another law was passed that raised the residency requirement to fourteen years. At the same time, the Alien Enemies Act and the Alien Friends Act gave the president powers to deport any alien whom he considered dangerous to the welfare of the nation. One proponent of these laws explained his support: "If no law of this kind was passed, it would be in the power of an individual State to introduce such a number of aliens into the country, as might not only be dangerous, but as

1795 Nat. Act.

5 yr +

(1798) 14 yrs

---

[1] More than 75 percent of this population was of British origin, another eight percent was German and the rest were mainly Dutch, French or Spanish. In addition, approximately a half million black slaves and perhaps as many Native Americans lived within the borders of the United States.

might be sufficient to overturn the Government, and introduce the greatest confusion in the country."

The xenophobia that gave rise to the Alien Acts of 1798 passed with the transfer of power from the Federalist to the Republican Party in 1800. The [Alien Friends Act was] permitted to expire,[b] and, in 1802, a new Naturalization Act re-established the provisions of the 1795 Act—what was to become a permanent five-year residency requirement for citizenship. While the Republicans were by no means free of suspicion of foreigners, they were not sufficiently fearful of the consequences of immigration to impose any restraints on the entry or practices of the foreign born. Instead, they pursued a policy that has been aptly described by Maldwyn Allen Jones in his history, *American Immigration*:

> Americans had to some degree reconciled the contradictory ideas that had influenced the thinking of the Revolutionary generation and had developed a clearly defined immigration policy. All who wished to come were welcome to do so; but no special inducements or privileges would be offered them.

For the next 75 years, the federal government did little about the regulation of immigration. It did establish procedures that made the counting of a portion of all immigrants possible. In 1819 Congress passed a law requiring ship captains to supply to the Collector of Customs a list of all passengers on board upon arrival at U.S. ports. This list was to indicate their sex, occupation, age and "country to which they severally belonged." At first only Atlantic and Gulf port information was collected; Pacific ports were added after 1850. Immigration information from Hawaii, Puerto Rico and Alaska dates only from the beginning of the twentieth century, as does the recording of information across land borders with Canada and Mexico.

Although a fully accurate picture of the level of all immigration cannot be made, the data available have enabled historians to sketch the general composition and trend of U.S. immigration. These data show a steadily increasing level of immigration. Immigrants arriving between the end of the Revolutionary War and the passage of the 1819 act are estimated to have totaled about 250,000. During the next ten years, over 125,000 came, and between 1830 and 1860, almost 4.5 million European immigrants arrived in the United States. Never before had the United States had to incorporate so large a number of newcomers into its midst. At first, the new arrivals were greeted with enthusiasm. With a nation to be built, peasants from Norway were as welcome as skilled craftsmen from Great Britain and experienced farmers from western, Protestant Germany. The novelist Herman Melville characterized this spirit:

---

[b]   The Alien Enemies Act is still on the books. 50 U.S.C.A. §§ 21–23.—eds.

There is something in the contemplation of the mode in which America has been settled, that, in a noble breast, should forever extinguish the prejudices of national dislikes.

Settled by the people of all nations, all nations may claim her for their own. You cannot spill a drop of American blood without spilling the blood of the whole world. . . .

We are the heirs of all time, and with all nations, we divide our inheritance. On this Western Hemisphere all tribes and people are forming into one federate whole; and there is a future which shall see the estranged children of Adam restored as to the old hearthstone in Eden.

Beginning in the 1830s, though, the composition of the groups entering the United States began to change, and few U.S. residents thought so romantically about the new immigrants.

Waves of Irish during the potato famines and German Catholic immigrants flowed into the country during the European depressions of the 1840s. These Catholics entered a country that was not only overwhelmingly Protestant, but that had been settled by some of the most radical sectarians, who prided themselves on their independence from the Pope's authority as well as from any king's. To begin with, U.S. residents had brought with them from Europe centuries of memories of the Catholic-Protestant strife that had so long dominated that continent's social and political life. Much anti-Irish feeling arose from these roots and was nourished by an oversimplified view of Catholicism which saw Catholics as unable to become good citizens—that is, independent and self-reliant—since they were subject to orders from the church. Even before the mass immigration of Catholics during the 1840s and 1850s, the xenophobic inventor Samuel F.B. Morse warned his fellow Americans:

How is it possible that foreign turbulence imported by shiploads, that riot and ignorance in hundreds of thousands of human priest-controlled machines should suddenly be thrown into our society and not produce turbulence and excess? Can one throw mud into pure water and not disturb its clearness?

It was easy to blame these new immigrants for many of the problems of the rapidly changing, increasingly urban nineteenth century U.S. society. Hostility against immigrants grew as they were accused of bringing intemperance, crime and disease to the new world. The first Select Committee of the House of Representatives to study immigration concluded:

that the number of emigrants from foreign countries into the United States is increasing with such rapidity as to jeopardize the peace and tranquility of our citizens, if not the permanency of the civil, religious, and political institutions of the United States. . . . Many of them are the outcasts of foreign countries; *paupers*, *vagrants*, and *malefactors* . . . sent hither at the expense of foreign governments, to relieve them from the burden of their maintenance.

A Protestant magazine sounded a further alarm by suggesting that "the floodgates of intemperance, pauperism and crime are thrown open by [immigrants], and if nothing be done to close them, they will carry us back to all of the drunkenness and evil of former times.["]

Out of these fears arose an alliance of those committed to saving the United States from the alleged dangers of immigration. Composed of social reformers who hoped to preserve the nation's institutions, some Protestant evangelicals who hoped to preserve the nation's morals and nativists who hoped to preserve the nation's ethnic purity, they formed associations, such as the secret Order of the Star-Spangled Banner, and political parties, such as the Know-Nothing Party.

These groups were committed to placing a curb on immigration itself and to ensuring that foreigners not be permitted to participate in the nation's political affairs. The naturalization statutes were a principal target of their concern. A pamphlet of the Know-Nothing Party warned of the inadequacy of these laws in protecting the nation against fraud:

> It is notorious that the grossest frauds have been practiced on our naturalization laws, and that thousands and tens of thousands have every year deposited votes in the ballot box, who could not only not read them, and knew nothing of the nature of the business in which they were engaged, but who had not been six months in the country, and, in many cases, hardly six days.

The party hoped to avoid these problems by eliminating the participation of even naturalized immigrants in the political process.

At its most vitriolic, nativism manifested itself in anti-Catholic riots against the Irish. New York, Philadelphia and Boston all saw such violence. Exposes revealing the "truth" about Catholic nunneries—that they were dens of iniquity and vice—precipitated the burning of convents and Catholic churches.[2] Although strident, nativist voices did not prevail. Attacks on ethnic groups usually came from a small, but vocal portion of the population that by no means represented the wishes of all Americans. Even during the times in which nativism reached its peak, there continued to be a variety of potent support for unlimited immigration. Economic needs, reinforced by the ideals of opportunity and freedom that were more deeply rooted in the country than was the anti-Catholic

---

[2] Not all convent-burning was indicative of anti-Catholicism per se. The burning of the Ursuline Convent at Charlestown, Massachusetts was due mainly to the local brickmakers' resentment of Irish economic competition.

heritage or fears of foreign takeover, worked against restricting immigration or making requirements for citizenship or voting more stringent.

After the Civil War, the country's desire for immigrants seemed insatiable * * * . Railroads were being laid across the nation, thus opening vast lands for settlement. Labor was needed to gouge the earth for coal and iron, to work in rapidly developing mills and to build cities.

labor

As demand for labor increased, so too did the number of immigrants. From 1860 to 1880, about 2.5 million Europeans entered this country each decade; during the 1880s the number more than doubled to 5.25 million. Another 16 million immigrants entered during the next quarter century, with 1.25 million entering in 1908.

Because the numbers of immigrants were so large, it appeared as if the United States had never before experienced immigration of this sort. Not only was there a change in the size of the flow, there was also a change, once more, in the source of immigration. The migration before the 1880s had been overwhelmingly from northern and western Europe. Even the hated Irish Catholics had come from a country where English was generally spoken and Irish immigration was now traditional. Less than three percent of the foreign-born population of the country had come from eastern or southern Europe. During the 1890s that pattern began to reverse itself, and during the first decade of the twentieth century, about 70 percent came from the new areas.

Just as the Irish and Germans had appeared to Americans to be more "foreign" than English Protestants, so too did the new immigrants appear to be more "foreign" than the old ones. In what may be an inevitable process, the old immigrants had become familiar and, therefore, respectable while the new ones were put under the closest possible scrutiny for signs of dissimilitude. And, alien characteristics are exactly what many Americans found—strange coloring, strange physiques, strange customs and strange languages.

The new immigrants were disliked and feared. They were considered culturally different and incapable of this country's version of self-government, and not because of their backgrounds but because they were thought to be biologically and inherently inferior. Influential professors of history, sociology and eugenics taught that some races could never become what came to be called "100 percent American."

A leading academic proponent of nativism, Edward Ross, wrote of Jews that they are "the polar opposite of our pioneer breed. Undersized and weak muscled, they shun bodily activity and are exceedingly sensitive to pain." He also lamented that it was impossible to make Boy Scouts out of them. Italians, he noted, "possess a distressing frequency of low foreheads, open mouths, weak chins, poor features, skewed faces, small or knobby crania and backless heads." According to Ross, Italians "lack the power to take rational care of themselves." * * *

Even though * * * mortality statistics do not support the contention that the new immigrants were inherently diseased or biologically inferior, such sentiments began to take their toll. In 1882 the United States passed its first racist, restrictionist immigration law, the Chinese Exclusion Act. From 1860 to 1880, Chinese immigration had grown from 40,000 to over 100,000. Chinese labor had been welcomed to lay railway lines and work in mining. However, with the completion of the transcontinental railroad, which was followed by a depression in the 1870s, intense anti-Chinese feelings developed, particularly in the West, where hard-working and ambitious Chinese had made lives for themselves.

The attacks upon the Chinese often focused upon their inability, in the eyes of their opponents, to assimilate. In 1876, a California State Senate Committee described the Chinese as follows:

> They fail to comprehend our system of government; they perform no duties of citizenship. . . . They do not comprehend or appreciate our social ideas. . . . The great mass of the Chinese . . . are not amenable to our laws. . . . They do not recognize the sanctity of an oath.

The supposed criminality of the Chinese was of particular concern. Although the crime statistics of the period do not bear out the accusations, the Chinese were believed to be criminals nevertheless. The state senate committee complained that "the Pacific Coast has become a Botany Bay to which the criminal classes of China are brought in large numbers and the people of this coast are compelled to endure this affliction." The Chinese were especially accused of bringing gambling and prostitution to the region. In 1876, *Scribner's Magazine* noted that "no matter how good a Chinaman may be, ladies never leave their children with them, especially little girls." The legislative committee concluded that "the Chinese are inferior to any race God ever made . . . [and] have no souls to save, and if they have, they are not worth saving."

Restrictionists—looking for justifications for closing other types of immigration—also eyed European immigrants as criminally inclined. The Police Commissioner of New York, Theodore Bingham, wrote in the *North American Review* that ["]85 percent of New York criminals were of exotic origin and half of them were Jewish." The author of an article in *Collier's Magazine* labeled Italians as "the most vicious and dangerous" criminals, and he suggested that "80 percent of the limited number of clever thieves" were Jewish.

Again, the crime statistics do not bear out the accusations. * * * The majority of immigrants were arrested for the petty crimes—vagrancy, disorderly conduct, breach of the peace, drunkenness—associated with poverty and difference in values. Immigrants were statistically more likely to commit minor offenses than were the native born who tended to commit property crimes and crimes of personal violence. According to the statistics, there was only one real cause for concern as far as immigrant crime was concerned. The children of the foreign born were the most likely group of all to commit crimes. Their crimes more often resembled those of the native born, though, than those of immigrants. This pattern indicates, more than anything else, that acculturation occurred even in the area of crime.

Despite the known evidence that immigrants were neither inherently criminal nor diseased, nativist arguments emphasizing the inferiority of immigrants were widely accepted. Restrictionists called for legislation that would decide whether the United States would be, as some put it, peopled by British, German and Scandinavian stock, or the new immigrants, "beaten men from beaten races; representing the worst failures in the struggle for existence."

Earlier, nativism had been offset by confidence that the United States had room for all, by a tradition of welcoming the poor and the oppressed and by belief that life in the New World would transform all comers into new Adams and Eves in the American Eden. At the end of the century, however, these ideas were affected by four historical developments:

- The official closing of the U.S. frontier;

- Burgeoning cities and increasing industrialization;

- The persistence of immigrants from southern and eastern Europe in maintaining their traditions; and

- The Catholic or Jewish religion of most of the new immigrants.

In the light of these developments, many Americans began to doubt the country's capacity to welcome and absorb the ever-increasing waves of new immigrants.

Evidence of this new feeling about European immigration could be seen as early as 1891. There had been earlier attempts at controlling the entry of immigrants to the United States—in the Act of 1875 that excluded prostitutes and alien convicts and in the Act of 1882 that barred the entry of lunatics, idiots, convicts and those liable to become a public charge—but these were not as comprehensive as the measure debated that year. One of the principal spokesmen for the bill, Henry Cabot Lodge, of Massachusetts, urged his fellow congressmen to establish new categories of admission to the United States in order to "sift . . . the chaff from the wheat" and prevent "a decline in the quality of American citizenship." The 1891 bill added new categories of exclusion that mirrored the concerns about the biological inferiority of immigrants. Those suffering from loathsome or contagious diseases and aliens convicted of crimes involving moral turpitude were barred from entry. The bill also provided for the medical inspection of all arrivals.[3]

Both houses of Congress quickly passed the measure; in the Senate, noted the *New York Times*, "the matter did not even occupy ten minutes." The measure did not go far enough for the quantitative restrictionists, though, since it did not succeed in stemming the flow of new entrants. In their efforts to change immigration policy, these restrictionists began to center their arguments upon one area of regulation—literacy.

As early as 1887, economist Edward W. Bemis gave a series of lectures in which he proposed that the United States prevent the entry of all male adults who were unable to read and write their own language. He argued that such a regulation would reduce by half or more those who were poor and undereducated. As awareness of the nature of the new immigration grew, nativists realized that a literacy test would also discriminate between desirable and undesirable nationalities, not just individuals. The proponents of the test saw it as an effective method of nationality restriction because, unlike the other "proofs" of cultural inferiority, literacy could easily and readily be measured.

The new immigrants were often attacked for their attachments to their native languages and what was perceived to be a failure to learn English. In an editorial, the *Nation* magazine proposed that a literacy test was insufficient and that English-language ability should be a requirement of entry. Recognizing that a proposal to make English a requirement of entry would effectively limit immigration to residents of the British Isles, the *Nation* declared in 1891 what other restrictionists believed—that "we are under no obligation to see that all races and nations enjoy an equal chance of getting here."

A literacy bill was first introduced in the Congress in 1895, and under the leadership of Senator Lodge passed both houses. In the last days of his administration, President Cleveland vetoed it, suggesting that the test was hypocritical. The House overrode his veto, but the Senate took no action and the proposal died. In a new wave of xenophobia that followed the assassination of President McKinley by an anarchist mistakenly believed to be an immigrant, a new bill passed the House. Despite the support of the new president, Theodore Roosevelt, the bill's sponsors were unable to gain a favorable vote in the Senate, and it too died.

---

[3]   Further grounds of exclusion similar in intent were added in 1903 and 1907.

In 1906, new, comprehensive legislation was proposed that included a literacy test for admission and both a literacy and an English-language requirement for naturalization. The restrictionists, now aided by labor unions wary of competition, were opposed in their endeavors by newly organized ethnic groups as well as business leaders opposed to any elimination of new labor sources. In all but one area, the restrictionists were triumphant. Once again, though, they were unsuccessful in gaining passage of a literacy requirement for either entry or naturalization. English-language proficiency was made a basis for citizenship, though, since most congressmen agreed with Representative Bonynge that "history and reason alike demonstrate that you cannot make a homogeneous people out of those who are unable to communicate with each other in one common language."

In 1907, after the restrictionist attempt to impose a literacy requirement failed, immigration to the United States reached a new high—with the arrival of 1,285,000 immigrants—and an economic depression hit the country. That same year, Congress passed legislation to establish a joint congressional presidential Commission to study the impact of immigrants on the United States. Its members appointed in 1909, the Dillingham Commission, as it is usually known, began its work convinced that the pseudoscientific racist theories of superior and inferior peoples were correct and that the more recent immigrants from southern and eastern Europe were not capable of becoming successful Americans. Although their own data contradicted these ideas, the Commission nevertheless held on to them. The Commission's recommendations were published in 1911 with 41 volumes of monographs on specific subjects, including discussions of immigrants and crime, changes in the bodily form of immigrants and the industrial impact of immigration. In the view of the Commission, their findings all pointed to the same conclusions:

- Twentieth century immigration differed markedly from earlier movements of people to the United States;

- The new immigration was dominated by the so-called inferior peoples—those who were physically, mentally and linguistically different, and, therefore, less desirable than either the native-born or early immigrant groups; and

- Because of the inferiority of these people, the United States no longer benefited from a liberal immigration admissions policy and should, therefore, impose new restrictions on entry.

The Commission endorsed the literacy test as an appropriate mechanism to accomplish its ends.

The demand for large-scale restriction still did not succeed, though, because of the continuing demand for labor, the growing political power of the new immigrant groups and the commitment of the nation's leaders to preserving the tradition of free entry. In 1912, Congress once more passed a literacy test, but President Taft successfully vetoed it, extolling the "sturdy but uneducated peasantry brought to this country and raised in an atmosphere of thrift and hard work" where they have "contributed to the strength of our people and will continue to do so." Another veto, this time by President Woodrow Wilson, defeated the work of the restrictionists in 1915. According to Wilson, the literacy test "seeks to all but close entirely the gates of asylum which have always been open to those who could find nowhere else the right and opportunity of constitutional agitation for what they conceived to be the natural and inalienable rights of men."

After the United States entered World War I in 1917, Congress finally overrode the presidential veto and enacted legislation that made literacy a requirement for entry. The bill also codified the list of aliens to be excluded, and it virtually banned all immigration from Asia. The efforts of the restrictionists were finally successful, in large measure because World War I brought nervousness about the loyalty and assimilability of the foreign born to a fever pitch. The loyalty of immigrants became a hot political issue. Theodore Roosevelt, for example, stormed against "hyphenated Americans," as he voiced his concern that the country was becoming little more than a "poly-glot boarding house." A frenzy of activity against German Americans (who only a short while before were thought, along with the English, Scots and Scandinavians to be the best qualified to enter) led to the closing of thriving German-language schools, newspapers and social clubs. The Governor of Iowa took what may have been the strongest measures; he decreed that the use of any language other than English in public places or over the telephone would be prohibited.

This agitation against the foreign born culminated in two efforts: a movement to "Americanize" immigrants and the development of immigration restrictions based on national origins quotas. The Americanization movement had had its start in 1915 when two government agencies, operating independently of each other, began assessing the number and efficacy of immigrant education programs operating in the country. * * * Lobbying efforts by the Bureau of Education led many states—twenty between 1919 and 1921—to pass legislation establishing Americanization programs to ensure that all immigrants would learn English, the "language of America," as a California commission called it.

Industry also joined the movement. It was frequently asserted that "ignorance of English is a large factor in [job] turnover" and similarly that "there is an important connection between ignorance of English and illiteracy to economic loss." The National Association of Manufacturers encouraged Americanization programs among its members. Henry Ford set up classes within his plants and required attendance of his 5,000 non-English-speaking employees. * * *

The success of the Americanization program in enrolling immigrants was not enough to satisfy the opponents of immigration. Still convinced that racial differences precluded the full assimilation of the new immigrants, some nativists doubted the ability of Americanization classes to transform immigrants into "100 percent Americans." Some were convinced that all immigrants should be compelled to learn English, and if they could not, should be subject to deportation. * * *

As the movement to compel assimilation of those already here progressed, those fearful of the consequences of immigration also sought new restrictions on entry. Restrictionists had learned that the literacy requirement which they believed held so much promise was not succeeding as had been expected. Immigration from southern and eastern Europe continued. The literacy rates of European countries showed increasing numbers eligible for entry; Italy even established schools in areas of high emigration to teach peasants to be literate so that they could pass the new U.S. test for entry.

To quantitative restrictionists, new measures were needed. The suspension of all immigration—an idea never before of any great appeal in U.S. immigration history—began to gain support. The two groups most associated with it, organized labor and "100 percenters," had little else in common. Labor supported suspension of immigration because of the competition for jobs that occurred with the entry of aliens.

The 100 percenters feared that European people and ideas—whether "bestial hordes" from conquered Germany or the "red menace" of Bolshevism—would contaminate U.S. institutions and culture. * * *

[T]he Senate proposed * * * legislation to reduce overall immigration and to change the ethnic composition of those permitted entry. The goal of the bill—similar to one originally proposed by Senator Dillingham of the earlier Immigration Commission—was to ensure that northern and western Europeans still had access to the United States while southern and eastern European immigration would be restricted. In 1921, Congress passed and President Harding signed into law the Senate-proposed legislation—a provisional measure which introduced the concept of national origins quotas. This act established a ceiling on European immigration and limited the number of immigrants of each nationality to three percent of the number of foreign-born persons of that nationality resident in the United States at the time of the 1910 census.

This first quota act was extended for two more years, but in 1924 came the passage of what was heralded as a permanent solution to U.S. immigration problems. The Johnson-Reed measure, more commonly known as the National Origins Act, provided for an annual limit of 150,000 Europeans, a complete prohibition on Japanese immigration, the issuance and counting of visas against quotas abroad rather than on arrival, and the development of quotas based on the contribution of each nationality to the overall U.S. population rather than on the foreign-born population.[c] This law was designed to preserve, even more effectively than the 1921 law, the racial and ethnic status quo of the United States. The national origins concept was also designed, as John Higham wrote in his study of U.S. nativism, *Strangers in the Land*, to give "comfort to the democratic conscience" by counting everyone's ancestors and not just the foreign born themselves.

Recognizing that it would take some time to develop the new quotas, as a stopgap measure the bill provided for the admission of immigrants according to annual quotas of two percent of each nationality's proportion of the foreign-born U.S. population in 1890 until 1927—amended to 1929—when the national origins quotas were established. The use of the 1890 census had been criticized as a discriminatory measure since it seemed to change the rules of European entry solely to lower the number of the so-called "new" immigrants. Use of the 1890 census instead of that of 1910 meant a reduction in the Italian quota from 42,000 to about 4,000, in the Polish quota from 31,000 to 6,000 and in the Greek quota from 3,000 to 100. The proponents of the new legislation argued, however, that use of the 1910 Census was what was really discriminatory since it underestimated the number of visas that should go to those from northern and western Europe. * * *

Despite the rhetoric of its supporters—and the exemption of members of the Western Hemisphere from its quotas—the Immigration Act of 1924 clearly represented a rejection of one of [the] longest-lived democratic traditions of the United States, represented by George Washington's view that the United States should ever be "an asylum to the oppressed and the needy of the earth." It also represented a rejection of cultural pluralism as a U.S. ideal. The Commissioner of Immigration could report, one year after this legislation took effect, that virtually all immigrants now "looked" exactly like Americans. Abraham Lincoln's fear that when the nativists gained control of U.S. policy they would rewrite the Declaration of Independence to read: "All men are created equal, except Negroes, and foreigners, and Catholics" seemed to be coming true.

---

[c] For purposes of calculating the national quotas, the 1924 legislation excluded the descendants of slaves from its definition of the population of the United States. Act of May 26, 1924, ch. 190, § 11(d), 43 Stat. 153, 159. African Americans constituted nine percent of the U.S. population, and European countries received the proportion of the quota that should have gone to Africa. For further discussion of the racial ramifications of the National Origins Act, see Mae M. Ngai, Impossible Subjects: Illegal Aliens and the Making of Modern America 21–55 (2004).— eds.

great depression

Immigration to the United States suffered still another blow with the Great Depression. During the 1930s, only 500,000 immigrants came to the United States, less than one-eighth of the number that had arrived in the previous decade. Most reduced in number were members of those nations jointly affected by the national origins quotas, and by economic conditions that made impossible their usual pattern of temporary migration for the purposes of work. * * * Temporary migration can be measured through data on emigration, the number of immigrants who leave the country some time after arrival. Throughout most of the early twentieth century, according to official statistics that were collected beginning in 1908, emigration stood at a minimum of 20 percent of immigration and, more commonly, at 30 to 40 percent. * * * In 1932, at the height of the Great Depression, the emigration figure stood at 290 percent of legal immigration. While 35,576 entered the country, over 100,000 left.

Those most tragically affected by the U.S. policy of restrictive immigration (and the economic problems that made U.S. citizens unwilling to alter it) were the refugees who tried to flee Europe before the outbreak of World War II. Although some efforts were made to accommodate them—in 1940 the State Department permitted consuls outside of Germany to issue visas to German refugees because the German quota sometimes remained unfilled—these measures were too few and came too late to help most of the victims of Nazi persecution. In what may be the cruelest single action in U.S. immigration history, the U.S. Congress in 1939 defeated a bill to rescue 20,000 children from Nazi Germany, despite the willingness of U.S. families to sponsor them, on the grounds that the children would exceed the German quota. Those refugees who were able to come in under existing quotas were still subject to all of the other requirements of entry, and a significant number were refused visas because of the public charge provisions in the grounds for exclusion.

Although the quota system of the 1920s stood substantially intact until 1965, U.S. immigration policy was affected by the events of World War II—in particular the shock this country received when it learned most graphically of the fate of the refugees refused entry. Even before that knowledge came, the war challenged long-held notions about U.S. traditions and needs. The United States realized that it once more needed the labor of aliens, for example. This country and Mexico then negotiated a large-scale temporary worker program—the bracero program—designed to fill the wartime employment needs of the United States. Also, in large part because of the alliance of the United States with China, Congress repealed the ban on all Chinese immigration, making it possible for a small number of Chinese once again to enter the country as legal immigrants. Notions of the inherent inferiority of certain groups [were] dispelled when those same groups became allies in the fight against other groups that were proving to be much stronger enemies than expected.

For a short period, the atmosphere was right for a liberalization of immigration policy. At the close of the war, especially after Americans learned of the Nazi atrocities, they seemed united in their appreciation of democracy and their commitment to renewing the U.S. role as a haven for the oppressed. An important first step was taken by President Harry S. Truman who issued a directive in December 1945 admitting 40,000 war refugees. Responding to the plight of U.S. soldiers who had married overseas, Congress passed the "War Brides Act" in 1946, which permitted 120,000 alien wives, husbands and children of members of the armed forces to immigrate to the United States.

In the years following the war, the executive branch continued to take an active role in reshaping immigration policy, even after the advent of the Cold War when public attitudes towards the issue turned more conservative. Most of these efforts, though, were in the area of refugee admissions and did not change the basic structure of U.S. immigration law. President Truman prodded the Congress to pass the Displaced Persons Act in 1948. After its expiration, Congress passed the Refugee Relief Act, under which 214,000 persons were admitted. Designed principally to expedite the admission of refugees fleeing Iron Curtain countries, the Act incorporated safeguards to prevent the immigration of undesirable aliens. Additional measures were passed in 1956 and 1957 to facilitate the entry of Hungarians displaced by the revolution in that country and "refugee-escapees" fleeing Communist or Communist-occupied or dominated countries and countries in the Middle East. In 1960, the Refugee Fair Share Law was passed to provide a temporary program for the admission of World War II refugees and displaced persons who remained in camps under the mandate of the United Nations High Commissioner for Refugees. This legislation gave the Attorney General a specific mandate to use his parole authority to admit eligible refugee-escapees. Although the statute was for a limited period of time, it was more comprehensive than other refugee admission programs and provided an ongoing mechanism to assist refugees.

Despite these strides in developing a policy that permitted refugees to escape from some of the restrictions of the national origins quota requirements, little else in the way of progress occurred in the immigration area until the 1960s. In fact the determination to preserve the quota system was so strong that the refugee measures provided that those entering under those provisions were to be charged to future quotas of their country of origin, as long as these did not exceed 50 percent of the quota of any one year. The refugee acts were seen as complements to the national origins policy; they made the 1924 law more responsive to emergencies but did not significantly alter immigration policy itself.

During the early 1950s, the climate was not ripe for any major liberalizing changes. Concern with communist expansion dominated U.S. thinking in the early 1950s, and the stand against communism often took the form of opposition to anything foreign. It was a period in which ethnic customs and values could easily be defined as "un-American."

It was in such an atmosphere that congressional hearings on a new immigration law took place. They were conducted under the leadership of Senator Patrick A. McCarran who, with his followers, believed that there were in the United States what he called "indigestible blocks" which would not assimilate into the American way of life. In 1952, the McCarran-Walter bill—passed into law as the Immigration and Nationality Act—consolidated previous immigration laws into one statute, but, in so doing, it preserved the national origins quota system. The Act also established a system of preferences for skilled workers and the relatives of U.S. citizens and permanent resident aliens, and tightened security and screening procedures.

It established a 150,000 numerical limitation on immigration from the Eastern Hemisphere; most Western Hemisphere immigration remained unrestricted,[d] although it established a subquota for immigrants born in the colonies or dependent areas of the Western Hemisphere. Finally, the Act repealed Japanese exclusion and established a small quota for the Asia-Pacific Triangle under which Orientals would be charged.

Congress passed the McCarran-Walter Act over the veto of President Truman who favored the liberalization of the immigration statutes and the elimination of national origins quotas. In his veto message, he strongly reaffirmed U.S. ideals.

> Such a concept [national origins quota] is utterly unworthy of our traditions and ideals. It violates the great political doctrine of the Declaration of Independence that "all men are created equal." It denies the humanitarian creed inscribed beneath the Statue of Liberty proclaiming to all nations: "Give me your tired your poor, your huddled masses, yearning to breathe free. . . ."

Truman's Commission

President Truman on September 4, 1952 appointed a commission to study and evaluate the immigration and naturalization policies of the United States. On January 1, 1953 the Commission issued its report, *Whom We Shall Welcome*, a statement of support for a nondiscriminatory, liberal immigration policy. The Commission summarized its findings:

---

[d] There was no overall numerical limitation on immigration from the Western Hemisphere, but labor certification and similar requirements placed substantial restrictions on legal avenues of migration.—eds.

The Commission believes that our present immigration laws flout fundamental American traditions and ideals, display a lack of faith in America's future, damage American prestige and position among other nations, ignore the lessons of the American way of life.

The Commission believes that laws which fail to reflect the American spirit must sooner or later disappear from the statute books.

The Commission believes that our present immigration laws should be completely rewritten.

It was not until 1965 that major changes—some urged as early as the Truman Commission—were actually made in the Immigration and Nationality Act. The election of John F. Kennedy, a descendent of Irish immigrants and the first Catholic president of the United States, marked a turning point in immigration history and focused attention again on immigration policy. As a senator, Kennedy had written *A Nation of Immigrants*, a book denouncing the national origins quota system. Now, as President, he introduced legislation to abolish the 40-year-old formula.

That a Catholic could be elected president signified the extent to which the United States had changed since the 1920s. Across the country came a lessening in anti-Catholic, anti-Asian and anti-Semitic sentiment, in part the result of a new tolerance of racial and ethnic differences stimulated by the civil rights movement. By the mid-1960s, Congress was ready for proposals to liberalize immigration policy, particularly after the assassination of President Kennedy and the Lyndon Johnson presidential landslide of 1964. The effort to eliminate the national origins quotas— begun many years earlier—culminated in the passage of the Immigration and Nationality Act Amendments of 1965.

The amendments accomplished the following:

- Abolished the national origins formula, replacing it with a per-country limit of 20,000 on every country outside the Western Hemisphere, and an overall ceiling of 160,000 for those countries;

- Placed a ceiling of 120,000 on immigration from the Western Hemisphere with no country limits; and

- Established Eastern Hemisphere preferences for close relatives, as well as those who had occupational skills needed in the United States under a seven-category preference system.

* * *

The new amendments * * * heralded in a new era in U.S. immigration policy. No longer would one nationality be given a larger quota than another in the Eastern Hemisphere. Preference would be given to reuniting families and to bringing those who had certain desirable or needed abilities. These were to be the goals of immigration policy, and the goal of preserving the racial and ethnic domination of northern and western Europe would no longer be an explicit part of U.S. immigration law.

The United States was, of course, far from free of prejudice at that time, and one part of the 1965 law reflected a change in policy that was in part due to antiforeign sentiments. Prejudice against dark-skinned people, particularly in social and economic life, remained strong. In the years after World War II, as the proportion of Spanish-speaking residents increased, much of the lingering nativism in the United States was directed against those from Mexico and Central and South America. The 1952 law—in keeping with the "Good Neighbor" policy, as it was described by Franklin Delano Roosevelt—had not placed any limitations on immigration from these regions, but by 1965 the pressure for such restrictions had mounted. Giving in to these pressures as a price to be paid for abolishing the national origins system, Congress put into the 1965 amendments a ceiling on immigration from the Western Hemisphere that was designed to close the last remaining open door of U.S. policy. This provision went into effect on July 1, 1968.

The legislation did not accomplish its goal regarding Western Hemisphere immigration without substantial costs. In 1976, the House Judiciary Committee reported on the effect of ending the Good Neighbor open door: a steadily increasing backlog of applicants from Latin America, with prospective immigrants waiting two years for a visa. * * *

In 1976 a new law was passed to make regulations regarding immigration the same for both hemispheres, applying to countries of the Western Hemisphere the 20,000-per-country limit and the preference system that was in effect in the Eastern Hemisphere. The only provision to cause any controversy in the 1976 Act was the application of the per-country ceiling provision to Mexico, which had exceeded the 20,000 limit every year since the enactment of the 1965 amendments. There was considerable support for the idea that special provisions should be permitted for contiguous countries, particularly Mexico, because of the special relationship that had developed as a result of shared borders. President Gerald Ford noted in his statement on signing the 1976 amendments into law that he would submit legislation to Congress to increase the immigration quotas for Mexicans desiring to come to the United States, and President Jimmy Carter endorsed similar legislation in 1977. No action, however, was taken to provide this special treatment for Mexico.

The 1976 law maintained two last vestiges of differential geographic treatment—the separate annual ceilings of 170,000 for the Eastern and 120,000 for the Western Hemisphere and the special ceiling (600 visas per year) assigned to colonies and dependencies. In 1978, new legislation combined the ceilings for both hemispheres into a worldwide total of 290,000 with the same seven-category preference system and per-country limits applied to both. * * *

Concern about Indochinese conditional entries was an important consideration in the establishment of a worldwide ceiling. The 1965 amendments to the Immigration and Nationality Act had included a permanent statutory authority for the admission of refugees, called the conditional entry provision, patterned after earlier legislation, especially the Fair Share Refugee Act of 1960. The seventh preference category was designated for these admissions and was allocated six percent of the Eastern Hemisphere ceiling of 170,000 visas, one-half of which could be used for aliens in the United States who were adjusting their status. In 1976 the preference system was extended to the Western Hemisphere, under a separate numerical ceiling with its own proportion of seventh-preference slots. * * * Western Hemisphere seventh-preference numbers—applicable only to Cubans who were then unable to leave in sizable numbers—were unused whereas Eastern Hemisphere demand was great. A worldwide ceiling would permit the visas to go where the refugee need was greatest without reference to hemisphere.

The 1978 amendments did not address the full range of issues raised by U.S. refugee policy, nor were they intended to do so. The working definition of a refugee—originally developed during the Cold War—still included considerations of national origins, even though the rest of immigration policy had dismissed this criteria.

In the Immigration and Nationality Act of 1952, a refugee was defined as a person who [feared persecution "on account of race, religion, or political opinion" and fled a Communist country or a country "within the general area of the Middle East."] * * * This definition did not permit the entry of those fleeing noncommunist persecution [elsewhere].

Problems also arose because of the inadequacy of the conditional-entry provisions in dealing with large-scale emergencies. * * * Under the [immigration law], the Attorney General has the discretion to parole any alien into the United States temporarily, under such conditions as the Attorney General may prescribe, in emergencies or for reasons deemed strictly in the public interest. During the 1960s, Cuban refugees were paroled into the United States; between 1962 and the end of May 1979, over 690,000 Cubans entered this country under that authority. In 1975, two parole programs were adopted to aid the resettlement of refugees from Indochina. Other major programs permitted the parole of still more

Indochinese between 1976 and 1979. In June 1979 President Carter announced that the number of Indochinese paroled into the country would be set at 14,000 per month. During the same period, the parole of about 35,000 Soviet refugees for the year was also authorized as was the entry of slightly more than a thousand Chilean and Lebanese parolees.

The parole authority had been used in these cases because the conditional entry provisions were too limited to deal with emergencies. Yet reliance on the parole authority seemed to be an inappropriate response to what were recurring situations. Attorney General Griffin B. Bell described one of the major problems with the use of the parole authority in refugee crises: "This . . . has the practical effect of giving the Attorney General more power than the Congress in determining limits on the entry of refugees into the country." * * * The concerns about refugees led to legislative action in 1979 and 1980. The Refugee Act of 1980 was designed to correct the deficiencies of U.S. refugee policy by providing ongoing mechanisms for the admission and aid of refugees. The legislation broadened the definition of refugee by removing the geographic and ideological limitations of the earlier conditional-entry provisions. It also established an allocation of 50,000 for normal refugee admissions, through 1982, and provided procedures through which the President in consultation with Congress could increase this number annually in response to unforeseen circumstances. It further provided for a special conditional entry status with adjustment to permanent resident alien status after one year in the United States.

In addition to making changes in admissions policy, the Refugee Act of 1980 also established the ongoing responsibility of the federal government for the resettlement of refugees accepted under the Act. The legislation included provision for up to 100 percent reimbursement to states for cash and medical assistance provided to refugees during their first 36 months in this country and for grants to voluntary agencies for some of their costs incurred in resettlement.

SUSAN F. MARTIN, A NATION OF IMMIGRANTS
1–2, 213–16, 218–19, 253–54, 265–68, 271–78, 280–81, 284–86 (2010).

The United States is in the midst of its fourth major wave of immigration. Today's wave is the largest in absolute numbers, although not as a proportion of the total population. Unlike in previous waves, today's immigrants come from every inhabited continent and represent just about every country in the United Nations. As in previous waves, there is a profound ambivalence about immigration among the American public.

* * *

Immigration has indeed been formative in making America what it is and what it will become. The phrase "a nation of immigrants," however, hides as much as it illuminates in lumping together all immigrants and all forms of immigration. In fact, [I argue], America has been settled from its very origins by three different models of immigration, all of which persist through the four waves * * * . Lawrence Fuchs[e] described each model in relationship to the colony in which it most thrived:

> * * * Pennsylvania sought immigrants who would be good citizens regardless of their religious background; Massachusetts wanted as members only those who were religiously pure; and Virginia, with its increasing reliance on a plantation economy, wanted workers as cheaply as it could get them, without necessarily welcoming them to membership in the community.

* * *

[Martin argues that the 1965 amendments abolishing the national origins quotas restored the Pennsylvania model by reopening immigration to those—no matter where they originated—who sought to make the United States their permanent home. She emphasizes that total immigration increased dramatically in the wake of the 1965 legislation, and that it shifted noticeably to immigrants from Asia and from the Caribbean. She then discusses the growth of undocumented migration in the 1970s and 1980s, and the legislative efforts to respond to this situation.]

[In 1986] the Immigration Reform and Control Act (IRCA) was signed into law. * * * [T]he intent was to reduce future illegal immigration through a combination of improved border enforcement and sanctions against employers who knowingly hired person without a work authorization, while bringing those who were illegally in the country out of the shadows and onto a path to citizenship. For the first time, IRCA made it illegal to hire an illegal alien but imposed sanctions[f] only if the employer knew the worker was in the country illegally. * * *

To address concerns about discrimination, IRCA authorized a new office within the Justice Department to investigate "unfair immigration-related employment practices." IRCA prohibited employers from discriminating * * * because of [an] individual's national origin, or * * * citizenship status. It was considered an unfair practice to seek different or additional documents from any newly hired employees, a provision designed to dissuade employers from setting up special procedures for foreign-appearing workers.

---

[e]   Lawrence H. Fuchs, The American Kaleidoscope: Race, Ethnicity, and the Civil Culture, Wesleyan University Press 8 (1990)—eds.

[f]   We will describe in Chapter Ten the other sanctions for failing to verify properly.—eds.

The legalization provisions included two separate programs. One program focused on undocumented immigrants who had been in the country since January 1, 1982. Initially, they obtained conditional legal status upon demonstrating their continued presence in the United States. After eighteen months, they could apply for legal permanent resident status upon showing that they had successfully completed a course in the English language and civics or had passed an examination that was comparable with the naturalization tests. * * * . The second program was the SAW (Special Agricultural Workers) program. Under its terms, persons who could demonstrate that they had worked unlawfully in agriculture for ninety days during the twelve month period ending on May 1, 1986, were eligible to be legalized. After demonstrating that they continued to work in agriculture during the following three years, they could become permanent residents. * * *

IRCA barred the newly legalized from most public benefit programs for the first five years after they received legal status. Exceptions were made for education and training programs, especially those, like Head Start, that helped children. * * *

In the years after enactment of IRCA, 1.6 million immigrants who were in the United States illegally were found eligible for legalization under the pre-1982 program and 1.1 million were found eligible under the SAW program. These numbers represented 90 percent of pre-1982 applicants and 86 percent of SAW applicants. * * * The number of [SAW] applications far exceeded estimates of the seasonal agricultural workforce. Several explanations have been offered for the wide discrepancy. SAW applications could be made from outside the country, meaning that people who had worked previously in agriculture (perhaps not during the period included in the law) could apply even if they had left the country. More seriously, there appeared to be many fraudulent applications by people who had never worked in agriculture but found someone to provide an affidavit or counterfeit documents showing that they had put in ninety days in the fields.

* * *

Two immediate issues were raised by the IRCA legalization program. First, it did not cover undocumented immigrants who had entered after January 1, 1982, unless they were seasonal agricultural workers. IRCA thus led to a large residual population that was still in the country illegally. Second, IRCA made no accommodations for the admission of the families of legalized immigrants. Once legalized immigrants had the opportunity, they began to petition for their spouses and children to obtain permanent residence. Some of these family members were in the home country while others were in the United States but did not meet the IRCA requirements for legalization or had entered after their "anchor" relative gained legalized status. Because the immigrants whose status was legalized under IRCA came from so few countries, and the per-country limits applied to immediate relatives of legal permanent residents, the backlog of applicants began to grow exponentially.

* * *

In 1988, action began on reform of the legal admissions system. [The Immigration Act of 1990 increased the number of immigrant visas, setting a nominal annual ceiling of 480,000 on family admissions, but actually allowing them to go much higher, because there is no cap on admission of spouses and children of U.S. citizens. In addition, the Act set annual quotas of 140,000 visas for employment-based immigration and 55,000 for diversity immigration. The statute also streamlined naturalization, but still allowed judicial ceremonies.]

* * *

[In sum, the] Immigration Act of 1990, and the massive legalization program under IRCA, [together with] the Refugee Act of 1980, * * * culminated a 25-year period in which there was a substantial return to the Pennsylvania model of immigration. The 1965 Amendments reversed the discriminatory national origins quotas, but the architects of the reform did not extol the benefits of immigration. Rather, they argued that national origins quotas were an anachronism in a period in which civil rights were flourishing. Eliminating the discriminatory provisions would enhance American prestige around the world, but they would not necessarily open the United States to increased immigration. By contrast, the 1990 legislation was promoted precisely because its supporters thought an expansion in immigration was in the national interest. Even those who favored controls on overall numbers, such as Senator Alan Simpson, were persuaded by the need to expand highly skilled immigration to meet the needs of a global economy. Moreover, Congress chose permanent admissions over temporary workers. In the spirit of the Pennsylvania model, immigrants would be welcomed as proto-citizens rather than as indentured laborers. IRCA had legalized millions of undocumented immigrants, putting them on a road to citizenship if they learned English and civics.

The 1990 legislation was intended to facilitate family reunification, with family unity visas and the lifting of per-country limits on spouses and minor children of legal permanent residents. This is not to say that everything about the 1990 legislation should be seen within this context. The legislation also expanded the grounds for deportation, including the creation of a category of aggravated felons that would become problematic in later years.[g] On balance, though, the Immigration Act of 1990 favored

---

[g] The Anti-Drug Abuse Act of 1988 created the aggravated felony category, which was expanded by legislation in 1990 and subsequent years.—eds.

a form of immigration that valued family, skills, and humanitarian interests and provided immigrants the opportunity to join the American community.

The consensus that led to passage of the Immigration Act of 1990 was short-lived. Within a few years of its passage, the reemergence of illegal immigration and concerns about the fiscal impact of legal immigration challenged the Pennsylvania model. * * *

By the early 1990s, unauthorized immigration was indeed on the rise.[h] In California, the concerns about illegal immigration were taking the shape of a political movement. The United States-Mexico border appeared to be a free entry zone with no controls over illegal migration. Photos of large numbers of migrants racing by foot up Interstate Highway 5, the major route which runs from the Mexican to the Canadian border, became stock footage on U.S. news reports. Reflecting growing dissatisfaction with the federal government's apparent inability to control the border, California activists responded by introducing Proposition 187. The preamble summarized their concerns: "The People of California find and declare as follows: That they have suffered and are suffering economic hardship caused by the presence of illegal aliens in this state. That they have suffered and are suffering personal injury and damage caused by the criminal conduct of illegal aliens in this state. That they have a right to the protection of their government from any person or persons entering this country unlawfully." Proposition 187 required state and local law enforcement agencies to cooperate with federal authorities in administering immigration law. * * *

Proposition 187 also barred undocumented immigrants from a range of public services, with the exception of emergency medical assistance. In what may have been the most controversial provision, the bar extended to public primary and secondary education. A 1982 Supreme Court decision, *Plyler v. Doe*, guaranteed the right of all children, including undocumented immigrants, to public education. The Supreme Court had determined that children should not be punished for the decisions of their parents to come to the United States illegally. Supporters of Proposition 187 felt they were sending a powerful message to the federal government to gain control over illegal immigration. Opponents saw the proposition as a mean-spirited assault on undocumented immigrants but not a serious effort to get at the underlying factors at work.

* * *

During the 1990s, as is the case today, unauthorized entry occurred in a number of different ways. Most of those illegally in the United States were believed to have entered clandestinely, largely across the land

---

[h] Relocated sentence—eds.

border with Mexico although others arrived by sea, often in makeshift boats or rafts. A sizable minority (estimated as high as 40–45 percent) entered through recognized ports of entry. Many did so having obtained legitimate visas, often as tourists, and then overstayed the period that the visa covered. Some obtained a border crossing card or longer-term visa that did not permit employment, and then worked in contravention of the terms of their admission. In still other cases, migrants entered as temporary workers but failed to leave when their period of work authorization ended. In some cases, migrants sought visas knowing that they planned to violate the terms. In other cases, the migrants had no initial intention of overstaying or working illegally, but circumstances changed, their stay was prolonged, and they entered into irregular status.

* * *

IRCA had attempted to deal with all of these forms of illegal migration, focusing on the one common element—the employment magnet. Employer sanctions had done little to curb employment of undocumented workers, however, because of a faulty employment verification system [that is easily defeated by false documents]. * * *

[In 1996 Congress enacted three laws, the Illegal Immigration Reform and Immigrant Responsibility Act (IIRIRA), the Anti-Terrorism and Effective Death Penalty Act (AEDPA), and the Personal Responsibility and Work Opportunity Reconciliation Act of 1996 (better known as welfare reform), that represent a distinct shift in U.S. law on the rights of legal immigrants.]

IIRIRA, in combination with the Anti-Terrorism Act, included provisions that weakened the due process rights of legal permanent residents. Passed in the aftermath of the Oklahoma City bombing, with the 1993 bombings of the World Trade Center still fresh in memory, the law went well beyond terrorism, including sections on the removal of immigrants who committed crimes. * * *

The Anti-Terrorism law redefined crimes of "moral turpitude" to include those punishable by imprisonment for one year or more, rather than those for which the aliens is actually sentenced to imprisonment for one year or more, and expanded the list of crimes that could be considered aggravated felonies. IIRIRA revised the definition of an aggravated felony to include far less serious crimes than those covered by the 1990 legislation or the Anti-Terrorism Act. Just about any offense that could result in a potential—not necessarily actual—custodial sentence of one year or more could render the alien deportable. The new rule was applied retroactively; crimes committed many years ago, even if there was no evidence of subsequent criminality, qualified as grounds for removal. * * *

Some of the most profound changes to occur in immigrant policy found their way into law through the welfare reform legislation passed in 1996. The Welfare Reform Act, in combination with IIRIRA, reduced substantially the access of legal immigrants to public benefit programs available to citizens. * * *

Until 1996, no federal benefit program denied eligibility to permanent resident aliens solely on the basis of alien status. * * * [In the past distinctions had been] made between aliens residing permanently and legally in this country and undocumented aliens. The former were generally determined eligible for federal assistance; the latter were generally barred from these programs.

The welfare reform bill moved the line. Now, the major distinction was between immigrants, regardless of their status, and citizens. The welfare act made legal immigrants ineligible for Supplementary Security Income (SSI) and food stamps until citizenship * * * .

Legal immigrants were made ineligible for federal, means-tested benefits during their first five years after entry. * * *

Under IIRIRA, all immigrants admitted under family-based categories must be sponsored by a relative who signs an affidavit of support and who can demonstrate an ability to support the immigrant and members of his or her immediate family at 125 percent of poverty level. The affidavits would be legally enforceable against the sponsor * * * .

In effect, 1996 legislative activities turned out to be pro-immigration but anti-immigrant, in the best tradition of the Virginia model. At a time when the United States was admitting record numbers of immigrants, and a sizable proportion lived and worked in poverty, restricting eligibility for safety-net programs made it clear that immigrants were welcomed as workers, but not as full members of the community. The welfare reforms said, in effect, that all obligations were one-sided: immigrants must continue to pay taxes, contribute to the U.S. economy, obey U.S. laws, and otherwise contribute to the public weal, but the broader society had no reciprocal obligations toward them. * * *

When President George W. Bush had his first meeting with President Vincente Fox of Mexico early in 2001, the two leaders pledged cooperation in solving the problem of unauthorized migration from Mexico to the United States. A series of high-level meetings, including presidential summits, began to outline a set of policies to be adopted by both countries. Mexico would enhance border controls to dissuade its nationals from exiting the country illegally, while the United States would provide a mechanism through which Mexicans could enter as temporary workers or regularize their status within the United States or both. Called "earned legalization," the idea was that Mexicans who had been working in the United States and paying their taxes had proven themselves worthy of regularization.

* * *

The negotiations between the United States and Mexico came to an almost complete halt after the terrorist attacks of September 11. * * * Attention turned instead to legislative and administrative actions to ensure that foreign terrorists did not pose a danger to the United States. Action focused on four principal issues: issuance of visas to terrorists, tracking foreign nationals in the United States, bars on entry and removal of suspected terrorists, and organizational roles and responsibilities.

* * *

In the aftermath of the attacks, the State Department took steps to tighten issuance of visas. All applicants from countries where visas were required had to come to embassies and consulates for a hearing. Most of the terrorists had obtained their visas in Saudi Arabia, where an expedited process had waived an interview for many applicants. * * *

A second prong of the response to 9/11 focused on identifying terrorists who might still be in the country. In the days following September 11, the government detained more than one thousand foreign nationals from Arab and other Muslim countries that have been linked to terrorism. Most of the detainees were found to have no ties to terrorist organizations. More than 750 were turned over to the Immigration and Nationalism Service, though, because they were found to have violated immigration laws. * * *

The administration then introduced a new registration system for nationals of more than 30 countries that are largely Arabic or Muslim, the National Security Entry-Exit Registration System (NSEERS). NSEERS was composed of a registration program conducted at various ports of entry and a special registration program for certain foreign nationals already in the county.

* * * Critics of the program were especially concerned about the targeting of Arab and Muslim foreign nationals for registration. * * *

Recognizing the controversy surrounding the special registration provisions, the administration moved forward with a universal entry-exit program, which had been mandated in IIRIRA but postponed because of the fears of businesses along the border between the United States and Canada that it would impede commerce. US-Visit (United States Visitor and Immigrant Status Indicator Technology) allowed the automated capture of basic information about each arriving and departing passenger. All arriving foreign visitors would have their photograph and fingerprints taken upon arrival and departure. The system would be introduced at air and sea ports of entry and then extended to the land ports of entry, which had far more crossing each day. As of this writing, US-Visit is operational on entry but exit controls have still not been introduced.

Because several hijackers had received student visas, movement in introducing a tracking system of foreign students and exchange visitors also accelerated. The Student and Exchange Visitor Information System (SEVIS) became operational in 2003. Schools report electronically to the Department of Homeland Security on the arrival of foreign students and exchange visitors and on the students' and visitors' change of address, changes in program of study, and other pertinent information.

The third area receiving post 9/11 attention related to bars on entry and grounds for removal of persons suspected of being foreign terrorists. * * *

The USA Patriot Act, passed after September 11, expanded the definition of terrorist activity [and] * * * expanded the grounds for detaining aliens who were barred from entering or could be removed because of suspected terrorist activities or membership.

* * *

Complicating the situation was the bar imposed by the USA Patriot Act on the admission of foreign nationals who provided material support to terrorist organizations. Terrorist organizations are defined broadly to include "groups of two or more individuals, whether organized or not," which engage in proscribed activities. There is no exception for providing material support under duress, which is particularly problematic for refugees. Even minimal support is prohibited. * * * The legislation permits admission only if the secretary of state and secretary of homeland security specifically waive the application of the material support bar.[i]

As applied, the law has had an unintended effect. The bar also applies to organizations that are working to overthrow governments that the United States has opposed militarily. * * *

In the aftermath of September 11, serious discussion of immigration reform languished in the United States although some progress was made in achieving agreements with Canada and Mexico on border security strategies. The summit of the Americas held in Monterrey, Mexico, January 12–13, 2004, provided the opportunity for President Bush to return to the issue of immigration reform. Less than a week before the summit, he unveiled his proposal for a new temporary worker program, titled the "Fair and Secure Immigration Reform." * * *

---

[i]   Either official can grant the waiver, after appropriate interagency consultation.—eds.

* * * Harsh public criticism of his plan came from both liberal and conservative camps, effectively blocking any comprehensive immigration reform.

* * *

Several legislative alternatives to President Bush's temporary worker proposal were introduced but not enacted. * * * Two bills, had bipartisan sponsorship in Congress. AgJOBS, was the principal legislative effort to reform the system for admitting temporary agricultural workers. * * *

The DREAM Act (Development, Relief, and Education for Alien Minors Act), * * * sought to facilitate the entry into institutions of higher education of those illegal immigrant minors who have obtained a high-school diploma. * * *

Despite their bipartisan support, AgJOBS and the DREAM Act languished as Congress considered more far-reaching reform. In the 109th Congress, the Senate and the House of Representatives took very different approaches to the issue. The House focused primarily on enhanced enforcement while the Senate tried for comprehensive reform. * * *

As the prospects for federal reform diminished, a number of states and localities took action to address what they perceived as the growing problem of illegal immigration. The National Council of State Legislators documented the trend: "State laws related to immigration have increased dramatically in recent years: In 2005, 300 bills were introduced and 38 laws were enacted. In 2006, activity doubled: 570 bills were introduced and 84 laws were enacted. In 2007, activity tripled: 1,562 bills were introduced and 240 laws were enacted." Some of these laws attempt to implement at the state level provisions that were debated at the federal level. For example, in 2008, nineteen laws were enacted in thirteen states to enforce sanctions against employers who hire unauthorized workers and to impose employment eligibility verification requirements and penalties.

Perhaps the most controversy was generated by an Arizona law (S.B. 1070) "requiring that a [law enforcement] officer make a reasonable attempt to determine the immigration status of a person stopped, detained or arrested if there is a reasonable suspicion that the person is unlawfully present in the United States, and requiring verification of the immigration status of any person arrested prior to releasing that person." The law, enacted in April 2010, further made it a criminal act if an unauthorized immigrant sought employment or failed to carry federal alien registration documents. It also allowed warrantless arrests "where there is probable cause to believe the person has committed a public offense that makes the person removable from the United States." And the legislation allowed people to sue local government or agencies if they believe the law is not being enforced. S.B. 1070 followed other Arizona initiatives to curb illegal immigration, including legislation that required employers in the state to use the E–Verify program[j] to determine authorization to work and made it a state offense to knowingly hire an unauthorized immigrant.

In signing the law, the Arizona governor called it a "tool for our state to use as we work to solve a crisis we did not create and the federal government has refused to fix." Proponents of the legislation cited what they described as increasing crime and border violence related to illegal immigration. The law was condemned immediately by civil rights and other groups that feared it would lead to racial and ethnic profiling. The governor's assurances that law enforcement could be trusted to implement the law in a nondiscriminatory manner did little to quell these concerns. The law was also criticized as an overreaction to concerns about border violence and crime, with opponents pointing out the crime rates had actually gone down in Arizona. Law enforcement officials were split, some favoring the legislation and others concerned that it would drive a wedge between the police and the communities they served. A number of legal suits followed, * * * [and] a federal judge enjoined Arizona from implementing several provisions of law * * * .

Just a few years after the liberalizing reforms of the Immigration Act of 1990 were enacted, immigration was in crisis. The country reacted with ambivalence. Public backlash against illegal immigration fueled efforts such as Proposition 187, but economic and humanitarian interests kept the back door open. The tension inherent in these two positions led to a return to the Virginia model. Foreign workers would be tolerated, even encouraged, but within restrictive frameworks that often precluded full membership in American society. An underclass of undocumented immigrants would pick the crops, process the food, garden and landscape, construct homes, manufacture garments, clean homes, take care of children and the elderly, and provide myriad other services. The immigrants benefited from higher wages than they could expect at home but were without the legal protections afforded to citizens in the labor market. Middle-and upper-class Americans benefited from having a workforce willing and able to do these jobs at low wages and under working conditions that most Americans would not accept.

At the same time, industries employing highly skilled workers benefited from the growth in temporary worker programs. A broken permanent immigration system could not keep up with demand for foreign science, information technology, and engineering professions.

---

[j] Employers use an internet link to a federal database to determine whether a new employee is authorized to work.—eds.

Rather than fix the permanent program to benefit from this human capital, Congress repeatedly tinkered with the H–1B program, increasing numbers and allowing workers to remain tied to an employer for longer and longer periods. As of July 2010, second-preference applicants (that is, persons with advanced degrees) from India and China must have applied before October 2005 because of large backlogs. The waiting times for family reunification for adult children of U.S. citizens, spouses, and minor children of Mexican legal permanent residents, and siblings of U.S. citizens, were even longer.[k]

The Massachusetts model also had a resurgence in the aftermath of the World Trade Center bombings in 1993 and 2001. Although most of the impetus for the 1996 Anti-Terrorism legislation was the Oklahoma bombings that were carried out by native-born U.S. citizens, Congress took the opportunity to institute restrictive measures affecting the rights of immigrants. September 11 quickly led to ethnic and religious profiling in the form of the NSEERs program. With passage of the USA Patriot Act, new ideological bars to admission were adopted, the most problematic being the provisions on persons providing material support to terrorist organizations even under significant duress. With an end to the Cold War, the ideological underpinnings of the refugee program disappeared, making it the first victim of the new preoccupation with terrorism.

The Pennsylvania model is not dead, but it is under severe challenge. Permanent immigration, with a route to citizenship, remains substantial but during the first half of the 2000 decade, the increase in unauthorized migrants exceeded the net increase in legal immigrants. This situation appears to be shifting as a result of the economic recession. In 2008, net growth in the unauthorized migrant population slowed down considerably because of fewer new arrivals. Demographers have found no evidence, as of the time of this writing, that returns to Mexico (the largest sources of unauthorized migration) have increased significantly.

Public concerns about immigration have not disappeared, however. [R]ecent years have seen a proliferation of initiatives at the state and local level to curb illegal immigration. Proponents argue that the federal government has abdicated its responsibility to manage movements of people into the country, creating a vacuum to be replaced by state and local efforts to deal with unresolved issues. Moreover, systemic problems in U.S. immigration policy remain, as do the underlying causes of migration. With economic recovery, illegal immigration is likely to resume at least at the same levels as were reached in the past decade. The

---

[k] The U.S. State Department's February 2016 visa bulletin reported that the waiting list for second-preference applicants from India reached back to August 2008, while second-preference applicants from China had been waiting since March 2012. Waiting times for some Mexican family reunification applications stretched back to 1994.—eds.

question will be whether the country will resume the pro-immigration, fundamentally anti-immigrant, policies of the past fifteen years or renew the covenant with immigrants, with mutual obligations, that long characterized the Pennsylvania model.

Immigration policy and laws continue to be hotly debated in the United States. The following excerpt from a Council of Foreign Relations report summarizes significant legislative proposals and executive actions of the past few years.

DANIELLE RENWICK & BRIANNA LEE, THE U.S IMMIGRATION DEBATE

Council on Foreign Relations Background Report (2015).

U.S. immigration policy has been a touchstone of political debate for decades as policymakers consider U.S. labor demands and border security concerns. Comprehensive immigration reform has eluded Congress for years, moving decisions into the executive and judicial branches of government and pushing the debate into the halls of state and municipal governments. Meanwhile, the fates of the estimated eleven million undocumented immigrants in the country, as well as future rules for legal migration, lie in the balance.

* * *

A 2013 Gallup poll found that the majority of Americans support various elements that would comprise comprehensive immigration reform, including creating a path to citizenship for undocumented immigrants (88 percent), requiring employers to check immigration status of workers (84 percent), tightening border security (83 percent), and expanding short-term visas for skilled workers (76 percent).

Many tech-industry leaders have become prominent supporters of immigration reform, arguing their companies rely on foreign talent, particularly in high-demand STEM (science, technology, engineering, and math) fields. They argue that if skilled workers—many of whom are educated in U.S. universities—are not permitted to work in the United States, some tech companies may be forced to move their operations offshore.

Meanwhile, the demographics of undocumented immigrants [have] changed. The number of undocumented immigrants living in the United States has leveled off since the 2008 economic crisis, which led some undocumented immigrants to return to their countries of origin and reduced the arrival of new migrants. More than half of this population has lived in the country for more than a decade. Nearly one third of undocumented immigrants in the United States are the parents of U.S.-born children, according to the Pew Research Center.

"[The United States' undocumented immigrant] population is not growing—it's more settled," says [Council on Foreign Relations] Senior Fellow Edward Alden. "Increasingly, people who are coming are Central Americans fleeing violence and seeking asylum—not Mexicans seeking work—and that's a very different policy problem. But I don't think Congress has caught up with that. The debate and the approaches still reflect the world of a decade ago."

* * *

IMMIGRATION REFORM LEGISLATION

* * * In June 2013, the Senate passed a comprehensive immigration reform bill [by a vote of 68–32] with bipartisan support. The bill would have provided a path to citizenship for undocumented immigrants in the country as well as tough border security provisions. But Speaker John Boehner (R-OH) did not put it before a vote in the House of Representatives.

Lawmakers have also offered piecemeal approaches to immigration reform. Legislation that Congress is considering includes:

- *Immigration Innovation Act:* A bipartisan bill introduced in the Senate in January 2015 that would nearly double the number of visas for temporary high-skilled workers, from 65,000 to 115,000, and eliminate annual per-country limits for employment-based green cards.

- *Start-Up Act:* A bipartisan bill introduced in the Senate in January 2015 (three prior versions had been introduced) that proposed creating an entrepreneurs' visa for immigrants and a STEM visa for U.S.-educated workers with advanced degrees in science, technology, engineering or mathematics, and eliminating per-country caps on employment-based immigration visas.

- *Secure Our Borders First Act*: A Republican bill that threatens penalties against senior Department of Homeland Security (DHS) officials whose departments fail to intercept a targeted number of crossings. The proposal would allow the Border Patrol to operate on all federal lands, provide funding for the National Guard to participate in securing the border, and authorize expanded use of surveillance drones along the border.

EXECUTIVE AUTHORITY

In light of congressional impasses, President Obama has resorted to executive action on immigration reform. In June 2012, Obama announced that the federal government would no longer deport undocumented immigrants who came to the United States before the age of sixteen and were younger than thirty at the time of the announcement, had been in the country for five continuous years, and had no criminal history. The executive action, known as the Deferred Action for Childhood Arrivals, or DACA, applied to an estimated 1.7 million people, granting them renewable two-year deportation deferrals and work permits. [By late 2015, approximately 700,000 people had obtained deferred action under this program.] The executive action was inspired by the Development, Relief, and Education for Alien Minors Act, known as the DREAM Act, a bill first introduced in 2001 that [passed the House in 2010 and won majority support in the Senate—but did not have enough votes to survive a filibuster].

In November 2014, shortly after the Republican Party took control of the Senate in midterm elections and prospects for a congressional vote on immigration reform waned, Obama announced a second executive action: the Immigration Accountability Executive Action, also known as Deferred Action for Parents of Americans, or DAPA. The move would affect as many as five million people, including an estimated four million undocumented immigrants who are the parents of U.S. citizens, deferring deportation and allowing them to work legally for three years. Those applying for this status would have to pass background checks. The executive action also [ended] Secure Communities, a 2008 program that * * * [involved the sharing of the fingerprints of local] arrestees with the federal Immigration and Customs Enforcement agency to examine their status and criminal history for possible deportation. [Under the replacement Priority Enforcement Program, such fingerprints, when sent to the FBI, are still immediately checked against DHS databases, but ICE is directed to initiate enforcement action through this channel only against those who are convicted of felonies or serious misdemeanors.]

* * *

Many in Congress lambasted the [DAPA] move, saying the president did not have legal authority to carry it out. Twenty-six states, led by Texas, sued the administration, alleging the president failed to enforce federal law and placed new financial burdens on the states. * * * On February 16, [2015], a federal judge in Texas placed an injunction against the executive order, delaying the expansion of DACA, which had been scheduled to enter into force that week. The administration has appealed to lift that injunction. [The Supreme Court granted certiorari in January 2016 and is expected to issue its decision in June.]

STATE AND LOCAL IMMIGRATION POLICIES

While immigration law is controlled at the federal level, states and cities vary widely in how they enforce federal immigration laws. In September 2013, California enacted some of the most immigrant-friendly policies on the books: Undocumented immigrants are eligible to apply for drivers' licenses, practice law, and receive in-state tuition at universities. Legal permanent residents may sit on juries and monitor polls, although they cannot vote.

At the other end of the spectrum, Arizona passed SB 1070 in April 2010, which made it illegal for immigrants not to carry their documents and authorized police to detain people they "reasonably" suspect are unauthorized.[1] * * * [S]everal other states have approved or considered similar legislation.

Existing laws are not enforced or implemented uniformly across the states, resulting [in] an uneven patchwork of standards. For example, the use of E–Verify, an electronic system used by businesses to verify employees' immigration statuses, varies widely across the country; the federal government has not passed a mandate for states [or most employers] to participate. Sixteen states have mandated its use by state agencies and [certain] employers, while California prohibits local municipalities from enforcing its use. [Meantime voluntary use of E–Verify by employers is steadily expanding.]

Cities have also taken some immigration-related policies into their own hands. In 2014, New York City limited its police's cooperation with federal authorities in deporting immigrants. Local law enforcement in New York City will now only cooperate with immigration authorities when the immigrants in question have committed a "violent or serious crime." Philadelphia, San Diego, Newark, Chicago, and Los Angeles have similar ordinances. In 2007, New Haven, CT, became the first city in the United States to offer municipal identification cards without requiring proof of immigration status. Several other cities, including New York City, Los Angeles, San Francisco, and Washington, DC, have followed suit.

* * *

PROSPECTS FOR COMPREHENSIVE REFORM

Given political polarization in Congress, particularly in the House of Representatives, prospects for legislation on immigration are dim, experts say. * * *

---

[1] The U.S. Supreme Court struck down three of the four major provisions of SB 1070. *Arizona v. United States,* 567 U.S. ___, 132 S.Ct. 2492, 183 L.2d.2d 351 (2012), discussed in Chapter Ten.—eds.

Talk of comprehensive reform in Congress has diminished. "If anything happens it will happen in pieces," Alden says. "I'm not particularly optimistic that anything will happen legislatively, but if it does it will be piecemeal."

In the meantime, the fates of millions of immigrants may lie with the courts as the Obama administration appeals the federal court decision [on DAPA].

———————

During the fall of 2015, the primary campaigns for the 2016 Republican presidential nomination unleashed intemperate anti-immigrant rhetoric from Donald Trump and several other candidates. Democratic candidates responded with ideas for expanding deferred action programs, plus further selective limits on enforcement. The ongoing civil war in Syria led to the arrival of almost one million asylum seekers in Europe in 2015, and to a modest 10,000 person increase in the U.S. refugee resettlement total planned for 2016. After terrorist attacks in Paris in November 2015, a majority of state governors objected to the resettlement of Syrian refugees in their states, though many other states continued to welcome refugees. Public pressure plus litigation later caused some of the objecting governors to relent. The December 2015 terrorist attack in San Bernardino, California, which involved a Pakistani citizen who had entered the United States on a fiancée visa, intensified security concerns. Calls to strengthen the screening of applicants for visas and visa waivers multiplied, as did criticisms of the U.S. government for failure to track noncitizens who overstay their visas. Ron Nixon, *U.S. Uncertain Of How Many Overstay Visas*, N. Y. Times, Jan. 2, 2016 at A1. In light of the more than 170 million[1] admissions of tourists, students, and other temporary visitors to the United States annually, *see* Katie Forman & Randall Monger, *Nonimmigrant Admissions to the United States: 2013*, DHS Office of Immigration Statistics (July 2014), this is a huge undertaking.

NOTES AND QUESTIONS ON U.S. IMMIGRATION HISTORY

1. Based on these readings, list the factors that have most shaped the immigration policy of the United States. What role do you think the economy has played? What about political ideas? Race, religion, and ethnic background? National security concerns? To what extent are the factors affecting migration different today from those a century ago?

2. The excerpts indicate that throughout the history of immigration to the United States, economic and social considerations have motivated many

———————

[1] The statistics reflect arrivals, not individuals; many individuals enter the United States multiple times within a year.

policy decisions. Frequently, however, their influences have been diametrically opposed to each other, as when the economic need for labor conflicted with restrictionist social concerns. How has the United States generally responded to these opposing perspectives on immigration?

3. The last paragraph of the Martin reading describes the Pennsylvania model as a covenant with immigrants, embodying mutual obligations. How do undocumented migrants fit that model? One can imagine many different versions of the respective obligations, but if a particular polity so chose, wouldn't the Pennsylvania model be consistent with a strong insistence that newcomers observe the nation's laws?

4. If the Pennsylvania model emphasizes the mutual agreement between the would-be immigrant and the United States, what is (or should be) the content of the agreement? Does the immigrant agree to anything more than observing the laws of the United States? Is there an implicit assumption, though no explicit requirement, that the immigrant will eventually become an American citizen? Is there an assumption that current citizens are free at any time to revoke the right of noncitizens to remain?

5. In order to become citizens, immigrants have historically been required to show some level of assimilation, by demonstrating proficiency in English and general civic knowledge. Should a showing of assimilation be required before an individual naturalizes? What about before a person is granted permanent residence? What are the justifications for a focus on assimilation in the naturalization process? What, if any, negative consequences might flow from a decision to de-emphasize assimilation?

6. As described further in Chapter Five, the terminology used to describe people who migrate from one society to another can be confusing, inconsistent, and offensive. The Immigration and Nationality Act uses the term "alien" to refer to all individuals, including those who live here permanently and lawfully, who are not citizens or nationals of the United States. We prefer the term "noncitizen," and will generally use that instead. In addition to being a less emotionally laden term, it emphasizes the importance of the concept of citizenship, the topic we turn to in Chapter Two.

7. Interested readers will find a wealth of additional informative and insightful treatments of American immigration history and policy in Louis DeSipio & Rodolfo O. de la Garza, U.S. Immigration in the Twenty-First Century: Making Americans, Remaking America (2015); Kunai M. Parker, Making Foreigners: Immigration and Citizenship Law in America, 1600–2000 (2015); Hiroshi Motomura, Immigration Outside the Law (2014); Susan F. Martin, A Nation of Immigrants (2010); Mary C. Waters & Reed T. Ueda (eds.), The New Americans: A Guide to Immigration Since 1965 (2007); Daniel Kanstroom, Deportation Nation: Outsiders in American History (2007); Hiroshi Motomura, Americans in Waiting: The Lost Story of Immigration and Citizenship in the United States (2006); Aristide R. Zolberg, A Nation by Design: Immigration Policy in the Fashioning of America (2006); Mae M. Ngai, Impossible Subjects: Illegal Aliens and the Making of Modern

America (2004); Roger Daniels, Guarding the Golden Door: American Immigration Policy and Immigrants Since 1882 (2004); Desmond S. King, Making Americans: Immigration, Race, and the Origins of the Diverse Democracy (2002); Douglas S. Massey, Jorge Durand & Nolan J. Malone, Beyond Smoke And Mirrors: Mexican Immigration In An Era Of Economic Integration (2002); Daniel J. Tichenor, Dividing Lines: The Politics of Immigration Control in America (2002); Roger Daniels, Coming to America: History of Immigration and Ethnicity in American Life (2d ed. 2002); Charles Hirschman, Philip Kasinitz & Josh DeWind (eds.), The Handbook of International Migration: The American Experience (1999); David M. Reimers, Still the Golden Door: The Third World Comes to America (2d ed. 1992); Michael C. LeMay, From Open Door to Dutch Door: An Analysis of U.S. Immigration Policy Since 1820 (1987); Thomas Muller & Thomas J. Espenshade, The Fourth Wave: California's Newest Immigrants (1985); Oscar Handlin, The Uprooted (2d ed. 1973); Maldwyn A. Jones, American Immigration (1960); John W. Higham, Strangers in the Land: Patterns of American Nativism, 1860–1925 (1955).

B. IMMIGRANTS IN THE UNITED STATES TODAY

The history of immigration to the United States reveals that the legal framework alternately encouraged and discouraged immigration, and it clearly encouraged and discouraged some immigrant groups more than others.

The first set of graphs reveals dramatic shifts in the numbers of immigrants admitted, their percentage of the U.S. population, and the countries from which they came during the past two centuries. Figure 1.1 reports the number of legal immigrants who have been admitted to the United States each year since 1820.

Figure 1.1
Legal Immigration to the United States,
1820–Present

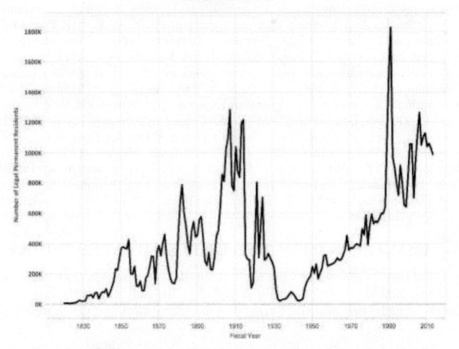

Source: Originally published on the Migration Policy Institute Data Hub,
www.migrationinformation.org/programs/data-hub/us-immigration-trends.

Figure 1.2 displays both the number of foreign-born individuals living in the United States and their percentage of the population. Thus, it is possible to identify readily both the absolute number of immigrants and how much of the population of the United States consisted of immigrants at any particular time. In 1850 the roughly two million foreign-born residents constituted 10 percent of the total population of the country. By 1870, the foreign-born population had doubled to five million, and they made up 15 percent of the U.S. population. One hundred years later, in 1970, ten million foreign-born residents constituted less than 4 percent of the total population. Today, the absolute number—42 million—of immigrants is high, and the percentage of the foreign-born is nearing the peaks experienced at the turn of the 20th century.

Figure 1.2
U.S. Immigrant Population and
Share over Time, 1850–Present

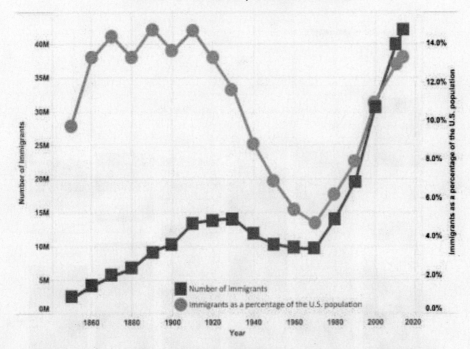

Source: Originally published on the Migration Policy Institute Data Hub,
www.migrationpolicy.org/programs/data-hub/charts/immigrant-population-over-time.

Figure 1.3 shows how the countries of origin have varied, with the diversity of immigrants changing over time. Before 1960, immigrants from three or four countries made up more than half of all immigrants. By 2000–2009, one must include thirteen source countries to account for fifty percent of the immigrants.

Figure 1.3
Top Sending Countries
(Comprising at Least Half of All LPRs): Selected Periods

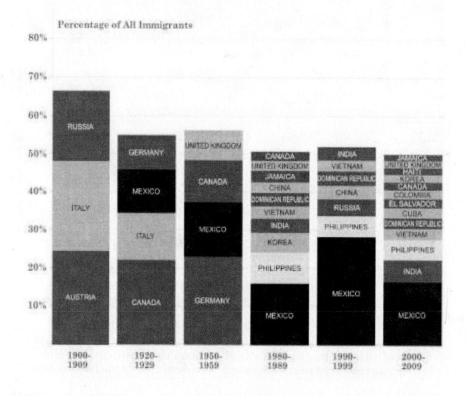

Source: U.S. DHS Yearbook of Immigration Statistics. Table 2 (2013).

Figure 1.4, from U.S. census data, reflects the U.S. population's views of their own immigrant heritage. For example, 48 million Americans reported that they had German heritage, more than claimed either Irish or British forebears, while 34 million looked to Mexican roots, and 4.4 million reported Chinese ancestry. (Respondents could list more than one country.) The right-hand column reports the number of current U.S. residents who were born in the listed country.

Figure 1.4
Estimates of the Top 20 Diaspora Groups
in the United States, 2011

Rank	Origin	Diaspora	Foreign Born
1	Germany	48,088,000	608,000
2	Ireland	39,285,000	133,000
3	Mexico	34,824,000	11,673,000
4	United Kingdom	33,243,000	685,000
5	Italy	17,433,000	374,000 .
6	Poland	9,472,000	462,000
7	France	8,635,000	161,000
8	Puerto Rico	5,410,000	1,602,000
9	Netherlands	4,462,000	81,000
10	China	4,398,000	1,866,000
11	Norway	4,391,000	27,000
12	Sweden	4,036,000	48,000
13	Philippines	3,627,000	1,814,000
14	India	3,472,000	1,857,000
15	Canada	3,176,000	786,000
16	El Salvador	2,271,000	1,265,000
17	Cuba	2,121,000	1,095,000
18	Vietnam	1,999,000	1,259,000
19	Korea	1,825,000	1,083,000
20	Dominican Republic	1,751,000	897,000

Source: Originally published on the Migration Policy Institute Data Hub, www.migrationinformation.org/programs/data-hub/us-immigration-trends#Diaspora.

Figure 1.5 highlights the countries from which the greatest numbers of new lawful permanent residents originate, showing the changes over roughly a decade. There is a diverse group of source countries, with no country, other than Mexico, contributing more than six or seven percent of the annual flow of immigrants. Note that, for this particular period, the source countries did not change in ranking, but the numbers and percentages of new immigrants have shifted.

Figure 1.5
New Lawful Permanent Residents by Country of Birth,
2000 and 2013

2000				2013			
Rank	Country of Birth	Number	Percent	Rank	Country of Birth	Number	Percent
1	Mexico	173,919	20.5	1	Mexico	135,028	13.6
2	China, People's Republic	45,652	5.4	2	China, People's Republic	71,798	7.2
3	Philippines	42,474	5.0	3	Philippines	68,458	6.9
4	India	42,046	4.9	4	India	54,446	5.5
5	Vietnam	26,747	3.1	5	Vietnam	41,311	4.2
6	Nicaragua	24,029	2.8	6	Nicaragua	32,219	3.3
7	El Salvador	22,578	2.7	7	El Salvador	27,101	2.7
8	Haiti	22,364	2.6	8	Haiti	23,166	2.3
9	Cuba	20,831	2.5	9	Cuba	21,131	2.1
10	Dominican Republic	17,536	2.1	10	Dominican Republic	20,351	2.1

Source: U.S. DHS Yearbook of Immigration Statistics, Table 3 (2013); U.S. DOJ Statistical Yearbook of the Immigration and Naturalization Service, Table 3 (2000).

Figure 1.6 illustrates the birthplaces of the total foreign-born population in the United States as of 2014. Mexico accounts for almost 30 percent, India for 5 percent, with the Philippines and China close behind at 4.5 percent each. Vietnam, El Salvador, and Cuba each constitutes 3 percent, followed by the Dominican Republic, Korea and Guatemala. These five Latin American countries and five Asian countries together comprise close to 60 percent of the current foreign-born population. In rough terms, 45 percent of the foreign-born have become citizens via the naturalization process. Another 30 percent are present in lawful status, and 25 percent are in unauthorized status. A small fraction, born abroad of U.S. citizen parents, have been citizens since birth.

Figure 1.6
Top 10 Largest U.S. Immigrant Groups
by Birthplace, 2014

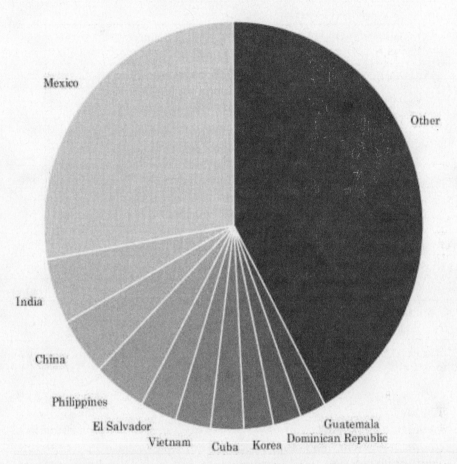

Source: Originally published on the Migration Policy Institute Data Hub,
www.migrationpolicy.org/programs/data-hub/us-immigration-trends#source.

CHAPTER TWO

CITIZENSHIP

• • •

Membership in a nation state is fundamental to protection under international law. States have laws defining who are full members—citizens—and who are not. The populations of states, of course, include many who are not citizens. These individuals, particularly if they are long-time residents, may also have large stakes in the society. Although not full members, they also claim legal rights and opportunities. Thus, the laws of immigration necessarily raise questions of membership and are inextricably linked to laws defining citizenship.

In this book we use two different schemes to represent membership. One model is represented by concentric circles: citizens form the innermost membership ring, with categories of noncitizens (residents, visitors, unauthorized migrants, aliens seeking entry) filling in outer rings. Under this representation, membership rights are assigned by category. The other model is chronological (or horizontal): immigrants begin the process (usually) by receiving a visa overseas, entering the United States, establishing residence and ultimately obtaining citizenship. Rights and opportunities (the privileges of membership) might be understood to accumulate over time as one moves along the process.

In identifying these two perspectives, we do not mean to imply that they necessarily define different conceptions of membership; we present them simply as heuristics. We think they help explain the basic themes and organization of this book. In a number of chapters, we will be looking at the concentric circles, asking what follows from being in one circle or another in terms of rights, benefits, and obligations. In other chapters we will be pursuing the chronological model by examining the rules for entry, residence, and removal of immigrants.

We start in this chapter with the topic at the core of the first model: the question of citizenship. We consider first the various ways by which individuals become citizens.

A. ACQUISITION OF NATIONALITY BY BIRTH

Two basic principles for the acquisition of nationality at birth are known to international practice: the *jus soli*, literally right of land or ground—conferral of nationality based on birth within the national territory; and the *jus sanguinis,* or right of blood—the conferral of nationality based on descent, irrespective of the place of birth. Anglo-American nationality law is fundamentally based on the *jus soli,* although both principles have played a role in the transmission of United States citizenship ever since the first nationality statute was passed. Act of March 26, 1790, Ch. 3, 1 Stat. 103.

Virtually all persons in the world possess citizenship of some state, and the vast majority acquired their citizenship at birth. In establishing birthright citizenship, polities effectively yield basic decisions about membership to the private decisions and acts of their populations. It might be thought sensible for a political community to grant children of citizens a provisional citizenship that ripens into full membership at the age of majority if certain criteria are met. But we are aware of no country that has taken this route. Why might this be so?

1. *JUS SANGUINIS*

a. Overview

We normally think of citizenship as a status of enormous significance. Chief Justice Warren described citizenship as "nothing less than the right to have rights." *Perez v. Brownell*, 356 U.S. 44, 64, 78 S.Ct. 568, 2 L.Ed.2d 603 (1958) (dissenting opinion). And the Supreme Court has stated that "[i]t would be difficult to exaggerate [the] value and importance" of American citizenship: "by many it is regarded as the highest hope of civilized men." *Schneiderman v. United States*, 320 U.S. 118, 122, 63 S.Ct. 1333, 87 L.Ed. 1796 (1943).

Yet the Constitution, as initially drafted, included no definition of citizenship. It is clear that the framers believed that the status had some significance: citizenship was made a qualification for the Presidency and election to Congress; and Congress was given the authority to adopt "an uniform Rule of Naturalization." But the original Constitution left unanswered basic questions about the acquisition, distribution and loss of citizenship and what rights pertained to citizenship. The *jus soli* principle, embodied in common law, statutes, and ultimately in the Fourteenth Amendment to the U.S. Constitution, has been the major mode of birthright citizenship in the United States, and will be discussed in greater detail below. Less noticed, U.S. law has also adopted the *jus sanguinis* approach to transmitting citizenship at birth.

The first Congress, at its second session, adopted legislation extending U.S. citizenship to children born abroad to U.S. citizen fathers. Act of March 26, 1790, Ch. 3, 1 Stat. 103. This transmission of U.S. nationality *jure sanguinis* to children born abroad to American parents can be considered a form of birthright citizenship; the children do not apply for naturalization or go through a naturalization proceeding because they are citizens at birth. In light of the absence of any definition of citizenship in the U.S. Constitution ratified in 1789, what authority did Congress have to adopt *jus sanguinis* rules for children born abroad? *See Rogers v. Bellei*, 401 U.S. 815, 823, 827–31, 91 S.Ct. 1060, 28 L.Ed.2d 499 (1971).

The current *jus sanguinis* rules are set forth in INA §§ 301(c), (d), (e), (g), (h); 308(2), (4); and 309. The most important relate to children born outside U.S. territory to parents either one or both of whom are U.S. citizens. If both are citizens, the child acquires citizenship at birth, provided only that one of the parents had a residence in the United States at some time prior thereto. INA § 301(c).[1] *See Weedin v. Chin Bow*, 274 U.S. 657, 47 S.Ct. 772, 71 L.Ed. 1284 (1927) (parental residence must precede birth of the child). If one parent is a noncitizen, however, then the citizen parent must have been physically present in the United States for a total of five years before the birth, including at least two years after the age of fourteen. Certain kinds of government and military service abroad count as physical presence in the United States for these purposes. INA § 301(g).

Congress has amended the *jus sanguinis* statutes on multiple occasions, and, in general, the law at the time of birth is the one that governs. To determine whether a person born outside the territorial jurisdiction is a United States citizen, therefore, it is not enough to consult the present INA, unless of course the birth occurred after enactment of the latest amendments. One must check carefully the precise requirements in effect at the time of the birth of the individual in question, and also see whether any requirements for later residence in the United States have been fulfilled. *See, e.g., Runnett v. Shultz*, 901 F.2d 782 (9th Cir.1990). For summaries of the relevant rules, broken down by date of birth, *see* USCIS Policy Manual—Nationality Charts 1–4, http://www.uscis.gov/policymanual/PDF/NationalityChart1.pdf (showing rules that apply to legitimate and illegitimate children [Charts 1 & 2], derivative citizenship [Chart 3] and children of U.S. citizens regularly residing abroad [Chart 4]).

b. Physical Presence in the United States

From the beginning, Congress has sought to avoid the creation of a class of expatriates who may transmit U.S. citizenship to their children

---

[1] The statute provides that the term "residence" means "the place of general abode; the place of general abode of a person means his principal, actual dwelling place in fact, without regard to intent." INA § 101(a)(33). This objective test of residence was adopted in reaction to administrative rulings which had found that even temporary sojourn in the United States, lasting no more than a few days, might fulfill the parental residence requirements of earlier statutes. *See, e.g., Matter of E-*, 1 I. & N. Dec. 40 (AG 1941); *Matter of V-*, 6 I. & N. Dec. 1 (AG 1953).

indefinitely, even though the family has had no close contact with actual life in the United States for generations. The issue has been what type of contact, on the part of the parents or the child, should be required.

Congress has employed two principal means toward this end. First, U.S. citizen parents lacking a specified period of historical residence in the United States have been unable to transmit citizenship to their children. Second, from 1934 until 1978, the child had to establish his or her own residence or extended physical presence in the United States for a specified number of years within stated periods, or else lose the citizenship acquired at birth. This rule applied to children born abroad when one of the child's parents was not a U.S. citizen. The length of residence and the ages during which residence had to be established—for parent or child—have been altered several times.

The first type of limitation, concerning parental residence before the child's birth, has raised few constitutional issues, and, as noted, remains part of current law. The second came under attack after *Afroyim v. Rusk,* 387 U.S. 253, 87 S.Ct. 1660, 18 L.Ed.2d 757 (1967), imposed strict constitutional limits on the power of Congress to deprive persons of U.S. citizenship involuntarily. But the Supreme Court, by a vote of five to four, eventually held that Congress retained the power to impose such a residence requirement as a "condition subsequent" on persons who are U.S. citizens by virtue of their birth abroad to one U.S. citizen parent. *Rogers v. Bellei,* 401 U.S. 815, 91 S.Ct. 1060, 28 L.Ed.2d 499 (1971). At the time of *Bellei*, the statute required the citizen *jure sanguinis* to be physically present in the United States for five years between the ages of 14 and 28, or else lose U.S. citizenship.

Despite the judicial endorsement of this type of post-acquisition residence requirement, Congress chose in 1978 to remove all such provisions from the immigration laws. Current law therefore relies solely on *parental* residence requirements to avoid the indefinite perpetuation of U.S. citizenship *jure sanguinis* within families that realistically have lost touch with their American roots. This change has considerably simplified the operation of current *jus sanguinis* rules, but Congress, as has been its usual (though not universal) practice when amending the citizenship rules, did not make its amendment retroactive. Persons who had already lost their citizenship under the earlier residency requirements thus remain denationalized, and those who did not acquire citizenship under the rules extant on the date of birth usually cannot benefit from later statutory liberalization.

Congress clearly aims to forestall the transmission of U.S. citizenship to multiple generations of families who have not maintained some physical connection with the territory of the United States. Do you think this is an appropriate goal?

If you think that there may be valid reasons to limit the role of *jus sanguinis* in some instances when children are born abroad, would you change the statutory scheme? Here are a few alternatives to consider:

- a rule that citizenship can be transmitted only to the first generation of persons born to U.S. citizens outside the United States (this is the rule in Mexico);

- a rule re-establishing the requirement that a person born outside the United States reside for some period of time in the United States in order to retain U.S. citizenship;

- a rule requiring that persons born to U.S. citizens abroad register with U.S. authorities at the age of majority in order to maintain (or attain?) U.S. citizenship;

- a rule mandating that a person having two nationalities based on birth abroad to U.S. citizen parents elect one or the other citizenship at the age of majority.

Turning from the rules adopted by some other countries, take a look at the INA provisions establishing citizenship *jure sanguinis*, INA §§ 301(c), (d), (g), (h), and at the provision detailing transmission of U.S. citizenship at birth to children born out of wedlock, INA § 309. These will help you analyze the problems below.

PROBLEMS

1. Your clients, a married couple, are Presbyterian missionaries in Ukraine. They are both children of missionaries; the husband was born in Poland and the wife in the Philippines, but both acquired U.S. citizenship at birth. They are expecting a baby next month, and it will be born in Ukraine. Will the child have U.S. citizenship?

   a. Would it matter if neither of your clients has ever spent more than one academic semester in the United States? One summer vacation? *yes, must have established residency (been in us sometime)*

   b. If you learn that one of your clients went to high school in the United States but the other has never been in the country, does it matter whether it is the husband or the wife? *No.*

2. Your client was born in the United States, but his parents moved to Switzerland when he was two, and he has spent most of his life in Europe. He has been living with a French woman in Paris for the past three years, and she recently discovered that she is pregnant. The child is due in five months. This event has prompted the couple to talk more earnestly about a subject they have discussed for a long time but never acted upon: whether they should get married. They haven't yet decided. In any event he wants to make sure that the child has U.S. citizenship. *Must have been in US for 5 yrs 2 yrs at least after 14. (pg. 51)*

a. He asks whether he has to move to the United States with his fiancée to accomplish this aim. He is not sure he could even arrange this in time because she has no passport and no U.S. visa. What do you advise?

b. The couple may decide anyway to stay in France, "to be absolutely certain," he says, "that the baby has French citizenship too." Is there any way that he can arrange for the child also to have U.S. nationality if it is born in Paris? Does he have to marry the mother to accomplish this? (Think about other factual information you might have to obtain to answer his questions.)

c. How, if at all, would your analysis change if the U.S. citizen in this problem were the mother, not the father?

c. Gender Discrimination and *Jus Sanguinis*

In addition to requirements of physical presence in the United States, the *jus sanguinis* statutes have had, and continue to have, gender-based elements. Frequently these rules have disadvantaged women; sometimes they have a discriminatory impact on men. Until 1934, federal statutes explicitly discriminated against women by allowing the transmission of citizenship *jure sanguinis* only by U.S. citizen fathers, not by U.S. citizen mothers.

This was but one form of gender discrimination in citizenship law. Congress adopted legislation in 1907 providing that U.S. citizen women who married non-citizen men lost their citizenship for so long as the marriage lasted. The Supreme Court expressly approved the constitutionality of these provisions. *Mackenzie v. Hare*, 239 U.S. 299, 36 S.Ct. 106, 60 L.Ed. 297 (1915) discussed in Section C.2 *infra*. The statute was partially repealed in the 1920s, but the result persisted for some women until 1934. Importantly, the 1920s legislation did not apply to U.S. citizen women who married Asian men ineligible for naturalization; such women continued to lose their citizenship upon marriage. Furthermore, women who lost their citizenship through marriage could not regain citizenship under the later law if they were racially ineligible to naturalize.

Although this discriminatory aspect of *jus sanguinis* rules is long gone, its impact lives on. Consider the case of Valerie Wauchope. Wauchope was born in Canada in 1911. Her mother was a U.S. citizen; her father was a Canadian citizen. In 1989, she applied to the State Department for a U.S. passport. If born today, Wauchope would be a U.S. citizen (provided her mother had met the requirements of residence in the United States). But under the rules in place in 1911, she was not a citizen at birth. And when Congress eliminated the gender-based rule in 1934, it did not make the change retroactive. Accordingly, she was denied a passport. Wauchope sued and won. *Wauchope v. U.S. Dep't of State*, 985 F.2d 1407 (9th Cir.1993). The court held that the gender discrimination violated modern equal protection principles in the Fifth Amendment's due process clause, and it ruled that its holding should be applied retroactively—that is, persons who could demonstrate that they would have been citizens prior to 1934 if the *jus sanguinis* rules had been written in gender-neutral terms would be deemed to have acquired U.S. citizenship at birth.

The United States chose not to appeal the court of appeals' decision. (Solicitor General Drew S. Days later explained that the United States did not seek Supreme Court review because it was convinced that the court's decision was "consistent with modern developments in the Supreme Court's jurisprudence concerning statutory distinctions based on gender." Drew S. Days, *The Solicitor General and the American Legal Ideal*, 49 S.M.U. L. Rev. 73, 81 (1995) .) In 1994, Congress accepted the ruling and adopted rules for implementing *Wauchope*. *See* INA § 301(h). The statute allows the children of the disadvantaged U.S. citizen mothers to take advantage of the retroactive change in the rules. Citizenship can be transmitted to future generations if the first generation mother has met the usual U.S. residence requirements.

In contrast to the *Wauchope* case, most of the more recent *jus sanguinis* litigation attacks statutory provisions that disadvantage men. Section 309 of the INA extends citizenship at birth to a child born out of wedlock outside of the United States to a U.S. citizen mother (provided the mother has at some point been physically present in the U.S. for a continuous period of one year); but a child born abroad and out of wedlock to a U.S. citizen father attains citizenship only if a number of additional conditions are met: (1) a blood relationship between the person and the father must be established by clear and convincing evidence; (2) the father must have had U.S. nationality at the time of the child's birth; (3) the father must have agreed in writing to provide financial support until the child reaches 18; and (4) while the child is under 18, (a) he or she must be legitimated under the law of his or her residence or domicile; (b) the father must acknowledge paternity of the child in writing under oath; or (c) the paternity of the child must be established by court adjudication. INA § 309(a).

During the past twenty years the Supreme Court has decided two cases involving children born overseas out of wedlock to U.S. citizen fathers and noncitizen mothers. *Miller v. Albright*, 523 U.S. 420, 118 S.Ct. 1428, 140 L.Ed.2d 575 (1998) (rejecting on justiciability grounds a challenge to requirement of legitimation before child reaches age of 18); *Nguyen v. INS*, 533 U.S. 53, 121 S.Ct. 2053, 150 L.Ed.2d 115 (2001) (upholding the requirement that the father acknowledge paternity before the child reaches 18). We include excerpts from the *Nguyen* majority and dissenting opinions, followed by an excerpt from a subsequent opinion by the Second Circuit.

NGUYEN V. INS

Supreme Court of the United States, 2001.
533 U.S. 53, 121 S.Ct. 2053, 150 L.Ed.2d 115.

JUSTICE KENNEDY delivered the opinion of the court:

[Tuan Ahn Nguyen was born in Vietnam in 1969. His father, a U.S. citizen, and his mother, a Vietnamese citizen, were not married. Nguyen lived with his father, Joseph Boulais, in Texas, where he arrived as a five year old child, and became a lawful permanent resident of the United States. Years later, based on his conviction on two criminal charges, Nguyen received a deportation order. While the immigration proceedings were pending, Nguyen's father had DNA testing to prove paternity, obtained a state court declaration that he was Nguyen's parent, and sought to establish on this basis that his then-28-year-old son must be considered a U.S. citizen and therefore not deportable.

The relevant statutory provision in force at Nguyen's birth required unwed U.S. citizen fathers of children born abroad to take one of three affirmative steps—legitimation, a declaration of paternity under oath, or a court order of paternity—before the child reached eighteen, for the child to be recognized as a U.S. citizen. This requirement did not apply to unwed U.S. citizen mothers of children born overseas. Nguyen, who was 28 years old at the time his father obtained the court order of paternity, filed an equal protection challenge to the statutory provisions imposing greater requirements on unwed citizen fathers than on unwed citizen mothers.

The Court analyzed the statutes under the heightened scrutiny standard, examining both whether the challenged classification served important governmental objectives and whether the means employed by the statute were substantially related to achieving those objectives.]

The first governmental interest to be served is the importance of assuring that a biological parent-child relationship exists. In the case of the mother, the relation is verifiable from the birth itself. The mother's status is documented in most instances by the birth certificate or hospital records and the witnesses who attest to her having given birth.

In the case of the father, the uncontestable fact is that he need not be present at the birth. If he is present, furthermore, that circumstance is not incontrovertible proof of fatherhood. Fathers and mothers are not similarly situated with regard to the proof of biological parenthood. The imposition of a different set of rules for making that legal determination with respect to fathers and mothers is neither surprising nor troublesome from a constitutional perspective. Section 309(a)(4)'s provision of three options for a father seeking to establish paternity—legitimation, paternity oath, and court order of paternity—is designed to ensure an acceptable documentation of paternity.

* * *

The second important governmental interest furthered in a substantial manner by § 309(a)(4) is the determination to ensure that the child and the citizen parent have some demonstrated opportunity or potential to develop * * * real, everyday ties that provide a connection between child and citizen parent and, in turn, the United States. In the case of a citizen mother and a child born overseas, the opportunity for a meaningful relationship between citizen parent and child inheres in the very event of birth * * * . The mother knows that the child is in being and is hers and has an initial point of contact with him. There is at least an opportunity for mother and child to develop a real, meaningful relationship.

The same opportunity does not result from the event of birth, as a matter of biological inevitability, in the case of the unwed father. Given the 9-month interval between conception and birth, it is not always certain that a father will know that a child was conceived, nor is it always clear that even the mother will be sure of the father's identity. This fact takes on particular significance in the case of a child born overseas and out of wedlock. One concern in this context has always been with young people, men for the most part, who are on duty with the Armed Forces in foreign countries. [In] 1969, the year in which Nguyen was born, there were 3,458,072 active duty military personnel, 39,506 of whom were female [, and] * * * 1,041,094 military personnel were stationed in foreign countries * * * .

When we turn to the conditions which prevail today, we find that the passage of time has produced additional and even more substantial grounds to justify the statutory distinction. The ease of travel and the willingness of Americans to visit foreign countries have resulted in numbers of trips abroad that must be of real concern when we contemplate the prospect of accepting petitioners' argument, which would mandate, contrary to Congress' wishes, citizenship by male parentage subject to no condition save the father's previous length of residence in this country. In 1999 alone, Americans made almost 25 million trips abroad, excluding trips to Canada and Mexico. * * *

Principles of equal protection do not require Congress to ignore this reality. To the contrary, these facts demonstrate the critical importance of the Government's interest in ensuring some opportunity for a tie between citizen father and foreign born child which is a reasonable substitute for the opportunity manifest between mother and child at the time of birth.

Indeed, especially in light of the number of Americans who take short
sojourns abroad, the prospect that a father might not even know of the
conception is a realistic possibility. Even if a father knows of the fact of
conception, moreover, it does not follow that he will be present at the
birth of the child. Thus, unlike the case of the mother, there is no
assurance that the father and his biological child will ever meet. Without
an initial point of contact with the child by a father who knows the child
is his own, there is no opportunity for father and child to begin a
relationship. Section 309 takes the unremarkable step of ensuring that
such an opportunity, inherent in the event of birth as to the mother-child
relationship, exists between father and child before citizenship is
conferred upon the latter.

* * *

[Justice Kennedy then turned to the question of whether the means
chosen by Congress were substantially related to these governmental
objectives.]

First, it should be unsurprising that Congress decided to require that
an opportunity for a parent-child relationship occur during the formative
years of the child's minority. In furtherance of the desire to ensure some
tie between this country and one who seeks citizenship, various other
statutory provisions concerning citizenship and naturalization require
some act linking the child to the United States to occur before the child
reaches 18 years of age. *See, e.g.,* INA § 320 (child born abroad to one
citizen parent and one noncitizen parent shall become a citizen if, *inter
alia*, the noncitizen parent is naturalized before the child reaches 18
years of age and the child begins to reside in the United States before he
or she turns 18); § 321 (imposing same conditions in the case of a child
born abroad to two alien parents who are naturalized).

Second, petitioners argue that § 309(a)(4) is not effective. In
particular, petitioners assert that, although a mother will know of her
child's birth, "knowledge that one is a parent, no matter how it is
acquired, does not guarantee a relationship with one's child." They thus
maintain that the imposition of the additional requirements of § 309(a)(4)
only on the children of citizen fathers must reflect a stereotype that
women are more likely than men to actually establish a relationship with
their children.

This line of argument misconceives the nature of both the
governmental interest at issue and the manner in which we examine
statutes alleged to violate equal protection. As to the former, Congress
would of course be entitled to advance the interest of ensuring an actual,
meaningful relationship in every case before citizenship is conferred. Or
Congress could excuse compliance with the formal requirements when an
actual father-child relationship is proved. It did neither here, perhaps

because of the subjectivity, intrusiveness, and difficulties of proof that might attend an inquiry into any particular bond or tie. Instead, Congress enacted an easily administered scheme to promote the different but still substantial interest of ensuring at least an opportunity for a parent-child relationship to develop. Petitioners' argument confuses the means and ends of the equal protection inquiry; § 309(a)(4) should not be invalidated because Congress elected to advance an interest that is less demanding to satisfy than some other alternative.

* * *

The difference between men and women in relation to the birth process is a real one, and the principle of equal protection does not forbid Congress to address the problem at hand in a manner specific to each gender.

The judgment of the Court of Appeals is affirmed.

JUSTICE O'CONNOR, joined by JUSTICES SOUTER, GINSBURG and BREYER, dissented:

* * *

The gravest defect in the Court's [analysis of the first governmental objective] is the insufficiency of the fit between § 309(a)(4)'s discriminatory means and the asserted end. Section 309(c) imposes no particular burden of proof on mothers wishing to convey citizenship to their children. By contrast, § 309(a)(1), which petitioners do not challenge before this Court, requires that "a blood relationship between the person and the father [be] established by clear and convincing evidence." Atop § 309(a)(1), § 309(a)(4) requires legitimation, an acknowledgment of paternity in writing under oath, or an adjudication of paternity before the child reaches the age of 18. It is difficult to see what § 309(a)(4) accomplishes in furtherance of "assuring that a biological parent-child relationship exists," that § 309(a)(1) does not achieve on its own. The virtual certainty of a biological link that modern DNA testing affords reinforces the sufficiency of § 309(a)(1).

* * *

The majority concedes that Congress could achieve the goal of assuring a biological parent-child relationship in a sex-neutral fashion, but then, in a surprising turn, dismisses the availability of sex-neutral alternatives as irrelevant. As the Court suggests, "Congress could have required both mothers and fathers to prove parenthood within 30 days or, for that matter, 18 years, of the child's birth." Indeed, whether one conceives the majority's asserted interest as assuring the existence of a biological parent-child relationship, or as ensuring acceptable documentation of that relationship, a number of sex-neutral arrangements—including the one that the majority offers—would better serve that end. * * * . While it is doubtless true that a mother's blood relation to a child is uniquely "verifiable from the birth itself" to those present at birth, the majority has not shown that a mother's birth relation is uniquely verifiable *by the INS,* much less that any greater verifiability warrants a sex-based, rather than a sex-neutral, statute.

* * *

Assuming, as the majority does, that Congress was actually concerned about ensuring a "demonstrated opportunity" for a relationship, it is questionable whether such an opportunity qualifies as an "important" governmental interest apart from the existence of an actual relationship. By focusing on "opportunity" rather than reality, the majority presumably improves the chances of a sufficient means-end fit. But in doing so, it dilutes significantly the weight of the interest. It is difficult to see how, in this citizenship-conferral context, anyone profits from a "demonstrated opportunity" for a relationship in the absence of the fruition of an actual tie. Children who have an "opportunity" for such a tie with a parent, of course, may never develop an actual relationship with that parent. If a child grows up in a foreign country without any postbirth contact with the citizen parent, then the child's never-realized "opportunity" for a relationship with the citizen seems singularly irrelevant to the appropriateness of granting citizenship to that child. Likewise, where there is an actual relationship, it is the actual relationship that does all the work in rendering appropriate a grant of citizenship, regardless of when and how the opportunity for that relationship arose.

Accepting for the moment the majority's focus on "opportunity," the attempt to justify § 309(a)(4) in these terms is still deficient. Even if it is important "to require that an opportunity for a parent-child relationship occur during the formative years of the child's minority," it is difficult to see how the requirement that *proof* of such opportunity be obtained before the child turns 18 substantially furthers the asserted interest. As the facts of this case demonstrate, it is entirely possible that a father and child will have the opportunity to develop a relationship and in fact will develop a relationship without obtaining the proof of the opportunity during the child's minority. * * *

* * *

Moreover, available sex-neutral alternatives would at least replicate, and could easily exceed, whatever fit there is between § 309(a)(4)'s discriminatory means and the majority's asserted end. According to the Court, § 309(a)(4) is designed to ensure that fathers and children have the same "opportunity which the event of birth itself provides for the mother and child." Even assuming that this is so, Congress could simply substitute for § 309(a)(4) a requirement that the parent be present at birth or have knowledge of birth. * * *

Indeed, the idea that a mother's presence at birth supplies adequate assurance of an opportunity to develop a relationship while a father's presence at birth does not would appear to rest only on an overbroad sex-based generalization. A mother may not have an opportunity for a relationship if the child is removed from his or her mother on account of alleged abuse or neglect, or if the child and mother are separated by tragedy, such as disaster or war, of the sort apparently present in this case. There is no reason, other than stereotype, to say that fathers who are present at birth lack an opportunity for a relationship on similar terms. The "[p]hysical differences between men and women," *Virginia*, 518 U.S., at 533, therefore do not justify § 309(a)(4)'s discrimination.

* * *

The question that then remains is the sufficiency of the fit between § 309(a)(4)'s discriminatory means and the goal of "establish[ing] . . . a real, practical relationship of considerable substance." If Congress wishes to advance this end, it could easily do so by employing a sex-neutral classification that is a far "more germane bas[i]s of classification" than sex, *Craig* [*v. Boren*, 429 U.S. 190, 198 (1976)]. For example, Congress could require some degree of regular contact between the child and the citizen parent over a period of time.

* * *

* * * I respectfully dissent.

The Second Circuit revisited some of these gender discrimination issues in 2015 in *Morales-Santana v. Lynch,* 792 F.3d 256 (2d Cir. 2015), and ruled that other gender-based differences in residence requirements in the derivative citizenship context violated the Equal Protection Clause.

MORALES-SANTANA V. LYNCH
United States Court of Appeals, Second Circuit, 2015.
792 F.3d 256.

LOHIER, CIRCUIT JUDGE:

[Luis Ramon Morales-Santana was born in the Dominican Republic in 1962 to unmarried parents. His mother was a citizen of the Dominican Republic. His father had acquired U.S. citizenship in 1917 pursuant to a 1917 statute, and had lived in Puerto Rico from birth until 20 days prior to his nineteenth birthday. The immigration statutes impose different requirements on unwed citizen fathers and unwed citizen mothers who wish to pass their citizenship to their children who are born outside the United States. At the time of Morales-Santana's birth, unwed citizen fathers must have been physically present in the United States or its possessions for ten years, five of which were after the age of fourteen.[a] This meant that unwed citizen fathers below the age of nineteen were unable to transmit U.S. citizenship to their children. In contrast, unwed citizen mothers needed to have been physically present for only one year at any time prior to the child's birth. Morales-Santana's father failed to satisfy the five year requirement by 20 days.

Morales-Santana was legitimated in 1970 when his parents married. He entered the United States as a lawful permanent resident in 1975; his father died in 1976. After conviction for several felonies, Morales-Santana was placed in removal proceedings in 2000, where he argued that he was not removable because he should be considered a U.S. citizen. Both the immigration judge and the BIA rejected his arguments. In reviewing his constitutional claim, the Second Circuit examined the statutory distinctions under heightened scrutiny, requiring the government to show that the statutory distinctions were substantially related to an actual and important governmental objective. The court emphasized that a hypothetical government objective would not suffice, and that the statutes could not rely on overbroad generalizations about the preferences and abilities of men and women.]

The Government asserts that Congress passed the 1952 Act's physical presence requirements in order to "ensur[e] that foreign-born children of parents of different nationalities have a sufficient connection to the United States to warrant citizenship." * * *

The Government invokes this important interest but fails to justify the 1952 Act's different treatment of mothers and fathers by reference to it. It offers no reason * * * that unwed fathers need more time than unwed mothers in the United States prior to their child's birth in order to assimilate the values that the statute seeks to ensure are passed on to citizen children born abroad.

* * *

* * * In *Nguyen*, the Court upheld the Immigration and Nationality Act's requirement that a citizen father seeking to confer derivative citizenship on his foreign-born child take the affirmative step of either legitimating the child, declaring paternity under oath, or obtaining a court order of paternity. The *Nguyen* Court determined that two interests supported the legitimation requirement for citizen fathers of children born abroad.

---

[a]   The statute now requires a minimum of five years of physical presence, at least two of which were after the age of fourteen. INA § 301(g).—eds.

The first interest, "assuring that a biological parent-child relationship exists," is irrelevant to the 1952 Act's physical presence requirements because derivative citizenship separately requires unwed citizen fathers to have legitimated their foreign-born children. Here, Morales-Santana's father established his biological tie to Morales-Santana by legitimating him. His physical presence in Puerto Rico for ten years as opposed to one year prior to Morales-Santana's birth would have provided no additional assurance that a biological tie existed.

The *Nguyen* Court identified a second interest in ensuring "that the child and the citizen parent have some demonstrated opportunity or potential to develop" a "real, meaningful relationship." * * * This interest in ensuring the "opportunity for a real, meaningful relationship" between parent and child is likewise not relevant to the 1952 Act's physical presence requirements. By legitimating his son, Morales-Santana's father took the affirmative step of demonstrating that an opportunity for a meaningful relationship existed. And again, requiring that Morales-Santana's father be physically present in Puerto Rico prior to Morales-Santana's birth for ten years instead of one year would have done nothing to further ensure that an opportunity for such a relationship existed.

So we agree that unwed mothers and fathers are *not* similarly situated with respect to the two types of parent-to-child "ties" justifying the legitimation requirement at issue in *Nguyen*. But unwed mothers and fathers *are* similarly situated with respect to *how long* they should be present in the United States or an outlying possession prior to the child's birth in order to have assimilated citizenship-related values to transmit to the child. Therefore, the statute's gender-based distinction is not substantially related to the goal of ensuring a sufficient connection between citizen children and the United States.

[In this case the Government argues that another important interest behind the different physical presence requirements is the congressional objective] to reduce the level of statelessness among newborns. For example, a child born out of wedlock abroad may be stateless if he is born inside a country that does not confer citizenship based on place of birth and neither of the child's parents conferred derivative citizenship on him.

The avoidance of statelessness is clearly an important governmental interest. Contrary to the Government's claim, though, avoidance of statelessness does not appear to have been Congress's actual purpose in establishing the physical presence requirements in the 1952 Act, and in any event the gender-based distinctions in the 1952 Act's physical presence requirements are not substantially related to that objective.

* * *

Neither the congressional hearings nor the relevant congressional reports concerning the [earlier immigration legislation] contain any reference to the problem of statelessness for children born abroad. The congressional hearings concerning the 1952 Act are similarly silent about statelessness as a driving concern. Notwithstanding the absence of relevant discussion concerning the problem of statelessness for children born abroad in the legislative history, the Government points to the Executive Branch's explanatory comments to * * * the proposed nationality code that * * * refer to a 1935 law review article [reporting that] approximately thirty countries had statutes assigning children born out of wedlock the citizenship of their mother. * * *

* * * The explanatory comments do not mention statelessness and do not refer to the [law review] article's discussion of statelessness. In any event, the * * * article itself does not support the Government's argument that the children of unwed citizen mothers faced a greater risk of statelessness than the children of unwed citizen fathers.

In sum, we discern no evidence (1) that Congress enacted the 1952 Act's gender-based physical presence requirements out of a concern for statelessness, (2) that the problem of statelessness was in fact greater for children of unwed citizen mothers than for children of unwed citizen fathers, or (3) that Congress believed that the problem of statelessness was greater for children of unwed citizen mothers than for children of unwed citizen fathers. We conclude that neither reason nor history supports the Government's contention that the 1952 Act's gender-based physical presence requirements were motivated by a concern for statelessness, as opposed to impermissible stereotyping.

Even assuming for the sake of argument that preventing statelessness was Congress's actual motivating concern when it enacted the physical presence requirements, we are persuaded by the availability of effective gender-neutral alternatives that [this] gender-based distinction * * * cannot survive intermediate scrutiny. As far back as 1933, Secretary of State Cordell Hull proposed * * * a gender-neutral alternative in a letter to the Chairman of the House Committee on Immigration and Naturalization. * * *

And unlike the legitimation requirement at issue in *Nguyen*, which could be satisfied by, for example, "a written acknowledgment of paternity under oath," the physical presence requirement that Morales-Santana challenges imposes more than a "minimal" burden on unwed citizen fathers. It adds to the legitimation requirement ten years of physical presence in the United States, five of which must be after the age of fourteen. In our view, this burden on a citizen father's right to confer citizenship on his foreign-born child is substantial.

For these reasons, the gender-based distinction at the heart of the 1952 Act's physical presence requirements is not substantially related to the achievement of a permissible, non-stereotype-based objective.

* * *

For the foregoing reasons, we reverse the BIA's decision and remand for further proceedings consistent with this opinion.

NOTES AND QUESTIONS ON
GENDER DISTINCTIONS AND JUS SANGUINIS

1.   In a brief to the Supreme Court in *Miller v. Albright,* 523 U.S. 420, 118 S.Ct. 1428, 140 L.Ed.2d 575 (1998), the government argued for "deference to congressional decisions concerning immigration and naturalization"— asserting that "policies toward the admission to this country, and most especially to full citizenship therein, of those not born here are uniquely political in character, dealing as they do with the threshold question of who is entitled to any share in the benefits, protections, and responsibilities of the democratic compact that the Constitution represents." Brief for the Respondent, at 22–23. (The Court in *Nguyen* didn't reach this issue because it concluded that the statute met the higher standard generally applied to gender-based distinctions.)

2.   Does the fact that a statute regulates the distribution of citizenship call for a higher level of scrutiny? Or, should usual norms regarding gender discrimination be relaxed in the face of regulations of citizenship and immigration?

3.   Several years prior to *Morales-Santana*, the Ninth Circuit upheld the statutory physical presence requirement for unwed citizen fathers against constitutional challenge. *United States v. Flores-Villar,* 536 F. 3d 990 (9th Cir. 2008), affirmed without opinion by an equally divided court, 564 U.S. 210, 131 S.Ct. 2312, 180 L.Ed.2d 222 (2011). The per curiam affirmance of the lower court decision upheld the statute's imposition of lengthier U.S. residency requirements on U.S. citizen fathers who wish to transmit citizenship to their out of wedlock children at birth. This leaves Justice Kennedy's *Nguyen* 5–4 majority opinion as the most recent Supreme Court analysis of the constitutionality of the legitimation or proof of paternity requirement set forth in § 309(a)(4).

Nguyen, Flores-Villar, and *Morales-Santana* all applied the heightened scrutiny standard, but they came to different conclusions as to whether the statutory gender-based discrimination was lawful. How did the Second Circuit distinguish Morales-Santana's circumstances from those of Nguyen? Do you find that reasoning convincing? Shortly after *Morales-Santana*, a federal district court in Texas also concluded that the gender distinction in the physical presence requirements was unconstitutional. *Villegas-Sarabia v. Johnson,* 2015 WL 4887462 (W.D. Tex. Aug. 17, 2015).

4. Relying on historical research into the role of race and gender in nationality law and family law, Kristin Collins challenges the *Nguyen* majority's assertions that the gender differences in derivative citizenship legislation are a "biologically inevitable" result of the differences in the reproductive roles of men and women. Instead, Collins argues, these differences arose out of a racially nativist nation-building policy. Reviewing correspondence by federal agency officials, judicial opinions, legislative history, and other historical documents, Collins concludes that derivative citizenship legislation reflects a conscious choice to limit recognition of nonwhite children as U.S. citizens. Kristin A. Collins, *Illegitimate Borders: Jus Sanguinis Citizenship and the Legal Construction of Family, Race, and Nation*, 123 Yale L.J. 2134 (2014).

EXERCISE

Assume that the President has decided that the gender discrimination should be purged from U.S. citizenship statutes. The Secretary of State has been instructed to draft gender-neutral revisions to the INA. You are an attorney in the Office of Legal Adviser in the State Department, and the Secretary of State has turned to you to eliminate the gender bias in § 309.

Note that simply eliminating § 309 would mean that nonmarital children would be granted equal treatment with marital children under § 301(g) but that U.S. citizen mothers of nonmarital children born overseas would be worse off than they are under § 309 (why?). But to give U.S. citizen fathers of non-marital children equal treatment with U.S. mothers under § 309 would give the parents of non-marital children advantages over U.S. citizen parents of marital children born overseas (under § 301(g)).

Prepare a draft of a gender-neutral statute, accompanied by an explanatory note that details how and why your proposal changes existing law. Would you make the changes retrospective in operation? If so, could second and third generation descendants claim citizenship?

---

2. *JUS SOLI*

As noted earlier, the *jus soli* principle is an important part of Anglo-American nationality laws, but the original Constitution of the United States did not define citizenship or the means of transmitting it. And though Congress enacted legislation in 1790 providing for naturalization of noncitizens in the United States and extending citizenship at birth to certain children born abroad, the early Congress did not define citizenship for persons born in the United States. This left the question of the citizenship of Indians, slaves, free blacks, and the children of immigrants to the various answers of the states and the courts. *See* James H. Kettner, The Development of American Citizenship, 1608–1870 (1978). The Supreme Court's attempt to solve the problem of the definition of U.S. citizenship—Chief Justice Taney's opinion in the *Dred*

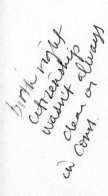
birth right citizenship wasn't clear or always in cons

[handwritten: Dred Scott was bad]

Scott case (holding that free blacks born in the U.S. were not citizens of the United States)—had tragic results, and ultimately occasioned legislative and constitutional change.

Congress acted quickly after the end of the Civil War to remove the stain of *Dred Scott*. The 1866 Civil Rights Act provided that "all persons born in the United States and not subject to any foreign power, excluding Indians not taxed, are hereby declared to be citizens of the United States." Act of Apr. 9, 1866, § 1, Ch. 31, 14 Stat. 27. Two years later, it wrote the definition of citizenship into the first sentence of the first section of the Fourteenth Amendment, thereby putting it beyond the power of shifting legislative majorities to alter. It reads: "All persons born or naturalized in the United States, and subject to the jurisdiction thereof, are citizens of the United States and of the State wherein they reside."

[handwritten: 14A citizenship clause]

Citizenship based on birth in the national territory is now rooted in the Constitution, but the constitutional text includes limiting language: persons must be "subject to the jurisdiction" of the United States. The Supreme Court's first holding on the subject suggested that the court would give a restrictive reading to the phrase, potentially disqualifying significant numbers of persons born within the physical boundaries of the nation. In *Elk v. Wilkins,* 112 U.S. 94, 5 S.Ct. 41, 28 L.Ed. 643 (1884), the Court ruled that native Indians were not U.S. citizens, even if they later severed their ties with their tribes. The words "subject to the jurisdiction thereof," the Court held, mean "not merely subject in some respect or degree to the jurisdiction of the United States, but completely subject to their political jurisdiction, and owing them direct and immediate allegiance." Most Indians could not meet the test. "Indians born within the territorial limits of the United States, members of, and owing immediate allegiance to, one of the Indian tribes, (an alien though dependent power,) although in a geographical sense born in the United States, are no more 'born in the United States and subject to the jurisdiction thereof,' * * * than the children of subjects of any foreign government born within the domain of that government * * * ." *Id.* at 102.

[handwritten: Elk - native americans not "citizens" b/c of jurisdiction clause]

[handwritten: Indians were not citizens even though born w/in us terr ↓ Amended and now all Indians born w/in US are citizens.]

Congress eventually passed legislation overcoming the direct effects of this holding. The Allotment Act of 1887 conferred citizenship on many Indians who resided in the United States, and later statutes expanded the scope of the grant. Since at least 1940 (and possibly since 1924—the application of the statute enacted that year to Indians born thereafter was unclear), all Indians born in the United States are U.S. citizens at birth. *See* INA § 301(b); Charles Gordon, Stanley Mailman, Stephen Yale-Loehr & Ronald Y. Wada, Immigration Law and Procedure (GMYW) § 92.03[3][e].

But in the meantime, the years following *Elk* saw the tightening of federal laws that excluded most Chinese immigrants from the United States. (Chapter Three will consider these Chinese exclusion laws in greater detail.) The question arose whether children born in the United States to Chinese parents would be citizens under *Elk*'s reading of the Fourteenth Amendment. After all, opponents of such citizenship pointed out, Chinese had always been excluded from naturalization.[2] As Section C of this chapter will explain, the original naturalization laws opened citizenship only to "free white persons." In 1870, in the wake of the Civil War, Congress extended naturalization eligibility to "persons of African nativity, or African descent." Western Hemisphere natives were included in 1940. Not until 1943 were Chinese made eligible for naturalization—a somewhat belated token of support extended to a World War II ally.

The Chinese exclusion laws themselves restated this racial bar to naturalization. Did the impossibility of their parents obtaining U.S. citizenship also somehow render such persons not subject to the jurisdiction of the United States, within the meaning of the Fourteenth Amendment, at the time of their birth?

The Supreme Court's answer came in a case involving Wong Kim Ark, who had been born in San Francisco to Chinese parents who had taken up residence in this country under treaties that initially had encouraged such migration. Excluded from entry in 1895 on returning from a brief visit to China, Wong Kim Ark claimed a right to admission as a citizen, based on the locus of his birth.

---

[2]   Only in 1952 were all racial and national origin bars eliminated from the naturalization laws. INA § 311. *See generally* GMYW §§ 94.01[2], 94.03[5].

Wong Kim Ark, from the file in his habeas corpus case in the
U.S. district court in San Francisco. (Photo: National Archives)

UNITED STATES V. WONG KIM ARK

Supreme Court of the United States, 1898.
169 U.S. 649, 18 S.Ct. 456, 42 L.Ed. 890.

MR. JUSTICE GRAY, after stating the case, delivered the opinion of the court.

The facts of this case, as agreed by the parties, are as follows: Wong Kim Ark was born in 1873 in the city of San Francisco, in the state of California and United States of America, and was and is a laborer. * * * Wong Kim Ark, ever since his birth, has had but one residence, to wit, in California * * * * In 1890 (when he must have been about 17 years of age) he departed for China on a temporary visit and with the intention of returning to the United States, and did return thereto by sea in the same year * * *.

* * *

The question presented by the record is whether a child born in the United States, of parents of Chinese descent, who, at the time of his birth are subjects of the Emperor of China, but have a permanent domicil and residence in the United States, and are there carrying on business, and are not employed in any diplomatic or official capacity under the Emperor of China, becomes at the time of his birth a citizen of the United States, by virtue of the first clause of the Fourteenth Amendment of the Constitution: "All persons born or naturalized in the United States, and subject to the jurisdiction thereof, are citizens of the United States and of the state wherein they reside."

[handwritten margin note: first line & how court will rule]

* * *

II. The fundamental principle of the common law with regard to English nationality was birth within the allegiance, also called "ligealty," "obedience," "faith," or "power," of the King. The principle embraced all persons born within the King's allegiance and subject to his protection. Such allegiance and protection were mutual—as expressed in the maxim, "protectio trahit subjectionem, et subjectio protectionem"—and were not restricted to natural-born subjects and naturalized subjects, or to those who had taken an oath of allegiance; but were predicable of aliens in amity, so long as they were within the kingdom. Children, born in England, of such aliens, were therefore natural-born subjects. But the children, born within the realm, of foreign ambassadors, or the children of alien enemies, born during and within their hostile occupation of part of the King's dominions, were not natural-born subjects, because not born within the allegiance, the obedience, or the power, or, as would be said at this day, within the jurisdiction, of the King.

* * *

III. The same rule was in force in all the English Colonies upon this continent down to the time of the Declaration of Independence, and in the United States afterwards, and continued to prevail under the Constitution as originally established.

* * *

The Supreme Judicial Court of Massachusetts, speaking by Mr. Justice (afterwards Chief Justice) Sewall, early held that the determination of the question whether a man was a citizen or an alien was "to be governed altogether by the principles of the common law," and that it was established, with few exceptions, "that a man, born within the jurisdiction of the common law, is a citizen of the country wherein he is born. By this circumstance of his birth, he is subjected to the duty of allegiance which is claimed and enforced by the sovereign of his native land; and becomes reciprocally entitled to the protection of that sovereign, and to the other rights and advantages which are included in the term 'citizenship.' " *Gardner v. Ward*, (1805) 2 Mass. 244, note. * * *

That all children, born within the dominion of the United States, of foreign parents holding no diplomatic office, became citizens at the time of their birth, does not appear to have been contested or doubted until more than 50 years after the adoption of the Constitution, when the matter was elaborately argued in the Court of Chancery of New York, and decided upon full consideration by Vice Chancellor Sandford in favor of their citizenship. *Lynch v. Clarke*, (1844) 1 Sandf. Ch. 583.

The same doctrine was repeatedly affirmed in the executive departments[.]

* * *

IV. It was contended by one of the learned counsel for the United States that the rule of the Roman law, by which the citizenship of the child followed that of the parent, was the true rule of international law as now recognized in most civilized countries, and had superseded the rule of the common law, depending on birth within the realm, originally founded on feudal considerations.

But at the time of the adoption of the Constitution of the United States in 1789, and long before, it would seem to have been the rule in Europe generally, as it certainly was in France, that, as said by Pothier, "citizens, true and native-born citizens, are those who are born within the extent of the dominion of France," and "mere birth within the realm gives the rights of a native-born citizen, independently of the origin of the father or mother, and of their domicil[.]" * * *

The later modifications of the rule in Europe rest upon the constitutions, laws or ordinances of the various countries, and have no important bearing upon the interpretation and effect of the Constitution of the United States. * * *

There is, therefore, little ground for the theory that, at the time of the adoption of the Fourteenth Amendment of the Constitution of the United States, there was any settled and definite rule of international law, generally recognized by civilized nations, inconsistent with the ancient rule of citizenship by birth within the dominion.

* * *

V.   In the fore front, both of the Fourteenth Amendment of the Constitution, and of the Civil Rights Act of 1866, the fundamental principle of citizenship by birth within the dominion was reaffirmed in the most explicit and comprehensive terms.

* * *

The first section of the Fourteenth Amendment of the Constitution begins with the words, "All persons born or naturalized in the United States, and subject to the jurisdiction thereof, are citizens of the United States and of the State wherein they reside." As appears upon the face of the amendment, as well as from the history of the times, this was not intended to impose any new restrictions upon citizenship, or to prevent any persons from becoming citizens by the fact of birth within the United States, who would thereby have become citizens according to the law existing before its adoption. It is declaratory in form, and enabling and extending in effect. Its main purpose doubtless was, as has been often recognized by this court, to establish the citizenship of free negroes, which had been denied in the opinion delivered by Chief Justice Taney in *Dred Scott v. Sandford*, (1857) 19 How. 393; and to put it beyond doubt that all blacks, as well as whites, born or naturalized within the jurisdiction of the United States, are citizens of the United States. *The Slaughter House Cases*, (1873) 16 Wall. 36, 73. But the opening words, "All persons born," are general, not to say universal, restricted only by place and jurisdiction, and not by color or race * * * .

* * *

The only adjudication that has been made by this court upon the meaning of the clause "and subject to the jurisdiction thereof," in the leading provision of the Fourteenth Amendment, is *Elk v. Wilkins*, 112 U. S. 94, 5 Sup. Ct. 41* * *

[John Elk was born on an Indian reservation to members of an Indian tribe. He later moved away from the reservation, renounced his allegiance to the tribe, and claimed he was a U.S. citizen although he had not been naturalized. At the time of the litigation, Indian tribes were considered alien nations, distinct political communities, the members of which owed immediate allegiance to their several tribes, and were not part of the people of the United States. Members of Indian tribes were not included in the population for purposes of apportioning representatives in Congress and direct taxes among the several states. They] were never deemed citizens, except when naturalized, collectively or individually, under explicit provisions of a treaty, or of an act of Congress; and, therefore, * * * "Indians born within the territorial limits of the United States, members of, and owing immediate allegiance to, one of the Indian tribes (an alien, though dependent, power), although in a geographical sense born in the United States, are no more 'born in the United States, and subject to the jurisdiction thereof,' " within the meaning of the first section of the Fourteenth Amendment, than the children of subjects of any foreign government born within the domain of that government, or the children born within the United States of ambassadors or other public ministers of foreign nations. * * *

* * *

The decision in *Elk v. Wilkins* concerned only members of the Indian tribes within the United States, and had no tendency to deny citizenship to children born in the United States of foreign parents of Caucasian, African, or Mongolian descent, not in the diplomatic service of a foreign country.

The real object of the Fourteenth Amendment of the Constitution, in qualifying the words "all persons born in the United States" by the addition "and subject to the jurisdiction thereof," would appear to have been to exclude, by the fewest and fittest words (besides children of members of the Indian tribes, standing in a peculiar relation to the national government, unknown to the common law,) the two classes of cases—children born of alien enemies in hostile occupation, and children of diplomatic representatives of a foreign state—both of which, as has already been shown, by the law of England, and by our own law, from the time of the first settlement of the English Colonies in America, had been recognized exceptions to the fundamental rule of citizenship by birth within the country.

* * *

The Amendment, in clear words and in manifest intent, includes the children born within the territory of the United States, of all other persons, of whatever race or color, domiciled within the United States. Every citizen or subject of another country, while domiciled here, is within the allegiance and the protection, and consequently subject to the jurisdiction, of the United States. His allegiance to the United States is direct and immediate, and, although but local and temporary, continuing only so long as he remains within our territory * * * .

To hold that the Fourteenth Amendment of the Constitution excludes from citizenship the children, born in the United States, of citizens or subjects of other countries, would be to deny citizenship to thousands of persons of English, Scotch, Irish, German or other European parentage, who have always been considered and treated as citizens of the United States.

VI. * * * It is true that Chinese persons born in China cannot be naturalized, like other aliens, by proceedings under the naturalization laws. But this is for want of any statute or treaty authorizing or permitting such naturalization, as will appear by tracing the history of the statutes, treaties, and decisions upon that subject—always bearing in mind that statutes enacted by Congress, as well as treaties made by the President and Senate, must yield to the paramount and supreme law of the Constitution.

* * *

The power of naturalization, vested in Congress by the Constitution, is a power to confer citizenship, not a power to take it away. * * * Congress having no power to abridge the rights conferred by the Constitution upon those who have become naturalized citizens by virtue of acts of Congress, *a fortiori* no act or omission of Congress, as to providing for the naturalization of parents or children of a particular race, can affect citizenship acquired as a birthright, by virtue of the Constitution itself, without any aid of legislation. * * *

* * *

The fact, therefore, that acts of Congress or treaties have not permitted Chinese persons born out of this country to become citizens by naturalization, cannot exclude Chinese persons born in this country from the operation of the broad and clear words of the constitution: "All persons born in the United States, and subject to the jurisdiction thereof, are citizens of the United States."

* * *

MR. JUSTICE MCKENNA, not having been a member of the court when this case was argued, took no part in the decision.

MR. CHIEF JUSTICE FULLER, with whom concurred MR. JUSTICE HARLAN, dissenting.

I cannot concur in the opinion and judgment of the court in this case.

* * *

* * * To be "completely subject" to the political jurisdiction of the United States is to be in no respect or degree subject to the political jurisdiction of any other government.

Now, I take it that the children of aliens, whose parents have not only not renounced their allegiance to their native country, but are forbidden by its system of government, as well as by its positive laws, from doing so, and are not permitted to acquire another citizenship by the laws of the country into which they come, must necessarily remain themselves subject to the same sovereignty as their parents, and cannot, in the nature of things, be, any more than their parents, completely subject to the jurisdiction of such other country.

* * *

These considerations lead to the conclusion that the rule in respect of citizenship of the United States prior to the Fourteenth Amendment differed from the English common law rule in vital particulars, and, among others, in that it did not recognize allegiance as indelible, and in that it did recognize an essential difference between birth during temporary, and birth during permanent, residence. If children born in the United States were deemed presumptively and generally citizens, this was not so when they were born of aliens whose residence was merely temporary, either in fact, or in point of law.

Did the Fourteenth Amendment impose the original English common law rule as a rigid rule on this country?

* * *

"Born in the United States, and subject to the jurisdiction thereof," and "naturalized in the United States, and subject to the jurisdiction thereof," mean born or naturalized under such circumstances as to be completely subject to that jurisdiction, that is, as completely as citizens of the United States who are of course not subject to any foreign power, and can of right claim the exercise of the power of the United States on their behalf wherever they may be. When, then, children are born the United States to the subjects of a foreign power, with which it is agreed by treaty that they shall not be naturalized thereby, and as to whom our own law forbids them to be naturalized, such children are not born so subject to the jurisdiction as to become citizens, and entitled on that ground to the interposition of our Government, if they happen to be found in the country of their parents' origin and allegiance, or any other.

* * *

In other words, the Fourteenth Amendment does not exclude from citizenship by birth children born in the United States of parents permanently located therein, and who might themselves become citizens; nor, on the other hand, does it arbitrarily make citizens of children born in the United States of parents who, according to the will of their native Government and of this government, are and must remain aliens.

Tested by this rule, Wong Kim Ark never became and is not a citizen of the United States, and the order of the district court should be reversed.

I am authorized to say that MR. JUSTICE HARLAN concurs in this dissent.

NOTES AND QUESTIONS ON WONG KIM ARK

1.   Consider *Wong Kim Ark* in its historical context. Two years earlier, the Supreme Court has placed its imprimatur on state-enforced segregation of the races by upholding a Jim Crow law in *Plessy v. Ferguson*, 163 U.S. 537, 16 S.Ct. 1138, 41 L.Ed. 256 (1896). America was on the verge of Empire, annexing Hawaii in 1898, occupying Cuba in the same year, and taking the Philippines and Puerto Rico from Spain under the terms of the 1899 Treaty of Paris. A renewed Anglo-Saxonism in the United States viewed the residents of these new possessions as generally unfit for full American citizenship. In this climate, a number of leading law professors of the day lent a hand in developing legal theories that would deny citizenship to children born to Chinese, and the Justice Department gave full support to that effort. (The full story of this background is set forth in Lucy Salyer, Wong Kim Ark: *The Contest Over Birthright Citizenship*, in Immigration Stories 51–85 (David A. Martin & Peter H. Schuck eds. 2005).) Against this background, the Court's holding in *Wong Kim Ark* is worthy of note. What accounts for its conclusion? Might the Court's recognition that reaching a contrary result "would be to deny citizenship to thousands of persons of English, Scotch, Irish, German or other European parentage, who have always been considered and treated as citizens of the United States" have something to do with it?

2.   Justice John Marshall Harlan, who penned the famous dissent in *Plessy v. Ferguson*, joined Chief Justice Fuller's dissent in *Wong Kim Ark*. How does one reconcile Harlan's attack on Jim Crow as a denial of equal citizenship with the conclusion of the dissent in *Wong Kim Ark* that the government has the power "notwithstanding the Fourteenth Amendment, to prescribe that all persons of a particular race, or their children, cannot become citizens"? *See* Gabriel J. Chin, *The* Plessy *Myth: Justice Harlan and the Chinese Cases*, 82 Iowa L. Rev. 151 (1996).

3.   Some of the language of the majority opinion in *Wong Kim Ark* seemed to leave open the status of children born within the United States to noncitizen parents only temporarily present within the national borders. What about children born to unauthorized migrants? Does the reasoning in the opinion require lawful presence before *jus soli* applies? Lawful and permanent presence? In fact, the decision has served to establish for the United States a general rule of citizenship by birth: birth in the territorial United States, even to tourists and undocumented migrants, results in U.S. citizenship. The only exceptions to this *jus soli* rule are exceedingly narrow:

birth to foreign sovereigns and accredited diplomatic officials;[3] birth on foreign public vessels—meaning essentially warships, not commercial vessels—even while they are located in U.S. territorial waters (we wonder: does this ever happen?); birth to alien enemies in hostile occupation of a portion of U.S. territory. *See* GMYW § 92.03[3][d].

4.   Special considerations may apply, however, in determining the effect of birth in an outlying territory of the United States. The issue is whether birth there results in full citizenship or only in status as a noncitizen national. Care must be taken to consult the relevant rules in effect for the particular territory at the time of the birth, and, if full citizenship was not granted, to track later developments affecting the status of the territory and its inhabitants. Filipinos, for example, were noncitizen nationals of the United States from 1899 to 1946, but lost their status as U.S. nationals when the Philippines became independent in 1946. In the early 1990s several deportation respondents from the Philippines defended on the basis that they were U.S. citizens, because their parents, born in the Philippines while it was a U.S. territory, were born "in the United States, and subject to the jurisdiction thereof" within the meaning of the Fourteenth Amendment. The Ninth Circuit rejected the claim, over a vigorous dissent. *Rabang v. INS*, 35 F.3d 1449 (9th Cir.1994).

Rabang v. INS.

5.   Sometimes the governing rules, in light of intervening changes in the political status of the territory, can be exceedingly complex. *See* GMYW § 92.04. As of today, the regular *jus soli* rules are in effect in all territories except American Samoa and Swains Island—meaning that children now born in any U.S. territorial possessions except those two become full citizens at birth. In 2015 individuals born in American Samoa relied on *Wong Kim Ark* to claim they were U.S. citizens at birth, rather than noncitizen nationals of the United States. The D.C. Circuit rejected their argument, concluding that *Wong Kim Ark* did not require the applicability of *jus soli* to partially self-governing territories. *Tuaua v. United States*, 788 F.3d 300 (D.C. Cir. 2015). In addition, the court noted that many residents of American Samoa prefer their status as U.S. non-citizen nationals; both the American Samoan government and the elected non-voting delegate to the U.S. House of Representatives intervened in the law suit to oppose the extension of full *jus soli* to American Samoa. *Id.*, at 302 n.3.

Tuaua v. US.

Children of Unauthorized Migrants and Temporary Lawful Visitors

Are children born to unauthorized migrants in the United States citizens at birth? Following the reasoning of *Wong Kim Ark*, it has usually been assumed so. But in 1985, Professors Peter Schuck and Rogers Smith

usually children of unauth. migr. are citizens

---

[3]   Birth on U.S. soil to a diplomat does entitle the child to permanent resident status in the United States, subject to certain administrative requirements. *See Nikoi v. Attorney General*, 939 F.2d 1065 (D.C.Cir.1991) (holding that absences of 11 and 16 years, though begun while the petitioners were minors, resulted in abandonment of resident status).

authored a book entitled *Citizenship Without Consent: Illegal Aliens in the American Polity*, which argued that *Wong Kim Ark* had not settled the question. They asserted that, properly read, "the Fourteenth Amendment's Citizenship Clause makes birthright citizenship for the children of illegal and temporary visitor aliens a matter of congressional choice rather than of constitutional prescription." *Id.* at 5. Schuck and Smith found room for congressional action in the Fourteenth Amendment's language that only persons "subject to the jurisdiction" of the United States are citizens at birth. According to the authors, this phrase limiting birthright citizenship is grounded in a "consensualist" understanding of citizenship. By this they mean that an individual's free choice, as well as the state's consent, not the historical circumstances of where and to whom she was born, should determine her citizenship.

A new dimension to the *jus soli* birthright citizenship debate came to the fore after Yaser Hamdi, captured by U.S. forces in Afghanistan in 2001 and held as an enemy combatant at the U.S. Naval Base at Guantánamo Bay, Cuba, disclosed that he had been born in Louisiana to parents from Saudi Arabia who were lawfully present on student visas. At the age of three, Hamdi had left the United States with his parents and had never returned. Based on his birth on U.S. soil, the U.S. government treated him as a U.S. citizen and transferred him to a military prison within the United States, from which he successfully filed a habeas corpus action to challenge his detention, *Hamdi v. Rumsfeld*, 542 U.S. 507, 124 S.Ct. 2633, 159 L.Ed.2d 578 (2004). Ultimately Hamdi was released to Saudi Arabia after he renounced his U.S. citizenship.

More recently, in the 2015 campaign for the Republican party presidential nomination, Donald Trump argued that babies born in the United States to undocumented immigrant parents are not U.S. citizens. Josh Barro, *Just What Do You Mean by 'Anchor Baby'?*, N.Y. Times, Aug. 28, 2015. Around the same time, political candidates discussed news reports of foreign nationals who obtain U.S. tourist visas in order to be in the United States when they give birth, thus assuring that their children are U.S. citizens. *Id.* An expose of underground birth tourism industry sites in southern California, Benjamin Carlson, *Welcome to Maternity Hotel, California*, Rolling Stone, Aug. 19, 2015, and government investigations into visa fraud, Victoria Kim & Frank Shyong, *'Maternity Tourism' Raids Target California Operations Catering to Chines*, L.A. Times, Mar. 3, 2015, kept this issue in the news. As a consequence, in recent years the *jus soli* birthright citizenship debate has focused on births to lawful temporary visitors to the United States as well as on births to unauthorized migrants. Congress held hearings on both of these issues in April 2015. *Birthright Citizenship: Is it the Right Policy for America?* Hearing before the Subcomm. on Immigration and Border

Security of the House Comm. on the Judiciary, 114th Cong., 1st Sess. 114–21 (2015).

We have included a selection from the Schuck and Smith book that, in effect, ignited the current debate. We then explore responses that counter the Schuck and Smith thesis, both as a matter of constitutional interpretation and as a matter of policy.

PETER H. SCHUCK & ROGERS M. SMITH, CITIZENSHIP WITHOUT CONSENT: ILLEGAL ALIENS IN THE AMERICAN POLITY
Pp. 2–5, 73–74, 76, 82–83, 85–87, 92–96, 99–100, 102, 113 (1985).

Despite the splendor of its constitutional pedigree * * * birthright citizenship is something of a bastard concept in American ideology. For all its appealing simplicity, it remains a puzzling idea. * * * [B]irthright citizenship originated as a distinctively feudal status intimately linked to medieval notions of sovereignty, legal personality, and allegiance. At a conceptual level, then, it was fundamentally opposed to the consensual assumptions that guided the political handiwork of 1776 and 1787. In a polity whose chief organizing principle was the idea of consent, mere birth within a nation's border seems to be an anomalous, inadequate measure or expression of an individual's consent to its rule and a decidedly crude indicator of the nation's consent to the individual's admission to political membership.

* * *

* * * [In] this book we elaborate an important but previously neglected dichotomy between two radically different conceptions of political community, which we call the "ascriptive" and the "consensual." In its purest form, the principle of *ascription* holds that one's political membership is entirely and irrevocably determined by some objective circumstance—in this case, birth within a particular sovereign's allegiance or jurisdiction. According to this conception, human preferences do not affect political membership; only the natural, immutable circumstances of one's birth are considered relevant.

The principle of *consent* advances radically different premises. It holds that political membership can result only from free individual choices. In the consensualist view, the circumstances of one's origins may of course influence one's preferences for political affiliation, but they need not do so and in any event are not determinative.

* * * [We] propose * * * an essentially consensual ideal of citizenship. Such a citizenship * * * would be more legitimate in theory, more flexible in meeting practical policy problems, and more likely to generate a genuine sense of community among all citizens than the existing scheme, while protecting the established human rights of aliens. To those ends, we

* * * advocate a combination of measures to render American citizenship law more consensual than it has previously been and to ameliorate what is the greatest contemporary threat to a consensually based political community—the massive presence of illegal aliens. We * * * propose four related reforms: first, more effective enforcement of existing immigration laws; second, a system of realistic, credible employer sanctions to remove the chief incentive to most illegal immigration; third, more generous legal admission policies, especially within this hemisphere, and fourth, a reinterpretation of the Fourteenth Amendment's Citizenship Clause to make birthright citizenship for the children of illegal and temporary visitor aliens a matter of congressional choice rather than of constitutional prescription.

THE FOURTEENTH AMENDMENT AND THE 1868 EXPATRIATION ACT

The framers of the [Fourteenth Amendment's citizenship clause] * * * did not write on a blank slate. * * * [T]he clause was adopted against a legal and ideological background in which the common-law view of political membership had found acceptance, a view in which (according to Lord Chief Justice Alexander Cockburn, a critic of the common-law rule writing at the time the clause was considered) "a merely casual birth in the country is to have the effect of conferring the character of a British Subject."[5] That view largely reflected its medieval English origins. But the context in which the clause was adopted was strikingly different. America was a more open, less insular society. Its central political ideas were not ascription and allegiance but consent and individual rights. And the clause was drafted with a very specific purpose in mind. It was designed to elevate to constitutional status the definition of citizenship adopted by statute over President Andrew Johnson's veto only two months earlier and by the very same Congress. A centerpiece of Reconstruction, the Civil Rights Act of 1866 had sought to guarantee blacks equal rights, privileges, and immunities under the law. At the same time, it created a new definition of United States citizenship, one that effectively overruled *Dred Scott*: "All, persons born in the United States, and not subject to any foreign power, excluding Indians not taxed, are hereby declared to be citizens of the United States."[7]

* * *

The greatest mystery surrounding the scope of the [Fourteenth Amendment's citizenship] clause * * * concerns the meaning of its phrase "and subject to the jurisdiction [of the United States]." We shall hereafter call this phrase the "jurisdiction requirement." Without that phrase, the clause would appear to demand a universal application, for it speaks of

---

[5] Sir A. Cockburn, *Nationality: or the Law relating to Subjects and Aliens considered with a View to Future Legislation* (1869).

[7] Ch. 31, 14 Stat. 27, sec. 1 (April 9, 1866).

"all" persons, not some, and it employs a geographical referent (birth "in the United States") rather than a legal one. The jurisdiction requirement's conjunctive form, however, clearly suggests that it was meant to narrow the scope of the birthright citizenship principle under the clause. Indeed, we shall argue that the jurisdiction requirement should be understood to impose a consensual qualification on that principle.

[After reviewing the congressional debates, Schuck and Smith conclude that the citizenship clause of the Fourteenth Amendment was clearly intended (1) to extend birthright citizenship to the American-born children of Chinese and other resident aliens, but (2) to deny birthright citizenship to children born to Indians who were living within tribal governmental structures.]

The debates over Indian citizenship did not merely resolve (at least for the time being) a nettlesome question of coverage under the Citizenship Clause, important as that resolution was. They also brought to the surface the central elements around which the 39th Congress organized its more general understanding of the scope and meaning of the jurisdiction requirement under the clause. In the clash between the rival conceptions of its scope that were articulated during the Senate debate, the more demanding formulation—the idea of "full and complete jurisdiction," a jurisdiction precluding "allegiance to anybody else"—was the one advanced by Senators Trumbull and Howard, the chief architects of the clause and indeed of the Fourteenth Amendment as a whole.

The jurisdiction requirement, then, can best be understood as having added to the ineradicably ascriptive birthright citizenship rule a transforming consensual conception of the necessary connection between an individual and his government—a conception that was * * * more profoundly *political* than one emphasizing the individual's mere presence on the soil at birth. The connection must be more than simply the individual's subjection to the government's police power and criminal jurisdiction, more even than the individual's manifest desire for membership in the political community and the absence of any similar allegiance (in Senator Trumbull's words) "to anyone else." It also demanded a more or less complete, direct power by government over the individual, and a reciprocal relationship between them at the time of birth, in which the government consented to the individual's presence and status and offered him complete protection. In the public-law view, * * * this protection and citizenship extended to the child, but only through the government's consent to the parents, whose consent was in turn taken provisionally to stand for that of the child. In this way, even birthright citizenship's inherently ascriptive nature flowed from consensualist commitments.

This more consensualist reading of the Citizenship Clause is supported by the fact that, although it imposed an obligation of allegiance upon the native-born citizen, Congress could not have conceived of that obligation as perpetual or indissoluble on his part. Only one day before the Fourteenth Amendment was ratified, Congress embraced the consensual conception of citizenship in a more direct and thoroughgoing way, affirming in the Expatriation Act of 1868 the fundamental right of all citizens voluntarily to withdraw their consent and to renounce their citizenship. That act clearly established the principle that membership in the political community must always reflect the individual citizen's consent, a consent that must remain vital and continuing lest the individual withdraw it.

* * *

THE PROBLEM OF ILLEGAL MIGRATION

When the framers of the Citizenship Clause adopted (in a significantly compromised form) the common-law rule of birthright citizenship, immigration to the United States was entirely unregulated. The nation maintained a policy of completely open borders for almost another decade, when the first exclusion law, barring prostitutes and vagabonds, was enacted. Indeed, until well into the first decade of this century, birthright citizenship could plausibly be understood as one ingredient of an integrated national strategy to encourage immigration in order to populate a vast, essentially empty continent with the need for more laborers, mechanics, and farmers than American society itself could produce. An open-border policy was also celebrated as a way to serve liberal, humanitarian values, to make America an "asylum" for the "oppressed and persecuted of all Nations and Religions," as George Washington had urged at the outset.

Today, of course, that strategy of open border is a distant memory, bearing about as much relationship to current immigration policy concerns as the horse-and-buggy does to contemporary modes of transportation. * * *

The number of illegal aliens presently in the United States is a matter of great and continuing controversy. * * * This reality and the fears that it has generated concerning its economic and social effects have transformed political discourse about American immigration policy in ways that * * * the Reconstruction framers of the Citizenship Clause could [not] have anticipated. "Control of our borders," not encouragement of immigration, now dominates contemporary policy discussion. * * *

If mutual consent is the irreducible condition of membership in the American polity, it is difficult to defend a practice that extends birthright citizenship to the native-born children of illegal aliens. The parents of such children are, by definition, individuals whose presence within the jurisdiction of the United States is prohibited by law. They are manifestly individuals, therefore, to whom the society has explicitly and self-consciously decided to deny membership. And if the society has refused to consent to their membership, it can hardly be said to have consented to that of their children who happen to be born while their parents are here in clear violation of American law.

unwanted in society

* * * [T]he present guarantee under American law of automatic birthright citizenship to the children of illegal aliens can only operate, at the margin, as one more incentive to illegal migration and violation by nonimmigrant (temporary visitor) aliens already here of their time limited visa restrictions. When this attraction is combined with the powerful lure of the expanded entitlements conferred upon citizen children and their families by the modern welfare state, the total incentive effect of birthright citizenship may well become significant. Certainly, it cannot be ignored. Needless to say, attempts to estimate the precise magnitude of this effect—the number of birthright citizens born to illegal alien parents who would not otherwise have come here—face insuperable data limitations. In addition to anecdotal evidence that many aliens do cross the border illegally to assure United States citizenship for their soon-to-be-born children, a very recent study illuminates two features of this phenomenon. First, the number of births in the United States to illegal alien parents is not trivial; a conservative estimate places the number as in excess of seventy-five thousand each year. Second, these births—and the public costs that they entail—seem to be disproportionately concentrated in a relatively few urban areas.

Congress is not impotent in the face of this challenge to consensualism. Although the Citizenship Clause of the Fourteenth Amendment has been assumed to guarantee birthright citizenship to such children *ex proprio vigore*, the evidence that we [have] reviewed suggests a rather different conclusion. First, the debates that preceded Congress's adoption of the clause establish that the 39th Congress neither considered, nor could have been expected to consider, this question. It legislated in a world in which unrestricted immigration to the United States was actually encouraged. The question of the citizenship status of the native-born children of illegal aliens never arose for the simple reason that no illegal aliens existed at that time, or indeed for some time thereafter.

arg. not Congress' intent

Second, the debates also establish that the framers of the Citizenship Clause had no intention of establishing a universal rule of birthright citizenship. To be sure, they intended to do more than simply extend citizenship to native born blacks by overruling the reasoning and result in *Dred Scott*. But they also intended, through the clause's jurisdiction requirement, to limit the scope of birthright citizenship. The essential limiting principle, discernible from the debates (especially those concerned with the citizenship status of Indians) was consensualist in nature. Citizenship, as qualified by this principle, was not satisfied by mere birth on the soil or by naked governmental power or legal jurisdiction over the individual. Citizenship required in addition the existence of conditions indicating mutual consent to political membership.

* * * [W]hatever the proper reach of the consent principle may be, it cannot logically be applied to include the native-born children of illegal aliens, to whom the nation's consent has expressly been denied.

* * *

* * * If Congress should conclude that the prospective denial of birthright citizenship to the children of illegal aliens would be a valuable adjunct of such national self-definition, the Constitution should not be interpreted in a way that impedes that effort. Illegal aliens, however admirable their initiative in seeking to come here, seem poorly situated, morally speaking, to contest that policy choice. They have migrated here, after all, in knowing defiance of American law, well aware that they may at any moment be obliged to return. If anybody may be said to have taken a calculated risk, they can. Moreover, almost all deported illegal aliens return to their own countries, of which they are still members. Although they would rather not do so—or would prefer to do so at a time of their own choosing—such preferences taken alone are ordinarily not morally compelling. Finally, citizenship status is not necessary to afford illegal aliens and their children at least minimal legal protection and public benefits, for they possess certain procedural and substantive rights under the Constitution merely by reason of their presence within the United States. We do not take any position here concerning what the precise nature and extent of those rights ought to be. It is enough for present purposes to affirm that the Constitution need not and should not be woodenly interpreted either to guarantee their children citizenship or to cast them into outer darkness.

* * *

It should be noted that all of the arguments that we have made against birthright citizenship for the children of illegal aliens apply with equal or greater force to the children of so-called nonimmigrants, aliens who have been allowed to enter under visa restrictions only for a limited period of time and for limited purposes. Unlike the situation with citizens and legal resident aliens, the government has declined to consent to their political membership or permanent presence in the society; indeed, it has admitted them on the express condition that they confine their activities and leave within a specified period. On the view of the Citizenship Clause that we have advanced, their children born here should not be regarded as having been born "subject to the jurisdiction" of the United States. * * *

In the end, the question of birthright citizenship for the children of illegal and nonimmigrant aliens probably should not turn on the conclusions that * * * revenue-cost analyses reach, important as those analyses may be for policy guidance. Instead, we believe, this question should be resolved in the light of broader ideals of constitutional meaning, social morality, and political community. These ideals militate against constitutionally ascribed birthright citizenship in these circumstances. As the earlier discussion suggests, the Citizenship Clause was never intended to guarantee citizenship for such individuals. Beyond the question of textual analysis, moreover, it is simply morally perverse to reward law-breaking by conferring the valued status of citizenship * * * .

STATEMENT OF PROF. GERALD L. NEUMAN
Societal and Legal Issues Surrounding Children Born in the United States to Illegal
Alien Parents, Joint Hearing before the Subcomm. on Immigration and Claims and the
Subcomm. on the Constitution of the House Comm. on the Judiciary,
104th Cong., 1st Sess. 105–09 (Dec. 13, 1995).

The historical purpose of [the Citizenship] Clause is well known: it was intended to overrule the most infamous decision in U.S. constitutional history, the *Dred Scott* decision. *Scott v. Sanford*, 60 U.S. (19 How.) 393 (1857). One of the holdings of that case was that the *jus soli* rule of citizenship applied only to whites: free persons of African descent could not be citizens of the United States, even if they were born in the United States.

The original text of the Constitution had failed to specify any criteria for citizenship in the United States, and the *jus soli* rule had been followed as part of our common law heritage. That omission had made the Dred Scott decision possible. After the Civil War, Congress sought to remedy that tragic error. * * *

The framers of the Fourteenth Amendment had strong reason for desiring a constitutional settlement of the issue of birthright citizenship. They had just overthrown a system founded on denial of political membership in the country to a hereditary category of inhabitants. The Citizenship Clause was designed to prevent that situation from ever happening again. Both the proponents and the opponents of the Citizenship Clause understood this. For example, Senator Cowan, a vehement opponent of the Fourteenth Amendment, complained that granting citizenship to the children of Chinese alien parents on the Pacific Coast would prevent the states from "dealing with [the Chinese] as in the wisdom they see fit." In response, the supporters of the Citizenship Clause expressly confirmed their intent to protect the children of Chinese parents by recognizing them as citizens. The legislative history of the Fourteenth Amendment provides strong confirmation that birth in the United States would suffice to confer citizenship on children of aliens of any race, as it had earlier done for children of unnaturalized European immigrants.

The legislative history also confirms that the framers of the Fourteenth Amendment intended to deny constitutionally mandated citizenship to a few categories of children, whom they regarded as not "subject to the jurisdiction" of the United States, and therefore not within the protection of the common law *jus soli* rule. * * *

The common law did not consider as subjects or citizens children born to aliens who did not enter the country as individuals, but rather entered under the auspices of their governments with legal or factual immunity from local law. Children born to ambassadors of foreign nations were covered by comity principles of international law that restrain the state's exercise of lawmaking power. Children born to parents accompanying an invading army enter under extraordinary circumstances that temporarily oust the operation of local law. The example repeatedly used in the congressional debates was the children of ambassadors. *See e.g.,* Cong. Globe, 39th Cong, 1st Sess. 2897 (1866) (remarks of Sen. Williams).

The framers of the Fourteenth Amendment also intended to deny constitutionally mandated citizenship to a category of children whose parents were neither citizens nor aliens: American Indians born within their own organized political communities. The tribes were separate, self-governing political communities whose sovereignty predated the Constitution. At the time of the adoption of the Fourteenth Amendment the federal government did not exercise legislative power directly over their members, but negotiated treaties with the tribes as sovereign powers. * * *

* * *

Nor is there anything in the language, legislative history, or traditional interpretation of the Citizenship Clause that would exclude children born in the United States to aliens who are not lawfully present here. Clearly, deportable aliens are subject to the jurisdiction of the United States—that is what makes them deportable, and often subject to criminal punishment as well. Their children born in the United States, though not themselves guilty of violating any law, have no immunity from the lawmaking power of the United States, and are fully subject to its jurisdiction.

The applicability of the constitutional *jus soli* rule to children of nonimmigrant aliens and illegal aliens finds confirmation in the similar interpretation of the rule by the United Kingdom and Canada. The

United Kingdom followed this interpretation until 1981, when a different rule was adopted by statute, and Canada still extends citizenship to all children born in the territory except the children of foreign diplomats.

Everything that I have said so far has been well-established for many years. This traditional understanding has been questioned today solely because of a contrary thesis argued in [*Citizenship Without Consent*, by Professors Schuck and Smith.] [T]hat book's argument for a revisionist interpretation of the Fourteenth Amendment is poorly reasoned and historically inaccurate.

* * *

First, the Citizenship Clause sets forth a constitutional rule guaranteeing citizenship to a category of persons. That rule itself expresses the consent of the community, and even on the book's own theory, there should be no need to look further. * * *

Second, the revisionist argument requires a new interpretation of the language "subject to the jurisdiction" of the United States, in order to reconcile the theory with the language of the Citizenship Clause. The authors claim that * * * a person is not "subject to the jurisdiction of the United States" unless the United States consents to the person's status as a citizen. This is completely circular, and so would really guarantee no one citizenship at birth. And it has no relation to any definition of "jurisdiction" that anyone else has ever proposed. * * *

Third, the book sometimes states that a person is "subject to the jurisdiction" of the United States only if that person owes no allegiance to any foreign country. But this claim contradicts the book's own thesis that children born to permanent resident aliens are U.S. citizens. It contradicts the legislative history of the Fourteenth Amendment, which emphasized the citizenship of the children of Chinese immigrants[.] * * *

* * *

Fourth, the authors characterize their interpretation of "subject to the jurisdiction" as adding "a transforming consensual conception" to the traditional *jus soli* rule. But the legislative history makes it very clear that the framers of the Fourteenth Amendment were not trying to adopt a transformative new conception of citizenship by consent. That was what the Supreme Court had done in the infamous *Dred Scott* decision, excluding African-Americans from the *jus soli* rule on the ground that whites did not consider them appropriate partners in the political community. The framers sought to overturn that innovation, and to reaffirm on a racially neutral basis the same principles that had always governed American citizenship for persons of European descent. * * *

Fifth, the book claims that the framers of the Fourteenth Amendment could not have contemplated conferring citizenship on children of illegal aliens "for the simple reason that no illegal aliens existed at the time, or indeed for some time thereafter." This too is a fallacy. The federal government was not actively engaged in regulating immigration from Europe before the Civil War, but many of the states were. And, more importantly, the federal government itself had been attempting to prohibit the international slave trade, a form of involuntary immigration. Under the revisionist theory, children born in the United States to illegally imported slaves would not have been guaranteed citizenship by the Fourteenth Amendment, because the United States government did not consent to their parents' presence in the country. This would contradict the clear purpose of the Civil Rights Act of 1886 and the Fourteenth Amendment to overturn the *Dred Scott* decision and to guarantee U.S. citizenship to all persons of African descent born in the United States.

* * *

If Congress attempts to amend the citizenship statutes without a constitutional amendment, it will be acting unconstitutionally. The courts are certain to invalidate such action and vindicate the children's citizenship just as the Supreme Court did in *Wong Kim Ark*. Unfortunately, however, the court's decision will come only after a period of severe uncertainty for the government and hardship for the children affected by the legislation. It is one thing for academics to propose a speculative new theory and submit it to professional refutation, but quite another thing to experiment with the rights of U.S. citizen children. * * *

DAVID A. MARTIN, MEMBERSHIP AND CONSENT: ABSTRACT OR ORGANIC?
11 Yale J. Int'l L. 278, 282–284, 291–94 (1985).

* * * [C]onsider what happens if the new citizenship rules [proposed by Schuck and Smith] are adopted, but [other measures for controlling illegal immigration] either are not implemented or fail to have an appreciable impact. * * * From the date of the change onward, we would find a growing class of people who were born and raised in the United States but who do not have, and presumably cannot easily obtain, U.S. citizenship. What would be the consequences? What would be the effect on their attitudes toward the country in which they live? What effect would this new and unfortunate status have on the attitudes of citizens, not only toward this new class but toward other "aliens" present?

These are not abstract questions. Many European countries are now struggling with the so-called problems of the second generation. Those countries imported foreign workers during the boom years of the 1950's and 1960's. * * * Over the years, those workers have produced children, born in their parents' European country of residence, but without immediate citizenship rights there, because broadly applicable birthright citizenship rules are not in force.

Those children (many now adults) have known only life in Europe, but in disturbingly large numbers resist identifying with it. Although naturalization is available, relatively few of the guest workers or their children pursue it. * * * Against this background, anti-foreigner political parties have enjoyed increasing success.

In these circumstances, beset with a kind of *"apartheid volontaire"* that resists new governmental programs and augurs continuing and deepening problems for those polities, some European observers look with envy at *"la formidable machine assimilatrice de la société américaine."*[24] Though the fabric of the United States is woven with diverse strands, the country has been notably successful in encouraging newcomers, or at least the children of newcomers, to identify closely with the polity. There are problems, to be sure, but by and large they come to be seen as problems to be solved within the polity, by Americans acting as Americans. That assimilative capacity (which need not entail obliteration of cultural heritage) represents a precious national asset, especially for so large and diverse a country. Its existence and value are sometimes overlooked because its maintenance has so far been relatively effortless. We have no European-style "second generation problem" here, in part because we cannot have second generation aliens. The children may have dual citizenship, of course, and they are free to choose to make the other allegiance their principal one. But if they stay here, a secure citizenship status forms a basic foundation for the shaping of identity and involvement in the polity. They are thereby encouraged to embrace life here as full participants, not as half-hearted, stand-offish "guests." Equally important, other citizens are induced to treat them as coequal members of the polity, not as intruders who stay too long.

* * *

Consent *is* basic to certain aspects of democracy, and especially American democracy, but it is not the only principle, and in any event it is more complex and nuanced than the authors acknowledge. * * *

Time and familiarity weave their way into the complex relationship we call citizenship. Their significance fits comfortably with ascriptive citizenship rules, at least as long as ascription is not irrevocable. Most of us were simply born into our most basic affiliations—family, religion, nation. Those ties are not only objects of choice; to a significant extent they are constitutive of one's basic identity, anterior to choice. They help shape the characteristics of mind, preference, and perception that one brings to any particular consensual decision. Later we may exercise a

---

[24] Julliard, *Comment on devient un "vrai" Français*, Le Nouvel Observateur, Aug. 30-Sept. 5, 1985, *reprinted in* Actualités Migrations, Sept. 16, 1985, at 13.

"consensual" power to change some of those affiliations or preferences, but such choices reflect an organic process, not the radical act of a sovereign individual able to sweep away all such prior attachments by one magisterial act of consent or non-consent.

Ascriptive citizenship rules, especially generous ones, recognize this reality. They anchor choice—the consensualist political process—in a realistic and protective framework. One does not come into the political world as a naked and lonely individual, wholly dependent for the honoring of one's claims on consensual arrangements that might or might not be worked out with other contracting individuals or associations. * * * Indeed, the very notion of basic human rights applicable to all, alien or citizen, is fundamentally ascriptive; it suggests a list of entitlements that one may claim simply by reason of birth as a human being and not by reason of compact. * * *

Certainly after a person's basic affiliative foundation is established, consent * * * guards the outer boundaries of legitimacy * * * by providing a fundamental check against abuses by the polity of which one finds oneself a member. Consent can be withdrawn either collectively through revolution or individually by renunciation of citizenship and removal from the society. However, it is illusory to think that such a radical withdrawal of consent can be made so rationalistic and apparently cost-free.

* * *

Professors Schuck and Smith sometimes disparage the ascriptive principle as "medieval," "feudal," a "bastard concept," or a "vestigial remnant." Ascription without an individual right to withdraw consent may deserve those epithets. But American citizenship rules had worked free of that taint by at least as early as 1868. Modern citizenship rules, through a painful process of trial and error in Congress and the Supreme Court, have now crystallized in a humane mixture of ascription and consent. The ascriptive elements that survive do so for good and protective reasons.

NOTES AND QUESTIONS ON UNDOCUMENTED MIGRANTS, TEMPORARY RESIDENTS, AND JUS SOLI

1. Schuck and Smith assert that citizenship for the children of undocumented migrants is not constitutionally compelled. They stop short of expressing a view as to how Congress ought to use the power that they believe it possesses. In testimony before Congress more than a decade after publication of the book, Schuck opposed pending legislation that would have limited birthright citizenship to the children of citizens and permanent resident aliens. He argued:

> [The] most important advantage [of a birthright citizenship rule] is that it provides a crude but pragmatic accommodation to a long-

standing, apparently intractable policy failure: the substantial ineffectiveness of our border and interior immigration enforcement programs. Our feckless enforcement policies have created a possibility, indeed a certainty, that a large group of illegal aliens are nevertheless long-term or even lifelong residents in the U.S. Without a birthright citizenship rule or other amnesty, these illegals, their children, and their children's children will continue to be outsiders mired in an inferior and illegal status and deprived of the capacities of self-protection and self-advancement. Whatever the disadvantages of birthright citizenship, it has the great virtue of limiting the tragic effects of this problem of inherited outlawry by confining illegal status to a single generation for each family.

Societal and Legal Issues Surrounding Children Born in the United States to Illegal Alien Parents, Joint Hearing before the Subcomm. on Immigration and Claims and Subcomm. on the Constitution, House Comm. on the Judiciary, 104th Cong., 1st Sess. 100 (1995).

Compare Subcommittee Chairman Lamar Smith's comment at the same hearing: "[T]he cost of the children of illegal aliens just in Los Angeles County is over a billion dollars, when you include welfare and education. There's other testimony that 16 percent of the births in all of California now are to the children of illegal aliens. The appearance there, let me say, is that law breakers are being rewarded, taxpayers are being cheated, and citizenship is being cheapened." *Id*. at 84.

2.   In his examination of the 1866 Senate debates regarding the Citizenship Clause of the Fourteenth Amendment, Garrett Epps highlighted the discussion of whether *jus soli* citizenship should extend to children born in the United States to Chinese laborers and to "Gypsies," a group he analogized to the "illegal immigrants" of contemporary debate. Epps also noted that the Senators carefully distinguished between the different legal statuses of Indians—some lived in towns and villages, some had settled on reservations, and some had not yet been subdued by U.S. military forces— and that the text "subject to the jurisdiction [of the United States]" referred to those in the first group. From his review of the legislative debates, Epps concluded that there was little evidence that the framers of the Fourteenth Amendment intended the citizenship clause to apply only to children born to parents with legal status. Garrett Epps, *The Citizenship Clause: A "Legislative History,"* 60 Am. U. L. Rev. 331 (2010).

3.   Is it relevant to the argument advanced by Schuck and Smith that the constitutional *jus soli* principle does not allow the parents of a child born in the United States to evade deportation based on a claim that it would amount to a de facto deportation of the citizen child? *See, e.g., Acosta v. Gaffney*, 558 F.2d 1153 (3d Cir. 1977). Nor does it permit the U.S. born citizen child to confer any immigration benefits on his or her parents until the child reaches the statutorily prescribed age of 21. INA § 201(b)(2)(A)(i). The parents' lack of immunity from removal proceedings, of course, may force

families to make difficult personal choices about how—and where—to raise their children. The *Acosta* court acknowledged that the parents there could leave the young child in foster care in the United States, though it expected them to take the child with them to Colombia. But if that was the choice, the child would retain full rights to return to the United States for residence whenever she chose. Residence abroad does not jeopardize citizenship, because there can be no requirement of subsequent presence in order to maintain U.S. nationality that is acquired *jure soli*.

All countries with expansive *jus soli* rules authorize deportation of noncitizen parents. *See* T. Alexander Aleinikoff & Douglas Klusmeyer, eds., Citizenship Policies for an Age of Migration 11 (2002). Do you think that this is a necessary corollary of a broad *jus soli* rule?

4. Assume Schuck and Smith are correct on the constitutional question. Should Congress adopt legislation denying birthright citizenship to children of undocumented migrants? To children of tourists and other temporary visitors to the United States? Multiple bills, with broad levels of co-sponsorship, have been introduced in recent years to eliminate birthright citizenship for children whose parents lack legal status. *See, e.g.,* the proposed Birthright Citizenship Act of 2011, H.R. 140, 112th Cong. (2011).

In addition, legislators in multiple states have introduced bills that would provide special birth certificates for children whose parents lack legal authorization to live in the United States. Julia Preston, *State Lawmakers Outline Plans to End Birthright Citizenship, Drawing Outcry*, N.Y. Times, Jan. 5, 2011. If enacted, would these state laws be constitutional?

In recent years Texas officials have refused to issue birth certificates for children born in Texas hospitals unless the parents can produce driver's licenses or certain other identification documents. Unauthorized immigrants frequently lack the specified documents and consequently many are unable to obtain the birth certificates if their children. Texas officials justify their practice on the need to protect the confidentiality of vital records. Manny Fernandez, *Immigrants Fight Texas' Birth Certificate Rules*, N.Y. Times, Sept. 17, 2015.

5. How would you evaluate the claims to birthright citizenship for children born to noncitizens who entered without authorization but have resided in the United States for a long time? Do you think their claims are more or less powerful than those of children born to noncitizens, such as Hamdi, who entered legally for a short time? What about children born to noncitizens who expect to be in the United States for six or possibly more years on an H–1B visa, one of the long-term nonimmigrant visas that will be discussed in Chapter Five?

6. As broad as the U.S. *jus soli* rule is, there are proposals to broaden citizenship acquisition rules even further. For example, foreign-born children who immigrate at an early age—sometimes called the "1.5 generation"—are hard to distinguish from children born and reared in the United States.

Granting them citizenship both reflects socialization realities and furthers integration, according to the Comparative Citizenship Project of the Carnegie Endowment for International Peace and the Migration Policy Institute. See T. Alexander Aleinikoff & Douglas Klusmeyer, eds., Citizenship Policies for an Age of Migration (2002). Is such a policy sensible? If integration is the goal, should the proposal apply to all children who have resided and attended school in the United States for a certain number of years? Or should it be limited to children of lawful permanent residents? This, of course, is just another context for the discussion that Schuck and Smith's book engendered.

Note also that President Obama's DACA program (Deferred Action for Childhood Arrivals) is based on a similar recognition of the claims of Generation 1.5. DACA, of course, does not grant citizenship. Rather it grants only a renewable reprieve from removal to its beneficiaries—undocumented persons who came to the United States before age 16 and have lived in the country for five years. DACA is mentioned in Chapter One and described in greater detail in Chapter Ten.

Towards Convergence?

The traditional line between *jus soli* states and *jus sanguinis* states is blurring. That is, some historically *jus soli* states are cutting back a bit, limiting *jus soli* citizenship to the children of lawfully residing noncitizens. Concomitantly, some historically *jus sanguinis* states have begun to recognize the citizenship of third or long-residing second-generation immigrants. For example, a law that took effect in Germany in 2000 introduced a limited form of *jus soli* citizenship: a child born in Germany acquires *jus soli* citizenship if one parent has lived in Germany for eight years with certain types of residence permits. Furthermore, the child must choose before his or her twenty-third birthday between German and any other citizenship that he or she may hold. *See Gesetz zur Reform des Staatsangehörigkeitsrechts, Bundesgesetzblatt*, I 1618 (1999), amending *Ausländergesetz* § 85.

These developments suggest, perhaps, that a unified theory of birthright citizenship could be developed by focusing on *generations* rather than *descent* or *residence*. Consider the following proposal, developed by the Comparative Citizenship Project of the Carnegie Endowment for International Peace and the Migration Policy Institute (and roughly patterned after current French citizenship rules):[4]

a. members of the third generation (the grandchildren of immigrants) would be automatically entitled to citizenship at birth;

b. members of the second generation (the children of immigrants) who are lawful residents or whose parents are lawful residents would be

---

[4] Aleinikoff & Klusmeyer, *supra*, Citizenship Policies for an Age of Migration.

entitled to citizenship after having resided in the state for a reasonably determined number of years;

c.   foreign-born children who immigrate at any early age should be considered members of the second generation and should be entitled to citizenship after residing in the state for ten years or completing six years in school.

How do these policies differ from current U.S. citizenship norms (note that they are both more and less generous)? Do they describe a sensible approach to citizenship acquisition norms?

3.   DUAL NATIONALITY

Under *jus soli* and *jus sanguinis* rules, some children at birth are citizens of more than one country, the state where they are born and the state of their parents' nationality. If the parents happen to be from different countries, the child may simultaneously possess citizenship in three states. For many years international law disfavored multiple nationality, allowing states to prevent or reduce instances of dual citizenship in a variety of ways. For example, when dual nationality is created at birth by the overlap of *jus soli* and *jus sanguinis* rules a state may require that a person elect one citizenship or the other at time of majority. For persons attaining citizenship through naturalization, which will be discussed in Section B below, the state of origin may deem such conduct expatriating; and the state granting naturalization may require renunciation of prior citizenship or even documentary proof that the other government recognizes the loss of its citizenship.

Some state-to-state arrangements tolerate dual citizenship but seek to ameliorate the complications it causes. For example, treaties may clarify military obligations of dual citizens. *See, e.g.,* the Articles 5 & 6 of the Council of Europe's Convention on Reduction of Cases of Multiple Nationality and Military Obligations in Cases of Multiple Nationality, 634 U.N.T.S. 221, *entered into force* Mar. 28, 1968. For a thorough discussion, *see* Stephen H. Legomsky, *Dual Nationality and Military Service: Strategy Number Two*, in Rights and Duties of Dual Nationals: Evolution and Prospects 79 (David A. Martin and Kay Hailbronner, eds., 2003).

In the past, many countries, including the United States, established policies and laws to prevent dual nationality, but the contemporary trend is decidedly in the other direction. *See* Charles Roth, *Worldwide Liberalization of Dual Citizenship Rules and Potential Side Effects on U.S. Citizenship*, 83 Interp. Rel. 2529 (2006); Michael Jones-Correa, *Dual Nationality in Latin America and its Consequences for Naturalization in the United States*, in Rights and Duties of Dual Nationals: Evolution and Prospects 303 (David A. Martin & Kay Hailbronner, eds., 2003). The next commentary surveys different scenarios giving rise to multiple citizenship in the United States and some of the implications of nationality in more than one state.

T. ALEXANDER ALEINIKOFF, BETWEEN PRINCIPLES AND POLITICS: THE DIRECTION OF U.S. CITIZENSHIP

From Migrants to Citizens: Membership in a Changing World,
T. Alexander Aleinikoff & Douglas Klusmeyer, eds., 137–41 (2000).

* * *

In the United States, the incidence of dual citizenship is far more widespread than is generally recognized. Plural citizenship may arise in four situations:

1. *Birth in the United States to immigrant parents.* A citizen of country A moves to the United States and has a child. The child is a dual citizen if country A has *jus sanguinis* rules that recognize the child as a citizen of country A. (Example: a German citizen has a child in Chicago. Note that if a German citizen marries a British citizen and they have a child in the United States, the child may be born with three nationalities.)

2. *Birth outside the United States to one parent who is a U.S. citizen and another who is a foreigner.* A citizen of the United States marries a citizen of country A and has a child in country A. If the U.S. citizen has maintained the ties to the United States necessary for the transmission of citizenship *jure sanguinis*, the child is a citizen of both country A and the United States. (Example: A native-born United States citizen marries a British citizen and has a child in the United Kingdom.)

3. *Naturalization with a renunciation requirement, but renunciation not recognized by country of origin.* A citizen of country A naturalizes in the United States. Even though the naturalization oath demands renunciation of other citizenships, country A does not deem naturalization elsewhere as expatriating the citizen. (Example: A Canadian citizen naturalizes in the United States. The U.S. oath requires renunciation, but Canada does not regard naturalization in the United States as expatriating unless the person specifically notifies Canadian authorities of an intent to renounce citizenship.)

4. *Naturalization, loss of citizenship, and resumption of citizenship.* A citizen of country A naturalizes in the United States. Country A deems the person to have lost citizenship but provides for the resumption of citizenship. (Example: Under Australian law, a citizen who naturalizes in the United States loses Australian citizenship. The person can, however, subsequently apply to resume Australian citizenship—this is not a

naturalization process—without losing U.S. citizenship unless he or she expresses the intent to do so.)[46]

The U.S. government does not record and has not estimated the number of U.S. dual citizens, but the total may be quite large. Any U.S.-born child of immigrants in the United States is likely at birth to be a citizen of both the United States and the parents' country of origin. Some of the largest "sending" countries to the United States—including Mexico, the Philippines, the Dominican Republic, Canada and India—recognize children born to their nationals here as citizens of their countries. The Census Bureau's March 1996 Current Population Survey provides data that can supply a rough estimate of the number of children born dual nationals in the United States each year. The study reports that there were 540,000 U.S.-citizen children less than one year of age living with at least one foreign-born parent who was not a naturalized U.S. citizen. It is reasonable to assume that most of these children are dual citizens, although the number is not a precise measure. It *under*counts, for example, the number of dual citizens by not including (1) U.S.-born children whose foreign parents left the United States within a year and (2) children of foreign-born parents who have naturalized in the United States but who are still able to transmit the citizenship under their home countries' *jus sanguinis* rules. The number may *over*count the number of dual nationals by including children of foreign-born parents whose home countries do not permit the transmission of citizenship overseas if the foreign-born child obtains another citizenship at birth (China is the most significant example). Nonetheless, half a million is probably an acceptable order of magnitude for the number of children who obtain dual citizenship at birth each year in the United States. Because most countries do not require dual citizens to elect one citizenship over the other, the status may continue for life, and, indeed, can be passed to generations beyond.

The rising incidence of dual citizenship is also due to the growing number of states that have altered their laws to permit their citizens to retain nationality despite naturalization elsewhere. Canada adopted such a policy in 1977, as have (more recently) Argentina, Colombia, Costa Rica, the Dominican Republic, El Salvador, France, Israel, Ireland, Italy, Panama, Switzerland and the United Kingdom.[48] Even in states that deem naturalization in the United States as constituting expatriation,

---

[46] In the late nineteenth century, the rule was generally that a wife took the citizenship of her husband. This is now almost universally rejected, the result being that individuals preserve their own nationality after marriage, although spouses are frequently given preferential treatment under the immigration quotas. See INA § 201(b). This twentieth-century development is a major contributing factor to increases in dual citizenship, since under *jus sanguinis* rules a child will obtain citizenship from each parent.

[48] This list is not all inclusive. [For a more recent list, *see* Dual Citizenship Countries, http://best-citizenships.com/dual-citizenship-countries.htm—eds.]

authorities are likely to be unaware of the U.S. naturalization and therefore may continue to treat naturalized individuals as citizens.

IS DUAL CITIZENSHIP A PROBLEM?

Both theoretically and symbolically, dual citizenship may appear problematic. A regime of nation-states arguably functions more smoothly when persons are assigned citizenship in just one state. Unitary citizenship not only resolves various state administrative problems but also, it might be claimed, provides for an indivisible loyalty that states are likely to seek and value.

But the world is more complicated than this ideal allows, and a desire for tidiness is often in conflict with the practicalities of human life. Migration, marriage, and birth ensure that neither states nor their citizenries are hermetically sealed. Indeed, dual citizenship cannot be attributed simply to the (intentional or unintentional) actions of individuals. The existence of plural citizenships is a function of the unwillingness of the international community to establish international norms on the acquisition and maintenance of citizenship; international law leaves such matters to the discretion of states, and the resulting welter of rules is wholly a product of state choices.

Although a post-national world still seems far away, it is clear that the world is increasingly transnational. Modern communications and transportation have brought the world to the United States' door as never before, and many of those coming are less willing to leave their countries of origin behind. This reluctance characterizes business elites who seek to take advantage of commercial opportunities in more than one country as well as lower-skilled workers who seek to improve their condition abroad but remain connected to home communities. And, as already noted, "sending" countries show an increasing interest in maintaining ties with their diaspora populations.

From one perspective, these developments represent a healthy development, making commercial and social ties between nations deeper and stronger, opening up new markets, and fostering appreciation of cultural diversity. Little evidence exists that wide-spread dual citizenship in the United States has been harmful to the national interest. While some dual citizens (and naturalized citizens) have committed espionage against the United States, so have persons of one nationality—either native-born citizens or immigrants. Similarly, while concerns have been voiced that dual nationals may vote the interests of their countries of origin ahead of the interests of the United States, the same would be possible whether or not the person officially retains the citizenship of his or her home country.

From another perspective, there is cause for concern. The growing interest of countries of origin in dual citizenship for their nationals may make it a different phenomenon than it was in the past. Furthermore, with the sovereignty of the nation-state being challenged both from within and without, the idea of citizenship may take on increasing importance. Insistence on unitary citizenship could serve as a brake on transnational developments that undermine the loyalty and commitment needed for the healthy functioning of a polyethnic state.

NOTES AND QUESTIONS ON DUAL NATIONALITY

1. Writing in 2000, Aleinikoff envisioned an increasingly transnational world, a growing demand for multiple citizenship, and the possibility that there would be renewed calls for unitary citizenship. More than fifteen years later, what is your assessment of these trends? Do you know many people who are citizens of more than one country? How do you think multiple citizenship is portrayed in the popular press?

2. U.S. Senator Ted Cruz, a candidate for the 2016 Republican Party presidential nomination, had multiple citizenships at birth. Born in Alberta, Canada, he was, under Canadian *jus soli* principles, a Canadian citizen. His mother was a U.S. citizen, while his father was a Cuban citizen who received asylum in the United States, later became a Canadian citizen, and ultimately obtained naturalization in the United States. Cruz, apparently unaware of his birthright Canadian citizenship until journalists reported it in 2014, took official steps to renounce his Canadian citizenship. Saeed Ahmed, *It's Official: Ted Cruz A Citizen of the U.S.—and the U.S. Only*, CNN News, Nov. 12, 2015. "Nothing against Canada, but I'm an American by birth and as a U.S. senator, I believe I should be only an American," Cruz reportedly said. Nolan Feeney, *Ted Cruz Renounces Newly Discovered Canadian Citizenship*, Time, June 10, 2014. During the 2016 Republican primaries both Senator Cruz and Senator Marco Rubio, who was born in the United States to Cuban parents who had not yet become U.S. citizens, faced criticism that dual nationality disqualified them from the presidency. *See, e.g.*, Bradford Richardson, *Trump: 'I'm Not Sure' if Rubio Is Eligible to Run for President*, The Hill, Feb. 21, 2016.

3. For further discussion of dual nationality, see Alfred Boll, Multiple Nationality and International Law (2007); Stanley A. Renshon, The 50% American: Immigration and National Identity in an Age of Terror (2005); Rights and Duties of Dual Nationals: Evolution and Prospect (David A. Martin & Kay Hailbronner, eds., 2003); Randall Hansen & Patrick Weil, eds., Dual Nationality, Social Rights and Federal Citizenship in the U.S. and Europe: The Reinvention of Citizenship (2002); Linda Bosniak, *Citizenship Denationalized*, 7 Ind. J. Global Legal Studies, 447 (2000); David A. Martin, *New Rules on Dual Nationality for a Democratizing Globe: Between Rejection and Embrace*, 14 Geo. Immigr. L.J. 1 (1999); Peter J. Spiro, *Dual Nationality and the Meaning of Citizenship*, 46 Emory L.F. 1411 (1997).

B. NATURALIZATION

In addition to acquiring citizenship at birth, individuals can seek a new citizenship later in life. Indeed, the Constitution of the United States, a country that envisioned itself as a new land attractive to settlers from other nations, expressly grants Congress the authority to create a "uniform Rule of Naturalization." The following selections first review the history of U.S. naturalization legislation and then turn the focus onto the racial restrictions that characterized those laws until 1952.

its in the const.

New York street corner next to the Federal Building where the U.S. Department of
Labor handled naturalization of immigrants (1939).
(Photo: National Archives)

CHARLES GORDON, STANLEY MAILMAN,
STEPHEN YALE-LOEHR & RONALD Y. WADA,
IMMIGRATION LAW AND PROCEDURE
Vol. 4, § 94.01[2] [b]–[f] (rev. ed. 2016).*

* * *

original statute on Naturalization

In the original statute of March 26, 1790, Congress prescribed that a free white alien who had resided in the United States for two years, including residence of one year in any State, might be naturalized by any common law court of record, provided the person was of good moral character and took an oath to support the Constitution. Five years later the 1790 statute was repealed by the Act of January 29, 1795, which re-enacted most of its provisions, with the following additions: The period of required residence in the United States increased to five years; federal courts were also able to grant naturalization; a formal declaration of intention three years before admission to citizenship was made a prerequisite; applicants were required to renounce their former allegiance and to swear allegiance to the United States; and applicants had to establish to the satisfaction of the court that they were attached to the Constitution of the United States and well disposed to the good order and happiness of the United States.

The statutory requirements for naturalization formulated at this time resembled very closely the substantive requirements now generally prescribed. However, the 1795 law was short-lived. The country entered a period of reaction characterized by outbursts against aliens. One product of this interlude of hysteria was the enactment of the Alien and Sedition acts. Another was the Act of June 18, 1798, which repealed the lenient provisions of the 1795 statute, and announced more restrictive naturalization requirements. The period of required residence was increased to 14 years in the United States and five years in a state; a declaration of intention at least five years before naturalization was prescribed; registration of aliens became mandatory; and residence for the purposes of naturalization could be proved only upon production of a certificate of registry. Naturalization of alien enemies was prohibited.

Fortunately this interval of reaction soon ended. The Act of April 14, 1802 repealed the 1798 statute and restored the reasonable requirements of the 1795 law, which have remained generally in effect through two centuries.

Although the early laws established acceptable substantive requirements, they were silent concerning the procedure to be followed. There were thousands of naturalization courts throughout the country, most of which were local courts in the various states. Each tribunal determined the procedure it would pursue in applications for naturalization. There was no centralized federal agency charged with the responsibility of enforcing the naturalization statutes.

This situation may have been adequate when there were few courts and a moderate quota of applicants for naturalization. With the expansion of immigration and the consequent increase in the number of aliens who sought naturalization, serious shortcomings in the naturalization process became evident. The absence of procedural standards and safeguards bred wide divergences in the practices of different naturalization courts, in the records they maintained, and in the type of evidence of citizenship they issued. The courts had no facilities to investigate the applications presented to them, and many of the court

officials were not scrupulous in insisting upon compliance with the
requirements fixed by law. As a result of these conditions, widespread
frauds developed, which frequently made a mockery of the naturalization
process.

led to fraud

On March 1, 1905 President Theodore Roosevelt appointed a
commission to investigate abuses in the naturalization process and to
recommend appropriate revisions. As the result of the report of this
commission, Congress enacted the Naturalization Act of June 29, 1906.
Under this statute the courts retained the ultimate authority to grant or
deny citizenship, but administrative supervision over naturalization was
vested in a federal agency (originally the Bureau of Immigration and
Naturalization in the Department of Commerce and Labor).

1905 – investigating abuses

1906 – Nat. Act.

* * *

Congress [later] enacted the Nationality Act of 1940 as a codification
and revision of all existing nationality laws. * * *

The next major milestone in the historical pattern was the
Immigration and Nationality Act of 1952, which is now the basic statute
for U.S. immigration and nationality law. * * * Among the major changes
effected by the 1952 Act were the following:

The racial qualifications for naturalization were completely
eliminated, and the statute specifically prohibited denial of
naturalization because of race or sex.

less discrimination

The statute, incorporating an enactment of 1950, specifically
prohibited the naturalization of certain members of subversive
groups. * * *

no subversive groups

Naturalization was precluded for aliens against whom a
deportation proceeding or order was outstanding. * * *

– none for any w/ order of depor.

The declaration of intention and the certificate of arrival were
eliminated as requirements for naturalization.

– no more decl. or cert.

The grounds for expatriation and denaturalization were
enlarged.

– more ways to get kicked out

The Immigration Act of 1990 (1990 Act) had a significant effect on
naturalization by transferring authority over naturalization from the
judiciary to the Attorney General. Consequently, the naturalization
process has evolved from a judicial framework to almost entirely an
administrative one * * * [—although federal judges are still normally
involved in administering the oath as part of the naturalization
ceremony. With the abolition of the INS and the transfer of functions to
the Department of Homeland Security in 2003, these administrative
responsibilities are now lodged in DHS' Bureau of Citizenship and
Immigration Services (USCIS).]

* * *

handwritten marginalia: DHS now makes decisions - same criteria as before

* * * Under administrative naturalization [DHS] now has the exclusive power to make decisions on naturalization applications. [Administrative] officers are no longer making recommendations to the judiciary. In actuality, the new procedures for handling naturalization applications on the administrative level are very similar to past procedures in judicial naturalization. [Administrative officers were] already responsible for most aspects of the naturalization process and established forms, systems, and procedures for handling virtually all phases of the process except the oath. [DHS] continues to evaluate applicants according to virtually the same criteria for eligibility that it used under the judicial system.

IAN F. HANEY LÓPEZ, RACIAL RESTRICTIONS IN THE LAW OF CITIZENSHIP

White By Law: The Legal Construction of Race, 37, 39, 42–46 (1996).

The racial composition of the U.S. citizenry reflects in part the accident of world migration patterns. More than this, however, it reflects the conscious design of U.S. immigration and naturalization laws.

* * *

handwritten marginalia: Race played a role until 1952.

* * * From this country's inception, the laws regulating who was or could become a citizen were tainted by racial prejudice. * * * Naturalized citizenship, the acquisition of citizenship by any means other than through birth, was conditioned on race until 1952. Like immigration laws, the laws of birthright citizenship and naturalization shaped the racial character of the United States.

handwritten marginalia: Congressional power via Constitution

Although the Constitution did not originally define the citizenry, it explicitly gave Congress the authority to establish the criteria for granting citizenship after birth. Article I grants Congress the power "To establish a[n] uniform Rule of Naturalization." From the start, Congress exercised this power in a manner that burdened naturalization laws with racial restrictions that tracked those in the law of birthright citizenship. In 1790, only a few months after ratification of the Constitution, Congress limited naturalization to "any alien, being a free white person who shall have resided within the limits and under the jurisdiction of the United States for a term of two years." * * * Though there would be many subsequent changes in the requirements for federal naturalization, racial identity endured as a bedrock requirement for the next 162 years. * * *

handwritten marginalia: white from the beginning

The history of racial prerequisites to naturalization can be divided into two periods of approximately eighty years each. The first period extended from 1790 to 1870, when only Whites were able to naturalize. In the wake of the Civil War, the "white person" restriction on naturalization came under serious attack as part of the effort to expunge *Dred Scott*. Some congressmen, Charles Sumner chief among them, argued that racial barriers to naturalization should be struck altogether. However, racial prejudice against Native Americans and Asians forestalled the complete elimination of the racial prerequisites. During congressional debates, one senator argued against conferring "the rank, privileges, and immunities of citizenship upon the cruel savages who destroyed [Minnesota's] peaceful settlements and massacred the people with circumstances of atrocity too horrible to relate." Another senator wondered "whether this door [of citizenship] shall now be thrown open to the Asiatic population," warning that to do so would spell for the Pacific coast "an end to republican government there, because it is very well ascertained that those people have no appreciation of that form of government; it seems to be obnoxious to their very nature; they seem to be incapable either of understanding or carrying it out." Sentiments such as these ensured that even after the Civil War, bars against Native American and Asian naturalization would continue. Congress opted to maintain the "white person" prerequisite, but to extend the right to naturalize to "persons of African nativity, or African descent." After 1870, Blacks as well as Whites could naturalize, but not others.

During the second period, from 1870 until the last of the prerequisite laws were abolished in 1952, the White-Black dichotomy in American race relations dominated naturalization law. During this period, Whites and Blacks were eligible for citizenship, but others, particularly those from Asia, were not. Indeed, increasing antipathy toward Asians on the West Coast resulted in an explicit disqualification of Chinese persons from naturalization in 1882. The prohibition of Chinese naturalization, the only U.S. law ever to exclude by name a particular nationality from citizenship, was coupled with [a] ban on Chinese immigration. * * *

World War II forced a domestic reconsideration of the racism integral to U.S. naturalization law. In 1935, Hitler's Germany limited citizenship to members of the Aryan race, making Germany the only country other than the United States with a racial restriction on naturalization. * * * Furthermore, the United States was open to charges of hypocrisy for banning from naturalization the nationals of many of its Asian allies. During the war, the United States seemed through some of its laws and social practices to embrace the same racism it was fighting. Both fronts of the war exposed profound inconsistencies between U.S. naturalization law and broader social ideals. These considerations, among others, led Congress to begin a process of piecemeal reform in the laws governing citizenship.

In 1940, Congress opened naturalization to "descendants of races indigenous to the Western Hemisphere." Apparently, this "additional limitation was designed 'to more fully cement' the ties of Pan-

Americanism" at a time of impending crisis.[40] In 1943, Congress replaced the prohibition on the naturalization of Chinese persons with a provision explicitly granting them this boon. In 1946, it opened up naturalization to persons from the Philippines and India as well. * * * In 1952, Congress moved towards wholesale reform, overhauling the naturalization statute to read simply that "[t]he right of a person to become a naturalized citizen of the United States shall not be denied or abridged because of race or sex or because such person is married."[44] Thus, in 1952, racial bars on naturalization came to an official end.

NOTES AND QUESTIONS ON
RACIAL CRITERIA FOR CITIZENSHIP

1.   As might be imagined, the statutory requirement that applicants for naturalization be "white" produced difficult questions of interpretation for administrative and judicial authorities. The Supreme Court adopted varying approaches for resolving the question. In *Ozawa v. United States,* 260 U.S. 178, 43 S.Ct. 65, 67 L.Ed. 199 (1922), the Court held that a "person of the Japanese race" is not "white" within the meaning of the statute because, as "sustained by numerous scientific authorities," Japanese are not members of "the Caucasian race." A year later in *United States v. Thind,* 261 U.S. 204, 43 S.Ct. 338, 67 L.Ed. 616 (1923), the Court concluded that "a high-caste Hindu of full Indian blood" was not eligible for naturalization. Whether or not Thind was classified as "Caucasian" by "certain scientific authorities," the word "white" was to be interpreted "in accordance with the understanding of the common man. * * * [W]hatever may be the speculations of the ethnologist, it does not include the body of people to whom [Thind] belongs." The Court noted: "It is very far from our thought to suggest the slightest question of racial superiority or inferiority. What we suggest is merely racial difference, and it is of such character and extent that the great body of our people instinctively recognize it and reject the thought of assimilation." 261 U.S. at 215.

2.   The history that Haney López recounts demonstrates that for most of this nation's history, our naturalization laws have excluded persons based solely on their race. The Court's assertion in *Thind* that these exclusions had nothing to do with notions of racial superiority strains credulity. As we shall see, similar notions marked the history of U.S. immigration law. Citizenship and immigration law, as gateways to membership, reflect deep-seated societal views of who belongs. Should we read the history as a progressive vindication of principles of equality and fairness; or is our history more cyclical, with nativist and exclusionary themes regularly coming to the fore? Rogers Smith has suggested that "the very success of liberalizing and democratizing reforms is to unsettle many, creating constituencies for

---

[40]   Note, *The Nationality Act of 1940*, 54 Harv.L.Rev. 860, 865 n.40 (1941).

[44]   Immigration and Nationality Act of 1952, ch. 2, § 311, 66 Stat. 239 (codified as amended at INA § 311).

rebuilding ascriptive inequalities in new forms. The overall pattern will be one of fluctuation between consensual and egalitarian and more ascriptive and in egalitarian arrangements, with the long-term trends being products of contingent politics more than inexorable cultural necessities." Rogers M. Smith, Civic Ideals: Conflicting Visions of Citizenship in U.S. History 9 (1997). Do the materials in this chapter tend to support or refute this claim?

3. Note that at the same time that persons were excluded from naturalizing on the basis of their race, their children born in the United States were citizens at birth by force of the Fourteenth Amendment. Is there a coherent theory of citizenship that explains the co-existence of these apparently conflicting rules?

[handwritten: irony that parents were barred from citizenship but children born in US = American]

1. A SNAPSHOT OF NATURALIZATION DEMOGRAPHICS

The number of individuals applying for naturalization in the United States increased significantly in the 1920s, again in the 1940s, and most dramatically in the last three decades. From 1946 to 1984, the number of persons naturalized exceeded 200,000 in any single year only once. Beginning in the late 1980s, the number of both applications and naturalizations increased substantially. Annual naturalizations averaged 141,000 in the 1970s, 205,000 in the 1980s, almost 500,000 in the 1990s, and 682,000 in the 2000s. Jie Zong & Jeanne Batalova, *Frequently Requested Statistics on Immigrants and Immigration in the United States*, Migration Policy Institute (2015).

At least three different factors contributed to the large increase in the 1990s. First, the cohort of immigrants legalized under the Immigration Reform and Control Act of 1986 (IRCA), Pub. L. 99–603, 100 Stat. 3359, became eligible for citizenship. (As we will examine below in Chapter Five, one additional inducement for naturalization is that it permits the new citizen to sponsor close family members for immigration on far more favorable terms than those that apply to lawful permanent resident (LPR) sponsors.) Second, there can be little doubt that the anti-immigrant rhetoric of the mid-1990s led some immigrants to seek the security of U.S. citizenship. Third, the welfare reform legislation of 1996, which severely limited eligibility of permanent resident aliens for most means-tested benefit programs, sparked a demand for naturalization as immigrants sought to preserve their access (at present or in the future) to the social safety net.

[handwritten margin notes: ① sponsor family ② anti-immigrant 1990s ③ welfare]

[handwritten: ↳ more narrative of fear of legal security that non-citizens do not have]

Figure 2.1
Persons Naturalized: 1907 to 2013

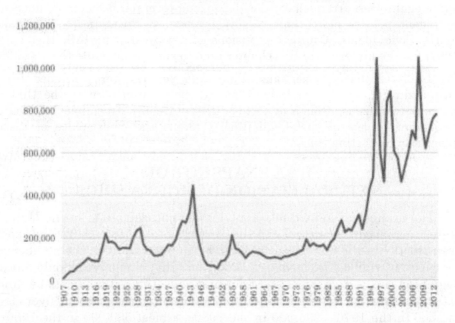

Source: U.S. DHS, 2013 Yearbook of Immigration Statistics, Table 20.

Naturalizations hit peaks of 1,040,991 in 1996 and 1,046,539 in 2008. Scheduled application fee increases and a naturalization campaign preceding the presidential election accounted for the 2008 surge. In recent years naturalizations have remained at levels that are high by historical standards. In 2011, 2012, and 2013, for example, 694,000, 757,000 and 780,000 lawful permanent residents became U.S. citizens, respectively.

In fiscal year 2013, the leading countries of origin of newly naturalized citizens were Mexico (approximately 100,000 or 13 percent of the total), India (almost 50,000), the Philippines (43,000), the Dominican Republic (40,000), China (35,000), and Cuba (30,000). These countries have been among the leading source countries of immigrants to the United States for some time. Together they account for approximately 40 per cent of the annual naturalizations. Gregory Auclair & Jeanne Batalova, *Naturalization Trends in the United States*, Migration Policy Institute (2013).

Currently, close to 47 percent of the foreign-born population (19.3 million of roughly 42 million immigrants) have naturalized. This amounts to six percent of the total U.S. population. Zong & Batalova, *Frequently Requested Statistics, supra.* Over the past two decades, there has been a large increase in the country's total foreign-born population; the percentage who have naturalized has risen during this time. From 1990 to 2013, the percentage of foreign-born persons who are naturalized U.S. citizens rose from 40.5 percent to 46.7 percent. During that same period, the total number of foreign-born persons living in the United States grew by 109 percent to reach a total of 41,348,066. *See* Table 1. Foreign-Born Population and World Region of Birth (1990, 2000, and 2013).

An interesting comparative perspective on the percentage of naturalizations in the United States is offered by Irene Bloemraad:

> In the mid-1900s, almost four of every five foreign-born U.S. and Canadian residents held citizenship in their adopted lands. Fifty years later, citizenship levels had changed little in Canada: about three quarters of the foreign-born had Canadian passports in 2001. In contrast, U.S. citizenship hovered at its lowest level in a century. Only two of every five foreign-born had naturalized in 2000.

Irene Bloemraad, *Becoming a Citizen in the United States and Canada: Structured Mobilization and Immigrant Political Incorporation*, 85 Social Forces 667 (2006).

"*unauthorized*"
→ no path to citizenship

The large unauthorized immigrant community in the United States accounts for some of the difference in naturalization rates because they cannot become citizens. Further, the 1990s witnessed a very large increase in immigration to the United States, and the naturalization rate in 2000 may not be representative of the overall naturalization process. Nonetheless, Bloemraad theorizes that additional factors may be at work. For example, she asserts that the proximity of the host country to the country of origin will likely have a negative effect, as the ease of return to nearby homelands may be a disincentive to naturalize. In contrast, she suggests that greater government assistance to immigrant groups is likely to increase the rate of naturalization. She notes that Canadian policy more actively fosters integration and citizenship, and that immigrant groups who have received United States government assistance, such as refugees and Cold War-era immigrants from the Soviet bloc, have also naturalized at an unusually high rate. Highlighting the greater political integration in Canada, she points to 45 (of 301) foreign-born members of Parliament in Canada, compared to 8 (of 435) in the U.S. House of Representatives in 2000. Irene Bloemraad, *Becoming a Citizen: Incorporating Immigrants and Refugees in the United States and Canada*, 2006, at 60–64; Irene Bloemraad, *Becoming a Citizen in the United States and Canada: Structured Mobilization and Immigrant Political Incorporation, supra*, at 684.

+ more gov' assistance

help post-war

2. THE BASIC STATUTORY PROVISIONS

Naturalization requirements continue along the general lines set by the 1795 Act. We explore the elements below. But first we take a quick look at the naturalization procedures.

The Immigration Act of 1990 transformed naturalization into almost entirely an administrative procedure under the authority of the Attorney General. Courts are still generally involved in administering the citizenship oath, however, and an especially powerful form of judicial review is available when the administrators deny a naturalization petition. These changes were accomplished primarily in INA § 310 (setting forth the basic administrative procedure and the judicial review provisions), § 335 (examination of application for naturalization), and § 336 (hearing before an immigration officer if application is denied at the examination stage).

Under the system established by the 1990 Act—as altered by the transfer of INS functions to DHS in 2003—an application for naturalization goes to a USCIS officer who examines the applicant and makes a formal determination to grant or deny. INA § 335. That examiner has authority to conduct a wide-ranging investigation and to subpoena witnesses and documents, but in the overwhelming majority of cases the examination consists primarily of an interview of the applicant. If the application is approved, the oath of allegiance can be administered by a court or by DHS, in accordance with INA § 310(b).

If the examiner denies the application, he or she must state the reasons. The applicant may then request a further hearing before an "immigration officer," who must be of equal or higher grade level to the examiner who initially denied the application. INA § 336(a); 8 C.F.R. § 336.2(b). This second officer has the discretion to schedule a full de novo hearing, or to "utilize a less formal review procedure, as he or she deems reasonable and in the interest of justice." *Id.* The latter course is likely if it appears that the problem can be resolved routinely—for example, by administering another test of English language capability or knowledge of U.S. government. If the full-fledged administrative hearing still results in a denial, the applicant can seek judicial review, in accordance with the general provisions of the Administrative Procedure Act, in the federal district court having jurisdiction over the place of his residence. INA § 310(c). The court's review "shall be *de novo,* and the court shall make its own findings of fact and conclusions of law." *Id.* The House committee explained that "citizenship is the most valued governmental benefit of this land and applicants should receive full recourse to the Judiciary when the request for that benefit is denied." H.R. Rep. No. 101–187, *supra,* at 14.

PROBLEMS

To help you dig into the statute and the summary of the substantive provisions that follow, imagine that you are an immigration attorney with the following clients. Before you meet with them, you should review the sections setting forth the substantive and procedural naturalization requirements, INA §§ 311–331, and 337, with special attention to §§ 312, 313, 316, 318, 319(a), 334, and 337. Section 101(f) is also important. What would you advise them? What additional information might you want to know before offering advice?

[handwritten marginalia: "Can choose either route"]

[handwritten marginalia: "3 years?"]

1.   Client A was lawfully admitted to the United States as a permanent resident 40 months ago as the spouse of another lawful permanent resident alien, B. B naturalized one year later. A wants to become a citizen as soon as possible. When is the earliest that she can apply? What are the procedural steps she needs to follow? Must she file any papers now?

[handwritten marginalia: "6 yrs ago", "5 years ago convicted", "how long?", "conviction", "now", "may be able to apply"]

2.   Client C, admitted to the United States nine years ago as a lawful permanent resident, committed burglary three years later and was convicted of the offense a year after that. He has now applied for naturalization. Is he eligible?

3.   Client D was admitted as a lawful permanent resident in 1985 and is interested in pursuing naturalization. D has from time to time volunteered for a charitable organization that raises money for hospitals and childcare centers in several Arab countries. The assets of the organization in the United States have been recently frozen by the U.S. government, based on a claim that some of the charity's funds were diverted to organizations that sponsored terrorism. The charity disputes the allegations, and D says that she has no knowledge of any activity by the organization that supported terrorism. She would like to know whether the government's allegations could affect her prospects for naturalization.

The substantive requirements for naturalization include age, residence and physical presence, good moral character, knowledge of U.S. history and government, English language proficiency, attachment to constitutional principles, and an oath of allegiance to the United States.

[handwritten marginalia: "Reqs."]

a. Age

[handwritten marginalia: "derivative citizenship"]

Applicants for naturalization must generally be at least 18 years old. INA § 334(b)(1). Most children who are naturalized obtain citizenship when one of their parents is naturalized. Known as "derivative citizenship," it occurs by operation of law. The child must have been admitted as a permanent resident and reside with the parent in the United States; there is no waiting period. INA § 320.

Until recently, children adopted overseas by U.S. citizen parents had to go through naturalization proceedings after entering the United States. Because their parents did not need to naturalize, the children did not benefit from derivative naturalization. In 2000, Congress made this process easier by enacting legislation that grants automatic citizenship to all children admitted as lawful permanent residents who are residing in the United States with a citizen parent. Child Citizenship Act of 2000, Pub. L. 106–395, 144 Stat. 1631 (amending INA § 320).

b. Residence and Physical Presence

Naturalization applicants must have been admitted as lawful permanent residents and have resided continuously in the United States for at least five years. During the five years immediately prior to applying for naturalization, the applicant must have been physically present in the United States for at least two and one half years. The applicant must have resided within the State in which the application is filed for at least three months and must reside continuously within the United States between the application and admission to citizenship. INA § 316(a).

Short trips out of the United States do not interrupt the residence requirement; absences between six months and one year are presumed to break the continuous residence requirement, but the presumption can be overcome by evidence that the applicant did not intend to abandon his or her residence. INA § 316(b). Applicants who leave the United States for a continuous period of one year or more will not satisfy the residency requirement; after they return to the United States they must begin anew to complete the residency requirement.

(i) U.S. Employment Abroad

Lawful permanent residents who lived in the United States for at least one year and then go abroad to work for the United States government, certain U.S. research institutions, certain U.S. companies, or certain public international organizations may receive an exception to the continuous residence requirement. INA § 316(b). Exceptions to the residency requirement do not waive the physical presence requirement, except for those employed overseas by the U.S. government, INA § 316(c), or certain religious organizations, INA § 317.

(ii) Spouses of U.S. Citizens

The residence requirement is reduced to three years for spouses of U.S. citizens. They must have been lawfully admitted as permanent residents and since admission have lived in "marital union" with their spouse for the three years immediately before filing their naturalization application. The special provisions applying to spouses and children who

have been battered by U.S. citizens also include a three-year continuous *battered. sec*
residence requirement. INA § 319.

(iii) Military Service

Naturalization applicants who have served honorably in the U.S.
armed forces for one year do not have to satisfy residency or physical
presence requirements. INA § 328. Most striking, noncitizens who serve
in active-duty status in the U.S. armed services during recognized periods
of military hostilities need not have been permanent resident aliens in   *can go*
order to be naturalized (if they were in the United States lawfully at the   *from*
time of their enlistment), and no period of residence or physical presence   *visa to*
is required. INA § 329(a).   *citizen ?*

In 2002 President Bush invoked his authority under § 329 to
designate "the period beginning on September 11, 2001" as a time in
which the United States is engaged in "armed conflict with a hostile
force." Executive Order 13269 (July 3, 2002). That period has not been
terminated. Accordingly, noncitizens serving in active-duty status—
including veterans of the 2003 Iraqi war—are eligible for naturalization
under the special provisions of § 329. As of late 2015, 109,321 members of
the armed forces had been granted expedited naturalization. USCIS, Fact
Sheet, Naturalization through Military Service, Nov. 6, 2015. There have
been 132 grants of posthumous citizenship for noncitizens killed while on
active duty during military hostilities. USCIS, Fact Sheet, Naturalization
through Military Service, Apr. 11, 2011.

Generally, enlistment is limited to lawful permanent residents or
U.S. citizens, but the Department of Defense has initiated a pilot program
to enlist noncitizens with special language, medical, or other skills. The
Military Accessions Vital to the National Interest (MAVNI) program
accepts noncitizens who are legally present, though not lawful permanent
residents. For example, asylees, refugees, students, and certain
nonimmigrants could seek to join the armed forces through the MAVNI
program. See 10 U.S.C. § 504(b)(2). For thorough examination of this
topic, see Margaret D. Stock, *Recent Developments in Military Enlistment
and Naturalization Law*, Imm. Briefings, March 2011.

c. Good Moral Character

Naturalization applicants must establish good moral character for
the five years preceding the date of application. INA § 316(a). The INA
does not directly define "good moral character"; rather, it provides a (non-
exclusive) list of acts that establish a lack of good moral character. INA
§§ 101(f), 316(e). Included in that list is a reference to most of the
criminal offenses enumerated in § 212(a)(2), including crimes involving
moral turpitude and controlled substance offenses. INA § 101(f)(3).
Naturalization applicants are asked whether they have ever been

arrested or convicted (you may wish to review Form N–400, available online). To verify the accuracy of their answers, both the applicant's fingerprints and biographical information are checked against FBI databases showing arrests and convictions.

Section 101(f)(3) applies only to crimes committed during the relevant period (usually five years), but paragraph (f)(8) applies to persons convicted at any time of the offenses it identifies, and it results in a permanent disqualification. Originally § 101(f)(8) listed only the crime of murder, but in 1990 it was amended to apply to any "aggravated felony," as defined in § 101(a)(43). The list of aggravated felonies, rather short in 1990, has expanded greatly over the years. Congress' largest set of additions to the definition, in 1996, was accompanied by a provision stating that the term, as amended, applies to a listed offense "regardless of whether the conviction was entered before, on, or after" the date of enactment. (For highly technical reasons, however, such an aggravated felony conviction before November 29, 1990, is not an automatic bar to good moral character for naturalization purposes. *See General Counsel Speaks on Aggravated Felonies and Good Moral Character*, 74 Interp. Rel. 1515 (1997).)

The effect of these amendments on the naturalization process should be apparent: applicants may be deemed to lack good moral character for crimes committed a number of years before, which were not considered to be aggravated felonies at the time of their commission. As we will see in Chapter Seven, retrospective application of immigration laws is not uncommon and is deemed not to raise a serious constitutional question. Did Congress go needlessly far here, or is the commission of a serious crime properly grounds for denying naturalization whether or not the person knew at the time that it could permanently deny him or her a chance to become a U.S. citizen?

d. Knowledge of Civics and History

Applicants for naturalization must demonstrate "a knowledge and understanding of the fundamentals of the history, and of the principles and form of government, of the United States." INA § 312(a)(2). The civics requirements are waived for persons with physical or developmental disabilities or mental impairments. Furthermore, the statute directs the Attorney General to give "special consideration" regarding compliance with the civics requirement to persons over 65 who have lawfully resided for at least 20 years. INA § 312(b). Regulations instruct naturalization examiners to choose questions and evaluate answers with "due consideration" to an applicant's "education, background, age, length of residence in the United States, opportunities available and efforts made to acquire the requisite knowledge, and any other elements or factors relevant to an appraisal of the adequacy of the applicant's knowledge and understanding." 8 C.F.R. § 312.2(c)(2).

The history and civics requirement is met by an oral test conducted by a DHS examiner during the naturalization interview. For many years, examiners relied upon (although were not limited to) a prepared list of 100 questions that had been informally generated by the INS. It included a range of basic questions about U.S. government ("How many representatives are there in Congress?" "What is the Bill of Rights?" "Who makes the laws in the United States?") and other questions such as "What are the colors of the flag?" and "What Immigration and Naturalization Service form is used to apply for naturalized citizenship?"

In September 2007, after several years of study, the USCIS Office of Citizenship announced a new naturalization test. Prepared in consultation with adult education experts, U.S. history and government scholars and experts on test development, the new test asks questions on American government, American history, and "integrated civics" (geography, symbols, and holidays). It includes questions from the old test (such as the names of one's representatives in Congress and freedoms protected by the First Amendment), as well as more conceptual questions ("What is freedom of religion?" "What is the economic system of the United States?" "What is the rule of law?" "Name one problem that led to the Civil War.") For further information, study materials, and lists of the questions, go to the USCIS website at http://www.uscis.gov/us-citizenship/naturalization-test.

What kinds of questions ought to be included in the naturalization test? Is knowledge of American history more important than, say, knowledge of American culture? How would one define, and test for, the latter?

e. English Language Proficiency

The INA requires that applicants for naturalization demonstrate "an understanding of the English language, including an ability to read, write, and speak words in ordinary usage in the English language." INA § 312(a)(1). The Act exempts from the English language requirement persons who, at the time of filing their petition, are (a) over the age of fifty and have been lawfully admitted for permanent residence for periods totaling twenty years, (b) over fifty-five and have been living in the United States in LPR status for at least fifteen years. Also exempt are persons who are "unable because of physical or developmental disability or mental impairment" to comply with the requirement. INA § 312(b).

A requirement of knowledge of spoken English first entered U.S. naturalization law in 1906. Act of June 29, 1906, ch. 3592, § 8, 34 Stat. 599. English literacy was added in 1950. Internal Security Act of 1950,

§ 30, 64 Stat. 1018. *See* Juan F. Perea, *Demography and Distrust: An Essay on American Languages, Cultural Pluralism, and Official English,* 77 Minn. L. Rev. 269, 337–40 (1992) . The wisdom of the English requirement has been hotly debated. We provide a small sample below. First, consider the statement of Cruz Reynoso, a Commissioner on the Select Commission for Immigration and Refugee Policy (SCIRP), commenting on the Commission's 1981 Final Report:

> The Commission report quotes favorably from Webster's notion of language—that it is a unifier of national bonds—and recommends continued use of the English-language requirement for citizenship. The Commission, unknowingly, misinterprets the character of our national union, the reality of our history, and the diversity of our people. Americans are not now, and never have been, *one* people linguistically or ethnically. American Indians (natives) are not now, and never have been like Europeans. By the treaty which closed the Mexican American war[,] our Country recognized its obligation to protect the property, liberty and religion of the new Americans. In short, America is a *political* union—not a cultural, linguistic, religious or racial union. It is acceptance of our constitutional ideals of democracy, equality and freedom which acts as the unifier for us as Americans.

With respect to language the California Supreme Court said it well in ruling that English may not be a requirement for voting among those who speak Spanish:

> "We cannot refrain from observing that if a contrary conclusion were compelled [that the California Constitution could require knowledge of the English language before a citizen could vote] it would indeed be ironic that petitioners [the Spanish-speaking citizens], who are the heirs of a great and gracious culture, identified with the birth of California and contributing in no small measure to its growth, should be disenfranchised in their ancestral land, despite their capacity to cast an informed vote." (Castro v. State of California [1970] 2 Cal.3d 223, 243.)

* * *

Of course, we as individuals would urge all to learn English for that is the language used by most Americans, as well as the language of the marketplace. *But,* we should no more demand English-language skills for citizenship than we should demand uniformity of religion. That a person wants to become a citizen and will make a good citizen is more than enough.

Every study I have read concludes that language requirements have been used to discriminate. Our early naturalization laws had no language requirement. We should do today as was done before the "nativism" (an early nice word to describe ethnic and racial prejudice) of the 19th Century set in; we should welcome the new arrivals with open arms, to all the obligations *and* the privileges of being full Americans.

SCIRP, *U.S. Immigration Policy and the National Interest* 403–04 (1981).

Now, contrast the following views:

"I have sympathy for the position that the integrating mechanism of a society is language," Henry Cisneros [former mayor of San Antonio and later Secretary of Housing and Urban Development] says. "The U.S. has been able to impose fewer such integrating mechanisms on its people than other countries, but it needs some tie to hold these diverse people, Irish, Jews, Czechs, together as a nation. Therefore, I favor people learning English and being able to conduct business in the official language of the country."

"The *unum* demands only certain things of the *pluribus,*" Lawrence Fuchs [Executive Director of the Select Commission] says. "It demands very little. It demands that we believe in the political ideals of the republic, which allows people to preserve their ethnic identity. Most immigrants come from repressive regimes; we say, we're asking you to believe that government should *not* oppress you. Then it only asks one other thing: that in the wider marketplace and in the civic culture, you use the official language. No other society asks so little."

"English is not just an instrument of mobility. It is a sign that you really are committed. If you've been here five years, which you must to be a citizen, and if you are reasonably young, you should be able to learn English in that time. The rest of us are entitled to that."

James Fallows, *Immigration—How It's Affecting Us*, The Atlantic Monthly 88–89 (Nov. 1983).

In light of these and other considerations, do you think the English-language requirement is sound policy? If so, how do you respond to the argument that the United States is a political, not a linguistic, union? If not, would you require the ability to communicate in some language in widespread use in the political domain?

f.　Oath of Allegiance

Since 1795, applicants have been required to swear an oath of allegiance to the United States. Here is the current version of the oath, as prescribed by regulation:

> I hereby declare, on oath, that I absolutely and entirely renounce and abjure all allegiance and fidelity to any foreign prince, potentate, state, or sovereignty, of whom or which I have heretofore been a subject or citizen; that I will support and defend the Constitution and laws of the United States of America against all enemies, foreign and domestic; that I will bear true faith and allegiance to the same; that I will bear arms on behalf of the United States when required by the law; that I will perform noncombatant service in the Armed Forces of the United States when required by the law; that I will perform work of national importance under civilian direction when required by the law; and that I take this obligation freely, without any mental reservation or purpose of evasion; so help me God.

8 C.F.R. § 337.1(a).[5] Most of this language comes rather directly from the statute, INA § 337(a). The portion of the statute defining the contents of the oath has changed relatively little since 1795.

The oath is regularly criticized for archaic and abstruse language. Recall that, to meet the statute's requirements, an applicant need only be able to "read or write simple words and phrases."[6] Do you think it should be rewritten? If so, would you simply use more modern language, or would you ask naturalizing citizens to affirm different commitments to their new country? Should native-born citizens be asked to take a similar oath—say at age 21? Should the oath requirement be eliminated, as some proponents of multiple citizenship propose? See the earlier discussion of dual nationality in Section A.3, *supra*.

The Commission on Immigration Reform proposed a new formulation for the oath in its 1997 Final Report. Written to "captur[e] the essence of naturalization," the Commission's revision would include the following language:

> Solemnly, freely, and without any mental reservation, I, (name) hereby renounce under oath [or upon affirmation] all

---

[5]　The statute permits conscientious objectors to military service to be exempted from the requirement to bear arms or perform noncombatant service. INA § 337(a).

[6]　Pub. L. 106–448, 114 Stat. 1939 (2000), amended § 337(a) of the INA to authorize the Attorney General to waive the oath requirement for those applicants whose physical or developmental disability or mental impairment prevents them from understanding the oath. A person for whom the oath is waived is considered "to have met the requirements of section 316(a)(3) with respect to attachment to the principles of the Constitution and well disposition to the good order and happiness of the United States."

former political allegiances. My sole political fidelity and allegiance from this day forward is to the United States of America.

U.S. Commission on Immigration Reform, Becoming an American: Immigration and Immigrant Policy 51 (1997). What work does the term "political" do in this proposal? Does it signal a change from the current oath in any material way?

g.   Attachment to Constitutional Principles

Applicants for naturalization must establish that they are "attached to the principles of the Constitution of the United States, and well disposed to the good order and happiness of the United States." INA § 316(a). Chief Justice Stone summarized his view of the constitutional tenets to which the statute refers:

> "the principle of constitutional protection of civil rights and of life, liberty and property, the principle of representative government, and the principle that constitutional laws are not to be broken down by planned disobedience. I assume also that all the principles of the Constitution are hostile to dictatorship and minority rule; and that it is a principle of our Constitution that change in the organization of our government is to be effected by the orderly procedures ordained by the Constitution and not by force or fraud."

Schneiderman v. United States, 320 U.S. 118, 181, 63 S.Ct. 1333, 1363, 87 L.Ed. 1796 (1943) (dissenting opinion).

Unquestionably, the Constitution to which an applicant must show "attachment" provides extraordinarily broad protection to political speech and thought—even, as Justice Holmes wrote in a famous dissent in a naturalization case, "for the thought we hate." *United States v. Schwimmer*, 279 U.S. 644, 654, 49 S.Ct. 448, 73 L.Ed. 889 (1929). "Surely," Holmes continued, "it cannot show a lack of attachment to the principles of the Constitution that [one] thinks that it can be improved." *Id*. at 653. But just as surely some calls for constitutional change evidence a rejection of the underlying principles of the Constitution. Imagine, for example, a claim that the United States is a "white person's country" and that the Constitution ought to mandate expulsion of non-whites. Or the view that the United States should be a theocracy, with the laws decreed by a clerical hierarchy. Even if such speech is protected—in the sense that the speaker could not be jailed for uttering it—may it form the basis for a finding that the speaker is not "attached to the Constitution" and therefore ineligible for naturalization?

In the case excerpted below, the Supreme Court addressed this issue during the middle of World War II. By a 5–3 vote, the Court ruled against expatriation.

SCHNEIDERMAN V. UNITED STATES

Supreme Court of the United States, 1943.
320 U.S. 118, 63 S.Ct. 1333, 87 L.Ed. 1796.

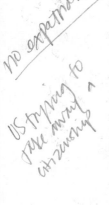

MR. JUSTICE MURPHY delivered the opinion of the Court:

[Schneiderman arrived in the United States from Russia at the age of three, joined the Young Workers League at sixteen, and two years later, in 1924, filed his declaration of intent to naturalize. He joined the Communist Party in 1925, and in 1927 he filed for and was granted naturalization. After his naturalization he attended the Sixth World Congress of the Communist International in Moscow, openly avowed his belief in Marxism as applied by the Communist Party of the United States, was the Communist Party's candidate for governor of Minnesota, and served as secretary of the Party in California.

Twelve years after he had become a citizen, the government filed suit to strip him of citizenship, claiming that he had been ineligible to naturalize at the time of the grant. At the time, membership in the Communist Party was not an express bar to naturalization, although Congress has since enacted statutes precluding naturalization—with minor exceptions—of members of the Communist Party, other totalitarian groups, and those who advocate the overthrow of the United States government by force or violence. *See* INA § 313. Nonetheless, the government argued that a member of the Communist Party could not be "attached to" the principles of the United States Constitution.]

The claim that petitioner was not in fact attached to the Constitution and well disposed to the good order and happiness of the United States at the time of his naturalization and for the previous five year period is twofold: First, that he believed in such sweeping changes in the Constitution that he simply could not be attached to it; Second, that he believed in and advocated the overthrow by force and violence of the Government, Constitution and laws of the United States.

In support of its position that petitioner was not in fact attached to the principles of the Constitution because of his membership in the League and the Party, the Government has directed our attention first to petitioner's testimony that he subscribed to the principles of those organizations, and then to certain alleged Party principles and statements by Party Leaders which are said to be fundamentally at variance with the principles of the Constitution. * * * [U]nder our traditions beliefs are personal and not a matter of mere association, and that men in adhering to a political party or other organization notoriously do not subscribe unqualifiedly to all of its platforms or asserted principles. Said to be among those Communist principles in 1927 are: the abolition of private property without compensation; the erection of a new proletarian state upon the ruins of the old bourgeois state; the creation of a dictatorship of the proletariat; denial of political rights to others than members of the Party or of the proletariat; and the creation of a world union of soviet republics. Statements that American democracy "is a fraud" and that the purposes of the Party are "utterly antagonistic to the purposes for which the American democracy, so called, was formed," are stressed.

* * *

The constitutional fathers, fresh from a revolution, did not forge a political strait-jacket for the generations to come. Instead they wrote Article V and the First Amendment, guaranteeing freedom of thought, soon followed. Article V contains procedural provisions for constitutional change by amendment without any present limitation whatsoever except that no State may be deprived of equal representation in the Senate without its consent. This provision and the many important and far-reaching changes made in the Constitution since 1787 refute the idea that attachment to any particular provision or provisions is essential, or that one who advocates radical changes is necessarily not attached to the Constitution. Criticism of, and the sincerity of desires to improve the Constitution should not be judged by conformity to prevailing thought because, "if there is any principle of the Constitution that more imperatively calls for attachment than any other it is the principle of free thought—not free thought for those who agree with us but freedom for the thought that we hate." [*United States v. Schwimmer*, 279 U.S. 644, 654, 49 S.Ct. 448, 73 L.Ed. 889 (1929) (Holmes, J., dissenting).] Whatever attitude we may individually hold toward persons and organizations that believe in or advocate extensive changes in our existing order, it should be our desire and concern at all times to uphold the right of free discussion and free thinking to which we as a people claim primary attachment. To neglect this duty in a proceeding in which we are called upon to judge whether a particular individual has failed to manifest attachment to the Constitution would be ironical indeed.

* * *

With regard to the constitutional changes he desired petitioner testified that he believed in the nationalization of the means of production and exchange with compensation, and the preservation and utilization of our "democratic structure * * * as far as possible for the advantage of the working classes." He stated that the "dictatorship of the proletariat" to him meant "not a government, but a state of things" in which "the majority of the people shall really direct their own destinies and use the instrument of the state for these truly democratic ends." None of this is necessarily incompatible with the "general political philosophy" of the Constitution as outlined above by the Government. It is true that the Fifth Amendment protects private property, even against taking for public use without compensation. But throughout our history many sincere people whose attachment to the general constitutional scheme cannot be doubted have, for various and even divergent reasons, urged differing degrees of governmental ownership and control of natural resources, basic means of production, and banks and the media of exchange, either with or without compensation. And something once regarded as a species of private property was abolished without compensating the owners when the institution of slavery was forbidden. Can it be said that the author of the Emancipation Proclamation and the supporters of the Thirteenth Amendment were not attached to the Constitution? We conclude that lack of attachment to the Constitution is not shown on the basis of the changes which petitioner testified he desired in the Constitution.

* * *

Apart from the question whether the alleged principles of the Party which petitioner assertedly believed were so fundamentally opposed to the Constitution that he was not attached to its principles in 1927, the Government contends that petitioner was not attached because he believed in the use of force and violence instead of peaceful democratic methods to achieve his desires. In support of this phase of its argument the Government asserts that the organizations with which petitioner was actively affiliated advised, advocated and taught the overthrow of the Government, Constitution and laws of the United States by force and violence, and that petitioner therefore believed in that method of governmental change.

* * *

There is a material difference between agitation and exhortation calling for present violent action which creates a clear and present danger of public disorder or other substantive evil, and mere doctrinal justification or prediction of the use of force under hypothetical conditions at some indefinite future time—prediction that is not calculated or intended to be presently acted upon, thus leaving opportunity for general discussion and the calm processes of thought and reason. *Cf. Bridges v. California*, 314 U.S. 252, 62 S.Ct. 190, 86 L.Ed. 192, and Justice Brandeis' concurring opinion in *Whitney v. California*, 274 U.S. 357, 372– 380, 47 S.Ct. 641, 647–650, 71 L.Ed. 1095. Because of this difference we may assume that Congress intended, by the general test of "attachment" in the 1906 Act, to deny naturalization to persons falling into the first category but not to those in the second. Such a construction of the statute

[handwritten: Court interprets statute to preserve freedom of thought]

is to be favored because it preserves for novitiates as well as citizens the full benefit of that freedom of thought which is a fundamental feature of our political institutions.

[handwritten: reversed + remanded]

* * *

The judgment is reversed and the cause remanded to the Circuit Court of Appeals for further proceedings in conformity with this opinion.

[JUSTICES DOUGLAS and RUTLEDGE filed concurring opinions. JUSTICE STONE, dissented, joined by JUSTICES ROBERTS and FRANKFURTER.]

———————

Compare the *Schneiderman* majority's full-throated exposition of freedom of thought under the First Amendment with the next case, which challenges as unconstitutional a question on the naturalization form asking applicants to detail past and present memberships and affiliations. Note that the litigation context is different. Price was an applicant for naturalization; Schneiderman was the defendant in an action seeking to take away his citizenship.

[handwritten: issue in Price]

PRICE V. INS

United States Court of Appeals, Ninth Circuit, 1991.
962 F.2d 836, cert. denied, 510 U.S. 1040, 114 S.Ct. 683, 126 L.Ed.2d 650 (1994).

BEEZER, CIRCUIT JUDGE:

[handwritten: Man applying for citizenship and challenging constitutionality of questions]

[John Price, a citizen of the United Kingdom, became a lawful permanent resident of the United States in 1960. In 1984 he applied for naturalization. He answered in the negative all parts of Question 19, which asked whether he was or had ever been a member of or associated with the Communist Party, had ever knowingly aided or supported it, or had ever "advocated, taught, believed in, or knowingly supported or furthered the interests of Communism." Relying on the First Amendment right of association, he refused to answer Question 18, which said: "List your present and past membership in or affiliation with every organization, association, fund, foundation, party, club, society or similar group in the United States or in any other country or place, and your foreign military service." The district court denied Price's petition for naturalization based on his refusal to list all organizations he had joined. Price appealed.]

[handwritten: refusal to answer question of association on 1st amend. grounds]

[handwritten: PH]

* * *

The Immigration and Naturalization Act [*sic*] gives the Attorney General the authority to "prescribe the scope and nature of the examination of petitioners for naturalization as to their admissibility to citizenship." INA § 332(a). The examination of petitioners must be limited to

> inquiry concerning the applicant's residence, physical presence in the United States, good moral character, understanding of and attachment to the fundamental principles of the Constitution of the United States, ability to read, write and speak English, and other qualifications to become a naturalized citizen as required by law.

Within these limits, the Attorney General has the authority to require an applicant for naturalization to aver to "*all facts which* in the opinion of the Attorney General *may be material to the applicant's naturalization*," INA § 335(a) (emphasis added), and to designate INS employees to take "testimony concerning *any matter touching or in any way affecting* the admissibility of any petitioner for naturalization." INA § 335(b) (emphasis added). Thus the Attorney General is given very broad authority to make inquiries as long as they are related in some way to the naturalization requirements.

* * *

The INS argues that limiting examination to asking petitioners whether they are members of organizations of the type described in section 313(a) [prohibiting naturalization of persons opposed to government or favoring totalitarian government—eds.] requires the INS to rely on petitioners' own determinations whether particular organizations are of the prohibited type, rather than allowing the Service to make that determination, and does not address the possibility that a petitioner may wrongly believe that an organization with which he is affiliated does not fall within section 313(a).

* * *

The INS also argues that membership in types of organizations not described in section 313(a) may be relevant to other requirements of naturalization such as duration of residence, good moral character or being "well disposed to the good order and happiness of the United States." "The government is entitled to know of any facts that may bear on an applicant's statutory eligibility for citizenship, so it may pursue leads and make further investigation if doubts are raised." *Berenyi v. District Director, INS*, 385 U.S. 630, 638, 87 S.Ct. 666, 671, 17 L.Ed.2d 656 (1967). It is completely reasonable to assume that knowing the organizations with which a petitioner is associated will be relevant to one or more of the requirements for citizenship. * * *

"[A]n alien seeking initial admission to the United States requests a privilege and has no constitutional rights regarding his application, for the power to admit or exclude aliens is a sovereign prerogative." *Landon* *v. Plasencia*, 459 U.S. 21, 32, 103 S.Ct. 321, 329, 74 L.Ed.2d 21 (1982). However, "once an alien gains admission to our country and begins to develop ties that go with permanent residence, his constitutional status changes accordingly." *Id.* It has long been recognized that resident aliens enjoy the protections of the First Amendment. * * *

However, the protection afforded resident aliens may be limited. The Supreme Court recently stated that the cases establishing constitutional protection for aliens within the territory of the United States "are constitutional decisions of this Court expressly according differing protection to aliens than to citizens * * * ." *United States v. Verdugo-Urquidez*, 494 U.S. 259, 110 S.Ct. 1056, 1064, 1065, 108 L.Ed.2d 222 (1990). Additionally, the Court has historically afforded Congress great deference in the area of immigration and naturalization. * * * *Fiallo v. Bell*, 430 U.S. 787, 792, 796, 97 S.Ct. 1473, 1477, 1480, 52 L.Ed.2d 50 (1977) (quotations omitted). * * *

The INS relies on *Kleindienst v. Mandel*, 408 U.S. 753, 92 S.Ct. 2576, 33 L.Ed.2d 683 (1972)[b] for the proposition that Price's first amendment rights invoke at most only limited judicial review. * * *

Price argues that because *Kleindienst* involved exclusion rather than naturalization, it does not control his case. However, the determination of who will become a citizen of the United States is at least as "peculiarly concerned with the political conduct of government," *Galvan v. Press*, 347 U.S. 522, 531, 74 S.Ct. 737, 743, 98 L.Ed. 911 (1954), as the decision of who will be allowed to enter, if not more so. While a resident alien may not participate in the process of governing the country, naturalized citizens may. Naturalization decisions, therefore, deserve at least as much judicial deference as do decisions about initial admission.[5] Furthermore, * * * the protection afforded [Price] under the First Amendment certainly is not greater than that of the citizen plaintiffs in *Kleindienst*. For these reasons, the *Kleindienst* standard is appropriate in this case.

Price argues that he is not challenging the political decision underlying the determination of the substantive requirements for naturalization, but that he challenges instead the method of inquiry, which, in the case of Question 18, chills his freedom of association.

---

[b] In *Kleindienst v. Mandel*, the Attorney General had denied a waiver of excludability for a Belgian scholar deemed inadmissible on the ground that he was a Communist. The Supreme Court announced that although First Amendment rights were implicated by the denial of the waiver, it would sustain the Attorney General's decision if it were based on a "facially legitimate and bona fide reason."—eds.

[5] The importance of the naturalization process was the basis for the district court's alternative holding that even under a more demanding First Amendment analysis, the government has a compelling interest in asking questions such as Question 18 that outweighs any First Amendment right a petitioner for naturalization may have.

Because of this posture, he contends, greater judicial scrutiny is appropriate.

A similar claim was rejected in *Kleindienst.* * * * The Court applied only limited judicial scrutiny and held that the requirements of the First Amendment were met because the reasons for refusing to grant the waiver were "facially legitimate and bona fide."

Applying this limited standard of review to the Attorney General's decision to ask Question 18 is also appropriate because "[n]o alien has the slightest right to naturalization unless all statutory requirements are complied with." *See Fedorenko v. United States,* 449 U.S. 490, 506, 101 S.Ct. 737, 747, 66 L.Ed.2d 686 (1981). Additionally, "the burden is on the applicant to show his eligibility in every respect." *See Berenyi,* 385 U.S. at 637, 87 S.Ct. at 671.[7]

* * *

Because a petitioner might be mistaken about whether an organization is of the type prohibited by section 313(a) and because Question 18 could reasonably reveal information relevant to other requirements for naturalization, the Attorney General's decision that Question 18 is relevant to determining qualification for naturalization is facially legitimate and bona fide.

The district court's denial of Price's petition for naturalization is affirmed.

NOONAN, CIRCUIT JUDGE, dissenting:

The Immigration Service propounds a question to persons seeking naturalization that would be intolerable if asked by a government agency of an American citizen. It is an intimidating question. It chills the right of free association guaranteed by the First Amendment.

The Immigration Service's answer is that aliens are different. They are second class people. No doubt for some purposes this characterization is the harsh truth. Since the abolition of slavery aliens are the only adults subject to treatment as second class people in the United States.

---

[7] In deportation hearings, the government must prove its case by "clear, unequivocal and convincing evidence." *Berenyi,* 385 U.S. at 636, 87 S.Ct. at 670 (quotation omitted). The fact that the alien carries the burden in naturalization proceedings helps to explain why, despite the sliding-scale theory of alien rights, [derived from *Johnson v. Eisentrager,* 339 U.S. 763, 771, 70 S.Ct. 936, 940, 94 L.Ed. 1255 (1950), which stated that an alien is "accorded a generous and ascending scale of rights as he increases his identity with our society,"] aliens at naturalization are not necessarily entitled to the full protection of the First Amendment arguably afforded in deportation hearings. *See Harisiades v. Shaughnessy,* 342 U.S. 580, 592, 72 S.Ct. 512, 520, 96 L.Ed. 586 (1952) (upholding the deportation of a member of the Communist Party under the then-applicable First Amendment test); *Parcham v. INS,* 769 F.2d 1001, 1005–06 (4th Cir.1985) (First Amendment protection applies in a deportation hearing); *American-Arab Anti-Discrimination Committee v. Meese,* 714 F.Supp. 1060 (C.D.Cal.1989) (same). Further support for this result is found in the fact that admission of an alien to citizenship is at least as fundamental to the identity of the nation as is the initial decision of whom to admit.

(handwritten margin note) This is a legitimate purpose to Question 18.

* * * [Deference to Congress over the admission of aliens] is defensible when the alien is outside the United States and seeking to enter this country. *Kleindienst*. It is also appropriate to give deference to Congress and the Executive Branch in matters which "may implicate our relations with foreign powers." *Fiallo*.

The case, however, is substantially different when the alien is a resident and a resident of long standing—in the present case 30 years. Realistically such a person has been conducting himself like an American for a very long time. His reactions to an intolerable inquiry are similar to those of a citizen. Rightly so. He has imbibed the air of freedom which permeates our culture. He insists upon a right not to be treated as a second class person where freedom of association is concerned.

* * *

The power of Congress to set standards for naturalization is very large, but like every other power of government it is circumscribed; it is not absolute. * * *

* * *

A narrowly tailored question could be asked of any petitioner without infringing on First Amendment rights. A petitioner could be asked if he had belonged to any organizations dedicated to the overthrow of the government or advocating or using terrorism or if he belonged to any foreign military, paramilitary or intelligence organization. Such a question would have an obvious relevance to the government's legitimate concerns. A question without bounds as to association has no relation to governmental concerns.

The Immigration Service says that the government is concerned with the petitioner's "character." Beyond excluding persons committed to subversion or terror or under the orders of a foreign government, there is no conceivable way that the government can measure a person's character. Persons of all kinds of character make up the United States. * * *

The statute is without rational purpose and, infringing severely on the right of free association, it is unconstitutional. I respectfully dissent.

NOTES AND QUESTIONS ON ATTACHMENT TO THE CONSTITUTION

1.   The majority's opinion *in Schneiderman v. United States*, according to Sanford Levinson, "tends to remove any real 'bite' from a decision to affirm one's attachment. The Constitution ends up seeming trivialized by the end of the opinion, even as the cause of civil liberties has probably been vindicated." Levinson raises the hypothetical case of an applicant for naturalization who had been a member of the Nationalist Party in South Africa and a fervent

supporter of apartheid. He asks whether the applicant should "be closely examined on his or her political views, and then be excluded if these views prove to oppose the post-Brown [v. Board of Education] reading of the Constitution as at the very least preventing state-mandated racial separation? To say 'yes' obviously rejects the Holmesian tolerance for thought we hate. A negative answer, though, in effect repeals the 'attachment' statute and brings to the surface the 'meaninglessness' that threatens any serious constitutional faith." Sanford Levinson, Constitutional Faith 148–49 (1988). See generally David Fontana, *A Case for the Twenty-First Century Constitutional Canon*: Schneiderman v. United States, 35 Conn. L. Rev. 35 (2002).

2.   The *Schneiderman* Court notes that "[t]his is not a naturalization proceeding in which the Government is being asked to confer the privilege of citizenship upon an applicant." 320 U.S. at 122. In a naturalization proceeding, "the burden is on the alien applicant to show his eligibility for citizenship in every respect. The Court has often stated that doubts 'should be resolved in favor of the United States and against the claimant.' " *Berenyi v. District Director*, 385 U.S. 630, 637, 87 S.Ct. 666, 17 L.Ed.2d 656 (1967). *Schneiderman* is actually a landmark decision in equal measure because the Court went on to hold for the first time that the government must prove its case in a denaturalization proceeding by evidence that is "clear, unequivocal and convincing," not "upon a bare preponderance of evidence which leaves the issue in doubt. This is so because rights once conferred should not be lightly revoked. And more especially is this true when the rights are precious and when they are conferred by solemn adjudication, as is the situation when citizenship is granted." 320 U.S. at 125.

Is this difference in burden of proof between naturalization and denaturalization justified? Does this difference, rather than varying levels of devotion to the First Amendment, better account for the diverse judicial outcomes in *Schneiderman* and *Price*? Should *Schneiderman* have been decided differently if it had arisen as an appeal of a denial of naturalization?

3.   In 1960 the Supreme Court struck down on First Amendment free association grounds an Arkansas statute requiring all public school teachers to file affidavits listing all organizations to which they had belonged during the prior five years. *Shelton v. Tucker*, 364 U.S. 479, 81 S.Ct. 247, 5 L.Ed. 2d 231 (1960). The *Shelton* court criticized the breadth of the statute. Despite the state's legitimate objective of assessing the competency and fitness of teachers, the Court ruled that compelling disclosure of every associational tie impairs the "right of free association, a right closely allied to freedom of speech and a right which, like free speech, lies at the foundation of a free society." *Id.* at 486. Why do you think the Ninth Circuit didn't apply the *Shelton* rationale in *Price*? Are there factors other than alienage that distinguish *Price* from *Shelton*?

4.   Turning from *Shelton* to immigration law precedents, is the *Price* majority correct to analogize applications for naturalization to applications

for immigrant admissions for the purpose of deciding what level of First Amendment scrutiny to apply? Should the requirement of a complete answer to question 18 be held to satisfy a higher standard in any event?

5.   In his dissent to *Price*, Judge Noonan seems to suggest that the government has no business deciding on the character of prospective citizens. Would this mean that the "attachment" and "good moral character" requirements are unconstitutional?

PROBLEMS

Suppose you were representing the following clients in their efforts to become U.S. citizens. In light of the judicial opinions above and the heightened concerns about immigrant terrorists after the December 2015 attack in San Bernardino, California, how would you analyze the issues their applications present?

1.   Malcolm, a practicing Muslim, states that while he is willing to take the oath of allegiance, he has reservations about bearing arms on behalf of the United States against persons of the Islamic faith or a predominantly Islamic country. He believes that if he kills, or is killed by, a member of the Islamic faith he would be condemned to hell, and he states that he would bear arms only when allowed under Islamic law. The USCIS examiner denies naturalization on the ground that, while the statute makes special provisions for conscientious objectors, it requires that such objection be to all wars. Here, according to the examiner, Malcolm is in effect seeking to reserve the right to choose which wars he will fight—a position that demonstrates a "mental reservation" about taking the oath as well as a lack of attachment to the Constitution because of the possibility that applicant will refuse to obey the law for certain kinds of conflicts. Malcolm seeks your advice as to the strengths and weaknesses of his claim. How would you assess his arguments and his likelihood of success?

2.   Jennifer, an applicant for naturalization, is a Jehovah's Witness who states under oath that she believes in the Constitution and the U.S. form of government but that her religious convictions prevent her from voting, serving on a jury, bearing arms, or participating in civilian service deemed to be of national importance. USCIS denies the naturalization application on the ground that she is not "attached to the principles of the Constitution." Jennifer wants to appeal and has asked you to evaluate her chances of success. What would you tell her?

C. LOSS OF CITIZENSHIP

The Naturalization Act of 1906 established a procedure to take away citizenship if a later judicial proceeding determined that that the naturalization was illegally or fraudulently acquired. For many years, it was also possible for naturalized citizens to lose their citizenship, not for defects in the original grant, but because of certain actions following naturalization—actions which had been declared by Congress to result in such forfeiture. Most of these grounds of expatriation applied equally to naturalized and native-born citizens, but a few imposed more stringent requirements on those who had gained citizenship by naturalization. Occasionally the loss of citizenship in this manner has also been called denaturalization, but we will avoid that terminology here. We will use the term "denaturalization" to mean only the revocation of the citizenship of a naturalized alien based on fraud or illegality in the original naturalization. Any other deprivation of citizenship, whether applied to native-born or naturalized citizens, will be called "expatriation."

1. DENATURALIZATION

Section 340 of the Act provides for denaturalization when naturalization was (a) illegally procured, or (b) procured by concealment of a material fact or by willful misrepresentation. The first appears straightforward: naturalization is illegally procured when the applicant did not in fact meet the statutory requirements at the time of naturalization. For example, an applicant might have illegally procured citizenship if he or she had been convicted of a disqualifying crime, and thus had lacked good moral character at the point of naturalization. See INA § 101(f)(6), (7), (8).

The concealment and willful misrepresentation grounds raise the obvious question of what constitutes a "material" fact. An interpretation that might occur to you—that a material fact is one that, if known, would have produced a denial of naturalization—has not been generally accepted. As discussed in the materials that follow, the Supreme Court has suggested a broader reading of the term.

The Supreme Court's initial standard on materiality was announced in *Chaunt v. United States*, 364 U.S. 350, 81 S.Ct. 147, 5 L.Ed.2d 120 (1960), which held that a misstatement was material if its disclosure would have justified denial of citizenship or might have led to the discovery of other facts that would warrant denial of citizenship. A divided Court struggled with the meaning of *Chaunt* in *Kungys v. United States*, 485 U.S. 759, 108 S.Ct. 1537, 99 L.Ed.2d 839 (1988). The various opinions of the Justices in *Kungys* are examined in the following case, which involves a criminal conviction for unlawful procurement of citizenship.

UNITED STATES V. PUERTA

United States Court of Appeals, Ninth Circuit, 1992.
982 F.2d 1297.

FLETCHER, CIRCUIT JUDGE:

Puerta was born in Almeria, Spain on January 20, 1956. He entered the United States on a student visa in 1981 and was admitted as a permanent resident in 1984. On February 26, 1990, he filed an application for naturalization. Question 5 asked him to list "[a]ny other names you have used (including maiden)." Puerta left this space blank. Questions 27 and 28 asked him to list any absences from the United States (for less or more than six months, respectively) since the time he entered for permanent residence. He wrote "None" in response to both questions.

On June 4, 1990, Puerta was interviewed by Immigration Examiner Robert Johnson. At trial, Johnson testified that he had no recollection of Puerta's interview. However, Johnson explained that his standard practice was to require every applicant to swear that the statements made on the application were true, and to review orally with the applicant the answer to each question. Johnson further explained that the slash marks on Puerta's application were his, undoubtedly made during his interview with Puerta. The slashes, Johnson said, indicated that Puerta orally answered questions 5, 27, and 28 the same way as he had done in writing: he had not used any other names and had never left the United States after entry. Puerta was naturalized shortly after his interview.

[In 1991, Puerta was arrested for attempting to defraud a bank in violation of California law. A search incident to the arrest revealed a number of driver's licenses in different names,] and a Spanish passport in the name Antonio Simon Palmer. The passport contained a United States non-immigrant visa obtained in Madrid, Spain on August 16, 1989, which was used to enter the United States on September 5, 1989. All pieces of identification were dated prior to February 26, 1990, the date Puerta filed his application for naturalization.

* * *

Puerta was convicted of violating 18 U.S.C. § 1425(a), which provides: "Whoever knowingly procures or attempts to procure, contrary to law, the naturalization of any person . . . [s]hall be fined not more than $5,000 or imprisoned not more than five years, or both." The statute does not define the phrase "contrary to law." Presumably the "law" referred to is the law governing naturalization, INA title III [§§ 301–362]. Puerta was prosecuted for false statements he made on his naturalization application and to an immigration examiner. No reported cases discuss whether § 1425(a) requires that false statements made to procure naturalization be material in order to be "contrary to law." We note, however, that INA § 340(a) permits denaturalization if citizenship was "procured by concealment of a *material* fact or by willful misrepresentation" (emphasis added). Further, the government agrees with Puerta that § 340(a) implies a materiality requirement similar to the one used in the denaturalization context. This position finds support in *Kungys v. United States*, 485 U.S. 759, 108 S.Ct. 1537, 99 L.Ed.2d 839 (1988), the leading denaturalization case: "While we have before us here a statute revoking citizenship rather than imposing criminal fine or imprisonment, neither the evident objective sought to be achieved by the materiality requirement, nor the gravity of the consequences that follow from its being met, is so different as to justify adoption of a different standard." *Id.* at 770, 108 S.Ct. at 1546. We therefore look to the standards governing materiality in the denaturalization context as a guide to determining what is "contrary to law" under 18 U.S.C. § 1425.

* * *

* * * After *Kungys*, however, it is no simple task to divine the meaning of "material" under the denaturalization statute. The eight Justices who decided *Kungys* (Justice Kennedy did not participate) wrote five separate opinions and offered three distinct tests for determining when a statement is material.[5]

Puerta claims that his false statements were not material because they were not shown to conceal actual ineligibility for naturalization. [The court reviewed the concurrence written by Justice Stevens, which attracted three votes, and a portion of the opinion written by Justice Scalia. Four members of the Court agreed that] the test for materiality in a denaturalization case would be "whether the misrepresentation or concealment had a natural tendency to produce the conclusion that the applicant was qualified" for citizenship. *Id.* at 771–72, 108 S.Ct. at 1547. Under Justice Scalia's test, Puerta's misrepresentations were without a doubt material, because they had a natural tendency to affect the decision by creating the appearance that no further investigation of Puerta's background was necessary.

* * *

Justice Scalia's test, as noted *supra*, was joined in full only by Chief Justice Rehnquist and Justices White and O'Connor (both of whom adopted the test but disagreed with the result of its application to the facts of the case). Justice Brennan, in a concurring opinion, restricted the application of Justice Scalia's test:

---

[5] Six Justices agreed that under their preferred tests, petitioner Kungys' statements regarding his date and place of birth were not material and did not provide a basis for denaturalization. Justices White and O'Connor dissented.

The Court holds that a misrepresentation is material if it has "a natural tendency to produce the conclusion that the applicant was qualified" for citizenship. A misrepresentation or concealment can be said to have such a tendency, the Court explains, if honest representations "would predictably have disclosed other facts relevant to [the applicant's] qualifications." Proof by clear, unequivocal, and convincing evidence that the misrepresentation had this tendency raises a presumption of ineligibility, which the naturalized citizen is then called upon to rebut.

I agree with this construction of the statute. I wish to emphasize, however, that in my view *a presumption of ineligibility does not arise unless the Government produces evidence sufficient to raise a fair inference that a statutory disqualifying fact actually existed....* Evidence that simply raises the possibility that a disqualifying fact might have existed does not entitle the Government to the benefit of a presumption that the citizen was ineligible. I therefore would not permit invocation of the presumption of disqualification in circumstances where it would not otherwise be fair to infer that the citizen was actually ineligible.

Because nothing in the Court's opinion is inconsistent with this standard, I join it.

Id. at 783–84, 108 S.Ct. at 1552 (Brennan, J., concurring) (emphasis added; citations omitted). This test appears to differ from Justice Stevens' "but for" test only in degree: Justice Stevens would denaturalize where false statements are coupled with a showing of actual ineligibility, whereas, by contrast, Justice Brennan would denaturalize where false statements are coupled with evidence giving rise to a "fair inference" of ineligibility. In any event, four members of the Court (Justices Brennan, Stevens, Marshall, and Blackmun) would require that the government prove more than Justice Scalia's bloc * * * would require.

Justice Brennan's view of materiality controls here. As a matter of construction, "[w]hen a fragmented Court decides a case and no single rationale explaining the result enjoys the assent of five Justices, 'the holding of the Court may be viewed as that position taken by those Members who concurred in the judgments on the narrowest grounds.'" *Marks v. United States*, 430 U.S. 188, 193, 97 S.Ct. 990, 993, 51 L.Ed.2d 260 (1977) (quoting *Gregg v. Georgia*, 428 U.S. 153, 169 n. 15, 96 S.Ct. 2909, 2923 n. 15, 49 L.Ed.2d 859 (1976) (opinion of Stewart, Powell, and Stevens, JJ.)). * * *

Whether a given quantum of evidence supports a fair inference of ineligibility (the *Kungys* test for the materiality of false statements, as announced by Justice Brennan) will vary with the facts of each case. *This* record contains no evidence from which any finder of fact could fairly infer that Puerta was actually ineligible for naturalization. All we know is that Puerta (1) denied the use of other names, yet carried many conflicting forms of identification, and (2) claimed not to have left the United States, yet carried a Spanish passport indicating at least one trip abroad. These discrepancies are certainly suspicious. But the government has offered no evidence linking them even tangentially to any statutory ground for disqualification. There is no basis for a trier of fact to conclude that Puerta was hiding a criminal record under one of his aliases. The suspicious banking transaction for which he was arrested is useless as proof of ineligibility, because it occurred after his naturalization and had not formed the basis of a state-court criminal conviction at the time of Puerta's federal trial [on the charge of unlawful procurement of citizenship.] Nor does Puerta's single proven absence from the United States fairly support an inference of ineligibility, given that the statute allows up to two and one-half years' absence during the five-year residency period, provided that no single absence exceeds six months (or more under certain circumstances). 8 U.S.C. § 316(a), (b). Under Justice Brennan's approach, "the defendant at least has the benefit of knowing specifically what disqualifying fact must be rebutted." *Kungys*, 485 U.S. at 793, 108 S.Ct. at 1558 (Stevens, J., concurring in judgment). Puerta did not have that opportunity because the existence of any disqualifying fact can only be postulated by indulging in the purest speculation. Under *Kungys*, Puerta's false statements were not material, and therefore may not form the basis of a criminal conviction under § 1425.

We recognize the potential anomaly in Justice Brennan's test in *Kungys*, which contemplates a higher standard of materiality in immigration law than does the criminal law generally. * * * Whatever attractions a unitary approach to materiality may have, its application to the immigration laws has failed to win an endorsement from a majority of the Supreme Court.

* * *

Reversed and remanded with instructions to enter a judgment of acquittal.

NOTES AND QUESTIONS ON "MATERIALITY" AND DENATURALIZATION

1.   Section 340(a) of the INA requires the government to institute proceedings to revoke the citizenship of individuals who procured naturalization "by concealment of a material fact." The Supreme Court's interpretation of this provision in *denaturalization proceedings* in two major cases, *Chaunt v. United States*, 364 U.S. 350, 81 S.Ct. 147, 5 L.Ed.2d 120

(1960) and *Kungys v. United States*, 485 U.S. 759, 108 S.Ct. 1537, 99 L.Ed.2d 839 (1988), forms the backdrop of the Ninth Circuit's *United States v. Puerta* analysis of a different statute, 18 U.S.C. § 1425(a), which imposes *criminal penalties* on unlawful acquisition of citizenship. *Kungys* relied on criminal law interpretations of materiality, and expressly stated that there was no reason "to justify adoption of a different standard" in denaturalization cases. *Kungys,* 485 U.S. at 770. Yet, *Puerta* appears to adopt a different standard. Can you articulate the difference in the standards in *Kungys* and *Puerta*, identify which one is harder to satisfy, and summarize the *Puerta* court's justification for the differences?

2.   In *Chaunt v. United States*, 364 U.S. 350, 81 S.Ct. 147, 5 L.Ed.2d 120 (1960), the Supreme Court suggested that misrepresentations are not material if (1) the truth would not have required the denial of citizenship or (2) the truth would not have led to other facts requiring the denial of citizenship. In three separate opinions, five members—Scalia, Rehnquist, Brennan, White, and O'Connor—of the splintered *Kungys v. United States* Court, 485 U.S. 759, 108 S.Ct. 1537, 99 L.Ed.2d 839 (1988), rejected this "but for" materiality test.

EXERCISE ON MISREPRESENTATION, MATERIALITY, AND INELIGIBILITY FOR NATURALIZATION

Persons A, B, C, D, and E have recently been naturalized. The fact situations described below all occurred prior to the filing of their naturalization applications, and none was disclosed in the applications. (Take another look at Form N–400 on the USCIS website to see where such information might have been indicated.)

a.   A was arrested 5 years ago and charged with disorderly conduct. The charges were dropped.

b.   B was convicted of arson and served 18 months in prison.

c.   C was convicted 4 years ago of possession of narcotics with intent to distribute, but was sent to a special community service and drug rehabilitation program instead of being incarcerated. Upon completion of the program, the trial judge entered an "order of expungement." He told C at that time that "your record has been wiped clean" and that C would "never have to worry about this episode again," provided C stay free of criminal activity. C has carefully abided by criminal laws since, not even incurring a traffic ticket.

d.   D fathered a child out of wedlock 8 years ago.

e.   E was a member of a radical right political group in the 1990s.

Assume that these facts have now become known to the government. Consider each fact situation from these perspectives: (a) You are the government attorney preparing the administrative revocation charges.

What do you charge? What are your chances of success? (b) You are the naturalized citizen's attorney. What are your best grounds of defense? What would you like to learn from your client to prepare the case? (c) You are the judge. What results under the applicable case law?

Procedures in Denaturalization Cases

Judicial denaturalization proceedings are initiated by U.S. attorneys, based on an affidavit prepared by DHS. INA § 340(a). The evidence supporting denaturalization must be "clear, unequivocal, and convincing." *Schneiderman v. United States*, 320 U.S. 118, 125, 63 S.Ct. 1333, 87 L.Ed. 1796 (1943). If the government seeks to prosecute the individual for illegally procuring citizenship, 18 U.S.C. § 1425, and obtains a conviction, the court shall cancel the certificate of naturalization. INA § 340(e).

In 1996, the Attorney General promulgated regulations establishing an administrative procedure for denaturalization, basing the rules on the 1990 statute that moved naturalization authority from the courts to the Attorney General. 61 Fed. Reg. 55550 (1996), adding 8 C.F.R. §§ 340.1–2. The process was intended to be used only for clear cases warranting denaturalization and had to be initiated within two years of the naturalization. The rules were challenged as beyond the Attorney General's statutory authority, and that claim was sustained by an en banc decision of the Ninth Circuit in *Gorbach v. Reno*, 219 F.3d 1087 (9th Cir.2000). The court rejected the government's argument that the power to denaturalize is inherent in the power to naturalize. "Citizenship in the United States of America is among our most valuable rights. * * * An executive department cannot simply decide, without express statutory authorization, to create an internal executive procedure to deprive people of those rights without even going to court." *Id.* at 1098. Subsequently, the court entered a permanent injunction prohibiting the government from invoking the administrative denaturalization procedures. *See* 78 Interp.Rel. 442 (2001).

2. EXPATRIATION

Denaturalization proceedings constitute one important way in which U.S. citizenship today may be taken away. In such proceedings, the government must establish, under a fairly stringent standard of proof, that the original naturalization was acquired illegally or through fraud. But through the years, Congress also added to the nationality statutes various provisions to deprive individuals of citizenship status based on specified behavior not related to defects in the acquisition process. Whether the citizen subjectively intended to surrender citizenship when the allegedly expatriating behavior occurred was usually irrelevant.

The Expatriation Act of 1907 was the first general statute specifying acts that resulted in the loss of U.S. citizenship. With the goal of preventing dual nationality, it removed U.S. citizenship from individuals who took an oath of allegiance to a foreign country or obtained naturalization in another country. It also removed U.S. citizenship from women who married foreigners. The Supreme Court upheld the latter provision in *Mackenzie v. Hare*, 239 U.S. 299, 36 S. Ct. 106, 60 L. Ed. 297 (1915), reasoning that the U.S. citizen in question had voluntarily renounced her citizenship by willingly taking actions that had the consequence of expatriation.

After World War II, the expatriation legislation's lack of regard for whether individuals actually desired to renounce their U.S. citizenship came under renewed attack. For several decades the Supreme Court wrestled with the constitutionality of the statutory grounds for involuntary expatriation. (We use the term "involuntary expatriation" here to mean a loss of citizenship imposed on persons based on certain chosen behavior, such as lengthy residence abroad or marriage to a foreign national, but without regard for whether they subjectively wished to surrender their citizenship.) The divisions among the Justices were bitter, and for a while, the results in the cases—sometimes sustaining the expatriation provisions, sometimes striking them down—traced an odd pattern.

In *Perez v. Brownell*, 356 U.S. 44, 78 S.Ct. 568, 2 L.Ed.2d 603 (1958), a Texas-born citizen voted in a political election in Mexico, where he had lived most of his life. Justice Frankfurter, writing for a majority of five, upheld the expatriation legislation as a legitimate exercise of the foreign relations power by Congress. In contrast, a 5–3 majority in *Schneider v. Rusk,* 377 U.S. 163, 84 S.Ct. 1187, 12 L.Ed.2d 218 (1964) struck down the provision that decreed loss of U.S. citizenship for a naturalized citizen who returned to reside in his native country for three years (implementing a practice quite common in 19th and early 20th century treaties meant to minimize dual nationality). Justice Douglas' brief majority opinion ruled unconstitutional the statute's "impermissible assumption that naturalized citizens as a class are less reliable and bear less allegiance to this country than the native born." From that date forward, expatriation provisions would have to apply equally to the naturalized and the native-born (though denaturalization, which is based on fraud or illegality in the initial grant, of course applies only to the former).

Three years after *Schneider*, in *Afroyim v. Rusk*, the Supreme Court revisited the ground of expatriation that it had upheld a decade earlier. The case involved the State Department's refusal to renew the U.S. passport of a naturalized U.S. citizen who moved to Israel and voted in an election for the Knesset, the national parliament. In another 5–4 decision, written by Justice Black, the Court overruled *Perez*:

> [W]e reject the idea expressed in *Perez* that, aside from the Fourteenth Amendment, Congress has any general power, express or implied, to take away an American citizen's citizenship without his assent. This power cannot, as *Perez* indicated, be sustained as an implied attribute of sovereignty possessed by all nations. Other nations are governed by their own constitutions, if any, and we can draw no support from theirs. In our country the people are sovereign and the Government cannot sever its relationship to the people by taking away their citizenship. * * *

> * * * [T]he unequivocal terms of the [Fourteenth] Amendment * * * [provide their] own constitutional rule in language calculated completely to control the status of citizenship. * * * There is no indication in these words of a fleeting citizenship, good at the moment it is acquired but subject to destruction by the Government at any time. Rather the Amendment can most reasonably be read as defining a citizenship which a citizen keeps unless he voluntarily relinquishes it.

* * *

Afroyim v. Rusk, 387 U.S. 253, 257, 262, 267–268, 87 S.Ct. 1660, 18 L.Ed.2d 757 (1967). For a full account of the background to the *Afroyim* case, see Peter J. Spiro, Afroyim: *Vaunting Citizenship, Presaging Transnationality,* in Immigration Stories 147 (David A. Martin & Peter H. Schuck eds. 2005).

The durability of *Afroyim* was called into question by another 5–4 ruling, handed down four years later after two Justices had retired and been replaced by new appointees. In *Rogers v. Bellei*, 401 U.S. 815, 91 S.Ct. 1060, 28 L.Ed.2d 499 (1971), the Court examined a challenge to the statutory requirement that children born abroad to one U.S. citizen parent must reside in the United States for at least five years between the ages of 14 and 28. Bellei, born in Italy in 1939 to an Italian father and an American mother, argued that this "condition subsequent" was unconstitutional under *Afroyim*. The majority, per Justice Blackmun, ruled for the government (401 U.S. at 827–28, 831, 834):

> The central fact, in our weighing of the plaintiff's claim to continuing and therefore current United States citizenship, is that he was born abroad. He was not born in the United States. He was not naturalized in the United States. * * * He simply is

not a Fourteenth-Amendment-first-sentence citizen. His posture contrasts with that of Mr. Afroyim, who was naturalized in the United States[.] * * *

* * *

[I]t is conceded here both that Congress may withhold citizenship from persons like plaintiff Bellei and may prescribe a period of residence in the United States as a condition *precedent* without constitutional question.

* * *

We feel that it does not make good constitutional sense, or comport with logic, to say, on the one hand, that Congress may impose a condition precedent, with no constitutional complication, and yet be powerless to impose precisely the same condition subsequent.

Nonetheless, Congress chose not long after the *Bellei* decision to repeal (without retroactive effect) all conditions subsequent applicable to persons gaining U.S. citizenship *jure sanguinis*. Under current law, someone born abroad in a situation like Bellei's need never establish residence in the United States in order to preserve his citizenship. He will probably have to do so, however, if he wishes to transmit citizenship to his own children.

Doubt about the vitality of *Afroyim* lingered after *Bellei*, but the following case seems to have brought relative stability to the constitutional doctrine governing expatriation.

VANCE V. TERRAZAS

Supreme Court of the United States, 1980.
444 U.S. 252, 100 S.Ct. 540, 62 L.Ed.2d 461.

MR. JUSTICE WHITE delivered the opinion of the Court.

Section 349(a)(2) of the Immigration and Nationality Act (Act) provides that "a person who is a national of the United States whether by birth or naturalization, shall lose his nationality by . . . taking an oath or making an affirmation or other formal declaration of allegiance to a foreign state or a political subdivision thereof." The Act also provides that the party claiming that such loss of citizenship occurred must "establish such claim by a preponderance of the evidence" and that the voluntariness of the expatriating conduct is rebuttably presumed. § 349(c), as added, 75 Stat. 656.[c] The issues in this case are whether, in establishing loss of citizenship under § 349(a)(2) a party must prove an intent to surrender United States citizenship and whether the United

---

c   This presumption now appears in § 349(b).—eds.

States Constitution permits Congress to legislate with respect to expatriation proceedings by providing the standard of proof and the statutory presumption contained in § 349(c).

I

[Laurence J. Terrazas was born in the United States to a Mexican citizen, and at birth acquired both United States and Mexican citizenship. At the age of 22, while a student in Mexico, Terrazas executed an application for a certificate of Mexican nationality, swearing "adherence, obedience, and submission to the laws and authorities of the Mexican Republic" and "expressly renounc[ing] United States citizenship, as well as any submission, obedience, and loyalty to any foreign government, especially to that of the United States of America, . . ." Terrazas read and understood the certificate. Soon thereafter Terrazas challenged the U.S. State Department's issuance of a certificate of loss of nationality, but the State Department's Board of Appellate Review concluded that he had voluntarily renounced his United States citizenship. Terrazas filed suit in federal district court.]

The District Court recognized that * * * every citizen has " 'a constitutional right to remain a citizen . . . unless he voluntarily relinquishes that citizenship.' " A person of dual nationality, the District Court said, "will be held to have expatriated himself from the United States when it is shown that he voluntarily committed an act whereby he unequivocally renounced his allegiance to the United States." * * * ." The District Court concluded that the United States had "proved by a preponderance of the evidence that Laurence J. Terrazas knowingly, understandingly and voluntarily took an oath of allegiance to Mexico, and concurrently renounced allegiance to the United States," and that he had therefore "voluntarily relinquished United States citizenship pursuant to § 349(a)(2) of the . . . Act."

* * *

The Court of Appeals reversed. * * * [It ruled that] Congress had no power to legislate the evidentiary standard contained in § 349(c) and that the Constitution required that proof be not merely by a preponderance of the evidence, but by "clear, convincing and unequivocal evidence." The case was remanded to the District Court for further proceedings.

The Secretary took this appeal under 28 U.S.C. § 1252. Because the invalidation of § 349(c) posed a substantial constitutional issue, we noted probable jurisdiction.

II

The Secretary first urges that the Court of Appeals erred in holding that a "specific intent to renounce U.S. citizenship" must be proved "before the mere taking of an oath of allegiance could result in an individual's expatriation." His position is that he need prove only the voluntary commission of an act, such as swearing allegiance to a foreign nation, that "is so inherently inconsistent with the continued retention of American citizenship that Congress may accord to it its natural consequences, *i.e.,* loss of nationality." We disagree.

* * *

The Secretary argues that [it is sufficient] to establish one of the expatriating acts specified in § 349(a) because Congress has declared each of those acts to be inherently inconsistent with the retention of citizenship. But *Afroyim* emphasized that loss of citizenship requires the individual's "assent," in addition to his voluntary commission of the expatriating act. It is difficult to understand that "assent" to loss of citizenship would mean anything less than an intent to relinquish citizenship, whether the intent is expressed in words or is found as a fair inference from proved conduct. * * * In the last analysis, expatriation depends on the will of the citizen rather than on the will of Congress and its assessment of his conduct.

* * *

[W]e are confident that it would be inconsistent with *Afroyim* to treat the expatriating acts specified in § 349(a) as the equivalent of or as conclusive evidence of the indispensable voluntary assent of the citizen. "Of course," any of the specified acts "may be highly persuasive evidence in the particular case of a purpose to abandon citizenship." *Nishikawa v. Dulles,* 356 U.S. 129, 139, 78 S.Ct. 612, 618, 2 L.Ed.2d 659 (1958) (Black, J., concurring). But the trier of fact must in the end conclude that the citizen not only voluntarily committed the expatriating act prescribed in the statute, but also intended to relinquish his citizenship.

* * *

III

With respect to the principal issues before it, the Court of Appeals held that Congress was without constitutional authority to prescribe the standard of proof in expatriation proceedings and that the proof in such cases must be by clear and convincing evidence rather than by the preponderance standard prescribed in § 349(c). We are in fundamental disagreement with these conclusions.

In *Nishikawa v. Dulles,* 356 U.S. 129, 78 S.Ct. 612, 2 L.Ed.2d 659 (1958), an American-born citizen, temporarily in Japan, was drafted into the Japanese Army. The Government later claimed that, under § 401(c) of the Nationality Act of 1940, 54 Stat. 1169, he had expatriated himself by serving in the armed forces of a foreign nation. The Government agreed that expatriation had not occurred if Nishikawa's army service had been involuntary. * * * This Court * * * required proof of a voluntary expatriating act by clear and convincing evidence.

Section 349(c) soon followed; its evident aim was to supplant the evidentiary standards prescribed by *Nishikawa.* The provision [places the burden of proof on the Government] to establish loss of citizenship by [a] preponderance of the evidence * * * . The presumption of voluntariness under the proposed rules of evidence, would be rebuttable—similarly—by preponderance of the evidence, . . ." H.R. Rep. No. 1086, 87th Cong., 1st Sess., 41, U.S. Code Cong. & Admin. News, p. 2985 (1961).

We see no basis for invalidating the evidentiary prescriptions contained in § 349(c). *Nishikawa* was not rooted in the Constitution. The Court noted, moreover, that it was acting in the absence of legislative guidance. Nor do we agree with the Court of Appeals that, because under *Afroyim* Congress is constitutionally devoid of power to impose expatriation on a citizen, it is also without power to prescribe the evidentiary standards to govern expatriation proceedings. * * * This power, rooted in the authority of Congress conferred by Art. 1, § 8, cl. 9, of the Constitution to create inferior federal courts, is undoubted and has been frequently noted and sustained.

* * * [S]ince Congress has the express power to enforce the Fourteenth Amendment, it is untenable to hold that it has no power whatsoever to address itself to the manner or means by which Fourteenth Amendment citizenship may be relinquished.

We are unable to conclude that the specific evidentiary standard provided by Congress in § 349(c) is invalid under either the Citizenship Clause or the Due Process Clause of the Fifth Amendment. It is true that in criminal and involuntary commitment contexts we have held that the Due Process Clause imposes requirements of proof beyond a preponderance of the evidence. *Mullaney v. Wilbur,* 421 U.S. 684, 95 S.Ct. 1881, 44 L.Ed.2d 508 (1975); *Addington v. Texas,* 441 U.S. 418, 99 S.Ct. 1804, 60 L.Ed.2d 323 (1979). * * * But expatriation proceedings are civil in nature and do not threaten a loss of liberty. Moreover, as we have noted, *Nishikawa* did not purport to be a constitutional ruling, and the same is true of similar rulings in related areas. *Woodby v. INS,* 385 U.S. 276, 285, 87 S.Ct. 483, 487, 17 L.Ed.2d 362 (1966) (deportation); *Schneiderman v. United States,* 320 U.S. 118, 125, 63 S.Ct. 1333, 1336, 87 L.Ed. 1796 (1943) (denaturalization). None of these cases involved a congressional judgment, such as that present here, that the preponderance standard of proof provides sufficient protection for the interest of the individual in retaining his citizenship. * * * [W]e have held that expatriation requires the ultimate finding that the citizen has committed the expatriating act with the intent to renounce his citizenship. This in itself is a heavy burden, and we cannot hold that

Congress has exceeded its powers by requiring proof of an intentional expatriating act by a preponderance of evidence.

IV

* * *

It is important at this juncture to note the scope of the statutory presumption. Section 349(c) provides that any of the statutory expatriating acts, if proved, are presumed to have been committed voluntarily. It does not also direct a presumption that the act has been performed with the intent to relinquish United States citizenship. That matter remains the burden of the party claiming expatriation to prove by a preponderance of the evidence. As so understood, we cannot invalidate the provision.[9]

* * *

Section 349(c) * * * and its legislative history make clear that Congress preferred the ordinary rule that voluntariness is presumed * * * . * * * To invalidate the rule here would be to disagree flatly with Congress on the balance to be struck between the interest in citizenship and the burden the Government must assume in demonstrating expatriating conduct. It would also constitutionalize that disagreement and give the Citizenship Clause of the Fourteenth Amendment far more scope in this context than the relevant circumstances that brought the Amendment into being would suggest appropriate. Thus we conclude that the presumption of voluntariness included in § 349(c) has continuing vitality.

V

In sum, we hold that in proving expatriation, an expatriating act and an intent to relinquish citizenship must be proved by a preponderance of the evidence. We also hold that when one of the statutory expatriating acts is proved, it is constitutional to presume it to have been a voluntary act until and unless proved otherwise by the actor. If he succeeds, there can be no expatriation. If he fails, the question remains whether on all the evidence the Government has satisfied its burden of proof that the expatriating act was performed with the necessary intent to relinquish citizenship.

The judgment of the Court of Appeals is reversed, and the case is remanded for further proceedings consistent with this opinion.

---

[9] The Secretary asserts that the § 349(c) presumption cannot survive constitutional scrutiny if we hold that intent to relinquish citizenship is a necessary element in proving expatriation. The predicate for this assertion seems to be that § 349(c) presumes intent to relinquish as well as voluntariness. We do not so read it. Even if we did, and even if we agreed that presuming the necessary intent is inconsistent with *Afroyim,* it would be unnecessary to invalidate the section insofar as it presumes that the expatriating act itself was performed voluntarily.

So ordered.

* * *

MR. JUSTICE MARSHALL, concurring in part and dissenting in part.

I agree with the Court's holding that a citizen of the United States may not lose his citizenship in the absence of a finding that he specifically intended to renounce it. I also concur in the adoption of a saving construction of INA § 349(a)(2) to require that the statutorily designated expatriating acts be done with a specific intent to relinquish citizenship.

I cannot, however, accept the majority's conclusion that a person may be found to have relinquished his American citizenship upon a preponderance of the evidence that he intended to do so. The Court's discussion of congressional power to "prescribe rules of evidence and standards of proof in the federal courts," is the beginning, not the end, of the inquiry. It remains the task of this Court to determine when those rules and standards impinge on constitutional rights. As my Brother Stevens indicates, the Court's casual dismissal of the importance of American citizenship cannot withstand scrutiny. * * *

For these reasons I cannot understand, much less accept, the Court's suggestion that "expatriation proceedings . . . do not threaten a loss of liberty." Recognizing that a standard of proof ultimately " 'reflects the value society places' "on the interest at stake, *Addington v. Texas*, 441 U.S. 418, 425, 99 S.Ct. 1804, 1809, 60 L.Ed.2d 333 (1979), I would hold that a citizen may not lose his citizenship in the absence of clear and convincing evidence that he intended to do so.

MR. JUSTICE STEVENS, concurring in part and dissenting in part.

The Court today unanimously reiterates the principle set forth in *Afroyim v. Rusk*, that Congress may not deprive an American of his citizenship against his will, but may only effectuate the citizen's own intention to renounce his citizenship. I agree with the Court that Congress may establish certain standards for determining whether such a renunciation has occurred. It may, for example, provide that expatriation can be proved by evidence that a person has performed an act that is normally inconsistent with continued citizenship and that the person thereby specifically intended to relinquish his American citizenship.

I do not agree, however, with the conclusion that Congress has established a permissible standard in § 349(a)(2). Since we accept dual citizenship, taking an oath of allegiance to a foreign government is not necessarily inconsistent with an intent to remain an American citizen. * * *

I also disagree with the holding that a person may be deprived of his citizenship upon a showing by a mere preponderance of the evidence that he intended to relinquish it. The Court reasons that because the proceedings in question are civil in nature and do not result in any loss of physical liberty, no greater burden of proof is required than in the ordinary civil case. Such reasoning construes the constitutional concept of "liberty" too narrowly.

* * * [A] person's interest in retaining his American citizenship is surely an aspect of "liberty" of which he cannot be deprived without due process of law. Because the interest at stake is comparable to that involved in *Addington v. Texas*, 441 U.S. 418, 425, 99 S.Ct. 1804, 1809, 60 L.Ed.2d 333 (1979) [which dealt with involuntary civil commitment], * * * I believe that due process requires that a clear and convincing standard of proof be met in this case as well before the deprivation may occur.

MR. JUSTICE BRENNAN, with whom MR. JUSTICE STEWART joins as to Part II, dissenting.

* * *

I

This case is governed by *Afroyim v. Rusk* [which] held unequivocally that a citizen has "a constitutional right to remain a citizen . . . unless he voluntarily relinquishes that citizenship." "[T]he only way the citizenship . . . could be lost was by the voluntary renunciation or abandonment by the citizen himself." The Court held that because Congress could not "abridge," "affect," "restrict the effect of," or "take . . . away" citizenship, Congress was "without power to rob a citizen of his citizenship" because he voted in a foreign election.

The same clearly must be true of the Government's attempt to strip appellee of citizenship because he swore an oath of allegiance to Mexico. Congress has provided for a procedure by which one may formally renounce citizenship.[2] In this case the appellant concedes that appellee has not renounced his citizenship under that procedure. Because one can lose citizenship only by voluntarily renouncing it and because appellee has not formally renounced his, I would hold that he remains a citizen. Accordingly, I would remand the case with orders that appellee be given a declaration of United States nationality.

II

I reach the same result by another, independent line of reasoning. Appellee was born a dual national. He is a citizen of the United States

---

2   INA § 349(a)(5) provides that "a national of the United States whether by birth or naturalization, shall lose his nationality by . . . making a formal renunciation of nationality before a diplomatic or consular officer of the United States in a foreign state, in such form as may be prescribed by the Secretary of State." The Secretary of State has prescribed such procedures in 22 CFR § 50.50 (1979). *See* Department of State, 8 Foreign Affairs Manual § 225.6 (1972). Congress also provided for renunciation by citizens while in the United States [during time of war. § 349(a)(6).] This last provision is not relevant to our case.

because he was born here and a citizen of Mexico because his father was Mexican. The only expatriating act of which appellee stands accused is having sworn an oath of allegiance to Mexico. If dual citizenship, *per se,* can be consistent with United States citizenship, *Perkins v. Elg,* 307 U.S. 325, 329, 59 S.Ct. 884, 887, 83 L.Ed. 1320 (1939), then I cannot see why an oath of allegiance to the other country of which one is already a citizen should create inconsistency. One owes allegiance to any country of which one is a citizen, especially when one is living in that country. *Kawakita v. United States,* 343 U.S. 717, 733–735, 72 S.Ct. 950, 960–961, 96 L.Ed. 1249 (1952). The formal oath adds nothing to the existing foreign citizenship and, therefore, cannot affect his United States citizenship.

NOTES AND QUESTIONS ON EXPATRIATION

1. Are the dissenters in *Terrazas* right concerning the procedural issue? Does the Court's approval of the preponderance standard and the presumption of voluntariness represent a significant retreat from its earlier judgments about the preciousness of U.S. citizenship? Why or why not?

2. Justice Brennan says that citizens may lose that status "only by formally renouncing it." Review the contents of Terrazas' oath of allegiance to Mexico. Why is Brennan in dissent?

3. Suppose Terrazas had been able to show that he executed the renunciation oath—after reading it—only because a Mexican citizenship certificate was required in order to secure a specific job in Mexico. He asserts that, subjectively, his strongest wish throughout the whole process was to retain his dual nationality. Suppose further that he spoke of this wish to many witnesses at the time; hence there is adequate factual support for his assertion. He was not motivated by a desire to surrender his U.S. affiliation, but instead by his desire to get a job. Could he then, consistently with the Constitution, be considered expatriated? What does it mean to find that an individual had a "specific intent to renounce U.S. citizenship"? *See Richards v. Secretary of State,* 752 F.2d 1413, 1421–22 (9th Cir.1985); *Parness v. Shultz,* 669 F.Supp. 7 (D.D.C.1987).

4. In the 1986 INA Amendments, Pub. L. 99–653, 100 Stat. 3655, Congress finally brought the language of § 349 into line with the Supreme Court's expatriation rulings. It changed the operative language of § 349(a), which contains the list of expatriating acts, to provide that U.S. citizens shall lose their nationality only by "voluntarily performing any of the following acts *with the intention of relinquishing United States nationality.*" (Emphasis added.)

5. Meir Kahane, a U.S. citizen by birth and a former activist with the militant Jewish Defense League who moved to Israel, challenged U.S. expatriation law on multiple occasions. Kahane became an Israeli citizen under the Law of Return—a process that does not require express renunciation of other allegiances. Kahane became active in politics, and in

1984 was elected to the Israeli Parliament, the Knesset, as head of the right-wing Kach party. Accepting an office under a foreign government was an expatriating act listed in INA § 349(a)(4). Aware of this, and apparently concerned that a 1971 conviction under U.S. firearms law would prevent even brief visits to the United States if he lost his U.S. citizenship, Kahane told the U.S. State Department that he did not intend to give up his U.S. citizenship. The State Department's Board of Appellate Review nonetheless found that he had committed the expatriating act with intent to relinquish U.S. citizenship. It examined other evidence of his actions, writings, and speeches, and concluded that he had shifted his allegiance to Israel; actions, the Board suggested, speak louder than words.

Kahane challenged this decision in court, which ruled rather readily against the State Department: "Since citizenship is 'beyond the power of any governmental unit to destroy,' [quoting *Afroyim*] it may well be that a declaration of intent to retain citizenship, made simultaneously with commission of the expatriating act, will suffice to preserve the actor's citizenship." *Kahane v. Shultz,* 653 F.Supp. 1486, 1493 (E.D.N.Y.1987). In early 1988, the Knesset passed a law providing that its members could be citizens only of Israel. To hold on to his seat, Kahane executed an express "Oath of Renunciation" of U.S. citizenship before a U.S. consul in Jerusalem. A few weeks later the Israeli Supreme Court barred the Kach party, on other grounds, from running in the November 1988 election. Kahane thereupon sought to revoke his renunciation. Getting nowhere with the State Department, he returned to federal district court, claiming that the Israeli law amounted to compulsion that vitiated the voluntariness of the expatriating act, namely, the oath of renunciation. The court ruled against him. *Kahane v. Secretary of State,* 700 F.Supp. 1162 (D.D.C.1988). Expatriation did not have the expected effect on Kahane's ability to travel to the United States, however—tragically, as it turned out. He was admitted in 1990 for a speaking tour, but he was assassinated while in New York City. N.Y. Times, Nov. 6, 1990, at A1. For a discussion of the first Kahane case, and further reflections on various theories that might underlie loss-of-citizenship doctrine, see T. Alexander Aleinikoff, *Theories of Loss of Citizenship,* 84 Mich. L. Rev. 1471 (1986).

Should there be room under our Constitution for rules that forbid assumption of an office under a foreign government, on pain of giving up U.S. citizenship? Could Congress constitutionally enforce such rules if it used only criminal or non-expatriating civil sanctions? Could Congress now forbid U.S. citizens from voting in foreign elections, using the same more limited range of sanctions? Should it?

6.   Senator Ted Cruz of Texas proposed the Expatriate Terrorist Act in order to strip U.S. citizenship from individuals who fight with Islamic State (ISIS) terrorists in Syria and Iraq. Mario Trujillo, *Cruz: Strip Citizenship from Americans in ISIS*, The Hill, Sept. 5, 2014. In the aftermath of the November 2015 terror attacks in Paris, President Hollande of France proposed revoking the citizenship of all dual nationals convicted of terrorism,

an expansion of the current law, which limits revocation to naturalized French citizens. *A Law To Strip Dual-Citizen Terrorists of French Nationality Moves a Step Forward*, The Economist, Feb. 11, 2016. After strenuous public opposition, Hollande withdrew this proposal. Adam Nossiter, *François Hollande Cancels Plan to Strip French Citizenship in Terrorism Cases*, N.Y. Times, Mar. 30, 2016. In December 2015, Australia enacted legislation to strip citizenship from dual nationals engaged in terrorism abroad or convicted of terrorism in Australia. Patrick Goodenough, *Australia to Strip Dual Citizens of Citizenship for Terror Activities*, CNS News, Dec. 4, 2015. Does current U.S. law provide for expatriation of individuals who bear arms with a non-state terrorist group? If not, could Congress constitutionally establish expatriation standards for terrorism-related activity?

Renunciation Outside the United States

In 1978, several inmates of a state prison in Lucasville, Ohio, wrote to the State Department renouncing their U.S. citizenship and claiming status as citizens of the Soviet Union. Apparently they believed that they might in this way secure the diplomatic interposition of their alleged new country of nationality to protect the human rights they claimed were violated by their incarceration. These letters were clearly meant to be direct expressions of specific intent to terminate U.S. nationality. Relying on the statutory requirement that the formal renunciation of nationality take place outside the United States, INA §§ 349(a)(5), 351(a), the State Department refused to consider the inmates as validly expatriated

The U.S. government has traditionally resisted accepting the surrender of citizenship by persons who are likely to retain residence in the United States. But *Kaufman v. Holder,* 686 F.Supp.2d 40 (D.D.C. 2010), may necessitate a change. Kaufman, a registered sex offender imprisoned in Wisconsin, invoked the statutory provision that allows formal renunciation within the United States when the United States is in a state of war. INA §§ 349(a)(6), 351(a). The government argued that this provision was triggered only by a formal declaration of war; the court found the current level of hostilities in Afghanistan and Iraq to be sufficient. *See* Mike Scarcella, *DOJ Abandons Challenge of Sex Offender's Desire to Renounce Citizenship*, National Law Journal, Aug. 18, 2010. The court mentioned only in passing the rather odious history of § 349(a)(6), which was initially adopted in 1944 in the (erroneous) expectation that it would result in widespread surrender of U.S. citizenship by Japanese-Americans interned in relocation camps. The proponents thought that such a change in status would provide a firmer legal footing for the detention, because internment of enemy nationals during wartime was well accepted in international law.

What policies are reflected in the provisions normally requiring that loss of citizenship occur only if the person is outside U.S. territory? Many have argued that concerns about preventing statelessness allow governments to limit renunciations of citizenship. Others have emphasized the importance of citizenship as an "international filing system," a mechanism important in a system of nation states because it allocates persons to states. Rogers Brubaker, *Citizenship As Social Closure*, Citizenship and Nationhood in France and Germany ch. 1 (1992). Do these policies make sense in the conditions of the modern world? Are they workable? However prudent they may be, are they constitutionally valid? That is, in light of the priority *Terrazas* places on the individual's voluntary decisions about his or her own citizenship status, is it permissible to require the commission of specified objective acts (which some persons may have difficulty performing) in addition to an unambiguous expression of intent to renounce? *See generally Davis v. District Director*, 481 F.Supp. 1178 (D.D.C.1979) (native-born citizen who formally renounced citizenship at U.S. consulate in Paris does not retain rights to enter and remain in this country without a proper visa).

Procedures in Expatriation Cases

Terrazas reflects the usual way in which a controversy over expatriation arises and is resolved. A U.S. consulate, upon learning that a potentially expatriating act has occurred, investigates the facts and files a report with the Department of State. If the Department agrees that expatriation has occurred, a copy of the consulate's Certificate of Loss of Nationality (CLN) is then sent to the individual and to immigration authorities. *See* INA § 358; 22 C.F.R. § 50.40(e).

Individuals may ask the State Department's Bureau of Consular Affairs to review the loss of nationality determination. *Id.* § 50.51. Alternatively, individuals may contest the issue in federal court. Under INA § 360(a), claimants within the United States may obtain a judicial determination of a citizenship claim by means of a declaratory judgment action in accordance with 28 U.S.C.A. § 2201. The action must be initiated within five years after the final administrative denial of a right or privilege of citizenship by any department or agency. Claimants outside the United States are granted by the INA a procedure permitting them to travel to this country in order to apply for admission. Judicial review then is available on habeas corpus. INA § 360(b), (c) .[7]

---

[7]   A claim of U.S. citizenship may also arise by way of a defense in a removal proceeding, in which case the issue is resolved by the immigration judge and, upon appeal, the BIA, without the direct involvement of the State Department. If the BIA rejects the claim and the alien files a petition for review in the court of appeals, INA § 242(b)(5) makes special provision for transfer, if the claim presents a genuine issue of material fact, to the district court for a new hearing.

The State Department's Approach

In 1990, the State Department adopted a new statement of evidentiary standards to be applied in expatriation cases. It reflects a wholly new attitude far more hospitable to dual citizenship than in earlier years, when the Department often tried to read as narrowly as possible any Supreme Court decisions that restricted expatriation. The standard, as currently posted on the Department's website, provides in part:

> [The actions listed in INA § 349(a)] will result in the loss of U.S. nationality if performed voluntarily and with the intention of relinquishing U.S. citizenship. The Department has a uniform administrative standard of evidence based on the premise that U.S. nationals intend to retain United States nationality when they obtain naturalization in a foreign state, subscribe to routine declarations of allegiance to a foreign state, or accept non-policy level employment with a foreign government.

* * *

> In light of the administrative premise discussed above, a person who:

> 1. is naturalized in a foreign country;

> 2. takes a routine oath of allegiance; or

> 3. serves in the armed forces of a foreign state not engaged in hostilities with the United States, or

> 4. accepts non-policy level employment with a foreign government,

> and in so doing wishes to retain U.S. nationality need not submit prior to the commission of a potentially expatriating act a statement or evidence of his or her intent to retain U.S. nationality since such an intent will be presumed.

> When, as the result of an individual's inquiry or an individual's application for registration or a passport it comes to the attention of a U.S. consular officer that a U.S. national has performed an act made potentially expatriating by Sections 349(a)(1), 349(a)(a)(2), 349(a)(3) or 349(a)(4), the consular officer will simply ask the applicant if there was intent to relinquish U.S. nationality when performing the act. If the answer is no, the consular officer will certify that it was not the person's intent to relinquish U.S. nationality, and consequently, find that the person has retained U.S. nationality.

* * *

An individual who has performed any of the acts made potentially expatriating by statute who wishes to lose U.S. nationality may do so by affirming in writing to a U.S. consular officer that the act was performed with an intent to relinquish U.S. nationality. Of course, a person always has the option of seeking to formally renounce U.S. nationality in accordance with Section 349(a)(5) INA.

The premise that a person intends to retain U.S. nationality is not applicable when the individual:

1. formally renounces U.S. nationality before a consular officer;

2. serves in the armed forces of a foreign state engaged in hostilities with the United States;

3. takes a policy level position in a foreign state;

4. is convicted of treason.

Cases in categories 2, 3, and 4 will be developed carefully by U.S. consular officers to ascertain the individual's intent toward U.S. nationality.

* * *

Advice about Possible Loss of U.S. Citizenship and Dual Nationality, http://travel.state.gov.

Are the provisions numbered (2) and (3) in the final quoted paragraph consistent with the Constitution as interpreted in *Afroyim* and *Terrazas?* How would the Department's evidentiary standards apply to someone who takes an oath of allegiance to another nation, including an express renunciation of U.S. nationality, as part of a naturalization ceremony before an administrative officer of that other nation, but who subjectively wishes to retain U.S. nationality as well?

EXERCISE

Suppose you are consulted by a client who wants to take a particular job overseas that requires the nationality of the host country. She finds that she can naturalize there, but must take a renunciatory oath in order to do so. She wants the job but also wishes to retain her U.S. citizenship and seems happy to know that the State Department apparently won't issue a CLN after the ceremony. How would you advise her? Is perjury a problem? Is the State Department's treatment of such oaths permissible under congressional enactments? Review the language of INA § 349(a)(1) and consider it in connection the wording of the naturalization oath, set forth in INA § 337.

CHAPTER THREE

FOUNDATIONS OF IMMIGRATION LAW

● ● ●

A. THE FEDERAL IMMIGRATION POWER

The historical overview in Chapter One makes clear that the United States, since its founding, has engaged in a national discussion over how many and what kind of immigrants should be permitted to enter and take up residence. What these debates have almost always taken for granted is the power of Congress to enact laws that regulate which noncitizens may enter the United States and under what conditions those that enter may remain. It is this issue—the source and scope of Congress' immigration power—that we explore in this section.

You may find it curious that the source and scope of Congress' power could be interesting questions. Surely the Framers would have endowed Congress explicitly with a power as important as that of controlling immigration. Yet the Constitution of the United States includes no language that expressly grants Congress such authority. The Supreme Court did not address the question until the second century of this country's existence, primarily because Congress did not enact significant limits on immigration until the 1880s. For most of the nineteenth century, Congress permitted open borders in an attempt to provide the developing nation with labor and capital. What immigration law existed was the creation of the states. Many states had laws that the modern eye may not readily recognize as immigration laws because they often restricted entry by other states' citizens as well as by foreigners, and because they regulated specific concerns, for example public health. In substance, however, these laws had much in common with modern immigration laws. *See* Gerald L. Neuman, *The Lost Century of American Immigration Law (1776–1875)*, 93 Colum. L. Rev. 1833 (1993).

This section will first examine the historical setting in which the major federal immigration cases were decided in the late nineteenth century. It will turn then to four landmark Supreme Court opinions, each involving a Chinese immigrant. The following discussion will explore the basic constitutional framework implicated by the government's regulation of immigration.

Were originally kept out.

1. CHINESE IMMIGRATION

The earliest federal statutes limiting immigration, enacted in 1875 and 1882, prohibited the entry of criminals, prostitutes, idiots, lunatics, and persons likely to become a public charge. Act of March 3, 1875, Ch. 141, 18 Stat. 477; Act of August 3, 1882, Ch. 376, 22 Stat. 214. There was a distinct anti-Chinese bias, as the 1875 statute specified that contract laborers from Asia were undesirable, as were Asian women who would engage in prostitution. Soon thereafter, in 1882, 1884, 1888 and 1892, Congress enacted the so-called Chinese exclusion laws, and these became the first federal immigration statutes to be subjected to judicial scrutiny.[8]

Chinese railroad workers in California, 1880s.
(Photo: Pajaro Valley Historical Association)

HIROSHI MOTOMURA, AMERICANS IN WAITING:
THE LOST STORY OF IMMIGRATION AND CITIZENSHIP
IN THE UNITED STATES*

16–17, 25–26 (2006).

Gold rush

Chinese immigrants first came to America in large numbers starting with the California Gold Rush in 1849, so drawn by the prospect of riches that among them California came to be called Gold Mountain. Few would

---

[8]   A fuller examination of the background of the first two judicial opinions excerpted in this section can be found in Chin, *Chae Chan Ping and Fong Yue Ting: The Origins of Plenary Power*, in Immigration Stories 7–23 (David A. Martin & Peter H. Schuck eds. 2005).

find that dream of quick wealth, but the growing economy in the western United States needed cheap labor. At first, most Chinese worked in mines; later they toiled to build the transcontinental railroad. The Central Pacific Railroad's workforce was 90 percent Chinese. Many were enticed by the allure of wages far surpassing what they could earn in China. During the 1860s, a worker could earn $30 per month on the railroad, six times what he could earn in southern China. In 1852, somewhere between 12,000 and 25,000 Chinese were in California. By 1870, this number had grown to about 63,000, and it exceeded 105,000 by 1880, when the U.S. Census reported the total population of California as 865,000. About 250,000 Chinese immigrated to the United States from 1850 until the 1882 Chinese Exclusion Act.

The U.S. government first addressed Chinese immigration when it negotiated and signed the Burlingame Treaty with China in 1868. At the time, the United States was interested in cheap labor and trade with China. By signing the treaty, the U.S. government accepted Chinese immigration, and the Chinese government accepted emigration, which would still remain a crime theoretically punishable by death until 1893. The treaty declared the "inherent and inalienable right of man to change his home and allegiance, and also the mutual advantage of free migration and emigration of [American and Chinese] citizens . . . for purposes of curiosity, of trade or as permanent residents."

Even when tens of thousands of Chinese workers were needed to lay the rails, anti-Chinese sentiment was strong throughout the West. "Anti-coolie" clubs depicted Chinese workers as indentured servants not unlike the slaves who had just been freed in the Southern states. There were also boycotts of Chinese-made goods, anti-Chinese newspaper editorials, and licensing requirements for Chinese miners and merchants. In 1852, California enacted a tax on Chinese miners to force them into other employment.

When the completion of the transcontinental railroad in 1869 put some ten thousand Chinese laborers out of work, they spread out into new occupations, depressing wages throughout the western United States. A severe recession from 1873 to 1878 further provoked popular sentiment in California and elsewhere in the American West to blame Chinese workers for American joblessness. During the 1870s, a rising tide of anti-Chinese fervor swept over the western states and gradually influenced national politics.

In 1876, a special joint congressional committee urged renegotiation of the Burlingame Treaty to curb Chinese immigration. In 1879, Congress passed a bill limiting arriving ships to only fifteen Chinese passengers, but President Rutherford Hayes vetoed it on the ground that it conflicted with the Burlingame Treaty. By the 1880 presidential election, however, both the Democratic and Republican Party platforms called for restrictions on Chinese immigration. That year, the two countries entered into a supplemental treaty that allowed the United States to "regulate, limit or suspend" immigration of Chinese laborers whenever their entry or residence in the United States "affects or threatens to affect the interests of that country, or to endanger the good order of [the United States] or of any locality within the territory thereof." But the supplemental treaty allowed those Chinese already in the United States in November 1880 to continue "to go and come of their own free will and accord."

The supplemental treaty did not quiet the crescendo of calls for further limits on Chinese immigration, and some states, impatient and unwilling to wait for federal action, acted on their own. An 1879 California statute required incorporated towns and cities to remove Chinese from their city limits. * * *

* * * [Several] years later, in the spring of 1882, Congress enacted a twenty-year moratorium on immigration of Chinese laborers, but President Chester Arthur vetoed it with a call for a shorter ban. Two months later, wide margins in both houses enacted a ten-year moratorium, which President Arthur signed into law—the first Chinese Exclusion Act. Congress declared that "the coming of Chinese laborers to this country endangers the good order of certain localities." Chinese exclusion was renewed several times and extended indefinitely in 1904, remaining the law of the land until 1943.

The Chinese Exclusion Act was hard to enforce, partly because it was not clear who was exempt as a returning Chinese immigrant who had originally arrived in the United States before the effective date of the ten-year moratorium. The act appeared to require Chinese laborers who were returning from China to show certificates, obtained from the U.S. government when they departed, to prove that they had first come to America before November 17, 1880. Chinese arriving in the United States were also exempt if they were merchants, teachers, students, or travelers. To prove this, they had to show a certificate to that effect, issued by the Chinese government.

At each port, a collector of customs decided whether a Chinese immigrant was barred or exempt. Working before the use of photographs became ordinary in processing, immigration inspectors relied on the certificates, which included "physical marks or peculiarities, and all facts necessary for . . . identification." Even after photographs came into widespread use by the end of the nineteenth century, government inspectors measured numerous body parts in great detail.

The collector often denied reentry even if the immigrants had certificates, but federal judges in San Francisco overturned many of these decisions and sometimes even allowed Chinese laborers to prove pre-November 1880 residency without a certificate at all. Federal judges also relaxed the entry requirements for Chinese merchants. In 1884, Congress reacted to these court decisions by making the certificate the "only evidence permissible to establish his right of re-entry." However, federal judges continued to show flexibility in the proof that they demanded, especially of Chinese who claimed to have left the United States before the certificate requirements took effect.

In 1888, Congress responded by changing the law yet again with the Scott Act, which barred a Chinese immigrant's return even with a certificate. This was the law that stranded Chae Chan Ping * * *.

* * *

Chae Chan Ping was a Chinese laborer who [had come] to the United States and settled in San Francisco in 1875, near the end of the first great wave of Chinese immigration. Twelve years later, he took a trip to China to visit his family, who had stayed behind in typical fashion. By the time Chae left on his journey, the Chinese Exclusion Act of 1882 had put a moratorium on the new immigration of laborers from China. Returning Chinese laborers would be readmitted only if they had a U.S. government certificate to prove they had been in America before the ban took effect. Chae left in 1887 with a certificate in hand, issued by the collector of customs in San Francisco.

2.   THE FOUNDATION CASES

For decades prior to Chae Chan Ping's odyssey, the Chinese had been the targets of discriminatory legislation in California. They were subjected to entry, license and occupation taxes, originally to raise money for the California treasury and later as a means to deter immigration. Chinese were denied the right to testify in court and prohibited from attending public schools with white children. San Francisco's Chinese community, which had a high degree of social organization and also had experience in dealing with government bureaucracy, filed court challenges to a number of the state laws. Judges declared many of them invalid, either as a violation of the Fourteenth Amendment or as conflicting with federal treaties. *See, e.g., Ho Ah Kow v. Nunan*, 12 F. Cas. 252, 5 Sawyer 552 (C.C.D. Cal.1879) (Mr. Justice Field on circuit) (invalidating San Francisco's "Queue Ordinance" which required that all prisoners have their hair cut to a maximum length of one inch); *People v. Downer*, 7 Cal. 169 (1857) (invalidating $50 tax on Chinese passengers); *Lin Sing v. Washburn*, 20 Cal. 534 (1862) (voiding capitation tax on

Chinese). *See generally* Lucy Salyer, Laws Harsh as Tigers: Chinese Immigrants and the Shaping of Modern Immigration Law (1995).[9]

Against this background, and with the help of the San Francisco Chinese community, Chinese immigrants brought a series of suits alleging that the federal statutes violated international law and the U.S. Constitution. As you read the four decisions below, it may help to keep in mind several different constitutional concerns. First, what provisions—or other features—of the United States Constitution authorize power to regulate immigration? Second, what roles do the respective branches of the federal government play with regard to immigration measures? Third, what authority do state governments have over immigration? And fourth, what restrictions, if any, do the rights-protecting provisions of the Constitution place on the exercise of the immigration control power?

a.   Exclusion at the Border

Chae Chan Ping argued that the U.S. Constitution and international law allowed him to re-enter the United States after his trip to China, but the Supreme Court ruled unanimously against him.

CHAE CHAN PING V. UNITED STATES
[CHINESE EXCLUSION CASE]
Supreme Court of the United States, 1889.
130 U.S. 581, 9 S.Ct. 623, 32 L.Ed. 1068.

MR. JUSTICE FIELD delivered the opinion of the Court.

* * *

* * * It must be conceded that the act of 1888 is in contravention of express stipulations of the [Burlingame] treaty of 1868 and of the supplemental treaty of 1880, but it is not on that account invalid or to be restricted in its enforcement. The treaties were of no greater legal obligation than the act of Congress. By the Constitution, laws made in pursuance thereof and treaties made under the authority of the United States are both declared to be the supreme law of the land, and no paramount authority is given to one over the other. A treaty, it is true, is in its nature a contract between nations and is often merely promissory in its character, requiring legislation to carry its stipulations into effect. Such legislation will be open to future repeal or amendment. If the treaty operates by its own force, and relates to a subject within the power of

---

[9]   Further examination of the impact of U.S. immigration law on Asian migrants can be found in Mae M. Ngai, Impossible Subjects: Illegal Aliens and the Making of Modern America (2004); Bill Ong Hing, Making and Remaking Asian America Through Immigration Policy, 1850–1990, at 19–26 (1993); Ronald Takaki, Strangers from a Different Shore: A History of Asian Americans 79–131 (1989); Charles J. McClain, *The Chinese Struggle for Civil Rights in Nineteenth Century America: The First Phase, 1850–1870*, 72 Calif. L. Rev. 529 (1984); Mary R. Coolidge, Chinese Immigration (1909).

Congress is elevated to same as Pres over immig [handwritten margin note]

Congress, it can be deemed in that particular only the equivalent of a legislative act, to be repealed or modified at the pleasure of Congress. In either case the last expression of the sovereign will must control.

The last one passed controls [handwritten margin note]

* * *

There being nothing in the treaties between China and the United States to impair the validity of the act of Congress of October 1, 1888, was it on any other ground beyond the competency of Congress to pass it? If so, it must be because it was not within the power of Congress to prohibit Chinese laborers who had at the time departed from the United States, or should subsequently depart, from returning to the United States. Those laborers are not citizens of the United States; they are aliens. That the government of the United States, through the action of the legislative department, can exclude aliens from its territory is a proposition which we do not think open to controversy. Jurisdiction over its own territory to that extent is an incident of every independent nation. It is a part of its independence. If it could not exclude aliens it would be to that extent subject to the control of another power. As said by this court in the case of *The Exchange*, 7 Cranch 116, 136, speaking by Chief Justice Marshall: "The jurisdiction of the nation within its own territory is necessarily exclusive and absolute. It is susceptible of no limitation not imposed by itself. Any restriction upon it, deriving validity from an external source, would imply a diminution of its sovereignty to the extent of the restriction, and an investment of that sovereignty to the same extent in that power which could impose such restriction. All exceptions, therefore, to the full and complete power of a nation within its own territories, must be traced up to the consent of the nation itself. They can flow from no other legitimate source."

We know US gov. can deny entry to U.S. — power to exclude is power of the sovereign [handwritten margin note]

While under our Constitution and form of government the great mass of local matters is controlled by local authorities, the United States, in their relation to foreign countries and their subjects or citizens are one nation, invested with powers which belong to independent nations, the exercise of which can be invoked for the maintenance of its absolute independence and security throughout its entire territory. The powers to declare war, make treaties, suppress insurrection, repel invasion, regulate foreign commerce, secure republican governments to the States, and admit subjects of other nations to citizenship, are all sovereign powers, restricted in their exercise only by the Constitution itself and considerations of public policy and justice which control, more or less, the conduct of all civilized nations. * * *

We may have a say in local matters, but immigration is part of our interactions w/ other countries and therefore are to be dealt w/ at fed. level. [handwritten margin note]

The control of local matters being left to local authorities, and national matters being entrusted to the government of the Union, the problem of free institutions existing over a widely extended country, having different climates and varied interests, has been happily solved.

For local interests the several States of the Union exist, but for national purposes, embracing our relations with foreign nations, we are but one people, one nation, one power.

To preserve its independence, and give security against foreign aggression and encroachment, is the highest duty of every nation, and to attain these ends nearly all other considerations are to be subordinated. It matters not in what form such aggression and encroachment come, whether from the foreign nation acting in its national character or from vast hordes of its people crowding in upon us. The government, possessing the powers which are to be exercised for protection and security, is clothed with authority to determine the occasion on which the powers shall be called forth; and its determination, so far as the subjects affected are concerned, are necessarily conclusive upon all its departments and officers. If, therefore, the government of the United States, through its legislative department, considers the presence of foreigners of a different race in this country, who will not assimilate with us, to be dangerous to its peace and security, their exclusion is not to be stayed because at the time there are no actual hostilities with the nation of which the foreigners are subjects. The existence of war would render the necessity of the proceeding only more obvious and pressing. The same necessity, in a less pressing degree, may arise when war does not exist, and the same authority which adjudges the necessity in one case must also determine it in the other. In both cases its determination is conclusive upon the judiciary. If the government of the country of which the foreigners excluded are subjects is dissatisfied with this action it can make complaint to the executive head of our government, or resort to any other measure which, in its judgment, its interests or dignity may demand; and there lies its only remedy.

* * *

The exclusion of paupers, criminals and persons afflicted with incurable diseases, for which statutes have been passed, is only an application of the same power to particular classes of persons, whose presence is deemed injurious or a source of danger to the country. As applied to them, there has never been any question as to the power to exclude them. The power is constantly exercised; its existence is involved in the right of self-preservation. * * *

The power of exclusion of foreigners being an incident of sovereignty belonging to the government of the United States, as a part of those sovereign powers delegated by the Constitution, the right to its exercise at any time when, in the judgment of the government, the interests of the country require it, cannot be granted away or restrained on behalf of any one. The powers of government are delegated in trust to the United States, and are incapable of transfer to any other parties. They cannot be abandoned or surrendered. Nor can their exercise be hampered, when needed for the public good, by any considerations of private interest. The exercise of these public trusts is not the subject of barter or contract. Whatever license, therefore, Chinese laborers may have obtained, previous to the act of October 1, 1888, to return to the United States after their departure, is held at the will of the government, revocable at any time, at its pleasure. Whether a proper consideration by our government of its previous laws, or a proper respect for the nation whose subjects are affected by its action, ought to have qualified its inhibition and made it applicable only to persons departing from the country after the passage of the act, are not questions for judicial determination. If there be any just ground of complaint on the part of China, it must be made to the political department of our government, which is alone competent to act upon the subject.

* * *

Order affirmed.

b.   From Exclusion to Deportation

In 1892, Congress again addressed the issue of Chinese immigration. Act of May 5, 1892, Ch. 60, 27 Stat. 25. The 1892 Act authorized the deportation of any Chinese alien unlawfully in the United States. It further required all Chinese laborers then living in the United States to acquire a "certificate of residence" from the Collector of Internal Revenue within one year after passage of the Act. Under regulations promulgated pursuant to the Act, the government would issue a certificate only on the "affidavit of at least one credible witness," which was construed as a white witness. *See* 149 U.S. at 701 n.1, 703, 731. An alien who failed to obtain the certificate could "be arrested * * * and taken before a United States judge, whose duty it shall be to order that he be deported from the United States." He could escape deportation only upon a demonstration "that by reason of accident, sickness or other unavoidable cause, he has been unable to procure his certificate, * * * and by at least one credible white witness, that he was a resident of the United States at the time of the passage of [the Act]." 27 Stat. 25–26.

We should note here that *deportation* has two meanings in the immigration laws. As in the 1892 legislation, it may mean the removal of noncitizens already within the United States—in contrast to the "exclusion" of noncitizens at the border who are seeking to enter. "Deportation" may also be used to mean the physical removal to another country of any noncitizen whether inside or at the border of the United States. Since 1996, the INA has used "removal" to refer to both exclusion and deportation, and we will follow that usage in this casebook.

The 1892 Act was challenged on numerous constitutional grounds.

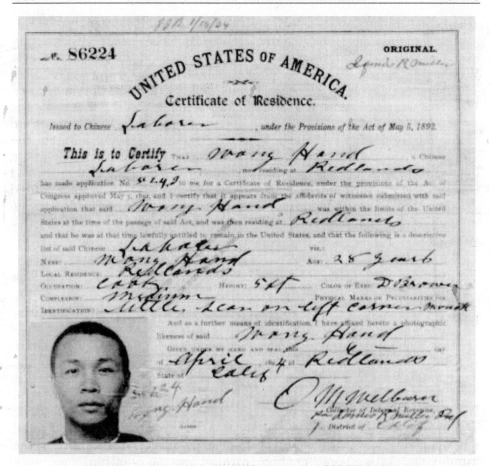

A typical residence certificate issued under the Chinese exclusion laws.
(Photo: Ethnic Studies Library, Asian American Studies Collections,
University of California at Berkeley)

FONG YUE TING V. UNITED STATES

Supreme Court of the United States, 1893.
149 U.S. 698, 13 S.Ct. 1016, 37 L.Ed. 905.

[Three Chinese laborers who were arrested and held by Federal authorities for not having certificates of residence petitioned for writs of habeas corpus. The Circuit Court for the Southern District of New York denied relief, and the Supreme Court consolidated the cases on appeal. The facts of one of the cases are stated in this edited excerpt.]

* * * On April 11, 1893, the petitioner applied to the collector of internal revenue for a certificate of residence; the collector refused to give him a certificate, on the ground that the witnesses whom he produced to prove that he was entitled to the certificate were persons of the Chinese race and not credible witnesses * * * . [There] was no person other than one of the Chinese race who knew and could truthfully swear that he was lawfully within the United States on May 5, 1892, and then entitled to remain therein; and because of such unavoidable cause he was unable to produce a certificate of residence, and was now without one. The petitioner was arrested by the marshal, and taken before the judge; and clearly established, to the satisfaction of the judge, that he was unable to procure a certificate of residence, by reason of the unavoidable cause aforesaid; and also established, to the judge's satisfaction, by the testimony of a Chinese resident of New York, that the petitioner was a resident of the United States at the time of the passage of the act; but having failed to [present] at least one credible white witness, as required by the statute, the judge ordered the petitioner to be remanded to the custody of the marshal, and to be deported from the United States, as provided in the act.

* * *

MR. JUSTICE GRAY, after stating the facts, delivered the opinion of the court.

The general principles of public law which lie at the foundation of these cases are clearly established by previous judgments of this court, and by the authorities therein referred to.

* * *

The right of a nation to expel or deport foreigners, who have not been naturalized or taken any steps towards becoming citizens of the country, rests upon the same grounds, and is as absolute and unqualified as the right to prohibit and prevent their entrance into the country.

* * *

The statements of leading commentators on the law of nations are to the same effect.

Vattel says: "Every nation has the right to refuse to admit a foreigner into the country, when he cannot enter without putting the nation in evident danger, or doing it a manifest injury. What it owes to itself, the care of its own safety, gives it this right; and in virtue of its natural liberty, it belongs to the nation to judge whether its circumstances will or will not justify the admission of the foreigner." "Thus, also, it has a right to send them elsewhere, if it has just cause to fear that they will corrupt the manners of the citizens; that they will create religious disturbances, or occasion any other disorder, contrary to the public safety. In a word, it has a right, and is even obliged, in this respect, to follow the rules which prudence dictates." Vattel's Law of Nations, lib. 1, c. 19, §§ 230, 231.

Ortolan says: "The government of each state has always the right to compel foreigners who are found within its territory to go away, by having them taken to the frontier. This right is based on the fact that, the foreigner not making part of the nation, his individual reception into the territory is matter of pure permission, of simple tolerance, and creates no obligation. The exercise of this right may be subjected, doubtless, to certain forms by the domestic laws of each country; but the right exists none the less, universally recognized and put in force. In France, no special form is now prescribed in this matter; the exercise of this right of expulsion is wholly left to the executive power." Ortolan, Diplomatie de la Mer, lib. 2, c. 14, (4th ed.) p. 297.

* * *

The right to exclude or to expel all aliens, or any class of aliens, absolutely or upon certain conditions, in war or in peace, being an inherent and inalienable right of every sovereign and independent nation, essential to its safety, its independence and its welfare, the question now before the court is whether the manner in which Congress has exercised this right in * * * the act of 1892 is consistent with the Constitution.

The United States are a sovereign and independent nation, and are vested by the Constitution with the entire control of international relations, and with all the powers of government necessary to maintain that control and to make it effective. The only government of this country, which other nations recognize or treat with, is the government of the Union; and the only American flag known throughout the world is the flag of the United States.

The Constitution of the United States speaks with no uncertain sound upon this subject. That instrument, established by the people of the United States as the fundamental law of the land, has conferred upon the President the executive power; has made him the commander-in-chief of the army and navy; has authorized him, by and with the consent of the Senate, to make treaties, and to appoint ambassadors, public ministers and consuls; and has made it his duty to take care that the laws be faithfully executed. The Constitution has granted to Congress the power to regulate commerce with foreign nations, including the entrance of ships, the importation of goods and the bringing of persons into the ports of the United States; to establish a uniform rule of naturalization; to define and punish piracies and felonies committed on the high seas, and offences against the law of nations; to declare war, grant letters of marque and reprisal, and make rules concerning captures on land and water; to raise and support armies, to provide and maintain a navy, and to make rules for the government and regulation of the land and naval forces; and to make all laws necessary and proper for carrying into execution these powers, and all other powers vested by the Constitution in the government of the United States, or in any department or officer thereof. And the several States are expressly forbidden to enter into any treaty, alliance or confederation; to grant letters of marque and reprisal; to enter into any agreement or compact with another State, or with a foreign power; or to engage in war, unless actually invaded, or in such imminent danger as will not admit of delay.

In exercising the great power which the people of the United States, by establishing a written Constitution as the supreme and paramount law, have vested in this court, of determining, whenever the question is properly brought before it, whether the acts of the legislature or of the executive are consistent with the Constitution, it behooves the court to be careful that it does not undertake to pass upon political questions, the final decision of which has been committed by the Constitution to the other departments of the government.

* * *

In Nishimura Ekiu's case [142 U.S. 651, 12 S.Ct. 336, 35 L.Ed. 1146 (1892)], it was adjudged that, although Congress might, if it saw fit, authorize the courts to investigate and ascertain the facts upon which the alien's right to land was made by the statutes to depend, yet Congress might intrust the final determination of those facts to an executive officer; and that, if it did so, his order was due process of law, and no other tribunal, unless expressly authorized by law to do so, was at liberty to re-examine the evidence on which he acted, or to controvert its sufficiency.

The power to exclude aliens and the power to expel them rest upon one foundation, are derived from one source, are supported by the same reasons, and are in truth but parts of one and the same power.

* * *

Chinese laborers * * * like all other aliens residing in the United States for a shorter or longer time, are entitled, so long as they are permitted by the government of the United States to remain in the country, to the safeguards of the Constitution, and to the protection of the laws, in regard to their rights of person and of property, and to their civil and criminal responsibility. But they continue to be aliens, having taken no steps towards becoming citizens, and incapable of becoming such under the naturalization laws; and therefore remain subject to the power of Congress to expel them, or to order them to be removed and deported from the country, whenever in its judgment their removal is necessary or expedient for the public interest.

[margin note: Chinese laborers enjoy certain const. protect. so long as here w/ permission]

* * *

* * * Congress, under the power to exclude or expel aliens, might have directed any Chinese laborer, found in the United States without a certificate of residence, to be removed out of the country by executive officers, without judicial trial or examination, just as it might have authorized such officers absolutely to prevent his entrance into the country. But Congress has not undertaken to do this.

The effect of the provisions of * * * the act of 1892 is that, if a Chinese laborer, after the opportunity afforded him to obtain a certificate of residence within a year, at a convenient place, and without cost, is found without such a certificate, he shall be so far presumed to be not entitled to remain within the United States, that an officer of the customs, or a collector of internal revenue, or a marshal, or a deputy of either, may arrest him, not with a view to imprisonment or punishment, or to his immediate deportation without further inquiry, but in order to take him before a judge, for the purpose of a judicial hearing and determination of the only facts which, under the act of Congress, can have a material bearing upon the question whether he shall be sent out of the country, or be permitted to remain.

* * *

If no evidence is offered by the Chinaman, the judge makes the order of deportation, as upon a default. If he produces competent evidence to explain the fact of his not having a certificate, it must be considered by the judge; and if he thereupon appears to be entitled to a certificate, it is to be granted to him. If he proves that the collector of internal revenue has unlawfully refused to give him a certificate, he proves an "unavoidable cause," within the meaning of the act, for not procuring one. If he proves that he had procured a certificate which has been lost or destroyed, he is to be allowed a reasonable time to procure a duplicate thereof.

The provision which puts the burden of proof upon him of rebutting the presumption arising from his having no certificate, as well as the requirement of proof, "by at least one credible white witness, that he was a resident of the United States at the time of the passage of this act," is within the acknowledged power of every legislature to prescribe the evidence which shall be received, and the effect of that evidence, in the courts of its own government. * * * The competency of all witnesses, without regard to their color, to testify in the courts of the United States, rests on acts of Congress, which Congress may at its discretion modify or repeal. The reason for requiring a Chinese alien, claiming the privilege of remaining in the United States, to prove the fact of his residence here, at the time of the passage of the act, "by at least one credible white witness," may have been the experience of Congress, as mentioned by Mr. Justice Field in [the *Chinese Exclusion Case*], that the enforcement of former acts, under which the testimony of Chinese persons was admitted to prove similar facts, "was attended with great embarrassment, from the suspicious nature, in many instances, of the testimony offered to establish the residence of the parties, arising from the loose notions entertained by the witnesses of the obligation of an oath." 130 U.S. 598, 9 S.Ct. 627. And this requirement, not allowing such a fact to be proved solely by the testimony of aliens in a like situation, or of the same race, is quite analogous to the provision, which has existed for seventy-seven years in the naturalization laws, by which aliens applying for naturalization must prove their residence within the limits and under the jurisdiction of the United States, for five years next preceding, "by the oath or affirmation of citizens of the United States." * * *

The proceeding before a United States judge * * * is in no proper sense a trial and sentence for a crime or offence. It is simply the ascertainment, by appropriate and lawful means, of the fact whether the conditions exist upon which Congress has enacted that an alien of this class may remain within the country. The order of deportation is not a punishment for crime. It is not a banishment, in the sense in which that word is often applied to the expulsion of a citizen from his country by way of punishment. It is but a method of enforcing the return to his own country of an alien who has not complied with the conditions upon the performance of which the government of the nation, acting within its constitutional authority and through the proper departments, has determined that his continuing to reside here shall depend. He has not, therefore, been deprived of life, liberty or property, without due process of law; and the provisions of the Constitution, securing the right of trial by jury, and prohibiting unreasonable searches and seizures, and cruel and unusual punishments, have no application.

The question whether, and upon what conditions, these aliens shall be permitted to remain within the United States being one to be determined by the political departments of the government, the judicial department cannot properly express an opinion upon the wisdom, the policy or the justice of the measures enacted by Congress in the exercise of the powers confided to it by the Constitution over this subject.

* * *

In the [case stated above], the petitioner had, within the year, applied to a collector of internal revenue for a certificate of residence, and had been refused it, because he produced and could produce none but Chinese witnesses to prove the residence necessary to entitle him to a certificate. Being found without a certificate of residence, he was arrested by the marshal, and taken before the United States District Judge, and established to the satisfaction of the judge, that, because of the collector's refusal to give him a certificate of residence he was without one by unavoidable cause; and also proved, by a Chinese witness only, that he was a resident of the United States at the time of the passage of the act of 1892. Thereupon the judge ordered him to be remanded to the custody of the marshal, and to be deported from the United States, as provided in that act.

It would seem that the collector of internal revenue, when applied to for a certificate, might properly decline to find the requisite fact of residence upon testimony which, by an express provision of the act, would be insufficient to prove that fact at a hearing before the judge. * * * [It was] within the constitutional authority of Congress to [require] the testimony of a credible white witness. And it was because no such testimony was produced, that the order of deportation was made.

Upon careful consideration of the subject, the only conclusion which appears to us to be consistent with the principles of international law, with the Constitution and laws of the United States, and with the previous decisions of this court, is that in each of these cases the judgment of the Circuit Court, dismissing the writ of habeas corpus, is right and must be

Affirmed.

MR. JUSTICE BREWER dissenting.

* * *

I rest my dissent on three propositions: First, that the persons against whom the penalties of * * * the act of 1892 are directed are persons lawfully residing within the United States; secondly, that as such they are within the protection of the Constitution, and secured by its guarantees against oppression and wrong; and, third, that [the Act] deprives them of liberty and imposes punishment without due process of law, and in disregard of constitutional guarantees, especially those found in the Fourth, Fifth, Sixth, and Eighth Articles of the Amendments.

And, first, these persons are lawfully residing within the limits of the United States. [Justice Brewer then discusses the Burlingame Treaty and the 1880 Treaty.]

* * *

While subsequently to [these treaties], Congress passed several acts to restrict the entrance into this country of Chinese laborers, and while the validity of this restriction was sustained in the *Chinese Exclusion* case, yet no act has been passed denying the right of those laborers who had once lawfully entered the country to remain, and they are here not as travellers or only temporarily. * * * There are 100,000 and more of these persons living in this country, making their homes here, and striving by their labor to earn a livelihood. They are not travellers, but resident aliens.

* * * They have lived in this country, respectively, since 1879, 1877, and 1874—almost as long a time as some of those who were members of the Congress that passed this act of punishment and expulsion.

That those who have become domiciled in a country are entitled to a more distinct and larger measure of protection than those who are simply passing through, or temporarily in it, has long been recognized by the law of nations. * * *

they should be protected.

* * *

* * * [W]hatever rights a resident alien might have in any other nation, here he is within the express protection of the Constitution, especially in respect to those guarantees which are declared in the original amendments. It has been repeated so often as to become axiomatic, that this government is one of enumerated and delegated powers, and * * * "the powers not delegated to the United States by the Constitution, nor prohibited by it to the States, are reserved to the States respectively, or to the people."

It is said that the power here asserted is inherent in sovereignty. This doctrine of powers inherent in sovereignty is one both indefinite and dangerous. Where are the limits to such powers to be found, and by whom are they to be pronounced? Is it within legislative capacity to declare the limits? If so, then the mere assertion of an inherent power creates it, and despotism exists. May the courts establish the boundaries? Whence do they obtain the authority for this? Shall they look to the practices of other nations to ascertain the limits? The governments of other nations have elastic powers—ours is fixed and bounded by a written constitution. The expulsion of a race may be within the inherent powers of a despotism. History, before the adoption of this Constitution, was not destitute of examples of the exercise of such a power; and its framers were familiar with history, and wisely, as it seems to me, they gave to this government no general power to banish. Banishment may be resorted to as punishment for crime; but among the powers reserved to the people and not delegated to the government is that of determining whether whole classes in our midst shall, for no crime but that of their race and birthplace, be driven from our territory.

Whatever may be true as to exclusion, * * * I deny that there is any arbitrary and unrestrained power to banish residents, even resident aliens. What, it may be asked, is the reason for any difference? The answer is obvious. The Constitution has no extraterritorial effect, and those who have not come lawfully within our territory cannot claim any protection from its provisions. And it may be that the national government, having full control of all matters relating to other nations, has the power to build, as it were, a Chinese wall around our borders and absolutely forbid aliens to enter. But the Constitution has potency everywhere within the limits of our territory, and the powers which the national government may exercise within such limits are those, and only those, given to it by that instrument. Now, the power to remove resident aliens is, confessedly, not expressed. Even if it be among the powers implied, yet still it can be exercised only in subordination to the limitations and restrictions imposed by the Constitution. * * *

* * *

In the case of *Yick Wo v. Hopkins*, 118 U.S. 356, 369, 6 Sup. Ct. Rep. 1070, it was said: "The Fourteenth Amendment of the Constitution is not confined to the protection of citizens. It says: 'Nor shall any State deprive any person of life, liberty, or property without due process of law; nor deny to any person within its jurisdiction the equal protection of the laws.' These provisions are universal in their application to all persons within the territorial jurisdiction, without regard to any differences of race, of color, or of nationality; and the equal protection of the laws is a pledge of the protection of equal laws." * * *

If the use of the word "person" in the Fourteenth Amendment protects all individuals lawfully within the State, the use of the same word "person" in the Fifth must be equally comprehensive, and secures to all persons lawfully within the territory of the United States the protection named therein; and a like conclusion must follow as to the Sixth.

* * * [The Act] deprives of "life, liberty, and property without due process of law." It imposes punishment without a trial, and punishment cruel and severe. It places the liberty of one individual subject to the unrestrained control of another. Notice its provisions: It first commands all to register. He who does not register violates that law, and may be punished; and so the section goes on to say that one who has not complied with its requirements, and has no certificate of residence, "shall be deemed and adjudged to be unlawfully within the United States," and then it imposes as a penalty his deportation from the country. Deportation is punishment. It involves first an arrest, a deprival of liberty; and, second, a removal from home, from family, from business, from property. * * *

* * * [I]t needs no citation of authorities to support the proposition that deportation is punishment. Every one knows that to be forcibly taken away from home, and family, and friends, and business, and property, and sent across the ocean to a distant land, is punishment; and that oftentimes most severe and cruel. * * *

But punishment implies a trial: "No person shall be deprived of life, liberty, or property, without due process of law." Due process requires that a man be heard before he is condemned, and both heard and condemned in the due and orderly procedure of a trial as recognized by the common law from time immemorial. * * * And no person who has once come within the protection of the Constitution can be punished without a trial. It may be summary, as for petty offences and in cases of contempt, but still a trial, as known to the common law. * * * But here, the Chinese are * * * arrested and, without a trial, punished by banishment.

Again, it is absolutely within the discretion of the collector to give or refuse a certificate to one who applies therefor. Nowhere is it provided what evidence shall be furnished to the collector, and nowhere is it made mandatory upon him to grant a certificate on the production of such evidence. It cannot be due process of law to impose punishment on any person for failing to have that in his possession, the possession of which he can obtain only at the arbitrary and unregulated discretion of any official. It will not do to say that the presumption is that the official will act reasonably and not arbitrarily. When the right to liberty and residence is involved, some other protection than the mere discretion of any official is required. * * *

* * *

It is true this statute is directed only against the obnoxious Chinese; but if the power exists, who shall say it will not be exercised tomorrow against other classes and other people? If the guarantees of these amendments can be thus ignored in order to get rid of this distasteful class, what security have others that a like disregard of its provisions may not be resorted to? * * *

* * *

In view of this enactment of the highest legislative body of the foremost Christian nation, may not the thoughtful Chinese disciple of Confucius fairly ask, Why do they send missionaries here?

MR. JUSTICE FIELD dissenting.

* * *

I had the honor to be the organ of the court in announcing [the] opinion and judgment [of the Court in the *Chinese Exclusion Case*]. I still adhere to the views there expressed in all particulars; but between legislation for the exclusion of Chinese persons—that is, to prevent them from entering the country—and legislation for the deportation of those who have acquired a residence in the country under a treaty with China, there is a wide and essential difference. The power of the government to exclude foreigners from this country, that is, to prevent them from entering it, whenever the public interests in its judgment require such exclusion, has been repeatedly asserted by the legislative and executive departments of our government and never denied; but its power to deport from the country persons lawfully domiciled therein by its consent, and engaged in the ordinary pursuits of life, has never been asserted by the legislative or executive departments except for crime, or as an act of war in view of existing or anticipated hostilities * * * .

* * *

[Justice Field then discusses the Alien and Sedition Acts of 1798, which among other things, authorized the President to remove aliens adjudged to be dangerous to the peace and safety of the United States.]

The duration of the act was limited to two years, and it has ever since been the subject of universal condemnation. In no other instance, until the law before us was passed, has any public man had the boldness to advocate the deportation of friendly aliens in time of peace. * * * And it will surprise most people to learn that any such dangerous and despotic power lies in our government—a power which will authorize it to expel at pleasure, in time of peace, the whole body of friendly foreigners of any country domiciled herein by its permission * * * . Is it possible that Congress can, at its pleasure, in disregard of the guarantees of the Constitution, expel at any time the Irish, German, French, and English who may have taken up their residence here on the invitation of the government, while we are at peace with the countries from which they came, simply on the ground that they have not been naturalized?

* * *

The purpose of [the 1892 law] was to secure the means of readily identifying the Chinese laborers present in the country and entitled to remain, from those who may have clandestinely entered the country in violation of its laws. * * *

This object being constitutional, the only question for our consideration is the lawfulness of the procedure provided for its accomplishment, and this must be tested by the provisions of the Constitution and laws intended for the protection of all persons against encroachment upon their rights. Aliens from countries at peace with us, domiciled within our country by its consent, are entitled to all the guaranties for the protection of their persons and property which are secured to native-born citizens. The moment any human being from a country at peace with us comes within the jurisdiction of the United States, with their consent—and such consent will always be implied when not expressly withheld, and in the case of the Chinese laborers before us was in terms given by the treaty referred to—he becomes subject to all their laws, is amenable to their punishment and entitled to their protection. Arbitrary and despotic power can no more be exercised over them with reference to their persons and property, than over the persons and property of native-born citizens. They differ only from citizens in that they cannot vote or hold any public office. As men having our common humanity, they are protected by all the guaranties of the Constitution. To hold that they are subject to any different law or are less protected in any particular than other persons, is in my judgment to ignore the teachings of our history, the practice of our government, and the language of our Constitution. Let us test this doctrine by an illustration. If a foreigner who resides in the country by its consent commits a public offence, is he subject to be cut down, maltreated, imprisoned, or put to death by violence, without accusation made, trial had, and judgment of an established tribunal following the regular forms of judicial procedure? If any rule in the administration of justice is to be omitted or discarded in his case, what rule is it to be? If one rule may lawfully be laid aside in his case, another rule may also be laid aside, and all rules may be discarded. In such instances a rule of evidence may be set aside in one case, a rule of pleading in another; the testimony of eye-witnesses may be rejected and hearsay adopted, or no evidence at all may be received, but simply an inspection of the accused, as is often the case in tribunals of Asiatic countries where personal caprice and not settled rules prevail. That would be to establish a pure, simple, undisguised despotism and tyranny with respect to foreigners resident in the country by its consent, and such an exercise of power is not permissible under our Constitution. Arbitrary and tyrannical power has no place in our system. * * *

I utterly dissent from and reject the doctrine expressed in the opinion of the majority, that "Congress, under the power to exclude or expel aliens, might have directed any Chinese laborer found in the United States without a certificate of residence to be removed out of the country by executive officers, without judicial trial or examination, just as it might have authorized such officers absolutely to prevent his entrance into the country." An arrest in that way for that purpose would not be a reasonable seizure of the person within the meaning of the Fourth Article of the amendments to the Constitution. It would be brutal and oppressive. The existence of the power thus stated is only consistent with the admission that the government is one of unlimited and despotic power so far as aliens domiciled in the country are concerned. According to its theory, Congress might have ordered executive officers to take the Chinese laborers to the ocean and put them into a boat and set them adrift; or to take them to the borders of Mexico and turn them loose there; and in both cases without any means of support; indeed, it might have sanctioned towards these laborers the most shocking brutality conceivable. I utterly repudiate all such notions, and reply that brutality, inhumanity, and cruelty cannot be made elements in any procedure for the enforcement of the laws of the United States.

The majority of the court have, in their opinion, made numerous citations from the courts and the utterances of individuals upon the power of the government of an independent nation to exclude foreigners from entering its limits, but none, beyond a few loose observations, as to its power to expel and deport from the country those who are domiciled therein by its consent. * * *

The government of the United States is one of limited and delegated powers. It takes nothing from the usages or the former action of European governments, nor does it take any power by any supposed inherent sovereignty. * * * Sovereignty or supreme power is in this country vested in the people, and only in the people. * * * When, therefore, power is exercised by Congress, authority for it must be found in express terms in the Constitution, or in the means necessary or proper for the execution of the power expressed. If it cannot be thus found, it does not exist.

* * * [A Chinese laborer's] deportation is thus imposed for neglect to obtain a certificate of residence, from which he can only escape by showing his inability to secure it from one of the causes named. That is the punishment for his neglect, and that being of an infamous character can only be imposed after indictment, trial, and conviction. * * *

The punishment is beyond all reason in its severity. It is out of all proportion to the alleged offence. It is cruel and unusual. As to its cruelty, nothing can exceed a forcible deportation from a country of one's residence, and the breaking up of all the relations of friendship, family, and business there contracted. The laborer may be seized at a distance from his home, his family and his business, and taken before the judge for his condemnation, without permission to visit his home, see his family, or complete any unfinished business. Mr. Madison well pictures its character in his powerful denunciation of the alien law of 1798 in his celebrated report upon the resolutions, from which we have cited, and concludes, as we have seen, that *if a banishment of the sort described be not a punishment, and among the severest of punishments, it will be difficult to imagine a doom to which the name can be applied.*

* * * [H]e is required * * * [to have] *at least one credible white witness.* Here the government undertakes to exact of the party arrested the testimony of a witness of a particular color, though conclusive and incontestible testimony from others may be adduced. The law might as well have said, that unless the laborer should also present a particular person as a witness who could not be produced, from sickness, absence, or other cause, such as the archbishop of the State, to establish the fact of residence, he should be held to be unlawfully within the United States.

* * *

I will not pursue the subject further. The decision of the court and the sanction it would give to legislation depriving resident aliens of the guaranties of the Constitution fills me with apprehensions. Those guaranties are of priceless value to every one resident in the country, whether citizen or alien. I cannot but regard the decision as a blow against constitutional liberty, when it declares that Congress has the right to disregard the guaranties of the Constitution intended for the protection of all men, domiciled in the country with the consent of the government, in their rights of person and property. How far will its legislation go? The unnaturalized resident feels it today, but if Congress can disregard the guaranties with respect to any one domiciled in this country with its consent, it may disregard the guaranties with respect to naturalized citizens. What assurance have we that it may not declare that naturalized citizens of a particular country cannot remain in the United States after a certain day, unless they have in their possession a certificate that they are of good moral character and attached to the principles of our Constitution, which certificate they must obtain from a collector of internal revenue upon the testimony of at least one competent witness of a class or nationality to be designated by the government?

What answer could the naturalized citizen in that case make to his arrest for deportation, which cannot be urged in behalf of the Chinese laborers of to-day?

* * *

MR. CHIEF JUSTICE FULLER dissenting.

I also dissent from the opinion and judgment of the court in these cases.

* * *

The argument is that friendly aliens, who have lawfully acquired a domicil in this country, are entitled to avail themselves of the safeguards of the Constitution only while permitted to remain, and that the power to expel them and the manner of its exercise are unaffected by that instrument. It is difficult to see how this can be so in view of the operation of the power upon the existing rights of individuals; and to say that the residence of the alien, when invited and secured by treaties and laws, is held in subordination to the exertion against him, as an alien, of the absolute and unqualified power asserted, is to import a condition not recognized by the fundamental law. Conceding that the exercise of the power to exclude is committed to the political department, and that the denial of entrance is not necessarily the subject of judicial cognizance, the exercise of the power to expel, the manner in which the right to remain may be terminated, rest on different ground, since limitations exist or are imposed upon the deprivation of that which has been lawfully acquired. * * * [The] act before us is not an act to abrogate or repeal treaties or laws in respect of Chinese laborers entitled to remain in the United States, or to expel them from the country, and no such intent can be imputed to Congress. As to them, registration for the purpose of identification is required, and the deportation * * * is by way of punishment to coerce compliance with that requisition. No euphuism can disguise the character of the act in this regard. It directs the performance of a judicial function in a particular way, and inflicts punishment without a judicial trial. It is, in effect, a legislative sentence of banishment, and, as such, absolutely void. Moreover, it contains within it the germs of the assertion of an unlimited and arbitrary power, in general, incompatible with the immutable principles of justice, inconsistent with the nature of our government, and in conflict with the written Constitution by which that government was created and those principles secured.

c.   Deportation and Punishment

The majority opinion in *Fong Yue Ting* held that an "order of deportation is not a punishment for crime"; therefore, "the provisions of the Constitution, securing the right of trial by jury, and prohibiting unreasonable searches and seizures, and cruel and unusual punishments, have no application." Does this mean that Congress could imprison noncitizens unlawfully residing in the United States without providing them the protections mandated by the Constitution in criminal proceedings?

The Supreme Court answered this question in the next case, which addressed a section of the 1892 immigration act not considered in *Fong Yue Ting.*

WONG WING V. UNITED STATES
Supreme Court of the United States, 1896.
163 U.S. 228, 16 S.Ct. 977, 41 L.Ed. 140.

MR. JUSTICE SHIRAS, after stating the facts * * *, delivered the opinion of the court.

[Wong Wing, Lee Poy, Lee You Tong, and Chan Wah Dong were imprisoned at hard labor for sixty days at the Detroit House of Corrections for being unlawfully within the United States. They filed a writ of habeas corpus challenging the legislation that any Chinese citizen judged to be in the United States illegally "shall be imprisoned at hard labor for a period of not exceeding one year and thereafter removed from the United States." Noncitizens charged under the section were not afforded a trial by jury. Act of May 5, 1892, Ch. 60, 27 Stat. 25. The federal circuit court in Michigan ruled against Wong Wing and his compatriots, and they appealed to the U.S. Supreme Court.]

The Chinese exclusion acts operate upon two classes—one consisting of those who came into the country with its consent, the other of those who have come into the United States without their consent and in disregard of the law. Our previous decisions have settled that it is within the constitutional power of Congress to deport both of these classes, and to commit the enforcement of the law to executive officers.

The question now presented is whether Congress can promote its policy in respect to Chinese persons by adding to its provisions for their exclusion and expulsion punishment by imprisonment at hard labor, to be inflicted by the judgment of any justice, judge or commissioner of the United States, without a trial by jury. * * *

We think it clear that detention, or temporary confinement, as part of the means necessary to give effect to the provisions for the exclusion or expulsion of aliens would be valid. Proceedings to exclude or expel would be vain if those accused could not be held in custody pending the inquiry into their true character and while arrangements were being made for their deportation. Detention is a usual feature of every case of arrest on a criminal charge, even when an innocent person is wrongfully accused; but it is not imprisonment in a legal sense.

So, too, we think it would be plainly competent for Congress to declare the act of an alien in remaining unlawfully within the United States to be an offence, punishable by fine or imprisonment, if such offence were to be established by a judicial trial.

But the evident meaning of the section in question * * * is that the detention provided for is an imprisonment at hard labor, which is to be undergone before the sentence of deportation is to be carried into effect, and that such imprisonment is to be adjudged against the accused by a justice, judge or commissioner, upon a summary hearing. * * *

* * *

Our views, upon the question thus specifically pressed upon our attention, may be briefly expressed thus: We regard it as settled by our previous decisions that the United States can, as a matter of public policy, by Congressional enactment, forbid aliens or classes of aliens from coming within their borders, and expel aliens or classes of aliens from their territory, and can, in order to make effectual such decree of exclusion or expulsion, devolve the power and duty of identifying and arresting the persons included in such decree, and causing their deportation, upon executive or subordinate officials.

But when Congress sees fit to further promote such a policy by subjecting the persons of such aliens to infamous punishment at hard labor, or by confiscating their property, we think such legislation, to be valid, must provide for a judicial trial to establish the guilt of the accused.

No limits can be put by the courts upon the power of Congress to protect, by summary methods, the country from the advent of aliens whose race or habits render them undesirable as citizens, or to expel such if they have already found their way into our land and unlawfully remain therein. But to declare unlawful residence within the country to be an infamous crime, punishable by deprivation of liberty and property, would be to pass out of the sphere of constitutional legislation, unless provision were made that the fact of guilt should first be established by a judicial trial. It is not consistent with the theory of our government that the legislature should, after having defined an offence as an infamous crime, find the fact of guilt and adjudge the punishment by one of its own agents.

* * *

[I]n the case of *Yick Wo v. Hopkins*, 118 U. S. 369, 6 Sup. Ct. 1064, it was said: "The fourteenth amendment to the constitution is not confined to the protection of citizens. It says: 'Nor shall any state deprive any person of life, liberty or property without due process of law; nor deny to any person within its jurisdiction the equal protection of the law.' These provisions are universal in their application to all persons within the territorial jurisdiction, without regard to any differences of race, of color, or nationality; and the equal protection of the laws is a pledge of the protection of equal laws." Applying this reasoning to the fifth and sixth amendments, it must be concluded that all persons within the territory of the United States are entitled to the protection guarantied by those amendments, and that even aliens shall not be held to answer for a capital or other infamous crime, unless on a presentment or indictment of a grand jury, nor be deprived of life, liberty, or property without due process of law.

* * *

The judgment of the Circuit Court is reversed * * * .

NOTES AND QUESTIONS ON
EXCLUSION, DEPORTATION, AND PUNISHMENT

1. **The Court's composition.** The Supreme Court decided *Chae Chan Ping*, *Fong Yue Ting*, and *Wong Wing* within a span of seven years. There were no dissents in the first or third, but there were only five votes for the *Fong Yue Ting* opinion. Two of the three *Fong Yue Ting* dissenters, Justice Field and Justice Brewer, had agreed with the *Chae Chan Ping* outcome. The third dissent was filed by Chief Justice Fuller, who joined the Court after *Chae Chan Ping* was decided. (Justice Harlan did not participate, as he was on leave from the Supreme Court to serve as the U.S. representative to the Bering Sea Arbitration, 149 U.S., at iii n.1.) Recent examinations of Justice Field's jurisprudential and political views can be found in Victor C. Romero, *Elusive Equality: Reflections on Justice Field's Opinions in* Chae Chan Ping *and* Fong Yue Ting, 68 Okla. L. Rev. 165 (2015) and David A. Martin, *Why Immigration's Plenary Power Doctrine Endures*, 68 Okla. L. Rev. 29 (2015).

2. **Are exclusion and deportation two sides of the same coin?**
Justice Gray stated that "[t]he right of a nation to expel or deport foreigners,
who have not been naturalized or taken any steps towards becoming citizens
of the country, rests upon the same ground, and is as absolute and
unqualified as the right to prohibit and prevent their entrance into the
country." Justice Field, who had written the opinion for the Court in *Chae
Chan Ping*, was not convinced that the exclusion case controlled the
deportation case. On what grounds did he and the other dissenters rely?

For Justice Brewer the answer was "obvious": "The Constitution has no
extraterritorial effect, and those who have not come lawfully within our
territory cannot claim any protection from its provisions. * * * But the
Constitution has potency elsewhere within the limits of our territory * * * ."
Does this adequately distinguish *Chae Chan Ping*? The noncitizen in that
case was detained upon a steamship within the port of San Francisco. How
was he not "within our territory"? Nor does Brewer's second ground (unlawful
entry) appear to apply. Chae Chan Ping was returning to his prior lawful
residence in this country.

Chief Justice Fuller seemed to view deportation as different from
exclusion because the former entails "deprivation of that which has been
lawfully acquired." Does this adequately distinguish *Chae Chan Ping*? Was
not Chae Chan Ping being deprived of that which he had lawfully acquired?
Does Fuller's analysis suggest that noncitizens who enter without inspection
are not entitled to the same constitutional protections against deportation as
noncitizens who enter lawfully?

We will see repeated efforts to draw a line between exclusion and
deportation based on the *location* (Brewer's ground) or *stake* (Fuller's ground)
of the noncitizen. To a twenty-first century reader, the location argument
appears highly arbitrary, at least as applied to Chae Chan Ping, though it
seems to have been highly congenial to nineteenth century jurists—in these
two cases and in others. On the other hand, taking the stakes argument
seriously might call for a fundamental rethinking of both *Chae Chan Ping*
and *Fong Yue Ting*.

There is no question that Justices Brewer, Field, and Fuller believed
that the Constitution imposes limits on the *exercise* of the deportation
power—limits that may not apply to the exclusion power. But did these
Justices doubt the *existence* of the power to deport noncitizens? Do the
constitutional sources of the exclusion power equally support a power to
deport noncitizens who have entered the country?

Congress repealed the Chinese Exclusion Act in 1943, and in 2011 and
2012 the U.S. Senate and the House of Representatives formally apologized
for the discriminatory legislation. S. Res. 201 (Oct. 6, 2011); H. Res. 683
(June 18, 2012). Under current law, noncitizens may be deported for a wide
variety of conduct, including (1) for conduct occurring prior to their entry
(e.g., INA § 237(a)(4)(D) (Nazis)); (2) if they were excludable at time of entry
(INA § 237(a)(1)(A)); and (3) for conduct occurring after a lawful entry (e.g.,

INA § 237(a)(2)(A) (conviction of a crime involving moral turpitude)). Does the apparent justification for the first two deportation categories—"delayed exclusion" of those who should not have been allowed to enter—apply to noncitizens in the third category? If not, what is an alternative rationale?

3. **Is all deportation punishment?** The three *Fong Yue Ting* dissenters were still on the Court in *Wong Wing.* They all thought that imprisonment at hard labor constituted punishment, just as they had earlier concluded that deportation of resident noncitizens for failure to procure a certificate of residence constituted punishment. Would they conclude that all deportations constitute punishment? What about the case of someone who came on a temporary visa and had been present only a few weeks before the deportation process began? A stakes analysis here might point toward a reduction in the constitutionally required procedural protections due, as compared to the case of a deportable lawful permanent resident—though not to its complete absence. *See* David A. Martin, *Graduated Application of Constitutional Protections for Aliens,* 2001 Sup. Ct. Rev. 47.

Consider the following characterization: The statute at issue in *Fong Yue Ting,* unlike that in *Wong Wing,* is an ordinary regulation of immigration. Noncitizens present in this country are asked to demonstrate that they are here lawfully. Those who do so are given a certificate which protects them against deportation; those unable to demonstrate that they are entitled to a certificate are presumed to be here illegally (or deemed to be here illegally), and hence deported. Perhaps the method of determining lawfulness of status is troubling (maybe even a violation of due process), but a defect of procedure does not make the resulting deportation "punishment." In principle it merely compels a person wrongfully present to go back "to his own country," as the majority phrases the point.[10]

3. THE CONSTITUTIONAL FRAMEWORK

This set of cases raises profound and complex questions of constitutional law. We will focus on four areas of inquiry. First, what are the sources of federal power to regulate immigration? Second, what roles do the respective branches of the federal government play with regard to immigration measures? Third, what authority do state governments have over immigration? And, fourth, what role does the principle of equal protection play?

---

[10] For further readings on deportation, punishment, and the increasing use of criminal sanctions in the immigration sphere, see Daniel Kanstroom, Deportation Nation: Outsiders in American History (2007); Stephen H. Legomsky, *The New Path of Immigration Law: Asymmetric Incorporation of Criminal Justice Norms,* 64 Wash. & Lee L. Rev. 469 (2007); Juliet Stumpf, *The Crimmigration Crisis: Immigrants, Crime, and Sovereign Power,* 56 Am. U. L. Rev. 367 (2006); Theresa A. Miller, *Blurring the Boundaries Between Immigration and Crime Control After September 11,* 25 Boston College Third World L. Rev. 81 (2005); Robert Pauw, *A New Look at Deportation As Punishment: Why At Least Some of the Constitution's Criminal Procedure Protections Must Apply,* 52 Admin. L. Rev. 305 (2000); Javier Bleichmar, *Deportation as Punishment: A Historical Analysis of the British Practice of Banishment and Its Impact on Modern Constitutional Law,* 14 Geo. Immigr. L.J. 115 (1999).

a. Sources of Federal Power

(i) Enumerated Powers

A fundamental principle of American constitutional law is that the federal government "is one of enumerated powers"; it can exercise "only the powers granted to it" and powers "necessary and proper" to the execution of delegated powers. *McCulloch v. Maryland*, 17 U.S. (4 Wheat.) 316, 324, 4 L.Ed. 579 (1819).

In *Chae Chan Ping*, what enumerated powers does Justice Field rely upon to support the conclusion that Congress had the authority to pass the Chinese exclusion laws? To what other powers explicit in Article I of the Constitution might he have appealed?

(a) The Commerce Power

Art. I, § 8, cl. 3 of the Constitution authorizes Congress "to regulate Commerce with foreign Nations, and among the several States." In the mid-1800's, the Supreme Court invalidated a number of state statutes that sought to regulate immigration through the imposition of taxes or other regulations on carriers. *See Chy Lung v. Freeman*, 92 U.S. (2 Otto) 275, 23 L.Ed. 550 (1876), discussed *infra*; *Henderson v. New York*, 92 U.S. (2 Otto) 259, 23 L.Ed. 543 (1876) (striking down New York requirement that ship masters pay $1.50 tax per passenger brought to New York or provide $300 bond to indemnify city for relief expenses for four years); *Passenger Cases*, 48 U.S. (7 How.) 283, 12 L.Ed. 702 (1849) (invalidating Massachusetts and New York taxes on immigrants). *Passenger Cases* yielded a 5–4 decision in which eight Justices wrote opinions. While it is difficult to discover a ground for the decision that a majority of the Court agreed upon, the commerce power received prominent attention in the opinions of Justices McLean, Wayne, Catron and Grier.

By 1884, in the *Head Money Cases*, 112 U.S. 580, 5 S.Ct. 247, 28 L.Ed. 798 (1884), the Supreme Court explicitly relied on Congress' Commerce Clause powers to uphold a federal statute, enacted in 1882, that imposed a tax of fifty cents on every noncitizen arriving in the United States. Said the Court: "Congress [has] the power to pass a law regulating immigration as a part of commerce of this country with foreign nations." *Id.* at 600, 5 S.Ct. at 254.

Can the commerce power be relied upon to uphold the regulation of noncitizens who do not come to the United States for commercial purposes? Is the migration of children, refugees, poor people, or spouses of permanent residents "commerce"? The Supreme Court, in at least one case, has concluded that migration is commerce. In *Edwards v. California*, 314 U.S. 160, 62 S.Ct. 164, 86 L.Ed. 119 (1941), a California statute that made it a crime to bring an indigent person into the state was struck down as an unconstitutional interference with Congress' power to regulate interstate commerce. The Court, through Justice Byrnes, stated that "it is settled beyond question that the transportation of persons is 'commerce.'" In a footnote, he added: "It is immaterial whether or not the transportation is commercial in character." *Id.* at 172 n. 1, 62 S.Ct. at 166 n.1.

(b) The Naturalization Power

Art. I, § 8, cl. 4 of the Constitution grants Congress the power to "establish an uniform Rule of Naturalization." This power was expressly delegated to Congress to prevent the confusion and controversy that could arise from separate state laws bestowing citizenship. *See* James H. Kettner, The Development of American Citizenship, 1608–1870, at 224–25 (1978).

Does the power to naturalize necessarily imply the power to regulate the admission of immigrants who may eventually be eligible for naturalization? Not obviously. One might well distinguish between regulation of the *physical entry* of noncitizens into the *territory* of the United States and regulation of the entry into the *political community* of the United States through the extension of full political rights to naturalized citizens. Can the Constitution be read as granting Congress only the latter power while reserving the former power to the States?

Interestingly, in the early years of the Republic, Congress viewed the naturalization power as a way to regulate immigration. In most states, noncitizens could not own or inherit land, vote or hold office—disabilities that were removed upon naturalization. Congress could thus encourage or discourage immigration by altering the prerequisites (such as length of residence) for naturalization. *See, e.g.*, 1 Annals of Cong. 1109–1125 (1790) (debate on Naturalization Act of 1790).

(c) The War Power

Art. I, § 8, cl. 11 grants Congress the power "to declare War." It is beyond dispute that the war power gives the federal government the authority to stop the entry of enemy aliens and to expel enemy aliens residing in the United States. This power was first granted to the President by one of the Alien and Sedition Acts and remains on the books today. *See* 50 U.S.C.A. §§ 21–23. The constitutionality of this provision has been consistently upheld. *See, e.g., Ludecke v. Watkins*, 335 U.S. 160, 68 S.Ct. 1429, 92 L.Ed. 1881 (1948). But is it possible to view the war power as authorizing the mass of statutes that presently regulate immigration—or even the statute challenged in *Chae Chan Ping*?

(d) The Migration and Importation Clause

Art. I, § 9, cl. 1 of the Constitution provides:

The Migration or Importation of such Persons as any of the States now existing shall think proper to admit, shall not be prohibited by the Congress prior to the Year one thousand eight hundred and eight.

slave trade ending in 1808

The denial of power to Congress *before* 1808 seems to imply the existence of such power *after* that year. Thus, this clause, at first reading, appears to authorize congressional power to *prohibit* immigration after 1808, and probably—by reasonable implication—to regulate it as well.

Unfortunately, things are not as clear as they seem. This clause is almost assuredly a veiled reference to an institution that the Founding Fathers could not bring themselves, in a charter of fundamental law, to recognize by name: slavery. *Passenger Cases*, 48 U.S. (7 How.) 283, 512–13, 12 L.Ed. 702 (1849) (opinion of Justice Daniel). Thus this clause has generally been interpreted as prohibiting congressional attempts to stop the slave trade before 1808. In fact, Congress passed a law prohibiting the importation of slaves on March 2, 1807, Ch. 22, 2 Stat. 426, which took effect January 1, 1808. *See generally* David Brion Davis, The Problem of Slavery in the Age of Revolution, 1770–1823, at 119–31 (1975); Walter Berns, *The Constitution and the Migration of Slaves*, 78 Yale L.J. 198 (1968).

unclear but mostly congress

(e) The Foreign Affairs Power

In *Chae Chan Ping*, Justice Field sought to associate the power to regulate immigration with the power to conduct foreign affairs: "[T]he United States, in their *relation to foreign countries* and their subjects or citizens, are one nation, invested with powers which belong to independent nations * * * . * * * [F]or national purposes, embracing our *relations with foreign nations*, we are but one people, one nation, one power." 130 U.S. at 604, 606 (emphasis supplied).

In modern constitutional terms, these words would be seen as an appeal to the foreign affairs power of the federal government. But like the immigration power, the foreign affairs power receives no explicit mention in the Constitution. Finding the constitutional basis of the power to conduct foreign relations has proven a vexing task, as Louis Henkin, a leading scholar on foreign affairs and the Constitution, has described:*

The Constitution does not delegate a "power to conduct foreign relations" to the federal government or confer it upon any of its branches. Congress is given power to regulate commerce with

---

*   Reprinted from *Foreign Affairs and the Constitution* by Louis Henkin, copyright © 1972, with permission of Foundation Press.

foreign nations, to define offenses against the law of nations, to declare war, and the President the power to make treaties and send and receive ambassadors, but these hardly add up to the power to conduct foreign relations. Where is the power to recognize other states or governments, to maintain or break diplomatic relations, to open consulates elsewhere and permit them here, to acquire or cede territory, to give or withhold foreign aid, to proclaim a Monroe Doctrine or an Open-Door Policy, indeed to determine all the attitudes and carry out all the details in the myriads of relationships with other nations that are "the foreign policy" and "the foreign relations" of the United States? * * * Congress can regulate foreign commerce but where is the power to make other laws relating to our foreign relations—to regulate immigration, or the status and rights of aliens, or activities of citizens at home or abroad affecting our foreign relations? These "missing" powers, and a host of others, were clearly intended for and have always been exercised by the federal government, but where does the Constitution say that it shall be so?

* * *

The attempt to build all the foreign affairs powers of the federal government with the few bricks provided by the Constitution has not been accepted as successful. It requires considerable stretching of language, much reading between lines, and bold extrapolation from "the Constitution as a whole," and that still does not plausibly add up to all the power which the federal government in fact exercises.

Louis Henkin, Foreign Affairs and the Constitution 16–18 (1972).

(ii) Inherent Power

Justice Field writes in *Chae Chan Ping* that "[t]he power of exclusion of foreigners [is] an incident of sovereignty belonging to the government of the United States, as a part of those sovereign powers delegated by the Constitution." Earlier in the opinion he states:

That the government of the United States * * * can exclude aliens from its territories is a proposition which we do not think open to controversy. Jurisdiction over its own territory to that extent is an incident of every independent nation. It is a part of its independence. If it could not exclude aliens, it would be to that extent subject to the control of another power.

Three years later, the Court's decision in *Nishimura Ekiu v. United States*, 142 U.S. 651, 12 S.Ct. 336, 35 L.Ed. 1146 (1892), upheld the immigration act of 1891, which codified existing exclusion laws and provided for exclusive inspection of arriving aliens by the federal government. Justice Gray, writing for the Court, stated:

> It is an accepted maxim of international law, that every sovereign nation has the power, as inherent in sovereignty, and essential to preservation, to forbid the entrance of foreigners within its dominions, or to admit them only in such cases and upon such conditions as it may see fit to prescribe. In the United States, this power is vested in the national government, to which the Constitution has committed the entire control of international relations, in peace as well as in war.

These powerful and oft-cited passages mask deep and unanswered puzzles. If the federal government is one of enumerated powers, how can it possess "inherent powers" that seem to owe their existence to sources outside the Constitution? Why should "maxims of international law" define the power of Congress? Isn't that what a (or at least our) Constitution is for? Even if we accept the idea that an attribute of sovereignty is the power to regulate immigration, why don't we discover that power in the States, which, under the Tenth Amendment, retain all governmental powers not delegated to the federal government?

In a non-immigration context, the Supreme Court found the foreign affairs power to derive, not from the Constitution, but from the fact of independence itself. *United States v. Curtiss-Wright Export Corp.*, 299 U.S. 304, 57 S.Ct. 216, 81 L.Ed. 255 (1936). *Curtiss-Wright's* theory is particularly troubling in the immigration area. If the power to regulate immigration is extra-constitutional, is it subject to any limits within the Constitution? May noncitizens be excluded without a guarantee of due process? Are noncitizens living in the United States not entitled to the protections of the First, Fourth, Fifth and Sixth Amendments? The Supreme Court has repeatedly stated that they are, at least outside the core immigration law issues of admission and expulsion. But how can these constitutional limits be applied to a power that exists outside the Constitution?

(iii) Constructional and Structural Arguments

Perhaps there is some source of power between enumerated powers and extra-constitutional powers. Let us suggest two.

(a) The Rule of Necessity

Judge Learned Hand has written:

For centuries it has been an accepted canon in interpretation of documents to interpolate into the text such provisions, though not expressed, as are essential to prevent the defeat of the venture at hand; and this applies with especial force to the interpretation of constitutions, which, since they are designed to cover a great multitude of necessarily unforeseen occasions, must be cast in general language, unless they are constantly amended.

Learned Hand, The Bill of Rights 14 (1958).

Is it possible to infer the immigration power using Hand's reasoning—"not [as] a logical deduction from the structure of the Constitution but only as a practical condition upon its successful operation"? *Id.* at 15. Justice Field hints at such a justification when he argues that if the federal government were not able to control immigration, the United States "would be to that extent subject to the control of another power." Foreign powers could send *agents provocateurs* or suicide bombers to disrupt American institutions; developing nations could send workers to take advantage of American jobs; other countries could seek to solve their problems of overpopulation by exporting people to the United States. Perhaps to lose control of one's borders is to "defeat the venture at hand" by losing our ability to achieve the objects for which the Constitution was established: "to insure domestic Tranquility, provide for the common defense, promote the general Welfare."

(b) Structural Justifications

Charles Black, a leading constitutional scholar, suggested that much of our constitutional law may be seen not as "the explication or exegesis of [a] particular textual passage," but rather as an "inference from the structures and relationships created by the constitution." Charles L. Black, Structure and Relationship in Constitutional Law 7 (1985). The primary purpose of the Constitution is to establish a system of government for a nation, a nation encompassing territory and members (*citizens*). *See* David A. Martin, *Why Immigration's Plenary Power Doctrine Endures*, 68 Okla. L. Rev. 29, 32–38 (2015) (arguing that Justice Field's opinion in *Chae Chan Ping* deploys *sovereignty* not in order to diminish rights but as a structural argument placing immigration control power in the national government, rather than the states). A system of government is the process by which citizens establish rules of conduct for persons within the territory. From these premises, two sorts of structural arguments may follow.

First, to be a sovereign nation, a people must have control over their territory. A nation of open borders runs the risk of not being able to govern itself because its sovereignty, to some extent, is in the hands of the other nations of the world. It seems reasonable to believe that the persons who wrote and ratified the Constitution thought (or hoped) they were creating a nation that would be able to take its place among other nations as an equal; one that would possess the powers of sovereignty generally possessed by all other nations. Second, the relationship of the citizen to the nation is crucial. Citizens, through the process of government, argue about, protect, and further values. Immigration decisions give citizens the ability to regulate who the participants in the discussion will be. By deciding whom we permit to enter the country, we say much about who we are as a nation. As the Chinese exclusion laws demonstrate, the process of self-definition can be ugly, short-sighted, wrong. But perhaps it is one power that every people must possess to be a sovereign people. As Michael Walzer has written:

> [T]he right to choose an admissions policy is * * * not merely a matter of acting in the world, exercising sovereignty, and pursuing national interests. At stake here is the shape of the community that acts in the world, exercises sovereignty, and so on. Admission and exclusion are at the core of communal independence. They suggest the deepest meaning of self-determination.

Michael Walzer, Spheres of Justice: A Defense of Pluralism and Equality 61–62 (1983).

Thus we have identified two kinds of structural arguments to justify the immigration power: one based on *self-preservation*, the other on *self-definition*. To what extent are U.S. immigration admission and expulsion rules in fact based on concerns of community self-definition? Consider the following argument:

> "[S]elf-definition" has rarely been a central aspect of immigration regulation. The vast majority of immigration decisions are not club membership rules carefully crafted to preserve a particular group identity. They are much closer to university admission policies than they are to rules regulating religious conversions. We choose how many aliens to admit based on economic, social and moral considerations, attempting to screen out individuals who are likely to threaten the public health, welfare, or security. * * * To be sure, immigration regulations reflect deep social norms and understandings. For example, family reunification policies are based on prevailing American definitions of "nuclear family." But our immigration laws are not primarily concerned with the construction or maintenance of a particular kind of community.

T. Alexander Aleinikoff, *Citizens, Aliens, Membership and the Constitution*, 7 Const. Comm. 9, 33–34 (1990).

b.   Plenary Power Doctrine

To generations of law students and lawyers raised on the theory of judicial review articulated in *Marbury v. Madison*, 5 U.S. 137, 2 L.Ed. 60 (1803), the words used by Justice Field in *Chae Chan Ping* are startling:

"If * * * [the] legislative department considers the presence of foreigners of a different race * * * to be dangerous to its peace and security, * * * its determination is conclusive upon the judiciary." 130 U.S. 581, 606 (1889). Known as the plenary power doctrine, this exceptional deference to Congress in matters concerning exclusion of noncitizens has been much critiqued in recent decades. As you proceed, you will see that the plenary power doctrine has undergone some erosion—both directly and indirectly—and courts have become more willing to hear constitutional claims.[11] Nonetheless, in immigration cases the federal judiciary frequently refers to the wide constitutional latitude that Congress enjoys.

Contrary voices continue to challenge the traditional view of plenary power. One scholar has expressed strong skepticism that there is a plenary power doctrine at all, see Gabriel J. Chin, *Is There a Plenary Power Doctrine? A Tentative Apology and Prediction for Our Strange But Unexceptional Constitutional Immigration Law*, 14 Geo. Immigr. L.J. 257, 258 (1999) :

> There is no need for a special plenary power doctrine or other constitutional rule to explain the cases, because the Court has rarely, if ever, tested discrimination against a group in the immigration context at a moment when it had already recognized that the Constitution prohibited discrimination on that ground against citizens. Typically, the Court has upheld discriminatory immigration laws during periods when domestic discrimination against citizens was permitted on the same basis.

Further, it is noteworthy that the concept of plenary power in immigration law developed in the highly racialized context in which the courts decided *Chae Chan Ping*, *Fong Yue Ting*, and other foundation cases. Indeed, these cases reached the courts in the same decade as the notorious *Plessy v. Ferguson*, 163 U.S. 537, 16 S. Ct. 1138, 41 L.Ed. 256 (1896), decision upholding "separate but equal" racial segregation. *See* Gabriel J. Chin, *Regulating Race: Asian Exclusion and the Administrative State*, 37 Harv. C.-R. C.-L. L. Rev. 1, 50–62 (2002); Gabriel J. Chin, *Segregation's Last Stronghold: Race, Discrimination and the Constitutional Law of Immigration*, 46 UCLA L. Rev. 1 (1998); Kevin R. Johnson, *Race, the Immigration Laws, and Domestic Race Relations: A "Magic Mirror" into the Heart of Darkness*, 73 Ind. L.J. (1998).

---

[11] *See* T. Alexander Aleinikoff, Semblances of Sovereignty: The Constitution, the State, and American Citizenship 153–65 (2002); Stephen H. Legomsky, Immigration and the Judiciary 177–222 (1987); Hiroshi Motomura, *The Curious Evolution of Immigration Law: Procedural Surrogates for Substantive Constitutional Rights*, 92 Colum. L. Rev. 1625 (1992); Hiroshi Motomura, *Immigration Law After a Century of Plenary Power: Phantom Constitutional Norms and Statutory Interpretation*, 100 Yale L.J. 545 (1990); Peter H. Schuck, *The Transformation of Immigration Law*, 84 Colum. L. Rev. 1 (1984). For a thorough treatment of the constitutional foundations of immigration law and noncitizens' rights in the United States, see Gerald L. Neuman, Strangers to the Constitution: Immigrants, Borders, and Fundamental Law (1996).

famous critique

Louis Henkin has harshly criticized the view that the Constitution imposes no limits on the plenary power of Congress to exclude or deport noncitizens.

> The doctrine that the Constitution neither limits governmental control over the admission of aliens nor secures the right of admitted aliens to reside here emerged in the oppressive shadow of a racist, nativist mood a hundred years ago. It was reaffirmed during our fearful, cold war, McCarthy days. It has no foundation in principle. It is a constitutional fossil, a remnant of a prerights jurisprudence that we have proudly rejected in other respects. Nothing in our Constitution, its theory, or history warrants exempting any exercise of governmental power from constitutional restraint. No such exemption is required or even warranted by the fact that the power to control immigration is unenumerated, inherent in sovereignty, and extraconstitutional.

> As a blanket exemption of immigration laws from constitutional limitations, *Chinese Exclusion* is a "relic from a different era." That era was one in which constitutional restraints were deemed inapplicable to actions by the United States outside its territory; when orotund generalities about sovereignty and national security were a substitute for significant scrutiny of governmental action impinging on individual rights; when the Bill of Rights had not yet become our national hallmark and the principal justification and preoccupation of judicial review. It was an era before United States commitment to international human rights; before enlightenment in and out of the United States brought an end both to official racial discrimination at home and to national-origins immigration laws; before important freedoms were recognized as preferred, inviting strict scrutiny if they were invaded and requiring a compelling public interest to uphold their invasion. Since that era, the Supreme Court has held that the Bill of Rights applies to foreign as well as to domestic affairs, in war as well as in peace, to aliens as well as to citizens, abroad as well as at home. The Court has left only immigration and deportation outside the reach of fundamental constitutional protections.

> The power of Congress to control immigration and to regulate alienage and naturalization is plenary. But even plenary power is subject to constitutional restraints. I cannot believe that the Court would hold today that the Constitution permits either exclusion on racial or religious grounds or

deportation of persons lawfully admitted who have resided peacefully here. * * *

Chinese Exclusion—its very name is an embarrassment— must go.

Louis Henkin, *The Constitution and United States Sovereignty: A Century of Chinese Exclusion and its Progeny*, 100 Harv. L. Rev. 853, 862–63 (1987).

David Martin argues that the plenary power doctrine has endured despite vociferous scholarly criticism because the Court sees strong connections between immigration control and the foreign affairs power. Given the relative scarcity of means to respond to unfavorable international developments—as compared to how government could deploy mature institutions to respond to a domestic crisis—the Court seeks to preserve leeway for the political branches to use a wide range of tools to address complex and uncertain global conditions. In his view the Supreme Court is unlikely to moderate the doctrine.

> [A] majority of the Justices harbor a deep skepticism that lower courts can be trusted to give sufficient weight to foreign policy concerns in making any such threshold assessment. The very nature of immigration litigation in the courts of appeals, with an actual and often sympathetic human being front and center, makes a reviewing judge far more likely to overvalue the individual interests at stake and undervalue the more subtle and complex reasons why a particular measure may be needed for system stability or to influence behavior beyond our borders— connections that often would not become fully apparent until broader damage is manifested months or years after an interventionist judicial decision.

David A. Martin, *Why Immigration's Plenary Power Doctrine Endures*, 68 Okla. L. Rev. 29, 48 (2015) . Martin sees the plenary power doctrine's survival as a call to reformers to roll up their sleeves and address objectionable practices through the political process. He notes significant successes achieved despite judicial quiescence, including repeal of the national-origins quota system. *Id.* at 54–56.

c.   **State, Local, and Federal Authority**

In recent years, as state laws (and state politicians) play a growing role in the national debate about immigration law and policy, it has become increasingly important to consider the exact contours of the federal government's power to control immigration, and the extent to which it displaces any analogous state power. In responding to these questions, consider the following.

Prior to the enactment of the first federal immigration legislation in 1875, states and localities had regulated immigration, sometimes directly, but more often indirectly through quarantine and health laws. *See* Gerald L. Neuman, *The Lost Century of American Immigration Law (1776–1875)*, 93 Colum. L. Rev. 1833 (1993). Federal courts, relying on the federal government's power to conduct foreign affairs, invalidated some of these state statutes. The classic statement of this position occurs in *Chy Lung v. Freeman*, 92 U.S. (2 Otto) 275, 23 L.Ed. 550 (1875). The case involved, in the Supreme Court's words, "a most extraordinary statute" that authorized the California Commissioner of Immigration to inspect aliens seeking to enter the United States. For any alien determined by the Commissioner to be deaf, dumb, blind, crippled, infirm, or a lunatic, idiot, pauper, convicted criminal or lewd or debauched woman, the master of the vessel was required to give a bond or pay an amount determined by the Commissioner to be sufficient to provide for the alien's care. In litigation filed by a Chinese woman denied entry at San Francisco, the Court relied in large part on the impact that such a regulation could have on American foreign policy.

Individual foreigners, however distinguished at home for their social, their literary, or their political character, are helpless in the presence of this potent commissioner. Such a person may offer to furnish any amount of surety on his own bond, or deposit any sum of money; but the law of California takes no note of him. It is the master, owner, or consignee of the vessel alone whose bond can be accepted; and so a silly, an obstinate, or a wicked commissioner may bring disgrace upon the whole country, the enmity of a powerful nation, or the loss of an equally powerful friend.

While the occurrence of the hypothetical case just stated may be highly improbable, we venture the assertion, that, if citizens of our own government were treated by any foreign nation as subjects of the Emperor of China have been actually treated under this law, no administration could withstand the call for a demand on such government for redress.

Or, if this plaintiff and her twenty companions had been subjects of the Queen of Great Britain, can anyone doubt that this matter would have been the subject of international inquiry, if not of a direct claim for redress? Upon whom would such a claim be made? Not upon the State of California; for, by our Constitution, she can hold no exterior relations with other nations. It would be made upon the government of the United States. If that government should get into a difficulty which would lead to war, or to suspension of intercourse, would California alone suffer, or all the Union? If we should conclude that a pecuniary indemnity was proper as a satisfaction for the injury, would California pay it, or the Federal government? If that government has forbidden the States to hold negotiations with any foreign nations, or to declare war, and has taken the whole subject of these relations upon herself, has the Constitution, which provides for this, done so foolish a thing as to leave it in the power of the States to pass laws whose enforcement renders the general government liable to just reclamations which it must answer, while it does not prohibit to the States the acts for which it is held responsible?

The Constitution of the United States is no such instrument. The passage of laws which concern the admission of citizens and subjects of foreign nations to our shores belongs to Congress, and not to the States. It has the power to regulate commerce with foreign nations: the responsibility for the character of those regulations, and for the manner of their execution, belongs solely to the national government. If it be otherwise, a single State can, at her pleasure, embroil us in disastrous quarrels with other nations.

Id. at 279–80.

Although Congress had not yet enacted extensive immigration legislation, *Chy Lung* struck down the California statute because it attempted to exercise power reserved to the national government. Despite *Chy Lung*'s ruling that the Constitution restricted the power of states to control immigration, the view developed that "some actions that might be regulated by Congress under its power over interstate or foreign commerce could also be regulated by a state under its power of police, so long as no actual conflict with federal legislation occurred." Gerald L. Neuman, *The Lost Century*, at 1887 (1993). For example, states might exercise their police power through quarantine and health laws in ways that amounted to immigration control. According to Neuman, several lower court decisions understood the Supreme Court decisions as approving broad state authority over immigration.

The immense increase in federal legislative activity in regulating immigration during the twentieth century overshadowed and extinguished most state efforts to control immigration directly, but the dawn of the twenty-first century witnessed renewed efforts by states to address immigration concerns. In 2012 the Supreme Court struck down three provisions of Arizona S.B. 1070 that criminalized unauthorized presence and unauthorized work in the United States, and authorized warrantless arrests of noncitizens believed to be removable from the United States. *Arizona v. United States*, 567 U.S. ___, 132 S.Ct. 2492, 183 L.Ed. 2d 351 (2012).

Due to the extensive federal regulation of immigration, courts have rarely confronted circumstances in which states have directly attempted to control immigration. Frequently, though, the courts review situations in which federal immigration legislation and state or local laws coexist. In these circumstances courts often inquire whether Congress intended federal legislation to occupy the field or intended to leave a sphere in which state and local governments could act. Federal preemption was the focus in *Hines v. Davidowitz*, 312 U.S. 52, 61 S.Ct. 399, 85 L.Ed. 581 (1941), in which the Supreme Court invalidated Pennsylvania's statute requiring noncitizens to register with the state and carry a state-issued identity card, even though Congress had not expressly forbidden state registration requirements when it enacted the federal scheme. The potential impact on foreign relations convinced the Court that preemption applied. When Congress enacted federal employer sanctions in 1986, it expressly preempted such state authority, with an exception for "licensing and similar laws." In 2011, the Supreme Court upheld an Arizona statute stripping a broad range of licenses from employers who knowingly hire noncitizens unauthorized to work, finding that the explicit exception applied and that this particular Arizona law was generally harmonious with the federal scheme. *Chamber of Commerce v. Whiting*, 563 U.S. 582, 131 S.Ct. 1968, 179 L.Ed.2d 1031 (2011). Preemption and related topics are featured in Chapter Ten.

d. Equal Protection

In its first major examination of the Fourteenth Amendment, the Supreme Court stated that it "doubt[ed] very much whether any action of a state not directed by way of discrimination against the negroes as a class, or on account of their race, will ever be held to come within the purview of [the equal protection clause]." *Slaughter-House Cases*, 83 U.S. (16 Wall.) 36, 21 L.Ed. 394 (1873). Yet in a case of major importance, decided thirteen years later—and three years before *Chae Chan Ping*—the Court addressed whether the equal protection clause protected Chinese nationals against discriminatory enforcement of a San Francisco ordinance regulating laundries.

YICK WO V. HOPKINS

Supreme Court of the United States, 1886.
118 U.S. 356, 6 S.Ct. 1064, 30 L.Ed. 220.

MR. JUSTICE MATTHEWS delivered the opinion of the court.

[Yick Wo came to California in 1861, ran a laundry business for twenty-two years, and was arrested for violating a newly enacted San Francisco ordinance outlawing laundries in wood buildings without prior approval by the Board of Supervisors. Most of the buildings in San Francisco were wood, as were 310 of the 320 laundries. The 240 Chinese families who operated laundries petitioned for approval, but all were denied. Similar laundries operated by non-Chinese remained in business. After Yick Wo was arrested, the California Supreme Court denied his petition for habeas corpus. The Court first addressed whether the plaintiffs could invoke the equal protection clause.]

The rights of the petitioners, * * * are not less, because they are aliens and subjects of the Emperor of China. * * *

The Fourteenth Amendment to the Constitution is not confined to the protection of citizens. It says: "Nor shall any state deprive any person of life, liberty, or property without due process of law; nor deny to any person within its jurisdiction the equal protection of the laws." These provisions are universal in their application, to all persons within the territorial jurisdiction, without regard to any differences of race, of color, or of nationality; and the equal protection of the laws is a pledge of the protection of equal laws. * * * The questions we have to consider and decide in these cases, therefore, are to be treated as involving the rights of every citizen of the United States equally with those of the strangers and aliens who now invoke the jurisdiction of the court.

[The petitioners contend] that the violations of which they are severally sentenced to imprisonment are void on their face, as being within the prohibitions of the fourteenth amendment, and, in the alternative, * * * that they are void by reason of their administration, operating unequally, so as to punish in the present petitioners what is permitted to others as lawful, without any distinction of circumstances— an unjust and illegal discrimination, it is claimed, which, though not made expressly by the ordinances, is made possible by them.

When we consider the nature and the theory of our institutions of government, the principles upon which they are supposed to rest, and review the history of their development, we are constrained to conclude that they do not mean to leave room for the play and action of purely personal and arbitrary power. * * * It is, indeed, quite true that there must always be lodged somewhere, and in some person or body, the authority of final decision; and in many cases of mere administration the responsibility is purely political, no appeal lying except to the ultimate tribunal of the public judgment, exercised either in the pressure of opinion, or by means of the suffrage. But the fundamental rights to life, liberty, and the pursuit of happiness, considered as individual possessions, are secured by those maxims of constitutional law which are the monuments showing the victorious progress of the race in securing to men the blessings of civilization under the reign of just and equal laws, so that, in the famous language of the Massachusetts Bill of Rights, the government of the commonwealth "may be a government of laws and not of men." For, the very idea that one man may be compelled to hold his life, or the means of living, or any material right essential to the enjoyment of life, at the mere will of another, seems to be intolerable in any country where freedom prevails, as being the essence of slavery itself.

* * *

* * * [T]he facts shown establish an administration directed so exclusively against a particular class of persons as to warrant and require the conclusion, that, whatever may have been the intent of the ordinances as adopted, they are applied by the public authorities charged with their administration, and thus representing the State itself, with a mind so unequal and oppressive as to amount to a practical denial by the State of that equal protection of the laws which is secured to the petitioners, as to all other persons, by the broad and benign provisions of the Fourteenth Amendment to the Constitution of the United States. * * *

The * * * petitioners have complied with every * * * precaution against injury to the public health. No reason whatever, except the will of the supervisors, is assigned why they should not be permitted to carry on, in the accustomed manner, their harmless and useful occupation, on which they depend for a livelihood. And while this consent of the supervisors is withheld from them and from two hundred others who have also petitioned, all of whom happen to be Chinese subjects, eighty others, not Chinese subjects, are permitted to carry on the same business under similar conditions. The fact of this discrimination is admitted. No reason for it is shown, and the conclusion cannot be resisted, that no reason for it exists except hostility to the race and nationality to which the petitioners belong, and which in the eye of the law is not justified. The discrimination is, therefore, illegal, and the public administration which enforces it is a denial of the equal protection of the laws and a violation of the Fourteenth Amendment of the Constitution. * * *

The judgment of the Supreme Court of California [is] reversed and the cases remanded * * * with directions to discharge the petitioners from custody and imprisonment.

_____

If the Fourteenth Amendment protected Chinese citizens operating laundries, why were not the Chinese exclusion laws similarly invalid—evidencing, as they did, hostility based on race and nationality?

The quick answer is that the Fourteenth Amendment applies only to the actions of the States, and not to the federal government. In the late nineteenth century, this formalistic answer probably explains why an equal protection challenge was not made in *Chae Chan Ping*, but that answer cannot suffice today. In *Bolling v. Sharpe*, 347 U.S. 497, 74 S.Ct. 693, 98 L.Ed. 884 (1954), a companion case to *Brown v. Board of Education*, the Court held that segregated schools in the District of

Columbia violated the due process clause of the Fifth Amendment. Since *Bolling*, it has usually been understood that "[e]qual protection analysis in the Fifth Amendment area is the same as that under the Fourteenth Amendment." *Buckley v. Valeo*, 424 U.S. 1, 93, 96 S.Ct. 612, 670, 46 L.Ed.2d 659 (1976) (per curiam). Does this mean that the Chinese exclusion laws would be invalid today? Not quite.

A more fundamental difficulty with applying the reasoning of *Yick Wo* to challenge Chae Chan Ping's exclusion would have been that *Chae Chan Ping* involved an immigration question—a noncitizen's right to enter the United States. *Yick Wo* involved an allegation of discrimination against noncitizens in the United States, but not a challenge to a decision to exclude or expel them. This aspect of *Yick Wo* suggests a tension that runs throughout the constitutional materials in this book. On the one hand, *Chae Chan Ping* is a seminal case for the "plenary power doctrine"—which severely limits noncitizens' constitutional rights when it comes to entering and remaining in this country. In contrast, *Yick Wo* suggests that noncitizens and citizens receive similar (but not necessarily identical) constitutional treatment in *nonimmigration* matters. Put differently, our constitutional law relating to *immigration* may differ from our constitutional law relating to noncitizen *immigrants*.

Federal preemption and stronger equal protection scrutiny of state and local laws add other complications to applying *Yick Wo* to challenge Chae Chan Ping's exclusion. Besides distinguishing immigration law from discrimination against noncitizens with respect to their rights and conduct as residents, one might also distinguish the federal law in *Chae Chan Ping* from the local law in *Yick Wo*. As we explore in detail in Chapter Eleven, later Supreme Court decisions recognized broad congressional authority to "make rules [regarding noncitizens] that would be unacceptable if applied to citizens," *Mathews v. Diaz*, 426 U.S. 67, 80, 96 S.Ct. 1883, 1891, 48 L.Ed.2d 478 (1976); but other court decisions vigorously scrutinized most state legislation that discriminates against noncitizens, *see, e.g., Graham v. Richardson*, 403 U.S. 365, 91 S.Ct. 1848, 29 L.Ed.2d 534 (1971).

NOTES AND QUESTIONS ON CONSTITUTIONAL CHALLENGES

1. **Framing the constitutional challenge.** Seven years before *Fong Yue Ting*, the Supreme Court had struck down the discriminatory municipal ordinance in *Yick Wo* and ruled that Chinese nationals in the United States came within the ambit of the equal protection clause. Surprisingly (to a modern observer), despite the vehemence of their opinions, the *Fong Yue Ting* dissenters paid little attention to Congress' decision to single out laborers of Chinese origin. Why do you think this was so? With this question in mind, look again at the opinions to see exactly what the dissenters found

objectionable about the statute. Why did they apparently find that objection more persuasive than a nationality or racial discrimination challenge?

2.   In both *Wong Wing* and *Yick Wo*, the Supreme Court relied upon generally applicable constitutional norms to invalidate governmental action that involved immigrants. *Wong Wing*, unlike *Yick Wo*, invalidated a *federal* statute—and one that was more closely related to the immigration power. In that respect it may stand more clearly than *Yick Wo* for the proposition that noncitizens are members of the constitutional community, apart from their right to enter and remain in this country.

————————

We close this section with an exercise that calls for applying the constitutional principles to a hypothetical counterterrorism statute.

EXERCISE

Assume that Congress, citing concerns about "terrorist activities by Islamic fundamentalists," passes (and that the President signs into law) the Immigration Counterterrorism Act, which includes the following:

Section 1. Notwithstanding any other provision of law, no Muslim refugees currently located overseas are eligible for resettlement in the United States as part of the U.S. Refugee Resettlement Program.

Section 2. Notwithstanding any other provision of law, aliens who present themselves at the border or within the territory of the United States are not eligible for asylum in the United States if they are nationals or citizens of countries in which the principal religion is Islam.

Section 3. Any alien who entered the United States as a refugee or who received asylum after arriving in the United States and has since participated in public activity criticizing the military or diplomatic policy of the United States shall be deportable; provided, however, that this section shall not apply to an alien who is the spouse, parent, or child of a citizen or national of the United States.

You are a lawyer writing a brief challenging the constitutionality of these provisions. Working just with what you have read so far—focusing on *Chae Chan Ping*, *Yick Wo*, *Wong Wing*, and *Fong Yue Ting*—what are the main arguments and authorities that you would rely on?

Now assume that you are a lawyer writing a brief defending these provisions as constitutional. Working with what you have read so far this semester, what are your main arguments and authorities?

[Handwritten annotations in margins:]

location matters
1A Est. Clause
← not specific enough
just a general religion which is motivated by animus toward Islam
no resettlement

14A EP

14A EP
← already at interior
14A protection triggered
no asylum

gov. has consented to them being here

(1) b/c protections at border
(2) right to close border
(3) more protections for LPRs and those here residing

B. THEORIES OF MIGRATION AND THE ECONOMIC IMPACT OF IMMIGRATION

After surveying the history of immigration to the United States and the evolving legal regime that has attempted to respond and regulate the flows of immigrants, it is useful to stand back for a moment and ask a more general question: Why do people migrate? A better understanding of the answers to this question should contribute substantially toward designing wise and effective policy. The selections in this section emphasize different perspectives on the migration phenomenon. The first excerpt argues that multiple factors working simultaneously, and sometimes in tension with each other, account for international migration.

DOUGLAS S. MASSEY, JORGE DURAND & NOLAN J. MALONE, BEYOND SMOKE AND MIRRORS: MEXICAN IMMIGRATION IN AN ERA OF ECONOMIC INTEGRATION

9–21 (2002).

* * *

WHY PEOPLE MIGRATE

* * *[According to *neoclassical economics*,] international migration stems from geographic differences in the supply of and demand for labor. Countries with large endowments of labor relative to capital have low wages, while those with limited endowments of labor relative to capital have high wages. The resulting international differential causes workers from low-wage countries to move to high-wage countries. As a result of this movement, the supply of labor falls and wages rise in the former while they do the opposite in the latter, leading, at equilibrium, to an international wage differential reflecting the costs of international movement, pecuniary and psychic.

Associated with the macro theory is an accompanying micro-economic model of decisionmaking. Rational actors choose to migrate through a cost-benefit calculation that leads them to expect positive net returns, usually monetary, from international movement. Migration is analogous to investment in human capital, where human capital consists of personal traits and characteristics that increase a worker's productivity. Early in their lives, people invest in education to make themselves more productive and later reap benefits in the form of higher earnings.

Where one lives can be viewed as an individual trait that rational actors change by investing in a move. Migrants seek to go to places where, given their skills, they can be more productive and earn more money. Before they can reap this benefit, however, they must undertake certain investments: the material costs of traveling, the costs of sustenance while moving and looking for work, the effort involved in learning a new language and culture, the difficulty experienced in adapting to a new labor market, and the psychological burden of cutting old ties and forging new ones. According to neoclassical theory, migrants estimate the costs and benefits of moving to various international locations and then go to wherever the expected net returns are greatest.

* * *

A variety of anomalous observations suggest, however, that motivations for migration go beyond such cost-benefit calculations. Under neoclassical theory, migration should not occur in the absence of a wage differential, yet such flows are frequently observed. Moreover, if there are no legal barriers to movement, migration should continue until the wage differential between two areas is eliminated, yet migration streams commonly end well before wage gaps disappear. Widely observed patterns of circular migration are also difficult to explain from a strict neoclassical viewpoint; each year thousands of undocumented migrants and even many legal immigrants decide to return to Mexico. * * *

These anomalies occur because the lifetime maximization of expected income is only one of several potential economic motivations for international migration, and not necessarily the most important. Neoclassical economics *begins* with the assumption that markets for goods and services exist, that they are complete and function well, that information and competition are perfect, and that rational individuals enter the market with exogenous tastes and preferences in order to maximize their utility (that is, they look out for number one). * * *

Yet reality is considerably more complex than the enabling assumptions of neoclassical economics. Markets for goods and services may not exist, they may be imperfect, and sometimes they may fail entirely, especially during the early phases of economic development. In addition, information is usually scarce and constrained by an individual's position on the social structure, and competition is far from perfect. Finally, even if individuals are rational and self-interested, they do not enter markets as atomized individuals but as members of families, households, and sometime larger communities, social groupings that allow for *collective* strategies, which at times may dovetail with those of individuals and at other times be at odds with them.

If we imagine a world where families and households face the prospect of poorly functioning, missing, or failed markets, we come to a very different line of theoretical reasoning known as the *new economics of labor migration*. Unlike the neoclassical model, it does not assume that migration decisions are made by isolated actors, but that they are taken within larger units of interrelated people, typically families or households but sometimes entire communities. Within these units, people not only act individually to maximize expected income but also work collectively to overcome failures in capital, credit, and insurance markets.

In most developed countries the risks to a household's material well-being are managed through private markets and government programs. Crop insurance and futures markets give farmers a means of protecting themselves against natural disasters and price fluctuations, and unemployment insurance and welfare programs protect workers against the vagaries of the business cycle and the dislocations of structural change. Private and government-sponsored pension systems allow citizens to minimize the risk of poverty in old age.

In relatively poor countries like Mexico, markets for futures and insurance are not well developed, and the Mexican government is in no position to fill the gap by offering substitutes. As a result, Mexicans are not only poorer than other North Americans; they are also exposed to substantially greater risk. * * *

Just as investors diversify risk by purchasing stocks across a range of firms, households diversify risks by sending out members to work in different labor markets. While some members (say, the wife and younger children) remain behind to work in the local economy, others (say, older sons and daughters) move to work elsewhere in Mexico, and still others (perhaps the household head and oldest son) migrate to work in the United States. As long as conditions in the various labor markets are negatively or weakly correlated, a household can manage risk through diversification. In the event that conditions at home deteriorate through rising unemployment, falling wages, failing crops, sagging prices, or high inflation, households can rely on migrant remittances as an alternative source of income.

In developing countries such as Mexico, markets for capital and credit are also weak or absent, preventing families from borrowing to smooth consumption or undertake productive activities. In the absence of an efficient banking system, international migration becomes a reasonable strategy that poor families can use to accumulate cash in lieu of formal borrowing for consumption or investment. Households simply send one or more workers abroad to take advantage of higher wages to build up savings over a short time horizon.

CONTEXTS OF DECISIONMAKING

* * *

* * * [A] variety of theorists have linked the origins of international migration not so much to the decisions of individuals or households as to the changing scope and structure of global markets, a line of reasoning that is generally known as *world systems theory*. In this scheme, the

expansion of markets into peripheral, nonmarket or pre-market societies creates mobile populations that are prone to migrate.

Driven by a desire for higher profits and greater wealth, owners and managers of large firms in developed nations enter poor countries on the periphery of the world economy in search of land, raw materials, labor, and markets. Migration is a natural outgrowth of the disruptions and dislocations that occur in the process of market expansion and penetration. As land, raw materials, and labor come under the control of markets, flows of migrants are generated. * * * The substitution of cash crops for staples undermines traditional social and economic relations, and the use of modern inputs, by producing high crop yields at low unit prices, drives out peasant farmers. All of these forces contribute to the creation of a mobile labor force: agricultural workers, displaced from the land, experience a weakened attachment to the community and become more prone to migrate internationally.

* * *

Economic globalization also creates cultural links between developed and developing nations. Sometimes the cultural links are long-standing, reflecting prior colonial relationships. Yet even in the absence of colonial history, the cultural consequences of economic penetration can be profound. Although Mexico was colonized by Spain, Mexicans increasingly study at U.S. universities, speak English, and follow U.S. consumer styles, reflecting America's global economic hegemony. These cultural links naturally dispose them to migrate to the United States rather than other places, including Spain.

* * *

THE DEMAND FOR IMMIGRANTS

The bifurcation of labor markets in global cities predicted by world systems theory dovetails with a larger line of theorizing known as *segmented labor market theory,* which grew out of institutional economics. Michael Piore has argued that international migration stems from a relatively permanent demand for unskilled labor that is built into the economic structure of developed nations. In his view, immigration is not caused by push factors in sending countries (such as low wages or high unemployment), but by pull factors in receiving societies (a chronic and unavoidable need for low-wage workers). The intrinsic demand for inexpensive labor stems from four fundamental problems faced by advanced industrial economies.

The first problem is *structural inflation.* Wages not only reflect conditions of supply and demand but confer status and prestige, social qualities inherent to specific jobs. In general, people believe that wages should reflect social status, and they have rather rigid notions about the correlation between occupational status and pay. As a result, wages offered by employers are not free to respond to changes in the supply of workers. A variety of informal social expectations and formal institutional mechanisms (such as union contracts, civil service rules, bureaucratic regulations, and human resource classifications) ensure that wages correspond to the hierarchies of prestige and status that people perceive.

If employers seek to attract workers for unskilled jobs at the bottom of an occupational hierarchy, they cannot simply raise wages for those jobs. Doing so would upset defined relationship between status and remuneration. If wages are increased at the bottom, employers will encounter strong pressure to raise wages at other levels of the job hierarchy. If the wages of busboys are raised in response to a labor shortage, for example, their wages may overlap with those of waitresses, thereby threatening the status of waitresses and prompting them to demand a corresponding wage increase, which threatens the position of cooks, who also pressure employers for a raise, and so on. As a result, the cost of raising wages to attract entry-level workers is typically more than the cost of those workers' wages alone. Thus, the prospect of structural inflation—the need to raise wages proportionately throughout the job hierarchy to maintain consistency with social expectation—provides employers with a strong incentive to seek easier and cheaper solutions, such as the importation of immigrants.

The demand for cheap, flexible labor is also augmented by the *social constraints on motivation* that are inherent to job hierarchies. Most people work not only to generate income but to accumulate social status. Acute motivational problems arise at the bottom of the job hierarchy because there is no status to be maintained and there are few avenues for upward mobility. * * * What employers need are workers who view bottom-level jobs simply as a means to the end of earning money and for whom employment is reduced solely to a matter of income, with no implications for status or prestige.

Immigrants satisfy this need on a variety of counts, at least at the beginning of their migratory careers. Migrants generally begin foreign labor as target earners: they are seeking to make money for a specific goal that will solve a problem or improve their status at home (such as building a new house, buying land, or acquiring consumer goods). Moreover, the disjuncture in living standards between developed and developing societies makes low wages abroad appear generous by the standards of the sending country. Finally, even though a migrant may realize that a foreign job carries low status, he does not view himself as a part of that society but as embedded within the status system of his home community, where hard-currency remittances buy considerable social status.

The demand for immigrant labor also stems from the *duality of labor and capital*. Capital is a fixed factor of production that can be idled by lower demand but not laid off; owners of capital bear the costs of its unemployment. Labor, in contrast, is a variable factor of production that can be released when demand falls, so that workers bear the costs of their own unemployment. Whenever possible, therefore, industrialists seek out the stable, permanent portion of demand and reserve it for the deployment of capital, leaving the variable portion of demand to be met by the addition and subtraction of labor, a dualism that creates distinctions among workers and leads to segmentation of the labor force.

Workers in the capital-intensive primary sector get stable, skilled jobs working with good tools and equipment. Employers are forced to invest in their human capital through training and education. Primary-sector jobs are complicated and require considerable knowledge and experience to perform, leading to the accumulation of firm-and job-specific knowledge. Primary-sector workers also tend to be unionized or highly professionalized, with contracts that require employers to bear a substantial share of the costs of layoffs (in the form of severance pay and unemployment benefits). Because of these costs and continuing obligations, workers in the primary sector become expensive to let go; they become more like capital.

The labor-intensive secondary sector, in contrast, is composed of poorly paid, unstable jobs from which workers may be laid off at any time with little or no cost to the employer. During down cycles an employer's first act is to shed such workers to cut the payroll. The resulting dualism thus yields a segmented labor market structure. Low wages, unstable conditions, and the lack of reasonable mobility prospects make it difficult to attract native workers into the secondary sector. They are instead drawn into the primary, capital-intensive sector, where wages are higher, jobs are more secure, and there is a possibility of occupational advancement. To fill the shortfall in demand within the secondary sector, employers turn to immigrants.

Taken together, motivation problems, structural inflation, and economic dualism create a demand for a particular kind of worker: one who is willing to labor under unpleasant conditions, at low wages, in jobs with great instability and little chance for advancement. In the past this demand was met by women, teenagers, and rural-to-urban migrants. * * *

* * *

In advanced industrial societies, however, these three sources of entry-level workers have drastically shrunk over time because of four fundamental demographic trends: the rise in female labor force participation, which has transformed women's work into a career pursued for social status as well an income; the rise in divorce rates, which has transformed women's employment into a source of primary support; the decline in birthrates and the extension of formal education, which have produced small cohorts of teenagers entering the labor force; and the urbanization of society, which has eliminated farms and rural communities as potential sources for new migrants to the city. The imbalance between the structural demand for entry-level workers and the limited domestic supply of such workers has generated an underlying, long-run demand for immigrants in developed countries.

WHY PEOPLE CONTINUE TO MIGRATE

Immigration may begin for a variety of reasons, but the forces that initiate international movement are quite different from those that perpetuate it. Although wage differentials, market failures, and structural change may motivate people to move in the first place, new conditions arise in the course of migration to make additional movement more likely, leading to the perpetuation of international migration across time and space. * * *

* * * Migrant networks are an important source of social capital for people contemplating a move abroad. They are sets of interpersonal ties that connect migrants, former migrants, and nonmigrants at place of origin and destination through reciprocal ties of kinship, friendship, and shared community origin. They increase the likelihood of international movement because they lower the costs and risks of movement and increase the expected net returns to migration.

* * *

The first migrants who leave for a new destination have no social ties to draw upon, and for them migration is costly, particularly if it involves entering another country without documents. After the first migrants have left, however, the potential costs of migration are substantially lowered for the friends and relatives left behind. * * *

Once international migration has begun, private institutions and voluntary organizations also arise to satisfy the demand created by the growing imbalance between the large number of people seek entry into capital-rich countries and the limited supply of visas they typically offer. This imbalance and the barriers that developed countries erect to keep people out create a lucrative niche for entrepreneurs dedicated to promoting international movement for profit, yielding a black market in migration services. As this underground market creates conditions conducive to exploitation and victimization, humanitarian organizations also arise to enforce the right and improve the treatment of both legal and undocumented migrants. * * *

* * * [The *cumulative causation of migration* occurs as] each act of migration alters the social context within which subsequent migration

decisions are made, thus increasing the likelihood of additional movement. Once the number of network connections in a community reaches a critical threshold, migration becomes self-perpetuating because each act of migration creates the social structure needed to sustain it.

In any bounded population, of course, processes of cumulative causation cannot continue ad infinitum. If migration continues long enough, networks eventually reach a point of saturation within any particular community. More and more community members reside in branch settlements overseas, and virtually all of those at home are connected to someone who lives abroad or has substantial foreign experience. When networks reach such a high level of elaboration, the costs of migration do not fall as sharply with each new migrant, and migration loses its dynamic momentum for growth. The prevalence of migration in the community approaches an upper limit, and migratory experience becomes so diffused that the stock of potential new migrants becomes very small and is increasingly composed of women, children, and the elderly.

If migration continues long enough, labor shortages and rising wages in the home community may further dampen the pressures for emigration, causing the rate of entry into the international migrant workforce to trail off. * * *

Because the theories discussed in this chapter posit causal mechanisms operating at multiple levels of aggregation, the various explanations are not logically contradictory. It is entirely possible for individuals to engage in cost-benefits calculations; for households to seek to minimize risk and overcome barriers to capital and credit; for both individuals and households to draw upon social capital to facilitate international movement; and for the socioeconomic context within which migration decisions are made to be determined by structural forces operating at the national and international levels, often influenced by migration itself. * * *

The next selection emphasizes the long-term historical processes at work in migration flows. It criticizes simple "push-pull" theories of migration, arguing that they ignore powerful political forces and they lack predictive power.

ALEJANDRO PORTES & JÓZSEF BÖRÖCZ, CONTEMPORARY
IMMIGRATION: THEORETICAL PERSPECTIVES ON ITS
DETERMINANTS AND MODES OF INCORPORATION

23 International Migration Review 606, 607–14 (1989).

ORIGINS

The most widely held approach to the origins of international migration—"push-pull" theories—see labor flows as an outcome of poverty and backwardness in the sending areas. Representatives of this perspective provide lists of "push factors"—economic, social and political hardships in the poorest parts of the world—and "pull factors"—comparative advantages in the more advanced nation-states—as causal variables determining the size and directionality of immigrant flows. These lists are invariably elaborated *post factum*, that is, after particular movements have already been initiated. The compilation of such lists is usually guided by two underlying assumptions: first, the expectation that the most disadvantaged sectors of the poorer societies are most likely to participate in labor migration; and second, the assumption that such flows arise spontaneously out of the sheer existence of inequalities on a global scale.

On the surface, these assumptions appear self-evident: workers migrate from Mexico to the United States and from Turkey to West Germany and not vice versa. However, the tendency of the push-pull model to be applied to those flows which are already taking place conceals its inability to explain why similar movements do not arise out of other equally "poor" nations or why sources of outmigration tend to concentrate in certain regions and not in others within the same sending countries.

Thus, the proclivity of these theories to the post hoc recitation of "obvious" causes makes them incapable of predicting the two principal differences in the origin of migration: 1) differences among collectivities—primarily nation-states—in the size and directionality of migrant flows; 2) differences among individuals within the same country or region in their propensities to migrate. The first question concerns macrostructural determinants of labor displacements while the second concerns their microstructural causes. The difference between these levels of analysis is also absent from most standard push-pull writings.

At the broader level of determination, the onset of labor flows does not arise out of invidious comparisons of economic advantage, but out of a history of prior contact between sending and receiving societies. History is replete with instances in which an absolute wage advantage in economically expanding areas has meant nothing to the population of more isolated regions; when their labor has been required, it has had to be coerced out of them. In general, the emergence of regular labor outflows of stable size and known destination requires the prior penetration by institutions of the stronger nation-state into those of the weaker sending ones. Political and economic conditions in the latter are then gradually molded to the point where migration to the hegemonic center emerges as a plausible option for the subordinate population. The process of external penetration and internal imbalancing of labor-exporting areas has taken very different forms, however, during the history of capitalism[, evolving from conquest and the slave trade, through migrant recruitment using economic inducements, to eventual self-initiated labor flows].

* * *

The various historical forms of penetration * * * form part of a progression guided by the initiatives of states at the center of the international economy and the changing interests of its dominant classes. The outcome of this progression has been to increase consistently the supply of pliable labor while decreasing its costs. The process has reached its culmination today when labor migrants assume the initiative and the full costs of the journey. This outcome is what economists now refer to as "inexhaustible supplies" of labor.

* * *

STABILITY

A second difficulty with standard push-pull theories is their inability to account for individual differences in patterns of migration. Given the same set of expelling forces and external inducements, why is it that some individuals leave while others stay? Why, in particular, given the lopsided "differentials of advantage" in favor of the receiving society, do only a minority of the source populations migrate? Descriptions of Mexican, Dominican or West Indian migration—including those at an exclusively macrostructural level—suggest that "everyone is leaving," which is far from being the case.

A related shortcoming is the inability of conventional theories to explain the resilience of migrant flows once the original economic inducements have disappeared or have been significantly lessened. According to the underlying economic rationale of the push-pull approach, migration should reflect, with some lag, ups and downs in the "differential of advantage" which gives rise to the process in the first place. In reality, migration flows, once established, tend to continue with relative autonomy from such fluctuations.

Contrary to the assertion that international labor migration is basically an outcome of economic decisions governed by the law of supply and demand, * * * the phenomenon is primarily social in nature. Networks constructed by the movement and contact of people across space are at the core of the microstructures which sustain migration over time. More than individualistic calculations of gain, it is the insertion of people into such networks which helps explain differential proclivities to move and the enduring character of migrant flows.

* * *

An important aspect of labor migration is the fact that the social channels which it creates open ways for entry and settlement of individuals who do not directly participate in the labor process. These dependent family members may enter the labor market subsequently. Opportunities may emerge, for example, for wives and for migrant children as they become of age. * * *

More than movement from one place to another in search of higher wages, labor migration should be conceptualized as a process of progressive network building. Networks connect individuals and groups distributed across different places, maximizing their economic opportunities through multiple displacements. Labor migration is thus a device through which individual workers and their households adapt to opportunities distributed unevenly in space. Hence, migration performs a dual function: for capital, it is a source of more abundant and less expensive labor; for the migrants, it is a means of survival and a vehicle for social integration and economic mobility.

NOTES AND QUESTIONS ON THEORIES OF MIGRATION

1.   Which theory of migration do you find most persuasive? Although the authors' emphases differ, can they be viewed as consistent with each other?

2.   What are the implications of their views for the kinds of immigration laws that Congress might consider enacting? For example, what would Massey and his co-authors think about a guest worker program? How would they design a program to control immigration from Mexico to the United States? How might legislators who agree with Massey or with Portes & Böröcz adopt different reforms of the immigrant admission categories?

———————

Economists have hotly disputed both why people migrate and the impact they have on the country of immigration. We conclude this section with selections from prominent voices in the contemporary debate concerning the impact of immigration on wages in the host country.

DAVID CARD, THE IMPACT OF THE MARIEL BOATLIFT ON THE MIAMI LABOR MARKET

43 Industrial and Labor Relations Review 245, 245–246, 256 (1990).

One of the chief concerns of immigration policy-makers is the extent to which immigrants depress the labor market opportunities of less-skilled natives. Despite the presumption that an influx of immigrants will substantially reduce native wages, existing empirical studies suggest that the effect is small. * * *

* * *

* * * From May to September 1980, some 125,000 Cuban immigrants arrived in Miami on a flotilla of privately chartered boats. Their arrival was the consequence of an unlikely sequence of events culminating in Castro's declaration on April 20, 1980, that Cubans wishing to emigrate to the United States were free to leave from the port of Mariel. The experiences of the Miami labor market in the aftermath of the Mariel Boatlift provide a natural experiment with which to evaluate the effect of unskilled immigration on the labor market opportunities of native workers.[a] Fifty percent of the Mariel immigrants settled permanently in Miami. The result was a 7% increase in the labor force of Miami and a 20% increase in the number of Cuban workers in Miami.

* * *

OVERVIEW OF THE MIAMI LABOR MARKET BEFORE THE BOATLIFT

For at least a decade prior to the Mariel Boatlift, Miami was the most immigrant intensive city in the country. Tabulations from the 1980 Census indicate that 35.5% of residents in the Miami Standard Metropolitan Statistical Area (SMSA) were foreign-born, compared to 22.3% in Los Angeles, the city with the next-highest immigrant fraction, and 6.1 % nationwide. At the time of the Census, 56% of immigrants in Miami were of Cuban origin. The remaining foreign-born residents, who accounted for 16% of the Miami population, included other Hispanic groups and a broad selection of Caribbean and European nationals. Miami also has a significant black population. The fraction of black residents was 15.0% in 1970 and had increased to 17.3% by the time of the 1980 Census. The large concentrations of both immigrants and blacks makes Miami ideal for studying the effect of increased immigration on the labor market opportunities of black natives.

* * *

The [data show that] Cubans and other Hispanics have very similar occupation distributions, with a higher representation in craft and operative occupations than either whites or blacks. Blacks are more

---

^a Relocated sentence.—eds.

highly concentrated in laborer and service-related occupations, and are significantly under-represented in managerial occupations.

* * *

THE MARIEL IMMIGRATION

* * *

* * * A recent Census Bureau report states that 126,000 refugees entered the United States as "Cuban Entrant" (the special immigration status awarded to the Mariel refugees) between April 1980 and June 1981. Based on the settlement of earlier Cubans, it is widely assumed that about one-half of these refugees settled permanently in Miami. The Census Bureau * * * shows an increase of 80,500 in the Dade County population between April 1 and July 1 of 1980; 59,800 of these new entrants were age 16–61. My own tabulations * * * indicate that the Cuban share of the 16–61 age group increased from 27% in 1979 to 33% in 1981. * * * Assuming that the Cuban share of the labor force would have remained constant between 1979 and 1981 in the absence of the Boatlift, these figures suggest that the Mariel immigration added approximately 45,000 to the Miami labor force—an increase of 7%.

* * * Contemporary reports indicate that the Mariels included a relatively high fraction of less-skilled workers and a high fraction of individuals with low English ability.

* * *

THE EFFECT OF THE MARIEL IMMIGRATION ON THE MIAMI LABOR MARKET

* * *

[A] widely cited indicator of the labor market pressure created by the Mariel influx is the Miami unemployment rate, which rose from 5.0% in April 1980 to 7.1% in July. Over the same period state and national unemployment rates followed a similar pattern, suggesting that the changes in Miami were not solely a response to the Mariel influx. Nevertheless, widespread joblessness of refugees throughout the summer of 1980 contributed to a perception that labor market opportunities for less-skilled natives were threatened by the Mariel immigrants.

[The author analyzes average wage rates and unemployment rates for whites, blacks, Cubans, and other Hispanics in the Miami labor market between 1979 and 1985 and in Atlanta, Los Angeles, Houston, and Tampa-St. Petersburg.] These four cities were selected both because they had relatively large populations of blacks and Hispanics and because they exhibited a pattern of economic growth similar to that in Miami over the late 1970s and early 1980s. * * * The wage data [show] that earnings are lower in Miami than in the comparison cities. The differentials in

1979 ranged from 8% for whites to 15% for blacks. More surprising is that real earnings levels of whites in both Miami and the comparison cities were fairly constant between 1979 and 1983. This pattern contrasts with the general decline in real wages in the U.S. economy over this period and underscores the relatively close correspondence between economic conditions in Miami and the comparison cities.

In contrast to the pattern for whites, the trends in earnings for nonwhites and Hispanics differ somewhat between Miami and the comparison cities. Black wages in Miami were roughly constant from 1979 to 1981, fell in 1982 and 1983, and rose to their previous level in 1984. Black earnings in the comparison cities, on the other hand, show a steady downward trend between 1979 and 1985. These data provide no evidence of a negative impact of the Mariel immigration on black wages in Miami. The data do suggest a relative downturn in black wages in Miami during 1982–83. It seems likely, however, that this downturn reflects an unusually severe cyclical effect associated with the 1982–83 recession.

Wage rates for non-Cuban Hispanics in Miami were fairly stable between 1979 and 1985, with only a slight dip in 1983. In contrast, Hispanic wage rates in the comparison cities fell about 6 percentage points over this period. Again, there is no evidence of a negative effect in Miami, either in the immediate post-Mariel period or over the longer run.

[There is indication of] a decline in Cuban wage rates relative to the wage rates of other groups in Miami. Relative to the wages of whites, for example, Cuban wages fell by 6–7 percentage points between 1979 and 1981. Assuming that the wages of earlier Cuban immigrants were constant, this decline is consistent with the addition of 45,000 Mariel workers to the pool of Cubans in the Miami labor force, and with the 34% wage differential between Mariels and other Cubans. * * *

The unemployment rates * * * lead to the same general conclusions * * * . There is no evidence that the Mariel influx adversely affected the unemployment rate of either whites or blacks. The unemployment rates a severe cyclical downturn in the black labor market in Miami in 1982–83. Black unemployment rates in Miami, which had been 2–4 points lower than those in comparison cities from 1979 to 1981, equalled or exceeded those in the comparison cities from 1982 to 1984. The 1985 data indicate a return to the pre-1982 pattern * * * .

Unlike the situation for whites and blacks, there was a sizable increase in Cuban unemployment rates in Miami following the Mariel immigration. Cuban unemployment rates were roughly 3 percentage points higher during 1980–81 than would have been expected on the basis of earlier (and later) patterns. Assuming that the unemployment rates of earlier Cuban immigrants were unaffected by the Mariel influx, this effect is consistent with unemployment rates of around 20% among the Mariels themselves. * * *

* * *

If the Mariel immigration reduced the wages of less-skilled natives, one would expect to observe a decline in the wage of workers in the lowest skill quartile, at least relative to workers in the upper quartile. The actual averages show no evidence of this effect. Apart from the temporary increase in relative wages of workers in the lowest quartile between 1979 and 1981, the distribution of non-Cubans' wages in the Miami labor market was remarkably stable between 1979 and 1985. Taken together * * * , these data provide little evidence of a negative effect of the Mariel influx on the earnings of natives.

* * *

CONCLUSIONS

* * * The Mariel immigrants increased the labor force of the Miami metropolitan area by 7%. Because most of these immigrants were relatively unskilled, the proportional increase in labor supply to less-skilled occupations and industries was much greater.

Yet, this study shows that the influx of Mariel immigrants had virtually no effect on the wage rates of less-skilled non-Cuban workers. Similarly, there is no evidence of an increase in unemployment among less-skilled blacks or other non-Cuban workers. Rather, the data analysis suggests a remarkably rapid absorption of the Mariel immigrants into the Miami labor force, with negligible effects on other groups. Even among the Cuban population there is no indication that wages or unemployment rates of earlier immigrants were substantially affected by the arrival of the Mariels.

* * *

GEORGE J. BORJAS, THE LABOR DEMAND CURVE *IS* DOWNWARD SLOPING: REEXAMINING THE IMPACT OF IMMIGRATION ON THE LABOR MARKET

118 Quarterly Journal of Economics 1335, 1335–43, 1349–51, 1370–71 (2003).[*]

Do immigrants harm or improve the employment opportunities of native workers? [T]he textbook model of a competitive labor market predicts that an immigrant influx should lower the wage of competing factors. Despite the intuitive appeal of this theoretical implication and despite the large number of careful studies in the literature, the existing evidence provides a mixed and confusing set of results. The measured impact of immigration on the wage of native workers fluctuates widely from study to study (and sometimes even within the same study), but seems to cluster around zero. * * *

This paper presents a new approach for thinking about and estimating the labor market impact of immigration. Most existing studies exploit the geographic clustering of immigrants and use differences across local labor markets to identify the impact of immigration. This framework has been troublesome because it ignores the strong currents that tend to equalize economic conditions across cities and regions. In this paper, I argue that by paying closer attention to the characteristics that define a skill group—and, in particular, by using the insight that both schooling and work experience play a role in defining a skill group—one can make substantial progress in determining whether immigration influences the employment opportunities of native workers.

* * *

The laws of supply and demand have unambiguous implications for how immigration should affect labor market conditions in the short run. The shift in supply lowers the real wage of competing native workers. Further, as long as the native supply curve is upward sloping, immigration should also reduce the amount of labor supplied by the native workforce.

* * *

In the United States [the typical study examines the labor market in a metropolitan area and calculates] a "spatial correlation" measuring the relation between the native wage in a locality and the relative number of immigrants in that locality. * * * [In his influential study of the Mariel flow,] Card compared labor market conditions in Miami and in other cities before and after the *Marielitos* increased Miami's workforce by 7 percent. Card's * * * estimate of the spatial correlation indicated that this sudden and unexpected immigrant influx did not have a discernable effect on employment and wages in Miami's labor market.

Recent studies have raised two questions about the validity of interpreting weak spatial correlations as evidence that immigration has no labor market impact. First, immigrants may not be randomly distributed across labor markets. If immigrants endogenously cluster in cities with thriving economies, there would be a spurious positive correlation between immigration and wages. Second, natives may respond to the wage impact of immigration on a local labor market by moving their labor or capital to other cities. These factor flows would re-equilibrate the market. As a result, a comparison of the economic opportunities facing native workers in different cities would show little or no difference because, in the end, immigration affected *every* city, not just the ones that actually received immigrants.

[Borjas recommends changing the focus from local labor markets to the national level. He also argues that for purposes of analysis workers should be aggregated into skill groups that take into account both their education levels and their work experience. In his terminology a five percent "supply shock" refers to an immigrant flow that increases the number of workers in a skill set by five percent.]

To see how this insight can provide a fruitful approach to the empirical analysis of the labor market impact of immigration, consider the following example. Recent immigration has increased the relative supply of high school dropouts substantially. The labor market implications of this supply shock clearly depend on how the distribution of work experience in the immigrant population contrasts with that of natives. After all, one particular set of native high school dropouts would likely be affected if all of the new low-skill immigrants were very young, and a very different set would be affected if the immigrants were near retirement age.

* * *

* * * There is a great deal of dispersion in [the supply shocks experienced by the different skill groups between 1960 and 2000] even within schooling categories. It is well known, for instance, that immigration greatly increased the supply of high school dropouts in recent decades. What is less well known, however, is that this supply shift did not affect equally all experience groups within the population of high school dropouts. Moreover, the imbalance in the supply shock changes over time. * * * [I]mmigrants made up half of all high school dropouts with 10 to 20 years of experience in 2000, but only 20 percent of those with less than 5 years. In 1960, however, the immigration of high school dropouts increased the supply of the most experienced workers [30 to 40 years of experience—eds.] the most. * * *

* * *

[A strong link] exists between * * * weekly wages and the immigrant share within schooling-experience cells. * * * [This] clearly illustrates a negative relation between wage growth and immigrant penetration into particular skill groups * * * . Put simply, the raw data show that weekly wages grew fastest for workers in those education-experience groups that were least affected by immigration.

* * *

* * * By 2000, immigration had increased the number of men in the labor force by 16.8 percent. * * * [My calculations indicate that] a 10 percent supply shock (i.e., an immigrant flow that increases the number of workers in the skill group by 10 percent) reduces weekly earnings by about 4 percent.

[I]mmigration has an even stronger effect on annual earnings, suggesting that immigration reduces the labor supply of native male workers. A 10 percent supply shock reduces annual earnings by 6.4 percent and the fraction of time worked by 3.7 percentage points. * * *

* * *

I also estimated the regression model within schooling groups to determine if the results are being driven by particular groups, such as the large influx of foreign-born high school dropouts. With only one exception, * * * the impact of immigration on the weekly earnings of particular schooling groups is negative and significant. The exception is the group of college graduates * * *. * * * It is probably not coincidental that the adjustment coefficient is positive for college graduates, the group that experienced perhaps the most striking change in the wage structure in recent decades.

* * *

* * * In contrast to the existing literature, the evidence reported in this paper consistently indicates that immigration reduces the wage and labor supply of competing native workers, as suggested by the simplest textbook model of a competitive labor market. Moreover, the evidence indicates that spatial correlations conceal around two-thirds of the national impact of immigration on wages.

* * * Between 1980 and 2000, immigration increased the labor supply of working men by 11.0 percent. Even after accounting for the beneficial cross-effects of low-skill (high-skill) immigration on the earnings of high-skill (low-skill) workers, my analysis implies that this immigrant influx reduced the wage of the average native worker by 3.2 percent. The wage impact differed dramatically across education groups, with the wage falling by 8.9 percent for high school dropouts, 4.9 percent for college graduates, 2.6 percent for high school graduates, and barely changing for workers with some college.

* * *

The adverse wage effects documented in this paper tell only part of the story of how the U.S. economy responded to the resurgence of large-scale immigration. The interpretation and policy implications of these findings require a more complete documentation and assessment of the many other consequences, including the potential benefits that immigrants impart on a host country.

GIANMARCO I. P. OTTAVIANO & GIOVANNI PERI, RETHINKING THE EFFECTS OF IMMIGRATION ON WAGES

National Bureau of Economic Research, Working Paper 12497 (2006)
http://www.nber.org/papers/w12497.

During the last three and a half decades the United States has experienced a remarkable surge in immigration. The share of foreign-born workers in the labor force has steadily grown from 5.3 % in 1970 to 14.7 % in 2005 * * * ; in the period between 1990 and 2005, almost one million immigrants entered the country every year. In parallel to this surge, the debate about the economic effects of immigration on U.S. natives, and particularly on their wages, has gained momentum * * * . * * * [T]he group of uneducated immigrants (without a high school degree) has become increasingly large among recent immigrants, while at the same time the real wage of uneducated U.S.-born workers has performed very poorly * * * . * * *

* * *

Our paper builds on [influential articles by Borjas], and takes a fresh look at some critical issues which imply significant revisions of several results. The key idea is that the effects of immigration on wages can only be measured within a *general equilibrium* framework. More specifically, a study on the effects of immigration on wages of different types of workers by education, experience and nativity should build on a production function that describes how these different types of workers interact with each other and with physical capital to produce output. Then, one can derive the demand for each type of labor, which depends on productivity and employment of the other labor types as well as on physical capital. Finally, market clearing conditions can be used to obtain wage equations from the labor demands and supplies, and use them to estimate the elasticities of substitution (relative wage elasticities) between workers empirically. Going back to the production function, these estimates can then be used to assess the effect of immigration (a change in the supply of different types of workers) on wages (the marginal productivity of different types of workers). In contrast, several existing empirical studies directly estimate a reduced-form wage equation for native workers with certain characteristics (such as educational or occupational groups) obtaining the elasticity of wages to new immigrants in the same group. Such an approach only provides the "partial" effect of immigration on wages (as it omits all cross-interactions with other types of workers and with capital) and as such is uninformative on the overall effect of immigrants on wages.

The *general equilibrium* approach is accompanied by two novel features of our analysis. First we remove the usual assumption that foreign- and U.S.-born workers are perfect substitutes within the same education- experience group. Be it because immigrants tend to choose a different set of occupations * * * , because they are a selected, motivated and generally talented group, or because they have some culture-specific skills it seems reasonable to allow them to be imperfect substitutes for natives even within an education-experience group and to let the data estimate the corresponding elasticities of substitution. * * * By modeling labor as a differentiated input in general equilibrium, we enlarge the picture to better capture the effects of immigration within and between different groups.

The second novel feature of our analysis is a more careful consideration of the response of physical capital to immigration. As physical capital complements labor it is important to account for its adjustment in the short and in the long run. * * * Immigration happens gradually over time * * * and investors respond continuously, although with sluggishness, to increased marginal productivity of capital caused by immigration. * * *

Once we account for the aforementioned effects, we deeply revise several commonly estimated effects of immigrants on the wages of U.S. natives. First, in the long-run the average wage of U.S.-born workers experienced a *significant increase* (+1.8%) as a consequence of immigration during the 1990–2004 period. Even in the short run (as of 2004) average wage of U.S. native workers had a moderate increase (+0.7%) because of immigration. This result stems from the imperfect substitutability between U.S.- and foreign-born workers so that immigration increases the wages of U.S.-born at the expenses of a decrease in wages of foreign-born workers (namely, previous immigrants). Second, the group of least educated U.S.-born workers *suffers a significantly smaller wage loss than previously calculated*. In the long run native workers only lost 1.1% of their real wage due to the 1990–2004 immigration. Even in the short run (as of 2004) the negative impact was a moderate 2.2% real wage loss. The methodology used in the previous literature would estimate much larger losses, around –8% in the short run and –4.2% in the long run. The fact that uneducated foreign-born do not fully and directly substitute for (i.e. compete with) uneducated natives, but partly complement their skills, is the reason for this attenuation. Third, *all other groups of U.S.-born workers* (with at least an [sic] high school degree) who accounted for 90% of the U.S.-born labor force in 2004, *gained from immigration*. Their real wage gains in the long run range between 0.7% and 3.4% while even in the short run they either gain (high school graduates) or have essentially no wage change (college graduates). * * * The group whose wage was *most negatively affected by immigration* is, in our analysis, *the group of previous immigrants*; however, it is they who probably have the largest non-economic benefits

from the immigration of spouses, relatives or friends making them willing
to sustain those losses.

* * *

NOTES AND QUESTIONS ON
THE IMPACT OF IMMIGRATION ON WAGES

1.   Borjas premises his analysis on the laws of supply and demand in
classical economic theory. How would he respond to the immigration
phenomena that Massey and his co-authors say the basic theory does not
explain? Does he view a greater supply of well-educated immigrants as
problematic for highly skilled U.S. workers?

2.   Card and Borjas have continued to draw conflicting conclusions
from the data on the impact of immigrant workers on the labor market. In
2012, Card revisited Borjas's 2003 paper excerpted above and asserted that
Borjas had made three incorrect assumptions that led to flawed results: (1)
Borjas failed to account for increased capital investment; (2) he divided
workers into four distinct education groups, rather than two, and (3) within
each group, Borjas viewed immigrant workers and U.S.-born workers as
perfect substitutes for each other. David Card, *Comment: The Elusive Search
for Economic Impact of Immigration,* 10 J. of Eur. Econ. Assn. 211 (2012). In
2015 Borjas responded, reiterating his 2003 conclusions. George J. Borjas,
The Wage Impact of Marielitos: A Reappraisal, National Bureau of Economic
Research Working Paper 21588 (Sept. 2015). Other economists participating
in this debate include Giovanni Peri & Vasil Yasenov, *The Labor Market
Effects of a Refugee Wave: Applying the Synthetic Control Method to the
Mariel Boatlift*, National Bureau of Economic Research Working Paper 21801
(Dec. 2015).

3.   Scholars who address the impact of immigrant women in the work
force and their effect on native-born women's professional careers include
Patricia Cortés & José Tessada, *Low-Skilled Immigration and the Labor
Supply of Highly Skilled Women,* 3 Am. Econ. J: Applied Econ. 88 (2011);
Howard F. Chang, *Immigration Restriction as Redistributive Taxation:
Working Women and the Costs of Protectionism in the Labor Market*, 5 J. L.
Econ. & Pol'y 1 (2009). Additional perspectives can be found in Alan Hyde,
The Law and Economics of Family Unification, 28 Geo. Immigr. L.J. 355
(2014), and Howard F. Chang, *The Economics of International Labor
Migration and the Case for Global Distributive Justice in Liberal Political
Theory*, 41 Cornell Int'l L. J. 1 (2008) (arguing that expanding immigration
will result in increased societal wealth). Many of the seminal articles of the
past two decades are collected in Law and Economics of Immigration
(Howard F. Chang ed., 2015).

C. MORAL CONSTRAINTS ON THE EXERCISE OF THE IMMIGRATION POWER

The differing perspectives on why people move and what impact they have on host countries do not lead to neat conclusions about what societies should do in response to migration. In the United States, as you know from having read *Chae Chan Ping* and *Fong Yue Ting,* Congress has broad constitutional authority to regulate immigration. How Congress should use this power poses difficult questions, whose disparate answers remain sharply contested. In beginning to formulate answers to those questions we believe that it is important first to explore possible moral bases for, or constraints upon, the exercise of the immigration power. If our presence in the United States is essentially an accident of birth, what gives us the right to keep others from entering? What is the nature of our moral claim to the territory of the United States? What is our responsibility to needy people living in other parts of the world? To needy people in the United States? The following materials are intended to help you focus on these questions.

BRUCE ACKERMAN,
SOCIAL JUSTICE IN THE LIBERAL STATE
93–95 (1980).[*]

* * * Quite unthinkingly, we have come to accept the idea that we have the right to exclude nonresidents from our midst. * * * [But] it is only a very strong empirical claim that can permit the American to justify exclusion of the foreign-born from "his" liberal state.

To simplify the argument, divide the world into two nation-states, the poor East and the rich West. Assume further that Western domestic institutions are organized in a liberalish way while the East is an authoritarian dictatorship in which a small elite explicitly declares its superiority over the masses they exploit. Assume, finally, that as part of its second-best response to this dark reality, the West has adopted a forthcoming immigration policy, admitting a large number, Z, of Easterners on a first-come, first-served basis. Indeed, Z is so large that it strains the capacity of Western institutions to sustain a liberal political conversation. Any more than Z and the West's standing as a liberal society will be endangered; the presence of so many alien newcomers will generate such anxiety in the native population that it will prove impossible to stop a fascist group from seizing political power to assure native control over the immigrant underclass. Nonetheless, the Easterners keep coming at an awesome rate; the scene takes place at the armed Western border:

Easterner: I demand recognition as a citizen of this liberal state.

Western Statesman: We refuse.

Easterner: What gives you the right to refuse me? Do you think I would fail to qualify as a citizen of an ideal liberal state?

Westerner: Not at all.

Easterner: Do you imagine you're better than me simply because you've been born west of this frontier?

Westerner: No. If that were all, I would not hesitate before admitting you.

Easterner: Well, then, what's the trouble?

Westerner: The fact is that we in the West are far from achieving a perfect technology of justice; if we admit more than Z newcomers, our existing institutions will be unable to function in anything but an explicitly authoritarian manner.

Easterner: But why am I being asked to bear the costs of imperfection?

Westerner: Sorry, we're doing everything we can. But Z is the limit on immigrants.

Easterner: But you're not doing everything. Why not expel some of your native-born Westerners and make room for me? Do you think they're better than I am?

Westerner: Z is the limit on our assimilative capacity only on the assumption that there exists a cadre of natives familiar with the operation of liberal institutions. If some of the natives were removed from the population, even Z would be too many.

Easterner: So what am I to do? I'll be dead before I get to the front of the line of immigrants.

Westerner: Go back among your own people and build your own liberal state. We'll try to help you out as best we can.

* * *

The *only* reason for restricting immigration is to protect the ongoing process of liberal conversation itself. Can our present immigration practices be rationalized on this ground?

MICHAEL WALZER, SPHERES OF JUSTICE: A DEFENSE OF PLURALISM AND EQUALITY

31–34, 37–40, 45, 47–49, 61–62 (1983).*

The idea of distributive justice presupposes a bounded world within which distributions [take] place: a group of people committed to dividing, exchanging, and sharing social goods, first of all among themselves. That world * * * is the political community, whose members distribute power to one another and avoid, if they possibly can, sharing it with anyone else. When we think about distributive justice, we think about independent cities or countries capable of arranging their own patterns of division and exchange, justly or unjustly. We assume an established group and a fixed population, and so we miss the first and most important distributive question: How is that group constituted?

I don't mean, How *was* it constituted? I am concerned here not with the historical origins of the different groups, but with the decisions they make in the present about their present and future populations. The primary good that we distribute to one another is membership in some human community. And what we do with regard to membership structures all our other distributive choices: it determines with whom we make those choices, from whom we require obedience and collect taxes, to whom we allocate goods and services.

* * *

* * * Since human beings are highly mobile, large numbers of men and women regularly attempt to change their residence and their membership, moving from unfavored to favored environments. Affluent and free countries are, like élite universities, besieged by applicants. They have to decide on their own size and character. More precisely, as citizens of such a country, we have to decide: Whom should we admit? Ought we to have open admissions? Can we choose among applicants? What are the appropriate criteria for distributing membership?

The plural pronouns that I have used in asking these questions suggest the conventional answer to them: we who are already members do the choosing, in accordance with our own understanding of what membership means in our community and of what sort of a community we want to have. Membership as a social good is constituted by our understanding; its value is fixed by our work and conversation; and then we are in charge (who else could be in charge?) of its distribution. But we don't distribute it among ourselves; it is already ours. We give it out to strangers. Hence the choice is also governed by our relationships with strangers—not only by our understanding of those relationships but also

---

by the actual contacts, connections, alliances we have established and the effects we have had beyond our borders. * * *

* * * In a number of ancient languages, Latin among them, strangers and enemies were named by a single word. We have come only slowly, through a long process of trial and error, to distinguish the two and to acknowledge that, in certain circumstances, strangers (but not enemies) might be entitled to our hospitality, assistance, and good will. This acknowledgment can be formalized as the principle of mutual aid, which suggests the duties that we owe, as John Rawls has written, "not only to definite individuals, say to those cooperating together in some social arrangement, but to persons generally." Mutual aid extends across political (and also cultural, religious, and linguistic) frontiers. The philosophical grounds of the principle are hard to specify (its history provides its practical ground). * * *

It is the absence of any cooperative arrangements that sets the context for mutual aid: two strangers meet at sea or in the desert or, as in the Good Samaritan story, by the side of the road. What precisely they owe one another is by no means clear, but we commonly say of such cases that positive assistance is required if (1) it is needed or urgently needed by one of the parties; and (2) if the risks and costs of giving it are relatively low for the other party. Given these conditions, I ought to stop and help the injured stranger, wherever I meet him, whatever his membership or my own. This is our morality; conceivably his, too. It is, moreover, an obligation that can be read out in roughly the same form at the collective level. Groups of people ought to help necessitous strangers whom they somehow discover in their midst or on their path. But the limit on risks and costs in these cases is sharply drawn. I need not take the injured stranger into my home, except briefly, and I certainly need not care for him or even associate with him for the rest of my life. My life cannot be shaped and determined by such chance encounters. Governor John Winthrop, arguing against free immigration to the new Puritan commonwealth of Massachusetts, insisted that this right of refusal applies also to collective mutual aid: "As for hospitality, that rule does not bind further than for some present occasion, not for continual residence." Whether Winthrop's view can be defended is a question that I shall come to only gradually. Here I only want to point to mutual aid as a (possible) external principle for the distribution of membership, a principle that doesn't depend upon the prevailing view of membership within a particular society. The force of the principle is uncertain, in part because of its own vagueness, in part because it sometimes comes up against the internal force of social meanings. And these meanings can be specified, and are specified, through the decision-making processes of the political community.

* * * [S]o long as members and strangers are, as they are at present, two distinct groups, admissions decisions have to be made, men and women taken in or refused. Given the indeterminate requirements of mutual aid, these decisions are not constrained by any widely accepted standard. That's why the admissions policies of countries are rarely criticized, except in terms suggesting that the only relevant criteria are those of charity, not justice. It is certainly possible that a deeper criticism would lead one to deny the member/stranger distinction. But I shall try, nevertheless, to defend that distinction and then to describe the internal and the external principles that govern the distribution of membership.

* * *

* * * The same writers who defended free trade in the nineteenth century also defended unrestricted immigration. They argued for perfect freedom of contract, without any political restraint. International society, they thought, should take shape as a world of neighborhoods, with individuals moving freely about, seeking private advancement. In their view, as Henry Sidgwick reported it in the 1890s, the only business of state officials is "to maintain order over [a] particular territory . . . but not in any way to determine who is to inhabit this territory, or to restrict the enjoyment of its natural advantages to any particular portion of the human race." Natural advantages (like markets) are open to all comers, within the limits of private property rights; and if they are used up or devalued by overcrowding, people presumably will move on, into the jurisdiction of new sets of officials.

Sidgwick thought that this is possibly the "ideal of the future," but he offered three arguments against a world of neighborhoods in the present. First of all, such a world would not allow for patriotic sentiment, and so the "casual aggregates" that would probably result from the free movement of individuals would "lack internal cohesion." Neighbors would be strangers to one another. Second, free movement might interfere with efforts "to raise the standard of living among the poorer classes" of a particular country, since such efforts could not be undertaken with equal energy and success everywhere in the world. And, third, the promotion of moral and intellectual culture and the efficient working of political institutions might be "defeated" by the continual creation of heterogeneous populations. Sidgwick presented these three arguments as a series of utilitarian considerations that weigh against the benefits of labor mobility and contractual freedom. But they seem to me to have a rather different character. The last two arguments draw their force from the first, but only if the first is conceived in non-utilitarian terms. It is only if patriotic sentiment has some moral basis, only if communal cohesion makes for obligations and shared meanings, only if there are members as well as strangers, that state officials would have any reason to worry especially about the welfare of their own people (and of *all* their own people) and the success of their own culture and politics. For it is at least dubious that the average standard of living of the poorer classes throughout the world would decline under conditions of perfect labor mobility. Nor is there firm evidence that culture cannot thrive in cosmopolitan environments, nor that it is impossible to govern casual aggregations of people. As for the last of these, political theorists long ago discovered that certain sorts of regimes—namely, authoritarian regimes—thrive in the absence of communal cohesion. That perfect mobility makes for authoritarianism might suggest a utilitarian argument against mobility; but such an argument would work only if individual men and women, free to come and go, expressed a desire for some other form of government. And that they might not do.

Perfect labor mobility, however, is probably a mirage, for it is almost certain to be resisted at the local level. Human beings, as I have said, move about a great deal, but not because they love to move. They are, most of them, inclined to stay where they are unless their life is very difficult there. They experience a tension between love of place and the discomforts of a particular place. While some of them leave their homes and become foreigners in new lands, others stay where they are and resent the foreigners in their own land. Hence, if states ever become large neighborhoods, it is likely that neighborhoods will become little states. Their members will organize to defend the local politics and culture against strangers. Historically, neighborhoods have turned into closed or parochial communities (leaving aside cases of legal coercion) whenever the state was open: in the cosmopolitan cities of multinational empires, for example, where state officials don't foster any particular identity but permit different groups to build their own institutional structures (as in ancient Alexandria), or in the receiving centers of mass immigration movements (early twentieth century New York) where the country is an open but also an alien world—or, alternatively, a world full of aliens. The case is similar where the state doesn't exist at all or in areas where it doesn't function. Where welfare monies are raised and spent locally, for example, as in a seventeenth-century English parish, the local people will seek to exclude newcomers who are likely welfare recipients. It is only the nationalization of welfare (or the nationalization of culture and politics) that opens the neighborhood communities to whoever chooses to come in.

Neighborhoods can be open only if countries are at least potentially closed. Only if the state makes a selection among would-be members and guarantees the loyalty, security, and welfare of the individuals it selects, can local communities take shape as "indifferent" associations, determined solely by personal preference and market capacity. Since individual choice is most dependent upon local mobility, this would seem to be the preferred arrangement in a society like our own. The politics and the culture of a modern democracy probably require the kind of largeness, and also the kind of boundedness, that states provide. I don't mean to deny the value of sectional cultures and ethnic communities; I mean only to suggest the rigidities that would be forced upon both in the absence of inclusive and protective states. To tear down the walls of the state is not, as Sidgwick worriedly suggested, to create a world without walls, but rather to create a thousand petty fortresses.

The fortresses, too, could be torn down: all that is necessary is a global state sufficiently powerful to overwhelm the local communities. Then the result would be the world of the political economists, as Sidgwick described it—a world of radically deracinated men and women. Neighborhoods might maintain some cohesive culture for a generation or two on a voluntary basis, but people would move in, people would move out; soon the cohesion would be gone. The distinctiveness of cultures and groups depends upon closure and, without it, cannot be conceived as a stable feature of human life. If this distinctiveness is a value, as most people (though some of them are global pluralists, and others only local loyalists) seem to believe, then closure must be permitted somewhere. At some level of political organization, something like the sovereign state must take shape and claim the authority to make its own admissions policy, to control and sometimes restrain the flow of immigrants.

* * *

* * * To say that states have a right to act in certain areas is not to say that anything they do in those areas is right. One can argue about particular admissions standards by appealing, for example, to the condition and character of the host country and to the shared understandings of those who are already members. * * * Decisions of this sort are subject to constraint, but what the constraints are I am not yet ready to say. It is important first to insist that the distribution of membership in American society, and in any ongoing society, is a matter of political decision. The labor market may be given free rein, as it was for many decades in the United States, but that does not happen by an act of nature or of God; it depends upon choices that are ultimately political. What kind of community do the citizens want to create? With what other men and women do they want to share and exchange social goods?

* * *

Can a political community exclude destitute and hungry, persecuted and stateless—in a word, necessitous—men and women simply because they are foreigners? Are citizens bound to take in strangers? Let us assume that the citizens have no formal obligations; they are bound by nothing more stringent than the principle of mutual aid. The principle must be applied, however, not to individuals directly but to the citizens as a group, for immigration is a matter of political decision. Individuals participate in the decision making, if the state is democratic; but they decide not for themselves but for the community generally. And this fact has moral implications. It replaces immediacy with distance and the personal expense of time and energy with impersonal bureaucratic costs. Despite John Winthrop's claim, mutual aid is more coercive for political communities than it is for individuals because a wide range of benevolent actions is open to the community which will only marginally affect its present members * * * . * * * These actions probably include the admission of strangers, for admission to a country does not entail the kinds of intimacy that could hardly be avoided in the case of clubs and families. Might not admission, then, be morally imperative, at least for these strangers, who have no other place to go?

* * *

* * * [Wealth, resources and territory] can be superfluous, far beyond what the inhabitants of a particular state require for a decent life (even as they themselves define the meaning of a decent life). Are those inhabitants morally bound to admit immigrants from poorer countries for as long as superfluous resources exist? Or are they bound even longer than that, beyond the limits of mutual aid, until a policy of open admissions ceases to attract and benefit the poorest people in the world? Sidgwick seems to have opted for the first of these possibilities; he proposed a primitive and parochial version of Rawls's difference principle: immigration can be restricted as soon as failure to do so would "interfere materially . . . with the efforts of the government to maintain an adequately high standard of life among the members of the community generally—especially the poorer classes." But the community might well decide to cut off immigration even before that, if it were willing to export (some of) its superfluous wealth. * * * [T]hey could share their wealth with necessitous strangers outside their country or with necessitous strangers inside their country. But just how much of their wealth do they have to share? Once again, there must be some limit, short (and probably considerably short) of simple equality, else communal wealth would be subject to indefinite drainage. The very phrase "communal wealth" would lose its meaning if all resources and all products were globally common. * * *

If we stop short of simple equality, there will continue to be many communities, with different histories, ways of life, climates, political structures, and economies. Some places in the world will still be more desirable than others, either to individual men and women with particular tastes and aspirations, or more generally. Some places will still be uncomfortable for at least some of their inhabitants. Hence immigration will remain an issue even after the claims of distributive justice have been met on a global scale—assuming, still, that global society is and ought to be pluralist in form and that the claims are fixed by some version of collective mutual aid. The different communities will still have to make admissions decisions and will still have a right to make them. If we cannot guarantee the full extent of the territorial or material base on which a group of people build a common life, we can still say that the common life, at least, is their own and that their comrades and associates are theirs to recognize or choose.

There is, however, one group of needy outsiders whose claims cannot be met by yielding territory or exporting wealth; they can be met only by taking people in. This is the group of refugees whose need is for membership itself, a non-exportable good. The liberty that makes certain countries possible homes for men and women whose politics or religion isn't tolerated where they live is also non-exportable: at least we have found no way of exporting it. These goods can be shared only within the protected space of a particular state. At the same time, admitting refugees doesn't necessarily decrease the amount of liberty the members enjoy within that space. The victims of political or religious persecution, then, make the most forceful claim for admission. If you don't take me in, they say, I shall be killed, persecuted, brutally oppressed by the rulers of my own country. What can we reply?

* * *

The distribution of membership is not pervasively subject to the constraints of justice. Across a considerable range of the decisions that are made, states are simply free to take in strangers (or not)—much as they are free, leaving aside the claims of the needy, to share their wealth with foreign friends, to honor the achievements of foreign artists, scholars, and scientists, to choose their trading partners, and to enter into collective security arrangements with foreign states. But the right to choose an admissions policy is more basic than any of these, for it is not merely a matter of acting in the world, exercising sovereignty, and pursuing national interests. At stake here is the shape of the community that acts in the world, exercises sovereignty, and so on. Admission and exclusion are at the core of communal independence. They suggest the deepest meaning of self-determination. Without them, there could not be *communities of character*, historically stable, ongoing associations of men and women with some special commitment to one another and some special sense of their common life.

But self-determination in the sphere of membership is not absolute. It is a right exercised, most often, by national clubs or families, but it is held in principle by territorial states. Hence it is subject both to internal decisions by the members themselves (*all* the members, including those who hold membership simply by right of place) and to the external principle of mutual aid. Immigration, then, is both a matter of political choice and moral constraint. * * *

JOSEPH H. CARENS, THE ETHICS OF IMMIGRATION
225–30, 260–62, 270–74, 277, 287 (2013).*

THE BASIC CHALLENGE OF OPEN BORDERS

In many ways, citizenship in Western democracies is the modern equivalent of feudal class privilege—an inherited status that greatly enhances one's life chances. To be born a citizen of a rich state in Europe or North America is like being born into the nobility (even though many of us belong to the lesser nobility). To be born a citizen of a poor country in Asia or Africa is like being born into the peasantry in the Middle Ages (even if there are a few rich peasants and some peasants manage to gain entry to the nobility). Like feudal birthright privileges, contemporary social arrangements not only grant great advantages on the basis of birth but also entrench these advantages by legally restricting mobility, making it extremely difficult for those born into a socially disadvantaged position to overcome that disadvantage, no matter how talented they are or how hard they work. Like feudal practices, these contemporary social arrangements are hard to justify when one thinks about them closely.

Reformers in the late Middle Ages objected to the way feudalism restricted freedom, including the freedom of individuals to move from one place to another in search of a better life— a constraint that was crucial to the maintenance of the feudal system. Modern practices of state control over borders tie people to the land of their birth almost as effectively. Limiting entry to rich democratic states is a crucial mechanism for protecting a birthright privilege. If the feudal practices protecting birthright privileges were wrong, what justifies the modern ones?

The analogy I have just drawn with feudalism is designed to give readers pause about the conventional view that restrictions on immigration by democratic states are normally justified. Now let me outline the positive case for open borders. I start from three basic interrelated assumptions. First, there is no natural social order. The institutions and practices that govern human beings are ones that human beings have created and can change, at least in principle. Second, in evaluating the moral status of alternative forms of political and social organization, we must start from the premise that all human beings are of equal moral worth. Third, restrictions on the freedom of human beings require a moral justification. These three assumptions are not just my views. They undergird the claim to moral legitimacy of every contemporary democratic regime.

* * *

Given these three assumptions there is at least a prima facie case that borders should be open, for three interrelated reasons. First, state control over immigration limits freedom of movement. The right to go where you want is an important human freedom in itself. It is precisely this freedom, and all that this freedom makes possible, that is taken away by imprisonment. Freedom of movement is also a prerequisite to many other freedoms. * * * [F]reedom of movement contributes to individual autonomy both directly and indirectly. * * *

Of course, freedom of movement cannot be unconstrained, but restrictions on freedom of movement require some sort of moral justification * * * . This justification must take into account the interests of those excluded as well as the interests of those already inside. It must make the case that the restrictions on immigration are fair to all human beings. There are restrictions that meet this standard of justification, as we shall see, but granting states a right to exercise discretionary control over immigration does not.

The second reason why borders should normally be open is that freedom of movement is essential for equality of opportunity. Within democratic states we all recognize, at least in principle, that access to social positions should be determined by an individual's actual talents and effort and not limited on the basis of birth-related characteristics such as class, race, or gender that are not relevant to the capacity to perform well in the position. * * * [Y]ou have to be able to move to where the opportunities are in order to take advantage of them. * * *

It is in the linkage between freedom of movement and equality of opportunity that the analogy with feudalism cuts most deeply. * * * In the modern world, we have created a social order in which there is a commitment to equality of opportunity for people within democratic states (at least to some extent), but no pretense of, or even aspiration to, equality of opportunity for people across states. Because of the state's discretionary control over immigration, the opportunities for people in one state are simply closed to those from another (for the most part). Since the range of opportunities varies so greatly among states, this means that in our world, as in feudalism, the social circumstances of one's birth largely determine one's opportunities. It also means that restrictions on freedom of movement are an essential element in maintaining this arrangement, that is, in limiting the opportunities of people with talents and motivations but the wrong social circumstances of birth. * * *

A third, closely related point is that a commitment to equal moral worth entails some commitment to economic, social, and political equality, partly as a means of realizing equal freedom and equal opportunity and partly as a desirable end in itself. Freedom of movement would contribute to a reduction of existing political, social, and economic inequalities. * * *

THE NATURE OF THE INQUIRY

* * *

From a political perspective, the idea of open borders is a nonstarter. * * *

Why make an argument that we should open our borders when there is no chance that we will? Because it is important to gain a critical perspective on the ways in which collective choices are constrained, even if we cannot do much to alter those constraints. Social institutions and practices may be deeply unjust and yet so firmly established that, for all practical purposes, they must be taken as background givens in deciding how to act in the world at a particular moment in time. The feudal system * * * was once deeply entrenched. So was the institution of slavery in the seventeenth and eighteenth centuries. For a long time, there was no real hope of transcending those arrangements. Yet criticism was still appropriate. Even if we must take deeply rooted social arrangements as givens for purposes of immediate action in a particular context, we should never forget about our assessment of their fundamental character. Otherwise we wind up legitimating what should only be endured.

* * *

The goal of this discussion then is to explore the implications of democratic principles for immigration when we treat the idea that states are entitled to control admissions as an open question rather than a presupposition. Any complex set of moral principles will contain tensions and trade-offs and will require a balancing of competing moral considerations, but even when these complexities are taken into account, the restrictions on immigration that we normally assume to be justifiable are in fact deeply at odds with our most fundamental moral principles.

COMMUNITIES OF CHARACTER

One famous effort to justify discretionary control over immigration is offered by Michael Walzer. * * * Without closure, he says, there can be no "communities of character, historically stable, ongoing associations of men and women with some special commitment to one another and some special sense of their common life." * * * If we insist that states be open, Walzer contends, the result will be * * * "a thousand petty fortresses" * * * .

* * *

[If Walzer] means that it is not possible to sustain a community of character unless there are people in the community who have lived there for most of their lives and who identify with the community and have a sense of its distinctiveness, he is probably right. But if he means that it is not possible to sustain a community of character unless it actively exercises control over the entrance into the community of people who are not born there, he is certainly wrong. Everything depends on how many are trying to get it. * * * Closure, in the sense of active, discretionary management of who gets in is not necessary to protect communities of character unless a lot of people are trying to get in (again relative to the size of the existing community).

* * *

Walzer himself asserts that people normally will not want to leave and will seek to do so (again, in large numbers) only if things are going very badly at home. Yet he also asserts that open borders between states will lead to "a world of deracinated men and women." He does not say why he expects this to happen, but the only plausible account is that he implicitly assumes that the differences between states will be so significant that many people will want to move despite the built-in attractions of staying at home. Despite his claims about the importance of communities of character, he is worried that too many people will be willing to leave their own community of character for an unfamiliar one that offers better life chances.

If that is an accurate description of the logic underlying Walzer's account, several more questions leap out. Why focus on the defensive measures (closure) needed to sustain a community under pressure from an unwanted influx of migrants rather than on the positive measures that would make closure unnecessary? Shouldn't our first concern be to identify the conditions that would enable all (or most) communities of character to flourish to such an extent that most members of those communities will have no desire to move elsewhere? Wouldn't that be the approach that would be best for most human beings? Wouldn't it be morally preferable for communities of character to flourish without closure (that is, without overtly excluding others)? Furthermore, if many people are seeking to leave their community of character to go somewhere else, don't we have to weigh their reasons for seeking entry elsewhere against the desires of those already present to maintain their community as it is? Walzer himself recognizes this elsewhere, setting almost no limits to entry in the case of refugees seeking asylum * * * . Why does he implicitly privilege the maintenance of communities of character above all else here?

Walzer's defense of discretionary control over immigration fails because he has no answer for these questions. Indeed, he does not even consider them. For arguments that attempt to do so, we have to look further.

* * *

SOVEREIGNTY

Another argument in defence of the state's discretionary control over immigration is that a norm of open borders would be intrinsically incompatible with state sovereignty. * * *

* * *

The assumption that controlling borders is essential to sovereignty is actually of relatively recent vintage. * * * States in the modern form date back to the seventeenth century, but they began to try to regulate entry and exit in a serious way only in the late nineteenth century. Passports were not introduced until World War I. As I have said before, having open borders is not the same as having no borders.

Sovereignty and control over admissions are linked in the popular imagination and in political discourse, but they are often disentangled in actual political arrangements in the real world. Sovereignty itself is less simple than some assume. Federal systems often have complex separate and shared sovereignty arrangements. * * * Like property, sovereignty is a bundle of rights that can be divided up in many different ways.

* * *

The fact that citizens of European Union states are largely free to move from one member state to another reveals starkly the ideological character of the claim that discretionary control over immigration is necessary for sovereignty. No one can seriously doubt that the European states are still real states today with most of the components of state sovereignty. * * * Nevertheless, with minor qualifications, European states that are members of the European Union do not claim that they may exercise discretionary control over the entry of immigrants from other EU states. They have agreed to limit their own sovereign power in this way. That is all that the open borders argument asks— only now in relation to the whole world and not just Europe. * * *

* * *

Having a right to migrate across state borders does not require people to move, any more than having a right to free mobility within a state requires people to move. Migration between states of the European Union is very low even though citizens of member states have a right to move (with minor qualifications).

* * *

In insisting that the principle of free movement is not intrinsically incompatible with state sovereignty, I do not mean to deny that there are circumstances under which immigration could threaten a state's capacity to govern itself. A massive inflow of migrants within a short time might indeed have this effect. But there is no necessary and inevitable link between sovereignty and restrictions on migration. * * *

PRIORITY FOR COMPATRIOTS

Some people try to justify both the inequalities between states and discretionary control over immigration as the morally legitimate result of our obligations to fellow members of our political community. These obligations, they say, rightly take precedence over the claims of strangers. * * *

I do not disagree with the claim that we are entitled to care more for our nearest and dearest than for distant strangers. * * *

I am not denying the moral relevance of particularistic attachments. Rather I am arguing that the moral claims of particularistic attachments are * * * constrained by considerations of justice. The question is not whether we may favor compatriots over outsiders but rather in what ways we may do so. * * * I am arguing that it is morally impermissible to favor current members of our community by excluding peaceful outsiders seeking to enter and settle. * * *

* * *

PUBLIC ORDER

* * *

Every human right and every liberty is subject in principle to some sort of public order restriction. * * *

Whether the public order constraint would require significant limitations on freedom of movement would depend primarily on how many people were trying to move, relative to the size of the receiving state (and perhaps the country of origin). In a world in which the inequalities between states were much more limited than they are today, the incentives to move would be much more limited. [C]itizens of the European Union have a right to freedom of movement among EU states, and this generates no public order problems. * * * So, in a more egalitarian world, it seems very unlikely that immigration would ever actually pose a threat to public order. For that reason we should see the public order constraint as only a minor qualification to the right of free movement, as it is for most other human rights.

NOTES AND QUESTIONS ON
MORAL PERSPECTIVES ON IMMIGRATION CONTROL

1.   To what extent are the positions of Ackerman, Walzer, and Carens reflected in the earlier discussion of the source of congressional authority to restrict immigration? (Recall particularly the structural justifications based on self-preservation and self-determination.)

2.   Carens asserts that there are no compelling moral arguments against open borders, but acknowledges there are circumstances in which societies can restrict immigration. In what settings would his open borders principle apply? From his perspective, what are the significant differences between feudal Europe and the European Union?

In an earlier essay on these subjects, Carens wrote: "What is *not* readily compatible with the idea of equal moral worth is the exclusion of those who want to join. If people want to sign the social contract, they should be permitted to do so." Joseph H. Carens, *Aliens and Citizens: The Case for Open Borders*, 49 Rev. of Politics 251, 269 (1987). What should a country be permitted to place into its social contract requirements? A demand to accept certain predominant cultural practices? To reject polygamy? A commitment to learn the national language and use it exclusively in public contexts? To accept the national religion? Maybe only a minimalist range of contract terms is acceptable in an already diverse democratic nation. Could a democracy's terms include a pledge to seek political change only through democratic and nonviolent means? A rejection of discrimination based on race, gender, religion, or national origin? In short, is it acceptable for a democratic society to be intolerant of intolerance when deciding on the criteria for admitting new members?

In The Ethics of Immigration, Carens also acknowledges that "[p]olitical communities require relatively stable, intergenerational populations in order to function effectively over time." *Id.* at 287. Does this acknowledgment justify numerical quotas as long as they are not stingy? Compare Ackerman's limited concession to the imperfect "technology of justice." Further, because stability, once lost, is hard for polities to restore, should both Carens and Ackerman afford more leeway for states to curtail migration so as to be sure to avert polarized backlash or authoritarian reaction?

3.   For an argument that eliminating U.S. border controls would "end the brutality inherent in enforcement of the current immigration controls," yield "economic benefits from free labor migration in a globalizing world economy," "recognize the economic and social reality of immigration," and lead to foreign policy benefits as well, see Kevin R. Johnson, Opening the Floodgates: Why America Needs to Eliminate its Borders and Rethink Immigration Law (2007).

4.   What is the relationship between admission to, and rights to membership in, a polity? That is, does our thinking about whom we admit to the United States depend in part on the rights and obligations (and opportunity for full membership) entailed by admission? Consider Michael Walzer's view:

> One might insist, as I shall ultimately do, that the same standards apply to naturalization as to immigration, that every immigrant and every resident is a citizen, too—or at least, a potential citizen. That is why territorial admission is so serious a matter. The members must be prepared to accept, as their own

equals in a world of shared obligations, the men and women they admit; the immigrants must be prepared to share the obligations.

Walzer, *supra*, at 52.

Walzer's view seems focused on assuring that citizenship is open, after a modest period of residence and integration, to those the polity has *chosen* to admit, even as ostensibly temporary workers. Linda Bosniak advocates a more expansive application of Walzer's principle of political inclusiveness, to cover virtually all migrants residing within a country's territory, which she calls "ethical territoriality."

> [T]he rights and recognition enjoyed by immigrants are usually understood to derive from either their formal status under law or their territorial presence. According to the status-based conception, a person's rights are determined by the specific legal category she occupies in the country's immigration and nationality regime. The status of citizenship is understood to represent membership's culmination—the moment the individual is entitled to enjoy full rights and entitlements and duties—whereas alienage status of various kinds entails lesser rights.

> * * *

> In contrast to the status-based approach, the territorial conception of rights for immigrants treats a person's geographical presence itself as a sufficient basis for core aspects of membership. * * * This presence is not necessarily tied to, or preceded by, political consent, although it may be. The territorial conception repudiates the notion of differential levels of inclusion, regarding the maintenance of partial membership statuses as illegitimate under liberal and democratic principles. * * *

> * * * It seems to me that ethical territoriality appropriately insists on treating membership as a matter of social fact rather than as a legal formality. And by opposing the imposition of less-than-complete-membership on classes of residents, ethical territoriality honors the egalitarian and anti-caste commitments to which liberal constitutionalism purports to aspire.

> * * *

> * * * [I]t is both anti-democratic and morally wrong in liberal terms to allow for treatment of a class of persons who are living among us as social and political outsiders. Territorialism embodies an ethic of inclusiveness and equality: it is the ground (both literally and figuratively) of national community belonging.

Linda Bosniak, *Being Here: Ethical Territoriality and the Rights of Immigrants,* 8 Theoretical Inquiries in Law 389, 390–392, 394 (2007). For a fuller exposition of these and related ideas, see Linda Bosniak, The Citizen and the Alien: Dilemmas of Contemporary Membership (2006).

Martin Ruhs offers a contrasting perspective. He argues that the wide gap between the rights of migrant workers in theory and practice may be due in part to an overly ambitious international treaty to protect migrant workers.*

[M]y research shows [that] labor immigration policies of high-income countries are characterized by a trade-off between openness and rights: More open admission policies tend to be associated with greater restrictions of migrant rights, especially in the case of lower-skilled workers.

We need to develop a new approach to the global protection of migrant workers that is based on a clear understanding about what has gone wrong with the 1990 [Convention on the Protection of All Migrant Workers and Members of their Families, which has gained very limited acceptance from migrant-receiving countries]. Specifically, we should consider the creation of a shorter list of universal "core rights" for migrant workers. This would have a higher chance of acceptance by a greater number of countries, thus increasing overall protection for migrant workers.

Exactly which rights should be on this shorter list is an important question to debate. In my view, the core rights should protect basic civil and labor rights, such as the right to keep your own identity documents, the right to equal access to the protections of the courts and the right to equal employment conditions.

But core rights do not need to include extensive social rights. Core rights should exclude, at least for a limited period of time, access to income-based benefits such as social housing and low-income support. In practice, these welfare benefits are already restricted under most labor immigration programs around the world.

* * *

In today's world, what migrants need most are core rights that are protected now. It might be counterintuitive, but given the reality of labor immigration policy, when it comes to protecting migrant rights, less is more.

Martin Ruhs, *Migrants Don't Need More Rights*, N.Y. Times, Dec. 19, 2013. He explores at length the trade-offs between liberalizing labor migration and expanding the social and economic rights of migrants in Martin Ruhs, The Price of Rights (2013).

CHAPTER FOUR

FEDERAL AGENCIES AND COURTS

∎ ∎ ∎

A person living abroad who decides she wants to come to the United States, temporarily or permanently, may well start the process by visiting the American official most easily accessible: the consular officer posted to her home country. If she looks carefully at the signs around the entrance to the consulate, she may learn that consuls are officers of the Department of State. And, in short order, if she pursues her application, she will come into contact with a rather bewildering variety of other U.S. agencies.

If she seeks to come for lawful permanent residence, she will probably need an approved visa petition from the Department of Homeland Security (DHS), through a process initiated by a close family member already in the United States, or by a prospective U.S. employer. If an employer is involved, the Department of Labor (DOL) may play an important role. If a family member's petition is denied, an appeal may take the case before the Board of Immigration Appeals (BIA), which is part of the Department of Justice (DOJ).

Once a visa petition is approved, the action shifts to the consulate for thorough screening before a visa issues. A doctor approved by the Public Health Service will probably perform a medical examination. At the port of entry, she will again encounter DHS (but a different component this time) in the person of the immigration inspector, who is entitled to rethink the screening determination of the consular officer. If a dispute arises over eligibility or admission, she might find herself in immigration court, also part of DOJ. If decisions go against her, litigation before the federal courts may be possible, but several types of agency decisions in the immigration arena are insulated from such review. Either on this visa petition or on alternative paths to admission, she might also encounter other governmental players.

To help understand the key players we will encounter in succeeding chapters as we explore the substantive provisions of the Immigration and Nationality Act, this chapter describes the agencies that implement the law and provides a brief introduction to the courts and the paths toward judicial review.

A. FEDERAL AGENCIES

U.S. practice has traditionally divided authority to administer the immigration laws among agencies based on whether the regulatory activity occurs outside the United States, on the one hand, or inside the country or at its borders and ports of entry, on the other. Authority outside the United States, in general, has been given to the Department of State, which has embassies or consulates in virtually all of the 195 other countries of the world. Authority exercised on U.S. soil has been placed in a succession of officers and departments over the past 120 years. Since the creation of the Department of Homeland Security in 2003, that authority now generally belongs to DHS. The Department of Justice, however, also plays an important role in the domestic sphere. DOJ is the institutional home to the immigration judges (IJs), who preside over removal hearings, and to the Board of Immigration Appeals, which reviews IJ decisions in removal cases as well as a select range of administrative decisions made by DHS officers.

Figure 4.1
Organization of DHS Immigration Functions

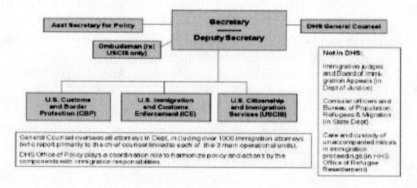

1. THE DEPARTMENT OF HOMELAND SECURITY AND ITS PREDECESSORS

a. History

Early federal regulation of immigration was under the authority of the Secretary of the Treasury, who initially had to act through state officials, usually designated by state governors. In 1891, Congress decided that such divided authority was unworkable. It created the federal post of Superintendent of Immigration within the Treasury Department, and federal officials shortly thereafter took over from the states full responsibility for administering the immigration laws. Federal immigration functions were seen as part of the regulation of labor from 1903 to 1940, and were accordingly housed in the departments holding that general authority. The Border Patrol was chartered in 1924 as part of the Bureau of Immigration in the Department of Labor. A 1940 Executive Order, motivated in part by security concerns as war engulfed Europe, transferred immigration and naturalization functions, which by then had been lodged for several years in a unified Immigration and Naturalization Service (INS) in DOL, to the Department of Justice. There they remained until 2003, when the Department of Homeland Security came into being. INS was thus the principal unit managing immigration functions for nearly 70 years, and it will still appear as the main governmental agency in some of the older cases and other readings presented in this book.

The Immigration and Nationality Act (INA), passed in 1952, also—and confusingly—still reflects this basic twentieth-century institutional structure. By its terms the statute still assigns most immigration authorities to the Attorney General (AG), the cabinet officer who heads DOJ, and specifies a few for "the Service" (INS). But the AG today retains only a fraction of these INA authorities, mostly having to do with matters decided by immigration courts, and INS has been abolished.

After the terrorist attacks of September 11, 2001, Congress passed new legislation, the Homeland Security Act (HSA), Pub. L. 107–296, 116 Stat. 2135 (2002), to create a new cabinet department and consolidate there a host of agencies whose functions relate to homeland security, including the Coast Guard, the Secret Service, the Federal Emergency Management Agency (FEMA), the Transportation Security Administration (responsible for screening airline passengers), and the Customs Service (responsible for regulating the international movement of goods in order to enforce import and export laws and collect taxes on imports).

Because the 9/11 attacks were carried out by noncitizens admitted on temporary visas, it is not surprising that most immigration control functions were also moved to the new Department of Homeland Security. The HSA did so through block transfers from DOJ of broadly described authorities, usually without directly amending the INA; hence the potential confusion in reading the statutory provisions on agency authority. Most of the authorities and powers described in the INA as exercised by the Attorney General—but not all—now actually belong to the Secretary of Homeland Security.

b.   The Components of DHS

Dismay at the failure to block the 9/11 terrorists' entry or to apprehend them later (after many had violated the terms of their initial admission) combined with other longstanding complaints about INS to win wide support for this reorganization. The HSA, however, did not simply transfer INS intact to the new department. Worried about potentially contradictory missions, Congress also directed a significant restructuring of immigration functions. In general, it divided INS's former authorities between different units, separating enforcement from services. The services function—also called adjudications or benefits—involves the approval or denial of applications filed by would-be migrants seeking admission to the United States or to modify their legal status here, or by their sponsors, as well as petitions for naturalization. Enforcement involves such activities as patrolling the border, investigating violations, arresting violators, and providing for their detention and removal.

As enacted, the HSA contemplated a two-way split between services and enforcement, but before this scheme took effect, the administration of President George W. Bush decided on a different approach to enforcement, which resulted in three new DHS units inheriting INS functions. In order to present "one face at the border," presidential directives essentially combined immigration enforcement with customs enforcement and then redivided these enforcement functions along geographical lines—in very rough terms, border vs. interior. Service functions remained with USCIS, as the HSA had provided. *See* David A. Martin, *Immigration Policy and the Homeland Security Act Reorganization: An Early Agenda for Practical Improvements,* 80 Interp.Rel. 601 (2003).

Obviously, the three bureaus of DHS with immigration responsibilities (known as CBP, ICE, and USCIS) still face many common or overlapping issues. Coordination remains a serious problem, probably exacerbated by the split of authority between DOJ and DHS, and by the three-way split within DHS. In any event, the transfer of immigration functions into DHS certainly has not resolved the longstanding concerns that contributed to Congress' decision to abolish INS.

(i) Customs and Border Protection (CBP)

The DHS component known as U.S. Customs and Border Protection (CBP) is responsible for the border enforcement mission and is intended to operate as a unified border agency. It screens both people and cargo, and it works to interdict both people and contraband (especially illicit drugs) entering the country at locations other than official ports of entry. In fiscal year (FY) 2015, CBP had 60,000 employees and a budget of $12.7 billion.

Inspections. The reorganizations that created the Department of Homeland Security combined the former INS inspector corps with customs inspectors transferred from the Department of Treasury. As of 2014, the agency had about 22,000 "CBP officers," as these inspectors are now formally called. That formal category does not include the Border Patrol (21,000 agents), CBP's air and marine officers (over 1,000), nor agriculture inspectors (over 2,000)—all functions that were also incorporated into CBP in 2003. (We will usually stick with the older terminology here, referring to "CBP officers" as "inspectors," for clarity and better differentiation among agency functions.)

Cars and pedestrians line up for inspection before entering the United States at the busy port of entry between Tijuana and San Diego. (Photo: David McNew/Getty Images).

The inspectors' role under the immigration laws is to examine the passports, visas, and other evidence of entitlement to admission presented by aliens and citizens arriving at the nation's 328 official ports of entry (at land borders, seaports, and also at international airports). As appropriate, they also consult other information available to the government in order to decide whether to admit or exclude. CBP also staffs preclearance stations in Canada, Ireland, and the Caribbean, which permit the completion of inspection before passengers board aircraft bound for the United States.

In recent years, roughly 350–400 million persons have been inspected and admitted annually, 50–60 percent of them noncitizens. (The total includes multiple counting of individuals who make multiple entries.) In a typical year, over 90 percent are admitted after what is called primary inspection, the brief encounter with the inspector at the initial booth. The others are referred to secondary inspection, in an office setting at the port of entry, for more detailed questioning. The overwhelming majority of them are found admissible at that point, perhaps after they or their friends present additional information to clear up apparent problems.

Of the small number denied entry after inspection (roughly 200–250,000), only about a quarter are removed pursuant to a formal removal order. Most of the rest are allowed to withdraw their applications for admission (this requires CBP permission), and so head home without the complications that ensue from formal removal. *See* Lisa Seghetti, *Border Security: Immigration Inspections at Ports of Entry* (Cong. Res. Serv. 2015); John F. Simanski, *Immigration Enforcement Actions: 2013* (DHS Office of Immigration Statistics, Sept. 2014); TRAC, *Immigration Inspections When Arriving in the U.S.* (2006), available at http://trac.syr.edu/immigration/reports/142/.

Border Patrol. The other major component of CBP is the Border Patrol. Its work focuses on the areas between ports of entry, in order to prevent or deter unauthorized entries or landings and to apprehend violators. The Border Patrol has its own distinctive geographic and bureaucratic organization pattern, broken down into 20 Sectors that ring the country, each headed by a Chief Patrol Agent. Strengthening border enforcement (as distinct from immigration enforcement in the interior of the United States) has drawn strong support from both Republicans and Democrats over the past two decades. Consequently, Congress has greatly increased funding, and the ranks of the Border Patrol have grown from just under 4,000 agents at the end of 1993 to 10,000 in 2004, to 21,000 in 2014.

The executive branch has also used this enhanced staffing to change strategies and thus make it harder to cross the southwestern border. Since the mid-1990s, the Border Patrol has emphasized "forward deployment," posting agents in visible locations within sight of each other along the border at all significant crossing regions, augmented by better fencing and more lighting. The purpose is to deter any attempt at entry rather than simply, as in the past, chasing and catching an erratic percentage of violators after they move across the line. The new strategy has succeeded in greatly reducing attempted crossings in former high-traffic places like San Diego and El Paso, but smugglers in response turned to guiding persons across more forbidding and remote desert areas. The Border Patrol makes use of technology, including nearly 250 CBP aircraft (some of them remote-operated pilotless planes) and increasingly sophisticated sensors, to locate such clandestine crossers. It has also augmented its search and rescue capacity, because the greater traffic through the deserts resulted in a higher death toll along the border among persons attempting entry.

Border Patrol apprehensions fluctuated between 800,000 and 1.7 million a year from 1983 to 2007. But enhanced deployments, coupled with the declining economy, reduced attempted crossings thereafter, dropping apprehensions dramatically to 487,000 in FY 2014 and 337,117 in FY 2015.

(ii) Immigration and Customs Enforcement (ICE)

Overview. Interior enforcement of both customs and immigration laws is the responsibility of U.S. Immigration and Customs Enforcement (ICE). This DHS component is responsible for locating and arresting or charging persons illegally in the country, representing the government in removal proceedings in immigration court, conducting efforts against fraud and smuggling (involving the movement of either human beings or goods), enforcing the laws against unauthorized employment of noncitizens, and also carrying out the former Customs Service's tasks in battling, for example, money laundering, child pornography, and international arms and drug trafficking. In FY 2015, Congress set ICE's budgetary resources at $6.3 billion. ICE is the principal investigative arm of DHS and the second largest investigative agency in the federal government, after the Federal Bureau of Investigation (FBI). It has 6,700 special agents in its Office of Homeland Security Investigations (HSI). HSI focuses primarily on complex criminal investigations, but also has responsibility for investigating violations of the employment verification laws and visa violations in the United States and abroad.

Enforcement and Removal Operations. ICE's civil immigration enforcement duties are handled primarily by its Office of Enforcement and Removal Operations (ERO), with nearly 8,000 officers and support staff, most based in field offices throughout the country. ERO handles the surprisingly complex logistics of taking custody of noncitizens detained during removal proceedings, assuring their presence every time they have a hearing in immigration court, and securing the ultimate removal of those (detained or not) who receive final removal orders or agree to depart under supervision. ERO also coordinates with state and local law enforcement to identify and detain criminal violators who are removable, and it pursues persons who fail to leave when ordered or who return without permission after being deported, among other duties.

Congress's steadily increased appropriations for immigration enforcement have resulted in ICE operating the largest detention and supervised release system in the country. In recent years, ICE has detained over 400,000 individuals per year, and has had approximately 34,000 detention beds at its disposal, in either its own detention facilities, contract facilities run by private corporations, or local jails that make space available for immigration detention pursuant to intergovernmental agreements.

A Border Patrol agent scouts the boundary fence near Yuma, Arizona.
(Photo: Department of Homeland Security)

Responding to major controversies over the previous decade regarding conditions of detention, detainee medical care, and access to family and counsel, among other matters, ICE embarked in 2009 on significant reforms to the detention system. The reforms emphasized consolidation of facilities into a smaller network, new facilities located close to major concentrations of noncitizen population, an online detainee locator system opened in 2010, increased use of "alternatives to detention" (which may include electronic monitoring—often with ankle bracelets—and supervised release during removal proceedings), revamped medical care, revised detention standards, new directives against sexual abuse and assault prevention, and especially new and better funded mechanisms for monitoring of detention facilities. *See* ICE, *Immigration Detention Overview and Recommendations* (report mapping reform plans, prepared by Dr. Dora Schriro, Oct. 6, 2009), http://www.ice. gov/doclib/about/offices/odpp/pdf/ice-detention-rpt.pdf; ICE, *Detention Reform Accomplishments*, http://www.ice.gov/detention-reform#tab1 (2015). Full implementation is still in process, and controversy over ICE detention continues. The controversy mounted in 2014, when DHS announced a severe plan to detain minors and families with children, in response to a sharp increase in such arrivals, mainly from Central America.

ICE reported over 400,000 removals and returns in FY 2012, but this total declined thereafter, reaching 316,000 in FY 2014 and 235,000 in FY 2015. ("Removals" take place under a formal removal order; "returns" result from ICE enforcement activity that did not involve a formal order, such as an individual's acceptance of voluntary departure under supervision.) *DHS releases end of year statistics* (ICE News Release, Dec. 18, 2014), https://www.ice.gov/news/releases/dhs-releases-end-year-statistics. The numerical decline stemmed in significant part from DHS changes in removal priorities and practices as part of a series of executive actions undertaken by the Obama administration during the President's second term.

In effectuating its mission, ICE arranges to transport roughly 300,000 people to their countries of nationality every year. For these purposes ERO operates its own system of daily or weekly bus routes (with a fleet as large as Greyhound), running, for example, from Minnesota to the southern Texas border, to accomplish the deportation of Mexicans. For other nationalities, deportation officers book air travel on commercial flights (sometimes with officer escorts) or chartered planes, or use DHS planes. A high percentage of non-Mexican removals require ERO to secure travel documents or other permission from the receiving country, in a labor-intensive case-by-case process. Some governments refuse or drag their feet in accepting return.

(iii)   Citizenship and Immigration Services (USCIS)

Overview. Consider now the service side of immigration management—adjudicating applications for various benefits. For example, when a grandfather from the old country who has come to visit decides he would like to stay a bit longer with his granddaughter, he must apply for an extension of stay as a tourist or, to use the technical term, a "temporary visitor for pleasure." When a student who has come to this country as a nonimmigrant marries a citizen and decides to settle here, she must apply for adjustment of her status to that of a lawful permanent resident. Later, after a specified period of residence, if she decides to become a U.S. citizen, she must petition for naturalization. And when a citizen decides to help her brother come from abroad to resettle here as an immigrant, the process does not formally start overseas where the brother is located. It begins instead with the citizen filing a visa petition with the immigration authorities in the United States. A USCIS examiner will review the petition in order to verify the claimed family relationship and establish prima facie qualification for preference immigration. (Before an immigrant visa will issue, several other steps must be completed, many of them by U.S. consular officials in the brother's home country.) In each such case (and there are many other examples), the USCIS officer who passes on the petition or request must decide whether the application is complete and bona fide, whether it meets the requirements set forth in the statute and the regulations, and in many cases whether the applicant further merits a favorable exercise of the discretion that the INA vests in DHS.

These decisions by examiners amount to adjudication, but in most cases, this is not the kind of "adjudication" that lawyers tend to think of— a formal hearing involving two contestants battling out the issues before a relatively passive decisionmaker. Much of the time the applicant does not even see in person the officer who will make the decision. The case must instead be made in writing on one of dozens of prescribed forms that work their way through the agency by the thousands each day. If personal contact does occur, it usually takes the form of a rather informal interview conducted by an examiner. Quite often, the individual applicant is not represented by counsel. In recent years, over six million applications and petitions for benefits under the INA (including naturalization applications) have been filed annually.

These immigration benefits are adjudicated by U.S. Citizenship and Immigration Services (USCIS), the third component within DHS to inherit a portion of the duties formerly performed by INS. USCIS had a budget of $3.2 billion in FY 2015. Congress has mandated that nearly all of the cost of its operations and capital investments come from fees imposed on applicants for immigration benefits; hence application fees are relatively high. USCIS is staffed by 19,000 employees and contract personnel.

Congress also created an Ombudsman's office in 2003, meant to help deal with customer questions or grievances about immigration services. That office has not been funded at a level that permits detailed investigation of each complaint, but it does draw upon the complaints it receives, plus other inquiry, to issue broader management review reports with suggestions for improvements in specific USCIS functions. The USCIS Ombudsman has no jurisdiction over immigration enforcement.

Offices and Processes. Nearly all immigration benefit applications are filed today by mail, and sometimes electronically, sent either to one of four Regional Service Centers, to the National Benefits Center, or to a specified centralized intake facility, called a "lockbox." The instructions for the relevant application form indicate precisely how and where it should be filed. (USCIS forms and instructions are available on its website, http://www.uscis.gov/forms.) The receipt staff performs initial functions such as checking for completeness of the papers and inclusion of the appropriate fee, logging in the application and generating a receipt to be mailed back to the applicant, creating the administrative file, sending it to the appropriate officer for decision, and scheduling an interview at a field office, if an interview is needed.

USCIS has a variety of different types of field offices, beyond the Service Centers. In addition to dozens of primary offices throughout the country (and in 25 international locations), where interviews are conducted, USCIS has approximately 130 Application Support Centers, designed to take the fingerprints now required for nearly all applications, in a secure and reliable fashion. Also, in recognition that asylum adjudications require unique skills and training, a separate asylum corps considers those applications. USCIS Asylum Offices are located in nine cities around the country, staffed by approximately 350 asylum officers. USCIS also manages two important computerized immigration status verification systems: Systematic Alien Verification for Entitlements (SAVE), which is checked by federal and state benefit-granting agencies, and E–Verify, which registered employers can use to check the employment authorization of their new hires.

USCIS is in the early stages of a multi-year revamping of all its business processes, in order to move from a paper-based to an electronic-based process. This change will also eventually benefit ICE and CBP as well, because all immigration functions have been dependent on paper files, known as A-files, which are often lost or delayed in transmission, thereby preventing or slowing both adjudications and enforcement actions. The change is known as USCIS Transformation, and it involves redesigning current processes, plus the gradual changeover, benefit by benefit (starting with nonimmigrant benefits) to the new electronic environment. See 88 Interp. Rel. 2065 (2011) (describing the first set of regulation changes to implement Transformation). Transformation has been plagued, however, by significant delays and cost overruns. Jerry Markon, *Delays in a DHS bid to go digital,* Wash. Post, Nov. 9, 2015, at A1.

In the meantime, USCIS launched in 2009 a new system, accessible at https://egov.uscis.gov/casestatus/landing.do, which allows all of its customers to check the status of their cases online using their receipt number. In addition, USCIS provides access to information about average case processing times by specific benefit and processing center, so that applicants can get an idea of how much longer they may have to wait for a decision. https://egov.uscis.gov/cris/processTimesDisplayInit.do.

c.   Regulations and Other Forms of Guidance

Immigration regulations are published in Title 8 of the Code of Federal Regulations, usually after notice-and-comment rulemaking in accordance with the Administrative Procedure Act (APA), 5 U.S.C. § 553. For guidance, immigration officers also have relied on "Operations Instructions" (OIs). Although many OIs read like regulations, they were issued without going through the APA rulemaking procedures, and they serve more as an internal operating manual. Unlike regulations, they do not have the force of law. Most such guidance has now been collected into a series of DHS field manuals, which are generally available to the public. (Sections containing classified or law-enforcement-sensitive information are withheld.)

Guidance of this type is reprinted in appendix volumes of immigration treatises, such as Charles Gordon, Stanley Mailman, Stephen Yale-Loehr & Ronald Y. Wada, *Immigration Law and Procedure* (Matthew Bender, rev. ed.). Many guidance documents can also be found on the USCIS website, Westlaw, and other online sources. The immigration agencies also communicate guidance to field offices by means of a variety of policy wires, cables, and memoranda. The important ones are carried in weekly reporting services like *Interpreter Releases* (Thomson Reuters) and *Bender's Immigration Bulletin* (Matthew Bender & Co., Inc., a member of the LexisNexis Group).

d.   A Glimpse of Front-Line Immigration Offices

The following reading conveys the atmosphere in immigration field offices and illustrates some of the challenges facing DHS officers and the individuals they encounter. In Philadelphia, as you will see, several key USCIS and ICE offices are located together in the same building, but this is not the dominant pattern.

MICHAEL MATZA, HOUSE OF DREAMS

Philadelphia Inquirer, Dec. 19, 2010, at A1.*

Bitten by winter wind, baked by summer sun, the impromptu parade of nations inches down 16th Street toward the door to thousands of dearly held dreams, and some bad endings. There are men in turbans, Irish flat caps, and berets, women in rainbow saris and African gele head ties. Their faces are white, black, and every hue between. Many clutch documents, skimming them again and again on the plodding approach to the entryway metal detector.

This is 1600 Callowhill St., Philadelphia—the address that binds a dizzyingly diverse and increasingly populous universe of at least three-quarter million immigrants in Pennsylvania, Delaware, and West Virginia. Here, at the District 5 [field] office of U.S. Citizenship and Immigration Services, the federal government decides who may live legally in America, under what conditions and for how long, and who must go home. * * *

District 5 does not teem with immigrants as do some of the other 25 USCIS districts, the most strained being in the South and West. With satellite centers in Pittsburgh, Dover, and Charleston and an $11.4 million budget, it turned out 17,000 new Americans last year, out of 750,000 nationwide, and issued about 6,000 of the 1.1 million green cards.

Also at 1600 Callowhill, [at the ICE office] on a floor just above the hoopla of twice-a-week swearing-in ceremonies, law enforcement nets are cast for deportation. District 5—home to an estimated 185,000 illegal immigrants—expelled a record-breaking 6,629 last year, up from 2,501 in 2001. * * *

WAITING THEIR TURN

In a second-floor alcove with neat rows of blue vinyl seats, 16 immigrants wait their turn to take citizenship tests on English usage and American civics. More than 125 will follow. From the walls, George Washington and the signers of the Declaration of Independence keep watch as Ismaila Adekunle nervously crams, studying a printout of 100 questions and answers from the USCIS website. The examiner will randomly pick 10. If Adekunle gets six right—and about 92 percent of immigrants do—he will be sworn in within a few weeks. If not, he can try again in 60 days.

But time suddenly is of the essence for the 20-year-old Nigerian, dressed for war in desert camouflage and combat boots. Born in Lagos, Adekunle was 3 when his father, Bunyamin, an airline clerk, and his mother, Deborah, immigrated to America for the classic reason: a better

---

life. He was raised near Broad Street and Olney Avenue in North Philadelphia, went to public schools, and last year enrolled at Lincoln University. He also, like older brother Ganiyu, joined the U.S. Army Reserve—"to show my appreciation," he says, "to play my part."

His unit is set to deploy to Afghanistan next year. He wants to go to war as a citizen, he says, to cement the bond with his "battle buddies." But there are other benefits to be reaped. While legal immigrants are welcome in the U.S. military—there are an estimated 45,000 across all branches—only citizens can become officers. Adekunle also would be eligible for federal student loans. * * *

Adekunle must swear to tell the truth, turn over a passel of identification and his Nigerian passport, and answer some pro-forma questions. They range from the quaint "Ever been a member of the Communist party?" to "Are you willing to defend the United States in an emergency?" The young soldier's response to the latter is to look down at his uniform and smile.

Civics proves a tougher challenge. Burroughs [the USCIS officer] fires off the questions: "What does the president's cabinet do?" Adekunle is stumped. "OK, we'll come back to that," she says. "How many judges on the Supreme Court?"

"Nine."

"What did the Declaration of Independence do?"

"Freed the United States from Great Britain."

"How many years does a United States senator serve?" Again, Adekunle draws a blank. He purses his lips. Burroughs moves on. "Who leads the United States if the president and vice president can't serve?"

"The House speaker."

"Name a branch of government."

"Legislative."

"When do we celebrate Independence Day?"

"July Fourth."

"Name the war between the North and the South."

"The Civil War."

It is his sixth correct answer. Finally, Burroughs is smiling. Next comes English usage. Adekunle clearly reads aloud the sentence: "What is the capital of the United States?" [Then, as requested, he] legibly writes: "Mexico is south of the United States."

"Congratulations! You have passed," Burroughs declares. A beaming Adekunle looks like he wants to hug her, but doesn't. * * *

MARRYING: A FAST TRACK

Marrying a U.S. citizen is a fast track to living legally ever after in America. The immigrant spouse can more readily get a green card and then is required to have it for only three years, instead of the standard five, before applying for citizenship. The break can be a reward for love and family values, or an opportunity to game the system. If prosecuted to conviction, phony marriages and other visa frauds are punishable by five years in prison and a $250,000 fine.

It's up to USCIS interviewers such as Lucy Noel to outwit the fakers. An immigration officer for seven years, she handles an average of seven cases a day, not all of them marriages, but all familial. It could be a naturalized citizen's immigrant nephew posing as a son to get benefits. Or a friend claiming to be a blood relative.

On this day, in a third-floor office overlooking the Vine Street Expressway, she [interviews a recently married couple in their fifties—a six-year visa overstayer and her U.S. citizen husband.] * * * The game of gotcha goes on nearly an hour. Were she to catch a whiff of fakery, Noel could separate the two for questioning. She could refer the case to a fraud investigator. But she sees no need. A month after [the wife's] application is approved, her green card should arrive in the mail, Noel tells them. * * *

FERRETING OUT FAKERS

The sixth-floor Fraud Detection and National Security Unit [of USCIS] is small and quiet, the antithesis of the bustle on lower floors where staff and immigrants intersect. Here, in relative seclusion, Michale Horn leads six investigators in ferreting out those who scam the system— typically for green cards and work permits—and those with far more nefarious deeds in mind.

Most of their cases are the mundane frauds. But there is no denying, 9/11 upped the stakes in the office. * * * It is here, for example, that investigators mine databases for immigrants who are known members of the 47 groups that the State Department defines as "designated terrorist organizations." Whether a case of benefit fraud or a suspected threat against the country, the unit exchanges fingerprints and other data with intelligence agencies to vet immigrants whose applications for legal status have been flagged.

Sometimes, Horn says, tips alleging crimes or terrorist ties come in the mail. Other times, as on this day, cases percolate up from the interview rooms below. Horn parts with details sparingly:

A "man from South America" applied for a green card, and managed to raise an examiner's suspicions. When Horn looks for a fingerprint match in a criminal database, he pops up as a convicted burglar. "Your fingerprints aren't going to lie," Horn says. "He appears to be removable." She sends the case to Immigration and Customs Enforcement—the immigration police unit known as ICE—for his arrest and deportation.

END OF THE JOURNEY

The [ICE/ERO office at the] end of a fifth-floor hallway has been the end of the American journey for legions of immigrants. There, two large cells—one for women, one for men, with a capacity of a dozen people each—await those whose crimes have caught up with them. On this day * * * each cell holds a single prisoner, barely visible through the small windows in the solid steel doors. Exactly why they are there, agents decline to say. * * *

The highest priority for ICE, officials say, is the expulsion of immigrants convicted of felonies. Some are in local jails. Others have served time and are back on the street. To round them up, ICE uses an undisclosed number of officers paired as "fugitive teams."[a]

At a noon meeting around a gray conference table, [ICE] field office director Thomas Decker confers with assistant director Dave O'Neill about one of the day's targets: "a Dominican female" convicted of cocaine possession in 1991. A team is on her trail in North Philadelphia. Sometime after her conviction, * * * [a]pparently thinking she can get away with it, she files for a green card, using either her own name or an alias. Her criminal history is revealed in the green-card interview and subsequent investigation. She is ordered deported in 2005. On this day, the fugitive team does not find her. But knowing her haunts, the agents are confident they will.

ONCE IN A LIFETIME

It happens once in a lifetime, every Wednesday and Friday afternoon.

The large reception room on the fourth floor can comfortably hold the 137 immigrants about to be sworn in as citizens this day—but not the more than 150 relatives and friends who have come along to witness a moment that has been years in the dreaming. Every folding chair is spoken for and the aisles are packed. English mingles with a Rosetta Stone catalogue of languages in a happy buzz.

Twenty-five years ago, the immigrants naturalized in District 5 were predominantly Vietnamese and Filipino. Now, the largest number of them are Indian, like Indrani Ray-Mukherji, 37, who was born in Calcutta, came to America in 2004, found work as an Amtrak sales agent, and now lives in Northeast Philadelphia. Of the 17,000 naturalizations last year, more than half were for people between the ages of 25 and 44.

---

[a] ICE counts as "fugitives" persons who have a final order of removal but who neither presented themselves to ICE for expulsion as required nor otherwise departed from the United States. In this usage, fugitives do not necessarily have a criminal charge or conviction.—eds.

Fewer than 300 were unemployed. About 2,100 held management or professional positions. * * *

[T]he group bounds to its feet for the national anthem, followed by the Oath of Allegiance. To a cacophony of cheers, naturalization certificates are handed out. But hold the kisses. Still to come is a short video narrated by President Obama, who intones, "This is now officially your country." * * * In the hall outside the reception room, volunteers help the new citizens register to vote.

Ray-Mukherji is one of the first to sign up. Her husband, Chandra Mukherji, who left India as a child and became a citizen in 1991, teases her for going about it with such solemnity. But she has her reasons, she says. "I feel some responsibility for the country now."

2. THE DEPARTMENT OF JUSTICE

a. Immigration Judges

We have not yet discussed the kind of immigration adjudication that probably generates the most drama and often draws the greatest attention. Certainly it has the highest potential for an immediate impact on the right of a noncitizen physically present in this country to remain. We are speaking, of course, of removal decisions. (Until 1996, these were known as exclusion or deportation decisions.)

Under the statute, a proceeding to remove a noncitizen must generally be conducted by an immigration judge (IJ). *See* INA §§ 101(b)(4); § 240(a)(1). (We explore in Chapters Six, Nine, and Ten exceptions permitting DHS officers to conduct less formal removal procedures in specified circumstances, usually involving either "arriving aliens" or noncitizens with serious criminal convictions who are not lawful permanent residents.) Throughout much of our history, the "special inquiry officers" conducting removal proceedings were simply experienced or senior immigration officers, who did not necessarily hold a law degree and who were designated to hold such hearings as part—but only part—of a range of responsibilities to administer and enforce the immigration laws. Often they would be the only federal official present for the proceedings. In the early decades of federal immigration controls, they might have inspected noncitizens at the border on one day, on another investigated violations, on yet another marshaled the case against a deportable noncitizen, and on still another served as a special inquiry officer to adjudicate the deportation of someone who had been investigated by their colleagues.

This mixture of roles weathered due process challenges, but eventually DOJ's interest in improving the quality and predictability of decisions resulted in the gradual evolution from hearing officers to specialized and professional immigration judges. During this same period, INS steadily expanded the deployment of specialized trial attorneys to represent the government in such proceedings, thus freeing the special inquiry officer for a more passive, judge-like decisionmaking role. *See* Sidney B. Rawitz, *From* Wong Yang Sung *to Black Robes,* 65 Interp. Rel. 453 (1988).

In 1983, the Department of Justice separated the hearing officers, by then regularly called "immigration judges," from INS, placing them in a new DOJ unit called the Executive Office for Immigration Review (EOIR) that reported directly to the Associate Attorney General. This did not mean that all the immigration judges moved to Washington; most remained physically in their old offices located in or near INS facilities throughout the country. But this different line of accountability provided a better structural assurance of adjudicative neutrality and fostered a strong spirit of professional independence among the judges. Nonetheless critics still sometimes maintained that an enforcement mentality pervaded all immigration-related agencies, and there have been recurrent calls for EOIR to become a wholly independent adjudicative body.

Congress responded, to a limited degree, to this line of criticism when it adopted the Homeland Security Act. Virtually all INS functions were transferred to DHS, but EOIR remained in the Department of Justice. *See* Martin, *supra,* 80 Interp. Rel. at 616; *see generally* Stephen H. Legomsky, *Forum Choices for the Review of Agency Adjudication: A Study of the Immigration Process,* 71 Iowa L. Rev. 1297 (1986) .

The major portion of an IJ's time is spent presiding over removal proceedings. Resolving the case involves not only deciding whether the noncitizen is covered by one of the grounds of inadmissibility or deportability, but also passing upon a wide variety of waivers and applications for relief that may be made in such proceedings, even by those (the vast majority) who concede removability. When considering such matters, the immigration judge often exercises the discretion the statute lodges formally in the Attorney General. Immigration judges also preside over bond redetermination proceedings for detained noncitizens— essentially an expedited appeal of the terms of release that are set initially by the enforcement agencies.

In fiscal year 1992, there were about 85 immigration judges, who received 110,000 deportation and exclusion cases. The number of judges doubled in the 1990s, as a result of Clinton administration initiatives to catch up with caseload and sustain respectable processing times. The corps grew unevenly thereafter, and Congress has often failed to add staffing to the courts, even while pumping up enforcement resources— which necessarily bring rapid increases in removal charges that need adjudication. As of February 2016, EOIR had 254 immigration judges serving in 57 immigration courts. In FY 2014 (the most recent statistics available), the judges received 226,000 new removal cases (a 10 percent increase over the previous year) and completed 184,000. Many of these were summary dispositions that did not require full hearings on the merits. The judges also ruled on nearly 60,000 bond redeterminations and disposed of over 19,000 other motions, primarily motions to reopen to consider new evidence. *See* EOIR, FY 2014 Statistics Year Book, at A7–A8.

Plainly, the workload of immigration judges is vast, and their staff support sparse. For example, there are few law clerks for all of EOIR. (In early 2016, the 254 judges were supported by 137 law clerks and other staff.) And there are no court stenographers; the judge operates the recording machine personally. Caseload pressures require that IJs almost always pronounce judgment orally, immediately at the conclusion of the hearing, to be captured on the recording device—and transcribed only if a party appeals the decision.

Figure 4.2
Immigration Court Backlogs, 1998–2015

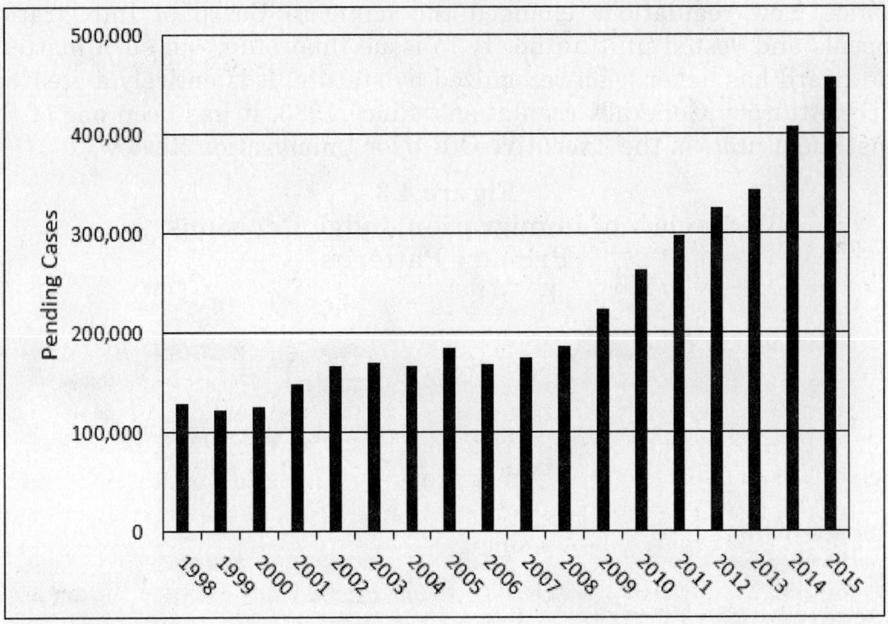

Source: TRAC Immigration, http://trac.syr.edu/phptools/immigration/court_backlog/.

In recent years, immigration court staffing and resources have fallen badly behind intake—a product of remarkable budgetary neglect on the part of both the executive and legislative branches as removal caseloads grew relentlessly. See Figure 4.2. Some courts are now calendaring cases for a full merits hearing four or five years in the future. *See* Walter Ewing, *Why Are Immigration Court Hearings Being Set Into 2019?* (Am. Immigr. Council, Feb. 3, 2015); Devlin Barrett, *U.S. Delays Thousands of Immigration Hearings by Nearly 5 Years*, Wall St. J., Jan. 28, 2015. The total backlog as of April 2015 exceeded 445,000, a record. TRAC, *Immigration Court Backlog Keeps Rising: Latest Figures as of April 2015*, http://trac.syr.edu/immigration/reports/385/.

b.   The Board of Immigration Appeals, Plus a Sketch of Other Administrative Appeal Procedures

(i) *Overview of the BIA*

Under 8 C.F.R. § 1003.1(b), noncitizens found removable by immigration judges have a right of appeal to the Board of Immigration Appeals (BIA), a multi-member review body appointed by the Attorney General. Since 1921, a Board of Review had existed in the Department of Labor, empowered to make recommendations to the Secretary regarding the disposition of appeals in exclusion and deportation cases. In 1940, following the transfer of immigration functions to the Department of Justice, new regulations changed the name to Board of Immigration Appeals and vested in it authority to issue final orders in such matters. The Board has never been recognized by statute; it is entirely a creature of the Attorney General's regulations. Since 1983, it has been one of the constituent units of the Executive Office for Immigration Review.

Figure 4.3
Review of Immigration Judge Decisions:
Primary Patterns

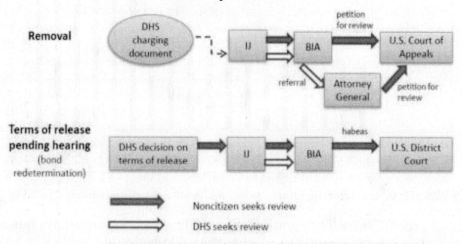

Note: AG may also take referral *suo sponte* or on BIA request. Referrals are quite infrequent.

The overwhelming majority of cases before the Board consist of appeals from immigration judge decisions in removal proceedings, including related rulings on bonds and motions. 8 C.F.R. § 1003.1(b)(3). In FY 2014, such appeals totaled 25,340 of 29,723 total BIA receipts. EOIR, FY 2014 Statistics Year Book at Q2. But the Board also hears appeals from specified DHS decisions, such as those imposing administrative fines and penalties on aircraft and vessels, refusing a limited class of waivers of inadmissibility, or denying certain kinds of visa petitions for intending immigrants. 8 C.F.R. § 1003.1(b)(4)–(7). The BIA's jurisdiction over visa petition denials reaches only those petitions based on a family relationship (other than adoptions); petitions based on occupational preferences follow a different avenue of appeal entirely, within DHS, to be discussed below.

Cases before the BIA are subject to further review by the Attorney General personally, although such review is infrequently invoked (rarely more than five per year; in some years, none). BIA cases may be "referred" to the Attorney General for a final authoritative decision, either before or after an initial ruling by the Board, in three circumstances (none at the noncitizen's behest): when the Attorney General so directs; when the Chair or a majority of the BIA decides that the case should be referred; or when the Secretary of Homeland Security requests referral. *See* 8 C.F.R. § 1003.1(h). In practice, referrals almost always take place after the BIA decides. For a comprehensive survey of referral practice, see Alberto R. Gonzales & Patrick Glen, *Advancing Executive Branch Immigration Policy through the Attorney General's Review Authority,* 101 Iowa L.Rev. 841 (2016) (written by someone who actually wielded the referral authority; Gonzales was AG 2005–2007).

What about all the other adjudications not directly reviewable by the BIA? A few are simply not appealable administratively—for instance, if a USCIS examiner denies an application to extend an admission period for a temporary visitor or to change from one nonimmigrant status to another (say, from student to tourist, or vice versa). *See* 8 C.F.R. §§ 214.1(c)(5), 248.3(g). A few other types of decisions are not subject to administrative appeal as such, but USCIS does not really have the final administrative word, because the noncitizen may renew the application once removal proceedings have begun. The immigration judge then considers the application *de novo,* followed by possible appeal to the BIA. The primary forms of benefit that follow this pattern are asylum, 8 C.F.R. §§ 208.14(c)(1), 1208.14(c)(1), and adjustment of status to lawful permanent resident, *id.* §§ 245.2(a)(5)(ii), 1245.2(a)(5)(ii).

(ii) Caseload Growth and EOIR's Responses

Originally, the BIA had five permanent members, including its chairman. In 1983, the Board received fewer than 4,000 appeals. It heard all cases *en banc*, although only a tiny proportion on the basis of oral argument. For most of the 1990s, although the Board's membership had increased and most cases were heard by three-member panels, case completions lagged well behind receipts, and a daunting backlog developed. The Department of Justice therefore implemented new streamlining regulations in 1999 and 2002 which shifted to far greater use of single-member decisionmaking. Today a case goes to a three-member panel only if it falls into one of six categories spelled out in 8 C.F.R. § 1003.1(e)(6), which cover only a minority of appeals. Single members usually issue an opinion explaining their ruling. But the member may affirm without opinion (AWO), in which case the IJ's opinion becomes the final agency determination for purposes of any further review. (Board members are assisted in their research and drafting functions by over 100 staff attorneys.)

Figure 4.4
BIA Appeal Receipts and Completions, FY 1996–2014

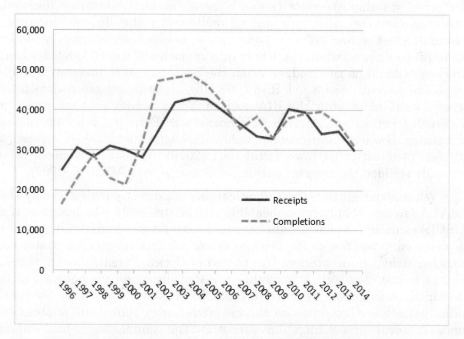

Sources: Executive Office for Immigration Review, 2000 Statistical Year Book (2001) (for 1996–1997); 2002 Statistical Year Book (2003) (for 1998–2001); 2006 Statistical Year Book (2007) (for 2002–2005); 2010 Statistical Year Book (2011) (for 2006–2009); FY 2014 Statistics Year Book, (2015) (for 2010–2014).

Implementation of the 2002 streamlining regulations largely eliminated a massive BIA case backlog. But one byproduct was a surge in immigration appeals to the federal courts. Not only did the BIA issue a great many more decisions during this period, but the rate of appeal to the courts rose from approximately 10 percent to 25 percent. *See* John R.B. Palmer, Stephen Yale-Loehr & Elizabeth Cronin, *Why are So Many People Challenging BIA Decisions in Federal Court? An Empirical Analysis of the Surge in Petitions for Review,* 20 Geo. Immigr. L.J. 1, 52–53 (2005). Some critics attributed the higher appeal rate to unhappiness with the new BIA procedures, including the greater use of affirmances without opinion, which accounted for one-third of BIA decisions in the initial period of operation under the 2002 reforms. Many federal judges expressed deep concern about EOIR's performance and their own burgeoning immigration caseload. They often remanded AWOs to the Board because they deemed an issue to be of such importance that the BIA itself needed to explain its understanding of the law and the facts, and not just rely on the IJ's opinion.

Later reforms responded to the judicial criticism, partly by expanding the Board's membership (to 17 as of early 2016) and augmenting its capacity through the use of temporary members (immigration judges or senior EOIR attorneys, who would be assigned to Board duties for up to one year). By 2011, AWOs had declined to two percent of decisions, and the BIA was publishing more precedent decisions than at any time since the 1990s. *EOIR Director Juan Osuna Discusses the Immigration Court System with the Senate Committee on the Judiciary,* 88 Interp.Rel. 1370–71 (2011). Reversals in the federal courts dropped from 17.5 percent in 2006 to 10.9 percent in 2014. John Guendelsberger, *Circuit Court Decisions for December 2014 and Calendar Year 2014 Totals,* EOIR Immigr. Law Advisor 5 (January 2015), https://www.justice.gov/sites/default/files/eoir/pages/attachments/2015/02/03/vol9no2ed.pdf.

This recent progress has not quieted calls for restructuring the Board (and usually the framework for the immigration courts as well). The critics' proposals range from an article I court, *see, e.g.,* Mark Metcalf, *Built to Fail: Deception and Disorder in America's Immigration Courts* (Center for Immigr. Studies Backgrounder, May 2011) at 13; Dana Leigh Marks, *An Urgent Priority: Why Congress Should Establish an Article I Immigration Court,* 13 Bender's Immigr. Bull. 3 (Jan. 1, 2008); Jaya Ramji-Nogales, Andrew Schoenholtz & Philip G. Schrag, *Refugee Roulette: Disparities in Asylum Adjudication,* 60 Stan. L. Rev. 295, 386 (2007); to a new article III Court of Immigration Appeals that would replace both the BIA and the federal courts of appeals in immigration cases, *see* Stephen H. Legomsky, *Restructuring Immigration Adjudication,* 59 Duke L.J. 1635 (2010).

(iii)   Review Within DHS: The Administrative Appeals Office (AAO)

One other important appeal pattern exists, involving review within DHS. For example, if an examiner denies a visa petition based on occupational grounds—for permanent workers under the employment-based preference categories or for nonimmigrant temporary workers or trainees—such decisions are reviewable within USCIS and not by immigration judges or the Board. Such appeals (there are about 50 specific types) are heard by USCIS's Administrative Appeals Office (AAO, also sometimes called the Administrative Appeals Unit), staffed by approximately 100 appeals officers as of 2016 (over three quarters of them are attorneys), divided among six branches that specialize by type of appeal. *See* 8 C.F.R. § 103.3; *The Administrative Appeals Office*, USCIS website. This website also gives access to the new AAO Practice Manual. The regulations further provide a possibility for "certification" of a case to higher officials for a definitive decision, at the initiative of the reviewing official or of the initial decisionmaker, when the case involves an unusually important, complex, or novel issue of law or fact. 8 C.F.R. § 103.4. Certification is quite infrequent.

Thus two main administrative appellate tribunals or decisionmakers now exist for immigration decisions issued within the United States: the BIA and the AAO. No easy rule of thumb differentiates between the two zones of appellate jurisdiction, except that appeals from removal orders issued by an immigration judge almost always go to the BIA. Beyond this, in order to appeal an adverse determination, consult the regulations to determine the forum. Title 8 C.F.R. §§ 1003.1(b) and 103.3 are the most important such regulations. More significantly, the document that communicates an agency's decision usually informs of any appeal rights, the forum that would hear the appeal, and time limits or other specifications governing review.

(iv) Precedent Decisions—And a Renewed Warning About Relying on the Statute to Determine Which Department Has Authority

A large volume of appellate decisions are handed down each month. Only a very few are designated as precedent decisions for inclusion in the official reports. *See* 8 C.F.R. §§ 103.3(c), 1003.1(i). These precedents are published in the multi-volume set known as "Administrative Decisions Under Immigration and Nationality Laws of the United States" (I & N Dec.). *See* 8 C.F.R. § 103.10(e). In these volumes, you will find reported decisions by the BIA and the AAO, a few rulings by other officials, and occasionally a decision by the Attorney General, when he or she takes a case on referral. The overwhelming majority, however, are BIA decisions. Today precedent decisions are also made available almost immediately via the Virtual Law Library on the EOIR website, with the final volume and page numbers already affixed. (The EOIR website also provides other useful information, including statistical reports and practice manuals, as well as easy access to local immigration court rules.) Under 8 C.F.R.

§ 1003.1(g), the interpretations of statute and regulations included in published BIA precedent decisions are binding on all other agencies, under the proviso in INA § 103(a)(1), which states that "determination and ruling by the Attorney General with respect to all questions of law shall be controlling."

Keep in mind that consulting the INA alone can give a highly misleading picture of institutional responsibilities as they currently exist. As indicated early in this chapter, the text of the INA still places most immigration authorities in the Attorney General. But because of generic transfers of authority in the statute that created DHS, most of the AG's stated INA powers, unless they relate to the formal adjudication handled by EOIR, are now wielded by the Secretary of Homeland Security and his or her delegates. Similarly confusing is the fact that relatively few regulations in 8 C.F.R. have been amended since 2003 to reflect the new allocation of responsibility to DHS.

c.　Other DOJ Units

Three other units in the Department of Justice should be mentioned. The first two were created because of the passage of the Immigration Reform and Control Act of 1986 (IRCA), Pub. L. No. 99–603, 100 Stat. 3359. As Chapter One indicated, IRCA enacted a system of employer sanctions to penalize those who knowingly hire undocumented noncitizens or fail to perform certain documentary verification at the time of hiring. INA § 274A. In an attempt to assure that this system did not increase discrimination against ethnic minorities, IRCA also added new provisions barring discrimination based on national origin or citizenship status. INA § 274B. Under the statute, allegations of employer violations of either of these provisions are heard by administrative law judges (ALJs) (who are not immigration judges) in the Department of Justice. Accordingly, the Department added a new unit to EOIR, the Office of the Chief Administrative Hearing Officer (OCAHO), who oversees the ALJs who carry out this function. See 28 C.F.R. Part 68. Several years later, Congress also bestowed authority on the ALJs to impose civil penalties for document fraud under INA § 274C. OCAHO's caseload remains small, however, in large part because the enforcement units have been fairly successful in negotiating settlements of complaints or charges. Receipts reached 91 cases in FY 2010, up from 23 in 2006, and later dropped to 74 in FY 2014. EOIR, FY 2014 Statistics Year Book at X1.

The principal investigating and charging responsibility under the employer sanctions and civil document fraud provisions rests with ICE. But the 1986 statute created a new office in the Department of Justice, the Office of Special Counsel for Immigration-Related Unfair Employment Practices, to fulfill these responsibilities under IRCA's antidiscrimination provisions. The Special Counsel is appointed by the

President, subject to the advice and consent of the Senate. *See* INA § 274B(c); 28 C.F.R. Part 44. After the creation of DHS, the Special Counsel's office remained in DOJ, where it is part of the Civil Rights Division.

Finally, the Federal Bureau of Investigation (FBI) plays an increasingly important but focused role in immigration decisions. Statutes and regulations over the last 25 years—and particularly since the 9/11 attacks in 2001—have imposed ever more stringent requirements for checking names and fingerprints against watchlists and various criminal and terrorist databases before immigration benefits can be issued. *See generally* DOJ Office of Inspector General, *The Federal Bureau of Investigation's Security Check Procedures for Immigration Applications and Petitions,* (June 2008). The FBI plays a crucial role in this process, drawing on information available from other agencies and the intelligence community. The system now produces clearances in most cases fairly quickly, but for those not promptly cleared, the security check process can cause delays lasting months or years.

3.   THE DEPARTMENT OF STATE

a.   The Bureau of Consular Affairs

For over 90 years, most persons wishing to travel to the United States, even for a short visit, have been required to secure preliminary documents known as visas from a U.S. official overseas. (Chapter Six will discuss this process and also describe the exceptions to the visa requirement.) State Department officials, called consular officers, are stationed at over 220 offices throughout the world to decide on applications for visas. *See* INA §§ 221, 222. In FY 2014, they issued over 9.9 million nonimmigrant visas, reflecting a steady and significant increase from the roughly six million issued annually in the first decade of the 21st century. (Consular officers typically reject about 15 percent of nonimmigrant visa applications.) From FY 2010 to 2014, the Department also issued just under 500,000 immigrant visas annually. *See* Dep't of State, Immigrant and Nonimmigrant Visas Issued at Foreign Service Posts: FY 2010–2014, Table I (2015), available on the State Department website.

Securing a visa, as arduous a process as it may be for some, does not guarantee admission to the United States—and many of the relevant documents bear a warning to this effect. Visas are essentially a form of permission to travel to the United States and apply for admission at the border. The inspector at the port of entry is entitled to disagree with the consular officer and thus to deny admission. (Denial is often, but not always, subject to further review by an immigration judge.) Fortunately, such disagreement is infrequent. Indeed, the system would break down if visas did not usually function to secure admission. But because airlines and other carriers are subject to substantial fines and other penalties if they bring noncitizens here without proper documents, INA § 273, a traveler cannot board unless the papers presented at the foreign ticket counter are all in order. A visa is therefore indispensable for noncitizens wishing to come here from most countries around the globe. (The citizens of 38 countries are eligible for visa-free travel for visits of up to 90 days.)

Although INA § 104 places these documentation responsibilities in officials of the Department of State, the formal authority of the Department head, the Secretary of State, is circumscribed. Note the curious language of § 104(a)(1), giving the Secretary broad authority, but excepting from that control "those powers, duties, and functions conferred upon the consular officers relating to the granting or refusal of visas." Can it really be intended to give consular officers autocratic power, immune from the supervision of their normal superiors, to decide whether to issue documents indispensable to noncitizens who wish to come to this country? Critics have often charged that the system operates this way. *See, e.g.,* Whom We Shall Welcome: Report of the President's Commission on Immigration and Naturalization 147 (1953). Their complaints are the more vehement because federal courts routinely hold that visa denials are not reviewable in court. But there is a different theory that underlies this provision: that such separation insulates what are meant to be routine bureaucratic decisions on admissibility from the high politics that are the stock-in-trade of the Secretary of State and his or her subordinates on the diplomatic side of the Department. *See, e.g.,* Alan Simpson, *Policy Implications of U.S. Consular Operations*, in The Consular Dimension of Diplomacy 11 (Martin F. Herz ed. 1983). Whether that purpose is truly advanced—and whether, even so, it justifies vesting so much power in the front-line consular officer—has often been questioned.

In any event, this putative insulating measure does serve to complicate the normal bureaucratic or managerial business of review and supervision to assure timeliness, consistency of outcomes, and legal validity. Nevertheless, these imperatives have still found expression through informal review mechanisms, crafted with close attention to § 104(a)(1). The regulations direct supervisors to review a random selection of visa decisions by consular officers. *See* 22 C.F.R. §§ 41.113(i), 41.121(c) (2015). Officially this review is done as "a significant management and instructional tool useful in maintaining the highest professional standards of adjudication and ensuring uniform and correct application of the law and regulations." 71 Fed. Reg. 37494 (2006) (explanatory statement accompanying new regulations). In some circumstances a second consular officer, upon disagreeing with the first, can issue a visa on his or her own authority despite an initial denial. A more complicated discussion process is involved if the first officer approved issuing the visa and the second disagrees. Cases can also be referred to Washington for what are carefully labeled advisory opinions, but which in fact are ordinarily given effect. *Legal* rulings in advisory opinions are binding on the consular officer. 22 C.F.R. § 41.121(d).

Visa issuance falls under the general responsibility of the Bureau of Consular Affairs, headed by an Assistant Secretary of State. In 2002, congressional concerns stemming from the receipt of visas by the September 11 hijackers prompted calls to remove the visa function from the State Department. The Homeland Security Act did not go quite that far. Visas are still issued by consular officers, who remain part of the Department of State, but authority over visa *policy*, including the issuance of regulations governing visas, was transferred to the Department of Homeland Security. DHS was also given significant authority to monitor the issuance of visas in foreign posts, and may even veto the issuance of an individual visa. DHS may not, however, direct the granting of a visa when the consular officer has refused it. HSA § 428. The two departments agreed upon a lengthy Memorandum of Understanding in September 2003 that carefully allocates their respective powers over visas and related matters. 80 Interp. Rel. 1365 (2003). In practice, State retains the lion's share of operational responsibility for the issuance of visas.

In 1994, the Department of State created a National Visa Center (NVC), based in New Hampshire, to take over from consuls the more routine functions involved in visa issuance. The Center checks visa requests for accuracy and completeness, creates immigrant visa files and computer records, and communicates necessary notices and requests for information to applicants or their attorneys, even though the actual visa will be issued at a consular post abroad. Over the last decade, the Department has progressively implemented new procedures allowing (and later requiring) the completion and submission of electronic visa applications, completed through an interactive online process. Today most nonimmigrant visa applications must be filed electronically. *See* 73 Fed. Reg. 23067–01 (2008).

In addition to Visa Services, the Bureau of Consular Affairs contains two other major divisions, Overseas Citizens Services and Passport Services. The former supervises consular protection and assistance provided to Americans in foreign countries (for example, in connection with foreign arrests, business transactions, or U.S. citizen deaths abroad). With regard to passports, through more than 25 domestic passport agencies and centers in the United States, and through State Department posts abroad, the Bureau has issued between 12 and 14 million passports per year from 2010 to 2014. Demand for passports has surged since 2004, largely because of a mandate Congress enacted that year to implement a recommendation of the 9/11 Commission. The law now requires that U.S.

citizens must have passports or comparably secure U.S. travel documents, including new "passport cards," for all foreign travel, even to Canada, Mexico, or the Caribbean. *See DHS and DOS Announce Issuance of Final Rule for Land and Sea Portion of WHTI,* 85 Interp.Rel. 1004 (2008); *Final Rules Issued Regarding Passport Requirements for WHTI Air Travel,* 83 Interp. Rel. 2573 (2006).

b. Other Bureaus

Another State Department bureau, the Bureau of Population, Refugees and Migration (PRM), plays the key role for the Department of State in connection with overseas refugee programs. PRM deals with both assistance to refugees in camps in first asylum countries (or occasionally displaced persons still within their countries of nationality) and admissions to the United States through the organized refugee resettlement program. It is also the principal point of contact with the Office of the United Nations High Commissioner for Refugees (UNHCR).

The Bureau of Educational and Cultural Affairs (ECA) manages a host of programs meant to enhance mutual understanding between Americans and the citizens of other countries. For immigration-law purposes, ECA's most important functions involve exchange arrangements, like the Fulbright program, that send Americans to other countries and bring several thousand foreign nationals here each year. Many such programs involve governmental or university exchanges, but others involve the private sector, including a program for *au pairs*. A specific nonimmigrant status (known as J–1) exists for "exchange visitors." *See* INA § 101(a)(15)(J). Although the participating programs take the lead in administering the exchange visitor arrangements, ECA oversees their functioning. The visa office in the Bureau of Consular Affairs also plays a role in deciding whether to waive statutory restrictions that may delay or prevent exchange visitors from becoming lawful permanent residents. *See* INA § 212(e).

c. Regulations and Other Guidance

The State Department publishes a Foreign Affairs Manual (FAM), certain chapters of which are devoted to interpretations and instructions relating to immigration and nationality questions, amplifying the Department's regulations appearing in 22 C.F.R. Parts 40–53. Portions of the FAM have been released to the public and are available in various immigration treatises, as well as online at http://www.state.gov/m/a/dir/regs/fam. In November 2015, the Department announced the forthcoming issuance of a reorganized electronic version of the FAM materials relating to immigration, to be known as 9 FAM-e.

Other immigration-related information is available from the Department of State's Visa Services website, http://travel.state.gov/

content/visas/english.html. Indispensable monthly charts on immigrant visa processing (showing visa allocation priority dates currently being processed—an indication of how far down the waiting list the Department is reaching) may be found at the Visa Bulletin site. Most of the documents and records involved in individual visa processing, however, are confidential under specific statutory direction. INA § 222(f).

4. OTHER FEDERAL AGENCIES

a. The Department of Labor

The INA requires USCIS to cooperate with the Department of Labor (DOL) in the process that leads to the granting of permanent resident status to persons who are subject to the labor certification requirement. If this requirement applies, DOL, through its Employment and Training Administration, must certify that American workers in the applicant's field are unavailable in the locality of the applicant's destination and that the applicant's employment will not adversely affect wages and working conditions of American workers. Labor certification is required for many immigrants who enter under the employment-based preference categories of INA § 203(b). If certification is denied, the employer may appeal to the Board of Alien Labor Certification Appeals (BALCA), which usually sits in panels of three administrative law judges, and has authority to affirm, reverse, or remand. We will examine the complicated and specialized process of labor certification in some detail in Chapter Five. The Department of Labor also has similar regulatory responsibilities in connection with several of the business-related categories for nonimmigrants, notably including those for temporary workers. DOL's Wage and Hour Division, which enforces the minimum wage, overtime, and child labor laws, also plays a limited role in monitoring employer compliance with the laws against the hiring of unauthorized workers.

b. The Public Health Service

The Public Health Service (PHS), headed by the Surgeon General, is an agency in the Department of Health and Human Services. Because several grounds of inadmissibility relate to medical conditions, PHS physicians and other authorized medical officials play a role under the Immigration and Nationality Act, both at ports of entry and overseas. PHS-designated doctors conduct medical examinations of intending immigrants, and some of their determinations are unreviewable except by a special medical review panel established pursuant to statute. *See* INA §§ 232, 240(c)(1)(B).

c. The Office of Refugee Resettlement

The INA and other statutes provide certain forms of assistance to refugees who are resettled within the United States. *See* INA § 412. Most of these programs are administered by the Office of Refugee Resettlement, another unit within the Department of Health and Human Services. INA § 411. The Homeland Security Act also gave that Office an important set of new authorities. As of early 2003, ORR took over from INS the responsibility for the care and custody of unaccompanied minors involved in immigration proceedings. HSA § 462. These authorities were expanded and refined in later statutes.

d. The Social Security Administration

The Social Security Administration (SSA) manages the nation's systems for monetary support to the elderly and disabled, including the crediting of payroll taxes to the individual account of the proper employee. Anyone employed in the United States must have a Social Security card. For this reason, Social Security records play a role in the databases used to verify work authorization or eligibility for public benefits. In addition, SSA sends "no-match" letters to employers when the combination of a particular name and social security number for which they report earnings does not match with information contained in agency records. Under some circumstances, such a letter may put the employer on notice that the employee is a noncitizen unauthorized to work in the United States—though SSA sends the letters to assure correct crediting of payments and not for immigration control purposes. More directly, SSA is closely involved with USCIS in the operation of the web-based employment verification system known as E–Verify, because a high percentage of new hires present social security card and a driver's license as their primary evidence of work authorization. We will consider verification procedures and employer obligations under the immigration laws in Chapter Ten.

B. COURTS

No overview of the government bodies involved with immigration and citizenship would be complete without a brief treatment of the role of the courts. We offer here a basic sketch, intended to supply a bit of background that may help understand how the cases in this book reached the courts. We defer full consideration of court review until Chapter Nine.

Before 1961, no immigration statute expressly permitted judicial review of exclusion and deportation orders or of other government decisions in immigration cases. The courts found a basis for jurisdiction, however, because exclusion and deportation require the government to take the noncitizen into physical custody at some point. A longstanding provision of the Judicial Code, 28 U.S.C. § 2241, gives federal district courts jurisdiction to issue writs of habeas corpus for persons "in custody in violation of the Constitution or laws * * * of the United States."

In 1961 Congress restructured judicial review by providing that noncitizens would obtain review of deportation orders, after exhausting administrative remedies, directly in the federal courts of appeals, under a procedure called a petition for review. If unsuccessful there, they could seek a writ of certiorari in the Supreme Court. Habeas corpus in the district court remained the avenue for review of exclusion orders for another 35 years, however. In 1996, Congress provided for a single form of "removal proceeding" at the administrative level, whether the respondent had been admitted or not, and then directed that virtually all judicial review should proceed to the court of appeals on petition for review. INA § 242 sets out the authorities and procedural requirements

Section 242 as enacted in 1996, however, purported to eliminate judicial review in several specific categories of cases, including most cases involving persons removable under the crime-related grounds of deportability and most cases involving discretionary waivers and discretionary relief from removal. INA § 242(a)(2)(B), (C). Some noncitizens denied judicial access challenged these 1996 restrictions, relying on the Suspension Clause, U.S. Const., Art. I, sec. 9, cl. 2. That clause states: "The privilege of the writ of habeas corpus shall not be suspended, unless when in Cases of Rebellion or Invasion the public Safety may require it." The Supreme Court's opinion suggested that the restrictions on judicial review raised serious constitutional questions. But the Court avoided a direct constitutional ruling by construing the 1996 amendments to leave open habeas review in the district courts, at least to consider "pure questions of law" that could not be heard in the courts of appeals. *INS v. St. Cyr*, 533 U.S. 289, 121 S.Ct. 2271, 150 L.Ed.2d 347 (2001).

Figure 4.5
Appeals to Federal Courts of Appeals of BIA Decisions, 1993–2014

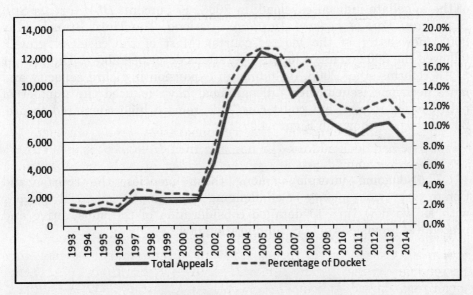

Source: Judicial Business of the U.S. Courts (1993–2014), http://www.uscourts.gov/ statistics-reports/analysis-reports/judicial-business-united-states-courts.

Congress responded to *St. Cyr* with legislation that reasserts in more precise language the exclusivity of the petition for review process in the courts of appeals, for noncitizens who want to get judicial review of a removal order. REAL ID Act of 2005, Pub. L. 109–13, Div. B, § 106, 119 Stat. 231, 302–05 (2005). But Congress also relented in some of its previous court-stripping ardor, in apparent recognition of the constitutional warnings in the *St. Cyr* decision. The REAL ID Act added a new INA § 242(a)(2)(D), which specifically preserves review in the courts of appeals of "constitutional claims or questions of law," notwithstanding virtually any other INA provision "which limits or eliminates judicial review." Today judicial review of removal-related matters flows directly to the courts of appeals, with the primary exception of challenges to detention that are unrelated to the merits of the removal case, which can be heard in district court. *See* Figure 4.3 *supra*.

Separate legislative provisions govern review of other decisions under the immigration laws that are not directly related to removal orders. Most significantly, under the general review provisions of the Administrative Procedure Act, 5 U.S.C. §§ 701–706 (2012), district courts hear challenges to USCIS benefit denials, at least in those circumstances where the issue is not open to consideration in a pending removal proceeding (which could raise an exhaustion-of-remedies barrier).

In the last 15 years, the federal courts experienced a dramatic rise in immigration cases. From calendar year 2001 to 2006, appeals from the BIA rose by 555 percent. In 2001 such appeals constituted three percent of the appellate judicial caseload; in 2006, 17 percent. *BIA Appeals Still Significant Part of Federal Appellate Caseload,* The Third Branch, May 2007 (newsletter of the federal courts). Most of the caseload growth followed the 2002 changes in BIA operations described above. The further EOIR reforms since 2008, including an expansion in Board capacity and more decisions issued with full opinions, have reduced the number of petitions for review, but court caseloads remain high compared to pre-2002 levels, as shown in Figure 4.5.

The ongoing interplay among these agencies, the courts, and Congress provides plenty of challenging and complex material to work with as we now turn to detailed consideration of the substantive and procedural provisions of U.S. immigration law.

CHAPTER FIVE

IMMIGRANTS AND NONIMMIGRANTS: ADMISSION CATEGORIES AND THE UNDOCUMENTED

∎ ∎ ∎

The American immigration system allows for the lawful admission of two broad groups of noncitizens: immigrants and nonimmigrants. Immigrants, as the label suggests, come to take up permanent residence, whereas nonimmigrants enter for a specific purpose to be accomplished during a temporary stay—which might nonetheless last for many years. A noncitizen in either group must show initially that he or she qualifies for admission by meeting one of several *categorical qualifying requirements*. He or she must also demonstrate that none of the many *inadmissibility grounds* in § 212(a) of the INA makes him or her ineligible.

This chapter examines the most common qualifying admission categories for both immigrants and nonimmigrants. It also looks at undocumented migration and the estimated 11 million persons now living in the United States without lawful immigration status. Later chapters will cover some topics closely related to admission categories. Chapters Six and Seven will describe discretionary measures, such as parole and deferred action, that may permit a noncitizen to be physically present with a form of legal blessing. Chapter Seven will consider the inadmissibility grounds, which may bar noncitizens even if they fit into an admission category. Chapter Eight will address the admission of refugees, as well as asylum, which can operate as an avenue of admission to the United States.

It is common to use the term *immigrant* to refer to all noncitizens who wish to stay in the United States indefinitely, legally or illegally. In contrast, this book will use *immigrant* as the statute does, to mean a noncitizen authorized to become *lawful permanent residents* (LPRs) of the United States. Informal lingo may refer to LPRs as *green card holders*, after the vernacular name for the chief document they receive. Permanent residents may stay as long as they wish, as long as they do not commit a crime or some other post-entry act that makes them deportable. Many immigrants choose to apply for naturalization after meeting the residence requirement—ordinarily five years—but they are not obligated to apply for citizenship. A person may remain in lawful permanent resident status indefinitely.

We will likewise follow the statute in using *nonimmigrant*; this term refers to noncitizens admitted to the United States for a temporary stay. One practical note, though: the line between nonimmigrants and immigrants is not as bright as you might think. Many immigrants first come to the United States as nonimmigrants, or even without any lawful immigration status at all, and then later become immigrants (that is, lawful permanent residents). This is especially true for noncitizens who become lawful permanent residents based on employment.

A. IMMIGRANTS

1. OVERVIEW

Assume that your client has been a lawful permanent resident of the United States for 10 years. Last month in Nairobi he married a national of Kenya who has a six-year-old child from a previous marriage, which was properly terminated by a valid divorce action. He wants to bring his wife and her child to this country as soon as possible.

This sort of scenario poses two basic questions. First, does this family relationship qualify your client's wife and her child to immigrate lawfully to the United States? To borrow language from current policy debates, does your client's wife and her child have an immigration line to stand in? Second, how long is that line—that is, how long must they wait? Consider this scenario as you read this Section A, and ask yourself how you would advise this client in light of admission categories and waiting periods.

a. Categories

Summary. Since 1921, the law has imposed annual numerical limitations—known in the immigration world as "quotas"—on most immigrant categories. The character of those limits changed considerably in 1965, when Congress abandoned the former national origins quota system. As Chapter One explained, that scheme, adopted in the 1920s, based quotas on country of origin, in order to preserve the ethnic composition of the United States at the turn of the twentieth century.

The current system has four main categories of immigrants:

(1) family-sponsored immigrants;

(2) employment-based immigrants;

(3) diversity immigrants; and

(4) humanitarian admissions.

Humanitarian admissions include the resettlement of refugees from outside the United States as well as persons who obtain asylum on U.S. soil. Over the past decade, overseas refugee admissions have run between 26,000 and 75,000 annually. Asylum grants have run between 20,000 and 40,000. Because these humanitarian admissions vary widely and are independent of developments in the other three categories, we will discuss the refugee and asylum provisions separately in Chapter Eight. In addition, the T and U nonimmigrant visa categories allow certain victims of human trafficking or of other specified forms of criminal abuse to become eligible for lawful permanent resident status. T and U visas can be considered types of humanitarian admissions, but because they generally operate as a form of relief from removal, we will cover them in Chapter Seven. This Section A focuses on the other three main categories.

The highest numbers of immigrant admissions are based on family ties. The admission of *immediate relatives* of U.S. citizens is numerically unlimited and recently has run about a half-million per year. In addition, about 226,000 family slots are allotted among four family-sponsored *preference* categories, which are based on specified relationships to citizens or lawful permanent residents. *See* INA §§ 201(b)(2)(A), 203(a).

Employment-based admissions are capped at about 140,000 annually, divided among five employment-based preference categories. *See* INA § 203(b). These workers' family members count against these ceilings. The workers themselves account for only about half of the 140,000 slots.

The third main admission category—diversity immigrants—accounts for about 50,000 individuals chosen by lottery each year from among applicants who meet the threshold requirements. In recent years, the annual lottery has attracted over 12 million applicants. Natives of about 15 to 20 countries that already send a high number of immigrants to the United States are not eligible.

Figure 5.1
Immigrant Admission Categories
(approximate number of annual admissions*)

- **Family-based** *Most common* [handwritten]
  - *[handwritten: immediate relatives]* Immediate relatives of U.S. citizens
    (no statutory ceiling; about 500,000 in recent years)
    - Spouses, children, and parents if petitioner is 21 or older
  - Preference categories (226,000 / year)
    - 1: unmarried sons and daughters of U.S. citizens
    - 2A: spouses and children of permanent residents
    - 2B: unmarried sons and daughters of permanent residents
    - 3: married sons and daughters of U.S. citizens
    - 4: brothers and sisters of U.S. citizens if citizen is 21 or older
- **Employment-based**
  - Preference categories (140,000 / year)
    - 1A: extraordinary ability
    - 1B: outstanding professors and researchers
    - 1C: multinational executives and managers
    - 2: advanced degrees or exceptional ability
    - 3: bachelor's degrees or shortage occupations
      (of these, 'unskilled workers' are capped at 5000 / year)
    - 4: special immigrants
    - 5: investors
- **Diversity immigrants (capped at 50,000 / year)**
- **Humanitarian**
    - overseas refugees
      (no statutory ceiling;
      between 56,000 and 75,000 refugee arrivals in 2009–2014)
    - asylum
      (no statutory ceiling;
      between 21,000 and 29,000 asylum grants in 2009–2014)

---

* Rough indicators, based on normal statutory ceilings, where applicable, or average of admissions in recent years, where no fixed ceiling applies. Annual numbers can vary significantly. For further explanation, see the material on Numerical Limits on pp. 281–282 later in this Section.

PROBLEMS

For each problem, assume you are an attorney approached for advice. What do you recommend? What further information do you need, if any?

There may be many ways to accomplish the client's aims; try to find the (most expeditious one,) paying attention to any backlogs in the preference categories for which your client may qualify. As to some, you should remember that a lawful permanent resident qualifies for naturalization, in most cases, after five years' residence in this country.

To analyze each problem, you will need to glean relevant information from the rest of this subsection A–1. For example, the latest monthly visa bulletin (a sample appears as Figure 5.7 below, p. 287) is indispensable.

1.) First, what is your advice to the client in this scenario from several pages ago: Your client has been a lawful permanent resident of the United States for 10 years. Last month in Nairobi he married a national of Kenya who has a six-year-old child by a previous marriage (which was properly terminated by a valid divorce action), and naturally he wants to bring his wife and her child to this country as soon as possible.

2.) Your client was admitted to the United States as a lawful permanent resident 15 years ago. He wants to bring his brother here from Greece.

3. Your client, a citizen of the Philippines, entered as a lawful permanent resident about ten months ago under the third family-sponsored preference, for married sons and daughters of U.S. citizens. At the time he brought with him his wife and three of his four children, leaving behind his eldest, a daughter who had already entered college and believed at the time that she did not want to emigrate. Now she has changed her mind, and would like to come to the United States and take up studies in this country as soon as possible. In answering, assume:

(a) that she is now three weeks short of her 21st birthday;

(b) that she turned 21 before you were consulted.

4. You have been contacted by a 20-year-old Swiss national who wishes to immigrate to the United States. He has heard that family ties are the key to immigration, and he tells you of his uncle in Chicago, who is a U.S. citizen and willing to do any necessary paperwork. He also reports that he has worked as a researcher for an engineering professor at his university, where he is completing his bachelor's degree in biomedical engineering.

5. Your client, a high school dropout, is the principal shareholder and chief executive officer of a Brazilian software firm with annual gross receipts equivalent to several million dollars. For many years, he has been thinking of establishing sales outlets in several other countries, possibly

including the United States. Whatever happens with the business, he wishes to take up permanent residence here. In advising him, what do you need to know about his educational background, and what difference would that information make?

b. Procedural Overview

Most immigration to the United States starts with a document called a *visa petition* filed by a person in the United States—usually a prospective employer, or a family member who is a U.S. citizen or lawful permanent resident. The relationship can qualify the noncitizen as an immigrant within an admission category. The employer or family member is known as the *petitioner;* the noncitizen who wishes to become a lawful permanent resident is the *beneficiary*.

For family categories, the relative in the United States typically files a visa petition with U.S. Citizenship and Immigration Services (USCIS), a part of the Department of Homeland Security (DHS). The petitioner must prove the necessary relationship with the noncitizen through birth or marriage certificates, or the like. In a limited set of other cases, noncitizens may petition for themselves. For example, victims of domestic violence at the hands of a citizen or lawful permanent resident spouse may do so. These noncitizens can qualify even if the abuser won't initiate the process.

For employment-based categories, the process often requires one preliminary step. The employer may first need to apply to the Department of Labor (DOL) for *labor certification*. This means that DOL certifies that the prospective lawful permanent resident will not be taking a job for which qualified U.S. workers (citizens or authorized noncitizens) are available. If DOL issues the certification, the employer then files a visa petition with USCIS, which verifies other qualifications, such as the employer's ability to pay the stated salary or wage. In some employment-based cases, the process is simpler—the employer can file the petition without first getting a labor certification. In other cases, no employer petition is needed; the prospective permanent resident may "self-petition" to initiate the process.

If USCIS is satisfied that the relationship is genuine and meets the legal requirements, it approves the visa petition. The next steps depend on the prospective permanent resident's location. If she is outside the United States, USCIS transmits the approval to the consulate in the country where the noncitizen will apply for the immigrant visa—normally the closest U.S. consulate in the immigrant's home country.

If the prospective permanent resident is already in the United States, she may not need to leave, get an immigrant visa, and reenter as a lawful permanent resident. In many cases, she may be eligible to apply to a

USCIS office in the United States for *adjustment of status*. *See* INA § 245. This means that her immigration status will be changed—*adjusted*—to immigrant, usually from a nonimmigrant status, such as a student.

[handwritten margin note: adjustment of status - if already in US. No need to leave]

c. Family-Sponsored Immigration

Immigrants may qualify as *immediate relatives* of U.S. citizens, INA § 201(b)(2)(A), or in one of the four family preference categories assigned to family reunification, *see* INA § 203(a). You may find it useful to consult these INA sections now and to refer to them as you read what follows.

Immediate relatives. "Immediate relative" is a term of art. It includes spouses and children, as well as parents of citizens who are over 21 years old. This limit on petitioning for parents reflects the United States' uniquely strong *jus soli* citizenship rules, under which virtually any child born on U.S. soil, even to parents who are present unlawfully, is a U.S. citizen. If not for the age requirement, newborns could immediately petition for their parents to become lawful permanent residents.

[handwritten margin note: 21 yrs age req'd avoid anchor babies"]

The statutory definition of "child," in INA § 101(b)(1) is long, complex, and precise. A "child" must be under 21 and unmarried. A stepchild may be a "child," if the marriage creating the stepparent-stepchild relationship took place before the stepchild's 18th birthday. An adopted child may be a child, if the adoption occurred before age 16. Children born out of wedlock may also count as children under the rules in § 101(b)(1)(D). A mother or father qualifies as a "parent" under the INA if the parental relationship was established while the offspring was a "child."

An unlimited number of immediate relatives can become lawful permanent residents, making this perhaps the most favored of all immigration categories. As Figure 5.2 shows, the number of immediate relatives (including both new arrivals and adjustments of status in the United States) is much higher than it was 40 years ago.

Figure 5.2
Immediate Relatives

Fiscal Year	Number
1970	79,213
1975	85,871
1980	145,992
1985	204,368
1990	231,680
1995	220,360 *> big jump*
2000	347,870
2005	436,115
2010	476,414
2011	453,158
2012	478,780 *– peak*
2013	439,460
2014	416,456

Sources: 1980 Statistical Abstract of the United States, Table 133 (for 1970–1975); 1980 INS Statistical Yearbook, Table 4 (for 1980); 1992 INS Statistical Yearbook, Table 4 (for 1985); 1996 INS Statistical Yearbook, Table 4 (for 1990); 2004 Yearbook of Immigration Statistics, Table 4 (for 1995, 2000); 2014 Yearbook of Immigration Statistics, Table 6 (for 2005–2014).

Family-sponsored preference categories. In contrast to immediate relatives, the family-sponsored preference categories have an annual cap, *see* INA § 203(a). With many more applicants than admission slots, backlogs develop. Admissions are processed within each family preference in chronological order, based on the filing date of the first document in the process. Actual annual admissions in each category may vary from the statutory ceiling, as explained in the material on Numerical Limits on pp. 281–282, later in this Section.

- **First preference**

    unmarried sons and daughters of U.S. citizens — over 21

    23,400 admissions annually

    Recall that unmarried children of citizens qualify as immediate relatives, not subject to numerical limits. Ask yourself: why then is this preference category necessary?

- **Second preference**

  spouses and unmarried sons and daughters of lawful permanent residents

  114,200 admissions annually

  Congress subdivided the second family-based preference into categories (A) and (B), with 77 percent of the slots reserved for spouses and minor children (category 2A): *[handwritten: spouses / unmarried children 18 & under]*

  87,934 annually

  Offspring 21 years of age or older (category 2B) may not claim more than 23 percent of this second preference: *[handwritten: unmarried children 21 & over]*

  26,266 annually

- **Third preference**

  married sons and daughters of U.S. citizens — *[handwritten: 21 & over? or 21 & under still?]*

  23,400 admissions annually

- **Fourth preference**

  brothers and sisters of U.S. citizens

  65,000 admissions annually

  Each sibling must have been the child of the same parent, and the petitioning citizen sibling must be at least 21 years old.

d. Employment-Based Immigration

The five employment-based (EB) categories have a total of 140,000 admissions annually, *see* INA § 203(b).

- **First preference**

  EB–1A: *extraordinary ability in the sciences, arts, education, business, or athletics* (requires "sustained national or international acclaim")

  EB–1B: *outstanding professors and researchers*

  EB–1C: *certain multinational executives and managers* (these two terms are defined in INA § 101(a)(44))

  40,000 admissions annually

- **Second preference**

  professionals with advanced degrees "or their equivalent" or who, "because of their exceptional ability in the sciences, arts, or business, will substantially benefit prospectively the national economy, cultural or educational interests, or welfare of the United States"

40,000 admissions annually

Their services must be sought by an employer, unless this requirement is waived "in the national interest."

- **Third preference**

professionals having only bachelor's degrees, and skilled and unskilled workers who would fill positions for which there is a shortage of American workers

40,000 admissions annually

As a compromise to put some pressure on employers with a need for unskilled labor to train or otherwise attract unemployed Americans, Congress capped the number of "unskilled" workers in the third employment-based preference to 5,000 annually.

- **Fourth preference**

"special immigrants," defined in INA § 101(a)(27)(C) through (M)

10,000 admissions annually

This preference category includes religious workers, former long-time employees of the U.S. government or of international organizations, and a host of other immigrants in miscellaneous categories. This category also includes immigrants in Special Immigrant Juvenile Status (SIJS), see Chapter Seven, p. 769.

- **Fifth preference**

investors

roughly 10,000 admissions annually

The investment must create a minimum of ten jobs in the U.S. economy. The minimum investment is $1,000,000, but less if the investment is in a rural area or high unemployment area, or if the money is invested through a "regional center" designated by USCIS based on an economic growth plan. See INA § 216A.

Petitioning. First, second and third employment-based preference immigrants generally cannot self-petition; an employer usually must petition for them. INA § 204(a)(1)(F). As exceptions, "aliens with extraordinary ability" (EB–1A), and second preference immigrants with a national-interest waiver can self-petition. Most fourth-and fifth-preference immigrants may also self-petition. *See* INA § 204(a)(1)(E), (G), (H).

Labor certification. Immigrants in the second employment-based preference also need a labor certification, unless the requirement is waived "in the national interest." Immigrants in the third employment-based preference always require a labor certification.

e. Diversity Immigration

When Congress ended national origins quotas in 1965, it anticipated that preference immigrants in the new system would not use all of the available slots. The excess would be open for "nonpreference" immigration, on a first-come first-served basis, to those who met certain minimal requirements. Such immigration did not require a petitioning family member in the United States, so it could include a more diverse group of immigrants. By 1978, however, demand in the preferences hit the overall preference ceiling, leaving no slots for nonpreference immigration.

Congress soon searched for ways to recapture some of the openness that nonpreference immigration signaled. Congress also sought to offset the steep reduction in European migration that occurred after the 1965 amendments to the INA. Supporters of the new provisions most often voiced concern about reduced immigration opportunities from Ireland.

After trying several different formulas for annual lotteries open to nationals of countries deemed underrepresented in admissions to the United States, Congress settled in 1990 on the diversity system in INA § 203(c). The statute decides which countries can share in the diversity admissions each year, applying an extraordinarily intricate formula based on immigration statistics from the preceding five years. Natives of "high admission countries" are ineligible to participate in the diversity lottery. For the FY 2017 lottery, this provision disqualified nationals from 19 countries: Bangladesh, Brazil, Canada, China (mainland-born), Colombia, Dominican Republic, Ecuador, El Salvador, Haiti, India, Jamaica, Mexico, Nigeria, Pakistan, Peru, Philippines, South Korea, United Kingdom (except Northern Ireland) and its dependent territories, and Vietnam.

Natives of all other countries qualify, but countries in low-admission regions get a larger share of the total number of diversity admissions; countries in high-admission regions get a smaller share. The 1990 legislation authorized 55,000 diversity admissions annually, but a later statute reduced the number to 50,000 for many years to come. Figure 5.3 shows the number of diversity admissions by region for fiscal year 2014.

Figure 5.3
Allocation of Diversity Admissions for FY 2014

Area	Number Admitted
Africa	23,199
Asia	16,355
Europe	11,713
Oceania	744
South America	837
North America	583
Unknown or not reported	59
Total	53,490

Source: 2014 Yearbook of Immigration Statistics, Table 10.

Qualifying for a diversity visa requires (1) a high school education or its equivalent, or (2) within five years preceding the application, at least two years of experience in an occupation that requires at least two years of training or experience. *See* INA § 203(c)(2). There is a separate application for each annual lottery, and only one application per year is allowed. Applications must be filed online, with digital photographs. Instructions are on the State Department's web page. A random lottery then selects the beneficiaries. A winner can bring a spouse and children; they count against the total diversity ceiling.

Registration for diversity admissions during FY 2015 was held from October 1 to November 2, 2013. From over 9.38 million qualified applications, the State Department selected 125,514 and notified them that they may be eligible and should gather the needed information. This figure far exceeds the annual 50,000 limit, anticipating that many of those notified will not pursue their cases or ultimately will not qualify. The Department provides each notified individual a rank-order number, and it then allows only those below a certain cut-off number to apply.

As the responses, qualification rate, and number of accompanying spouse and children become clear, the Department adjusts the cut-off number monthly, so that more lottery winners further down the list can apply for a visa or adjustment of status. This process involves agonizing uncertainty for those whose rank-order number is reached only late in the fiscal year. If a notified person is tardy with an application or the processing is slow, an apparent lottery winner can become a loser at midnight on September 30, when the fiscal year expires, or earlier, if the 50,000 ceiling is reached.

The top recipient countries for FY 2015, based on notifications rather than admissions, were: Cameroon, Liberia, Iran, Nepal, Ethiopia, Egypt,

Democratic Republic of the Congo, Ukraine, Uzbekistan, and Russia, in that order. *See* Department of State, DV 2015 - Selected Entrants.

f. Family Members: "Derivatives"

Suppose a noncitizen qualifies in the third family preference as a married daughter of a U.S. citizen, but that the noncitizen's husband and children do not personally meet the third preference requirements and have no other way of directly qualifying for admission to the United States. Must they wait until she becomes a lawful permanent resident and then successfully petitions for them in the second family preference?

The answer is no. Section 203(d)—which also applies to employment-based and diversity immigration—is designed to avoid such separation of nuclear families. It provides that the spouse or child may be admitted in the same preference category and in the "same order of consideration" as the principal immigrant. This means at the same spot on the waiting list, when there is a backlog. The admissions of these family members—known as *derivative beneficiaries*—are charged against the ceiling for the principal's preference category. This feature has prompted the criticism that most of the 140,000 slots nominally for employment-based immigration are actually used by derivatives and not by the workers themselves.

Section 203(d) applies to both accompanying family members and those "following to join." Administrative practice treats derivatives as "following to join" at any time after the principal becomes a lawful permanent resident, as long as the derivative is still a spouse or child. The benefits of § 203(d) are available only if the specified relationship existed when the principal became a lawful permanent resident. A lawful permanent resident's "after-acquired" spouse or child must use the second preference. *See Matter of Naulu*, 19 I & N Dec. 351, 352 n.1 (BIA 1986).

Section 203(d) has one major limitation. As written, it applies only to a spouse or child of a noncitizen who becomes a lawful permanent resident under § 203(a), (b), or (c). What if a noncitizen becomes a lawful permanent resident as a U.S. citizen's immediate relative? Immediate relatives qualify as immigrants under § 201(b)(2)(A)(i), so a spouse or child cannot use § 203(d). A child in such cases will usually qualify in his own right as the petitioning citizen's immediate relative, typically as a stepchild who is a "child" under § 101(b)(1). But can you identify scenarios where an immediate relative's spouse or child will not qualify on his own and so cannot become a permanent resident at the same time?

g. Numerical Limits

Overall caps. At first glance, INA § 201(c) seems to put an annual ceiling of 480,000 on all family-sponsored immigration, including immediate relatives. But there is no such cap in practice. To explain:

immediate relative admissions are unlimited. Congress was concerned that if the statute capped overall family-based immigration but immediate relative admissions grew, then the number of admissions in the family preference categories would necessarily shrink. Rather than simply eliminate a nominal overall ceiling, Congress adopted the complex formula in INA § 201(c). It guarantees an annual minimum of 226,000 admission slots for the family-sponsored preference categories. When combined with the number of immediate relative admissions—about 500,000 in recent years—total family-based immigration is well above 480,000.

Figure 5.4 shows admission totals, by major categories, for selected years since 1995. The totals are sometimes higher or lower (or much lower) than the statutory allotment, even though waiting lists are long. Most of the fluctuation is due to processing bottlenecks that reflect resource allocations within federal government agencies, coupled with catch-up numbers the following year, as explained below. Current processing times for specific types of applications are available on the USCIS website.

Admission spaces that go unused in the preference categories in one year are added to the next year's totals. These spaces are distributed in a highly complex fashion and often go into a different category than the one that fell short the year before. For explanation of this distribution, see Seton Stapleton, *Immigrant Visa Availability under the Immigration Act of 1990: Initial Observations from the Visa Office*, 68 Interp. Rel. 373 (1991); Jeffrey A. Devore & Xiomara M. Hernandez, *Priority Dates: More Important Than Ever,* 11–20 Bender's Immigr. Bull. 2 (2006).

Figure 5.4
Immigrants Admitted by Major Category of Admission, Selected Years, FY 1995–2014

	1995	2000	2005	2010	2012	2013	2014
All Immigrants	720,461	841,002	1,122,257	1,042,625	1,031,631	990,553	1,016,518
Immediate relatives	220,360	346,350	436,115	476,414	478,780	439,460	416,456
Family-sponsored preferences	238,122	235,092	212,970	214,589	202,019	210,303	229,104
1st preference	15,182	27,003	24,729	26,998	20,660	24,358	25,686
2nd preference	144,535	112,015	100,139	92,088	99,709	99,115	105,641
3rd preference	20,876	24,830	22,953	32,817	21,752	21,294	25,830
4th preference	57,529	67,851	65,149	62,686	59,898	65,536	71,947
Employ-ment-based preferences	85.336	106,642	246,865	148,343	143,998	161,110	151,596
1st preference	17,339	27,566	64,731	41,055	39,316	38,978	40,554
2nd preference	10,475	20,255	42,597	53,946	50,959	63,026	48,801
3rd preference	50,245	49,589	129,070	39,762	39,229	43,632	43,156
4th preference	6,737	9,014	10,121	11,100	7,866	6,931	8,362
5th preference	540	218	346	2,480	6,628	8,543	10,732
Diversity Immigrants	40,301	50,920	46,234	49,763	40,320	45,618	53,490
Refugees & Asylees*	114,664	62,928	142,962	136,291	150,614	119,630	134,242
Other**	17,411	39,070	37,111	17,225	15,900	14,432	31,630

* Refugees and asylees are counted in the year when they adjust status to lawful permanent resident (at least one year after the initial admission or asylum grant).

** Noncitizens granted cancellation of removal are the largest group in this category.

Sources: 2004 Yearbook of Immigration Statistics, Table 4 (for 1995);
2009 Yearbook of Immigration Statistics, Table 6 (for 2000);
2014 Yearbook of Immigration Statistics, Table 6 (for 2005–2014).

Figure 5.5
Lawful Permanent Residents by Major Category, FY 2014

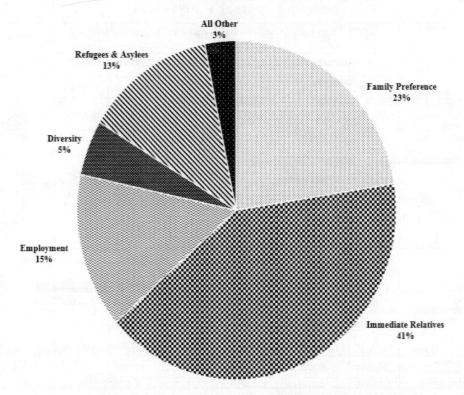

Source: 2014 Yearbook of Immigration Statistics, Table 6.

Figure 5.5 shows major categories of new lawful permanent residents in FY 2014. Family categories were over 63 percent of the total, and of the family categories, immediate relatives were about two-thirds. Figure 5.6 then shows how immigration from the top ten sending countries—which together accounted for 48 percent of new lawful permanent residents—breaks down by category. The patterns are strikingly different among populations—for example, a vast predominance of family-based immigration for Mexico, heavy refugee-type immigration for Cuba, and major concentrations of employment-based immigration from India and South Korea, followed by China and the Philippines.

Per-country ceilings. Applying the annual category ceilings is complicated enough, but further complexity comes from per-country ceilings under INA § 202. After Congress repealed the national origins quotas, it added these ceilings as their own kind of diversity provision, assuring that no single country received over 20,000 admissions annually in all preference categories combined. The ceilings had especially harsh effects on Mexico and the Philippines, where demand for U.S.

immigration is particularly strong due to geographical, historical, and economic ties.

Figure 5.6
Top Ten LPR-Sending Countries, FY 2014

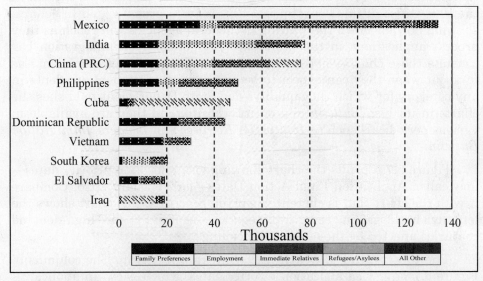

Source: 2014 Yearbook of Immigration Statistics, Table 10.

The per-country ceilings apply only to the family-based and employment-based preference categories. The number of immediate relatives who become lawful permanent residents do not count against a country's ceiling. Diversity immigrants are subject to a separate per-country ceiling provision (currently 3,500). *See* INA § 203(c)(1)(E)(v).

The current per-country ceiling is at least 25,620. It may be somewhat higher depending on fluctuations in the number of visas issued in a given fiscal year. The statute exempts some preference admissions under limited circumstances. *See, e.g.*, INA § 202(a)(5). Admissions are charged to a country based on the immigrant's birthplace, not nationality, with a few exceptions designed primarily to keep families together. INA § 202(b).

The per-country limit is sometimes misunderstood. It does not mean that each country may send about 25,000 preference immigrants each year to the United States. Instead, the provision kicks in only if the system's normal operation would push annual preference immigration from any country over the ceiling. Countries at the per-country ceiling are subject to special allocation rules, which divide up that country's preference immigrant slots among all of its preferences. *See* INA § 202(e). As a result, the monthly visa bulletin in Figure 5.7 shows separate cut-off dates for China, India, Mexico, and the Philippines.

h.   In Practice: Visa Charts, Conversion, and Aging Out

Visa allocation priority date charts. Fortunately, practicing immigration lawyers never need to attempt the ceiling calculations required under §§ 201, 202, and 203. That complex task falls to officials of the Visa Office of the Department of State, who prepare monthly charts showing how far down the waiting list federal agencies will reach as they process applications in the preference categories. The immigration bar consults those charts—not the statutory sections—in advising clients as to about when they can expect to become lawful permanent residents in any category for which they qualify. The State Department publishes the charts in its *Visa Bulletin* and on its website, and they are available in various periodicals such as *Interpreter Releases* and *Benders' Immigration Bulletin*.

Figure 5.7 reprints the chart showing visa allocation priority dates—now called Application Final Action Dates—for February 2016. Compare it with the chart that is current when you read this. The chart shows the lengthy backlogs in several categories, especially for high-demand countries affected by the per-country ceilings.

The charts and allocation system in operation. The columns in Figure 5.7 have visa allocation priority dates, which show an applicant's approximate position on the waiting list. Within each preference, visas are issued in chronological order of application. Until a preference immigrant's priority date is current—that is, *before* the date shown—she may not receive a visa or adjust to lawful permanent resident status.

The priority date is the date when the first required document was properly filed with the appropriate federal agency. This is the visa petition for the family categories and some employment preferences, and the application for labor certification for the employment preferences that require it. Note that even when an applicant reaches the front of the line—no visa will issue until all eligibility determinations are concluded.

Figure 5.7
Application Final Action Dates for February 2016

	All chargeability areas except those listed	CHINA-mainland born	INDIA	MEXICO	PHILIPPINES
Family-Sponsored Preferences					
1st Preference	July 8, 2008	July 8, 2008	July 8, 2008	January 1, 1995	November 1, 2003
2nd Preference (A)	September 1, 2014	September 1, 2014	September 1, 2014	June 8, 2014	September 1, 2014
2nd Preference (B)	May 15, 2009	May 15, 2009	May 15, 2009	September 8, 1995	February 1, 2005
3rd Preference	October 1, 2004	October 1, 2004	October 1, 2004	September 8, 1994	November 22, 1993
4th Preference	June 8, 2003	June 8, 2003	June 8, 2003	April 1, 1997	August 8, 1992
Employment-Based Preferences					
1st Preference	C	C	C	C	C
2nd Preference	C	March 1, 2012	August 1, 2008	C	C
3rd Preference	October 1, 2015	October 1, 2012	June 15, 2004	October 1, 2015	January 8, 2008
Other workers	October 1, 2015	December 22, 2006	June 15, 2004	October 1, 2015	January 8, 2008
4th Preference	C	C	C	C	C
Certain Religious Workers	C	C	C	C	C
5th Preference	C	January 15, 2014	C	C	C

Source: Department of State, Visa Bulletin No. 89, Volume IX (February 2016).

Assume, for example, that an employer applies for labor certification for a stated job on April 1, 2014, and that the Department of Labor issues the certification on March 1, 2015. The employer then files a visa petition with USCIS for the appropriate employment-based preference category. The visa petition is approved on September 1, 2015. The approval is communicated to the U.S. consulate where the immigrant will apply for an immigrant visa, or to the USCIS office where he will apply to adjust status.

In this scenario, the immigrant's priority date is April 1, 2014. As of February 2016, was his priority date current, allowing him to pursue the last stages of processing? The fact that he needs a labor certification tells you that he applied in one of two possible employment categories. Figure

5.7 shows that the second employment-based preference is current (unless the immigrant was born in China or India), so he may be scheduled for his final consular interview, or, if in the United States, he may apply to adjust status. But if he is in the third preference and was born in China, he must wait. In February 2016, only Chinese natives with a priority date before October 1, 2012, could be processed in that category. In February 2016, most employment-based categories were current, but the third preference had a backlog, and processing required a priority date before October 1, 2015. "Other workers"—the "unskilled," whose admissions are limited to a fraction of the EB–3 slots—often face longer delays.

The family categories are chronically backlogged because of high qualifying demand. As an example in a family-sponsored preference, assume that on February 7, 2014, a U.S. citizen father files a first preference petition with USCIS for his 26-year-old daughter, a native of Brazil. He is required to file additional evidence to confirm the authenticity of his daughter's birth certificate, and the petition is not approved until April 20, 2015. Approval is soon communicated to the U.S. consulate in Rio de Janeiro. The daughter's priority date is February 7, 2014. Qualifying in the family-sponsored first preference, she still faces a lengthy wait. As of February 2016, family first preference is current only if the immigrant's priority date is before July 8, 2008. You can check the prior visa bulletins to see how much any category has advanced over time.

There is one more wrinkle in working with the monthly Visa Bulletin. It includes separate charts with a second set of dates—called Dates for Filing Applications—that allow some family-sponsored and employment-based preference immigrants to initiate their applications earlier, to make up for some of the time that the application process will take.

Conversion. If the Brazilian daughter in this scenario marries before admission to the United States, she no longer qualifies for the first preference. But she can keep the same priority date for the category in which she now qualifies: the third family-sponsored preference. The visa petition automatically *converts* to a petition in the newly relevant family category, with her original priority date. She need not go to the end of a new line. Agency regulations allow conversion for some other changes in the petitioner or beneficiary's status. *See* 8 C.F.R. § 204.2(i).

Most important may be when a petitioner files a family 2A preference petition for his spouse and children, and then naturalizes. The petition converts automatically to an immediate relative petition for the spouse and minor children. For unmarried sons and daughters over 21, the petitioner's naturalization converts the petition from family 2B

[handwritten margin note: if daughter marries petition is converted]

[handwritten margin note: naturalization may speed up the process]

preference to first preference. Normally conversion is advantageous, but if the first preference backlog is longer, the son or daughter may choose to continue to be treated in the family 2B preference. *See* INA § 204(k).

Aging out. Immigration law usually treats sons and daughters under 21 more favorably than those who have turned 21. But what date counts for calculating the child's age? Possibilities include: (a) when the petitioner files the visa petition, (b) when the petition is approved, (c) when the beneficiary applies for an immigrant visa or adjustment of status, (d) when the visa issues, and (e) when actual admission or adjustment occurs. Until 2002, the pertinent date was the latest—the actual date of admission or adjustment. This maximized the chances of "aging out." Children who turned 21 before admission or adjustment fell into a less favorable category or became completely ineligible.

In 2002, Congress responded with the Child Status Protection Act (CSPA), Pub. L. No. 107–208, 116 Stat. 927 (2002) (codified principally in INA §§ 201(f), 203(h), and 204(k)). For immediate relatives, the child's age is deemed to be the age when the parent files the visa petition. *See Matter of Avila-Perez,* 24 I & N Dec. 78 (BIA 2007). If the petition begins as a second preference petition but converts to an immediate relative petition when the parent naturalizes, what counts is the child's age when naturalization occurs. *See* INA § 201(f).

The rules are more complicated for the family 2A preference and for derivative beneficiaries under § 203(d). Recall that offspring in these groups becomes ineligible on their 21st birthday. The CSPA determines the child's age is in two steps. First, how old is the child when the relevant preference category becomes current? This could take over ten years for the fourth preference—or over twenty years for the fourth preference for the Philippines. Second, reduce that age by the period of time that the visa petition was pending between filing and the USCIS decision. This reduction is *only* for adjudicating of the visa petition itself. Delays in visa processing or adjustment of status do not matter. Finally, the beneficiary must seek to acquire the visa or adjustment within one year after the category becomes current, or else lose the benefit of these rules. *See* INA § 203(h).

To illustrate: a U.S. citizen petitions for his noncitizen brother. The brother has a daughter who is ten at that time. His fourth preference priority date becomes current 13 years later. Is the daughter, now 23, too old to be admitted under § 203(d) as a derivative? If the federal government took three years to approve the petition for her father, the three years is now deducted from her age. She is treated as 20 years old. She qualifies for derivative status—*if* her father applies for an immigrant visa or adjustment of status within a year after fourth preference becomes current. As a variation, what if the visa petition for her father had been approved more quickly, one year after filing? Now only one year is deducted from her age. She is treated as 22 and is ineligible. For more on how these rules work, see 79 Interp. Rel. 1433, 1503, 1520 (2002); 80 *id.* 243 (2003).

You may want to return to Problem 3 on p. 273 and consider one nuance in the Child Status Protection Act. INA § 203(h)(3) addresses cases in which "the age of an alien is determined . . . to be 21 years of age or older." It provides:

> the alien's petition shall automatically be converted to the appropriate category and the alien shall retain the original priority date issued upon the receipt of the original petition.

Will this clause help the daughter in Problem 3 if she has aged out of derivative status in spite of the application of INA § 203(h)? She is too old for admission as a derivative under § 203(d). Her father must file a family 2B preference petition for her. What is her priority date for this petition? Normally, it is the date when the *father* files the family 2B petition, not the petitioning date when her grandparent filed the long-ago third preference petition that was the basis for the admission of the rest of her family. But § 203(h)(3) says that "the alien shall retain the original priority date." Does this let the daughter use the priority date from the original third preference petition on her father's behalf? If so, her wait in the long family 2B preference line will be much shorter; in fact she would almost surely qualify immediately with such an early priority date.

The BIA interpreted § 203(h)(3) not to let the intending immigrant use the older, more advantageous priority date in such cases. *See Matter of Wang,* 25 I & N Dec. 28 (BIA 2009). After the federal courts of appeals split on the issue, the U.S. Supreme Court ruled 5–4 in 2014 to uphold the BIA's reading of § 203(h)(3). *See Scialabba v. Cuellar de Osorio,* 134 S.Ct. 2191 (2014). The plurality, in an opinion by Justice Kagan, found § 203(h)(3) to be "through and through perplexing," *id.* at 2200, and that it was sufficiently contradictory and ambiguous to warrant deference to the BIA under the landmark Supreme Court decision in *Chevron, U.S.A., Inc. v. Natural Resources Defense Council, Inc.,* 467 U.S. 837, 104 S.Ct. 2778, 81 L.Ed.2d 694 (1984).

Chevron established a two-step analysis for courts to apply when they review an agency's reading of a statute that the agency administers:

> First, always, is the question whether Congress has directly spoken to the precise question at issue. If the intent of Congress is clear, that is the end of the matter; for the court, as well as the agency, must give effect to the unambiguously expressed intent of Congress. If, however, the court determines Congress has not

directly addressed the precise question at issue, the court does not simply impose its own construction of the statute, as would be necessary in the absence of an administrative interpretation. Rather, if the statute is silent or ambiguous, the question for the court is whether the agency's answer is based on a permissible construction of the statute.

467 U.S. at 842–43, 104 S.Ct. at 2781–82.

In *Cuellar de Osorio*, Justice Kagan explained:

The argument [against the BIA's interpretation] assumes that the respondents' sons and daughters should "receive credit" for all the time the respondents themselves stood in line. * * * But if the parent had died while waiting for a visa, or had been found ineligible, or had decided not to immigrate after all, the derivative would have gotten nothing for the time spent in line. Similarly, the Board could reasonably conclude, he should not receive credit for his parent's wait when he has become old enough to live independently. In the unavoidably zero-sum world of allocating a limited number of visas, the Board could decide that he belongs behind any alien who has had a lengthier stand-alone entitlement to immigrate. * * *

This is the kind of case *Chevron* was built for. Whatever Congress might have meant in enacting § 203(h)(3), it failed to speak clearly. Confronted with a self-contradictory, ambiguous provision in a complex statutory scheme, the Board chose a textually reasonable construction consonant with its view of the purposes and policies underlying immigration law. Were we to overturn the Board in that circumstance, we would assume as our own the responsible and expert agency's role. We decline that path, and defer to the Board.

Id. at 2213.

Justices Roberts and Scalia concurred in the judgment, objecting to the plurality's view that self-contradictory statutes receive *Chevron* deference, but still finding this statute ambiguous enough to reach the same result. Justice Alito and Justice Sotomayor each wrote a dissent, the latter joined by Justice Breyer and (except for one footnote) Justice Thomas. According to Sotomayor, before courts find ambiguity they are called upon to interpret statutes as a "coherent regulatory scheme," fitting, if possible, all parts into a "harmonious whole." *Id.* at 2217. She emphasized that Congress's clear intent was to preserve the earlier priority date, no matter when or how an "appropriate category" becomes available.

Note on Administrative Law:
The *Chevron* Doctrine, *Mead,* and *Brand X*

The rationale. In *Chevron*, the U.S. Supreme Court explained some of the reasons for deference to agency interpretation of statutes:

> "The power of an administrative agency to administer a congressionally created . . . program necessarily requires the formulation of policy and the making of rules to fill any gap left, implicitly or explicitly, by Congress." *Morton v. Ruiz*, 415 U.S. 199, 231, 94 S.Ct. 1055, 1072, 39 L.Ed.2d 270 (1974). If Congress has explicitly left a gap for the agency to fill, there is an express delegation of authority to the agency to elucidate a specific provision of the statute by regulation. Such legislative regulations are given controlling weight unless they are arbitrary, capricious, or manifestly contrary to the statute. Sometimes the legislative delegation to an agency on a particular question is implicit rather than explicit. In such a case, a court may not substitute its own construction of a statutory provision for a reasonable interpretation made by the administrator of an agency.

467 U.S. at 842–44, 104 S.Ct. at 2781–83.

Such deference may also be justified on additional grounds. First, the agency works with the statute on a daily basis and is likely to better understand the operational implications of construing a statute in a certain way. The agency will also better understand how possible constructions would affect or fit with other provisions in ways that a generalist court may not appreciate; this may especially be true with a statute as complex as the INA. Second, the agency may have aided in drafting of the statute and therefore have greater insight than the courts into the intent behind the provision and the language chosen. Finally, deference to agency interpretation may create greater uniformity in application of the statute than would be achieved under different opinions among courts of appeals.

Mead. The Supreme Court limited the application of the *Chevron* doctrine in *United States v. Mead Corp.*, 533 U.S. 218, 121 S.Ct. 2164, 150 L.Ed.2d 292 (2001). The Court ruled that not all instances of "administrative implementation of a particular statutory provision" receive *Chevron* deference. There are two prerequisites. First, Congress must have "delegated authority to the agency generally to make rules carrying the force of law." Second, the agency interpretation must have been "promulgated in the exercise of that authority." 533 U.S. at 227, 121 S.Ct. at 2171.

Mead suggests that interpretations would ordinarily meet this test if they result from formal agency decisionmaking—such as notice-and-comment rulemaking, or adjudications in a "relatively formal administrative procedure." Less formal agency interpretations receive the lower level of deference outlined in *Skidmore v. Swift & Co.*, 323 U.S. 134, 139–40, 65 S.Ct. 161, 89 L.Ed. 124 (1944). Under *Skidmore*, courts look "to the degree of the agency's care, its consistency, formality, and relative expertness, and to the persuasiveness of the agency's position," and then decide how much to defer to the agency. *Mead*, 533 U.S. at 228. Most agency interpretations of immigration statutes appear either in regulations issued after notice and comment, or in Board of Immigration Appeals (BIA) precedent decisions. Because such interpretations emerge from a formal procedure, they generally merit *Chevron* rather than *Skidmore* deference.

Brand X. The BIA, like other administrative agencies, generally yields to a court interpretation in any circuit where the legal question has been settled. This can mean, for example, that it applies one interpretation in the Eleventh Circuit and the contrary interpretation in the Ninth Circuit—a practice known as "intra-circuit acquiescence." When the BIA faces the same question in a case arising in a circuit that has not yet ruled on the issue, the BIA will choose what it believes is the better interpretation, to be applied by immigration judges and the DHS in any circuit that has not adopted a conflicting interpretation. In such circumstances, making national law uniform would seem to require a U.S. Supreme Court decision. Indeed, resolving circuit splits is one important function of the Court. But a 2005 Supreme Court decision applied *Chevron* in a way that opens up another path toward nationwide uniformity.

In *National Cable & Telecommunications Assn. v. Brand X Internet Services*, 545 U.S. 967, 125 S.Ct. 2688, 162 L.Ed.2d 820 (2005), the circuit court had overruled the Federal Communications Commission's interpretation of a statute. The court of appeals had already construed the statute, reaching a different result before the FCC had occasion to decide the issue. The court of appeals held that its earlier judicial interpretation bound the FCC. The Supreme Court disagreed:

> A court's prior judicial construction of a statute trumps an agency construction otherwise entitled to *Chevron* deference only if the prior court decision holds that its construction follows from the unambiguous terms of the statute and thus leaves no room for agency discretion. This principle follows from *Chevron* itself. *Chevron* established a "presumption that Congress, when it left ambiguity in a statute meant for implementation by an agency, understood that the ambiguity would be resolved, first and foremost, by the agency, and desired the agency (rather than the

courts) to possess whatever degree of discretion the ambiguity allows." *Smiley [v. Citibank (South Dakota), N.A.,* 517 U.S. 735, 740–41 (1996)]. Yet allowing a judicial precedent to foreclose an agency from interpreting an ambiguous statute, as the Court of Appeals assumed it could, would allow a court's interpretation to override an agency's. *Chevron's* premise is that it is for agencies, not courts, to fill statutory gaps. The better rule is to hold judicial interpretations contained in precedents to the same demanding *Chevron* step one standard that applies if the court is reviewing the agency's construction on a blank slate: Only a judicial precedent holding that the statute unambiguously forecloses the agency's interpretation, and therefore contains no gap for the agency to fill, displaces a conflicting agency construction.

A contrary rule would produce anomalous results. It would mean that whether an agency's interpretation of an ambiguous statute is entitled to *Chevron* deference would turn on the order in which the interpretations issue: If the court's construction came first, its construction would prevail, whereas if the agency's came first, the agency's construction would command *Chevron* deference. Yet whether Congress has delegated to an agency the authority to interpret a statute does not depend on the order in which the judicial and administrative constructions occur. The Court of Appeals' rule, moreover, would "lead to the ossification of large portions of our statutory law," *Mead, supra,* at 247 (Scalia, J., dissenting), by precluding agencies from revising unwise judicial constructions of ambiguous statutes. Neither *Chevron* nor the doctrine of *stare decisis* requires these haphazard results.

The dissent answers that allowing an agency to override what a court believes to be the best interpretation of a statute makes "judicial decisions subject to reversal by Executive officers." ([O]pinion of Scalia, J.). It does not. Since *Chevron* teaches that a court's opinion as to the best reading of an ambiguous statute an agency is charged with administering is not authoritative, the agency's decision to construe that statute differently from a court does not say that the court's holding was legally wrong. Instead, the agency may, consistent with the court's holding, choose a different construction, since the agency remains the authoritative interpreter (within the limits of reason) of such statutes. In all other respects, the court's prior ruling remains binding law (for example, as to agency interpretations to which *Chevron* is inapplicable). The precedent has not been "reversed" by the agency, any more than a federal court's interpretation of a State's law can be said to have been "reversed" by a state court that adopts a conflicting (yet authoritative) interpretation of state law.

545 U.S., at 982–85. For examples of the BIA's exercise of the authority recognized in *Brand X,* see *Matter of Diaz-Castaneda,* 25 I & N Dec. 188 (BIA 2010); *Matter of Guevara Alfaro,* 25 I & N Dec. 417 (BIA 2011).

Inconsistent agency interpretations. *Brand X* helped to clarify this dictum from the Supreme Court decision in *INS v. Cardoza-Fonseca,* 480 U.S. 421, 447 n.30, 107 S.Ct. 1207, 1221 n.30, 94 L.Ed.2d 434 (1987):

> An agency interpretation of a relevant provision which conflicts with the agency's earlier interpretation is "entitled to considerably less deference" than a consistently held agency view.

Though this sentence seems to call for reduced deference when an agency changes its initial interpretation, *Brand X* explained to the contrary:

> Agency inconsistency is not a basis for declining to analyze the agency's interpretation under the *Chevron* framework. Unexplained inconsistency is, at most, a reason for holding an interpretation to be an arbitrary and capricious change from agency practice under the Administrative Procedure Act. For if the agency adequately explains the reasons for a reversal of policy, "change is not invalidating, since the whole point of *Chevron* is to leave the discretion provided by the ambiguities of a statute with the implementing agency." *Smiley* v. *Citibank (South Dakota), N. A.,* 517 U.S. 735, 742 (1996). "An initial agency interpretation is not instantly carved in stone. On the contrary, the agency ... must consider varying interpretations and the wisdom of its policy on a continuing basis," *Chevron,* [467 U.S.] at 863–864, for example, in response to changed factual circumstances, or a change in administrations.

545 U.S. at 981.

Does the *Chevron* approach—as modified by *Mead* and *Brand X*—give too much authority to administrative agencies in the federal executive branch? This fundamental question and the precise application of *Chevron* as modified are well worth keeping in mind throughout your study of immigration law, for they are core issues in many immigration law decisions in the courts.

2. CONSTITUTIONAL STANDARDS FOR EVALUATING ADMISSION CATEGORIES

The preference categories and the other provisions of the INA governing immigrant admissions inevitably draw a host of fine distinctions among categories of noncitizens who might wish to immigrate to the United States. The fairness and desirability of such distinctions are open to much debate. Is it fair or desirable, for example, to burden citizens of Mexico or the Philippines with inordinately long waiting lists, solely because the per-country ceiling provisions fail to take account of the substantial historical or economic ties between the United States and those nations? Is it fair or desirable to hold India or the People's Republic of China, with over a billion people, to the same per-country ceiling as Belize? Should marriage disqualify the offspring of permanent residents?

Questions like these are the stuff of wide-ranging debates over legislative reform of the U.S. immigration system. But to what extent are they constitutional questions, subject to policing by the federal courts? The U.S. Supreme Court considered this in the following case. The litigation challenged the definition of "child" in INA § 101(b)(1)(D) as it read before Congress amended it in 1986. At the time of the decision, the statute recognized only the relationship between children born out of wedlock and their natural *mothers*, excluding such relationships with natural *fathers*.

FIALLO V. BELL

Supreme Court of the United States, 1977.
430 U.S. 787, 97 S.Ct. 1473, 52 L.Ed.2d 50.

MR. JUSTICE POWELL delivered the opinion of the Court.

This case brings before us a constitutional challenge to §§ 101(b)(1)(D) and 101(b)(2) of the Immigration and Nationality Act of 1952 (Act).

I

The Act grants special preference immigration status to aliens who qualify as the "children" or "parents" of United States citizens or lawful permanent residents. Under § 101(b)(1), a "child" is defined as an unmarried person under 21 years of age who is a legitimate or legitimated child, a stepchild, an adopted child, or an illegitimate child seeking preference by virtue of his relationship with his natural mother. The definition does not extend to an illegitimate child seeking preference by virtue of his relationship with his natural father. Moreover, under § 101(b)(2), a person qualifies as a "parent" for purposes of the Act solely on the basis of the person's relationship with a "child." As a result, the natural father of an illegitimate child who is either a United States citizen or permanent resident alien is not entitled to preferential treatment as a "parent."

The special preference immigration status provided for those who satisfy the statutory "parent-child" relationship depends on whether the immigrant's relative is a United States citizen or permanent resident alien.[a] A United States citizen is allowed the entry of his "parent" or "child" without regard to *either* an applicable numerical quota *or* the labor certification requirement. On the other hand, a United States permanent resident alien is allowed the entry of the "parent" or "child" subject to numerical limitations but without regard to the labor certification requirement.

Appellants are three sets of unwed natural fathers and their illegitimate offspring who sought, either as an alien father or an alien child, a special immigration preference by virtue of a relationship to a citizen or resident alien child or parent. In each instance the applicant was informed that he was ineligible for an immigrant visa unless he qualified for admission under the general numerical limitations and, in the case of the alien parents, received the requisite labor certification.

* * * At the outset, it is important to underscore the limited scope of judicial inquiry into immigration legislation. This Court has repeatedly emphasized that "over no conceivable subject is the legislative power of Congress more complete than it is over" the admission of aliens. *Oceanic Navigation Co. v. Stranahan*, 214 U.S. 320, at 339, 29 S.Ct. 671, at 676 (1909). Our cases "have long recognized the power to expel or exclude aliens as a fundamental sovereign attribute exercised by the Government's political departments largely immune from judicial control." *Shaughnessy v. Mezei*, 345 U.S. 206, at 210, 73 S.Ct. 625, at 628 (1953). Our recent decisions have not departed from this long-established rule. Just last Term, for example, the Court had occasion to note that "the power over aliens is of a political character and therefore subject only to narrow judicial review." *Hampton v. Mow Sun Wong*, 426 U.S. 88, at 101 n. 21, 96 S.Ct. 1895, at 1904–1905, (1976), *citing Fong Yue Ting v. United States*, 149 U.S. 698, at 703, 13 S.Ct. 1016, at 1022 (1893). And we observed recently that in the exercise of its broad power over immigration and naturalization, "Congress regularly makes rules that would be unacceptable if applied to citizens." *Id.*, at 80, 96 S.Ct., at 1891.

Appellants apparently do not challenge the need for special judicial deference to congressional policy choices in the immigration context,[5] but

---

[a]   Before the 1976 amendments to the INA, most Western Hemisphere immigration was subject to an annual ceiling of 120,000, but the preference system did not apply. Noncitizens who were not excludable simply queued up for available numbers. However, all were subject to the labor certification requirement, unless it was waived because of specified family relationships. The Court treats the *Fiallo* case under pre-1976 law, but you should keep in mind that parents of lawful permanent residents—unlike parents of U.S. citizens—no longer receive any special immigration benefits.—eds.

[5]   The appellees argue that the challenged sections of the Act, embodying as they do "a substantive policy regulating the admission of aliens into the United States, [are] not an appropriate subject for judicial review." Our cases reflect acceptance of a limited judicial responsibility under the Constitution even with respect to the power of Congress to regulate the admission and exclusion of aliens, and there is no occasion to consider in this case whether there

instead suggest that a "unique coalescing of factors" makes the instant case sufficiently unlike prior immigration cases to warrant more searching judicial scrutiny.

Appellants first observe that since the statutory provisions were designed to reunite families wherever possible, the purpose of the statute was to afford rights not to aliens but to United States citizens and legal permanent residents. Appellants then rely on our border-search decisions * * * for the proposition that the courts must scrutinize congressional legislation in the immigration area to protect against violations of the rights of citizens. At issue in the border-search cases, however, was the nature of the protections mandated by the Fourth Amendment with respect to Government procedures designed to stem the illegal entry of aliens. Nothing in the opinions in those cases suggests that Congress has anything but exceptionally broad power to determine which classes of aliens may lawfully enter the country.

Appellants suggest a second distinguishing factor. They argue that none of the prior immigration cases of this Court involved "double-barreled" discrimination based on sex and illegitimacy, infringed upon the due process rights of citizens and legal permanent residents, or implicated "the fundamental constitutional interests of United States citizens and permanent residents in a familial relationship." But this Court has resolved similar challenges to immigration legislation based on other constitutional rights of citizens, and has rejected the suggestion that more searching judicial scrutiny is required. In *Kleindienst v. Mandel* [408 U.S. 753, 92 S.Ct. 2576 (1972), considered in Chapter Seven, p. 589 below], for example, United States citizens challenged the power of the Attorney General to deny a visa to a noncitizen who, as a proponent of "the economic, international, and governmental doctrines of World communism", was ineligible to receive a visa * * * absent a waiver by the Attorney General. The citizen-appellees in that case conceded that Congress could prohibit entry of all noncitizens falling into the class defined by [that section]. They contended, however, that the Attorney General's statutory discretion to approve a waiver was limited by the Constitution and that their First Amendment rights were abridged by the denial of Mandel's request for a visa. The Court held that "when the Executive exercises this [delegated] power negatively on the basis of a facially legitimate and bona fide reason, the courts will neither look behind the exercise of that discretion, nor test it by balancing its justification against the First Amendment interests of those who seek personal communication with the applicant." We can see no reason to review the broad congressional policy choice at issue here under a more

---

may be actions of the Congress with respect to aliens that are so essentially political in character as to be nonjusticiable.

exacting standard than was applied in *Kleindienst v. Mandel,* a First Amendment case.[6]

Finally, appellants characterize our prior immigration cases as involving foreign policy matters and congressional choices to exclude or expel groups of aliens that were "specifically and clearly perceived to pose a grave threat to the national security," * * * "or to the general welfare of this country." * * * We find no indication in our prior cases that the scope of judicial review is a function of the nature of the policy choice at issue. To the contrary, "[s]ince decisions in these matters may implicate our relations with foreign powers, and since a wide variety of classifications must be defined in the light of changing political and economic circumstances, such decisions are frequently of a character more appropriate to either the Legislature or the Executive than to the Judiciary," and "[t]he reasons that preclude judicial review of political questions also dictate a narrow standard of review of decisions made by the Congress or the President in the area of immigration and naturalization." * * *

III

As originally enacted in 1952, § 101(b)(1) of the Act defined a "child" as an unmarried legitimate or legitimated child or stepchild under 21 years of age. The Board of Immigration Appeals and the Attorney General subsequently concluded that the failure of this definition to refer to illegitimate children rendered ineligible for preferential nonquota status both the illegitimate alien child of a citizen mother, and the alien mother

---

[6] The thoughtful dissenting opinion of our Brother Marshall would be persuasive if its basic premise were accepted. The dissent is grounded on the assumption that the relevant portions of the Act grant a "fundamental right" to American citizens, a right "given only to the citizen" and not to the putative immigrant. The assumption is facially plausible in that the families of putative immigrants certainly have an interest in their admission. But the fallacy of the assumption is rooted deeply in fundamental principles of sovereignty.

We are dealing here with an exercise of the Nation's sovereign power to admit or exclude foreigners in accordance with perceived national interests. Although few, if any, countries have been as generous as the United States in extending the privilege to immigrate, or in providing sanctuary to the oppressed, limits and classifications as to who shall be admitted are traditional and necessary elements of legislation in this area. It is true that the legislative history of the provision at issue here establishes that congressional concern was directed at "the problem of keeping families of United States citizens and immigrants united." * * * To accommodate this goal, Congress has accorded a special "preference status" to certain aliens who share relationships with citizens or permanent resident aliens. But there are widely varying relationships and degrees of kinship, and it is appropriate for Congress to consider not only the nature of these relationships but also problems of identification, administration, and the potential for fraud. In the inevitable process of "line drawing," Congress has determined that certain classes of aliens are more likely than others to satisfy national objectives without undue cost, and it has granted preferential status only to those classes.

As Mr. Justice Frankfurter wrote years ago, the formulation of these "[p]olicies pertaining to the entry of aliens . . . is entrusted exclusively to Congress". *Galvan v. Press,* 347 U.S., at 531, 74 S.Ct., at 743. This is not to say, as we make clear in n. 5, *supra,* that the Government's power in this area is never subject to judicial review. But our cases do make clear that despite the impact of these classifications on the interests of those already within our borders, congressional determinations such as this one are subject only to limited judicial review.

of a citizen born out of wedlock. The Attorney General recommended that the matter be brought to the attention of Congress, and the Act was amended in 1957 to include what is now § 101(b)(1)(D). Congress was specifically concerned with the relationship between a child born out of wedlock and his or her natural mother, and the legislative history of the 1957 amendment reflects an intentional choice not to provide preferential immigration status by virtue of the relationship between an illegitimate child and his or her natural father.

This distinction is just one of many drawn by Congress pursuant to its determination to provide some—but not all—families with relief from various immigration restrictions that would otherwise hinder reunification of the family in this country. In addition to the distinction at issue here, Congress has decided that children, whether legitimate or not, cannot qualify for preferential status if they are married or are over 21 years of age. Legitimated children are ineligible for preferential status unless their legitimation occurred prior to their 18th birthday and at a time when they were in the legal custody of the legitimating parent or parents. Adopted children are not entitled to preferential status unless they were adopted before the age of 14 and have thereafter lived in the custody of their adopting or adopted parents for at least two years.[b] And stepchildren cannot qualify unless they were under 18 at the time of the marriage creating the stepchild relationship.

With respect to each of these legislative policy distinctions, it could be argued that the line should have been drawn at a different point and that the statutory definitions deny preferential status to parents and children who share strong family ties. But it is clear from our cases that these are policy questions entrusted exclusively to the political branches of our Government, and we have no judicial authority to substitute our political judgment for that of the Congress.

Appellants suggest that the distinction drawn in § 101(b)(1)(D) is unconstitutional under any standard of review since it infringes upon the constitutional rights of citizens and legal permanent residents without furthering legitimate governmental interests. Appellants note in this regard that the statute makes it more difficult for illegitimate children and their natural fathers to be reunited in this country than for legitimate or legitimated children and their parents, or for illegitimate children and their natural mothers. And appellants also note that the statute fails to establish a procedure under which illegitimate children and their natural fathers could prove the existence and strength of their family relationship. Those are admittedly the consequences of the congressional decision not to accord preferential status to this particular

---

[b] Later amendments raised the age limit for adoption to 16 and deleted "thereafter" from the definition, thus recognizing two years' custody whether it occurred before or after formal adoption. *See* current INA § 101(b)(1)(E).—eds.

class of aliens, but the decision nonetheless remains one "solely for the responsibility of the Congress and wholly outside the power of this Court to control." Congress obviously has determined that preferential status is not warranted for illegitimate children and their natural fathers, perhaps because of a perceived absence in most cases of close family ties as well as a concern with the serious problems of proof that usually lurk in paternity determinations.[8] In any event, it is not the judicial role in cases of this sort to probe and test the justifications for the legislative decision.[9] *Kleindienst v. Mandel,* 408 U.S., at 770, 92 S.Ct., at 2585.

IV

We hold that §§ 101(b)(1)(D) and 101(b)(2) of the Immigration and Nationality Act of 1952 are not unconstitutional by virtue of the exclusion of the relationship between an illegitimate child and his natural father from the preferences accorded by the Act to the "child" or "parent" of a United States citizen or lawful permanent resident.

Affirmed.

MR. JUSTICE MARSHALL, with whom MR. JUSTICE BRENNAN joins, dissenting.

Until today I thought it clear that when Congress grants benefits to some citizens, but not to others, it is our duty to insure that the decision comports with Fifth Amendment principles of due process and equal protection. Today, however, the Court appears to hold that discrimination among citizens, however invidious and irrational, must be tolerated if it occurs in the context of the immigration laws. Since I cannot agree that Congress has license to deny fundamental rights to citizens according to the most disfavored criteria simply because the Immigration and Nationality Act is involved, I dissent.

* * *

* * * The definitions [in § 101(b)] cover virtually all parent-child relationships except that of biological father-illegitimate child. Thus while

---

[8] The inherent difficulty of determining the paternity of an illegitimate child is compounded when it depends upon events that may have occurred in foreign countries many years earlier. Congress may well have given substantial weight, in adopting the classification here challenged, to these problems of proof and the potential for fraudulent visa applications that would have resulted from a more generous drawing of the line. Moreover, our cases clearly indicate that legislative distinctions in the immigration area need not be as " 'carefully tuned to alternative considerations,' " * * * as those in the domestic area.

[9] Appellants insist that the statutory distinction is based on an overbroad and outdated stereotype concerning the relationship of unwed fathers and their illegitimate children, and that existing administrative procedures, which had been developed to deal with the problems of proving paternity, maternity, and legitimation with respect to statutorily recognized "parents" and "children," could easily handle the problems of proof involved in determining the paternity of an illegitimate child. We simply note that this argument should be addressed to the Congress rather than the courts. Indeed, in that regard it is worth noting that a bill introduced in the 94th Congress would have eliminated the challenged distinction.

all American citizens are entitled to bring in their alien children without regard to either the numerical quota or the labor certification requirement, fathers are denied this privilege with respect to their illegitimate children. Similarly, all citizens are allowed to have their parents enter without regard to the labor certification requirement, and, if the citizen is over 21, also without regard to the quota. Illegitimate children, however, are denied such preferences for their fathers.

The unfortunate consequences of these omissions are graphically illustrated by the case of appellant Cleophus Warner. Mr. Warner is a naturalized citizen of the United States who * * * petitioned the Attorney General for an immigrant visa for his illegitimate son Serge, a citizen of the French West Indies. Despite the fact that Mr. Warner acknowledged his paternity and registered as Serge's father shortly after his birth, has his name on Serge's birth certificate, and has supported and maintained Serge since birth, the special dispensation from the quota and labor certification requirements was denied because Serge was not a "child" under the statute. It matters not that, as the Government concedes, Serge's mother has abandoned Serge to his father and has, by marrying another man, apparently rendered impossible, under French West Indies law, Mr. Warner's ever legitimating Serge. Mr. Warner is simply not Serge's "parent."

* * * This case, unlike most immigration cases that come before the Court, directly involves the rights of citizens, not aliens. "[C]oncerned with the problem of keeping families of United States citizens and immigrants united", Congress extended to American citizens the right to choose to be reunited in the United States with their immediate families. The focus was on citizens and their need for relief from the hardships occasioned by the immigration laws. The right to seek such relief was given only to the citizen, not the alien. INA § 204. If the citizen does not petition the Attorney General for the special "immediate relative" status for his parent or child, the alien, despite his relationship, can receive no preference. It is irrelevant that aliens have no constitutional right to immigrate and that Americans have no constitutional right to compel the admission of their families. The essential fact here is that Congress did choose to extend such privileges to American citizens but then denied them to a small class of citizens. When Congress draws such lines among citizens, the Constitution requires that the decision comport with Fifth Amendment principles of equal protection and due process. The simple fact that the discrimination is set in immigration legislation cannot insulate from scrutiny the invidious abridgment of citizens' fundamental interests.

* * * Once it is established that this discrimination among citizens cannot escape traditional constitutional scrutiny simply because it occurs

in the context of immigration legislation, the result is virtually foreordained. One can hardly imagine a more vulnerable statute.

The class of citizens denied the special privilege of reunification in this country is defined on the basis of two traditionally disfavored classifications—gender and legitimacy. Fathers cannot obtain preferred status for their illegitimate children; mothers can. Conversely, every child except the illegitimate—legitimate, legitimated, step-, adopted—can obtain preferred status for his or her alien father. The Court has little tolerance for either form of discrimination.

gender bias

* * * In view of the legislation's denial of this right to these classes, it is clear that, whatever the verbal formula, the Government bears a substantial burden to justify the statute. * * *

The legislative history, however, gives no indication of why these privileges were absolutely denied illegitimate children and their fathers. The Government suggests that Congress may have believed that "such persons are unlikely to have maintained a close personal relationship with their offspring." If so, Congress' chosen shorthand for "closeness" is obviously overinclusive. No one can dispute that there are legitimate, legitimated, step-, and adoptive parent-child relationships and mother-illegitimate child relationships that are not close and yet are accorded the preferential status. Indeed, the most dramatic illustration of the overinclusiveness is the fact that while Mr. Warner can never be deemed a "parent" of Serge, nevertheless, if he should marry, his wife could qualify as a stepparent, entitled to obtain for Serge the preferential status that Mr. Warner cannot obtain. *Andrade v. Esperdy,* 270 F. Supp. 516 (S.D.N.Y. 1967); *Nation v. Esperdy,* 239 F. Supp. 531 (S.D.N.Y. 1965). Similarly, a man who, in an adulterous affair, fathers a child outside his marriage cannot be the "parent" of that child, but his wife may petition as stepparent. *Matter of Stultz,* 15 I & N Dec. 362 (1975).

If serge's dad got married, woman could petition serge?!

That the statute is underinclusive is also undisputed. Indeed, the Government could not dispute it in view of the close relationships exhibited in appellants' cases, recognized in our previous cases, and established in numerous studies.

The Government suggests that Congress may have decided to accept the inaccurate classifications of this statute because they considered a case-by-case assessment of closeness and paternity not worth the administrative costs. This attempted justification is plainly inadequate. In *Stanley v. Illinois,* [405 U.S. 645, 92 S.Ct. 1208, 31 L.Ed.2d 551 (1972) (which found unconstitutional a state statute that automatically treated children born out of wedlock as wards of the state upon the death of the mother, without any hearing on the father's fitness)], we expressed our low regard for the use of "administrative convenience" as the rationale for interfering with a father's right to care for his illegitimate child.

"Procedure by presumption is always cheaper and easier than individualized determination. But when, as here, the procedure forecloses the determinative issues of competence and care, when it explicitly disdains present realities in deference to past formalities, it needlessly risks running roughshod over the important interests of both parent and child. It therefore cannot stand." 405 U.S., at 656–657, 92 S.Ct., at 1215.

This Court has been equally intolerant of the rationale when it is used to deny rights to the illegitimate child. While we are sensitive to " 'the lurking problems with respect to proof of paternity,' " we are careful not to allow them to be " 'made into an impenetrable barrier that works to shield otherwise invidious discrimination.' " We require, at a minimum, that the statute [be] " 'carefully tuned to alternative considerations' ", and not exclude all illegitimates simply because some situations involve difficulties of proof.

Given such hostility to the administrative-convenience argument when invidious classifications and fundamental rights are involved, it is apparent that the rationale is inadequate in the present case. As I observed earlier, since Congress gave no indication that administrative costs were its concern we should scrutinize the hypothesis closely. The likelihood of such a rationale is diminished considerably by the comprehensive and elaborate administrative procedures already established and employed by the INS in passing on claims of the existence of a parent-child relationship. All petitions are handled on a case-by-case basis with the petitioner bearing the burden of proof. Moreover, the INS is no stranger to cases requiring proof of paternity. When, for example, a citizen stepmother petitions for the entrance of her husband's illegitimate child, she must necessarily prove that her husband is the child's father. Indeed, it is ironic that if Mr. Warner marries and his wife petitions for Serge, her proof will, in fact, be one step more complex than his would be—not only must she prove his paternity, but she must also prove their marriage. Nevertheless, she would be entitled to an opportunity to prove those facts; he is not.

Nor is a fear of involvement with foreign laws and records a persuasive explanation of the omission. In administering the Act with respect to legitimated children, for example, the critical issue is whether the steps undertaken are adequate under local law to render the child legitimate, and the INS has become expert in such matters. I note, in this connection, that where a child was born in a country in which all children are legitimate, proof of paternity is the critical issue and the proof problems are identical to those involved with an illegitimate child.

Given the existence of these procedures and expertise, it is difficult indeed to give much weight to the hypothesized administrative-convenience rationale. Moreover, as noted previously, this Court will not allow concerns with proof to justify "an impenetrable barrier that works to shield otherwise invidious discrimination." As the facts of this case conclusively demonstrate, Congress has "failed to consider the possibility of a middle ground between the extremes of complete exclusion and case-by-case determination of paternity." Mr. Warner is a classic example of someone who can readily prove both paternity and closeness. Appellees concede this. The fact that he is denied the opportunity demonstrates beyond peradventure that Congress has failed to " 'carefully tun[e] [the statute] to alternative considerations.' " That failure is fatal to the statute.

When Congress grants a fundamental right to all but an invidiously selected class of citizens, and it is abundantly clear that such discrimination would be intolerable in any context but immigration, it is our duty to strike the legislation down. Because the Court condones the invidious discrimination in this case simply because it is embedded in the immigration laws, I must dissent.

MR. JUSTICE WHITE also dissents, substantially for the reasons stated by MR. JUSTICE MARSHALL in his dissenting opinion.

NOTES AND QUESTIONS ON
CONSTITUTIONAL CHALLENGES TO ADMISSION CATEGORIES

1. In 1986, Congress amended the § 101(b)(1)(D) definition of "child" to cover some relationships like those in *Fiallo*. It now reads:

> a child born out of wedlock, by, through whom, or on whose behalf a status, privilege, or benefit is sought by virtue of the relationship of the child to its natural mother or to its natural father if the father has or had a bona fide parent-child relationship with the person.

Should this amendment be considered a vindication of the majority's 1977 position in *Fiallo*: that changes in arguably objectionable immigration provisions should be left to the political branches? Or does it give you pause that the title of the subsection of the 1986 legislation that enacted this amendment—"Equal Treatment of Fathers"—is not quite accurate? What does the final clause, beginning with "if the father," mean? Why did Congress add it? How should the immigration authorities apply it?

The regulations that implemented the amended statute referred to sophisticated blood tests that had been developed between 1977 and 1986, allowing far more reliable determinations of paternity. *See* 54 Fed. Reg. 36753 (1989) (implementing regulations, amending 8 C.F.R. § 204.2(c)); *Matter of Pineda*, 20 I & N Dec. 70 (BIA 1989). If *Fiallo* had arisen after reliable paternity tests became available, should the Court have approached the issue differently? Should it do so today with even more precise DNA testing available? Are courts better positioned than Congress to act based on such scientific developments?

2. Should biological paternity be required at all? If the family reunification provisions are meant to let U.S. citizens and lawful permanent residents live in the United States with close family members, why doesn't the law simply test for the actual "closeness" of ties among family members, as Justice Marshall's dissent suggests? Why shouldn't aunts, uncles, or cousins be given family reunification immigration benefits if the petitioner shows that in his ethnic group—or perhaps in his own family—such ties are as close as the average ties among members of the usual suburban American nuclear family? Indeed, why require biological relationships at all? Why not adopt a system allowing family reunification-type immigration benefits based on proof of functional family ties, whatever the biological relationship? On a different plane, should a receiving country apply its own predominant cultural conceptions of family in deciding who should receive immigration benefits? Why or why not?

3. What are the administrative implications of inquiries into closeness? What kinds of evidence would be relevant to prove closeness? What criteria and internal agency procedures could help assure uniformity in deciding if a relationship is close enough?

In *Nguyen v. INS*, 533 U.S. 53, 121 S.Ct. 2053, 150 L.Ed.2d 115 (2001), in Chapter Two, p. 56, *supra*, the Supreme Court addressed some of the reasons to prefer a bright-line rule over some type of "closeness" determination. *Nguyen* rejected a gender discrimination challenge to a statutory distinction similar to that in *Fiallo*. The rule at issue made it harder for unwed fathers than unwed mothers to transmit U.S. citizenship at birth to a child born outside the United States. The statute accomplished this by requiring concrete acts of unwed fathers but not unwed mothers in order to transmit citizenship, such as legitimation or a formal acknowledgment of paternity before the child turns 18. The plaintiffs in *Nguyen* argued that Congress could and should instead have conferred citizenship on any out-of-wedlock child of a U.S. citizen father born outside the United States whenever "an actual father-child relationship is proved." The Court observed with approval that Congress rejected this approach, "perhaps because of the subjectivity, intrusiveness, and difficulties of proof that might attend an inquiry into any particular bond or tie," opting instead for "an easily administered scheme." 533 U.S. at 69, 121 S.Ct. at 2064.

On the other hand, bright-line tests make some arbitrary outcomes inevitable. Striking the right balance is difficult, but administrators may have incentives for erring in favor of fixed rules. By the same token, judges may be too quick to dismiss as "administrative convenience" some real concerns that are far more complex than simply adding to the annual agency budget. For a useful discussion of these issues, see Colin S. Diver, *The Optimal Precision of Administrative Rules*, 93 Yale L.J. 65 (1983). *See also Fook Hong Mak v. INS*, 435 F.2d 728, 730 (2d Cir. 1970) (Friendly, J.) ("an administrator, vested with discretionary power, [may] determine by appropriate rulemaking that he will not use it in favor of a particular class on a case-by-case basis, if his determination is founded on considerations rationally related to the statute he is administering. * * * This may be an even 'juster justice' than to accord different treatment because of trivial differences of fact"); *American Hospital Ass'n v. NLRB*, 899 F.2d 651, 660 (7th Cir. 1990) (Posner, J.) ("The decision how much discretion to eliminate from the decisional process is itself a discretionary judgment, entitled to broad judicial deference").

4. Justice Marshall states that if Cleophus Warner were now to marry, his wife could petition to bring in Serge Warner as her stepchild, citing *Andrade v. Esperdy,* 270 F. Supp. 516 (S.D.N.Y. 1967). At the time of the *Fiallo* decision, some judicial decisions had indeed held that the statutory definition of stepchild, INA § 101(b)(1)(B), is to be applied in this literal (if anomalous) fashion. The Board of Immigration Appeals initially resisted this interpretation, reasoning that the statutory purpose could be fulfilled by granting petitions for stepchildren only where there is evidence of a pre-existing family unit or equivalent ties. *Matter of Moreira,* 17 I & N Dec. 41, 46–47 (BIA 1979).

In *Palmer v. Reddy,* 622 F.2d 463 (9th Cir. 1980), the Ninth Circuit explicitly rejected the *Moreira* standards and directed that the "stepchild" provision be construed literally to require only marriage to the natural parent, whether or not there was a showing of "active parental interest." Which approach is more consistent with the congressional plan? Which better honors Justice Marshall's principle of closeness? The Board eventually—but "with some reluctance"—applied the *Palmer* result nationwide. *See Matter of McMillan,* 17 I & N Dec. 605, 605 (BIA 1981). *See also Medina-Morales v. Ashcroft,* 371, F.3d 520, 531–32 (9th Cir. 2004).

5. Justice Marshall's dissent suggests that the Court can apply more rigorous constitutional review to the classifications in *Fiallo* without necessarily having to apply such scrutiny in most other immigration cases. "This case," he writes, "unlike most immigration cases that come before the Court, directly involves the rights of citizens." But does this factor distinguish most other immigration cases? The vast majority of permanent immigration to the United States begins with a petition filed with USCIS by a U.S. citizen. (The family-sponsored second preference calls for a lawful permanent resident to file a visa petition, but the circle of beneficiaries is limited: a spouse or unmarried son or daughters.) The employment-based preferences and many nonimmigrant admissions usually start with a petition filed by a prospective U.S. employer. *See generally* Hiroshi Motomura, *Whose Immigration Law?: Citizens, Aliens, and the Constitution*, 97 Colum. L. Rev. 1567 (1997) (suggesting more serious consideration of citizens' constitutional rights in deciding the constitutionality of immigration laws); Hiroshi Motomura, *Whose Alien Nation?: Two Models of Constitutional Immigration Law*, 94 Mich. L. Rev. 1927 (1996) (same).

6. After *Fiallo,* could Congress amend the INA to make only members of the Caucasian race eligible for immigration? By what standard should a court consider an equal protection challenge to such a statute? Before the 1965 amendments to the INA did away with the national-origins quota system, courts easily disposed of constitutional challenges to the lines Congress had drawn. An example is *Hitai v. INS,* 343 F.2d 466 (2d Cir. 1965), which applied the purely racial theories reflected in the INA at that time. Hitai was born in Brazil to naturalized Brazilian citizens. But because his parents had been born Japanese citizens, he came within the small Japanese quota under the INA at that time. He argued that it was constitutional to discriminate

> between native-born Brazilians for the purpose of granting permanent residence in the United States, by assigning those Brazilians whose ancestry is attributable to certain 'Asiatic races' to a quota area, which has a definite limit, and permitting other Brazilians whose ancestry is not so attributable to enter the United States as permanent residents without any quota area limit

Id. at 467.

The Second Circuit summarily upheld the statute as constitutional, citing *Chae Chan Ping v. United States,* 130 U.S. 581, 9 S. Ct. 623, 32 L. Ed. 1068 (1889). A decade later, in *Dunn v. INS,* 499 F.2d 856 (9th Cir. 1974), *cert. denied,* 419 U.S. 1106, 95 S.Ct. 776, 42 L.Ed.2d 801 (1975), the Ninth Circuit applied the "rational basis" test to reject an equal protection challenge to a provision that disqualified only Mexican nationals from adjusting their status from nonimmigrant to immigrant while within the United States. (The INA was later amended to remove this bar.)

Against the backdrop of cases like *Hitai* and *Dunn,* consider the significance of the statement in *Fiallo* (in footnote 5) that "[o]ur cases reflect acceptance of a limited judicial responsibility" to review Congress' line-drawing, rather than no responsibility at all. Does the Court speak of a "limited responsibility" precisely to preserve the possibility that it might strike down any modern immigration legislation that based admission categories explicitly on racial distinctions?

As a judge, how would you evaluate a special security screening regulation that explicitly applies only to nationals of countries in the Middle East? Is line-drawing based on nationality—a durable but not necessarily immutable trait—constitutionally the same as line-drawing based on national origin in the domestic context? If strict scrutiny applies in such cases, is it constitutional to have specially favorable procedures or substantive provisions for some nationalities—such as the admission of Canadian nationals, as has been true on the northern border for decades? What about rules that treat Cubans differently—especially given steps toward normalizing U.S.-Cuba relations? Could U.S. treaties confer special immigration benefits on nationals of those treaty countries only?

A related question is whether statutes that draw nationality distinctions should be upheld as long as they rest on a "rational basis"? As indicated in *Fiallo,* the Supreme Court's decision in *Kleindienst v. Mandel*, 408 U.S. 753, 92 S. Ct. 2576, 33 L. Ed. 2d 683 (1972), in Chapter Seven, establishes an alternative test—a "facially legitimate and bona fide reason"— that may be even less demanding. Are there other tests that could help decide when an explicit nationality or religion distinction should be seen as a pretext for impermissible racial discrimination? If the government claims that foreign policy concerns justify the use of these immigration restrictions, how should a court evaluate the genuineness and strength of such factors? Are courts institutionally capable of such review? *Fiallo* implicates all of these questions, which we will again consider in different contexts in other chapters.

7. *Jean v. Nelson,* 472 U.S. 846, 105 S. Ct. 2592, 86 L. Ed. 2d 664 (1985), involved the influx of Haitians, most of whom sought asylum, into south Florida during the early 1980s. The U.S. government adopted a general practice of detaining rather than releasing these Haitians on parole pending decisions on their asylum claims. The plaintiffs alleged that this policy denied equal protection because it discriminated on the basis of national origin and race against these Haitians.

When the Supreme Court eventually decided the case, it did not reach the constitutional issue. Instead, it found that any discrimination against the Haitians based on race or national origin would be unlawful as contrary to the statute and regulations. Though the statute and regulations contained nothing that expressly barred consideration of race or national origin in deciding whether to grant parole, the Court found that they required the government to give the Haitians "nondiscriminatory parole consideration." 472 U.S. at 855, 105 S. Ct. at 2997.

According to one analysis, an antidiscrimination norm guided the Court's reading of the statute and regulations—thus applying the canon that courts should interpret statutes to avoid serious constitutional doubt— without actually deciding that the statute was unconstitutional. *See* Hiroshi Motomura, *Immigration Law After a Century of Plenary Power: Phantom Constitutional Norms and Statutory Interpretation*, 100 Yale L.J. 545, 546– 48, 587–93, 604–05 (1990). Should statutory interpretation play this role in limiting government decisions, or is it more conceptually sound to decide either that a statute is constitutional or that it is not?

3. FAMILY REUNIFICATION: A CLOSER LOOK AT IMMIGRATION BASED ON MARRIAGE

The dominant feature of permanent immigrant admissions to the United States today is family reunification. Immediate relatives of U.S. citizens, as we have seen, can immigrate without numerical limits. Of the numerically limited immigration slots, well over half are reserved for family members who qualify under the family-sponsored preferences.

Consider which family relationships are recognized by the statute and which are not. What sorts of family ties should count for immigration benefits? What basic values should inform the statute's categories and the rules used to administer them? How have agencies dealt with the tension between the objectives of family unification and of avoiding fraud or abuse? To explore these questions, we take a closer look at immigration based on marriage, which is the basis for immigration by well over a third of the new lawful permanent residents each year.

a. What Marriages Are Recognized by the INA?

(i) General Principles

Marriage is a legal concept, established and regulated by law. But whose law applies? Suppose a foreign country permits marriages between first cousins or between uncles and nieces or aunts and nephews, or allows persons to marry at age 12. Should USCIS recognize such marriages for purposes of the INA? Answering this question turns out to be an extraordinarily complex undertaking that involves not only what marriages "count," but also the role of multiple government agencies and officials in making such decisions in a wide variety of situations.

The general rule is that "the validity of a marriage ordinarily is judged by the law of the place where it is celebrated." Charles Gordon, Stanley Mailman, Stephen Yale-Loehr & Ronald Y. Wada, *Immigration Law and Procedure* § 36.02[2][a] (rev. ed. 2015). This rule applies for marriages in foreign countries or in a U.S. state or territory. It includes common-law marriages if they are recognized under the law of the state where the couple lives. But there are exceptions. As we explore below, otherwise valid marriages entered into solely for the purpose of obtaining immigration benefits are not recognized for immigration purposes. Moreover, the INA expressly limits the recognition of so-called proxy marriages—defined as marriages "where the contracting parties thereto are not physically present in the presence of each other, unless the marriage shall have been consummated." INA § 101(a)(35). On proxy marriages, see Kerry Abrams, *Peaceful Penetration: Proxy Marriage, Same-Sex Marriage, and Recognition*, 2011 Mich. St. L. Rev. 141 (2011).

Marriages that may be valid in the country of origin may not be recognized for immigration purposes if they are deemed to conflict with public policy. This rule is generally understood to mean that the marriage must be lawful in the intended place of residence in the United States. *See Matter of Darwish*, 14 I & N Dec. 307 (BIA 1973) (polygamous marriage not recognized for immigration purposes even though valid under Jordanian law; plural marriages violate U.S. public policy); *Matter of Zappia*, 12 I & N Dec. 439 (BIA 1967) (marriage between first cousins resident in Wisconsin but entered into during a brief visit to South

Carolina, where such marriages are legal, is invalid for immigration purposes because void in Wisconsin).

What if only the U.S. citizen is in the United States and the couple has not yet married? One option is the K–1 fiancé visa, which allows the noncitizen to be admitted to the United States, on the condition that the parties marry within 90 days of the noncitizen's admission. Once married, the noncitizen can adjust status to lawful permanent resident. *See generally* Jonathan S. Greene, *The Tricky Triangle: Marriage, Divorce, and Permanent Residence*, 15–03 Immigr. Briefings (2015).

(ii) Same-Sex Marriages

The recognition of same-sex marriages in U.S. immigration law has evolved rapidly in the past generation, and especially since 2010, culminating in the U.S. Supreme Court's decisions in *United States v. Windsor*, 133 S. Ct. 2675, 186 L.Ed.2d 808 (2013), and then in *Obergefell v. Hodges*, 135 S. Ct. 2584 (2015). These decisions, combined with policies and decisions within the federal executive branch, mean that same-sex marriages are now recognized for immigration purposes.

But the law was not always that way. In fact, the rule seemed clear until June 2013 that same-sex marriages were *not* recognized for immigration purposes. The story of these developments offers several important lessons for immigration law, especially for the relationship between state and federal law, for the interplay between legislative bodies (Congress and state legislatures) and federal administrative agencies (the Department of Homeland Security and the Department of Justice), and for the practical challenges of managing significant changes in doctrine.

As you read about these developments, ask yourself what new legal issues emerged at each stage, and what advocates on both sides might have done at each stage to work for or against the recognition of same-sex marriages in the immigration law setting.

(a) The Traditional Case Law

May a same-sex spouse of a U.S. citizen qualify for lawful immigrant status as an immediate relative? The following judicial decision captured prevailing doctrine and its rationale until at least 1990.

ADAMS V. HOWERTON

United States Court of Appeals, Ninth Circuit, 1982.
673 F.2d 1036, cert. denied, 458 U.S. 1111, 102 S.Ct. 3494, 73 L.Ed.2d 1373.

WALLACE, CIRCUIT JUDGE:

Adams, a male American citizen, and Sullivan, a male alien, appeal from the district court's entry of summary judgment for Howerton, Acting District Director of the Immigration and Naturalization Service (INS). The district court held that their homosexual marriage did not qualify Sullivan as Adams's spouse pursuant to section 201(b) of the Immigration and Nationality Act of 1952, as amended (the Act). We affirm.

I

Following the expiration of Sullivan's visitor's visa, Adams and Sullivan obtained a marriage license from the county clerk in Boulder, Colorado, and were "married" by a minister. Adams then petitioned the INS for classification of Sullivan as an immediate relative of an American citizen, based upon Sullivan's alleged status as Adams's spouse. The petition was denied, and the denial was affirmed on appeal by the Board of Immigration Appeals. * * *

II

* * *

Cases interpreting the Act indicate that a two-step analysis is necessary to determine whether a marriage will be recognized for immigration purposes. The first is whether the marriage is valid under state law. The second is whether that state-approved marriage qualifies under the Act. * * *

* * *

It is not clear * * * whether Colorado would recognize a homosexual marriage. There are no reported Colorado cases on the subject. The Colorado Attorney General in an informal, unpublished opinion addressed to a member of the Colorado legislature three days after the alleged marriage in question occurred, stated that purported marriages between persons of the same sex are of no legal effect in Colorado. Colorado statutory law, however, neither expressly permits nor prohibits homosexual marriages. Some statutes appear to contemplate marriage only as a relationship between a male and a female.

While we might well make an educated guess as to how the Colorado courts would decide this issue, it is unnecessary for us to do so. We decide this case solely upon construction of section 201(b), the second step in our two-step analysis.

III

* * * So long as Congress acts within constitutional constraints, it may determine the conditions under which immigration visas are issued. Therefore, the intent of Congress governs the conferral of spouse status under section 201(b), and a valid marriage is determinative only if Congress so intends.

It is clear to us that Congress did not intend the mere validity of a marriage under state law to be controlling. Although the 1965 amendments do not define the term "spouse," the Act itself limits the persons who may be deemed spouses. Section 101(a)(35) of the Act specifically provides that the term "spouse" does not include

> a spouse, wife, or husband by reason of any marriage ceremony where the contracting parties thereto are not physically present in the presence of each other, unless the marriage shall have been consummated.

Furthermore, valid marriages entered into by parties not intending to live together as husband and wife are not recognized for immigration purposes. Therefore, even though two persons contract a marriage valid under state law and are recognized as spouses by that state, they are not necessarily spouses for purposes of section 201(b).

* * * Where a statute has been interpreted by the agency charged with its enforcement, we are ordinarily required to accord substantial deference to that construction, and should follow it "unless there are compelling indications that it is wrong." *New York Dept. of Social Services v. Dublino*, 413 U.S. 405, 421, 93 S.Ct. 2507, 2517, 37 L.Ed.2d 688 (1973). Thus, we must be mindful that the INS, in carrying out its broad responsibilities, has interpreted the term "spouse" to exclude a person entering a homosexual marriage.

While we do accord this construction proper weight, we base our decision primarily on the Act itself. Nothing in the Act, the 1965 amendments or the legislative history suggests that the reference to "spouse" in section 201(b) was intended to include a person of the same sex as the citizen in question. It is "a fundamental canon of statutory construction" that, "unless otherwise defined, words will be interpreted as taking their ordinary, contemporary, common meaning." The term "marriage" ordinarily contemplates a relationship between a man and a woman. *See* Webster's Third New International Dictionary 1384 (1971); Black's Law Dictionary 876 (5th ed. 1979). The term "spouse" commonly refers to one of the parties in a marital relationship so defined. Congress has not indicated an intent to enlarge the ordinary meaning of those words. In the absence of such a congressional directive, it would be inappropriate for us to expand the meaning of the term "spouse" for immigration purposes. Our role is only to ascertain and apply the intent of Congress.

Our conclusion is supported by a further review of the 1965 amendments to the Act. These amendments not only added section 201(b) in its present form, but also amended the mandatory exclusion provisions of section 212(a) of the Act. Yet, both * * * the amendments and the accompanying Senate Report clearly express an intent to exclude homosexuals. *See Boutilier v. INS*, 387 U.S. 118, 121, 87 S.Ct. 1563, 1565, 18 L.Ed.2d 661 (1967). As our duty is to ascertain and apply the intent of Congress, we strive to interpret language in one section of a statute consistently with the language of other sections and with the purposes of the entire statute considered as a whole. We think it unlikely that Congress intended to give homosexual spouses preferential admission treatment under section 201(b) of the Act when, in the very same amendments adding that section, it mandated their exclusion. * * *

* * *

IV

We next consider the constitutionality of the section 201(b) so interpreted. Adams and Sullivan contend that the law violates the equal protection clause because it discriminates against them on the bases of sex and homosexuality. They also argue that review of this claimed violation must be pursuant to a strict standard because the federal law abridges their fundamental right to marry. We need not and do not reach the question of the nature of the claimed right or whether such a right is implicated in this case. Even if it were, we would not apply a strict scrutiny standard of review to the statute. Congress has almost plenary power to admit or exclude aliens, *see Fiallo v. Bell*, 430 U.S. 787, 792, 97 S.Ct. 1473, 1478, 52 L. Ed.2d 50 (1977); *Kleindienst v. Mandel*, 408 U.S. 753, 765–67, 92 S.Ct. 2576, 2583–84, 33 L.Ed.2d 683 (1972), and the decisions of Congress are subject only to limited judicial review.

We need not * * * delineate the exact outer boundaries of this limited judicial review. We hold that Congress's decision to confer spouse status under section 201(b) only upon the parties to heterosexual marriages has a rational basis and therefore comports with the due process clause and its equal protection requirements. There is no occasion to consider in this case whether some lesser standard of review should apply.

* * *

* * * Congress has determined that preferential status is not warranted for the spouses of homosexual marriages. Perhaps this is because homosexual marriages never produce offspring, because they are not recognized in most, if in any, of the states, or because they violate traditional and often prevailing societal mores. In any event, having

found that Congress rationally intended to deny preferential status to the spouses of such marriages, we need not further "probe and test the justifications for the legislative decision." [*Fiallo v. Bell*, 430 U.S.] at 799, 97 S.Ct. at 1481.

* * *

Affirmed.

(b) Federal Statutory Changes: The 1990 Immigration Act and the Defense of Marriage Act (DOMA)

In a general overhaul of the INA's exclusion grounds in 1990, Congress repealed the statutory provision under which homosexuality was treated as a ground for exclusion. Pub. L. 101–649, § 601(a), 104 Stat. 4978 (1990). Congress did not amend the definition of spouse.

Questions: Did the repeal of this exclusion ground allow for a convincing new argument that the reasoning in *Adams* was no longer sound? As a practical matter, would it have been better to make this sort of argument to a federal court or to a federal executive branch agency, or both? What is your reasoning in weighing these options? If you had been on the opposite side, which forum would you have preferred, and why?

If the 1990 changes to the exclusion grounds opened any opportunity to revisit *Adams*, it seemed to close in 1996, when Congress enacted the Defense of Marriage Act (DOMA). Section 3 of that statute provided:

> In determining the meaning of any Act of Congress, or of any ruling, regulation, or interpretation of administrative bureaus and agencies of the United States, the word "marriage" means only a legal union between one man and one woman as husband and wife, and the word "spouse" refers only to a person of the opposite sex who is a husband or wife.

Pub. L. 104–199, 110 Stat. 2419 (1996).

Question: Did DOMA leave open any avenues for a presidential administration—if it were sympathetic to same-sex marriages—to allow some immigration benefits for same-sex partners in a marriage or a similar nonmarital status such as a civil union or domestic partnership? How would such an administration have accomplished this?

(c) Constitutional Law: Bowers and Lawrence

To the extent that the *Adams* rule relied on societal mores, it gained support in the U.S. Supreme Court's decision in *Bowers v. Hardwick*, 478 U.S. 186, 106 S.Ct. 2841, 92 L.Ed.2d 140 (1986). In upholding a Georgia statute criminalizing homosexual sodomy, the Court found the "belief of a majority of the electorate in Georgia that homosexual sodomy is immoral and unacceptable" a sufficient rational basis for the statute.

The Court overruled *Bowers* in *Lawrence v. Texas,* 539 U.S. 558, 123 S.Ct. 2472, 156 L.Ed.2d 508 (2003), finding that a state law punishing homosexual conduct violates substantive due process. Justice Kennedy's majority opinion explained:

> [The *Bowers* Court failed] to appreciate the extent of the liberty at stake. To say that the issue in *Bowers* was simply the right to engage in certain sexual conduct demeans the claim the individual put forward, just as it would demean a married couple were it to be said marriage is simply about the right to have sexual intercourse. The laws involved in *Bowers* and here are, to be sure, statutes that purport to do no more than prohibit a particular sexual act. Their penalties and purposes, though, have more far-reaching consequences, touching upon the most private human conduct, sexual behavior, and in the most private of places, the home. The statutes do seek to control a personal relationship that, whether or not entitled to formal recognition in the law, is within the liberty of persons to choose without being punished as criminals.

> This, as a general rule, should counsel against attempts by the State, or a court, to define the meaning of the relationship or to set its boundaries absent injury to a person or abuse of an institution the law protects. It suffices for us to acknowledge that adults may choose to enter upon this relationship in the confines of their homes and their own private lives and still retain their dignity as free persons. When sexuality finds overt expression in intimate conduct with another person, the conduct can be but one element in a personal bond that is more enduring. The liberty protected by the Constitution allows homosexual persons the right to make this choice.

> * * *

> The petitioners are entitled to respect for their private lives. The State cannot demean their existence or control their destiny by making their private sexual conduct a crime. Their right to liberty under the Due Process Clause gives them the full right to engage in their conduct without intervention of the government. "It is a promise of the Constitution that there is a realm of personal liberty which the government may not enter." [*Planned Parenthood v. Casey,* 505 U.S. 833, 847, 112 S.Ct. 2791, 2805, 120 L. Ed. 2d 674 (1992)]. The Texas statute furthers no legitimate state interest which can justify its intrusion into the personal and private life of the individual.

539 U.S. at 567, 578, 123 S.Ct. at 2478, 2484.

A few months later, the Massachusetts Supreme Judicial Court barred the state from excluding same-sex couples from marriage. *Goodridge v. Department of Public Health*, 440 Mass. 309, 798 N.E. 2d 941 (2003). Though informed by the *Lawrence* Court's reasoning, *Goodridge* relied solely on the state constitution's liberty and equality guarantees.

Both before and after *Lawrence* and *Goodridge* were decided in 2003, many states adopted provisions reaffirming that marriage consists of a union between one man and one woman. While many states initially did so only through legislation, most of these states eventually adopted a constitutional amendment, ratified by voters, to prohibit same-sex marriage. Other states moved in the opposite direction. By 2013, same-sex marriages came to be recognized as a matter of state law in 13 states plus the District of Columbia. While the earlier instances of recognition came through state court decisions, eventually some states accepted marriage equality through legislation or popular vote. These changes in state law focused renewed attention on the wisdom and constitutional validity of the 1996 federal Defense of Marriage Act.

Questions: Did *Lawrence* allow for a convincing new argument that the reasoning in *Adams* was no longer sound? As a practical matter, would it have been better to make this sort of argument to a federal court or to a federal executive branch agency, or both? What is your reasoning in weighing these options? If you had been on the opposite side, which forum would you have preferred, and why? What would have happened if a case with facts identical to *Adams* had returned to the Ninth Circuit or reached the U.S. Supreme Court after *Lawrence*?

(d) Managing Change

On February 23, 2011, Attorney General Holder announced a new Department of Justice policy regarding litigation over DOMA. The federal government would no longer defend the constitutionality of DOMA in federal circuits where precedent had not already determined that rational-basis review, instead of heightened scrutiny, applies. Holder explained:

> President [Obama] and I have concluded that classifications based on sexual orientation warrant heightened scrutiny and that, as applied to same-sex couples legally married under state law, Section 3 of DOMA is unconstitutional. * * *

> As you know, the Department has a longstanding practice of defending the constitutionality of duly-enacted statutes if reasonable arguments can be made in their defense, a practice that accords the respect appropriately due to a coequal branch of

government. However, the Department in the past has declined to defend statutes despite the availability of professionally responsible arguments, in part because the Department does not consider every plausible argument to be a "reasonable" one. * * * This is the rare case where the proper course is to forgo the defense of this statute. * * *

In light of the foregoing, I will instruct the Department's lawyers to immediately inform the district courts in [two pending cases in the Second Circuit, including the *Windsor* litigation] of the Executive Branch's view that heightened scrutiny is the appropriate standard of review and that, consistent with that standard, Section 3 of DOMA may not be constitutionally applied to same-sex couples whose marriages are legally recognized under state law. If asked by the district courts in the Second Circuit for the position of the United States in the event those courts determine that the applicable standard is rational basis, the Department will state that, consistent with the position it has taken in prior cases, a reasonable argument for Section 3's constitutionality may be proffered under that permissive standard. Our attorneys will also notify the courts of our interest in providing Congress a full and fair opportunity to participate in the litigation in those cases. * * *

Letter from the Attorney General to Congress on Litigation Involving the Defense of Marriage Act, Feb. 23, 2011.

Congress proceeded to make arrangements to defend DOMA in court, hiring former Solicitor General Paul Clement. *See* Michael D. Shear & John Schwartz, *Law Firm Won't Defend Marriage Act*, N.Y. Times, Apr. 25, 2011.

Even as the federal government changed its position on defending DOMA in court, federal agencies continued to enforce DOMA. According to the Holder letter:

> [T]he President has instructed Executive agencies to continue to comply with Section 3 of DOMA, consistent with the Executive's obligation to take care that the laws be faithfully executed, unless and until Congress repeals Section 3 or the judicial branch renders a definitive verdict against the law's constitutionality. This course of action respects the actions of the prior Congress that enacted DOMA, and it recognizes the judiciary as the final arbiter of the constitutional claims raised.

Letter from the Attorney General, supra. USCIS announced that it would continue to apply DOMA to deny applications for immigration benefits.

At the same time, the administration started to keep track of immigration cases in which the validity of a same-sex marriage might affect the ultimate outcome. Signs also emerged that DHS would exercise prosecutorial discretion so as not to remove noncitizens who would have a solid claim to status if DOMA were to be struck down. In addition, Attorney General Holder accepted review of a BIA decision that had applied DOMA to deny immigration benefits, *Matter of Dorman,* 25 I & N Dec. 485 (AG 2011). He vacated and remanded the decision in April 2011 with a brief opinion that directed the Board to "make such findings as may be necessary to determine whether and how the constitutionality of DOMA is presented in this case, including, but not limited to: 1) whether the respondent's same-sex partnership or civil union qualifies him to be considered a 'spouse' under New Jersey law; 2) whether absent the requirements of DOMA, respondent's same-sex partnership or civil union would qualify him to be considered a 'spouse' under the Immigration and Nationality Act." 25 I & N Dec. at 485. Administrative bodies like the BIA do not have the authority to declare statutes unconstitutional. Holder was evidently directing the creation of a more complete record in an immigration law case that would facilitate federal court engagement with the constitutional issue setting.

Question: Suppose that the President of the United States had asked for your views in February 2011 on how to manage the prospect of court-ordered changes in law. Would you have advised taking the opposite approach: to continue to defend the constitutionality of DOMA in all courts, but to stop applying DOMA to applications for immigration benefits? What is your response and reasoning?

(e)   Constitutional Recognition of Same-Sex Marriage: Windsor *and* Obergefell

In June 2013, the Supreme Court ruled that section 3 of DOMA is unconstitutional. *See United States v. Windsor,* 133 S.Ct. 2675, 2696 (2013). On the same day, it avoided reaching the merits of an appeal from a district court ruling that had struck down California's law banning recognition of same-sex marriages. The Court reasoned that the state had not filed an appeal and the remaining appellants lacked standing. *See Hollingsworth v. Perry,* 133 S.Ct. 2652, 2668 (2013). The district court ruling negating the California law therefore remained operative, but the constitutional validity of similar laws in other states was left open to further litigation.

Three weeks after these decisions, the BIA ruled that it would recognize legally valid same-sex marriages as a basis for federal immigration benefits. The Board stated in *Matter of Zeleniak,* 26 I & N Dec. 158, 159–60 (2013):

The Supreme Court's ruling in *Windsor* has . . . removed section 3 of the DOMA as an impediment to the recognition of lawful same-sex marriages and spouses if the marriage is valid under the laws of the State where it was celebrated. This ruling is applicable to various provisions of the Act, including, but not limited to, sections 101(a)(15)(K) (fiancé and fiancée visas), 203 and 204 (immigrant visa petitions), 207 and 208 (refugee and asylee derivative status), 212 (inadmissibility and waivers of inadmissibility), 237 (removability and waivers of removability), 240A (cancellation of removal), and 245 (adjustment of status).

* * * The [DHS] Director has already determined that the petitioner's February 24, 2010, marriage is valid under the laws of Vermont, where the marriage was celebrated. Thus, the sole remaining inquiry is whether the petitioner has established that his marriage to the beneficiary is bona fide[, which is to be determined on remand].

After *Windsor* and *Zeleniak*, the relevant federal government agencies announced that they would treat same-sex marriages the same as opposite-sex marriages for immigration law purposes. Same-sex marriages celebrated in jurisdictions that allowed same-sex couples to marry would be recognized regardless of the laws and policies on same-sex marriage in the couple's domicile state. In addition, USCIS announced that it would reopen petitions or applications that had been denied solely because of DOMA section 3. *See* Victor C. Romero, *Reading (Into)* Windsor*: Presidential Leadership, Marriage Equality, and Immigration Policy*, 23 S. Cal. Rev. L. & Soc. Just. 1, 22–27 (2013).

In June 2015, the U.S. Supreme Court decided *Obergefell v. Hodges*, 135 S.Ct. 2584 (2015), with a 5–4 majority opinion authored by Justice Anthony Kennedy, who had also written for the majorities in *Lawrence* and *Windsor*. In *Obergefell*, Kennedy wrote:

> the right to marry is a fundamental right inherent in the liberty of the person, and under the Due Process and Equal Protection Clauses of the Fourteenth Amendment couples of the same-sex may not be deprived of that right and that liberty. The Court now holds that same-sex couples may exercise the fundamental right to marry.

135 S.Ct. at 2604–05.

With the federal government already having recognized same-sex marriages for immigration purposes after *Windsor*, the principal immigration consequence of *Obergefell* is that same-sex couples living in states that had not allowed same-sex marriages not need leave their state to marry and receive immigration benefits. They may now marry throughout the United States in their states of residence.

Questions: Would it be constitutional for a future Congress to limit the definition of "marriage," for immigration law purposes only, to marriage between a man and woman? Could a federal agency adopt a regulation or policy that similarly restricted the definition of "spouse" in establishing the relationship with a U.S. citizen or lawful permanent resident that the INA requires for some forms of discretionary relief from removal?

(f) Adams v. Howerton: *Epilogue*

After Adams and Sullivan lost their effort to have the INS recognize their marriage, Sullivan applied for suspension of deportation—a form of discretionary relief that was then available under the INA. This, too, was unsuccessful. Sullivan lost the last round of his attempt to stay lawfully in the United States when the Ninth Circuit upheld the denial of his suspension application, in a majority opinion by then-Circuit Judge Anthony Kennedy. *See Sullivan v. INS*, 772 F.2d 609 (9th Cir. 1985).

Adams and Sullivan left the United States in 1985, after holding what a 2004 article on the two men called a painful "deportation sale" of many of their prized possessions. Then, the article continued, "their first port of call was England. From there, they began traveling across Europe looking for a country that would accept them as a couple. Eventually, they alighted in Ireland, where they stayed six months." The article reported that they were still a couple—still married, in their view, since the 1975 marriage had never been declared invalid and remains of record in the Colorado archives. By 2004, they had been back in the United States for several years, a place they considered home. *See* James B. Meadows, *A Marriage Made in Boulder,* Rocky Mountain News, April 3, 2004.

Richard Adams died of cancer in 2012, at the age of 65. On what would have been their 39th wedding anniversary, April 21, 2014, Sullivan filed a petition with USCIS to become a lawful permanent resident based on his marriage to Adams. *See* Hailey Branson-Potts, *A Decades-Old Same-Sex Marriage Complicates a Green Card Case*, L.A. Times, Jul. 1, 2014. Sullivan relied on INA § 201(b)(2)(A)(i), which recognizes the surviving spouse of a U.S. citizen as an "immediate relative" for two years after the citizen's death, as long as the surviving spouse doesn't remarry. Sullivan became a lawful permanent resident in April 2016.

Concluding questions: How should administrative agencies manage the prospect of a significant court-ordered change in immigration law? If and when the change occurs, how—if at all— should administrative agencies allow cases decided under the old rules to be reopened if they might come out differently under the new rules?

b. Sham Marriages

Because a high percentage of immigrant admissions are based on marriage, policing against sham marriages has been an ongoing concern for legislators, administrators, and courts. But what exactly is a sham marriage? The answer is more complex than might first appear. For a marriage to be considered valid for immigration purposes, something more is required than simple validity under the law of the jurisdiction where the marriage was performed. The case law, statute, regulations, and administrative practice have used many different formulations to describe just what that extra might be.

All three branches of the federal government have wrestled with a related administrative question: how can we fashion procedures that maintain respect for human dignity and privacy, while still providing efficient means for effective detection and enforcement against bogus marriages? Another important concern is the possibility that any scheme to test the bona fides of a marriage might enhance the power of an abusive spouse who, as a U.S. citizen or lawful permanent resident, would be able to control the process. On marriage fraud generally, see Kerry Abrams, *Marriage Fraud*, 100 Cal. L. Rev. 1 (2012).

We introduce these issues with a case that reflects the early efforts of courts and administrators to develop standards for judging the validity of a marriage for immigration purposes, followed by a brief article that illustrates what can happen in an interview for adjustment of status based on marriage. We then consider legislation on the topic.

DABAGHIAN V. CIVILETTI
United States Court of Appeals, Ninth Circuit, 1979.
607 F.2d 868.

CHOY, CIRCUIT JUDGE:

Dabaghian appeals from the district court's judgment upholding a decision of the Immigration and Naturalization Service which stripped him of permanent-resident status. We reverse and remand with instruction to enter judgment for Dabaghian.

Dabaghian is a native and citizen of Iran. He entered the United States as a visitor in 1967 and obtained student status in 1968. In September 1971 he married a United States citizen. In October 1971 he applied for adjustment of status to "alien lawfully admitted for permanent residence" under § 245 of the Immigration and Nationality Act. The adjustment of status was granted on January 13, 1972, a date on which there is contested evidence to show that he was separated from his wife. On January 28, 1972, Dabaghian filed for divorce, which was granted seven months later. In September 1973 he married an Iranian citizen.

In August 1974 the Attorney General moved under § 246 of the Act, to rescind the adjustment of status on the ground that Dabaghian had not in fact been eligible for it at the time it was granted. The Immigration Judge revoked Dabaghian's status as a permanent resident; a split Board of Immigration Appeals dismissed Dabaghian's appeal. His action for review and relief in the district court was then dismissed on summary judgment.

Attrny Gen wants to revoke status saying sham marriage

The INS, it is important to note, never has claimed or proved that Dabaghian's first marriage was a sham or fraud when entered. Instead, the INS moved to rescind on the ground that on January 13, 1972, when the adjustment of status was granted, his marriage was dead in fact even though it was still legally alive. Thus, says the INS, he was not the "spouse" of a United States citizen and was ineligible for the adjustment of status.

INS has not proven sham, but claim marriage was "dead"

We reject the INS' legal position. If a marriage is not sham or fraudulent from its inception, it is valid for the purposes of determining eligibility for adjustment of status under § 245 of the Act until it is legally dissolved.

Rule

The INS contention has no support in any statute or federal decision. Indeed, it has been rejected time and again in recent immigration cases.

In *Bark v. INS*, 511 F.2d 1200 (9th Cir. 1975), the applicant married a woman who was a resident alien. She filed a petition on his behalf under § 204 of the Act to qualify him for preference as the spouse of a resident alien under § 203(a)(2). He then applied for adjustment of status to that of a permanent resident under § 245 of the Act. The INS denied the adjustment on the ground that the marriage was a sham, primarily on evidence of separation. This court held that the key issue in a sham marriage case is "Did the petitioner and his wife intend to establish a life together at the time of their marriage?" Since the later separation was alone insufficient to answer this question, the case was reversed and remanded.

courts test intend to establ. life together

The court stated,

Aliens cannot be required to have more conventional or more successful marriages than citizens. . . . Evidence that the parties separated after their wedding is relevant in ascertaining whether they intended to establish a life together when they exchanged marriage vows. But evidence of separation, standing alone, cannot support a finding that a marriage was not bona fide when it was entered. The inference that the parties never intended a bona fide marriage from proof of separation is arbitrary unless we are reasonably assured that it is more probable than not that couples who separate after marriage never intended to live together.... Common experience is directly to the contrary. Couples separate, temporarily and permanently, for all kinds of reasons that have nothing to do with any preconceived intent not to share their lives, such as calls to military service, educational needs, employment opportunities, illness, poverty, and domestic difficulties.

Id. at 1201–02.

* * * The court in *Chan* [*v. Bell,* 464 F. Supp. 125, 130 (D.D.C. 1978),] stated that the INS "has no expertise in the field of predicting the stability and growth potential of marriages—if indeed anyone has—and it surely has no business operating in that field." Moreover, the very effort to apply the "factually-dead" test would trench on constitutional values; it "would inevitably lead the INS into invasions of privacy which even the boldest of government agencies have heretofore been hesitant to enter." * * *

Dabaghian's purported ineligibility turns upon whether he was the "spouse" of an American citizen at the time of adjustment of status. If he was, he was eligible then to receive permanent-resident status, not subject to any quota. The word "spouses" in § 201(b) includes the parties to all marriages that are legally valid and not sham. There is no exception for marriages that the INS thinks are "factually dead" at the time of adjustment. For the INS to give such an interpretation to "spouses" and for the Attorney General to be satisfied that Dabaghian was not a "spouse" are abuses of discretion. Since no other reason for ineligibility under § 245 of the Act has been alleged or proven, there can be no rescission of Dabaghian's permanent-resident status.

Reversed and Remanded to the district court with instruction to enter a judgment directing the INS to reinstate Dabaghian as a permanent resident.

MELISSA NANN BURKE,
TO HAVE AND HOLD A GREEN CARD

Legal Affairs, January/February, 2006, at 10.

* * * When Lavinia, 24 years old, a waitress, and a nonresident alien [from Romania], married Cristian [Popoiu], a 27-year-old truck driver and a United States citizen, she instantly became eligible for a green card—the coveted documentation granting her the right to live and work in the U.S. It had been nine months since she applied for her green card when the two came to [Andrew] Garcia's interview room to clear one of the last hurdles in the application process: to convince him, as an official of the

U.S. Citizenship and Immigration Services, that their marriage was the genuine article and not a union designed to win Lavinia U.S. residency.

The most common way for immigrants to settle legally in the United States is to marry a U.S. citizen. It's a process that last year made legal residents of 252,193 spouses of U.S. citizens—each one of them interviewed by a CIS officer. But not surprisingly, this path to legal residency has been (littered with fraud) and more than a few sham marriages. Sniffing out the illegitimacy of these unions falls to immigration officers like Garcia. He's one of 12 officers in Philadelphia who each interview between 10 and 18 green card applicants a day—many of them married couples—in an effort to root out the pretenders.

fraud & shams

Though sham marriages that lead to green cards have been used as comedic Hollywood tropes (see, for instance, the Gérard Depardieu romp, *Green Card*), CIS officials say the job of sizing up immigrants is always serious business. * * *

In the last year, the federal government has scored big wins in the fight against fraudulent marriages, breaking up nuptial scam rings in South Florida, Chicago, Des Moines, and Seattle. In those cases, ring leaders are said to have paid U.S. citizens to marry aliens so that the aliens could earn permanent residency. The implicated U.S. citizens who went along with the scheme earned several thousand dollars each. * * *

Officer Garcia didn't waste time with pleasantries when he met the Popoius. He * * * launched into questions that got very personal, very fast. He asked the two about their tax filings and about the day they first met. Perhaps curious about whether she had demonstrated any proclivity to mix money with affection, he also asked Lavinia if she had ever worked as a prostitute.

very personal

Lavinia, her palms laid in her lap, took deep, calming breaths as she worked through Garcia's questions. In a voice that was commanding but soft, Garcia asked to see the couple's passports, which Lavinia removed from a fat file folder she had placed on Garcia's desk. It held birth certificates, bank statements, copies of an apartment lease, tax returns, even photos from their vacations to Key West, Fla., and Washington, D.C.—evidence of a life together.

folder of proof

The law doesn't detail what makes a marriage valid for immigration purposes, and immigration officers like Garcia aren't long on specifics about what exactly they're looking for when testing a marriage's validity. But they say that they keep their eyes peeled for inconsistencies that creep into stories or tax documents or green card application forms. Husbands and wives who haven't known each other for very long or who don't live together tend to raise eyebrows. Couples whose nuptials weren't attended by family often have some explaining to do. Even more suspicious are weddings that families aren't aware of. * * *

subjective

Meeting with couples gives immigration officers a chance to see how the husband and wife treat each other. Donald J. Monica, who heads the Philadelphia CIS office, explained that the interviewers ask themselves, "Does it look like the people interact with each other normally?" When the answer isn't yes, or when things seem not to add up, the immigration officer will take one of the pair across the hall into a separate room where the questions get more specific. Is there a washer-dryer in the house? Who does the grocery shopping? What did you give your wife for her birthday?

Fishy stories sometimes encourage an interviewer to call for a deeper look into a couple's life, through a visit to their home or interviews with their bosses. But that's not always necessary to smoke out a fraud. One husband and wife recently exposed during a visit to the Philadelphia office couldn't agree on the color of their bedroom walls or carpet. Or the number of siblings each other had, or where they met. An even more brazen pair saw its faux marriage come apart when officials found that the husband and wife couldn't speak the same language.

For Lavinia and Cristian, there were no snags. They'd hired an immigration lawyer to give them a sense of what they should expect at their meeting with Garcia, and the lawyer told them not to be shy if they were asked questions about lingerie—or even more intimate details. What they encountered in their 25-minute session was tame compared with what they were ready for. * * *

After [several detailed questions and] a few clicks of his mouse, Garcia looked at them both. "Lavinia, it's my pleasure to grant you lawful permanent residence today," he said. "You should get your green card in the mail in 10 days."

NOTES AND QUESTIONS ON SHAM MARRIAGES

1.   INS and the BIA traditionally sought to deny visa petitions for alleged spouses in two distinct situations. The first is when the underlying marriage was sham or fraudulent—that is, when the parties "did not intend to establish a life together at the time they were married," *Bark, supra.* The second is when the underlying marriage was nonviable or "factually dead" at the time the immigration benefit was granted. The agencies persisted in using both grounds for denial for many years after the early court decisions that invalidated the second test. In 1980, the Board finally capitulated and ruled that visa petitions would not be denied based solely on a finding that the underlying marriage is not viable. *Matter of McKee,* 17 I & N Dec. 332 (BIA 1980).

The BIA emphasized in *McKee,* however, that adjudicators would still scrutinize evidence of current separation in order to determine whether the initial marriage was sham or fraudulent. This position is consistent with *Bark,* as is apparent from the long quote from *Bark* in *Dabaghian.* The *Bark* court continued: "[o]f course, the time and extent of separation, combined with other facts and circumstances, can and have adequately supported the conclusion that a marriage was not bona fide." 511 F.2d at 1202.

In 1986, as we will consider below, Congress adopted a statutory scheme and standard to address the sham marriage issue. The parties must show that the marriage "was not entered into for the purpose of procuring an alien's admission as an immigrant." INA § 216(d)(1)(A)(i)(III). *See also* INA § 204(a)(2)(A)(ii) ("was not entered into for the purpose of evading any provision of the immigration laws"). This standard will usually—but not always—overlap with the *Bark* test. Despite this standard and related statutory provisions, courts continue to use the *Bark* test in judging the validity of marriages for immigration purposes. *See, e.g., Aran v. Napolitano,* 2010 WL 4906549 (D. Ariz. 2010).

not a fraudulent marriage

2.   In *Dabaghian,* could the government have defended the rescission of lawful permanent resident status more effectively if it had already fully accepted the *Bark* test, but then applied it to a later point in time? That is, instead of applying *Bark* only to the parties' intentions when they married, should the government have argued that an examiner should also consider the parties' intent to sustain a life together at the time the noncitizen is poised to receive the immigration benefit?

Such an approach, the government might have contended, would be more consistent with what many cases have held is the "foremost policy" of our permanent immigration provisions—family unification. All of 15 days elapsed between Dabaghian's adjustment of status and his filing for divorce from the U.S. citizen wife who had petitioned for him. Why should Dabaghian benefit when his family—at the time when the benefit took effect—manifestly had no interest in unifying? Why not reserve admission spaces (a politically scarce resource) for family members who really want to live together? Could the federal government have argued convincingly in *Dabaghian* that the "factually dead" standard, if it simply applied *Bark* at a later time, is most consistent with Congress' basic purpose?

3.   One reason for the *Dabaghian* court's rejection of the *Bark* "factually dead" test was the court's concern about the potentially intrusive questioning that examiners might conduct to see if the marriage were still alive. But isn't a similarly intrusive inquiry necessary to decide if a marriage is a sham? Consider the questioning process as described in the Burke article above, and this from another journalist's account:

> In the modern jambalaya of online dating, arranged weddings, bicoastal relationships, open marriages and serial divorce, a bona fide union can be harder than ever to discern, leaving lovers who are unable to produce a land-line telephone bill facing questions about birth control. That Tuesday . . . , one couple volunteered that the wife was eight weeks pregnant only to have the husband be asked: "Is it yours?"

"The latitude that officers have is broad, and one that has to be exercised with a lot of care," said Andrea Quarantillo, the immigration agency's district director for New York. "Is it perfect? No. It's judgmental."

Nina Bernstein, *Do You Take This Immigrant?*, N.Y. Times, June 12, 2010.

4.   The BIA has held that applications may not be granted on the basis of marriages that have been *legally* terminated as of the date that the immigration benefit is to be conferred. *See Matter of Boromand,* 17 I & N Dec. 450, 453 (BIA 1980). Nor may immigration benefits be granted if the spouses have legally separated under a formal, written separation agreement. *See Paez-Basto v. Acting Sec'y*, 2014 WL 4809528 (M.D. Fla. Sep. 26, 2014) (applying *Matter of Lenning,* 17 I & N Dec. 476 (BIA 1980)).

5.   There are also sham divorces—formal dissolution of marriage for the sole purpose of claiming benefits that are available only to unmarried persons, such as family-sponsored second preference visas for sons and daughters. In *Matter of Aldecoaotalora,* 18 I & N Dec. 430 (BIA 1983), the Board ruled that such a divorce would not be recognized for immigration purposes, where the former spouses continued to live together and to hold property jointly. It based this conclusion on:

> the intent of Congress in providing for preference status for unmarried sons and daughters of lawful permanent residents was to reunite with their parents unmarried children who, although not minors, were still part of a family unit. * * * By her own admissions, the beneficiary has established that, although divorced from her husband, she has neither severed her relationship with him nor returned to the family unit of her parents.

Is this an accurate reading of congressional intent? Could DHS deny second preference benefits to otherwise eligible, never married persons, on the ground that they have long lived apart from the parents' family unit?

c.   IMFA and VAWA: The Immigration Marriage Fraud Amendments and the Violence Against Women Act

The principles and concepts in *Bark* and *Dabaghian* remain valid as guideposts, but the practical framework for government scrutiny of marriages consists of provisions added to the INA by the Immigration Marriage Fraud Amendments of 1986 (IMFA), Pub. L. 99–639, 100 Stat. 3537, and later amended several times, most notably by the Violence Against Women Act of 1994 and successor VAWA enactments.

The most important of these provisions is INA § 216. It provides that all persons who obtain lawful permanent resident status based on a marriage that is less than two years old at the time—whether under the second preference or as an immediate relative—receive such status "on a conditional basis," valid only for two years, though DHS may act before then to terminate the noncitizen's conditional resident status. The thinking behind the two-year waiting period is that sham marriages are unlikely to be sustainable for that period of time. This conditional period counts fully toward the residence period required for naturalization. *See* INA § 216(e). Before the noncitizen spouse can get full, unconditional lawful permanent resident status, USCIS requires additional information.

It is not only spouses who may obtain conditional permanent residence. Sometimes a child from a prior marriage of the noncitizen spouse will also become a conditional permanent resident as an "alien son or daughter." Look closely at § 216 to see how this might happen.

You should be able to answer the next set of Problems after reading the materials that follow them and familiarizing yourself with § 216. That section is awkwardly drafted and requires careful attention. Some problems also require a close look at INA § 204(a)(2), (c), (g) and § 245(d), (e).

PROBLEMS

1. Noncitizens A and B both live in Venezuela after marrying a year ago. A is granted a visa under the employment-based third preference and plans to move with B to the United States. B receives a visa in the same preference category, as a derivative beneficiary under INA § 203(d). Will B's permanent resident status be granted on a conditional basis?

2. Noncitizen C marries U.S. citizen D and is admitted as an immediate relative under INA § 201(b).

   (a) Eighteen months later, C separates from D. Six months pass, and the couple has not reconciled. What are C's options to remain in the United States as a lawful permanent resident?

   (b) Suppose instead that C and D are legally divorced after twenty months. What result?

   (c) What if D instead had died after twenty months?

3. Noncitizen E marries U.S. citizen F and is admitted as an immediate relative.

   (a) One year later, a daughter is born. Six months after that, F walks out and refuses to help E in any further immigration proceedings. What are E's options to remain in the United States as a lawful permanent resident?

   (b) Suppose instead that noncitizen E leaves with the child after 18 months of marriage, because F had become angry and moody after losing his job. He frequently spent the evenings berating her, finding fault with her decisions, and occasionally threatening to strike her. What are E's options? → U–VISA.

4. Noncitizen G is admitted as a nonimmigrant and does not leave the United States at the end of her authorized stay, remaining without lawful status. One month after her admission period expires, DHS locates her and starts removal proceedings. G then marries U.S. citizen H.

(a) H files a visa petition on her behalf so that she may adjust her status under INA § 245. What are G's options to remain in the United States as a lawful permanent resident?

(b) Suppose instead that after the marriage she obtains agreement from DHS to depart voluntarily, the removal proceedings are dropped, and she leaves the country in the fifth month after her admission period expires. How soon can G return to the United States with an immigrant visa based on her marriage to H?

5. Noncitizen I marries U.S. citizen J and is admitted as a conditional lawful permanent resident. The conditional basis is removed two years later. Six months later, they divorce. One year after that, I marries K, a noncitizen not admitted to the United States, and files a second preference petition on K's behalf. What result?

(i) Petitions, "Termination," and "Removal" of the Condition

To have the conditional basis "removed," the general rule is that both spouses must file a joint petition to DHS on Form I–751 within the last 90 days of the two-year period. Once the petition is filed, DHS has statutory authority to call both spouses for an interview, although the interview is often waived, thus reserving examiners' time for those cases where the papers raise a question that merits further inquiry. *See* 8 C.F.R. §§ 216.4, 216.5. Under certain circumstances, however, the noncitizen may be able to secure a hardship waiver of the requirement of a joint filing and file the petition without the spouse. *See* INA § 216(c)(4). And when the citizen or LPR spouse has died, joint filing is not required. INA § 216(c)(1)(A).

The terminology in INA § 216 may be confusing. DHS "terminates" permanent resident status if it finds that the underlying marriage was improper (as defined in the INA) or other conditions are met. *See* INA § 216(b)(1); § 216(c)(2) (termination for failure to file timely removal petition). If termination occurs, the noncitizen is deportable under INA § 237(a)(1)(D). But if DHS finds that a proper petition has been filed and the underlying marriage was valid, DHS "removes" the conditional basis at the end of the two years. *See id.* § 216(c), (d)(1). Removal, as the term is used by IMFA, signifies the end of the conditional period and the noncitizen's acquisition of full permanent resident status. Noncitizens will want removal (in this specific sense); they will hope to avoid termination.

If removal of the conditional basis is denied (or if no petition for removal is filed), the noncitizen becomes deportable, but in removal proceedings the immigration judge can reconsider the determinations relevant to termination of the permanent resident status. On most of the issues tied to termination, the government bears the burden of proof in immigration court, under a "preponderance of the evidence" standard. DHS must show, for example, that the marriage has been annulled or that the marriage was entered into for the purpose of procuring immigration benefits. *See* INA § 216(b)(2), (c)(2), (c)(3).

(ii) Waivers of the Joint Petition Requirement

A noncitizen who wants to file the petition alone—typically because the petitioning spouse will not cooperate—must seek a waiver under § 216(c)(4) of the joint petition requirement. The noncitizen bears the burden of proof and must present the waiver request to USCIS. Extreme hardship waivers under INA § 216(c)(4)(A) impose a fairly demanding standard. Somewhat easier to obtain, assuming that the noncitizen meets the basic threshold requirements, are the good faith/not at fault waiver in § 216(c)(4)(B) and the battered spouse waiver in INA § 216(c)(4)(C).

The "good faith/not at fault" waiver in INA § 216(c)(4)(B) makes it possible for a noncitizen spouse to have the conditional basis removed, even if the sponsoring spouse refuses to join in the joint petition ordinarily required for removal of the conditional basis. This waiver requires actual termination of the marriage, not just separation. Despite the caption for § 216(c)(4)), applicant need not also show extreme hardship. *See generally Matter of Balsillie*, 20 I & N Dec. 486 (BIA 1992).

What if the couple is in the process of obtaining a divorce, but final judicial proceedings will not occur until well after the two-year mark and the sponsoring spouse (at least for now) appears willing to cooperate in the process for removal of the conditional basis? For a discussion of the options and dilemmas in this scenario, see Robert C. Divine & R. Blake Chisam, Immigration Practice § 14–7(a)(5)(i) (2014–15 ed.).

The (c)(4)(C) waiver requires domestic violence or extreme cruelty. Congress added it in 1990 to recognize that the two-year waiting period could contribute to the problem of domestic violence by giving the sponsoring spouse significant power over the noncitizen spouse. Victims of abuse may be deterred from going to authorities for fear that the abuser will retaliate by preventing removal of the victim spouse's conditional status. For example, the abuser might refuse to join in a petition to remove the conditional basis, or claim that the marriage was a sham. Abusers could also control (and misrepresent to the other spouse) information about the immigration process. Together these factors could put immigrant spouses at serious risk and make them feel compelled to accept an abusive relationship in order to attain lawful status in the United States.

Since 1990, INA § 216 has been amended several times to further protect victims of domestic abuse who have received conditional permanent resident status. For example, the Violence Against Women Reauthorization Act of 2013, § 806, Pub. L. 113–14, 127 Stat. 54, added a new INA § 216(c)(4)(D). It makes a waiver of the joint petition requirement available in some cases involving domestic violence after a marriage ceremony that later proves to be ineffective because of bigamy. This waiver complements an earlier provision, explained at p. 334 *infra*, to address bigamy when the abuser has not filed an immigrant petition.

Section 216(c)(4) may not provide a waiver in all situations where the marriage was initially genuine and valid under the *Bark* test but later fell apart. Whether waiver is available in such a situation will depend on the examiner's or immigration judge's exercise of the discretion explicitly granted by § 216(c)(4) in applying the waiver requirements Should the possibility of losing permanent residence in this fashion be considered a defect in the statute? Is loss of permanent residence overly harsh? Consider these comments from Senator Alan Simpson, who chaired the key Senate subcommittee when IMFA was considered (quoted in 65 Interp.Rel. 1339 (1988)):

> [W]e realize that there could be cases in which the alien spouse was not primarily responsible for the failure of the marriage, and during debate, some pointed out that this would give rise to an opportunity for "unfairness." However, if we all understand that the only real purpose in giving the substantial immigration benefit our laws provide to an alien spouse is to keep the family together, then we would wish that all will further understand that if the marriage just simply doesn't work—for whatever reason—even when the alien spouse is not at fault, there is no longer a family to "keep together."

65 Interp.Rel. 1339 (1988).

(iii)   IMFA's Other Provisions

IMFA also stiffens a few other provisions meant to prevent or punish marriage fraud. For example, it tightened the requirements for the K nonimmigrant category for fiancées and fiancés, *see* INA §§ 214(d), 245(d). It strengthened restrictions on future immigration of persons who have ever been involved in marriage fraud, INA § 204(c). It also established criminal penalties for involvement in marriage fraud, up to five years imprisonment and a fine of $250,000, *see* INA § 275(c).

INA § 204(a)(2) makes it harder for a person who immigrated on the basis of a first marriage to sponsor a second spouse later, following divorce from the first. Either five years must have passed since the initial grant of lawful permanent resident status to the current petitioner, or the petitioner must show by clear and convincing evidence that the initial marriage was valid. What policy underlies the imposition of this more stringent burden of proof? What kinds of evidence might be offered to satisfy it? *See Matter of Patel*, 19 I & N Dec. 774 (BIA 1988); *cf. Matter of Pazandeh*, 19 I & N Dec. 884 (BIA 1989). This test for sham marriages is like, but not identical to, the basic IMFA test in § 216, *see, e.g.,* § 216(b)(1)(A)(i). How does the approach in § 204(a)(2) differ from the sham marriage standard set forth in *Bark* and *Dabaghian*?

Another provision makes it harder for noncitizens in removal proceedings to cure their immigration status problems by means of "eleventh hour" marriages, entered into while those proceedings were pending. Such a marriage cannot be the basis for adjustment of status, unless the noncitizen proves the genuineness of the marriage by clear and convincing evidence—a more demanding burden of proof than the usual preponderance of the evidence standard. *See* INA §§ 204(g), 245(e).

(iv)   Concluding Question on IMFA

Does IMFA exacerbate or alleviate the problems that concerned the courts in *Bark* and *Dabaghian*? Compare the kinds of investigation and questioning required before IMFA (as allowed by those two cases) to the kinds of inquiry required or facilitated by IMFA.

d.   Self-Petitioning: Widow(er)s and VAWA Cases

(i)   Beneficiaries of Deceased Petitioners

In 1991, Congress amended the INA to allow widows and widowers of U.S. citizens to self-petition for immediate relative status, if they had been married to the citizen for two years, had not remarried, and filed within two years after the citizen spouse's death. *See* Pub. L. 102–232, 105 Stat. 1733 (1991). In 2009, after litigation and publicity regarding poignant cases of widows who had not been married for two years when the citizen died, Congress enlarged the category of eligible spouses, by essentially eliminating the requirement of two years of marriage. Congress also provided that if a citizen had in fact filed an immediate relative petition for a noncitizen spouse, and the citizen petitioner then died, the noncitizen spouse remains a "spouse" as far as the petition is concerned. *See* Pub. L. No. 111–83, § 568, 123 Stat. 2142 (2009); codified in INA § 201(b)(2)(A)(i) (second and third sentences) and § 204(a)(1)(A)(ii).

The 2009 amendments also let certain other categories of relatives continue with the immigration process despite the death of the petitioner or, for derivatives, the death of the principal beneficiary. But this rule applies only if the beneficiary already resides in the United States and seeks adjustment of status (not admission on an immigrant visa), and only if the relevant visa petition had been filed before the sponsor or principal died. *See* INA § 204(*l*).

B 204(1)

Question: These 2009 amendments suggest underlying purposes for the family-based immigration provisions that differ from the ones reflected in Senator Simpson's statement quoted in the discussion of IMFA waivers on p. 332. Considering who can benefit from the 2009 amendments, how would you describe the differences between these goals? How weighty are the goals of the 2009 amendments as compared to the family unity purposes mentioned by Simpson—which are often the purposes highlighted in congressional speeches and judicial decisions like *Fiallo*? What effect do these amendments have on other family-based immigration beneficiaries waiting overseas, given the "unavoidably zero-sum world of allocating a limited number of visas" (to use Justice Kagan's phrase from *Cuellar de Osorio)*?

(ii) Self-Petitions Under VAWA

We have seen that INA § 216(c)(4)(C) allows a waiver of the IMFA joint petition requirement in cases involving domestic violence or extreme cruelty. This waiver presupposes, however, that the noncitizen spouse has already become a conditional lawful permanent resident on the basis of an immigrant visa petition filed by the sponsoring spouse. A related but separate problem arises when an abusive spouse refuses to file the initial immigrant visa petition or threatens to withdraw a pending petition.

Congress has addressed this problem on several occasions. The Violence Against Women Act of 1994 (VAWA), Pub. L. 103–322, 108 Stat. 1902–1955, allowed a battered spouse, if eligible for immigration based on marriage, to self-petition for lawful permanent resident status without the abusive partner's involvement. Self-petitioning initially required findings that the marriage was bona fide and that removal of the self-petitioner would result in extreme hardship to the self-petitioner or to his or her children. Six years later, the Battered Immigrant Women Protection Act of 2000 (often called VAWA 2000), eliminated the extreme hardship requirement. VAWA 2000 also treated a noncitizen as a spouse if he or she married in good faith but later found that the marriage was invalid because of bigamy by the sponsoring spouse. *See* INA § 204(a)(1)(A)(iii), (A)(iv), (A)(v), (B)(ii), (B)(iii), (B)(iv). In addition, VAWA 2000 gave examiners the discretion to find that a self-petitioner, despite certain criminal convictions, has the "good moral character" sometimes required in the INA. The crimes must have been "connected to the alien's having been battered or subjected to extreme cruelty." INA § 204(a)(1)(C).

USCIS centralizes all handling of VAWA self-petitions in the Vermont Service Center, in order to help assure appropriate sensitivity and confidentiality. Successful self-petitioners in the second family-sponsored preference category—who, unlike "immediate relatives," may have to wait several years before their priority date becomes current—are routinely given deferred action status as a temporary reprieve from removal, plus work authorization. These benefits go far toward allowing them to remain in the United States until they can adjust to lawful permanent resident status. For a summary of the self-petitioning process, see Dree K. Collopy, *Thwarting the Intent Behind VAWA? USCIS' Interpretation of Good Moral Character*, Immigr. Briefings (2014).

(iii)   *Related Protective Provisions*

Over the past two decades, Congress has passed other measures to reduce immigration-law obstacles to the protection of domestic violence victims and certain other threatened noncitizens. Later in this casebook we will examine these provisions more fully, but here is a brief overview.

Domestic abuse in other situations. Under various INA sections, some grounds of inadmissibility and deportability can be waived or overcome if the petitioner shows that the ground had "a connection" to the battery or cruelty. *See, e.g.,* INA §§ 212(a)(6)(A)(ii), 212(a)(9)(B)(iii)(IV), 212(a)(9)(C)(ii), 237(a)(7). Caveat: these provisions—which sometimes refer to such victims as "VAWA self-petitioners"—are often couched in cryptic language, or they are sometimes overlooked or mistakenly believed to provide waivers for a wider class of intending immigrants.

VAWA also expanded the special avenue of relief from removal known as cancellation of removal as it applies to the victims of battery by a family member who is a U.S. citizen or lawful permanent resident. *See* INA § 240A(b)(2). Congress also bolstered the INA's provisions against domestic violence by adding a strict deportation ground for noncitizens convicted of a crime of domestic violence or found in violation of protection orders. *See* INA § 237(a)(2)(E).

Trafficking and crime victims. So far, our consideration of provisions addressing domestic abuse has addressed situations involving an abuser who is a U.S. citizen or a lawful permanent resident. VAWA 2000 expanded the possibilities for relief for persons victimized by nonrelatives or by persons who themselves lack durable immigration status. Two new nonimmigrant visa categories, T and U, significantly expanded the possibilities to help protect victims of gender-related abuse, though both categories have a broader reach.

T visas are for victims of "a severe form of human trafficking" who show that removal would result in extreme hardship. U visas are for persons who "have suffered substantial physical or mental abuse" as victims of certain kinds of crimes—a broad and varied statutory list. *See* INA §§ 101(a)(15)(T), (U); 214(*o*), (p). Both T and U visas initially provide temporary status, but then foresee adjustment to lawful permanent resident status after a few years, once modest further requirements are satisfied.

"Mail order brides." Congress acted in 2005 to address another potential source of domestic violence, based on evidence that "mail-order brides" from other countries are vulnerable to abuse by the men who select them and then file the visa petition to allow the bride to immigrate. *See* International Marriage Brokers Regulation Act (IMBRA), Subtitle D, Title VIII, Violence Against Women and Department of Justice Reauthorization Act of 2005 (VAWA 2005), Pub. L. 109–162, 199 Stat. 2960 (2006); Violence Against Women Reauthorization Act of 2013, §§ 807, 808, Pub. L. 113–14, 127 Stat. 54, codified at 8 U.S.C. § 1375a.

IMBRA requires international marriage brokers, if covered, to do extensive background checks on their U.S. clients, including checking sex offender public registries. The brokers must provide the noncitizen with broad disclosures before immigration processing begins. The Act spells out which matchmaking organizations are covered; religious organizations and certain services (including most internet dating sites) that do not specialize in international matches are exempt. For an overview of issues arising in the implementation of IMBRA, see Government Accountability Office, *Immigration Benefits: Improvements Needed to Fully Implement the International Marriage Broker Regulation Act* (2014).

e.   Marriage-Based Immigration and Professional Ethics

The article by Melissa Burke earlier in these materials on marriage-based immigration makes clear that federal immigration agencies and federal prosecutors regard marriage fraud as a serious problem. The benefits from successful fraud are high, and the risk of detection is perceived to be relatively low, even though prosecution of organizers has become a higher priority in recent years. *See, e.g.,* Department of Homeland Security (DHS) Office of Inspector General (OIG), *U.S. Citizenship and Immigration Services' Tracking and Monitoring of Potentially Fraudulent Petitions and Applications for Family-Based Immigration Benefits* (June 2013); Cathy Locke, *Sacramento Man Draws Two-Year Prison Sentence for Marriage Fraud Scheme*, Sacramento Bee, May 11, 2015; Jay Weaver, *Feds Charge 27 With Marriage Fraud*, Miami Herald, Apr. 21, 2015.

Attorneys representing persons seeking immigration benefits based on marriage may encounter situations where the relationship somehow appears questionable. What, then, is the attorney's ethical obligation to determine the *bona fides* of the client's marriage? Relatedly, what is the attorney's ethical obligation to disclose to a tribunal, such as USCIS or an immigration court, any information suggesting that the client is attempting to take advantage of a sham marriage? A different sort of problem arises when there is no doubt about the *bona fides* of the marriage, and the attorney is representing a married couple. What if the individual interests of the petitioning citizen and noncitizen intending immigrant spouse appear to diverge?

To guide your reading of the following brief overview of relevant American Bar Association Model Rules of Professional Conduct and federal provisions, consider the following scenarios:

1. A couple comes to you for representation in connection with either immigration based on marriage or removal of conditional status under INA § 216. What would you do if you suspected that the marriage is a sham?

2. A couple comes to you for representation in connection with immigration based on marriage. What would you do if you suspected that the noncitizen was using the citizen (sometimes called a 'gigolo marriage') to gain lawful permanent residence?

3. A couple comes to you for representation in connection with immigration based on marriage. What if, after the couple had a heated argument, the citizen spouse wants you to withdraw the visa petition?

4. A couple comes to you for representation in connection with removal of conditional status under INA § 216. What if the noncitizen spouse tells you that the citizen spouse is beating her?

Besides evaluating the options available to address these situations, consider how you might prevent or minimize these problems.

ABA Model Rules. Several provisions of the Model Rules of Professional Conduct (as adopted by the American Bar Association) are especially relevant to ethical dilemmas that can arise in immigration law practice. The Model Rules have served as the template for ethics rules in all states except California, though states following the Model Rules have done so with variations in text and interpretation.

In addition to state ethics rules, federal immigration-related statutes and regulations specifically address the ethical obligations of attorneys in dealings with the federal government. What follows is an overview of the most relevant Model Rules and federal provisions.

One type of ethical duty is maintaining client confidentiality. Model Rule 1.6 provides that with certain narrow exceptions,

> (a) "A lawyer shall not reveal information relating to representation of a client unless the client gives informed consent . . . ."

Another part of Model Rule 1.6 provides:

> (b) A lawyer may reveal information relating to the representation of a client to the extent the lawyer reasonably believes necessary:
>
> . . .
>
> > (3) to prevent, mitigate or rectify substantial injury to the financial interests or property of another that is reasonably certain to result or has resulted from the client's commission of a crime or fraud in furtherance of which the client has used the lawyer's services . . .

The Comments accompanying Model Rule 1.6 explain that "the confidentiality rule . . . applies not merely to matters communicated in confidence by the client but also to all information relating to the representation, whatever its source."

But the confidentiality obligation is not absolute. The Comments accompanying Model Rule 1.6 make clear that information otherwise protected by that rule must sometimes be disclosed under Model Rule 3.3, which provides in part:

> (a) A lawyer shall not knowingly:
>
> > (1) make a false statement of fact or law to a tribunal or fail to correct a false statement of material fact or law previously made to the tribunal by the lawyer;
> >
> > (2) fail to disclose to the tribunal legal authority in the controlling jurisdiction known to the lawyer to be directly adverse to the position of the client and not disclosed by opposing counsel; or
> >
> > (3) offer evidence that the lawyer knows to be false. If a lawyer, the lawyer's client, or a witness called by the lawyer, has offered material evidence and the lawyer comes to know of its falsity, the lawyer shall take reasonable remedial measures, including, if necessary, disclosure to the tribunal. A lawyer may refuse to offer evidence, other than the testimony of a defendant in a criminal matter, that the lawyer reasonably believes is false.

(b) A lawyer who represents a client in an adjudicative proceeding and who knows that a person intends to engage, is engaging or has engaged in criminal or fraudulent conduct related to the proceeding shall take reasonable remedial measures, including, if necessary, disclosure to the tribunal.

Immigration judges and USCIS adjudicators appear to meet the definition of 'tribunal.'

In addition, Model Rule 3.1 requires that claims be meritorious:

A lawyer shall not bring or defend a proceeding, or assert or controvert an issue therein, unless there is a basis in law and fact for doing so that is not frivolous, which includes a good faith argument for an extension, modification or reversal of existing law.

Also relevant is Model Rule 1.2(d), which provides:

(d) A lawyer shall not counsel a client to engage, or assist a client, in conduct that the lawyer knows is criminal or fraudulent, but a lawyer may discuss the legal consequences of any proposed course of conduct with a client and may counsel or assist a client to make a good faith effort to determine the validity, scope, meaning or application of the law.

Interestingly, an earlier 1981 draft version of Rule 1.2(d) would have swept more broadly by prohibiting a lawyer from assisting a client "in conduct that the lawyer knows or *reasonably should know* is criminal or fraudulent." Model Rules of Professional Conduct, Rule 1.2(d) (emphasis added). Despite the ABA's obvious effort to strengthen client confidentiality and reduce attorney obligations unilaterally to reveal or rectify questionable practices, some state bars enforce a conception of ethical responsibility more in line with the 1981 draft. The following appeared in the Texas Bar Journal, reprinted at 61 Interp. Rel. 442 (1984):

The District 10 Grievance Committee issued a private reprimand to an attorney of San Antonio on Dec. 22, 1983. The committee found that the attorney failed to undertake an adequate investigation into the marital status of his client before assisting him in an application for temporary status with the Immigration and Naturalization Service. The attorney knew, or should have known, that his client's marital status was questionable. Also, the attorney failed to timely advise the Immigration and Naturalization Service as to false information given to it at the time of the application for temporary status. Shortly thereafter, the attorney knew that false information had been given.

Another area of ethical issues is dual representation, addressed in Model Rule 1.7:

(a) Except as provided in paragraph (b), a lawyer shall not represent a client if the representation involves a concurrent conflict of interest. A concurrent conflict of interest exists if:

(1) the representation of one client will be directly adverse to another client; or

(2) there is a significant risk that the representation of one or more clients will be materially limited by the lawyer's responsibilities to another client, a former client or a third person or by a personal interest of the lawyer.

(b) Notwithstanding the existence of a concurrent conflict of interest under paragraph (a), a lawyer may represent a client if:

(1) the lawyer reasonably believes that the lawyer will be able to provide competent and diligent representation to each affected client;

(2) the representation is not prohibited by law;

(3) the representation does not involve the assertion of a claim by one client against another client represented by the lawyer in the same litigation or other proceeding before a tribunal; and

(4) each affected client gives informed consent, confirmed in writing.

Federal statutes and regulations. INA § 274C(a)(5) makes it unlawful for any person or entity knowingly:

to prepare, file, or assist another in preparing or filing, any application for benefits under this chapter, or any document required under this chapter, or any document submitted in connection with such application or document, with knowledge or in reckless disregard of the fact that such application or document was falsely made or, in whole or in part, does not relate to the person on whose behalf it was or is being submitted . . .

The definition of "falsely made" includes 'fail[ure] to state a fact which is material to the purpose for which it was submitted.' INA § 274C(f).

A federal regulation calls for the Department of Justice to impose disciplinary sanctions on any attorney who:

Knowingly or with reckless disregard makes a false statement of material fact or law, or willfully misleads, misinforms, threatens, or deceives any person (including a party to a case or an officer or employee of the Department of Justice), concerning any material and relevant matter relating to a case, including knowingly or with reckless disregard offering false evidence.

The provision continues:

If a practitioner has offered material evidence and comes to know of its falsity, the practitioner shall take appropriate remedial measures . . . .

8 C.F.R. § 1003.102(c) (2015), *applied in Matter of Shah*, 24 I & N Dec. 282 (BIA 2007). *See also United States v. Zalman*, 870 F.2d 1047 (6th Cir.), *cert. denied*, 492 U.S. 921, 109 S.Ct. 3248, 106 L.Ed. 2d 594 (1989) (sustaining attorney's conviction for fraud and failing to disclose sham marriages when clients applied for adjustment of status).

For further reading, see Elizabeth Keyes, *Zealous Advocacy: Pushing Against the Borders in Immigration Litigation*, 45 Seton Hall L. Rev. 475 (2015); Reid F. Trautz, *When a Client Lies: Balancing Candor and Confidentiality* (American Immigr. Lawyers Ass'n Practice & Professionalism Center 2012); Anna Marie Gallagher, Ethics, Professionalism, and Immigration Law, 11–12 Immigr. Briefings (Dec. 2011); Lauren Gilbert, *Facing Justice: Ethical Choices in Representing Immigrant Clients*, 20 Geo. J. Legal Ethics 219 (2007).

f. A Broader Perspective on Immigration and Family Law

Kerry Abrams has described the surprisingly extensive ways in which today's immigration law winds up intruding into the traditional state family-law domain—a phenomenon that she believes is insufficiently considered by either immigration lawyers or family lawyers. After considering the federal statutory scheme for family-sponsored immigration and analyzing the impact of immigration law at four separate stages of the marital relationship—(1) regulating courtship, (2) entry into marriage, (3) the intact marriage, and (4) exit from marriage—she observes:

In each of the four stages, immigration law regulates marriage very differently than family law does. In the first and third—courtship and the intact marriage—it regulates even where state family law has an explicitly hands-off attitude toward regulation. In the second and fourth stages—entry and exit—it regulates more intrusively and extensively than does state family law.

Sometimes this regulation of marriage, as with IMFA, appears to be an unintentional side effect of implementing immigration policy. In the case of IMFA, Congress was attempting to police the fraud that was the inevitable by-product of an immigration system that privileges spouses of citizens over other potential immigrants. Congress's goal of fraud prevention necessarily required it to spell out what kinds of marriages would qualify as legitimate. In other cases, Congress is engaged in a kind of backpedaling, attempting to intervene in marriage because of problems caused by immigration law itself. The provisions of VAWA that exempt battered spouses from the joint petition requirement, for example, make sense as an attempt to mitigate the harshness of the usual immigration rules. Finally, a third type of regulation intervenes in marriage because of congressional disapproval of certain relationships. IMBRA makes exceptions for "cultural" or "religious" matchmaking organizations not because matchmaking through these organizations has been proven to result in a better, smarter, or wealthier immigrant population, but rather because it believes the marriages emerging from these entities are exempt from the unacceptable power dynamics it believes most "mail-order bride" marriages possess. In each case, regardless of Congress's intent, immigration law is functioning as a form of family law for those who are regulated by it.

* * * The plenary power doctrine has been chipped away at, modified, criticized, and debated by courts, scholars, and lawyers for over a hundred years, but its tension with state control over family law has never before been explored. Lawmakers might decide that principles of federalism mandate that laws be drafted in a way that will least intrude on state family law's policy objectives while still fulfilling the goals of federal immigration policy. Courts interpreting these laws might construe them narrowly, so that minimal damage would be done to state law understandings of marriage.

Even in cases where Congress is clearly regulating immigration, and the impact on marriage is an incidental or unintended by-product of its immigration goals, Congress might do well to acknowledge the effect that immigration law has on marriage and consider the wealth of experience and information that state family law might provide. Family law offers organizing principles and theoretical models that would help us to understand the effects immigration law has on families. Immigration scholars and lawmakers should examine state family law to see how and why various doctrines have developed. They would then be in a better position to calibrate the effects of immigration law on the family. * * *

Kerry Abrams, *Immigration Law and the Regulation of Marriage*, 91 Minn. L. Rev. 1625, 1707–08 (2007).

Is there is anything wrong with an immigration law that—as Abrams puts it—"regulates marriage very differently than family law does"? Are the differences between the purposes of family law and immigration law significant enough that differences in the regulation of marriage in an immigration context are sometimes justified and even advisable?

4. INVESTORS AS IMMIGRANTS

Until 1990, U.S. law had no specific provisions favoring the immigration of prospective investors in the U.S. economy, even if investors and their lawyers sometimes found ways to use an investment as the basis for admission in another category. Proponents of an admission category for investors often argued along these lines: we have preferences for those who come to *fill* jobs for which U.S. workers are unavailable; why not a preference for noncitizens who would *create* jobs? The Select Commission on Immigration and Refugee Policy, which issued its report in 1981, was persuaded that we should do so. SCIRP, Final Report 131–32. Father Theodore M. Hesburgh, the Commission's chair, dissented, arguing that "the rich should not be able to buy their way into this country." *Id.* at 336.

A Migration Policy Institute report in 2014 identified four general reasons why immigrant investor programs may be attractive to persons with financial resources:

- *Traditional immigration*: these programs can provide another path to immigration and perhaps later to citizenship.

- *Insurance policy*: residence rights in another country in case of political or economic upheaval.

- *Ease of travel*: citizenship or residence in another country (and perhaps consequently in the European Union) may allow travel free of visa requirements or other encumbrances associated with the person's current citizenship.

- *Lower taxes*: residence in a low-tax country may allow the wealthy to reduce their overall tax obligations.

See Madeleine Sumption & Kate Hooper, *Selling Visas and Citizenship: Policy Questions from the Global Boom in Investor Immigration* 5 (Migration Policy Inst. 2014).

In 1990, Congress adopted an investor provision in INA § 203(b)(5), namely a fifth employment-based (EB–5) preference with 10,000 annual spaces. The investment must create at least 10 jobs for U.S. workers, not counting the investor and his or her family. The baseline investment is $1 million, but it can be reduced to $500,000 for "targeted employment areas"—rural communities or designated high-unemployment regions.

To guard against misuse or manipulation, all EB–5 immigrants and their families receive permanent residence on a two-year conditional basis under INA § 216A, which is closely modeled on conditional residence for noncitizen spouses in § 216. *See* INA § 216A(d)(1). But, as we will see, other fundamental criticisms of the EB–5 category have emerged, including the potential for fraud on investors, as well as doubts about the economic benefits of the program.

Figure 5.8
Admissions of Immigrant Investors (EB–5), FY 1992–2014

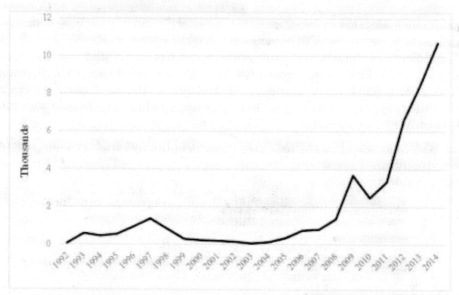

Source: 1999 INS Statistical Yearbook (2002) (for years 1992–1994);
2004 Yearbook of Immigration Statistics, table 4 (for years 1995–2000);
2010 Yearbook of Immigration Statistics, table 6 (for years 2001–2010);
2014 Yearbook of Immigration Statistics, table 6 (for years 2011–2014).

Figure 5.8 shows that until about 2007, annual use of the investor category was quite modest—only a few hundred admissions. This changed dramatically starting in 2008, rising to 10,723 in 2014, slightly exceeding the formal annual limit of 10,000. *See* 2014 Yearbook of Immigration Statistics, Table 6. For applicants from China, who are now about 85 percent of all EB–5 immigrants, the February 2016 Visa Bulletin showed a two-year backlog to January 15, 2014. The program is not a permanent part of the INA; it has a sunset provision, though the program has regularly been extended. In December 2015, Congress extended the EB–5 category until September 30, 2016. This is a relatively short extension, because Congress is expected to consider many pending proposals for reforming or even abolishing EB–5, in view of reported problems and recent scandals.

The post-2007 increase was due in part to a more stable, centralized, and welcoming regulatory process at USCIS for EB–5 applications. At least as important was the greatly expanded use of a provision allowing investments in a business entity known as a "regional center" located in a targeted employment area. Investing in an approved regional center lets the investor count indirect job creation from his investment—not just the construction worker building the building, for example, but a portion of the jobs at the restaurants where he eats, at the gas station where he buys fuel, and so forth.

One example of a heavily advertised regional center is a long-established ski and golf resort called Jay Peak in northern Vermont. The resort is in a targeted employment area, and the Vermont Agency of Commerce and Community Development operates a regional center there to invest in a multi-phase expansion and renovation of resort lodging and conference facilities. By late 2012, it had attracted 550 EB–5 investors. *See* Katharine Q. Seelye, *Lure of Green Cards Brings Big Investments for Remote Resort in Vermont*, N.Y. Times, Dec. 31, 2012.

The Jay Peak website listed the benefits of this type of EB–5 investment, in these words:

- A direct route to a Green Card

- No day-to-day business management

- Permanent residency in the United States for you, your partner and any children under 21

- Live, work and retire anywhere in the United States

- Become a U.S. citizen after 5 years of being a green card holder

- The investor is not required to live in the place of investment; rather, he or she can live wherever he/she wishes in the United States. * * *

An earlier version of the website described plans for an "exit strategy" after a minimum of two years:

Upon removal of temporary green card conditions for all eligible limited partners in the project, there is an exit strategy available whereby the limited partners will own individual fractional residential units within the deeded real property of the partnership. Jay Peak will manage the sale or rental of those units on behalf of the limited partners with all sales or rental proceeds being paid to the limited partner less any closing cost, realtor commission or management fee.

And this enticement: "Become a part of the excitement[.] EB–5 Visa Investors benefit from *2 weeks complimentary vacation* at Jay Peak Resort each year."

Two attorneys explained the attractions of regional centers to potential investors—especially as other employment-based preferences have become backlogged—as follows:

> Rewind to 2003. Options for immigrant investors were scarce, unattractive, non-existent, or exceptionally difficult to manage within the confines of the Immigration and Nationality Act (INA). Investors who would have previously considered the $1 million EB–5 option are now assessing whether this option makes any sense. Potential immigrant investors are questioning whether they should invest a minimum of $1 million in a "new" enterprise and then be burdened with the stress of needing to create 10 new "full-time" jobs within a two-year period for qualifying employees, when the same result (obtaining permanent residence and developing a successful business) can be achieved concurrently by passively investing $500,000 in a Regional Center project (which effectively outsources the job creation stress to the Regional Center operators), while engaging in either full-time employment or developing a separate business entity. An effective Regional Center program allows such investors to decouple their efforts in obtaining permanent residence from their efforts to continue their ongoing employment or develop their business interests as they see fit.

See Brandon Meyer & Karen Caco, *Spreading Like Wildfire!: What Explains the Explosive Growth of EB–5 Regional Centers?*, 10–02 Immigr. Briefings 3 (2010).

The EB–5 program, both in its basic form and through regional centers, has been a challenge for agency implementation, requiring detailed examination of complex business plans and transactions that are not typically part of its regulatory domain. The EB–5 program also presents many snares and pitfalls for immigration law practitioners. *See* Angelo A. Paparelli & Ted J. Chiappari, *Dollars and Jobs for EB–5 Green Cards: A Challenging Route to U.S. Residency*, 17 Bender's Immigr. Bull. (Oct. 1, 2012); Brandon Meyer & Karen Caco, *Now for the Hard Part: Attracting Investors to EB–5 Regional Centers,* 10–03 Immigr. Briefings (2010).

Critics have questioned whether the investments result in a significant level of enduring job creation, noting that USCIS does not track these cases in a way that readily provides information about business longevity or the number of jobs actually created. A report by the DHS Office of Inspector General observed:

> USCIS is unable to demonstrate the benefits of foreign investment into the U.S. economy. Although USCIS requires documentation that the foreign funds were invested in the investment pool by the foreign investor, the [Code of Federal Regulations] does not provide USCIS the authority to verify that the foreign funds were invested in companies creating U.S. jobs. Additionally, the CFR allows foreign investors to take credit for jobs created by U.S. investors. As a result, USCIS has limited oversight of regional centers' business structures and financial activities.

DHS Office of Inspector General, *U.S. Citizenship and Immigration Services' Employment-Based Fifth Preference (EB–5) Regional Center Program* 7–9 (Dec. 2013). *See also* Audrey Singer & Camille Galdes, *Improving the EB–5 Investor Visa Program: International Financing for U.S. Regional Economic Development* (Brookings-Rockefeller 2014). Moreover, the minimum investment level, set forth in the INA in 1990, has never been adjusted for inflation or other changes in the U.S. economy. (It would require over $900,000 in the year 2015 to make an investment equivalent to $500,000 in 1990 dollars.)

Other concerns involve the potential for fraud on potential investors and others. In 2013, the Securities and Exchange Commission and USCIS jointly issued an "Investor Alert" warning individual investors about fraudulent investment scams that exploit the EB–5 Program. *See* 90 Interp. Rel. 1992 (2013). According to one critical account:

> because the EB–5 industry is virtually unregulated, it has become a magnet for amateurs, pipedreamers, and charlatans, who see it as an easy way to score funding for ventures that banks would never touch. They've been encouraged and enabled by an array of dodgy middlemen, eager to cash in on the gold rush. Meanwhile, perhaps because wealthy foreigners are the main potential victims, U.S. authorities have seemed inattentive to abuses.

Peter Elkind & Marty Jones, *The Dark, Disturbing World of the Visa-For-Sale Program*, Fortune, July 24, 2014. In April 2016, the federal Securities and Exchange Commission and the Vermont Attorney General filed civil complaints against the two businessmen with lead roles in the Jay Peak Resort, alleging that they had engaged in a "massive eight-year fraudulent scheme" in raising funds for projects related to Jay Peak. *See* Katharine Q. Seelye, *Fraud Charges Mar a Plan to Aid a Struggling Vermont Region*, N.Y. Times, May 10, 2016.

Though a growing number of countries have immigrant investor programs offering lawful residence or even citizenship, Canada ended its nationwide program in 2014. The Minister of Citizenship and Immigration explained: "Research shows that immigrant investors pay less in taxes than other economic immigrants, are less likely to stay in Canada over the medium- to long-term and often lack the skills, including official language proficiency, to integrate as well as other immigrants from the same countries do." Press Release, Government of Canada, *Building a Fast and Flexible Immigration System* (Feb. 11, 2014). For an analysis of immigrant investor programs worldwide, see Sumption & Hooper, *supra,* at 19 (Migration Policy Inst. 2014).

EXERCISE: DESIGNING AN IMMIGRANT INVESTOR PROGRAM

You are an advisor to the democratically elected President of the newly independent European country of Meridian, which was once part of the former Soviet Union. Meridian currently has no immigrant investor program. It is your task to design one to enhance the economy of Meridian by attracting funds from wealthy individuals around the world.

The President would like you to design the new immigrant investor program with several general goals in mind. The program should:

- channel foreign funds reliably into the Meridian economy where the funds can do the most good;

- insure that investors acquire any immigration and citizenship benefits only if they fulfill program requirements;

- minimize the cost of administering the program; and

- counter the perception, both domestically and internationally, that residency rights or citizenship in Meridian are "for sale."

How would you design the program to meet these goals? Some aspects of program design are general. For example, must the funds be invested in private sector projects, or would the program require a direct payment to the Meridian government? Other aspects of program design are specific. For example, how much would be required, and how would you determine that amount?

The President would also like you to consider, as a variation on an investor program, whether it would be better to auction the same number of immigrant admission slots to the highest bidders, with the proceeds to go to a public works fund for highway construction and maintenance or for other job-creation purposes.

Are there other goals that a program should bear in mind, or other issues that you would need to address? Would more information about Meridian affect your analysis? If so, how?

5. EMPLOYMENT-BASED IMMIGRATION

Employment-based immigration involves complex standards and an elaborate, multi-agency process. We start our consideration with a snapshot from a *New Yorker* article written by Calvin Trillin after he spent several weeks examining the practice of immigration law in Houston. Though many details of the labor certification procedure that he describes have changed since he wrote, the article's lively depiction of the process' dynamics, tensions, and even contradictions remains timely. After that, we will examine the employment-based immigration categories, the labor certification process, and ways to avoid labor certification.

As you study this material, a key practical reality is that most noncitizens who qualify for employment-based immigration are already in the United States when they apply for lawful permanent resident status. In FY 2014, about 130,000 immigrants in the employment-based categories adjusted status to lawful permanent resident status from inside the United States, and only 22,000 were new arrivals. This means that an understanding of the employment-based immigration categories will be crucial when you continue on to Section B on Nonimmigrants.

CALVIN TRILLIN, MAKING ADJUSTMENTS
The New Yorker, May 28, 1984, at 61–62, 65–66.

The process of getting labor certification amounts to staging a sort of sham employment offer. The lawyer writes a job description that complies with the Department of Labor's standards, and the potential employer of the alien actually advertises such a job through the state employment commission. If someone shows up who is a citizen and has the qualifications outlined in the ad and is willing to work for the stated wage, the labor certification is not granted—although the employer has no obligation to give the citizen a job. If the lawyer who wrote the job description has been skillful, there is a good chance that no qualified citizen will show up. Writing job descriptions that pass the Department of Labor but attract no other potential employees is what Ed Prud'homme calls "one of the few art forms in the business," and Beaumont Martin is considered one of the artists. One of the Chinese students had managed to get a job in the accounting department of a small oil company, and, since the job required some computer expertise, Martin decided to write a job description that nudged her over a bit from accounting to computer analysis. ("There are a lot of people running around with accounting degrees.") When he had typed it up, he handed it to her:

SYSTEMS ANALYST 020.067–018

Conduct analyses of accounting, management, and operational problems and formulate mathematical models for solution by IBM computer system, using FORTRAN, COBOL, and PASCAL. Analyze problems in terms of management information. Write computer programs and devise and install accounting system and related procedures. Masters or equal in management information systems. $1667/month.

She read it over. "It's beautiful," she said. * * *

Along with the forms and folders on the floor next to Beaumont Martin's lounge chair was a worn copy of a fourteen-hundred-page government book called Dictionary of Occupational Titles—known to immigration lawyers as the D.O.T. For anyone who wants to make labor certification into an art form, the D.O.T. is an essential piece of equipment. It contains one-paragraph descriptions of virtually every occupation practiced by anybody in the United States. It describes the task of a neurosurgeon and it describes the task of a fibre-glass-container-winding operator. In a consistently direct style, it says what a leak hunter does ("Inspects barrels filled with beer or whisky to detect and repair leaking barrels") and what a sponge buffer does ("Tends machine that buffs edges of household sponges to impart rounded finish") and what an airline pilot does ("Pilots airplane"). Using the D.O.T. as a guide, an immigration lawyer tries to give the client an occupational title in the least crowded field available and then describe the job in a paragraph that sounds pretty much like a paragraph in the D.O.T. but happens to describe almost nobody but the client in question. "Immigration law is taking a short-order cook and making him into an executive chef," Pete Williamson told me. "What we're talking about here is a matter of focus."

When I was discussing labor certification with Pete Williamson one afternoon, he mentioned a young woman he had seen that day who wanted to stay in the country but did not fall into any of the categories of family reunification. She obviously did not qualify for any of the non-immigrant visas available to businessmen or investors. She was already married—to someone who, as it happened, had more or less the same visa problems that she did. Her only hope for a green card was labor certification. Her only occupation was looking after the children of a neighbor.

I said that it didn't sound promising. A few days with immigration lawyers had greatly broadened my view of how the employment sections of the immigration law were actually used. I was no longer under the delusion that the law worked to bring to this country people who had rare skills or worked in fields where there were serious shortages of American workers. "It's a matter of nudging the client's situation over a bit one way or another in order to make it fit into a category that's eligible," one lawyer had told me. "And sometimes, if you want to stay in the United States, you have to shape your career to fit the immigration law." Williamson had explained that it was possible for, say, a South American shirt manufacturer who wanted to resettle here to come in on a visitor's visa or a business visa, establish a corporation, have the personnel department of the corporation file an application to have him labor-certified as the president of a shirt firm doing business with Latin America ("Must know Spanish. Must be familiar with South American cottons . . ."), apply for a green card through the labor certification, and settle in for life. Still, it seemed unlikely that being a mother's helper in Texas was a job "for which a shortage of employable and willing persons exists."

There were two other important elements in the case, Williamson said. The young woman in question was a college graduate. Also, both she and the children she looked after were Muslims—all from Pakistan. Williamson intended to nudge her over from a nanny to a tutor—a tutor qualified to instruct the children in their own culture and religion. He thought it unlikely that any citizen with similar qualifications would respond to the ad. Williamson takes some satisfaction in such focusing—enough, he says, to offset the repetitiousness of certain aspects of the practice and the frustrations of dealing with the Immigration and Naturalization Service. "It's a competent, involved, technical job in which, if you're successful, you can see the consequences of your actions," he told me when I asked what appealed to him about practicing immigration law. "Also, I don't like the government."

---

a. Introduction

In fiscal year 2014, the employment-based categories—surveyed earlier in this chapter at pp. 277–279—accounted for 151,596 new lawful permanent residents of the United States. (This number includes the principal immigrants' spouses and children.) Of these, the vast majority are skilled workers, usually members of a profession, in the second and third employment-based preferences. To be sure, many immigrants come to this country each year to take up unskilled or low-skilled work, but they are more typically admitted in the family-based categories, or they may be unauthorized migrants.

Employers seeking the services of most immigrants who qualify in the employment-based categories are subject to a market test. They must show, usually by obtaining a labor certification, that no domestic workers are available to perform such work and that the immigrant will not adversely affect the wages and working conditions of similarly employed U.S. workers. INA § 212(a)(5)(A)(i). Labor certification is always required for immigrants in the third employment-based preference (EB–3). Labor certification is required in the second employment-based preference (EB–2), unless a waiver is obtained, as explored in Section A5c below.

No market test is required for the first preference category (EB–1): immigrants who have "extraordinary ability in the sciences, arts, education, business, or athletics," are professors or researchers "recognized internationally as outstanding in a specific academic area," or are managers or executives in multinational corporations. For this group, which represents about 25 percent of all employment-based immigration, the apparent reasoning is that either such immigrants have talents beyond compare, or that their contributions are so manifest that their admission is desirable whether or not they compete with domestic workers.

No need for labor certification

As we examine the employment categories, ask yourself how Congress has sought to balance the interests of employers in accessing a labor supply at low cost versus the interests of U.S. workers in protecting wages and working conditions. More fundamentally, why do we have special admission categories for workers who fill high-paying and prestigious jobs? Is the country unable to educate and train its own population for such jobs? Or does the United States seek to take advantage of the costs that other countries have incurred in training skilled workers and professionals? Are no U.S workers able and willing to take the jobs filled annually by 5,000 immigrants "performing unskilled labor"? INA § 203(b)(3)(A)(iii).

The next Exercise may help to guide your reading of the materials that follow, which examine the various legal requirements and their policy implications.

EXERCISE: LABOR CERTIFICATION

A local sociology professor comes to your law office for help. "I met the finest young student at a recent conference in Switzerland," he tells you. "His thoughtful comments at a seminar where I was a guest speaker attracted my attention. He's about to complete his bachelor's degree in sociology, and he wants to move to the United States. I told him I'd help him, and he said gratefully he'd be happy to serve as my research assistant. I could pay him minimum wage, and he'd drive me to work and mow my lawn as well. Surely it's easy to get a visa for an educated and upstanding young man like this." In your subsequent conversation with the professor, you learn that the young man is 23 years old and is fluent in English, German, French and Turkish.

What do you advise? How could you best construct a situation that might lead to the student's admission as an immigrant? What additional information do you need? What parts of the professor's and the student's plans would need to be altered to qualify the latter for an immigrant visa? What exactly are the procedural steps that must be followed, all the way from the initial job description to the student's admission at a port of entry (if that can be accomplished)?

b. Labor Certification

The impulse to protect American workers against immigrant competition has long played a role in U.S. immigration laws. Just ten years after Congress adopted first sustained federal immigration controls in 1875, it enacted the first labor-related immigration measure, the Contract Labor Law of 1885. Act of Feb. 26, 1885, Ch. 164, 23 Stat. 332. Congress strengthened its enforcement provisions two years later. Act of Feb. 23, 1887, Ch. 220, 24 Stat. 414. Described by a later congressional committee as "aimed at the practice of certain employers importing cheap labor from abroad," H.R. Rep. No. 1365, 82d Cong., 2d Sess. 12–13 (1952), the Act made it "unlawful to import aliens or assist in importation or migration of aliens . . . under contract, made previous to the importation or migration, for the performance of labor or service of any kind in the United States.

By the mid-twentieth century, support grew for selective efforts to fill gaps in the U.S. workforce with immigrant workers. Other measures, such as the National Labor Relations Act and the Fair Labor Standards Act, were thought to protect U.S. workers adequately against employer abuses. In 1952, Congress repealed the 1885 law, adopting in its place the first labor certification provision. It allowed the Secretary of Labor to block persons seeking to enter for the purpose of skilled or unskilled labor if their entry would displace or "adversely affect" the wages and working conditions of U.S. workers similarly employed. But the initiative rested with the Secretary of Labor, and the provision was seldom invoked.

In 1965, responding to effective lobbying led by the AFL-CIO, Congress reversed the operation of the labor certification process. Since then, the law has essentially presumed that foreign workers are not needed; the noncitizen and her intending employer must secure affirmative certification. The current labor certification provision is in INA § 212(a)(5).

(i) Overview

The absence of labor certification appears in § 212(a)(5) as an inadmissibility ground, but certification is more usefully viewed as a requirement for all immigrants in the employment-based third preference and some in the employment-based second preference. Section 204(b) makes this effect more explicit. Certification by the Department of Labor (DOL) establishes that a shortage of available and qualified workers exists in the noncitizen's field at the place of intended employment, and that her hiring on the offered terms would not adversely affect the wages or working conditions of similarly employed U.S. workers. In contrast, immigrants in family-based categories do not need labor certification, even if they intend to work in fields already well supplied with U.S. workers.

Employers apply for labor certification through a process known as Program Electronic Review Management, or PERM. *See* 20 C.F.R. Parts 655 and 656. In contrast to the system used before PERM was adopted in 2005, PERM relies primarily on attestations by employers that they have complied with regulatory requirements, subject to audit and to supervised recruitment in situations where noncompliance with requirements is more likely. Previously, employers had to document several stages of recruitment efforts in a voluminous file, which a DOL regional certifying officer (CO) would review. PERM was intended to alleviate the backlogs that had plagued decisionmaking in that system, with employers waiting two or three years for a decision.

Labor certification requires employers to make a good-faith recruitment effort—between 30 and 180 days before filing an application—to find qualified U.S. workers who are able and willing to work at the place of intended employment. Labor certification will be denied if such workers are available, or if the recruitment or documentation is inadequate. The job requirements—as set forth in the job descriptions used in recruiting—must not be unduly restrictive. Employers may reject interested U.S. workers only for lawful, job-related reasons. Employers must offer the "prevailing wage."

INA § 212(a)(5) lays out some of the basics, but many practical questions are left for the regulations to answer. How far must an employer search for U.S. workers? What if qualified workers are available in the state's largest city but they don't want to work at the employer's place of business 200 miles away? What if one U.S. worker would do so, provided he received a 20 percent boost in salary over the employer's initial offer? In what circumstances may the employer reject a U.S. applicant because he is not equally qualified with the noncitizen, even though he is minimally qualified for the job? When does the availability of an "equally qualified" U.S. worker *not* preclude certification?

Labor certification applications are filed directly with DOL on Form ETA 9089 (reprinted in the Statutory Supplement). The form includes sworn employer attestations under penalty of perjury that, among other things, the position has been and is open to any U.S. worker without discrimination, that the job opportunity did not become available as a result of a strike or lockout, and that the employer has the financial ability to pay the stated compensation. Form ETA 9089 also requires detailed information about the noncitizen whom the employer wishes to hire. The noncitizen must also sign the form under penalty of perjury and further declare that she intends to take the job if labor certification is approved.

In reality, most labor certifications applications are filed for employees who are already working for the applying employer in some type of nonimmigrant status with work authorization. This scenario explains a common reason for denial—that some of the noncitizen's required work experience was acquired while working for the same employer. This fact raises doubts about the job requirements, since the employer could equally well hire a U.S. worker with lower skills than advertised and then provide equivalent on-the-job training.

The regulations, as amended in 2007, forbid substitution of a different noncitizen as beneficiary after the application is filed. *See* 20 C.F.R. § 656.11(a). This limitation reflects DOL's judgment that the possibility of substitution had led to considerable abuse. Some employers or attorneys would obtain certification, DOL reported, then essentially auction or sell the approved position to another employee. 72 Fed. Reg. 27904, 27905 (2007). The regulations also expressly prohibit (1) barter or sale of applications and approved certifications; and (2) payments by or on behalf of the employee to reimburse the employer's costs for obtaining certification. *See* 20 C.F.R. § 656.12.

The Department of Labor Certifying Officer will either approve the application, require additional information, notify the employer that the application has been selected for audit, or deny the application if clearly deficient. Denials may be appealed to the Board of Alien Labor Certification Appeals (BALCA). After the employer has exhausted administrative remedies, judicial review of a denial is normally available in federal district court under the Administrative Procedure Act. Employers who misuse the system or violate the regulations can find their right to file future certifications suspended, be required to use supervised recruitment for future applications, or suffer criminal sanctions for willful falsehoods.

Assuming that the application is approved, the employer must file the labor certification with USCIS along with the employer's visa petition on Form I–140 within 180 days, or else the certification expires. *See* 20 C.F.R. § 656.30(b). The DOL certification is conclusive as to labor market conditions, but USCIS can deny a visa petition on other grounds, for example that the noncitizen is not qualified for the certified job, the employer is unable to pay the stated compensation, or the employee or employer has engaged in misrepresentation or fraud. USCIS transmits visa petition approvals to the USCIS office that will handle the noncitizen's adjustment of status, or less commonly to a Department of

State consular officer outside the United States for the issuance of an immigrant visa.

(ii) Job Requirements

How can the Labor Department guard against the obvious incentives, evident in the Trillin article, for employers and attorneys to write job descriptions that are tailored so precisely to the background of the noncitizen intended as a beneficiary that it would be nearly impossible that qualified U.S. workers will be found? Consider the creative lawyering at work in *Oriental Rug Importers v. E.T.A.*, 696 F.2d 47 (6th Cir. 1982). The employer, a rug importer and vendor, sought the services of an experienced buyer. The required qualifications, drawn neatly to fit the intended beneficiary, included 30 years' experience and training, proficiency in French and German, and possession of tools for reweaving rugs. The certifying officer found the qualifications unduly restrictive and denied the application for labor certification. The court affirmed.

Controversies over an employer's job requirements are a significant part of practice in this field. The next case remains the leading BALCA precedent on this issue. The application process and regulations have since been reorganized, but the basic requirements remain the same.

IN THE MATTER OF INFORMATION INDUSTRIES, INC.

Board of Alien Labor Certification Appeals, 1989.
1989 WL 103627, 88–INA–82.

* * *

STATEMENT OF THE CASE

The Employer, Information Industries, Inc., is a nationwide computer consulting business headquartered in Aurora, Colorado. Employer's business consists of hiring technical and professional computer specialists and contracting out their services to other companies. The job in question in this case was entitled a "Systems Engineer" by Employer. The employee hired for this position was to be contracted out to AT & T in Denver. The application for certification filed on December 15, 1986 listed the duties of the job as follows:

> Use UNIX and IBM operating systems to develop, implement and service scientific based operating systems for engineering firms and other clients. Includes converting symbolic statements of administrative data or business problems to detailed logical flow charts of coding into computer language. Analyzing business problems by applying knowledge of computer capabilities, subject matter, algebra, and symbolic logic to develop sequence of program steps. Analyzing, reviewing, and

rewriting programs to increase operating efficiency or adapt to new requirements. Compiling documentation of program development and subsequent revisions.

The only requirements for the job listed by Employer were a B.S. in Engineering and an M.S. in Computer Science.

In a Notice of Findings ("NOF") issued on August 10, 1987, the Certifying Officer ("CO") found that Employer's application had not met the requirements of the regulations. Employer filed a lengthy rebuttal on October 13, 1987. Certification was denied by a Final Determination issued on October 19, 1987, on the ground that the requirement of two degrees, a B.S. in Engineering and an M.S. in Computer Science, is unduly restrictive in violation of [20 C.F.R.] § 656.21(b)(2). * * *

DISCUSSION

* * *

b. *Business Necessity*

In 20 C.F.R. Part 656, DOL has set out procedures through which an employer, on behalf of an alien, can establish the factors required for certification. The regulations contain detailed requirements for the employer to advertise the job, recruit through the local job service office and otherwise, and offer terms and conditions of employment that match those prevailing in the relevant job market. If, after complying with these regulations, the employer can establish that there are no U.S. workers both qualified for the job and available to perform it, certification will be granted.

In advertising and recruiting for the job, § 656.21(b)(2)[c] requires that:

The employer shall document that the job opportunity has been and is being described without unduly restrictive job requirements:

(i) The job opportunity's requirements, unless adequately documented as arising from business necessity:

(A) Shall be those normally required for the job in the United States;

(B) Shall be those defined for the job in the Dictionary of Occupational Titles (D.O.T.) including those for subclasses of jobs;

(C) Shall not include requirements for a language other than English.

---

[c] The current regulation at 20 C.F.R. § 656.17(h) is substantially similar to the language that BALCA applies here, with further language addressing (a) business necessity justifications for foreign language requirements and (b) job opportunities that combine occupations.—eds.

What constitutes business necessity in the context of alien labor certification cases has produced some of the most controversial and diverse decisions in this area of the law. Since this is the first case in which the Board is attempting to address this issue in a definitive manner, it will be analyzed in great detail below.

In labor certification cases, judges have viewed business necessity from different perspectives. These different focuses have led to the development of inconsistent business necessity standards. The case law shows that those judges who have upheld the denial of labor certifications have often disregarded the employer's need to effectively operate its business, by focusing exclusively on the stated legislative purpose of protecting the U.S. workers. Courts following this rationale have adopted stringent business necessity standards. For instance, in *Pesikoff v. Secretary of Labor*, 501 F.2d 757 (D.C.Cir.1974), *cert. denied*, 419 U.S. 1038 (1974), the court stressed in its decision denying certification that the 1965 legislative shift in [the INA] was intended to protect the U.S. labor market from an influx of aliens. The court reasoned, therefore, that the Secretary has discretion ". . . to ignore employer specifications which he [the Secretary] deems in accordance with his labor market expertise, to be irrelevant to the basic job which the employer desires performed." *Id.* at 762. In a subsequent decision upholding a denial of certification in which it followed *Pesikoff*, the D.C. Circuit rejected a District Court's holding that "[e]very employer is entitled to hire persons who have qualifications that can be utilized in a manner that will contribute to the efficiency and quality of the business." *Acupuncture Center of Washington v. Dunlop*, 543 F.2d 852, 858 (D.C.Cir.1976).

Additionally, some judges have focused on how the term "business necessity" has been interpreted under Title VII of the Civil Rights Act of 1964 (42 U.S.C. § 2000e), adopting the strict business necessity standard set out in an early Title VII case, *Diaz v. Pan Am. World Airways, Inc.*, 442 F.2d 385 (5th Cir.1971). In the preamble to the Notice of Proposed Rulemaking for the current labor certification regulations, DOL defined "business necessity" as something the absence of which would undermine the essence of the business operation. 45 F.R. 4920 (Jan. 22, 1980).

This definition was substantively identical to the definition set out in *Diaz*. However, DOL and the Certifying Officer no longer contend that this definition should be adopted, conceding that it is not necessary that an entire business be undermined before certification can be granted. Rather, they agree that business necessity must be measured "in the context of the employment opportunity for which certification is being sought." In any event, the inappropriateness to alien labor certification cases of *Diaz* or similar standards holding business necessity to have been established "only when the essence of the business operation is undermined" (*Diaz, supra*, at 388) is readily apparent. For under this standard, business necessity could rarely, if ever, be established by any sizeable business entity. As an example, it is doubtful that a company such as AT & T could ever establish that the inability to fill a single job would undermine the essence of its business. Having created a procedure by which alien labor certification can be obtained, and allotting [a specific number of] visas yearly for this purpose, it is illogical to believe that Congress intended it would be virtually impossible for employers to obtain such certification. Therefore, since none of the parties advocate the *Diaz* test, and we believe it is inherently inappropriate to apply this standard in labor certification cases, that test will not be adopted by the Board.

In contrast, judges who have refused to substitute their own business judgments for those of the employer have often accepted any offered business justification for hiring an alien. As a result, courts which have focused on the needs of employers have adopted a more lenient business necessity standard. The court, in granting labor certification in *Silva v. Secretary of Labor*, 518 F.2d 301 (1st Cir.1975), concluded that the legislative intent after 1965 was not to confer on the Secretary a right to treat as irrelevant the employer's job preferences. *Id.* at 310. Similarly, the court in *Ratnayake v. Mack*, 499 F.2d 1207 (8th Cir.1974), in its grant of certification, reasoned that some deference must be accorded to employers in setting forth the needed employment qualifications, because an employer is in the best position to judge what is needed for its business. The court held that "the job requirements of an employer are not to be set aside if they are shown to be reasonable and tend to contribute to or enhance the efficiency and quality of the business." *Id.* at 1212. In that same vein, the court in *Jadeszko v. Brennan*, 418 F. Supp. 92, 95 (E.D.Pa.1976), stated that "Congress has not given [the Secretary] the authority to say that one who wants to employ a baker in the morning must be content with a candle stick maker who is willing to work in the afternoon."

c. Business Necessity Standard

Having analyzed the legislative history of the Act, the applicable regulations, and the relevant case law, it is the Board's opinion that in adopting a business necessity standard, consideration must be given both to the preference system which recognizes that the United States can benefit from alien labor, and to the purpose of labor certification, i.e., the protection of the American worker. Since the statutory burden is on the employer to justify certification, emphasis should be placed on protecting the American worker; but Congress's recognition that alien labor can benefit the United States should not be ignored.

Our task is somewhat easier following oral argument, since the more extreme positions have been rejected by the parties. Not only has the

Certifying Officer disaffirmed a strict "essence of the business operation" test, but conversely both Employer and amicus agree that more can be required in establishing business necessity then merely "tend[ing] to contribute to or enhance the efficiency and quality of the business." *See* Statement of American Immigration Lawyer's Association's Alternative Business Necessity Test, at 3, quoting *Ratnayake, supra*, at 1212. * * *

We hold that, to establish business necessity under § 656.21(b)(2)(i), an employer must demonstrate that the job requirements bear a reasonable relationship to the occupation in the context of the employer's business and are essential to perform, in a reasonable manner, the job duties as described by the employer. This standard, in assuring both that the job's requirements bear a reasonable relationship to the occupation and are essential to perform the job duties, gives appropriate emphasis to the Act's presumption that qualified U.S. workers are available. An employer cannot obtain alien labor certification by showing that the job requirements merely "tend to contribute to or enhance the efficiency and quality of the business."[9] On the other hand, this standard is not impossible to meet. An employer has the discretion, within reason, to obtain certification for any job whose requirements are directly related to its business, and does not have to establish dire financial consequences if the job is not filled or is filled by a U.S. worker who is not fully qualified.

Turning to the facts of this case, the Certifying Officer denied certification because she found that Employer's job requirements were unduly restrictive, in violation of § 656.21(b)(2). It is Employer's position that its requirements are normal for this job in the United States, and conform to the D.O.T. If Employer is correct, then it is not required to establish that the job requirements arise from business necessity.

In addressing Employer's contention, first, the specific title of the job must be determined. The CO contends that the position is that of "Programmer, Engineering and Scientific;" D.O.T. Code 020.167–022; Employer states that the position is that of "Systems Engineer," D.O.T. Code 003.167–062. Until the correct job title is determined, it cannot be decided whether the job requirements are normal for the job in the United States. That the requirements conform to the D.O.T. is clear, for the only job requirement for either job title in the D.O.T. is a Specific Vocational Preparation rating ("SVP") of 8. An SVP of 8 means that it is permissible for the Employer to require up to 10 years of education and experience; thus, the two-degree requirement in this case does not conflict

_____

[9]   For example, for a position as a lawyer, a job requirement of the ability to play golf usually cannot be justified as a business necessity even if the employer listed playing golf as a job duty on the Form 750–A. Although it may "tend to contribute to or enhance the efficiency and quality of the business" socially and perhaps even economically, playing golf generally does not bear a reasonable relationship to the occupation of practicing law.

with the D.O.T. Moreover, the position does not require fluency in a foreign language.

In regard to whether the job requirements are normal for this job in the U.S., neither party's position is established by the record. Although the duties of the job are set out in the [application form], they are expressed in technical jargon which cannot be precisely understood by laymen. Neither party attempted to explain these job duties in lay terms. That a so-called expert body offered an opinion which was relied upon by the CO is insufficient, since that evidence contains little more than the conclusions of that body, without explanation or reasoning. Nor did either party attempt to analyze the job's requirements in terms of the job duties, as required under our business necessity test. Thus Employer has not explained which job duties require its systems engineers to have a B.S. in Engineering, and the CO has not explained why this degree, or a Masters in Computer Science, are not bona fide requirements for the position regardless of which title best suits it.

Moreover, as counsel for the CO apparently admitted at the oral argument, it cannot be determined exactly which job requirement the CO alleged to be unduly restrictive—the requirement that the applicant have a B.S. specifically in engineering, or the requirement of having both a Bachelor's and a Master's degree.

Under these circumstances, this case must be remanded to the Certifying Officer. On remand, the CO shall determine which job title best describes this job, and further determine whether the job requirements are normal for that job title in the U.S. If the CO finds that the job requirements are not normal, and are unduly restrictive, a Notice of Findings clearly setting out her findings and the reasoning behind them shall be issued. Employer shall than have the opportunity to file an appropriate rebuttal addressing, inter alia, the business necessity standard set out in this decision.

ORDER

The Certifying Officer's denial of certification is vacated, and the case is remanded to the CO for further proceedings consistent with this decision.

[Concurring opinions of JUDGES LITT and BRENNER omitted.]

NOTES AND QUESTIONS ON JOB REQUIREMENTS

1. On remand, the certifying officer again denied labor certification, still unconvinced that the two-degree requirement was justifiable. The CO's opinion noted:

The two-degree requirement is found to be unduly restrictive as it exceeds those defined for the occupation in the DOT and is not normally required for similar jobs in the U.S.

This finding is based on a comparison with other labor certification applications processed by the Certifying Officer, including those previously filed and currently pending by the employer. * * *

It appears employer has structured the requirements around the alien's qualifications, thus they do not represent the actual minimum requirements for the job * * * .

Notice of Findings, Nov. 6, 1989. The noncitizen subsequently moved to Michigan, where his employer obtained labor certification and ultimately permanent residence for him. (This outcome illustrates the regional variation that the PERM system tries to remedy through greater centralization and standardization.)

2.   The Dictionary of Occupational Titles, a standard part of labor certification practice for decades, has been replaced by a new computerized database system called O*NET, "the system developed by the Department of Labor, Employment and Training Administration, to provide to the general public information on skills, abilities, knowledge, work activities, interests and specific vocational preparation levels associated with occupations." 20 C.F.R. § 656.3. O*NET occupational category descriptions list such things as the tasks typically performed, the knowledge, skills and abilities engaged, and—significantly for labor certification—the specific vocational preparation (SVP) normally required. The regulations define SVP as "the amount of lapsed time required by a typical worker to learn the techniques, acquire the information, and develop the facility needed for average performance in a specific job-worker situation." 20 C.F.R. 656.3.

3.   As proposed in 2002, the PERM regulations would have made significant changes in the business necessity test. The explanatory material accompanying the notice of proposed rulemaking gave this rationale:

The business necessity standard, currently at 20 CFR 656.21(b), often works to the disadvantage of U.S. workers. This regulation has been difficult to administer and has generated a greater amount of litigation than any other regulatory provision in the current regulations. Since the position for which certification is sought is usually held by an alien worker who is the beneficiary of the application, job requirements tend to be manipulated to favor the selection of the alien. The existing business necessity standard requires the CO to evaluate the unique standards of an employer's business. In highly technical areas this is an extremely difficult undertaking and may be subject to employer manipulation since we are in no position to second guess the employer in such circumstances.

We have concluded that any business necessity standard that may be adopted would present similar problems. Therefore, the proposed rule would not retain a business necessity standard as a justification for employer's job requirements that exceed requirements that are normal to jobs in the United States.

67 Fed. Reg. 30466, 30472 (2002).

The proposed rules would have let employers deviate from normal requirements only in limited circumstances that DOL believed more readily lent themselves to objective determination. Foreign language requirements would have been allowed only if clearly required for the job (for example, a translator) or if the employer documented that a large majority of its customers or contractors cannot communicate in English and that the job requires frequent contact with them. For other nonstandard requirements, the employer would have to show either that it had employed a U.S. worker for the position on those terms within the two years preceding the filing, or that the requirements are "normal to the occupation" and routinely required by other employers in the industry.

The final regulations did not incorporate these proposed changes. Instead, the regulations incorporate the *Information Industries* business necessity standard. *See* 20 C.F.R. § 656.17(h)(1). Does it provide workable and effective guidelines that are consistent with the basic policies underlying the statute? BALCA cases since *Information Industries* have tended to show that the first prong of the test, requiring a "reasonable relationship" between job requirements and the occupation is relatively easy to satisfy. Of greater importance in most cases is the second prong, requiring that the job requirements "are *essential* to perform, in a reasonable manner, the job duties." (Emphasis added.) What are the advantages and disadvantages of the changes proposed in 2002, as compared to the business necessity standard in *Information Industries*?

4.   When are foreign language requirements allowed? Consider these facts: employer applies for a labor certification for a "cleaning manager" to manage the company's "home cleaning division which cleans and maintains residences occupied by handicapped and aged customers unable to attend to their own needs." The job requirements included the ability to speak Spanish. Employer asserts that it is virtually impossible to find U.S. workers willing to take janitorial jobs and therefore it is essential that the supervisor of the employees, most of whom are new immigrants, be Spanish-speaking. Is the requirement permissible? *See Matter of Home Assistance, Inc.*, 1997 WL 580520, No. 95–INA–391 (BALCA 1997) (affirming denial of certification for failure to provide sufficient documentation of need).

The current regulations include specific criteria to be met if the employer wants to require foreign language skills:

(2) A foreign language requirement can not be included, unless it is justified by business necessity. Demonstrating business

necessity for a foreign language requirement may be based upon the following:

(i) The nature of the occupation, e.g., translator; or

(ii) The need to communicate with a large majority of the employer's customers, contractors, or employees who can not communicate effectively in English, as documented by:

(A) The employer furnishing the number and proportion of its clients, contractors, or employees who can not communicate in English, and/or a detailed plan to market products or services in a foreign country; and

(B) A detailed explanation of why the duties of the position for which certification is sought requires frequent contact and communication with customers, employees or contractors who can not communicate in English and why it is reasonable to believe the allegedly foreign-language-speaking customers, employees, and contractors can not communicate in English.

20 C.F.R. § 656.17(h)(2).

5. On another recurring issue—combining duties in one job—the regulations provide:

(3) If the job opportunity involves a combination of occupations, the employer must document that it has normally employed persons for that combination of occupations, and/or workers customarily perform the combination of occupations in the area of intended employment, and/or the combination job opportunity is based on a business necessity. Combination occupations can be documented by position descriptions and relevant payroll records, and/or letters from other employers stating their workers normally perform the combination of occupations in the area of intended employment, and/or documentation that the combination occupation arises from a business necessity.

20 C.F.R. § 656.17)(h)(3).

6. On the responsibilities of the Department of Labor and the Department of Homeland Security in assessing job requirements and whether an individual worker satisfies those requirements, see *Hoosier Care, Inc. v. Chertoff*, 482 F.3d 987 (7th Cir. 2007).

(iii)   The Prevailing Wage Requirement

The Labor Department's regulations, *see* 20 C.F.R. § 656.40, require employers to pay the certified noncitizen at least the prevailing wage, even if she would be willing to work for less. Prevailing wage determinations are administered by the Office of Foreign Labor Certification (OFLC) National Prevailing Wage and Helpdesk Center

(NPWHC) in Washington, D.C. This part of labor certification reflects the statutory directive that employment of the noncitizen not "adversely affect the wages and working conditions of the workers in the United States similarly employed." But what wage level is "prevailing"? What is the relevant group for comparison, and how much discretion should the Secretary have in making such decisions?

Is the prevailing wage determined differently for different types of employers even if the work performed is the same? In 1988, a divided BALCA held that Tuskegee University could use the 43 schools in the United Negro College Fund—not all nearby colleges—as its comparison group. See *Matter of Tuskegee University*, 5 Imm. L. & Proc. Rep. B3–172 (BALCA 1988). In 1994, unanimously overruling *Tuskegee*, BALCA declined to let a nonprofit treatment center for handicapped children hire a "maintenance repairer" at a prevailing wage determined in reference to wages at other United Way nonprofit agencies. *See Matter of Hathaway Children's Services*, 1994 WL 29778, 91–INA–388 (BALCA, 1994). Part of BALCA's reasoning was that the INA and the regulations allow no waivers of the prevailing wage requirement based on employer hardship.

In 1998, Congress overruled *Hathaway* as it applies to employees of institutions of higher education and of affiliated nonprofit entities, and to employees of all nonprofit and governmental research organizations. The prevailing wage for such positions is now determined by reference to comparable nonprofit institutions, not by comparison to researchers at private, for-profit employers. INA § 212(p). The regulations maintain this approach. But an employer like Hathaway is still covered by the wider economy's prevailing wage. Should it be? What policy is served if the job goes unfilled because Tuskegee or Hathaway cannot pay that wage?

The "prevailing wage" requirement raises deeper issues. Insisting on such wages prevents a *deterioration* of pay scales, but there are other possible adverse effects. Should the Department of Labor be equally concerned about retarding increases in wages that might otherwise occur in times of labor shortage?

Consider a concrete example. Professional nurses are in such short supply that licensed nurses are exempt from individual labor certification under the provisions of Schedule A as explained below. But a large number of U.S. workers who are trained nurses do not practice that profession because wages are low and they have better opportunities for higher pay in other fields. If hospitals could not hire immigrant nurses at current wages, what would likely happen? Would employers bid up wages, drawing many qualified workers back into the labor pool, and inducing more people to develop the necessary skills and training? Or does this depend on other factors? How would an inability to hire immigrants affect wages and working conditions in the restaurant or hotel business, in factories, in marginal small businesses, or in agriculture? Does your answer suggest that the Department of Labor's time horizon is too short or its vision too restricted, given how a free-market system works? Or is the DOL approach a justified way to keep down hospital costs or to keep marginally profitable hospitals open and functioning? Is DOL the appropriate government agency to make such a policy decision?

(iv)   *Labor Certification and the Lawyer's Role*

The Trillin article that opened our consideration of employment-based immigration describes the certification process in language, such as "sham employment offer," that obviously departs from the way practicing attorneys would think of—or would want others to think of—their role. (Those characterizations were Trillin's, not those of the attorneys he had observed, and the article was sharply criticized by the immigration bar.) A focal point is the lawyer's role in an employer's recruitment and hiring process. The DOL regulations provide:

(b) Representation.

(1) Employers may have agents or attorneys represent them throughout the labor certification process. If an employer intends to be represented by an agent or attorney, the employer must sign the statement set forth on the Application for Permanent Employment Certification form: That the attorney or agent is representing the employer and the employer takes full responsibility for the accuracy of any representations made by the attorney or agent. Whenever, under this part, any notice or other document is required to be sent to the employer, the document will be sent to the attorney or agent who has been authorized to represent the employer on the Application for Permanent Employment Certification form.

(2)(i) It is contrary to the best interests of U.S. workers to have the alien and/or agents or attorneys for either the employer or the alien participate in interviewing or considering U.S. workers for the job offered the alien. As the beneficiary of a labor certification application, the alien can not represent the best interests of U.S. workers in the job opportunity. The alien's agent and/or attorney can not represent the alien effectively and at the same time truly be seeking U.S. workers for the job opportunity. Therefore, the alien and/or the alien's agent and/or attorney may not interview or consider U.S. workers for the job offered to the alien, unless the agent and/or attorney is the employer's representative, as described in paragraph (b)(2)(ii) of this section.

(ii) The employer's representative who interviews or considers U.S. workers for the job offered to the alien must be the person who normally interviews or considers, on behalf of the employer, applicants for job opportunities such as that offered the alien, but which do not involve labor certifications.

20 C.F.R. § 656.10(b)(1), (2). These provisions suggest that an attorney must perform a difficult balancing act in advising on legal requirements while not improperly distorting the labor market test that recruitment is supposed to accomplish.

DOL announced in June 2008 that it would audit over 2,500 labor certification applications filed by Fragomen Del Ray Bernsen & Loewy LLP, a leading U.S. immigration law firm. The impetus for the audit was DOL's belief that Fragomen may have violated the governing regulation by directing some clients to consult with the law firm before hiring U.S. workers. Fragomen responded in August by suing DOL in federal court to stop the audit, asserting that DOL had improperly adopted a new interpretation of the regulation, in violation of statutes and the U.S. Constitution. *See Fragomen Fires Back at Department of Labor*, 85 Interp. Rel. 2349 (2008).

Later in August 2008, responding to "considerable feedback from employers and employer representatives including attorneys and agents, that regularly practice in or make use of the PERM program," DOL issued new guidance on attorney involvement in the recruitment and hiring process. The new guidance, which DOL explained would supersede the documents that DOL issued when it initiated the Fragomen audits, provides in part:

> The Department has long held the view that good faith recruitment requires that an employer's process for considering U.S. workers who respond to certification-related recruitment closely resemble the employer's normal consideration process. In most situations, that normal hiring process does not involve a role for an attorney or agent * * * in assessing the qualifications of applicants to fill the employer's position. It also does not involve any role for the foreign worker or foreign national in any aspect of the consideration process. However, given that the permanent labor certification program imposes recruitment standards on the employer that may deviate from the employer's normal standards of evaluation, the Department understands and appreciates the legitimate role attorneys and agents play in the permanent labor certification process. Additionally, the Department respects the right of employers to consult with their attorney(s) or agent(s) during that process to ensure that they are complying with all applicable legal requirements.

By prohibiting attorneys, agents, and foreign workers from interviewing and considering U.S. workers during the permanent labor certification process, * * * the Department does not thereby prohibit attorneys and agents from performing the analyses necessary to counsel their clients on legal questions that may arise with respect to this process. The employer, and not the attorney or agent, must be the first to review an application for employment, and must determine whether a U.S. applicant's qualifications meet the minimum requirements for the position, unless the attorney or agent is the representative of the employer who routinely performs this function for positions for which labor certifications are not filed. * * * Attorneys (and, to the extent it is consistent with state rules governing the practice of law, agents) may, however, provide advice throughout the consideration process on any and all legal questions concerning compliance with governing statutes, regulations, and policies.

* * * Attorneys and agents may receive resumes and applications of U.S. workers who respond to the employer's recruitment efforts; however, they may not conduct any preliminary screening of applications before the employer does so, other than routine clerical or ministerial organizing of resumes which does not include any assessment of, or comments on, the qualifications of any applicants, unless the attorney or agent is the representative of the employer who routinely performs this function for positions for which labor certifications are not filed. The attorney or agent may not withhold from the employer any resumes or applications that it receives from U.S. workers.

Attorneys and agents may not participate in the interviewing of U.S. worker applicants, unless the attorney or agent is the representative of the employer who routinely performs this function for positions for which labor certifications are not filed. Such involvement has resulted in an impermissible "chilling effect" on the interests of U.S. worker-applicants in the position.

U.S. Department of Labor, Restatement of PERM Program Guidance Bulletin on the Clarification of Scope of Consideration Rule in 20 C.F.R. § 656.10(b)(2) (Aug. 29, 2008).

In September 2008, DOL suspended the audit as part of a settlement between DOL and the Fragomen law firm in October 2008. *See* Erin Marie Daly, *DOL Drops Audit of Fragomen's Green Card Cases*, Law 360,

Sept. 18, 2008; *Fragomen Firm and DOL File Joint Stipulation of Settlement and Order*, 85 Interp. Rel. 3034 (2008).

(v) Assessing Labor Certification

The labor certification process appears to rely on a straightforward model: when an employer who is looking to fill an existing job cannot find a qualified U.S. worker to take it, he or she should be able to tap into the foreign labor market to fill a job important to the conduct of the business. But as you now know, this is not how it works in practice. Because of the rule barring substitution of beneficiaries, the employer already must know the noncitizen he or she would like to employ. Indeed, usually the noncitizen is already working for the employer—legally in a nonimmigrant category or unlawfully. The employer then describes the job in a manner tailored, to the extent legally possible, to the specific qualifications of the would-be immigrant and attempts to demonstrate to the Department of Labor that no U.S. worker is available with those particular qualifications to perform the carefully defined job duties.

As might be expected, this system has been thoroughly criticized. An early example is an audit of the labor certification process in 1996 by DOL's Office of Inspector General (OIG). The audit found that for the 24,150 noncitizens for whom labor certification applications were approved during the audit period, 99 percent were in the United States when the application was filed; 74 percent were working for the U.S. employer at the time of application (16 percent of whom were working illegally); 11 percent never worked for the petitioning employer after adjustment to lawful permanent resident status; and 17 percent left the employer within six months after becoming lawful permanent residents. In examining 600 randomly selected cases, the OIG also found that in almost a quarter of the cases, the employers received no resumes in response to their advertising of the job; for the three-quarters of the cases that did generate applications from U.S. workers, only 0.08 percent of such workers were hired—and then to fill other jobs with the employer, not to take the job for which the noncitizen's services were sought.

The audit concluded that the labor certification process was "perfunctory at best and a sham at worst," a "time-consuming paper shuffle that employers endure to give the appearance of complying with the law." It is "ineffective in ensuring that qualified, willing, and available U.S. workers are given a fair opportunity to compete for the jobs for which aliens are hired." U.S. Department of Labor, Office of the Inspector General, The Department of Labor's Foreign Labor Certification Programs: The System is Broken and Needs To Be Fixed, Rep. No. 06–96–002–03–321, at 2, 7, 12 (1996). For a strong critique of the audit's methodology and conclusions, see Steven C. Bell, *Analysis of the Inspector General's Audit of the Department of Labor's Foreign Labor*

Certification Programs (NAFSA Working Paper No. 63, 1999), summarized at 76 Interp. Rel. 1494 (1999).

For a different sort of criticism of the labor certification process, see Ben A. Rissing & Emilio J. Castilla, *House of Green Cards: Statistical or Preference-Based Inequality in the Employment of Foreign Nationals*, 79 Am. Soc. Rev. 1226 (2014) (concluding that labor certification approvals differ significantly depending on a worker's country of citizenship, with workers from Latin America less likely to receive approvals than workers from Canada or Asian countries, even after controlling for key factors).

Other developments regarding H–1B temporary workers undermine the rationale of the labor certification system in another way. In a typical pattern, a noncitizen is in H–1B temporary worker status, and the employer applies for labor certification for that employee. When processing backlogs grew in the 1990s, Congress responded with the American Competitiveness in the Twenty-first Century Act ("AC21") § 106, Pub. L. 106–313, 114 Stat. 1251 (2000). This legislation raised the ceiling on H–1B admissions (later reduced), and it eased the situation of H–1B workers awaiting permanent residence status. It let H–1B workers switch jobs more readily while waiting, and it allowed extensions of H–1B status beyond the normal six-year limit.

Noteworthy for labor certification is that AC 21 also adopted new INA § 204(j). This section allows some employment-based adjustment applicants to remain eligible for adjustment of status, even if they change jobs or employers. Adjustment applicants may do so if their application has been pending for 180 days or more, and the new job is in "the same or similar" field as the job for which the originating visa petition was filed. The labor certification remains valid under INA § 212(a)(5)(A)(iv).

This "portability" provision for H–1B workers calls into question many of the labor protections once thought (at least formally) to be hallmarks of the traditional labor certification system. Changing jobs or employers is allowed, as long as the job is "similar." This makes irrelevant any protection to U.S. workers ostensibly provided by the labor certification, which was premised on a finding that there were no U.S. workers available *at the place* mentioned in the original application. *See* INA § 212(a)(5)(A)(i)(I). Prevailing wages are also determined, in most instances, according to a specific geographic market. If the employee's new job is in a higher-wage region, should the new employer be allowed to pay the lower wage where the employee had been working?

Further, in adjudicating the related I–140 petitions, USCIS has traditionally paid close attention to whether the petitioning employer is capable of paying the wage or salary stated in the labor certification process. Will this requirement apply to the subsequent employer? Suppose that the original employer, around the time the employee is switching jobs, withdraws the I–140 visa petition—an unsurprising reaction in such circumstances. Should that prevent the noncitizen from gaining lawful permanent resident status? Why—if Congress already contemplated that he might not work for that employer anyway? Section § 204(j) subtly but fundamentally challenges many underlying protection premises of labor certification. For more on how USCIS is addressing these issues, see USCIS, Policy Memorandum on Determining Whether a New Job is in "the Same or a Similar Occupational Classification" for Purposes of Section 204(j) Job Portability, Mar. 18, 2016.

c. Easing or Avoiding Labor Certification

As should be clear by now, labor certification is a time-consuming, highly technical, and expensive process. For these reasons, good immigration lawyers seek to avoid labor certification whenever possible. Use the following Exercise, along with the materials following it, to gain greater familiarity with the available options. (The Exercise refers to the key regulations, which are reprinted in the Statutory Supplement).

EXERCISE

An American university seeks to hire a promising young scientist from India for the physics department, with the rank of assistant professor. Even though he obtained his Ph.D. degree just three years ago, the university's interest was sparked by a "brilliant" article he published in an international journal. University officials have not decided just how much teaching they would want him to perform, because they are primarily interested in his joining a high-powered research team that they hope will win large foundation and government grants for the university. The employment-based second preference would seem to fit, but that category ordinarily requires labor certification, and the university is concerned that the process will take years.

The university has engaged you as its lawyer to secure the approval of his immigration papers. What do you advise? Consider at least:

- the "equally qualified" provisions of INA § 212(a)(5)(A)(ii) (*see* 20 C.F.R. § 656.18)

- Schedule A (*see* 20 C.F.R. §§ 656.5(b)(1), 656.15)

- the national interest waiver of the employer petition requirement (*see* § 203(b)(2)(B)(i))

- the "priority worker" (EB–1) categories of INA § 203(b)(1) (the preference) (*see* 8 C.F.R. § 204.5(g)–(*l*))

What would each of these options accomplish for your client? Which would allow you to avoid the individual labor certification process?

(i) Schedule A

DOL's Schedule A, 20 C.F.R. § 656.5, lists occupations judged short of qualified U.S. workers. It amounts to a blanket determination that anyone seeking that kind of work in the United States will not displace U.S. workers or adversely affect wages and working conditions. The Schedule has been reduced over the years, because Congress has moved some of its former categories into the first or fourth employment-based preferences, which do not require labor certification. As of February 2016, Schedule A includes only licensed nurses, physical therapists, and certain noncitizens "of exceptional ability" in the sciences, arts, or performing arts. If the occupational category appears on Schedule A, the employer can skip DOL and go directly to USCIS with Form ETA 9089 and its I–140 visa petition.

(ii) National Interest Waivers

Under INA § 203(b)(2)(B), the requirement that a second-preference immigrant's services be sought by an employer in the United States, may be waived, if waiver is deemed "in the national interest." The regulations, without further elaboration of the "national interest" standard, provide that such a waiver also exempts the individual from labor certification. 8 C.F.R. § 204.5(k)(4)(ii).

The current standard is a three-pronged test set out in 1998 in the precedent decision of *Matter of New York State Dept. of Transportation (NYSDOT)*, 22 I & N Dec. 215 (Assoc. Comm'r 1998), discussed in 75 Interp. Rel. 1289–99 (1998). *NYSDOT* requires the petitioner to show first that the noncitizen will be employed "in an area of substantial intrinsic merit," and second that "the proposed benefit will be national in scope." The third prong requires that "[t]he petitioner seeking the waiver must persuasively demonstrate that the national interest would be adversely affected if a labor certification were required for the alien." 22 I & N Dec. at 217–18.

What do national interest waiver cases look like in practice? One practitioner offers this sketch of some representative cases involving the second prong, that "the proposed benefit that will be national in scope":

> In April 2012, [the Administrative Appeals Office (AAO) of USCIS] ruled that the work of an acupuncturist could not be considered national in scope since "direct impact of patient treatment is limited to the patients themselves." In May 2011, the AAO ruled that a speech language pathologist could not demonstrate national scope since the benefits of her work were so attenuated and there was no evidence that the beneficiary would be developing national standards or curricula. * * *

Through these decisions the AAO has established that important regional impact cannot stand in the place of national influence.

In a January 2010 decision for a cardiologist, the AAO reviewed the matter of "national scope" and distinguished between national impact and purely local effect. The cardiologist not only worked as a physician but also performed clinical research. In its decision, the AAO noted, "While cardiac treatment as a whole serves the national interest, the impact of a single cardiologist at the national level is negligible ... Nevertheless, the petitioner is involved in ongoing clinical research that he publishes and presents at conferences. There is no evidence that he seeks to abandon his clinical research to work solely as a physician. Thus, we are satisfied that the proposed benefits of his research would be national in scope." Here, the AAO validates scientific research as a means for fulfilling the "national scope" requirement.

Paul Herzog, *The National Interest Waiver: Understanding Its History and Navigating Its Terrain*, 90 Interp. Rel. 1955, 1956 (2013).

Herzog has illustrations for the third, typically most difficult prong:

The AAO has repeatedly made the point that the petitioner satisfies this criterion when he or she can "demonstrate a past history of achievement with some degree of influence on the field as a whole." For researchers, an effective way of demonstrating this is through extensive citation of published work. For example, in an April 22, 2011, decision, the AAO reversed a denial by the service center in the case of a chemist, noting that her scholarly articles had been cited hundreds of times. * * * In a November 2011 decision, the AAO noted that, while the letters of reference seemed to have all been written by the same person and the petitioner had only four published articles, those four articles had been cited over 400 times.

By contrast, in two decisions issued on the same day, the AAO upheld denials. In one case involving an international relations scholar, the AAO noted that, while the petitioner had authored articles and presented his work, the case lacked evidence that these articles actually had influence on the field as a whole. The AAO specifically referred to the absence of citations. Lack of citation was also a factor in the other case involving a materials engineer. In upholding the denial, the AAO noted the paucity of citations to the petitioner's published work and the absence of evidence demonstrating that the petitioner's work had influence upon the field as a whole.

Id. at 1957. For further guidance, see Megan Kludt, Anna Angel & Kelsey Camire, *Recent Trends in National Interest Waiver Cases*, 18–12 Bender's Immigr. Bull. 01 (2013).

(iii)   Aliens of Extraordinary Ability (EB–1A)

The first subcategory of priority workers, individuals with "extraordinary ability in the sciences, arts, education, business, or athletics" (who also meet certain other stipulations) occupies a highly favored position. Such workers are exempt from labor certification and need not persuade an employer to file on their behalf. Instead, they may self-petition, filing Form I–140 directly with USCIS.

Picture yourself as the USCIS examiner considering the petition. How do you decide whether the petitioner's abilities are extraordinary? Exactly what is the difference between extraordinary ability and merely exceptional ability (the stuff of the second employment-based preference)?

The agencies have adopted regulations that try to translate these broad statutory phrases into administrable form. *See* 8 C.F.R. § 204.5(g)–(*l*) (in the Statutory Supplement) (giving operational content to some of the vague terms used for EB–1 and EB–2 categories). The regulations tend to use a menu approach, requiring the petitioner to present evidence in a certain number of categories set forth in the regulation. But controversies arise, as the next case shows.

VISINSCAIA V. BEERS
United States District Court, District of Columbia, 2013.
4 F. Supp. 3d 126.

BOASBERG, UNITED STATES DISTRICT JUDGE.

This case calls on the Court to decide whether Plaintiff Svetlana Visinscaia is a great ballroom dancer or merely a very good one. Visinscaia, a native and citizen of Moldova, was admitted to the United States on August 5, 2011, on an F–1 visa to attend community college in Virginia. Toward the end of her first year in this country, she filed a petition asking the United States Citizenship and Immigration Service to reclassify her as an "alien of extraordinary ability," a status that would allow her to remain here as a competitive dancer and coach. As evidence of her ability and renown as a dancer, Visinscaia submitted a number of published reports about her performances, as well as awards and letters from colleagues and students attesting to her leading role in the international "Dance Sport" community. USCIS nonetheless denied her application on the ground that she did not satisfy the statutory requirements for an extraordinary-ability visa.

After exhausting her administrative options, Visinscaia filed suit in this Court under the Administrative Procedure Act, alleging that the agency's denial was arbitrary and capricious and an abuse of discretion. * * * Although Visinscaia has produced impressive evidence of her successful career as a dancer and dance instructor, the Court cannot overturn the agency's reasoned judgment.

Visinscaia was born in Moldova. Showing promise as a dancer from a young age, she began to compete—and do very well—in competitions throughout her country and in Eastern Europe generally. By 2005, the 15-year old had achieved a world-class ranking in the field of ballroom dance, and in that year she won her first—and, to this point, only—world championship in the World Dance Sport Federation Junior II Ten category. Having reached the end of the road on the juniors' circuit, Visinscaia continued to compete but also began serving as an instructor at a local dance academy. In 2011, she came to the United States to study in Sterling, Virginia.

Visinscaia began her quest for a new, long-term visa in May 2012, when she filed an I–140 petition for classification as an alien of extraordinary ability in the field of ballroom dance. That Visinscaia would seek such status is unsurprising: federal law assigns applicants of extraordinary ability the highest priority among employment-based visa applicants, *see* INA § 203(b)(1)(A), and such aliens need not present evidence of a job offer from an American employer before they are granted a visa. *Kazarian v. USCIS,* 596 F.3d 1115, 1120 (9th Cir. 2010).

* * *

USCIS does not disagree that Visinscaia has been a successful competitive dancer for more than a decade. Merely achieving success, however, is insufficient for someone to be granted extraordinary-ability status. Instead, to determine whether Visinscaia qualifies, the agency—and this Court—must interpret and apply § 203(b)(1)(A) of the Immigration and Nationality Act. Although the INA does not define "extraordinary ability" beyond the general recognition that abilities in the "sciences, arts, education, business, or athletics" may qualify, the statute does provide some oblique guidance. "Sustained national or international acclaim" is a hallmark of extraordinary ability, for example, as are achievements that "have been recognized in the field through extensive documentation." Federal regulations explain, further, that "extraordinary ability" can be defined as "a level of expertise indicating that the individual is one of that small percentage who have risen to the very top of the field of endeavor." 8 C.F.R. § 204.5(h)(2).

The "extraordinary ability" designation is thus "extremely restrictive" by design. *See Lee v. Ziglar,* 237 F. Supp.2d 914, 919 (N.D. Ill. 2002); *see also id.* at 915, 918 (finding that "arguably one of the most famous baseball players in Korean history" did not qualify for visa as baseball coach for Chicago White Sox). Still, evidence of extraordinary ability is not impossible to come by. *See, e.g., Muni v. INS,* 891 F. Supp. 440 (N.D. Ill. 1995) (finding that agency improperly discounted evidence for NHL hockey player who had won Stanley Cup three times, won "most underrated defenseman," and been paid more than average NHL player); *Matter of Price,* 20 I. & N. Dec. 953, 955–56 (BIA 1994) (granting visa petition of professional golfer who won 1983 World Series of Golf and 1991 Canadian Open, ranked 10th in 1989 PGA Tour, collected $714,389 in 1991, and received widespread major media coverage).

To meet this strict definition, an alien must submit evidence that she has sustained national or international acclaim and that her achievements have been recognized in the field of expertise. That evidence must include documentation of either (1) "a one-time achievement (that is, a major, international [*sic*] recognized award)," 8 C.F.R. § 204.5(h)(3); or (2) at least three of the ten types of lesser achievements enumerated in the regulations. The Ninth Circuit—the only federal court of appeals to address the substance of an "extraordinary-ability" challenge—has held that the regulations set out a two-step test. If the alien satisfies her initial evidentiary burden—that is, if she proves that she has met either of the requirements of § 204.5(h)(3)—USCIS must then decide, in a "final merits determination" and weighing the documentation offered, whether the evidence demonstrates extraordinary ability. See *Kazarian,* 596 F.3d at 1120–21. In practice, USCIS has endorsed that holding.

* * *

A. ONE-TIME ACHIEVEMENT

In extraordinary-ability cases, the burden is on the petitioner to provide sufficient evidence of, among other things, a "one-time achievement (that is, a major, international [*sic*] recognized award)." 8 C.F.R. § 204.5(h)(3). Plaintiff claims that her first-place finish at the 2005 World Dance Sport Federation Championship in the Junior II Ten Dance category constitutes such a one-time achievement that can satisfy her burden at this stage. In its January 2013 decision, however, the AAO concluded that the 2005 Championship did not qualify as a major achievement within the meaning of the agency's regulations. The AAO disagreed with Visinscaia's argument, in part because its reading of the legislative history behind § 204 of the INA—which mentioned the Nobel Prize as an example of a major, one-time achievement—suggested that "the award must be internationally recognized in the alien's field as one of the top awards in that field." Because (1) Visinscaia failed to produce evidence that her award was "reported in top international media" and (2) "the competition was limited to those younger than 15 years of age and was not open to the petitioner's entire field," the AAO determined that the award was neither internationally recognized nor one of the top awards in the field. In those circumstances, it could not qualify as a major international award for the purpose of the § 204 inquiry.

* * *

The parties, it is clear, disagree not about whether Visinscaia won the award she claims to have won, but rather about what constitutes a "major" international award for the purpose of the statute. Neither the plain meaning of the statute's words nor even common sense, unfortunately, is of much help to a court attempting to draw a line between "major" and "lesser" awards. Critically, furthermore, nothing in the case law, the INA, or the regulations implementing the statute explains how USCIS or a reviewing court is to differentiate between the two classes of award. To be sure, in the debates leading to passage of the statute, one member of Congress named the Nobel Prize as an example of a major, internationally recognized award that would by itself demonstrate "extraordinary ability." But not even USCIS claims that an alien must win a Nobel Prize to qualify. (Nor, for the record, does Plaintiff suggest that the 2005 Junior II Ten Championship is equivalent to the Nobel.) Which of humanity's thousands of other awards qualify as major international awards, then, is "a question that the law does not answer." *Rijal v. U.S. Citizenship & Immigration Servs.*, 772 F.Supp.2d 1339, 1345 (W.D.Wash.2011), *affirmatively adopted by* 683 F.3d 1030 (9th Cir.2012). It is, instead, a question that Congress—in classic form—entrusted to the administrative process to answer.

In reviewing that process, the Court looks for evidence that USCIS considered the relevant factors and articulated a rational connection between the facts it found and the choice it made. The agency did just that. * * * First, it discounted the media coverage of the award, which amounted to one mention in a newspaper whose circulation is unknown (save for a self-promotional letter from the publisher). * * * Adding to its case, the agency reasoned that an age-limited award in an esoteric field did not, on its face, look like a major award. Indeed, if an adult alien were seeking a visa based on his previous world-class performance at pre-teen chess tournaments, USCIS would hardly be arbitrary in determining that such achievement was too limited.

* * *

B. ALTERNATIVE CRITERIA

Having failed to demonstrate a single major achievement, then, for Plaintiff to prevail, she must prove that she satisfies at least three of the ten other criteria listed in the regulations. Visinscaia asserts that she clears the bar on four of those criteria: (1) "[o]riginal artistic and athletic contributions of major significance in the field"; (2) "perform[ance] in a leading or critical role for organizations or establishments that have a distinguished reputation"; (3) "display of the alien's work . . . at artistic exhibitions or showcases"; and (4) "receipt of lesser nationally or internationally recognized prizes or awards." * * *

* * *

1. Original Contribution

Visinscaia first objects to USCIS's conclusion that she failed to prove that she has made an original contribution to her field. In support of her claim at the agency level, Visinscaia cited letters of support from numerous dance professionals outlining her purported original contributions, including her use of "certain weight transfer techniques which allow her to preserve her sterling technique and form, particularly through individual transition pieces." She also provided documentation claiming generally that her technique is "now being widely adopted by other competitors," and by her students.

The agency, however, concluded that none of these letters provided specific information relating to the impact of Visinscaia's dance technique on the field as a whole. The AAO noted that the regulatory requirement that the petitioner demonstrate the "major significance" of any original contributions means that the petitioner's work must significantly affect her field of endeavor. It agreed that many of Visinscaia's support letters remarked on her unique dance technique, but it also observed that none— even those submitted in response to the agency's request for further evidence—provided any detail as to whether specific studios or academies now use the technique or whether specific top competitors have adopted it.

* * * In these circumstances, the Court cannot conclude that the agency's decision was arbitrary.

2. Leading or Critical Role

Similarly, the AAO concluded that Visinscaia failed to prove that she had played a leading or critical role as an instructor at Dance Sport Club Codreanca, which Plaintiff claims is an organization of distinguished reputation in Moldova. Visinscaia points to a letter from Petru Gozun, the founder of Dance Sport Club Codreanca, as well as two articles discussing the history and prestige of the club. The AAO questioned Visinscaia's evidence, concluding that it did not establish that she had served in a leading or critical role for the organization. It observed, further, that Visinscaia had been an "instructor" at the Club and that the Gozun letter did not specify how she had "contributed to the organization in a way that is significant to the organization's outcome" in that role. In addition, just because this club may have a distinguished reputation in Moldova does not necessarily mean that its renown spreads much beyond the country's borders.

* * *

* * * Without sufficient detail regarding Plaintiff's role at the organization, it was eminently reasonable for the AAO to conclude that Visinscaia could not satisfy this criterion on the basis of the letter alone.

3. Exhibitions or Showcases

The AAO also rejected Visinscaia's argument that her work has been displayed at artistic exhibitions or showcases. Visinscaia submitted documents showing that she had performed numerous times at the National Palace of Moldova, which, she claims, "correspond[s] to the Kennedy Center in Washington, D.C." The AAO, however, concluded that dance performances could not satisfy this requirement. Instead, the agency asserted, "artistic exhibitions or showcases" are "limited to [presentations of] the visual arts," where "tangible pieces of art . . . were on display." Because Visinscaia's performances did not constitute that sort of presentation, they could not be used to meet her burden under this criterion.

Visinscaia responds that "there is no such language in the statute, implementing regulations, the legislative history, or agency memos to support the conclusion that this criterion be restricted in this sense." If she is right, though, this simply means that there is a gap for the agency to fill. Where that is the case, it is blackletter law that the agency's interpretation of its own regulation deserves deference. * * *

4. Lesser Awards

Finally, Visinscaia claims that she satisfies the "lesser national and international awards" criterion on the basis of her 2005 World Championship and her numerous other awards (usually placement in the top two or three at a given event). Although the original USCIS adjudicator refused to allow that the World Championship constituted a lesser international award, the AAO did. The AAO concluded, however, that none of Visinscaia's other awards was nationally recognized, as the record "contain[ed] no documentary evidence demonstrating that the petitioner's competition placements are recognized beyond the presenting organizations . . . and are therefore commensurate with nationally or internationally recognized prizes or awards for excellence in the field." As the AAO noted, the record contained no evidence that the other awards had "garner[ed] national or international recognition from the competition in which it is awarded." There was no evidence, for example, that the newspaper and web sites to which Plaintiff pointed as evidence of international attention had a large readership—or, indeed, any readership at all. Without evidence of how a larger audience viewed

Plaintiff's awards, there was no way for the agency to evaluate whether those awards were recognized widely enough to satisfy this criterion.

* * *

Despite the Court's admittedly thin expertise in the field of competitive ballroom dancing, it has little doubt that Svetlana Visinscaia is a very good ballroom dancer. But that is a different question from whether USCIS acted arbitrarily when it denied her application for an extraordinary-ability visa. Since the answer to that query is that the agency did not, USCIS must prevail in this matter. * * *

NOTES AND QUESTIONS ON "EXTRAORDINARY ABILITY"

1.   The other categories of the first employment-based preference, for outstanding professors and researchers and for multinational executives and managers, share with the EB–1A category the important feature of avoiding labor certification. But those categories do require that the noncitizen seeking to immigrate has a job offer from a U.S. employer.

2.   *Visinscaia* applied the Ninth Circuit's approach to EB–1 petitions as set forth in *Kazarian v. USCIS,* 596 F.3d 1115, 1120 (9th Cir. 2010). On application of *Kazarian* by USCIS to EB–1 adjudications in the "outstanding professor/researcher" category, see Paul Herzog, *Winning an EB–1B Outstanding Professor/Researcher Case After* Kazarian, 92 Interp. Rel. 141 (2015). As background, Herzog explains: "With the lengthy backlogs in the EB–2 category for Chinese and Indian immigrants, and no prospects of any relief from Congress, many immigrants in the scientific and academic communities are casting a covetous eye on the outstanding professor/researcher category. This option is tempting because a petition approval in this category allows the beneficiary to bypass the labor certification process and immigrate without being subject to visa backlog."

3.   Is there a better approach to adjudicating EB–1 petitions than the menu approach in the regulations? Would it help if the menu were more specific? Would more specificity have made the application of the statute to Visinscaia more predictable?

B. NONIMMIGRANTS

1. INTRODUCTION

A nonimmigrant, generally speaking, is a noncitizen who seeks admission to the United States for a temporary stay and for a specific purpose. The categories range from tourists, who are now generally granted an admission period of six months (even if they intend a shorter visit); to students and various business-related categories, which may allow entry for longer periods; to diplomats and employees of foreign governments or affiliated with international organizations, whose stay may be extended indefinitely and who are exempted from several other requirements because of their official status. *See, e.g.,* INA § 102.

The nonimmigrant categories are set out, perhaps surprisingly, as part of the definition of "immigrant" in INA § 101(a)(15). The reason for this placement is evident from § 214(b), which presumes that noncitizens coming to the United States are coming as immigrants, with the intent to remain permanently. In turn, noncitizens who seek admission in one of the nonimmigrant categories, which are generally less restrictive, must carry the burden to show that they qualify. Section 101(a)(15) mirrors this presumption by defining "immigrant" as "every alien except" those who qualify in one of the nonimmigrant categories in § 101(a)(15). INA § 214 sets out further requirements for specific categories. Most nonimmigrant categories have no fixed numerical limits, but some important ones have annual caps, as discussed below.

The Visa Office of the Department of State has developed a set of visa symbols for the various nonimmigrant categories, generally tracking the alphabetical subparagraphs in § 101(a)(15), and sometimes subdividing the categories further than the statutory language suggests. For example, a tourist enters as a "temporary visitor for pleasure" on a B–2 visa. A noncitizen here temporarily on business, perhaps to negotiate a contract with a U.S. supplier, will enter on a B–1 visa as a "temporary visitor for business." A student headed for an academic institution receives an F–1 visa; the student's spouse and children receive F–2 visas.

You can gain a sense of the wide array of the nonimmigrant categories and the demand for them by examining Figure 5.9, which shows total admissions for selected admission categories in FY 2014. The table counts admissions, not individuals; a single individual can be admitted multiple times in a year. This table also excludes most short-term admissions along U.S. land borders, which totaled about 58 percent of the 180 million total nonimmigrant admissions in FY 2014.

Of the over 73 million nonimmigrant admissions in the categories in Figure 5.9 for FY 2014, over 90 percent were visitors for business or pleasure. Of these visitors, about 32 percent were admissions under the visa waiver program (described below and more fully in Chapter Six). For this reason, and because most visas permit multiple entries, the annual number of nonimmigrant *admissions* greatly exceeds the number of nonimmigrant *visas* issued each year by the State Department.

admissions, not individuals

Figure 5.9
Nonimmigrant Admissions (Selected Categories), Fiscal Year 2014

Visitors for business	B1	4,755,509
Visitors for business—Visa Waiver Program		2,976,445
Visitors for pleasure	B2	40,457,847
Visitors for pleasure—Visa Waiver Program		18,161,646
Transit aliens	C	1,004,916
Treaty traders and investors, plus spouses/children	E	422,025
Academic students	F	1,737,927
Vocational students	M	20,534
Spouses/children of academic/vocational students	F, M	79,203
Exchange visitors, plus spouses/children	J	557,760
Diplomats and other representatives	A, G, N, NATO	421,144
Temporary workers and trainees, spouses/children	H, O, P, Q, R, TN	2,095,175
Foreign media, plus spouses/children	I	46,054
Fiancé(e)s of U.S. citizens, and their children	K	41,778
Intra-company transferees, plus spouses/children	L	835,707

Source: 2014 DHS Yearbook of Immigration Statistics, Table 25.

There are four basic procedural paths to nonimmigrant status. (Chapter Six will treat admission procedures more fully.)

- The noncitizen applies for a nonimmigrant visa at a U.S. consulate outside the United States. The visa authorizes travel to the United States, but it does not guarantee admission, which is a decision made at the port of entry. After admission, the category and expiration date shown in the admission documents, electronically generated at the border or later modified at a DHS office in the United States, determine the conditions and category of admission, no matter what the visa facilitating admission indicates.

- Citizens of 38 countries (predominantly but not all of them in Europe) may be admitted without a visa as a business visitor or tourist for up to 90 days. About 21 million admissions took place under the Visa Waiver Program in FY 2014.

- A noncitizen who has been lawfully admitted as a nonimmigrant, and who is maintaining that status, may change to a different nonimmigrant status under INA § 248.

- Other rules apply to noncitizens from Canada or Mexico. Citizens of Canada may generally be admitted as nonimmigrants without a visa for up to six months.

Noncitizens who are citizens and residents of Mexico may be admitted with a Border Crossing Card, which allows a stay of up to 30 days, within 25 to 75 miles of the U.S.-Mexico border depending on the port of entry.

Whichever procedure is used, some nonimmigrant admissions require preliminary steps to acquire supporting documents. For some employment-related categories, the employer must gain approval of a preliminary petition filed with USCIS. Prospective students and scholars must present documents from the school or exchange program, most typically a Form I–20. (The Statutory Supplement includes a copy.) These supporting requirements are discussed more fully later in this section.

Short-term B–1 or B–2 visitors and students account for the lion's share of nonimmigrant admissions each year. In general, these admissions are fairly straightforward and usually do not demand the attention of an attorney. But the procedures for business categories—also a substantial segment of total nonimmigrant admissions—are more complex and frequently require legal counsel to navigate successfully. Accordingly, after examining the general issue of nonimmigrant intent and student statuses, we will focus primarily on selected business and employment-based nonimmigrant categories.

For many immigration lawyers, a staple of practice is advice on nonimmigrant categories for a given business situation. Key factors in such counseling include:

- Basic requirements (e.g., academic degrees or licensure, past work for employer or affiliates, admission to an accredited school)

- Any required labor market test or attestation

- Duration of stay, including renewal options

- Scope of work authorization, if any

- Treatment of family members, including their work authorization

- Procedural steps and fees required

- Options for later becoming a lawful permanent resident

This last factor—eventual lawful permanent resident status—links these materials on nonimmigrants back to Section A of this chapter on immigrant admission categories. Consider this: in FY 2014, about 480,000 of the over one million new lawful permanent residents were new arrivals in the United States. In contrast, about 535,000 noncitizens became lawful permanent residents through adjustment of status, so by definition were already in the United States. The percentage of noncitizens who became lawful permanent residents through adjustment was dramatically higher in the employment-based categories, where about 134,000 were adjustments, and only 22,000 were new arrivals. Although some of these adjustments involved noncitizens who lacked lawful immigration status, these new immigrants generally had been in valid nonimmigrant status when they became lawful permanent residents.

This pattern reflects a growing trend: the practical blurring of the line between immigrant and nonimmigrant status. Traditionally, U.S. immigration law has sharply distinguished between persons admitted as permanent resident aliens—admitted for an indefinite stay and entitled to most of the opportunities available to citizens—and nonimmigrants, admitted for a specific time and a specific purpose. Nonimmigrants were permitted to adjust under INA § 245 to lawful permanent resident status if they qualified under one of the appropriate categories, but nonimmigrants were generally not admitted with the expectation that they would become lawful permanent residents. (An obvious but numerically minor exception is the long-standing K nonimmigrant category for fiancé(e)s.)

Though many noncitizens who become lawful permanent residents still are new arrivals, these developments move U.S. immigration law in the direction of European-style policies. Many European countries allow permanent settled status to be acquired only over time. The scope of rights, opportunities, and responsibilities might grow as a noncitizen's ties to the country of residence mature, but the general approach is not to grant permanent resident status upon arrival. U.S. law could evolve in this direction, by offering lawful permanent resident only after some period of nonimmigrant status, and by allowing or even assuming dual intent for all nonimmigrants. What are the benefits and costs in this shift in conceptualization of immigration categories? *See generally* Hiroshi Motomura, Americans in Waiting: The Lost Story of Immigration and Citizenship in the United States 139–42 (2006).

Consider these attributes and implications of nonimmigrant status as you examine the facts in the next Exercise. It gives you a chance to synthesize, from a practical planning perspective, a broad range of materials in this chapter: (1) on immigrant admissions in Section A of this chapter; and (2) on nonimmigrant categories in the rest of this Section B.

EXERCISE

Shoshi Productions, Inc. (SPI), a Japanese corporation based in Tokyo, manufactures computer microchips. Its subsidiary, Shoshi Foreign Distributions (SFD), is responsible for selling and distributing the parent's products outside of Japan. SPI owns fifty percent of SFD. SPI has recently purchased a small American computer company, New World Chips.

For each of the individuals mentioned below, what nonimmigrant categories are available? Among these nonimmigrant options, which is best for each? What further information would you need to respond fully?

Assume that each of the individuals in this Exercise may also be interested in staying permanently in the United States. How would that possibility affect the advice that you give about nonimmigrant options? What is the prognosis for eventual lawful permanent resident status for each individual?

- *Engineer*: To enable New World to manufacture the microchips currently being produced in Japan, SPI would like its top engineer to come to the United States to supervise the retooling of New World's factory. He holds a degree from a first-rate Japanese engineering school.

- *Vice President*: SPI also wants its Vice President for Personnel to come to the United States to run New World temporarily while he trains New World supervisors and employees in Japanese-style management techniques. The Vice President began working for SPI ten years ago in the sales department. He has no college degree.

- *Vice President's wife*: The Vice President's spouse would like to accompany him to the United States. She is a concert violinist who has a national reputation within Japan, but whose work is not widely known outside her home country.

- *Vice President's child*: The Vice President has a daughter, age 17, who wants to accompany him to the United States. She will soon graduate from high school in Japan. She wants to attend college in the United States, but she would like to visit several campuses before deciding where to apply. She hopes to work for her father at New World while in college, but her long-term ambition is to attend graduate school in the United States to study biomedical engineering, eventually earn a Ph.D., and live and work in the United States indefinitely.

- *French architects and landscapers*: SPI would like to redesign the New World workspace, and has hired a French industrial architecture firm to do the job. That firm has informed SPI that its architects will have to spend at least six months on site, drawing up blueprints and later returning to supervise the reconstruction. The French firm would like to bring its landscaping crew to install the plants and irrigation system called for in the design.

- ***Start-up staff for SFD's U.S. office***: SFD wants to open a U.S. office from which it could sell and distribute SPI's microchips. SFD would like to send to the United States a three-person delegation that could scout out a location for the office. SFD hopes to assign some of its sales staff from its Japanese operations to work in the office temporarily until U.S. workers can be found.

2. "IMMIGRANT INTENT"— AND STUDENTS AND EXCHANGE VISITORS

For many of the nonimmigrant categories, the most important requirement is that the noncitizen "has a residence in a foreign country which he has no intention of abandoning." *See, e.g.,* INA § 101(a)(15)(B), (F), (J), (M), (O), (P). In deciding whether to issue nonimmigrant visas, State Department consular officers tend to be especially careful in this regard, particularly in countries known for a high incidence of visa overstays. This care reflects the concern that the noncitizen is not a bona fide nonimmigrant, but in fact intends to remain in the United States indefinitely. According to estimates, nonimmigrant overstayers constitute perhaps one third to one half of the unauthorized population. *See* Ruth Ellen Wasem, *Nonimmigrant Overstays: Brief Synthesis of the Issue* 1, 7 (Cong. Res. Serv. 2014); David A. Martin, *Eight Myths About Immigration Enforcement*, 10 N.Y.U. J. Legis. & Pub. Pol'y 525, 544 (2007).

Noncitizens are not bona fide nonimmigrants if they intend from the beginning to remain in the United States permanently by any means possible, legal or otherwise. But many cases have held that "a desire to remain in this country permanently in accordance with the law, should the opportunity to do so present itself, is not necessarily inconsistent with lawful nonimmigrant status." *Matter of Hosseinpour*, 15 I & N Dec. 191, 192 (BIA 1975). *See also Lauvik v. INS*, 910 F.2d 658, 660–61 (9th Cir. 1990). This is the "dual intent" doctrine, which may make the permanent foreign residence requirement less rigid than it might first appear. The doctrine applies in principle to any nonimmigrant, and some courts have frowned on efforts to deport noncitizens who are admitted as nonimmigrants but then apply to become lawful permanent residents based on marriage or a new job, allegedly revealing that they were never bona fide nonimmigrants. *See, e.g., Garavito v. INS*, 901 F.2d 173, 177 (1st Cir. 1990) (filing of immigrant visa petition naming respondent as beneficiary does not negate nonimmigrant intent).

At the front end, however, if an applicant for a student or tourist visa appears before a consular officer overseas and expresses a strong desire to seek and obtain lawful permanent residence, the likely result is denial of the nonimmigrant visa. In practice, therefore, the dual intent doctrine is principally of use in other categories where the INA and the regulations expressly allow dual intent. For example, this is true for the H–1B and L categories, which are prominently used by businesses, as explored below. In categories that do not clearly recognize dual intent, difficult practical problems arise as consular officers and other government personnel try to decide if an applicant for a visa or admission as a nonimmigrant should be denied because of her immigrant intent.

To consider how this works in practice, assume that you are a consular officer tasked with granting or denying applications for student visas. How would you decide whether to issue a student visa to an applicant? The next selection lays out the basics of the nonimmigrant categories that may be available to a noncitizen who wants to study in the United States. The second reading sets out State Department guidelines on applying the nonimmigrant intent requirement to students.

CHAD C. HADDAL, FOREIGN STUDENTS IN THE UNITED STATES: POLICIES AND LEGISLATION

Congressional Research Service Report for Congress 1–4 (2008).

There are three main avenues for students from other countries to temporarily come to the United States to study, and each involves admission as a nonimmigrant. * * * The three visa categories used by foreign students are F visas for academic study; M visas for vocational study; and J visas for cultural exchange.

F Visa

The most common visa for foreign students is the F–1 visa. It is tailored for international students pursuing a full-time academic education. The F–1 student is generally admitted as a nonimmigrant for the period of the program of study, referred to as the duration of status. The law requires that the student have a foreign residence that they have no intention of abandoning. Their spouses and children may accompany them as F–2 nonimmigrants.

To obtain an F–1 visa, prospective students also must demonstrate that they have met several criteria:

- They must be accepted by a school that has been approved by the Attorney General.

- They must document that they have sufficient funds or have made other arrangements to cover all of their expenses for 12 months.

- They must demonstrate that they have the scholastic preparation to pursue a full course of study for the academic level to which they wish to be admitted and must have a sufficient knowledge of English (or have made arrangements with the school for special tutoring, or study in a language the student knows).

Once in the United States on an F visa, nonimmigrants are generally barred from off-campus employment. Exceptions are for extreme financial hardship that arises after arriving in the United States and for employment with an international organization. F students are permitted to engage in on-campus employment if the employment does not displace a U.S. resident. In addition, F students are permitted to work in practical training that relates to their degree program, such as paid research and teaching assistantships. An alien on an F visa who otherwise accepts employment violates the terms of the visa and is subject to removal and other penalties * * * .

J Visa

Foreign students are just one of many types of aliens who may enter the United States on a J–1 visa * * * . Others admitted under this cultural exchange visa include scholars, professors, teachers, trainees, specialists, foreign medical graduates, international visitors, au pairs, and participants in student travel/work programs. Those seeking admission as a J–1 nonimmigrant must be participating in a cultural exchange program that the U.S. Department of State's Bureau of Educational and Cultural Affairs (BECA) has designated. They are admitted for the period of the program. Their spouses and children may accompany them as J–2 nonimmigrants.

* * * The programs that wish to sponsor J visas also must satisfy the following criteria:

- be a bona fide educational and cultural exchange program, with clearly defined purposes and objectives;

- have at least five exchange visitors annually;

- provide cross-cultural activities;

- be reciprocal whenever possible;

- if not sponsored by the government, have a minimum stay for participants of at least three weeks (except for those designated as "short term" scholars);

- provide information verifying the sponsoring program's legal status, citizenship, accreditation, and licensing;

- show that they are financially stable, able to meet the financial commitments of the program, and have funds for the J nonimmigrant's return airfare;

- ensure that the program is not to fill staff vacancies or adversely affect U.S. workers;

- assure that participants have accident insurance, including insurance for medical evacuations; and

- provide full details of the selection process, placement, evaluation, and supervision of participants.

As with F visas, those seeking J visas must have a foreign residence they have no intention of abandoning. However, many of those with J visas have an additional foreign residency requirement in that they must return abroad for two years if they wish to adjust to any other nonimmigrant status or to become a legal permanent resident in the United States. This foreign residency requirement applies to J nonimmigrants who meet any of the three following conditions:

- An agency of the U.S. government or their home government financed in whole or in part—directly or indirectly—their participation in the program.

- The BECA designates their home country as clearly requiring the services or skills in the field they are pursuing.

- They are coming to the United States to receive graduate medical training.

There are very few exceptions to the foreign residency requirement for J visa holders who meet any of these criteria—even J visa holders who marry U.S. citizens are required to return home for two years. Although many aliens with J–1 visas are permitted to work in the programs in which they are participating, the work restrictions for foreign students with a J–1 visa are similar to those for the F visa.

M Visa

Foreign students who wish to pursue a non-academic (e.g., vocational) course of study apply for an M visa. This visa is the least used of the foreign student visas. Much as the F students, those seeking an M visa must show that they have been accepted by an approved school, have the financial means to pay for tuition and expenses and otherwise support themselves for one year, and have the scholastic preparation and language skills appropriate for the course of study. Their spouses and children may accompany them as M–2 nonimmigrants. As with all of the student visa categories, they must have a foreign residence they have no intention of abandoning. Those with M visas are also barred from working in the United States, including in on-campus employment.

* * *

NOTES ON STUDENT STATUS

1.   DHS reported in November 2015 that almost 1.2 million students in the F or M categories, 8 percent more than in November 2014, were enrolled at nearly 9000 U.S. schools. Seventy-seven percent of all international students are from Asia. The top ten sending countries of citizenship are China, India, South Korea, Saudi Arabia, Canada, Vietnam, Japan, Taiwan, Brazil, and Mexico, in that order. Fifty-seven percent were male. Thirty-nine percent of international students studying in the U.S., or about 467,000, are enrolled in STEM (science, technology, engineering and mathematics) coursework. Eighty-seven percent of these STEM students are from Asia. *See* U.S. Immigration and Customs Enforcement, *SEVIS By the Numbers* (Nov. 2015).

2.   Schools must use an automated web-based system known as SEVIS (Student and Exchange Visitor Information System), managed by ICE, to share information about foreign students and scholars. This information is available to consular officers, inspectors at the border, and other immigration officers. When a school approves admission of an F–1 student, it must post the key initial I–20 form on SEVIS. The school must later provide ongoing reports about the student's address and satisfaction of requirements (such as arriving for the term, maintaining a full load of courses, changing degree programs, on-campus employment, off-campus employment during or after completion of studies—known as "practical training," or transferring to another school), and withdrawal or completion of studies.

3.   Under long-standing administrative practice (but without express statutory authorization), F–1 students can engage in "optional practical training" (OPT). This training allows work for an off-campus employer in a field related to their studies during term breaks or for a period after finishing the course of study. This period has often served as a stepping stone to longer-term employment in the United States with that employer, perhaps under the H–1B category followed by eventual employment-based permanent immigration. The standard maximum OPT period is 12 months, but a 2008 regulation extended this to 29 months, under specific conditions, for persons working in the so-called STEM fields: science, technology, engineering, or mathematics.

4. Critics have attacked OPT for harming injuring U.S. workers who compete for jobs in STEM fields. In August 2015, a federal district court, in response to a lawsuit filed by a labor organization representing U.S. STEM workers, vacated the regulation for failure to comply with the Administrative Procedure Act's notice and comment procedures. The court stayed its order to allow DHS to submit the regulation for notice and comment, which it did in October 2015 with a new proposed maximum OPT period of 36 months in STEM fields. *See Washington Alliance of Technology Workers v. Dept. of Homeland Security*, 2015 WL 9810109 (D.D.C. Aug. 12, 2015); 80 Fed. Reg. 63,376 (2015). DHS issued final regulations in March 2016 with the 36-month STEM maximum. *See* 81 Fed. Reg. 13,040 (2016).

STUDENTS AND IMMIGRANT INTENT

U.S. Department of State cable (No. 2005 State 274068),
reprinted in 82 Interp. Rel. 1762 (2005).

1. *Summary*: This cable provides some guidance for consular officers in how to interpret the immigrant intent provisions when adjudicating student visa applications. Consular officers adjudicating student visa applications should evaluate the applicant's requirement to maintain a residence abroad in the context of the student's present circumstances; they should focus on the student applicant's immediate and near-term intent. * * *

2. *Residence abroad requirement in general terms*: * * * [T]he immigrant intent requirement applies in only certain nonimmigrant visa classifications. Most of these visa classifications require the visa applicant to satisfactorily demonstrate that s/he possesses a residence abroad that s/he has no intention of abandoning. This residence abroad requirement is found in the B, F, J, M, O–2, P, and Q visa classifications.

3. The purpose of travel is always the controlling criterion for determining a proper visa classification. Each classification differs fundamentally in terms of activities permitted and time period contemplated in the United States. Student visa adjudication is made more complex by the fact that students typically stay in the U.S. longer than do many other non-immigrant visitors. In these circumstances, it is important to keep in mind that the applicant's intent is to be adjudicated based on present intent—not on contingencies of what might happen in the future, during a lengthy period of study in the United States.

4. *Context of residence abroad for students*: While the concept of "ties" is very useful in evaluating many nonimmigrant visa applicants, it is relatively less useful in assessing the present intent of a student. The typical student is young, without employment, without family dependents, and without substantial personal assets. Students may have only general rather than specific plans for the future. These personal circumstances differ greatly from those of persons usually qualifying for B–1's or P visas for example. The residence abroad requirement for a student should therefore be considered in a broader light, focusing on the student applicants' immediate intent. While students may not be able to demonstrate strong "ties", their typical youth often conveys a countervailing major advantage in establishing their bona fides: they don't necessarily have a long-range plan, and hence are relatively less likely to have formed an intent to abandon their homes.

5. *Intended course of study*: The fact that the alien plans on studying a subject for which there is no or little employment opportunity in his country of residence is not a basis for denying the visa; because circumstances may change, this fact should not be deemed a negative

factor in adjudicating the case. Nor, on the other hand, is the fact that the country of residence can provide the equivalent quality courses in the same subject matter. The student has the right to choose where s/he will obtain an education if accepted by the school.

6. *Visa renewal during course of study*: Some students have to apply for new visas if they go home or travel during their period of study. Returning student applications should generally be reissued in the normal course of business, unless circumstances have changed significantly from the time of previous issuance. Students should be encouraged to travel home during their studies in order to maintain ties to their country of origin. If students feel that they will encounter difficulties in seeking a new student visa or that a visa will not be issued to them so they can continue their studies, they may be less inclined to leave the United States during their studies and hence may distance themselves culturally from their homeland. Posts should facilitate the reissuance of student visas so that these students can travel freely back and forth between the homeland and the United States.

7. *Student visa reminders*:

A. *Educational qualifications*: The I–20 is evidence that the school has accepted the applicant as a student. The choice of the subject matter is not determinative of the applicant's scholastic aptitude. Consular officers should not go behind the I–20 to adjudicate the alien's qualifications as a student for that institution. If the consular officer has reason to believe that the applicant engaged in fraud or mis[re]presentation to garner acceptance into the school as laid out in 9 FAM 41.61 Note 8, then that information is an important factor to consider in determining if the applicant has a bona fide intent to engage in study in the United States. * * *

B. *Community colleges or lesser-known schools*: All legitimate schools must be accorded the same weight under the law. The INA does not distinguish among schools qualifying for I–20 authorization based on size or recognition. There is no legal difference between community colleges, English language schools and four-year institutions. Applicants should be adjudicated on their bona fides as students regardless of institution of program of study. * * *

NOTES AND QUESTIONS ON NONIMMIGRANT INTENT

1. Assume that you are working as a consular officer in the U.S. Department of State. Does this cable provide you with enough guidance to determine if any given applicant for a student visa is a bona fide nonimmigrant? If not, what more would you, as a consular officer, want by way of guidance?

2.   How wise or administrable is the formulation in the statute, "having a residence in a foreign country which he has no intention of abandoning"? The phrasing dates from a time when international travel was less frequent and more expensive. Today, for example, a foreign national may be engaged to a U.S. citizen and have firm plans to settle here in three years after finishing an advanced degree in her home country—but may wish first to make several short-term lawful visits.

Would it be better in the modern era of frequent and multi-layered international contacts to replace the quoted language with something like "possessing the intent to leave the United States at the end of his or her period of authorized stay"? If so, should this requirement apply to all nonimmigrant categories, not just to those categories in § 101(a)(15) that now have the "no intention of abandoning" requirement? As compared to the current provision, would this standard be easier or harder for consular officers to administer? Can you come up with a better formulation to distinguish nonimmigrants from immigrants?

may be better to question intent to leave US.

— harder.

3.   For contrasting criticism of the application of nonimmigrant intent requirement, see Daniel Walfish, *Student Visas and the Illogic of the Intent Requirement*, 17 Geo. Immigr. L.J. 473 (2003); Jessica Vaughan, *Shortcuts to Immigration: The "Temporary" Visa Program Is Broken* (Center for Imm. Studies Backgrounder, Jan. 2003).

3.   BUSINESS AND ENTREPRENEURIAL NONIMMIGRANTS

The U.S. economic system—the largest of any nation in the world—attracts millions of noncitizens a year interested in pursuing business and work opportunities. Some come as temporary laborers, picking apples and lettuce, harvesting tobacco, even herding sheep. Others come to drum up business for foreign corporations. Multinational corporations send employees to receive training and to manage U.S. subsidiaries. Foreign investors may come to investigate opportunities for purchasing U.S. businesses and property or for opening businesses of their own. Professional athletes enter for a sports season. Entertainers may plan a U.S. tour.

An increasingly interdependent world combined with significant waits for some employment-based immigrant visas has guaranteed an exceptionally high demand for nonimmigrant work visas. Naturally, this demand comes largely from the nonimmigrants themselves, but it also comes from the many U.S.-based employers who believe that the domestic labor force is inadequate for their needs.

Much of immigration practice concerns these nonimmigrants. Practitioners must understand the needs of the client (the noncitizen, the sponsoring organization, or both) and be able to assess the availability and implications of various possible avenues. Moreover, the INA leaves important concepts and terms undefined, and administrative agencies and courts can provide conflicting guidance. It is not as if noncitizens walk into an attorney's office with "H–1" or "E–2" stamped on their heads. Commercial relations are extraordinarily complex and varied, and a client's business and migration objectives may be served under a variety of categories—each with its own advantages and disadvantages.

One fundamental tension runs through these materials on business and entrepreneurial nonimmigrants. U.S. employers often seek to hire foreign employees. It may be sensible national policy to admit noncitizens who are needed by domestic employers, and noncitizen entrepreneurs who will help grow the domestic economy. Since the earliest immigration laws, however, immigration policy has sought to protect U.S. workers from competition from foreign workers. An employer's claimed need may simply reflect a desire for more workers at a lower wage or salary.

For noncitizens seeking admission as immigrants, the labor certification process mediates these two goals—even if its actual success in doing so remains uncertain. But the immigrant categories may be unsuitable for business and entrepreneurial nonimmigrants. First, the employer may need workers immediately. It takes time to process labor certification and immigrant visa applications, and immigrant admission categories may be backlogged. Second, the labor certification process can be complex and expensive. Or the needed stay may be only for a limited duration—truly seasonal workers like ski lift operators in Vermont or farmworkers in Minnesota. Some of the INA's nonimmigrant categories allow relatively quick entry for particular purposes and limited periods. To ensure that employers and workers do not use nonimmigrant visas to circumvent restrictions on immigrant admissions that are intended to protect U.S. workers, the Department of Homeland Security, the Department of Labor, and the Department of State patrol the categories carefully.

a. B–1 Visitors for Business

Noncitizens who are "visiting the United States temporarily for business"—the B–1 category—are the largest category of business-related nonimmigrants. In FY 2014, DHS recorded over 7.7 million B–1 admissions, about 3.0 million of which were under the Visa Waiver Program. One can easily imagine a wide range of business activities that would qualify for B–1 status. Individual entrepreneurs and representatives of foreign corporations might seek admission to find U.S. customers, investigate potential investments, engage in a sports competition, attend an industry conference, look for locations to establish a U.S. subsidiary, arrange international deals, or negotiate contracts. Indeed, it has become a catch-all provision, used to admit nonimmigrants for business purposes when other nonimmigrant classifications do not apply.

The B–1 classification offers advantages over other business-related nonimmigrant categories. A noncitizen initiates the process in her home country; no petition on her behalf need be filed with USCIS in the United States. No labor certification is required, in contrast to the H–2A and H–2B temporary worker categories.

But there are important limitations. First, the noncitizen must receive no remuneration from a U.S. source other than reimbursement for expenses incident to the temporary stay. *See* 22 C.F.R. § 41.31. More importantly, the statute excludes from the B–1 category noncitizens "coming for the purpose * * * of performing skilled or unskilled labor." INA § 101(a)(15)(B). Likewise, State Department regulations provide: "The term 'business,' as used in INA 101(a)(15)(B), refers to conventions, conferences, consultations and other legitimate activities of a commercial or professional nature. It does not include local employment or labor for hire." 22 C.F.R. § 41.31(b)(1). Yet this conceptual distinction between B–1s and the H categories can be hard to apply in the real world.

Consider, for example, a foreign corporation that wants to send its employees to the United States to help perform a contract on U.S. soil. The firm may prefer B–1 classification over H–1B or H–2B. How should USCIS decide which nonimmigrant category is appropriate in such a case? Should it view the noncitizens as employees of the foreign corporation whose labor in the United States enables the overseas firm to enter into such contracts? If so, B–1 might be a sensible classification. Or should USCIS see them as engaging in labor in the United States that U.S. workers might be able to perform? If so, H–2B with its labor certification requirement might be the only appropriate category. The next case explores these difficult definitional questions and the sometimes conflicting purposes of the nonimmigrant categories.

INTERNATIONAL UNION OF BRICKLAYERS AND ALLIED CRAFTSMEN V. MEESE

United States District Court for the Northern District of California, 1985.
616 F. Supp. 1387.

LEGGE, DISTRICT JUDGE.

* * * Homestake [Mining Company] began construction in early 1984 on its McLaughlin Gold Project in order to open a new gold mine. Due to metallurgical problems in the Lake County region, Homestake concluded that it was necessary to employ technology not used previously in the gold mining industry. * * *

[It later] agreed to purchase a newly-designed gold ore processing system from Didier-Werke ("Didier"), a West German manufacturing company. Although the purchase agreement required Didier to supply an integrated processing system, it was not possible to premanufacture the entire system in West Germany. The purchase agreement was therefore made contingent upon Didier's West German employees completing the work on the system at the project site in Lake County.

In September 1984, Didier submitted B–1 "temporary visitor for business" visa petitions on behalf of ten of its West German employees to United States consular officers in Bonn, West Germany. Relying upon INS Operations Instruction 214.2(b)(5), consular officers approved the petitions and issued B–1 visas to the West Germans. In January 1985, the West Germans entered the United States to work on the processing system. The work involves the installation of the interior linings of the system's autoclaves, and requires certain technical bricklaying skills. * * *

Plaintiffs allege that the federal defendants' practice of issuing B–1 "temporary visitor for business" visas under the authority of INS Operations Instruction 214.2(b)(5) violates two provisions of the Act. First, plaintiffs allege that the practice violates section 101(a)(15)(B) of the Act, because the issuance of B–1 visas to aliens coming to the United States to perform skilled or unskilled labor is expressly prohibited by section 101(a)(15)(B). Second, plaintiffs allege that the practice violates section 101(a)(15)(H)(ii) of the Act, because aliens have been permitted to bypass the labor certification requirements contained in the regulations under section 101(a)(15)(H)(ii). * * *

THE VALIDITY OF THE OPERATIONS INSTRUCTION UNDER THE ACT

* * *

The Language of the Act and the Operations Instruction

* * * [The] Operations Instruction * * * provides that an alien may be classified as a "temporary visitor for business" nonimmigrant if:

> *he/she is* to receive no salary or other remuneration from a United States source (other than an expense allowance or other reimbursement for expenses incidental to the temporary stay) ... [and is] *coming to install, service, or repair commercial or industrial equipment or machinery purchased from a company outside the U.S.* or to train U.S. workers to perform such service. ...

INS Operations Instruction 214.2(b)(5) (emphasis added).

* * * Section 101(a)(15)(B) [of the INA] unequivocally excludes from the B–1 "temporary visitor for business" classification an alien who is

"coming for the purpose of . . . performing skilled or unskilled labor." * * * INS Operations Instruction 214.2(b)(5), however, does not contain an exclusion for an alien seeking to enter the United States to perform skilled or unskilled labor. The Operations Instruction provides that an alien may be classified as a "temporary visitor for business" if the alien is "coming to install, service, or repair commercial or industrial equipment or machinery." The effect of this language is to authorize the issuance of a B-1 visa to an alien coming to this country to perform skilled or unskilled labor. In the present case, for example, the West Germans undeniably are performing labor—whether it be deemed skilled or unskilled—in connection with the installation of the gold ore processing system at the McLaughlin Gold Project.

Similarly, a comparison of the language of section 101(a)(15)(H)(ii) of the Act with the language of INS Operations Instruction 214.2(b)(5) shows that the Operations Instruction also contravenes that section of the Act. Section 101(a)(15)(H)(ii) classifies an H-2 "temporary worker" as an alien "coming . . . to perform temporary services or labor, if unemployed persons capable of performing such service or labor cannot be found in this country." Because the Act requires the Attorney General to consult other agencies of the government concerning "temporary worker" visas, see INA § 214(c), the Attorney General has established H-2 labor certification procedures. Thus, an H-2 visa petition cannot be approved unless the alien's employer obtains either "*[a] certification from the Secretary of Labor . . . stating that qualified persons in the United States are not available and that the employment of the beneficiary will not adversely affect wages and working conditions of workers in the United States similarly employed . . . [or] notice that such certification cannot be made.*" 8 C.F.R. § 214.2(h)(3) (1985) (emphasis added).

In contrast, * * * the Operations Instruction authorizes the issuance of a nonimmigrant visa to an alien performing skilled or unskilled labor, though qualified Americans may be available to perform the work involved. The Operations Instruction therefore lacks the safeguards contained in section 101(a)(15)(H)(ii) of the Act and the regulation promulgated under that section. Again, the present case illustrates this point, because the parties have stipulated that neither the West Germans nor their employer was required to seek labor certification from the Secretary of Labor prior to the issuance of the visas to the West Germans. * * *

The Intent of Congress

* * * [The court summarizes the history of labor-protective immigration provisions since the Contract Labor Act of 1885.] In taking these actions, Congress evidenced a continuing concern for the protection of American workers from unnecessary foreign competition. The House

Report accompanying the 1952 Act explained that the purpose of section 101(a)(15)(H)(ii) was to:

> grant the Attorney General sufficient authority to admit *temporarily certain alien workers,* industrial, agricultural, or otherwise, *for the purpose of alleviating labor shortages as they exist or may develop* in certain areas or certain branches of American productive enterprises. . . .

H.R. Rep. No. 1365, 82d Cong., 2d Sess., *reprinted in* 1952 U.S. Code Cong. & Ad. News 1653, 1698 (emphasis added). * * *

The foregoing legislative history demonstrates that one of Congress' central purposes in the Act was the protection of American labor. The legislative history also demonstrates that sections 101(a)(15)(B) and 101(a)(15)(H)(ii) of the Act were intended to restrict the influx of aliens seeking to perform skilled or unskilled labor in the United States. Thus, to the extent that INS Operations Instruction 214.2(b)(5) permits aliens to circumvent the restrictions enacted by Congress in those sections, the Operations Instruction is inconsistent with both the language and the legislative intent of the Act. * * *

Defendants' Arguments

Defendants contend that INS Operations Instruction 214.2(b)(5) should be upheld because it embodies a reasonable administrative interpretation of the Act.

Defendants' argument centers on the purposes Congress sought to achieve in sections 101(a)(15)(B) and 101(a)(15)(H)(ii) of the Act. Defendants contend that those sections evidence Congress' intent to foster multiple purposes. Although defendants acknowledge that one such purpose was the protection of American labor, they argue that another was the promotion of international commerce. Further, defendants assert that the language in sections 101(a)(15)(B) and 101(a)(15)(H)(ii) reveals a tension between American labor interests and international commerce interests; that the Operations Instruction seeks to minimize the tension; and that the Operations Instruction is therefore consistent with the multiple purposes in the Act.

Defendants rely primarily upon the decision of the Board of Immigration Appeals in *Matter of Hira,* 11 I. & N. Dec. 824 (BIA 1966). In *Hira,* an alien employed by a Hong Kong custom-made clothing manufacturer had entered the United States under the authority of a B–1 "temporary visitor for business" visa. While in this country, the alien took orders on behalf of his employer from prospective customers, and took the measurements of those customers. Prior to the expiration of the alien's visa, the INS commenced deportation proceedings against him. The INS concluded that the alien's activities involved the performance of skilled labor, and ordered that the alien be deported for failure to maintain his B–1 "temporary visitor for business" status. On appeal, the Board of Immigration Appeals focused its analysis on the term "business" within section 101(a)(15)(B) of the Act. Adopting the Supreme Court's definition from an earlier version of the Act, the Board held that "business," for purposes of section 101(a)(15)(B) of the Act, "contemplate[s] only 'intercourse of a commercial character.'" *Id.* at 827 (quoting *Karnuth v. United States ex rel. Albro,* 279 U.S. 231, 49 S.Ct. 274, 73 L.Ed. 677 (1929)). In support of that definition, the Board alluded to prior administrative cases in which aliens were found eligible for "temporary visitor for business" status because "there was involved international trade or commerce and the employment was a necessary incident thereto." *Id.* at 830 (citations omitted). The Board also elaborated upon the underlying requirements for eligibility as a "temporary visitor for business" nonimmigrant:

> The significant considerations to be stressed are that there is a clear intent on the part of the alien to continue the foreign residence and not to abandon the existing domicile; the principal place of business and the actual place of eventual accrual of profits, at least predominantly, remains in the foreign country; the business activity itself need not be temporary, and indeed may long continue; the various entries into the United States made in the course thereof must be individually or separately of a plainly temporary nature in keeping with the existence of the two preceding considerations.

Id. at 827 (footnote omitted).

Applying those principles the Board in *Hira* concluded that the alien's business was intercourse of a commercial character, even though he took prospective customers' measurements in connection with the business. Thus, the Board held that the alien was entitled to B–1 "temporary visitor for business" status. The Attorney General subsequently affirmed the Board's decision, and certified it as controlling.

* * * Defendants argue that here the West Germans came to this country only as a necessary incident to the purchase and sale of the gold-ore processing system, rather than as individuals hired expressly as laborers. * * *

Defendants' arguments are answered primarily by the language of the Act. * * * [T]he language of section 101(a)(15)(B) of the Act, which *excludes* an alien "coming for the purpose of . . . performing skilled or unskilled labor," precludes defendants' purported distinction between business and labor in this case; so does the expressed congressional intent of protecting American labor. * * *

The interpretation of a federal statute by the officials responsible for its administration is entitled to deference. A court, however, must reject an administrative interpretation "that [is] inconsistent with the statutory mandate or that frustrate[s] the policy that Congress sought to implement." *Securities Industry Ass'n v. Board of Governors*, 468 U.S. 137, 143, 104 S.Ct. 2979, 2983, 82 L.Ed.2d 107 (1984).

The court concludes from both the language and legislative intent of the Act that the federal defendants' interpretation embodied in the Operations Instruction contravenes the Act. The court therefore decides that INS Operations Instruction 214.2(b)(5) violates sections 101(a)(15)(B) and 101(a)(15)(H)(ii) of the Act. * * *

ORDER

* * * INS Operations Instruction 214.2(b)(5) is declared unlawful and in violation of sections 101(a)(15)(B) and 101(a)(15)(H)(ii) of the Immigration and Nationality Act. * * * [Defendants] are permanently enjoined from issuing B–1 "temporary visitor for business" visas under the authority of INS Operations Instruction 214.2(b)(5).

NOTES AND QUESTIONS ON THE "PERFORMING LABOR" PROHIBITION

1. An appeal in *Bricklayers* was dropped when the parties agreed on a new regulation on the admission of building and construction workers. In announcing the amended rule, INS reported the reaction of foreign countries and corporations to the court's opinion:

> Following the District Court's order, which precluded the admission of even the most highly specialized technicians, the Service and the Department of State received communications from U.S. industries and foreign governments which indicated a problem of crisis proportions. Industry predicted that equipment under warranty would not be repaired or serviced, with resultant losses of investment and lay-offs of American workers, and that access to state-of-the-art foreign technology would be limited with resultant losses of competitive position. Foreign governments generally viewed this new restriction as a constraint on trade and hinted at reciprocal actions.

51 Fed. Reg. 44266 (1986).

The post-litigation regulation, still in effect, provides:

> Aliens seeking to enter the country to perform building or construction work, whether on-site or in-plant, are not eligible for classification or admission as B–1 nonimmigrants * * *. However, alien nonimmigrants otherwise qualified as B–1 nonimmigrants may be issued visas and may enter for the purpose of supervision or training of others engaged in building or construction work, but not

for the purpose of actually performing any such building or construction work themselves.

8 C.F.R. § 214.2(b)(5); *see also* 22 C.F.R. § 41.31(b)(1) (State Department regulation to the same effect).

This rule was apparently premised on a narrow reading of *Bricklayers*—that the decision reached no further than the situation of building or construction workers. But the court's reasoning casts doubt on the validity of several other categories for which B–1 admissions are allowed.

2. The BIA's *Hira* precedent permits certain activities that might appear to be the performance of skilled or unskilled labor if "the employment was a necessary incident" to intercourse of a commercial character, and the labor is minimal and tied to a business principally based elsewhere. Does *Bricklayers* distinguish or overrule *Hira*? Which is the better test for dealing with short-term business situations? The next Exercise provides one context in which to consider the applicable tests.

EXERCISE ON B–1 VISA ELIGIBILITY

Gordon Rogers, a clerk employed by a Canadian railroad, seeks to enter the United States on a daily basis. On a typical workday, he reports to work in Niagara Falls, Ontario, where he obtains documents related to the train shipment bound for Canada he is to monitor. He then drives to Niagara Falls, New York, where he checks the train for safety and for compliance with documentation requirements. He fills out customs paperwork and enters information about the shipment into the railroad's computer system. He then leaves the documentation for the train crew and returns to Canada.

Rogers spends about one-third of his work day in the United States. He uses the rest on additional paperwork for these shipments, and on checking the train when it arrives from the United States. If U.S. Customs and Border Protection wants to inspect the train leaving the United States, he returns from Canada to the border to open the cars.

Rogers is the only employee regularly assigned to this duty. Customary railroad practices, both in the United States and Canada, prohibit these functions from being performed by the train's operating crew.

Is Rogers eligible for a B–1 visa?

---

b. H–1B Temporary Workers

The H–1B classification covers noncitizens coming temporarily to the United States to provide services in a "specialty occupation," loosely meaning professional positions. More precisely, INA § 214(i) defines "specialty occupation" as one requiring "theoretical and practical application of a body of highly specialized knowledge," as well as attainment of a bachelor's or higher degree as a minimum for entry into the occupation. In principle, the H–1B program is meant to complement and not displace U.S. workers, but controversy exists over whether, in structure and especially in application, the regulatory regime effectively accomplishes this aim. We will first outline the basic requirements and procedures, then take a closer look at this controversy later in this Section.

Employers initiate the H–1B petitioning process. Before filing the visa petition (Form I–129) with USCIS, the employer must first file a Labor Condition Application (LCA), also known as an "attestation," with the Department of Labor. A prospective H–1B employer need show only that it filed an attestation and DOL accepted it (after a review for "completeness and obvious inaccuracies"). DOL approval of the LCA is not required.

In the LCA, the employer must attest, among other things, that it has notified the appropriate bargaining representative of its employees of the filing, with job details including salary. Or if there is no union, it must post notice of the filing "in conspicuous locations at the place of employment." The employer must also attest that the job is being offered at the prevailing wage or actual wage paid to similar individuals (whichever is greater), and that it will provide working conditions for the noncitizen that will not adversely affect the working conditions of similarly employed workers. Attestations are subject to potential review later, under a set of procedures that circumscribe DOL's investigatory authority. See INA §§ 101(a)(15)(H), 212(n), (t).

Additional obligations apply to "H–1B dependent" employers— meaning firms of more than 50 employees for which H–1B workers constitute at least 15 percent of the workforce, or specified higher percentages for smaller firms. Such employers generally pay higher fees and must provide additional assurances. They must attest that they have taken good-faith steps to recruit U.S. workers, such as advertising or participating in industry job fairs, and have made an offer to any U.S. worker with equal or better qualifications. See INA § 212(n)(1). H–1B dependent firms must also attest that the H–1Bs do not displace U.S. workers—meaning that no one in an equivalent job was or will be laid off—but only for 90 days before and after a visa petition is filed. Employers that are not H–1B dependent need not attest to either recruitment or non-displacement.

Once USCIS has approved the visa petition, a noncitizen applying for H–1B classification must demonstrate that she is qualified to work in the particular specialty occupation, usually by having the required bachelor's or advanced degree. Qualification may also be established by professional licensure, when that is required for the field, or by experience in the specialty equivalent to the completion of such a degree and "recognition of expertise in the specialty through progressively responsible positions relating to the specialty." 8 C.F.R. § 214.2(h)(4)(iii)(C)(4).

H–1B temporary workers are currently limited, by statute, to 65,000 per fiscal year. The category has been severely oversubscribed in recent years. For FY 2016, USCIS reached the cap five business days after the filing season opened. Skeptics see the cap as the one effective method for minimizing the H–1B category's negative impact on U.S. workers and their wage scales. But Congress has adopted and refined a series of significant exemptions from the cap. Employees of institutions of higher education or affiliated nonprofit entities, or nonprofit or governmental research organizations do not count toward the H–1B cap at all. In addition, up to 20,000 H–1B workers with at least a master's degree from a U.S. institution of higher education are exempt. H–1B extensions and petitions for a current H–1B worker to change to a different employer also do not count against the ceiling.

All of these exemptions make H–1B usage far higher than the caps suggest. Admissions of H–1B nonimmigrants admissions reached 511,773 in FY 2014. India had the largest share with about 43 percent of the total, with Canada second at about 13 percent. *See* 2014 Yearbook of Immigration Statistics, Table 32. However, the number of admissions indicates usage only very roughly, because an H–1B worker who travels internationally could be admitted dozens of times over the course of the H–1B admission period, which frequently extends to six years. A better indicator of H–1B is the number of visas issued, which reached 161,369 in FY 2014. *See* Department of State, Report of Visa Office 2014, Table XVI(B).

Besides the cap, other measures address some concerns of the H–1B category's critics. An extra $1500 fee over and above the regular processing fee is required to file an initial petition or an extension of stay, or to hire an H–1B worker from another U.S. employer. (It is $750 for employers with 25 or fewer workers in the United States.) *See* INA § 214(c)(9). These funds are channeled to the National Science Foundation and the Department of Labor, to be used primarily for job training programs for U.S. workers, college scholarships for low-income students in engineering, math, and computer science, and certain other science enrichment courses. Colleges, universities, and nonprofit research institutions are exempt from this fee. Additional fees may be required up to $4500, depending the employer's total number of employees and the number who are H–1B temporary workers or L intracompany transferees (discussed below). *See* INA §§ 214(c)(12), 286(v); Pub. L. 114–113, 129 Stat. 2242, Div. O, tit. IV, § 402(f).

An H–1B nonimmigrant need not have "a foreign residence which he has no intention of abandoning," and the regulations allow an H–1B nonimmigrant to be admitted and, "at the same time, lawfully seek to become a permanent resident." 8 C.F.R. § 214.2(h)(16)(i). Spouses and children can be admitted as H–4 nonimmigrants. Spouses of those H–1B nonimmigrants who are seeking lawful permanent resident status in the employment-based categories are eligible for work authorization.

The standard rule is that H–1B nonimmigrants can be admitted for up to three years initially, extendable up to six years. *See* INA § 214(g)(4), 8 C.F.R. § 214.2(h)(9)(iii)(A), 8 C.F.R. § 214.2(h)(15)(ii)(B). In 2000, Congress adopted a significant exception: the six-year limit does not apply if an employment-based application for an immigrant visa petition or adjustment of status has been filed on the H–1B nonimmigrant's behalf, and 365 days or more have elapsed since the filing of the labor certification application or the employment-based preference petition. *See* American Competitiveness in the Twenty-first Century Act ("AC 21"), § 106(a), Pub. L. 106–313, 114 Stat. 1251 (2000). In such cases, the period of stay can be extended in one-year increments "until such time as a final decision is made on the alien's lawful permanent residence." AC 21, § 106(b).

Suppose a worker in H–1B status wants to apply for adjustment of status in an employment-based preference category, but there is a waiting period in that category due to per-country limits. In this common situation, the AC 21 legislation allows three-year extensions of H–1B status. AC 21, § 104(c). Another provision of AC 21 lets H–1B nonimmigrants start working for a new employer once that employer files a new "non-frivolous" H–1B petition, rather than having to wait for USCIS to approve the new petition. *See* AC 21, § 105(a), codified at INA § 214(n).

Another significant provision in AC 21 allows "H–1B portability." If an H–1B nonimmigrant has an adjustment of status application pending for 180 days or more—not considered long in this context—he may change jobs. His adjustment application remains valid "if the new job is in the same or a similar occupational classification as the job for which the petition was filed." AC 21, § 106(c) , codified at INA § 204(j). The labor certification likewise remains valid. *See* INA § 212(a)(5)(A)(iv).

Congress enacted these provisions in response to processing backlogs for labor certification and adjustment of status applications. The package of changes has great practical and policy significance by making it easier for H–1B temporary workers to adjust to lawful permanent resident status while working in the United States. Importantly, H–1B temporary workers who qualify in employment-based immigration category that is backlogged—as has happened more recently with the EB–2 preference for natives of China and India—can continue to work in the United States while waiting for their priority dates to become current. Other potential adjustment applicants have no similar option while waiting.

c.   O and P Nonimmigrants

The O–1 nonimmigrant category is available as an admission avenue for noncitizens who can show "extraordinary ability . . . demonstrated by sustained national or international acclaim" in "sciences, arts, education, business, or athletics." INA § 101(a)(15)(O). The statute eases this standard for one of the covered fields by defining "extraordinary ability" simply as "distinction" for O–1 purposes "in the case of the arts." INA § 101(a)(46). The O–1 category allows performing artists, entertainers, athletes, chefs, and business persons to be admitted as nonimmigrants, even if they would not qualify for H–1B status because they lack academic degrees.

In practice, the "extraordinary ability" required for EB–1A immigrants, *see* INA § 203(b)(1)(A), is generally more demanding than what the same phrase requires for O–1 nonimmigrants, so O–1 admission does not always establish EB–1A eligibility. Persons who accompany O–1 nonimmigrants, such as supporting actors and stage crew, may be admitted in the O–2 category. Spouses and children of O–1 and O–2 nonimmigrants may be admitted in O–3 status, but this does not authorize them to work.

The P–1 category is for less accomplished or less prominent entertainers and athletes who meet a basic standard of international recognition, defined as "a high level of achievement in the field evidenced by a degree of skill and recognition substantially above that ordinarily encountered, to the extent that such achievement is renowned, leading, or well known in more than one country." 8 C.F.R. § 214.2(p)(3). Entertainers and athletes who may not meet the P–1 requirements may use the P–2 and P–3 categories as part of certain exchange programs or as "culturally unique" artists and entertainers. *See* INA § 101(a)(15)(P). All P categories include "essential support" personnel. Spouses and children of all P nonimmigrants may be admitted in P–4 status, but this does not authorize work.

The O and P categories contrast with the H–1B category in ways that offer options for noncitizens who qualify for multiple admission vehicles. In contrast to the H–1B category, the number of O and P nonimmigrant admissions is not capped. Before approving an O or P petition, the federal government must consult with a labor organization representing U.S. peer workers to obtain an advisory opinion, *see* INA § 214(c)(3), (4), but there is no mechanism that specifically regulates the wage paid. Admission in the P and O categories is limited to the duration of a specific competition, event, or activity, *see* INA § 214(a)(2). But this can be defined broadly, for example as an initial three-year admission period for a scientist who qualifies an O–1 nonimmigrant. Moreover, there is no overall limit on how long an O nonimmigrant may spend in that category, and some P nonimmigrants may extend their stay up to ten years.

These advantages of O–1 status can combine to make it much more attractive than H–1B status, even if it is initially harder for a scientist or educator to qualify for O–1 status under the "extraordinary ability" standard. As for acquisition of lawful permanent resident status, as is true with H–1B admissions, an O–1 or P–1 nonimmigrant may come to the United States and "at the same time, lawfully seek to become a permanent resident." 8 C.F.R. § 214.2(o)(13), (p)(15) .

d.   L–1 Intracompany Transferees

Persons granted L visas are generally referred to as "intracompany transferees." The category is used extensively by foreign corporations to transfer employees of a certain rank or with certain qualifications to work in its U.S. branch or subsidiary. The number of L nonimmigrant visas (including spouses and children) has increased steadily over the past 30 years—from 26,535 in FY 1980 to 149,621 in FY 2014. India accounted for about 30 percent of the L visas issued in FY 2014, with 44,954, followed by the United Kingdom (11,274), Japan (10,916), and Mexico (9,923). See Department of State, Report of Visa Office 2014, Tables XVI(B), XVII. These are numbers of visas, not admissions. For FY 2013, L–1 admissions (the principal workers) totaled 503,206, close to that year's total of H–1B admissions, and spouses and children of L–1 nonimmigrants accounted for another 220,435 admissions. These figures include multiple counts of single individuals who travel in and out of the United States.

The key requirement for the L category is that the person "render his services * * * in a capacity that is managerial, executive, or involves specialized knowledge." INA § 101(a)(44) defines "managerial" and "executive" capacity. "Specialized knowledge" is defined as "special knowledge of the company product and its application in international markets or * * * an advanced level of knowledge of processes and procedures of the company." INA § 214(c)(2)(B). The statute stipulates that a noncitizen seeking L classification must have been employed by the sponsoring firm for at least one year within the three years preceding the date of his application for entry. The H categories have no such prior employment requirement.

The L–1 category requires the employer to file a preliminary petition with DHS. Large corporations meeting certain size and prior L–1 usage requirements may file blanket petitions, rather than petitions for individual noncitizens. See 8 C.F.R. § 214.2(l)(4). L–1 nonimmigrants may be admitted initially for up to three years, extendable for up to seven years for managers and executives and five years for those with "specialized knowledge." *See* INA § 214(c)(2)(D), 8 C.F.R. § 214.2(*l*)(7), 8 C.F.R. § 214.2(*l*)(15)(ii). Spouses and children are classified as L–2 nonimmigrants. Spouses are allowed to work, *see* INA § 214(c)(2)(E), unlike the spouses of many H–1B nonimmigrants.

An L–1 nonimmigrant is expressly permitted to have dual intent; she may come to the United States as an L–1 nonimmigrant and, "at the same time, lawfully seek to become a permanent resident." 8 C.F.R. § 214.2(*l*)(16). Because the definitions of "managerial" and "executive" for L–1 status also apply to managers and executives under the first employment-based immigrant preference (EB–1C), managerial and executive L–1 nonimmigrants can readily qualify for an immigrant visa as well. *See* INA § 203(b)(1)(C). L–1s with "specialized knowledge" lack such a direct route to lawful permanent resident status but often can qualify for EB–2 or EB–3 admission.

Two areas of potential misuse of the L–1 category have attracted the attention of the administering agencies. In one scenario, a small business owner overseas buys or starts a small U.S. firm solely to allow the business to petition for the transfer of its president or sole stockholder. The regulations impose special requirements if the noncitizen is being transferred to the United States to open or work in a new office. *See* 8 C.F.R. § 214.2(*l*)(3)(v), (vi). They also require that the foreign entity continue doing business during the noncitizen's stay in the United States. *See* 8 C.F.R. § 214.2(*l*)(1)(ii)(G). This prevents the owner from liquidating the business to which he supposedly would have returned.

Another concern is that businesses can use the "specialized knowledge" branch of the L–1 category (L–1B) to get around the statutory cap on H–1B admissions and perhaps evade the (modest) worker protections that come from the H–1B attestation requirements. The DHS Inspector General warned in 2006 that the term "specialized knowledge" has no meaningful limits that adjudicators can apply to deny petitions. *See* Office of Inspector General, Department of Homeland Security, Review of Vulnerabilities and Potential Abuses of the L–1 Visa Program 4–9 (2006). Consider this example:

> Fogo de Chao (Holdings), Inc., operates numerous Brazilian steakhouse restaurants, known as *churrascarias,* in Brazil and the United States. According to Fogo de Chao, a critical component of its success has been the employment in each of its restaurants of genuine gaucho chefs, known as *churrasqueiros,* who have been raised and trained in the particular culinary and festive traditions of traditional barbecues in the Rio Grande do Sul area of Southern Brazil.

> * * * From 1997 to 2006, the Department of Homeland Security granted Fogo de Chao over 200 L–1B visas for its

churrasqueiros. In 2010, Fogo de Chao sought to transfer another *churrasqueiro* chef, Rones Gasparetto, to the United States, reasoning that his distinctive cultural background and extensive experience cooking and serving meals in the *churrasco* style constitute " specialized knowledge."

Fogo de Chao (Holdings) Inc. v. U.S. Dept. of Homeland Security, 769 F.3d 1127, 1129–30 (D.C. Cir. 2014).

Does this meet the "specialized knowledge" requirement? USCIS concluded that "[t]he inherent knowledge a person gains as a result of his or her upbringing, family and community traditions, and overall assimilation to one's native culture necessarily falls into the realm of general knowledge, even if an individual's specific culture itself is limited to a relatively small population or geographic location." *Id.* at 1139.

The D.C. Circuit found that "nothing in the regulations or previous guidance explains why informational knowledge, experience, and skills that would otherwise be considered specialized lose that status just because they were originally acquired through one's upbringing, family traditions, and life experience outside the workplace." The court explained:

> it is for the agency in the first instance to formulate a rule that articulates whether and when cultural knowledge can be a relevant component of specialized knowledge. It likewise is for the agency to articulate, if deemed appropriate, a line between, on the one hand, actual skills and knowledge derived from an employee's traditions and upbringing, and, on the other hand, the simple status of being from a particular region.

Id. at 1142. In 2015, USCIS released a policy memorandum that sets forth two basic ways to show "specialized knowledge":

> **special knowledge**, which is knowledge of the petitioning organization's product, service, research, equipment, techniques, management, or other interests and its application in international markets that is distinct or uncommon in comparison to that generally found in the particular industry; or

> **advanced knowledge**, which is knowledge of or expertise in the petitioning organization's specific processes and procedures that is not commonly found in the relevant industry and is greatly developed or further along in progress, complexity and understanding than that generally found within the employer.

See USCIS Releases Final Guidance on L–1B Adjudications, 92 Interp. Rel. 1520 (2015).

As an adjudicator at USCIS, how would you apply these tests to a *churrasqueiro* chef? What further evidence would you need?

e.   E Treaty Traders and Treaty Investors

The discussion of H–1B visas assumed that a U.S. employer seeks foreign workers. But L visas suggest that much of the demand for nonimmigrant visas comes from foreign enterprises that seek to create or exploit business and investment opportunities here. As international trade and investment opportunities in the United States have grown, E status has also become a prominent vehicle for nonimmigrant admissions.

INA § 101(a)(15)(E) establishes two distinct E classifications. The crucial requirement for both categories is that the United States and the noncitizen's country of nationality have an international agreement under whose terms an E nonimmigrant seeks to carry on activities in this country. The E–1 category is for a "treaty trader"; the E–2 category is for a "treaty investor." As the next reading explains, both categories can include employees of the investor or trader. In FY 2014, 44,155 E visas were issued, including visas for spouses and children. *See* Department of State, Report of the Visa Office 2014, Table XVI(B).

An E nonimmigrant may be admitted for up to two years initially, with two-year extensions, *see* 8 C.F.R. § 214.2(e)(19), and may remain in the United States as long as he or she continues to undertake the activities for which entry was initially granted. Thus, E status offers a distinct advantage over H–1B and L classifications, which are subject to a five, six, or seven-year cap. Another advantage over the H and L categories is that an E visa does not require a preliminary petition by a sponsoring entity in the United States. The noncitizen initiates the process by applying for an E visa at a consular office overseas, or by applying for a change of nonimmigrant status in the United States.

Like H–1B and L nonimmigrants, E nonimmigrants need not show that they intend to retain their foreign residence. *See* 8 C.F.R. § 214.2(e)(5). Spouses of E nonimmigrants may work. *See* 8 C.F.R. § 214.2(e)(6). The following excerpt explains the basics of the E category.

CHARLES GORDON, STANLEY MAILMAN, STEPHEN YALE-LOEHR & RONALD Y. WADA, IMMIGRATION LAW AND PROCEDURE

§§ 17.01, 17.03, 17.05, 17.06 (2015).[*]

A nonimmigrant classification which most closely approximates the status of an immigrant is that of treaty trader (E–1) or treaty investor

---

(E–2). * * * So long as eligibility continues, "E" status not only permits the alien to engage in the qualifying trade or investment, but permits incidental activities, as well, and a stay of indefinite duration. It also allows the spouse and children to join the principal alien in the same status, and the accompanying spouse to have work authorization * * *. An indispensable requirement, however, is that the principal alien be a national of a country with which the United States has a treaty of commerce and navigation, providing for the trade or investor activity. The nationality of the accompanying spouse or children is immaterial to their "E" status.

The treaty trader must carry on trade of a substantial nature that is international in scope and principally between the United States and the treaty country. The treaty investor must have invested or be in the process of investing a substantial amount of capital in an enterprise which he or she will develop and direct and which will not be a marginal enterprise entered into solely to earn a living.

Employees of qualified treaty persons or business organizations may be classified as treaty traders or investors if they have the treaty nationality. They must be engaged, however, in an executive or supervisory capacity, or have special qualifications essential to the enterprise. An agent of a qualified foreign person or organization, may also qualify for E–1. * * *

The statute specifies that the agreement, under which the nonimmigrant may enter for the specified trade or investor purposes, is to be "a treaty of commerce and navigation." The agreements recognized by the State Department as treaties of "friendship, commerce, and navigation" (FCN) and listed in the Visa Office, Foreign Affairs Manual are by and large so entitled or similarly named.[1] Not all such agreements, however, are strictly FCNs. * * * Authorization for treaty status (E–1 and E–2) was accomplished, in the case of the Philippines, Mexico and Canada by diplomatic agreements that are not formally treaties, after specific statutory authorization.

Bilateral investment treaties (BITs) negotiated by the United States with other countries are also recognized as FCNs, but only for purposes of conferring E–2 authorization. * * *

Prototypical of FCN language authorizing both treaty trader and treaty investor classification is the text of the 1953 treaty with Japan, at Article I, paragraph 1:

> *Nationals* of either Party shall be permitted to enter the territories of the other Party and to remain therein: (a) for the purpose of carrying on trade between the territories of the two

---

[1]   *See* 9 FAM § 41.51 n.2, Exhibit I * * *.

Parties and engaging in related commercial activities; (b) for the purpose of developing and directing the operations of an enterprise in which they have invested, or in which they are actively in the process of investing, a substantial amount of capital; and (c) for other purposes subject to the laws relating to the entry and sojourn of aliens.[8]

* * * [The United States has entered in treaties with about 80 countries authorizing treaty trader (E–1) and treaty investor (E–2) classifications to their nationals.] For citations, effective dates, geographic coverage and other useful details relating to the treaties, generally, consult the [State Department's] Foreign Affairs Manual (FAM).

* * *

Although the treaty trader (E–1) and treaty investor (E–2) classifications are identical in most of their characteristics, inherent in their definition are marked differences. Distinguishing the treaty trader, in terms of the required commercial activity, is the operative phrase "solely to carry on substantial trade, including trade in services or trade in technology, principally between the United States and the foreign state of which he is a national. . . . " Under a rule that is both old and questionable, the trade must already exist at the time classification is sought; this means binding contracts, that "call for the immediate exchange of qualifying items of trade," not merely negotiations.

The concept of "trade," which had been largely restricted in the past to transactions involving goods and certain few quasi-services, has * * * been expanded by regulation to include services more generally and by statute to include services and technology. The Immigration Act of 1990 further solidified this expansion by specifically including "trade in services or trade in technology" within the definition of a treaty trader at INA § 101(a)(15)(E)(i). What is meant by "substantial trade" has never been defined by regulation, but interpretations have emphasized a regularity of transactions in amounts sufficient to support the trader and his or her family. * * * More than half of the trade must be between the United States and the treaty country. The trade must constitute an exchange; it must be international in scope; and it must involve qualifying activities. * * *

The statutory language which speaks directly to the E–2 investor is: "solely to develop and direct the operations of an enterprise in which he has invested, or of an enterprise in which he is actively in the process of investing, a substantial amount of capital; . . ." Issues suggested by this language relate to the extent the investment must be committed before status is granted, the nature of the capital investment permitted, the

---

[8]   4 U.S.T. 2063, 2066 (1953).

meaning of "substantial" in this context and the special significance, if any, of the phrase "solely to develop and direct the operations. . . ." * * *

In the State Department's view, a hallmark of the investment intended by the statute is the placing of funds or other capital assets at risk to generate a profit. The nature of the asset invested ordinarily does not matter so long as it is subject to loss. According to the 1952 House report, Congress contemplated investments in "commercial enterprises," and that the new status would be for "aliens who will be engaged in . . . a real operating enterprise and not a fictitious paper operation."

Being "actively in the process of investment" involves something more than a mere intention to invest. How much more, can be hard to assess. According to the State Department, "the alien must be close to the start of actual business operations, not merely in the stage of signing contracts (which may be broken) or scouting for suitable locations and property. Mere intent to invest, or possession of uncommitted funds in a bank account, or even prospective investment arrangements entailing no present commitment, will not suffice."

---

f. H–2 Temporary Workers

The employment-related nonimmigrant visas discussed so far allow admission for limited periods, though they are not usually tied to work or other economic activity that itself is of limited duration. But other temporary work is more seasonal or intermittent. These jobs generally do not require a college degree or other formal credentials. Examples include a host of agricultural jobs tied to the planting and harvesting cycle, plus other seasonal jobs, such as ski instructors or ski lift operators. Now we examine these nonimmigrant categories—H–2A and H–2B temporary workers—the ones often given the shorthand label, "guest workers."

(i) H–2A Workers

Agriculture may be the paradigmatic case of a short-term labor need. Crops ripen and must be harvested quickly, but then labor may not be needed again until the next growing season. Not surprisingly, temporary worker programs have operated for decades in the agricultural industry. Historically the most important example may be the Mexican Bracero program from 1942 to 1964. "Bracero" literally means one who works with his arms; the closest English equivalent is probably "field hand." Beginning in 1942, the United States entered into a series of agreements with Mexico for the employment of temporary agricultural workers, under a variety of authorizing statutes. Between four and five million Mexican workers worked in this program before Congress allowed the statutory authority to lapse in 1964. Many observers believe that the Bracero program contributed significantly to unauthorized migration in later decades, because the migration patterns established under the Bracero program simply continued even after the legal authority ended.

In 1986, when Congress adopted employer sanctions as part of its efforts to staunch the flow of undocumented labor, growers argued that without a large-scale temporary worker program crops would rot in the fields. Some early versions of the legislation included a massive temporary worker program. The program in the enacted statute was more modest, though still intended to assure growers of an adequate supply of workers. First, the 1986 Act included a special legalization program open only to persons who had worked for 90 days in agriculture during the year preceding enactment. Then it divided the former H–2 category into H–2A for temporary workers in agriculture, and H–2B for temporary workers in other fields. Streamlined labor certification procedures apply to H–2A temporary agricultural workers. See INA §§ 101(a)(15)(H)(ii), 218.

There is no statutory ceiling on H–2A visas. As Figure 5.10 shows, their use has grown considerably since the early 1990s, from under 7,000 in 1990 to over 90,000 in FY 2014. See Department of State, Report of the Visa Office 2014, Table XVI(B). In 2014, the United States had 761,000 agricultural jobs, and the Department of Labor certified about 117,000 H–2A jobs. See Office of Foreign Labor Certification, Department of Labor, Annual Report 2014, at 43 (2015); Bureau of Labor Statistics, U.S. Department of Labor, Occupational Outlook Handbook, 2016–17 Edition, Agricultural Workers.

Usage of the statutory H–2A program was once heavily concentrated in the southeastern quadrant of the country, reflecting heavy reliance on undocumented agricultural labor instead in the southwest and California. H–2A usage is now more widespread, but Southeastern states still lead in the number of certifications requested and granted. In FY 2014, seven states—North Carolina, Florida, Georgia, Washington, Louisiana, Kentucky, and California—accounted for about 68,000 H–2A jobs out of the total of about 117,000 nationwide. See Office of Foreign Labor Certification, Department of Labor, Annual Report 2014, at 43 (2015).

Figure 5.10
H–2A Visas Issued, FY 1992–2014

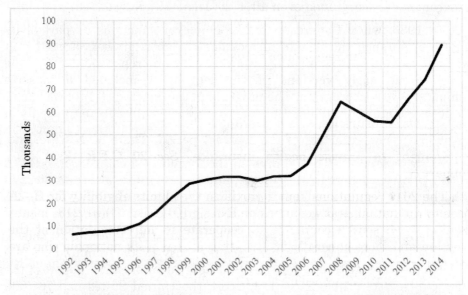

Source: Department of State, Report of the Visa Office 2014, Table XVI(B).

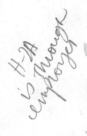

To bring in H–2A agricultural workers, an employer must first file a labor certification application with the Department of Labor, to show that "(A) there are not sufficient workers who are able, willing and qualified, and who will be available at the time and place needed, to perform the [agricultural] labor or services involved in the petition, and (B) the employment of the alien in such labor or services will not adversely affect the wages and working conditions of workers in the United States similarly employed." INA § 218(a)(1). If the labor certification is granted, the employer must next have a petition approved by USCIS before the individual workers can obtain visas for entry.

As with labor certification for employment-based immigrant categories, the employer must undertake efforts to recruit U.S. workers. *See* INA § 218(b)(4), 20 C.F.R. §§ 655.150–655.158. In recent years, the governing regulations have changed dramatically several times. In the early 2000s, the George W. Bush administration supported significant expansion of temporary worker programs. When broad legislation to this end failed in Congress, the administration pursued this objective through new H–2A regulations that streamlined the labor certification process by reducing review by DOL officials in favor of employer attestations backed by audits and penalties. The regulations also changed the long-standing formula for computing the "adverse effect wage rate" (AEWR) that employers must pay in the agricultural area where the work will take place.

The Obama administration's Labor Department concluded that the reliance on attestation had caused significant erosion in worker protections. New regulations in 2010 returned to greater DOL oversight of labor certification and restored the previous AEWR methodology after DOL determined that the new formula cost workers an average of one dollar per hour. The regulations enhanced other worker protections, with greater pre-employment disclosures, assured transportation reimbursement, better standards and monitoring for employer-provided housing, the provision of meals or convenient cooking facilities, workers compensation insurance, and a guarantee that employment will continue for at least three-quarters of the contract period. There is, however, no requirement to provide health insurance. *See* 20 C.F.R. Part 655, Subpart B.

The 2010 regulations kept a provision that limits eligibility for H–2A visas to the nationals of countries on a designated list. This rule is meant to incentivize source countries to cooperate in implementation of the program and more generally in accepting return of its nationals who are ordered removed from the United States. The list is updated annually, adding and subtracting based on prior cooperative experience. For 2016, 84 countries were on the H–2A list. *See Identification of Foreign Countries Whose Nationals Are Eligible to Participate in the H–2A and H–2B Nonimmigrant Worker Programs*, 80 Fed. Reg. 72,079 (2015). The same list applies to H–2B workers as well, though some variance is possible.

DOL also used the 2010 regulations to act on long-standing complaints from advocates for U.S. farmworkers that the agency would insist on good terms and conditions of employment for foreign workers, but that it failed to make sure that H–2A employers offer the same terms and conditions to potential domestic recruits. Some critics charged that this failure was a reason (or even a deliberate strategy by growers) for the low recruitment and retention of agricultural workers among the domestic workforce. The 2010 regulations impose far more detailed requirements for domestic recruitment, with most recruitment to occur before the employer files the labor certification application. *See* 20 C.F.R. §§ 655.150–655.158. DOL also created a new electronic job registry to facilitate the job hunt by available workers. The regulations basically require parity among comparable workers, foreign or domestic, on the terms and conditions of employment, generally including housing arrangements and transportation, plus pay at a rate at least equal to the AEWR rate. Employers must remain open to hiring U.S. workers until 50 percent of the contract period has passed. *See, e.g., id.* § 655.122(a), (d)(1). § 655.150(b).

The back-and-forth in the regulations in the Bush and Obama administrations illustrate the competing needs in agriculture of employers, U.S. workers, and the H–2A workers themselves, who work under typically harsh and sometimes exploitative conditions. *See, e.g.,* Ilan Brat, *On U.S. Farms, Fewer Hands for the Harvest*, Wall St. J., Aug. 12, 2015; Ron Nixon, *Farm Group Seeks Immigration Changes*, N.Y. Times, Feb. 11, 2014; Joseph Berger, *Long Days in the Fields, Without Earning Overtime*, N.Y. Times, Aug. 8, 2014; Southern Poverty Law Center, Close to Slavery: Guestworker Programs in the United States (2013).

In addressing these tensions, there is this basic question: why treat agriculture separately? Are the workforce needs for agricultural labor more pressing or different in some other way from needs that arise in other sectors of the U.S. economy? What else might explain the persistence of agricultural temporary worker programs as distinct from programs of more general application? And how would a large-scale temporary agricultural worker program affect U.S. farms and U.S. farmworkers? According to U.S. census data, 55 percent of those employed in farming (including forestry and fishing) are native-born. Because this percentage does not include naturalized citizens or lawful permanent residents, it understates the involvement of authorized workers in agriculture. *See* David A. Martin, *Eight Myths About Immigration Enforcement*, 10 N.Y.U. J. Legis. & Pub. Pol'y 525, 539 (2007).

(ii) H–2B Workers

Temp. nonagricultural workers

The H–2B category is for temporary nonagricultural workers. In FY 2014, DOL approved the most H–2B labor certifications in these occupations: landscaping workers (accounting for 37 percent of positions certified), forestry workers, maids and housekeeper cleaners, amusement and recreation attendants, meat, poultry, and fishery workers, and construction workers, in that order. *See* Office of Foreign Labor Certification, Department of Labor, Annual Report 2014, at 49 (2015). DOL certified almost 94,000 H–2B jobs, but the number actually filled by H–2B workers is limited by the annual cap of 66,000, split equally into the two halves of the fiscal year. *See* INA §§ 214(g)(1)(B), (g)(2), (g)(10). Some H–2B admissions do not count against the cap.

The H–2B category has a double requirement of temporariness, as well as a requirement for a labor market test: H–2B is open to a noncitizen "who is coming *temporarily* to the United States to perform [nonagricultural] *temporary* service or labor if unemployed persons capable of performing such service or labor cannot be found in this country." INA § 101(a)(15)(B)(ii)(b) (emphasis added).

What makes service or labor temporary? In *Matter of Artee Corp.*, 18 I & N Dec. 366 (Comm'r 1982), the INS Commissioner ruled that "[i]t is not the nature or the duties of the position which must be examined to determine the temporary need. It is the nature of the need for the duties to be performed which determines the temporariness of the position." The regulation restates this requirement as a job "in which the petitioner's need for the duties to be performed by the employee(s) is temporary, whether or not the underlying job can be described as permanent or temporary." 8 C.F.R. § 214.2(h)(6)(ii).

Consider this case. A company provides highly skilled personnel to the nuclear power industry. For each of the past five years, it successfully petitioned for nuclear start-up technicians to perform temporary services for nuclear power plants around the United States. The agency then denied a petition for 30 more technicians, citing the five-year history and the lack of evidence that the demand for the start-up technicians would be "non-recurring or infrequent." Upholding this denial, a federal district court in *Volt Technical Services Corp. v. INS*, 648 F. Supp. 578, 581 (S.D.N.Y. 1986) rejected as "nonsensical" the idea that positions "are temporary merely because a single task or assignment is temporary."

How temporary must a temporary job be? The regulations state that the "employer must establish that the need for the employee will end in the near, definable future." Generally that period "will be limited to one year or less, but in the case of a one-time event could last up to 3 years." 8 C.F.R. § 214.2(h)(6)(ii)(B). Also, the need must be "a one-time occurrence, a seasonal need, a peak load need, or an intermittent need." *Id.* These rules make it very difficult to use the H–2B category for certain types of workers—nannies, for example.

Processing of H–2B applications follows a now-familiar three-step pattern for admission categories that require a labor market test. The employer must first secure labor certification from DOL and then win approval of a visa petition filed with USCIS. Thereafter the worker obtains the visa at a U.S. consulate (though in some circumstances, the worker can gain the status in the United States). H–2B workers are generally admitted for up to one year at first, but they can continue working, for the same or a different employer, for up to three years in the United States.

The H–2B labor certification process has been an arena for considerable controversy. The substantive areas of disagreement include the wages that must be paid to H–2B workers and the date of the employer's labor market test. But the larger disagreement—and litigation—has focused on the role of the Department of Labor in H–2B labor certification. Employers and organizations representing H–2B workers and U.S. workers have sued the federal government, arguing that the Department of Homeland Security impermissibly delegated its decisionmaking authority to DOL on wage determinations and the ultimate decision to issue or deny labor certification. The controversy forced DOL and DHS to issue regulations jointly to replace regulations originally issued by DOL alone. As we go to press, litigation on DOL authority is pending in several federal courts of appeals. *See G.H. Daniels III & Associates, Inc. v. Perez*, 626 Fed. Appx. 205 (10th Cir. 2015); *Bayou Lawn & Landscape Services v. Secretary, U.S. Department of Labor*, 621 Fed. Appx. 620 (11th Cir. 2015); *Comite de Apoyo a los Trabajadores Agricolas (CATA) v. Perez*, 774 F.3d 173 (3d Cir. 2014); *Louisiana Forestry Ass'n, Inc. v. Secretary, U.S. Dept. of Labor*, 745 F.3d 653 (3d Cir. 2014).

Figure 5.11 shows H–2B admissions since 1992. The increase in admissions for 2005–2007 reflected special provisions in the Save Our Small and Seasonal Business Act (SOSSBA) of 2005, Pub. L. No. 109–13, 119 Stat. 318 (2005), that exempted returning H–2B workers from the cap. Congress did not extend that provision beyond 2007, but then revived it in December 2015 for fiscal year 2016. *See* INA § 214(g)(9)(A).

Many H–2B workers have been victims of serious labor abuses. *See* Southern Poverty Law Center, Close to Slavery: Guestworker Programs in the United States (2013). In one notorious case, a federal jury in Louisiana in February 2015 awarded $14 million in compensatory and punitive damages to five Indian H–2B workers. The jury found after a four-week trial that Signal International (a marine services company), a New Orleans immigration lawyer, and India-based labor recruiter lured about 500 hundred workers to repair oil facilities in Mississippi and Texas, and then defrauded and forced them to live in inhuman conditions. *See* Liam Stack, *Indian Guest Workers Awarded $14 Million*, N.Y. Times, Feb. 19, 2015. Signal International later filed for bankruptcy under terms that included a $20 million settlement to resolve 11 similar lawsuits by over 200 other workers. *See In Bankruptcy Filings, Maritime Company Says It Settled Labor Case*, N.Y. Times, July 17, 2015.

Figure 5.11
H–2B Visas Issued, FY1992–2014

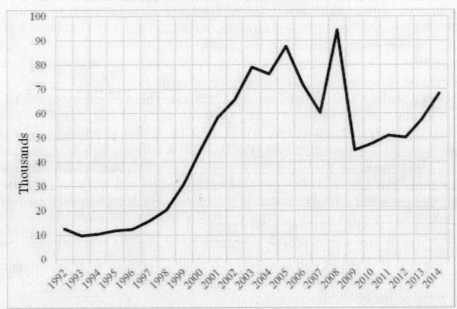

Source: Department of State, Report of the Visa Office 2014, Table XVI(B).

If the harm is severe enough to be trafficking, the workers may qualify for T visas that may make them eligible to adjust to lawful permanent resident status. This is a nonimmigrant category for victims of a "severe form of trafficking in persons," including the legal categories of forced commercial sex and forced labor. The definition generally requires the use of "force, fraud, or coercion" by the trafficker. *See* 8 C.F.R. § 214.11(a). The statute also requires finding that the individual "would suffer extreme hardship involving unusual and severe harm upon removal," and that the individual (unless under 18 years of age) "has complied with any reasonable request for assistance in the Federal, State, or local investigation or prosecution of acts of trafficking or the investigation of crime where acts of trafficking are at least one central reason for the commission of that crime." *See* INA §§ 101(a)(15)(T), 214(*o*).

Exploited workers may also qualify for U visas—which are for victims of certain crimes—with similar eligibility to adjust to lawful permanent resident status. Because T and U visas are often used as a form of relief from removal from the United States, we defer full treatment of them until Chapter Seven.

g.　Nonimmigrant Categories and Free Trade Agreements

Other international agreements besides treaties of commerce and navigation can bear directly on nonimmigrant admissions. Free trade agreements are the primary example. Though the United States is not a party to any free trade treaty as ambitious as those that created the European Union, which led to a broad regime of free movement of labor and capital among contracting states, some of its trade compacts have specific provisions facilitating the migration of designated categories of workers.

Most prominently, the North American Free Trade Agreement (NAFTA), which took effect January 1, 1994, brought Mexico into the free trade zone that had existed since 1988 by virtue of the U.S.-Canadian Free Trade Agreement (FTA), 27 I.L.M. 293 (1988). NAFTA makes no provision for permanent immigration, but it allows four categories of Canadian and Mexican citizens to enter the United States as nonimmigrants if they are "businesspersons"—defined as those "engaged in trade in goods, the provision of services or the conduct of investment activities." NAFTA, ch.16, Annex 1603. These categories are labeled business visitors, traders and investors, intra-company transferees, and professionals. The first three categories roughly correspond to the B–1, E–1 and E–2, and L–1 categories, respectively. The professionals category appears to correspond to the H–1B category, but has a carefully negotiated list of eligible occupations.

For business visitors and intra-company transferees, admission under NAFTA is accommodated under the existing INA. For E visas, the implementing legislation allows access by Canadians and Mexicans. *See* Pub. L. 103–182, § 341(a), 107 Stat. 2057 (1993); INA § 214(e). NAFTA also led to the creation of a new TN category for professionals. The TN procedure parallels that for H–1Bs, except that employers of Canadian citizens need not file a labor attestation nor a preliminary petition with DHS. TN professionals are not subject to the H–1B cap of 65,000. Similar country-specific arrangements have become part of the INA as a result of free trade agreements with Chile and Singapore, which not only provide for E visas but also created a new H–1B1 "fast track" category, which dispenses with some of the substantive and procedural requirements for H–1B visas. *See* INA §§ 101(a)(15)(H)(i)(b1), 214(g)(8).

To the extent that Congress considers reforms to the business nonimmigrant provisions in the INA, it becomes highly relevant that free trade agreements incorporate formal promises by the United States to refrain from certain types of changes to such categories, as applied to nationals of the treaty partner. For example, the U.S.-Singapore Free Trade Agreement states that the United States shall not require labor certification or other similar procedures as a condition of entry and shall not impose any numerical limits on intracompany transfers from Singapore. *See* Chapter 11, § 3 of the U.S.-Singapore Free Trade Agreement, Annex 11A, signed May 6, 2003. *See also* Chapter 14, § 3 of the U.S.-Chile Free Trade Agreement, Annex 14.3, signed June 6, 2003.

Similarly, no party to NAFTA may impose numerical limits or labor market tests as a condition of entry for intracompany transferees. *See* Chapter 16, of the North American Free Trade Agreement, Annex 1603 § C, signed Dec. 17, 1992.

4. CONTROVERSIES OVER TEMPORARY WORKERS

The desirability and the contours of any temporary worker program have been hotly debated in this generation as they have been in earlier times. Several themes are perennially at the core of the legislative and public discussion. First, is there truly a shortage of U.S. workers in any given sector of the economy or is any apparent shortage just a product of stubbornly low wages? Second, even assuming that the economic need exists, is a temporary worker program preferable to the alternatives? One alternative is expanding the pool of U.S. workers in various ways, including better wages and working conditions for workers. Another alternative is restructuring the relevant economic sector to be less reliant on labor. Or that sector might relocate some or all of its activities outside the United States where a labor force may be more readily available. Another alternative, in practice, is unauthorized migration.

In June 2013, by a vote of 68–32, U.S. Senate passed S. 744, the Border Security, Economic Opportunity, and Immigration Modernization Act, a comprehensive immigration reform bill. Among its many provisions, the legislation included new temporary worker provisions—known as W visas—with separate branches for agricultural and nonagricultural workers. S. 744 would have provided higher admission numbers, with specific formulas for later adjustments in annual ceilings. It would have raised the annual H–1B caps, with new measures meant to minimize displacement or wage reduction for U.S. workers. S. 744 also would have simplified the process by which a temporary worker might adjust to lawful permanent resident status after a number of years as a nonimmigrant in the United States. The House of Representatives took no action on S. 744.

The readings below pull out a few of the main issues and arguments in the debate over temporary workers. That debate remains robust, especially because temporary worker provisions have featured prominently in the broader deliberations over comprehensive immigration reform, which we will consider in Chapter 10D. The readings are divided into two parts—first on H–1B and L–1 nonimmigrants, and second on H–2A and H–2B temporary workers, but there are strong conceptual and political parallels between the arguments offered in both arenas.

a.   H–1B and L–1 Nonimmigrants

There is an ongoing policy debate over the H–1B and L–1 nonimmigrant categories, with the contending camps often taking diametrically opposing positions. Proponents of these categories see the restrictions on high-level business immigration, particularly the cap on H–1Bs, as limiting the nation's ability to compete globally and actually inducing companies to move offshore. This camp has similar criticisms of the constraints on the L category and on permanent employment-based immigration. Their opponents see these visas as reducing salaries in high-tech fields, making such vocations less attractive to young U.S. workers choosing a field, and even facilitating the offshoring of high-level U.S. jobs.

The next two readings below reflect strong differences, not only in assessing the benefits and harms attributable to these categories, but also in the scope of the inquiry into those benefits and harms.

RONIL HIRA, IMMIGRATION REFORMS NEEDED TO PROTECT SKILLED AMERICAN WORKERS

Testimony before the U.S. Senate Judiciary Committee, March 17, 2015.

* * *

The clear intent of the law * * * is that hiring foreign workers will not harm American workers. Yet the H–1B program is most definitely harming American workers, harming them badly, and on a large scale. *Most* of the H–1B program is now being used to import cheaper foreign guestworkers, replacing American workers, and undercutting their wages. So, contrary to intent of the INA, the use of the program is indeed "adversely affecting American workers' wages and working conditions." The scale of this damage is large and its effects long lasting, adversely impacting: the careers of hundreds of thousands of American workers; future generations of students; and, America's future capacity to innovate. This is not just adversely affecting a few workers. The H–1B program is very large with approximately 120,000 new workers admitted annually. Once admitted those workers can remain in the U.S. up to six years. While no one knows exactly how many H–1Bs are currently in the country, analysts estimate the stock of H–1B workers at 600,000.

There are hundreds of thousands of additional guestworkers admitted on L–1 and OPT visas, and they too are harming the job prospects of American workers. Because Congress never expected L–1 and OPT workers to be potential competition to American workers those programs have virtually no rules to protect American workers. That expectation was incorrect. As with the H–1B program, these guestworker visa programs are now being used too to replace and undercut American workers.

* * *

The recent case of Southern California Edison (SCE) illustrates the most flagrant abuses of the H–1B program and exposes the flaws in the protections for American workers. As reported by *Computer World* and the *Los Angeles Times,* SCE is replacing its American workers with H–1B workers hired by outsourcers Tata and Infosys. To add insult to injury, SCE forced its American workers to train their H–1B replacements as a condition of receiving their severance packages. There could not be a clearer case of the H–1B program being used to harm American workers' wages and working conditions. And no clearer example demonstrating that the protections for American workers in the H–1B program are woefully inadequate. The SCE case is flagrant but isn't an isolated case. Disney in Florida reportedly did something similar to 500 American workers a few weeks ago. Many other cases have been documented such as Cargill in Minnesota, Harley Davidson in Wisconsin, and Northeast Utilities and Pfizer both in Connecticut. In addition to directly replacing American workers, H–1Bs are also widely being used instead of recruiting and hiring Americans. There are countless other examples, some reported and some not. Even when they are not replacing American workers, employers turn to H–1B workers without ever considering American workers. Recent news reports indicate that Deloitte Consulting is using exclusively foreign workers to upgrade the State of California's unemployment insurance computer systems. It is a sad irony that firms are importing guestworkers to service the unemployment system when hundreds of thousands of Americans who have the skills to do this work are unemployed and underemployed. And this isn't the first time H–1Bs have worked on an unemployment insurance system. The state of Indiana gave a similar contract to India-based Tata a decade ago and it too hired only guestworkers to do the work.

* * *

Myth: Employers must prove there are no qualified American workers before hiring an H–1B.

Reality: There are no requirements to demonstrate a shortage of Americans prior to hiring an H–1B. Employers do not need to recruit American workers for a job filled by an H–1B. In fact, a job can, and often is, earmarked for an H–1B worker. The SCE case demolishes the myth of H–1Bs only being hired when no American worker can be found— American workers were already doing the job and being replaced by H–1Bs. * * *

Solution: Prior to hiring an H–1B, all employers should be required to actively recruit American workers and required to hire qualified American applicants. Explicitly ban all displacement of American workers by all employers. This would ensure that the H–1B program is being used as it is intended, to complement the American labor force.

* * *

Myth: H–1B workers cannot be cheaper than Americans because employers must pay the "prevailing wage."

Reality: Congress' intent of requiring that a legally defined "prevailing wage" be paid to H–1B workers was to ensure that H–1B workers were not pushing down the wages of American workers. To fulfill that, H–1B wages are supposed to be set at least at the market rate. But most H–1Bs are paid below that market wage, and they are hired because they are cheaper than American workers. And this is perfectly legal. Why? Because the "prevailing wage" rules, in statute and regulations, are poorly designed and written. *Employers can easily hire an H–1B worker at wages far below what an American worker is paid.* Simply put, the H–1B program has become a cheap labor program. * * *

* * *

Infosys and Tata Consultancy have been top H–1B employers for a number of years. These two India-based IT firms specialize in outsourcing and offshoring, are major publicly traded companies with a combined market value of about $115 billion, and are the top two H–1B employers in the United States. In Fiscal Year (FY) 2013, Infosys ranked first with 6,269 H–1B petitions approved by the government, and Tata ranked second with 6,193. As with the SCE scandal, these leading offshore outsourcing firms use the H–1B program to replace American workers and to facilitate the offshoring of American jobs. Because of this, Americans lost more than 12,000 jobs to H–1B workers in just one year to those two companies alone.

Most of the top H–1B employers employ the exact same business model as Tata and Infosys. Hundreds of thousands of American workers have lost their jobs due to H–1B program misuse and hundreds of thousands more are losing wages.

Solution: Raise the minimum "prevailing wage" to at least the average (mean) wage. If the H–1B workers we would like to target have specialized skills, shouldn't they be paid at least the average wage? This will not completely eliminate the use of H–1B workers as cheaper labor but it would help clean up some of the most flagrant abuses. * * *

Myth: Compliance with the program's rules that protect American workers is robust.

Reality: Compliance with the H–1B program depends almost exclusively on a whistle blower coming forward to flag violations. This is the worst and most ineffective method of ensuring compliance. Whistle blowers are almost always retaliated against if they come forward. Further, many workers, foreign and American, do not even know when violations are being made. Even in those cases where they are aware of a violation it is difficult for them to gather evidence that could prove it. * * *

* * *

Outsourcing firms received more than half of the H–1B visas issued in FY13. The list is a who's who in the Indian outsourcing industry. In fact, Indian Government officials refer to the H–1B as the "Outsourcing Visa." Tata and Infosys, the two outsourcing companies hired by Southern California Edison to replace its American workers, were the *top 2* H–1B recipients in 2013. The rest of the outsourcing firms use the program the same way—for cheap labor and to facilitate the offshoring of American jobs.

H–1B advocates often conflate the H–1B with a legal permanent residence (a greencard). The H–1B program is a temporary non-immigrant work permit. * * * The employer holds the visa, not the worker, and if the H–1B worker is laid off he must leave the U.S. This provides enormous leverage over the H–1B worker.

The employer, not the worker, has the discretion of applying for a greencard for an H–1B worker. And most of the top H–1B employers don't sponsor their H–1B workers for greencards. By my estimates less than half of H–1Bs are being sponsored for greencards. * * * [M]ost of the top H–1B employers are using the program for cheaper temporary labor—as a vehicle to outsource jobs overseas rather than as a bridge to permanent immigration. Just to use one example—Accenture received 3,321 H–1Bs yet applied for a mere 4 greencards for its H–1B workers in FY13. That is a 0.1% rate, or 1 greencard application for every 830 H–1B workers. * * *

The L–1 visa and F–1 visa Optional Practical Training (OPT) programs are in many ways more harmful to American workers than the H–1B program. They have no protections for American workers or foreign workers. There are no recruitment or non-displacement requirements for either program. American workers can and are replaced by these workers. The scandalous case of Siemens, of Lake Mary Florida, forcing its American workers to train foreign L–1 visa replacements hired by Tata has been well documented.

Neither the L–1 nor the OPT have *any wage floor,* a cap, recruitment requirements, or non-displacement. Further, both programs are subject to virtually no federal scrutiny or oversight. We have no idea how many L–1 visa holders are here at any one time, and unlike the H–1B, we don't even know how many are approved for each company because of blanket petitions (for which no publicly available government data exist). * * *

With no wage floor, the L–1 visa program offers wage arbitrage opportunities even greater than with the H–1B. Workers can be paid home country wages. * * *

* * *

Professional jobs have been an important rung on the ladder to the middle class. Computer occupations in particular have been a traditional path from working class to the middle class. Exploitation of the H–1B and other guestworker programs is shutting that pathway down and as we see in the case of Southern California Edison, many are being forcibly sent down from the middle class.

This is especially troubling since the technology industry has a terrible track record on diversity. There are very low rates of hiring of African-Americans and Hispanics as well as women. And age discrimination is an open secret in the technology industry. The SCE workers are typically in their 40s and 50s and are men and women of all races. While the H–1Bs being imported for IT occupations are almost all Indian men in their 20s and 30s.

* * *

GIOVANNI PERI, KEVIN SHIH, CHAD SPARBER & ANGIE MAREK ZEITLIN, CLOSING ECONOMIC WINDOWS: HOW H1–B VISA DENIALS COST U.S.-BORN TECH WORKERS JOBS AND WAGES DURING THE GREAT RECESSION

Partnership for New American Economy, June 2014, at 4, 8, 12, 14–16, 20, 23.

In six of the last nine years, the H–1B visa cap has been met within 90 days of the government opening up the application window; and in 2007, 2008, 2013, and 2014, so many applications came in during the first week that officials had to hold a lottery to determine which ones to process. That meant that tens of thousands of potential workers were denied the ability to come to the U.S. * * *

Some policymakers, however, worry about whether relying on foreign-born workers here on U.S. soil might impact or displace tech workers born and trained in America. In this report, we examine this question using a uniquely strong research approach. Taking advantage of the randomness created by the 2007 and 2008 H–1B visa lotteries, we determine how the denial of H–1B visas for computer workers in that period impacted job and wage growth for U.S.-born tech workers in the years that followed. * * *

The results of our analysis are clear. Cities whose employers faced large numbers of denials in the H–1B visa lotteries experienced considerably less job creation and wage growth for American-born computer workers in the two years that followed. Denying H–1B visas didn't help the economies of America's cities or their U.S.-born workers. Instead, it cost their tech sectors hundreds of thousands of jobs and billions in missed wages.

* * *

The vast majority of scholarly articles examining the impact of H–1B visa holders have found no evidence that such workers crowd out employment or innovation. Still, drawbacks in the methodology used for those papers make it impossible to make such conclusions unequivocally. The true innovation of this paper is that it leverages the natural experiment generated by the 2007 and 2008 H–1B visa lotteries to build a model that identifies the true causal impact that H–1B visa workers in computer-related fields have on U.S.-born workers living in the same metropolitan area and working in the same occupations—the very group that critics worry would be adversely impacted by an influx of foreign-born talent. To do this, we use data from the United States Citizenship and Immigration Services and the U.S. Department of Labor to calculate how the demand for computer workers in 236 metropolitan areas across the country went unmet as a result of the 2007 and 2008 H–1B visa lotteries. We then use data from the American Community Survey to examine how that unsatisfied demand for workers impacted the number of jobs created for U.S.-born computer workers and the wages paid to them in the two years that followed.

Our findings present clear evidence of the powerful impact that H–1B workers have on the growth of tech sectors in American cities. In areas that had a large number of unsuccessful H–1B lottery petitions relative to the size of their computer workforce in 2007 and 2008, the expansion of the tech sector and the growth in wages paid to local computer workers slowed considerably. In Washington, DC, the large number of local H–1B visa applications that didn't make it through the lottery caused local companies to lose out on creating as many as 30,222 computer jobs for U.S.-born workers in the period between 2005–2006 and 2009–2010. * * *

* * *

To understand what sort of outcomes we might see in the data, it's useful to consider two different scenarios involving the possible role of foreign-born high-skilled workers in the computer workforce. In a situation where high-skilled, foreign-born, workers are being hired even though similarly qualified, U.S.-born workers are available, we would expect a sudden shock in the supply of H–1B workers to cause employers to promptly hire local, U.S.-born workers instead. In this case, the employment of U.S.-born, computer workers would rapidly rise in metropolitan areas that had bad luck in the H–1B visa lottery. We would also expect to see the wages of those U.S.-born, high-skilled computer workers go up as well, reflecting the fact that their skills are now in shorter supply. Less-skilled workers playing support roles would potentially be relatively unaffected by such a situation: They would still be supporting the same number of workers. The only difference would be that the high-skilled employees would be U.S.-born instead of foreign-born.

A second scenario paints a starkly different picture. In this environment, instead of H–1B workers being substitutes for available American ones, they are complementary to them. These foreign-born workers contribute unique skills or fill different roles in the computer-related firms that hire them. Their work, in some cases, results in innovations that raise corporate revenues overall, or allow firms to pursue new lines of business. By potentially contributing to innovations that save the firm time and improve performance, these workers also have the potential to contribute to increased productivity in the workplace. In this scenario, a sudden decrease in the supply of H–1B workers would lead computer-related firms to grow more slowly in the coming years and potentially scale back their ambitions in the more immediate term. This would cause the growth of new jobs created for U.S.-born workers in the computer-related industries to slow down as a result of the lottery. Wage growth would slow as well, as workers faced a less robust market for their services.

* * *

Our work also breaks down all employment and wage growth data to consider the impact the H–1B lotteries had on U.S.-born tech workers both with and without college degrees. While many Americans think of computer-related industries as employing mostly high-skilled workers, a substantial number of less-skilled individuals also work in the field: In 2006, about two out of every five U.S.-born individuals working in technology did not have a four-year college degree— at most they had only some college education. For our purposes, it is useful to look at these two groups separately. Critics, who worry that H–1B workers displace American high-skilled workers, would expect U.S.-born, high-skilled computer workers to benefit when they have fewer foreign-born programmers and computer experts to compete with. By breaking the two groups down separately, we are able to show clearly that this is not the case.

* * *

* * * In every one of our models, cities that had larger H–1B shocks experienced slower growth in the number of jobs available for U.S.-born computer workers—both high- and low-skilled—in the years that followed. Specifically, we found that every time a city experienced a 1 percent shock in the available supply of computer workers (as a result of the H–1B visa lotteries in 2007 and 2008), the growth in the number of jobs available for non-college educated, U.S.-born workers slowed as much as 7.1 percent between the 2005–2006 and 2009–2010 time periods. For equivalent U.S.-born college-educated workers, it slowed by as much as 1.3 percent during that time. We also found that employers who were denied H–1B visas were not able to respond by hiring high-skilled, U.S.-born workers in their place.

* * *

Our low estimate predicts that by 2009–2010, the 2007 and 2008 H–1B visa lotteries had caused U.S. metropolitan areas to miss out on creating roughly 60,000 new jobs for U.S.-born IT workers. Our higher estimate, however, predicts that the H–1B lotteries cost city-based U.S.-born tech workers as many as 231,200 new jobs during that period—a figure more than three times higher than the actual number of new jobs created for those workers during that time frame. Our figures also indicate that the majority of the jobs for U.S.-born workers described above would not have gone to the high-skilled computer workers, that companies say they have trouble recruiting but rather to the less-skilled, non-college educated workers who often support their work. More than four out of five jobs that would have been created for U.S.-born computer workers (using our high estimates) would have gone to U.S.-born computer workers without a college degree. That translates into almost 189,000 additional jobs that could have been created by 2009–2010—a figure that would have grown U.S.-born, less-skilled employment in the computer related fields by almost 28 percent over actual 2010 levels.

* * *

The figures above detailing the number of tech jobs "lost" from our economy as a direct result of the 2007 and 2008 visa lotteries is in some ways an underestimate. As mentioned above, the coefficients our models produced indicate that employers were not able to fill the roughly 178,000 positions set aside for H–1B employees with U.S.-born workers instead. Instead, the vast majority of those jobs were done away with altogether or left unfilled, meaning they too can be counted as jobs "lost" as a direct result of the large number of H–1B visa denials in 2007 and 2008. Altogether, that means that U.S. employers in computer-related fields would have had as many as 409,000 additional jobs of all backgrounds (US-born and foreign-born) by 2009–2010 if not for the H–1B visa lottery—a substantially larger employment base that would have expanded the U.S. income tax revenue and potentially contributed to innovation and patenting levels at America's tech firms.

* * *

One particularly interesting city impacted by recent H–1B trends was Detroit. After being the center of the American automobile industry for decades, the area's economy has struggled in more recent years to adapt to America's innovative, knowledge-driven economy.

In January 2010, more than one in seven adults over the age of 16 in the Detroit metropolitan area were unemployed. The 700,000-person city, once the fourth largest in the country, had also seen its population shrink by more than 1 million people since its peak in 1950. Heavy financial troubles led the city government to file for Chapter 9 bankruptcy in 2013.

In the midst of all these developments, computer industry employers in the Detroit metropolitan area were particularly hard hit by the H–1B lotteries. Our figures show that in 2007 and 2008, employers in Detroit trying to expand their operations saw an average of more than 5,300 H–1B applications eliminated in the lottery each year. Simply approving those visas—before even considering any other boost to employment that would have resulted—would have expanded the number of technology jobs in the city by almost 27 percent above 2005–2006 levels. It also would have created numerous, potentially well-compensated positions in Detroit's economy for U.S.-born workers as well. We estimate that approving the H–1B applications would have generated as many as 14,999 jobs for U.S.-born workers in computer-related fields. By 2009–2010, the annual wages of already existent U.S.-born, college-educated computer workers would have been between $44 million and $135 million higher per year as well.

NOTES AND QUESTIONS ON THE H–1B AND L–1 VISA SYSTEM

1. In his congressional testimony, Hira mentions how Southern California Edison not only replaced U.S. workers with H–1B workers, but "to add insult to injury" also "forced its American workers to train their H–1B replacements as a condition of receiving their severance packages." A similar, highly publicized episode involved Walt Disney World. *See* Julia Preston, *Pink Slips at Disney, But First, Training Foreign Replacements*, N.Y. Times, June 4, 2015. If you were a federal official looking into what happened at Southern California Edison, what would you want to know to decide if violations of the rules for H–1B status occurred, or to determine if the episode reflects deeper problems with the H–1B category? Two laid-off former Disney employees later sued Disney and the two companies that brought in the H–1B workers, claiming collusion to violate the law governing H–1B status. *See*

Julia Preston, *Lawsuits Claim Disney Colluded to Replace U.S. Workers With Immigrants*, N.Y. Times, Jan. 26, 2016.

2. In another highly publicized episode, H–1B workers hired by Tata Consultancy Services shadowed U.S. workers at Toys 'R' Us, produced training manuals for those jobs, then returned to India to train Tata employees there to perform the same work. The U.S. workers were then laid off. *See* Julia Preston, *Toys 'R' Us Brings Temporary Foreign Workers to U.S. to Move Jobs Overseas,* N.Y. Times, Sept. 30, 2015. What, if anything, went wrong at Toys 'R' Us? As a policy matter, is there a difference between the H–1B workers who replace U.S. workers in the United States and H–1B workers who facilitate outsourcing of the work to other countries? If a U.S. company is free to outsource its operations to a foreign location, with U.S. employees laid off as a result, what is troubling about having U.S. employees helping to make that transition as cost-effective as possible?

3. What explains the wide gulf between the views expressed by Hira and by Peri *et al.*? Is it a matter of assumptions, study design, time horizon, some combination of these factors, or something else?

4. Would Hira's proposals address the situations at Southern California Edison and Toys 'R' Us effectively and without unintended negative consequences? Should the cap be lowered, raised, or eliminated? Another possible change would focus on the attestation requirement, which ostensibly tries to protect U.S. workers while keeping H–1B hiring flexible and expeditious. Should a full labor certification process be required? Is it a problem that a small number of firms "win" a very high percentage of H–1B admission slots in the annual lottery? How would you design changes to the H–1B nonimmigrant category?

5. L–1s, especially in the specialized knowledge category, raise similar concerns, as do J–1 exchange visitors and F–1 students in Optional Practical Training (OPT). Should Congress adopt a labor certification requirement, a higher skills threshold, wage requirements, or an annual cap on the specialized knowledge category or perhaps all L–1s? But if employees have specialized knowledge, foreign financial backing, and the required prior employment by the firm (which is not required for H–1B workers), why doesn't that eliminate any need for a labor market test or numerical cap? What are the analogous concerns—and possible responses—for J–1 exchange visitors and F–1 students in the labor market?

6. Should special rules be provided to facilitate the H–1B hiring of graduates (or "top graduates"?) of U.S. science and engineering schools? Should they cover all academic degrees or only at the masters or doctoral level? *See* Liz Robbins, *Should Foreign Graduates Get a Visa Edge?*, N.Y. Times, Nov. 1, 2015. Australia had such a program but abandoned it out of concern that it had stimulated the creation of questionable educational programs for persons with marginal qualifications. *See House Subcommittee Addresses H–1B Visas*, 86 Interp. Rel. 1139 (2011).

b. H–2A and H–2B Temporary Workers

The basic issues in debates over H–1B and L–1 nonimmigrants reappear, though in different form, in debates over H–2A and H–2B temporary workers. Speaking directly to farm labor in the 1990s, the Commission on Immigration Reform chaired by former Congresswoman Barbara Jordan addressed both of these issues when it "unanimously and strongly agree[d]" that a guest worker program "would be a grievous mistake." U.S. Commission on Immigration Reform, Legal Immigration: Setting Priorities 172 (1995). The Commission expressed skepticism that farm labor is in short supply, and then it made a more fundamental point:

> Even if labor shortages develop, the Commission would be cautious about recommendations for a guestworker program to address them. Guestworker programs effectively expand rural poverty. Moreover, guestworker programs are predicated on limitations on the freedom of those who are invited to enter and work. Experience has shown that such limitations are incompatible with the values of democratic societies worldwide. For that very reason, "temporary" guestworkers tend to become permanent residents, *de facto* or even *de jure*. We cannot ignore the inconsistency between the stated intent of guestworker programs and their actual consequences.

Id. at 173.

We start with this framework for understanding the debate, in which many views reflect some combination of four perspectives:

> One perspective considers temporary workers as substitutes for unauthorized workers. A second evaluates the effects of temporary worker programs and unauthorized migration as similar forces in the U.S. economy—benefiting many citizens and permanent residents, but perhaps disadvantaging others. A third perspective compares the roles that temporary worker admissions and unauthorized migration play in international economic development. A fourth assesses temporary admissions and unauthorized migration in the context of citizenship and of the integration of immigrants. Each of these four perspectives says something different about temporary workers * * * .

Hiroshi Motomura, *Immigration Outside the Law* 211–12 (2014).

———

The following readings explore the economic, social, and philosophical dimensions of this debate, which will revive in earnest whenever Congress re-engages on immigration reform.

JORGE DURAND & DOUGLAS S. MASSEY, BORDERLINE SANITY

The American Prospect, Sept. 24, 2001, at 28.

* * * [I]mmigration from Mexico * * * is going to continue. We are talking, after all, about two countries with more than just a 2,000-mile border in common. * * * [B]ilateral trade has grown to $200 billion per year, and the border is now marked by a string of rapidly growing twin cities and a booming manufacturing sector. The two nations also share a 60-year history of uninterrupted migration. The Mexican-born population of the United States now stands at eight million. * * *.

But if the international flow of workers is inevitable, other empirical data suggest how it might be better managed. Our own research, for instance, which involved interviews with close to 5,000 immigrants over the last 15 years, shows that when migrants first enter a developed country, most are not motivated, as Americans tend to imagine, by a desire to live where they can maximize earnings. In reality, most migrants move in an attempt to solve economic problems at home. They are leaving countries with inadequate capital, credit, and mortgage markets—countries also without unemployment insurance, crop insurance, futures markets, and other protections against sudden losses of family income. Initially, most migrants seek to work abroad only temporarily, and mainly in order to diversify family-income risks, to accumulate cash unavailable at home (most often so they can build a house), or to finance a small business or a consumer purchase (such as a car).

In other words, international migration is often less influenced by conditions in labor markets than conditions in other kinds of markets. So U.S. policies, which to date have chiefly aimed to make the American labor market less attractive to Mexican migrants, have been of little use. Programs designed to improve the performance and accessibility of a sending country's credit and insurance markets are far more likely to affect migration decisions. * * *

Our first proposal is to [increase substantially] * * * the U.S. immigration quota for Mexico. * * * But our research shows that not all immigrants do want to move here permanently. To a great extent, Mexicans seek permanent-resident visas because that is the only door open to them. If another option were available—such as a temporary-worker program—more people would opt for it. Indeed, an enlightened policy, rather than making it difficult for migrants to come and go, would support their evident desire to return home by granting them temporary-work visas that allow them to enter, leave, live, and work in the United States without restriction for a period of, say, two years. We propose such visas as the mainstay of U.S.-Mexican immigration management. They would be renewable once in the lifetime of the migrant, but only after the worker returned home for at least a year. A binational agency managed by the U.S. and Mexican governments, to which aspiring migrants would apply directly, would distribute the temporary-worker visas, thus getting employers out of the corruption-prone business of labor recruitment. And if these visas were generously available, they would go a long way toward reducing undocumented migration and the ills that accompany it.

In order to guarantee labor rights, these visas would not be tied to specific employers or jobs but issued directly to the migrants themselves. Whenever a work visa is tied to a particular job, as in the current guest-worker program, the migrant is left vulnerable to exploitation, unable to exercise the most fundamental right a worker can have: the right to withhold his or her labor. Granting migrants the right to change jobs would free them to participate in unions and to report violations of their labor rights. It would also make it more difficult for unscrupulous employers to use immigrants to lower the wages of native workers or cut corners on ensuring their health and safety.

If something on the order of 300,000 two-year visas were issued annually, the temporary migrants working in the United States at any time would constitute only a small share of the U.S. workforce but a large fraction of those who presently migrate with permanent visas they don't really want or with no papers at all. What's more, we have historical evidence of the efficacy of such programs. In the 1950s, the United States issued 450,000 temporary visas annually to Mexicans [as part of the Bracero program]—and reduced undocumented migration to near zero.

* * * [A substantial portion of the funds raised through special fees for these visas] should be used to facilitate the improvement of markets and the social infrastructure in Mexico. The integration of Spain and Portugal into the European Union offers a successful model. During the 1960s and 1970s, hundreds of thousands of emigrants left those two nations for work in the wealthier countries of northern Europe (particularly Germany), and northern officials worried that admitting Spain and Portugal into the European labor market would unleash even larger waves of emigration. But in preparation for their integration into the union, EU members invested substantial funds in Spain and Portugal. Transportation, communication, banking, and social-welfare networks were all upgraded. As a result, when unification finally occurred, in 1986, there was no rise in emigration. On the contrary, Spain and Portugal immediately began to experience large net return migrations, despite the fact that per capita income in both countries was (and still is) well below that in Germany.

* * * Immigrant flows do not last forever. Historical data indicate that most European nations in the course of economic development

underwent an "emigration transition" from low-to high-to low-emigration rates. In Europe this process took eight or nine decades, but recent experience suggests that the transition time is now considerably shorter. Take South Korea. In 1965 it ranked among the world's poorest nations; by 1998 it was one of the wealthy industrialized nations. In the interim, some 780,000 Koreans emigrated to the United States. Yet by the end of South Korea's transition, gross emigration was only 13,000 a year and net migration was near zero. The goal of U.S. policy should be to help Mexico move as quickly as possible through its own emigration transition and assume its place as a full and equal partner in the North American market. * * *

bolster Mexico in the NA market

DANIEL T. GRISWOLD, WILLING WORKERS: FIXING THE PROBLEM OF ILLEGAL MEXICAN MIGRATION TO THE UNITED STATES

Cato Institute, Center for Trade Policy Studies,
Trade Policy Analysis No. 19 (Oct. 15, 2002) at 20–22.

good for citiz + UPs bad for owners?

The number of [temporary worker visas (TWVs)] issued should be sufficient to meet demand in the U.S. labor market. Using the current estimated net inflow of undocumented workers, 300,000 visas per year would be a reasonable starting point. Distribution of visas could be rationed through a one-time application fee. The fee should be set high enough to offset costs and regulate demand, but low enough to undercut smugglers, perhaps in the range of $1,000. If a black market in smuggling reappeared or persisted, that would signal that the number of legal visas should be increased or the fee lowered. * * *   *← directly counter smuggling*

1 time appl. fee of $1000

A program should be created to allow undocumented workers already in the United States to earn legal status based on years of work and other productive behavior. Undocumented workers already in the United States should be issued TWVs immediately provided they register with the government and do not pose a threat to our internal or national security. Those who have lived and worked in the United States for more than a certain period should be eligible to apply for permanent residence status and, ultimately, citizenship. * * *

legalize those here

As a compromise for those concerned about future migration, the ability of temporary workers to sponsor relatives could be curtailed. Workers with TWVs should be able to sponsor their spouses and minor children to enter the country temporarily while the TWV is still valid. Keeping families together is not only just and humane; it also encourages more responsible social behavior. But those objectives would not require that temporary workers be allowed to sponsor relatives outside their nuclear family, such as siblings, parents, and adult children. With modern communications and transportation available, it is easier for immigrants to keep in touch and visit their extended families in the home

no "anchor"

fams together

country. The multiple-entry nature of the TWV would allow immigrants to easily visit their extended families back in their home country.

PHILIP L. MARTIN & MICHAEL S. TEITELBAUM, THE MIRAGE OF MEXICAN GUEST WORKERS

80 Foreign Affairs 118–21 (2001).

U.S. and Mexican advocates promote temporary worker programs as a "win-win" game. According to their arguments, U.S. employers would benefit from a guest worker program because they would obtain legal access to workers who would accept low wages and be unlikely to unionize. At the same time, the temporary Mexican workers would win jobs at wages far higher than those available at home. * * * [Many] assume they could design a guest worker program to make the Mexican workers "temporary" and "returnable," ineligible for social services, and unable to gain citizenship. For their part, Mexico's politicians hope to gain votes by providing a new source of jobs to the country's underemployed work force. In addition, the government hopes to gain economic benefits from the extra dollars their workers send back home, and to increase its political leverage in the United States.

The only problem with this "win-win" scenario is that it will not work. * * * [V]irtually no low-wage "temporary worker" program in a high-wage liberal democracy has ever turned out to be genuinely temporary. On the contrary, most initially small (and often "emergency") temporary worker programs have grown much larger, and lasted far longer, than originally promised.

This tendency toward permanence is easily explained—guest worker programs are virtual recipes for mutual dependence between employers and the migrants who work for them. Employers naturally grow to depend on the supply of low-wage and compliant labor, relaxing their domestic recruitment efforts and adjusting their production methods to take advantage of the cheap labor. History has shown that in agriculture (where many Mexican guest workers would be employed), a pool of cheap workers gives farm owners strong incentives to expand the planting of labor-intensive crops rather than invest in mechanized labor-saving equipment and the crops suitable for it. Thus, although the labor supply is supposed to be available only temporarily, farmers adapt in ways that ensure their continued need for workers willing to accept such low wages. On the other side of the coin, those bargain wages for employers are a boon for the "temporary" workers, who earn much more than they could at home. For instance, laborers in U.S. fruit and vegetable agriculture make between $5 and $7 an hour, as opposed to 50 cents an hour in Mexico. Past guest worker programs have shown that the participants and their families grow accustomed to the increased income; they therefore have no incentive to return home unless rapid economic and job growth there creates commensurate opportunities. As the workers' "temporary" sojourns extend over time, the odds of their ever returning to their homeland diminish, and young people in the home country come to regard employment abroad as normal.

Meanwhile, the promised "win-win" outcomes for politicians have often turned out to be as illusory as the temporary nature of the work. For the countries that send their surplus labor abroad, the eagerly awaited worker remittances bring decidedly mixed economic blessings: the country receives needed capital, some of which is productively invested, but the influx of cash drives up real estate prices, stimulates conspicuous consumption of imported goods, and is unevenly distributed. The remittances also tend to decline over time, unless the number of new emigrants continues to grow. So the source country earns capital temporarily but loses many emigrant workers permanently. To make matters worse, the anticipated enhancement of political influence in the destination country has proved disappointing and often double-edged. * * *

For the host country, the permanent settlement of guest workers also tends to require greater spending on social services than the government initially anticipated. Many workers find ways to bring their families to join them, creating a large pool of poorly paid and often undereducated people. They, along with any children born in the host country, require government-financed services such as public education and health care. In the United States specifically, the settlement of millions of Mexicans would increase the numbers of U.S. residents who lack health insurance and rely on publicly financed clinics and other safety nets. Finally, political leaders have often belatedly discovered that admitting temporary low-wage workers unnaturally sustains industries with low productivity and wages, such as garment manufacturing, labor-intensive agriculture, and domestic services. In consequence, the economy's overall productivity and growth suffer. * * *

CRISTINA M. RODRÍGUEZ, GUEST WORKERS AND INTEGRATION: TOWARD A THEORY OF WHAT IMMIGRANTS AND AMERICANS OWE ONE ANOTHER

2007 U. Chi. Legal Forum 219, 221–23.

* * * [W]e should resist the temptation to adopt a large-scale guest worker program, because such a program is likely to fail on two interrelated counts: It will fail to achieve the short-term objectives supporters claim for it, and it will thwart what should be the long-term goals of our immigration policy. On the first count, the implicit promise of the guest worker program is that it will satisfy the United States' labor

needs while reducing illegal immigration, thus restoring the rule of law to the system and enabling the government to better track immigrants to the U.S. As studies of guest worker programs consistently reveal, however, though a guest worker program may address labor market demands, it will do so at the risk of compounding the illegal immigration problem and perpetuating the poor treatment of migrant workers.

But second, and more importantly, though a guest worker program may satisfy many short-term interests, in the long term it will compromise our ability to integrate immigrants effectively into the American body politic, in large part precisely because it will fail to prevent the emergence of a new undocumented population. This insight has not been clearly articulated in the debate over the guest worker idea, but it should be central to the discussion. Important participants in the current immigration debate have emphasized that the United States can no longer do without a meaningful integration policy to complement our immigration control measures. But whether the U.S. should adopt a separate integration policy or not, it is critical that the system of immigrant admissions and controls itself reflects integrationist aspirations. Proposed reforms should be judged in part by whether they will facilitate the incorporation of immigrants and their descendants into American social and civic life. * * *

Temporary worker programs ultimately thwart this incorporation objective, because they erect undesirable and otherwise avoidable obstacles to the integration process by constraining the two key mechanisms of immigrant integration: mobility and reciprocity. Incorporation depends on immigrants having mobility—the ability to move freely among society's various sectors as well as in and out of ethnic communities. Receiving societies logically and rightly expect immigrants to adapt to their new surroundings, but immigrants cannot make good on that obligation without mobility. This mobility depends on immigrants' ability to emerge from immigrant sectors of the economy and to develop the social and cultural capital necessary for interacting with people and institutions at large—both of which depend on the security of what I call the right to remain, or the security of a continued presence in the U.S. that guest worker programs do not provide.

Incorporation also depends on extant members of the receiving society displaying a reciprocal willingness to adapt to the presence of immigrant communities. A society's failure to adapt blocks immigrant assimilation by preventing immigrants from becoming part of important social institutions and community relations. The failure to treat immigrants as potential members also reflects an absence of the spirit of social cooperation that should characterize a democratic society. * * *

MICHAEL WALZER, SPHERES OF JUSTICE: A DEFENSE OF PLURALISM AND EQUALITY

Pp. 58–60 (1983).[*]

[W]hat are we to make of the host country as a political community? Defenders of the guest-worker system claim that the country is now a neighborhood economically, but politically still a club or a family. As a place to live, it is open to anyone who can find work; as a forum or assembly, as a nation or a people, it is closed except to those who meet the requirements set by the present members. The system is a perfect synthesis of labor mobility and patriotic solidarity. But this account somehow misses what is actually going on. The state-as-neighborhood, an "indifferent" association governed only by the laws of the market, and the state-as-club-or-family, with authority relations and police, do not simply coexist, like two distinct moments in historical or abstract time. The market for guest workers, while free from the particular political constraints of the domestic labor market, is not free from all political constraints. State power plays a crucial role in its creation and then in the enforcement of its rules. Without the denial of political rights and civil liberties and the ever present threat of deportation, the system would not work. Hence guest workers can't be described merely in terms of their mobility, as men and women free to come and go. While they are guests, they are also subjects. They are ruled, like the Athenian metics, by a band of citizen-tyrants.

But don't they agree to be ruled? Isn't the contractualist argument effective here, with men and women who actually come in on contracts and stay only for so many months or years? Certainly they come knowing roughly what to expect, and they often come back knowing exactly what to expect. But this kind of consent, given at a single moment in time, while it is sufficient to legitimize market transactions, is not sufficient for democratic politics. Political power is precisely the ability to make decisions over periods of time, to change the rules, to cope with emergencies; it can't be exercised democratically without the ongoing consent of its subjects. And its subjects include every man and woman who lives within the territory over which those decisions are enforced. * * *

* * *

The relevant principle here is not mutual aid but political justice. The guests don't need citizenship—at least not in the same sense in which they might be said to need their jobs. Nor are they injured, helpless, destitute; they are able-bodied and earning money. Nor are they standing, even figuratively, by the side of the road; they are living among the

---

citizens. They do socially necessary work, and they are deeply enmeshed in the legal system of the country to which they have come. Participants in economy and law, they ought to be able to regard themselves as potential or future participants in politics as well. And they must be possessed of those basic civil liberties whose exercise is so much preparation for voting and office holding. They must be set on the road to citizenship. They may choose not to become citizens, to return home or stay on as resident aliens. Many—perhaps most—will choose to return because of their emotional ties to their national family and their native land. But unless they have that choice, their other choices cannot be taken as so many signs of their acquiescence to the economy and law of the countries where they work. And if they do have that choice, the local economy and law are likely to look different: a firmer recognition of the guests' civil liberties and some enhancement of their opportunities for collective bargaining would be difficult to avoid once they were seen as potential citizens. * * *

HIROSHI MOTOMURA, IMMIGRATION OUTSIDE THE LAW[*]
Pp. 227–29 (2014).

* * * [A]ny system that treats temporary workers as potential permanent residents—and then as potential citizens—is open to the charge that it is really a system of permanent admissions. Skeptics might argue that it is more honest and transparent to evaluate whether and how to increase the number of lawful permanent residents admitted to the United States.

* * *

* * * One goal is to respond to the economy's needs with temporary workers rather than increased permanent admissions. The second goal is to keep temporary workers from becoming a servant underclass. The tension between these goals—and the way to resolve that tension—is captured in the idea that temporary workers should have a path to citizenship. This idea may seem counterintuitive, but any sound immigration policy must pursue these two goals simultaneously.

Doing so requires giving temporary workers some reasons to leave the United States that are not incentives or penalties tied directly to the individual worker or his work. The emphasis should instead be on international economic development initiatives that help to create general conditions in locales of origin that will give temporary workers, as a group, strong reasons to return, thus keeping migration

---

[*]   Copyright © 2014 by Oxford University Press, Inc. Reprinted by permission of Oxford University Press, Inc.

temporary or circular for many of them. Some sending countries, notably but not only the Philippines, already try actively to entice emigrants to return. Programs by the US government could have the same aim. Some initiatives could concentrate on specific communities that have historically sent significant numbers of migrants to the United States and have built up strong migration networks over generations.

* * *

Working without self-contradiction toward both temporary migration and integration, and toward creating a realistic path to citizenship for temporary workers, means turning both temporary work and permanent immigration into normal, government-fostered choices for individual migrants. The common element is treating temporary workers with dignity by offering them real choices. Doing so may be difficult and may even seem utopian, but the undertaking can start by respecting something obvious yet often overlooked—that many who come to the United States have no initial intent to stay permanently. Many do stay, but the first decision is typically to leave home temporarily, often under dire circumstances that push migrants to leave.

give them choice

This approach—temporary workers with a path to citizenship— has its limits. It would be troubling to turn the acquisition of permanent residence by temporary workers into the dominant approach to selecting immigrants and thus future citizens. It would better enhance US society's capacity to integrate newcomers and to maximize their contributions if most immigrants arrive as permanent residents. * * * [T]he welcome that is inherent in treating newcomers as future citizens makes them much more likely to integrate in ways that satisfy them and those who came to the United States before them. But it is not objectionable if some temporary workers become lawful permanent residents by exercising a choice. Overall, this approach to temporary worker programs from a citizenship and integration perspective would make them far more viable as part of a sound response to unauthorized migration.

NOTES AND QUESTIONS ON GUEST WORKER PROGRAMS

1.   What responses might the supporters of guest worker programs offer to the critiques of Rodriguez and Walzer?

2.   The article by Durand and Massey premises some of its conclusions on the understanding that high migration from Mexico is "inevitable." But Mexican migration dropped considerably in 2008 and has remained low, as we discuss in the next Section. In fact, the unauthorized population from Mexico continues to shrink modestly. What differences does this new and

apparently enduring pattern make to the analyses offered in this set of readings, especially by Durand and Massey, and by Griswold?

3.   Howard Chang supports guest-worker programs as a second-best policy in light of political constraints. (Best, in his view, would be elimination or drastic reduction of barriers to free movement of labor.) He comments: "Through guest-worker programs, natives enjoy the benefits of unskilled alien workers in the labor market but do not bear the fiscal burden of providing the full set of public benefits that these workers would receive if they had ready access to permanent residence and ultimately citizenship." Howard F. Chang, *Liberal Ideals and Political Feasibility: Guest-Worker Programs as Second-Best Policies*, 27 N.C.J. Int'l L. & Commercial Reg. 465, 466 (2002).

4.   Eleanor Brown argues that guest worker programs could be far better managed to greatly improve the workers' compliance with the temporary terms of their visas, if we would move away from "the dominant uninational conceptualization of immigration law" toward a greater use of binational cooperation treaties. Based on field research, she describes in detail a binational program for importing temporary workers from Jamaica to Canada, explaining why that program enjoys a far higher compliance rate than do comparable (and largely unilateral) programs bringing temporary workers from Jamaica to the United States. She summarizes the reasons, pointing to an information screening component, a legal compliance component, and a collective sanctions component:

> The information screening component argues that persons who are proximate to visa applicants may be incentivized to share with officials inside information as to which persons are likely to be law-abiding short-term guests. The legal compliance component contends that, among the subjects of this study, visa compliance is dominant even when they leave their home countries because their communal norms prioritize visa compliance, and they lose status in their communities if they deviate from these norms. The collective sanctions component contends that astute officials utilize group accountability rules to send signals to community members about the costs associated with breaking immigration laws, which incentivize them to enforce these norms.

> * * * [A] central role [is] played by the community screener [in the community of origin of the workers]. She functions as an "intermediary in trust" who stands to lose her primary currency, namely, the credibility of her advice, if those who she recommends abscond. Building on Richard McAdams's esteem-based model and Eric Posner's signaling model of norms promulgation, * * * there is a persuasive case that governmental policy can amplify visa-compliance norms in the communities from which guest workers originate [through the stigmatization of visa violators].

Eleanor Marie Lawrence Brown, *Outsourcing Immigration Compliance,* 77 Fordham L. Rev. 2475, 2482 (2009).

Brown describes further advantages of the binational model:

> [S]ource-labor countries are also well-placed to aid in sanctioning noncompliant aliens, even when those aliens are already on American soil, through their influence on communities from which aliens originate. Thus, the United States also stands to benefit from partially outsourcing the sanctioning function. Can the United States expect other countries to reliably meet their screening and sanctioning commitments? This Article argues that the answer is yes. In a competitive globalized context in which developing countries prize the access that their nationals have to the American labor market, the repeated game-like nature of their interactions with the United States increases the likelihood that source-labor countries will actually meet their commitments and will incentivize their nationals to do the same.

Id. at 2481.

5.   The apparent acceptance of a guest worker plan in the 2006–2007 debates by certain labor and Latino interest groups came as something of a surprise. They had historically opposed such plans, in part because of the problematic history of the most prominent of earlier large-scale guest worker programs, the bracero program, in effect from 1942 to 1964. One explanation of the changed position was offered by Janet Murguia, president of the National Council of La Raza, in 2007:

> Many Latinos still have searing memories of the infamous bracero program, which more than 50 years ago became synonymous with worker abuse. * * * [Such guest-worker programs risk creating] a permanent, sizable subclass of workers who endure harsh treatment while simultaneously undercutting their American co-workers.

> Despite these concerns, * * * my organization and many Latino leaders find ourselves in the interesting position of being principal advocates for a significant new worker visa program as part of comprehensive immigration reform. * * * [We believe that this proposal will] do what previous reforms did not: Acknowledge that there will continue to be a flow across the border and that we will do everything we can to control and regulate it. * * *

> The immigration reform bill the Senate passed last year contains a much different model of a worker visa program than the unjust model we have lived with for decades. Workers would not be at the mercy of abusive employers in that they could change jobs and alert the authorities to mistreatment. Rather than becoming a permanent second-class workforce, they would have the opportunity to earn a path to permanent status—and ultimately citizenship—as

one of the only classes of migrants able to petition for themselves rather than relying on an employer or relative to petition for them. There are important labor protections for immigrant workers as well as for their American co-workers, including a requirement that immigrant workers be paid the prevailing wage in an industry to avoid undercutting the wages of American workers employed there.

* * *

Janet Murguia, *A Change of Heart on Guest Workers*, Wash. Post, Feb. 11, 2007.

6.   How effective are the labor protections that Murguia and other authors highlight? What enforcement measures do they require? How much does support by her and others depend on assuming that enforcement of immigration limits is impossible? If that assumption is true, why would the contemplated labor-law enforcement be expected to work in the face of the same economic pressures for low-wage labor? Or if labor-law enforcement could work—presumably with greater resources and better institutional design—why couldn't a more amply resourced enforcement regime be expected to work against future unauthorized migration or against the hiring of unauthorized migrants?

EXERCISE ON GUEST WORKER PROGRAMS

You have been asked to design a guest worker program to avoid the problems that have plagued earlier such schemes, in both the United States and Mexico, as described by Martin and Teitelbaum. What sort of program would you propose? What enforcement assumptions would go into such a design—regarding both labor law enforcement and future immigration law enforcement?

C. UNAUTHORIZED MIGRANTS IN THE UNITED STATES

1. INTRODUCTION

Unauthorized migrants obviously do not constitute an admission category, but unauthorized migration has been a significant feature of the immigration landscape for several decades, with a major impact on both the substance and tone of public discourse over immigration. Because facts and perceptions (including misperceptions) about the undocumented population feature prominently in policy debates, and in decisions regarding institutional design and the allocation of resources, we devote a few introductory pages here to the underlying history and current facts. We will revisit some of the key issues later, especially in the discussion of immigration law enforcement in Chapter Ten, Section A.

We start by addressing the terminology. The terms "illegal aliens," "undocumented aliens," and "unauthorized migrants" are all in common usage. Some object to "illegal aliens" as insensitive, noting that many persons unlawfully in the United States may ultimately qualify for legal status or obtain discretionary relief from deportation; it is also argued that the United States has tolerated and even encouraged the presence of persons deemed "illegal." But others counter that "undocumented" is a euphemism for entry or continuing presence that violates federal law; moreover, many aliens not authorized to be in the United States possess documents (although they may be fraudulent).

In 2013, several major news media organizations, including *The Los Angeles Times* and *Associated Press*, abandoned the term "illegal immigrant." *The New York Times* limited its use, encouraging reporters and editors "to consider alternatives when appropriate to explain the specific circumstances of the person in question, or to focus on actions." *See* Christine Haughney, *The Times Shifts on "Illegal Immigrant," but Doesn't Ban the Use*, N.Y. Times, Apr. 23, 2013. One study found that the news media's use of the term "illegal alien" declined significantly since 1996. *See* Emily Guskin, *"Illegal," "Undocumented," "Unauthorized": News Media Shift Language on Immigration*, Pew Research Center (June 17, 2013). For a journalist's reflections, see Jeffrey Toobin, *Should I Use the Term "Illegal Immigrant"?*, The New Yorker, Aug. 5, 2015.

Courts sometimes explain their use of terms. *See, e.g., Texas v. United States*, 787 F.3d 733, 745 n.15 (5th Cir. 2015); *Martinez v. Regents of the Univ. of Calif.*, 50 Cal. 4th 1277, 1288, 241 P.2d 855, 862, 117 Cal. Rptr. 359, 362 (2010). Here, we generally adopt the term "unauthorized" (used by the Mexico/United States Binational Study on Migration) or "undocumented" to describe a person whose presence in the United States is in violation of law.

This Section continues with two narratives of unauthorized migration, written by the same reporter but on opposite sides of the U.S.-Mexico border—and thus looking not only at unauthorized migrants in the United States, but also at the places that they leave to cross the border.

DAMIEN CAVE, AN AMERICAN LIFE, LIVED IN SHADOWS
New York Times, June 8, 2014.*

Tulsa, Okla.—Ignacio, a father of four, bounces along in his pickup truck, driving at exactly the speed limit through an aging suburb. The clock says 6:44 a.m. Religious pendants hang off the mirror. His teenage son sits beside him, chatty if half-awake, as they approach an apartment building for a day of roofing in dire heat.

A police cruiser suddenly appears to the right. Ignacio stays quiet, hands on the wheel, but in his mind he repeats the prayer that covers his 12 years living here illegally: "No me pare, no me pare"—"Don't stop me, don't stop me."

"We used to have such a comfortable life, money to pay for our house, the car, to go wherever we wanted," Ignacio says, referring to a time before Oklahoma's 2007 law against illegal immigrants forced him to close his successful hair salon. "Now we are biting our nails, trying to make enough money every month."

The routines of life as an immigrant in the country illegally now vary widely by location—perhaps more than ever. Last year 11 states, including California and Utah, passed laws permitting illegal immigrants to obtain drivers licenses, while 15 states now let immigrant students pay in-state tuition regardless of legal status, up from 11 in 2012.

Some other states have followed a different path. Oklahoma led the way in 2007 with legislation that made it a crime to knowingly shelter or transport unauthorized immigrants, while preventing them from obtaining licenses, credentials and public benefits. It was the first sweeping state effort to discourage illegal immigration, and advocates for the approach—which has been expanded here and exported to a few other states—argue that it improves quality of life for legal residents and citizens.

"Every time you have people coming over from different cultures that don't assimilate with the American culture, they develop an underground culture," said Maj. Shannon Clark, a spokesman for the Tulsa County Sheriff's Office. "These people will try to generate revenue and gain money and do things that are in total conflict with the law."

But Oklahoma's restrictions did not reduce Oklahoma's illegal immigrant population, census figures show. While some families fled, others came and tens of thousands more—like Ignacio and his family, who requested that only their first names be used—have stayed put, hiding and striving in the shadows.

Tulsa is an especially tough place to pull that off. Even by Oklahoma's standards, it is known as a vigilant city, with a suburban lifestyle that requires driving to work and a sheriff's office that has made immigration enforcement a high priority.

Legal immigrants and criminals here have also found ways to use the law to their advantage. Ignacio says he has lost more than $100,000 to frauds he never reported to the police, fearing deportation. And it was a former employer and new competitor—a Mexican woman with legal status—who forced him to shut down his salon by reporting to inspectors that he lacked a Social Security number.

"The legal ones without compassion are the worst," said Maria, Ignacio's wife.

Dad

The alarm clock honks at 6 a.m.—and for a few minutes more—before Ignacio comes out of his bedroom in baggy shorts and a T-shirt. Groggy and darkly tanned from long days on rooftops, he collapses into a kitchen chair as Maria collects 10 cans of V8 energy drinks to keep him and their oldest son, José, hydrated at work.

"Coffee?" she asks. Ignacio shakes his head. He grabs a bag of bean and cheese sandwiches on wheat bread and heads to his truck, which is just a few years old. Despite the fact that money is tight, nice cars and cellphones are important. "If you have a nice car, they treat you well," he says, referring to the police. "If you drive an old, ugly car, they stop you and arrest you."

The journey to the job site lasts less than 20 minutes. A police officer is looking at his cellphone as they drive past, leaving Ignacio and José to meet up with a crew of eight other Hispanic men. A maintenance supervisor from the apartment complex waves good morning.

"This is the best crew you can have," he says.

Ignacio and José climb a tall ladder, then get to work cleaning the roof. They are sweating within the first hour. "It's tough work, especially with the heat," Ignacio says. He turns away from the sun and yells for someone to bring him shears to cut the heavy-duty plastic they are laying down over the old tar.

He would much rather be trimming hair. Ignacio, 40, comes from a long line of barbers in Zacatecas, an old silver city in central Mexico, and he often says he has "hair-cutting in his blood." He used to make a good living at it here in Tulsa, working first at a salon on the heavily Hispanic east side, then opening his own shop where he and his wife together made up to $700 a day.

But then they ran into trouble. Ignacio said that his boss at the first salon had refused to give him a 1099 form so he could pay his taxes, so when he opened his own salon in January of 2004, and voluntarily paid the taxes he owed, he attracted attention to his previous employer who, in retaliation, directed state inspectors to his new business.

When Oklahoma's illegal-immigrant law arrived three years later, the visits intensified. He tried to renew his barber's license, but was rebuffed; the Oklahoma Cosmetology Board had ruled that proof of legal status was required for every credential the state issued.

Ignacio shut down the shop in 2008. He said he turned to roofing only after being cheated by other immigrants in other ways. His secondhand toy store ran aground when a supplier took his money and never delivered a trailer full of merchandise. A promised shipment of Christmas trees arrived after Christmas. The couple considered returning to Mexico, but decided they would stay for the children's education.

In 2009, he said, life's burdens and failures began to make him suicidal. When his mother died that year, and he could not go home because he knew he could not return the way he came in, with a tourist visa, he wrote a note to his wife asking her to take good care of the children.

"You are the only one they have," he wrote. "Pray to God for me."

Mom and the Children

Sitting at a table outside the one-story house the couple bought nine years ago, Maria holds up the note. It is on the back of a sign, and the children have colored over parts of the writing. "I don't know why I kept it," she says, trying to laugh.

There are other documents as well: a scrap of paper with the name and phone number of the person who was supposed to get them visas; a letter from an inspector with the state Board of Cosmetology naming Ignacio's former employer as the source of a complaint; another from the Oklahoma Tax Commission indicating, seven months later, that he had complied with all state income tax requirements.

The photos in the pile show the couple's old salon—Maria and Ignacio on the day it opened, then later, when snapshots of satisfied clients covered the wall. She pulls out a picture of a new Hummer. "He was going to paint it over with the name of the salon," she says.

She laughs again. "Vámonos, hijas," she says, calling to her three daughters. The younger two, Michelle, 10, and Cointa, 6, are American citizens born in Tulsa. They pile into the family S.U.V. as Maria rolls down the windows, making a joke about avoiding air-conditioning to save money. The temperature is over 90.

Her first stop is the grocery store where—after parking carefully within the yellow lines—Maria spends $16.41 on bread and other items. Most of the customers are Hispanic or Asian.

Next, she stops at a store with a sign out front that says "pay your bills here." She hands cash to a woman in a Western Union shirt, for cable and electricity. "I used to pay by check," she says afterward, holding two of her daughters' hands, "back when we had a bank account."

Into the S.U.V. yet again, for a short drive to Dollar Tree for cleaning supplies, including soap to make sure the vehicles look good as new, then to Walgreen's for Gatorade. This is the only store that requires English and Alejandra, 16, translates. The first thing she does is make sure the clerk complies with the sale prices of six bottles for $5.

At home, after a roundabout route to avoid the police, Alejandra shows off her immaculate bedroom. The closet is well organized; the bed made. She plays the violin, and like her mother, she keeps important records: her membership in the National Honor Society, a "student of the month" certificate from sixth grade.

Like many other children of parents who are in the country illegally, she seems to feel that doing well will help make the United States more accepting.

"My parents can only take us a certain part of the way," Alejandra says, warming up lunch for her father and brother. "We have to go the extra mile."

But there are limits. A group of boys threw bottles of urine at her and a friend a few months ago, and the family decided not to press charges because it would have meant a trip to court. When José, 19, who was born in Mexico, recently asked a military recruiter to find out if he could join now that he has the right to work with the deferred action program that applies to some children brought here illegally, the recruiter never called back.

For José in particular, the past few years have been a rough introduction to American law and order. He had gotten used to having money, time, a girlfriend—not thinking about his illegal status—until he accompanied his mother to an appointment at a hospital affiliated with Oklahoma State University.

She needed to have her gall bladder removed, and an emergency room doctor had referred her to a specialist. But the hospital refused, the family said, because it received state funds and Oklahoma's 2007 immigration law bars immigrants without legal status from receiving benefits.

Even when José explained that his father would pay cash, they did not admit her. "What I expected from reality," José said, "it's not what happened."

Maria eventually got the surgery at a private hospital—with a bill of $11,000. Ignacio says they are still paying it off, $50 a month. A spider bite he suffered on a rooftop a few months ago added another medical bill of about $4,000.

Ignacio is proud to be paying these, just as he is proud not to have asked for food stamps for his citizen children.

And at times now, the family can see reason for hope. José has secured a scholarship for the local community college. At night, they all usually trickle into the sanctuary of St. Thomas More Catholic Church for choral practice. Ignacio smiles more with a songbook in his hand. José sings a few solos, raising his voice to the ceiling, his dark eyes at peace.

But the relief is never permanent. Tomorrow means another stressful drive to a 13-hour day on a scorching rooftop. Winter will eventually come again, the outdoor work will end. And the worry about being deported lingers.

"You think about it all the time," Ignacio said. "You are always aware of that danger."

DAMIEN CAVE, BETTER LIVES FOR MEXICANS CUT ALLURE OF GOING NORTH[h]

New York Times, July 6, 2011.[*]

Agua Negra, Mexico.—The extraordinary Mexican migration that delivered millions of illegal immigrants to the United States over the past 30 years has sputtered to a trickle, and research points to a surprising cause: unheralded changes in Mexico that have made staying home more attractive. A growing body of evidence suggests that a mix of developments—expanding economic and educational opportunities, rising border crime and shrinking families—are suppressing illegal traffic as much as economic slowdowns or immigrant crackdowns in the United States.

Here in the red-earth highlands of Jalisco, one of Mexico's top three states for emigration over the past century, a new dynamic has emerged. For a typical rural family like the Orozcos, heading to El Norte without papers is no longer an inevitable rite of passage. Instead, their homes are filling up with returning relatives; older brothers who once crossed illegally are awaiting visas; and the youngest Orozcos are staying put.

"I'm not going to go to the States because I'm more concerned with my studies," said Angel Orozco, 18. Indeed, at the new technological institute where he is earning a degree in industrial engineering, all the students in a recent class said they were better educated than their parents—and that they planned to stay in Mexico rather than go to the United States.

Douglas S. Massey [of Princeton] * * * said his research showed that interest in heading to the United States for the first time had fallen to its lowest level since at least the 1950s. "No one wants to hear it, but the flow has already stopped," Mr. Massey said, referring to illegal traffic. "For the first time in 60 years, the net traffic has gone to zero and is probably a little bit negative." * * *

The question is why. Experts and American politicians from both parties have generally looked inward, arguing about the success or failure of the buildup of border enforcement and tougher laws limiting illegal immigrants' rights—like those recently passed in Alabama and Arizona. Deportations have reached record highs as total border apprehensions and apprehensions of Mexicans have fallen by more than 70 percent since 2000.

But Mexican immigration has always been defined by both the push (from Mexico) and the pull (of the United States). * * * In simple terms, Mexican families are smaller than they had once been. The pool of likely migrants is shrinking. * * * [B]irth control efforts have pushed down the fertility rate to about 2 children per woman from 6.8 in 1970, according to government figures. So while Mexico added about one million new potential job seekers annually in the 1990s, since 2007 that figure has fallen to an average of 800,000, according to government birth records. By 2030, it is expected to drop to 300,000. * * * At the same time, educational and employment opportunities have greatly expanded in Mexico. Per capita gross domestic product and family income have each jumped more than 45 percent since 2000, according to one prominent economist, Roberto Newell. Despite all the depictions of Mexico as "nearly a failed state," he argued, "the conventional wisdom is wrong."

A significant expansion of legal immigration—aided by American consular officials—is also under way. * * * State Department figures show that Mexicans who have become American citizens have legally brought in 64 percent more immediate relatives, 220,500 from 2006 through 2010, compared with the figures for the previous five years. Tourist visas are also being granted at higher rates of around 89 percent, up from 67 percent, while American farmers have legally hired 75 percent more temporary workers since 2006. * * *

Hard Years in Jalisco

When Angel Orozco's grandfather considered leaving Mexico in the 1920s, his family said, he wrestled with one elemental question: Will it be worth it? At that point and for decades to come, yes was the obvious answer. * * * [T]he wages paid by the railroads, where most early migrants found legal work, were five times what could be earned on farms in Arandas, the municipality that includes Agua Negra.

* * * When Angel's father, Antonio, went north to pick cotton in the 1950s and '60s with the Bracero temporary worker program, which accepted more than 400,000 laborers a year at its peak, working in the United States made even more sense. The difference in wages had reached 10 to 1. Arandas was still dirt poor. * * *

Legal status then meant little. After the Bracero program ended in 1964, Antonio said, he crossed back and forth several times without documentation. Passage was cheap. Work lasting for a few months or a year was always plentiful. So when his seven sons started to become adults in the 1990s, he encouraged them to go north as well. Around 2001, he and two of his sons were all in the United States working—part of what is now recognized as one of the largest immigration waves in American history.

But even then, illegal immigration was becoming less attractive. In the mid-1990s, the Clinton administration added fences and federal agents to what were then the main crossing corridors beyond Tijuana and Ciudad Juárez. The enforcement push, continued by President George W. Bush and President Obama, helped drive up smuggling prices from around $700 in the late 1980s to nearly $2,000 a decade later, and the costs continued to climb * * * . It also shifted traffic to more dangerous desert areas near Arizona.

Antonio said the risks hit home when his nephew Alejandro disappeared in the Sonoran Desert around 2002. A father of one and with a pregnant wife, Alejandro had been promised work by a friend. It took years for the authorities to find his body in the arid brush south of Tucson. Even now, no one knows how he died. * * *

A Period of Progress

Another important factor is Mexico itself. Over the past 15 years, this country once defined by poverty and beaches has progressed politically and economically in ways rarely acknowledged by Americans debating immigration. Even far from the coasts or the manufacturing sector at the border, democracy is better established, incomes have generally risen and poverty has declined.

* * * [By 2003, research showed that the wage disparity between Arandas and] the United States had narrowed: migrants in the north were collecting 3.7 times what they could earn at home.

That gap has recently shrunk again. The recession cut into immigrant earnings in the United States, * * * even as wages have risen in Mexico * * * . Jalisco's quality of life has improved in other ways, too. About a decade ago, the cluster of the Orozco ranches on Agua Negra's outskirts received electricity and running water. New census data shows a broad expansion of such services: water and trash collection, once unheard of outside cities, are now available to more than 90 percent of Jalisco's homes. * * *

Still, education represents the most meaningful change. The census shows that throughout Jalisco, the number of senior high schools or preparatory schools for students aged 15 to 18 increased to 724 in 2009, from 360 in 2000, far outpacing population growth. The Technological Institute of Arandas, where Angel studies engineering, is now one of 13 science campuses created in Jalisco since 2000—a major reason professionals in the state, with a bachelor's degree or higher, also more than doubled to 821,983 in 2010, up from 405,415 in 2000.

* * * If these trends—particularly Mexican economic growth—continue over the next decade, [Jeffrey] Passel [of the Pew Hispanic Center] said, changes in the migration dynamic may become even clearer. "At the point where the U.S. needs the workers again," he said, "there will be fewer of them." * * *

How did this happen? Partly, emigrants say, illegal life in the United States became harder. Laws restricting illegal immigrants' rights or making it tougher for employers to hire them have passed in more than a dozen states since 2006. The same word-of-mouth networks that used to draw people north are now advising against the journey. "Without papers all you're thinking about is, when are the police going to stop you or what other risks are you going to face," said Andrés Orozco. Andrés, a horse lover who drives a teal pickup from Texas, is one of many Orozcos now pinning their hopes on a visa. And for the first time in years, the chances have improved.

Mexican government estimates based on survey data show not just a decrease in migration overall, but also an increase in border crossings with documents. In 2009, the most recent year for which data is available, 38 percent of the total attempted crossings, legal and illegal, were made with documents. In 2007, only 20 percent involved such paperwork.

* * * Advocates of limited immigration worry that the issuing of more visas creates a loophole that can be abused. Between 40 and 50 percent of the illegal immigrants in the United States entered legally with visas they overstayed, as of 2005, according to the Pew Hispanic Center. More recent American population data, however, shows no overall increase in the illegal Mexican population. That suggests that most of the temporary visas issued to Mexicans—1.1 million in 2010—are being used legitimately even as American statistics show clearly that visa opportunities have increased.

Easing a Chaotic Process

One man, [Edward] McKeon, the minister counselor who oversees all consular affairs in Mexico, has played a significant role in that expansion.

* * * Working within administrative rules, State Department officials say, he re-engineered the visa program to de-emphasize the affordability standard that held that visas were to be denied to those who could not prove an income large enough to support travel to the United States. * * * This led to an almost immediate decrease in the rejection rate for tourist visas. Before he arrived, around 32 percent were turned down. Since 2008, the rate has been around 11 percent.

Mr. McKeon—praised by some immigration lawyers for bringing consistency to a chaotic process—was also instrumental in expanding the temporary visa program for agricultural workers. * * * For H–2As, Mexican workers can now receive their documents the same day that they apply.

Mr. McKeon also pushed to make the program more attractive to Mexicans who might otherwise cross the border illegally. * * * Specifically, consulate workers dealing with H–2A applicants who were once illegal—making them subject to 3-or 10-year bans depending on the length of their illegal stay—now regularly file electronic waiver applications to the United States Customs and Border Patrol. About 85 percent of these are now approved, Mr. McKeon said, so that in 2010 most of the 52,317 Mexican workers with H–2A visas had previously been in the United States illegally. * * *

A Divisive Topic

* * * On the other side, Steven A. Camarota, a demographer at the Center for Immigration Studies in Washington, which favors reduced immigration, said that increasing the proportion of legal entries did little good. "If you believe there is significant job competition at the bottom end of the labor market, as I do, you're not fixing the problem," Mr. Camarota said. "If you are concerned about the fiscal cost of unskilled immigration and everyone comes in on temporary visas and overstays, or even if they don't, the same problems are likely to apply." By his calculations, unskilled immigrants like the Orozcos have, over the years, helped push down hourly wages, especially for young, unskilled American workers. Immigrants are also more likely to rely on welfare, he said, adding to public costs.

The Orozco clan, however, may point to a different future. * * * After graduating, [Angel Orozco] hopes to work for a manufacturing company in Arandas, which seems likely because the director of his school says that nearly 90 percent of graduates find jobs in their field. Then, Angel said, he will be able to buy what he really wants: a shiny, new red Camaro.

NOTES AND QUESTIONS ON UNAUTHORIZED MIGRATION

1. If the changed trends in Mexican migration described in Cave's second article continue, what are the implications for future policy toward unauthorized migration? For guest worker programs?

2. "It is popularly believed," wrote Wayne Cornelius, "that undocumented immigrant workers toil in the informal or 'underground' economy, where employers pay sub-minimum wages and escape government regulation of labor standards. But field research in California and Illinois has found that most *indocumentados* work in relatively small or medium-sized 'formal sector' firms that are very much part of the mainstream economy. They tend to concentrate in firms and industries that are under intense foreign and/or domestic competitive pressures and that suffer from sharp fluctuations in demand for the goods or services they produce." He continued:

> For such firms, the principal advantage of undocumented immigrant labor is not its cheapness but its *flexibility* (or *disposability,* in the more critical view of many academics and labor-union leaders). The immigrant work force is more willing than U.S.-born workers to accept high variability in working hours, working days per week, and months per year, and low job security. * * * Immigrant workers are ideal "shock absorbers," enabling businesses to adapt more quickly and easily to rapidly changing market conditions and consumer preferences. * * * Thus, the U.S. labor markets in which Mexican undocumented workers typically participate are not so much *illegal* as they are *fluid* and *volatile.*

Wayne A. Cornelius, *Mexican Migration to the United States: Introduction*, in Mexican Migration to the United States: Origins, Consequences, and Policy Options 1, 4–8 (Wayne A. Cornelius & Jorge A. Bustamante eds., 1989). Later in this Section, we will look more closely at the labor market participation of unauthorized migrants.

2. CHARACTERISTICS OF THE UNAUTHORIZED POPULATION IN THE UNITED STATES

Not surprisingly, it is difficult to gauge the number of unauthorized migrants in the United States. Demographer Jeffrey Passel of the Pew Research Center has been a pioneer in developing a widely respected method for estimating this population and identifying a wealth of further detailed information.

hard to know #

Figure 5.12
Estimates of the U.S. Unauthorized Immigrant Population
1990–2014

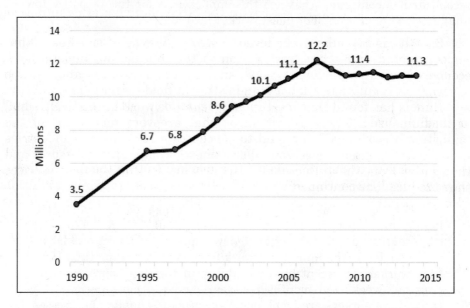

Source: Pew Research Center, U.S. Unauthorized Immigrant Population Levels Off
(July 21, 2015), http://www.pewresearch.org/fact-tank/2015/07/22/unauthorized-
immigrant-population-stable-for-half-a-decade/ft_15-07-23_unauthimmigrants/;
supplemented by earlier Pew data, available on the Pew website: http://www.pew
research.org/data-trend/society-and-demographics/immigrants/.

JEFFREY S. PASSEL,
WRITTEN TESTIMONY SUBMITTED TO THE U.S. SENATE
COMMITTEE ON HOMELAND SECURITY AND
GOVERNMENTAL AFFAIRS, MARCH 26, 2015

Pew Research Center, March 26, 2015.

* * *

The unauthorized immigrant population in the U.S. peaked at 12.2
million in 2007 after growing steadily by about half a million per year
from 3.5 million in 1990. After 2007, the trend changed abruptly and the
numbers dropped dramatically by about 1 million over the next two years
to 11.3 million in 2009 as the number of new unauthorized immigrants
arriving plummeted and large numbers left the country. Since 2009, the
national unauthorized immigrant population has remained essentially
unchanged as arrivals and departures have come into rough balance.

* * *

From 1990 to 2007, the number of unauthorized immigrants increased in every state, but growth was slower in the six states with the largest unauthorized immigrant populations than in the rest of the nation as a whole. California, the state with the largest number of unauthorized immigrants in all years, experienced the largest numerical growth, but its 88% increase from 1990 to 2007 was slower than that of other large states and nearly all smaller states. As a group, the other five largest states (Florida, Illinois, New Jersey, New York and Texas) experienced growth in their unauthorized immigrant population at the national average of 250% over the period. Meanwhile, the unauthorized immigrant population in the rest of the country increased almost sevenfold, from 700,000 in 1990 to 4.7 million in 2007.

These growth differentials led to a marked shift in the distribution of unauthorized immigrants across the country. The share in California dropped to 23% in 2007 from 42% in 1990. The share in the other five large states was unchanged at 38%, but the share in the rest of the country essentially doubled, to 39% in 2007 from 20% in 1990. With the overall decreases in the unauthorized immigrant population since 2007, these shifts came to a halt.

Post-Recession Trends in Unauthorized Immigrant Populations

* * *

The differential growth across states is related to patterns of change in Mexican and non-Mexican unauthorized immigrant populations. According to a Pew Research analysis, the losses in 13 of the 14 states were due to drops in the number of unauthorized immigrants from Mexico, who make up the majority of unauthorized immigrants. * * *

In six of the seven states where populations of unauthorized immigrants grew from 2009 to 2012, it was because the number of non-Mexicans increased; the number of Mexicans declined or did not change. * * *

There is wide variety in state populations of unauthorized immigrants, according to the Pew Research estimates. More than half the 2012 unauthorized immigrant population (60%) lived in the six states with the largest numbers of such immigrants—California, Florida, Illinois, New Jersey, New York and Texas. At the opposite end, six states (Maine, Montana, North Dakota, South Dakota, Vermont and West Virginia) had fewer than 5,000 unauthorized immigrants each in 2012. Unauthorized immigrants accounted for 3.5% of the 2012 U.S. population of nearly 316 million and 26% of the nation's 42.5 million foreign-born residents, according to the center's estimates. Both shares were larger in 2007, the peak year for the nation's unauthorized immigrant population, at 4.0% and 30%, respectively.

* * *

In addition to unauthorized immigrants, the nation's foreign-born population of 42.5 million people in 2012 consisted of 11.7 million legal permanent residents, 17.8 million naturalized citizens and 1.9 million legal residents with temporary status (including students, diplomats and "high-tech guest workers").

Origins of Unauthorized Immigrants

Mexicans are a majority of unauthorized immigrants (52% in 2012), but both their numbers and share have declined in recent years, according to Pew Research estimates. Although the U.S. population of unauthorized immigrants was stable from 2009 to 2012, the number of Mexicans in this population fell by about half a million people during those years. According to the Pew Research Center estimates, there were 5.9 million Mexican unauthorized immigrants in 2012, compared with 6.4 million in 2009 and 6.9 million in 2007. The decline likely resulted from both an increase in departures to Mexico and a decrease in arrivals from Mexico (Passel, Cohn and Gonzalez-Barrera, 2012).

After top-ranked Mexico, there is a large drop in the numbers of unauthorized immigrants from other specific countries. El Salvador, with 675,000 unauthorized immigrants in 2012, is the second-largest source. It is followed by Guatemala (525,000), India (450,000), Honduras (350,000), China (300,000) and the Philippines (200,000). Rounding out the top 10 in 2012 are Korea (180,000), the Dominican Republic (170,000) and Colombia (150,000).

As the Mexican numbers continued to drop between 2009 and 2012, unauthorized immigrant populations from South America and from a grouping of Europe and Canada held steady. Unauthorized immigrant populations from Asia, the Caribbean, Central America and the rest of the world grew slightly from 2009 to 2012.

Among the 44 states (and District of Columbia) for which data about national origin are available, Mexicans make up the majority of all unauthorized immigrants in 26 of them. The four states where Mexicans make up more than eight-in-ten unauthorized immigrants are all in the West—New Mexico (89%), Arizona (84%), Idaho (83%) and Wyoming (82%).

* * *

Unauthorized Immigrants in the Labor Force

The 8.1 million unauthorized immigrants who were working or looking for work in 2012 made up 5.1% of the labor force or about one-in-twenty U.S. workers. Both of those estimates are unchanged from 2009. The number in the labor force has remained between 8.1 million and 8.3

million since 2007. (The share of unauthorized immigrants in the workforce peaked in 2007, at 5.4%.

The share is markedly higher in some states, especially those with high shares of unauthorized immigrants in the population. Among adults ages 16 and older who are working or looking for work, unauthorized immigrants represent the highest share in Nevada (10.2% in 2012); Nevada also has the highest share of unauthorized immigrants in the overall population (7.6%). The share in the labor force also is relatively high in California (9.4%) and Texas (8.9%), which rank second and third in the unauthorized immigrant share of the total population.

Unauthorized immigrants are more likely than the overall U.S. population to be of working age and less likely to be young or older. That is one reason that the unauthorized immigrant share of the labor force is higher than its share of the population overall.

Unauthorized immigrants of working age have substantially different patterns of labor force participation than do people born in the U.S. Unauthorized immigrant men of working age are considerably more likely to be in the workforce than U.S.-born men (91% versus 79%). For women, the opposite is true; only 61% of unauthorized immigrant women are in the labor force, compared with 72% of U.S.-born women. For both genders, substantial portions of the U.S.-born population of working age are not in the labor force because they are attending school, retired or disabled, but that is true for only a small share of unauthorized immigrants. A major difference for women is that a higher share of unauthorized immigrant women say they are not working and have young children at home (22%) compared with other immigrants (13%) and U.S.-born women (7%). While there have been some modest changes in labor force participation rates over the past 20 years, the participation of unauthorized immigrant men and women, relative to the U.S.-born population and legal immigrants, has remained essentially unchanged since 2005.

Concentrations of Unauthorized Immigrants: Industries

Because unauthorized immigrants tend to have less education than people born in the U.S. or legal immigrants, they are more likely to hold low-skilled jobs and less likely to be in white-collar occupations; further, their status limits job opportunities. Consequently, unauthorized immigrants tend to be overrepresented in certain sectors of the economy. Of all unauthorized immigrant workers, 22% are in services (professional, business and other), 18% in the leisure and hospitality sector and 16% in construction (Table 1). These three industry sectors encompass 55% of unauthorized workers but only 31% of U.S.-born workers. Manufacturing (13%) and agriculture (5%) also have relatively large shares of the unauthorized immigrant workforce.

Looked at using another metric—the unauthorized-immigrant share of the total workforce—it becomes clear that they are particularly concentrated in some subsets of each major industry. In 2012, they represented 24% of workers in the landscaping industry, 23% of those in private household employment, 20% of those in apparel manufacturing, 20% in crop production, 19% in the dry cleaning and laundry industry and 19% of those in building maintenance. These figures are much larger than unauthorized immigrants' share of the overall workforce—5.1%. (Figure 4 below shows major industry concentrations. * * *)

* * *

Concentrations of Unauthorized Immigrants: Occupations

Industry classifications tend to contain occupations requiring a range of education levels, whereas occupation classifications tend to include jobs requiring similar skill levels or certifications. Because unauthorized immigrants tend to cluster in low-skilled jobs, they tend to be even more concentrated in specific occupation groups than in specific industries.

Among unauthorized immigrants in the labor force, 33% are service workers, 15% are construction workers and 14% are production and installation workers. Almost two-thirds (62%) of unauthorized immigrant workers have occupations in these three broad categories; by contrast, only half that share (31%) of U.S.-born workers have such occupations. (See Table 2. * * *)

Because they are so concentrated in certain major occupation groups, unauthorized immigrants are a high proportion of workers in some more detailed categories. For example, 26% of farmworkers are unauthorized immigrants, as are 17% of building, groundskeeping and maintenance workers, and 14% of construction workers. Unauthorized immigrants also are overrepresented as a share of food preparation workers and servers (11%), production workers (9%) and transportation and material moving workers (7%) compared with their overall presence in the labor force.

* * *

NOTES ON THE UNAUTHORIZED POPULATION

1. **Children of undocumented immigrants.** Another report from the Pew Research Center addressed births to undocumented parents:

> About 295,000 babies were born to unauthorized-immigrant parents in 2013, making up 8% of the 3.9 million U.S. births that year, according to a new, preliminary Pew Research Center estimate based on the latest available federal government data. This was a decline from a peak of 370,000 in 2007.

Births to unauthorized-immigrant parents rose sharply from 1980 to the mid-2000s, but dipped since then, echoing overall population trends for unauthorized immigrants. In 2007, an estimated 9% of all U.S. babies were born to unauthorized-immigrant parents, meaning that at least one parent was an unauthorized immigrant.

* * *

There were an estimated 11.3 million unauthorized immigrants living in the U.S. in March 2013, according to a preliminary Pew Research estimate. They make up 4% of the population, but their share of births is higher because the immigrants include a higher share of women in their childbearing years and have higher birthrates than the U.S. population overall.

* * *

Most children of unauthorized immigrants in the U.S. are born here, and therefore are citizens. In 2012, there were 4.5 million U.S.-born children younger than 18 living with unauthorized-immigrant parents. There also were 775,000 children younger than 18 who were unauthorized immigrants themselves and lived with unauthorized-immigrant parents. These totals do not count U.S.-born children of unauthorized immigrants who do not live with their parents.

The nation's unauthorized immigrants are more likely than in the past to be long-term residents of the U.S., and are increasingly likely to live with U.S.-born children. In 2012, there were 4 million unauthorized-immigrant adults who lived with their U.S.-born children, both minor and adult. They made up 38% of unauthorized immigrant adults. By comparison, in 2000, 2.1 million unauthorized-immigrant adults, or 30% of this group, lived with their U.S.-born children, minor and adult.

Jeffrey S. Passel & D'Vera Cohn, *Number of Babies Born in U.S. to Unauthorized Immigrants Declines* (Pew Research Center 2015). Another Pew Research Center report offered this observation on students with unauthorized parents:

Children with at least one unauthorized immigrant parent made up 6.9% of students enrolled in kindergarten through 12th grade in 2012. Most (5.5% of all students) are U.S.-born children who are U.S. citizens at birth. The rest (1.4%) are unauthorized immigrants themselves.

* * *

The share of students with unauthorized immigrant parents varies widely by state. The 2012 share was in double digits in four states—Nevada (17.7%), California (13.2%), Texas (13.1%) and

Arizona (11.0%). In seven states, the share in 2012 was less than 1%.

Jeffrey S. Passel, D'Vera Cohn & Molly Rohal, *Unauthorized Immigrant Totals Rise in 7 States, Fall in 14*, at 17 (Pew Res. Center 2014). *See also* Robert Warren, US-Born Children of Undocumented Residents: Numbers and Characteristics in 2013 (Center for Migration Studies 2015).

2. **Education, income, and health insurance.** A 2009 Pew report included these findings on the unauthorized:

- Adult unauthorized immigrants are disproportionately likely to be poorly educated. Among unauthorized immigrants ages 25–64, 47% have less than a high school education. By contrast, only 8% of U.S.-born residents ages 25–64 have not graduated from high school.

- An analysis of college attendance finds that among unauthorized immigrants ages 18 to 24 who have graduated from high school, half (49%) are in college or have attended college. The comparable figure for U.S.-born residents is 71%.

- The 2007 median household income of unauthorized immigrants was $36,000, well below the $50,000 median household income for U.S.-born residents. In contrast to other immigrants, undocumented immigrants do not attain markedly higher incomes the longer they live in the United States.

- A third of the children of unauthorized immigrants and a fifth of adult unauthorized immigrants lives in poverty. This is nearly double the poverty rate for children of U.S.-born parents (18%) or for U.S.-born adults (10%).

- More than half of adult unauthorized immigrants (59%) had no health insurance during all of 2007. Among their children, nearly half of those who are unauthorized immigrants (45%) were uninsured and 25% of those who were born in the U.S. were uninsured.

Jeffrey S. Passel & D'Vera Cohn, *A Portrait of Unauthorized Immigrants in the United States* iv–v (Pew Hispanic Center 2009).

3. **Fiscal impact.** Significant debate over the fiscal impact of unauthorized migration has existed for decades. Unauthorized migrants are not eligible for most means-tested benefit programs, including Temporary Assistance for Needy Families, food stamps (now known as SNAP, Supplemental Nutrition Assistance Program), Supplemental Security Income, non-emergency Medicaid, public housing, and legal services. *See, e.g.,* 7 U.S.C.A. § 2015(f) (SNAP); 42 U.S.C.A. § 1382c (SSI). Nor are they eligible for unemployment compensation, postsecondary financial aid, or job training. These bars were reaffirmed in the 1996 welfare legislation. Personal

Responsibility and Work Opportunity Reconciliation Act of 1996 (PRWORA), Pub. L. 104–193, 110 Stat. 2105, §§ 402(b), 431(b).

But unauthorized migrants are eligible for some public benefits, including emergency Medicaid, school meal programs, and immunization for and treatment of communicable diseases. PRWORA §§ 562, 742. Most importantly, the 1982 Supreme Court decision in *Plyler v. Doe*, 457 U.S. 202, 102 S.Ct. 2382, 72 L.Ed.2d 786 (1982), considered in detail in Chapter Ten, held that Texas could not deny undocumented children access to public elementary and secondary education, under the equal protection clause of the Fourteenth Amendment.

A 2007 study by the Congressional Budget Office on this subject provided the following summary of its findings:

> In preparing its analysis, the Congressional Budget Office (CBO) reviewed 29 reports published over the past 15 years that attempted to evaluate the impact of unauthorized immigrants on the budgets of state and local governments. * * * The estimates—whether from formal studies, analyses of data on particular topics, or less-formal inquiry—show considerable consensus regarding the overall impact of unauthorized immigrants on state and local budgets. However, the scope and analytical methods of the studies vary, and the reports do not provide detailed or consistent enough data to allow for a reliable assessment of the aggregate national effect of unauthorized immigrants on state and local budgets. * * * After reviewing the estimates, CBO drew the following conclusions:

> • State and local governments incur costs for providing services to unauthorized immigrants and have limited options for avoiding or minimizing those costs. * * * Rules governing many federal programs, as well as decisions handed down by various courts, limit the authority of state and local governments to avoid or constrain the costs of providing services to unauthorized immigrants. * * *

> • The amount that state and local governments spend on services for unauthorized immigrants represents a small percentage of the total amount spent by those governments to provide such services to residents in their jurisdictions. * * * Costs were concentrated in programs that make up a large percentage of total state spending—specifically, those associated with education, health care, and law enforcement. In most of the estimates that CBO examined, however, spending for unauthorized immigrants accounted for less than 5 percent of total state and local spending for those services.

> • The tax revenues that unauthorized immigrants generate for state and local governments do not offset the total cost

of services provided to those immigrants. Most of the estimates found that even though unauthorized immigrants pay taxes and other fees to state and local jurisdictions, the resulting revenues offset only a portion of the costs incurred by those jurisdictions for providing services related to education, health care, and law enforcement. Although it is difficult to obtain precise estimates of the net impact of the unauthorized population on state and local budgets * * * , that impact is most likely modest.

- Federal aid programs offer resources to state and local governments that provide services to unauthorized immigrants, but those funds do not fully cover the costs incurred by those governments.

Congressional Budget Office, The Impact of Unauthorized Immigrants on the Budgets of State and Local Governments 2–3 (Dec. 2007). For a survey of studies of the fiscal impact of unauthorized immigration, see William A. Kandel, Fiscal Impacts of the Foreign-Born Population 28–42 (Cong. Res. Serv. 2011).

3.   UNAUTHORIZED MIGRATION AS A HISTORICAL AND SOCIAL PROCESS

People enter the United States unlawfully for varied reasons. Some come to join family members, some to flee persecution in their homeland, some to go to school. Virtually all scholars agree, however, that economic factors—jobs—provide the most important incentive for illegal entry and residence. America offers jobs to unemployed or underemployed laborers from less developed nations at wages that are generally substantially above prevailing wages in the aliens' countries of origin (even if the wages the migrants receive here are below wages normally paid to U.S. citizens or legal immigrants).

But as noted in the readings in Chapter Three, Section C, simple economic disparity offers a very incomplete account of actual migration patterns. Several factors have played a major role. One consists of past private efforts at the promotion of work-based migration to the major receiving states, often augmented by explicit government policy (whether or not that role was officially acknowledged). Another factor is the eventual creation of social networks linking particular source communities and receiving communities. The following readings provide additional insight into these dynamics and the lingering effects of government policies.

KITTY CALAVITA, THE IMMIGRATION POLICY DEBATE: CRITICAL ANALYSIS AND FUTURE OPTIONS

Mexican Migration to the United States: Origins, Consequences, and
Policy Options 151, 155–59 (W. Cornelius & J. Bustamante, eds., 1989).

MEXICAN MIGRATION AS A BACKDOOR LABOR SOURCE

Mexican immigration to the United States gained momentum in the pre-World War I period, as policymakers and even some employers reassessed the costs versus the benefits of European immigration. The European immigrant was a reputed troublemaker who frequently became a permanent member of American society and was increasingly the backbone of labor strikes. In 1911, the Dillingham Commission, responding to these concerns, noted the special advantages of Mexican migration:

> Because of their strong attachment to their native land ... and the possibility of their residence here being discontinued, few become citizens of the United States. The Mexican migrants are providing a fairly adequate supply of labor.... While they are not easily assimilated, this is of no very great importance as long as most of them return to their native land. In the case of the Mexican, he is less desirable as a citizen than as a laborer.

The most significant restrictions of the early twentieth century exempted Mexicans from their orbit. A response to warnings from Southwestern growers that successful harvests depended on abundant Mexican labor excluded Mexicans from the literacy test requirement of 1917 for the duration of the war. As World War I came to a close, the labor secretary and immigration commissioner extended the exemptions. As a result of these policies and employers' recruitment efforts, legal immigration from Mexico soared from eleven thousand in 1915 to fifty-one thousand in 1920. Industries as far north as Chicago drew labor from this back door. By 1926, 35 percent of Chicago Inland Steel's labor force was Mexican.

The passage of the quotas in the 1920s again exempted Mexicans. The argument against restricting Mexican immigration was strong:

> The Mexican, they pointed out, was a vulnerable alien living just a short distance from his homeland.... He, unlike Puerto Ricans or Filipinos ... could easily be deported. No safer or more economical unskilled labor force was imaginable.[*]

The shift from European to Mexican migration as a source of labor did enhance flexibility, as evidenced by the repatriation of thousands of Mexican workers and their families during the depression of the 1930s.

---

[*] Mark Reisler, By the Sweat of their Brow: Mexican Immigrant Labour in the United States, 1900–1940, at 181 (1976).

As World War II refueled the U.S. economy, the United States again needed and used Mexican contract laborers imported through the Bracero Program, whose formal and informal policies contributed to the rise of the undocumented nature of Mexican migration that characterizes the contemporary period. The program attempted to institutionalize the primary virtue of this labor supply, its flexibility.

The Bracero Agreement of 1949 provided that "illegal workers, when they are located in the United States, shall be given preference under outstanding U.S. Employment Service Certification." Illegals, or "wetbacks," were "dried out" by the U.S. Border Patrol which escorted them to the Mexican border, had them step to the Mexican side, and brought them back as braceros. Employers often accompanied their undocumented workers back to the border and contracted them there as legal workers. In some cases, the border patrol "paroled" illegals directly to employers. In 1951 the President's Commission on Migratory Labor estimated that between 1947 and 1949 the United States legalized more than 142,000 undocumented Mexicans in this way, while recruiting only 74,600 new braceros from Mexico.

In addition to these more or less official policies of encouraging illegal migration, Immigration and Naturalization Service (INS) district chiefs enhanced, at their discretion, the supply of undocumented workers for seasonal employment. The chief inspector at Tucson, for example, reported to the President's Commission on Migratory Labor that he "received orders from the District Director at El Paso each harvest to stop deporting illegal Mexican labor." In other cases, Border Patrol officials told agents to stay away from designated ranches and farms in their district. The implicit message from Congress to the Border Patrol was consistent with this laissez-faire approach. Congress was "splendidly indifferent" to the rising number of illegals during the bracero period, reducing the budget of the Border Patrol just as undocumented migration increased.

By the time the United States terminated the Bracero Program in 1964, the symbiosis between Mexican migrants and employers in the Southwest was well entrenched, the product of over fifty years of formal and informal policy-making. Almost five million Mexican workers had been brought to the United States as braceros; more than five million illegal aliens were apprehended during the same period.

While policies associated with the Bracero Program were instrumental in enhancing the appeal of illegal migration from the migrants' point of view, a key congressional decision immunized employers from any risk involved in their employment. In 1952, the McCarran-Walter Act made it illegal to "harbor, transport, or conceal illegal entrants." An amendment to the provision, referred to as the Texas

Proviso after the Texas growers to whom it was a concession, excluded employment per se from the category of "harboring." Whether or not "knowing" employment of undocumented workers would constitute harboring remained ambiguous despite congressional discussion. Nonetheless, the amendment was interpreted by the INS as carte blanche to employ undocumented workers.

Of course, the U.S. attitude toward Mexican migrants has not been unequivocal. Mass expulsions and roundups of Mexican workers and their families during Operation Wetback in 1954 and 1955 were reminiscent of the depression policies of the 1930s. In part, these mass deportations reflected the militaristic approach of the new INS commissioner, Joseph Swing, a former U.S. Army general known within the INS bureaucracy as "The General," in apparent reference both to his former military career and to his leadership style. More generally, however, they represented the long-held view of Mexican labor as eminently flexible—welcomed during periods of high demand and deported when the demand had waned. In any case, such periodic deportations neither significantly interrupted the now-institutionalized patterns of migration nor reflected any fundamental change in the perception of Mexico as a backdoor source of labor.

———————

Given the historical pattern, the following excerpt provides a model for understanding how, as one leading scholar put it, "Mexican migration to the United States represents a deeply institutionalized, multigenerational social process." Wayne A. Cornelius, Mexican Migration to the United States: The Limits of Government Intervention 2–4 (Working Papers in U.S.-Mexican Studies, 5; 1981). For an insightful and influential history of U.S. treatment of undocumented migrants in the first half of the 20th century, see Mae M. Ngai, Impossible Subjects: Illegal Aliens and the Making of Modern America, ch. 2 (2004).

DOUGLAS S. MASSEY, LUIN GOLDRING & JORGE DURAND, CONTINUITIES IN TRANSNATIONAL MIGRATION: AN ANALYSIS OF NINETEEN MEXICAN COMMUNITIES

99 American Journal of Sociology 1492, 1496–1502 (1994).*

Transnational labor migration may originate for a variety of complementary reasons. Migrants may observe wage differentials between origin and destination areas and respond to expected positive returns to foreign labor. Households may seek to diversify risks to their

———————

economic well-being by sending family members to work in different regional labor markets, one of which is foreign. Migrants may be recruited by foreign employers seeking to import workers for specific tasks. People may be impelled to move because structural transformations in the local economy eliminate traditional sources of sustenance or because political upheavals cause people to fear for their physical safety.

No matter how international migration begins, the first migrants from a community are likely to experience it as a very costly and risky enterprise, both in monetary and psychological terms. They have little or no knowledge of conditions in the host country and are ignorant of its culture, language, and ways of life. In most cases, they incur the expenses of the trip and absorb the opportunity costs of income forgone while moving and looking for work. They arrive having to pay off these overhead expenses and are thus relatively dependent on their first employer. Given their lack of knowledge about prevailing wage rates, work habits, legal conventions, and social expectations, they are vulnerable to exploitation and mistreatment, especially if they are undocumented and do not speak the language of the host country.

Given these costs and risks, the first transnational labor migrants usually come not from the bottom of the socioeconomic hierarchy but from the lower middle ranges. Such people have enough resources to absorb the costs and risks of the trip but are not so affluent that foreign labor is unattractive. * * *

[T]he earliest migrants leave their families and friends behind and strike out for solitary work in an alien land. Most transnational migrants begin as target earners, seeking to earn as much money as possible as quickly as possible in order to recoup their initial investment, attain a predetermined income goal, and return home to family and friends. They have little interest in permanent settlement abroad.

Once one or more people have come and gone in this fashion, however, the situation in the sending community does not return to the status quo ante. Each act of migration generates a set of irreversible changes in individual motivations, social structures, and cultural values that alter the context within which future migration decisions are made. These changes accumulate across time to create conditions that make additional migration more likely. * * *

At the individual level, participation in a high-wage economy induces changes in tastes and motivations that turn people away from target earning and toward persistent migration. Satisfaction of the wants that originally led to migration creates new wants. Access to high wages and the goods they buy creates new standards of material well-being, and first-hand experiences in an affluent society raise expectations and create new ambitions for upward mobility. As migrants earn high wages and alter their consumption patterns, they adopt new lifestyles and local economic pursuits become less attractive.

The first-hand experience gained from migration makes the satisfaction of these new wants increasingly feasible. Once someone has migrated and returned, that person has direct knowledge of employment opportunities, labor-market conditions, and ways of life in the destination country; they use these understandings to migrate again with fewer risks and costs than before. Once it has been experienced, therefore, migration becomes a familiar and reliable socioeconomic resource that can be employed again and again as new needs arise and motivations change.

Empirical research in Mexico shows conclusively that once a man has migrated to the United States, the odds are extremely high that he will migrate again. Indeed, the probability of taking an additional trip rises monotonically as the number of trips increases. The more a man migrates, the more he is likely to continue migrating, a pattern that has proved to be remarkably persistent in the face of restrictive immigration policies.

Given their status as target earners, during the first few trips and in the early history of migration from a community, migrants tend to live under rather spartan conditions, sleeping in barracks or sharing apartments with other men and sleeping in shifts to save money. They work long hours and have little social life. In some cases they work two eight-hour shifts in the same day. Most of their earnings are repatriated in the form of savings or remittances. Migrants see themselves as members of their home communities and not as participants in the host society.

As migrants spend increasing time abroad, however, this form of social life becomes more and more problematic. As stays abroad lengthen and the number of trips rises, pressure from family members wanting to migrate grows. The first relatives to accompany a married migrant are typically unmarried sons of working age, since they have the greatest earnings potential after the father and their migration is consistent with prevailing gender roles. Over time, however, unmarried working-age daughters, wives, and younger children are likely to accompany him as well. Other relatives, such as nephews, nieces, and cousins, eventually join experienced migrants. As increasing numbers of young men acquire migrant experience, they also begin to travel north in groups based on friendship as well as kinship. As a result, the demographic base of migration steadily widens and the mean age of migration drops.

The act of migration not only induces changes within individual migrants that make further movement more likely, it also initiates changes in social structures that spread migration through the community. Each migrant is inevitably linked to a set of nonmigrants through a variety of social ties that carry reciprocal obligations for assistance based on shared understandings of kinship, friendship, and common community origin. Given the expectations and practices associated with kinship and friendship, each act of migration creates a set of people with social ties to the receiving country. Nonmigrants draw upon these ties to gain access to employment and assistance abroad, substantially reducing the costs and risks of movement compared to earlier migrants.

Every new migrant thus reduces the costs and risks and increases the attractiveness and feasibility of migration for a set of friends and relatives. With these lowered costs and risks, additional people are induced to migrate for the first time, which further expands the set of people with ties abroad. This additional migration reduces costs and risks for a new set of people, causing some of them to migrate, and so on. Once the number of network connections reaches a critical threshold, migration becomes self-perpetuating because each act of movement creates the social structure necessary to sustain it. Empirical studies in Mexico clearly show that having network connections greatly increases the likelihood of international movement.

As migrants make successive trips, they accumulate foreign experience and knowledge that render ties to them increasingly valuable. As information about the destination country and its socioeconomic resources accumulates in the population, the costs of migration steadily drop to make the cost-benefit calculation positive for an increasingly large set of people, while the risks of movement steadily fall to render migration a feasible risk-diversification strategy for a growing number of households. Over time, therefore, migration becomes progressively less selective and more representative of the community as a whole.

Migration also changes the cultural context within which decisions are made, and international movement becomes increasingly attractive for reasons that are not purely economic. Migrants evince a widely-admired lifestyle that others are drawn to emulate. Although some of its attractiveness is material—based on the ability to consume goods and purchase property—the lifestyle also acquires a strong normative component. In communities where foreign wage labor has become fully integrated into local values and expectations, people contemplating entry into the labor force literally do not consider other options: they expect to migrate frequently in the course of their lives and assume they can go whenever they wish.

As migration assumes a greater role in the community, it becomes increasingly important as a rite of passage for young men, providing an accepted means of demonstrating their worthiness, ambition, and manhood to others. Moreover, as women become more integrated within postindustrial society, they begin to push for more egalitarian gender roles and encourage activities that lead to longer stays abroad, such as investing in household goods and buying property in the destination country.

Over time and with extensive movement back and forth, communities of origin and destination increasingly come to comprise transnational circuits—social and geographic spaces that arise through the constant circulation of people, money, goods, and information. As these circuits develop, practices and values that once demarcated distinct societies begin to have a transformative influence on each other. Over time, migrant communities become culturally "transnationalized," incorporating ideologies, practices, expectations, and political claims from both societies to create a "culture of migration" that is distinct from the culture of both the sending and receiving nation.

As migration is increasingly taken for granted, the demographic composition and socioeconomic role of the place of origin undergo a dramatic transformation. In many places, women, children, and older people dominate a reduced population except during the few weeks or months when migrants return for holidays and celebrations. In economically marginal agricultural areas, farming and other traditional activities lose importance. As the place of origin becomes a site of rest and recreation, in sharp contrast to the routine of work abroad, its social meaning undergoes changes. Migrants spend money collectively on infrastructure and other community projects aimed at transforming the landscape into a place of leisure, a place where migrants and their families can display their status and exercise political claims and power.

The first migrants from a community typically go to a specific niche in the destination country's political economy, yielding little diversity with respect to destination, occupation, or strategies of movement. Early migrants follow the path of the first migrant because that is where the costs and risks of migration are lowest and the chances of success greatest. Once they have identified a promising migrant worker, moreover, labor recruiters and contractors tend to use them as vehicles to recruit additional workers from their circle of friends and relatives. As experience in the host country accumulates, however, and as more people are drawn into the process, some migrants inevitably seek out better opportunities in new places and occupations. In this way the diversity of foreign destinations, jobs, and strategies increases.

As the migration process proceeds, however, typically someone from the sending community achieves a position of responsibility that enables him or her to channel employment, housing, and other resources to fellow townspeople. The position may be a crew boss in a railroad, a foreman in a factory, a union representative in a company, a majordomo in a restaurant, a labor contractor for a grower, or perhaps even a business owner. Although it is impossible to predict where or how it will occur, sooner or later someone attains such a position and begins to recruit fellow townspeople for work. * * *

As migrants make repeated trips and accumulate more time abroad, as wives and children join the migrant workforce, as more people become involved in the migration process, and as stronger links are formed with specific employers in particular locations, a growing number of migrants and families settle in the host society. They acquire informal ties to its inhabitants and establish formal links with institutions such as banks, government, and schools. They learn the host-country language and become permanent legal residents. Empirical studies show that the probability of settlement rises steadily as migrant experience increases.

As families settle around specific places of employment, branch communities of long-term and permanent out-migrants begin to form. These communities anchor the networks and further reduce the costs and risks of movement by providing a secure and familiar environment within which new migrants can arrive, find housing and employment, and learn the ropes in the receiving country. Increasingly, migration is channeled to these communities and the diversity of destinations associated with a place of origin is further reduced.

As migrants become part of established communities in the host country, they adapt themselves to the local setting. Whether or not they have legal documents, they send their children to school, learn a minimum of the host country's language, and use financial institutions and social services. Over time the local landscape of the receiving community is transformed. Whether or not they are immigrant entrepreneurs, the migrants contribute to the creation and growth of a market for specialized foods, entertainment, and cultural products. The formation of ethnic neighborhoods represents a process of socioeconomic adaptation and transformation that permits many "foreign" practices to be maintained in the new setting.

How have the patterns examined by Massey, Goldring, and Durand persisted in spite of enforcement of federal immigration laws against violators? The next excerpt gives one answer to this question.

HIROSHI MOTOMURA, IMMIGRATION OUTSIDE THE LAW[*]
Pp. 43–55 (2014).

The coalitions that won repeal of the national origins system also secured other important civil rights legislation, most prominently the Civil Rights Act of 1964 and the Voting Rights Act of 1965. For Latin America, however, the repeal of the national origins system came at significant cost, by introducing numerical limits. Previously, the national origins system had set a numerical limit for overall immigration from the Eastern Hemisphere. The number of immigrants from the Western Hemisphere was not capped, even if individuals could be barred if they fell within certain exclusion grounds, such as those for immigrants without sufficient financial means.

The 1965 [immigration] amendments changed this. Some legislators pressed for a cap on immigration from Latin America, expressing concerns that it would otherwise increase dramatically. Reform-minded legislators could not fend off the argument that ending the national origins system, with its discriminatory caps, meant that all countries and regions should be treated equally. Congress decided to limit Western Hemisphere immigration to 120,000 per year starting in 1968. Similar pressures led in 1976 to a new annual limit of 20,000 per year on immigration from any single country. These per-country limits exempted spouses and unmarried minor children of all US citizens and the parents of adult US citizens, but they applied to all other categories, including other relatives and all immigrants in employment categories. Further amendments folded the Western Hemisphere cap into an annual worldwide cap of 270,000 immigrants. Long lines soon formed for populous countries where the desire to go to the United States was strong due to geographical, historical, or economic ties.

The post-1965 per-country and overall caps on the number of immigrants only partly explain the growth of the unauthorized population to over 11 million today. Another crucial contributing factor has been that the qualifying categories for admission as a lawful immigrant have been defined narrowly and limited in number. The admissions system forces many qualifying immigrants to wait years or even decades. The system completely shuts out many other immigrants who have neither qualifying family ties nor a high level of formal education. * * *

* * *

The end of the Bracero program in 1964 blocked the broadest lawful official employer access to cheap, flexible, temporary labor from Latin

---

America. Soon afterward, three new features of the admission scheme—the new Western Hemisphere cap, per-country limits, and restrictive employment-based immigration categories—combined to make it very hard for workers from Mexico to come as permanent residents.

* * *

A combination of historical migration patterns, strong transnational networks, and robust demand for foreign workers has sustained patterns of immigration to the United States, much of it unauthorized, and all in spite of restrictions on lawful immigration. With the unauthorized population far exceeding federal enforcement capacity, enforcement must also be selective, both in the interior and at the border.

* * *

The best way to analyze why immigration law operates as it does is to consider what it would take to transform it. * * *

Any fundamental change of this sort cannot be durable unless two things both happen, and if that is improbable, then it is fair to consider the current state of affairs to be a system that operates by design. First, the system for admitting new immigrants and temporary workers lawfully needs to expand dramatically. Or, enforcement could intensify to a level that would seriously reduce unauthorized migration. Several factors suggest strongly that the second option is not politically sustainable.

The wages, working conditions, and even the jobs of citizens and lawful permanent residents throughout the US economy can depend on the availability of unauthorized coworkers to fill out an employer's workforce. Domestic economic growth in many sectors depends on the availability of workers to fill informal, temporary, low-wage jobs. This is not just a matter of employer preferences. The demands originate throughout the population of the United States. Consumers want lower prices, which depend on minimizing labor costs, even if they seldom stop to consider what keeps prices low. The result is broad, if controversial, acquiescence in unauthorized migration. Though they are in the United States without lawful permission, they are tolerated as workers at first, though over time they make lives, families, and communities. As the Swiss writer Max Frisch wrote about the northern European experience: "we asked for workers, but people came."

Acquiescence in a flexible unauthorized workforce also reflects deeper rationales. The pragmatic reality is that good workers are essential to the economy but are hard to identify in advance. The US immigration system seems to reflect the temptation—messy and cruel—to let them come and work unlawfully, and then later to grant lawful status to some who can show strong histories of work, integration, and other contributions to US society. In the meantime, they serve what amounts to a probationary period when they are paid less, are laid off more easily, work with fewer protections than US citizens or permanent residents, and suffer other indignities. * * *

Unauthorized migration also gives the US government a flexible option for addressing international economic development issues. Unauthorized workers send substantial amounts of money to their home countries. These remittances are an essential part of those economies, especially in developing countries with substantial numbers of expatriates in the United States. Preserving these streams is an essential part of US international economic policy. If immigration enforcement constricts remittances, the US government may need to foster development more directly in migrants' home countries, or to safeguard political stability there by other means. Such initiatives might be inflexible, unfeasible, or less politically attractive than allowing remittances from unauthorized workers to continue.

Similarly, unauthorized migration functions as a safety valve for political and economic pressures in sending countries, including the consequences of US government actions that generate migration to the United States. For example, the North American Free Trade Agreement (NAFTA) transformed the Mexican economy in ways that have disrupted the livelihoods of many small-scale farmers. Prices for some crops have tumbled to levels that make farming unsustainable. Feeling that they have no choice, many of these farmers become migrants. Some go elsewhere in Mexico, while others come to the United States, many of them unlawfully. If immigration enforcement were to become much stricter and cut off the option to leave Mexico for the United States, NAFTA's political consequences for the Mexican government, and in turn for the US government, would be much more serious and hard to contain.

NOTES AND QUESTIONS ON UNAUTHORIZED MIGRATION AS A HISTORICAL AND SOCIAL PROCESS

1.   Economist Gordon Hanson writes of "the underlying economic reality that despite its faults, illegal immigration has been hugely beneficial to many US employers, often providing benefits that the current legal immigration system does not." He explains:

> Not only do unauthorized immigrants provide an important source of low-skilled labor, they also respond to market conditions in ways that legal immigration presently cannot, making them particularly appealing to US employers. Illegal inflows broadly track economic performance, rising during periods of expansion and stalling during downturns (including the present one). By contrast, legal flows for low-skilled workers are both very small and relatively unresponsive to economic conditions.

Despite all this, illegal immigration's overall impact on the US economy is small. Low-skilled native workers who compete with unauthorized immigrants are the clearest losers. US employers, on the other hand, gain from lower labor costs and the ability to use their land, capital, and technology more productively. * * * [T]he small net gain that remains after subtracting US workers' losses from US employers' gains is tiny. And if we account for the small fiscal burden that unauthorized immigrants impose, the overall economic benefit is close enough to zero to be essentially a wash.

* * * Because the net impact of illegal immigration on the US economy does not appear to be very large, one would be hard pressed to justify a substantial increase in spending on border and interior enforcement, at least in terms of its aggregate economic return.

Gordon H. Hanson, The Economics and Policy of Illegal Immigration in the United States 1–2 (Migration Policy Inst. 2009). For a contrasting view that enforcement is both worthwhile and politically feasible, especially if accompanied and reinforced by a broad legalization program, see David A. Martin, *Resolute Enforcement is Not Just for Restrictionists: Building a Stable and Efficient Immigration Enforcement System,* 30 J.L. & Pol. 411 (2015).

2.   Is it a persuasive advantage of unauthorized immigration that it effectively functions as an ex post screening mechanism—supplying low-skilled workers, removing those who commit criminal offenses after entry, and eventually granting lawful status to unauthorized migrants who prove to be productive workers? *See* Adam B. Cox & Eric Posner, *The Second-Order Structure of Immigration Law, 59 Stan. L. Rev. 809 (2007).*

3.   How would you evaluate the following concerns that some have voiced about unauthorized migration?:

- Undocumented migrants work for lower wages and tolerate worse working conditions than native workers (or at least find themselves unable to complain effectively owing to their status), thereby undermining labor standards in the United States, particularly in times of high unemployment.

- Businesses may win from illegal migration, but significant segments of the labor force lose. It is not a coincidence that average worker wages have stagnated over the last decade, a period of massive illegal migration, while the business executives in top brackets have claimed a much larger share of overall income.

- The presence of large numbers of undocumented migrants creates disrespect for the law and in effect penalizes noncitizens who wait many years for lawful entrance.

- Undocumented migrants cost states and localities money due to their use of hospitals and their children's enrollment in public schools. Higher overall tax revenues benefit mainly the federal government.

- Because they live in the shadow of the law, undocumented migrants are less likely to assimilate. They are also less likely to report crimes or cooperate with criminal investigations.

If you find these concerns persuasive, what follows? Tougher border enforcement? Better interior enforcement? Legalization for unauthorized migrants in the United States? An increase in legal immigration? All of the above? We return to some of these questions in Chapter Ten.

CHAPTER SIX

ADMISSION PROCEDURES

■ ■ ■

The efforts of Congress, agencies, and courts to implement the complex substantive provisions outlined in Chapter Five have resulted in an elaborate set of admission procedures and a distinctive due process jurisprudence. We begin with a word about terminology. Immigration legislation distinguishes between immigrants, individuals who intend to remain in the United States permanently, and nonimmigrants, individuals who travel to the United States for a temporary period. In general, all noncitizens, whether immigrants or nonimmigrants, must present valid passports and visas in order to enter the United States. The passport is issued by the traveler's home country and attests to citizenship and identity. In contrast, the visa is issued by the United States and is evidence that the individual has permission to enter. Under certain international agreements, the United States and other countries waive the visa requirement for citizens of certain nations.

In discussing admission to the United States, we generally use the term noncitizen, but our discussion of admission procedures will sometimes include references to an "arriving alien." Under the regulations an arriving alien is "an applicant for admission coming or attempting to come into the United States at a port-of-entry." 8 C.F.R. § 1.2. Would-be immigrants, as well as nonimmigrants, who present themselves at a U.S. port of entry are deemed arriving aliens. In contrast, noncitizens who entered the United States surreptitiously are not viewed as arriving aliens. And immigrants already admitted as lawful permanent residents who are returning to the United States from a subsequent short trip abroad are generally not regarded as arriving aliens. INA § 101(a)(13)(C).

We begin this chapter on admission procedures with a snapshot of the visa processing that occurs at U.S. consulates overseas. U.S. State Department officials abroad review hundreds of thousands of requests annually from non-U.S. citizens who wish to visit the United States temporarily as nonimmigrants or permanently as immigrants. Though the basic patterns of consular processing are standardized, each consulate has its own unique procedures and folkways. This excerpt describes the U.S. Consulate in Mumbai India.

A. ADMISSION PROCEDURES UNDER THE STATUTE AND REGULATIONS

POORVI CHOTHANI, CERTAIN U.S. IMMIGRANT AND NONIMMIGRANT VISA PROCESSES AND OTHER SERVICES AVAILABLE AT THE U.S. CONSULATE GENERAL IN MUMBAI

83 Interp. Rel. 1597 (2006).

INTRODUCTION

In the last fiscal year, U.S. Consulates in India issued more than 350,000 nonimmigrant visas. About one-third of a total of 122,981 intra-company transfer visas (L visas) issued by the U.S. were issued in India for the same fiscal year. Of the total student visas issued this year, 18,600 were issued to Indian students, and there are about 81,000 Indian students presently studying in the U.S.

The U.S. Embassy in India, which has a visa section, is located in New Delhi. There are three additional consular posts: Mumbai (Bombay), Kolkata (Calcutta) and Chennai (Madras). The U.S. Department of State (DOS) recently announced that it would open a new post at Hyderabad, which is an important center of several Information Technology (IT) and IT Enabled Services (ITES) companies.

* * * The Mumbai Post is one of the busiest consulates and is reported to receive a large number of fraudulent cases and also sees a high incidence of forged documents. Forged documents are often presented by NIV applicants[, thus] reducing the value of documentary proof of assets.

* * *

Due to space constraints and security reasons, only the visa applicant is allowed at any interview; attorneys, relatives or other "interested parties" are not allowed into the Mumbai Post. Since 9/11, the security measures in and around the Mumbai Post have increased. In exceptional cases, a relative who is a U.S. citizen may be permitted to accompany an IV applicant.

Most applicants prefer to conduct their visa interview in English. However, the Mumbai Post does provide interpreters for regional languages including Hindi, Gujarati and Marathi.

NONIMMIGRANT VISA PROCESSING

Persons applying for nonimmigrant visas at the Mumbai Post include visitors, students, participants in exchange programs, religious workers, temporary workers, persons with extraordinary abilities, performing artists, professional journalists, and representatives of foreign governments. Applicants are required to apply at the consular office responsible for the consular district in which they live. * * *

Subsequent to the U.S. Visitor and Immigrant Status Indicator Technology (US-VISIT) program that requires applicants to provide biometric information, all posts in India have discontinued the "drop box" facility for submitting U.S. visa applications. All posts in India collect fingerprint impressions and photographs from all visa applicants, except those traveling on official government business or those who are under age 14 or over age 79.

At the time of the visa interview, applicants are asked to electronically scan the index (second) finger of each hand. Applicants who are required to be fingerprinted, who have a cut or blister or other temporary skin injury on their index fingers may not be issued a visa until their finger heals and they can be fingerprinted. The scanned fingerprint data collected at the time of the visa application will be compared with fingerprint scans at the U.S. port of entry to prevent the use of U.S. visas by imposters and by those wanted for more serious offenses.

Persons already in possession of valid U.S. visas acquired before the implementation of US-VISIT may travel to the U.S. on their current visas and are not required to reapply for new visas until their current ones expire. They will be fingerprinted at the border or port of arrival.

BOOKING AN APPOINTMENT FOR THE VISA INTERVIEW

All nonimmigrant visa applicants are required to schedule an appointment with the Visa Facilitation Services (VFS), which is an organization retained by the U.S. Consulate as the off-site interview scheduler. There are significant delays in obtaining visa interview appointments. However, all consular posts in India are working towards reducing appointment wait times.

Applicants can schedule appointments online on the VFS website or by visiting the VFS Center closest to the applicant. * * *

It is advisable to apply very early for an appointment for the visa interview. The U.S. Consulate at Mumbai's website provides typical waiting periods for NIV visa appointments (as of June 28, 2006): [visitors: 157 days; students and exchange visitors: 18 days; others: 21 days].

* * *

* * * Prior to booking an appointment online or in person at any VFS Application Center, it is necessary to pay the fees and obtain a visa fee receipt [at a designated bank]. The fee receipt is issued with a unique barcode number, which is required when booking an online interview.

The bank requires each applicant to present a photocopy of the first page of the passport when paying the fees.

* * * After booking an appointment the applicant should submit copies of the passport, one photograph, the appointment letter (generated online), original fee receipt (which contains two barcode stickers) obtained from the HDFC Bank, duly completed visa application forms and a signed copy of the checklist that is generated online, to the VFS Center. The photograph has to conform to the requirements stipulated by the U.S. government. It is important that these documents be submitted five working days before the appointment date. The applicant should then report to the Mumbai Post as per the details in the appointment letter. The applicant should carry copies of the documents presented to the VFS Center and all supporting documents to help him or her prove ability to finance the visit to the U.S., nonimmigrant intent and purpose of visit. Students should also submit the SEVIS fee receipt with the documents. * * * Applicants should be forthcoming about their purpose and plans in visiting the U.S.; applicants should prepare for the interview by being able to clearly and concisely describe their intentions.

At the time of granting an appointment for visa interview the VFS Center checks the documents, retains the visa application forms and returns the passport along with a photocopy of the applicant's passport page with the VFS' stamp.

* * *

All consular posts in India, including the Mumbai Post[,] have set aside some appointment slots for emergency applications involving humanitarian or medical emergencies; students with valid Form I–20s; returning H or L visa applicants; and certain unforeseen business related needs. Weddings, graduation ceremonies and other foreseeable events are not considered emergencies. * * *

VISA INTERVIEW

Visa applicants should be at the U.S. Consulate 15 minutes before the scheduled appointment. The interviewing officer retains the passport for stamping after he or she has determined that a visa will be issued. The passport is then couriered to the applicant and usually reaches the applicant within the next two working days.

Some applications, however, may require additional processing that could delay visa issuance for an extended period of time. The applicant will be notified if there is any delay in his or her case and if the applicant requires any security or additional checks or tests. * * * The Mumbai Post usually conducts additional checks within 30 days of the interview. However, some applicants face longer delays.

* * *

FAMILY BASED IMMIGRANT VISA PROCESSING

The Mumbai Post ranks among the busiest posts for immigrant visa [IV] issuance including family-based and employment-based visas. Persons born in India are ineligible to participate in the Diversity Visa Program.

* * *

Family-based cases require that a petition be filed with and approved by USCIS before any U.S. Consulate can take action. Petitions approved by USCIS are generally forwarded to the National Visa Center (NVC) in Portsmouth, New Hampshire for processing and are then sent to the U.S. Embassy or Consulate where the applicant lives. Most of the immigrant visa petitions for Indian nationals are subject to numerical limitations and are assigned a priority date. Cases with priority dates are kept at the National Visa Center until the priority date is nearly current and only then are sent to the Embassy or Consulate.

* * *

IV Visa Appointment

After an Embassy or Consulate has received an approved petition from the National Visa Center or the U.S. Embassy in New Delhi, an appointment is scheduled and the applicant is notified. The applicant is requested to fill out form DS 230 Part II and submit it with other documents, before the interview date, to a VFS Center * * * .

* * *

Fees must be paid for each intending immigrant regardless of age and are not refundable. Fees should be sent to the consular office only if they have not been paid to the National Visa Center or if the petition was approved by the U.S. Embassy at New Delhi. It is necessary to carry proof of payment of fees to the interview. It is necessary to pay the VFS courier fees when submitting the documents at a VFS Center.

* * *

Every IV applicant, regardless of age, must undergo a medical examination before he or she goes for the visa interview. The Mumbai Post has designated certain doctors and institutes to conduct the examination. Costs for such examinations must be borne by the applicant in addition to the visa fees.

* * *

Police Clearance

All IV visa applicants, over the age of 16 years, are required to produce police clearance certificates from the passport office and from the local police station where the applicant resides. Police certificates must cover the entire period of the applicant's residence in any area. The term "police certificate" means a certification by appropriate police authorities stating what their records show concerning each applicant, including all arrests, the reasons for the arrests, and the disposition of each case of which there is a record. Police certificates are not required for periods spent in the U.S. Police certificates from certain countries are considered unobtainable. All police certificates are considered to be valid for one year from the date of issuance and must be valid on the day the immigrant visa is issued.

* * * It sometimes takes a long time to process [police certificates], and the procedure should be initiated well in advance.

* * *

IV applicant interviews are sometimes scheduled as early as 7:30 a.m. Attorneys can help the visa applicant prepare for the interview by explaining the nature of information required from the applicants. The posts in India do not permit attorneys to accompany the applicants. However, an attorney may represent the client via e-mail or letters. It is sometimes possible to make e-mail inquiries with members in the office. In our experience we have found that the Mumbai Post responds promptly to e-mails.

Fraud

Officers at the Mumbai Post have indicated that they very often have to determine whether the visa applications are based on genuine relationships or not. They have also found on many occasions that documents presented as proof of a relationship may be forged or may not reflect the true nature of the relationship. On occasion, the Mumbai Post sends its officers to conduct field visits where they personally interview the applicant's family members and/or neighbors to determine the genuineness of the relationship claimed.

NOTE ON VISA PROCESSING

Visa processing at all U.S. Consulates overseas has much in common, but different issues may be highlighted in certain locations (e.g., is visa fraud seen as a major problem in that location?), shaping each office's approaches. An effective immigration attorney will want to identify the unique approaches of the consulate where her client's visa request will be processed. For a variety of portraits of the day-to-day workings of consular processing, see 83 Interp. Rel. 1553 (2006) (Madrid); 82 Interp. Rel. 105 (2005) (Taiwan); 77 Interp. Rel. 1153 (2000) (Tokyo & Osaka-Kobe); 75 Interp. Rel. 1469 (1998)

(Tel Aviv); 75 Interp. Rel. 1009 (1998) (Ciudad Juarez); 75 Interp. Rel. 37 (1998) (London).

1. IMMIGRANT ADMISSIONS

Today, the process of securing status as a lawful permanent resident in the United States is elaborate and time-consuming. First, a visa petition is generally required. After approval of the petition, there are two different paths toward permanent residence: (1) obtaining an immigrant visa at a U.S. consulate and then traveling to the United States; or (2) becoming a permanent resident through adjustment of status while remaining in the United States. (Concurrent requests for consular processing and adjustment of status are treated as withdrawal of the adjustment application.) We will focus first on immigrant visa processing at a consulate outside the United States.

a. The Visa Petition

Obtaining an immigrant visa typically involves two steps: (1) filing a visa petition with the Department of Homeland Security in the United States, and (2) completing the visa process at a U.S. consulate abroad. As you recall from Chapter Five, generally a family member or an employer in the United States begins the process by filing a visa petition on behalf of the noncitizen beneficiary. The petition, Form I–130 for family reunification and Form I–140 for employment, serves to verify the underlying relationship and to demonstrate that the beneficiary satisfies all the requirements of the appropriate immigrant category. (Remember that many of the employment-based visas require the employer to secure labor certification from the Department of Labor before filing the I–140.) Some noncitizens, such as most special immigrants (fourth preference), investors (fifth), and individuals of extraordinary ability (first), do not need an employer and can petition directly on their own. *See* INA § 204(a)(1). VAWA petitioners, women or children who have been battered or subjected to abuse, can self-petition in some circumstances. INA § 101(a)(51).

Petitioners usually file visa petitions by mail with the U.S. Citizenship and Immigration Services (USCIS), accompanied by the appropriate fee. Once a visa petition is approved, USCIS forwards the endorsed visa petition to the State Department's National Visa Center (NVC) in Portsmouth, New Hampshire (unless the petitioner has indicated that the beneficiary will adjust status within the United States). The NVC creates a case file, provides instructions to petitioners and beneficiaries, and receives fees and many of the required documents. When the NVC has checked for completeness of all the information submitted, and completed the administrative processing, it determines whether the visa priority date is current. If a visa is not immediately available, the officer notifies the noncitizen that the petition has been received and will be held until one is.

b. Overseas Processing

When the priority date is current and the visa file is complete, the NVC sends the visa file to the consulate where the beneficiary will complete the application process in person. Noncitizens (other than those using the adjustment process, discussed below) are ordinarily expected to complete the visa process at a U.S. consulate in their home countries. In limited circumstances, they may persuade a consulate elsewhere to process the case and issue the visa, especially if they can demonstrate that returning to their homeland would be a hardship due to factors such as physical infirmity, advanced age, the presence of war or widespread civil disturbance, or the unavailability of U.S. visa services there. Such cases are sometimes known as "orphan visa" or "homeless visa" cases.

The NVC sends the applicant the "Appointment Package for Immigrant Visa Applicants," containing the date of the visa appointment, the visa application form, instructions regarding the required medical examination by an approved physician, and instructions for fee payments. Usually the consulate directly schedules the medical appointment shortly before the interview.

Prior USCIS approval of the visa petition does not mean that the applicant has been found admissible; that issue, based on application of the § 212(a) inadmissibility grounds discussed in Chapter Seven, is decided by the consul—or by the examiner considering an adjustment application. If the consular officer finds the applicant admissible, she issues an immigrant visa, valid for six months. *See* INA § 221(c). Unlike a nonimmigrant visa, an immigrant visa is not affixed to the applicant's passport. It consists instead of a set of documents to be presented in a special envelope to the admitting immigration officer at the port of entry.

c. At the Port of Entry

When the intending immigrant arrives in the United States, the responsibility switches from the State Department back to the Department of Homeland Security. The Customs and Border Protection (CBP) officer at the port of entry inspects the set of visa documents prepared at the consulate and may question the visa holder. If that officer finds no disqualifications, he will keep the immigrant visa, make a notation of admission as a lawful permanent resident in the passport, and forward the necessary papers for issuance of the Permanent Resident Card, Form I–551.

The I–551 is the celebrated "green card." I–551 cards issued today are valid for ten years and contain counterfeit-resistant optical patterns.

The system also allows government computers to store and transmit images of the photo, fingerprint, and signature on the card, to thwart impostors claiming to have lost an earlier card. The green card was introduced initially to serve as evidence of compliance with the INA's fingerprinting and registration requirements, *see* INA § 264(d), and for many years was formally known as the "Alien Registration Receipt Card." *§ 246(d)*

If a permanent resident will be gone from the United States no longer than 12 months, the green card can supply the documentation needed at re-entry. But a returning permanent resident may sometimes be regarded as "seeking admission" to the United States, making all the inadmissibility grounds of § 212(a) apply afresh, as Chapter Seven will explain. *See* INA § 101(a)(13)(C). Possession of a green card thus will not assure readmission; it merely dispenses with certain documentary requirements. *inadmissibility grounds § 212(a)* *§ 101(a)(13)(c)*

2. NONIMMIGRANT ADMISSIONS

a. Nonimmigrant Visas

Most individuals who wish to come to the United States for a temporary stay must first secure a nonimmigrant visa from a U.S. consular officer in a foreign country. Many visitors make multiple visits on the same visa. Consular officers, relying on their individualized judgment, can issue visas valid for a single admission or multiple entries; they can also issue visas for a short duration or a multi-year period. In addition, as described below, many visitors require no visa at all for admission.

The noncitizen bears the burden of proving that he qualifies for the visa, and the most important issue in the high-demand categories (especially B–1 and B–2 visitors, F and M students, and J exchange visitors) will often be whether he has a home in a foreign country to which he intends to return. The consular officer has discretion to require any kind of documentary support she deems necessary. *See* INA §§ 221(g), 222(c)–(d).

Since 2004, as a security measure, Congress has required an in-person interview before the issuance of a visa for all applicants aged 14 to 79, subject only to highly limited waivers. INA § 222(h). At the interview, the consular officer makes sure that all the information has been correctly supplied on the application and then proceeds to question the applicant, especially on any matters that raise doubts about admissibility.

If the consular officer finds that any of the inadmissibility grounds apply, she may deny the visa. Or if a waiver of the applicable ground is available, the officer usually assists with that application, to be forwarded for adjudication, along with the officer's report of any pertinent information bearing on the waiver and developed during the interview. If the visa application is approved, the consular officer affixes a nonimmigrant visa into the applicant's passport. Unless otherwise specified, the visa is good for multiple entries before its expiration.

b. Exceptions to the Visa Requirement

(i) Mexico and Canada

The United States issues combined Border Crossing Cards (BCCs) and B–1/B–2 visas to Mexican nationals. The BCC is sufficient immigration documentation for Mexican nationals at a southern land border port of entry. Canadian nationals benefit from a long-time exception that admits them to study or visit temporarily on their passports without a visa or BCC.

(ii) Visa Waiver Program

Until 1986, the United States required citizens of all countries other than Canada or Mexico to obtain visas from U.S. consulates overseas. This policy continued long after most other countries allowed Americans to visit temporarily without a visa. Congress authorized a visa waiver pilot program in 1986, and made it permanent in 2000. The Visa Waiver Program applies only to temporary visitors in the B–1 or B–2 nonimmigrant categories who seek admission for up to 90 days from selected countries that meet specified statutory criteria, such as reciprocal rights for U.S. citizens, issuance of machine readable passports, and low visa refusal rates. INA § 217.

Since 2009, those who want to travel on a visa waiver have been required to obtain advance clearance through a web-based system known as the Electronic System for Travel Authorization (ESTA). The traveler provides biographic information that allows DHS to check him or her against databases to identify security- or crime-based concerns.

As of early 2016, the nationals of 38 countries are eligible for the program: Andorra, Australia, Austria, Belgium, Brunei, Chile, Czech Republic, Denmark, Estonia, Finland, France, Germany, Greece, Hungary, Iceland, Ireland, Italy, Japan, Latvia, Liechtenstein, Lithuania, Luxembourg, Malta, Monaco, the Netherlands, New Zealand, Norway, Portugal, San Marino, Singapore, Slovakia, Slovenia, South Korea, Spain, Sweden, Switzerland, Taiwan, and the United Kingdom.

The visitor who enters under the visa waiver program waives significant rights. She cannot extend her stay, change nonimmigrant status under § 248, or adjust to permanent resident status under § 245(a) once she is in the United States (except as an immediate relative of a U.S.

citizen). *See* INA §§ 245(c); 248. She also waives her right to a removal hearing, except that she may apply for and have a hearing on asylum. INA § 217(b). These waivers have been sustained against constitutional challenges. *See, e.g., Bingham v. Holder,* 637 F.3d 1040 (9th Cir. 2011).

c. At the Port of Entry

Without a visa (or a showing that she is visa-exempt), a noncitizen probably will not be able to board a plane or other vessel for the United States. Carriers are subject to fines and other expenses for bringing passengers without adequate documentation. *See* INA §§ 241(c), (e), 273.

At the port of entry, a CBP officer inspects the noncitizens. The consul's prior decisions on admissibility do not bind the immigration officers at the border checkpoint or port of entry. Most arrivals are admitted after a few quick and routine questions. If any questions about admissibility cannot be readily cleared up, the person is referred to secondary inspection for more questioning, usually conducted in offices or cubicles nearby at the port of entry but away from the primary inspection booths. Of those noncitizens who are not admitted, the vast majority are turned back without ever seeing an immigration judge, in part because noncitizens believed inadmissible are usually given a chance to withdraw their applications for admission. There is no right to withdraw; both the inspector and the applicant must consent. *See* INA § 235(a)(4).

As of mid-2013, CPB has a new automated procedure to replace the traditional Form I–94 card, the Arrival-Departure Record, for arrivals by air. Arrival and departure information is recorded electronically based on information from the carrier's manifest, from the ESTA (for visa waiver cases) system, or from the visa-issuing consulate, supplemented by information obtained at the port of entry. Individuals who need a hard-copy I–94 can print one from a new I–94 website. Responding to complaints that admitted persons would no longer have ready access to key information, such as admission date, category, and end date, CBP announced that it would stamp passports with that information at admission. Paper I–94s will still be used at land borders and in other limited circumstances.

Although people often speak of a noncitizen being here "on a tourist visa" or "on a student visa," this usage is technically incorrect—and potentially misleading. The visa only helps move the noncitizen to the port of entry. The type and length of her actual admission will be reflected in what is written on the I–94 or, more likely now, an admission stamp in the passport.

Say a noncitizen has a B–2 visa that expires on September 1, 2018. She is admitted to the United States on January 1, 2018. If her I–94 indicates admission in B–2 status until March 1, 2018, she must leave by

March 1. If she does nothing to extend her authorized stay, it will do her no good on March 2 to point out that her visa is valid until September 1. In fact, a nonimmigrant visa holder generally voids her visa if she overstays her authorized admission period. *See* INA § 222(g).

Suppose she does not extend or change her status but instead leaves in late February before the end of her authorized stay. She can then use the visa to return to the United States at any time before it expires on September 1 (unless it was a single-entry visa). If she returns on August 1 and the admitting officer determines that the new visit is bona fide, she would receive a new I–94 that is valid, for example, for three months, until November 1, 2018. She may stay for that full period, even though her visa expires one month after admission.

Alternatively, while she still is in lawful status based on the January 1 admission, she can apply to DHS to have her admission period extended, or to have her nonimmigrant classification changed under INA § 248 (*e.g.,* from B–2 tourist to F–1 student). If permission is granted, she need not have the visa amended, as long as she plans no further travel outside the United States before the new admission period expires.

PROBLEMS

1.   Beatrice, a British national, is interested in traveling to the East Coast of the United States to visit several college campuses. She has been accepted at three U.S. universities, but she is not sure if she would like to enroll. What kind of visa should she seek and where should she apply for it? (You may wish to consult Chapter Five, Section B again. Do not consider inadmissibility grounds, which will be discussed in Chapter Seven.) Is she eligible for the visa waiver program? If she has a choice between seeking a visa or traveling under the visa waiver program, what factors should she consider in deciding how to proceed?

2.   Beatrice's cousins, Clark, a Canadian citizen, and Mariana, a Mexican citizen, would like to meet her in the United States and visit the colleges together. Assuming they are not prospective students and that no inadmissibility grounds apply to them, can they rely on the visa waiver program for entry into the United States? What other options do they have?

3.   Suppose that Mariana, a Mexican citizen, has been accepted at a college in Dallas, Texas. Will Mariana's border crossing card allow her entry to the United States to attend classes for the fall semester?

---

3. PAROLE

Suppose a noncitizen is detained at the border and ultimately ruled inadmissible under § 212 on a nonwaivable ground. What happens if she becomes gravely ill before the government can remove her? Can officials send her to the hospital without admitting her and thus violating the Act? Must the government instead condemn a portion of the hospital and make it technically a part of the detention facility?

Immigration authorities developed the concept of parole, which allows an inadmissible noncitizen to travel away from the border and the detention facilities, in order to cope with such emergencies. Originally parole was a purely administrative invention, but in 1952 it was given statutory sanction. Parole is now permissible "for urgent humanitarian reasons or significant public benefit." Once the purposes of the parole have been served, or upon a revocation of parole, the person "shall forthwith return or be returned to the custody from which he was paroled," and continues to be treated as an applicant for admission. INA § 212(d)(5)(A). The statutes creating the Department of Homeland Security in 2003 essentially transferred the parole-granting authority to DHS. It is now exercised by specified officials in USCIS, ICE, and CBP. Immigration judges have no general authority to grant parole.

Parole has been used in a variety of circumstances. In some instances, it serves as a mechanism to release individuals from detention while they await a final decision on their cases. In other instances, it functions as an alternative to admission to the United States.

Within the admission setting, it is sometimes used for general humanitarian reasons, such as allowing a noncitizen into the United States for urgent medical care. It has also been used to assist families of members of the U.S. Armed Forces, to speed the entry of refugees, and to allow U.S. noncitizen residents to leave and return to the United States while their applications for lawful status are pending.

Recently, parole has been used to assist unauthorized immigrant family members of U.S. citizens on active duty in the U.S. military. In 2013 USCIS outlined circumstances in which parole would be available for military personnel's family members who had entered without inspection (EWI) and thus had not been lawfully admitted to the United States. Policy Memorandum, PM–602–0091, *Parole of Spouses, Children and Parents of Active Duty Members of the U.S. Armed Forces* (Nov. 15, 2013). This step, known as *parole in place*, gives the beneficiaries a form of legal permission to remain. In addition, it allows them to adjust status without leaving the United States (and thus without triggering the three- or ten-year bar of INA § 212(a)(9)(B)). Eligibility for adjustment of status will be discussed in the section below.

In the refugee context, parole has proved to be a flexible tool in the hands of the executive branch, allowing Presidents to rely on parole to bring in large groups of refugees in compelling circumstances. The practice began when the Soviet Union sent tanks into Hungary to put down a revolution there in 1956. Hungarian quotas were full, but the Eisenhower administration came under increasing pressure to admit large numbers of Hungarian refugees. The President ultimately decided to make innovative use of the parole power to bring some 30,000 refugees to this country.

Thus started a long and controversial practice of paroling in refugees when ordinary statutory provisions proved inadequate. Hundreds of thousands of people fleeing Cuba and Indochina, along with a few from other countries, were later beneficiaries. Many in Congress protested, insisting that parole was supposed to be temporary, whereas the refugees were clearly coming for an indefinite stay, and that it was supposed to be used for individual cases, not large groups. When Congress enacted the Refugee Act of 1980, it added a provision barring parole for refugees except in individual cases for individually compelling reasons, INA § 212(d)(5)(B).

Nonetheless, the executive branch again invoked the parole authority to respond to mass exoduses from Cuba in 1980 and again in 1994. In 1980 parole may have been technically consistent with § 212(d)(5)(B) because the Cubans had not been determined to be refugees when they were paroled into the United States, and they were not being paroled as part of an official refugee program. In 1994 there was a sudden and dangerous increase of Cubans escaping Cuba in small boats or homemade rafts. The United States responded by negotiating an agreement with Cuba to curtail the outflow in return for a U.S. commitment to accept at least 20,000 Cubans annually through regular channels. This program, still in existence, involves parole of several thousand Cubans selected through an annual lottery. *See* Cuban Family Reunification Parole Program, 72 Fed. Reg. 65,588 (Nov. 21, 2007).

Another use of parole, known as *advance parole*, has also assumed importance in contemporary practice. Under this concept, officials allow applicants to leave the United States while applications are pending, and assure them that they will be able to return without jeopardizing their situation. As discussed below, advance parole frequently provides vital flexibility for individuals in the adjustment of status process.

4. ADJUSTMENT OF STATUS

a. Historical Background

As noted at the outset of this Chapter, governments issue visas to noncitizens to authorize admission and to set the terms of the visit. Typically, governments issue visas at their embassies and consulates abroad. In 1935 the U.S. government developed a "pre-examination" process that simplified the acquisition of immigrant status for some nonimmigrants already in the United States. Administrators concluded that many nonimmigrants could show that they qualified for permanent immigration—perhaps through permanent employment or marriage to a U.S. citizen—and that a costly trip overseas would be a burden.

Clearly qualified noncitizens could complete most of the necessary paperwork in this country, and then travel briefly to a U.S. consulate in Canada to secure the immigrant visa, bolstered by a letter from U.S. authorities assuring Canada that the person would be allowed to travel back into the United States in any event. Except for a brief period, pre-examination was unavailable to Mexican and Caribbean migrants, first by practice, then by regulation. Mae Ngai has cited this administrative willingness to facilitate the adjustment of certain out-of-status noncitizens—primarily Europeans—but not others, as evidence for racialization of the notion of the "illegal alien." *See* Mae M. Ngai, *Impossible Subjects: Illegal Aliens and the Making of Modern America* 84–87, 90 (2004).

The administrative innovation of pre-examination eventually led Congress to amend the statute. In 1952, with the new Immigration and Nationality Act, Congress adopted § 245, which authorizes *adjustment of status* from nonimmigrant to immigrant for noncitizens who meet certain requirements. This whole process is carried out in the United States.

saves trouble of having to travel abroad to American consulate.

b.   Overview of § 245

Adjustment of status replaces traveling overseas to obtain an immigrant visa from a consular officer. The statute gives DHS discretion to grant adjustment of status to noncitizens who fulfill the requirements for an immigrant visa, who are not inadmissible, and for whom an immigrant visa is immediately available. Adjustment does not eliminate the need for a visa petition in those immigrant categories where it is required. Generally, the visa petition must first be submitted to USCIS, and the adjustment application can be filed only after that visa petition is approved. (In some circumstances the petition can be submitted at the same time as the application for adjustment. *See* 8 C.F.R. § 245.2(a)(2)(C).)

In adjustment cases, a USCIS examiner makes all the same determinations as a consular officer would in considering an immigrant visa applicant—that is, whether any of the inadmissibility grounds apply. For this process, the applicant for adjustment, although physically present in the United States, is considered as though he were at the border applying for initial admission. The examiner also must apply additional criteria for adjustment, some of which are specified by §§ 245(a) and (c), considered below. Adjustment applicants may be scheduled for an interview, conducted by a USCIS examiner, but the interview is often waived, especially for those in the employment-based categories. Adjustment applicants are routinely given work authorization while the application is pending.

The adjustment process may take several months. Leaving the United States is treated as abandonment of the adjustment application, and in any event could lead to difficulty gaining readmission on the earlier visa, owing to the nonimmigrant intent doctrine. Acknowledging this dilemma, the agencies allow applicants to apply for a grant of *advance parole*, which provides solid assurance (though not a guarantee) that they can depart and return to the United States without jeopardizing their adjustment application or their eligibility for work authorization. DHS now expects that adjustment applicants will need advance parole, and the fee for adjustment of status also covers applications for advance parole and work authorization.

As mentioned earlier, the deciding officer has discretion to allow applicants to adjust to immigrant status without going overseas. Factors relevant to the exercise of discretion have included family ties in the United States, hardship in traveling abroad, length of residence in the United States, preconceived intent to remain, and any repeated violations of immigration law. If adjustment of status is granted to an applicant who qualifies in one of the preference categories, the applicant counts toward the quota for that preference for the current fiscal year. *See* INA § 245(b).

Although discretionary, and occasionally characterized as extraordinary, adjustment of status has become an increasingly popular, frequently used avenue toward permanent residence. In FY 2013, adjustments of status accounted for 54 percent of all new immigrants. The percentage of adjustments varied greatly by type of immigrant. They accounted for 87 percent of those granted lawful permanent residence based on employment-based preferences, 53 percent for immediate relatives, 13 percent for family-based preferences, and only 3 percent for diversity immigrants. *See* DHS 2013 Yearbook of Immigration Statistics, Table 6.

In addition to allowing would-be immigrants to avoid the expense and disruption of traveling overseas for visa processing, adjustment of status has become significant in a much more substantive way. As Chapter Seven will detail, key inadmissibility grounds for unlawful presence are triggered only if the noncitizen *leaves* the United States. A noncitizen who has been unlawfully present for a period longer than 180 days is barred for three years. A period of unlawful presence of one year or more can mean a ten-year bar. INA § 212(a)(9)(B)(i). As a consequence, for individuals unlawfully present for more than 180 days, adjustment of status has become the only route to permanent residence without a delay of many years (though waivers of the three- and ten-year bars are possible).

For noncitizens placed in removal proceedings in the United States, adjustment of status can also work as a form of relief from removal. Once a visa petition on behalf of the noncitizen has been filed with USCIS, the noncitizen can request the immigration judge in the removal proceeding to grant adjustment to lawful permanent resident status. The noncitizen must then introduce evidence at the removal hearing to show that she has a basis for becoming an immigrant, for example as an immediate relative, and meets the statutory requirements for adjustment of status. If USCIS approves the visa petition and the judge determines the applicant is eligible to adjust, the judge will exercise discretion as to whether to grant this relief.

c.   Adjustment Under § 245(a) and (c)

INA § 245(a) sets forth the requirements for adjustment of status, and § 245(c) sets out disqualifications. Besides proving eligibility for an immigrant visa and the absence of any inadmissibility grounds, noncitizens seeking adjustment must have been inspected and admitted or paroled. Noncitizens allowed to enter the United States after presenting themselves for admission and inspection are deemed admitted, even if they were inadmissible but that fact was not known to the border inspector who allowed them into the United States. For example, if a U.S. border inspector waves through a car driven by a U.S. citizen and there is a young noncitizen child sitting in the back seat, the child has effectively been admitted and, accordingly, later may be eligible for adjustment of status.

Persons who entered without inspection do not qualify for adjustment under § 245(a). However, as noted above, in certain circumstances individuals who entered without inspection can qualify for parole while they are in the United States. Those who receive the benefit of *parole in place* may then be able to adjust their status.

Even for those previously inspected and admitted, § 245(c) bars adjustment of status in some circumstances. For example, noncitizens initially admitted under the visa waiver program are ineligible for adjustment unless they are now immediate relatives of U.S. citizens.

Paragraph (c)(2) provides that adjustment is unavailable to noncitizens who worked without authorization before filing, unless they are immediate relatives of U.S. citizens. The same prohibition applies to noncitizens who are "in unlawful immigration status on the date of filing the application for adjustment of status or who [have] failed (other than through no fault of [their] own or for technical reasons) to maintain continuously a lawful status since entry into the United States." Suppose a nonimmigrant went out of status while waiting for action on a request to extend his nonimmigrant status. Is he now ineligible to adjust? The answer is no, according to the regulations. *See* 8 C.F.R. § 245.1(d)(2)(ii).

Such failure to maintain status is considered to have happened for a technical reason. Similarly, expiration of nonimmigrant status while an adjustment application is pending does not run afoul of (c)(2).

Paragraph (c)(7) expands the ineligible group beyond § 245(c)(2), by prohibiting adjustment for parolees and others allowed to be present in the United States without nonimmigrant status. (Note that this paragraph does not affect adjustments in the family categories.) Paragraph (c)(8) bars from adjustment noncitizens who have worked without authorization or "otherwise violated the terms of a nonimmigrant visa." There is no express exception in (c)(8) for immediate relatives, but the government position has been that (c)(8) does not supersede the more specific language of (c)(2) exempting immediate relatives (and a few specified groups of "special immigrants") from the bar to adjustment because of unauthorized work or a status violation. *See* Memorandum From Associate Commissioner Crocetti, Dec.20, 1996, *reprinted in* 74 Interp. Rel. 123 (1997).

Another subsection, § 245(k), provides a safe haven that overcomes disqualification under (c)(2), (7), or (8) in limited circumstances. It protects only persons applying in the employment-based categories, and only if their defaults lasted no longer than 180 days in the aggregate.

Now that you have seen the outlines of the adjustment of status process, test your understanding by applying the statutory framework to the situations presented in the next set of problems, which require you to consult INA § 245. You also will need to look at the inadmissibility ground regarding entry without inspection, INA § 212(a)(6)(A)(i), and the unlawful presence ground with its three- and ten-year bars that is triggered when a noncitizen leaves the United States, INA § 212(a)(9)(B)(i).

PROBLEMS

4.   Gary has obtained labor certification for a child tutor, Nora, a British national, who has actually been working for the family for the past few years after entering on a B–2 tourist visa. Gary filed the labor certification application several years ago. Nora's priority date has just been reached. Nora has never been authorized to work in the United States. Is Nora eligible to adjust status to assume lawful permanent residence in the United States?

5.   Nora has two siblings in the United States. One is her brother, Dennis, who has worked without authorization as a cook in a restaurant since being admitted as a B–1 business visitor four months ago. His authorized stay expired 30 days ago. Dennis has just married Vera, a U.S. citizen, who wants to help him get a green card. Can Dennis adjust status? If not, what are his prospects for becoming a permanent resident of the

United States by returning to the United Kingdom in order to obtain an immigrant visa from the U.S. consulate there?

6. Nora also has a sister, Zelda, who was admitted in F–1 status several years ago to study at Duke University, where she graduated with a master's degree a few months ago. Zelda was then authorized by DHS to undertake 12 months of "practical training" with a firm in Durham, (an authorized complement to her schooling, which is often granted to F–1 students). After a few weeks, however, she quit following a dispute with her boss. She then took a job with a local restaurant and has been working without authorization ever since. Before graduation, Zelda accepted a permanent job offer from a U.S. biomedical engineering firm, contingent upon proper immigration approvals. The firm filed for a labor certification for Zelda a few months ago, and that application has just been approved. Can Zelda adjust status now? If not, can she receive an immigrant visa at a U.S. consulate in the United Kingdom?

7. Nora's friend Isabel, a citizen of Guyana, entered the United States without inspection six years ago. Since that time Isabel has supported herself by working for various landscaping companies. George, a Jamaican national who is a lawful permanent resident of the United States, wants to marry Isabel. Will Isabel be able to adjust her status and become a lawful permanent resident? If George were a U.S. citizen, would that change Isabel's ability to obtain adjustment of status?

8. Isabel's sister Maria, also a citizen of Guyana, came to live with Isabel three years ago. Maria brought her two-year old son Michael with her, and they both entered without inspection. Maria has worked as a nanny for the past two years. Maria is engaged to marry James, a U.S. citizen who is a career soldier in the U.S. Marines. Will Maria and Michael be able to adjust their status?

d. Adjustment Under § 245(i)

In August 1994, Congress introduced a three-year trial program that significantly liberalized adjustment of status. Many people eligible for an immigrant visa who did not fall within any of the inadmissibility grounds were able to overcome their entry without inspection or the disqualifications in § 245(c) by paying a penalty fee ($1000 on top of the normal fee). INA § 245(i).

When § 245(i) opened up adjustment to many more noncitizens, it was primarily intended as a convenience. In 1994, ineligibility for adjustment did not keep a noncitizen from becoming a permanent resident. He simply had to leave the United States to obtain a visa. In 1996, however, Congress added inadmissibility grounds for unlawful presence, along with the three- and ten-year bars to readmission, which apply only to a person who has *departed* the United States after accruing either 180 days or one year of unlawful presence. From then on, adjustment of status (or a waiver) became the only way to avoid those bars.

As the initial § 245(i) provision neared its expiration in 1997, opponents argued that it amounted to an amnesty that allowed unauthorized immigrants to avoid the three- and ten-year bars. Proponents called it a sensible approach to regularize the status for noncitizens who had qualified and waited in line under the immigrant quota system. Congress adopted a compromise, allowing § 245(i) to lapse but with a broad grandfather clause, benefiting people on whose behalf a visa petition or labor certification application was filed on or before January 14, 1998. Congress later extended the grandfather provision to cover persons who were in the United States on December 21, 2000, and who had a visa petition or labor certification application filed for them by April 30, 2001. Section 245(i) remains on the books, but it provides relief for a small number of beneficiaries for whom approvable initial papers— not necessarily the application they are pursuing now—were filed by this date.

PROBLEMS

9. Suppose that Nora, the British national in Problem 4, had entered without inspection from Canada in November 2000. She has never left the United States since that time. In March 2001 she began working as a nanny for Gary's family. Gary applied for labor certification for Nora as a child tutor the next month, and the application was denied. Gary appealed to the Board of Alien Labor Certification Appeals (BALCA), and ultimately prevailed. Gary then applied for an immigrant visa for Nora, and the visa application was denied. Again, Gary appealed, this time to the USCIS Administrative Appeals Office. After several remands, reversals, and submission of additional information, the immigrant visa was approved. Finally, Nora's priority date has been reached. During her years in the United States, Nora has never been authorized to work. Is Nora eligible to adjust her status to assume lawful permanent residence in the United States? — yes

10. Suppose that Gary's wife died while the immigrant visa petition was pending, and that Gary then married Nora. If Gary petitions for her as his spouse, would this affect Nora's eligibility to adjust her status? priority

— No —

5. REVIEW OF ADMISSIONS DECISIONS

Seeking lawful admission to the United States is a multi-step process, and a noncitizen may receive a negative decision at different points in the proceedings. Application rejections may occur in very different geographical and political spaces—in the United States, in a foreign country, or at the border of the United States.

a. Denials in the United States

(i) Visa Petition Denials

Visa petition denials in the United States are reviewable in court under the Administrative Procedure Act, after exhaustion of administrative remedies. As you may recall from Chapter Four, the administrative appellate procedures vary depending on the type of visa petition. Denials of employment-based visa petitions are heard by the USCIS Administrative Appeals Office, 8 C.F.R. § 103.3, while denials of family-based visa petitions are heard by the BIA, 8 C.F.R. § 1003.1(b)(5).

(ii) Adverse Adjustment Decisions

An applicant denied adjustment of status by USCIS has no appeal, but may renew her adjustment application before the immigration judge conducting her removal proceedings (assuming such proceedings occur). 8 C.F.R. §§ 245.2(a)(5)(ii), 1245.2(a)(1), (a)(5)(ii). The earlier USCIS denial does not bind the immigration judge, who applies the statutory grounds and exercises discretion anew, based on any information in the appropriate forms or developed at the removal hearing. Adjustment may also be sought from the immigration judge during proceedings even if the noncitizen had not applied for it earlier before USCIS.

The immigration judge's decision—unlike USCIS's—is appealable to the Board of Immigration Appeals. Judicial review of the BIA's decision is limited to "constitutional claims or questions of law" upon review of a final order of removal. INA § 242(a)(2)(D). In Chapter Nine, we will explore the reach of the review-stripping provision and the review-preserving exception.

(iii) Rescission of Adjustment

INA § 246(a) provides for rescission of adjustment of status acquired under § 245 if, at any time within five years after adjustment, "it shall appear to the satisfaction of the Attorney General that the person was not in fact eligible for such adjustment of status." When the ineligibility for adjustment is discovered more than five years have adjustment, the adjusted permanent resident may still be removed. *See Matter of Belenzo*, 17 I & N Dec. 374 (BIA 1980; AG 1981). Moreover, a removal order rescinds lawful permanent resident status, whenever issued, without a separate, prior rescission proceeding. *See* INA § 246(a). The Third Circuit has reached a contrary conclusion, *Garcia v. Attorney General,* 553 F.3d 724 (3d Cir. 2009), but no other circuit agrees, and the BIA has reaffirmed *Belenzo* for application elsewhere. *Matter of D-R-*, 25 I & N Dec. 445, 462–63 (2011).

b. Rejection at the Consulate

As noted earlier in this chapter, beneficiaries of immigrant visa petitions ordinarily complete the visa process at the U.S. consulate in their home countries. Moreover, most nonimmigrants obtain their visas from U.S. consulates abroad. As noted in Chapter Four, there is an unusual provision in INA § 104(a) that exempts individual visa determinations from the supervision and control of the Secretary of State. Nonetheless the State Department developed a *de facto* internal review mechanism, which provided that denials would be considered by another officer within the consulate, who could not, strictly speaking, reverse the initial decision, but instead could issue the visa in his or her own name upon a judgment that the person was eligible. This was an internal control measure rather than an appeal the applicant could seek.

In 2006, the State Department revised the regulations and the Foreign Affairs Manual to make explicit the selective nature of this review and also to direct more supervisory attention to visa decisions—a byproduct of enhanced security concerns. Supervisors must review a random selection of both positive and negative visa decisions by consular officers. 9 FAM § 41.113 PN 17.1 (2010); *see also* 22 C.F.R. §§ 41.113(i), 41.121(c); 9 FAM § 41.121 PN 18.1–2, *id.* 41.121 PN 1.2–8 (2011). In addition, applicants may also submit additional information to overcome a visa refusal, and in many circumstances are entitled to reconsideration upon doing so. *See, e.g.*, 22 C.F.R. § 41.121(c), 42.81(e). Insights into effective advocacy on behalf of clients faced with consular visa denials can be found in Anna Marie Gallagher, *Guiding Your Client Through the Fog: Administrative Processing and the Visa Application Process*, 13–10 Immigr. Briefings 1 (2013); Andrew T. Chan & Robert A. Free, *The Lawyer's Role in Consular Visa Refusals*, 08–04 Immigr. Briefings 1 (2008).

The Department's headquarters Visa Office may request a report on a specific case or class of cases, and sometimes issues an advisory opinion "to the consular officer for assistance in considering the case further." Suggestions in such opinions regarding factual determinations are advisory, in keeping with INA § 104, but rulings on matters of law are binding on the consular officer. 22 C.F.R. §§ 41.121(d), 42.81(d).

There is no procedure, however, that permits the applicant to appeal a consular visa denial to a higher administrative authority. Nor is there an explicit statutory provision regarding judicial review. Consular decisions made overseas have generally been held to be beyond the jurisdiction of the courts. This rule has been applied not only to a person seeking a visa for a short vacation or business trip to the United States, but also to a person seeking an immigrant visa based on his or her relation to a U.S. citizen or permanent resident—and equally to a suit filed by the citizen or LPR sponsor seeking to challenge the family member's immigrant visa denial. *See, e.g., Pena v. Kissinger,* 409 F.Supp. 1182 (S.D.N.Y. 1976).

Some courts have found jurisdiction to consider underlying questions regarding the constitutionality of the statute under which the consul acted, despite the consular nonreviewability doctrine. *See, e.g., Martinez v. Bell,* 468 F.Supp. 719 (S.D.N.Y.1979) (sustaining the government on the merits). Others have found jurisdiction when the key decisions were actually made not by the consular officer overseas but by officials in the United States. *See,* e.g., *American Academy of Religion v. Napolitano,* 573 F.3d 115, 123–25 (2d Cir. 2009) (sustaining judicial review of failure to issue visa to Tariq Ramadan, a Swiss citizen and Islamic scholar).

In 2015 the Supreme Court reviewed a U.S. citizen's challenge to the consular denial of an immigrant visa for her husband. *Kerry v. Din,* 576 U.S.___, 135 S.Ct. 2128, 192 L.Ed.2d 183, discussed in Section B below, The district court dismissed the case on consular nonreviewability grounds, but the Ninth Circuit reversed. *Din v. Kerry,* 718 F.3d 856 (9th Cir. 2013). The Supreme Court, in turn, vacated the Ninth Circuit's judgment and remanded the case for dismissal. Although the Supreme Court upheld the consular visa denial, the Court extensively examined the constitutional claims raised by the U.S. citizen visa petitioner.

Visa revocations have also traditionally been considered immune from judicial review. In 2004 Congress amended INA § 221(i) to bar judicial review of visa revocations and to make revocation a ground of deportability. Intelligence Reform and Terrorism Prevention Act, § 5304, Pub. L. 108–458, 118 Stat. 3638, 3735 (2004) (amending INA § 237(a)(1)(B)). This change in the grounds of deportability could have a drastic impact, particularly if visa revocation is unreviewable. Perhaps for that reason, the 2004 legislation provided that judicial review of the visa revocation, normally barred, is permitted as part of the review of a removal order, when revocation is the sole ground of deportability. *See* INA § 221(i).

NOTES AND QUESTIONS ON REVIEW OF CONSULAR DECISIONS

1.   The APA presumptively makes administrative decisions reviewable in the courts on the suit of anyone "aggrieved" by the agency action. Why shield consular officers? Are there functional reasons to support the doctrine of consular nonreviewability? Foreign affairs implications? The sheer number of disappointed visa applicants? Other factors?

2.   The U.S. Commission on Immigration Reform, a blue-ribbon commission chartered by Congress to consider reforms to the immigration

system, issued wide-ranging recommendations in the late 1990s on our overall immigration system, after a multi-year study and nationwide hearings. The Commission proposed a system for review of certain visa denials and revocations by consular officers. The Commission recommended review of all immigrant visas and of nonimmigrant visas in which an individual or entity in the United States has petitioned for the admission of the noncitizen. U.S. Commission on Immigration Reform, Becoming an American: Immigration and Immigrant Policy 181–82 (1997). Neither Congress nor the executive branch has acted on this recommendation.

3. The *American Academy of Religion* case distinguishes between decisions made by consular officers and by DHS officials. If a decision is not reviewable when reached by a consular officer, why should the same decision be reviewable once an officer from a different department (or indeed the Secretary of State personally) becomes involved? Do you think the location of the officer making the decision—overseas versus within the United States—is a more significant distinction than the category of decisionmaker?

The *American Academy of Religion* litigation continued for several more years. After ruling that the consular nonreviewability doctrine did not prevent the federal courts from considering the visa denial, the Second Circuit considered the merits and concluded that the case must be remanded to afford Tariq Ramadan an opportunity to respond to the charge that he had knowingly contributed to a terrorist organization. 573 F.3d at 128–34 (2d Cir. 2009). Subsequently, Ramadan obtained an exemption from the terrorist grounds of inadmissibility and successfully applied for a ten-year multiple entry visa. *American Academy of Religion v. Napolitano*, 2011 WL 1157698 (S.D.N.Y.) Litigation continued over attorney fees, which the court denied in March 2011. *Id.* For further discussion of this case, see Chapter Seven, pp. 615–616.

4. Assume that you are a staffer to the Senate Judiciary Committee, assigned to rethink the overall system for review of visa denials. What would you propose? If it is appropriate to subject only a subset of visa decisions to judicial review, how would you select the subset? Or better, what mix of more formalized administrative review plus judicial review would be optimal for our complex admissions system? What objectives do you take into account in making that choice?

c.   Rejection at the Border

Noncitizens who arrive in the United States generally must present visas at the border or show that they are exempt from the visa requirement. The immigration officer at the port of entry ordinarily assesses admissibility through a quick inspection of the entry documents and the screening databases described earlier in this chapter. If the officer has doubts that the noncitizen should be admitted, another immigration officer asks more extensive questions, known as secondary inspection. Noncitizens may be allowed, at the discretion of the immigration officer, withdraw their application for admission during primary or secondary inspection and return to the country they left. INA § 235(a)(4).

Noncitizens refused entry to the United States who do not withdraw their applications have the right to a removal hearing before an immigration judge. The noncitizen bears the burden of proving admissibility, INA § 291, and the statute requires applicants for admission to prove "clearly and beyond doubt" that they are entitled to be admitted. INA § 240 (c)(2)(A). Individuals fearing persecution, torture, or threats to their lives and freedom can apply for asylum or withholding of removal at the hearing. INA § 208. These issues will be discussed in Chapter Eight.

Removal proceedings in immigration court are discussed at greater length in Chapter Nine. Such proceedings are adversarial, and both the noncitizen and the government have the right to present evidence and to examine and cross-examine witnesses. INA § 240. Immigration judges preside; noncitizens have the right to be represented by counsel at their own expense. *Id.* Obtaining counsel can be difficult, especially for respondents with limited means, and the statute requires that the noncitizen shall have at least 10 days before the hearing date in order to attempt to secure legal representation. INA § 239(b)(1). An unsuccessful challenge to a border official's refusal of entry has serious consequences, as removal pursuant to the formal order of an immigration judge results in a five-year bar to readmission to the United States. INA § 212(a)(9)(A)(i), discussed in Chapter Seven. Noncitizens can appeal the immigration judge's order to the Board of Immigration Appeals and, in multiple instances noted in Chapter Nine, to the federal courts.

6. EXPEDITED REMOVAL

In 1996 Congress enacted an expedited removal procedure that generally applies to arriving aliens who seek admission to the United States but (1) have no documents, (2) have fraudulent or invalid documents, or (3) have committed immigration fraud in the past. *See* INA § 235(b)(1). Mandatory detention during the initial portion of the procedure, often followed by detention as a matter of discretion during later stages, constitutes an important component of the process.

Large numbers of noncitizens are subject to expedited removal. In 2011, there were approximately 120,000 expedited removals; they accounted for roughly 30 percent of the total removals from the United States. In 2012, there were more than 163,000 expedited removals, comprising 40 percent of all removals. In 2013, there were 193,000 expedited removals, and they amounted to 44% of all removals. John F.

Simanski, *Enforcement Actions: 2013*, DHS Office of Immigration Statistics, Table 7.

a. At Ports of Entry

The law applies expedited removal at all times to arriving aliens (except Cubans arriving by air), if they are judged inadmissible under INA § 212(a)(6)(C) (relating to attempts to obtain admission or other immigration benefits through fraud or misrepresentation), or § 212(a)(7) (lack of a valid passport, visa, or other required document).[12] The expedited removal statute authorizes an immigration officer who finds an arriving alien inadmissible on the specified grounds to order him removed *"without further hearing or review* unless the alien indicates either an intention to apply for asylum under section 208 or a fear of persecution." INA § 235(b)(1)(A)(i) (emphasis added). Under the regulations and operating manuals, such an order may be issued only after an extended interview in secondary inspection, followed by supervisory review of the officer's conclusion that the person meets the criteria for expedited removal. *See* 8 C.F.R. § 235.3.

Departure under an expedited removal order carries the same consequences as that based on a removal order issued by an immigration judge. In particular, when issued to an arriving alien, the order makes the person inadmissible for five years. *See* INA § 212(a)(9)(A)(i). The statute does, however, grant DHS officers broad discretion to waive the five-year bar later, if the noncitizen wishes to return before the period has run. *See* INA § 212(a)(9)(A)(iii). Immigration officers interviewing persons who initially seem subject to expedited removal also have discretion to allow them to withdraw their applications for admission. *See* INA § 235(a)(4), 8 C.F.R. § 235.4(a). The individual has no absolute right to withdraw the application; withdrawal must be approved by the officer. The stakes are high in this decision, because withdrawal, though it ordinarily entails immediate return to the country of departure, is not considered removal under a formal order. Thus the person incurs no bar to reapplying for admission later—for example, after returning home and correcting any technical problem with the visa he or she initially presented.

b. Expansion Beyond Ports of Entry

In addition to applying expedited removal automatically to all arriving noncitizens, the statute gives the Secretary of Homeland Security (formerly the Attorney General) the "sole and unreviewable discretion" to apply expedited removal to noncitizens who have not been admitted or paroled into the United States, if they do not "affirmatively

---

[12] An obscurely worded exception exempts Cubans arriving by air from the coverage of expedited removal. INA § 235(b)(1)(F).

show[ ], to the satisfaction of an immigration officer," that they have been continuously present in the United States for the preceding two years. INA § 235(b)(1)(A)(iii), 8 C.F.R. § 235.3(b)(1). This means that expedited removal can, but need not, be applied to all noncitizens who entered the United States without inspection and have been present less than two years. In the interior, as well as at the border, expedited removal is applicable only to noncitizens deemed inadmissible who lack valid entry documents or are using false or invalid admission documents.

In 2002 Attorney General John Ashcroft first applied expedited removal provisions beyond the border to those (other than Cuban nationals) who arrive by sea. 67 Fed. Reg. 68924 (2002). Two years later, the Department of Homeland Security again relied on the expansive statutory authority to announce another major enlargement of the expedited removal program. It applies to noncitizens who entered without inspection and who are stopped within 100 miles of the U.S.-Mexico border or the U.S.-Canada border, unless they can show that they have been continuously present in the United States for more than 14 days. 69 Fed. Reg. 48877 (2004). In 2006, DHS announced that it would also apply expedited removal on these terms within 100 miles of the maritime borders.

c. Judicial Review

Judicial review of expedited removal orders is available, through habeas corpus, only in extremely limited circumstances. A person subject to an expedited removal order may go to court with an identity challenge—i.e., the petitioner alleges that she is not the person named in the expedited removal order, a highly unlikely eventuality. Status claimants (persons who claim under oath that they are U.S. citizens, lawful permanent residents, or previously admitted asylees or refugees) may also secure court review of that particular allegation after exhausting administrative review. See INA §§ 235(b)(1)(C), 242(e)(2).

The statute also provides for expedited hearing of challenges to "the validity of the system." INA § 242(e)(3). Such cases may be filed only in the federal district court in the District of Columbia and must be filed within 60 days of the implementation of the challenged regulation, procedure, or policy. Standing and other jurisdictional obstacles are considerable. See American Immigration Lawyers Assn. v. Reno, 18 F.Supp.2d 38 (D.D.C. 1998), aff'd, 199 F.3d 1352 (D.C.Cir.2000).

d. Asylum Seekers

As noted earlier, the expedited removal statute directs the removal of the noncitizen "without further hearing or review," but includes an express exception for noncitizens who indicate "an intention to apply for asylum * * * or a fear of persecution." INA § 235(b)(1)(A)(i). This provision makes it clear that individuals subject to expedited removal proceedings, whether at the border or in the interior, can prevent the immediate issuance of a removal order by claiming asylum or asserting a fear of return. In such cases, the immigration inspector must complete the interview, make a summary record of the results, and then arrange for the noncitizen to be sent to a detention facility where he will be interviewed by a specially trained asylum officer.

(i) Identifying Asylum Seekers

One major concern has been that persons wishing to claim asylum would not be able to do so effectively. They might be too intimidated in the expedited removal setting, and so might not even voice a fear of return before being hurried back across the border or onto a return flight. Or expressions of such fear might be ignored or overridden. Or the noncitizens might not realize that the words exchanged with the immigration inspectors would be their only opportunity to request protection.

The regulation requires an extensive initial interview by the inspector in every expedited removal case, whether or not asylum was requested. 8 C.F.R. § 235.3. Early in the interview, in a language that the noncitizen can understand, the officer must read the following:

> U.S. law provides protection to certain persons who face persecution, harm or torture upon return to their home country. If you fear or have a concern about being removed from the United States or about being sent home, you should tell me so during the interview because you will not have another chance. You will have the opportunity to speak privately and confidentially to another officer about your fear and concern. That officer will determine if you should remain in the United States and not be removed because of that fear.

The officer must record a sworn statement, which the individual initials on each page and signs at the end. That statement, written out by the inspector (in English) as the interview proceeds, summarizes the person's story but is not a verbatim transcript. The regulations also mandate review of the file by a high-ranking supervisor before an expedited removal order is issued. *See* David A. Martin, *Two Cheers for Expedited Removal in the New Immigration Laws,* 40 Va. J. Int'l L. 673 (2000).

(ii) The Credible Fear Interview

All noncitizens who ask for asylum or express a fear of return are supposed to be scheduled for an interview with an asylum officer. The asylum officer's duty is to determine whether the individuals has a "credible fear of persecution," which the statute defines as follows:

> a significant possibility, taking into account the credibility of the statements made by the alien in support of the alien's claim and such other facts as are known to the officer, that the alien could establish eligibility for asylum under section 208.

INA § 235(b)(1)(B)(v).

Concerns that asylum seekers would not have a fair opportunity to tell their stories during the credible fear process, owing to fatigue after a long journey or predictable reticence deriving from the fact of detention or from interrogation by officials in a wholly unfamiliar setting, led to guidelines that the credible fear interview should not take place earlier than 48 hours after the person's arrival in a detention center following referral from secondary inspection. *See* 62 Fed. Reg. 10,312, 10,320 (1997).

By statute, the noncitizen may consult with anyone of his choosing after secondary inspection and before the credible fear interview, so long as it is at no expense to the government and does not cause "unreasonable delay." The delay built in to the schedule allows the possibility of consultation with counsel or with accredited NGO representatives prior to the interview, but access to legal assistance is difficult in these circumstances.

If the asylum officer finds that a credible fear exists, the noncitizen is scheduled for a full merits hearing in immigration court in which to develop the asylum claim. The noncitizen may be released on parole while the merits hearing is pending. If the asylum officer does not find a credible fear, she issues an expedited removal order. The noncitizen may request review of the credible fear issue by an immigration judge in a special procedure that must be completed within seven days. If unsuccessful, the noncitizen is subject to immediate removal on the basis of the order previously issued. If the immigration judge finds a credible fear, the noncitizen is scheduled for a full merits hearing, and may be released on bond pending the hearing.

From 2006 through 2009, approximately 5,000 were referred for credible fear interviews each year; this constituted roughly five percent of those in expedited removal. Larger numbers—9,000 and 11,000 respectively—were referred for credible fear screening in 2010 and 2011. Between 2006 and 2011, asylum officers found credible fear, on average, in 80 percent of the individuals they interviewed. DHS, USCIS, Asylum Division, Briefing Paper on Expedited Removal and Credible Fear Process, Oct. 19, 2011. The numbers of referrals for credible fear interviews continued to increase—approximately 13,000 in 2012, 19,000 in 2013, and 11,000 in 2014—and the asylum officers concluded that 80 percent of the individuals screened during those years had a credible fear.

The pattern changed in FY 2015; the number of credible fear decisions skyrocketed to 48,000, and the rate of finding credible fear dropped to 70 percent. Of the total credible fear decisions, 14,000 were at ports of entry and 34,000 at inland locations. Asylum officers concluded the fear was credible in 64 percent of the cases at the ports of entry and 73 percent of the inland cases. *See* USCIS, Credible Fear Workload Report Summary, FY 2015. The surge in credible fear interviews coincided with the arrival of thousands of unaccompanied Central American children and families at the southern U.S. border in mid-2014. DHS took an enforcement-minded approach to the crisis and applied the expedited removal provisions to the mothers and children.

(iii)   *Detention*

The expedited removal statute and regulations expressly require detention, with very limited exceptions (for medical emergency or "legitimate law enforcement reasons"), throughout the initial stages of consideration by the inspector and the asylum officer. 8 C.F.R. § 235.3(b)(2)(iii). Release on parole is permitted, however, for those who pass the credible fear test, in the discretion of the director of the appropriate DHS field office. *See* 62 Fed. Reg. 10312, 10320 (1997) (supplemental information accompanying the main 1996 Act rulemaking).

Within seven days of finding a credible fear of persecution or torture, an ICE officer must interview the asylum seeker and assess her eligibility for parole using a standardized worksheet. DHS policy is that the interviewing officer should recommend for parole those persons whose identity is established, who do not pose a flight risk or a danger to the community, and who have no other risk factors weighing against release. Officials who do not recommend parole must explain their denial in writing. ICE Directive 11002.1, Parole of Arriving Aliens Found to Have a Credible Fear of Persecution or Torture (Dec. 8, 2009).

When DHS applied expedited removal procedures to the Central Americans arriving at the U.S. southern border in 2014, DHS began detaining mothers and children. DHS established a temporary facility, and expanded already existing facilities. The capacity for family detention increased from 100 beds to more than 3,000. Julia Preston, *Detention Center Presented as Deterrent to Border Crossings*, N.Y. Times, Dec. 15, 2014. As discussed further in Chapter Nine, Section B, these detention policies fueled controversy and have generated ongoing litigation.

(iv)   Administrative and Judicial Review

Noncitizens whose interviews with an asylum officer result in negative credible fear determinations may challenge the determination before an immigration judge in an oral procedure generally completed within 24 hours, and in all cases in no longer than seven days. INA § 235(b)(1)(B)(iii)(III). Those who pass the credible fear screening, either based on the asylum officer's interview or on review before the immigration judge, are referred for full hearing of their asylum claims in immigration court; they have access to the BIA and federal court for review if asylum is denied.

Noncitizens who are not referred by immigration inspectors for a credible fear interview have no right to appeal. As mentioned earlier, a high-ranking supervisor must review all files before an expedited removal order is issued. 8 C.F.R. § 235.3(b)(7).

NOTES AND QUESTIONS ON EXPEDITED REMOVAL

1.   Critics suggest that the expedited removal is constitutionally infirm because arriving aliens are turned away by an immigration officer without a hearing in immigration court. We will defer discussion of this issue to Section C below, which presents the constitutional framework for admissions decisions. Whether or not constitutionally mandated, should there be judicial review of expedited removal orders? Could the procedure remain truly expedited if judicial review were involved?

2.   What is your assessment of the expansions of expedited removal beyond ports of entry? Is there a stronger case for applying summary procedures to persons who attempt to enter clandestinely than to arriving aliens who are, after all, presenting themselves for inspection in the regular setting at the border? What are the advantages and disadvantages in each setting?

What additional risks of misapplication arise when expedited removal is expanded beyond ports of entry? Beyond the immediate vicinity of the border? Consider, in this regard, reports that Border Patrol agents routinely board trains between New York and Chicago and ask passengers to produce immigration papers and identification. See NYCLU & NYU Immigrant Rights Clinic, *Justice Derailed: What Raids on New York's Trains and Buses Reveal about Border Patrol Interior Enforcement Practices*, Nov. 2011. *See also* Dina Kleyman, *Protecting the Border, One Passenger Interrogation At a Time,* 77 Brooklyn L. Rev. 1557 (2012) .

3.   Turning to those who are fleeing persecution, there are four levels of screening for asylum seekers in the expedited removal process: initial inspection (by an immigration officer), secondary inspection, asylum officer, immigration judge. Do these furnish sufficient safeguards for asylum seekers? If not, what additional procedures would you recommend? In what

ways would those additional safeguards reduce errors and how much would they cost, both in terms of efficiency and in financial terms?

4.   A 2005 report by the U.S. Commission on International Religious Freedom (CIRF), a bipartisan independent government body, found significant implementation deficiencies by DHS field offices (such as failures to provide all required advisories or to refer cases to an asylum officer when the person mentioned a fear of return), prompting calls for the abolition of expedited removal. CIRF offered several recommendations intended to assure more consistent implementation of existing regulations and guidance and to facilitate monitoring by managers, so as to detect and correct departures from policy.

The CIRF Report also noted that only a small percentage of arriving noncitizens who are referred to asylum officers are found to lack a credible fear. Do you think this suggests that individuals who mention fear to an inspector at the border should go straight to a full removal hearing in immigration court, bypassing the credible fear screening? That the expedited removal legislation should be amended to delete the credible fear screening and instead require a removal hearing for all who say they fear persecution? Or does the very presence of credible fear screening, even with a low formal screen-out rate, provide a deterrent to ill-founded or fraudulent claims—the original concern that led Congress to adopt expedited removal in the first place.

5.   The U.S. Commission on Immigration Reform concluded in the late 1990s that expedited removal should apply only during migration emergencies, as had been proposed in some earlier versions of the 1996 legislation, and urged Congress to amend the law accordingly. Though the Commission criticized the credible fear screening as an inappropriate standard for deciding who will have access to the full procedure, the Commission stated that the current credible fear procedure is an appropriate standard for deciding which asylum seekers should be released during the pendency of full-fledged immigration court proceedings. Continued confinement of those who could not show credible fear would provide a justifiable deterrent against future abuse of the asylum system. U.S. Commission on Immigration Reform, U.S. Refugee Policy: Taking Leadership 30–32 (1998). Do you agree with this assessment?

EXERCISE: EXPEDITED REMOVAL

Chen was apprehended by Border Patrol officers while hiding in a remote area on the beach at the eastern end of Long Island, New York. He admits that he is a Chinese national. He has no identification or travel documents. Chen has refused to talk about how he arrived in the United States, but he was discovered two weeks after a freighter ran aground on a sandbar around 1:45 AM several hundred yards offshore, about a half-mile from where Chen was found. About 300 Chinese nationals tried to swim ashore. Most made it, but a few drowned in the choppy waters. Of those who reached shore, almost all were apprehended within several hours, but a few remain unaccounted for. Chen has only a small satchel of clothes and a bedroll with him. He seems to have been surviving by scavenging food from dumpsters behind nearby restaurants.

You are a DHS attorney and have been asked by your supervisor to analyze whether it is lawful to put Chen into expedited removal proceedings. Your supervisor charges you to consult INA § 235(b)(1)(A)(iii) and the notices that Attorney General Ashcroft and DHS published in the Federal Register concerning the circumstances in which expedited removal can apply. For the purposes of this analysis, do not address constitutional issues.

B. NATIONAL SECURITY AND SCREENING SYSTEMS

One of the many consequences of the September 11, 2001 terrorist attacks, and more recently the 2015 terror assaults in Paris and the December 2015 mass shootings in San Bernardino, California, has been much closer scrutiny of both nonimmigrant and immigrant visa applications. National security concerns surface in many facets of immigration law. The Supreme Court's 2015 *Kerry v. Din* opinion, discussed in the prior section, began when the husband of a U.S. citizen was denied an immigrant visa on unspecified terrorism and national security grounds. More recently, governors of many states have voiced concerns that terrorists might slip into the United States through the refugee resettlement process. Ashley Frantz & Ben Brumfield, *More Than Half the Nation's Governors Say Syrian Refugees Not Welcome*, CNN News, Nov. 19, 2015. Representatives in Congress have raised national security alarms concerning the visa-free travel program. Kristina Peterson, *Visa Waiver Program Gets Scrutiny*, Wall St. J., Nov. 29, 2015. The San Bernardino assailant who entered the United States as the fiancée of a U.S. citizen has prompted heightened concerns about other visa programs. *See, e.g.*, Julia Preston, *Legislator Questions San Bernardino Suspect's Visa*, N.Y. Times, Dec. 19, 2015, at A3.

Greater scrutiny has heightened the inherent tension between national security and the expeditious processing of immigration-related applications. Moreover, the sheer magnitude of the many security-related tasks facing the government necessarily requires choices about law-enforcement priorities, and such selective enforcement can raise discrimination issues. Not surprisingly, some of the enhanced national security measures triggered sharp controversy.

The major post-2001 statutory and regulatory initiatives to enhance the government's capacity to keep out dangerous individuals or to locate dangerous persons already in the United States built on systems already in place.

1. ENTRY-EXIT CONTROLS

Congress first called for the development of a comprehensive entry-exit control system in the 1996 Act. Early plans for this system sparked strong opposition from border communities on both sides of the frontiers (particularly in Canada), which feared a damaging impact on cross-border trade and tourism, and opponents won modifications of the mandate and a stretch-out of the timetable. *See President Signs Entry/Exit Control Legislation*, 77 Interp. Rel. 828 (2000). But the September 11 attacks renewed interest and led to several pieces of new legislation imposing new requirements and stronger deadlines. DHS deployed the first major components of the permanent system, known as US-VISIT (Visitor and Immigrant Status Indicator Technology), in international airports in 2003. Its originally stated objective was "to create an integrated, automated entry and exit system * * * that records the arrival and departure of aliens; verifies the identities of aliens; and authenticates travel documents presented by such aliens through the comparison of biometric identifiers." 69 Fed. Reg. 53318 (2004) (also describing the statutory provisions governing the system).

The early focus of US-VISIT was on entry processing, to capture biometric information (photo and fingerprints) on noncitizens who are admitted, so as to facilitate checking that information against coordinated databases, and, for persons entering on visas, to use the biometrics to verify that the person presenting the visa is the same individual to whom it was issued. Noncitizens at the primary inspection booth are photographed, and they also place their fingers on an electronic reader which both makes a permanent record of the prints and also compares identity against information contained in the visa. Since October 2004 the Department of State has issued only machine-readable visas with encoded biometric information that can be readily compared in this fashion.

Certain categories, including individuals traveling on diplomatic visas, children under 14, and travelers over 79, are exempt from the US-VISIT screening. Furthermore, universal use of the fingerprinting process would present logistical complications at land borders. Partially in response, most Canadian nationals are not required to be fingerprinted, and Mexican nationals using "laser visas" as a Border Crossing Card (BCC), discussed earlier in this chapter, are also exempt. Mexicans using a BCC to travel beyond the border zone, however, are supposed to be processed through the biometric entry system. And most persons referred to secondary inspection at the land borders are likewise fingerprinted and photographed.

DHS completed deployment of this entry system in international airports in 2004, and in all fixed port-of-entry facilities by the end of 2005. Biometric exit systems have presented immense logistical and financial challenges, and there are questions as to whether a full exit system is cost effective. The report excerpted below summarizes key points.

ENTRY-EXIT SYSTEM:
PROGRESS, CHALLENGES, AND OUTLOOK

Immigration Task Force, Bipartisan Policy Center 3–5 (May 2014).

* * *

About 40 percent of unauthorized immigrants entered the country legally but remained after their legal status expired. Entry-exit systems were originally conceived as a tool to identify overstays—in other words, to track when foreign nationals enter the country and whether they leave in accordance with the terms of their admission. A complete entry-exit system would track all arrivals and departures at all land, air, and sea ports of entry (POE).

Over the past 18 years, Congress passed several laws requiring the implementation of an entry-exit system that does not inhibit the free flow of legitimate commerce and travel. After the events of September 11, 2001, an entry-exit system was also viewed as a national security asset. In response, Congress added biometric identifiers (such as fingerprints) to the statutory requirements, in addition to previously-required biographic identifiers (such as names and birthdates).

PROGRESS

The entry capability is fully deployed. Historically, millions of travelers admitted to the United States each year were not subject to any sort of document check; today, Customs and Border Protection (CBP) screens 100 percent of entering travelers. Nearly all noncitizens entering at air and sea ports are now subject to ten-fingerprint biometric enrollment. At land borders, CBP collects biometrics from nearly all foreigners who are not from Canada or Mexico.

The exit capability is not complete. Exit systems are more challenging because the United States did not construct its land, air, or sea POE infrastructure with departure inspections in mind. DHS operates a complete biographic system in the air and sea environments, and through a new data-exchange partnership with Canada, collects biographic exit data on the northern land border. At the southern land border, no systematic or mandatory exit collection exists. This is a large gap, as about 45 percent of all entry inspections—land, air, or sea—occur at the southern land border.

CHALLENGES

Significant challenges stand in the way of completing the exit system, particularly for vehicles exiting at land borders. Insufficient space on the U.S. side of the border precludes construction of an exit infrastructure that would be similar to the entry process at most POEs. Factor in personnel costs and logistical constraints, as well as the impact on travel and commerce, and it quickly becomes clear that a "mirror" infrastructure is impractical for tracking travelers who exit the country by land. DHS is working to establish a data-sharing partnership with Mexico similar to the current partnership with Canada. Unlike Canada, however, Mexico does not collect data on all inbound travelers or have the infrastructure to do so. Other possible methods of completing the land exit system face compliance concerns and appear vulnerable to fraud.

At airports, seaports, and land pedestrian crossings, the necessary technology is available and a biometric solution appears within reach. However, only real-world testing can prove a solution's viability. Previous DHS pilots provided valuable information, but matches based on the biometric data collected were *less* accurate than what DHS currently achieves with biographic data. DHS is currently engaged in another round of technical and logistical assessments * * * .

IMPLICATIONS

Improvements to law enforcement ultimately determine an entry-exit system's value for both immigration and national security purposes. Because the entry capability is complete, analysis of the potential benefits focus on completing the exit system, including the value of biographic versus biometric data.

With respect to immigration, exit data would make some enforcement practices more efficient. Notably, however, exit records would provide little benefit for the removal of current overstays encountered through routine contact with law enforcement—the dominant mechanism by which unauthorized immigrants are currently located and removed. Law enforcement officers do not need exit records to determine whether an individual in custody has exited the United States. The potential benefits of an exit system for immigration enforcement break down as follows:

Statistical Purposes. An entry-exit system can generate statistics that help the government determine the effectiveness of its enforcement efforts, the size of the overstay population, and country eligibility for special admission programs like the Visa Waiver Program. Biographic data would be sufficient for these purposes

Denial of Admission or Visas. The ability of DHS and the U.S. Department of State (DOS) to deny admission or visas to people who overstayed in the past would improve. Biometrics would enhance this capability by increasing confidence in these denials.

More Efficient Enforcement. A complete exit system would reduce the need to pursue leads for individuals who already departed or adjusted status. Compared to biographic capability, biometrics would add a modest amount of additional efficiency through more accurate matches.

Additional Interior Enforcement. In theory, DHS could use an accurate overstay identification capability as part of stepped-up interior enforcement. However, although exit records would indicate that individuals had not left the country, they would not help law enforcement locate the individual, nor would they ensure the substantial increase in enforcement resources that such a strategy would require.

For criminals and terrorists, the entry capability is most important because it enables the Department of State (DOS) and CBP to ensure that known dangerous individuals never enter the country in the first place. Depending on the accompanying immigration enforcement strategy, exit capability would also enable DHS to sweep up some dangerous individuals whose malicious intent is not known at the time of entry. The major potential benefit of exit records is information about whether a dangerous criminal or terrorist has left the country. In order for this information to be trustworthy, however, confidence in it would have to be extraordinarily high—if the system was too susceptible to fraud, criminals could disguise their presence in the country by creating a false record of exit.

Based on our review of the entry-exit system's current state of implementation, challenges, and options for moving forward, several key observations can be made:

- Biometric identifiers have greater potential for accuracy than biographic, but this benefit has not been proven in real-world settings. Additional testing and piloting will be needed to prove capability.

- Exit records offer little value for overstays who come into contact with law enforcement—the dominant way unauthorized immigrants are currently identified and removed. The key benefits of exit records would be to (1) enable the government to deny future visas or admission on the basis of past overstays and (2) improve the efficiency of enforcement by reducing the number of dead-end overstay investigations for individuals who already left the country. A biographic system could provide the bulk of these benefits.

- The southern land border presents a significant barrier to completing the exit system. These challenges will be difficult to overcome in the near- or medium-term.

- If DHS were to implement a biometric exit system before all logistical and technical questions are answered, it would be unlikely to provide the full benefits it is designed to achieve.

* * *

———————

In 2013 Customs and Border Patrol (CBP) became responsible for the collection of biographic and biometric entry and exit data. Immigration and Customs Enforcement (ICE) assumed responsibility for identifying overstays, and a new DHS Office of Biometric Identity Management (OPIM) took over the other US-VISIT operations. Immigration Task Force, *Entry-Exit System: Progress, Challenges, and Outlook*, Bipartisan Policy Center 5 (May 2014). In January 2016 ICE issued a long awaited report on noncitizens who overstay their visas. Ron Nixon, *Few Foreign Visitors to U.S. Overstay Visa, Federal Report Says*, N.Y. Times, Jan. 21, 2016, at A18. Based on records of the 45 million noncitizens who had entered the United States as visitors for business or pleasure via air or sea port of entry in FY 2015, ICE concluded that 1.17 percent (527,000) appeared to have overstayed. DHS, Entry/Exit Overstay Report: FY 2015 (Jan. 19, 2016). Concerns about monitoring noncitizens in the United States remained strong, and Congress scheduled hearings on these issues in January 2016. *Why Is the Biometric Exit Tracking System Still Not in Place?* Hearing before the Subcomm. on Immigration and the National Interest of the Senate Comm. on the Judiciary. 114th Cong., 2nd Sess. (2016).

2. STUDENT MONITORING: SEVIS

Another initiative finalized since 2001 is the Student and Exchange Visitor Information System (SEVIS), meant to monitor students and exchange visitors in the F, J, and M categories from the time they receive their documentation to study until they graduate or leave school. It is an internet-based system overseen by ICE that allows for quick transmission of relevant information to and from schools where the student is registered (such as the student's arrival and enrollment, graduation or other departure, or signing up for an insufficient number of courses). The SEVIS rules impose extensive reporting requirements on schools and also require the use of SEVIS communications in connection with visa issuance. *See* 22 C.F.R. §§ 41.61–41.62; 8 C.F.R. §§ 214.2(f) and (j)). The

SEVIS fee for students is $200, as of early 2016; the fee for most exchange visitors is $180.

The 1996 Act had required a student tracking system, partly in response to the discovery that one of the 1993 bombers at the World Trade Center had been admitted as an F–1 student. *See* Pub. L. 104–208, § 641, 110 Stat. 3009. Resistance from universities and colleges staved off implementation, but that resistance dissolved after the September 11 attacks. *See House Subcommittees Mull Need for Closer Monitoring of Student Visas*, 78 Interp. Rel. 1710 (2001). Congress responded by requiring full implementation of SEVIS, as well as an interim version in the meantime. *See* Enhanced Border Security and Visa Entry Reform Act, §§ 501, 502, Pub. L. 107–173, 116 Stat. 434 (2002); USA PATRIOT Act § 416, Pub. L. 107–56, 115 Stat. 354–55 (2001); 67 Fed. Reg. 76256 (2002) (final regulation). For more information about implementation and improvements to the SEVIS system, see, e.g., *ICE Addresses Designated School Officials' "Anxieties, Concerns, and Misconceptions" Regarding SEVIS II,* 88 Interp. Rel. 1376 (2011).

3. DATABASES AND SCREENING SYSTEMS

For several decades the immigration agencies have relied on lookout systems meant to flag cases of potentially dangerous or otherwise ineligible individuals, but different agencies maintained their own separate systems and tended to share information only on a limited basis. After the 9/11 attacks, Congress enacted several statutes calling for greatly improved sharing of information among U.S. agencies, the development of interoperable systems to facilitate such sharing, and the consolidation of databases in many circumstances. Meanwhile, it mandated completion of specified checks before most types of immigration benefits could be granted. In part to fulfill these requirements, USCIS operates a system of Application Support Centers throughout the country. Their primary function is to provide a venue for accurate taking of digital fingerprints and photographs, after a reliable identity check, of persons who are applying or have been preliminarily approved for immigration benefits. The ASCs replaced an earlier system that relied largely on manual fingerprint cards prepared by local law enforcement agencies. Those arrangements frequently resulted in the federal screener's receipt of inadequate images, and it was vulnerable to identity fraud.

The post 9/11 screening requirements initially outstripped the capacities of the implementing agencies, particularly the FBI, and immigration checks often fell to a low priority for completion. Thousands of cases languished for a year, and hundreds for multiple years. The delays often triggered lawsuits seeking a court order simply requiring the agency to make a decision on the benefit.

Those systems that were fingerprint-based were better able to adjust to the new demands because biometrics can connect the subject with high accuracy to any derogatory information. But most of the lookout systems have been name check systems (which usually use both name and date of birth), and they are far less exact. Because names written in foreign alphabets or scripts can be transliterated in different ways, because many people might have the same name and date of birth, and because other inaccuracies can exist, such systems check for name variations and often also use a range of dates near the stated birth date. An apparent match—a "hit"—thus does not necessarily mean that the noncitizen is disqualified. Further manual investigation is required to establish whether this applicant is the same person as the one in the database, and perhaps also to decide whether the negative information makes the person legally inadmissible.

By 2011, real progress had been made in staffing the screening systems, improving the technological systems, and assuring better sharing of information, though additional resources and further improvements are needed. For useful summaries, see DHS Office of Inspector General, Information Sharing on Foreign Nationals: Overseas Screening (OIG–11–68, April 2011) [hereafter "Overseas Screening"]; Department of Justice, Office of the Inspector General, Follow-Up Audit of the Terrorist Screening Center i, v (Audit Report 07–41, Sept. 2007). For an examination of database screening and digital watchlist systems, including the Terrorist Watchlist and the No Fly List, *see* Margaret Hu, *Big Data Blacklisting*, 67 Fla. L. Rev. 1735 (2015).

4. REGULAR AND SPECIAL REGISTRATION

The INA requires all noncitizens in the United States for more than 30 days to be registered and fingerprinted, but permits waiver of some of the requirements. INA §§ 261–266. A comprehensive federal alien registration system of this sort was first adopted in 1940, spurred by concerns about security risks as World War II broke out in Europe. *See Hines v. Davidowitz,* 312 U.S. 52, 61 S.Ct. 399, 85 L.Ed. 581 (1941) (striking down a state alien registration scheme because pre-empted by the federal law). Because of workload concerns, by the 1980s INS had adopted regulations and notices waiving most nonimmigrant fingerprinting requirements and counting the normal processing documents, particularly the I–94 form and the alien registration receipt card (green card) carried by permanent residents, as sufficient to comply with the registration mandate.

The INA also required an annual report of address by all noncitizens until 1982, but then replaced that provision with a requirement for them simply to report when they changed addresses. INA § 265. That requirement was widely ignored, but failures rarely triggered any follow up enforcement—until the new enforcement push generated by the September 11 attacks spurred sporadic use of such a charge against certain suspects. Possible penalties for noncompliance with the registration requirements can be severe. They include removal from the United States, a fine, and imprisonment. *See* INA §§ 237(a)(3)(A), 266.

In addition to the "regular registration" requirements, INA § 263 permits the Attorney General (now DHS) to require specified classes of noncitizens to submit to special registration and fingerprinting. In response to the September 11 attacks, Attorney General John Ashcroft deployed this authority with respect to both arriving aliens and persons already in the United States, by adopting a controversial program known as the National Security Entry-Exit Registration System, or NSEERS. Starting on September 11, 2002, the INS began requiring certain nonimmigrants from listed countries (and some nonimmigrants from other countries as well, identified by individual characteristics deemed to signal risk) who arrive at U.S. ports of entry to undergo "special registration" under NSEERS. They were photographed, fingerprinted, and subjected to a more intensive interview under oath about their background and the purpose and itinerary of their visit to the United States. They were then obligated to report to INS after 30 days and thereafter annually, and to report changes of address, employment, or educational institution (as applicable) within ten days of a change. When departing the United States, they were required to appear personally before an immigration officer at designated ports of entry. *See* 67 Fed. Reg. 52584 (2002); 79 Interp. Rel. 899 (2002).

Over the next several months the list of designated countries grew to 25, all predominantly Muslim except for North Korea. Furthermore, a significant number of arriving aliens from *other* countries were also subject to special registration, according to individualized criteria set out in an INS memorandum. *See* 79 Interp. Rel. 1481 (2002). These criteria include, among other things, whether the noncitizen has made unexplained trips to any of several listed countries, whether he had previously overstayed an authorized period of admission, or whether "the nonimmigrant alien's behavior, demeanor, or answers indicate that alien should be monitored in the interest of national security." *Id.*

In November 2002, the INS expanded its NSEERS special registration program to reach individuals inside the United States through what is sometimes termed "call-in registration." Male nationals of the designated 25 countries, who were at least 16 years of age and were admitted to the United States as nonimmigrants before special registration took effect at ports of entry, had a six-week window (later extended in some cases) to report to a designated government office to be photographed, fingerprinted, and interviewed under oath. Failure to comply was deemed a failure to maintain nonimmigrant status and thus a deportability ground under INA § 237(a)(1)(C)(i), as well as a criminal violation under § 266. This program raised issues regarding the use of nationality, ethnicity, religion, and race in immigration enforcement, which we consider from constitutional and policy perspectives in Chapter Ten, Section B.

In December 2003, DHS announced a major scaling back of the special registration, while retaining authority to impose new programs as needed. The call-in portion ended, and persons in the program no longer had to report after 30 days or annually. Instead they would be notified individually whenever additional reporting was required. *See Special Registration to End, be Replaced by Upcoming 'U.S. VISIT' Monitoring Program for All Visitors,* 80 Interp. Rel. 690 (2003).

In April 2011, DHS formally terminated the NSEERS registration requirements. The Department explained that US-VISIT and other automated screening systems developed since 2002 now provide sufficient information to meet security objectives without the need to impose burdensome requirements on whole categories of nonimmigrant travelers. 76 Fed. Reg. 23830 (2011).

NOTES AND QUESTIONS ON NATIONAL SECURITY AND SCREENING SYSTEMS

1.   After the September 11, 2001 terrorist attacks, top-level officials quickly became aware of the negative effects of inefficient processing or security procedures that are seen as inhospitable. Worried that such situations create diplomatic ill will or damage the competitiveness of U.S. businesses or universities, Secretary of State Condoleeza Rice and Secretary of Homeland Security Michael Chertoff announced broad new steps in 2006 to facilitate travel while honoring security needs. *See Rice-Chertoff Joint Conference on Secure Borders and "Open Doors,"* 83 Interp. Rel. 161 (2006). The number of student visas has continued to increase steadily, with 295,000 new F student visas issued in 2006, 410,000 in 2010, 565,000 in 2013, and 625,000 in 2014. *See* DOS Visa Office Report 2010, table XVI(A); DOS Visa Office Report 2015, table XVI(A).

The number of student visa admissions at ports of entry has also expanded significantly each year. (Recall from Chapter Five that many visas are valid for multiple entries and for multiple years.) DHS reported that 740,000 individuals were admitted on F visas in 2006; 840,000 in 2007; 940,000 in 2008; 950,000 in 2009; and 1,595,000—an increase of 600,000 over the prior year—in 2010. *See* DHS Yearbook 2010, table 25. From 2011 through 2013, the most recent data available when we went to press, DHS recorded more than 1,500,000 F-vis admissions per year. Katie Foreman & Randall Monger, *Nonimmigrant Admissions to the United States: 2013*, DHS Office of Immigration Statistics, table 1.

2.   The NSEERS special registration program generated controversy, with some critics particularly troubled that all of the designated countries, with the sole exception of North Korea, had predominantly Muslim populations. Others protested that many nonimmigrants within the United States were arrested for immigration status violations after appearing promptly for the "call-in registration." Supporters noted that the September 11 attacks by individuals with nonimmigrant visas highlighted the importance of keeping track of noncitizens. They emphasized that special registration procedures at the border also applied to individuals from many non-Muslim countries. How would you weigh the various arguments concerning NSEERS registration? What additional facts would be important to know in order to evaluate the program? We will revisit the NSEERS program and examine challenges to the use of race and ethnicity in enforcement in Chapter Ten, Section B.

C. THE CONSTITUTIONAL REQUIREMENT OF DUE PROCESS

We turn now to the constitutional framework. Under the Due Process Clause of the Fifth Amendment, the government must use fair procedures when a person may be "deprived of life, liberty or property." Early in the twentieth century the Supreme Court faced a due process challenge from a Japanese citizen who had arrived in Seattle. *Yamataya v. Fisher (The Japanese Immigrant Case)*, 189 U.S. 86, 23 S.Ct. 611, 47 L.Ed. 721 (1903). Kaoru Yamataya was a 16-year old girl sent by her parents to the United States for education. Four days after Yamataya landed, an immigration officer ruled that she was deportable because she had been excludable at entry as a pauper and as likely to become a public charge. Her uncle, Masataro Yamataya, who lived in the United States, filed a habeas corpus petition on her behalf. The petition contended that Kaoru Yamataya's hearing was inadequate because she did not understand English, was not provided an opportunity to contest her deportability, and was not assisted by counsel. Justice Harlan spoke for the court:

Ps arg for inadeq. process

> * * * That Congress may exclude aliens of a particular race from the United States; prescribe the terms and conditions upon which certain classes of aliens may come to this country; establish regulations for sending out of the country such aliens as come here in violation of law; and commit the enforcement of such provisions, conditions and regulations exclusively to executive officers, without judicial intervention, are principles firmly established by the decisions of this court.

congressional power

* * *

Leaving on one side the question whether an alien can rightfully invoke the due process clause of the Constitution who has entered the country clandestinely, and who has been here for too brief a period to have become, in any real sense, a part of our population, before his right to remain is disputed, we have to say that the rigid construction of the acts of Congress suggested by the [government] are not justified. Those acts do not necessarily exclude opportunity to the immigrant to be heard, when such opportunity is of right. * * *

* * *

* * * [T]his court has never held, nor must we now be understood as holding, that administrative officers, when executing the provisions of a statute involving the liberty of persons, may disregard the fundamental principles that inhere in "due process of law" as understood at the time of the adoption of the Constitution. One of these principles is that no person shall be deprived of his liberty without opportunity, at some time, to be heard, before such officers, in respect of the matters upon which that liberty depends—not necessarily an opportunity upon a regular, set occasion, and according to the forms of judicial procedure, but one that will secure the prompt, vigorous action contemplated by Congress, and at the same time be appropriate to the nature of the case upon which such officers are required to act. Therefore, it is not competent for * * * any executive officer * * * arbitrarily to cause an alien, who has entered the country, and has become subject in all respects to its jurisdiction, and a part of its population, although alleged to be illegally here, to be taken into custody and deported without giving him all opportunity to be heard upon the questions involving his right to be and remain in the United States. No such arbitrary power can exist where the principles involved in due process of law are recognized.

This is the reasonable construction of the acts of Congress here in question, and they need not be otherwise interpreted. * * *

Id. at 97, 100–101.

Procedural due process cases pose two distinct questions. First, does the due process clause apply? And if so, what process was due (or fair) for that decision? Though *Yamataya* stands for the general principle that the due process clause applies to deportation procedures—at least for lawfully admitted noncitizens—the Court went on to uphold her deportation, even though she had had no formal hearing, alleged that she could neither speak nor understand English, and claimed that she was unaware of the nature of the proceedings.

In the mid-twentieth century, the Supreme Court again examined the reach and mandate of the Due Process Clause in immigration cases. When government officials inspected noncitizens at U.S. borders to the United States, would refusing admission to a foreign national be a deprivation of life, liberty, or property? In *United States ex rel. Knauff v. Shaughnessy*, 338 U.S. 537, 544, 70 S.Ct. 309, 313, 94 L.Ed. 317 (1950), Ellen Knauff sought admission under the War Brides Act of 1945, Pub. L. 79–271, 59 Stat. 659, which gave preferential immigration status (and in turn, naturalization eligibility) to the foreign spouses and children of U.S. World War II veterans. Knauff, however, was turned away without a hearing, based a regulation that provided, as the Court described it, "that the Attorney General might deny an alien a hearing * * * where he determined that the alien was excludable under the regulations on the basis of information of a confidential nature, the disclosure of which would be prejudicial to the public interest." *Id.* at 541.

The Supreme Court rejected the constitutional challenge brought by Knauff, then detained at Ellis Island, to the lack of an opportunity to hear and rebut negative information about her.

> At the outset we wish to point out that an alien who seeks admission to this country may not do so under any claim of right. Admission of aliens to the United States is a privilege granted by the sovereign United States Government. Such privilege is granted to an alien only upon such terms as the United States shall prescribe.

Id. at 542. Justice Minton continued:

> [B]ecause the power of exclusion of aliens is also inherent in the executive department of the sovereign, Congress may in broad terms authorize the executive to exercise the power, e.g., as was done here, for the best interests of the country during a time of national emergency. Executive officers may be entrusted with the duty of specifying the procedures for carrying out the congressional intent. Whatever the procedure authorized by Congress is, it is due process as far as an alien denied entry is concerned.

Id. at 544.

Several years later, in *Kwong Hai Chew v. Colding*, 344 U.S. 590, 73 S.Ct. 472, 97 L.Ed. 576 (1953), the Supreme Court ruled that a Chinese seaman who had married a U.S. citizen and become a permanent resident could not be detained and excluded from the United States without a hearing upon his return to the United States from a voyage working on a U.S-flag merchant ship. The government invoked the same regulation that it had used in *Knauff* to issue an exclusion order without a hearing.

Chew argued that his detention and exclusion were not authorized by that regulation, or if so, were unconstitutional.

> The case of *Knauff v. Shaughnessy*, relied upon below, is not in point. It relates to the rights of an alien entrant and does not deal with the question of a resident alien's right to be heard. For purposes of his constitutional right to due process, we assimilate petitioner's status to that of an alien continuously residing and physically present in the United States.

> It is well established that if an alien is a lawful permanent resident of the United States and remains physically present there, he is a person within the protection of the Fifth Amendment. He may not be deprived of his life, liberty or property without due process of law. * * *

>   * * *

> Petitioner's * * * contention is that if an alien is a lawful permanent resident of the United States and also is a seaman who has gone outside of the United States on a vessel of American registry, with its home port in the United States, and, upon completion of such voyage, has returned on such vessel to the United States and is still on board, he is still, from a constitutional point of view, a person entitled to procedural due process under the Fifth Amendment. We do not regard the constitutional status which petitioner indisputably enjoyed prior to his voyage as terminated by that voyage. From a constitutional point of view, he is entitled to due process without regard to whether or not, for immigration purposes, he is to be treated as an entrant alien, and we do not now reach the question whether he is to be so treated.

> Section 175.57(b)'s authorization of the denial of hearings raises no constitutional conflict if limited to 'excludable' aliens who are not within the protection of the Fifth Amendment. * * *

>   * * *

> [W]e conclude that the detention of petitioner, without notice of the charges against him and without opportunity to be heard in opposition to them, is not authorized by [the regulation].

Id. at 596–603.

One month after *Chew* appeared to ameliorate the harshness of *Knauff*, the Supreme Court returned to the applicability of the Due Process Clause to noncitizens at the border.

SHAUGHNESSY V. UNITED STATES EX REL. MEZEI

Supreme Court of the United States, 1953.
345 U.S. 206, 73 S.Ct. 625, 97 L.Ed. 956.

MR. JUSTICE CLARK delivered the opinion of the Court.

This case concerns an alien immigrant permanently excluded from the United States on security grounds but stranded in his temporary haven on Ellis Island because other countries will not take him back. [The trial court had concluded that the government's continued exclusion of Mezei without a hearing amounted to an unlawful detention, and allowed him to enter the United States temporarily after posting a bond.]

Respondent's present dilemma springs from these circumstances: Though, as the District Court observed, "[t]here is a certain vagueness about [his] history," respondent seemingly was born in Gibraltar of Hungarian or Rumanian parents and lived in the United States from 1923 to 1948. In May of that year he sailed for Europe, apparently to visit his dying mother in Rumania. Denied entry there, he remained in Hungary for some 19 months, due to "difficulty in securing an exit permit." Finally, armed with a quota immigration visa issued by the American Consul in Budapest, he proceeded to France and boarded the *Ile de France* in Le Havre bound for New York. Upon arrival on February 9, 1950, he was temporarily excluded from the United States by an immigration inspector acting pursuant to the Passport Act as amended and regulations thereunder. [The same statute and regulations at issue in the *Knauff* and *Chew* cases applied in *Mezei*.]

Pending disposition of his case he was received at Ellis Island. After reviewing the evidence, the Attorney General on May 10, 1950, ordered the temporary exclusion to be made permanent without a hearing before a board of special inquiry, on the "basis of information of a confidential nature, the disclosure of which would be prejudicial to the public interest." That determination rested on a finding that respondent's entry would be prejudicial to the public interest for security reasons. But thus far all attempts to effect respondent's departure have failed: Twice he shipped out to return whence he came; France and Great Britain refused him permission to land. The State Department has unsuccessfully negotiated with Hungary for his readmission. Respondent personally applied for entry to about a dozen Latin American countries but all turned him down. So in June 1951 respondent advised the Immigration and Naturalization Service that he would exert no further efforts to depart. In short, respondent sat on Ellis Island because this country shut him out and others were unwilling to take him in.

Asserting unlawful confinement on Ellis Island, he sought relief through a series of habeas corpus proceedings. After four unsuccessful efforts on respondent's part, the United States District Court for the

Southern District of New York on November 9, 1951, sustained the writ. The District Judge, vexed by the problem of "an alien who has no place to go," did not question the validity of the exclusion order but deemed further "detention" after 21 months excessive and justifiable only by affirmative proof of respondent's danger to the public safety. When the Government declined to divulge such evidence, even *in camera*, the District Court directed respondent's conditional parole on bond. By a divided vote, the Court of Appeals affirmed. Postulating that the power to hold could never be broader than the power to remove or shut out and that to "continue an alien's confinement beyond that moment when deportation becomes patently impossible is to deprive him of his liberty," the court found respondent's "confinement" no longer justifiable as a means of removal elsewhere, thus not authorized by statute, and in violation of due process. Judge Learned Hand, dissenting, took a different view: The Attorney General's order was one of "exclusion" and not "deportation"; respondent's transfer from ship to shore on Ellis Island conferred no additional rights; in fact, no alien so situated "can force us to admit him at all."

* * *

It is true that aliens who have once passed through our gates, even illegally, may be expelled only after proceedings conforming to traditional standards of fairness encompassed in due process of law. *The Japanese Immigrant Case (Kaoru Yamataya v. Fisher)*, 1903, 189 U.S. 86, 100–101, 23 S.Ct. 611, 614, 47 L.Ed. 721; *Wong Yang Sung v. McGrath*, 1950, 339 U.S. 33, 49–50, 70 S.Ct. 445, 453–454, 94 L.Ed. 616; *Kwong Hai Chew v. Colding*, 1953, 344 U.S. 590, 598, 73 S.Ct. 472, 478. But an alien on the threshold of initial entry stands on a different footing: "Whatever the procedure authorized by Congress is, it is due process as far as an alien denied entry is concerned." *United States ex rel. Knauff v. Shaughnessy, supra.* And because the action of the executive officer under such authority is final and conclusive, the Attorney General cannot be compelled to disclose the evidence underlying his determinations in an exclusion case; "it is not within the province of any court, unless expressly authorized by law, to review the determination of the political branch of the Government." *United States ex rel. Knauff v. Shaughnessy.* In a case such as this, courts cannot retry the determination of the Attorney General.

Neither respondent's harborage on Ellis Island nor his prior residence here transforms this into something other than an exclusion proceeding. Concededly, his movements are restrained by authority of the United States, and he may by habeas corpus test the validity of his exclusion. But that is true whether he enjoys temporary refuge on land, or remains continuously aboard ship. In sum, harborage at Ellis Island is not an entry into the United States. For purposes of the immigration laws, moreover, the legal incidents of an alien's entry remain unaltered whether he has been here once before or not. He is an entering alien just the same, and may be excluded if unqualified for admission under existing immigration laws.

To be sure, a lawful resident alien may not captiously be deprived of his constitutional rights to procedural due process. *Kwong Hai Chew v. Colding*, 1953, 344 U.S. 590, 601, 73 S.Ct. 472, 479; *cf. Delgadillo v. Carmichael*, 1947, 332 U.S. 388, 68 S.Ct. 10, 92 L.Ed. 17. Only the other day we held that under some circumstances temporary absence from our shores cannot constitutionally deprive a returning lawfully resident alien of his right to be heard. *Kwong Hai Chew v. Colding, supra.* Chew, an alien seaman admitted by an Act of Congress to permanent residence in the United States, signed articles of maritime employment as chief steward on a vessel of American registry with home port in New York City. Though cleared by the Coast Guard for his voyage, on his return from four months at sea he was "excluded" without a hearing on security grounds. On the facts of that case, including reference to § 307(d)(2) of the Nationality Act of 1940, we felt justified in "assimilating" his status for constitutional purposes to that of continuously present alien residents entitled to hearings at least before an executive or administrative tribunal. Accordingly, to escape constitutional conflict we held the administrative regulations authorizing exclusion without hearing in certain security cases inapplicable to aliens so protected by the Fifth Amendment.

But respondent's history here drastically differs from that disclosed in Chew's case. Unlike Chew who with full security clearance and documentation pursued his vocation for four months aboard an American ship, respondent, apparently without authorization or reentry papers,[9] simply left the United States and remained behind the Iron Curtain for 19 months. Moreover, while § 307 of the 1940 Nationality Act regards maritime service such as Chew's to be continuous residence for naturalization purposes, that section deems protracted absence such as respondent's a clear break in an alien's continuous residence here. In such circumstances, we have no difficulty in holding respondent an entrant alien or "assimilated to [that] status" for constitutional purposes. That being so, the Attorney General may lawfully exclude respondent without a hearing as authorized by the emergency regulations promulgated pursuant to the Passport Act. Nor need he disclose the evidence upon which that determination rests. *United States ex rel. Knauff v. Shaughnessy*, 1950, 338 U.S. 537, 70 S.Ct. 309, 94 L.Ed. 317.

---

9 * * * Of course, neither a reentry permit, issuable upon proof of prior lawful admission to the United States, nor an immigration visa entitles an otherwise inadmissible alien to entry. An immigrant is not unaware of this; [the statute] directs those facts to be "printed conspicuously upon every immigration visa." * * *

There remains the issue of respondent's continued exclusion on Ellis Island. Aliens seeking entry from contiguous lands obviously can be turned back at the border without more. While the Government might keep entrants by sea aboard the vessel pending determination of their admissibility, resulting hardships to the alien and inconvenience to the carrier persuaded Congress to adopt a more generous course. By statute it authorized, in cases such as this, aliens' temporary removal from ship to shore. But such temporary harborage, an act of legislative grace, bestows no additional rights. Congress meticulously specified that such shelter ashore "shall not be considered a landing" nor relieve the vessel of the duty to transport back the alien if ultimately excluded. And this Court has long considered such temporary arrangements as not affecting an alien's status; he is treated as if stopped at the border.

Thus we do not think that respondent's continued exclusion deprives him of any statutory or constitutional right. It is true that resident aliens temporarily detained pending expeditious consummation of deportation proceedings may be released on bond by the Attorney General whose discretion is subject to judicial review. *Carlson v. Landon*, 1952, 342 U.S. 524, 72 S.Ct. 525, 96 L.Ed. 547. By that procedure aliens uprooted from our midst may rejoin the community until the Government effects their leave. An exclusion proceeding grounded on danger to the national security, however, presents different considerations; neither the rationale nor the statutory authority for such release exists. Ordinarily to admit an alien barred from entry on security grounds nullifies the very purpose of the exclusion proceeding; Congress in 1950 declined to include such authority in the statute. That exclusion by the United States plus other nations' inhospitality results in present hardship cannot be ignored. But, the times being what they are, Congress may well have felt that other countries ought not shift the onus to us; that an alien in respondent's position is no more ours than theirs. Whatever our individual estimate of that policy and the fears on which it rests, respondent's right to enter the United States depends on the congressional will, and courts cannot substitute their judgment for the legislative mandate.

Reversed.

MR. JUSTICE BLACK, with whom MR. JUSTICE DOUGLAS concurs, dissenting.

Mezei came to this country in 1923 and lived as a resident alien in Buffalo, New York, for twenty-five years. He made a trip to Europe in 1948 and was stopped at our shore on his return in 1950. Without charge of or conviction for any crime, he was for two years held a prisoner on Ellis Island by order of the Attorney General. Mezei sought habeas corpus in the District Court. He wanted to go to his wife and home in Buffalo. The Attorney General defended the imprisonment by alleging that it would be dangerous to the Nation's security to let Mezei go home even temporarily on bail. Asked for proof of this, the Attorney General answered the judge that all his information was "of a confidential nature" so much so that telling any of it or even telling the names of any of his secret informers would jeopardize the safety of the Nation. Finding that Mezei's life as a resident alien in Buffalo had been "unexceptional" and that no facts had been proven to justify his continued imprisonment, the District Court granted bail. The Court of Appeals approved. Now this Court orders Mezei to leave his home and go back to his island prison to stay indefinitely, maybe for life.

Mr. Justice Jackson forcefully points out the danger in the Court's holding that Mezei's liberty is completely at the mercy of the unreviewable discretion of the Attorney General. I join Mr. Justice Jackson in the belief that Mezei's continued imprisonment without a hearing violates due process of law.

* * *

MR. JUSTICE JACKSON, whom MR. JUSTICE FRANKFURTER joins, dissenting.

Fortunately it still is startling, in this country, to find a person held indefinitely in executive custody without accusation of crime or judicial trial. Executive imprisonment has been considered oppressive and lawless since John, at Runnymede, pledged that no free man should be imprisoned, dispossessed, outlawed, or exiled save by the judgment of his peers or by the law of the land. The judges of England developed the writ of habeas corpus largely to preserve these immunities from executive restraint.

Under the best tradition of Anglo-American law, courts will not deny hearing to an unconvicted prisoner just because he is an alien whose keep, in legal theory, is just outside our gates. Lord Mansfield, in the celebrated case holding that slavery was unknown to the common law of England, ran his writ of habeas corpus in favor of an alien, an African Negro slave, and against the master of a ship at anchor in the Thames.

I.

What is our case?[2] In contemplation of law, I agree, it is that of an alien who asks admission to the country. Concretely, however, it is that of a lawful and law-abiding inhabitant of our country for a quarter of a century, long ago admitted for permanent residence, who seeks to return home. After a foreign visit to his aged and ailing mother that was

---

[2] I recite facts alleged in the petition for the writ. Since the Government declined to try the case on the merits, I think we must consider the question on well-pleaded allegations of the petition. Petitioner might fail to make good on a hearing; the question is, must he fail without one?

prolonged by disturbed conditions of Eastern Europe, he obtained a visa for admission issued by our consul and returned to New York. There the Attorney General refused to honor his documents and turned him back as a menace to this Nation's security. This man, who seems to have led a life of unrelieved insignificance, must have been astonished to find himself suddenly putting the Government of the United States in such fear that it was afraid to tell him why it was afraid of him. He was shipped and reshipped to France, which twice refused him landing. Great Britain declined, and no other European country has been found willing to open its doors to him. Twelve countries of the American Hemisphere refused his applications. Since we proclaimed him a Samson who might pull down the pillars of our temple, we should not be surprised if peoples less prosperous, less strongly established and less stable feared to take him off our timorous hands. With something of a record as an unwanted man, neither his efforts nor those of the United States Government any longer promise to find him an abiding place. For nearly two years he was held in custody of the immigration authorities of the United States at Ellis Island, and if the Government has its way he seems likely to be detained indefinitely, perhaps for life, for a cause known only to the Attorney General.

Is respondent deprived of liberty? The Government answers that he was "transferred to Ellis Island on August 1, 1950 for safekeeping," and "is not being detained in the usual sense, but is in custody solely to prevent him from gaining entry into the United States in violation of law. He is free to depart from the United States to any country of his choice." Government counsel ingeniously argued that Ellis Island is his "refuge" whence he is free to take leave in any direction except west. That might mean freedom, if only he were an amphibian! Realistically, this man is incarcerated by a combination of forces which keeps him as effectually as a prison, the dominant and proximate of these forces being the United States immigration authority. It overworks legal fiction to say that one is free in law when by the commonest of common sense he is bound. Despite the impeccable legal logic of the Government's argument on this point, it leads to an artificial and unreal conclusion. We must regard this alien as deprived of liberty, and the question is whether the deprivation is a denial of due process of law.

The Government on this point argues that "no alien has any constitutional right to entry into the United States"; that "the alien has only such rights as Congress sees fit to grant in exclusion proceedings"; that "the so-called detention is still merely a continuation of the exclusion which is specifically authorized by Congress"; that since "the restraint is not incidental to an order [of exclusion] but is itself the effectuation of the exclusion order, there is no limit to its continuance" other than statutory, which means no limit at all. The Government all but adopts the words of one of the officials responsible for the administration of this Act who testified before a congressional committee as to an alien applicant, that "He has no rights."

The interpretations of the Fifth Amendment's command that no person shall be deprived of life, liberty or property without due process of law, come about to this: reasonable general legislation reasonably applied to the individual. The question is whether the Government's detention of respondent is compatible with these tests of substance and procedure.

II. SUBSTANTIVE DUE PROCESS.

Substantively, due process of law renders what is due to a strong state as well as to a free individual. It tolerates all reasonable measures to insure the national safety, and it leaves a large, at times a potentially dangerous, latitude for executive judgment as to policies and means.[5]

After all, the pillars which support our liberties are the three branches of government, and the burden could not be carried by our own power alone. Substantive due process will always pay a high degree of deference to congressional and executive judgment, especially when they concur, as to what is reasonable policy under conditions of particular times and circumstances. Close to the maximum of respect is due from the judiciary to the political departments in policies affecting security and alien exclusion. *Harisiades v. Shaughnessy*, 342 U.S. 580, 72 S.Ct. 512, 96 L.Ed. 586.

Due process does not invest any alien with a right to enter the United States, nor confer on those admitted the right to remain against the national will. Nothing in the Constitution requires admission or sufferance of aliens hostile to our scheme of government.

Nor do I doubt that due process of law will tolerate some impounding of an alien where it is deemed essential to the safety of the state. Even the resident, friendly alien may be subject to executive detention without bail, for a reasonable period, pending consummation of deportation arrangements. *Carlson v. Landon*, 342 U.S. 524, 72 S.Ct. 525, 96 L.Ed. 547. The alien enemy may be confined or his property seized and administered because hostility is assumed from his continued allegiance to a hostile state.

If due process will permit confinement of resident aliens friendly in fact because of imputed hostility, I should suppose one personally at war with our institutions might be confined, even though his state is not at war with us. In both cases, the underlying consideration is the power of our system of government to defend itself, and changing strategy of attack by infiltration may be met with changed tactics of defense.

---

[5] *Korematsu v. United States*, 323 U.S. 214, 65 S.Ct. 193, 89 L.Ed. 194.

* * *

I conclude that detention of an alien would not be inconsistent with substantive due process, provided—and this is where my dissent begins—he is accorded procedural due process of law.

III. PROCEDURAL DUE PROCESS.

Procedural fairness, if not all that originally was meant by due process of law, is at least what it most uncompromisingly requires. Procedural due process is more elemental and less flexible than substantive due process. It yields less to the times, varies less with conditions, and defers much less to legislative judgment. Insofar as it is technical law, it must be a specialized responsibility within the competence of the judiciary on which they do not bend before political branches of the Government, as they should on matters of policy which compromise substantive law.

If it be conceded that in some way this alien could be confined, does it matter what the procedure is? Only the untaught layman or the charlatan lawyer can answer that procedures matter not. Procedural fairness and regularity are of the indispensable essence of liberty. Severe substantive laws can be endured if they are fairly and impartially applied. Indeed, if put to the choice, one might well prefer to live under Soviet substantive law applied in good faith by our common-law procedures than under our substantive law enforced by Soviet procedural practices. Let it not be overlooked that due process of law is not for the sole benefit of an accused. It is the best insurance for the Government itself against those blunders which leave lasting stains on a system of justice but which are bound to occur on ex parte consideration. *Cf. United States ex rel. Knauff v. Shaughnessy*, 338 U.S. 537, 70 S.Ct. 309, 94 L.Ed. 317, which was a near miss, saved by further administrative and congressional hearings from perpetrating an injustice. *See* Knauff, *The Ellen Knauff Story* (New York) 1952.

Our law may, and rightly does, place more restrictions on the alien than on the citizen. But basic fairness in hearing procedures does not vary with the status of the accused. If the procedures used to judge this alien are fair and just, no good reason can be given why they should not be extended to simplify the condemnation of citizens. If they would be unfair to citizens, we cannot defend the fairness of them when applied to the more helpless and handicapped alien. This is at the root of our holdings that the resident alien must be given a fair hearing to test an official claim that he is one of a deportable class. *Wong Yang Sung v. McGrath*, 339 U.S. 33, 70 S.Ct. 445, 94 L.Ed. 616.

The most scrupulous observance of due process, including the right to know a charge, to be confronted with the accuser, to cross-examine informers and to produce evidence in one's behalf, is especially necessary where the occasion of detention is fear of future misconduct, rather than crimes committed.

* * *

Because the respondent has no right of entry, does it follow that he has no rights at all? Does the power to exclude mean that exclusion may be continued or effectuated by any means which happen to seem appropriate to the authorities? It would effectuate his exclusion to eject him bodily into the sea or to set him adrift in a rowboat. Would not such measures be condemned judicially as a deprivation of life without due process of law? Suppose the authorities decide to disable an alien from entry by confiscating his valuables and money. Would we not hold this a taking of property without due process of law? Here we have a case that lies between the taking of life and the taking of property; it is the taking of liberty. It seems to me that this, occurring within the United States or its territorial waters, may be done only by proceedings which meet the test of due process of law.

Exclusion of an alien without judicial hearing, of course, does not deny due process when it can be accomplished merely by turning him back on land or returning him by sea. But when indefinite confinement becomes the means of enforcing exclusion, it seems to me that due process requires that the alien be informed of its grounds and have a fair chance to overcome them. This is the more due him when he is entrapped into leaving the other shore by reliance on a visa which the Attorney General refuses to honor.

It is evident that confinement of respondent no longer can be justified as a step in the process of turning him back to the country whence he came. Confinement is no longer ancillary to exclusion; it can now be justified only as the alternative to normal exclusion. It is an end in itself.

The Communist conspiratorial technique of infiltration poses a problem which sorely tempts the Government to resort to confinement of suspects on secret information secretly judged. I have not been one to discount the Communist evil. But my apprehensions about the security of our form of government are about equally aroused by those who refuse to recognize the dangers of Communism and those who will not see danger in anything else.

Congress has ample power to determine whom we will admit to our shores and by what means it will effectuate its exclusion policy. The only limitation is that it may not do so by authorizing United States officers to take without due process of law the life, the liberty or the property of an alien who has come within our jurisdiction; and that means he must meet a fair hearing with fair notice of the charges.[9]

It is inconceivable to me that this measure of simple justice and fair dealing would menace the security of this country. No one can make me believe that we are that far gone.

NOTES AND QUESTIONS ON DUE PROCESS

1. **The rest of the story**. Congressional and public pressure eventually secured the release of both Knauff and Mezei. Ellen Knauff was ultimately granted a full hearing at which the adverse information was revealed. Although the special inquiry officer ruled against her, the BIA reversed that result on appeal and admitted her to the United States, in a lengthy opinion setting forth in detail the slender evidence that had formed the basis for the Justice Department's initial judgment that she was dangerous. The BIA opinion is reprinted as an appendix to the book she wrote about her experience. Ellen Raphael Knauff, *The Ellen Knauff Story* (1952).

Ignatz Mezei also received a hearing, at which the government sought to exclude him not only for communist associations, but also for giving false information to consular officers to obtain an immigrant visa, and for a petty larceny conviction in 1935 for receipt of seven bags of stolen flour. With the conviction alone enough to exclude him, Mezei sought discretionary relief by presenting character witnesses and evidence that he had never been a Communist Party member. He was initially unsuccessful, but Mezei later secured his release under a special clemency measure after nearly four years in detention on Ellis Island. He was paroled into the United States, but unlike Knauff, was not formally admitted. For rich accounts of the lives and cases, see Charles D. Weisselberg, *The Exclusion and Detention of Aliens: Lessons from the Lives of Ellen Knauff and Ignatz Mezei*, 143 U. Pa. L. Rev. 933, 954–85 (1995).

2. **The rule in *Mezei***. *Mezei* could be read as stating, in dicta, that clandestine entrants receive the full panoply of due process rights in deportation proceedings (that is, that they fall under *Yamataya v. Fisher*). *See* Henry M. Hart, Jr., *The Power of Congress to Limit the Jurisdiction of the Federal Courts: An Exercise in Dialectic*, 66 Harv. L. Rev. 1362, 1392–96 (1953). *Yamataya, supra* p. 521, you may remember, expressly stated that clandestine entry was not before the Court. Reading *Mezei* in this broad

---

[9] The trial court sought to reconcile due process for the individual with claims of security by suggesting that the Attorney General disclose *in camera* enough to enable a judicial determination of the legality of the confinement. The Attorney General refused. I do not know just how an *in camera* proceeding would be handled in this kind of case. If respondent, with or without counsel, were present, disclosures to them might well result in disclosures by them. If they are not allowed to be present, it is hard to see how it would answer the purpose of testing the Government's case by cross-examination or counter-evidence, which is what a hearing is for. The questions raised by the proposal need not be discussed since they do not call for decision here.

fashion creates an obvious inducement to enter without inspection, for the noncitizen then acquires a better constitutional position than the unfortunate soul who does as he should and presents himself for inspection at the port of entry. Such a result is at best ironic, but it is the traditional understanding of *Mezei*: that a noncitizen's entitlement to constitutional due process depends on whether he stands at the border trying to get in (even if he has been here before), or instead has already made an entry and must be removed. In other words, due process depends on the traditional statutory category in which the noncitizen finds himself—exclusion or deportation—thus largely (but not entirely) on location, rather than on the stakes involved for him.

But does *Mezei* have to be read that way? The Court describes the constitutionally preferred class as "aliens who have once passed through our gates, even illegally." Aliens who enter without inspection would seem to have jumped the fence, rather than passing through the gates. Maybe the Court meant to protect only those who were inspected at entry and who are later brought into deportation proceedings because of some defect—some illegality—that comes to light thereafter, revealing that the original entry was illegal, despite compliance with the formalities of inspection. Should such a distinction be made?

3. **Drawing the line.**

a.   This brings us to a related, fundamental question. The constitutional doctrine relating to admission developed for over a century within the traditional exclusion-deportation framework that was fundamental to the INA until 1996. As Chapter Seven explains more fully, before the 1996 Act noncitizens who had entered the United States—even surreptitiously—were subject to deportation grounds. Noncitizens who had not entered were subject to exclusion grounds. The 1996 Act shifted the structure so that the most important statutory line is now admission (that is, inspection by an officer and authorization to establish presence in the United States) rather than entry. The inadmissibility grounds in § 212 apply to noncitizens who have not been admitted. The deportability grounds in § 237 apply only after admission.

The main effect is to alter the treatment of clandestine border crossers. Before 1996, they would have been deportable; hence their constitutional rights were determined under the rubric of rights of deportable noncitizens. Now, they are considered inadmissible. Does this mean that their due process rights will be decided by applying *Mezei*, and not the more generous due process analysis of *Yamataya*? Would such a result make sense in light of the considerations outlined in Note 2 above? Twenty years after the 1996 Act, courts have yet to answer this question with any clarity. What should the answer be? Now that the statutory line has shifted, should we reconsider the traditional reading of *Mezei* and adopt a new constitutional due process doctrine as well?

b.   For people at the border, what is the constitutional dividing line between protected permanent residents like *Chew* and unprotected noncitizens like *Mezei*—length of absence, nature of activities while outside the United States, types of preclearance before departure? In *Mezei*, Justice Clark mentions several factors but does not reveal which was decisive.

———————

Thirty years after *Chew* and *Mezei,* a lawful permanent resident, refused admission to the United States after a brief stay in Mexico, again filed a constitutional challenge to the procedures that led to her rejection. How much of the *Mezei* doctrine survives the following decision?

LANDON V. PLASENCIA

Supreme Court of the United States, 1982.
459 U.S. 21, 103 S.Ct. 321, 74 L.Ed.2d 21.

JUSTICE O'CONNOR delivered the opinion of the Court.

* * *

Respondent Maria Antonieta Plasencia, a citizen of El Salvador, entered the United States as a permanent resident alien in March, 1970. She established a home in Los Angeles with her husband, a United States citizen, and their minor children. On June 27, 1975, she and her husband travelled to Tijuana, Mexico. During their brief stay in Mexico, they met with several Mexican and Salvadoran nationals and made arrangements to assist their illegal entry into the United States. She agreed to transport the aliens to Los Angeles and furnished some of the aliens with alien registration receipt cards that belonged to her children. When she and her husband attempted to cross the international border at 9:27 on the evening of June 29, 1975, an INS officer at the port of entry found six nonresident aliens in the Plasencias' car. The INS detained the respondent for further inquiry pursuant to § 235(b) of the Immigration and Nationality Act of 1952. In a notice dated June 30, 1975, the INS charged her under § 212(a)(31) of the Act, which provides for the exclusion of any alien seeking admission "who at any time shall have, knowingly and for gain, encouraged, induced, assisted, abetted, or aided any other alien to enter or to try to enter the United States in violation of law,"[a] and gave notice that it would hold an exclusion hearing at 11:00 a.m. on June 30, 1975.

An immigration law judge conducted the scheduled exclusion hearing. After hearing testimony from the respondent, her husband, and three of the aliens found in the Plasencias' car, the judge found "clear, convincing and unequivocal" evidence that the respondent did "knowingly

————————

[a] In 1990, Congress eliminated the "for gain" requirement in this exclusion ground, which now appears as INA § 212(a)(6)(E). Section 212(d)(11) allows a discretionary waiver if only close family members were smuggled in.—eds.

and for gain encourage, induce, assist, abet, or aid nonresident aliens" to enter or try to enter the United States in violation of law.

* * *

[Plasencia first argued that, as a returning resident absent only briefly, she should have been placed in deportation proceedings rather than exclusion proceedings under the statute. The Court rejected this contention.]

* * * Plasencia [also] argued * * * that she was denied due process in her exclusion hearing. We agree with Plasencia that under the circumstances of this case, she can invoke the Due Process Clause on returning to this country, although we do not decide the contours of the process that is due or whether the process accorded Plasencia was insufficient.

This Court has long held that an alien seeking initial admission to the United States requests a privilege and has no constitutional rights regarding his application, for the power to admit or exclude aliens is a sovereign prerogative. *See, e.g., United States ex rel. Knauff v. Shaughnessy*, 338 U.S. 537, 542, 70 S.Ct. 309, 312, 94 L.Ed. 317 (1950); *Nishimura Ekiu v. United States*, 142 U.S. 651, 659–660, 12 S.Ct. 336, 338, 35 L.Ed. 1146 (1892). Our recent decisions confirm that view. *See, e.g., Fiallo v. Bell*, 430 U.S. 787, 792, 97 S.Ct. 1473, 1477, 52 L.Ed.2d 50 (1977); *Kleindienst v. Mandel*, 408 U.S. 753, 92 S.Ct. 2576, 33 L.Ed.2d 683 (1972). As we explained in *Johnson v. Eisentrager*, 339 U.S. 763, 770, 70 S.Ct. 936, 939, 94 L.Ed. 1255 (1950), however, once an alien gains admission to our country and begins to develop the ties that go with permanent residence his constitutional status changes accordingly. Our cases have frequently suggested that a continuously present resident alien is entitled to a fair hearing when threatened with deportation, and, although we have only rarely held that the procedures provided by the executive were inadequate, we developed the rule that a continuously present permanent resident alien has a right to due process in such a situation.

The question of the procedures due a returning resident alien arose in *Kwong Hai Chew v. Colding*. There, the regulations permitted the exclusion of an arriving alien without a hearing. We interpreted those regulations not to apply to Chew, a permanent resident alien who was returning from a five-month voyage abroad as a crewman on an American merchant ship. We reasoned that, "For purposes of his constitutional right to due process, we assimilate petitioner's status to that of an alien continuously residing and physically present in the United States." Then, to avoid constitutional problems, we construed the regulation as inapplicable. Although the holding was one of regulatory interpretation, the rationale was one of constitutional law. Any doubts that *Chew* recognized constitutional rights in the resident alien returning from a brief trip abroad were dispelled by *Rosenberg v. Fleuti*, [374 U.S. 449, 83 S.Ct. 1804, 10 L.Ed.2d 1000 (1963),] where we described *Chew* as holding "that the returning resident alien is entitled as a matter of due process to a hearing on the charges underlying any attempt to exclude him."

If the permanent resident alien's absence is extended, of course, he may lose his entitlement to "assimilat[ion of his] status," *Kwong Hai Chew v. Colding, supra*, 344 U.S., at 596, 73 S.Ct., at 477, to that of an alien continuously residing and physically present in the United States. In *Shaughnessy v. United States ex rel. Mezei*, 345 U.S. 206, 73 S.Ct. 625, 97 L.Ed. 956 (1953), this Court rejected the argument of an alien who had left the country for some twenty months that he was entitled to due process in assessing his right to admission on his return. We did not suggest that no returning resident alien has a right to due process, for we explicitly reaffirmed *Chew*. We need not now decide the scope of *Mezei*; it does not govern this case, for Plasencia was absent from the country only a few days, and the United States has conceded that she has a right to due process.

The constitutional sufficiency of procedures provided in any situation, of course, varies with the circumstances. * * * In evaluating the procedures in any case, the courts must consider the interest at stake for the individual, the risk of an erroneous deprivation of the interest through the procedures used as well as the probable value of additional or different procedural safeguards, and the interest of the government in using the current procedures rather than additional or different procedures. *Mathews v. Eldridge*, 424 U.S. 319, 334–335, 96 S.Ct. 893, 902–903, 47 L.Ed.2d 18 (1976). Plasencia's interest here is, without question, a weighty one. She stands to lose the right "to stay and live and work in this land of freedom." Further, she may lose the right to rejoin her immediate family, a right that ranks high among the interests of the individual. The government's interest in efficient administration of the immigration laws at the border also is weighty. Further, it must weigh heavily in the balance that control over matters of immigration is a sovereign prerogative, largely within the control of the executive and the legislature. The role of the judiciary is limited to determining whether the procedures meet the essential standard of fairness under the Due Process Clause and does not extend to imposing procedures that merely displace congressional choices of policy. Our previous discussion has shown that Congress did not intend to require the use of deportation procedures in cases such as this one. Thus, it would be improper simply to impose deportation procedures here because the reviewing court may find them preferable. Instead, the courts must evaluate the particular circumstances and determine what procedures would satisfy the minimum requirements of due process on the re-entry of a permanent resident alien.

Plasencia questions three aspects of the procedures that the government employed in depriving her of these interests. First, she contends that the immigration law judge placed the burden of proof upon her. [The BIA had generally placed the burden on the government when the noncitizen was a lawful permanent resident. The regulations were silent on the issue and the opinions below had not directly addressed the question.]

Second, Plasencia contends that the notice provided her was inadequate. She apparently had less than eleven hours' notice of the charges and the hearing. The regulations do not require any advance notice of the charges against the alien in an exclusion hearing, and the BIA has held that it is sufficient that the alien have notice of the charges at the hearing. The United States has argued to us that Plasencia could have sought a continuance. It concedes, however, that there is no explicit statutory or regulatory authorization for a continuance.

Finally, Plasencia contends that she was allowed to waive her right to representation,[8] without a full understanding of the right or of the consequences of waiving it. Through an interpreter, the immigration law judge informed her at the outset of the hearing, as required by the regulations, of her right to be represented. He did not tell her of the availability of free legal counsel, but at the time of the hearing, there was no administrative requirement that he do so. The Attorney General has since revised the regulations to require that, when qualified free legal services are available, the immigration law judge must inform the alien of their existence and ask whether representation is desired. As the United States concedes, the hearing would not comply with the current regulations.

If the exclusion hearing is to ensure fairness, it must provide Plasencia an opportunity to present her case effectively, though at the same time it cannot impose an undue burden on the government. It would not, however, be appropriate for us to decide now whether the new regulation on the right to notice of free legal services is of constitutional magnitude or whether the remaining procedures provided comport with the Due Process Clause. Before this Court, the parties have devoted their attention to the entitlement to a deportation hearing rather than to the sufficiency of the procedures in the exclusion hearing.[9] Whether the

---

[8]   The statute provides a right to representation without expense to the government. Section 292. Plasencia has not suggested that she is entitled to free counsel.

[9]   Thus, the question of Plasencia's entitlement to due process has been briefed and argued, is properly before us, and is sufficiently developed that we are prepared to decide it. Precisely what procedures are due, on the other hand, has not been adequately developed by the briefs or argument. The dissent undertakes to decide these questions, but, to do so, must rely heavily on an argument not raised by Plasencia: to wit, that she was not informed at the hearing that the

several hours' notice gave Plasencia a realistic opportunity to prepare her case for effective presentation in the circumstances of an exclusion hearing without counsel is a question we are not now in a position to answer. Nor has the government explained the burdens that it might face in providing more elaborate procedures. Thus, although we recognize the gravity of Plasencia's interest, the other factors relevant to due process analysis—the risk of erroneous deprivation, the efficacy of additional procedural safeguards, and the government's interest in providing no further procedures—have not been adequately presented to permit us to assess the sufficiency of the hearing. We remand to the Court of Appeals to allow the parties to explore whether Plasencia was accorded due process under all of the circumstances.

Accordingly, the judgment of the Court of Appeals is

Reversed and remanded.

JUSTICE MARSHALL, concurring in part and dissenting in part.

I agree that the Immigration and Nationality Act permitted the INS to proceed against respondent in an exclusion proceeding. The question then remains whether the exclusion proceeding held in this case satisfied the minimum requirements of the Due Process Clause. While I agree that the Court need not decide the precise contours of the process that would be constitutionally sufficient, I would not hesitate to decide that the process accorded Plasencia was insufficient.

The Court has already set out the standards to be applied in resolving the question. Therefore, rather than just remand, I would first hold that respondent was denied due process because she was not given adequate and timely notice of the charges against her and of her right to retain counsel and to present a defense.[2]

While the type of hearing required by due process depends upon a balancing of the competing interests at stake, due process requires "at a minimum . . . that deprivation of life, liberty or property by adjudication be preceded by notice and opportunity for hearing." *Mullane v. Central Hanover Bank & Trust Co.*, 339 U.S. 306, 313, 70 S.Ct. 652, 656, 94 L.Ed. 865 (1950). Permanent resident aliens who are detained upon reentry into this country clearly are entitled to adequate notice in advance of an exclusion proceeding.

---

alleged agreement to receive compensation and the meaningfulness of her departure were critical issues. Also, the dissent fails to discuss the interests that the government may have in employing the procedures that it did. The omission of arguments raised by the parties is quite understandable, for neither Plasencia nor the government has yet discussed what procedures are due. Unlike the dissent, we would allow the parties to explore their respective interests and arguments in the Court of Appeals.

   [2]   Because Plasencia did not receive constitutionally sufficient notice, I find it unnecessary to address the other constitutional deficiencies she asserts.

To satisfy due process, notice must "clarify what the charges are" in a manner adequate to apprise the individual of the basis for the government's proposed action. Notice must be provided sufficiently in advance of the hearing to "give the charged party a chance to marshal the facts in his defense." * * *

[Plasencia received less than 24 hours' notice of the hearing, and only received notice in Spanish at the beginning of the hearing of the charges against her, her right to retain counsel, and her right to present evidence.]

The charges against Plasencia were also inadequately explained at the hearing itself. The immigration judge did not explain to her that she would be entitled to remain in the country if she could demonstrate that she had not agreed to receive compensation from the aliens whom she had driven across the border. Nor did the judge inform respondent that the meaningfulness of her departure was an issue at the hearing.

These procedures deprived Plasencia of a fair opportunity to show that she was not excludable under the standards set forth in the Immigration and Nationality Act. Because Plasencia was not given adequate notice of the standards for exclusion or of her right to retain counsel and present a defense, she had neither time nor opportunity to prepare a response to the government's case. The procedures employed here virtually assured that the Government attorney would present his case without factual or legal opposition.

When a permanent resident alien's substantial interest in remaining in this country is at stake, the Due Process Clause forbids the Government to stack the deck in this fashion. Only a compelling need for truly summary action could justify this one-sided proceeding. In fact, the Government's haste in proceeding against Plasencia could be explained only by its desire to avoid the minimal administrative and financial burden of providing her adequate notice and an opportunity to prepare for the hearing. Although the various other government interests identified by the Court may be served by the exclusion of those who fail to meet the eligibility requirements set out in the Immigration and Nationality Act, they are not served by procedures that deny a permanent resident alien a fair opportunity to demonstrate that she meets those eligibility requirements.

I would therefore hold that respondent was denied due process.

NOTES AND QUESTIONS ON
DUE PROCESS FOR RETURNING PERMANENT RESIDENTS

1.   **The rest of the story.** For a detailed history of the Plasencias' trip to Mexico, Maria Plasencia's heartfelt (though legally naive) *pro se* defense in the exclusion proceedings, including the candid testimony offered by her and

her husband, and the aftermath of the ruling, see Kevin R. Johnson, *Maria and Joseph Plasencia's Lost Weekend: The Case of* Landon v. Plasencia, *in* Immigration Stories 221 (David A. Martin & Peter H. Schuck eds. 2005). Johnson reports that Mrs. Plasencia was paroled into the United States for the duration of the court proceedings, and that the government did not pursue the case after the remand to the district court. "The government presumably decided not to proceed against Maria because of the pro-immigrant due process law that the courts might have created if they had addressed her due process claims." *Id.* at 239. Her attorneys lost touch with her after the Supreme Court's decision, but speculated that she might still be living in the United States as a lawful permanent resident. *Id.* at 238–39.

2. *Plasencia, Mezei,* **and** *Fleuti. Plasencia* distinguishes *Mezei* but does not purport to overrule it. Nonetheless, the Court has now alleviated much of the threat that *Mezei* seemed to pose to permanent residents who travel (though *Mezei* continue to cast a large shadow for all other inadmissible noncitizens). Henceforth, full due process entitlement seems to be the norm for nearly all returning permanent residents, even those seeking admission, and *Mezei* marks out an imprecisely defined exception.

How should we draw the line that distinguishes these exceptional cases? The Court says only that a permanent resident may lose his protected status if his "absence is extended." Presumably this provides more protection than the standard that the U.S. Supreme Court announced in *Rosenberg v. Fleuti*, 374 U.S. 449, 83 S.Ct. 1804, 10 L.Ed.2d 1000 (1963), a decision which Justice O'Connor notes in *Plasencia*.

In *Fleuti*, the issue was whether George Fleuti, a native and citizen of Switzerland and a permanent resident since 1952, was reentering the United States upon his return from a short trip of "about a couple hours" to Ensenada, Mexico in 1956. This mattered because in 1959 the INS tried to deport him as an alien "excludable by the law existing at the time of . . . entry." The exclusion ground in question (based on Fleuti's homosexuality) had not been on the books when Fleuti initially entered the United States in 1952, but it had become law by 1956.

In *Fleuti*, the Court found that a noncitizen was not making an entry when returning from a temporary absence that was not "meaningfully interruptive" of permanent residence. The Court read into the statute an exception for "innocent, casual, and brief" trips. Congress later modified the *Fleuti* exception in 1996, but it was the law when the Court decided *Plasencia* in 1982. The Court held that even if Maria Plasencia's trip to Mexico fell outside the *Fleuti* exception because she was engaged in smuggling individuals across the border, and was therefore seeking a new entry into the United States when she returned, she was still entitled to procedural due process protection as a returning permanent resident.

Fleuti made clear that a lawful permanent resident's return can pose several related but distinct issues. First is whether he seeks entry or admission to the United States in the sense that exclusion or inadmissibility grounds might apply. Even if the answer is yes, he is not necessarily relegated to the same constitutional status as a first-time entrant; that is a separate second issue. A third issue is whether the noncitizen can use his green card as a re-entry or re-admission document. Not if he has been absent for more than one year, according to 8 C.F.R. § 211.1(a)(2). A fourth issue is whether he has lost lawful permanent resident status by virtue of the absence. The BIA uses a multiple factor test to answer this question. *See Matter of Huang*, 19 I & N Dec. 749, 752–54 (BIA 1988). In *Plasencia*, for example, the issue addressed by the Court was constitutional treatment. The Court assumed that Plasencia was seeking entry, that she was still a lawful permanent resident status, and that her green card was sufficient documentation.

If any subjective intent test is ultimately employed, the Court probably could not avoid *de facto* overruling *Mezei*. According to the facts as Mezei pleaded them, he had no intention of making a lengthy journey, much less of abandoning his U.S. home. And the fact that his family remained behind in Buffalo while he traveled lends a strong measure of plausibility to these claims.

On the first issue, INA § 101(a)(13) now says that a returning permanent resident is not seeking admission—that is, inadmissibility grounds do not apply—unless certain facts are present: for example, a continuous absence in excess of 180 days, abandonment or relinquishment of the permanent resident status, or the commission of a crime that would make a noncitizen inadmissible. Are these guidelines a sensible way of defining those returning permanent residents who receive heightened due process protection based on prior attachments to the United States (and notwithstanding their physical departure)? If so, should *Plasencia* come out the same way today, under the current INA? The larger question here is whether Congress, even if it cannot define constitutional rights by statute, might nonetheless create categories that influence how the Court draws constitutional lines.

3. **Who gets due process, and what process is due?** So far, we have considered whether due process applies to a given case, but we have not examined closely what specific procedures due process might require. This is the point of contention in *Plasencia* between the majority's decision to remand for decision on whether Maria Plasencia received due process, and Justice Marshall, who "would not hesitate to decide that the process accorded Plasencia was insufficient."

To decide what process is due and to understand how the Court approaches this question in *Plasencia*, it is important to note that in the 1970s the Supreme Court initiated a major reconceptualization of due process analysis in civil cases. The Court first asks whether a claimant possesses a "liberty" or "property" interest under the Fifth Amendment's Due Process Clause. If there is such an interest, the second analytical step is to decide on a case-by-case basis exactly what procedural protections due process requires.

A long-time lawful permanent resident with a family in the United States, like Plasencia or Mezei, can argue that prohibition of reentry implicates their liberty to carry on their established life, but what about a first-time applicant for admission like Ellen Knauff? What is the liberty interest noncitizens have as they seek to enter the United States for the first time? To be sure, exclusion imposes bodily restraints on their freedom of movement, but do all non-U.S. citizens in the world who might happen to present themselves at our borders have a legitimate claim of entitlement to free movement in this very potent sense?

If we think of their claims under the property rubric, do they have more than a unilateral expectation or hope that they would be permitted to enter the United States? Does the U.S. immigration law provide the independent source for a "legitimate claim of entitlement"? If so, do all first-time applicants for admission who have a visa have a property interest? What if they do not have a visa? When someone who has never been in the United States is denied admission, has there been a *deprivation* of liberty or property? Or to put the questions in functional terms, can the United States afford to provide due process to everyone in the world who simply presents himself or herself at a port of entry? If so, how much process? If not, how should we decide when due process rights attach?

If a noncitizen has a liberty or property interest, the next question is what process is due. Modern cases stress the flexibility of the concept of due process; procedures acceptable in some settings may be wholly unacceptable in others. The prevailing mode of inquiry is a three-part balancing test set forth in the landmark case of *Mathews v. Eldridge*, 424 U.S. 319, 96 S.Ct. 893, 47 L.Ed.2d 18 (1976). The test requires courts to consider (1) the interests at stake for the individual, (2) the interest of the government, and (3) the gain to accurate decisionmaking that can be expected from the procedural protection sought. *Id.* at 335, 96 S.Ct. at 903.

4. **National security and admission procedures after *Mezei*.** In 1952, Congress provided explicit statutory authority for the kinds of secret procedures that had been employed against Knauff and Mezei on the authority of regulations alone. INA § 235(c) permits the government to order removal of an arriving alien on most of the national security inadmissibility grounds without a further hearing if it acts on the basis of "confidential information," the disclosure of which "would be prejudicial to the public interest, safety, or security." The section 235(c) procedure was invoked less frequently as the Cold War thawed than it was in the 1950s, but it was still employed, and not only against suspected Soviet bloc sympathizers.

Since the terrorist attacks of September 11, 2001, the government has invoked various enforcement measures based on national security. Several of them pose significant questions about the fairness of using secret information not shared with the alien in removal proceedings.

In 2015, the Supreme Court again faced many of the issues raised in the preceding Notes and Questions on Due Process for Returning Permanent Residents: the effect of family ties and location in evaluating procedural due process requirements, the presence of national security interests, the use of secret evidence to determine admissibility, and more. Fauzia Din, a citizen and resident of the United States, alleged that a consular official's denial of her husband's visa application violated her constitutional right to live in the United States with her husband. The government provided no explanation other than that the denial was based on the provision of the INA that prohibits the issuance of visas to those who engage in terrorist activities. *See* INA § 212(a)(3)(B). The Court ruled against Din, issuing three separate opinions.

KERRY V. DIN

Supreme Court of the United States, 2015.
576 U.S. ___, 135 S.Ct. 2128, 192 L.Ed.2d 183.

Justice SCALIA announced the judgment of the Court and delivered an opinion, in which THE CHIEF JUSTICE and Justice THOMAS join.

Fauzia Din is a citizen and resident of the United States. Her husband, Kanishka Berashk, is an Afghan citizen and former civil servant in the Taliban regime who resides in that country. * * *

The state action of which Din complains is the denial of *Berashk's* visa application. Naturally, one would expect him—not Din—to bring this suit. But because Berashk is an unadmitted and nonresident alien, he has no right of entry into the United States, and no cause of action to press in furtherance of his claim for admission. See *Kleindienst v. Mandel,* 408 U.S. 753, 762, 92 S.Ct. 2576, 33 L.Ed.2d 683 (1972). So, Din attempts to bring suit on his behalf, alleging that the Government's denial of her *husband's* visa application violated *her* constitutional rights. In particular, she claims that the Government denied her due process of law when, without adequate explanation of the reason for the visa denial, it deprived her of her constitutional right to live in the United States with her spouse. There is no such constitutional right. What Justice Breyer's dissent strangely describes as a "deprivation of her freedom to live together with her spouse in America," is, in any world other than the artificial world of ever-expanding constitutional rights, nothing more than a deprivation of her spouse's freedom to immigrate into America.

For the reasons given in this opinion and in the opinion concurring in the judgment, we vacate and remand.

* * * Before issuing a visa, the consular officer must ensure the alien is not inadmissible under any provision of the INA. § 291. One ground for inadmissibility, § 212(a)(3)(B), covers "[t]errorist activities." In addition to the violent and destructive acts the term immediately brings to mind, the

INA defines "terrorist activity" to include providing material support to a terrorist organization and serving as a terrorist organization's representative. § 212(a)(3)(B)(i), (iii)–(vi).

* * *

* * * A consular officer informed Berashk that he was inadmissible under § 212(a)(3)(B) but provided no further explanation.

* * * The first question that we must ask * * * is whether the denial of Berashk's visa application deprived Din of [a Due Process interest]. Only if we answer in the affirmative must we proceed to consider whether the Government's explanation afforded sufficient process.

* * *

[Justice Scalia rejected the claim that the denial of Berashk's visa deprived either Din or Berashk of liberty, noting that neither had been forcibly detained or arrested. He further rejected Din's argument that there was an implied fundamental right to marry and that the immigration law's impact on her fundamental right necessitated robust procedural protections.]

Din describes the denial of Berashk's visa application as implicating, alternately, a "liberty interest in her marriage," a "right of association with one's spouse," "a liberty interest in being reunited with certain blood relatives," and "the liberty interest of a U.S. citizen under the Due Process Clause to be free from arbitrary restrictions on his right to live with his spouse." * * *

* * * [T]he Federal Government here has not attempted to forbid a marriage. * * *

* * *

[A] long practice of regulating spousal immigration precludes Din's claim that the denial of Berashk's visa application has deprived her of a fundamental liberty interest. Although immigration was effectively unregulated prior to 1875, as soon as Congress began legislating in this area it enacted a complicated web of regulations that erected serious impediments to a person's ability to bring a spouse into the United States. *See* Abrams, *What Makes the Family Special?* 80 U. Chi. L. Rev. 7, 10–16 (2013).

* * *

Although Congress has tended to show "a continuing and kindly concern . . . for the unity and the happiness of the immigrant family," E. Hutchinson, Legislative History of American Immigration Policy 1798–1965, p. 518 (1981), this has been a matter of legislative grace rather than fundamental right. Even where Congress has provided special privileges to promote family immigration, it has also "written in careful checks and qualifications." *Ibid.* This Court has consistently recognized that these various distinctions are "policy questions entrusted exclusively to the political branches of our Government, and we have no judicial authority to substitute our political judgment for that of the Congress." *Fiallo v. Bell,* 430 U.S. 787, 798, 97 S.Ct. 1473, 52 L.Ed.2d 50 (1977). Only by diluting the meaning of a fundamental liberty interest and jettisoning our established jurisprudence could we conclude that the denial of Berashk's visa application implicates any of Din's fundamental liberty interests.

Justice Breyer suggests that procedural due process rights attach to liberty interests that either are (1) created by nonconstitutional law, such as a statute, or (2) "sufficiently important" so as to "flow 'implicit[ly]' from the design, object, and nature of the Due Process Clause."

The first point is unobjectionable, at least given this Court's case law. But it is unhelpful to Din * * * .

Justice Breyer's second point—that procedural due process rights attach even to some nonfundamental liberty interests that have *not* been created by statute—is much more troubling. He [divines] a "right of spouses to live together and to raise a family," along with "a citizen's right to live within this country."

* * *

Justice Breyer [would] vastly expand[ ] the scope of our implied-rights jurisprudence by setting it free from the requirement that the liberty interest be "objectively, deeply rooted in this Nation's history and tradition, and implicit in the concept of ordered liberty." * * *

Neither Din's right to live with her spouse nor her right to live within this country is implicated here. * * * The Government has not refused to recognize Din's marriage to Berashk, and Din remains free to live with her husband anywhere in the world that both individuals are permitted to reside. And the Government has not expelled Din from the country. It has simply determined that Kanishka Berashk engaged in terrorist activities within the meaning of the Immigration and Nationality Act, and has therefore denied him admission into the country. This might, indeed, deprive Din of something "important," but if that is the criterion for Justice Breyer's new pairing of substantive and procedural due process, we are in for quite a ride.

* * *

Because Fauzia Din was not deprived of "life, liberty, or property" when the Government denied Kanishka Berashk admission to the United States, there is no process due to her under the Constitution. To the extent that she received any explanation for the Government's decision, this was more than the Due Process Clause required. The judgment of the

Ninth Circuit is vacated, and the case is remanded for further proceedings.

Justice KENNEDY, with whom Justice ALITO joins, concurring in the judgment.

* * *

Today's disposition should not be interpreted as deciding whether a citizen has a protected liberty interest in the visa application of her alien spouse. The Court need not decide that issue, for this Court's precedents instruct that, even assuming she has such an interest, the Government satisfied due process when it notified Din's husband that his visa was denied under the immigration statute's terrorism bar, § 212(a)(3)(B).

I

The conclusion that Din received all the process to which she was entitled finds its most substantial instruction in the Court's decision in *Kleindienst v. Mandel,* 408 U.S. 753, 92 S.Ct. 2576, 33 L.Ed.2d 683 (1972). There, college professors—all of them citizens—had invited Dr. Ernest Mandel, a self-described " 'revolutionary Marxist,' " to speak at a conference at Stanford University. Yet when Mandel applied for a temporary nonimmigrant visa to enter the country, he was denied. * * * In a letter regarding this decision, the INS explained Mandel had exceeded the scope and terms of temporary visas on past trips to the United States, which the agency deemed a " 'flagrant abuse of the opportunities afforded him to express his views in this country.' " 408 U.S., at 759, 92 S.Ct. 2576.

* * *

T]he Court limited its inquiry to the question whether the Government had provided a "facially legitimate and bona fide" reason for its action. Finding the Government had proffered such a reason— Mandel's abuse of past visas—the Court ended its inquiry and found the Attorney General's action to be lawful. The Court emphasized it did not address "[w]hat First Amendment or other grounds may be available for attacking an exercise of discretion for which no justification whatsoever is advanced." *Ibid.*

The reasoning and the holding in *Mandel* control here. That decision was based upon due consideration of the congressional power to make rules for the exclusion of aliens, and the ensuing power to delegate authority to the Attorney General to exercise substantial discretion in that field. *Mandel* held that an executive officer's decision denying a visa that burdens a citizen's own constitutional rights is valid when it is made "on the basis of a facially legitimate and bona fide reason." *Id.,* at 770, 92 S.Ct. 2576. Once this standard is met, "courts will neither look behind the exercise of that discretion, nor test it by balancing its justification against" the constitutional interests of citizens the visa denial might implicate. *Ibid.* This reasoning has particular force in the area of national security, for which Congress has provided specific statutory directions pertaining to visa applications by noncitizens who seek entry to this country.

Like the professors who sought an audience with Dr. Mandel, Din claims her constitutional rights were burdened by the denial of a visa to a noncitizen, namely her husband. And as in *Mandel,* the Government provided a reason for the visa denial: It concluded Din's husband was inadmissible under § 212(a)(3)(B)'s terrorism bar. Even assuming Din's rights were burdened directly by the visa denial, the remaining question is whether the reasons given by the Government satisfy *Mandel* 's "facially legitimate and bona fide" standard. I conclude that they do.

Here, the consular officer's determination that Din's husband was ineligible for a visa was controlled by specific statutory factors. The provisions of § 212(a)(3)(B) establish specific criteria for determining terrorism-related inadmissibility. The consular officer's citation of that provision suffices to show that the denial rested on a determination that Din's husband did not satisfy the statute's requirements. Given Congress' plenary power to "suppl[y] the conditions of the privilege of entry into the United States," *United States ex rel. Knauff v. Shaughnessy,* 338 U.S. 537, 543, 70 S.Ct. 309, 94 L.Ed. 317 (1950), it follows that the Government's decision to exclude an alien it determines does not satisfy one or more of those conditions is facially legitimate under *Mandel.*

* * *

The Government, furthermore, was not required, as Din claims, to point to a more specific provision within § 212(a)(3)(B). To be sure, the statutory provision the consular officer cited covers a broad range of conduct. And Din perhaps more easily could mount a challenge to her husband's visa denial if she knew the specific subsection on which the consular officer relied. Congress understood this problem, however. The statute generally requires the Government to provide an alien denied a visa with the "specific provision or provisions of law under which the alien is inadmissible," § 212(b)(1); but this notice requirement does not apply when, as in this case, a visa application is denied due to terrorism or national security concerns. § 212(b)(3). Notably, the Government is not prohibited from offering more details when it sees fit, but the statute expressly refrains from requiring it to do so.

Congress evaluated the benefits and burdens of notice in this sensitive area and assigned discretion to the Executive to decide when more detailed disclosure is appropriate. This considered judgment gives additional support to the independent conclusion that the notice given was constitutionally adequate, particularly in light of the national security concerns the terrorism bar addresses. * * *

For these reasons, my conclusion is that the Government satisfied any obligation it might have had to provide Din with a facially legitimate and bona fide reason for its action when it provided notice that her husband was denied admission to the country under § 212(a)(3)(B). * * *

Justice BREYER, with whom Justice GINSBURG, Justice SOTOMAYOR, and Justice KAGAN join, dissenting.

I

* * *

The liberty interest that Ms. Din seeks to protect consists of her freedom to live together with her husband in the United States. She seeks *procedural,* not *substantive,* protection for this freedom.

* * * As this Court has long recognized, the institution of marriage, which encompasses the right of spouses to live together and to raise a family, is central to human life, requires and enjoys community support, and plays a central role in most individuals' "orderly pursuit of happiness," *Meyer v. Nebraska,* 262 U.S. 390, 399, 43 S.Ct. 625, 67 L.Ed. 1042 (1923). Similarly, the Court has long recognized that a citizen's right to live within this country, being fundamental, enjoys basic procedural due process protection.

* * *

Justice Scalia's more general response—claiming that I have created a new category of constitutional rights—misses the mark. I break no new ground here. [Here the dissent cites cases granting procedural protection to a list of liberty interests that include a prisoner's right to maintain "goodtime" credits shortening a term of imprisonment, a right to certain aspects of reputation, a student's right not to be suspended from school class, a prisoner's right against involuntary commitment, a mentally ill prisoner's right not to take psychotropic drugs, and a right to welfare benefits.] How could [the] Constitution * * * not also offer some form of procedural protection to a citizen threatened with governmental deprivation of her freedom to live together with her spouse in America? * * *

II

A

The more difficult question is the nature of the procedural protection required by the Constitution. * * *

* * *

We have often held that [a statement of reasons], permitting an individual to understand *why* the government acted as it did, is a fundamental element of due process. * * * Properly apprised of the grounds for the Government's action, Ms. Din can then take appropriate action—whether this amounts to an appeal, internal agency review, or (as is likely here) an opportunity to submit additional evidence and obtain reconsideration.

* * * [I]n the absence of some highly unusual circumstance (not shown to be present here), the Constitution requires the Government to provide an adequate reason why it refused to grant Ms. Din's husband a visa. That reason, in my view, could be either the factual basis for the Government's decision or a sufficiently specific statutory subsection that conveys effectively the same information.

B

1

Justice Kennedy, without denying that Ms. Din was entitled to a reason, believes that she received an adequate reason here. * * * I do not see how [a reference to the statutory provision or to "terrorism and national security bars"] could count as adequate.

For one thing, the statutory provision to which it refers, § 212(a)(3)(B), sets forth, not one reason, but dozens. It is a complex provision with 10 different subsections, many of which cross-reference other provisions of law. Some parts cover criminal conduct that is particularly serious, such as hijacking aircraft and assassination. §§ 212(a)(3)(B)(iii)(I), (IV). Other parts cover activity that, depending on the factual circumstances, cannot easily be labeled "terrorist." * * *

For another thing, the State Department's reason did not set forth any factual basis for the Government's decision. Perhaps the Department denied the visa because Ms. Din's husband at one point was a payroll clerk for the Afghan Government when that government was controlled by the Taliban. But there is no way to know if that is so.

The generality of the statutory provision cited and the lack of factual support mean that here, the reason given is analogous to telling a criminal defendant only that he is accused of "breaking the law" * * * . It does not permit Ms. Din to assess the correctness of the State Department's conclusion; it does not permit her to determine what kinds of facts she might provide in response; and it does not permit her to learn whether, or what kind of, defenses might be available. In short, any "reason" that Ms. Din received is not constitutionally adequate.

2

[Justice Kennedy] says that ordinary rules of due process must give way here to national security concerns. But just what are those concerns? And how do they apply here? * * *

[W]hen faced with the need to provide public information without compromising security interests, the Government has found ways to do so, for example, by excising sensitive portions of documents requested by the press, members of the public, or other public officials. Moreover, agencies and courts have found ways to conduct proceedings in private, through internal review or *in camera* proceedings, and thereby protect sensitive information. * * *

I do not deny the importance of national security, the need to keep certain related information private, or the need to respect the determinations of the other branches of Government in such matters. But protecting ordinary citizens from arbitrary government action is fundamental. * * *

Justice Kennedy also looks for support to the fact that Congress specifically exempted the section here at issue, § 212(a)(3)(B), from the statutory provision requiring the State Department to provide a reason for visa denials. § 212(b)(3). An exception from a statutory demand for a reason, * * * leaves open the question whether other law requires a reason. Here that other law is the Constitution, not a statute.

* * *

For these reasons, with respect, I dissent.

NOTES AND QUESTIONS ON KERRY V. DIN

1. What exactly is the disagreement between Justice Kennedy's concurrence and Justice Breyer's dissent? What if the government had cited a particular clause or subclause of § 212(a)(3)(B)? Or suppose the Solicitor General had explained the national security concerns more fully. Would Justice Breyer then have found that the government satisfied the Constitution's procedural due process requirements?

2. The U.S. Supreme Court split three ways; the dissenting opinion had the most signatures, but no rationale had the support of more than four Justices. The standard rule in such multiple-opinion decisions is that "the holding of the Court may be viewed as that position taken by those Members who concurred in the judgments on the narrowest grounds." *Marks v. United States*, 430 U.S. 188, 193 (1977). The D.C. Circuit later elaborated that the holding in such cases must be "a position implicitly approved by at least five Justices who support the judgment." *See King v. Palmer*, 950 F.2d 771, 781 & n.6 (D.C. Cir. 1991) (en banc). Do five Justices agree on anything in *Kerry v. Din* beyond reversing the Ninth Circuit decision?

3. Is this decision essentially one in which the Court revisits *Knauff* and *Mezei*'s analysis of procedural due process when noncitizens are outside the United States? Are there ways to distinguish *Din* from those cases?

As a final way of pulling together the many strands in *Yamataya, Knauff, Chew, Mezei, Plasencia, and Din,* consider the following scenario.

EXERCISE: DUE PROCESS AT THE BORDER

Mohammed Adawallah was born in Yemen in 1982. He has been a lawful permanent resident of the United States since 2001. He currently lives near Cincinnati, Ohio, with his wife and child, both of whom are U.S. citizens, and has 34 other relatives in the United States. Adawallah is a graduate of Ohio State University. He has been politically active while living in this country, being particularly outspoken in his opposition to U.S. policies in the Middle East. Eleven months ago, Adawallah filed a naturalization application, which is still pending.

Eight months ago, Adawallah applied for and obtained a reentry permit from the government, as is the standard procedure when a permanent resident plans an extended trip abroad. He stated on his application for the permit that he wished to go to Cyprus to be with his mother while she underwent and recuperated from "major heart surgery."

Approximately 26 weeks after departing, Adawallah arrived at Kennedy Airport in New York on a flight from Heathrow Airport in London. His itinerary showed that he had flown to London from Beirut, Lebanon. When questioned by inspectors, Adawallah said that he had not gone to Cyprus because his mother's surgery had been cancelled as not medically necessary. The government asserted during the questioning that Adawallah went instead to Egypt with two other men, with whom he attended a gathering of Hamas, which the U.S. government has officially designated as a terrorist organization. Adawallah categorically denied that he has ever been affiliated with Hamas or any other terrorist group, or that he has ever engaged in any terrorist activity. After the questioning, he was detained for removal proceedings. To what sort of procedures is he entitled under the statute? Is he an arriving alien?

Shortly thereafter, DHS charged Adawallah with being inadmissible to the United States on national security grounds, citing INA § 212(a)(3)(B), on the basis of confidential information. DHS also instituted summary exclusion proceedings under § 235(c), but gave Adawallah no indication of the details of the confidential information that supported their conclusion that he is affiliated with a terrorist organization.

Is a constitutional due process challenge to the government's use of this confidential information likely to be successful?

CHAPTER SEVEN

INADMISSIBILITY, DEPORTABILITY, AND RELIEF FROM REMOVAL

■ ■ ■

Chapter Five explained the categories for admission to the United States, and Chapter Six addressed the procedures for administering them. But there is more to the story. Noncitizens who fit into an admission category will be barred if they are inadmissible under INA § 212(a). For example, someone who qualifies for an immigrant visa as an immediate relative may be inadmissible if she is a member of a terrorist organization. And even after admission, an admitted noncitizen might become deportable under INA § 237(a). For example, a criminal conviction might mean that a lawful permanent resident is deportable.

Inadmissible and deportable noncitizens are the two subcategories of removable noncitizens. Because the basic issue is being able to come to or stay in the United States lawfully, inadmissibility and deportability are often hotly contested. To explore this key area of immigration law, this chapter covers the inadmissibility grounds in INA § 212, the deportability grounds in INA § 237, as well as discretionary waivers and various forms of relief from removal. Inadmissibility and deportability grounds are often parallel. They share the fundamental idea that some noncitizens should not be admitted or allowed to stay in the United States, even if they meet the most basic underlying criteria for doing so. But inadmissibility and deportability grounds are rarely identical, with inadmissibility generally broader in coverage. This makes intuitive sense, since taking away something a person already enjoys—lawful presence in the United States—generally has greater impact than withholding initial admission.

Removal under a formal order carries several negative consequences for the noncitizen beyond expulsion itself. Noncitizens previously removed are generally inadmissible for five or ten years unless the federal government permits an earlier application for admission, but the bar can be longer or even permanent. See INA § 212(a)(9)(A). Once ordered removed, a noncitizen who later reenters without permission is subject to summary removal through reinstatement of the earlier order and to criminal punishment. See INA §§ 241(a)(5), 276. Removal also may end a noncitizen's eligibility for social security benefits. See 42 U.S.C.A § 402(n). And noncitizens who fail to depart are subject in theory to fines up to

$500 per day under INA § 274D, though no such fines have yet been imposed.

When do inadmissibility grounds apply, and when do deportability grounds apply? The key is whether the noncitizen has been *admitted* to the United States or instead is seeking "admission," which INA § 101(a)(13)(A) defines as lawful entry "after inspection and authorization by an immigration officer." What matters is whether the noncitizen complied with procedures for admission by presenting herself for inspection and admission—not whether she should have been admitted under the governing immigration law. For the purpose of drawing the line between inadmissibility and deportability, then, an erroneous admission is still an admission. This means that a noncitizen who presents themselves at the border for inspection and who is "waved in" by a border official has been admitted, regardless of whether she was admitted in a particular immigrant or nonimmigrant status. *See Matter of Quilantan*, 25 I & N Dec. 285 (BIA 2010).

Inadmissibility grounds apply to any noncitizen who has not been admitted. Deportability grounds apply only after a noncitizen has been admitted. As examples, a noncitizen who crosses the border without inspection at a port of entry is inadmissible, not deportable, even if she has lived in the United States for many years. A noncitizen who is in the United States unlawfully after overstaying a period of admission is deportable, not inadmissible.

What about a lawful permanent resident who travels outside the United States? When she returns, is she seeking admission and thus subject to the inadmissibility grounds? Under the general rule in INA § 101(a)(13)(C)—which the BIA has held is a presumption—a lawful permanent resident "shall not be regarded as seeking an admission into the United States." This provision sets out significant exceptions, but the government must show that at least one applies, if it asserts that a returning permanent resident is seeking admission. *See* 78 Interp. Rel. 523 (2001) (nonprecedent decision).[13]

In case you see the terms "exclusion" and "deportation" in immigration cases, a glance at history may help avoid confusion. Until 1996, noncitizens who had made an "entry" were subject to deportation grounds, and those who had not made an entry were subject to exclusion grounds. Of course, inspection and admission was an entry, but so was a surreptitious border crossing. Entrants without inspection (EWIs) escaped the more demanding exclusion grounds and enjoyed modestly

---

[13] Section 101(a)(13)(C) supersedes pre-1996 cases, especially *Rosenberg v. Fleuti*, 374 U.S. 449, 462, 83 S.Ct. 1804, 1812, 10 L.Ed.2d 1000 (1963), holding that permanent residents were not seeking "entry" when returning from an "innocent, casual, and brief excursion" outside the United States. *See, e.g., Camins v. Gonzales*, 500 F.3d 872, 878 (9th Cir. 2007) (holding that § 101(a)(13)(C) supersedes *Fleuti*, at least for prospective application).

greater procedural protections. The 1996 Act abandoned this entry-based line between exclusion and deportation. Exclusion grounds are now called inadmissibility grounds, deportation grounds are now deportability grounds, and the new line is based on admission. The law still sometimes distinguishes among inadmissible aliens for certain purposes, treating "arriving aliens" (basically port-of-entry cases—those formerly known as excludable aliens) differently from "other inadmissible aliens" —that is, entrants without inspection.

A. INADMISSIBILITY GROUNDS

Section 212(a) lists groups of "aliens who are ineligible to receive visas and ineligible to be admitted to the United States." This language is a practical reminder that a noncitizen who seeks admission may be screened on several occasions. Suppose, for example, that she applies for an immigrant visa at a U.S. consulate in her home country. The inadmissibility grounds will be first applied to her by the consular officer—an employee of the Department of State—who decides whether to issue any visa that may be required for admission. But when the immigrant next arrives at a port of entry bearing a duly issued visa, the inspector at the port of entry—an officer of the U.S. Customs and Border Protection (CBP) of the Department of Homeland Security—has full authority to consider anew whether any inadmissibility ground applies to her. *See* INA § 221(h). Or consider another noncitizen who was admitted several years ago as a student in F–1 status. If he applies to become a lawful permanent resident through adjustment of status under INA § 245(a), USCIS within the Department of Homeland Security will apply the inadmissibility grounds to him before considering him eligible to adjust.

1. OVERVIEW

INA § 212(a) contains the inadmissibility grounds themselves. In addition, INA § 237(a)(1)(A) makes any noncitizen deportable if he was inadmissible at the time of entry or adjustment of status. Simply put, any inadmissibility ground can become a deportability ground later, if the inadmissibility goes undetected at the port of entry. The rest of § 212 consists primarily of waiver provisions that cut back in intricate ways on the inadmissibility grounds in subsection (a). These waiver provisions set out statutory prerequisites (which can be quite daunting) but also require a favorable exercise of discretion from a federal government official. Though the application of statutory requirements is subject to judicial review, discretionary decisions generally are not. *See* INA § 242(a)(2)(B).

For noncitizens seeking admission to the United States as nonimmigrants, INA § 212(d)(3) provides DHS with discretionary power to waive nearly all the inadmissibility grounds. Noncitizens seeking admission as immigrants have far fewer waiver opportunities, but those with a spouse, child, or parent who is a U.S. citizen or lawful permanent resident are most likely to be eligible. Each waiver for immigrants has its own precise requirements.

Sprinkled through the rest of § 212 are additional requirements that must be met to avoid inadmissibility in certain defined circumstances. For example, § 212(n) describes in detail the labor condition attestation process required for H–1B nonimmigrants. One provision provides a more sweeping authority for inadmissibility: § 212(f) authorizes the President to issue a proclamation suspending the entry of specific classes of noncitizens or all noncitizens, when he or she finds that entry "would be detrimental to the interests of the United States."

Of course, you are not expected to memorize the inadmissibility grounds, but you should become familiar with the general structure of § 212, and know where to find the answers to specific questions that a client might pose. The problems in this Section will help establish that familiarity with both the inadmissibility grounds and the waivers. As you work through them, carefully read §§ 212(a) and 221(g), as well as the key waivers, which are: § 212(d)(3), (d)(5), (d)(11), (e), (g), (h), and (i). If the facts provided do not allow you to answer some of the problems completely, identify what else you would need to learn by interviewing the client or otherwise investigating.

2. CRIMES

The next three problems introduce you to the basic rules on crime-related inadmissibility under § 212(a)(2) and possible waivers under § 212(h). The application of these provisions depends on how certain terms are defined, such as "crime involving moral turpitude," "aggravated felony," and "conviction." The INA does not define "crime involving moral turpitude"—a key concept for both inadmissibility and deportability. The statute defines "aggravated felony," *see* INA § 101(a)(43), which is principally a deportability ground. An aggravated felony does not make a noncitizen inadmissible under § 212, but a crime that is an aggravated felony can disqualify a person from an inadmissibility waiver, and it may also be a crime involving moral turpitude. Section 101(a)(48) defines conviction and the length of sentence for immigration purposes.

Most of the cases defining these terms have arisen in the deportability context, so we will defer a closer look at their meaning until the materials on deportability in Section B of this chapter. In working through these problems, you should assume a valid conviction (where the problem speaks of a conviction) and identify what difference it would make if an offense is a crime involving moral turpitude or an aggravated felony.

PROBLEMS

1. Your client, A, qualifies for the family-sponsored first preference, but was convicted of petty larceny seven years ago and sent to prison for a total of three months. Is A inadmissible? What if she had been convicted of two counts of petty larceny? What if the conviction was for grand theft? What if it was for possession of 150 grams of marijuana? If an inadmissibility ground applies, what waivers might be available?

2. A German national employed in the U.S. consulate in Frankfurt recognizes an individual, B, who comes in to apply for a B–2 visa. She takes the consular officer aside and says that B is well known on the streets for running an illegal gambling operation in the region; she wouldn't be surprised if B means to set up a similar operation in Minneapolis, where he says he will visit friends. Is B inadmissible? Should he be?   NO·

3. C, a native and citizen of the Dominican Republic, became a lawful permanent resident of the United States in 1986, when he was 11 years old. In 1994, when C was 19 years old, he pled guilty to statutory rape after his underage girlfriend's mother discovered their relationship. He received a suspended sentence as part of the plea agreement and served no jail time. This conviction was not a ground of deportation at the time. He has had a spotless criminal record thereafter, operates a successful business with 20 employees, and is now married to a U.S. citizen and has three U.S. citizen children. Recently he took a two-week trip to his native country. Upon his return from this trip, is he inadmissible? Are any waivers available?

3. IMMIGRATION CONTROL

The immigration control grounds appear principally in paragraphs (6), (7), and (9) of § 212(a). Their evolution reflects Congress' attempts to attach more serious consequences to a wider range of immigration-related violations. To start developing an understanding of these grounds, consider the following problem.

PROBLEM

Two Border Patrol officers come across D, a national of Costa Rica, on a Florida beach at night, tugging a small vessel up away from the waterline. One officer thinks he saw other figures rushing away into nearby brush as their car approached, but a later search discovers nothing. Undaunted, D tells the officers that he is glad to see them and wishes to apply for admission as a tourist. He presents his passport. Is D inadmissible? On what ground? Are any waivers available?

a.   Fraud and Willful Misrepresentation of Material Facts

Inadmissibility based on fraud and willful misrepresentation is a long-standing feature of the INA, and now appears in INA § 212(a)(6)(C)(i). In 1996, Congress added clause (ii) specifically targeting false claims of U.S. citizenship (and a related inadmissibility ground for unlawful voting in § 212(a)(10)(D)). INA § 212(i) provides a waiver, but it is limited to inadmissibility under § 212(a)(6)(C)(i). Along with this substantive expansion, § 212(a)(6)(C) became procedurally pivotal in 1996, in that inadmissibility for fraud or willful misrepresentation—or inadmissibility under § 212(a)(7) for lack of proper documents—can trigger expedited removal under INA § 235(b)(1), as Chapter Six discussed, pp. 503–511.

Interpreting the inadmissibility grounds, like many provisions of the INA, often requires consulting agency interpretations of the statutory provisions. The next readings are, first, relevant sections of the Foreign Affairs Manual, a Department of State document that gives consular officers more precise guidance for carrying out their functions under the INA, followed by a BIA decision that applies the inadmissibility ground and decides on a waiver.[14] Then try assessing the fact patterns in the problems that follow.

U.S. DEPARTMENT OF STATE, FOREIGN AFFAIRS MANUAL

9 Foreign Affairs Manual Section 40.63, Notes, as amended through February 2015.[a]

* * *

APPLICATION OF INA 212(a)(6)(C)(I)

* * *

Not a Substitute for Other INA 212(a) Inadmissibility. INA 212(a)(6)(C)(i) was not intended by Congress * * * to be a substitute for the other grounds of inadmissibility provided by the INA nor for grounds that do not exist in the INA. It should not be used to accomplish indirectly that which cannot be accomplished directly. The section was not intended to permit and must not become a device for entrapment of aliens whom you might suspect to be ineligible on some other ground(s) for which there is not sufficient evidence to sustain a finding of inadmissibility. You should always assess an applicant's eligibility for a visa in accordance with all INA provisions governing the eligibility for a visa or inadmissibility of certain specifically described classes. Bear in mind that

---

[14] The Supreme Court has also struggled with the issue of deciding what misrepresentations and concealments are "material." *See* Chapter Two, pp. 128–132, discussing *Kungys v. United States,* 485 U.S. 759, 108 S.Ct. 1537, 99 L.Ed.2d 839 (1988).

[a]   Internal numbering for headings and subheadings is omitted here.—eds.

aliens may not be refused visas simply because they do not seem particularly desirable individuals as either immigrants or nonimmigrants.

Nature of Penalty. In applying the provisions of INA 212(a)(6)(C)(i), keep in mind the severe nature of the penalty the alien incurs: lifetime inadmissibility, unless a waiver is available. (See 9 FAM 40.63 N9.) When considering whether to impose such a dire penalty, keep in mind the words quoted by the Attorney General in his landmark opinion on this matter. (The *Matter of S- and B-C-*, 9 I & N Dec. 436, at [446 (A.G. 1961)]): "Shutting off the opportunity to come to the United States actually is a crushing deprivation to many prospective immigrants. Very often it destroys the hopes and aspirations of a lifetime, and it frequently operates not only against the individual immediately but also bears heavily upon his family in and out of the United States."

* * *

INTERPRETATION OF THE TERM "MISREPRESENTATION"

Misrepresentation Defined. As used in INA 212(a)(6)(C)(i), a misrepresentation is an assertion or manifestation not in accordance with the facts. Misrepresentation requires an affirmative act taken by the alien. A misrepresentation can be made in various ways, including in an oral interview or in written applications, or by submitting evidence containing false information.

Differentiation Between Misrepresentation and Failure to Volunteer Information. In determining whether a misrepresentation has been made, it is necessary to distinguish between misrepresentation of information and information that was merely concealed by the alien's silence. Silence or the failure to volunteer information does not in itself constitute a misrepresentation for the purposes of INA 212(a)(6)(C)(i).

Misrepresentation Must Have Been Before U.S. Official. For a misrepresentation to fall within the purview of INA 212(a)(6)(C)(i), it must have been practiced on an official of the U.S. Government, generally speaking, a consular officer or a Department of Homeland Security (DHS) officer.

Misrepresentation Must Be Made on Alien's Own Application. The misrepresentation must have been made by the alien with respect to the alien's own visa application. Misrepresentations made in connection with some other person's visa application do not fall within the purview of INA 212(a)(6)(C)(i). Any such misrepresentations may be considered with regard to the possible application of INA 212(a)(6)(E).

Misrepresentation Made by Applicant's Attorney or Agent. The fact that an alien pursues a visa application through an attorney or travel agent does not serve to insulate the alien from liability for misrepresentations made by such agents, if it is established that the alien was aware of the action being taken in furtherance of the application. This standard would apply, for example, where a travel agent executed a visa application on an alien's behalf. Similarly, an oral misrepresentation made on behalf of an alien at the port of entry by an aider or abettor of the alien's illegal entry will not shield the alien in question from inadmissibility under INA 212(a)(6)(C)(i), irrespective of what penalties the aider or abettor might incur, if it can be established that the alien was aware at the time of the misrepresentation made on his or her behalf.

* * *

INTERPRETATION OF THE TERM "WILLFULLY"

"Willfully" Defined. The term "willfully" as used in INA 212(a)(6)(C)(i) is interpreted to mean knowingly and intentionally, as distinguished from accidentally, inadvertently, or in an honest belief that the facts are otherwise. In order to find the element of willfulness, it must be determined that the alien was fully aware of the nature of the information sought and knowingly, intentionally, and deliberately made an untrue statement.

Misrepresentation Is Alien's Responsibility. An alien who acts on the advice of another is considered to be exercising the faculty of conscious and deliberate will in accepting or rejecting such advice. It is no defense for an alien to say that the misrepresentation was made because someone else advised the action unless it is found that the alien lacked the capacity to exercise judgment.

* * *

MATTER OF CERVANTES-GONZALEZ
Board of Immigration Appeals, 1999.
22 I & N Dec. 560.

GRANT, BOARD MEMBER:

In an oral decision dated January 21, 1997, an Immigration Judge denied the respondent's requests for a waiver of inadmissibility and adjustment of status pursuant to sections 212(i) and 245 of the Immigration and Nationality Act. * * *

* * *

In determining whether to grant the application for a section 212(i) waiver, the Immigration Judge found that the respondent had failed to establish extreme hardship to his spouse in the event he is deported. Additionally, the Immigration Judge denied the respondent's application for adjustment of status as a matter of discretion.

On appeal, the respondent argues that the Immigration Judge erred in finding no extreme hardship and that he also gave improper weight to the negative factors in this case.

* * *

WHETHER A WAIVER IS REQUIRED
UNDER SECTION 212(i) OF THE ACT

The respondent first argues that he does not require a waiver of inadmissibility under section 212(i) of the Act because he is not inadmissible under section 212(a)(6)(C)(i) of the Act. Specifically, he states that his sole conviction for possession of a false identification document (namely, a counterfeit Texas birth certificate) with the intent to defraud the United States (by obtaining a United States passport) does not fall within the definition of fraud in the Act. As he was convicted only of possession, he asserts that it is error to find him guilty of seeking to procure a fraudulent document. We disagree. Section 212(a)(6)(C)(i) of the Act states:

> [A]ny alien who, by fraud or willfully misrepresenting a material fact, seeks to procure (or has sought to procure or has procured) a visa, other documentation, or admission into the United States or other benefit provided under this Act is inadmissible.

Obviously, the respondent admits to *procuring* one document in the form of a fraudulent birth certificate. The respondent testified that he purchased the birth certificate in Los Angeles, California, for approximately $400 or $500 so that he could obtain employment. He then used the birth certificate to procure by fraud a social security number, and he used both documents to *seek to procure* a passport. The latter document was necessary in order for the respondent to be able to travel into and out of the United States and to aid him in obtaining employment.

We note also that in finding the respondent's conviction fell within section 212(a)(6)(C) of the Act, the Immigration Judge and the Immigration and Naturalization Service did not improperly "go behind" the conviction record as contended by the respondent. Rather, they were merely establishing the facts regarding the respondent's fraud, which would have constituted grounds for inadmissibility whether or not the respondent had been convicted. *See* section 212(a)(6)(C) of the Act (no conviction is required in order to establish inadmissibility).

In sum, we agree with the Immigration Judge that the respondent's activities clearly fall within the purview of section 212(a)(6)(C)(i) of the Act. By fraud and by willful misrepresentation of a material fact, he sought to procure both "documentation" and "other benefits" under the Act. * * *

* * *

EXTREME HARDSHIP

* * *

1. Factors To Be Considered

The factors deemed relevant in determining extreme hardship to a qualifying relative include, but are not limited to, the following: the presence of lawful permanent resident or United States citizen family ties to this country; the qualifying relative's family ties outside the United States; the conditions in the country or countries to which the qualifying relative would relocate and the extent of the qualifying relative's ties to such countries; the financial impact of departure from this country; and, finally, significant conditions of health, particularly when tied to an unavailability of suitable medical care in the country to which the qualifying relative would relocate.

While not all of the foregoing factors need be analyzed in any given case, we will now apply those factors to the present case to the extent they are relevant in determining extreme hardship to the respondent's spouse. We emphasize again, however, that the list of factors noted above is not exclusive and also that the Attorney General and her delegates have the authority to construe extreme hardship narrowly. *INS v. Jong Ha Wang*, [450 U.S. 139, 144 (1981)]. In addition, we note that establishing extreme hardship does not create any entitlement to relief. Although extreme hardship is a requirement for section 212(i) relief, once established, it is but one favorable discretionary factor to be considered.

2. Analysis

The respondent is a 24-year-old native and citizen of Mexico. He has resided in the United States since 1989 and was recently married in 1995. At the time of the marriage, the respondent's wife was a lawful permanent resident; she became a naturalized United States citizen in 1996. Both the respondent and his wife reside with her family and provide them some financial support in return for room and board. Most of the respondent's family, however, resides in Mexico.

The respondent testified that he and his wife have very little money. Therefore, if forced to accompany the respondent to Mexico, the respondent's wife would be unable to travel back and forth to visit her family in the United States. In addition, the respondent's wife testified that she would have difficulty in obtaining employment in Mexico.

Having fully weighed the factors mentioned above, we find that the respondent has failed to establish extreme hardship to his spouse.[4] As

---

4   IIRIRA § 349 amended section 212(i) of the Act [in 1996] to require a showing of extreme hardship to an alien's United States citizen or permanent resident alien spouse or parent. This

noted in the Immigration Judge's decision, the respondent's wife knew that the respondent was in deportation proceedings at the time they were married. In contrast to the respondent's assertions on appeal, this factor is not irrelevant. Rather, it goes to the respondent's wife's expectations at the time they were wed. Indeed, she was aware that she may have to face the decision of parting from her husband or following him to Mexico in the event he was ordered deported. In the latter scenario, the respondent's wife was also aware that a move to Mexico would separate her from her family in California. We find this to undermine the respondent's argument that his wife will suffer extreme hardship if he is deported. *See Perez v. INS*, 96 F.3d 390, 392 (9th Cir. 1996) (stating that " '[e]xtreme hardship' is hardship that is 'unusual or beyond that which would normally be expected' upon deportation. 'The common results of deportation are insufficient to prove extreme hardship.' "); *Shooshtary v. INS*, [39 F.3d 1049, 1051 (9th Cir. 1994)] (holding that the uprooting of family and separation from friends does not necessarily amount to extreme hardship but rather represents the type of inconvenience and hardship experienced by the families of most aliens being deported); *Silverman v. Rogers*, 437 F.2d 102, 107 (1st Cir. 1970) (stating that "[e]ven assuming that the federal government had no right either to prevent a marriage or destroy it, we believe that here it has done nothing more than to say that the residence of one of the marriage partners may not be in the United States"), *cert. denied*, 402 U.S. 983 (1971).

Additionally, at no time during the hearing did the respondent's wife suggest that she would suffer any particular hardship, let alone extreme hardship, by moving to Mexico. Furthermore, although the respondent's spouse would lose the physical proximity to her family, she speaks Spanish and the majority of her family is originally from Mexico. Therefore, she should have less difficulty adjusting to life in a foreign country.

In addition, neither the respondent nor his wife have any real financial ties to the United States. The respondent's wife is currently unemployed. Although the respondent is a musician in a band, he provided no evidence to prove that it had experienced success such that deportation would cause him to relinquish a lucrative career and, therefore, plunge his wife into unaccustomed poverty. Even if this were the case, we have generally not found financial hardship alone to amount to extreme hardship.

In sum, the respondent has failed to show that his spouse would suffer extreme hardship over and above the normal economic and social disruptions involved in the deportation of a family member. Therefore, we

---

section of the IIRIRA also limited the availability of section 212(i), which had previously allowed aliens to establish eligibility if they were parents of United States citizens or lawful permanent resident aliens. [footnote relocated—eds.]

agree with the Immigration Judge's decision denying the respondent a waiver of inadmissibility under section 212(i) of the Act.

Having found the respondent statutorily ineligible for relief, we decline to discuss whether or not he merits a waiver as a matter of discretion. * * *

* * *

Based on the foregoing, we conclude that the respondent has failed to establish statutory eligibility for a waiver of inadmissibility under section 212(i) of the Act. Therefore, he is also ineligible for adjustment of status. * * * Accordingly, his appeal will be dismissed.

VILLAGELIU, BOARD MEMBER, concurring:

* * *

While I generally concur with both the result and reasoning of the majority opinion, I write separately to address briefly [certain] minor points in the majority's precedent opinion that may be misinterpreted.

* * *

* * * [T]he majority's opinion may be read to imply that the time the respondent and his spouse wed is determinative as to whether to discount the spouse's hardship because of diminished expectations when marrying an alien in deportation proceedings. I disagree with that implication. Such diminished expectations clearly must relate to the actual circumstances, both of the marriage, and of the pending deportation proceedings, and the totality of the circumstances is paramount. Moreover, we only "discount" equities acquired after a final order of deportation. *See Matter of Correa*, 19 I & N Dec. 130 (BIA 1984). In this case no final order was entered since an appeal was pending. *See Matter of Lok*, 18 I & N Dec. 101 (BIA 1981) (stating that an order is final when the Board renders its decision on appeal).

Here, such a discount was appropriate, as the majority properly pointed out that the respondent's spouse at no time suggested that she would suffer any particular hardship if she moved to Mexico with the respondent. A different situation would arise, for instance, where the marriage takes place after proceedings are initiated, but was preceded by a long-term cohabitative relationship; where the alien was in protected status and deportation was neither imminent nor likely in the foreseeable future; or where eligibility for adjustment of status without the need for a discretionary waiver of inadmissibility has been established. A respondent's relationship to his spouse's offspring may also be an appropriate consideration in the extreme hardship determination. Any hardship to a qualifying spouse must always be considered. In short, as we have often stated, extreme hardship is not a definable term of fixed and inflexible meaning, and the elements to establish extreme hardship are dependent upon the facts and circumstances of each case. Under the specific facts of this case extreme hardship was not established, and this case should not be misinterpreted as requiring a discount of the hardships present in all cases where the wedding ceremony takes place after proceedings are initiated.

* * * [T]he majority's opinion correctly notes that in purchasing the fraudulent birth certificate, using it to procure a fraudulent social security card, and subsequently using these documents to seek to procure a United States passport in order to travel into and out of the United States and seek employment, the respondent sought to procure both "documentation" and "other benefits" under the Act. The majority's finding is consistent with the close scrutiny of such a finding required by *Matter of Healy and Goodchild*, 17 I & N Dec. 22 (BIA 1979), because of its harsh consequences. However, a small clarification is needed. The other benefits under the Act the respondent sought to procure are the right to travel with a United States passport pursuant to section 215(b) of the Act. The majority's language may be misinterpreted as suggesting that using the fraudulent passport to obtain employment is obtaining a benefit under the Act.

Although the use or possession of such document is punishable under section 274C of the Act, working in the United States is not "a benefit provided under this Act," and we have specifically held that a violation of section 274C and fraud or misrepresentation under section 212(a)(6)(C)(i) of the Act are not equivalent. *See Matter of Lazarte*, [21 I & N Dec. 214] (BIA 1996). It is long settled that inadmissibility for immigration fraud does not ensue from the mere purchase of fraudulent documents, absent an attempt to fraudulently use the document for immigration purposes.

Finally, the majority points out that the Supreme Court has indicated that we may permissibly construe the element of extreme hardship narrowly. However, such permissibility does not require a narrow construction of extreme hardship, and we have recently declined to do so, choosing instead to rely on our precedents for guidance in our case-by-case determinations. * * *

[The opinion of ROSENBERG, BOARD MEMBER, concurring and dissenting, is omitted.]

* * *

In 2001, the Ninth Circuit denied Cervantes-Gonzalez' petition for review, holding that it lacked jurisdiction to review the BIA's decision regarding discretionary waivers. *Cervantes-Gonzales v. INS*, 244 F.3d 1001, 1006 (9th Cir. 2001).

PROBLEMS

1. Noncitizen E, a high-school teacher from Istanbul, presents a fraudulent Turkish passport, bearing his picture and what appears to be a legitimate B–2 visa affixed thereto (nonimmigrant visitor for pleasure), at the Turkish Airlines check-in counter at the Istanbul airport. E states that he obtained it for a fee from someone who held himself out as a travel agent, that he never appeared before a U.S. consular officer, that he believed this procedure to be the proper way to obtain a passport and visa, and that he thought his documents were perfectly valid. The airline refused to let him board, and E did not come to the United States on that occasion. Later, E applies in proper fashion for a visa to come to the United States. Is E inadmissible under INA § 212(a)(6)(C)(i)? If he is inadmissible, is a waiver available? Would it make a difference if E were instead a farmer from rural Turkey who had only a fourth-grade education?

2. Noncitizen F used a bogus green card to secure entry into the United States, successfully, one time eight years ago, and then left after five months. Now he has developed a substantial international import-export business and seeks to enter the United States lawfully as a nonimmigrant E–1 treaty trader. Is F inadmissible? F's widowed mother already lives in the United States and recently became a U.S. citizen. They have been estranged and he is not sure whether she would petition for his permanent residence. If she will, would that make any difference in F's possible admissibility? Are any waivers available? Would it make a difference if he and his mother were on better terms? If the mother were afflicted with a chronic illness? If he were?

b. Bars Based on Other Immigration Violations

(i) Entrants Without Inspection (EWIs)

The central inadmissibility ground based on immigration violations is INA § 212(a)(6)(A)(i), which makes inadmissible "an alien present in the United States without being admitted or paroled, or who arrives in the United States at any time or place other than as designated by the Attorney General." Simply put, this provision covers EWIs (entrants without inspection).

(ii) Prior Removal

Also important is INA § 212(a)(9)(A), which bars readmission for any noncitizen who has been ordered removed. The current bar is ten years for a person removed from inside the United States, or five years for removal at the border or a port of entry. The government may consent in advance to the admission of a noncitizen who was removed previously— essentially a discretionary waiver, with virtually no other statutory prerequisites. Consent has been granted sparingly but is possible, given the right showing, in a balancing process that loosely resembles the reasoning applied to determine "extreme hardship" in *Cervantes-Gonzalez*.

(iii)   Unlawful Presence

Before 1996, a noncitizen's prior unlawful stay generally did not bar her lawful admission later, not even as a permanent resident—so long as no formal exclusion or deportation order was issued against her. Today, three provisions adopted in 1996 impose more serious consequences for prior unlawful presence, even if she has never been ordered removed. Of these, INA § 212(a)(9)(B) has drawn the most attention. As interpreted and applied, this subsection provides that a noncitizen who has been unlawfully present for a single period of more than 180 days but less than one year, and then voluntarily departs, is inadmissible for three years. If she has been unlawfully present for a single period of one year or more, a ten-year bar applies, triggered once she departs or is removed.

Section 212(a)(9)(B)(ii) defines "unlawful presence" to cover noncitizens who entered without inspection or stayed beyond the expiration date of a nonimmigrant admission. But suppose a temporary worker, who is still within her admission period, violates the terms of her nonimmigrant status by working for a different employer? She is certainly unlawfully present in the sense that DHS could initiate a removal proceeding. But is she unlawfully present for purposes of the three- or ten-year bar? Generally not, as explained in guidance issued by USCIS, summarized and reprinted at 86 Interp. Rel. 1393, 1420 (2009). The rationale is that though overstays are easy to determine and accrue unlawful presence, violations of other conditions of admission are sometimes quite technical and do not necessarily notify noncitizens that they are running "bad time."

Other than overstayers, nonimmigrants accrue unlawful presence only after the government gives them notice that they have violated the conditions of their admission, as might appear in a ruling denying an extension or change of status. A combination of administrative and statutory exceptions has carved out categories of noncitizens who lack formal immigration status but nonetheless do not accrue unlawful presence. These include minors, asylum seekers, beneficiaries of family unity, battered women and children, and victims of trafficking, as well as noncitizens granted voluntary departure, stays of removal, deferred action, or deferred enforced departure. USCIS Adjudicator's Field Manual ch. 40.9.2 (b)(2)–(3), https://www.uscis.gov/ilink/docView/AFM/HTML/AFM/0-0-0-1.html. In sum, "a person can only accrue unlawful presence if he or she is in unlawful status, but . . . a person can be in unlawful status without accruing unlawful presence." Lauren Gilbert, *Obama's Ruby*

Slippers: Enforcement Discretion in the Absence of Immigration Reform, 116 W. Va. L. Rev. 255, 304 (2013).

Generally, the government's initiation of removal proceedings against a noncitizen has no effect on the accrual of unlawful presence. A noncitizen who was already accruing unlawful presence when removal proceedings began will continue to accrue unlawful presence. A noncitizen, such as a lawful permanent resident, who was not accruing unlawful presence will likewise not begin running "bad time" after the initiation of removal proceedings. *See* USCIS Adjudicator's Field Manual ch. 40.9.2 (b)(5), https://www.uscis.gov/iframe/ilink/docView/AFM/HTML/AFM/0-0-0-1.html (citing 8 C.F.R. § 239.3.).

Section 212(a)(9)(B) does not apply to noncitizens in the United States, if they have not *departed* the United States after accumulating 180 days or one year of unlawful presence. The policy behind this limitation is obscure at best, but this feature makes it highly desirable for any noncitizen who qualifies for permanent residence to adjust status without leaving the United States, as Chapter Six discussed.

Another inadmissibility ground, INA § 212(a)(9)(C), penalizes unlawful presence, by making any noncitizen inadmissible who has been unlawfully present for an *aggregate* period of more than one year or has been ordered removed, and thereafter enters or attempts to enter without being admitted—that is, crosses or tries to cross the border clandestinely. This bar is permanent, but after ten years outside the United States, a discretionary advance consent procedure is available like the one in § 212(a)(9)(A).

The third provision added in 1996 that attaches tough consequences to immigration violations is INA § 222(g). It says that if a noncitizen is admitted on a nonimmigrant visa and stays longer than the authorized time period, that visa is void at the conclusion of his authorized period of stay. He is not necessarily barred from a later nonimmigrant admission, but for the rest of his life such admissions must be on the basis of a new visa issued in his home country, with an exception for "extraordinary circumstances." The State Department has explained that this requirement is meant to assure knowledgeable special scrutiny of a past violator's qualifications before any new visa issues. 75 Interp. Rel. 45 (1998).

The following problems will acquaint you with the statutory basics of these inadmissibility grounds relating to immigration control.

PROBLEMS

1. G, a Honduran national, recently married an American citizen in Tegucigalpa, but three years ago G was removed from the United States for overstaying her admission as a B–2 visitor for pleasure. Is G inadmissible? If so, how long before she becomes admissible again? Can you speed up her access? Are any waivers available?

2. H, who seeks to come as an F–1 nonimmigrant student, admits that he entered the United States from Mexico, his home country, without inspection three times over the last five years. Each time, H stayed for about five months and left of his own accord. Is he inadmissible? What if he came a fourth time for another five month stay? What if he came only once but stayed eight months? What if H traveled with his brother at the time of his second entry, with H serving as a kind of guide because he already knew the route? Are any waivers or exceptions available?

3. J, a citizen of Korea, was admitted on a business visitor (B–1) visa, with an authorized period of stay that expired on May 1 of last year. J did not return to Korea at the time. Instead, he stayed in the United States until January 1 of the current year, working without authorization for much of that time. J is now back in Korea. An immigrant visa has finally become available to him based on a family fourth preference petition that his U.S. citizen sister filed for him many years ago. Is J inadmissible? Are any waivers or exceptions available? Would it be different if he had never left the United States?

c. Self-Enforcement and Immigration Control

Is an inadmissibility ground for prior unlawful presence (with waivers) a good or bad idea? Both the three-year and ten-year bars and the voiding of visas for nonimmigrant overstays can be seen as attempts to build a measure of self-enforcement into the immigration laws. Their drafters evidently meant to give noncitizens a real incentive to leave the United States voluntarily when their admission period is over, rather than stay unlawfully. But consider these comments on the bars, written by one of the co-authors of this book who was initially inclined to favor the provision:

> [E]xperience has shown that the bars are ill-designed to promote self-enforcement. Those who have no prospects for immigration benefits when Day 180 rolls around are totally untouched. If they leave then, they can be virtually certain they'll never qualify for U.S. residence. If they stay, there's just a chance they might get lucky. Maybe they'll find a U.S. spouse or qualifying employer. And [maybe they'll find a loophole or Congress will change the rules, as has already happened twice, but only for limited groups of beneficiaries.]

[handwritten margin note: - 3/10 yr ban not as effective as one thinks]

But there's a deeper reason why the bars aren't a credible part of enforcement * * * . The bars carry real consequences only when individual aliens are finally poised for immigration benefits. At that point, they invariably have U.S. citizens or permanent residents deeply invested in their staying. It is exactly the moment when enforcement will seem maximally cruel and controversial. However attractive the bars may seem in the abstract, they have to be implemented one individual or family at a time. * * *

* * * We need to repeal the three- and 10-year bars.

David A. Martin, *Waiting for Solutions*, Legal Times, May 29, 2001, at 66.

d. Waivers of the Unlawful Presence Bar

Noncitizens who qualify for permanent resident status but who are ineligible to adjust status must leave the United States to obtain an immigrant visa through consular processing. They thus trigger a three- or ten-year bar if they have been unlawfully present for the specified length of time. The key decision will often be the grant or denial of a waiver under § 212(a)(9)(B)(v). That provision authorizes waiver of the bars if "refusal of admission * * * would result in extreme hardship to the citizen or lawfully resident spouse or parent of such alien." Note that hardship to citizen or LPR children does not count for these purposes, at least not directly.

A crucial practical consideration has been that, until 2013, no noncitizen could apply for a waiver of inadmissibility (which is decided by USCIS) until she left the United States to undergo consular processing. That locational requirement confronted the noncitizen with what was often an agonizing, high-risk gamble. She could choose to remain in the United States without lawful immigration status. If she left the United States to apply for a waiver, she might face a long wait for a decision. If her application won approval, she could return to the United States as a lawful permanent resident. But if her application were denied, she faced an even longer separation due to the three- or ten-year bar.

In 2013, DHS implemented a new procedure that allowed a subset of those potentially eligible for waiver to apply for provisional unlawful presence waivers before they leave the United States for their consular interview, so long as no other inadmissibility ground applies. 90 Interp. Rel. 4 (2013). The new regulation opened up that possibility only for immediate relatives of U.S. citizens. This pre-approval process was meant to reduce the amount of time that U.S. citizens are separated from their immediate relatives while those family members travel abroad to obtain an immigrant visa (and also to alleviate the gamble described above). If the provisional waiver application is approved, the beneficiary departs the United States to undergo consular processing. Assuming the official uncovers no other ground of inadmissibility, the immigrant visa can issue immediately. *See* Julia Preston, *Immigration Change to Ease Family Separations*, N.Y. Times, Jan. 3, 2013, at A12. In July 2015, DHS published proposed rules that would significantly expand the availability of the advance provisional waiver, by including persons prima facie eligible for family-sponsored or employment-based immigration if granted a waiver of the three- and ten-year bars. 92 Interp. Rel. 1339 (2015).

DHS waiver decisions under § 212(a)(9)(B) have often drawn by analogy on the § 212(i) standards in *Cervantes-Gonzalez* and similar cases. Compare these two excerpts from two decisions separated by less than two months, both involving appeals from denials of a waiver to the spouse of a U.S. citizen. As you review them, consider the choices each applicant made in marshaling the facts of each case:

> The record contains, in addition to the Applicant's letter on appeal, two letters from the [U.S. consulate in the Dominican Republic]; an affidavit from the Applicant's spouse; a letter from a licensed mental health counselor; and medical records. The entire record was reviewed and considered in rendering a decision on the appeal.

* * *

> In her affidavit, the Applicant's spouse asserted that separation from the Applicant would be very straining on her mental state and she would be isolated and alone. She indicated that she is worried about the impact of separation on her children. The Applicant provided a letter from a licensed mental health counselor, which indicates that the Applicant's spouse has received individual outpatient therapy since August 31, 2011, to stabilize her mood and deal with family stressors. Although this qualifies as evidence of emotional hardship to his spouse, the Applicant has not demonstrated that his spouse's hardship, as a result of remaining in the United States without him, is unusual or beyond that which is normally to be expected upon an applicant's bar to admission to the United States.

> The Applicant's spouse claimed medical and educational hardship if she relocated to the Dominican Republic. The Applicant's spouse declared that she wants her children to have the best education possible, which would not be available in the Dominican Republic. She claimed that she and her children have excellent medical care in the United States and would not have comparable medical care in the Dominican Republic. The Applicant provided a letter dated January 20, 2014, from a licensed practical nurse stating that his child had a bilateral

ureteral re-implant on July 31, 2013. Although the Applicant's spouse claims that the quality of medical care would be significantly lower than in the United States, the Applicant has not provided any documents to support her claim. Nor has the Applicant provided documentation to show that the educational system in the Dominican Republic would be inadequate for his children. Furthermore, * * * hardship to the Applicant's children will not be separately considered, except as it may affect the Applicant's spouse.

* * * The Applicant states that he attends church, has accepted his mistakes, and is remorseful for having violated U.S. immigration laws, but his statement does not describe any hardship to his spouse.

* * * The Applicant has not established that refusal of admission to the United States would result in extreme hardship to his U.S. citizen spouse. As the Applicant has not demonstrated that a qualifying relative will experience extreme hardship, we will not determine whether the Applicant merits a favorable exercise of discretion.

Matter of J-L-R-M-, ID# 14048, 2015 WL 6735249 (Admin. App. Office 2015). Now compare the second excerpted case:

With the appeal the Applicant submits statements from his spouse and him, financial documentation, medical information for his spouse, a psychological evaluation of the spouse, a letter from the Applicant's employer, letters of support from the Applicant's children, and country information for Mexico. The entire record was reviewed and considered in rendering a decision on the appeal.

* * *

On appeal the Applicant asserts that his spouse will suffer economically and emotionally with debts, bills and family obligations. The Applicant's spouse states that because of the Applicant's waiver denial she is experiencing insomnia, restlessness, stress, high blood pressure, anxiety, and heart palpitations for which she is taking medication. The Applicant's spouse further maintains that she cannot provide for her family, meet expenses, and pay debts with her income alone. She asserts that she would have to close her business to get a regular job, which she contends would be difficult due to her age and the unemployment rate. She further maintains that the Applicant may get a job in Mexico, but wages are low and he would not be able to send money.

With respect to the emotional hardship referenced, a psychological evaluation of the Applicant's spouse submitted on appeal diagnoses her with major depressive disorder, single episode, general anxiety disorder, sleep disorder, and hypertension. The evaluation states that the spouse reports feeling stressed about possibly being separated from the Applicant, and describes the Applicant as attentive to the physical, social and psychological needs of the family. It further states that the spouse shows symptoms of depression, social withdrawal, decreased appetite, negative thinking, and poor concentration, plus neck, head and stomach pain, lethargy, and heart palpitations. The evaluation opines that the Applicant's presence, motivation and emotional support are paramount for his spouse's stability and social functioning, and states that the Applicant's spouse fears being unable to deal with anxiety and depression if separated from the Applicant. It further states that the spouse worries about the consequences on her children if separated from the Applicant and that their financial situation will become exacerbated. The evaluator recommends that the Applicant's spouse continue individualized counseling sessions.

more health issues for wife

children

finances

In addition, financial documentation in the record includes bills and information related to the spouse's business and income, showing that she has significant financial obligations. The documentation in the record also establishes that the Applicant is gainfully employed and his income plays an important role in the financial well-being of the family. Based on a totality of the circumstances, the record establishes that the Applicant's spouse will experience extreme hardship if she remains in the United States while the Applicant relocates abroad.

We also find the record to establish that the Applicant's spouse would experience extreme hardship if she were to relocate to Mexico to reside with the Applicant. The Applicant asserts violence and lack of safety in Mexico make it impossible for his family to go there. The spouse maintains that she and her children are terrified of living in Mexico due to high crime. She cites submitted country information and news accounts of murders, drug traffickers, and kidnappings in Mexico. We note that the U.S. Department of State recommends deferred non-essential travel to [some parts] of the Applicant's home state.

no Spanish

The spouse also asserts that she and her children, whom she states do not read or write Spanish, have never lived anywhere but the United States and that relocating would disrupt her children's education. The spouse contends that she and the

Applicant would not have money to pay for education nor be able to obtain loans if they were unemployed in Mexico. She states that she and the Applicant are paying on a home and vehicles for her children to drive to school, and maintains that if they relocated they would have to sell the home and vehicles. The spouse also contends that the Applicant has no home, vehicle, connections or family in Mexico for support.

* * *

The record establishes that the Applicant's U.S. citizen spouse was born and raised in the United States, that her parents, siblings, children, and grandchild are in the United States, and that she has no ties to Mexico. She would have to leave her family and her community, give up her business and possibly lose her home and she would be concerned about her safety as well as her financial well-being in Mexico. The Applicant has thus establishe[d] that his spouse would suffer extreme hardship were she to relocate abroad to reside with the Applicant due to his inadmissibility.

* * * We now turn to a consideration of whether the Applicant merits a waiver of inadmissibility as a matter of discretion.

* * *

The favorable factors in this matter are the extreme hardship the Applicant's U.S. citizen spouse would face, regardless of whether she accompanies the Applicant or stays in the United States; hardship to the Applicant's children; letters of support for the Applicant; community ties; gainful employment in the United States; home ownership; and the Applicant's lack of a criminal record other than a 2010 arrest for DUI. The negative factors are the Applicant's [procuring admission to the United States through] fraud or misrepresentation * * * and periods of unlawful presence and employment in the United States. Although the Applicant's immigration violations are serious, the record establishes that the positive factors in this case outweigh the negative factors and a favorable exercise of discretion is warranted.

Matter of J-A-S-G-, ID # 14320, 2015 WL 9426308 (Admin. App. Office 2015).

What explains the difference in outcomes between the denial in the first case and the approval in the second, both decided by the Administrative Appeals Office?

If you were the lawyer for the first applicant, J-L-R-M-, is there any information you might seek or actions that you might take to try to arrive at a different outcome?

4. PUBLIC CHARGE

Concern about an influx of paupers underlay many of the earliest attempts—then by the state governments—to restrict immigration. *See generally* Gerald L. Neuman, *The Lost Century of American Immigration Law (1776–1875)*, 93 Colum. L. Rev. 1833, 1846–59 (1993). In 1882, Congress enacted the first federal provision barring from entry "any person unable to take care of himself or herself without becoming a public charge." Act of Aug. 3, 1882, ch. 376, § 2, 22 Stat. 214. There has been a public charge excludability or inadmissibility ground ever since.

INA § 237(a)(5) also makes deportable any "alien who, within five years from the date of entry, has become a public charge from causes not affirmatively shown to have arisen since entry." But case law has limited this deportability ground to the rare cases where (1) the public assistance program imposed on the noncitizen or other persons an obligation to repay the agency; and (2) the agency's demand for reimbursement has not been satisfied. *See Matter of B-*, 3 I & N Dec. 323 (BIA 1948). Only eight public charge deportations occurred from 1961 through 1970, and only 31 from 1971 through 1980, when the government stopped publishing the figures.

In contrast, the public charge *inadmissibility* ground—now in INA § 212(a)(4)—is highly significant for the number of visa applicants that it disqualifies. The administering officer has broad discretion, since any alien is inadmissible who *"in the opinion of the consular officer . . . or in the opinion of the Attorney General . . .* is likely at any time to become a public charge" (emphasis added).

Much of the recent history of this inadmissibility concerns the sponsor's affidavit of financial support, which, in an early informal form, became a standard method of overcoming the public charge exclusion ground. *See, e.g., Matter of Kohama*, 17 I & N Dec. 257 (Assoc. Comm'r 1978). Concerned by numerous state court cases holding that affidavits of support were not legally binding on the sponsor as a matter of state law, however, Congress later modified federally funded assistance programs such as food stamps, Assistance to Families with Dependent Children (AFDC), and Supplemental Security Income (SSI) by adding new "deeming provisions." For purposes of determining public assistance eligibility, a sponsor's income and assets were deemed to be available to the sponsored noncitizen, with exemptions for refugees and certain other groups.

The 1996 Immigration Act and the Personal Responsibility and Work Opportunity Reconciliation Act, Pub. L. 104–193, 110 Stat. 2105 (1996) (1996 Welfare Act), took the next step by requiring formal affidavits of support for most immigrants and making the affidavits enforceable, while also leaving the deeming mechanism in place. One of the legislative reports on an early version of the 1996 Act, noting the increasing use of public assistance by recent immigrants, explained: "In effect, immigrants make a promise to the American people that they will not become a financial burden." S. Rep. No. 249, 104th Cong., 2d Sess. 6 (1996).

An enforceable affidavit of support on Form I–864 is now required for all immigrants qualifying as immediate relatives of citizens or under the family-based preferences—regardless of the immigrant's own assets or earning potential, with exceptions for surviving spouses of citizens, battered spouses and children, and certain others. *See* INA § 212(a)(4), 213A. The affidavit requirement also applies to employment-based immigrants where the employer is a relative or an entity in which the relative has a five-percent ownership interest. (For admission categories not requiring an affidavit, the assessment of public charge inadmissibility is discretionary.)

The sponsor must show the ability to support all sponsored immigrants *plus his or her own household* at a minimum of 125 percent of the federal poverty line. *See* INA § 213A(a)(1)(A). In 2015, this minimum for four persons was $30,312.50, which amounts to one wage-earner working full-time at $15.16 per hour. (Higher levels apply to Hawaii and Alaska. Active-duty U.S. military personnel need show only 100 percent of the federal poverty line.)

In addition to the sponsor's income, the assets of the sponsor may also be counted if they can be converted to cash within one year. If so, one-fifth of their value is added to annual income, or one-third if only a spouse and minor children are sponsored. The sponsor generally must be the petitioner, but another person who meets the minimum may accept joint and several liability with a petitioner whose income and assets are insufficient. The intending immigrant's past or prospective income is counted only if he or she (a) has income at the time of filing, (b) will continue to receive income from the same source upon approval of the petition, and (c) will live with the sponsor.

The sponsor must be eighteen years of age and domiciled in the United States. Each sponsor must file an affidavit of support on Form I–864. If the sponsor needs to count the income of other household members to meet the minimum, the other members have to execute similar pledges on Form I–864A. (All these forms appear in the Statutory Supplement.)

The affidavit is quite durable—enforceable until the sponsored immigrant is credited with work for 40 Social Security quarters (*i.e.,* usually ten years), naturalizes, leaves the United States and relinquishes permanent resident status, or dies. If a citizen or permanent resident sponsors a spouse and they later divorce, the support obligation survives. *See Wenfang Lui v. Mund*, 686 F.3d 418 (7th Cir. 2012) (holding that a noncitizen's failure to seek work does not relieve a sponsor from her duty of support).

To put the affidavit requirement in context, first consider that the 1996 Welfare Act's limits on noncitizen eligibility for public benefits provide that new lawful immigrants are ineligible for five years for any "federal means-tested public benefits"—food stamps, SSI, and nonemergency Medicaid. *See* Welfare Act § 403, 8 U.S.C. § 1613. (Chapter Eleven will discuss these restrictions.) Even after five years, the deeming provisions carried over from prior law will bar most sponsored immigrants until they naturalize or work 40 quarters without receiving federal means-tested public benefits. *See* Welfare Act § 421, 8 U.S.C. § 1631.

Suppose that, despite the initial five-year ineligibility period and the deeming provisions, a new immigrant receives means-tested benefits, for example from a state or local government. The government entity that pays out those benefits may rely on the affidavit to sue the immigrant's sponsor for reimbursement. Moreover, sponsored immigrants themselves may enforce the support obligation against their sponsors. *See* INA § 213A(b), (e).

EXERCISE ON AFFIDAVITS OF SUPPORT

Advise the sponsor and others who might potentially assume financial responsibility on the following facts. Most of these questions can be addressed by consulting INA §§ 212(a)(4) and 213A, but you should also examine Forms I–864 and I–864A on the USCIS Forms web page, as well as the latest federal poverty level guidelines in Form I–864P.

Juan gained lawful permanent resident status in the United States and then naturalized 12 years ago. Soon after becoming a citizen, he filed an immigrant visa petition for his brother Antonio, a Mexican citizen. His brother's priority date has just become current, and Juan has been informed that he must complete an affidavit of support. Juan earns $33,000 a year, and his wife, who works part-time and was recently laid off, earned $6,000 last year. They have three children, the oldest of whom is in high school. Although their means are modest, they live comfortably in a small community in south Texas where the cost of living is among the lowest in the United States. They have $1,000 in savings and own their own house. Their equity interest in the home is $30,000.

Antonio has been a successful small farmer in Mexico and has $5,000 in savings. Juan works for a landscaping service, and his boss is interested in hiring Antonio after he arrives. Antonio would initially be paid $10.00 an hour ($20,000 annually), but the boss says he can advance quickly to $12.00 per hour ($24,000 annually) if he proves to be a hard worker. Antonio is married and has one son, four years old. He speaks little English. He told Juan in a recent phone call that he suffered a back injury, but he is sure it is nothing serious.

What advice can you give Juan about how he might help Antonio and Antonio's family immigrate to the United States?

QUESTIONS ON PUBLIC CHARGE INADMISSIBILITY

1. Might the 125 percent requirement bar too many immigrants who could achieve economic self-sufficiency, if not real prosperity?

2. Was it necessary *both* to require support affidavits and to restrict immigrant eligibility for public benefits? If new immigrants are barred from the major federal welfare programs for their first five years (and longer in most cases due to the deeming provisions), why also require an affidavit of support? Or if an affidavit is required, why is it necessary to restrict immigrant eligibility? Or should Congress take a different approach and make the public-charge *deportability* ground easier to enforce? Which approach most closely reflects the idea that immigrants likely to become a public charge should not be admitted?

---

5. PUBLIC HEALTH

From early on, U.S. immigration law has had an exclusion ground for persons with dangerous contagious diseases. *See* INA § 212(a)(1)(A)(i). The spread of AIDS (acquired immune deficiency syndrome) in the 1980s prompted statutory and regulatory bars to the admission of noncitizens with AIDS or the associated human immunodeficiency virus (HIV). In 2008, Congress deleted the specific enumeration of HIV infection from INA § 212(a)(1)(A)(i). But the governing regulation excluding noncitizens with HIV did not change until January 2010, when the Department of Health and Human Services removed HIV from the list of communicable diseases of public health significance. 74 Fed. Reg. 56547 (2009).

As of early 2016, nine diseases are on the list. Active tuberculosis is the most important, especially with the appearance of treatment-resistant strains, but the list also includes infectious leprosy and several sexually transmitted diseases. In addition, two other categories of diseases could lead to inadmissibility: (1) quarantinable diseases designated by Presidential Executive Order and (2) diseases constituting a public health emergency of international concern. *See* 42 C.F.R. § 34.2(b). In 2014, DHS imposed travel restrictions on passengers arriving from certain West African countries affected by Ebola. DHS required passengers on flights originating in those countries to land at designated airports in order to undergo additional screening and protocols before admission, including having their temperature taken. 91 Interp. Rel. 1928 (2014).

Ebola/ coronavirus

Three related inadmissibility grounds also deserve mention. One requires immigrants to document vaccination against certain vaccine-preventable diseases. *See* § 212(a)(1)(A)(ii). Another makes noncitizens inadmissible if they have a mental or physical disorder with accompanying threatening behavior. *See* § 212(a)(1)(A)(iii). And INA § 212(a)(1)(A)(iv) makes drug abusers or addicts inadmissible.

Waivers of these public health-related inadmissibility grounds may be available under INA § 212(g) or, for nonimmigrants, 212(d)(3)(A). A final practical note: even if § 212(a)(1)(A) does not bar noncitizens with medical issues, the public charge ground, § 212(a)(4), may pose a problem if they face significant future medical expenses.

6. NATIONAL SECURITY, FOREIGN POLICY, AND THE CONSTITUTION

The terrorist attacks of September 11, 2001, were carried out by foreigners, mostly nationals of Saudi Arabia, all of whom had been admitted to the United States as nonimmigrants. At least two had violated their student status but had not been the subjects of any enforcement action.

After the attacks, the connection between immigration controls and national security drew a great deal of attention. The Department of Justice made unprecedented use of immigration powers as a major part of its immediate response. Citing immigration law violations, it detained without bond over 700 noncitizens deemed to be "of interest" on security grounds. It delayed the filing of charges or slowed hearings or final removal in many cases to allow further FBI investigation into the person's possible terrorist connections. DOJ closed many removal hearings to the public, sometimes relying on classified evidence not shared with the noncitizen respondent. The Department of State tightened consular screening of visa issuance. Far more thorough and time-consuming background checks against security databases came to be required.

changes post-9/11

Congress also got into the act. The USA PATRIOT Act, passed about seven weeks after September 11, made significant changes to immigration-related statutes. *See* Pub. L. 107–56, 115 Stat. 349 (2001). And in 2002, the Enhanced Border Security and Visa Entry Reform Act further amended immigration processes to assure better databases and better database integration, with the goal of generating timely lookout

Patriot Act

information for those suspected of terrorist or criminal connections. *See* Pub. L. 107–173, 116 Stat. 543 (2002). Congress also set a tight timetable for the completion of a comprehensive entry-exit monitoring system that could quickly identify nonimmigrant overstays, though it never provided significant funding for the infrastructure needed to complete a comprehensive system. The new laws also required a variety of documents and records to include biometric identifiers such as fingerprints.

The Homeland Security Act abolished the INS as of March 2003 and moved most of its functions into separate units of the new Department of Homeland Security. *See* Pub. L. 107–296, 116 Stat. 2135 (2002). And in 2005, the REAL ID Act, to combat fraud of a type used by several 9/11 hijackers to obtain driver's licenses, essentially required states to standardize and restrict the issuance of state identity documents. (Because Congress cannot directly command states to implement such changes, the REAL ID Act sets conditions that must be met if states want their IDs to remain valid for use in federal or federally-regulated activities, including air travel.) *See* Pub. L. 109–13, Div. B, §§ 201–202, 119 Stat. 231, 302–05.

As this brief account indicates, national security concerns have strongly influenced immigration law in both procedure and substance. This subsection focuses on inadmissibility grounds related to national security and foreign policy. We start by surveying the history of measures that target noncitizens believed to be subversives or terrorists. The survey also introduces the constitutional issues that national-security measures can pose in immigration law. Though our detailed consideration of national security and foreign policy will start with inadmissibility and defer deportability until later in this chapter, this introductory subsection provides background that is common to both.

a. Background and Constitutional Framework

BRIAN N. FRY, RESPONDING TO IMMIGRATION: PERCEPTIONS OF PROMISE AND THREAT

Chapter 3: American Nativism in Historical Perspective Pp. 64–74 (2001).

* * *

Anti-Catholicism was the most prevalent form of nativism in the colonial period. Distilled from "No-Popery" laws and a series of real and imagined Catholic conspiracies in seventeenth century England, English settlers tried to limit the immigration and rights of Catholics. Religious intolerance varied from one colony to the next, but Catholics were routinely barred from entering certain colonies, holding public office and voting. Even though it is impossible to chronicle and characterize every

Catholics viewed as a threat

instance of anti-Catholicism, colonial nativists generally viewed Roman Catholicism as an "authoritarian" religion endangering the political stability of their settlements. To guard against this presumed danger, colonists strove to minimize their numbers and participation in civic affairs.

Catholics were prohibited from naturalizing throughout much of the colonial era, and until 1806, did not assume public office in most states, largely because of objectionable oaths. England's Glorious Revolution of 1689 (where Parliament overthrew the Catholic King, James II) exacerbated anti-Catholic nativism in the colonies, precipitating rumors that Catholics were conspiring with Indians to massacre the Protestants. In 1690, during the French and Spanish Wars, Catholics were viewed as potential saboteurs, a fifth column.[13] "Every Catholic within the colonies was looked upon as a potential enemy who might let his papal allegiance supersede his loyalty to the crown by co-operating with the armies of French Canada and the Spanish Florida against the settlers."[2] As a result, Catholics were—in some of the colonies—burdened with additional taxes, forbidden to settle in large groups, and disarmed. Later, in 1755, Britain deported more than six thousand Acadians (French-speaking Catholic peasants from Nova Scotia) to the southern colonies. Their reception was a hostile one, and some even became indentured servants.

* * *

Jews, French Huguenots, Protestant Irish and Germans also faced native hostility. Like the Catholics, Jews were often barred from voting and holding office. The Protestant French Huguenots seemed more French than Protestant to the colonists, particularly during the Anglo-French wars in 1689. * * *

* * *

[N]ativist societies born in the 1840s, such as the Order of the United Americans (OUA) and Order of United American Mechanics (OUAM), carried the nativist "seed" into the fifties, facilitating the development of what later became known as the Know Nothing movement. In 1850, the Order of the Star Spangled Banner was founded in New York, and their ranks quickly swelled, often with OUA members. Instructed to say they "know nothing" when outsiders asked about their society, Horace Greeley of the New York Tribune contemptuously labeled them as such in 1853. At one time, the Know Nothings had over 1.25 million members and ten

---

[13] The origin of the fifth column metaphor stems from the "column of supporters which General Mola declared himself to have in Madrid, when he was besieging it in the Spanish Civil War, in addition to the four columns of his army outside the city" (Oxford English Dictionary 1989: 890).

[2] [Ray Allen Billington, The Protestant Crusade 1800–1860: A Study of the Origins of American Nativism 9 (1963).] [reference reformatted and relocated.—eds.]

thousand councils. Most effective as a local movement, their council system doubled as a political system for the American Party (the official name of Know Nothings) to elect seven governors, eight U.S. senators, and 104 U.S. Representatives by 1856. So effective and popular was the American Party in 1855 that the *New York Herald* unhappily predicted a presidential victory in 1856. But the very issue which helped unite the American Party in the early 1850s—slavery—proved too divisive just a few years later.

Unable to ignore the slavery crisis in their own national meetings between 1854 and 1856, and accentuated by regional differences in group membership and objectives, consensus in the American Party began to wane. * * *

In 1856, the party's candidate for President, Millard Fillmore, came in a distant third, bringing the party's activities to a close in most states. Except in a few border states, the Know Nothings were little more than a shell by 1860. It would take a Civil War, one fought by Catholics and immigrants alike, to expunge the anti-immigrant and anti-Catholic sentiment of the sixties. * * *

* * *

* * * [T]he depression in the 1890s contributed to a resurgence of nativist activities. European aliens found themselves ineligible for certain jobs and Catholics increasingly became the targets of the American Protective Association. The APA, over a half-million strong in 1894, was particularly active in the Midwest. They accused Catholics of intentionally disrupting the economy for the purpose of facilitating a Roman takeover, boycotted their businesses, and were involved in two Protestant-Catholic riots. They helped re-elect William McKinley as governor of Ohio and aided sympathizers in their bids for Congress. But by the latter part of 1894, internal dissension racked the organization, and the religious fervor of the organization carried less weight with a changing middle-class. * * *

Anti-radical nativism also surfaced in the nineties, but in a much more violent show of force. In 1897, deputies opened fire on a group of unarmed Hungarian and Polish strikers in Pennsylvania, injuring forty immigrants and killing twenty-one. In 1891, eleven Italians were lynched in New Orleans. However, an improving economy and the swift defeat of Spain in the 1898 Spanish-American War seemed to dam the current of restriction for a short while, but another crisis would shortly reappear.

The twentieth century began on the restrictionist foot with the Immigration Acts of 1903 and 1907. In response to the assassination of President McKinley in 1901 by Leo Czolgosz, a native-born anarchist of obvious foreign extraction, Congress pushed for the exclusion and deportation of alien anarchists. This objective was incorporated into the more general 1903 bill, which expanded the criteria for excluding and deporting aliens, and for the first time since the Aliens Act of 1798, penalized immigrants for their political beliefs. * * *

* * *

* * * [In 1917] the war with Germany [directed] the public's attention to another "fifth column"—German-Americans. The German-American Alliance's bold support for Germany, the virtually unanimous pro-Germany stance of the German-American press, and a few blundered attempts at sabotage by a group of Germans, was intolerable to a country drunk on "100 per cent Americanism." Federal agents used the 1798 Alien Enemies Act to arrest 6,300 Germans ("enemy aliens"), of whom 2,300 were interned. Congress also enacted the 1917 Espionage Act and 1918 Sedition Act to prosecute U.S. citizens of German origin who [criticized the war effort or obstructed the draft.] * * * During the war, German-Americans not only "swatted" the hyphen, but also Americanized names—for example, Schmidt became Smith, East Germantown, Indiana was renamed Pershing, and sauerkraut became "liberty cabbage." Nonetheless, these last minute demonstrations of loyalty did little to pacify official or public sentiment. Volunteer "spy-hunting" organizations, such as the American Protective League, continued to harass German Americans, and by early 1915, fifteen states passed laws requiring that English be the language of instruction in all public and private schools.

* * *

The Alien and Sedition Acts of 1798

Fry mentions the Alien and Sedition Acts of 1798, passed at a time of wide public concern about subversion stemming from revolutionary France. Those laws constitute a highly important chapter in the history of U.S. legal responses to perceived national security threats posed by immigration.

The Alien Act (often called the Alien Friends Act), ch. 58, 1 Stat. 570 (1798), gave the President the power "at any time during the continuance of this act, to order all such aliens as he shall judge dangerous to the peace and safety of the United States, or shall have reasonable grounds to suspect are concerned in any treasonable or secret machinations against the government thereof, to depart out of the territory of the United States, within such time as shall be expressed in such order." The Act was never directly applied to any alien, but some foreigners departed to avoid its application, and President Adams signed a small number of arrest warrants, whose targets either went into hiding or left before being caught. James Morton Smith, Freedom's Fetters: The Alien and Sedition Laws and American Civil Liberties 159–76 (1956).

The Alien Act stimulated one of the nation's first extended debates about the constitutional rights of noncitizens. Against the claim that aliens enjoyed no such rights because not parties to the compact, Madison and Jefferson contended that because aliens owed a temporary allegiance during their stay, they were entitled to certain protections as a matter of mutuality. *See* Gerald L. Neuman, Strangers to the Constitution: Immigrants, Borders, and Fundamental Law 52–63 (1996). The Aliens Act was allowed to expire in 1800, and the Jeffersonian view of its invidiousness has generally carried the day in the court of history.

A second law—the Alien Enemies Act—passed in 1798 in response to public fears about foreign machinations, was accepted by the Jeffersonians and survives with little change today. *See* ch. 66, 1 Stat. 577 (1798), now codified at 50 U.S.C. §§ 21–23. It authorizes the internment and removal of nationals of states with which the United States is at war, after a congressional declaration of war or in certain other circumstances involving threatened hostilities, upon the public proclamation of the President. As the Fry excerpt indicates, it has been used during many conflicts, including World War II, although always selectively. Presidents have stopped short of rounding up all citizens of the foreign state present in the United States. During World War II, German and Japanese nationals were only selectively detained. The notorious internment of Japanese-Americans removed from the West Coast—over 60 percent of whom were U.S. citizens—was ordered on the basis of general military powers, not the Alien Enemies Act, which applies only to foreign nationals.

———

We now pick up the historical thread where the Fry account leaves off. The 1903 Act had provided for the exclusion of specified subversives but authorized deportation only for those who should have been excluded on this ground when they entered. In 1917, Congress extended the deportation grounds to include *post-entry* subversive conduct. Any "alien who at any time after entry shall be found advocating or teaching [subversion]" could be deported. Immigration Act of 1917, ch. 29, § 19, 39 Stat. 889. As World War I continued, this deportation ground expanded further to cover aliens who were "members of or affiliated with any organization that entertains a belief in" violent overthrow of the government or anarchism. Anarchist Act of 1918, ch. 186, § 1, 40 Stat. 1012. Aliens who wrote, published, circulated or possessed subversive literature also became deportable. Act of June 5, 1920, ch. 251, § 1, 41 Stat. 1008.

The aftermath of World War I and the rise of the Bolshevik regime in Russia soon brought the Palmer Raids, a repressive campaign to deport noncitizens affiliated with allegedly subversive organizations. Thousands were imprisoned, and over five hundred were eventually deported. What follows is a portion of historian John Higham's account of the Raids.

A new [U.S.] Attorney General, A. Mitchell Palmer, took over * * * in March 1919. * * * Palmer created a new division of the Bureau of Investigation for [a] war against radicalism. In anticipation of a peacetime sedition law, the division proceeded to assemble data on all revolutionary activities * * * . * * * [T]he Union of Russian Workers * * * was chosen as the first target.

On November 7, 1919, the second anniversary of the Bolshevik régime in Russia, Palmer's men descended on Russian meeting places in eleven cities and seized hundreds of members of the organization. Screening for once was swift. Little more than a month later 249 aliens, most of them netted in the November raids, were on a specially chartered transport en route to Finland. From there they traveled overland to Russia through snows and military lines. Some had to leave behind in America their wives and children, at once destitute and ostracized.

* * *

Basking in the popularity of his anti-Russian raid, Palmer now prepared a mightier blow. On January 2 the Department of Justice, aided by local police forces in thirty-three cities, carried out a vast roundup of alien members of the two communist parties. Officers burst into homes, meeting places and pool rooms, as often as not seizing everyone in sight. The victims were loaded into trucks, or sometimes marched through the streets handcuffed and chained to one another, and massed by the hundreds at concentration points, usually police stations. There officials tried to separate out the alien members of radical organizations, releasing the rest or turning them over to the local police. * * * Altogether, about three thousand aliens were held for deportation, almost all of them eastern Europeans.

John Higham, Strangers in the Land: Patterns of American Nativism 1860–1925, at 229–31 (1955).

The January 1920 raids in Boston and other New England towns netted about 1000 persons. Twenty who had been arrested and ordered deported brought suit challenging the proceedings' legality. Judge George Weston Anderson, in setting aside most of the deportations on due process grounds, described the raids and their aftermath:

Pains were taken to give spectacular publicity to the raid, and to make it appear that there was great and imminent public danger, against which these activities of the Department of Justice were directed. The arrested aliens, in most instances perfectly quiet and harmless working people, many of them not long ago Russian peasants, were handcuffed in pairs, and then, for the purposes of transfer on trains and through the streets of Boston, chained together. * * * The Department of Justice agents in charge of the arrested aliens appear to have taken pains to have them * * * exposed to public photographing.

Private rooms were searched in omnibus fashion; trunks, bureaus, suit cases, and boxes broken open; books and papers seized. I doubt whether a single search warrant was obtained or applied for. * * *

* * *

At Deer Island the conditions were unfit and chaotic. No adequate preparations had been made to receive and care for so large a number of people. Some of the steam pipes were burst or disconnected. The place was cold; the weather was severe. The cells were not properly equipped with sanitary appliances. There was no adequate number of guards or officials to take a census of and properly care for so many. For several days the arrested aliens were held practically incommunicado. * * * Inevitably the atmosphere of lawless disregard of the rights and feelings of these aliens as human beings affected, consciously or unconsciously, the inspectors who shortly began at Deer Island the hearings, the basis of the records involving the determination of their right to remain in this country.

In the early days at Deer Island one alien committed suicide by throwing himself from the fifth floor and dashing his brains out in the corridor below in the presence of other horrified aliens. One was committed as insane; others were driven nearly, if not quite, to the verge of insanity.

After many days of confusion, the aliens themselves, under the leadership of one or two of the most intelligent and most conversant with English, constituted a committee, and represented to Assistant Commissioner Sullivan that, if given an opportunity, they would themselves clean up the quarters and arrange for the orderly service of food and the distribution of mail. * * * It is not without significance that these aliens, thus arrested under charges of conspiracy to overthrow our government by force and violence, were, while under arrest, many of them illegally, found to be capable of organizing amongst themselves, with the consent of and in amicable co-operation with their keepers, an effective and democratic form of local government.

Colyer v. Skeffington, 265 Fed. 17, 44–45 (D. Mass. 1920), *reversed in part sub nom. Skeffington v. Katzeff*, 277 Fed. 129 (1st Cir. 1922).

b. Constitutional Limits on National Security Inadmissibility

The leading modern precedent on the constitutionality of inadmissibility grounds is the 1972 U.S. Supreme Court decision in *Kleindienst v. Mandel.* In reading *Mandel*, you may find it useful to know that the Supreme Court has long struggled—in many contexts not involving immigration and citizenship—to define First Amendment limits on government restrictions or punishments for subversive activities or for advocacy of unlawful action. An early twentieth century milestone was Justice Holmes' "clear and present danger" test in *Schenck v. United States*, 249 U.S. 47, 39 S.Ct. 247, 63 L.Ed. 470 (1919).

[handwritten margin note: Mandel 1st Amend.]

Several years before *Mandel*, the Court seemed to have reached an important landmark by providing the tightest limits yet on government action. In *Brandenburg v. Ohio*, 395 U.S. 444, 89 S.Ct. 1827, 23 L.Ed.2d 430 (1969) (per curiam), the Court ruled that because of the First Amendment, the government cannot ban advocacy "except where such advocacy is directed to inciting or producing imminent lawless action and is likely to incite or produce such action." *Brandenburg* led some to think that the Court might substantially limit exclusion based on writings or speech when *Mandel* appeared on its docket.

[handwritten margin note: Schenck Test clear + present danger]

[handwritten margin note: Brandenburg]

KLEINDIENST V. MANDEL
Supreme Court of the United States, 1972.
408 U.S. 753, 92 S.Ct. 2576, 33 L.Ed.2d 683.

MR. JUSTICE BLACKMUN delivered the opinion of the Court.

[Ernest Mandel was a well-known Belgian author who described himself as "a revolutionary Marxist" but not a member of the Communist party. His writings and activities rendered him excludable under the pre-1990 version of INA § 212(a)(28), which set forth a long list of excludable aliens, including "anarchists," "those who advocate or teach . . . opposition to all organized government," and members of any branch of the Communist Party. Mandel had visited the United States twice before filing the unsuccessful visa application that led to this litigation. Both times, apparently unbeknownst to him, he had been adjudged excludable under § 212(a)(28) as one who advocates or teaches or publishes material advocating or teaching "the economic, international, and governmental doctrines of world communism." Both times he had been the beneficiary of a waiver under INA § 212(d)(3). Then in 1969 he applied for a nonimmigrant visa to attend conferences in the United States. He was informed of his excludability, and after several rounds of correspondence, he was told that the Attorney General would not grant a waiver this time, because, in the Attorney General's view, he had violated the terms of his earlier admissions by deviating from the stated purposes of those trips. Mandel and several of those who had invited him to this country filed suit. The District Court ruled for the plaintiffs.]

II

Until 1875 alien migration to the United States was unrestricted. The Act of March 3, 1875, 18 Stat. 477, barred convicts and prostitutes. Seven years later Congress passed the first general immigration statute. * * * Section 2 of [a 1903] Act made ineligible for admission "anarchists, or persons who believe in or advocate the overthrow by force or violence of the Government of the United States or of all government or of all forms of law." * * * [In 1918,] Congress expanded the provisions for the exclusion of subversive aliens. Title II of the Alien Registration Act of 1940, 54 Stat. 671, amended the 1918 Act to bar aliens who, at any time, had advocated or were members of or affiliated with organizations that advocated violent overthrow of the United States Government.

In the years that followed, after extensive investigation and numerous reports by congressional committees, Congress passed the Internal Security Act of 1950, 64 Stat. 987. This Act dispensed with the requirement of the 1940 Act of a finding in each case, with respect to members of the Communist Party, that the party did in fact advocate violent overthrow of the Government. These provisions were carried forward into the Immigration and Nationality Act of 1952.

We thus have almost continuous attention on the part of Congress since 1875 to the problems of immigration and of excludability of certain defined classes of aliens. The pattern generally has been one of increasing control with particular attention, for almost 70 years now, first to anarchists and then to those with communist affiliation or views.

III

It is clear that Mandel personally, as an unadmitted and nonresident alien, had no constitutional right of entry to this country as a nonimmigrant or otherwise. *United States ex rel. Turner v. Williams,* 194 U.S. 279, 292, 24 S.Ct. 719, 723, 48 L.Ed. 979 (1904); *United States ex rel. Knauff v. Shaughnessy,* 338 U.S. 537, 542, 70 S.Ct. 309, 312, 94 L.Ed. 317 (1950); *Galvan v. Press,* 347 U.S. 522, 530–532, 74 S.Ct. 737, 742–743, 98 L.Ed. 911 (1954); *see Harisiades v. Shaughnessy,* 342 U.S. 580, 592, 72 S.Ct. 512, 520, 96 L.Ed. 586 (1952).

The appellees concede this. Indeed, the American appellees assert that "they sue to enforce their rights, individually and as members of the

American public, and assert none on the part of the invited alien." "Dr. Mandel is in a sense made a plaintiff because he is symbolic of the problem."

The case, therefore, comes down to the narrow issue whether the First Amendment confers upon the appellee professors, because they wish to hear, speak, and debate with Mandel in person, the ability to determine that Mandel should be permitted to enter the country or, in other words, to compel the Attorney General to allow Mandel's admission.

IV

In a variety of contexts this Court has referred to a First Amendment right to "receive information and ideas":

It is now well established that the Constitution protects the right to receive information and ideas. "This freedom [of speech and press] . . . necessarily protects the right to receive. . . ."

Stanley v. Georgia, 394 U.S. 557, 564, 89 S.Ct. 1243, 1247, 22 L.Ed.2d 542 (1969).

* * *

In the present case, the District Court majority held:

The concern of the First Amendment is not with a non-resident alien's individual and personal interest in entering and being heard, but with the rights of the citizens of the country to have the alien enter and to hear him explain and seek to defend his views * * *.

The Government disputes this conclusion on two grounds. First, it argues that exclusion of Mandel involves no restriction on First Amendment rights at all since what is restricted is "only action—the action of the alien in coming into this country." Principal reliance is placed on *Zemel v. Rusk*, 381 U.S. 1, 85 S.Ct. 1271, 14 L.Ed.2d 179 (1965), where the Government's refusal to validate an American passport for travel to Cuba was upheld. The rights asserted there were those of the passport applicant himself. The Court held that his right to travel and his asserted ancillary right to inform himself about Cuba did not outweigh substantial "foreign policy considerations affecting all citizens" that, with the backdrop of the Cuban missile crisis, were characterized as the "weightiest considerations of national security." *Id.*, at 13, 16, 85 S.Ct., at 1279. The rights asserted here, in some contrast, are those of American academics who have invited Mandel to participate with them in colloquia debates, and discussion in the United States. In light of the Court's previous decisions concerning the "right to receive information," we cannot realistically say that the problem facing us disappears entirely or is nonexistent because the mode of regulation bears directly on physical movement. * * *

The Government also suggests that the First Amendment is inapplicable because appellees have free access to Mandel's ideas through his books and speeches, and because "technological developments," such as tapes or telephone hook-ups, readily supplant his physical presence. This argument overlooks what may be particular qualities inherent in sustained, face-to-face debate, discussion and questioning. While alternative means of access to Mandel's ideas might be a relevant factor were we called upon to balance First Amendment rights against governmental regulatory interests—a balance we find unnecessary here in light of the discussion that follows in Part V—we are loath to hold on this record that existence of other alternatives extinguishes altogether any constitutional interest on the part of the appellees in this particular form of access.

V

Recognition that First Amendment rights are implicated, however, is not dispositive of our inquiry here. In accord with ancient principles of the international law of nation-states, the Court in *The Chinese Exclusion Case,* 130 U.S. 581, 609, 9 S.Ct. 623, 631, 32 L.Ed. 1068 (1889), and in *Fong Yue Ting v. United States,* 149 U.S. 698, 13 S.Ct. 1016, 37 L.Ed. 905 (1893), held broadly, as the Government describes it, that the power to exclude aliens is "inherent in sovereignty, necessary for maintaining normal international relations and defending the country against foreign encroachments and dangers—a power to be exercised exclusively by the political branches of government. . . ." Since that time, the Court's general reaffirmations of this principle have been legion. The Court without exception has sustained Congress' "plenary power to make rules for the admission of aliens and to exclude those who possess those characteristics which Congress has forbidden." *Boutilier v. Immigration and Naturalization Service,* 387 U.S. 118, 123, 87 S.Ct. 1563, 1567, 18 L.Ed. 2d 661 (1967). "[O]ver no conceivable subject is the legislative power of Congress more complete than it is over" the admission of aliens. *Oceanic Navigation Co. v. Stranahan,* 214 U.S. 320, 339, 29 S.Ct. 671, 676, 53 L.Ed. 1013 (1909). * * *

We are not inclined in the present context to reconsider this line of cases. Indeed, the appellees, in contrast to the *amicus,* do not ask that we do so. The appellees recognize the force of these many precedents. In seeking to sustain the decision below, they concede that Congress could enact a blanket prohibition against entry of all aliens falling into the class defined by §§ 212(a)(28)(D) and (G)(v), and that First Amendment rights could not override that decision. But they contend that by providing a waiver procedure, Congress clearly intended that persons ineligible under the broad provision of the section would be temporarily admitted when appropriate "for humane reasons and for reasons of public interest." S. Rep. No. 1137, 82d Cong., 2d Sess. 12 (1952). They argue that the Executive's implementation of this congressional mandate through decision whether to grant a waiver in each individual case must be limited by the First Amendment rights of persons like appellees. Specifically, their position is that the First Amendment rights must prevail, at least where the Government advances no justification for failing to grant a waiver. They point to the fact that waivers have been granted in the vast majority of cases.

Appellees' First Amendment argument would prove too much. In almost every instance of an alien excludable under § 212(a)(28), there are probably those who would wish to meet and speak with him. The ideas of most such aliens might not be so influential as those of Mandel, nor his American audience so numerous, nor the planned discussion forums so impressive. But the First Amendment does not protect only the articulate, the well known, and the popular. Were we to endorse the proposition that governmental power to withhold a waiver must yield whenever a bona fide claim is made that American citizens wish to meet and talk with an alien excludable under § 212(a)(28), one of two unsatisfactory results would necessarily ensue. Either every claim would prevail, in which case the plenary discretionary authority Congress granted the Executive becomes a nullity, or courts in each case would be required to weigh the strength of the audience's interest against that of the Government in refusing a waiver to the particular alien applicant, according to some as yet undetermined standard. The dangers and the undesirability of making that determination on the basis of factors such as the size of the audience or the probity of the speaker's ideas are obvious. Indeed, it is for precisely this reason that the waiver decision has, properly, been placed in the hands of the Executive.

Appellees seek to soften the impact of this analysis by arguing, as has been noted, that the First Amendment claim should prevail, at least where no justification is advanced for denial of a waiver. The Government would have us reach this question, urging a broad decision that Congress has delegated the waiver decision to the Executive in its sole and unfettered discretion, and any reason or no reason may be given. This record, however, does not require that we do so, for the Attorney General did inform Mandel's counsel of the reason for refusing him a waiver. And that reason was facially legitimate and bona fide.

* * *

In summary, plenary congressional power to make policies and rules for exclusion of aliens has long been firmly established. In the case of an alien excludable under § 212(a)(28), Congress has delegated conditional exercise of this power to the Executive. We hold that when the Executive exercises this power negatively on the basis of a facially legitimate and bona fide reason, the courts will neither look behind the exercise of that discretion, nor test it by balancing its justification against the First Amendment interests of those who seek personal communication with the applicant. What First Amendment or other grounds may be available for attacking exercise of discretion for which no justification whatsoever is advanced is a question we neither address or decide in this case.

Reversed.

MR. JUSTICE DOUGLAS, dissenting.

Under *The Chinese Exclusion Case*, 130 U.S. 581, 9 S.Ct. 623, 32 L.Ed. 1068, rendered in 1889, there could be no doubt but that Congress would have the power to exclude any class of aliens from these shores. The accent at the time was on race. Mr. Justice Field, writing for the Court, said: "If, therefore, the government of the United States, through its legislative department, considers the presence of foreigners of a different race in this country, who will not assimilate with us, to be dangerous to its peace and security, their exclusion is not to be stayed because at the time there are no actual hostilities with the nation of which the foreigners are subjects." *Id.,* at 606, 9 S.Ct., at 630.

An ideological test, not a racial one, is used here. But neither, in my view, is permissible, as I have indicated on other occasions. Yet a narrower question is raised here. * * *

* * *

As a matter of statutory construction, I conclude that Congress never undertook to entrust the Attorney General with the discretion to pick and choose among the ideological offerings which alien lecturers tender from our platforms, allowing those palatable to him and disallowing others. The discretion entrusted to him concerns matters commonly within the competence of the Department of Justice—national security, importation of drugs, and the like.

I would affirm the judgment of the three-judge District Court.

MR. JUSTICE MARSHALL, with whom MR. JUSTICE BRENNAN joins, dissenting.

* * *

I, too, am stunned to learn that a country with our proud heritage has refused Dr. Mandel temporary admission. I am convinced that Americans cannot be denied the opportunity to hear Dr. Mandel's views in person because their Government disapproves of his ideas. Therefore, I dissent from today's decision and would affirm the judgment of the court below.

* * *

Today's majority apparently holds that Mandel may be excluded and Americans' First Amendment rights restricted because the Attorney General has given a "facially legitimate and bona fide reason" for refusing to waive Mandel's visa ineligibility. I do not understand the source of this unusual standard. Merely "legitimate" governmental interests cannot override constitutional rights. Moreover, the majority demands only "facial" legitimacy and good faith, by which it means that this Court will never "look behind" any reason the Attorney General gives. No citation is given for this kind of unprecedented deference to the Executive, nor can I imagine (nor am I told) the slightest justification for such a rule.

Even the briefest peek behind the Attorney General's reason for refusing a waiver in this case would reveal that it is a sham. The Attorney General informed appellees' counsel that the waiver was refused because Mandel's activities on a previous American visit "went far beyond the stated purposes of his trip . . . and represented a flagrant abuse of the opportunities afforded him to express his views in this country." But, as the Department of State had already conceded to appellees' counsel, Dr. Mandel "was apparently not informed that [his previous] visa was issued only after obtaining a waiver of ineligibility and therefore [Mandel] may not have been aware of the conditions and limitations attached to the [previous] visa issuance." There is *no* basis in the present record for concluding that Mandel's behavior on his previous visit was a "flagrant abuse"—or even willful or knowing departure—from visa restrictions. For good reason, the Government in this litigation has *never* relied on the Attorney General's reason to justify Mandel's exclusion. In these circumstances, the Attorney General's reason cannot possibly support a decision for the Government in this case. But without even remanding for a factual hearing to see if there is *any* support for the Attorney General's determination, the majority declares that his reason is sufficient to override appellees' First Amendment interests.

Even if the Attorney General had given a compelling reason for declining to grant a waiver under § 212(d)(3)(A), this would not, for me, end the case. As I understand the statutory scheme, Mandel is "ineligible" for a visa, and therefore inadmissible, solely because, within the terms of § 212(a)(28), he has advocated communist doctrine and has published writings advocating that doctrine. The waiver question under § 212(d)(3)(A) is totally secondary and dependent, since it is triggered here only by a determination of (a)(28) ineligibility. * * *

Accordingly, I turn to consider the constitutionality of the sole justification given by the Government here and below for excluding Mandel—that he "advocates" and "publish[es] . . . printed matter . . .

advocating ... doctrines of world communism" within the terms of § 212(a)(28).

Still adhering to standard First Amendment doctrine, I do not see how (a)(28) can possibly represent a compelling governmental interest that overrides appellees' interests in hearing Mandel. Unlike (a)(27) or (a)(29), (a)(28) does not claim to exclude aliens who are likely to engage in subversive activity or who represent an active and present threat to the "welfare, safety, or security of the United States." Rather, (a)(28) excludes aliens solely because they have advocated communist doctrine. Our cases make clear, however, that government has no legitimate interest in stopping the flow of ideas. It has no power to restrict the mere advocacy of communist doctrine, divorced from incitement to imminent lawless action. For those who are not sure that they have attained the final and absolute truth, all ideas, even those forcefully urged, are a contribution to the ongoing political dialogue. The First Amendment represents the view of the Framers that "the path of safety lies in the opportunity to discuss freely supposed grievances and proposed remedies; and that the fitting remedy for evil counsels is good ones"—"more speech." *Whitney v. California*, 274 U.S., at 375, 377, 47 S.Ct., at 648, 649, 71 L.Ed. 1095 (Brandeis, J., concurring). * * *

* * *

The heart of Appellants' position in this case * * * is that the Government's power is distinctively broad and unreviewable because "[t]he regulation in question is directed at the admission of aliens." Thus, in the appellants' view, this case is no different from a long line of cases holding that the power to exclude aliens is left exclusively to the "political" branches of Government, Congress, and the Executive.

These cases are not the strongest precedents in the United States Reports, and the majority's baroque approach reveals its reluctance to rely on them completely. They include such milestones as *The Chinese Exclusion Case*, 130 U.S. 581, 9 S.Ct. 623, 32 L.Ed. 1068 (1889), and *Fong Yue Ting v. United States*, 149 U.S. 698, 13 S.Ct. 1016, 37 L.Ed. 905 (1893), in which this Court upheld the Government's power to exclude and expel Chinese aliens from our midst.

But none of these old cases must be "reconsidered" or overruled to strike down Dr. Mandel's exclusion, for none of them was concerned with the rights of American citizens. All of them involved only rights of the excluded aliens themselves. At least when the rights of Americans are involved, there is no basis for concluding that the power to exclude aliens is absolute. "When Congress' exercise of one of its enumerated powers clashes with those individual liberties protected by the Bill of Rights, it is our 'delicate and difficult task' to determine whether the resulting restriction on freedom can be tolerated." *United States v. Robel*, 389 U.S. 258, 264, 88 S.Ct. 419, 424, 19 L.Ed.2d 508 (1967). * * *

* * *

I do not mean to suggest that simply because some Americans wish to hear an alien speak, they can automatically compel even his temporary admission to our country. Government may prohibit aliens from even temporary admission if exclusion is necessary to protect a compelling governmental interest.[6] Actual threats to the national security, public health needs, and genuine requirements of law enforcement are the most apparent interests that would surely be compelling. But in Dr. Mandel's case, the Government has, and claims, no such compelling interest. Mandel's visit was to be temporary. His "ineligibility" for a visa was based solely on § 212(a)(28). The only governmental interest embodied in that section is the Government's desire to keep certain ideas out of circulation in this country. This is hardly a compelling governmental interest. Section (a)(28) may not be the basis for excluding an alien when Americans wish to hear him. Without any claim that Mandel "live" is an actual threat to this country, there is no difference between excluding Mandel because of his ideas and keeping his books out because of their ideas. Neither is permitted.

* * *

NOTES AND QUESTIONS ON MANDEL

1.   The *Mandel* majority takes an unusual approach. It works hard to find that a First Amendment issue exists, because of the interests of prospective U.S. citizen listeners, even though the circulation of Mandel's books and ideas was not hindered, but then adopts a novel standard for resolving First Amendment questions in some immigration settings.

If the First Amendment is implicated, why not apply strict scrutiny, as the First Amendment rights of citizens normally require? Recall that in *Fiallo v. Bell,* 430 U.S. 787, 97 S.Ct. 1473, 52 L.Ed.2d 50 (1977), in Chapter Five, p. 296 *supra*, the Court rejected a citizens' rights argument, but in a setting that did not involve the First Amendment. Consider these comments on approaching the constitutional aspects of immigration law by asking how immigration decisions affect citizens:

> Looking at constitutional immigration law by focusing on citizens' rights might seem to banish aliens from the constitutional fold. In fact, however, a citizens' rights focus leaves considerable room for treating aliens fairly within our constitutional traditions. Poor

---

[6]   I agree with the majority that courts should not inquire into such things as the "probity of the speaker's ideas." Neither should the Executive, however. Where Americans wish to hear an alien, and their claim is not a demonstrated sham, the crucial question is whether the Government's interest in excluding the alien is compelling.

treatment of aliens often means poor treatment of citizens. For example, if we discriminate on the basis of race in selecting immigrants, we may be hurting citizens in several ways. We may deprive them of reunification with family members, and we may cast a stigma upon members of particular groups as being less worthy of inclusion in our immigrant stream. We may also hurt citizens by adopting discriminatory principles that can be applied detrimentally to citizens in other contexts.

Hiroshi Motomura, *Whose Immigration Law?: Citizens, Aliens, and the Constitution*, 97 Colum. L. Rev. 1567, 1572 (1997).

On the other hand, would a focus on the rights of citizens who wish to meet and talk with the noncitizen really distinguish the "old cases" that Justice Marshall says "involved only rights of the excluded aliens themselves"? Many of those noncitizens could have found citizen co-plaintiffs, had that been seen as crucial.

2.   What does it mean that the Court asks the government for a "facially legitimate and bona fide reason" for its action? *Mandel* may be significant not for its deference to the government, but rather for suggesting that the courts might have any role at all in reviewing immigration decisions of this type. Perhaps it makes little difference to unsuccessful plaintiffs whether they lose on the merits because the court defers so much to the government, or because no real First Amendment issue exists when the government merely refuses admission, or they lose because the court lacks jurisdiction. But the differences among these rationales may matter for the ultimate development of a sound body of law.

This view that Mandel carved out a new role for the courts received a boost in 1977, when the Court stated in *Fiallo* that past cases "reflect acceptance of a limited judicial responsibility under the Constitution even with respect to the power of Congress to regulate the admission and exclusion of aliens." More recently, the concurring and dissenting opinions of Justices Kennedy and Breyer in *Kerry v. Din*, in Chapter 6 at pp. 548–552, suggest that the "facially legitimate and bona fide reason" test has two components: whether the government provided a legal basis for the decision, and whether it identified a factual basis for concluding that the legal standard was not met. The point of contention between the two Justices became how much information the government must provide about the legal and factual basis for its decision.

Several federal appeals courts have treated the "facially legitimate and bona fide reason" test as the same as rational basis review. *See, e.g., Johnson v. Whitehead*, 647 F.3d 120, at 127 (4th Cir. 2011); *Ablang v. Reno*, 52 F.3d 801, 804 (9th Cir. 1995); *Azizi v. Thornburgh*, 908 F.2d 1130, 1133 n.2 (2d Cir. 1990). There is some support for viewing the standard as even more deferential to the political branches than rational basis review. *See Bangura v. Hansen*, 434 F.3d 487, 495 (6th Cir. 2006) (citing *Fiallo v. Bell*, 430 U.S. 787, 798–99, 97 S.Ct. 1473, 52 L.Ed.2d 50 (1977)).

If courts are at least considering these constitutional arguments, can they refine the substantive test without intruding unduly on national security concerns or upsetting U.S. foreign relations? Could courts fashion standards that would defer less to the government than the "facially legitimate and bona fide reason," and better serve First Amendment values while still attending to the needs of an efficient immigration system? Or is more deference to the executive branch necessary to be very certain that terrorists and other truly dangerous foreigners may not enter the country?

A thorough account of how *Mandel* led to curtailing ideological exclusion, through both litigation and the decisions of the political branches—and of the lawyers' battle in *Mandel* itself—appears in Peter H. Schuck, *Kleindienst v. Mandel: Plenary Power v. the Professors,* in Immigration Stories 169 (David A. Martin & Peter H. Schuck eds. 2005).

3. Alternatively, imagine a different way that *Mandel* might have been litigated. Consider the array of potential plaintiffs. Might any of them have been more successful if they had framed the case not as a first amendment issue at all, but as a denial of procedural due process? Would it have made a difference, for example, if they had challenged the lack of an opportunity to present evidence to overcome the waiver denial? Does *Kerry v. Din*, on p. 545, answer these questions?

4. Chapter Six, p. 500, explained that consular decisions made overseas are generally not reviewable in court. What is the relevance of *Mandel* for this consular nonreviewability? Does *Mandel* endorse consular nonreviewability, or does asking the government for a "facially legitimate and bona fide reason" cast doubt on complete insulation of consular decisions? *Does Kerry v. Din* resolve the constitutionality of the consular nonreviewability doctrine?

Who is most affected by consular nonreviewability? One commentator on *Kerry v. Din* has suggested that the doctrine "will disproportionately impact racial and ethnic minorities, the persons most likely to be seeking a visa for a noncitizen spouse and the persons most likely to be denied the visa on terrorism or other grounds." M. Isabel Medina, *When It Comes to Immigration, Neither Marriage Nor Citizenship Matter*, http://lawprofessors. typepad.com/immigration/2015/06/symposium-on-kerry-v-din-when-it-comes-to-immigration-neither-marriage-nor-citizenship-matter-by-m-i.html (June 19, 2015).

5. Justice Douglas would overturn the visa denial based solely on his reading of the statute and the underlying congressional intent. Apparently he would find that the Attorney General, under the statute, *must* waive excludability unless he finds that the noncitizen's presence would raise concerns "commonly within the competence of the Department of Justice—national security, importation of drugs, and the like." Can this possibly have been the intent of Congress in enacting paragraph (28) and making it waivable under subsection (d)(3)? Why would Congress have added

paragraph (28) when other subsections addressed security and criminal concerns directly?

c.   Terrorism-Related Inadmissibility Grounds

After the fall of the Berlin Wall, Congress used the Immigration Act of 1990, Pub. L. 101–649, 104 Stat. 4978, to completely recast the national security-related exclusion grounds, now in INA § 212(a)(3). (INA § 237(a)(4) reflects similar reworking of the analogous deportability grounds.) Congress repealed or greatly curtailed exclusion or deportation grounds for anarchists, members of the Communist Party and other totalitarian parties, as such—replacing those grounds with removal based on terrorism and foreign policy findings. This approach did not explicitly cover organized terrorist "threats" or activities involving "terrorist organizations."

In the wake of the 1993 bombing of New York City's World Trade Center and the 1995 bombing of a federal building in Oklahoma City, Congress passed the Antiterrorism and Effective Death Penalty Act of 1996, Pub. L. No. 104–132, 110 Stat. 1214 (AEDPA), which forbade all material support to a foreign terrorist organization. Material support included humanitarian aid, based on a congressional finding that "foreign organizations that engage in terrorist activity are so tainted by their criminal conduct that any contribution to such an organization facilitates that conduct." *Id.* at § 301, 110 Stat. 1247.

Current INA § 212(a)(3)(B) reflects significant post-9/11 expansion by the USA PATRIOT Act, Pub. L. No. 107–56, 115 Stat. 272 (2001), and the REAL ID Act of 2005, Pub. L. No. 109–13, 119 Stat. 231. The PATRIOT Act made three significant changes. First, it broadened the scope of "terrorist activity" to add the use of "any weapon or dangerous device" to the previous list of biological agents, chemical agents, nuclear weapons or devices, explosives, or firearms. The inadmissibility ground applies only if the use of the weapon or device was not for "mere personal monetary gain" and was "intended to endanger, directly or indirectly, the safety of one or more individuals or to cause substantial damage to property." USA PATRIOT Act, § 411 (codified at INA § 212(a)(3)(B)(iii)(V)(bb)).

Second, the PATRIOT Act made inadmissible representatives of "terrorist organizations" and those likely to advocate terrorism, defining "terrorist organizations" to include not only groups that the Secretary of State designated as terrorist organizations but also any group of two or more individuals that committed, planned, or prepared to commit terrorist activities. *Id.* at § 212(a)(3)(B)(vi)(III). Finally, the PATRIOT Act made a significant evidentiary change, shifting the burden of proof to noncitizens to show that they did not know or reasonably should not have known that their actions materially supported a terrorist activity.

Similarly, a noncitizen who provided material support to or solicited funds or members for a designated terrorist organization was inadmissible, unless the individual could "demonstrate that he did not know, and should not reasonably have known, that the act would further the organization's terrorist activity." *Id.* at § 212(a)(3)(B)(iv). In 2001, the Bush Administration froze the assets of the largest Muslim charity in the United States based on allegations that the charity supported Hamas, a Palestinian group that had been implicated in several terrorist attacks in Israel. Under the PATRIOT Act, noncitizens who solicited contributions for the charity had to show that they did not know and did not have reason to know of the charity's terrorist connections.

The REAL ID Act of 2005 continued the expansion of removal grounds related to terrorism and further limited defenses to those grounds. The Act expanded the scope of the deportability grounds to match the inadmissibility grounds for providing material support to a terrorist organization. It expanded the definition of "material support" to include financial contributions to an organization which the contributor should reasonably have known had a subgroup that engages in terrorist activity. These changes put pressure on the issues of whether de minimis activities or actions taken under duress could constitute material support. Last, the Act increased the evidentiary burden on noncitizens charged as removable under these grounds, requiring proof by clear and convincing evidence of a lack of knowledge that an action would further terrorist activity or that a non-designated group was a terrorist organization. *See* REAL ID Act of 2005, Pub. L. No. 109–13, 119 Stat. 231 (amending 8 U.S.C. §§ 1182(a)(3)(B)(iv)(VI) & 1182(a)(3)(B)(vi)(III)).

Studying the terrorism inadmissibility grounds is best approached in three phases: first, by navigating the complex statutory provisions that define what connections to terrorist activity and organizations render a noncitizen inadmissible; second, by delving into the most significant issues that this definition raises, namely, what constitutes material support for terrorism, and whether there are exceptions for de minimis activity and actions taken under duress. Third, the government has carved out a set of exemptions that ameliorate some of the consequences of these broadly drawn inadmissibility provisions.

(i) Defining Terrorism

Terrorism is notoriously hard to define. Gerald Neuman, writing before September 11, 2001, summarized the difficulties:

> One [difficulty] is identifying the forms of violent action that are sufficiently extreme, whether because of the methods employed or because of the victims targeted, that they deserve condemnation as terrorism. Another is the problem of distinguishing terroristic acts performed by governments—"state

terrorism"—from other acts of governmental force. A third is the justifiability of acts otherwise characterized as terrorism when they are performed by "national liberation" movements vindicating the right of a people to self-determination. International cooperation against terrorism has attempted to finesse this difficulty of definition by focusing piecemeal on particular forms of violence employed by terrorists, and agreeing upon measures addressed to those forms of violence as objectively defined, regardless of any characterization as "terrorist" and regardless of the political motivations of the actors. Thus, conventions concern themselves with unlawful acts against the safety of aircraft, and unlawful acts against the safety of ships, as well as violence against international protected persons (such as heads of states and representatives of states). The International Convention Against the Taking of Hostages includes the intention of compelling a third party to perform an action as an element of its definition of hostage-taking, but does not require that the purpose be political rather than economic or personal.

Gerald L. Neuman, *Terrorism, Selective Deportation and the First Amendment after* Reno v. AADC, 14 Geo. Immigr. L.J. 313, 322–23 (2000). For a comprehensive survey, see Nicholas J. Perry, *The Breadth and Impact of the Terrorism-Related Grounds of Inadmissibility of the INA*, 06–10 Immigr. Briefings (2006).

Noncitizens are inadmissible if, among other things, they have engaged in terrorist activity, or if a consular officer has reasonable ground to believe they are likely to engage in such activity after entry. Also inadmissible are a wide group of individuals and representatives of organizations who publicly endorse or espouse terrorist activities.

Terrorist Activity. "Terrorist activity" is defined in terms of violent acts committed or planned. These acts include any unlawful use of a weapon or dangerous device "other than for mere personal monetary gain." INA § 212(a)(3)(B)(iii)(V)(bb). Spouses and children of persons barred under this ground may also be inadmissible. INA § 212(a)(3)(B)(i), (ii). "Engage in terrorist activity" is defined broadly in § 212(a)(3)(B)(iv) to include providing "material support" for terrorist activity or organizations.

Terrorist Organizations. Key to these inadmissibility grounds is the definition of "terrorist organization" in § 212(a)(3)(B)(vi). INA § 219 sets out a procedure for the Secretary of State to designate terrorist organizations. Organizations so designated appear on the Designated Foreign Terrorist Organizations (FTO) list, and are now known as "Tier I" organizations. Designation under § 219 has major ramifications beyond immigration. Any person—citizen or noncitizen—who provides material support to a § 219 organization is subject to severe criminal penalties, and the Secretary of the Treasury may freeze the organization's assets. 18 U.S.C. § 2339B; INA § 219(a)(2)(C). In December 2015, there were 58 Tier I terrorist organizations. Several lawsuits by organizations challenging these designations have established that the State Department's designation procedures must conform to due process. *See National Council of Resistance of Iran v. Department of State,* 251 F.3d 192 (D.C. Cir. 2001). Courts also review the findings that an organization is a foreign organization and that it engages in terrorist activity. But the third requirement for § 219 designation—that an organization's terrorist activity threatens U.S. security—is considered a nonjusticiable political question. *See People's Mojahedin Organization of Iran v. Department of State,* 327 F.3d 1238 (D.C. Cir. 2003).

A second, more streamlined procedure allows the Secretary of State to designate additional organizations, to appear on the Terrorist Exclusion List (TEL). They are also known as "Tier II" organizations. A Tier II designation has only immigration consequences and does not trigger criminal sanctions or asset forfeiture. A third part of the terrorist organization definition, known as Tier III, expansively includes any "group of two or more individuals, whether organized or not," which engages in committing a terrorist activity or (with certain limitations) inciting it, preparing or planning a terrorist activity, and gathering information on potential targets.

Even before their post-9/11 expansion, Neuman commented: "the statutory definitions of 'terrorist activity' and 'engag[ing] in terrorist activity' are extraordinarily broad, so broad that Congress surely never intended that they be enforced against all aliens who come within them. Congress has cast a very broad net in order to facilitate the effective enforcement of restrictions against a narrower class of terrorists on a discretionary basis." Neuman, 14 Geo. Immigr. L.J. at 321–22. For example, in 1997 the Department of State issued a visitor's visa to Gerry Adams, the leader of Sinn Fein, the political wing of the Irish Republican Army. Adams was classified as a terrorist in view of his association with the IRA, but he was granted a waiver—as on past occasions—in view of the prevailing cease-fire in Northern Ireland. *See* Associated Press, *Sinn Fein leader granted U.S. visa,* Aug. 15, 1997. Adams was later a key figure accepting a comprehensive April 1998 agreement that ultimately led to the restoration of the Northern Ireland Assembly, the creation of a broad government structure involving both Catholics and Protestants, and the decommissioning of armed militias in the country. Is there anything wrong with making visa decisions in these ways, giving broad discretion to the executive branch?

To better understand these provisions, try applying INA § 212(a)(3) to the following problems. Then assess, based on the constitutional decisions that you have considered thus far, whether a finding of inadmissibility under the statute would withstand a constitutional challenge.

PROBLEMS

1. W was convicted in the United Kingdom 23 years ago for his involvement, as a 19-year-old, with an attack on a British military base in Northern Ireland. Three soldiers were injured, but no one was killed. W was later caught and convicted, serving a seven-year sentence in a British prison. After his release he found work as a skilled mechanic, severed ties with the Irish Republican Army, and later became a local leader with an ecumenical peace group seeking to build channels of communication and friendship between Catholics and Protestants.

Two years ago he married a woman, a U.S. citizen, whom he had met at an NGO conference. Her visa petition for his admission as an immediate relative has been approved. Is W inadmissible? If so, are any waivers available?

2. You are a consular officer considering the issuance of a student visa to graduate student Y under § 101(a)(15)(F). A check of government lookout databases reveals intelligence information about Y, which the analyst says is well-corroborated. It states that Y has attended six meetings of a front organization for a clandestine group believed to be responsible for recent bombings in Y's home country.

A check with local police authorities in Y's home country reveals no convictions or even arrests for any offenses. They believe him to be a legitimate student. During his interview with you, Y presents a thorough and complete story about his bachelor's and master's degree programs, where he had a strong record. Recommendation letters from his professors and employers vouch for the seriousness of his academic pursuits, and the prominent U.S. university in which he has enrolled has sent messages to you, bolstered by letters from that state's congressional delegation, about how eager they are to receive him. Nothing in the interview suggests any affiliation with the organization, despite several lines of questions meant to probe for weaknesses in his account.

What should you do? If you are uncertain about whether he is a risk, should you approve or disapprove the visa? Is Y inadmissible? On what ground or grounds? Are there other steps that you or the State Department must pursue before applying the ground?

3. You are an immigration attorney recently contacted by Z, admitted to the United States in H–1B status five years ago from Ruritania. Shortly after his departure, a violent civil war broke out in

Ruritania, and Z's ethnic group, the Rodolfians, has suffered greatly from damage to structures and the economy of the region and from government crackdowns, because the group is identified with the insurgents. Three years ago Z sent a $1,000 contribution in response to an appeal from the Rodolfian Liberation League (RLL), which has always billed itself as a political party and mutual aid society. It had invited successful Rodolfians living abroad to contribute to a special fund meant to support families that had suffered during the conflict and to rebuild communities damaged in the fighting. Z also persuaded other U.S. citizen and immigrant friends to send similar contributions. He sent a smaller donation the following year, but then ceased support, because he read that the RLL had become directly involved in the violent struggle.

Z's employer has now obtained approval of an employment-based visa petition for him, and his priority date is current. He is ready to apply for adjustment of status, but he is deeply worried that these gifts may disqualify him. What is his risk? What grounds of inadmissibility might apply to him?

NOTES AND QUESTIONS ON
POLICY ASPECTS OF TERRORISM-BASED INADMISSIBILITY

1.　The preceding problems highlight the discretion of immigration authorities to act against noncitizens on the basis of speech or association. Is such discretion a necessary tool in protecting the nation against terrorism and other threats? Or is it instead a worrisome grant of power to the executive branch? Could the statute be drawn more narrowly and still afford adequate diplomatic tools and protection against terrorist entry?

2.　In 1987, without amending the INA itself, Congress responded to objections to "ideological exclusion" with a temporary measure prohibiting exclusion or deportation "because of any past, current, or expected beliefs, statements, or associations which, if engaged in by a United States citizen in the United States, would be protected under the Constitution of the United States." Foreign Relations Authorization Act, Fiscal Years 1988 and 1989, Pub. L. No. 100–204, 101 Stat. 1331 (1987).

Would this approach better serve First Amendment values? Or could consular officers no longer act on the basis of reasonable but imperfect information suggesting that a visa applicant has engaged or is likely to engage in terrorism? Short of a past conviction or an unlikely confession during an interview to violent activities or plans, what can a consular officer or intelligence officer rely on in determining whether a person is involved in terrorism *besides* past associations or statements? Given that such judgments will almost always be uncertain, how should we allocate the risk of error—in favor of admission or in favor of exclusion?

3.　Membership in a Communist or "other totalitarian party" remains an inadmissibility ground, but only for noncitizens coming as immigrants.

INA § 212(a)(3)(D). What views of free speech and membership in the national community—or any other rationales—underlie this distinction between immigrants and nonimmigrants? More generally, can a society based on tolerance validly bar prospective members based solely on a disapproved ideology, or on affiliation with a disapproved organization? Or may democratic societies legitimately be intolerant of Communists, fascists, white supremacists, believers in theocracy, or others who do not accept the basic principle of tolerance itself? Does the answer vary depending on how serious a threat the alternative ideology happens to pose at the time?

(ii) Material Support to Terrorism

It plainly makes sense to bar admission to persons who knowingly and voluntarily provide funds or other support to violent terrorist activity. But achieving that goal raises several separate questions that flow from the common issue of how broadly the prohibition against material support of terrorism sweeps.

Terrorist activity. If the recipient of the noncitizen's support is an organization to which the U.S. Government is sympathetic, has the noncitizen provided material support to terrorist activity? Answering that question will often implicate questions of foreign policy. Should immigration judges make that determination, or is it better left to other components of the executive branch?

Mens rea. What *mens rea* does the material support bar require? Must the person intend that the funds support violence, or is it enough that person intends to support political or charitable activities carried out by organizations with terrorist wings? Inadmissibility grounds that are sweeping, with a low *mens rea* threshold and a broad definition of terrorist organizations or activities, may bar admission based on utterly innocent acts—a classic case of overbreadth. But narrowly tailored inadmissibility grounds may let some truly dangerous terrorism supporters into the country—where they might go beyond fundraising to help perpetrate violent acts. Similarly, what degree of intent is required—mere negligence or some other level of knowledge, awareness, or intent?

If the law requires proof of intent to support violent activities, the government's task in marshaling the necessary information is obviously more daunting. It can be hard enough to follow the money, as it passes to largely clandestine organizations, in order to show that the person's contributions actually went to a questionable recipient. It can be quite difficult to prove the donor's intent, especially as to organizations with both violent and nonviolent purposes.

"Material" support. When is the support "material"? Is there a de minimis level of support for terrorism that will not trigger exclusion?

DHS and the Department of Justice have regularly argued against a de minimis standard. Does the government work on a tip-of-the-iceberg theory: small contributions may be all we can prove, out of what could be much more extensive support in the past? Or someone who has given small-scale help may be willing to foster more lethal activities in the future, should a better opportunity arise (such as through admission to U.S. territory).

There are at least two ways to approach this question. One is to interpret the statute to exclude from its coverage a de minimis category of support that is not significant enough to be "material." An unpublished BIA decision reflects this approach, holding that providing terrorists a packed lunch and the equivalent of about $4.00 for beer did not rise to the level of material support. *In re H-A-*, 2009 WL 9133770 (BIA 2009) ("Even if this could be deemed "support" for the terrorists, it cannot be said to be material"). The second is to determine that any level of support for terrorist activity constitutes "material support," but rely on the discretion that Congress gave to the executive branch to carve out specific exemptions. The BIA's primary decision on the material support bar, excerpted below, takes that pathway. More information on the discretionary exemptions, including one for insignificant support, appears later in this section.

Duress. What if support is given at the point of a gun or due to other sorts of coercion? In a society riven by civil war, people might be forced to provide food, supplies, or the payment of "revolutionary taxes" to guerrillas coming through the village. In fact, the violence or threats used to coerce such support may be precisely the reason that unwilling donors flee and seek asylum. Even more graphically, children are kidnapped to join an armed band, then forced (and often drugged) to commit atrocities or lead armed attacks as child soldiers. Are such actions "terrorist activity" that should disqualify the coerced person from admission or refugee status? Does the text of the statute give answers to these questions?

Though courts and commentators have addressed various aspects of the material support bar, the following case, decided in 2006, remains the BIA's primary decision on the material support bar. The issue was whether the noncitizen, a national of Burma, qualified for asylum or withholding of removal. (As Chapter Eight will explain, these are forms of protection against return to a country where persecution is threatened.) Because persons inadmissible under many of the terrorism-related grounds are ineligible for asylum or withholding of removal, the BIA had to decide if the noncitizen's admitted donation of $685 to the Chin National Front amounted to material support for a terrorist organization.

MATTER OF S-K-

Board of Immigration Appeals, 2006.
23 I & N Dec. 936.

PAULEY, BOARD MEMBER:

* * *

The respondent, a native and citizen of Burma, is a Christian and an ethnic Chin. According to the respondent, she faces persecution and/or torture if returned to Burma because the Government, currently a military dictatorship ruled by the majority Burman ethnic group, regularly commits human rights abuses against ethnic and religious minorities and, in fact, arrested and detained both the respondent's brother and fiancé, the latter ultimately being killed by the military.

In 2001, the respondent became acquainted with an undercover agent for the Chin National Front ("CNF") who was a friend of her deceased fiancé, became sympathetic to the CNF's goal of securing freedom for ethnic Chin people and donated money to the organization for approximately 11 months. In addition, she attempted to donate some other goods, such as a camera and binoculars, to the CNF, but they were confiscated after she had given them to the undercover agent. The agent informed the respondent that she should flee Burma because the Burmese military, known to torture anyone affiliated with the CNF, had seen a letter written by the respondent to the CNF; the military knew that the respondent was the person who had attempted to provide the material goods. The respondent was actually residing in Singapore at the time, but since her temporary work visa was about to expire and she could not return to Burma, she fled to the United States in order to request asylum.

Although the Immigration Judge found that the respondent had established a well-founded fear of persecution in order to qualify for asylum, he denied her application for relief because, by providing money and other support to the CNF, an organization which uses land mines and engages in armed conflict with the Burmese Government, the respondent provided material support to an organization or group of individuals who she knew, or had reason to know, uses firearms and explosives to endanger the safety of others or to cause substantial property damage. Therefore, she was statutorily barred from asylum and from withholding of removal * * * .

* * * We granted the respondent's request for oral argument in order for the parties to address what we viewed as the major questions arising in the case: (1) what standards or definition should be used to assess whether the term "material support" should be defined narrowly or more broadly; whether it should take into consideration the mens rea of the

provider, as proposed by the respondent; and whether it includes the type of support provided by the respondent to the CNF; and (2) to what extent, in light of our precedent, we should factor in an organization's purpose and goals in order to assess whether an organization, like the CNF, is engaged in terrorist activity. In other words, we asked the parties to address whether the use of justifiable force against an illegitimate regime and the right of people to self-determination, which the respondent argues is the CNF's purpose, is a valid purpose, which would not fall within the definition of terrorist activity under the Act. We will address these issues in reverse order.

II. ANALYSIS

A. *Terrorist Organization*

During oral argument and on appeal, the respondent argued that the Burmese Government is not legitimate because the military junta rules the country under martial law and crushes any attempts at democratic reform. According to the respondent, the United States does not recognize the Burmese Government's legislative acts, and therefore the CNF's actions are not unlawful under Burmese law. Rather, she asserts, the organization's actions are similar to those of forces fighting the Taliban in Afghanistan or forces rebelling against Saddam Hussein in Iraq, which are supported by the United States. Its goals are democracy and it uses force only in self-defense. Moreover, the CNF is allied with the National League of Democracy, which the United States has recognized as a legitimate representative of the Burmese people and is recognized by the United Nations. Therefore, the respondent contends that the Immigration Judge erred in concluding that the CNF is a terrorist organization.

Whether the CNF's actions are lawful in Burma is a question of foreign law and is a factual issue on which the respondent bears the burden of proof, inasmuch as the "evidence indicates" that the terrorism bar to asylum may apply. * * *

During oral argument, the respondent pointed to testimony from the Assistant Secretary of State describing the Burmese military as a "group of thugs," as well as to the fact that the United States Government has passed the Burmese Freedom and Democracy Act of 2003, acknowledging that the National League of Democracy is the legitimate representative of the Burmese people. * * *

* * * [T]he respondent acknowledged, upon questioning, that the United States does maintain a diplomatic relationship with the Burmese Government and maintains an embassy there. Therefore, in some sense or degree, the United States recognizes as legitimate the Burmese Government, which appears to consider the activities of the CNF unlawful.

Although the respondent urges us to determine that the Burmese Government is illegitimate and argues that we have such authority, we are unable to agree with the respondent's argument. While there may have been cases in which we determined that certain acts by foreign governments were unlawful in terms of harming individuals who sought asylum here, we have not gone so far as to determine that a foreign sovereignty would not be recognized by the United States Government. Such a determination is beyond our delegated authority and is a matter left to elected and other high-level officials in this country.

Furthermore, the respondent cites to past case law interpreting asylum applicants' claims and granting relief where aliens have attempted to overthrow governments that do not allow citizens to change the political structure and therefore exercise illegitimate power when prosecuting such individuals. In other words, she asserts that the motivation of the group seeking to effect change in a country must be analyzed in order to determine whether the harm produced is persecution or, as claimed in this case, terrorist activity. *See Matter of Izatula*, 20 I & N Dec. 149 (BIA 1990) (holding, in a case involving an alien who actively assisted the mujahedin in Afghanistan, that the general rule that prosecution for an attempt to overthrow a lawfully constituted government does not constitute persecution is inapplicable in countries where a coup is the only means of effectuating political change). During oral argument, counsel for the respondent acknowledged that by utilizing such factors to determine whether an organization falls within section 212(a)(3) of the Act, he was advocating that we apply a "totality of the circumstances" test.

We are unable to find any support for the respondent's assertion that such a test should be utilized. Our past case law is not inconsistent with some of the respondent's arguments. However, that case law does not address the bar to relief in section 212(a)(3)(B)(i)(I) of the Act. In this case, we are dealing with specific statutory language, which we read as applying to the respondent.

* * * [H]aving reviewed the statutory sections, we find that Congress intentionally drafted the terrorist bars to relief very broadly, to include even those people described as "freedom fighters," and it did not intend to give us discretion to create exceptions for members of organizations to which our Government might be sympathetic. Rather, Congress attempted to balance the harsh provisions set forth in the Act with a waiver [in INA § 212(d)(3)(B)], but it only granted the power to make exemptions to the Attorney General and the Secretaries of State and Homeland Security, who have not delegated such power to the Immigration Judges or the Board of Immigration Appeals.

* * * [T]here is no exception in the Act to the bar to relief in cases involving the use of justifiable force to repel attacks by forces of an illegitimate regime. As noted by the Immigration Judge, there was sufficient evidence in the record to conclude that the CNF uses firearms and/or explosives to engage in combat with the Burmese military, and the respondent has not provided evidence that would rebut this conclusion or lead us to interpret the Act differently. Moreover, the record shows that the respondent knew or should have known of the CNF's use of arms. Thus, assuming the respondent provided material support to the CNF, her sole remedy to extricate herself from the statutory bar appears to lie in the waiver afforded by Congress for this purpose, for which the DHS stated at oral argument she is eligible to apply. However, the Immigration Judges and the Board have no role in the adjudication of such a waiver.

B. Materiality of Support Provided

The respondent also argues that the type and amount of support which she provided to the CNF was not material. She asserts that the Immigration Judge failed to take into consideration whether the funds and goods she provided were relevant to the planning or implementation of a terrorist act, as allegedly required by the United States Court of Appeals for the Third Circuit in *Singh-Kaur v. Ashcroft*, [385 F.3d 293 (3d Cir. 2004)]. Since no evidence was submitted to support a conclusion that the respondent's contributions were relevant to a specific terrorist goal, the respondent asserts that finding that her contributions were material goes against the congressional intent to tie materiality to terrorist activity.[7] * * *

* * *

We are unaware of any legislative history which indicates a limitation on the definition of the term "material support." * * * Rather, the statute is clearly drafted in this respect to require only that the provider afford material support to a terrorist organization, with the sole exception being a showing by clear and convincing evidence that the actor

---

[7] * * * While it is clear that our government leaders have taken a strict approach to dealing with suspected terrorists and have attempted to make it more difficult for those involved in terrorism to gain relief of any kind, they also have expressly provided a waiver that may be exercised in cases where the result reached under the terrorist bars to relief would not be consistent with our international treaty obligations or where, as a matter of discretion, the Secretary of State or the Secretary of Homeland Security determines that the facts of a specific case warrant such relief. Accordingly, while the Immigration Judges and the Board do not have the authority to grant the respondent or similarly situated aliens a discretionary waiver, other officials, including the Secretary of State, prior to the instigation of removal proceedings, or the Secretary of Homeland Security, at any time upon consultation with other agency officials, have been granted this power. [INA § 212(d)(3)(B).] We find no reason to assume they will not act consistently with our international treaty obligations [under the UN Convention and Protocol relating to the Status of Refugees] in exercising their power to grant such a waiver. [relocated footnote—eds.]

did not know, and should not reasonably have known, that the organization was of that character. Section 212(a)(3)(B)(iv)(VI)(dd) of the Act. We thus reject the respondent's assertion that there must be a link between the provision of material support to a terrorist organization and the intended use by that recipient organization of the assistance to further a terrorist activity. Especially where assistance as fungible as money is concerned, such a link would not be in keeping with the purpose of the material support provision, as it would enable a terrorist organization to solicit funds for an ostensibly benign purpose, and then transfer other equivalent funds in its possession to promote its terrorist activities.

We turn then to the respondent's claim that the statute's requirement of material support means that trivial or unsubstantial amounts of assistance, such as she allegedly provided, are not within the statutory bar. In *Singh-Kaur v. Ashcroft, supra,* the Third Circuit found that the provision of very modest amounts of food and shelter to individuals who the alien reasonably should have known had committed or planned to commit terrorist activity did constitute material support. The court also found that the listed examples in section 212(a)(3)(B)(iv)(VI) of the Act were not exhaustive but were "intended to illustrate a broad concept rather than narrowly circumscribe a term with exclusive categories." *Id.* at 298.

* * *

As the DHS contends, it is certainly plausible in light of the decision in *Singh-Kaur v. Ashcroft,* and recent amendments to the Act, that the list in section 212(a)(3)(B) was intended to have an expanded reach and cover virtually all forms of assistance, even small monetary contributions. Congress has not expressly indicated its intent to provide an exception for contributions which are de minimis. Thus the DHS asserts that the term "material support" is effectively a term of art and that all of the listed types of assistance are covered, irrespective of any showing that they are independently "material."

On the other hand, the respondent's contrary argument that "material" should be given independent content is by no means frivolous. However, we find it unnecessary to resolve this issue now, inasmuch as we agree with the DHS that based on the amount of money the respondent provided, her donations of S$1100 (Singapore dollars) constituted material support.[15] Specifically, the respondent testified that she contributed approximately S$100 per month over an 11-month period, representing approximately one-eighth of her monthly income. This was

---

[15] We take administrative notice that this corresponded at the time to approximately US$685. By contrast, the average annual per capita income in Burma was approximately US$225.

sufficiently substantial by itself to have some effect on the ability of the CNF to accomplish its goals, whether in the form of purchasing weaponry or providing routine supplies to its forces, for example. We therefore agree with the Immigration Judge that the respondent provided material support to the CNF.

III. CONCLUSION

Based on the foregoing, we agree with the Immigration Judge's decision that the respondent is statutorily ineligible for asylum and withholding of removal for having provided material support to a terrorist organization. [The case is remanded because she was nonetheless still eligible for protection under the Convention Against Torture.] * * *

OSUNA, ACTING VICE CHAIRMAN, concurring:

* * *

We are finding that a Christian member of the ethnic Chin minority in Burma, who clearly has a well-founded fear of being persecuted by one of the more repressive governments in the world, one that the United States Government views as illegitimate, is ineligible to avail herself of asylum in the United States despite posing no threat to the security of this country. It may be, as the majority states, that Congress intended the material support bar to apply very broadly. However, when the bar is applied to cases such as this, it is difficult to conclude that this is what Congress intended.

* * *

In enacting the material support bar, Congress was rightly concerned with preventing terrorists and their supporters from exploiting this country's asylum laws. It is unclear, however, how barring this respondent from asylum furthers those goals. The respondent provided funds and some equipment to a member of the CNF, an organization that has *not* been designated by the Department of State as a terrorist organization under section 212(a)(3)(B)(vi) of the Act. The available information in the record indicates that the CNF engages in violence primarily as a means of self-defense against the Burmese Government, a known human rights abuser that has engaged in systematic persecution of Burmese ethnic minorities, including the Chin Christians. * * *

The CNF, however, is a group that has resorted to violence in self-defense, including the use of explosives. The Immigration Judge was thus correct to find that the assistance that the respondent provided to the CNF constituted material support to any individual who the respondent knew, or should have known, "has committed or plans to commit a terrorist activity." Section 212(a)(3)(B)(iv)(VI)(bb) of the Act. The fact that this language goes beyond common notions of "terrorism" is immaterial in the context of this case.

Yet, the statutory language is breathtaking in its scope. * * * [T]he DHS conceded at oral argument that an individual who assisted the Northern Alliance in Afghanistan against the Taliban in the 1990s would be considered to have provided "material assistance" to a terrorist organization under this statute and thus would be barred from asylum. This despite the fact that the Northern Alliance was an organization supported by the United States in its struggle against a regime that the United States and the vast majority of governments around the world viewed as illegitimate.

It also includes groups and organizations that are not normally thought of as "terrorists" per se. Read literally, the definition includes, for example, a group of individuals discharging a weapon in an abandoned house, thus causing "substantial damage to property." Section 212(a)(3)(B)(iii)(V) of the Act. This may constitute inappropriate or even criminal behavior, but it is not what we normally think of as "terrorist" activity.

The broad reach of the material support bar becomes even starker when viewed in light of the nature of the Burmese regime, and how it is regarded by the United States Government. In 2003, Congress passed the Burmese Freedom and Democracy Act of 2003, Pub. L. No. 108–61, 117 Stat. 864, which, among other things, imposes sanctions on the Burmese Government as a result of its deplorable human rights record. The Secretary of State has designated Burma as one of a handful of "countries of particular concern" in light of this record, including its treatment of ethnic and religious minorities. Bureau of Democracy, Human Rights and Labor, U.S. Dep't of State, Burma—International Religious Freedom Report 2003 (Dec. 18, 2003) available at http://www.state.gov/g/drl/rls/irf/2003/23823.htm. In particular, the Burmese Government has engaged in arrests of Christian clergy, destruction of churches, prohibition of religious services and proselytizing by Christians, and forced conversions of Christians. These efforts are part of a larger effort to "Burmanize" the Chin ethnic minority.

* * *

In sum, what we have in this case is an individual who provided a relatively small amount of support to an organization that opposes one of the most repressive governments in the world, a government that is not recognized by the United States as legitimate and that has engaged in a brutal campaign against ethnic minorities. It is clear that the respondent poses no danger whatsoever to the national security of the United States. Indeed, by supporting the CNF in its resistance to the Burmese junta, it is arguable that the respondent actually acted in a manner consistent with United States foreign policy. And yet we cannot ignore the clear language that Congress chose in the material support provisions; the statute that we are required to apply mandates that we find the respondent ineligible for asylum for having provided material support to a terrorist organization.

* * *

NOTES AND QUESTIONS ON MATERIAL SUPPORT

1. **Navigating the statutory language.** Exactly why does the text of § 212(a)(3)(B) cover a situation like S-K-'s? Which part of clause (i), the primary list of disqualifying criteria, makes her inadmissible? Focusing on the definitions in § 212(a)(3)(B), is she barred for giving to a terrorist organization? For supporting terrorist activity? In what terrorist activity did the CNF engage? What actions were "unlawful" in the sense required? Whose laws apply?

2. **Terrorist or freedom fighter?** Why doesn't the Board have enough information, particularly in the form of U.S. legislative or executive branch condemnations of the Burmese regime, to decide that the CNF should be considered freedom fighters rather than terrorists? Should judgments about the legitimacy of the goals of an organization that uses violence be made by judicial or quasi-judicial officers, or instead by the executive branch?

In the 1980s and 1990s, the executive branch fairly consistently regarded as terrorists the members of the Irish Republican Army who had been involved in violence in Northern Ireland. But many judges explicitly or implicitly regarded IRA actions as justifiable support of Irish independence, and so ruled against British government extradition requests or found IRA members eligible for asylum despite analogous bars for terrorist activity. What are the advantages and disadvantages to assigning such judgments about legitimacy of goals to judges? To the executive branch?

3. **Mens rea?** What level of knowledge of a connection to terrorism does the case seem to require, and who bears the burden of proof regarding knowledge of the nature of a terrorist organization? Are these standards reasonable? Consider this critique from Tariq Ramadan, a Swiss citizen and Muslim scholar, denied a visa in 2004 as he was preparing to assume a position at the University of Notre Dame as a professor of religion.

> For more than two years now, the U.S. government has barred me from entering the United States to pursue an academic career. The reasons have changed over time, and have evolved from defamatory to absurd, but the effect has remained the same: I've been kept out.

> First, I was told I couldn't enter because I had endorsed terrorism and violated the USA Patriot Act. It took a lawsuit for the government eventually to abandon this baseless accusation. * * * [This latest time] U.S. authorities offered a new rationale for turning me away: Between 1998 and 2002, I had contributed small

sums of money to a French charity supporting humanitarian work in the Palestinian territories. * * *

I should note that the investigation did not reveal these contributions. As the department acknowledges, I brought this information to its attention myself two years earlier, when I reapplied for a visa.

In its letter, the U.S. Embassy claims that I "reasonably should have known" that the charities in question provided money to Hamas. But my donations were made between December 1998 and July 2002, and the United States did not blacklist the charities until 2003. How should I reasonably have known of their activities before the U.S. government itself knew? I donated to these organizations for the same reason that countless Europeans—and Americans, for that matter—donate to Palestinian causes: not to help fund terrorism, but to provide humanitarian aid to people who desperately need it.

Tariq Ramadan, *Why I'm Banned in the USA*, Wash. Post, Oct. 1, 2006, at B1. A federal appeals court later ruled that the government had to provide Ramadan with an opportunity to show that he lacked actual or constructive knowledge that his contributions went to a terrorist organization. The court added: "The need to confront Ramadan with a claim that he knew ASP [Association de Secours Palestinien] funded Hamas is especially important in this case because of the timing of Ramadan's contributions." *American Academy of Religion v. Napolitano*, 573 F.3d 115, 133 (2d Cir. 2009). In January 2010, Secretary of State Hillary Clinton, after the required interagency consultation, signed an exemption under INA § 212(d)(3)(B) that allowed a visa to be issued to Ramadan. In April 2010, he visited the United States for five days of meetings and public appearances. *See* Kirk Semple, *At Last Allowed, Muslim Scholar Visits*, N.Y. Times, Apr. 8, 2010, at A29.

4.   **De minimis?** Besides arguing the legitimacy of the CNF's actions, S-K- also contended that small amounts of aid should not be considered *material* support. Because the BIA judged her donation large enough to cross any such threshold, it did not resolve this question.

5.   **Duress?** Most courts that have considered the issue have held that there is no duress exception to the material support inadmissibility bar, relying on the availability of a discretionary agency exemption for duress to ameliorate unduly harsh outcomes. *See Sesay v. U.S. Att'y Gen.*, 787 F.3d 215, 224 (3rd Cir. 2015); *Annachamy v. Holder*, 733 F.3d 254, 260 (9th Cir. 2013); *Alturo v. U.S. Att'y Gen.*, 716 F.3d 1310, 1314 (11th Cir. 2013); *Barahona v. Holder*, 691 F.3d 349, 354 (4th Cir. 2012). One circuit has declined to follow this trend, instead calling on the BIA to issue a precedential decision on the question. *Ay v. Holder*, 743 F.3d 317, 320 (2d Cir. 2014) ("Remand is especially appropriate in this case because of the frequency with which this issue arises, and the grave consequences that applying the material support bar carries for many applicants for relief.").

The government has maintained that no such defense exists. This stance drew sustained criticism for its impact on refugees. *E.g.*, Teresa Pham Messer, *Barred from Justice: The Duress Waiver to the Material Support Bar*, 6 Hous. L. Rev.: Off the Record 63, 71 (2015); *see also Sesay*, 787 F.3d at 223 (noting that "almost ten years after Congress granted the Executive Branch the power to grant waivers, there remains no published process for requesting one, although * * * numerous requests have been granted through ad hoc submissions to * * * the Department of Homeland Security.")

(iii) *Discretionary Exemptions*

The sheer breadth of the terrorism-related inadmissibility grounds almost inevitably requires some mechanism to decide on cases that should not be barred even though they fall within the broad wording. Congress has provided and gradually expanded one such mechanism, a purely discretionary authority to exempt certain groups of people and categories of conduct from most, but not all, of the parts of § 212(a)(3)(B). This provision appears in INA § 212(d)(3)(B), which is only slightly less complicated than the provisions for which it can provide a waiver. Exemptions from the terrorism-related inadmissibility grounds are usually either group-based or conduct-based.

Group-based exemptions. In February 2007, DHS employed its discretionary authority to make the material support bar inapplicable, with certain qualifications, to a list of eight specific groups, including the CNF, the Burmese group at issue in *Matter of S-K-, supra*. Exercise of Authority under Section 212(d)(3)(B)(i) of the Immigration and Nationality Act, 72 Fed. Reg. 9954 (2007). A year later, the Consolidated Appropriations Act (CAA) of 2008 provided legislatively that certain specified groups, including the CNF, would not be considered a terrorist organization on the basis of any act or event before enactment of the legislation. The same enactment expanded the power of the Secretary of State and the Secretary of Homeland Security to waive the application of § 212(a)(3)(B), though not in several enumerated situations. *See* Consolidated Appropriations Act, 2008, Pub. L. No. 110–161, 121 Stat. 1844 (2007). After these developments, the BIA issued a decision indicating that S-K- would be granted asylum, but that the 2006 decision in her case would retain its precedential effect as to the application and interpretation of the material support provisions. *See Matter of S-K-*, 24 I & N Dec. 475 (B.I.A. 2008).

Conduct-based exemptions. Beginning in 2007, DHS began to create conduct-based exemptions that responded to several of the controversies described earlier in this section: for example, the applicability of the bar to de minimis levels of support. Other DHS orders issued in February 2007 authorized conduct-based exemptions for "material support provided under duress" to terrorist organizations. The order established a case-by-case process, administered by USCIS, to decide whether the evidence showed that the support was provided under duress and also to apply a range of other requirements set forth in the order. Exemptions issued in 2011 essentially expanded the 2007 material support duress exemption to reach noncitizens who, under duress, received military-type training from a terrorist organization, or solicited funds or members for a terrorist organization. (Such actions could not be the subject of a waiver before the CAA of 2008.) A separate directive allowed exemption for persons who had provided medical care to individuals associated with terrorist organizations or terrorist activities. Policy Memorandum, Implementation of New Discretionary Exemption under INA Section 212(d)(3)(B)(i) for the Solicitation of Funds or Members under Duress, U.S. Citizenship and Immigration Services (Feb. 23, 2011); Exercise of Authority under the Immigration and Nationality Act, 76 Fed. Reg. 70463 (2011); *see also USCIS Issues Two More Memoranda on Exemptions from Certain Terrorism-Related Grounds of Inadmissibility*, 88 Interp. Rel. 584 (2011).

In August 2012, DHS authorized case-by-case exemptions for anyone who had been admitted as an asylee or refugee, or granted Temporary Protected Status (TPS) or certain other specialized benefits (not including nonimmigrant visas), and who might otherwise be disqualified because of support for, or certain other acts connected with, Tier III organizations. Exercise of Authority under the Immigration and Nationality Act, 77 Fed. Reg. 49821 (2012). Many such persons had initially been properly admitted before Congress expanded the terrorist-related inadmissibility grounds. They had then become potentially eligible for adjustment of status to lawful permanent resident, but the intervening expansion of the Tier III bars had left them in limbo. This exemption alleviated the situation and allowed adjustment to proceed.

In February 2014, the Secretaries of State and of Homeland Security jointly issued two more exemptions under INA § 212(d)(3)(B)(i) that potentially benefit a wide range of persons otherwise barred by the provisions relating to support for or activities with Tier III terrorist organizations or their members. The first deals with the provision of "insignificant material support," and the other covers "certain routine commercial * * * or social transactions," "certain humanitarian assistance," and certain assistance provided "under substantial pressure that does not rise to the level of duress." Exercise of Authority under Section 212(d)(3)(B)(i) of the Immigration and Nationality Act, 79 Fed. Reg. 6913 (2014).

Who decides? The fountainhead exemptions in 2007, one of which is excerpted below, established the substantive and procedural framework for the conduct-based exemption process. Note the additional requirements, such as full disclosure of the individual's contacts with the terrorist organization plus passage of background checks, which a noncitizen seeking an exemption must meet. The individualized exemption decisions by USCIS are discretionary and not subject to review by immigration judges, the BIA, or the courts.

DEPARTMENT OF HOMELAND SECURITY
OFFICE OF THE SECRETARY

Exercise of Authority Under Sec. 212(d)(3)(B)(i) of the Immigration and Nationality Act
72 Fed.Reg. 9958 (2007).

Following consultations with the Secretary of State and the Attorney General, I hereby conclude, as a matter of discretion in accordance with the authority granted to me by Sec. 212(d)(3)(B)(i) of the Immigration and Nationality Act ("the Act"), considering the national security and foreign policy interests deemed relevant in these consultations, that subsection 212(a)(3)(B)(iv)(VI) of the Act shall not apply with respect to material support provided under duress to a terrorist organization as described in subsection 212(a)(3)(B)(vi)(III) if warranted by the totality of the circumstances.

This exercise of authority as a matter of discretion shall apply to an alien who satisfies the agency that he:

(a) Is seeking a benefit or protection under the Act and has been determined to be otherwise eligible for the benefit or protection;

(b) Has undergone and passed relevant background and security checks;

(c) Has fully disclosed, in all relevant applications and interviews with U.S. Government representatives and agents, the nature and circumstances of each provision of such material support; and

(d) Poses no danger to the safety and security of the United States.

Implementation of this determination will be made by U.S. Citizenship and Immigration Services (USCIS), in consultation with U.S. Immigration and Customs Enforcement (ICE). USCIS has discretion to determine whether the criteria are met.

When determining whether the material support was provided under duress, the following factors, among others, may be considered: whether the applicant reasonably could have avoided, or took steps to avoid, providing material support, the severity and type of harm inflicted or threatened, to whom the harm was directed, and, in cases of threats alone, the perceived imminence of the harm threatened and the perceived likelihood that the harm would be inflicted.

When considering the totality of the circumstances, factors to be considered, in addition to the duress-related factors stated above, may include, among others: the amount, type and frequency of material support provided, the nature of the activities committed by the terrorist organization, the alien's awareness of those activities, the length of time since material support was provided, the alien's conduct since that time, and any other relevant factor.

* * * Any determination made under this exercise of authority as set out above shall apply to any subsequent benefit or protection application, unless it has been revoked.

This exercise of authority shall not be construed to prejudice, in any way, the ability of the U.S. Government to commence subsequent criminal or civil proceedings in accordance with U.S. law involving any beneficiary of this exercise of authority (or any other person).

* * *

Dated: February 26, 2007.

Michael Chertoff,

Secretary of Homeland Security.

Figure 7.1 illustrates the impact of the exemption policies. Note that a high proportion of the waivers of the material support bar were granted to refugees overseas seeking resettlement in the United States, not to asylum seekers already in the United States.

Figure 7.1
Material Support Waivers
Cumulative, April 2014

Total Exemptions Granted	17,321
Refugees	**12,518**
Group Exemptions	7,056
Burmese cases	6,643
Cuba	281
Iraq	112
Iraqi Uprising	4
Medical Care	33
Tier III Duress Exemptions	4,870
Tier I/II Duress Exemptions	555
Adjustment of Status/I–730 SCOPS*	**4,152**
Group Exemptions	1,173
Duress Exemptions	2,400

Individual Exemptions	18
Medical Care	18
LGE**	427
Iraqi Uprising	116
Adjustment of Status-Field Offices	**46**
Asylum	**513**
Tier III Duress Exemptions	206
Tier I/II Duress Exemptions	266
Group Exemptions	21
Medical Care	20
NACARA	**92**

Total Exemptions Denied	**146**
Refugees	**86**
Asylum Division	**25**
Asylum (I–589)	25
NACARA (I–881)	0 (0)
SCOPS*	**27**
Field Offices	**8**

*   Service Center Operations

** Limited General Exemption (signed Aug. 2012)

Source: USCIS TRIG Working Group, Asylum Division.

Some members of Congress have proposed amending the INA to reduce the impact of the "material support" provision on refugees, but without undermining its use (and that of a related criminal provision, 18 U.S.C. § 2339A) to deal with real supporters of dangerous terrorist organizations or activities. What are the key issues that such legislation should address, both as to substantive criteria and the procedures for deciding what is a terrorist organization? How would you change the statute to provide a more targeted inadmissibility provision? Or do the DHS memoranda on exemptions overcome objections to the current statute?

(iv) Designated Terrorist Groups—Guilt by Association?

Having navigated the maze of terrorism-related inadmissibility provisions and exemptions, the question arises whether there are constitutional limitations on their scope. Advocates and noncitizens in removal cases have contended for many years that provisions like § 212(a)(3)(B) impose "guilt by association," and that the wide discretion applied to their enforcement violates the First Amendment. The First

Amendment doctrine on which these critics rely is captured in the following passage from *NAACP v. Claiborne Hardware Co.,* 458 U.S. 886, 918–20, 102 S.Ct. 3409, 3428–29, 73 L.Ed.2d 1215 (1982):

> The First Amendment * * * restricts the ability of the State to impose liability on an individual solely because of his association with another. In *Scales v. United States,* 367 U.S. 203, 229, 81 S.Ct. 1469, 1486, 6 L.Ed.2d 782 [1961], the Court noted that a "blanket prohibition of association with a group having both legal and illegal aims" would present "a real danger that legitimate political expression or association would be impaired." The Court suggested that to punish association with such a group, there must be "clear proof that a defendant 'specifically intend[s] to accomplish [the aims of the organization] by resort to violence.' " * * *

> * * * "The government has the burden of establishing a knowing affiliation with an organization possessing unlawful aims and goals, and a specific intent to further those illegal aims." [Citing *Healy v. James,* 408 U.S. 169, 186, 92 S.Ct. 2338, 2348, 33 L.Ed.2d 266.]

HOLDER V. HUMANITARIAN LAW PROJECT

Supreme Court of the United States, 2010.
561 U.S. 1, 130 S.Ct. 2705, 177 L.Ed.2d 355.

CHIEF JUSTICE ROBERTS delivered the opinion of the Court.

[The plaintiffs were organizations and individuals who wished to donate to two Tier I organizations designated under INA § 219: the Kurdistan Workers Party (PKK) and the Liberation Tigers of Tamil Eelam. The plaintiffs argued that their donations, which consisted of training group members on how to use humanitarian and international law and the United Nations petition process to peacefully resolve disputes, would aid only nonviolent humanitarian and political activities. They asserted, therefore, that the broad ban on support was impermissibly vague and violated their freedoms of speech and association under the First Amendment. The precise issue was the constitutionality of the criminal penalties in 18 U.S.C. § 2339B for contributing material support to organizations designated as foreign terrorist organizations under § 219—a setting where the constitutional restrictions are arguably more stringent than in the immigration context.

The U.S. Supreme Court first declined to interpret the statute narrowly so as not to cover the plaintiffs' intended activities, and then rejected the argument that the statute was unconstitutionally vague. The Court then reached the First Amendment argument.]

The First Amendment issue before us is more refined than either plaintiffs or the Government would have it. It is not whether the Government may prohibit pure political speech, or may prohibit material support in the form of conduct. It is instead whether the Government may prohibit what plaintiffs want to do—provide material support to the PKK and LTTE in the form of speech.

* * *

* * * Congress considered and rejected the view that ostensibly peaceful aid would have no harmful effects.

We are convinced that Congress was justified in rejecting that view. * * *

Material support meant to "promot[e] peaceable, lawful conduct," can further terrorism by foreign groups in multiple ways. "Material support" is a valuable resource by definition. Such support frees up other resources within the organization that may be put to violent ends. It also importantly helps lend legitimacy to foreign terrorist groups—legitimacy that makes it easier for those groups to persist, to recruit members, and to raise funds—all of which facilitate more terrorist attacks. * * *

* * *

In analyzing whether it is possible in practice to distinguish material support for a foreign terrorist group's violent activities and its nonviolent activities, we do not rely exclusively on our own inferences drawn from the record evidence. We have before us an affidavit stating the Executive Branch's conclusion on that question. The State Department informs us that "[t]he experience and analysis of the U.S. government agencies charged with combating terrorism strongly suppor[t]" Congress's finding that all contributions to foreign terrorist organizations further their terrorism. McKune Affidavit, App. 133, ¶ 8. In the Executive's view: "Given the purposes, organizational structure, and clandestine nature of foreign terrorist organizations, it is highly likely that any material support to these organizations will ultimately inure to the benefit of their criminal, terrorist functions—regardless of whether such support was ostensibly intended to support non-violent, non-terrorist activities." McKune Affidavit, App. 133, ¶ 8.

That evaluation of the facts by the Executive, like Congress's assessment, is entitled to deference. This litigation implicates sensitive and weighty interests of national security and foreign affairs. The PKK and the LTTE have committed terrorist acts against American citizens abroad, and the material-support statute addresses acute foreign policy concerns involving relationships with our Nation's allies. We have noted that "neither the Members of this Court nor most federal judges begin the day with briefings that may describe new and serious threats to our

Nation and its people." *Boumediene v. Bush,* 553 U.S. 723, 797, 128 S.Ct. 2229, 171 L.Ed.2d 41 (2008). It is vital in this context "not to substitute . . . our own evaluation of evidence for a reasonable evaluation by the Legislative Branch." *Rostker v. Goldberg,* 453 U.S. 57, 68, 101 S.Ct. 2646, 69 L.Ed.2d 478 (1981).

Our precedents, old and new, make clear that concerns of national security and foreign relations do not warrant abdication of the judicial role. We do not defer to the Government's reading of the First Amendment, even when such interests are at stake. We are one with the dissent that the Government's "authority and expertise in these matters do not automatically trump the Court's own obligation to secure the protection that the Constitution grants to individuals." But when it comes to collecting evidence and drawing factual inferences in this area, "the lack of competence on the part of the courts is marked," *Rostker,* 453 U.S. at 65, 101 S.Ct. 2646, and respect for the Government's conclusions is appropriate.

One reason for that respect is that national security and foreign policy concerns arise in connection with efforts to confront evolving threats in an area where information can be difficult to obtain and the impact of certain conduct difficult to assess. The dissent slights these real constraints in demanding hard proof—with "detail," "specific facts," and "specific evidence"—that plaintiffs' proposed activities will support terrorist attacks. That would be a dangerous requirement. In this context, conclusions must often be based on informed judgment rather than concrete evidence, and that reality affects what we may reasonably insist on from the Government. The material-support statute is, on its face, a preventive measure—it criminalizes not terrorist attacks themselves, but aid that makes the attacks more likely to occur. The Government, when seeking to prevent imminent harms in the context of international affairs and national security, is not required to conclusively link all the pieces in the puzzle before we grant weight to its empirical conclusions.

* * *

At bottom, plaintiffs simply disagree with the considered judgment of Congress and the Executive that providing material support to a designated foreign terrorist organization—even seemingly benign support—bolsters the terrorist activities of that organization. * * *

[The Court also addressed the plaintiffs' freedom of association claim:]

The Court of Appeals correctly rejected this claim because the statute does not penalize mere association with a foreign terrorist organization. * * *

Plaintiffs also argue that the material-support statute burdens their freedom of association because it prevents them from providing support to designated foreign terrorist organizations, but not to other groups. Any burden on plaintiffs' freedom of association in this regard is justified for the same reasons that we have denied plaintiffs' free speech challenge. * * *

* * *

Justice BREYER, with whom Justices GINSBURG and SOTOMAYOR join, dissenting.

[The dissent urged a narrow interpretation of the statute to avoid the constitutional issues, but then addressed them:]

* * * I cannot agree with the Court's conclusion that the Constitution permits the Government to prosecute the plaintiffs criminally for engaging in coordinated teaching and advocacy furthering the designated organizations' lawful political objectives. In my view, the Government has not met its burden of showing that an interpretation of the statute that would prohibit this speech- and association-related activity serves the Government's compelling interest in combating terrorism.

d. Inadmissibility Grounds Based on Foreign Policy

Closely related to the terrorism-related inadmissibility grounds are the foreign policy grounds in INA § 212(a)(3)(C). The conference committee report accompanying the 1990 Act explained this provision as follows.

> Under current law there is some ambiguity as to the authority of the Executive Branch to exclude aliens on foreign policy grounds * * *. The foreign policy provision in this title would establish a single clear standard for foreign policy exclusions (which is designated as 212(a)(3)(C) of the INA). The conferees believe that granting an alien admission to the United States is not a sign of approval or agreement and the conferees therefore expect that, with the enactment of this provision, aliens will be excluded not merely because of the potential signal that might be sent because of their admission, but when there would be a clear negative foreign policy impact associated with their admission.

> This provision would authorize the executive branch to exclude aliens for foreign policy reasons in certain circumstances. Specifically, under this provision, an alien could be excluded only if the Secretary of State has reasonable ground to believe an alien's entry or proposed activities within the United States would have potentially serious adverse foreign

policy consequences. However, there are two exceptions to this general standard.

First, an alien who is an official of a foreign government or a purported government, or who is a candidate for election to a foreign government office (and who is seeking entry into the United States during the period immediately prior to the election) would not be excludable under this provision solely because of any past, current or expected beliefs, statements or associations which would be lawful in the United States. The word "solely" is used in this provision to indicate that, in cases involving government officials, the committee intends that exclusions not be based merely on, for example, the possible content of an alien's speech in this country, but that there be some clear foreign policy impact beyond the mere fact of the speech or its content, that would permit exclusion.

possible

In particular, the conferees expect that the authority to exclude aliens with a government connection would apply primarily to senior government officials (or candidates for senior government posts). While, as a general matter, admitting foreign government officials is not necessarily a signal of approval, the conferees recognize that in cases involving senior officials it may be difficult to avoid conveying that impression.

The second exception, which applies to all other aliens, would prevent exclusion on the basis of an alien's past, current or expected beliefs, statements or associations which would be lawful within the United States unless the Secretary of State personally determines that the alien's admission to the United States would compromise a compelling United States foreign policy interest, and so certifies to the relevant Congressional Committees. It is the intent of the conference committee that this authority would be used sparingly and not merely because there is a likelihood that an alien will make critical remarks about the United States or its policies.

compelling

Furthermore, the conferees intend that the "compelling foreign policy interest" standard be interpreted as a significantly higher standard than the general "potentially serious adverse foreign policy consequences standard." In particular, the conferees note that the general exclusion standard in this provision refers only to the "potential" for serious adverse foreign policy consequences, whereas exclusion under the second exception (under which an alien can be excluded because of his beliefs, statements or associations) must be linked to a "compelling" foreign policy interest. The fact that the Secretary of State personally must inform the relevant Congressional Committees when a determination of excludability is made under this provision is a further indication that the conferees intend that this provision be used only in unusual circumstances.

With regard to the second exception, the following include some of the circumstances in which exclusion might be appropriate: when an alien's mere entry into the United States could result in imminent harm to the lives or property of United States persons abroad or to property of the United States government abroad (as occurred with the former Shah of Iran), or when an alien's entry would violate a treaty or international agreement to which the United States is party.

H.R. Rep. 101–955, 101st Cong., 2d Sess. 128–31 (1990).

In July 2014, the United States relied on § 212(a)(3)(C) to impose restrictions on travel to the U.S. by Venezuelan government officials responsible for human rights abuses relating to large-scale protests in Venezuela against deteriorating economic, social, and political conditions. The State Department cited instances of arbitrary detentions, excessive use of force, efforts to repress dissent through judicial intimidation, limit freedom of the press, and silence members of the political opposition. 91 Interp. Rel. 1377 (2014).

A closely comparable ground of deportability is in INA § 237(a)(4)(C). The major BIA precedent applying INA § 237(a)(4)(C) is *Matter of Ruiz-Massieu*, 22 I & N Dec. 833 (1999). The case grew out of the U.S. government's effort to deport Mario Ruiz-Massieu, a former Deputy Attorney General of Mexico, to his native country. One major issue throughout the litigation was just who has authority under § 237(a)(4)(C)(i) to decide which version of events to credit—the Secretary of State, the immigration judge, or perhaps the federal courts. Here is the BIA's answer:

> [T]he Secretary of State's reasonable determination in this case should be treated as conclusive evidence of the respondent's deportability. The Immigration Judge thus erred in holding that the [INS] is obliged to present clear, unequivocal, and convincing evidence in support of the Secretary of State's belief. [This evidentiary] requirement * * * is met by the Secretary's facially reasonable and bona fide determination that the respondent's presence here would cause potentially serious adverse foreign policy consequences for the United States.

22 I & N Dec. at 842.

PROBLEMS

1.   X, the Dutch head of a right-wing, anti-foreigner party in the Netherlands that has been gaining strength recently, is planning a two-week trip to the United States to make speeches and raise funds for an upcoming election campaign. Because the Netherlands is a visa waiver program country, he will not need a visa. You are an Under Secretary of State and are concerned that X's admission will give the impression that the U.S. government supports him. At the very least you do not want to do anything that helps his fundraising. Can you block his admission? Should you? What grounds might apply, and what would you have to establish to invoke them?

2.   Could the State Department:

(a) prevent the French deputy foreign minister (and his extended family members?) from vacationing at Lake Winnipesaukee in New Hampshire, because of U.S. anger at France's position at the United Nations regarding an uprising in the Middle East? ‾ No.

(b) bar specific members of the Turkish parliament who have publicly criticized or insulted prominent members of the U.S. Congress for their support of a congressional resolution condemning the Armenian genocide that occurred in the Ottoman Empire in 1915–17? ‾ No.

(c) block the admission of anti-globalization protesters coming to Washington, D.C., to participate in demonstrations during an annual meeting of the World Bank? Past demonstrations of this sort have often turned violent. ‾ Yes.

(d) bar any official, at any level, of the government of Burma (Myanmar), as well as selected businessmen who have supported the regime, in retaliation for another government crackdown on the Burmese democracy movement? ‾ yes.

In September 1995 the United States used the foreign policy exclusion provisions to revoke the visa of General Hector Gramajo, then a candidate for the Guatemalan Presidency, based on allegations of atrocities committed while he had served as Guatemalan defense minister. The revocation followed a $47.5 million federal court judgment against Gramajo in a suit brought by an American nun who had been tortured and eight Guatemalans who had been terrorized by the Guatemalan military while Gramajo served as defense minister. *See* 73 Interp. Rel. 293 (1996).

Compare the refusal of a visa for Markus Wolf, who had been deputy minister of state security and head of the foreign espionage branch of former East Germany. Wolf wanted to travel to New York to meet with his editors at Random House, the publisher of his autobiography. A State Department official explained that Wolf's agency "actively abetted and fostered state-supported terrorism." *See* Marc Fisher, *Ex-East German Spymaster Is Barred From U.S.*, Wash. Post, March 12, 1997.

B. DEPORTABILITY GROUNDS

Deportation statutes are nearly as old as the Republic. As mentioned in Section A of this chapter, the Alien and Sedition Acts of 1798 authorized the President to deport (1) resident aliens who were citizens of nations at war with the United States, Act of July 6, 1798, ch. 66, 1 Stat. 577 (Alien Enemies Act) and (2) aliens whom the President judged "dangerous to the peace and safety of the United States," Act of June 25, 1798, ch. 58, 1 Stat. 570 (Alien Friends Act). The Alien Friends Act was allowed to expire in 1801, while the Alien Enemies Act survives to this day.

[handwritten margin note: We still have Alien Enemies Act]

For most of the nineteenth century, federal law had no general deportation statute. Noncitizens who entered the country were allowed to remain as long as they wished. But in the late 1800s, as the federal government began to restrict who could enter, it recognized the need to remove those whose entry had violated those restrictions. At first, then, deportation statutes were meant primarily to supplement exclusion laws.

[handwritten margin note: deportations began in late 1800s]

For example, contract labor laws enacted in 1885 and 1887 prohibited the "importation or migration" of persons who had pre-existing contracts to perform most kinds of labor or services in the United States. Act of Feb. 26, 1885, ch. 164, 23 Stat. 332; Act of Feb. 23, 1887, ch. 220, 24 Stat. 414. (The statutes did not apply to skilled jobs for which American workers could not be found, domestic servants, professional actors, artists, singers or lecturers.) These laws were amended in 1888 to authorize the *deportation* of an immigrant who had been "allowed to land contrary to the prohibition" in the earlier laws. Act of Oct. 19, 1888, ch. 1210, 25 Stat. 566. Similarly, the 1892 statute at issue in *Fong Yue Ting,* p. 160, *supra,* which authorized the deportation of Chinese laborers who failed to obtain certificates of residence, was enacted to help enforce the earlier Chinese exclusion laws. Sweeping more broadly, the 1891 amendments to the immigration laws, while adding new exclusion grounds, broadened the deportation provision of the 1888 Act to encompass "any alien who shall come into the United States in violation of law." Act of Mar. 3, 1891, ch. 551, § 11, 24 Stat. 1086.

[handwritten margin note: 1891 deportation def.]

In 1907, Congress amended the immigration laws to authorize deportation of a noncitizen who was a prostitute "at any time within three years after she shall have entered the United States." Act of Feb. 20, 1907, ch. 1134, § 3, 34 Stat. 899–900. For the first time since the Alien and Sedition Acts, this statute authorized the deportation of a noncitizen based on conduct in the United States *after* a lawful entry.

[handwritten margin note: prostitution became deportable offense]

[handwritten note at bottom: deportation based on post-lawful entry conduct]

In the century since then, Congress has added considerably to the list of post-entry acts by a lawfully admitted noncitizen that can render her deportable. This chapter devotes attention to a number of these provisions, but it is helpful to step back and look at key concepts reflected in the deportability grounds. Daniel Kanstroom's history of deportation in the United States suggests two different models:

> [Th]ere are two basic types of deportation laws: *extended border control* and *post-entry social control.* The extended border control model implements basic features of sovereign power: the control of territory by the state and the legal distinction between citizens and noncitizens. Extended border control deportation laws have two variants, each of which has been a part of U.S. law for many years. First, there are laws that mandate the deportation of persons who have evaded border controls, either by surreptitious entry or by fraud or misrepresentation. These laws most directly support the border control regime, and their legitimacy, such as it is, is most closely linked to that of sovereignty itself.

> There are also laws that permit the deportation of persons who violate an explicit condition on which they were permitted to enter the country. For example, a person who enters the United States as a student must maintain a full course load, and a person with a work visa must work for a particular employer. The legitimacy of such laws, also derived from border control and sovereignty, is enhanced by the contractual aspect of the deal that permitted entry.

* * *

> [Other] deportation laws * * * combine extended border control with a rather different goal: post-entry social control. Deportation laws routinely govern conduct for a specific period following the time of admission. The purest post-entry social control laws, however, proscribe criminal or political conduct within the United States, often without time limit. They are often not directly connected to visa issuance, admission, or immigration processes at all. There is no requirement that a noncitizen be informed of them at entry. Indeed, they may be changed retroactively: a noncitizen may be deported for conduct that was not a deportable offense when it occurred.

> Such post-entry social control deportation laws derive from what might be termed an "eternal probation" or an "eternal guest" model. The strongest version of this model would suggest that the millions of noncitizens among us, including long-term lawful permanent residents, are harbored subject to the whim of

[Handwritten margin notes:]

post-entry acts deeming someone deportable

① extended border control
• control of territory by state
a) laws for deport. of people who evaded surreptitiously or by fraud or misrep
b) deportation for violation of condition of entrance

② post-entry social control
• govern conduct post-entry
– eternal probation or eternal guest
1) visa holders or LPRs

the government and may be deported for any reason. The earliest federal post-entry social control law, the 1798 Aliens Act, authorized highly discretionary executive deportation power to be used against noncitizen dissidents. A fierce debate arose not only over the politics of the law, but also over its basic legal legitimacy. As James Madison put it, "it can not be a true inference, that because the admission of an alien is a favor, the favor may be revoked at pleasure."[16]

Madison

Daniel Kanstroom, Deportation Nation: Outsiders in American History 5–6 (2007). For additional thought-provoking perspectives on the evolution of grounds of deportability amid the maelstrom of American political, economic, and social changes, see Aristide R. Zolberg, A Nation by Design: Immigration Policy in the Fashioning of America (2006).

§ 237
*list of
deport.
grounds*

Section 237 of the INA lists deportability grounds. A single individual might be deportable under more than one. The numerically significant broad categories are noncitizens who: (1) were inadmissible at time of entry or later violated their immigration status; or (2) were convicted of criminal offenses. Also noteworthy but much less numerous are noncitizens who: (3) falsified documents or failed to register; (4) engaged in activity raising national security or foreign policy concerns; (5) became a public charge; or (6) voted unlawfully. But of course, many deportable noncitizens are not removed, because they are eligible for relief from removal, as explained later in this chapter, or because they are not identified or located by immigration authorities, a pattern influenced by enforcement priorities, as addressed in Chapter Ten.

As you read the statutory provisions, ask yourself: If you were a member of Congress, would you vote to maintain, modify, or delete any of the deportability grounds in § 237(a)? Would you add grounds that subject those who violate civil rights laws to removal? Those who decide not to naturalize within a certain number of years? What principles and values should guide your choices? Would you remove a noncitizen for conduct (or a trait) that is not unlawful for a U.S. citizen—e.g., poverty or drug addiction? Should we insist that those who want to immigrate to the United States and join the American community have fewer faults or be less of a burden on society than persons born here? Is Congress using immigration laws to protect its image of ideal members of our community—an ideal that citizens sometimes fail to fulfill?

More generally, consider whether these ~~deportability~~ grounds function as an extension of the border, or post-entry social control, or some blend of the two models. Do you detect a trend toward one or the other of these approaches? If so, does it matter? If the statutes reflect one

---

[16] Report to the General Assembly of Virginia (Jan. 7, 1800), 4 *Elliot's Debates on the Federal Constitution* 541, 546 (Lippincott, 2d ed. 1097).

model or the other, does it affect their constitutionality? Should the distinction affect whether relief from removal is available?

1. IMMIGRATION CONTROL

Immigration control deportability grounds embody what Kanstroom calls extended border control. In analyzing these grounds, recall that inadmissibility grounds apply to noncitizens who arrive at a port of entry, or who are in the United States but have not been admitted (because they entered without inspection or were paroled into the country). As a close look at the first sentence of § 237(a) makes clear, deportability grounds apply only to noncitizens who have been admitted.

a. Inadmissible at Time of Entry or Adjustment of Status

applies even if you're not let you in but lied?

Under INA § 237(a)(1)(A), a noncitizen is deportable if she was inadmissible when she entered the United States or when she adjusted her status to permanent resident. This provision turns *all* the inadmissibility grounds in § 212(a) into potential deportability grounds even after noncitizens have been inspected and admitted. Section 237(a)(1)(A) applies, for example, if she presented herself for inspection and was admitted, but she did not actually meet all the admission requirements because, perhaps, she made some misrepresentations to obtain an immigrant visa. Being admitted refers to procedural regularity—whether she presented herself for inspection and admission. *See Matter of Quilantan*, 25 I & N Dec. 285 (BIA 2010). If erroneous admission did not count as an admission, then noncitizens would remain subject to the inadmissibility grounds, and § 237(a)(1)(A) would serve no purpose.

Because § 237(a)(1)(A) has no statute of limitations, acts long ago can come back to haunt someone after decades living in the United States, if it is later determined that she fell short of full qualification for admission. Moreover, this provision applies not just to a lawful permanent resident's initial admission to the United States, but to later admissions as well (though the law provides that an LPR's entry after inspection will not always count as an admission). *See* INA § 101(a)(13)(C), discussed in Section A of this chapter.

waiver of deportability may be requested by close family

Recognizing the potential harshness of § 237(a)(1)(A), Congress provided a discretionary waiver for noncitizens who are deportable because they were inadmissible for fraud or misrepresentation in obtaining an immigrant visa or admission. INA § 237(a)(1)(H). A spouse, parent, son, or daughter of a U.S. citizen or lawful permanent resident may apply for this waiver of deportability. In contrast, Congress chose to authorize the analogous inadmissibility waiver in § 212(i) only for a narrower class of family members: the parent of a citizen or LPR is ineligible.

b. Presence in the United States in Violation of Law

If a noncitizen is admitted after inspection, but then overstays his authorized period of admission, he is deportable under INA § 237(a)(1)(B) for being unlawfully present in the United States. (He is also deportable under § 237(a)(1)(C), as explained immediately below.) Before the 1996 Act abandoned an entry-based line between exclusion and deportation in favor of one based on admission, this ground was necessary to deport EWIs. Now, EWIs face inadmissibility grounds.

overstaying

c. Failure to Maintain Nonimmigrant Status

If a noncitizen fails to maintain his status or violates the conditions of his admission, he is deportable under INA § 237(a)(1)(C)(i). This ground can be applied to nonimmigrants who stay beyond their authorized admission period. But it also covers nonimmigrants who work without authorization, students who leave school, and temporary workers who abandon their authorized employment, and deportation charges can be filed even before the initial period of stay has ended.

ex: student visa and leaves school

d. Registration Requirements and Change of Address

Noncitizens who stay in the United States for more than 30 days must register, be fingerprinted, and provide their U.S. address and written notice of any address changes, *see* INA §§ 262, 265(a). As a practical matter, most lawfully present noncitizens satisfy the registration requirements by means of the documentation they receive relating to their immigration status. *See* 8 C.F.R. § 264.1. In addition, the INA authorizes requirements for special registration of groups of non-permanent residents, and for additional information from noncitizens (or a subgroup) from particular countries, *see* INA §§ 263, 265(b). These provisions have been part of federal immigration statutes since 1940. Failure to provide notice of a change of address is both a deportability ground and a criminal offense, *see* INA §§ 237(a)(3), 266.

e. Fraud and Misrepresentation

A noncitizen who commits fraud or misrepresentation to gain admission, documentation, or some other immigration benefit is typically deportable under INA § 237(a)(1)(A) for being inadmissible under § 212(a)(6)(C).

The use of fraudulent immigration documents can also make a noncitizen deportable under § 237(a)(3)(C), but only after an extra procedural step. INA § 274C imposes civil and criminal penalties on persons and entities that engage knowingly in certain types of immigration-related document fraud. The § 274C adjudication does not occur in the removal proceeding, but rather through a process supervised by an administrative law judge who is part of the office of the Chief Administrative Hearing Officer in EOIR. A final order under § 274C makes a noncitizen deportable under § 237(a)(3)(C).

PROBLEMS

With the foregoing overview in mind, apply the text of the immigration control deportability grounds to the problems below.

1. A is a lawful permanent resident living in Detroit. She crossed the border to Canada and picked up B, a Pakistani national, in Toronto. When A drove B back across the border to Detroit, B showed the immigration inspector someone else's green card. (B looks enough like the other person to escape detection.) The government later discovers that B entered the United States in this way. Both A and B are put in removal proceedings. What immigration charges may be lodged against A? Against B?

2. C, a Canadian national, was admitted to the United States to attend UCLA. After successfully completing his first year, he took a reduced sophomore course load to devote considerable time to surfing. The next year, he dropped out and now works full-time at a souvenir shop in Santa Monica, believing that he has no immigration law worries because he has been in the United States for less than the four years it usually takes to get a college degree. DHS has begun removal proceedings. Is C deportable?

---

2. IDEOLOGY, NATIONAL SECURITY, AND THE CONSTITUTION

The plenary power doctrine enunciated in the *Chinese Exclusion Case* and *Fong Yue Ting* arose in an era of rampant anti-Chinese sentiment in the United States in the late nineteenth century. Are the constitutional perspectives articulated in those opinions a relic of a bygone age, or have they retained their influence over several generations? To answer this question, we look at twentieth-century constitutional challenges to deportability based on noncitizen speech and association.

Recall the historical overview in the inadmissibility materials in Section A of this chapter; it also provides essential background on deportability up through the 1920s. In the period between the World Wars, U.S. citizens who joined the Communist Party did not violate the law. Indeed, the Communist Party ran candidates for public office throughout the United States. But noncitizen members could be accused of belonging to an organization that advocated the violent overthrow of the U.S. government, thus exposing them to deportation.

A 1918 deportation law made aliens deportable who were "members of or affiliated with any organization that entertains a belief in" violent overthrow of the government or anarchism. Anarchist Act of 1918, ch. 186, § 1, 40 Stat. 1012. In 1938, the government invoked this statute to put Harry Bridges, a well-known radical labor organizer, into deportation proceedings, asserting that he was a member of, or had been affiliated with, the Communist Party of the United States. The U.S. Supreme Court quashed the deportation order in *Bridges v. Wixon,* 326 U.S. 135, 65 S.Ct. 1443, 89 L.Ed. 2103 (1945). Writing for the majority, Justice Douglas concluded on statutory grounds that the evidence against Bridges did not sustain a deportability finding. In a widely quoted concurrence, Justice Murphy wrote:

> The Bill of Rights is a futile authority for the alien seeking admission for the first time to these shores. But once an alien lawfully enters and resides in this country he becomes invested with the rights guaranteed by the Constitution to all people within our borders. Such rights include those protected by the First and the Fifth Amendments and by the due process clause of the Fourteenth Amendment. None of these provisions acknowledges any distinction between citizens and resident aliens. They extend their inalienable privileges to all "persons" and guard against any encroachment on those rights by federal or state authority. * * *

> Since resident aliens have constitutional rights, it follows that Congress may not ignore them in the exercise of its "plenary" power of deportation. * * * [T]he First Amendment and other portions of the Bill of Rights make no exception in favor of deportation laws or laws enacted pursuant to a "plenary" power of the Government. Hence the very provisions of the Constitution negative the proposition that Congress, in the exercise of a "plenary" power, may override the rights of those who are numbered among the beneficiaries of the Bill of Rights.

> Any other conclusion would make our constitutional safeguards transitory and discriminatory in nature. Thus the Government would be precluded from enjoining or imprisoning an alien for exercising his freedom of speech. But the Government at the same time would be free, from a constitutional standpoint, to deport him for exercising that very same freedom. The alien would be fully clothed with his constitutional rights when defending himself in a court of law, but he would be stripped of those rights when deportation officials encircle him. I cannot agree that the framers of the Constitution meant to make such an empty mockery of human freedom.

Id. at 161–62, 65 S.Ct. 1443, 1455–56, 89 L.Ed. 2103 (1945).

In 1939, while Bridges' case was pending, the U.S. Supreme Court dropped a bombshell on Congress. In *Kessler v. Strecker*, 307 U.S. 22, 59 S.Ct. 694, 83 L.Ed. 1082 (1939), the Court ruled that under the applicable statute a noncitizen who had joined the Communist Party after entering the United States, but was no longer a member when arrested, was not deportable based on subversive connections. After *Kessler*, radical organizations expelled noncitizen members to protect them from deportation.

In response, Congress overrode *Kessler* by enacting the Alien Registration Act of 1940, ch. 439, § 23(b), 54 Stat. 673. It made deportable any alien who had been a member of a subversive group "at any time" after entering the United States. The statute applied to noncitizens "irrespective of the time of their entry into the United States," and according to the Senate Report, it was intended to apply to all aliens who were associated with subversive organizations "for no matter how short a time or how far in the past." S. Rep. No. 1796, 76th Cong., 3d Sess. (1940).[17]

With the onset of the Cold War in the late 1940s, these deportation grounds broadened substantially. *See, e.g.,* Act of May 25, 1948, ch. 338, § 1, 62 Stat. 268. In contrast to earlier deportation statutes that had required the government to prove in each membership case that the organization advocated the violent overthrow of the government, a 1950 statute identified the Communist Party by name and based deportation on mere membership in, or affiliation with, the party. Subversive Activities Control Act, Title I of the Internal Security Act of 1950, ch. 1024, § 22, 64 Stat. 1006 (1950).

The Immigration and Nationality Act of 1952 synthesized into one codified statute a host of earlier immigration control statutes that included numerous deportation grounds for subversive activities. The INA became law over a veto by President Truman, who objected, among other things, to the breadth and vagueness of the subversion-related deportation grounds. *See* Veto Statement of President Truman, June 25, 1952, *reprinted in* President's Commission on Immigration and Naturalization, Whom We Shall Welcome 281–82 (1953).

All of this supplied the political setting for the next case. Deportation orders had been issued against Peter Harisiades, a labor organizer and active member of the Communist Party until expelled by the party

---

[17] For further historical background, see Burt Neuborne, *Harisiades v. Shaughnessy: A Case Study in the Vulnerability of Resident Aliens,* in Immigration Stories (David A. Martin & Peter H. Schuck eds., 2005), Daniel Kanstroom, Deportation Nation: Outsiders in American History 46–63, 136–155, 186–206 (2007); Kevin R. Johnson, *The Antiterrorism Act, the Immigration Reform Act and Ideological Regulation in the Immigration Laws: Important Lessons for Citizens and Noncitizens,* 28 St. Mary's L.J. 833, 834–60 (1997).

following *Kessler*, Luigi Mascitti, and Dora Coleman. These permanent residents gave new meaning to the word "long-term." They had lived in the United States for a combined total of 106 years.

HARISIADES V. SHAUGHNESSY

Supreme Court of the United States, 1952.
342 U.S. 580, 72 S.Ct. 512, 96 L.Ed. 586.

MR. JUSTICE JACKSON delivered the opinion of the Court.

The ultimate question in these three cases is whether the United States constitutionally may deport a legally resident alien because of membership in the Communist Party which terminated before enactment of the Alien Registration Act, 1940.

Harisiades, a Greek national, accompanied his father to the United States in 1916, when thirteen years of age, and has resided here since. He has taken a wife and sired two children, all citizens. He joined the Communist Party in 1925, when it was known as the Workers Party, and served as an organizer, Branch Executive Committeeman, secretary of its Greek Bureau, and editor of its paper "Empros." The party discontinued his membership, along with that of other aliens, in 1939, but he has continued association with members. He was familiar with the principles and philosophy of the Communist Party and says he still believes in them. He disclaims personal belief in use of force and violence and asserts that the party favored their use only in defense. A warrant for his deportation because of his membership was issued in 1930 but was not served until 1946. The delay was due to inability to locate him because of his use of a number of aliases. After hearings, he was ordered deported on the grounds that after entry he had been a member of an organization which advocates overthrow of the Government by force and violence and distributes printed matter so advocating. * * *

Mascitti, a citizen of Italy, came to this country in 1920, at the age of sixteen. He married a resident alien and has one American-born child. He was a member of the Young Workers Party, the Workers Party and the Communist Party between 1923 and 1929. His testimony was that he knew the party advocated a proletarian dictatorship, to be established by force and violence if the capitalist class resisted. He heard some speakers advocate violence, in which he says he did not personally believe, and he was not clear as to the party policy. He resigned in 1929, apparently because he lost sympathy with or interest in the party. A warrant for his deportation issued and was served in 1946. After the usual administrative hearings he was ordered deported on the same grounds as Harisiades. * * *

Mrs. Coleman, a native of Russia, was admitted to the United States in 1914, when thirteen years of age. She married an American citizen and has three children, citizens by birth. She admits being a member of the Communist Party for about a year, beginning in 1919, and again from 1928 to 1930, and again from 1936 to 1937 or 1938. She held no office and her activities were not significant. She disavowed much knowledge of party principles and program, claiming she joined each time because of some injustice the party was then fighting. The reasons she gives for leaving the party are her health and the party's discontinuance of alien memberships. She has been ordered deported because after entry she became a member of an organization advocating overthrow of the Government by force and violence. * * *

* * *

I.

These aliens ask us to forbid their expulsion by a departure from the long-accepted application to such cases of the Fifth Amendment provision that no person shall be deprived of life, liberty or property without due process of law. Their basic contention is that admission for permanent residence confers a "vested right" on the alien, equal to that of the citizen, to remain within the country, and that the alien is entitled to constitutional protection in that matter to the same extent as the citizen. Their second line of defense is that if any power to deport domiciled aliens exists it is so dispersed that the judiciary must concur in the grounds for its exercise to the extent of finding them reasonable. The argument goes on to the contention that the grounds prescribed by the Act of 1940 bear no reasonable relation to protection of legitimate interests of the United States and concludes that the Act should be declared invalid. Admittedly these propositions are not founded in precedents of this Court.

For over thirty years each of these aliens has enjoyed such advantages as accrue from residence here without renouncing his foreign allegiance or formally acknowledging adherence to the Constitution he now invokes. Each was admitted to the United States, upon passing formidable exclusionary hurdles, in the hope that, after what may be called a probationary period, he would desire and be found desirable for citizenship. Each has been offered naturalization, with all of the rights and privileges of citizenship, conditioned only upon open and honest assumption of undivided allegiance to our Government. But acceptance was and is not compulsory. Each has been permitted to prolong his original nationality indefinitely.

So long as one thus perpetuates a dual status as an American inhabitant but foreign citizen, he may derive advantages from two sources of law—American and international. He may claim protection against our Government unavailable to the citizen. As an alien he retains a claim upon the state of his citizenship to diplomatic intervention on his behalf, a patronage often of considerable value. The state of origin of each of these aliens could presently enter diplomatic remonstrance against these deportations if they were inconsistent with international law, the prevailing custom among nations or their own practices.

The alien retains immunities from burdens which the citizen must shoulder. By withholding his allegiance from the United States, he leaves outstanding a foreign call on his loyalties which international law not only permits our Government to recognize but commands it to respect. * * *

Under our law, the alien in several respects stands on an equal footing with citizens,[9] but in others has never been conceded legal parity with the citizen.[10] Most importantly, to protract this ambiguous status within the country is not his right but is a matter of permission and tolerance. The Government's power to terminate its hospitality has been asserted and sustained by this Court since the question first arose.[11]

* * *

That aliens remain vulnerable to expulsion after long residence is a practice that bristles with severities. But it is a weapon of defense and reprisal confirmed by international law as a power inherent in every sovereign state. Such is the traditional power of the Nation over the alien and we leave the law on the subject as we find it.

This brings us to the alternative defense under the Due Process Clause—that, granting the power, it is so unreasonably and harshly exercised by this enactment that it should be held unconstitutional.

In historical context the Act before us stands out as an extreme application of the expulsion power. There is no denying that as world convulsions have driven us toward a closed society the expulsion power has been exercised with increasing severity, manifest in multiplication of grounds for deportation, in expanding the subject classes from illegal entrants to legal residents, and in greatly lengthening the period of residence after which one may be expelled. This is said to have reached a

---

[9] This Court has held that the Constitution assures him a large measure of equal economic opportunity. *Yick Wo v. Hopkins*, 118 U.S. 356, 6 S.Ct. 1064, 30 L.Ed. 220; *Truax v. Raich*, 239 U.S. 33, 36 S.Ct. 7, 60 L.Ed. 131; he may invoke the writ of habeas corpus to protect his personal liberty, *Nishimura Ekiu v. United States*, 142 U.S. 651, 660, 12 S.Ct. 336, 338, 35 L.Ed. 1146; in criminal proceedings against him he must be accorded the protections of the Fifth and Sixth Amendments, *Wong Wing v. United States*, 163 U.S. 228, 16 S.Ct. 977, 41 L.Ed. 140; and, unless he is an enemy alien, his property cannot be taken without just compensation. *Russian Volunteer Fleet v. United States*, 282 U.S. 481, 51 S.Ct. 229, 75 L.Ed. 473.

[10] He cannot stand for election to many public offices. For instance, Art. I, § 2, cl. 2, § 3, cl. 3, of the Constitution respectively require that candidates for election to the House of Representatives and Senate be citizens. See Borchard, Diplomatic Protection of Citizens Abroad, 63. The states, to whom is entrusted the authority to set qualifications of voters, for most purposes require citizenship as a condition precedent to the voting franchise.

[11] *Fong Yue Ting v. United States*, 149 U.S. 698, 707, 711–714, 730, 13 S.Ct. 1016, 1019, 1021–1022, 1028, 37 L.Ed. 905.

point where it is the duty of this Court to call a halt upon the political branches of the Government.

It is pertinent to observe that any policy toward aliens is vitally and intricately interwoven with contemporaneous policies in regard to the conduct of foreign relations, the war power, and the maintenance of a republican form of government. Such matters are so exclusively entrusted to the political branches of government as to be largely immune from judicial inquiry or interference.[16]

These restraints upon the judiciary, occasioned by different events, do not control today's decision but they are pertinent. It is not necessary and probably not possible to delineate a fixed and precise line of separation in these matters between political and judicial power under the Constitution. Certainly, however, nothing in the structure of our Government or the text of our Constitution would warrant judicial review by standards which would require us to equate our political judgment with that of Congress.

Under the conditions which produced this Act, can we declare that congressional alarm about a coalition of Communist power without and Communist conspiracy within the United States is either a fantasy or a pretense? This Act was approved by President Roosevelt June 28, 1940, when a world war was threatening to involve us, as soon it did. Communists in the United States were exerting every effort to defeat and delay our preparations. Certainly no responsible American would say that there were then or are now no possible grounds on which Congress might believe that Communists in our midst are inimical to our security.

Congress received evidence that the Communist movement here has been heavily laden with aliens and that Soviet control of the American Communist Party has been largely through alien Communists. It would be easy for those of us who do not have security responsibility to say that those who do are taking Communism too seriously and overestimating its danger. But we have an Act of one Congress which, for a decade, subsequent Congresses have never repealed but have strengthened and extended. We, in our private opinions, need not concur in Congress' policies to hold its enactments constitutional. Judicially we must tolerate what personally we may regard as a legislative mistake.

We are urged, because the policy inflicts severe and undoubted hardship on affected individuals, to find a restraint in the Due Process Clause. But the Due Process Clause does not shield the citizen from conscription and the consequent calamity of being separated from family, friends, home and business while he is transported to foreign lands to stem the tide of Communism. If Communist aggression creates such

---

[16] *United States v. Curtiss-Wright Export Corp.*, 299 U.S. 304, 319–322, 57 S.Ct. 216, 220–222, 81 L.Ed. 255.

hardships for loyal citizens, it is hard to find justification for holding that the Constitution requires that its hardships must be spared the Communist alien. When citizens raised the Constitution as a shield against expulsion from their homes and places of business, the Court refused to find hardship a cause for judicial intervention.[17]

We think that, in the present state of the world, it would be rash and irresponsible to reinterpret our fundamental law to deny or qualify the Government's power of deportation. However desirable world-wide amelioration of the lot of aliens, we think it is peculiarly a subject for international diplomacy. It should not be initiated by judicial decision which can only deprive our own Government of a power of defense and reprisal without obtaining for American citizens abroad any reciprocal privileges or immunities. Reform in this field must be entrusted to the branches of the Government in control of our international relations and treaty-making powers.

We hold that the Act is not invalid under the Due Process Clause. These aliens are not entitled to judicial relief unless some other constitutional limitation has been transgressed, to which inquiry we turn.

II.

The First Amendment is invoked as a barrier against this enactment. The claim is that in joining an organization advocating overthrow of government by force and violence the alien has merely exercised freedoms of speech, press and assembly which that Amendment guarantees to him.

The assumption is that the First Amendment allows Congress to make no distinction between advocating change in the existing order by lawful elective processes and advocating change by force and violence, that freedom for the one includes freedom for the other, and that when teaching of violence is denied so is freedom of speech.

Our Constitution sought to leave no excuse for violent attack on the status quo by providing a legal alternative—attack by ballot. To arm all men for orderly change, the Constitution put in their hands a right to influence the electorate by press, speech and assembly. This means freedom to advocate or promote Communism by means of the ballot box, but it does not include the practice or incitement of violence.[18]

True, it often is difficult to determine whether ambiguous speech is advocacy of political methods or subtly shades into a methodical but prudent incitement to violence. Communist governments avoid the inquiry by suppressing everything distasteful. Some would have us avoid

---

[17] *Hirabayashi v. United States*, 320 U.S. 81, 63 S.Ct. 1375, 87 L.Ed. 1774 (1943); *Korematsu v. United States*, 323 U.S. 214, 65 S.Ct. 193, 89 L.Ed. 194 (1944). [These cases upheld discriminatory wartime measures, including internment, taken against U.S. citizens of Japanese descent on the West Coast.—eds.]

[18] *Dennis v. United States*, 341 U.S. 494, 71 S.Ct. 857, 95 L.Ed. 1137.

the difficulty by going to the opposite extreme of permitting incitement to violent overthrow at least unless it seems certain to succeed immediately. We apprehend that the Constitution enjoins upon us the duty, however difficult, of distinguishing between the two. Different formulae have been applied in different situations and the test applicable to the Communist Party has been stated too recently to make further discussion at this time profitable.[19] We think the First Amendment does not prevent the deportation of these aliens.

III.

The remaining claim is that this Act conflicts with Art. I, § 9, of the Constitution forbidding *ex post facto* enactments. An impression of retroactivity results from reading as a new and isolated enactment what is actually a continuation of prior legislation.

During all the years since 1920 Congress has maintained a standing admonition to aliens, on pain of deportation, not to become members of any organization that advocates overthrow of the United States Government by force and violence, a category repeatedly held to include the Communist Party. These aliens violated that prohibition and incurred liability to deportation. They were not caught unawares by a change of law. There can be no contention that they were not adequately forewarned both that their conduct was prohibited and of its consequences.

In 1939, this Court decided *Kessler v. Strecker,* 307 U.S. 22, 59 S.Ct. 694, 83 L.Ed. 1082, in which it was held that Congress, in the statute as it then stood, had not clearly expressed an intent that Communist Party membership remained cause for deportation after it ceased. The Court concluded that in the absence of such expression only contemporaneous membership would authorize deportation.

The reaction of the Communist Party was to drop aliens from membership, at least in form, in order to immunize them from the consequences of their party membership.

The reaction of Congress was that the Court had misunderstood its legislation. In the Act here before us it supplied unmistakable language that past violators of its prohibitions continued to be deportable in spite of resignation or expulsion from the party. It regarded the fact that an alien defied our laws to join the Communist Party as an indication that he had developed little comprehension of the principles or practice of representative government or else was unwilling to abide by them.

However, even if the Act were found to be retroactive, to strike it down would require us to overrule the construction of the *ex post facto* provision which has been followed by this Court from earliest times. It

---

[19] *Ibid.*

always has been considered that that which it forbids is penal legislation which imposes or increases criminal punishment for conduct lawful previous to its enactment. Deportation, however severe its consequences, has been consistently classified as a civil rather than a criminal procedure. Both of these doctrines as original proposals might be debatable, but both have been considered closed for many years and a body of statute and decisional law has been built upon them.

* * *

It is contended that this policy allows no escape by reformation. We are urged to apply some doctrine of atonement and redemption. Congress might well have done so, but it is not for the judiciary to usurp the function of granting absolution or pardon. We cannot do so for deportable ex-convicts, even though they have served a term of imprisonment calculated to bring about their reformation.

When the Communist Party as a matter of party strategy formally expelled alien members en masse, it destroyed any significance that discontinued membership might otherwise have as indication of change of heart by the individual. Congress may have believed that the party tactics threw upon the Government an almost impossible burden if it attempted to separate those who sincerely renounced Communist principles of force and violence from those who left the party the better to serve it. Congress, exercising the wide discretion that it alone has in these matters, declined to accept that as the Government's burden.

We find none of the constitutional objections to the Act well founded. * * *

MR. JUSTICE CLARK took no part in the consideration or decision of these cases.

MR. JUSTICE FRANKFURTER, concurring.

It is not for this Court to reshape a world order based on politically sovereign States. In such an international ordering of the world a national State implies a special relationship of one body of people, *i.e.,* citizens of that State, whereby the citizens of each State are aliens in relation to every other State. Ever since national States have come into being, the right of people to enjoy the hospitality of a State of which they are not citizens has been a matter of political determination by each State. (I put to one side the oddities of dual citizenship.) Though as a matter of political outlook and economic need this country has traditionally welcomed aliens to come to its shores, it has done so exclusively as a matter of political outlook and national self-interest. This policy has been a political policy, belonging to the political branch of the Government wholly outside the concern and the competence of the Judiciary.

* * *

The Court's acknowledgment of the sole responsibility of Congress for these matters has been made possible by Justices whose cultural outlook, whose breadth of view and robust tolerance were not exceeded by those of Jefferson. In their personal views, libertarians like Mr. Justice Holmes and Mr. Justice Brandeis doubtless disapproved of some of these policies, departures as they were from the best traditions of this country and based as they have been in part on discredited racial theories or manipulation of figures in formulating what is known as the quota system. But whether immigration laws have been crude and cruel, whether they may have reflected xenophobia in general or anti-Semitism or anti-Catholicism, the responsibility belongs to Congress. Courts do enforce the requirements imposed by Congress upon officials in administering immigration laws * * *. But the underlying policies of what classes of aliens shall be allowed to enter and what classes of aliens shall be allowed to stay, are for Congress exclusively to determine even though such determination may be deemed to offend American traditions and may, as has been the case, jeopardize peace.

In recognizing this power and this responsibility of Congress, one does not in the remotest degree align oneself with fears unworthy of the American spirit or with hostility to the bracing air of the free spirit. One merely recognizes that the place to resist unwise or cruel legislation touching aliens is the Congress, not this Court.

I, therefore, join in the Court's opinion in these cases.

MR. JUSTICE DOUGLAS, with whom MR. JUSTICE BLACK concurs, dissenting.

There are two possible bases for sustaining this Act:

> (1) A person who was once a Communist is tainted for all time and forever dangerous to our society; or

> (2) Punishment through banishment from the country may be placed upon an alien not for what he did, but for what his political views once were.

Each of these is foreign to our philosophy. We repudiate our traditions of tolerance and our articles of faith based upon the Bill of Rights when we bow to them by sustaining an Act of Congress which has them as a foundation.

The view that the power of Congress to deport aliens is absolute and may be exercised for any reason which Congress deems appropriate rests on *Fong Yue Ting v. United States,* 149 U.S. 698, 13 S.Ct. 1016, 37 L.Ed. 905, decided in 1893 by a six-to-three vote. That decision seems to me to be inconsistent with the philosophy of constitutional law which we have developed for the protection of resident aliens. We have long held that a resident alien is a "person" within the meaning of the Fifth and the Fourteenth Amendments. * * * He is entitled to habeas corpus to test the legality of his restraint, to the protection of the Fifth and Sixth Amendments in criminal trials, and to the right of free speech as guaranteed by the First Amendment.

An alien, who is assimilated in our society, is treated as a citizen so far as his property and his liberty are concerned. He can live and work here and raise a family, secure in the personal guarantees every resident has and safe from discriminations that might be leveled against him because he was born abroad. Those guarantees of liberty and livelihood are the essence of the freedom which this country from the beginning has offered the people of all lands. If those rights, great as they are, have constitutional protection, I think the more important one—the right to remain here—has a like dignity.

The power of Congress to exclude, admit, or deport aliens flows from sovereignty itself and from the power "To establish an uniform Rule of Naturalization." U.S. Const., Art. I, § 8, cl. 4. The power of deportation is therefore an *implied* one. The right to life and liberty is an *express* one. Why this *implied* power should be given priority over the *express* guarantee of the Fifth Amendment has never been satisfactorily answered. * * *

The right to be immune from arbitrary decrees of banishment certainly may be more important to "liberty" than the civil rights which all aliens enjoy when they reside here. Unless they are free from arbitrary banishment, the "liberty" they enjoy while they live here is indeed illusory. Banishment is punishment in the practical sense. It may deprive a man and his family of all that makes life worth while. Those who have their roots here have an important stake in this country. Their plans for themselves and their hopes for their children all depend on their right to stay. If they are uprooted and sent to lands no longer known to them, no longer hospitable, they become displaced, homeless people condemned to bitterness and despair.

This drastic step may at times be necessary in order to protect the national interest. There may be occasions when the continued presence of an alien, no matter how long he may have been here, would be hostile to the safety or welfare of the Nation due to the nature of his conduct. But unless such condition is shown, I would stay the hand of the Government and let those to whom we have extended our hospitality and who have become members of our communities remain here and enjoy the life and liberty which the Constitution guarantees.

Congress has not proceeded by that standard. It has ordered these aliens deported not for what they are but for what they once were.

Perhaps a hearing would show that they continue to be people dangerous and hostile to us. But the principle of forgiveness and the doctrine of redemption are too deep in our philosophy to admit that there is no return for those who have once erred.

NOTES AND QUESTIONS ON
THE IMPLICATIONS OF HARISIADES

1. Despite the broad wording of the deportation grounds for subversion, they were used infrequently. In the 1950s, 230 noncitizens were deported on these grounds. The number declined to 15 in the 1960s, and to 18 in the 1970s. The federal government then stopped publishing separate statistics for this ground. 2001 INS Statistical Yearbook, table 67.

2. *Harisiades* was sorely disappointing to those who thought the Supreme Court rulings in *Kessler* and *Bridges* foretold more robust constitutional protections for lawful permanent residents. But both decisions had relied on statutory grounds, allowing the Court to avoid constitutional issues. *Harisiades*, facing the constitutional challenges head on, was different in tone and result. The times had changed. In the seven years between *Bridges* and *Harisiades*, World War II had ended, the U.S.-U.S.S.R. alliance had dissolved, and the Cold War had begun. Moreover, the Communist Party's effort to take advantage of *Kessler* by expelling noncitizen members had provoked a widespread negative reaction.

3. Justice Jackson wrote for the *Harisiades* majority more than 60 years ago. The Cold War has since ended, and the Soviet Union dissolved in 1992. Yet, the references to perilous global politics and world-wide hostile movements may sound eerily familiar in the United States post-September 11. But do fundamental changes in international law, which now acknowledges the rights of individuals as well as the rights of states, undermine the *Harisiades* rationale? What about the substantial rise in the number of states, including the United States, that accept dual nationality? What is the impact of later Supreme Court decisions that have distinguished between procedural due process guarantees at the border and in the interior? Does the analysis in *Harisiades* allow room for analogous distinctions suggesting closer constitutional scrutiny if deportability, not inadmissibility, is at issue? What view of permanent residence does *Harisiades* reflect, and is that view persuasive today?

These questions may become less daunting as we work through the next subsection, which addresses several themes that they raise, including how removal is related to (a) punishment, (b) retroactivity, (c) statutory interpretation, (d) the meaning of permanent residence, (e) the passage of time, and (f) constitutional liberties.

3. THE CONCEPT OF DEPORTABILITY

a. Removal and Punishment

Justice Jackson summarily dismissed the idea that expulsion is punishment for constitutional purposes. But it is doubtful that he really meant that deportation is not punishment in the sense of harm or sanctions for misconduct or violation of law. James Madison forcefully made this argument long ago against the Alien and Sedition Acts:

> If the banishment of an alien from a country into which he has been invited as the asylum most auspicious to his happiness,—a country where he may have formed the most tender connections; where he may have invested his entire property, and acquired property of the real and permanent, as well as the movable and temporary kind; where he enjoys, under the laws, a greater share of the blessings of personal security, and personal liberty, than he can elsewhere hope for; * * *—if a banishment of this sort be not a punishment, and among the severest of punishments, it will be difficult to imagine a doom to which the name can be applied.

4 Elliot's Debates 555 (Philadelphia, J.B. Lippincott & Co., 1881 ed.). Rather, it seems clear that Jackson was distinguishing civil from criminal punishments to protect immigration statutes from the substantive and procedural limits the Constitution places on criminal proceedings.

The Court's distinction between deportation and punishment is most evident in contrasting the landmark cases of *Fong Yue Ting v. United States*, 149 U.S. 698, 13 S.Ct. 1016, 37 L.Ed. 905 (1893), and *Wong Wing v. United States,* 163 U.S. 228, 16 S.Ct. 977, 41 L.Ed. 140 (1896), pp. 160, 174, *supra.* Recall that *Fong Yue Ting* upheld the deportation of Chinese noncitizens under the 1892 immigration statute for lack of a residence certificate that could be obtained only on the basis of testimony from a white witness. The decision also held that the constitutional protection against cruel and unusual punishment does not apply to deportation. In contrast, the Court in *Wong Wing* struck down, in the same statute, a section that authorized imprisonment, without a judicial trial, of noncitizens found deportable. *Wong Wing* sharply distinguished deportation from punishment:

> No limits can be put by the courts upon the power of Congress to protect, by summary methods, the country from the advent of aliens whose race or habits render them undesirable as citizens, or to expel such if they have already found their way into our land and unlawfully remain therein. But to declare unlawful residence within the country to be an infamous crime, punishable by deprivation of liberty and property, would be to

pass out of the sphere of constitutional legislation, unless provision were made that the fact of guilt should first be established by a judicial trial.

Id. at 237.

Though the doctrine persists that removal from the United States is not punishment for constitutional purposes, we will see later in this chapter that the Supreme Court has been more receptive to arguments for greater constitutional protection in some settings based on the sheer severity of removal. *See Padilla v. Kentucky,* 559 U.S. 356, 130 S.Ct. 1473, 176 L.Ed.2d 284 (2010), p. 668, *infra; see also Vartelas v. Holder,* 132 S. Ct. 1479, 1487, 182 L.Ed.2d 473 (2012) (noting the "severity of [the] sanction" when "banishment" is applied to lawful permanent residents).

b.   Retroactivity

The ex post facto clause. By reaffirming that removal is not punishment for constitutional purposes, *Harisiades* was able to invoke the well-established corollary that the Constitution's prohibition against ex post facto laws does not apply to deportation statutes. A noncitizen may be deported for past conduct that did not render the noncitizen deportable at the time the act was committed. Part III of Justice Jackson's opinion addressed the ex post facto challenge briefly, noting that Congress had given notice, via anti-subversive speech statutes, that membership in certain organizations could lead to deportation, and that in any event the ex post facto clause is implicated only in criminal proceedings.

Two years later, the Supreme Court rejected an ex post facto challenge to the deportation of Juan Galvan, who had lived in the United States since arriving from Mexico in 1918. Applying the Subversive Activities Control Act of 1950, an INS hearing officer ordered Galvan deported after finding that he had belonged to the Communist Party from 1944 to 1946. Writing for the Court, Justice Frankfurter explained:

> In light of the expansion of the concept of substantive due process as a limitation upon all powers of Congress, * * * much could be said for the view, were we writing on a clean slate, that the Due Process Clause qualifies the scope of political discretion heretofore recognized as belonging to Congress in regulating the entry and deportation of aliens. And since the intrinsic consequences of deportation are so close to punishment for crime, it might fairly be said also that the *ex post facto* Clause, even though applicable only to punitive legislation, should be applied to deportation.

> But the slate is not clean. As to the extent of the power of Congress under review, there is not merely "a page of history,"

New York Trust Co. v. Eisner, 256 U.S. 345, 349, 41 S.Ct. 506, 507, 65 L.Ed. 963, but a whole volume. Policies pertaining to the entry of aliens and their right to remain here are peculiarly concerned with the political conduct of government. * * * [T]hat the formulation of these policies is entrusted exclusively to Congress has become about as firmly imbedded in the legislative and judicial tissues of our body politic as any aspect of our government. And whatever might have been said at an earlier date for applying the *ex post facto* Clause, it has been the unbroken rule of this Court that it has no application to deportation.

Galvan v. Press, 347 U.S. 522, 530–31, 74 S.Ct. 737, 742, 98 L.Ed. 911 (1954).

JUSTICE BLACK dissented, joined by JUSTICE DOUGLAS:

* * * [D]uring the period of his membership * * * [Communist] Party candidates appeared on California election ballots, and no federal law then frowned on Communist Party political activities. * * *

For joining a lawful political group years ago—an act which he had no possible reason to believe would subject him to the slightest penalty—[Galvan] now loses his job, his friends, his home, and maybe even his children, who must choose between their father and their native country.

Id. at 532–33, 74 S.Ct. at 743–44 (BLACK, J., dissenting).

The Supreme Court has consistently rejected ex post facto challenges to other deportability grounds. *See, e.g., Mahler v. Eby,* 264 U.S. 32, 44 S.Ct. 283, 68 L.Ed. 549 (1924) (upholding the retroactive application of a 1920 statute to a 1918 conviction under the Selective Draft and the Espionage Acts of 1917); *Marcello v. Bonds,* 349 U.S. 302, 75 S.Ct. 757, 99 L.Ed. 1107 (1955) (upholding the retroactive application of a 1952 deportation statute to a 1938 marijuana-related conviction).

Similar retroactivity issues arose from Congress' efforts in the 1990s to add new criminal deportability grounds and expand existing ones. Under § 321(b) of the 1996 Act, the expanded definition of aggravated felony in INA § 101(a)(43) applies "regardless of whether the conviction was entered before, on, or after the date of enactment." Ex post facto challenges to retroactive applications of this sort have consistently failed. *See, e.g., Morris v. Holder,* 676 F.3d 309, 316–17 (2d Cir. 2012) (expanded definition of "aggravated felony"); *United States v. Yacoubian,* 24 F.3d 1, 9–10 (9th Cir. 1994) (deportation ground for firearms offenses).

The due process clause. The Supreme Court has applied the due process clause to scrutinize legislation that imposes new civil duties or liabilities based on past acts, but it has demanded no more than a rational basis for the retroactive application. In one decision, the Court added:

> Our decisions, however, have left open the possibility that legislation might be unconstitutional if it imposes severe retroactive liability on a limited class of parties that could not have anticipated the liability, and the extent of that liability is substantially disproportionate to the parties' experience.

Eastern Enterprises v. Apfel, 524 U.S. 498, 524–28, 118 S.Ct. 2131, 2146–49, 141 L.Ed.2d 451 (1998). The Court's recent receptivity to greater constitutional protection based on the severity of removal—*see Padilla v. Kentucky*, 559 U.S. 356, 130 S.Ct. 1473, 176 L.Ed.2d 284 (2010), p. 668, *infra*—may signal an opening for a due process argument against retroactive deportability grounds.

c. Statutory Interpretation Doctrines: Clear Statement Requirements, the Rule of Lenity, and the Avoidance of Constitutional Doubt.

Though retroactive deportability grounds have been sustained, concerns about retroactivity can play a significant role in statutory interpretation. For example, when *Galvan* rejected the ex post facto challenge, the Court seemed to read any *scienter* requirement out of the deportation ground. Communist Party membership could lead to deportation, regardless of the member's attitude toward violent change or his understanding of the Party's mission or tactics. Yet, applying that deportability ground retroactively may have led to second thoughts. Three years later, Justice Frankfurter construed the deportation statute to require a "meaningful association" with the Party. *See Rowoldt v. Perfetto,* 355 U.S. 115, 120, 78 S.Ct. 180, 183, 2 L.Ed.2d 140 (1957).

More recently, and more directly on the retroactivity issue, the Supreme Court addressed legislation in 1996 that tightened eligibility for discretionary relief from removal. The Court held that the changes were not retroactive, because there is a presumption against retroactivity that only a clear congressional statement could overcome. *See INS v. St. Cyr*, 533 U.S. 289, 121 S.Ct. 2271, 150 L.Ed.2d 347 (2001). But so long as Congress has explicitly provided for retroactivity, courts have deferred.

Reaching beyond retroactivity to the interpretation of deportation statutes generally, a classic approach has been to read such statutes narrowly. Justice Douglas penned the classic statement of this canon of interpretation, sometimes called the "rule of lenity":

> We resolve the doubts in favor of that construction [urged by the noncitizen] because deportation is a drastic measure and at times the equivalent of banishment or exile * * * . It is the

forfeiture for misconduct of a residence in this country. Such a forfeiture is a penalty. To construe this statutory provision less generously to the alien might find support in logic. But since the stakes are considerable for the individual, we will not assume that Congress meant to trench on his freedom beyond that which is required by the narrowest of several possible meanings of the words used.

Fong Haw Tan v. Phelan, 333 U.S. 6, 10, 68 S.Ct. 374, 376, 92 L.Ed. 433 (1948). In *Fong Haw Tan*, the government sought to deport a lawful permanent resident on the basis of a criminal record; the Supreme Court ultimately interpreted the statute not to establish deportability.

Does this canon of statutory interpretation surprise you, in light of the obstacle that the plenary power doctrine presents to challenging the government's immigration decisions? Or does the canon make sense in light of that doctrine? That is, though the Court recognizes broad congressional authority, deportation's harsh consequences lead it to insist that Congress state clearly when noncitizens are deportable. This "clear statement" rule imposes a duty on Congress to consider carefully the scope of deportation grounds—an indirect means for the Court to help make sure the legislators and the public are explicit about what is at issue, so that the political check is fully operative. It also helps clarify for noncitizens what specific acts may carry harsh consequences.

Paralleling *Fong Haw Tan*'s rule of lenity, courts have sometimes construed immigration-related statutes in the noncitizen's favor because the statute might otherwise tread close to—or possibly transgress—constitutional limits. This is an application of the doctrine of constitutional avoidance—the principle that statutes should be read to avoid interpretations that raise serious constitutional questions. As noted in Chapter Six's discussion of procedural due process, courts sometimes read a statute in the noncitizen's favor even when the plenary power doctrine could preclude constitutional challenge. *See* Hiroshi Motomura, *Immigration Law After a Century of Plenary Power: Phantom Constitutional Norms and Statutory Interpretation*, 100 Yale L.J. 545 (1990). Phantom norms may be one way to explain why statutes relating to deportability are not retroactive unless Congress clearly says so.

d.   Deportability Grounds and the Passage of Time

Suppose a noncitizen was convicted of a crime many years after being admitted to the United States. Suppose she was admitted as an infant and committed the offense as an adult. Or suppose she committed a crime twenty years ago that could have led to her deportation, but she has led an exemplary life since then, and only now is the government taking steps to enforce the law against her. Or suppose a new deportability ground applies retroactively to something that she did long ago. Should the passage of time affect removal? If so, how?

(i) Time Before the Initiation of Removal Proceedings

In criminal law, a statute of limitations normally begins running when a crime has been committed. The rationales include: (1) the desirability that prosecutions be based on fresh evidence; (2) the likelihood that a person who has refrained from further criminal activity for a period of time has reformed; (3) the decline of the retributive impulse over time; (4) the desirability of lessening the possibility of blackmail based on a threat to prosecute or disclose evidence to law enforcement officials; and (5) the promotion of repose. American Law Institute, Model Penal Code and Commentaries, Comment Part I § 1.06 (1985). A similar rule in immigration law could require removal proceedings to be initiated a certain number of years after the act that is the basis for deportability.

The "excludable at entry" deportation ground once had a statute of limitations. The 1903 Act provided: "any alien who shall come into the United States in violation of law * * * shall be deported * * * at any time within two years after arrival." Act of March 3, 1903, ch. 1012, § 20, 32 Stat. 1218. This period later became three years, and then five years. See Act of Feb. 20, 1907, ch. 1134, § 20, 34 Stat. 904; Immigration Act of 1917, ch. 29, § 19, 39 Stat. 889. When Congress repealed the limitation in 1952, the Senate Judiciary Committee explained: "If the cause for exclusion existed at the time of entry, it is believed that such aliens are just as undesirable at any subsequent time as they are within the five years after entry." S. Rep. No. 1515, 81st Cong., 2d Sess. 389 (1950).

Historian Mae M. Ngai argues that some of the policies underlying statutes of limitations in criminal law apply to the initiation of removal proceedings against noncitizens who are in the United States unlawfully. (As a technical matter, some of them would be inadmissible, and some deportable.) Referring to the statutes of limitations in some early federal immigration statutes, she explains:

> * * * This policy recognized an important reality about illegal immigrants: They settle, raise families and acquire property—in other words, they become part of the nation's economic and social fabric. * * *

> * * *

> A statute of limitations on unlawful entry is * * * consistent with basic legal and moral principles. It does not condone or reward illegal immigration: Unauthorized presence would remain a violation of the law and continue to carry the risk of apprehension and removal, at least for some period of time. But

it would allow us to recognize that the undocumented become, for better or worse, members of the community, and to accept them as such.

Restoring the statute of limitations would not solve our immigration problems. But it would go a long way toward stemming the accretion of a caste population that is easily exploitable and lives forever outside the polity.

Mai M. Ngai, *We Need A Deportation Deadline*, Wash. Post, June 14, 2005, at A21. *See also* T. Alexander Aleinikoff, *Illegal Employers*, American Prospect, Dec. 19, 2001 (proposing a ten-year statute of limitations for unauthorized migrants).

But consider the rebuttal that the concept of a statute of limitations does not apply as Ngai urges. Even if the unlawful entry was long ago, the noncitizen is unlawfully present today. Faced with a related issue, the Supreme Court held in 2006 that it was not retroactive to apply a newly enacted removal procedure to a noncitizen who had unlawfully entered many years before. Justice David Souter's majority opinion explained that the relevant time was not the original entry, but unlawful presence today:

> While the law [INA § 241(a)(5)] looks back to a past act in its application to "an alien [who] has reentered . . . illegally," the provision does not penalize an alien for the reentry (criminal and civil penalties do that) * * * . [I]t is the conduct of remaining in the country after entry that is the predicate action; the statute applies to stop an indefinitely continuing violation that the alien himself could end at any time by voluntarily leaving the country. It is therefore the alien's choice to continue his illegal presence, after illegal reentry and after the effective date of the new law, that subjects him to the new and less generous legal regime, not a past act that he is helpless to undo up to the moment the Government finds him out.

Fernandez-Vargas v. Gonzales, 548 U.S. 30, 44, 126 S.Ct. 2422, 165 L.Ed.2d 323 (2006). By this reasoning, how can any statute of limitations even *start* to run while the noncitizen is in the United States unlawfully?

One current INA section operates somewhat like a statute of limitations. Noncitizens who entered before January 1, 1972, and have been continuously resident since then may become lawful permanent residents—as a matter of government discretion—via registry under § 249. This cutoff date was set in 1986, replacing the previous cutoff date of 1948, but has not been moved forward since then. A registry applicant is ineligible if found to lack good moral character or to be covered by certain inadmissibility and deportability grounds. With the cutoff date so far in the past, it is unsurprising that only 104 noncitizens became permanent residents through registry in fiscal year 2013. DHS, 2013 Yearbook of Immigration Statistics 24, table 7.

Note the difference between registry and a regular statute of limitations, which typically blocks government sanctions unless initiated within a stated period after the specific violation by the individual. What are the advantages and disadvantages, in the immigration context, of using a fixed statutory cutoff date, infrequently changed by Congress, versus the more common individualized time limitation?

As a member of Congress, would you support advancing the registry cutoff date? Would you support a five-year (or ten-year?) statute of limitations for all deportability grounds? Some grounds and not others?

(ii) Time Between Admission and a Deportable Act

The deportability ground based on conviction of a crime involving moral turpitude applies to a noncitizen "convicted of a crime involving moral turpitude committed within five years * * * after admission." INA § 237(a)(2)(A)(i). Should the same idea—that acts should no longer make a noncitizen deportable after certain period of residence in the United States—be applied to other deportability grounds? For some grounds but not others, or different time periods for different grounds, such as a longer period for deportability based on a violent crime as compared to a nonviolent one?

For an exploration of time-based limitations on deportability, *see* Juliet P. Stumpf, *Doing Time: Crimmigration Law and the Perils of Haste*, 58 UCLA L. Rev. 1705, 1745–46 (2011) (observing that "statutes and common law place time limitations on the pursuit of stale claims, through statutes of limitations, statutes of repose, and laches. Perhaps it is time to revive the notion of a time limit on deportability grounds.").

e. The First Amendment and Other Constitutional Liberties

Another theme in *Harisiades* is the link between deportability and constitutional liberties. Are deportability statutes limited by constitutional guarantees, such as Fifth Amendment due process and equal protection, or First Amendment freedom of speech and association?

Under *Yamataya v. Fisher,* 189 U.S. 86, 23 S.Ct. 611, 47 L.Ed. 721 (1903), discussed in Chapter Six, the Fifth Amendment's guarantee of procedural due process applies in deportation, but *Yamataya* did not address substantive deportability grounds. In contrast, *Harisiades* did not involve a challenge to deportation procedures. Rather, the Court rejected a First Amendment constitutional challenge to a statutory deportation ground based on Communist Party membership. Does this mean that Congress could pass a law ordering the removal of any noncitizen who marches in a parade supporting legalization of marijuana, or who joins the Ku Klux Klan? Perhaps you could read Justice Jackson's opinion that way, but the constitutional reasoning deserves a closer look.

Justice Jackson seemed to say that the speech in question was not protected and thus deportation based on such speech could not offend the First Amendment. He cited *Dennis v. United States*, 341 U.S. 494, 71 S.Ct. 857, 95 L.Ed. 1137 (1951), decided the year before *Harisiades*. *Dennis* sustained the criminal convictions of Communist organizers under the Smith Act, a 1940 statute (passed as a rider to the statute in *Harisiades*) that prohibited knowingly or willfully advocating the overthrow of the United States government. *Dennis* held that speech is not protected by the First Amendment "where there is a 'clear and present danger' of the substantive evil which the legislature had the right to prevent." 341 U.S. 494, 515, 71 S.Ct. 857, 870, 95 L.Ed. 1137 (1951).

In 1969, *Brandenburg v. Ohio*, 395 U.S. 444, 89 S.Ct. 1827, 23 L.Ed.2d 430 (1969) (per curiam), cast substantial doubt on the continuing vitality of *Dennis* by striking down a statute similar to the Smith Act. Applying a standard less deferential to the government, the Court effectively expanded First Amendment protections. *Brandenburg* held that the government may not "forbid or proscribe advocacy of the use of force or of law violation except where such advocacy is directed to *inciting or producing imminent lawless action* and is likely to incite or produce such action." 395 U.S. at 447, 89 S.Ct. at 1829 (emphasis added).

Did *Brandenburg* change what *Harisiades* says about First Amendment protections for noncitizens? Consider how you would respond to the following argument: The First Amendment as construed in *Dennis* did not protect what Harisiades, Mascitti, and Coleman did, and this conclusion did not depend on whether they were citizens or noncitizens. Thus, *Harisiades* stands for the proposition that the First Amendment protects citizens and noncitizens equally. Now that *Brandenburg* has expanded the scope of the First Amendment beyond what it was in *Dennis*, noncitizens should enjoy the same expanded coverage as citizens. Thus, *Brandenburg*, by superseding *Dennis*, in effect overrules *Harisiades*.

See generally T. Alexander Aleinikoff, *Federal Regulation of Aliens and the Constitution*, 83 Am. J. Int'l L. 862, 868–69 (1989).

The meaning of *Harisiades* became central to convoluted litigation that fought efforts to deport eight noncitizens for their associations with the Popular Front for the Liberation of Palestine. The government charged the two lawful permanent residents under the antiterrorist deportability provisions in INA § 237(a)(4)(B) that make deportable any alien covered by the terrorism-related inadmissibility grounds in §§ 212(a)(3)(B) or (F), discussed earlier in this chapter. Against the six who were not lawful permanent residents, the government charged deportation grounds based on overstaying or otherwise violating their terms of admission. All of the noncitizens claimed that the government had engaged in unlawful selective prosecution based on their political associations. *Reno v. American-Arab Anti-Discrimination Committee* [*AADC*], 525 U.S. 471, 119 S.Ct. 936, 142 L.Ed.2d 940 (1999).

After four trips through the district court and the Ninth Circuit, the Supreme Court ruled for the government on jurisdictional grounds, finding that the limits on judicial review in INA § 242 did not allow the noncitizens to raise their claims in court, at least not before there was a final removal order. Writing for the Court, Justice Scalia rejected the noncitizens' argument that jurisdiction was necessary because delaying review of their selective prosecution claim would chill their First Amendment rights.

Three of the opinions in the case addressed three themes that have run consistently through cases that raise constitutional claims against immigration enforcement: (1) the tension between constitutional liberties and the scope of government power in controlling immigration, (2) the relationship between criminal punishment and removal, and (3) the significance of lawful permanent residence, addressed in the subsection that follows.

Justice Scalia raised the first two themes in his majority opinion. On constitutional liberties and government power, he wrote:

> [A]n alien unlawfully in this country has no constitutional right to assert selective enforcement as a defense against his deportation * * *. Because such claims invade a special province of the Executive—its prosecutorial discretion—we have emphasized that the standard for proving them is particularly demanding * * *.

> These concerns are greatly magnified in the deportation context * * *. Postponing justifiable deportation (in the hope that the alien's status will change—by, for example, marriage to an American citizen—or simply with the object of extending the alien's unlawful stay) is often the principal object of resistance to a deportation proceeding, and the additional obstacle of selective-enforcement suits could leave [DHS] hard pressed to enforce routine status requirements. And as for "chill[ing] law enforcement by subjecting the prosecutor's motives and decisionmaking to outside inquiry": What will be involved in deportation cases is not merely the disclosure of normal domestic law enforcement priorities and techniques, but often the disclosure of foreign-policy objectives and (as in this case) foreign-intelligence products and techniques. The Executive should not have to disclose its "real" reasons for deeming

nationals of a particular country a special threat—or indeed for simply wishing to antagonize a particular foreign country by focusing on that country's nationals—and even if it did disclose them a court would be ill equipped to determine their authenticity and utterly unable to assess their adequacy.

Id. at 488–91. On the second theme, the relationship between removal and punishment, he stated:

> Moreover, the consideration on the other side of the ledger in deportation cases—the interest of the target in avoiding "selective" treatment—is less compelling than in criminal prosecutions. While the consequences of deportation may assuredly be grave, they are not imposed as a punishment.

Id. at 489–92.

Justice Ginsburg, concurring, agreed that the First Amendment did not require immediate judicial review of the selective enforcement claim. But she wrote that she was "not persuaded" that the selective enforcement of deportation laws would survive a properly presented First Amendment challenge, citing *Bridges v. Wixon*:

> It is well settled that "[f]reedom of speech and of press is accorded aliens residing in this country." *Bridges v. Wixon,* 326 U.S. 135, 148, 65 S.Ct. 1443, 89 L.Ed. 2103 (1945). Under our selective prosecution doctrine, "the decision to prosecute may not be deliberately based upon an unjustifiable standard such as race, religion, or other arbitrary classification, including the exercise of protected statutory and constitutional rights." *Wayte v. United States,* 470 U.S. 598, 608, 105 S.Ct. 1524, 84 L.Ed.2d 547 (1985) (internal citations and quotation marks omitted). I am not persuaded that selective enforcement of deportation laws should be exempt from that prescription.

525 U.S. at 497–98, 119 S.Ct. at 950 (Ginsburg, J., concurring in part and concurring in the judgment).

On the theme of deportation as a form of punishment, she wrote: "If the Government decides to deport an alien "for reasons forbidden by the Constitution, it does not seem to me that redress for the constitutional violation should turn on the gravity of the governmental sanction. Deportation, in any event, is a grave sanction." *Id.* at 950 (citation and quotations omitted).

In dissent, Justice Souter asserted that "[t]he interest in avoiding selective enforcement of the criminal law . . . is that prosecutorial discretion not be exercised to violate constitutionally prescribed guaranties of equality or liberty. This interest applies to the like degree in immigration litigation, and is not attenuated because the deportation is not a penalty for a criminal act or because the violation is ongoing." *Id.* at 511.

f.   The Significance of Permanent Residence

AADC's third theme is the significance of permanent residence. The majority and the concurrence divide around the distinction between lawful permanent residents and de facto residents—noncitizens with ties created through long-term residence but who are present in violation of immigration law.

The following passage provides a useful framework for considering these questions:

> * * * [F]or much of its history, America treated lawful immigrants as future citizens, and immigration as a transition to citizenship. Lawful immigrants—or as I will outline later, *some* lawful immigrants—could become "intending citizens." For more than a century and a half—from 1795 to 1952—every applicant for naturalization had to file a declaration of intent several years in advance. This declaration gave any noncitizen who was eligible to naturalize a precitizenship status that elevated him, even from his first day in America, well above those who had not filed declarations and therefore were not seen as on the citizenship track. Many statutes throughout this period expressly preferred intending citizens. The Homestead Act of 1862, the key to settling the western frontier, made noncitizens eligible for grants of land once they filed declarations. The U.S. government sometimes extended diplomatic protection to intending citizens who got into trouble overseas. And until the early twentieth century, many intending citizens could vote.

> * * *

> To capture this way of viewing immigration, I have coined the term *immigration as transition*. It treats lawful immigrants as Americans in waiting, as if they would eventually become citizens of the United States, and thus confers on immigrants a *presumed equality*. * * *

> * * *

> * * * [Another view] of immigration is what I call *immigration as contract*. [L]awful immigrants [may] have "promised" to stay out of trouble with the law, on pain of deportation. Or even if they do not commit any crimes, their admission to this country may be just a temporary grant of permission that the government can revoke at any time. Or perhaps [they] promised to support themselves financially. On

the other hand, the U.S. government may have promised not to change the rules governing their vulnerability to deportation, or the rules governing their access to public benefits. These similar ideas appear frequently in the making of law and policy, past and present.

* * *

[B]y contract I mean a certain way of making immigration decisions. The offer that immigrants accept by coming to America may be a take-it-or-leave-it proposition. Their bargaining power is very weak, and there is no real negotiation. And yet, immigration as contract is accurate to describe this view of immigration because it adopts ideas of fairness and justice often associated with contracts. The core idea is thinking about coming to America as a set of expectations and understandings that newcomers have of their new country, and their new country has of newcomers.

Underlying this way of talking about fairness and justice in our treatment of lawful immigrants is a certain way of thinking about equality in immigration and citizenship. Immigration as contract is based on the sense that fairness and justice for lawful immigrants does not require us to treat them as the equals of citizens. Though immigration as contract is a model of justice, it is a model of *unequal justice* that turns not on conferring equality itself, but on giving notice and protecting expectations.

* * *

[A] third view of immigration alongside transition and contract * * * I call *immigration as affiliation*. This is the view that the treatment of lawful immigrants and other noncitizens should depend on the ties that they have formed in this country. Newcomers put down roots. Immigration as affiliation is the foundation for the argument that lawful immigrants * * * should be treated just like citizens, now that they have paid taxes, have children who are U.S. citizens, and have shown themselves to be reliable and productive workers.

As a way of thinking and talking about fairness and justice in immigration, affiliation drives arguments that lawful immigrants—though convicted of crimes that make them deportable—should be allowed to stay in the United States, if they have been here for a long time and have strong family and community ties. The longer they are here, and the more they become enmeshed in the fabric of American life, the more these lawful immigrants and citizens should be treated equally. This view of immigration is not based on the justice without equality of immigration as contract, nor on the presumed equality of immigration as transition, but rather on an *earned equality*.

Hiroshi Motomura, Americans in Waiting: The Lost Story of Immigration and Citizenship in the United States 9–11 (2006). *

It often seems unusually harsh to remove some who has spent most of her life in the United States, even if removal proceedings start promptly after the deportability ground arises. These considerations are even more powerful for children who came to the United States at an early age and have been socialized here. This group—sometimes called the 1.5 generation—is most likely to have deep social and cultural ties in the United States, and unlikely to have many ties to rely on if they are forced to return to their country of origin. In these situations, the "immigration as affiliation" perspective would support the view that these long-term residents, like citizens, should not be banished from their homes.

Justice Ginsburg's concurrence and the Ninth Circuit's opinion in *AADC* reflect this sense that long-term residence, regardless of whether it is authorized, provides a foundation for constitutional protections against deportability. Raising doubts about whether the selective enforcement of deportation laws could withstand a First Amendment challenge, Justice Ginsburg emphasized *Bridges*' statement that " '[f]reedom of speech and of press is accorded aliens residing in this country.' " 525 U.S. at 497–98, 119 S.Ct. at 950 (Ginsburg, J., concurring in part and concurring in the judgment). Her concurrence referred to deportation as "uprooting the alien from home, friends, family, and work," reflecting a view of immigration as affiliation. *AADC*, 525 U.S. at 497–98, 119 S.Ct. at 950 (quoting Gerald Neuman, Strangers to the Constitution: Immigrants, Borders, and Fundamental Law 162 (1996)).

The Ninth Circuit's opinion, vacated by the Supreme Court, quoted Justice Murphy's concurrence in *Bridges*: "[s]ince resident aliens have constitutional rights, it follows that Congress may not ignore them in the exercise of its 'plenary' power of deportation." *Bridges*, 326 U.S. at 161, 65 S.Ct. at 1455 (Murphy, J., concurring). The Ninth Circuit expressed concern that "If aliens do not have First Amendment rights at deportation, then their First Amendment rights in other contexts are a nullity, because the omnipresent threat of deportation would permanently chill their expressive and associational activities." *American-Arab Anti-Discrimination Committee v. Reno*, 70 F.3d 1045, 1065–66 (9th Cir. 1995).

The Ninth Circuit's opinion and Justice Ginsburg's concurrence overlook the fact that six of the noncitizens had overstayed their authorization to be in the United States. Contrast this approach with Justice Scalia's majority opinion, which did not draw distinctions between the two permanent residents and the other noncitizens and emphasizes the overstayers' violation of immigration law.

> To resolve the present controversy, we need not rule out the possibility of a rare case in which the alleged basis of discrimination is so outrageous that the foregoing considerations can be overcome. * * * [However, w]hen an alien's continuing presence in this country is in violation of the immigration laws, the Government does not offend the Constitution by deporting him for the additional reason that it believes him to be a member of an organization that supports terrorist activity.

AADC, 525 U.S. at 491.

One might read the majority opinion in *AADC* as applying a version of "immigration as contract" to argue that permanent residence is granted with the understanding that it remains revocable, and that the law clearly signaled at the time of contracting (admission) that criminal misconduct could jeopardize residence or in any event that no noncitizen in the United States enjoys complete security of residence.

Is the proper distinction one based on lawfulness of residence? Compare Justice Murphy's reasoning in *Bridges v. Wixon*, p. 635, *supra*: "once an alien *lawfully enters and resides* in this country he becomes invested with the rights guaranteed by the Constitution to all people within our borders." (Emphasis supplied.)

Are there reasons that lawful permanent residence is still insufficient? Justice Murphy's concurrence reflects a view of permanent resident status that contrasts sharply with Justice Jackson's emphasis in *Harisiades* that Harisiades, Coleman, and Mascitti lived in the United States for decades without embracing the Constitution, becoming citizens, and renouncing their foreign allegiances. One response to Justice Murphy might be that long-term lawful permanent residents can avoid removal by becoming citizens. This echoes *Harisiades v. Shaughnessy*, p. 637, *supra*, where Justice Jackson emphasized that the three longtime residents had failed to pursue their opportunity to naturalize. This may reflect an "immigration as transition" perspective that would confer on lawful permanent residents a presumed equality with citizens that would not continue if they failed to apply for citizenship once eligible.

For Justice Jackson, any presumed equality would have vanished when the noncitizens had lived in the United States long enough to naturalize and had failed to do so. In contrast, Justice Murphy implied that affiliation was key: that they resided lawfully, paid taxes, raised U.S. citizen children, and were members of the U.S. community.

NOTES AND QUESTIONS ON
DEPORTABILITY AND THE CONSTITUTION

1.   There is an epilogue to the story in *AADC*. Though the Court ruled against the noncitizens on both the jurisdictional and selective prosecution issues, it did not rule on the constitutionality of the terrorism-related deportability ground invoked against the two permanent residents. In 2007, eight years after the Court's ruling and 21 years after the case began, immigration judge Bruce Einhorn dismissed the immigration charges, holding that the government's failure to disclose potentially exculpatory evidence as to the noncitizens' alleged PFLP activities violated the two permanent residents' due process rights. In the meantime, Aiad Barakat, one of the six nonimmigrants when the story started, prevailed on the status violation charge, became a lawful permanent resident, and naturalized in 2006. *See* Henry Weinstein, *20-Year Bid to Deport 2 Is Dismissed*, L.A. Times, Jan. 31, 2007.

2.   To consolidate your understanding of any First Amendment limits on the government's power to define deportability, how would the U.S. Supreme Court decide a First Amendment challenge to removing lawful permanent residents based on membership in a terrorist organization? In answering this question, consider the following paragraph from *Holder v. Humanitarian Law Project*, 561 U.S. 1, 130 S.Ct. 2705, 177 L.Ed. 2d 355 (2010).

> Our precedents, old and new, make clear that concerns of national security and foreign relations do not warrant abdication of the judicial role. We do not defer to the Government's reading of the First Amendment, even when such interests are at stake. We are one with the dissent that the Government's "authority and expertise in these matters do not automatically trump the Court's own obligation to secure the protection that the Constitution grants to individuals." But when it comes to collecting evidence and drawing factual inferences in this area, "the lack of competence on the part of the courts is marked," *Rostker [v. Goldberg,* 453 U.S. 57, 65, 101 S.Ct. 2646, 69 L.Ed. 2d (1981)], and respect for the Government's conclusions is appropriate.

130 S.Ct. at 2727.

Does it make a difference that the Court in *Humanitarian Law Project* focused on the constitutionality of potential criminal penalties under 18 U.S.C. § 2339B for providing material support to organizations formally designated as foreign terrorist organizations under INA § 219 (so-called Tier I organizations), rather than on the immigration consequences? The suit was filed by U.S. persons who wished to donate to two Tier I organizations in a way, they argued, that would aid only the nonviolent humanitarian and political activities of the organization.

3. Should lawfully present nonimmigrants have the same First Amendment protections against removal based on deportability as lawful permanent residents? Or is it the length of residence that matters more than lawful presence? What about long-term residents who are unlawfully present? Does Justice Murphy's dictum apply to the six nonimmigrants involved in *AADC*, who were admitted as B, F, and H–1 nonimmigrants and so were not lawful permanent residents of the United States? If the dictum did apply initially, would it continue to apply once they overstayed their admission periods?

4. In your view, what is the difference between being a lawful permanent resident and being a U.S. citizen? What is the difference between being an LPR and another type of noncitizen in the United States—for example, a lawfully present nonimmigrant, or a long-term resident who lacks lawful immigration status? For reflections on these issues from a different analytical perspective, see David A. Martin, *Graduated Application of Constitutional Protections for Aliens: the Real Meaning of* Zadvydas v. Davis, 2001 Supreme Court Review 47 (2002).

5. Justice Murphy also wrote that if the First Amendment prohibits the government from imprisoning a noncitizen for protected speech, it also must prohibit the government from deporting the noncitizen. Do you agree? Would recognizing that immigration decisions are intimately tied to national self-definition suggest that the nation may deport noncitizens on political grounds, even if it is unable to control the conduct of citizens? Is it persuasive to distinguish imprisonment from deportation because the latter is simply the withdrawal of a privilege to remain in the United States? What about a deportability ground for noncitizens who advocate changing the United States into a theocracy? What about a deportability ground for noncitizens who advocate, but do not imminently incite, suicide bombing to achieve that goal?

6. Another related deportability ground is potentially very broad, though it has been invoked quite sparingly. Section 237(a)(4)(C) makes removable noncitizens whom the Secretary of State has reasonable grounds to believe would, by their presence or activities, have potentially serious adverse foreign policy consequences for the United States. This ground is parallel to the inadmissibility ground discussed in Section A of this chapter, and is subject to the same limits and exceptions.

7. The number of cases filed in immigration court in which the government relies on terrorism-related deportability is very small. Only 12 such cases were filed in fiscal years 2004–2006, and 114 cases relied on national security deportability grounds, out of a total 814,073 cases in that period. Transactional Records Access Clearinghouse (TRAC), *Immigration Enforcement: The Rhetoric, The Reality*, May 28, 2007, trac.syr.edu/immigration/reports/178/. (TRAC reports deportability under § 237(a)(4)(A)

as national security-related and under § 237(a)(4)(B) as terrorism-related.) But does tallying the deportability grounds actually charged accurately measure the impact of DHS enforcement that is undertaken to diminish the risk of terrorist activity? If you were an ICE investigator and had substantial evidence of a noncitizen's terrorist involvement, when would you seek removal on a terrorism charge? Would it matter that the individual was admitted as a nonimmigrant? Entered without inspection? Think about the evidence you are likely to have and what you would present in immigration court.

8.   Now consider other constitutional protections, such as equal protection. Could Congress order the removal of all noncitizen males of Arab descent? All Jewish noncitizens? All noncitizens from North Korea? Recall the *Chinese Exclusion Case*, p. 156, *supra*, *Fiallo v. Bell*, p. 296, *supra*, and this from Justice Frankfurter's *Harisiades* concurrence: "the underlying policies of what classes of aliens shall be allowed to enter and what classes of aliens shall be allowed to stay, are for Congress exclusively to determine even though such determination may be deemed to offend American traditions and may, as has been the case, jeopardize peace."

EXERCISE: RETHINKING DEPORTABILITY

Before we examine the crime-related grounds of deportability, consider all of the deportability grounds in § 237(a) that are not crime-related.

Which of these grounds would you keep? Which would you delete? What grounds would you add? Would you add a ground for violations of civil rights laws?

Would you reword deportability grounds to differ more from any analogous inadmissibility grounds? Would you distinguish more sharply between lawful permanent residents and other noncitizens? Should it matter that a permanent resident has not naturalized after a certain number of years?

Would you deport a noncitizen for conduct (or a trait) which is not unlawful for a U.S. citizen—e.g., drug addiction or poverty? What principles and values guide your choices?

---

4. CRIMES

In fiscal year 2013, approximately 45% percent of all removals based on formal removal orders were of noncitizens with criminal convictions (198,394 removals versus 438,421 total removals). DHS reports as a criminal removal any noncitizen with a criminal conviction, even if a crime-based deportability grounds was not the formal legal basis for removal. The following table shows the recent trend:

Figure 7.2

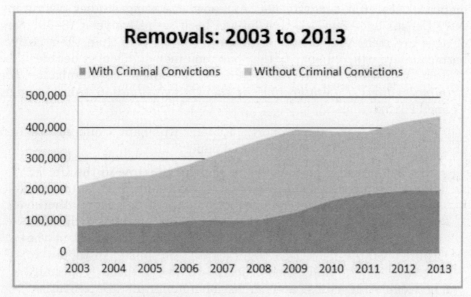

Source: DHS, 2013 Yearbook of Immigration Statistics 107–15, table 41.

The 198,394 removals in 2013 of noncitizens with criminal convictions include removals based on both inadmissibility and deportability grounds. Of this total, about 62,000 had convictions for immigration-related crimes (including entry, reentry, false claims to citizenship, and alien smuggling). DHS Office of Immigration Statistics, Immigration Enforcement Actions: 2013, at 7, tbl. 9 (2014).

Keep in mind as you read the cases in this Section that most of the doctrine relating to the crime-based deportability grounds is developed in, and has primary relevance for, cases involving lawful permanent residents. The government only infrequently relies on a criminal ground of deportability for noncitizens who have deportable convictions but are not lawful permanent residents. Citing the conviction to prove deportability would be an unnecessary complication for DHS. If the noncitizen is an entrant without inspection or an overstay and also involved in crime, DHS typically charges the more accessible immigration control ground, which usually can be readily proven based solely on DHS records. Even if the noncitizen committed the crime while in lawful nonimmigrant status, that status will often have expired or been violated by the end of the criminal proceedings. Though the conviction is relevant to DHS's charging priorities and to eligibility for possible relief (treated in Section C), it need not be made the basis of the deportability charge.

Part of the impetus in the 1990s to adopt stricter rules for deportation of noncitizens convicted of crimes drew on a public perception that there was greater criminality among the foreign-born. But are

lower incarceration rates

immigrants more likely than citizens to commit crimes? Current empirical research suggests not. A report collecting studies examining 2010 Census data revealed that foreign-born males between 18–39 years of ages are incarcerated at a significantly lower rate than their native-born counterparts, a disparity that has remained stable over decades. *See* Walter A. Ewing, Daniel E. Martinez & Rubén G. Rumbaut, *The Criminalization of Immigration in the United States* 6 (Am. Immigr. Council 2015).

An author of the report, Rubén Rumbaut, offered related observations in a separate co-authored paper:

> [I]nstead of being responsible for increasing crime in the United States, immigrants may be a factor in reducing it. Since the early 1990s, when the immigrant population (and especially the undocumented population) was increasing sharply to historic highs, the overall rates of property and violent crimes in the United States decreased significantly, in many instances to historic lows, and those decreases have been especially noticeable in cities and areas of immigrant concentration. Additionally, survey data from the Los Angeles metropolitan area showed lower rates of arrest and incarceration among the foreign born (including the groups with the highest proportion of undocumented immigrants) than among native born young men. The problem of crime in the United States is not caused by immigration, and never has been. That is largely a bogus claim, albeit a persistent one—an enduring stereotype.

M. Kathleen Dingeman & Rubén G. Rumbaut, *The Immigration-Crime Nexus and Post-Deportation Experiences: En/Countering Stereotypes in Southern California and El Salvador*, 31 U. La Verne L. Rev. 363, 400 (2010); see also Marjorie S. Zatz & Hilary Smith, *Immigration, Crime, and Victimization: Rhetoric and Reality*, 8 Ann. Rev. L. Soc. Sci. 141, 151–52 (2012) (noting that immigrants are far more likely to be incarcerated in Europe than in the United States and exploring explanations, including the criminalization of immigration in both areas and the overt racialization of immigrants in Europe).

In light of the facts that Dingeman and Rumbaut describe, the increasing number of criminal removals over the past decade reflects not increased crime by immigrants, but rather greater government resources and better technical means devoted to identifying those noncitizens (most of them already lacking a legal status) who commit crimes. Similarly, the 2010 census data showed a recent rise in incarceration rates for immigrant men, which the authors of the 2015 report attributed to changes in immigration enforcement as well as increased incarceration of immigrant men "as Congress redefined more and more immigration offenses as criminal (such as unauthorized entry or re-entry into the country), thus triggering criminal incarceration before deportation." Ewing *et al, supra,* at 6.

a. The Criminal Justice System and Immigration Law *Crimigration*

Juliet Stumpf offers an observation that helps to frame the issues:

> While criminal law is animated by the idea that the punishment must be proportionate to the crime, proportionality is scarce in immigration law. Criminal law embodies proportionality in punishment schemes that impose milder sanctions such as short or suspended sentences for lesser crimes, and harsher sanctions for graver crimes. In contrast, the statutory sanction for every immigration violation is removal from the country.

The distinction in treatment between crim laws and immig violation

Juliet Stumpf, *Fitting Punishment*, 66 Wash. & Lee L. Rev. 1683, 1687–88 (2009). Are you troubled by the largely binary nature of immigration punishment? What would a better, more proportional approach look like? How would it apply, if at all, to non-LPRs who have a criminal conviction and are then placed in removal proceedings, since their removability normally is not dependent on the criminal conduct? *Cf.* Gabriel J. Chin, *Illegal Entry as Crime, Deportation as Punishment: Immigration Status and the Criminal Process*, 58 UCLA L. Rev. 1417 (2011) (proposing that immigration status play a more substantial role in the criminal prosecution and sentencing of noncitizens for nonimmigration crimes).

What interests are served by removing noncitizens who have completed judge-imposed criminal sentences? Should lawful permanent residents receive the same treatment as citizens, who cannot be banished? Or should permanent residents be subject to removal as an added penalty for crimes? Should it matter how long they have lived in the United States? What about comparable protections for long-term unauthorized residents? Or for those who arrived in the United States as small children and have never lived elsewhere?

In 2010, the U.S. Supreme Court issued *Padilla v. Kentucky*, a decision with implications for the characterization of deportation as a matter of constitutional law, and for the relationship between criminal and immigration law, especially the immigration consequences of convictions. It also has prompted lawyers in the criminal justice system to seek more immigration law training and assure consideration of immigration consequences in plea bargaining. *Padilla* shows how immigration law and criminal law are closely intertwined when the defendant in a criminal case is not a U.S. citizen, at least when the defendant is a lawful permanent resident.

PADILLA V. KENTUCKY

Supreme Court of the United States, 2010.
559 U.S. 356, 130 S.Ct. 1473, 176 L.Ed.2d 284.

JUSTICE STEVENS delivered the opinion of the Court.

Petitioner Jose Padilla, a native of Honduras, has been a lawful permanent resident of the United States for more than 40 years. Padilla served this Nation with honor as a member of the U.S. Armed Forces during the Vietnam War. He now faces deportation after pleading guilty to the transportation of a large amount of marijuana in his tractor-trailer in the Commonwealth of Kentucky.[1]

In this postconviction proceeding, Padilla claims that his counsel not only failed to advise him of this consequence prior to his entering the plea, but also told him that he " 'did not have to worry about immigration status since he had been in the country so long.' " Padilla relied on his counsel's erroneous advice when he pleaded guilty to the drug charges that made his deportation virtually mandatory. He alleges that he would have insisted on going to trial if he had not received incorrect advice from his attorney.

* * *

While the [Immigration and Nationality Act of 1917] was "radical" because it authorized deportation as a consequence of certain convictions, the Act also included a critically important procedural protection to minimize the risk of unjust deportation: At the time of sentencing or within 30 days thereafter, the sentencing judge in both state and federal prosecutions had the power to make a recommendation "that such alien shall not be deported." [39 Stat.] at 890. This procedure, known as a judicial recommendation against deportation, or JRAD, had the effect of binding the Executive to prevent deportation; the statute was "consistently ... interpreted as giving the sentencing judge conclusive authority to decide whether a particular conviction should be disregarded as a basis for deportation," *Janvier v. United States,* 793 F.2d 449, 452 (C.A.2 1986). Thus, from 1917 forward, there was no such creature as an automatically deportable offense. Even as the class of deportable offenses expanded, judges retained discretion to ameliorate unjust results on a case-by-case basis.

* * *

However, the JRAD procedure is no longer part of our law. Congress first circumscribed the JRAD provision in the 1952 Immigration and Nationality Act (INA); and in 1990 Congress entirely eliminated it. In 1996, Congress also eliminated the Attorney General's authority to grant

---

[1] Padilla's crime, like virtually every drug offense except for only the most insignificant marijuana offenses, is a deportable offense under INA § 237(a)(2)(B)(i).

discretionary relief from deportation, an authority that had been exercised to prevent the deportation of over 10,000 noncitizens during the 5-year period prior to 1996. Under contemporary law, if a noncitizen has committed a removable offense after the 1996 effective date of these amendments, his removal is practically inevitable but for the possible exercise of limited remnants of equitable discretion vested in the Attorney General to cancel removal for noncitizens convicted of particular classes of offenses. Subject to limited exceptions, this discretionary relief is not available for an offense related to trafficking in a controlled substance.

These changes to our immigration law have dramatically raised the stakes of a noncitizen's criminal conviction. The importance of accurate legal advice for noncitizens accused of crimes has never been more important. These changes confirm our view that, as a matter of federal law, deportation is an integral part—indeed, sometimes the most important part—of the penalty that may be imposed on noncitizen defendants who plead guilty to specified crimes.

Before deciding whether to plead guilty, a defendant is entitled to "the effective assistance of competent counsel." *McMann v. Richardson,* 397 U.S. 759, 771, 90 S.Ct. 1441, 25 L.Ed.2d 763 (1970); *Strickland [v. Washington,* 466 U.S. 668, 686, 104 S.Ct. 2052, 80 L.Ed.2d 674 (1984)]. The Supreme Court of Kentucky rejected Padilla's ineffectiveness claim on the ground that the advice he sought about the risk of deportation concerned only collateral matters, *i.e.,* those matters not within the sentencing authority of the state trial court. In its view, "collateral consequences are outside the scope of representation required by the Sixth Amendment," and, therefore, the "failure of defense counsel to advise the defendant of possible deportation consequences is not cognizable as a claim for ineffective assistance of counsel." 253 S.W.3d, at 483. The Kentucky high court is far from alone in this view.

We, however, have never applied a distinction between direct and collateral consequences to define the scope of constitutionally "reasonable professional assistance" required under *Strickland,* 466 U.S., at 689, 104 S.Ct. 2052. Whether that distinction is appropriate is a question we need not consider in this case because of the unique nature of deportation.

We have long recognized that deportation is a particularly severe "penalty," *Fong Yue Ting v. United States,* 149 U.S. 698, 740, 13 S.Ct. 1016, 37 L.Ed. 905 (1893); but it is not, in a strict sense, a criminal sanction. Although removal proceedings are civil in nature, deportation is nevertheless intimately related to the criminal process. Our law has enmeshed criminal convictions and the penalty of deportation for nearly a century. And, importantly, recent changes in our immigration law have made removal nearly an automatic result for a broad class of noncitizen offenders. Thus, we find it "most difficult" to divorce the penalty from the conviction in the deportation context. *United States v. Russell,* 686 F.2d 35, 38 (C.A.D.C.1982). Moreover, we are quite confident that noncitizen defendants facing a risk of deportation for a particular offense find it even more difficult.

Deportation as a consequence of a criminal conviction is, because of its close connection to the criminal process, uniquely difficult to classify as either a direct or a collateral consequence. The collateral versus direct distinction is thus ill-suited to evaluating a *Strickland* claim concerning the specific risk of deportation. We conclude that advice regarding deportation is not categorically removed from the ambit of the Sixth Amendment right to counsel. *Strickland* applies to Padilla's claim.

III

Under *Strickland,* we first determine whether counsel's representation "fell below an objective standard of reasonableness." 466 U.S., at 688, 104 S.Ct. 2052. Then we ask whether "there is a reasonable probability that, but for counsel's unprofessional errors, the result of the proceeding would have been different." *Id.,* at 694, 104 S.Ct. 2052. The first prong—constitutional deficiency—is necessarily linked to the practice and expectations of the legal community * * * .

The weight of prevailing professional norms supports the view that counsel must advise her client regarding the risk of deportation. * * *

We too have previously recognized that " '[p]reserving the client's right to remain in the United States may be more important to the client than any potential jail sentence.' " *St. Cyr,* 533 U.S., at 323, 121 S.Ct. 2271 (quoting 3 Criminal Defense Techniques §§ 60A.01, 60A.02[2] (1999)). * * *

In the instant case, the terms of the relevant immigration statute are succinct, clear, and explicit in defining the removal consequence for Padilla's conviction. See INA § 237(a)(2)(B)(i). Padilla's counsel could have easily determined that his plea would make him eligible for deportation simply from reading the text of the statute, which addresses not some broad classification of crimes but specifically commands removal for all controlled substances convictions except for the most trivial of marijuana possession offenses. Instead, Padilla's counsel provided him false assurance that his conviction would not result in his removal from this country. This is not a hard case in which to find deficiency: The consequences of Padilla's plea could easily be determined from reading the removal statute, his deportation was presumptively mandatory, and his counsel's advice was incorrect.

Immigration law can be complex, and it is a legal specialty of its own. Some members of the bar who represent clients facing criminal charges, in either state or federal court or both, may not be well versed in it. There will, therefore, undoubtedly be numerous situations in which the deportation consequences of a particular plea are unclear or uncertain. The duty of the private practitioner in such cases is more limited. When the law is not succinct and straightforward (as it is in many of the scenarios posited by Justice Alito), a criminal defense attorney need do no more than advise a noncitizen client that pending criminal charges may carry a risk of adverse immigration consequences. But when the deportation consequence is truly clear, as it was in this case, the duty to give correct advice is equally clear.

* * *

The Solicitor General has urged us to conclude that *Strickland* applies to Padilla's claim only to the extent that he has alleged affirmative misadvice. In the United States' view, "counsel is not constitutionally required to provide advice on matters that will not be decided in the criminal case . . . ," though counsel is required to provide accurate advice if she chooses to discusses these matters.

US argues

* * *

A holding limited to affirmative misadvice would invite two absurd results. First, it would give counsel an incentive to remain silent on matters of great importance, even when answers are readily available. Silence under these circumstances would be fundamentally at odds with the critical obligation of counsel to advise the client of "the advantages and disadvantages of a plea agreement." *Libretti v. United States,* 516 U.S. 29, 50–51, 116 S.Ct. 356, 133 L.Ed.2d 271 (1995). When attorneys know that their clients face possible exile from this country and separation from their families, they should not be encouraged to say nothing at all. Second, it would deny a class of clients least able to represent themselves the most rudimentary advice on deportation even when it is readily available. It is quintessentially the duty of counsel to provide her client with available advice about an issue like deportation and the failure to do so "clearly satisfies the first prong of the *Strickland* analysis." *Hill v. Lockhart,* 474 U.S. 52, 62, 106 S.Ct. 366, 88 L.Ed.2d 203 (1985) (White, J., concurring in judgment).

* * *

no retroactive impact.

It seems unlikely that our decision today will have a significant effect on those convictions already obtained as the result of plea bargains. For at least the past 15 years, professional norms have generally imposed an obligation on counsel to provide advice on the deportation consequences of a client's plea. We should, therefore, presume that counsel satisfied their obligation to render competent advice at the time their clients considered pleading guilty.

Likewise, although we must be especially careful about recognizing new grounds for attacking the validity of guilty pleas, in the 25 years since we first applied *Strickland* to claims of ineffective assistance at the plea stage, practice has shown that pleas are less frequently the subject of collateral challenges than convictions obtained after a trial. Pleas account for nearly 95% of all criminal convictions. But they account for only approximately 30% of the habeas petitions filed. The nature of relief secured by a successful collateral challenge to a guilty plea—an opportunity to withdraw the plea and proceed to trial—imposes its own significant limiting principle: Those who collaterally attack their guilty pleas lose the benefit of the bargain obtained as a result of the plea. Thus, a different calculus informs whether it is wise to challenge a guilty plea in a habeas proceeding because, ultimately, the challenge may result in a *less favorable* outcome for the defendant, whereas a collateral challenge to a conviction obtained after a jury trial has no similar downside potential.

Finally, informed consideration of possible deportation can only benefit both the State and noncitizen defendants during the plea-bargaining process. By bringing deportation consequences into this process, the defense and prosecution may well be able to reach agreements that better satisfy the interests of both parties. As in this case, a criminal episode may provide the basis for multiple charges, of which only a subset mandate deportation following conviction. Counsel who possess the most rudimentary understanding of the deportation consequences of a particular criminal offense may be able to plea bargain creatively with the prosecutor in order to craft a conviction and sentence that reduce the likelihood of deportation, as by avoiding a conviction for an offense that automatically triggers the removal consequence. At the same time, the threat of deportation may provide the defendant with a powerful incentive to plead guilty to an offense that does not mandate that penalty in exchange for a dismissal of a charge that does.

In sum, we have long recognized that the negotiation of a plea bargain is a critical phase of litigation for purposes of the Sixth Amendment right to effective assistance of counsel. The severity of deportation—"the equivalent of banishment or exile," *Delgadillo v. Carmichael*, 332 U.S. 388, 390–391, 68 S.Ct. 10, 92 L.Ed. 17 (1947)—only underscores how critical it is for counsel to inform her noncitizen client that he faces a risk of deportation.[15]

It is our responsibility under the Constitution to ensure that no criminal defendant—whether a citizen or not—is left to the "mercies of incompetent counsel." *Richardson*, 397 U.S., at 771, 90 S.Ct. 1441. To

---

[15] To this end, we find it significant that the plea form currently used in Kentucky courts provides notice of possible immigration consequences. Further, many States require trial courts to advise defendants of possible immigration consequences. [The Court cited 22 such state statutes.]

satisfy this responsibility, we now hold that counsel must inform her client whether his plea carries a risk of deportation. Our longstanding Sixth Amendment precedents, the seriousness of deportation as a consequence of a criminal plea, and the concomitant impact of deportation on families living lawfully in this country demand no less.

Taking as true the basis for his motion for postconviction relief, we have little difficulty concluding that Padilla has sufficiently alleged that his counsel was constitutionally deficient. Whether Padilla is entitled to relief will depend on whether he can demonstrate prejudice as a result thereof, a question we do not reach because it was not passed on below.

* * *

JUSTICE ALITO, with whom THE CHIEF JUSTICE joins, concurring in the judgment.

I concur in the judgment because a criminal defense attorney fails to provide effective assistance within the meaning of *Strickland v. Washington,* 466 U.S. 668, 104 S.Ct. 2052, 80 L.Ed.2d 674 (1984), if the attorney misleads a noncitizen client regarding the removal consequences of a conviction. In my view, such an attorney must (1) refrain from unreasonably providing incorrect advice and (2) advise the defendant that a criminal conviction may have adverse immigration consequences and that, if the alien wants advice on this issue, the alien should consult an immigration attorney. I do not agree with the Court that the attorney must attempt to explain what those consequences may be. * * *

I

* * *

The Court tries to downplay the severity of the burden it imposes on defense counsel by suggesting that the scope of counsel's duty to offer advice concerning deportation consequences may turn on how hard it is to determine those consequences. Where "the terms of the relevant immigration statute are succinct, clear, and explicit in defining the removal consequence[s]" of a conviction, the Court says, counsel has an affirmative duty to advise the client that he will be subject to deportation as a result of the plea. But "[w]hen the law is not succinct and straightforward . . ., a criminal defense attorney need do no more than advise a noncitizen client that pending criminal charges may carry a risk of adverse immigration consequences." This approach is problematic * * *.

First, it will not always be easy to tell whether a particular statutory provision is "succinct, clear, and explicit." How can an attorney who lacks general immigration law expertise be sure that a seemingly clear statutory provision actually means what it seems to say when read in isolation? What if the application of the provision to a particular case is not clear but a cursory examination of case law or administrative decisions would provide a definitive answer?

Second, if defense counsel must provide advice regarding only one of the many collateral consequences of a criminal conviction, many defendants are likely to be misled. To take just one example, a conviction for a particular offense may render an alien excludable but not removable. If an alien charged with such an offense is advised only that pleading guilty to such an offense will not result in removal, the alien may be induced to enter a guilty plea without realizing that a consequence of the plea is that the alien will be unable to reenter the United States if the alien returns to his or her home country for any reason, such as to visit an elderly parent or to attend a funeral. Incomplete legal advice may be worse than no advice at all because it may mislead and may dissuade the client from seeking advice from a more knowledgeable source.

Third, the Court's rigid constitutional rule could inadvertently head off more promising ways of addressing the underlying problem—such as statutory or administrative reforms requiring trial judges to inform a defendant on the record that a guilty plea may carry adverse immigration consequences. As *amici* point out, "28 states and the District of Columbia have *already* adopted rules, plea forms, or statutes requiring courts to advise criminal defendants of the possible immigration consequences of their pleas." Brief for State of Louisiana et al. 25. A nonconstitutional rule requiring trial judges to inform defendants on the record of the risk of adverse immigration consequences can ensure that a defendant receives needed information without putting a large number of criminal convictions at risk; and because such a warning would be given on the record, courts would not later have to determine whether the defendant was misrepresenting the advice of counsel. Likewise, flexible statutory procedures for withdrawing guilty pleas might give courts appropriate discretion to determine whether the interests of justice would be served by allowing a particular defendant to withdraw a plea entered into on the basis of incomplete information.

* * *

* * * [S]everal considerations support the conclusion that affirmative misadvice regarding the removal consequences of a conviction may constitute ineffective assistance.

First, a rule prohibiting affirmative misadvice regarding a matter as crucial to the defendant's plea decision as deportation appears faithful to the scope and nature of the Sixth Amendment duty this Court has recognized in its past cases. * * * [T]horough understanding of the intricacies of immigration law is not "within the range of competence demanded of attorneys *in criminal cases*." By contrast, reasonably competent attorneys should know that it is not appropriate or responsible to hold themselves out as authorities on a difficult and complicated subject matter with which they are not familiar. * * *

Second, incompetent advice distorts the defendant's decisionmaking process and seems to call the fairness and integrity of the criminal proceeding itself into question. When a defendant opts to plead guilty without definitive information concerning the likely effects of the plea, the defendant can fairly be said to assume the risk that the conviction may carry indirect consequences of which he or she is not aware. That is not the case when a defendant bases the decision to plead guilty on counsel's express misrepresentation that the defendant will not be removable. * * *

Third, a rule prohibiting unreasonable misadvice regarding exceptionally important collateral matters would not deter or interfere with ongoing political and administrative efforts to devise fair and reasonable solutions to the difficult problem posed by defendants who plead guilty without knowing of certain important collateral consequences.

Finally, the conclusion that affirmative misadvice regarding the removal consequences of a conviction can give rise to ineffective assistance would, unlike the Court's approach, not require any upheaval in the law. As the Solicitor General points out, "[t]he vast majority of the lower courts considering claims of ineffective assistance in the plea context have [distinguished] between defense counsel who remain silent and defense counsel who give affirmative misadvice." * * *

In concluding that affirmative misadvice regarding the removal consequences of a criminal conviction may constitute ineffective assistance, I do not mean to suggest that the Sixth Amendment does no more than require defense counsel to avoid misinformation. When a criminal defense attorney is aware that a client is an alien, the attorney should advise the client that a criminal conviction may have adverse consequences under the immigration laws and that the client should consult an immigration specialist if the client wants advice on that subject. By putting the client on notice of the danger of removal, such advice would significantly reduce the chance that the client would plead guilty under a mistaken premise.

* * *

JUSTICE SCALIA, with whom JUSTICE THOMAS joins, dissenting.

In the best of all possible worlds, criminal defendants contemplating a guilty plea ought to be advised of all serious collateral consequences of conviction, and surely ought not to be misadvised. The Constitution, however, is not an all-purpose tool for judicial construction of a perfect world; and when we ignore its text in order to make it that, we often find ourselves swinging a sledge where a tack hammer is needed.

The Sixth Amendment guarantees the accused a lawyer "for his defense" against a "criminal prosecutio[n]"—not for sound advice about the collateral consequences of conviction. For that reason, and for the practical reasons set forth in Part I of Justice Alito's concurrence, I dissent from the Court's conclusion that the Sixth Amendment requires counsel to provide accurate advice concerning the potential removal consequences of a guilty plea. For the same reasons, but unlike the concurrence, I do not believe that affirmative misadvice about those consequences renders an attorney's assistance in defending against the prosecution constitutionally inadequate; or that the Sixth Amendment requires counsel to warn immigrant defendants that a conviction may render them removable. * * *

* * *

The Sixth Amendment as originally understood and ratified meant only that a defendant had a right to employ counsel, or to use volunteered services of counsel. We have held, however, that the Sixth Amendment requires the provision of counsel to indigent defendants at government expense, *Gideon v. Wainwright,* 372 U.S. 335, 344–345, 83 S.Ct. 792, 9 L.Ed.2d 799 (1963), and that the right to "the assistance of counsel" includes the right to *effective* assistance, *Strickland v. Washington,* 466 U.S. 668, 686, 104 S.Ct. 2052, 80 L.Ed.2d 674 (1984). Even assuming the validity of these holdings, I reject the significant further extension that the Court, and to a lesser extent the concurrence, would create. * * *

There is no basis in text or in principle to extend the constitutionally required advice regarding guilty pleas beyond those matters germane to the criminal prosecution at hand—to wit, the sentence that the plea will produce, the higher sentence that conviction after trial might entail, and the chances of such a conviction. * * * Because the subject of the misadvice here was not the prosecution for which Jose Padilla was entitled to effective assistance of counsel, the Sixth Amendment has no application.

* * *

The Court's holding prevents legislation that could solve the problems addressed by today's opinions in a more precise and targeted fashion. If the subject had not been constitutionalized, legislation could specify which categories of misadvice about matters ancillary to the prosecution invalidate plea agreements, what collateral consequences counsel must bring to a defendant's attention, and what warnings must be given. Moreover, legislation could provide consequences for the misadvice, nonadvice, or failure to warn, other than nullification of a criminal conviction after the witnesses and evidence needed for retrial have disappeared. Federal immigration law might provide, for example, that the near-automatic removal which follows from certain criminal convictions will not apply where the conviction rested upon a guilty plea induced by counsel's misadvice regarding removal consequences. Or legislation might put the government to a choice in such circumstances: Either retry the defendant or forgo the removal. But all that has been precluded in favor of today's sledge hammer.

* * *

NOTES AND QUESTIONS ON PADILLA

1. Consider the immediate implications of *Padilla*. How should an immigration lawyer advise a defense attorney or prosecutor about the immigration consequences of various possible plea agreements? How will defense counsel or a court know when, as Justice Stevens puts it for the majority, "deportation consequence is truly clear"? If the deportation consequence is not clear, what is defense counsel's duty?

2. Failure to advise amounting to ineffective assistance of counsel is not enough to establish relief after *Padilla*. The defendant must also show actual prejudice. Can a judicial warning about the potential for removal cure the failure of defense counsel to advise about immigration consequences? As both the *Padilla* majority and Justice Alito's concurrence point out, a number of states already had statutes requiring a trial judge, before accepting a plea of guilty (or nolo contendere in most states), to inform defendants that if they are not United States citizens a criminal conviction may lead to their removal from the United States.

What is the relationship between advisals under such state statutes and the duties recognized by the U.S. Supreme Court in *Padilla*? If a trial judge gives such an advisal to a defendant, how if at all, are the defense attorney's obligations under *Padilla* affected? To what extent can a defense attorney fulfill her obligations under *Padilla* by reading such an advisal to her client? Do the answers to these questions depend on whether it is truly clear, not just possible, that the consequence of conviction is deportability?

3. Jenny Roberts argues that the traditional inquiry into prejudice— whether the defendant would have rejected the plea and proceeded to trial— is too narrow in the *Padilla* context because it fails to account for how ineffective assistance of counsel affects plea negotiations. She urges courts to broaden the traditional understanding of ineffective counsel and recognize that, for example, failure to negotiate an attainable plea can deprive noncitizen defendants of other options:

> First, counsel might re-negotiate, leading to a likely second plea structured to avoid imposition of the consequence (even if it means a higher penal sentence). Second, counsel might secure a sentence that is significantly discounted to account for the harshness of the

collateral consequence. Third, a defendant might make a different risk calculation in deciding whether to plead guilty or go to trial.

Jenny Roberts, *Proving Prejudice, Post*-Padilla, 54 How. L.J. 693, 698 (2011). *See Commonwealth v. Lavrinenko*, 38 N.E.3d 278, 294–95 (Mass. 2015) (holding that refugee status is entitled to particularly substantial weight in determining whether ineffective counsel prejudiced the defendant).

4. How does *Padilla* modify the traditional rule (or its practical consequences) that deportation or removal is not "punishment" for constitutional purposes? Even as *Padilla* proves to be a very important decision, should its impact be confined to the precise questions presented by the case?

5. The Supreme Court ruled in *Chaidez v. United States*, 133 S.Ct. 1103, 185 L.Ed.2d 149 (2013), that *Padilla* would not be applied retroactively to cases already final on direct review when *Padilla* was decided on March 31, 2010. The defendant in *Chaidez*, a lawful permanent resident since 1977, had pleaded guilty to two counts of federal mail fraud committed about twenty years after she moved to the United States. She was sentenced to four years of probation and ordered to pay restitution. The Court first addressed retroactivity generally:

> *Teague* [*v. Lane,* 489 U.S. 288, 109 S.Ct. 1060, 103 L.Ed.2d 334 (1989)], makes the retroactivity of our criminal procedure decisions turn on whether they are novel. When we announce a "new rule," a person whose conviction is already final may not benefit from the decision in a habeas or similar proceeding. Only when we apply a settled rule may a person avail herself of the decision on collateral review. Here, Chaidez filed her *coram nobis* petition five years after her guilty plea became final. Her challenge therefore fails if *Padilla* declared a new rule.

The Court then applied this framework to *Padilla*:

> So when we decided *Padilla*, we answered a question about the Sixth Amendment's reach that we had left open, in a way that altered the law of most jurisdictions—and our reasoning reflected that we were doing as much. * * * Deportation, we stated, is "unique." It is a "particularly severe" penalty, and one "intimately related to the criminal process"; indeed, immigration statutes make it "nearly an automatic result" of some convictions. We thus resolved the threshold question before us by breaching the previously chink-free wall between direct and collateral consequences: Notwithstanding the then-dominant view, "*Strickland* applies to Padilla's claim."
>
> If that does not count as "break[ing] new ground" or "impos[ing] a new obligation," we are hard pressed to know what would * * * *Padilla*'s holding that the failure to advise about a non-criminal consequence could violate the Sixth Amendment would not have

been—in fact, was not—"apparent to all reasonable jurists" prior to our decision. *Padilla* thus announced a "new rule."

After *Chaidez*, the question remains whether state courts might apply *Padilla* retroactively as a matter of state procedural law. In *Commonwealth v. Sylvain*, 466 Mass. 422 (2013), the Massachusetts Supreme Judicial Court concluded that *Padilla* does operate retroactively in that state. The Court noted that "long before *Padilla* was decided, it was customary for practitioners in Massachusetts to warn their clients of the possible deportation consequences of pleading guilty." As a result of that Massachusetts practice, *Padilla* did not announce a "new" rule, and the defendant, whose conviction was final at the time *Padilla* was decided, could raise the ineffective assistance argument recognized in *Padilla*. The states have split, with some joining *Sylvain* to hold that *Padilla* operates retroactively, *e.g., Ramirez v. State*, 333 P.3d 240 (N.M. 2014), and others concluding that it does not, *e.g., Thiersaint v. Commissioner*, 111 A.3d 829 (Conn. 2015) (joining three other states).

b. The Basics of Crime-Related Deportability

Padilla underscores what is at stake and shows that accurate assessment of the immigration consequences of criminal convictions is essential over a long period of time—from plea negotiations in the criminal case all the way through determinations about deportability in a later removal proceeding in immigration court as well as post-conviction relief in the criminal justice system. With issues so framed, we now consider the immigration consequences of criminal convictions.

The major categories of crime-based deportability grounds in INA § 237(a)(2) are: crimes involving moral turpitude, aggravated felonies, drug crimes, firearms offenses, crimes of domestic violence, and several miscellaneous offenses. These categories often overlap in that a particular conviction may trigger multiple grounds. Moreover, the same conviction can be the basis of both deportability and inadmissibility. After the following overview of the most common grounds, several problems will allow you to check your understanding of the statutory basics.

(i) Crimes Involving Moral Turpitude

For most of the past century, conviction of a "crime involving moral turpitude" was the chief deportability ground based on crimes. Though the aggravated felony ground has prompted more litigation recently, the archaic-sounding moral turpitude ground remains basic to the statute.

One conviction of a crime involving moral turpitude makes a noncitizen deportable if he committed it within five years after the date of admission and a sentence of one year or longer may be imposed. INA § 237(a)(2)(A)(i). What counts as the date of admission? The BIA has held this provision refers to the admission by virtue of which a noncitizen is present in the United States. If, for example, a noncitizen is admitted as a nonimmigrant and later adjusts status to lawful permanent resident without ever leaving the United States, the adjustment does not restart the five years. *See Matter of Alyazji*, 25 I & N Dec. 397 (BIA 2011). Adjustment of status can sometimes count as admission for purposes of starting the five-year clock, such as when a parolee adjusts to lawful permanent resident status. Convictions of two or more crimes involving moral turpitude (arising out of more than a single criminal scheme) make a noncitizen deportable regardless of the date of commission or length of sentence. INA § 237(a)(2)(A)(ii).

But what exactly is a crime involving moral turpitude? This term is maddeningly vague and the cases just as maddeningly intricate. The leading immigration practice treatise observes, "[a]ttempts to arrive at a workable definition of moral turpitude never have yielded entire satisfaction. * * * [T]his term defies a precise definition because its limits are charted by human experience." Charles Gordon, Stanley Mailman, Stephen Yale-Loehr & Ronald Y. Wada, Immigration Law and Procedure [GMYW] § 71.05[1][d][i] (2015). The case law has adopted various definitions, including this one from Black's Law Dictionary: "an act of baseness, vileness, or depravity in the private and social duties which a man owes to his fellow men, or to society in general, contrary to the accepted and customary rule of right and duty between man and man."[18]

Moral turpitude provides a standard of conduct in other areas of law, such disbarment of attorneys, revocation of licenses, and impeachment of witnesses. In immigration law, there is broad agreement as to whether the generic versions of many crimes—phrased in commonplace terms like "theft," "fraud," or "assault"—involve moral turpitude. Three broad categories of crimes are deemed to involve moral turpitude: serious crimes against persons (e.g., murder, voluntary manslaughter, rape, aggravated assault, kidnapping), serious property crimes (e.g., arson, burglary, embezzlement), and crimes with an element of fraud. Leading authorities publish long lists that report whether convictions under particular statutes have been have been held to involve or not involve moral turpitude. *See, e.g.,* GMYW § 71.05[1][d][ii]; Mary E. Kramer, Immigration Consequences of Criminal Activity: A Guide to Representing Foreign-Born Defendants 245–62 (6th ed. 2015).

(ii) Aggravated Felonies

Section 237(a)(2)(A)(iii) makes deportable any noncitizen who has been convicted of an aggravated felony at any time after admission. INA § 101(a)(43) defines aggravated felony in broad terms that ensures that a

---

[18] *See, e.g., United States v. Smith*, 420 F.2d 428, 431 (5th Cir.1970).

wide range of state criminal offenses fall within the definition—imagine the difficulty of listing in a statute all relevant offenses from all states.

The Anti-Drug Abuse Act of 1988 added "aggravated felony" to the INA in an effort to target crimes committed by participants in the drug trade, defining it at that time to include only murder, drug trafficking and firearms trafficking. Legislative amendments in 1990, 1994, 1996, and 2001 greatly expanded the term in two dimensions. First, the statutory definition of aggravated felony is now much broader, with over 20 separate categories. Under INA § 101(a)(43)(M), for example, an offense that involves fraud or deceit is an aggravated felony if the loss to the victim(s) exceeds $10,000. Until 1996, this part of the aggravated felony definition required a loss exceeding $200,000. (Are all the crimes described in § 101(a)(43) appropriately labeled *aggravated* felonies?) Second, the definition is retroactive, though not all consequences of an aggravated felony conviction reach back into the indefinite past.

An aggravated felony conviction has severe consequences beyond deportability. Aggravated felons are ineligible for most forms of relief from removal (discussed in Section C of this chapter). They may not obtain asylum, INA §§ 208(b)(2)(B)(i), cancellation of removal, § 240A(a)(3), or voluntary departure, § 240B(a)(1), (b)(1)(C). They are barred for life from re-entering the United States, unless they obtain consent to apply for readmission, § 212(a)(9)(A)(iii). Under INA § 238(b), aggravated felons who are not lawful permanent residents are subject to administrative removal without an immigration judge hearing. See p. 949 *infra*. Aggravated felony convictions can also have major non-immigration-law consequences, such as substantially enhancing the severity of a sentence. (Such sentence enhancement applies to both citizens and noncitizens.) *See* U.S. Sentencing Commission, Guidelines Manual § 2L1.2 (2010). This is why many judicial decisions interpreting the aggravated felony statute are criminal cases with no immigration law implications.

An aggravated felony conviction is not an explicit basis for inadmissibility, but it may also be a conviction for a crime involving moral turpitude or make a noncitizen inadmissible on some other ground. Whether the offense is an aggravated felony may also still be relevant because of the effect this may have on eligibility for waivers or relief from removal.

(iii) Drug Offenses

For more than half a century, the INA has made persons deportable if convicted of most drug offenses. The Anti-Drug Abuse Act of 1988 expanded the provision to cover any conviction "relating to a controlled substance." Pub. L. 100–690, § 1751(b), 102 Stat. 4181. (Of course, such crimes may also trigger another deportability ground, such as the aggravated felony category.) The deportation ground for any "narcotic drug addict" includes any alien who is a "drug abuser or addict," whether or not there has been a criminal conviction. INA § 237(a)(2)(B)(ii).

The current version of this ground, INA § 237(a)(2)(B), applies to a conviction for violating *any* law, including that of a foreign country, relating to a controlled substance. The sole exception is narrow—for a single offense of possession of 30 grams or less of marijuana for personal use.

(iv) Crimes of Domestic Violence

In 1996, Congress added crimes involving domestic violence as a deportability ground. Noncitizens are deportable for convictions that occur at any time after admission on a list of specific crimes: domestic violence, stalking, child abuse, child neglect, or child abandonment, INA § 237(a)(2)(E)(i). It also includes those who have violated protection orders by making threats of violence, causing bodily injury, or engaging in repeated harassment, § 237(a)(2)(E)(ii).

The statutory definition of domestic violence includes two aspects: (1) the crime must be a crime of violence within the meaning of 18 U.S.C. § 16; and (2) the crime must be committed against a person who is a current or former spouse, or someone in a relationship similar to that of a spouse, § 237(a)(2)(E)(i). The statute also covers attacks against persons protected under federal or local domestic or family violence laws.

In 2000, Congress added a waiver for domestic violence victims. The Attorney General may waive the domestic violence deportability ground for a noncitizen victim of battering or extreme cruelty if the noncitizen was acting in self-defense or other extenuating circumstances exist. *See* § 237(a)(7); The Violence Against Women Act of 2000 (VAWA), Victims of Trafficking and Violence Protection Act of 2000, Pub. L. No. 106–386, 114 Stat. 1464.

As a practical matter, noncitizens convicted of domestic violence might be charged under three grounds of deportability: crime of domestic violence, § 237(a)(2)(E), crime involving moral turpitude, § 237(a)(2)(A)(i), and, if it was a crime of violence and the prison term was one year or more, aggravated felony, §§ 101(a)(43)(F), 237(a)(2)(A)(iii).

PROBLEMS

Evaluate whether the following noncitizens fall under the crime-based deportability grounds:

1. E was admitted as a permanent resident seven years ago. Three years ago, he committed and was convicted of embezzlement and sentenced

to six months to two years in prison, with all but six months of the sentence suspended. *may want to negotiate lesser charge that has < 1yr jail potential*

2. F was admitted as a permanent resident seven years ago. Five years ago, he committed and was convicted of cocaine trafficking and sentenced to five years in prison. *Drug offense (anytime) → no diff in LPR time b/c it's aggravated felony*

3. G was admitted as a permanent resident ten years ago. Three years ago, he was convicted of tax fraud committed a year before the conviction. Two years ago, he committed and was convicted of money-laundering. *— Aggravated*

4. H, admitted as a permanent resident eight years ago, committed and was convicted of alien smuggling last year.

7 yrs
8 yrs
Multiple convictions

c. What Is a "Conviction"?

Most of the INA § 237(a)(2) deportability grounds require a conviction, defined in § 101(a)(48)(A):

> The term "conviction" means, with respect to an alien, a formal judgment of guilt of the alien entered by a court or, if adjudication of guilt has been withheld, where—
>
> (i) a judge or jury has found the alien guilty or the alien has entered a plea of guilty or nolo contendere or has admitted sufficient facts to warrant a finding of guilt, and
>
> (ii) the judge has ordered some form of punishment, penalty, or restraint on the alien's liberty to be imposed.

Under this definition, a conviction can occur without the entry of an adjudication of guilt, if defendant pleads nolo contendere or admits to facts sufficient to warrant a finding of guilt. The BIA has held, and courts have agreed, that deferred adjudications are convictions for immigration purposes, if the defendant pled guilty but later had the charge dismissed upon successful completion of community service or probation. *See Matter of Punu*, 22 I & N Dec. 224 (BIA 1998); *Madriz-Alvarado v. Ashcroft*, 383 F.3d 321 (5th Cir. 2004). But a similar procedure in Virginia does not lead to a conviction where the defendant pled not guilty, and the judge found facts justifying a finding of guilt but did not actually reach a finding of guilt. *See Crespo v. Holder*, 631 F.3d 130, 133–36 (4th Cir. 2011). The growing use of deferred adjudications during the 1980s and 1990s was in fact the motivation for Congress to adopt § 101(a)(48)(A) in 1996. The section obviously favors imposing negative immigration consequences even where the state or local criminal justice system has tried to find room to foster rehabilitation.

INA § 101(a)(48)(A) does not address probation, but the BIA has ruled that probation can be punishment and is at least a restraint on liberty for purposes of applying the definition of conviction. *See Matter of Punu*, 22 I & N Dec. 224 (BIA 1998). As for the length of a sentence, § 101(a)(48)(B) provides that a suspended sentence counts as a term of imprisonment.

If a conviction is reversed on appeal for procedural or substantive defects, the underlying crime cannot be the basis for removal. *Matter of Adamiak*, 23 I & N Dec. 878 (BIA 2006); *Alim v. Gonzales*, 446 F.3d 1239 (11th Cir. 2006). But it remains effective for removal purposes if it was vacated to avoid immigration consequences. *Matter of Pickering*, 23 I & N Dec. 621 (BIA 2003). The BIA has held that the noncitizen has the burden to prove that a conviction was vacated on substantive or procedural grounds. *Matter of Chavez-Martinez*, 24 I & N Dec. 272 (BIA 2007). However, the federal courts are split on this issue. *Compare Nath v. Gonzales*, 467 F.3d 1185, 1188–89 (9th Cir. 2006) (DHS bears burden of proving that the conviction remains valid for removal purposes); *with Rumierz v. Gonzales*, 456 F.3d 31, 40–41 (1st Cir. 2006) (noncitizen bears burden of proving that the conviction was vacated for substantive or procedural error).

(i) Expungements

State and federal laws permit courts to expunge criminal records in certain circumstances. Under many statutes, courts may set aside or expunge a conviction and seal the criminal record after a certain amount of time has passed, the sentence has been served, and the defendant has satisfied other obligations.

An expungement differs in effect from the reversal of a conviction on appeal for legal error. A conviction reversed on appeal for substantive or procedural error cannot be the basis for removal because it was not lawful, but expungement merely limits a lawful conviction's subsequent effect. The BIA has applied § 101(a)(48)(A) to hold that expungement pursuant to a state rehabilitative statute has no impact on a conviction's immigration consequences. *Matter of Roldan-Santoyo*, 22 I & N Dec. 512 (BIA 1999). The courts that have addressed the issue have generally agreed. *See, e.g., Nath v. Gonzales*, 467 F.3d 1185, 1188–89 (9th Cir. 2006); *Pickering v. Gonzales*, 465 F.3d 263 (6th Cir. 2006). The BIA has made one exception: an expungement under a state statute that is analogous to federal juvenile delinquency laws will eliminate immigration consequences. *Matter of Devison-Charles*, 22 I & N Dec. 1362 (BIA 2000).

(ii) Sentence Reductions

Suppose a noncitizen successfully petitioned a court to vacate his one-year sentence and impose a 360-day sentence instead. The BIA has ruled that the new sentence replaces the old one for determining any immigration law consequences. *Matter of Song*, 23 I & N Dec. 173 (BIA 2001). The new sentence determines the immigration consequences even if the noncitizen sought to vacate the original sentence for the express purpose of avoiding removal and asserts no substantive or procedural defect in the original sentence. *Matter of Cota-Vargas*, 23 I & N Dec. 849 (BIA 2005). Why should a sentence reduction of this type succeed in negating deportation, whereas a judicial order vacating the sentence is ineffective (*see Matter of Pickering, supra*) if done for the purpose of preventing removal?

(iii)   Pardons

A pardon is more effective than judicial expungement of a criminal conviction, at least for some crime-related deportability grounds. By statute a "full and unconditional pardon" by a state governor or the President of the United States eliminates the immigration consequences of convictions for crimes involving moral turpitude, aggravated felonies, and high speed flight from an immigration checkpoint. *See* INA § 237(a)(2)(A)(vi).

Under § 237(a)(2), should pardons of domestic violence crimes be treated differently from pardons of controlled substance convictions? *See Matter of Suh*, 23 I & N Dec. 626, 627 (BIA 2003) (pardon does not eliminate deportability for domestic violence or controlled substance crime). At least two federal circuits have held the pardon provision applies only to grounds of deportability, not inadmissibility. *Aguilera-Montero v. Mukasey*, 548 F.3d 1248, 1251–52 (9th Cir. 2008); *Balogun v. U.S. Attorney General*, 425 F.3d 1356, 1362–63 (11th Cir. 2005).

(iv)   Other Post-Conviction Relief

A noncitizen who seeks to vacate a prior conviction that is the basis of deportability has a variety of potential procedural vehicles. The appropriate court filing might be a writ of habeas corpus, or one of several possible common law writs, especially *coram nobis*. These procedural vehicles and their availability to raise ineffective assistance claims in general and *Padilla* claims in particular vary from state to state. Some states have restrictions that may make it impossible for some noncitizens facing removal to file *Padilla* claims because they missed a filing deadline, or because they has served out the criminal sentence and therefore are no longer in custody. *See, e.g., People v. Carrera*, 239 Ill.2d 241, 245–59, 940 N.E.2d 1111, 346 Ill. Dec. 507 (2010) (post-conviction relief is unavailable to an individual who has served his criminal sentence). The constitutionality of such limitations, if they eliminate or severely restrict the practical possibility of relief based on *Padilla* in certain cases, is an open question.

(v) Waivers

Recall from Section A of this chapter that INA § 212(h) authorizes a waiver of inadmissibility based on criminal convictions if certain requirements are met. Though the statute refers only to inadmissibility, the BIA has extended its application to some deportability situations. If a lawful permanent resident departed from and has been readmitted to the United States after committing a deportable offense, § 212(h) is available. *Matter of Sanchez*, 17 I & N Dec. 218 (BIA 1980).

What if she has stayed in the United States since committing the offense? If she qualifies for an immigrant visa, for example as an immediate relative, she can file for adjustment of status as relief from removal and seek a § 212(h) waiver. *Matter of Parodi*, 17 I & N Dec. 608 (BIA 1980). What if she stayed in the United States and has no basis for adjustment, but wants to use § 212(h)? The circuits have split on this issue. *Compare Malagon de Fuentes v. Gonzales*, 462 F.3d 498 (5th Cir. 2006) (§ 212(h) not available); *with Yeung v. INS*, 76 F.3d 337 (11th Cir. 1995) (§ 212(h) available).

Consider another limitation on § 212(h) waivers. In 1996, Congress made aggravated felons not only deportable but also ineligible for a form of relief from removal called cancellation of removal, discussed in Section C of this chapter. Congress also apparently anticipated that lawful permanent residents convicted of aggravated felonies might circumvent these new restrictions by obtaining § 212(h) waivers of crime-based inadmissibility and then adjusting their status to permanent resident as a form of relief from removal. To block this option, Congress limited waiver eligibility by adding the following proviso to the end of § 212(h):

> No waiver shall be granted under this subsection in the case of an alien who has previously been admitted to the United States as an alien lawfully admitted for permanent residence if either since the date of such admission the alien has been convicted of an aggravated felony or the alien has not lawfully resided continuously in the United States for a period of not less than 7 years immediately preceding the date of initiation of proceedings to remove the alien from the United States.

The BIA has ruled that the proviso bars a lawful permanent resident no matter how he became one—whether through adjustment or an immigrant visa admission—but at least two circuits have held the proviso inapplicable to permanent residents by adjustment. *Compare Lanier v. U.S. Atty. Gen.*, 631 F.3d 1363 (11th Cir. 2011); *Martinez v. Mukasey*, 519 F.3d 532, 546 (5th Cir. 2008); *with Matter of Koljenovic*, 25 I & N Dec. 219 (BIA 2010).

To the extent that the proviso treats a noncitizen who is not a permanent resident better than one who is, courts have found no equal protection violation. The Seventh Circuit explained:

> We find that a rational basis exists for Congress' decision to declare only those aggravated felons who have previously been admitted as LPRs ineligible for § 212(h) relief. One of Congress' purposes in enacting reforms to the INA through IIRIRA was to expedite the removal of criminal aliens from the United States. Eliminating the availability of § 212(h) relief for LPR aggravated felons would eradicate one source of delay that might thwart this effort. * * * LPRs enjoy rights and privileges by virtue of their status which are not shared by non-LPRs, and they typically have closer and long-standing ties to the United States through employment and family relationships. Therefore, Congress may rationally have concluded that LPRs who commit serious crimes despite these factors are uniquely poor candidates for relief from removal through the "backdoor" of waiver of inadmissibility. * * * Congress might have reasoned that LPR aggravated felons were a higher risk of recidivism, and were generally less deserving of a second chance than were non-LPR aggravated felons.

Lara-Ruiz v. INS, 241 F.3d 934, 947–48 (7th Cir. 2001).

As an alternative to a waiver, noncitizens who are deportable due to a criminal conviction may also be eligible for relief from removal that is more general in scope and not specifically tailored to crime-based removability. Section C of this chapter explores those forms of relief.

d. Classifying Convictions

Crime-based deportability grounds pose a challenge: how to classify a particular federal, state, or local conviction as falling within one of the criminal grounds for removal in federal immigration law. Alina Das frames the issue and introduces the "categorical approach" to classifying crimes as deportable offenses:

> Consider, for example, an immigrant with a state assault conviction. According to case law, to constitute a "crime involving moral turpitude" under the federal immigration statute, an assault offense generally must involve immoral intent, i.e., intentional physical injury rather than, for example, negligent or unintentional injury. Applying a categorical analysis to the assault conviction, an immigration official would begin by looking to the statutory definition of the [state] assault offense to determine if it requires an intentional physical injury.

Alina Das, *The Immigration Penalties of Criminal Convictions: Resurrecting Categorical Analysis in Immigration Law*, 86 N.Y.U. L. Rev. 1669, 1674–75 (2011).

The traditional "categorical approach" to classifying a conviction requires the immigration official to evaluate whether the state statute defining the crime of conviction fits categorically within the federal definition of a corresponding deportability ground. The categorical approach regards as immaterial the noncitizen's particular conduct in committing the crime, instead focusing on comparing the range of conduct that the elements of the criminal statute cover.

To take up Das' example, the categorical approach would compare the elements of the state assault statute with the elements of a federal assault statute that would constitute a crime involving moral turpitude. Usually this is done by comparing the elements of the crime of conviction with elements of a "generic" federal offense that constitutes a deportability ground. Per Das, the generic assault offense will constitute a crime involving moral turpitude only if it includes proof of an intentional physical injury as an element of the offense. If the state assault statute does not require as an element of conviction an intentional physical injury, then it does not categorically fit within the deportability ground of crimes involving moral turpitude. Under a pure categorical approach, if the statute of conviction is broad enough to support a conviction for a criminal act that does not involve moral turpitude, then the noncitizen has not been convicted of a crime involving moral turpitude. *See, e.g., Goldeshtein v. INS*, 8 F.3d 645 (9th Cir. 1993).

The categorical approach, with its emphasis on comparing the definitions of the criminal and immigration statutes, raises the question of whether and how to use information about a particular conviction to determine a noncitizen's deportability. What steps can an immigration court take to determine whether a particular conviction fits the removal ground? Suppose the assault statute does not require a finding of intentional physical injury. Can the immigration judge turn to facts outside the record of conviction, such as testimony or police reports, to determine whether there was, in fact, intentional physical injury? Should the immigration judge hold an evidentiary hearing or search the criminal record to find facts that would establish or rule out deportability?

- If the record of conviction showed that the immigrant was convicted of intentional physical injury under the criminal statute, could an immigration official consider testimony that the immigrant instead acted negligently?

- On the other hand, if the record of conviction demonstrated that the immigrant was convicted of negligent physical injury under the criminal statute, can the immigration

> judge rely on a police report alleging that the immigrant actually committed an intentional offense?

- Or should the categorical approach limit an immigration official to assessing the statutory offense, forbidding retrial of any of the facts?

See id.

An early attempt to resolve these questions arose when the Attorney General decided *Matter of Silva-Trevino.* The decision broadened the traditional categorical approach by permitting agency inquiry into the facts of the criminal case to determine whether the noncitizen had committed a deportable crime. *See Matter of Silva-Trevino,* 24 I & N Dec. 687 (2008), *vacated, Silva-Trevino v. Holder,* 742 F.3d 197 (5th Cir. 2014). As you will see, *Moncrieffe v. Holder,* along with *Mellouli v. Lynch, infra,* undercut the Attorney General's expansion of the categorical approach to classifying crimes, disapproving of the free rein *Silva-Trevino* had given immigration judges to reach beyond the record of conviction to inquire into the facts of the criminal case.

A second issue follows from the differences between criminal and immigration law:

> [A strict categorical approach] with its emphasis on comparing the elements of a crime with the elements of a generic sentencing term, does not apply neatly to the immigration statute. The immigration statute contains numerous grounds of removal that are not easily defined in terms of strict elements. Some of the provisions in immigration law include more ambiguous terminology. Noting these and other differences, federal courts and the agency began to carve out exceptions to categorical analysis for certain immigration law provisions that appear to include "non-elements" or "qualifiers."

Das, 86 N.Y.U. L. Rev. at 1677–78.

If Congress has defined some crime-related removal grounds to include circumstances specific to immigration law, will an approach that requires a complete match between the criminal statute and the removal ground suffice, or can an immigration official adjudicate whether those circumstances were met?

When the Supreme Court addressed this issue in *Nijhawan v. Holder,* 557 U.S. 29, 129 S.Ct. 229, 4174 L.Ed.2d 22 (2009), it threw the categorical classification of crimes into disarray. In *Nijhawan,* the Court addressed how to classify crimes when the removal ground includes a requirement that operates largely outside of criminal law. The case concerned the "aggravated felony" removal ground that includes "an offense that * * * involves fraud or deceit *in which the loss to the victim or* *victims exceeds $10,000.*" § 101(a)(43)(M)(i) (emphasis added)." Only three criminal fraud statutes had a comparable monetary threshold requirement.

The Court distinguished the removal ground from criminal statutes and introduced a circumstance-specific approach to classifying crimes as deportable offenses:

> [T]he "aggravated felony" statute differs from [the criminal sentencing statute] in that it lists certain other "offenses" using language that almost certainly does not refer to generic crimes but refers to specific circumstances. For example, subparagraph (P), after referring to "an offense" that amounts to "falsely making, forging, counterfeiting, mutilating, or altering a passport," adds, *"except in the case of a first offense for which the alien * * * committed the offense for the purpose of assisting . . . the alien's spouse, child, or parent . . . to violate a provision of this chapter"* (emphasis added). The language about (for example) "forging . . . passport[s]" may well refer to a generic crime, but the italicized exception cannot possibly refer to a generic crime. That is because there is no such generic crime; there is no criminal statute that contains any such exception. Thus if the provision is to have any meaning at all, the exception must refer to the particular circumstances in which an offender committed the crime on a particular occasion.

Id. at 37–38. The Court explained:

> The interpretive difficulty before us reflects the linguistic fact that in ordinary speech words such as "crime," "felony," "offense," and the like sometimes refer to a generic crime, say, the crime of fraud or theft in general, and sometimes refer to the specific acts in which an offender engaged on a specific occasion, say, *the* fraud that the defendant planned and executed last month. The question here, as we have said, is whether the italicized statutory words "offense that involves fraud or deceit *in which the loss to the . . . victims exceeds $10,000*" should be interpreted in the first sense (which we shall call "categorical"), *i.e.,* as referring to a generic crime, or in the second sense (which we shall call "circumstance-specific"), as referring to the specific way in which an offender committed the crime on a specific occasion. If the first, we must look to the statute defining the offense to determine whether it has an appropriate monetary threshold; if the second, we must look to the facts and circumstances underlying an offender's conviction.

Id. at 33–34. *Nijhawan* seemed to offer an alternative to the categorical approach, one that permitted assessing the factual circumstances of the crime.

Recent Supreme Court decisions considering how to classify crimes as deportable offenses have addressed some of the questions raised here. The first, *Moncrieffe v. Holder,* 569 U.S. ___, 133 S.Ct. 1678, 185 L.Ed.2d 727 (2013), involved a guilty plea under the Georgia state offense of possession of marijuana with intent to distribute.

MONCRIEFFE V. HOLDER

Supreme Court of the United States, 2013.
569 U.S. ___, 133 S.Ct. 1678, 185 L.Ed.2d 727.

JUSTICE SOTOMAYOR delivered the opinion of the Court.

* * *

The INA defines "aggravated felony" to include a host of offenses. Among them is "illicit trafficking in a controlled substance." INA § 101(a)(43)(B). This general term is not defined, but the INA states that it "includ[es] a drug trafficking crime (as defined in section 924(c) of title 18)." In turn, 18 U.S.C. § 924(c)(2) defines "drug trafficking crime" to mean "any felony punishable under the Controlled Substances Act," or two other statutes not relevant here. The chain of definitions ends with [18 U.S.C.] § 3559(a)(5), which provides that a "felony" is an offense for which the "maximum term of imprisonment authorized" is "more than one year." The upshot is that a noncitizen's conviction of an offense that the Controlled Substances Act (CSA) makes punishable by more than one year's imprisonment will be counted as an "aggravated felony" for immigration purposes. A conviction under either state or federal law may qualify, but a "state offense constitutes a 'felony punishable under the Controlled Substances Act' only if it proscribes conduct punishable as a felony under that federal law." *Lopez v. Gonzales,* 549 U.S. 47, 60, 127 S.Ct. 625, 166 L.Ed.2d 462 (2006).

Petitioner Adrian Moncrieffe is a Jamaican citizen who came to the United States legally in 1984, when he was three. During a 2007 traffic stop, police found 1.3 grams of marijuana in his car. This is the equivalent of about two or three marijuana cigarettes. Moncrieffe pleaded guilty to possession of marijuana with intent to distribute, a violation of Ga. Code Ann. § 16–13–30(j)(1) (2007). Under a Georgia statute providing more lenient treatment to first-time offenders, § 42–8–60(a) (1997), the trial court withheld entering a judgment of conviction or imposing any term of imprisonment, and instead required that Moncrieffe complete five years of probation, after which his charge will be expunged altogether.

* * *

When the Government alleges that a state conviction qualifies as an "aggravated felony" under the INA, we generally employ a "categorical approach" to determine whether the state offense is comparable to an offense listed in the INA. Under this approach we look "not to the facts of the particular prior case," but instead to whether "the state statute defining the crime of conviction" categorically fits within the "generic" federal definition of a corresponding aggravated felony. By "generic," we mean the offenses must be viewed in the abstract, to see whether the state statute shares the nature of the federal offense that serves as a point of comparison. Accordingly, a state offense is a categorical match with a generic federal offense only if a conviction of the state offense " 'necessarily' involved . . . facts equating to [the] generic [federal offense]." Whether the noncitizen's actual conduct involved such facts "is quite irrelevant."

Because we examine what the state conviction necessarily involved, not the facts underlying the case, we must presume that the conviction "rested upon [nothing] more than the least of th[e] acts" criminalized, and then determine whether even those acts are encompassed by the generic federal offense. But this rule is not without qualification. First, our cases have addressed state statutes that contain several different crimes, each described separately, and we have held that a court may determine which particular offense the noncitizen was convicted of by examining the charging document and jury instructions, or in the case of a guilty plea, the plea agreement, plea colloquy, or " 'some comparable judicial record' of the factual basis for the plea." Second, our focus on the minimum conduct criminalized by the state statute is not an invitation to apply "legal imagination" to the state offense; there must be "a realistic probability, not a theoretical possibility, that the State would apply its statute to conduct that falls outside the generic definition of a crime."

* * *

The aggravated felony at issue here, "illicit trafficking in a controlled substance," is a "generic crim[e]." So the categorical approach applies. * * * [T]o satisfy the categorical approach, a state drug offense must meet two conditions: It must "necessarily" proscribe conduct that is an offense under the CSA, and the CSA must "necessarily" prescribe felony punishment for that conduct.

Moncrieffe was convicted under a Georgia statute that makes it a crime to "possess, have under [one's] control, manufacture, deliver, distribute, dispense, administer, purchase, sell, or possess with intent to distribute marijuana." We know from his plea agreement that Moncrieffe was convicted of the last of these offenses. We therefore must determine whether possession of marijuana with intent to distribute is "necessarily" conduct punishable as a felony under the CSA.

We begin with the relevant conduct criminalized by the CSA. There is no question that it is a federal crime to "possess with intent to . . . distribute . . . a controlled substance," 21 U.S.C. § 841(a)(1), one of which is marijuana, § 812(c). So far, the state and federal provisions correspond. But this is not enough, because the generically defined federal crime is "any felony punishable under the Controlled Substances Act," 18 U.S.C. § 924(c)(2), not just any "offense under the CSA." Thus we must look to what punishment the CSA imposes for this offense.

Section 841 is divided into two subsections that are relevant here: (a), titled "Unlawful acts," which includes the offense just described, and (b), titled "Penalties." Subsection (b) tells us how "any person who violates subsection (a)" shall be punished, depending on the circumstances of his crime (e.g., the type and quantity of controlled substance involved, whether it is a repeat offense). Subsection (b)(1)(D) provides that if a person commits a violation of subsection (a) involving "less than 50 kilograms of marihuana," then "such person shall, except as provided in paragraphs (4) and (5) of this subsection, be sentenced to a term of imprisonment of not more than 5 years," i.e., as a felon. But one of the exceptions is important here. Paragraph (4) provides, "Notwithstanding paragraph (1)(D) of this subsection, any person who violates subsection (a) of this section by distributing a small amount of marihuana for no remuneration shall be treated as" a simple drug possessor, 21 U.S.C. § 844, which for our purposes means as a misdemeanant. These dovetailing provisions create two mutually exclusive categories of punishment for CSA marijuana distribution offenses: one a felony, and one not. The only way to know whether a marijuana distribution offense is "punishable as a felony" under the CSA, is to know whether the conditions described in paragraph (4) are present or absent.

* * * [T]he fact of a conviction for possession with intent to distribute marijuana, standing alone, does not reveal whether either remuneration or more than a small amount of marijuana was involved. It is possible neither was; we know that Georgia prosecutes this offense when a defendant possesses only a small amount of marijuana, and that "distribution" does not require remuneration. So Moncrieffe's conviction could correspond to either the CSA felony or the CSA misdemeanor. Ambiguity on this point means that the conviction did not "necessarily" involve facts that correspond to an offense punishable as a felony under the CSA. Under the categorical approach, then, Moncrieffe was not convicted of an aggravated felony.

* * *

Recognizing that its approach leads to consequences Congress could not have intended, the Government hedges its argument by proposing a remedy: Noncitizens should be given an opportunity during immigration proceedings to demonstrate that their predicate marijuana distribution convictions involved only a small amount of marijuana and no remuneration, just as a federal criminal defendant could do at sentencing. * * *

This solution is entirely inconsistent with both the INA's text and the categorical approach. As noted, the relevant INA provisions ask what the noncitizen was "convicted of," not what he did, and the inquiry in immigration proceedings is limited accordingly. * * *

Moreover, the procedure the Government envisions would require precisely the sort of *post hoc* investigation into the facts of predicate offenses that we have long deemed undesirable. The categorical approach serves "practical" purposes: It promotes judicial and administrative efficiency by precluding the relitigation of past convictions in minitrials conducted long after the fact. Yet the Government's approach would have our Nation's overburdened immigration courts entertain and weigh testimony from, for example, the friend of a noncitizen who may have shared a marijuana cigarette with him at a party, or the local police officer who recalls to the contrary that cash traded hands. And, as a result, two noncitizens, each "convicted of" the same offense, might obtain different aggravated felony determinations depending on what evidence remains available or how it is perceived by an individual immigration judge. The categorical approach was designed to avoid this "potential unfairness."

Furthermore, the minitrials the Government proposes would be possible only if the noncitizen could locate witnesses years after the fact, notwithstanding that during removal proceedings noncitizens are not guaranteed legal representation and are often subject to mandatory detention, where they have little ability to collect evidence. A noncitizen in removal proceedings is not at all similarly situated to a defendant in a federal criminal prosecution. The Government's suggestion that the CSA's procedures could readily be replicated in immigration proceedings is therefore misplaced.

The Government defends its proposed immigration court proceedings as "a subsequent step *outside the categorical approach* in light of Section 841(b)(4)'s 'circumstance-specific' nature." This argument rests upon *Nijhawan,* in which we considered another aggravated felony, "an offense that . . . involves fraud or deceit in which the loss to the victim or victims exceeds $10,000." INA § 101(a)(43)(M)(i). We held that the $10,000 threshold was not to be applied categorically as a required component of a generic offense, but instead called for a "circumstance-specific approach" that allows for an examination, in immigration court, of the "particular circumstances in which an offender committed the crime on a particular occasion." *Nijhawan,* 557 U.S., at 38–40, 129 S.Ct. 2294. The Government suggests the § 841(b)(4) factors are like the monetary threshold, and thus similarly amenable to a circumstance-specific inquiry.

We explained in *Nijhawan,* however, that unlike the provision there, "illicit trafficking in a controlled substance" is a "generic crim[e]" to which the categorical approach applies, not a circumstance-specific provision. That distinction is evident in the structure of the INA. The monetary threshold is a limitation, written into the INA itself, on the scope of the aggravated felony for fraud. And the monetary threshold is set off by the words "in which," which calls for a circumstance-specific examination of "the conduct involved '*in*' the commission of the offense of conviction." *Nijhawan,* 557 U.S., at 39, 129 S.Ct. 2294. Locating this exception in the INA proper suggests an intent to have the relevant facts found in immigration proceedings. But where, as here, the INA incorporates other criminal statutes wholesale, we have held it "must refer to generic crimes," to which the categorical approach applies.

* * *

Finally, the Government suggests that the immigration court's task would not be so daunting in some cases, such as those in which a noncitizen was convicted under the New York statute previously discussed or convicted directly under § 841(b)(4). True, in those cases, the record of conviction might reveal on its face that the predicate offense was punishable only as a misdemeanor. But most States do not have stand-alone offenses for the social sharing of marijuana, so minitrials concerning convictions from the other States, such as Georgia, would be inevitable. * * *

* * *

* * * If a noncitizen's conviction for a marijuana distribution offense fails to establish that the offense involved either remuneration or more than a small amount of marijuana, the conviction is not for an aggravated felony under the INA. * * *

* * *

[The dissenting opinions of JUSTICES THOMAS and ALITO are omitted.]

NOTES AND QUESTIONS ON CLASSIFYING CRIMES

1. *Moncrieffe* defends the categorical approach on practical grounds, as (1) promoting efficiency by precluding the relitigation of past convictions in mini-trials in immigration court, (2) promoting uniformity in removal determinations by ensuring that noncitizens who are convicted of the same offense obtain the same aggravated felony determinations, and (3) avoiding the problem of the cold case that requires the noncitizen to locate witnesses and evidence years after the fact, without guaranteed counsel and perhaps

while detained. *See also Matter of R-*, 6 I & N Dec. 444, 447–48 (BIA 1954) (adding to this list that the categorical approach "eliminates the situation where a nonjudicial agency retries a judicial matter").

Are you persuaded? Should a noncitizen who commits a serious crime with "evil" intent escape deportation simply because some conduct condemned by the statute would not constitute a crime involving moral turpitude? Or, conversely, should the need for administrative efficiency, convenience, and uniformity condemn to deportation a noncitizen whose moral blameworthiness is greatly reduced in light of the particular circumstances of the offense?

2.   On the basic issue of how to classify a conviction, a fundamental question is whether it is accurate or fair to rely on facts that appear in the criminal file but were not necessary to convict. *Cf.* Restatement of Judgments (Second) § 27 & comment j (issue preclusion is limited to matters that were actually litigated and determined in the prior case and essential to the judgment). Consider how, in practice, the information that becomes available about any given criminal case is generated. A defense attorney who heeds the call in *Padilla* to anticipate possible immigration consequences will try to keep out of the criminal file any facts that might establish deportability later, even if those facts are irrelevant to the outcome in the criminal case.

Rebecca Sharpless provides this helpful overview:

> The charging document in a criminal case must allege the elements, the "essential facts constituting the offense charged." A conviction is subject to reversal if the prosecutor has failed to charge all of the elements of the crime. But not all facts that appear in a charging document are essential facts. While alleging the essential elements of a crime is the most important function of the charging document, it is not its sole function. A second function of a charging document is to give the defendant sufficient notice in ordinary language of the crime being alleged. The charging document must "provide the accused with a sufficient description of the acts he is alleged to have committed to enable him to defend himself adequately." [5 W.R. LaFave et al., Criminal Procedure § 19.3(a), at 249 (3d ed. 2007).] This requirement has been described as mandating that the charging document describe the "who . . ., what, where, and how" of the crime. For example, in an assault case, a charging document typically identifies the alleged victim. In a crime against property, the charging document typically describes the type of property that was involved. Courts have found a federal constitutional violation when pleadings in state cases lack specificity.

> Nonessential facts also typically appear in the factual basis for a plea. The federal criminal rules of procedure and many states require a factual basis as a condition of pleas to guard against defendants pleading guilty to crimes they could not have committed.

There are typically no, or virtually no, standards governing them. A statement of factual basis, even more so than a charging document, contains a broad range of facts, typically using everyday language to describe the manner in which the crime was allegedly carried out.

To prevail at trial, the prosecution does not have to prove every fact in the charging document. Nor would the prosecution have needed to prove every fact that later appears in a statement of factual basis. In a Florida battery case, for example, guilt would not turn on whether the victim was the defendant's spouse or whether the battery was carried out by a blow to the victim's head or by a de minimis unwanted touching. In a Florida theft case, guilt would not depend on showing that the property at issue was gum or a shopping cart.

A conviction does not exist apart from its elements. To say that a person has been found guilty of a crime is simply to say that he or she has been found guilty of each element of the crime. Another way of expressing this point is to say that a conviction consists of only facts that are necessarily decided by the criminal justice system * * * Extraneous facts need not be proven at all and therefore certainly are not proven beyond a reasonable doubt. A defendant therefore has no reason to dispute (or to exclude from the record) nonelement facts.

Rebecca Sharpless, *Toward a True Elements Test: Taylor and the Categorical Analysis of Crimes in Immigration Law*, 62 U. Miami L. Rev. 979, 983–85 (2008).

3. In April 2015, Attorney General Eric Holder vacated his predecessor's decision in *Silva-Trevino*, reasoning that an intervening circuit split and Supreme Court decisions had cast doubt on the validity of an inquiry into evidence outside the record of conviction. Noting that he did not disapprove of every aspect of the opinion, the Attorney General charged the Board of Immigration Appeals with adopting a uniform standard for applying a modified categorical approach. *Matter of Silva-Trevino*, 26 I & N Dec. 550 (Att'y Gen. 2015).

4. After *Moncrieffe,* how much of the circumstance-specific approach from *Nijhawan* is left? How far does the circumstance-specific analysis go toward an open-ended inquiry into the facts in the criminal prosecution?

Regarding what evidence may be used in an immigration court hearing to decide deportability based on a prior conviction, *Nijhawan* concluded: "We can find nothing unfair about the immigration judge's having here relied upon earlier sentencing-related material." Does *Moncrieffe* permit an immigration judge to go further, allowing DHS, in any removal proceeding charging deportability under *any* provision of § 237(a)(2), to introduce evidence on the facts in the criminal case and require the immigration judge to decide if those facts have been established by clear and convincing evidence?

5. Recall that in *Nijhawan*, the U.S. Supreme Court distinguished, within the aggravated felony definition, between two types of crimes, observing that it "contains some language that refers to generic crimes and some language that almost certainly refers to the specific circumstances in which a crime was committed." It went on to identify "murder, rape, or sexual abuse of a minor" as offenses listed in that definition in "language that must refer to generic crimes." Into which of these two categories does a "crime of domestic violence" fall?

EXERCISE ON CLASSIFYING CRIMES

Bianco, a citizen of Venezuela, was admitted to the United States as a nonimmigrant and became a lawful permanent resident four years later. Almost two years later, she was convicted in Pennsylvania of an aggravated assault. Bianco admitted in the criminal case that the victim was her husband. The sentencing sheet shows that she was sentenced to make restitution to her husband and was ordered to participate in a domestic violence program. A year after the conviction, the Department of Homeland Security filed a Notice to Appear alleging that Bianco is deportable.

A "crime of domestic violence" includes "any crime of violence (as defined in section 16 of Title 18) against a person committed by a current or former spouse of the person." INA § 237(a)(2)(E)(i). Under 18 U.S.C. § 16(a), "crime of violence" includes "an offense that has as an element the use, attempted use, or threatened use of physical force against the person or property of another."

The state statute under which Bianco was convicted provided seven alternative methods by which the offense could be committed. Bianco was charged under a subsection providing that a person who "attempts to cause or intentionally or knowingly causes bodily injury to another with a deadly weapon" is guilty of aggravated assault. This statute does not require any domestic relationship between perpetrator and victim.

The immigration judge found that Bianco was convicted of aggravated assault, a crime that satisfied the definition of a "crime of violence" under 18 U.S.C. § 16(a), and ordered Bianco removed based on INA § 237(a)(2)(E)(i) for having been convicted of a crime of domestic violence.

On appeal, Bianco does not challenge the conclusion that she was convicted of a crime of violence, nor does she deny that the victim was her husband. But she argues that on these facts the offense does not make her deportable under INA § 237(a)(2)(E)(i) as a domestic violence crime. Will her argument succeed?

Recall Alina Das' description of a statute "that defines assault in subparts, some of which require intentional physical injury and some of which do not." In that case, she instructs, "an immigration official would examine [a limited set of documents that constitute] the record of conviction to determine which part of the assault statute was applied in the noncitizen's criminal case." Das, *supra,* at 1674–75 (2011). Then the immigration judge matches the elements of the assault statute she has just identified with the elements of the deportability ground. This two-step process has been dubbed the "modified categorical approach."

Moncrieffe explained further that when state statutes "contain several different crimes, each described separately," then "a court may determine which particular offense the noncitizen was convicted of by examining the charging document and jury instructions, or in the case of a guilty plea, the plea agreement, plea colloquy, or 'some comparable judicial record'." This passage referred to the rule that a "modified categorical approach" applies to "divisible" statutes. By severely curtailing the use of the record of conviction when statutes are not divisible, *Moncrieffe* made the concept of a "divisible statute" crucial, but the decision shed no further light on definition of this term.

The U.S. Supreme Court addressed this issue in *Descamps v. United States*, 133 S. Ct. 2276 (2013). As with some other leading decisions on classifying crimes, the context was criminal sentencing, but the Court analyzes the classification of crimes as if the same approaches and definitions apply in both criminal law and immigration law. *See Matter of Chairez-Castrejon*, 26 I & N Dec. 349, 352–55 (BIA 2014) (applying *Descamps* to the removal context).

As background, the federal Armed Career Criminal Act (ACCA) increases the sentences of some federal defendants who have three prior convictions for certain crimes, including "burglary, arson, or extortion." In deciding whether a prior conviction under California law was a conviction for "burglary," the Supreme Court addressed when a statute is subject to the modified categorical approach.

DESCAMPS V. UNITED STATES

Supreme Court of the United States, 2013.
133 S.Ct. 2276, 186 L.Ed.2d 438.

JUSTICE KAGAN delivered the opinion of the Court.

* * *

Descamps argued that his prior burglary conviction could not count as an ACCA predicate offense under our categorical approach. He had pleaded guilty to violating California Penal Code Ann. § 459, which provides that a "person who enters" certain locations "with intent to commit grand or petit larceny or any felony is guilty of burglary." That statute does not require the entry to have been unlawful in the way most burglary laws do. Whereas burglary statutes generally demand breaking and entering or similar conduct, California's does not: It covers, for example, a shoplifter who enters a store, like any customer, during normal business hours. In sweeping so widely, the state law goes beyond the normal, "generic" definition of burglary. According to Descamps, that asymmetry of offense elements precluded his conviction under § 459 from serving as an ACCA predicate, whether or not his own burglary involved an unlawful entry that could have satisfied the requirements of the generic crime.

* * *

Our caselaw explaining the categorical approach and its "modified" counterpart all but resolves this case. In those decisions, as shown below, the modified approach serves a limited function: It helps effectuate the categorical analysis when a divisible statute, listing potential offense elements in the alternative, renders opaque which element played a part in the defendant's conviction. So understood, the modified approach cannot convert Descamps' conviction under § 459 into an ACCA predicate, because that state law defines burglary not alternatively, but only more broadly than the generic offense.

* * *

* * * *Taylor [v. United States*, 495 U.S. 575, 110 S.Ct. 2143, 109 L.Ed.2d 607 (1990)], recognized a "narrow range of cases" in which sentencing courts—applying what we would later dub the "modified categorical approach"—may look beyond the statutory elements to "the charging paper and jury instructions" used in a case. *Id.,* at 602, 110 S.Ct. 2143. To explain when courts should resort to that approach, we hypothesized a statute with alternative elements—more particularly, a burglary statute (otherwise conforming to the generic crime) that prohibits "entry of an automobile as well as a building." One of those alternatives (a building) corresponds to an element in generic burglary, whereas the other (an automobile) does not. In a typical case brought under the statute, the prosecutor charges one of those two alternatives, and the judge instructs the jury accordingly. So if the case involves entry into a building, the jury is "actually required to find all the elements of generic burglary," as the categorical approach demands. But the statute alone does not disclose whether that has occurred. Because the statute is "divisible"—*i.e.,* comprises multiple, alternative versions of the crime—a later sentencing court cannot tell, without reviewing something more, if the defendant's conviction was for the generic (building) or non-generic (automobile) form of burglary. Hence *Taylor* permitted sentencing courts, as a tool for implementing the categorical approach, to examine a limited

class of documents to determine which of a statute's alternative elements formed the basis of the defendant's prior conviction.

* * *

* * * In *Nijhawan v. Holder,* 557 U.S. 29, 129 S.Ct. 2294, 174 L.Ed.2d 22 (2009), we discussed another Massachusetts statute, this one prohibiting " 'Breaking and Entering at Night' " in any of four alternative places: a "building, ship, vessel, or vehicle." *Id.,* at 35, 129 S.Ct. 2294. We recognized that when a statute so "refer[s] to several different crimes," not all of which qualify as an ACCA predicate, a court must determine which crime formed the basis of the defendant's conviction. *Ibid.* That is why, we explained, *Taylor* and *Shepard* developed the modified categorical approach. By reviewing the extra-statutory materials approved in those cases, courts could discover "which statutory phrase," contained within a statute listing "several different" crimes, "covered a prior conviction." 557 U.S., at 41, 129 S.Ct. 2294. * * *

Applied in that way—which is the only way we have ever allowed— the modified approach merely helps implement the categorical approach when a defendant was convicted of violating a divisible statute. The modified approach thus acts not as an exception, but instead as a tool. It retains the categorical approach's central feature: a focus on the elements, rather than the facts, of a crime. And it preserves the categorical approach's basic method: comparing those elements with the generic offense's. All the modified approach adds is a mechanism for making that comparison when a statute lists multiple, alternative elements, and so effectively creates "several different . . . crimes." *Nijhawan,* 557 U.S., at 41, 129 S.Ct. 2294. If at least one, but not all of those crimes matches the generic version, a court needs a way to find out which the defendant was convicted of. That is the job, as we have always understood it, of the modified approach: to identify, from among several alternatives, the crime of conviction so that the court can compare it to the generic offense.

The modified approach thus has no role to play in this case. The dispute here does not concern any list of alternative elements. Rather, it involves a simple discrepancy between generic burglary and the crime established in § 459. The former requires an unlawful entry along the lines of breaking and entering. The latter does not, and indeed covers simple shoplifting, as even the Government acknowledges. In *Taylor's* words, then, § 459 "define[s] burglary more broadly" than the generic offense. And because that is true—because California, to get a conviction, need not prove that Descamps broke and entered—a § 459 violation cannot serve as an ACCA predicate. Whether Descamps *did* break and enter makes no difference. And likewise, whether he ever admitted to breaking and entering is irrelevant. Our decisions authorize review of the plea colloquy or other approved extra-statutory documents only when a statute defines burglary not (as here) overbroadly, but instead alternatively, with one statutory phrase corresponding to the generic crime and another not. In that circumstance, a court may look to the additional documents to determine which of the statutory offenses (generic or non-generic) formed the basis of the defendant's conviction. But here no uncertainty of that kind exists, and so the categorical approach needs no help from its modified partner. We know Descamps' crime of conviction, and it does not correspond to the relevant generic offense. Under our prior decisions, the inquiry is over.

* * *

[The opinion of JUSTICE THOMAS, concurring in the judgment, and the dissenting opinion of JUSTICE ALITO are omitted.]

NOTES AND QUESTIONS ON DESCAMPS

How would the analysis in *Descamps* differ if the Court had held that the modified categorical approach applied? What documents would a court review to determine whether Descamps had committed the "generic" form of burglary, and for what purpose?

Rebecca Sharpless describes the modified categorical approach as follows: "if a statute is divisible and only some offenses trigger removal, an adjudicator is permitted to look at the record of conviction, but only to determine whether the noncitizen was convicted of the statutory elements that trigger removal." Sharpless, *supra*, 62 U. Miami L. Rev. at 997–1000. Both *Moncrieffe* and *Descamps* limit the use of the modified categorical approach to look beyond the statute of conviction to the facts in the criminal record of conviction. Why is the Court so stingy about allowing use of the modified categorical approach, which itself limits immigration courts to a prescribed set of documents in the criminal record? *See Moncrieffe, supra,* at p. 692.

_____

In the next case, Court applied the categorical approach to decide whether a state drug paraphernalia conviction is a conviction "relating to a controlled substance" as defined in a specified federal statute, when the state criminal law sweeps more broadly than the federal law.

MELLOULI V. LYNCH

Supreme Court of the United States, 2015.
135 S.Ct. 1980, 192 L.Ed.2d 60.

JUSTICE GINSBURG delivered the opinion of the Court.

This case requires us to decide how immigration judges should apply a deportation (removal) provision, defined with reference to federal drug laws, to an alien convicted of a state drug-paraphernalia misdemeanor. * * *

We hold that Mellouli's Kansas conviction for concealing unnamed pills in his sock did not trigger removal under INA § 237(a)(2)(B)(i). * * *

I

A

This case involves the interplay between several federal and state statutes. * * * The question presented is whether a Kansas conviction for using drug paraphernalia to store or conceal a controlled substance subjects an alien to deportation under INA § 237(a)(2)(B)(i), which applies to an alien "convicted of a violation of [a state law] relating to a controlled substance (as defined in [§ 802, the federal controlled substance statute])." [The criminal deportability ground, INA § 237(a)(2)(B)(i), incorporates the federal controlled substances statute, 21 U.S.C. § 802, which limits the term "controlled substance" to a "drug or other substance" included in one of five federal schedules.] Kansas defines "controlled substance" as any drug included on its own schedules, and makes no reference to § 802 or any other federal law. At the time of Mellouli's conviction, Kansas' schedules included at least nine substances not included in the federal lists. * * *

B

Mellouli, a citizen of Tunisia, entered the United States on a student visa in 2004. He attended U.S. universities, earning a bachelor of arts degree, *magna cum laude,* as well as master's degrees in applied mathematics and economics. After completing his education, Mellouli worked as an actuary and taught mathematics at the University of Missouri-Columbia. In 2009, he became a conditional permanent resident and, in 2011, a lawful permanent resident. Since December 2011, Mellouli has been engaged to be married to a U.S. citizen.

In 2010, Mellouli was arrested for driving under the influence and driving with a suspended license. During a postarrest search in a Kansas detention facility, deputies discovered four orange tablets hidden in Mellouli's sock. According to a probable-cause affidavit submitted in the state prosecution, Mellouli acknowledged that the tablets were Adderall and that he did not have a prescription for the drugs. Adderall, the brand name of an amphetamine-based drug typically prescribed to treat attention-deficit hyperactivity disorder, is a controlled substance under both federal and Kansas law. Based on the probable-cause affidavit, a criminal complaint was filed charging Mellouli with trafficking contraband in jail.

Ultimately, Mellouli was charged with only the lesser offense of possessing drug paraphernalia, a misdemeanor. The amended complaint alleged that Mellouli had "use[d] or possess[ed] with intent to use drug paraphernalia, to-wit: a sock, to store, contain, conceal, inject, ingest, inhale or otherwise introduce into the human body a controlled substance." The complaint did not identify the substance contained in the sock. Mellouli pleaded guilty to the paraphernalia possession charge; he also pleaded guilty to driving under the influence. For both offenses, Mellouli was sentenced to a suspended term of 359 days and 12 months' probation.

In February 2012, several months after Mellouli successfully completed probation, Immigration and Customs Enforcement officers arrested him as deportable under § 237(a)(2)(B)(i) based on his paraphernalia possession conviction. * * * Mellouli was deported in 2012.

Under federal law, Mellouli's concealment of controlled-substance tablets in his sock would not have qualified as a drug-paraphernalia offense. Federal law criminalizes the sale of or commerce in drug paraphernalia, but possession alone is not criminalized at all. Nor does federal law define drug paraphernalia to include common household or ready-to-wear items like socks; rather, it defines paraphernalia as any "equipment, product, or material" which is "primarily *intended or designed for use*" in connection with various drug-related activities. 21 U.S.C. § 863(d) (emphasis added). In 19 States as well, the conduct for which Mellouli was convicted—use of a sock to conceal a controlled substance—is not a criminal offense. At most, it is a low-level infraction, often not attended by a right to counsel.

The Eighth Circuit denied Mellouli's petition for review. We granted certiorari, and now reverse the judgment of the Eighth Circuit.

II

We address first the rationale offered by the BIA and affirmed by the Eighth Circuit, which differentiates paraphernalia offenses from possession and distribution offenses. Essential background, in evaluating the rationale shared by the BIA and the Eighth Circuit, is the categorical approach historically taken in determining whether a state conviction renders an alien removable under the immigration statute. Because Congress predicated deportation "on convictions, not conduct," the approach looks to the statutory definition of the offense of conviction, not to the particulars of an alien's behavior. The state conviction triggers removal only if, by definition, the underlying crime falls within a category of removable offenses defined by federal law. An alien's actual conduct is irrelevant to the inquiry, as the adjudicator must "presume that the conviction rested upon nothing more than the least of the acts criminalized" under the state statute. *Moncrieffe v. Holder,* 133 S.Ct. 1678, 1684–1685, 185 L.Ed.2d 727 (2013).[4]

The categorical approach has a long pedigree in our Nation's immigration law. *Id.,* 133 S.Ct., at 1685. As early as 1913, courts examining the federal immigration statute concluded that Congress, by tying immigration penalties to *convictions,* intended to "limi[t] the immigration adjudicator's assessment of a past criminal conviction to a legal analysis of the statutory offense," and to disallow "[examination] of the facts underlying the crime." [Alina Das, *The Immigration Penalties of Criminal Convictions: Resurrecting Categorical Analysis in Immigration Law,* 86 N.Y.U. L. Rev. 1669, 1688, 1690 (2011).]

Rooted in Congress' specification of conviction, not conduct, as the trigger for immigration consequences, the categorical approach is suited to the realities of the system. Asking immigration judges in each case to determine the circumstances underlying a state conviction would burden a system in which "large numbers of cases [are resolved by] immigration judges and front-line immigration officers, often years after the convictions." Jennifer Lee Koh, *The Whole Better than the Sum: A Case for the Categorical Approach to Determining the Immigration Consequences of Crime,* 26 Geo. Immigr. L.J. 257, 295 (2012). By focusing on the legal question of what a conviction *necessarily* established, the categorical approach ordinarily works to promote efficiency, fairness, and predictability in the administration of immigration law. In particular, the approach enables aliens "to anticipate the immigration consequences of guilty pleas in criminal court," and to enter " 'safe harbor' guilty pleas [that] do not expose the [alien defendant] to the risk of immigration sanctions." Koh, *supra,* at 307. *See* Das, *supra,* at 1737–1738.[5]

The categorical approach has been applied routinely to assess whether a state drug conviction triggers removal under the immigration statute. As originally enacted, the removal statute specifically listed

---

[4] A version of this approach, known as the "modified categorical approach," applies to "state statutes that contain several different crimes, each described separately." *Moncrieffe v. Holder,* 133 S.Ct. 1678, 1684 (2013). In such cases, "a court may determine which particular offense the noncitizen was convicted of by examining the charging document and jury instructions, or in the case of a guilty plea, the plea agreement, plea colloquy, or some comparable judicial record of the factual basis for the plea." *Ibid.* Off limits to the adjudicator, however, is any inquiry into the particular facts of the case. Because the Government has not argued that this case falls within the compass of the modified-categorical approach, we need not reach the issue.

[5] Mellouli's plea may be an example. In admitting only paraphernalia possession, Mellouli avoided any identification, in the record of conviction, of the federally controlled substance (Adderall) his sock contained.

covered offenses and covered substances. It made deportable, for example, any alien convicted of "import[ing]," "buy[ing]," or "sell[ing]" any "narcotic drug," defined as "opium, coca leaves, cocaine, or any salt, derivative, or preparation of opium or coca leaves, or cocaine." Ch. 202, 42 Stat. 596–597. Over time, Congress amended the statute to include additional offenses and additional narcotic drugs. Ultimately, the Anti-Drug Abuse Act of 1986 replaced the increasingly long list of controlled substances with the now familiar reference to "a controlled substance (as defined in [§ 802])." In interpreting successive versions of the removal statute, the BIA inquired whether the state statute under which the alien was convicted covered federally controlled substances and not others.

Matter of Paulus, 11 I. & N. Dec. 274 (1965), is illustrative. At the time the BIA decided *Paulus,* the immigration statute made deportable any alien who had been "convicted of a violation of . . . any law or regulation relating to the illicit possession of or traffic in narcotic drugs or marihuana." California controlled certain "narcotics," such as peyote, not listed as "narcotic drugs" under federal law. The BIA concluded that an alien's California conviction for offering to sell an unidentified "narcotic" was not a deportable offense, for it was possible that the conviction involved a substance, such as peyote, controlled only under California law. Because the alien's conviction was not necessarily predicated upon a federally controlled "narcotic drug," the BIA concluded that the conviction did not establish the alien's deportability.

Under the *Paulus* analysis, * * * Mellouli would not be deportable. Mellouli pleaded guilty to concealing unnamed pills in his sock. At the time of Mellouli's conviction, Kansas' schedules of controlled substances included at least nine substances—*e.g.,* salvia and jimson weed—not defined in § 802. The state law involved in Mellouli's conviction, therefore, like the California statute in *Paulus,* was not confined to federally controlled substances; it required no proof by the prosecutor that Mellouli used his sock to conceal a substance listed under § 802, as opposed to a substance controlled only under Kansas law. Under the categorical approach applied in *Paulus,* Mellouli's drug-paraphernalia conviction does not render him deportable. In short, the state law under which he was charged categorically "relat[ed] to a controlled substance," but was not limited to substances "defined in [§ 802]."[9]

* * * Denying Mellouli's petition for review, the Eighth Circuit deferred to the BIA's decision in [*Matter of Martinez Espinoza,* 25 I & N Dec. 118 (2009)], and held that a Kansas paraphernalia conviction

---

[9]   The dissent maintains that it is simply following "the statutory text." It is evident, however, that the dissent shrinks to the vanishing point the words "as defined in [§ 802]." If § 237(a)(2)(B)(i) stopped with the words "relating to a controlled substance," the dissent would make sense. But Congress did not stop there. It qualified "relating to a controlled substance" by adding the limitation "as defined in [§ 802]." If those words do not confine § 237(a)(2)(B)(i)'s application to drugs defined in § 802, one can only wonder why Congress put them there.

"'relates to' a federal controlled substance because it is a crime . . . 'associated with the drug trade in general.'" 719 F.3d, at 1000.

The disparate approach to state drug convictions, devised by the BIA and applied by the Eighth Circuit, finds no home in the text of § 237(a)(2)(B)(i). The approach, moreover, "leads to consequences Congress could not have intended." *Moncrieffe,* 133 S.Ct., at 1690. * * * Drug possession and distribution convictions trigger removal only if they necessarily involve a federally controlled substance, *see Paulus,* 11 I & N Dec. 274, while convictions for paraphernalia possession, an offense less grave than drug possession and distribution, trigger removal whether or not they necessarily implicate a federally controlled substance, see *Martinez Espinoza,* 25 I & N Dec. 118. The incongruous upshot is that an alien is *not* removable for *possessing* a substance controlled only under Kansas law, but he *is* removable for using a sock to contain that substance. Because it makes scant sense, the BIA's interpretation, we hold, is owed no deference under the doctrine described in *Chevron U.S.A. Inc. v. Natural Resources Defense Council, Inc.,* 467 U.S. 837, 843, 104 S.Ct. 2778, 81 L.Ed.2d 694 (1984).

III

Offering an addition to the BIA's rationale, the Eighth Circuit reasoned that a state paraphernalia possession conviction categorically relates to a federally controlled substance so long as there is "nearly a complete overlap" between the drugs controlled under state and federal law. The Eighth Circuit's analysis, however, scarcely explains or ameliorates the BIA's anomalous separation of paraphernalia possession offenses from drug possession and distribution offenses.

Apparently recognizing this problem, the Government urges, as does the dissent, that the overlap between state and federal drug schedules supports the removal of aliens convicted of *any* drug crime, not just paraphernalia offenses. * * * As this case illustrates, however, the Government's construction of the federal removal statute stretches to the breaking point, reaching state-court convictions, like Mellouli's, in which "[no] controlled substance (as defined in [§ 802])" figures as an element of the offense. * * *

The historical background of § 237(a)(2)(B)(i) demonstrates that Congress and the BIA have long required a direct link between an alien's crime of conviction and a particular federally controlled drug. The Government's position here severs that link by authorizing deportation any time the state statute of conviction bears some general relation to federally controlled drugs. * * *

In sum, construction of § 237(a)(2)(B)(i) must be faithful to the text, which limits the meaning of "controlled substance," for removal purposes, to the substances controlled under § 802. * * * [T]o trigger removal under

§ 237(a)(2)(B)(i), the Government must connect an element of the alien's conviction to a drug "defined in [§ 802]."

* * * For the reasons stated, the judgment of the U.S. Court of Appeals for the Eighth Circuit is reversed.

Justice THOMAS, with whom Justice ALITO joins, dissenting.

* * * Because the statute renders an alien removable whenever he is convicted of violating a law "relating to" a federally controlled substance, I would affirm.

I

With one exception not applicable here, § 237(a)(2)(B)(i) makes removable "[a]ny alien who at any time after admission has been convicted of a violation of (or a conspiracy or attempt to violate) any law or regulation of a State, the United States, or a foreign country relating to a controlled substance (as defined in section 802 of title 21)." * * * The critical question, which the majority does not directly answer, is what it means for a law or regulation to "relat[e] to a controlled substance (as defined in section 802 of title 21)." * * * [A] state law regulating various controlled substances may "relat[e] to a controlled substance (as defined in section 802 of title 21)" even if the statute also controls a few substances that do not fall within the federal definition. * * *

* * *

True, approximately three percent of the substances appearing on Kansas' lists of "controlled substances" at the time of Mellouli's conviction did not fall within the federal definition, meaning that an individual convicted of possessing paraphernalia may never have used his paraphernalia with a federally controlled substance. But that fact does not destroy the relationship between the *law* and federally controlled substances. * * *

* * *

* * * True, faithfully applying [the statutory] text means that an alien may be deported for committing an offense that does not involve a federally controlled substance. Nothing about that consequence, however, is so outlandish as to call this application into doubt. An alien may be removed only if he is convicted of violating a law, and I see nothing absurd about removing individuals who are unwilling to respect the drug laws of the jurisdiction in which they find themselves.

The majority thinks differently, rejecting the only plausible reading of this provision and adopting an interpretation that finds no purchase in the text. I fail to understand why it chooses to do so, apart from a gut instinct that an educated professional engaged to an American citizen should not be removed for concealing unspecified orange tablets in his sock. Or perhaps the majority just disapproves of the fact that Kansas, exercising its police powers, has decided to criminalize conduct that Congress, exercising its limited powers, has decided not to criminalize. Either way, that is not how we should go about interpreting statutes, and I respectfully dissent.

NOTES AND QUESTIONS ON MELLOULI

1. As a review of the "conviction" element in crime-related deportability grounds, why was Mellouli's sentence a "conviction" under the INA?

2. *Mellouli* represents a strict application of the categorical approach. Using Mellouli's paraphernalia offense, check your understanding of how the categorical approach operates to limit the potential breadth of the drug-related deportability ground at issue:

    a. Suppose Kansas' list of controlled substances exactly mirrored the federal controlled substances list. Explain why under the categorical approach the case might have turned out differently.

    b. Suppose all of the substances on Kansas's controlled substance list are also on the federal controlled substance list, and that the federal list contained nine substances that Kansas's list does not. Explain why the analysis of this scenario is the same as in part (a) of this Question.

3. Applying a strict categorical approach allowed the majority to turn a blind eye to Mellouli's admission that the orange tablets in his sock were Adderall, a controlled substance on both the federal and state lists. The dissent took issue with the majority's interpretation of the deportability provision to require a "*direct link* between an alien's crime of conviction and a particular federally controlled drug," which rendered Mellouli's paraphernalia conviction a non-deportable offense.

Is the dissent right? Does *Mellouli* undermine efforts to stem the drug trade, including initiatives to curb trade in illicit pharmaceuticals? *See, e.g.,* National Methamphetamine & Pharmaceuticals Initiative, https://www.white house.gov/ondcp/hidta-initiatives. Or is it an example of the Court's implicit use of the rule of lenity to interpret the deportability grounds in a noncitizen's favor? *See Fong Haw Tan v. Phelan,* 333 U.S. 6, 9–10, 68 S.Ct. 374, 92 L.Ed. 433 (1948) (establishing that ambiguities in deportation statutes should be construed in a noncitizen's favor).

4. Section 237(a)(2)(B)(i) refers to other provisions of federal law to define "controlled substance." *See* 21 U.S.C. §§ 802, 811–812. Under 21 U.S.C. § 811, the Attorney General can add or remove drugs or substances from the "controlled substance" lists. If the Attorney General adds another item, how will an individual have notice that the deportability ground has expanded?

Section 237(a)(2)(B)(ii) raises a similar issue by rendering deportable any noncitizen drug abuser and addict. The provision applies to those who currently fall into these categories or who did at any time after admission, even if they no longer do. The statute does not define "drug abuser" or "addict." How can immigration authorities decide what constitutes drug abuse? Is an abuser of alcohol a drug abuser? Would this scheme survive a challenge that it fails to provide adequate notice, or that it is void for vagueness?

5.   Perhaps *Mellouli* is a way of enforcing *Padilla*'s suggestion that the criminal plea negotiation can function to avoid deportation consequences of a criminal conviction. *See Padilla v. Kentucky*, 559 U.S. 356, 373, 130 S. Ct. 1473, 1486, 176 L. Ed. 2d 284 (2010):

> [Defense counsel] may be able to plea bargain creatively with the prosecutor in order to craft a conviction and sentence that reduce the likelihood of deportation, as by avoiding a conviction for an offense that automatically triggers the removal consequence. At the same time, the threat of deportation may provide the defendant with a powerful incentive to plead guilty to an offense that does not mandate that penalty in exchange for a dismissal of a charge that does.

Mellouli's plea bargain ensured that the controlled substance was not the basis of the conviction and that the name of the drug was not in the criminal complaint. If Mellouli's plea is the result of an agreement between defense counsel and prosecutor that achieved what *Padilla* envisioned—a guilty plea in exchange for a conviction that does not automatically trigger removal—immigration authorities arguably should not be able to undo the benefit to Mellouli of that bargain.

On the other hand, doesn't that turn the relationship between criminal law and immigration law on its head? Deferring to a plea bargain struck in order to avoid deportation consequences means that criminal justice actors, usually in state court, are making decisions about deportation. Isn't that the job of federal immigration officials and judges? Or should those with contemporaneous knowledge of the circumstances surrounding the conviction have a say in how severe the consequences of that conviction should be? *See United States v. Diaz Aguilar,* 2015 WL 4774507, 21 (E.D.N.Y. Aug. 14, 2015) (issuing as part of a criminal sentence a recommendation to the immigration judge against deportation).

NOTES AND QUESTIONS ON THE CATEGORICAL AND MODIFIED CATEGORICAL APPROACHES

1.   The troika of Supreme Court cases—*Moncrieffe, Descamps,* and *Mellouli*—put significant limits on classifying criminal convictions as deportability grounds. They severely restrict the circumstances in which a

judge may examine the underlying facts, and relegate the modified categorical approach to the role of sorting which offense within the statute of conviction may trigger deportability. Does this triad of cases run counter to Congress's intent to use the deportability grounds to combat crime?

2. The cases nevertheless retain some leeway under *Nijhawan* to inquire into the facts surrounding a crime under the "circumstance-specific" approach. Do deviations from the categorical approach raise concerns about arbitrariness (or unpredictability) in enforcement? Or do they raise due process concerns more generally, especially if the facts that may emerge to establish deportability in an immigration removal proceeding were not essential—and thus perhaps not seriously contested—in the prior criminal prosecution?

3. How, if at all, does *Padilla v. Kentucky* affect your answer to the preceding question? Does the possible reliance in an immigration proceeding on the various aspects of the file in a prior criminal case affect the meaning of "effective assistance of counsel"?

EXERCISE: CRIMINAL DEPORTABILITY GROUNDS

How should Congress define the criminal conduct that would justify a noncitizen's removal from the United States?

(A) On substance:

Should all of the crimes now in § 237(a)(2) make a noncitizen deportable? Is there other criminal activity you would add?

How much should Congress rely on a broad term like "crime involving moral turpitude," and how much on the kind of detailed listing in INA § 101(a)(43)'s aggravated felony provision?

How might a statute effectively address what information in the prior criminal proceeding may be used to decide deportability?

(B) On procedure:

Should Congress restore the judicial recommendation against deportation (JRAD) discussed in *Padilla*, p. 668 *supra*?

Should Congress go further and make criminal sentencing the exclusive venue for deciding the immigration law consequences of a conviction?[19]

---

[19] *See* Margaret H. Taylor & Ronald F. Wright, *The Sentencing Judge as Immigration Judge*, 51 Emory L.J. 1131 (2002).

e.   Defining "Aggravated Felony"

Our emphasis up to this point has been the fundamental issue of how to classify convictions. We now take a closer look at the definition of aggravated felony, which has been the question presented in several recent Supreme Court decisions. As explained earlier in this section, an aggravated felony conviction renders a noncitizen deportable, and also ineligible for asylum, cancellation of removal, and voluntary departure. Noncitizens with an aggravated felony conviction are also barred for life from re-entering the United States, unless they obtain consent to apply for readmission.

(i)   Crimes of Violence

The case below analyzes the portion of the aggravated felony definition that includes "crime of violence." Does a state DUI offense qualify as a crime of violence, if it requires only a showing of negligence in operating a motor vehicle or completely lacks a *mens rea* component?

LEOCAL V. ASHCROFT

Supreme Court of the United States, 2004.
543 U.S. 1, 125 S.Ct. 377, 160 L.Ed.2d 271.

• IS DUI – "crime of violence"

CHIEF JUSTICE REHNQUIST delivered the opinion of the Court.

* * *

1980
1987

• 2000

Petitioner immigrated to the United States in 1980 and became a lawful permanent resident in 1987. In January 2000, he was charged with two counts of DUI causing serious bodily injury under Fla. Stat. § 316.193(3)(c)(2), after he caused an accident resulting in injury to two people. He pleaded guilty to both counts and was sentenced to two and a half years in prison.

* * * Section 101(a)(43) of the INA defines "aggravated felony" to include, *inter alia*, "a crime of violence (as defined in section 16 of title 18, but not including a purely political offense) for which the term of imprisonment [is] at least one year." Title 18 U.S.C. § 16, in turn, defines the term "crime of violence" to mean:

> (a) an offense that has as an element the use, attempted use, or threatened use of physical force against the person or property of another, or
>
> (b) any other offense that is a felony and that, by its nature, involves a substantial risk that physical force against the person or property of another may be used in the course of committing the offense.

* * *

Florida Stat. § 316.193(3)(c)(2) makes it a third-degree felony for a person to operate a vehicle while under the influence and, "by reason of such operation, caus[e] . . . [s]erious bodily injury to another." The Florida statute, while it requires proof of causation of injury, does not require proof of any particular mental state. * * * The question here is whether § 16 can be interpreted to include such offenses.

* * * The plain text of § 16(a) states that an offense, to qualify as a crime of violence, must have "as an element the use, attempted use, or threatened use of physical force against the person or property of another." We do not deal here with an *attempted* or *threatened* use of force. Petitioner contends that his conviction did not require the "use" of force against another person because the most common employment of the word "use" connotes the *intentional* availment of force, which is not required under the Florida DUI statute. The Government counters that the "use" of force does not incorporate any *mens rea* component, and that petitioner's DUI conviction necessarily includes the use of force. To support its position, the Government dissects the meaning of the word "use," employing dictionaries, legislation, and our own case law in contending that a use of force may be negligent or even inadvertent.

Whether or not the word "use" alone supplies a *mens rea* element, the parties' primary focus on that word is too narrow. Particularly when interpreting a statute that features as elastic a word as "use," we construe language in its context and in light of the terms surrounding it. The critical aspect of § 16(a) is that a crime of violence is one involving the "use . . . of physical force *against the person or property of another*." (Emphasis added.) * * * The key phrase in § 16(a)—the "use . . . of physical force against the person or property of another"—most naturally suggests a higher degree of intent than negligent or merely accidental conduct. Petitioner's DUI offense therefore is not a crime of violence under § 16(a).

Neither is petitioner's DUI conviction a crime of violence under § 16(b). Section 16(b) sweeps more broadly than § 16(a), defining a crime of violence as including "any other offense that is a felony and that, by its nature, involves a substantial risk that physical force against the person or property of another may be used in the course of committing the offense." But § 16(b) does not thereby encompass all negligent misconduct, such as the negligent operation of a vehicle. It simply covers offenses that naturally involve a person acting in disregard of the risk that physical force might be used against another in committing an offense. The reckless disregard in § 16 relates *not* to the general conduct or to the possibility that harm will result from a person's conduct, but to the risk that the use of physical force against another might be required in committing a crime. * * *

Thus, while § 16(b) is broader than § 16(a) in the sense that physical force need not actually be applied, it contains the same formulation we found to be determinative in § 16(a): the use of physical force against the person or property of another. Accordingly, we must give the language in § 16(b) an identical construction, requiring a higher *mens rea* than the merely accidental or negligent conduct involved in a DUI offense. This is particularly true in light of § 16(b)'s requirement that the "substantial risk" be a risk of using physical force against another person "in the course of committing the offense." In no "ordinary or natural" sense can it be said that a person risks having to "use" physical force against another person in the course of operating a vehicle while intoxicated and causing injury.

In construing both parts of § 16, we cannot forget that we ultimately are determining the meaning of the term "crime of violence." The ordinary meaning of this term, combined with § 16's emphasis on the use of physical force against another person (or the risk of having to use such force in committing a crime), suggests a category of violent, active crimes that cannot be said naturally to include DUI offenses. * * *

Section 16 therefore cannot be read to include petitioner's conviction for DUI causing serious bodily injury under Florida law. * * *

This case does not present us with the question whether a state or federal offense that requires proof of the *reckless* use of force against a person or property of another qualifies as a crime of violence under 18 U.S.C. § 16. DUI statutes such as Florida's do not require any mental state with respect to the use of force against another person, thus reaching individuals who were negligent or less. Drunk driving is a nationwide problem, as evidenced by the efforts of legislatures to prohibit such conduct and impose appropriate penalties. But this fact does not warrant our shoehorning it into statutory sections where it does not fit. * * *

NOTES AND QUESTIONS ON CRIMES OF VIOLENCE

1.   *Leocal,* decided in 2004, applied a categorical approach to an aggravated felony provision, limiting its analysis to what the statute covers and not looking at the facts of the particular case. *Moncrieffe,* in 2013, approved this strict categorical approach as the general method for determining whether a state criminal conviction constitutes an aggravated felony. *Moncrieffe, supra,* at p. 692.

2.   Would the outcome of *Leocal* have differed if the government had chosen to charge a different deportability ground, such as a crime involving moral turpitude? The history of litigation around the question of whether DUIs are crimes of moral turpitude illustrates the convolutions that classifying crimes can create. In 1999, the BIA held that a DUI offense

punishing driving under the influence while knowing that driving was forbidden was a crime involving moral turpitude. *See Matter of Lopez Meza*, I & N Dec. 1188 (BIA 1999). Two years later, the BIA held in *Matter of Torres-Varela*, 23 I & N Dec. 78 (BIA 2001) (en banc), that driving under the influence with two prior DUI offenses was not a crime of moral turpitude because the Arizona statute of conviction did not require a culpable mental state. The Ninth Circuit held in *Hernandez-Martinez v. Ashcroft*, 329 F.3d 1117 (9th Cir. 2003), that driving under the influence is not a crime involving moral turpitude because the conviction was under an Arizona statute that is divisible and covers conduct that is not base, vile, or depraved. Six years later, however, the Ninth Circuit, applying the same statute as in *Hernandez-Martinez*, held that DUI *is* a crime involving moral turpitude by applying a modified categorical approach. *Marmolejo-Campos v. Holder*, 558 F.3d 903 (9th Cir. 2009).

3.   The *Leocal* Court concluded that the "crime of violence" definition in 18 U.S.C. § 16 was clear, but in a footnote added that it would have had to resolve any ambiguity in the noncitizen's favor:

> Although here we deal with § 16 in the deportation context, § 16 is a criminal statute, and it has both criminal and noncriminal applications. Because we must interpret the statute consistently, whether we encounter its application in a criminal or noncriminal context, the rule of lenity applies.

534 U.S. 1, 11 n.8. Both *Leocal* and *Fong Haw Tan*, p. 651, *supra*, involved a criminal statute relevant to an immigration case. Should the rule of lenity apply in an immigration case with no criminal law component?

4.   The Supreme Court has since taken up several issues that *Leocal* raised. We discuss one constitutional challenge in the section that follows. In addition, the Court explicitly left untouched the requirement that a "crime of violence" encompass "violent force" for purposes of the aggravated felony and domestic violence deportability grounds. *United States v. Castleman*, ___ U.S. ___, 134 S.Ct. 1405, 188 L.Ed.2d 426, n. 4 (2014). Finally, in *Kawashima v. Holder*, 565 U.S. ___, 132 S.Ct. 1166, 182 L.Ed.2d 1 (2012), the Court held that convictions under 26 U.S.C. § 7206(1) and (2) for filing, and aiding and abetting in filing, a false statement on a corporate tax return are aggravated felonies. That rendered the lawful permanent resident respondents subject to removal if a $10,000 statutory loss threshold was met. The Court also granted certiorari in *Torres v. Lynch* in June 2015. The issue is whether, using the categorical approach, a state offense constitutes an aggravated felony under INA § 101(a)(43), on the ground that the state offense is "described in" a specified federal statute, but the federal statute includes an interstate commerce element that the state offense lacks.

(ii) Constitutional Challenges

Do the rule of lenity and the clear statement rule, tools of statutory interpretation that require courts to construe statutes in favor of noncitizens, sufficiently guard against statutory overbreadth? Or is stronger medicine required to ensure that deportability grounds are sufficiently clear? In 2015, the Supreme Court struck down as unconstitutionally vague a sentencing enhancement provision for multiple convictions for a "violent felony," a residual clause that includes any felony that "involves conduct that presents a serious potential risk of physical injury to another." *See Johnson v. United States*, 576 U.S. ___, 135 S.Ct. 2551, 192 L.Ed.2d 569 (2015). *Johnson* raises the potential for similar "void for vagueness" challenges to deportability provisions, because the voided clause closely resembles a provision of the aggravated felony deportability ground that includes a "crime of violence," and is broader than the "crime of violence" provision in section 16(a) upheld in *Leocal.*

Since *Johnson*, several Courts of Appeals have concluded that the phrase "crime of violence" as defined in § 16(b) is void for vagueness. *Dimaya v. Lynch*, 803 F.3d 1110 (9th Cir. 2015); *United States v. Vivas-Ceja*, 808 F.3d 719 (7th Cir. 2015); *but see United States v. Taylor,* 814 F.3d 340 (6th Cir. 2016) (upholding a virtually identical statutory provision against a vagueness challenge in the death penalty context).

In *Dimaya,* the Ninth Circuit first determined that a vagueness challenge is available outside of criminal law in a civil removal proceeding, reasoning that:

> [A] necessary component of a non-citizen's right to due process of law is the prohibition on vague deportation statutes. Recently, the Supreme Court noted the need for "efficiency, fairness, and predictability in the administration of immigration law." *Mellouli v. Lynch,* 135 S.Ct. 1980, 1987, 192 L.Ed.2d 60 (2015). Vague immigration statutes significantly undermine these interests by impairing non-citizens' ability to "anticipate the immigration consequences of guilty pleas in criminal court." *Id.* (internal quotation marks omitted); *see also Padilla v. Kentucky,* 559 U.S. 356, 364, 130 S.Ct. 1473, 176 L.Ed.2d 284 (2010) ("[A]ccurate legal advice for noncitizens accused of crimes has never been more important" because "deportation is an integral part—indeed, sometimes the most important part—of the penalty that may be imposed on noncitizen defendants who plead guilty to specified crimes.")

Dimaya, 803 F.3d at 1114. The court then relied on *Johnson* to conclude that section 16(b) was unconstitutionally vague, after concluding that the statutory provision in *Johnson* was similar to section 16(b):

> In *Johnson,* the Supreme Court recognized two features of ACCA's residual clause that "conspire[d] to make it unconstitutionally vague." 135 S.Ct. at 2557. First, the Court

explained, the clause left "grave uncertainty" about "deciding what kind of conduct the 'ordinary case' of a crime involves." *Id.* That is, the provision "denie[d] fair notice to defendants and invite[d] arbitrary enforcement by judges" because it "tie[d] the judicial assessment of risk to a judicially imagined 'ordinary case' of a crime, not to real-world facts or statutory elements." *Id.* Second, the Court stated, ACCA's residual clause left "uncertainty about how much risk it takes for a crime to qualify as a violent felony." *Id.* at 2558. By combining these two indeterminate inquiries, the Court held, "the residual clause produces more unpredictability and arbitrariness than the Due Process Clause tolerates." *Id.* On that ground it held the residual clause void for vagueness. The Court's reasoning applies with equal force to the similar statutory language and identical mode of analysis used to define a crime of violence for purposes of the INA. The result is that because of the same combination of indeterminate inquiries, § 16(b) is subject to identical unpredictability and arbitrariness as ACCA's residual clause.

Id. at 1115.

These cases raise a larger question of whether other crime-based deportability grounds adequately warn noncitizens of what may make them deportable. But is that the right question? Addressing vagueness doctrine outside of immigration law, the U.S. Supreme Court has explained: "The more important aspect of vagueness doctrine 'is not actual notice, but the other principal element of the doctrine—the requirement that a legislature establish minimal guidelines to govern law enforcement.'" *Kolender v. Lawson*, 461 U.S. 352, 358, 103 S.Ct. 1855, 1858, 75 L.Ed.2d 903 (1983), *quoting Smith v. Goguen*, 415 U.S. 566, 574, 94 S.Ct. 1242, 1247, 39 L.Ed.2d 605 (1974). From this perspective, and given the decades of case law under the categorical approach that had placed specific offenses in or out of the CIMT characterization, it is unsurprising that the Court has rejected a "void for vagueness" challenge to the statutory phrase "crime involving moral turpitude." *Jordan v. DeGeorge*, 341 U.S. 223, 71 S.Ct. 703, 95 L.Ed. 886 (1951). Moreover, the cases invalidating 18 U.S.C. § 16(b)'s definition of crime of violence do not address the constitutionality of § 16(a), the provision at issue in *Leocal*.

Why isn't the case law on crime of violence just as susceptible as CIMTs to clarification through case law, especially administrative decisions (that are accessible even if formally unpublished)?

(iii) State Felonies That Are Federal Misdemeanors

State offenses may be aggravated felonies under INA § 101(a)(43), yet some states may criminalize behavior that other states do not, or one state may punish as a felony what other states call a misdemeanor. These disparities may make noncitizens deportable for acts in one state that would not have the same consequence if committed in another.

Moncrieffe declared that "a state offense constitutes a 'felony punishable under the Controlled Substances Act' [and therefore an aggravated felony] only if it proscribes conduct punishable as a felony under that federal law" (citing *Lopez v. Gonzales*, 549 U.S. 47, 60, 127 S.Ct. 625, 166 L.Ed.2d 462 (2006)). Requiring that the state offense proscribe conduct punishable as a felony under federal law puts a premium on uniformity. Does it do so, however, at the cost of devaluing federalism? Jurisdictions have different criminal laws, and individuals can live where they agree with those judgments. Federalism counsels that a jurisdiction's residents should follow its norms of behavior even if another state or the federal government adopts different norms.

One counter might be that even if such considerations support differing degrees of criminal punishment, federal immigration law should adopt a national standard on the level of offensiveness of criminal conduct that warrants removal from the United States. This rationale resonated with the Court in *Lopez*:

> [T]he Government's reading would render the law of alien removal, and the law of sentencing for illegal entry into the country, dependent on varying state criminal classifications even when Congress has apparently pegged the immigration statutes to the classifications Congress itself chose. It may not be all that remarkable that federal consequences of state crimes will vary according to state severity classification when Congress describes an aggravated felony in generic terms, without express reference to the definition of a crime in a federal statute (as in the case of "illicit trafficking in a controlled substance"). But * * * [w]e cannot imagine that Congress took the trouble to incorporate its own statutory scheme of felonies and misdemeanors if it meant courts to ignore it whenever a State chose to punish a given act more heavily.

Lopez, 549 U.S. at 58.

Lopez held that only a crime that is punishable as a federal felony can be an aggravated felony under INA § 101(a)(43)(B), which expressly refers to federal law in defining "illicit trafficking in a controlled substance" as an aggravated felony. *Lopez* left open the meaning of "punishable as a federal felony," as the next case explains.

CARACHURI-ROSENDO V. HOLDER

Supreme Court of the United States, 2010.
560 U.S. 563, 130 S.Ct. 2577, 177 L.Ed.2d 68.

JUSTICE STEVENS delivered the opinion of the Court.

Petitioner Jose Angel Carachuri-Rosendo, a lawful permanent resident who has lived in the United States since he was five years old, faced deportation under federal law after he committed two misdemeanor drug possession offenses in Texas. For the first, possession of less than two ounces of marijuana, he received 20 days in jail. For the second, possession without a prescription of one tablet of a common antianxiety medication, he received 10 days in jail. After this second offense, the Federal Government initiated removal proceedings against him. He conceded that he was removable, but claimed he was eligible for discretionary relief from removal under INA § 240A(a).

To decide whether Carachuri-Rosendo is eligible to seek cancellation of removal or waiver of inadmissibility under § 240A(a), we must decide whether he has been convicted of an "aggravated felony," a category of crimes singled out for the harshest deportation consequences. * * *

Under the Immigration and Nationality Act (INA), a lawful permanent resident subject to removal from the United States may apply for discretionary cancellation of removal if, *inter alia,* he "has not been convicted of any aggravated felony," § 240A(a)(3). The statutory definition of the term "aggravated felony" includes a list of numerous federal offenses, one of which is "illicit trafficking in a controlled substance . . . including a drug trafficking crime (as defined in section 924(c) of title 18)." § 101(a)(43)(B). Section 924(c)(2), in turn, defines a "drug trafficking crime" to mean "any felony punishable under," *inter alia,* "the Controlled Substances Act (21 U.S.C. 801 et seq.)." A felony is a crime for which the "maximum term of imprisonment authorized" is "more than one year." 18 U.S.C. § 3559(a).

* * * Except for simple possession of crack cocaine or flunitrazepam, a first-time simple possession offense is a federal misdemeanor; the maximum term authorized for such a conviction is less than one year. However, a conviction for a simple possession offense "after a prior conviction under this subchapter [or] under the law of any State . . . has become final"—what we will call recidivist simple possession—may be punished as a felony, with a prison sentence of up to two years. Thus, except for simple possession offenses involving isolated categories of drugs not presently at issue, only *recidivist* simple possession offenses are "punishable" as a federal "felony" under the Controlled Substances Act. And thus only a conviction within this particular category of simple possession offenses might, conceivably, be an "aggravated felony" under INA § 101(a)(43).

For a subsequent simple possession offense to be eligible for an enhanced punishment, *i.e.,* to be punishable as a felony, the Controlled Substances Act requires that a prosecutor charge the existence of the prior simple possession conviction before trial, or before a guilty plea. Notice, plus an opportunity to challenge the validity of the prior conviction used to enhance the current conviction are mandatory prerequisites to obtaining a punishment based on the fact of a prior conviction. And they are also necessary prerequisites under federal law to "authorize" a felony punishment, for the type of simple possession offense at issue in this case.

* * * [I]n *Lopez v. Gonzales,* 549 U.S. 47, 56, 127 S.Ct. 625, 166 L.Ed.2d 462 (2006), we determined that, in order to be an "aggravated felony" for immigration law purposes, a state drug conviction must be punishable as a felony under *federal* law. * * *

In the case before us, the Government argues that Carachuri-Rosendo, despite having received only a 10-day sentence for his Texas misdemeanor simple possession offense, nevertheless has been "convicted" of an "aggravated felony" within the meaning of the INA. This is so, the Government contends, because had Carachuri-Rosendo been prosecuted in federal court instead of state court, he *could have been* prosecuted as a felon and received a 2-year sentence based on the fact of his prior simple possession offense. * * *

* * *

* * * This type of petty simple possession offense is not typically thought of as an "aggravated felony" or as "illicit trafficking." * * *

The same is true for the type of penalty at issue. We do not usually think of a 10-day sentence for the unauthorized possession of a trivial amount of a prescription drug as an "aggravated felony." A "felony," we have come to understand, is a "serious crime usu[ally] punishable by imprisonment for more than one year or by death." Black's Law Dictionary 694 (9th ed. 2009) (hereinafter Black's). An "aggravated" offense is one "made worse or more serious by circumstances such as violence, the presence of a deadly weapon, or the intent to commit another crime." *Id.,* at 75, 127 S.Ct. 625. The term "aggravated felony" is unique to Title 8, which covers immigration matters; it is not a term used elsewhere within the United States Code. * * *

* * *

The Government's position, like the Court of Appeals' "hypothetical approach," would treat all "conduct punishable as a felony" as the equivalent of a "conviction" of a felony whenever, hypothetically speaking, the underlying conduct could have received felony treatment under federal law. We find this reasoning—and the "hypothetical approach" itself—unpersuasive for the following reasons.

First, and most fundamentally, the Government's position ignores the text of the INA, which limits the Attorney General's cancellation power only when, *inter alia,* a noncitizen "has . . . been *convicted* of a[n] aggravated felony." INA § 240A(a)(3) (emphasis added). The text thus indicates that we are to look to the conviction itself as our starting place, not to what might have or could have been charged. * * *

* * * Although a federal immigration court may have the power to make a recidivist finding in the first instance, it cannot, *ex post,* enhance the state offense of record just because facts known to it would have authorized a greater penalty under either state or federal law. Carachuri-Rosendo was not actually "convicted," § 240A(a)(3), of a drug possession offense committed "after a prior conviction . . . has become final," § 844(a), and no subsequent development can undo that history.

* * *

Second, and relatedly, the Government's position fails to give effect to the mandatory notice and process requirements contained in 21 U.S.C. § 851. For federal law purposes, a simple possession offense is not "punishable" as a felony unless a federal prosecutor first elects to charge a defendant as a recidivist in the criminal information. The statute * * * speaks in mandatory terms, permitting "[n]o person" to be subject to a recidivist enhancement—and therefore, in this case, a felony sentence— "unless" he has been given notice of the Government's intent to prove the fact of a prior conviction [and] an opportunity to challenge the fact of the prior conviction itself. The Government would dismiss these procedures as meaningless, so long as they may be satisfied during the immigration proceeding.

But these procedural requirements have great practical significance with respect to the conviction itself and are integral to the structure and design of our drug laws. They authorize prosecutors to exercise discretion when electing whether to pursue a recidivist enhancement. * * *

* * *

Third, the Court of Appeals' hypothetical felony approach is based on a misreading of our decision in *Lopez*. . . . [T]he "hypothetical approach" employed by the Court of Appeals introduces a level of conjecture at the outset of this inquiry that has no basis in *Lopez*. * * *

Fourth, it * * * is quite unlikely that the "conduct" that gave rise to Carachuri-Rosendo's conviction would have been punished as a felony in federal court. Under the United States Sentencing Guidelines, Carachuri-Rosendo's recommended sentence, based on the type of controlled substance at issue, would not have exceeded one year and very likely would have been less than 6 months. * * *

Finally, as we noted in *Leocal v. Ashcroft,* 543 U.S. 1, 11 n.8, 125 S.Ct. 377, 160 L.Ed.2d 271 (2004), ambiguities in criminal statutes referenced in immigration laws should be construed in the noncitizen's favor. * * *

* * *

In sum, the Government is correct that to qualify as an "aggravated felony" under the INA, the conduct prohibited by state law must be punishable as a felony under federal law. But as the text and structure of the relevant statutory provisions demonstrate, the defendant must *also* have been *actually convicted* of a crime that is itself punishable as a felony under federal law. The mere possibility that the defendant's conduct, coupled with facts outside of the record of conviction, could have authorized a felony conviction under federal law is insufficient to satisfy the statutory command that a noncitizen be "convicted of a[n] aggravated felony" before he loses the opportunity to seek cancellation of removal. INA § 240A(a)(3). * * *

* * *

[The concurring opinions of JUSTICE SCALIA and JUSTICE THOMAS are omitted.]

(iv) State Misdemeanors as Aggravated Felonies

Lopez tells us that a state felony is not an aggravated felony under INA § 101(a)(43)(B)—which defines "illicit trafficking in a controlled substance" by referring to another federal statute—when the corresponding federal offense is a misdemeanor. But can a state misdemeanor be an aggravated felony? Many states define as a misdemeanor any criminal offense for which the sentence is one year or less. For example, New York classifies certain assaults as misdemeanors with a maximum one-year prison term. *See, e.g.,* N.Y. Penal Code, §§ 120.00, 70.15. Would such an assault be an aggravated felony under INA § 101(a)(43)(F) because it is "a crime of violence * * * for which the term of imprisonment [is] at least one year"?

What about a guilty plea by a nineteen-year-old lawful permanent resident to a misdemeanor charge based on sexual intercourse with a fifteen-year-old female? Is this a conviction for the aggravated felony of sexual abuse of a minor, which would make the permanent resident ineligible for cancellation of removal under INA § 240A? Faced with these facts, the Seventh Circuit reasoned:

> * * * Congress decided to broaden INA § 101(a)(43)(A) from just murder to include rape and sexual abuse of a minor,

implicitly signaling that it felt both of these latter two crimes were of similar severity and import. Murder and rape are widely recognized as felony crimes. Thus, grouping sexual abuse of a minor with these two acts, without explicitly limiting sexual abuse of a minor to the status of a misdemeanor, is a fairly strong indication, albeit a limited one because of the lack of definite legislative commentary on the subject, that Congress intended both misdemeanor and felony convictions for sexual abuse of a minor to be considered aggravated felonies.

* * * [R]ather than leave the question of what constitutes an aggravated felony open-ended, Congress said, "The term 'aggravated felony' means— . . ." and proceeded to list what crimes would be considered aggravated felonies. It is important to note that the term aggravated felony is placed within quotation marks and Congress then used the word "means" after this term. What is evident from the setting aside of aggravated felony with quotation marks and the use of the term "means" is that INA § 101(a)(43) serves as a definition section. * * * Congress had the discretion to use whatever term it pleased and define the term as it deemed appropriate. The statute functions like a dictionary, in that it provides us with Congress' definition of the term "aggravated felony." There is no explicit provision in the statute directing that the term "aggravated felony" is limited only to felony crimes. We therefore are constrained to conclude that Congress, since it did not specifically articulate that aggravated felonies cannot be misdemeanors, intended to have the term aggravated felony apply to the broad range of crimes listed in the statute, even if these include misdemeanors.

Guerrero-Perez v. INS, 242 F.3d 727, 736–37 (7th Cir. 2001). The BIA ultimately acceded to the Seventh Circuit's view in *Matter of Small*, 23 I & N Dec. 448 (BIA 2002), applying the rule nationwide.

C. RELIEF FROM REMOVAL

1. OVERVIEW

In most removal proceedings, the noncitizen does not seriously challenge removability. Instead, the major issue to be contested is usually an application for relief from removal. For example, DHS records can prove an overstay violation. Proof of identity and alienage, plus a certification of the lack of a DHS record of valid admission, can establish entry without inspection. Criminal grounds of inadmissibility or deportability can be based on the record of conviction, which generally cannot be attacked collaterally in immigration court. Noncitizens often concede removability at the outset of the hearing and then request one or more forms of relief.

The longer a noncitizen has lived in the United States—with or without authorization—the greater the ties she is likely to have established and the greater the hardship that removal will entail. The burdens do not fall solely on the noncitizen: family and friends may be deprived of significant personal relationships, employers may lose productive employees, and neighborhoods may lose valued residents. Not surprisingly, then, a number of avenues of relief are available to noncitizens, especially those who have lived in the United States for a substantial period of time and have close relatives who are U.S. citizens or permanent residents.

One of us has observed that the availability of relief influences public perceptions about the legitimacy of the immigration enforcement system as a whole:

> Resolute enforcement is important, but it must also be prudent. * * * There is a good case to be made for the law's imposition of measured prohibitions on free migration, in the nation-state-dominated world order we inhabit. But because ordinary immigration violations—entries without inspection and overstaying of temporary admissions—are not regarded as inherently evil, particularly when the press focuses on individually sympathetic cases, the system needs a carefully designed statutory capacity to soften the harshest edges of enforcement. That capacity helps over time to build or sustain public faith in the overall justice and proportionality of the system.

David A. Martin, *Resolute Enforcement is Not Just for Restrictionists: Building a Stable and Efficient Immigration Enforcement System*, 30 J.L. & Pol. 411, 458 (2015).

a. The Origins of Relief: Private Bills

Because of its historical significance, we begin with the private bill, one of the original forms of relief. In earlier periods of federal immigration law—unlike today—private bills were the primary form of relief from deportation. They were enacted in order to create humanitarian flexibility in a law that, if applied as written, would have produced harsh results.

Private bills frequently were the forerunners of significant legislative amendments. A flood of private bill requests in the 1930s inspired Congress to make the first in a series of broad delegations to the Executive Branch to grant deportation relief in meritorious cases. *See*

Alien Registration Act of 1940, Pub. L. 76–670, 54 Stat. 670, 672. Here is another example:

> Before the Immigration and Nationality Act accorded "nonquota" status to spouses of American citizens irrespective of their ancestry, Asian spouses of American citizens were subject to quota restrictions. The stationing of American servicemen in the Far East and the resulting marriages between American citizens and alien spouses of Asian ancestry led to the introduction and passage of a considerable number of private bills according the individual Asian spouse "nonquota" status. The increasing volume of this type of private bills led eventually to public legislation giving "nonquota" status to the spouses of American servicemen irrespective of their ancestry and later led to the provision in the Immigration and Nationality Act which placed alien spouses of all American citizens on equal footing irrespective of race.

Elizabeth J. Harper, *et al.*, Immigration Laws of the United States 657–59 (1975). Today, when there is no other way to prevent removal, relief may still possible through federal legislation granting permanent resident status to one specific individual, but it is rare. In recent years, private bills have been enacted in a tiny number of cases. *See* Margaret Mikyung Lee, *Private Immigration Legislation*, Congressional Research Service Report to Congress (2007). As of early 2016, only two private bills have been signed into law since 2005. *See Congress Passes Two Private Immigration Relief Bills*, 87 Interp. Rel. 2414 (2010).

One reason for the decline is that mere introduction of a private bill no longer automatically guarantees, as in earlier decades, a stay of removal for a considerable period irrespective of the private bill's ultimate chance for passage. Now, after introduction of a private bill, a stay of removal occurs only if the House or Senate Judiciary Committee asks the executive branch for a report on the noncitizen, and Committee rules impose high procedural barriers before such a request can be issued. If that happens, the immigration agencies will generally authorize a stay of removal. *See* Anna Gallagher, *Remedies of Last Resort: Private Bills and Pardons*, 06–02 Immigr. Briefings (2006); Rules of Procedure and Statement of Policy for Private Immigration Bills, H. Comm. on the Judiciary, Subcomm. on Immigr. and Border Security (April 22, 2015) (identifying multiple procedural bars to the consideration of private bills).

b. Statutory Eligibility and Executive Discretion

Most forms of relief rooted in the statute have two key components: (1) statutory eligibility criteria that form the threshold for a grant of relief by the agency, and (2) a favorable exercise of discretion, after the threshold criteria are met, to determine whether to grant or deny the specific relief.

This chapter divides relief into four parts. It first canvasses the statutory eligibility requirements for the main forms of relief. Then, assuming that a noncitizen meets those threshold criteria, it examines the exercise of discretion in granting or denying relief. It then takes up statutory schemes that have broadened the availability of relief for victims of violence and crime. The section closes with an examination of prosecutorial discretion, which allows noncitizens to avoid expulsion and often to get work authorization, but without durable formal lawful immigration status.

As you study these materials on relief, ask yourself whether the system provides the proper level of relief from removal. What policies and goals have led to the development of these avenues for some noncitizens to avoid expulsion? Should agency officials or immigration judges have more discretion to confer relief in individual cases, or will more generous relief invite higher levels of immigration law violation? Is there a better way to organize and define these provisions? We will return to these fundamental questions later in this section.

2. STATUTORY ELIGIBILITY FOR RELIEF

This section examines the threshold statutory requirements that a noncitizen must meet to be eligible for a particular form of relief. As we will discuss in subsection 3, at that point the agency must still decide whether to exercise discretion to grant the requested relief.

We start with the eligibility criteria for forms of relief that are most desirable from the noncitizen's perspective because they retain—or lead to—lawful permanent resident status. Next are types of relief from removal that do not confer permanent resident status and typically do not eliminate the underlying deportability ground. (We defer until Chapter Eight our consideration of relief from removal based on protection from persecution and torture.)

a. An Overview of Cancellation of Removal

Section 240A of the INA allows noncitizens, through a mechanism called cancellation of removal, to regularize their status as lawful permanent residents of the United States, in spite of their removability. This version of relief for permanent residents was enacted in 1996, but it has precursors that date back to the early 1900s.

One recent precursor is relief under § 212(c). Before 1996, lawful permanent residents could seek what was known as "§ 212(c) relief." If they had seven years of lawful domicile in the United States, permanent residents who were deportable—typically due to criminal convictions—

could show countervailing equities to the immigration judge to ask for relief from deportation. *See Francis v. INS,* 532 F.2d 268 (2d Cir.1976); *see generally* T. Alexander Aleinikoff, David A. Martin & Hiroshi Motomura, Immigration: Process and Policy 689–714 (3d ed. 1995). Relief under § 212(c) still can be invoked by some noncitizens convicted before April 1997. *See INS v. St. Cyr,* 533 U.S. 289, 121 S.Ct. 2271, 150 L.Ed.2d 347 (2001) (holding that § 212(c) remains available to noncitizens who pled guilty before April 1, 1997, even if their removal proceedings began after that date).

Under § 240A, the Attorney General—typically acting through an immigration judge—may cancel the removal of a noncitizen and allow the noncitizen to remain as a permanent resident. There are two separate channels of cancellation. For noncitizens who are already permanent residents, cancellation maintains that status in spite of their removability (usually due to a criminal conviction). Cancellation of removal confers permanent resident status for the first time on noncitizens who entered without inspection or who were admitted as nonimmigrants. For all noncitizens, cancellation of removal effectively erases the prior personal history for removability purposes, though that history may still impair naturalization eligibility.[20]

b. Cancellation of Removal for Permanent Residents

If lawful permanent residents who are either inadmissible or deportable satisfy certain statutory prerequisites, § 240A(a) provides that the Attorney General *may* cancel their removal.

Eligibility for § 240A(a) cancellation for lawful permanent residents has two requirements concerned with time. A noncitizen must have (1) resided in the United States continuously for seven years after lawful admission, and (2) been a lawful permanent resident for at least five years. Individuals who have resided continuously in the United States since admission as a permanent resident seven or more years ago would satisfy both elements. So, too, would someone who has resided continuously in the United States since being admitted as a student seven years ago, adjusting to permanent resident status at least five years ago. For members of the military, the continuous residence requirement may not apply, *see* INA § 240A(d)(3).

Calculating the time period is pivotal for many applicants. Until 1996, time during deportation and exclusion proceedings counted toward the requirement. Now, the service of a notice to appear (NTA) in a

---

[20] Another form of relief from removal is adjustment of status, which a noncitizen can invoke in immigration court proceedings. We considered adjustment in Chapter Six on admission procedures, because adjustment is sought most typically not defensively by noncitizens in removal proceedings, but rather affirmatively by noncitizens as a way of gaining permanent resident status without traveling abroad to obtain an immigrant visa at a U.S. consulate.

stop-1

removal proceeding stops the accrual of continuous residence, applying what is often called the stop-time rule in § 240A(d)(1)(A). (Prosecutorial discretion in the form of "repapering" may be exercised to cancel a notice to appear and then reissue it after the required time has accrued, but repapering is entirely within the discretion of DHS.)

The stop-time rule also applies "when the alien has committed an offense referred to in section 212(a)(2) that renders the alien inadmissible to the United States under section 212(a)(2) or removable from the United States under section 237(a)(2) or (4)." INA § 240A(d)(1)(B).

> ### *PROBLEMS ON QUALIFYING TIME PERIODS*
>
> Try applying the statutory provisions on residence and the accrual of time to the following situations.
>
> 1.   J lawfully entered the United States as a nonimmigrant employee of the United Nations exactly eight years ago. Exactly three years later, she became a permanent resident. One month ago, she was served a notice to appear in a removal proceeding based on a deportability ground. (Assume that she committed no offense that under INA § 240A(d)(1)(B) would stop the accrual of qualifying time.) Is J eligible to apply for cancellation of removal?
>
> 2.   K was admitted as a lawful permanent resident eight years ago. Two years ago, she was charged with a crime involving moral turpitude, and two months thereafter she was convicted. Three months ago, K was served with a notice to appear in a removal proceeding. Is K eligible to apply for cancellation of removal?
>
> 3.   Now assume that the crime involving moral turpitude that K was charged with in the previous problem is within the petty offense exception of § 212(a)(2)(A)(ii)(II), making K deportable under § 237(a)(2), but not inadmissible under § 212(a)(2). When does the clock stop?

c.   Cancellation of Removal for Nonpermanent Residents

240A(b)

INA § 240A(b) outlines another form of cancellation of removal that is designed primarily to afford relief to noncitizens who have lived in the United States for an extended period, but who are not lawful permanent residents. An earlier version of this relief was known as "suspension of deportation," authorized by former INA § 244.

Cancellation of removal pursuant to § 240A(b) allows a noncitizen to become a lawful permanent resident. There is no requirement that the noncitizens have been admitted to the United States or that they be lawfully present, so unauthorized migrants may be eligible. Despite the provision's caption in the INA, which refers to nonpermanent residents, nothing bars permanent residents from seeking cancellation under

§ 240A(b). They may wish to do so if they are ineligible for § 240A(a) cancellation. The threshold requirements for this form of cancellation resemble those for cancellation for lawful permanent residents, but overall are much more demanding.

(i) Continuous Physical Presence

Ten years of continuous physical presence (not residence) is the minimum time period for § 240A(b) cancellation of removal. The INA does not define "presence," but § 240A(d) sets out two rules that determine if physical presence is "continuous." First, the stop-time rule in § 240A(d)(1) applies to the accrual of continuous physical presence under § 240A(b). In addition, accrual stops if the nonpermanent resident "departed from the United States for any period in excess of 90 days or for any periods in the aggregate exceeding 180 days." *See* § 240A(d)(2). For members of the military, the continuous physical presence requirement may not apply, *see* INA § 240A(d)(3).

PROBLEMS ON QUALIFYING TIME PERIODS

1.   L was admitted to the United States on a student visa twelve years ago, and became a permanent resident two years ago. She has returned home to France for the month of August every year since she first arrived as a student. Three months ago, L was served with a notice to appear (based on a deportability ground unrelated to any crime). Do the summer trips render L ineligible for cancellation of removal?

2.   M has been working without authorization since clandestinely crossing the border from Mexico twelve years ago. Seven years ago, she took a two-month trip to Mexico to visit her dying grandmother. Three months ago, M was served with a notice to appear based on being in the United States without admission or parole. Does the two-month trip make M ineligible for § 240A(b) cancellation?

(ii) Good Moral Character

Under INA § 240A(b)(1)(B), a noncitizen who applies for cancellation must have been of "good moral character" for ten years immediately preceding the date of application. INA § 101(f), which Chapter Two discussed in the naturalization context, lists some persons who are *not* of "good moral character" (such as anyone convicted of an aggravated felony), but it does not define what "good moral character" is. Unsurprisingly, criminal activities constitute the major grounds for finding that a person lacks good moral character.

(iii)   *Exceptional and Extremely Unusual Hardship*

For § 240A(b) cancellation, noncitizens must show that removal would result in "exceptional and extremely unusual hardship to the alien's spouse, parent, or child, who is a citizen of the United States or an alien lawfully admitted for permanent residence."

Is it sound policy to limit the class of qualifying relationships? The 1996 amendments eliminated a noncitizen's ability under prior law to meet the hardship requirement by showing hardship to herself. The statute also seems to preclude consideration of harm to extended family members (such as a grandparent or nephew) or to others for whom the noncitizen has acted like an immediate family member.

Does the specific list of individuals rule out an expansive reading of the language? In a pre-1996 suspension of deportation case, the Supreme Court held that the statute's plain meaning controls, declining to embrace an interpretation that would include an aunt as the "functional equivalent" of a "parent" for purposes of showing hardship to the child. The Court reasoned that "Congress has specifically identified the relatives whose hardship is to be considered, and then set forth unusually detailed and unyielding provisions defining each class of included relatives," precluding a functional approach to defining the term "child." *INS v. Hector,* 479 U.S. 85, 88, 90, 107 S.Ct. 379, 93 L.Ed.2d 326 (1986) (per curiam).

Despite the formal placement of "exceptional and extremely unusual hardship" within the eligibility requirements, courts generally consider the assessment of hardship in cancellation cases to be a discretionary determination beyond judicial review. *See Romero-Torres v. Ashcroft*, 327 F.3d 887, 889–92 (9th Cir. 2003). This hardship standard is discussed in detail in the section on discretion, *infra* at p. 733.

(iv) Numerical Limits on Cancellation

INA § 240A(e) caps—at 4000 per fiscal year—the number of persons who may be granted cancellation of removal under INA § 240A(b) (and suspension of deportation where the old rules apply). Looking at the statutory text, can you see why the cap does not apply to § 240A(a)?

The Executive Office for Immigration Review has a procedure for reserving decisions in cancellation cases when, as in 2010, the number of grants approaches the cap. *See* Randall Monger & James Yankay, U.S. Legal Permanent Residents: 2010, at 3, table 2 (DHS Office of Immigration Statistics 2011). Once 3,800 cases have been granted, immigration judges and the BIA are instructed to delay final decisions until October 1 of the following fiscal year, unless specifically authorized by EOIR to go ahead before then (so as to use all 4,000 of the year's spaces). *See Chief IJ O'Leary Issues Guidance on Handling Applications for Suspension or Cancellation when FY Numbers Used Up*, 88 Interp. Rel. 1302 (2011). The cap has been reached every year since 2010, each time earlier in the fiscal year, causing a growing backlog of cases with delayed cancellation determinations. *See* Margaret H. Taylor, *What Happened to Non-LPR Cancellation? Rationalizing Immigration Enforcement by Restoring Durable Relief from Removal*, 30 J.L. & Pol. 527 (2015).

Recall that applicants for § 240A(b) cancellation must establish that their removal would impose "exceptional and extremely unusual hardship" on certain U.S. citizen or permanent resident family members. Why would Congress cut off relief for persons who have met this very high hardship requirement and otherwise fully qualify for cancellation? Margaret Taylor recommends doing away with the cap altogether:

> Imposing an annual limit on those who may receive humanitarian relief from removal is, quite simply, a bad idea, particularly when the numerical limit is vastly disproportionate to the number of individuals who are eligible to apply. The cap does not depress the number of individuals who apply for relief each year and in no way impacts the number who can establish that they qualify. Instead, a statutory cap requires the administering agency to hold off granting the applications of deserving individuals, creating intolerable delays that keep these applicants in legal limbo. And * * * the work authorization provided to non-LPR cancellation applicants [while their applications are pending] can serve as a magnet to draw weak or unfounded cases into the severely backlogged immigration court system.

Id. at 548–49.

———————

Having worked through the basics of cancellation, now assess the following facts and identify any other relevant information that you need.

EXERCISE

Patricio Hernandez-Cordero and Maria Guadalupe Ortega de Hernandez are citizens of Mexico. The Hernandezes are married and have four children: Victor (age 14), Patricio, Jr. (7), Lisa (5), and Veronica (2). Victor is a Mexican citizen; the youngest three children are United States citizens. Twelve years ago, Mr. Hernandez entered the United States without inspection and has not left the country since. Seven years ago, Ms. Hernandez was lawfully admitted as a permanent resident. Two years after becoming a permanent resident, she returned to Mexico for four weeks, and three years after that, she took a trip to Mexico for five months.

Last month, Mr. and Ms. Hernandez were served with notices to appear (NTA). The NTA against Ms. Hernandez alleges that she helped a cousin enter the United States illegally six months ago. (She is not facing criminal charges.) The NTA against Mr. Hernandez states that he is present in the United States without being admitted or paroled.

DHS has stipulated that, but for the immigration violations, the couple is "industrious, law-abiding, and the type of people that anyone would desire as next-door neighbors." The family lives in Georgetown, Texas, where Mr. Hernandez built a home on a lot purchased six years ago. Mr. Hernandez is a self-employed carpenter, earning about $30,000 a year; he has, through hard work and thrift, accumulated assets having a value of approximately $125,000. These assets include the family's home, a car, Mr. Hernandez's tools, and another piece of unimproved real estate for which they have paid in full.

The Hernandezes say that they would suffer hardship if removed to Mexico based on the following considerations:

(1) They would be forced to sell their home at a loss.

(2) The family would lose economic self-sufficiency because Mr. Hernandez would be unable to find in Mexico the kind of work at the same rate of remuneration that he has obtained in the United States. The evidence of economic hardship is supported by an affidavit from an economist who specializes in Latin America.

(3) The four children speak Spanish, but they are currently enrolled in American schools, and none reads or writes Spanish. Three of the children have never visited or lived in Mexico. Six teachers have provided affidavits detailing the diminished educational opportunities available in Mexico and the serious emotional difficulty that the children would suffer if their parents were removed and they accompanied the family to Mexico.

(4) An affidavit from a licensed psychologist also concludes that the family would suffer severe emotional and psychological consequences if forced to return to Mexico.

(5) Lisa has a blood disorder that requires treatment every four months. The family has, so far, been unable to identify a hospital in Mexico that could provide the necessary treatments.

(6) The family would leave behind many friends and relatives, a number of whom are prepared to vouch for the honesty and decency of the family. For example, Dan Johnson, the vice president of the bank that financed construction of the Hernandez home, would testify that "Patricio Hernandez and his family would be an asset to any country in which they chose to live. He takes pride in his work, and his word is his bond." And

[handwritten top margin: Patricia 240A(b)]

[handwritten top margin: Maria – 240 A(a) – subject to discretion]

John Bryan, a ranch owner who employed both Mr. and Ms. Hernandez in the past, would state: "I have had continuous contact with the Hernandez family over the past decade. I consider them to be outstanding people who would be a great asset to American society. They are hard working, and persons of the highest moral caliber. They have assimilated themselves well into our society."

In response, DHS argues:

(1) Economic opportunities in Mexico may not be as favorable in Mexico as in the United States, but Mr. Hernandez is an able-bodied skilled craftsman. Also, mere economic hardship cannot constitute "exceptional and extremely unusual hardship" under the statute.

[handwritten right margin: not same opportunities but they'll figure it out]

(2) The hardships of loss of friends and schooling opportunities are real, but they are hardly exceptional or extreme. Such hardship is likely to attend the removal of any alien who has resided unlawfully in the United States for a number of years. Moreover, the Hernandezes have significant family ties in Mexico where their parents and most of their brothers and sisters live. The children are bilingual, which should significantly help them integrate into Mexican life.

[handwritten right margin: family is in Mexico]

You are the immigration judge. Do the Hernandezes meet the threshold statutory eligibility criteria to apply for cancellation of removal? You do not need to address the exceptional and extremely unusual hardship standard here.

3. MERITING DISCRETION

Once threshold eligibility is established under the statutory criteria, a grant of any form of relief from removal still requires the favorable exercise of discretion by the Attorney General, delegated to an immigration judge presiding over a removal proceeding. As you read through these materials, consider the function that discretion plays in determining which noncitizens merit a grant of relief even after they have satisfied the legislated criteria. As we have seen, BIA decisions guide discretionary decisions, but administrative agencies could instead adopt regulations for this purpose, or Congress could provide guidance by statute.

Daniel Kanstroom has described discretion as "the flexible shock absorber of the administrative state. It is a venerable and essential component of the rule of law that recognizes the inevitable complexities of enforcement of laws by government agencies." He also describes it as a two-edged sword: "It can cut toward harsh enforcement or it can cut toward mercy." Daniel Kanstroom, Aftermath: Deportation Law and the New American Diaspora 215 (2012).

This section surveys the approaches to discretion that immigration judges may take when determining whether to grant or deny relief. Keep an eye on how the scope of discretion changes across the diverse forms of relief.

a. Cancellation of Removal for Permanent Residents: Discretionary Considerations

Long-term lawful permanent residents do not need to establish a particular degree of hardship to be eligible for cancellation under § 240A(a), although of course hardship is likely to figure into the exercise of discretion. In 1998, the BIA announced that the standards previously used in cases under its predecessor provision, former INA § 212(c), would guide the exercise of discretion for cancellation under § 240A(a):

> * * * [T]here is no inflexible standard for determining who should be granted discretionary relief, and each case must be judged on its own merits. Within this context, the Board ruled in *Matter of Marin*, [16 I & N Dec. 581 (BIA 1978),] that in exercising discretion under section 212(c) of the Act, an Immigration Judge, upon review of the record as a whole, "must balance the adverse factors evidencing the alien's undesirability as a permanent resident with the social and humane considerations presented in his (or her) behalf to determine whether the granting of . . . relief appears in the best interest of this country." We find this general standard equally appropriate in considering requests for cancellation of removal under section 240A(a) of the Act.

> We also find that the factors we have enunciated as pertinent to the exercise of discretion under section 212(c) are equally relevant to the exercise of discretion under section 240A(a) of the Act. For example, favorable considerations include such factors as family ties within the United States, residence of long duration in this country (particularly when the inception of residence occurred at a young age), evidence of hardship to the respondent and his family if deportation occurs, service in this country's armed forces, a history of employment, the existence of property or business ties, evidence of value and service to the community, proof of genuine rehabilitation if a criminal record exists, and other evidence attesting to a respondent's good character. Among the factors deemed adverse to an alien are the nature and underlying circumstances of the grounds of exclusion or deportation (now removal) that are at issue, the presence of additional significant violations of this country's immigration laws, the existence of a criminal record and, if so, its nature, recency, and seriousness, and the presence of other evidence

indicative of a respondent's bad character or undesirability as a permanent resident of this country.

In some cases, the minimum equities required to establish eligibility for relief under section 240A(a) (i.e., residence of at least 7 years and status as a lawful permanent resident for not less than 5 years) may be sufficient in and of themselves to warrant favorable discretionary action. However, as the negative factors grow more serious, it becomes incumbent upon the alien to introduce additional offsetting favorable evidence, which in some cases may have to involve unusual or outstanding equities.

With respect to the issue of rehabilitation, a respondent who has a criminal record will ordinarily be required to present evidence of rehabilitation before relief is granted as a matter of discretion. However, applications involving convicted aliens must be evaluated on a case-by-case basis, with rehabilitation a factor to be considered in the exercise of discretion. We have held that a showing of rehabilitation is not an absolute prerequisite in every case involving an alien with a criminal record.

Matter of C-V-T-, 22 I & N Dec. 7, 11–12 (BIA 1998).

b. Cancellation of Removal for Nonpermanent Residents: Exceptional and Extremely Unusual Hardship

Distinguishing eligibility requirements and discretion. Nonpermanent residents seeking cancellation are also subject to a general exercise of the Attorney General's discretion like the one discussed in *Matter of C-V-T-*, once they have been found to meet the statutory eligibility requirements of INA § 240A(b). But administrative decisions on two of those eligibility factors themselves are usually treated by the courts as discretionary, and hence subject only to highly deferential judicial review—if indeed to any judicial review at all. (As Chapter Nine will develop, INA § 242(a)(2)(B) bars judicial review of discretionary denials of relief, with only a narrow exception established by § 242(a)(2)(D), preserving review for "questions of law.")

Those two cancellation factors are "exceptional and extremely unusual hardship" and "good moral character." This section of the casebook primarily explores the hardship factor, but we open with a passage from a "good moral character" case that explains the reasons why courts often treat these sorts of determinations as discretionary, even though the statute structures them as part of the statutory eligibility threshold. Judge Frank Easterbrook wrote:

"Good moral character" is a statutory requirement—that is, a condition of eligibility—for cancellation of removal. But the Immigration and Nationality Act does not define "good moral character." Hence the decision *whether* an alien has the required character reflects an exercise of administrative discretion. * * * Neither the immigration judge nor the Board compared Portillo-Rendon's driving record against a rule. For the purpose of § 242(a)(2)(D), "law" means a dispute about the meaning of a legal text, so that the alien wins if the text means one thing and loses if it means something else. * * * There is no dispute about a controlling text here; there is only a (potential) dispute about whether Portillo-Rendon's driving infractions are serious and frequent enough to show that he lacks good moral character, as opposed to making isolated mistakes. The IJ and BIA thought that this record shows poor moral fiber; that is a discretionary call and thus is not subject to judicial review.

Portillo-Rendon v. Holder, 662 F.3d 815, 817 (7th Cir. 2011).

Exceptional and extremely unusual hardship. For noncitizens who are not permanent residents to win cancellation, § 240A(b) requires a showing that removal would result in "exceptional and extremely unusual hardship to the alien's spouse, parent, or child, who is a citizen of the United States or an alien lawfully admitted for permanent residence." This demanding requirement, adopted in 1996, was largely a response to the BIA decision in *Matter of O-J-O-*, 21 I & N Dec. 381 (BIA 1996), which granted suspension of deportation under former INA § 244 based on the pre-1996 "extreme hardship" standard. The applicant, a 24-year-old from Nicaragua, had lived in the United States since the age of thirteen. According to the Board:

> This is a close case on the issue of "extreme hardship" but one which, in the final analysis, meets the requirement of significant hardships over and above the normal economic and social disruptions involved in deportation. The respondent has lived in the United States during his critical formative years. He has significant church and community ties in the United States. He is fully assimilated into American culture and society. This assimilation makes the prospect of readjustment to life in Nicaragua much harder than would ordinarily be the case. He would also face difficult economic and political circumstances in his native country, including the possible loss of an ongoing business concern.

Id. at 387. Against this backdrop, the legislative history of § 240A(b) explained the 1996 change:

> The managers have deliberately changed the required showing of hardship from "extreme hardship" to "exceptional and extremely unusual hardship" to emphasize that the alien must provide evidence of harm to his spouse, parent, or child

substantially beyond that which ordinarily would be expected to result from the alien's deportation. The "extreme hardship" standard has been weakened by recent administrative decisions holding that forced removal of an alien who has become "acclimated" to the United States would constitute a hardship sufficient to support a grant of suspension of deportation. *See Matter of O-J-O-* (BIA 1996). Such a ruling would be inconsistent with the standard set forth in new section 240A(b)(1). Similarly, a showing that an alien's United States citizen child would fare less well in the alien's country of nationality than in the United States does not establish "exceptional" or "extremely unusual" hardship and thus would not support a grant of relief under this provision. Our immigration law and policy clearly provide that an alien parent may not derive immigration benefits through his or her child who is a United States citizen. The availability in truly exceptional cases of relief under section 240A(b)(1) must not undermine this or other fundamental immigration enforcement policies.

H.R. Conf. Rep. 104–828, 104th Cong. 2d Sess. 230 (1996).

The BIA applies the new language in the next case.

MATTER OF RECINAS

Board of Immigration Appeals, 2002.
23 I & N Dec. 467.

VILLAGELIU, BOARD MEMBER:

The respondents have appealed from the decision of an Immigration Judge dated December 18, 2000, denying their application for cancellation of removal pursuant to section 240A(b) of the Immigration and Nationality Act. The appeal will be sustained.

I. FACTUAL BACKGROUND

The adult respondent is a 39-year-old native and citizen of Mexico. She is the mother of four United States citizen children, aged 12, 11, 8, and 5, and the two minor respondents, aged 15 and 16, both of whom are natives and citizens of Mexico. Her parents are lawful permanent residents and her five siblings are United States citizens. She is divorced and has no immediate family in Mexico.

The three respondents entered the United States in 1988 on nonimmigrant visas and stayed longer than authorized. Except for a brief absence in 1992, they have remained in this country since their initial entry.

II. Issue

The sole issue on appeal is whether the Immigration Judge erred in finding that the respondent failed to demonstrate that her removal would result in exceptional and extremely unusual hardship to her four United States citizen children and/or her lawful permanent resident parents.[1]

III. Analysis

* * *

A. Exceptional and Extremely Unusual Hardship Standard

In *Matter of Monreal,* 23 I & N Dec. 56 (BIA 2001), we first considered the "exceptional and extremely unusual" hardship standard in a precedent decision in the case of a 34-year-old Mexican national who was the father of three United States citizen children. We held that to establish exceptional and extremely unusual hardship under section 240A(b) of the Act, an alien must demonstrate that his or her spouse, parent, or child would suffer hardship that is substantially beyond that which would ordinarily be expected to result from the person's departure. We specifically stated, however, that the alien need not show that such hardship would be "unconscionable." We also noted that, in deciding a cancellation of removal claim, consideration should be given to the age, health, and circumstances of the qualifying family members, including how a lower standard of living or adverse country conditions in the country of return might affect those relatives.

After reviewing the case, we dismissed the respondent's appeal, finding that he had not satisfied the new hardship standard. We noted that the respondent had been working for 10 years at his uncle's business, but had a brother living in Mexico who also worked for the same business. Our decision emphasized that the respondent was in good health and would be able to work and support his United States citizen children in Mexico. We further found that, upon his return to Mexico, the respondent would be reunited with family members, including his wife (the mother of their three children), who had already returned to Mexico with one of the children. Finally, we noted that the respondent's children were in good health and that the eldest, who was 12 years old, could speak, read, and write Spanish.

We revisited the issue in *Matter of Andazola,* 23 I & N Dec. 319 (BIA 2002), finding that the exceptional and extremely unusual hardship standard was not met in the case of a single Mexican woman. The respondent had two United States citizen children, who were 11 and 6 years old. Their father (who apparently had authorization to remain in the United States) contributed financially to the family, was a presence in

---

[1] As the Immigration Judge noted, the minor respondents do not have a qualifying relative for purposes of cancellation of removal. See section 240A(b)(1)(D) of the Act.

the lives of the children, and could continue to help support the family upon their return to Mexico. All of the respondent's siblings were living in the United States, but were without documentation. The respondent had not shown that her United States citizen children would be deprived of all schooling, or of an opportunity to obtain any education. In denying relief, we considered it "significant" that the respondent had accumulated assets, including $7,000 in savings and a retirement fund, and owned a home and two vehicles. We noted that these assets could help ease the family's transition to Mexico. Accordingly, we found that the case presented a common fact pattern that was insufficient to satisfy the exceptional and extremely unusual hardship standard.

While any hardship case ultimately succeeds or fails on its own merits and on the particular facts presented, *Matter of Andazola* and *Matter of Monreal* are the starting points for any analysis of exceptional and extremely unusual hardship. Cancellation of removal cases coming before the Immigration Judges and the Board must therefore be examined under the standards set forth in those cases.

B. Hardship Factors

In the present case, the adult respondent is a single mother of six children, four of whom are United States citizens. The respondent and her children have no close relatives remaining in Mexico. Her entire family lives in the United States, including her lawful permanent resident parents and five United States citizen siblings. As in *Matter of Andazola*, the respondent's mother serves as her children's caretaker and watches the children while the respondent manages her own motor vehicle inspection business.

The respondent is divorced from the father of her United States citizen children. Although the respondent's former husband at one point was paying $146.50 per month in child support, there is no indication that he remains actively involved in their lives. He is currently out of status and was in immigration proceedings in Denver as of the date of the respondent's last hearing.

The respondent has been operating her own business performing vehicle inspections for 2 years. The business has two employees. She reported having $4,600 in assets, which is apparently the value of an automobile she owns. The respondent testified that after 2 months in business her proceeds were $10,000 a month, but she was also repaying her mother and brother money that she and her former husband had borrowed from them. After meeting expenses, her net profits were $400–500 per month.

The respondent's four United States citizen children have all spent their entire lives in this country and have never traveled to Mexico. She and her family live 5 minutes away from her mother, with whom they have a close relationship. According to the respondent, her children, particularly two of her United States citizen children, experience difficulty speaking Spanish and do not read or write in that language.

Finally, the respondent has no alternative means of immigrating to the United States in the foreseeable future. There is a significant backlog of visa availability to Mexican nationals with preference classification. Therefore, the respondent has little hope of immigrating through her United States citizen siblings, or even her parents, should they naturalize.

C.   Assessment of Hardship

While this case presents a close question, we find it distinguishable from both *Matter of Monreal* and *Matter of Andazola*. As we noted in those decisions, the exceptional and extremely unusual hardship standard for cancellation of removal applicants constitutes a high threshold that is in keeping with Congress' intent to substantially narrow the class of aliens who would qualify for relief. Nevertheless, the hardship standard is not so restrictive that only a handful of applicants, such as those who have a qualifying relative with a serious medical condition, will qualify for relief. We consider this case to be on the outer limit of the narrow spectrum of cases in which the exceptional and extremely unusual hardship standard will be met. Keeping in mind that this hardship standard must be assessed solely with regard to the qualifying relatives in this case, we find the following factors to be significant.

The respondent has raised her family in the United States since 1988, and her four United States citizen children know no other way of life. The respondent's children do not speak Spanish well, and they are unable to read or write in that language.

Unlike the children in *Monreal* and *Andazola*, the respondent's four United States citizen children are entirely dependent on their single mother for support. The respondent is divorced from the children's father, and there is no indication that he remains involved in their lives in any manner. This increases the hardship the children would face upon return to Mexico, as they would be completely dependent on their mother's ability, not only to find adequate employment and housing, but also to provide for their emotional needs.

The respondent has been able to leave her children in the care of her lawful permanent resident mother while she attended courses to obtain a vehicle inspector's certificate and established a business. This assistance from her mother has enabled her to support her children within a stable environment. The respondent's ability to provide for the needs of her family will be severely hampered by the fact that she does not have any family in Mexico who can help care for her six children. As a single mother, the respondent will no doubt experience difficulties in finding work, especially employment that will allow her to continue to provide a safe and supportive home for her children.

From the perspective of the United States citizen children, it is clear that significant hardship will result from the loss of the economic stake that their mother has gained in this country, coupled with the difficulty she will have in establishing any comparable economic stability in Mexico. We emphasize that the respondent is a single parent who is solely responsible for the care of six children and who has no family to return to in Mexico. These are critical factors that distinguish her case from many other cancellation of removal claims.

In addition to the hardship of the United States citizen children, factors that relate only to the respondent may also be considered to the extent that they affect the potential level of hardship to her qualifying relatives. In *Andazola* we found that similar factors were not sufficient to meet the high standard of exceptional and extremely unusual hardship. However, in this case, there are additional factors that we find raise the level of hardship, by a close margin, to that required to establish eligibility for relief.

The respondent's lawful permanent resident parents also are qualifying relatives. While we have not considered their hardship in assessing the respondent's claim, her parents form part of the strong system of family support that the respondent and the minor qualifying relatives would lose if they are removed from the United States.

Although the minor respondents lack a qualifying relative for purposes of cancellation of removal, their existence also cannot be ignored. In a family such as this, headed by a single parent, the hardship of their parent inherently translates into hardship on the rest of the family, in this case to all six children. In considering the hardship that the United States citizen children would face in Mexico, we must also consider the totality of the burden on the entire family that would result when a single mother must support a family of this size. Unlike the situation in *Monreal* and *Andazola*, all of the respondent's family, including her siblings, resides *lawfully* in the United States. We find this significant because they are unlikely to be subject to immigration enforcement and will probably remain in the United States indefinitely. The respondent's family members are very close and have been instrumental in helping her raise her children and obtain the necessary funds to establish her business. The loss of this support would further increase the hardship that she, and therefore her United States citizen children, would suffer if they are compelled to return to Mexico, where no support structure exists.

Finally, we note that the respondent's prospects for lawful immigration through her United States citizen siblings or lawful permanent resident parents are unrealistic due to the backlog of visa availability for Mexican nationals with preference classification. There are no other apparent methods of adjustment available to any of the respondents. These are factors we have previously found to be significant when considering an identical hardship standard for suspension of deportation.

The hardship factors present in this case are more different in degree than in kind from those present in *Monreal* and *Andazola*. For this reason, we see no need to depart from the analysis set forth in those cases. Part of that analysis requires the assessment of hardship factors in their totality, often termed a "cumulative" analysis. Here, the heavy financial and familial burden on the adult respondent, the lack of support from the children's father, the United States citizen children's unfamiliarity with the Spanish language, the lawful residence in this country of all of the respondent's immediate family, and the concomitant lack of family in Mexico combine to render the hardship in this case well beyond that which is normally experienced in most cases of removal. The level of hardship presented here is higher than that established in either *Monreal* or *Andazola* and, in our view, is sufficient to be considered exceptional and extremely unusual.

We emphasize, in conclusion, that this decision cannot be read in isolation from *Monreal* and *Andazola*. Those cases remain our seminal interpretations of the meaning of "exceptional and extremely unusual hardship" in section 240A(b)(1)(D) of the Act. The cumulative factors present in this case are indeed unusual and will not typically be found in most other cases, where respondents have smaller families and relatives who reside in both the United States and their country of origin.

IV. CONCLUSION

Given the unusual facts presented in this case, we find that the adult respondent has shown that her United States citizen children will suffer exceptional and extremely unusual hardship if she is removed from the United States. Accordingly, her appeal will be sustained and she will be granted cancellation of removal.

As the adult respondent has been granted relief and appears to have no impediment to adjusting her status, the minor respondents are likely to soon have a qualifying relative for purposes of establishing eligibility for cancellation of removal. Given this fact, we find it appropriate to remand their records to the Immigration Judge for their cases to be held in abeyance pending a disposition regarding the adult respondent's status.

NOTES AND QUESTIONS ON
HARDSHIP IN CANCELLATION OF REMOVAL

1. First, address the statutory eligibility criteria. In *Recinas*, the BIA notes that the two noncitizen children lack a "qualifying relative" for purposes of § 240A(b). How can the mother have such a relationship while her children do not? (Read § 240A(b)(1)(D) closely.)

2. Now turn to the immigration judge's assessment of hardship. What would you add to or delete from the list of favorable and unfavorable factors identified in *C-V-T-* for cancellation of removal for lawful permanent residents under § 240A(a)? What weight should be given to the listed factors? Should an adjudicator seek evidence on each factor?

3. Suppose you were an immigration judge to whom the power of discretion is assigned. How would you go about exercising your "two-edged sword?" Is it a grand power to dispense justice as you see fit? If it is the ultimate power to bestow mercy, can you act on hunches or your personal reaction to the noncitizen? How far does your discretion go? Can you grant relief to persons whose cases you find sympathetic, even if they do not meet the statutory eligibility criteria?

To what extent will evaluation of the discretionary factors depend on the perspective of the particular adjudicator? What mechanisms exist (or could be constructed) to promote uniformity among decisionmakers? Is Judge Easterbrook's perspective, quoted before *Recinas,* an obstacle to such uniformity?

4. What mechanisms are available to address implicit bias in exercising that discretion? One immigration judge has shared her own experience from the bench:

> As I observe his testimony, I notice the witness is not looking me in the eye, making me begin to suspect that I am not being told the truth. I note my concern while the testimony continues. As his story comes out in a confusing jumble, with bits and pieces that are not firmly grounded in a chronological timeline, I am again plagued by doubts about his veracity. * * * After a few more minutes, I catch myself and remember that it is not culturally appropriate in many cultures to look an authority figure in the eye. Okay, discount that factor. Then I remember that rigid timelines and linear storytelling are not necessarily common or expected in all cultures. Okay, another factor must be discounted or minimized.

* * *

> Implicit biases are those automatic attitudes or stereotypes that affect our understanding, actions, or decisions in an unconscious manner. They are attributed to acquired associations, favorable and unfavorable, learned from an early age after continued exposure to direct and indirect messages—the essence of

socialization in our modern communities. They reflect a national consciousness created by our media, history, news, and political policy. * * * Because implicit bias has been learned, these beliefs can also be unlearned. * * *

Judge Dana Leigh Marks, *Who, Me? Am I Guilty of Implicit Bias?*, 54 ABA Judges J. 1 (2015).

As one component of a larger solution, Judge Marks offers this suggestion: "To help reduce the impact of implicit bias, it has * * * been suggested that we identify the sources of ambiguity in the decision-making context and endeavor to establish more concrete, tangible standards." *Id.* at 5.

Is Judge Marks right? Won't more concrete standards reduce the flexibility that is the hallmark of discretion? Or does implicit bias already cabin discretion in undesirable ways?

EXERCISE

Return to the Exercise on p. 731–733. Assuming the Hernandezes have met the statutory eligibility requirements, how would you evaluate hardship and exercise your discretion in ruling on their applications?

c. Discretionary Waivers

Recall from Sections A and B of this chapter that INA § 212(h) can provide a waiver of inadmissibility or deportability based on criminal convictions. This provision poses a general question about agency discretion in deciding on waivers of inadmissibility and deportability. A regulation, 8 C.F.R § 212.7(d), addresses discretion in § 212(h) waivers:

> The Attorney General, in general, will not favorably exercise discretion under section 212(h)(2) of the Act to consent to an application or reapplication for a visa, or admission to the United States, or adjustment of status, with respect to immigrant aliens who are inadmissible under section 212(a)(2) of the Act in cases involving violent or dangerous crimes, except in extraordinary circumstances, such as those involving national security or foreign policy considerations, or cases in which an alien clearly demonstrates that the denial of the application for adjustment of status or an immigrant visa or admission as an immigrant would result in exceptional and extremely unusual hardship. Moreover, depending on the gravity of the alien's underlying criminal offense, a showing of extraordinary circumstances might still be insufficient to warrant a favorable exercise of discretion under section 212(h)(2) of the Act.

Former BIA Member Lory Rosenberg criticized this regulation for "limit[ing] access to a waiver where Congress expressly provided that a waiver would be available." She reasoned that the regulation "violates the principle that every discretionary determination requires a weighing and balancing of the relevant factors." Lory Rosenberg, *Where Have All the Waivers Gone: An Examination of Extremely and Exceptionally Unusual Discretionary Standards*, 8 Bender's Immigr. Bull. 185 (Feb. 2003).

Are you persuaded? Compare *Fook Hong Mak v. INS*, 435 F.2d 728 (2d Cir. 1970), which upheld a regulation precluding discretionary relief for noncitizens who failed to leave after being allowed to transit the United States without a visa. Judge Friendly explained:

> We are unable to understand why there should be any general principle forbidding an administrator, vested with discretionary power, to determine by appropriate rulemaking that he will not use it in favor of a particular class on a case-by-case basis, if his determination is founded on considerations rationally related to the statute he is administering. The legislature's grant of discretion to accord a privilege does not imply a mandate that this must inevitably be done by examining each case rather than by identifying groups.

Id. at 730. The circuits addressing the validity of 8 C.F.R § 212.7(d) have upheld it. *See, e.g., Samuels v. Chertoff*, 550 F.3d 252, 257 (2d Cir. 2008).

d. Perspectives on Discretionary Relief

Daniel Kanstroom frames the role of discretion as follows:

> The roots of the deportation discretion problem are deeply intertwined with our understanding of the nature of law. One might distinguish discretion from rules: the core of the "rule of law." * * * Discretion, as Ronald Dworkin once famously put it, "like the hole in a doughnut, does not exist except as an area left open by a surrounding belt of restriction." A rough, pragmatic definition is simply "power to make a choice between alternative courses of action." The implication in either case is that there is no such thing as a uniquely correct discretionary decision. There may, however, certainly be *incorrect* discretionary decisions, such as those that are unauthorized or arbitrary. The most basic theoretical problems of discretion are thus how to define and restrain its abuse without destroying its non-rulelike character.

* * *

One of the most well-known and best attempts to grapple with this problem is that of Judge Henry Friendly in a 1966 case, *Wong Wing Hang v. INS*. The case was an appeal from a denial of suspension of deportation relief. Judge Friendly * * * offered a useful formula: "The denial of suspension to an eligible alien would be an abuse of discretion if it were made without a rational explanation, inexplicably departed from established policies, or rested on an impermissible basis such as an invidious discrimination against a particular race. * * *

Daniel Kanstroom, Deportation Nation: Outsiders in American History 231–32 (2007). For further analysis of the levels, stages, and significance of enforcement discretion, *see* Hiroshi Motomura, Immigration Outside the Law 129–30 (2014).

Judge Friendly's reasoning in *Wong Wing Hang* offers further guidance on the exercise of discretion to grant relief from removal. The case raised questions of judicial review in light of the apparent tension between two provisions of the Administrative Procedure Act:

> Here we encounter the familiar conflict between the preamble of [5 USC § 701(a)(2) of the Administrative Procedure Act, *excepting from judicial review*] "*agency action [that] is by law committed to agency discretion*," and the command of [§ 706(a)(2)] that *the reviewing court shall "set aside agency action * * * found to be (1) arbitrary, capricious, an abuse of discretion*, or otherwise not in accordance with law." (Emphasis supplied.) Some help in resolving the seeming contradiction may be afforded by the distinction drawn by Professors Hart and Sacks between a discretion that "is not subject to the restraint of the obligation of reasoned decision and hence of reasoned elaboration of a fabric of doctrine governing successive decisions" and discretion of the contrary and more usual sort, see The Legal Process 172, 175–177 (Tent. ed. 1958); only in the rare—some say non-existent—case where discretion of the former type has been vested, may review for "abuse" be precluded. An argument could be made that the change from the earlier versions of the suspension provision, "the Attorney General may suspend if he finds," 54 Stat. 672 (1940), 62 Stat. 1206 (1948), to its present form affords an indication that Congress meant to accord the Attorney General or his delegate ad hoc discretion of that sort. But the Attorney General himself has not thought so; applications for suspension of deportation * * * have long been subjected to various administrative hearing and appeal procedures, see the history recounted in *Jay v. Boyd*, 351 U.S. 345, 351–352, 76 S.Ct. 919, 100 L.Ed. 1242 (1956), with their concomitants of "the obligation of reasoned decision."

Wong Wing Hang v. INS, 360 F.2d 715, 717–18 (2d Cir.1966) (Friendly, J.).

Shifting from the judicial to the legislative role, how much could you do in drafting statutes or regulations to resolve the tension between (a) avenues of relief flexible enough to respond to the particular facts, and (b) rules to enhance predictability and limit executive branch discretion? In assessing the optimal degrees of flexibility and precision, consider the arguments by

Maurice Roberts, former Chairman of the BIA, for more guidelines for the exercise of discretion:

> It should be possible to achieve greater uniformity of decision, while at the same time minimizing the opportunities for result-oriented adjudication based on an adjudicator's subjective feelings, by defining with greater precision not only the policies to be served but also the elements to be considered. * * * Great [precision] need not completely strait-jacket the adjudicator or limit the range of elements which may properly be considered.

* * *

> Uniformity of decision with mathematical precision is, of course, possible. Specific point values could be prescribed for each element deemed relevant, *e.g.,* so many minus points for a preconceived intent, so many for a wife abroad, so many for each minor child abroad, so many for being responsible for the break-up of the foreign marriage, so many for each intentional misstatement to the Service, etc. Plus points could be assigned for an American citizen or permanent resident wife, for each American child, for each year of the alien's residence here, and the like. An appropriate plus score could be fixed as a prerequisite to the favorable exercise of discretion. * * *

> Any notion of such mechanical jurisprudence would, of course, be summarily rejected if seriously suggested. Yet, unless more realistic and specific guidelines are laid down, the opposite extreme becomes possible if it is left to each individual adjudicator to determine for himself, on the basis of his own subjective experiences and beliefs, just what factors in the alien's life should be determinative in exercising discretion and how much weight should be accorded each factor. An intolerant adjudicator could deny relief to aliens whose cultural patterns, political views, moral standards or life styles differed from his own. Worse still, a hostile or xenophobic adjudicator could vent his spleen on aliens he personally considered offensive without articulating the actual basis for his decision.

> Unless standards are laid down which are not illusory and can be uniformly applied in the real world, we depart from even-handed justice and the rule of law. * * *

Maurice Roberts, *The Exercise of Administrative Discretion Under the Immigration Laws*, 13 San Diego L. Rev. 144, 164–65 (1975).

Several years after Roberts urged greater guidance, the INS issued proposed regulations to identify factors to be considered in the exercise of discretion under various INA provisions, 44 Fed. Reg. 36187–93 (1979), but abandoned the project a year and a half later. The agency explained: "It is impossible to list or foresee all of the adverse or favorable factors which may be present in a given set of circumstances," citing the danger that such a list posed "that the use of the guidelines may become so rigid as to amount to an abuse of discretion." 46 Fed. Reg. 9119 (1981).

Would guidance—whether in regulations, a precedent decision of the BIA, or in the statute itself—hamper the free exercise of discretionary authority? If discretion is meant to be exercised under a decisionmaking process that develops a "fabric of doctrine," isn't some hampering of an individual immigration judge's decisions inevitable? Is it desirable?

Now consider the legislative proposals in the following Exercise.

EXERCISE

Consider this hypothetical legislative proposal:

§ 1. Except as provided in Section 2, all provisions for relief from removal are hereby repealed.

§ 2. The Secretary of Homeland Security may waive any ground of inadmissibility or deportability and adjust the status of an alien on whose behalf the ground is waived to that of lawful permanent resident if the Secretary determines that such waiver and adjustment are justified by humanitarian concerns or are otherwise in the national interest.

§ 3. A determination by the Secretary under Section 2 shall not be set aside by a court unless it is arbitrary or capricious.

Now consider an alternate (or additional) proposal:

§ 1. There shall be a five year statute of limitations on removal.

§ 2. All provisions for relief from removal are hereby repealed.

If you were a member of Congress, would you support these provisions by themselves or in some combination? If not, what amendments might win your support?

Would you distinguish between immigrants and nonimmigrants? Between noncitizens who were admitted and noncitizens who entered without inspection? Between noncitizens who have resided here for a short while and those who are long-time residents? How exactly would a statute of limitations apply to *presence* in the United States in violation of law (INA § 237(a)(1)(B)?

Would you provide for judicial review of a final administrative decision regarding relief under the first provision?

Would you provide guidance for the exercise of discretion in the statute, or would you prefer guidance to come from the agency administering the statute? If the latter option is preferable, what form(s) should that guidance take?

a "relief" from removal that is actually a form of removal

4. VOLUNTARY DEPARTURE

Voluntary departure is a form of relief from removal that does not permit a noncitizen to stay in the United States indefinitely as cancellation of removal does, or prosecutorial discretion may. Relatively few removable noncitizens are eligible to maintain or establish permanent resident status, but many can obtain more limited forms of relief, and voluntary departure is by far the most common. It allows the noncitizen a certain period of time, not exceeding 120 days, to leave the United States.

rule.

As with other forms of relief, voluntary departure requires both statutory eligibility and a favorable exercise of discretion. For example, noncitizens removable for aggravated felonies or terrorist activities are not eligible to seek voluntary departure. INA § 240B(a)(1).

Reqs.

Though voluntary departure is typically considered a form of relief from removal, the Executive Office for Immigration Review counts voluntary departure as a form of removal, presumably because the practical result is supposed to be the noncitizen's departure. Between fiscal years 2012 and 2014, an average of about 18% of total removal decisions in immigration courts—close to 20,000 per year—were grants of voluntary departure, as compared with about 108,000 removal orders in each year. Executive Office for Immigration Review, FY 2014 Statistics Yearbook at O1, table 17. It is also important to put formal voluntary departure of this type into the broader context of the number of noncitizens who are compelled in some way to leave the United States. In a much larger number of cases—178,371 in 2013—noncitizens are returned to the home country without a removal order or a formal order of voluntary departure. DHS Office of Immigration Statistics, Immigration Enforcement Actions: 2013, at 7 (2014). Most of these cases, counted as "returns" rather than "removals," are accomplished by CBP or ICE based on apprehension at or near the border.

a lot of people "return" voluntarily

Return v. Removal

returns rather than Removal.

There are three types of voluntary departure. The first two types, governed by § 240B(a), authorize the agency to permit voluntary departure either in lieu of being subject to § 240 proceedings, or prior to the completion of those proceedings. These forms of voluntary departure are available before the conclusion of removal proceedings under terms more favorable than the third type, governed by § 240B(b), that permits a grant of voluntary departure at the completion of proceedings but imposes more stringent criteria. All three types of voluntary departure allow noncitizens to avoid a formal removal order.

240B(a) - 2

240B(b) - 3

volunt. dep. = no formal order of removal

*quid pro
quo*

*- avoid the
expense of
deport.*

The Supreme Court has described voluntary departure as a *quid pro quo*:

> From the Government's standpoint, the alien's agreement to leave voluntarily expedites the departure process and avoids the expense of deportation—including procuring necessary documents and detaining the alien pending deportation. The Government also eliminates some of the costs and burdens associated with litigation over the departure. With the apparent purpose of assuring that the Government attains the benefits it seeks, the Act imposes limits on the time for voluntary departure, and prohibits judicial review of voluntary departure decisions.
>
> Benefits to the alien from voluntary departure are evident as well. He or she avoids extended detention pending completion of travel arrangements; is allowed to choose when to depart (subject to certain constraints); and can select the country of destination. And, of great importance, by departing voluntarily the alien facilitates the possibility of readmission. * * * Under the current Act, an alien involuntarily removed from the United States is ineligible for readmission for a period of 5, 10, or 20 years, depending upon the circumstances of removal. * * * An alien who makes a timely departure under a grant of voluntary departure, on the other hand, is not subject to these restrictions—although he or she otherwise may be ineligible for readmission based, for instance, on an earlier unlawful presence in the United States.

Dada v. Mukasey, 554 U.S. 1, 11, 128 S.Ct. 2307, 171 L.Ed.2d 178 (2008).

212(a)(9)(B)
↓
*① removal bar
differs from
departure bar*
276 / 275

Dada notes that the negative consequences of a formal removal order include inadmissibility for ten years, unless the noncitizen obtains advance permission to reapply for admission. INA § 212(a)(9)(A). The value of escaping this ten-year inadmissibility may be limited, however, now that mere departure often triggers a different ten-year bar under INA § 212(a)(9)(B). Noncitizens with formal removal orders who later reenter unlawfully are also subject to a felony prosecution, *see* INA § 276, whereas simple entry without inspection is a misdemeanor under § 275.

If the noncitizen fails to meet the conditions of an immigration judge's grant of voluntary departure, an alternate order of removal takes effect. That is, immigration court procedure accounts efficiently for the not infrequent situation where the noncitizen remains past the specified deadline. The immigration judge grants voluntary departure in an order that automatically becomes a fully enforceable removal order, without the need for further court proceedings, if the individual fails to depart in timely fashion. A noncitizen who fails to leave on time also faces a potential fine and a ten-year ineligibility period for voluntary departure, cancellation, registry, or adjustment of status. *See* INA § 240B(d). Further, if he leaves under voluntary departure embodied in an immigration court order, but later returns without advance permission, he can be quickly removed through a process called reinstatement of removal. *See* INA § 241(a)(5).

a. Statutory Eligibility for Voluntary Departure

Matter of Arguelles-Campos, 22 I & N Dec. 811 (BIA 1999) contrasted applying for voluntary departure before or during removal proceedings (under INA § 240B(a)) versus requesting it at the conclusion of the proceeding (under § 240B(b):

> An alien who wishes to voluntarily depart the United States instead of being subject to removal proceedings may apply for voluntary departure [under INA § 240B(a)] with the Service. The authorized Service officer, in his or her discretion, shall specify the period of time permitted for voluntary departure. * * *

> The Service may attach to the granting of voluntary departure any conditions it deems necessary to ensure the alien's timely departure from the United States, including the posting of a bond, continued detention pending departure, and removal under safeguards. * * *

> * * *

> If an alien applies for voluntary departure before the conclusion of the removal proceedings, no additional relief may be requested. If additional relief has been requested, such a request must be withdrawn. The alien must also have conceded removability, waived appeal of all issues, and not been convicted of an aggravated felony or be deportable on national security grounds. INA § 240B(a)(1).

> The Immigration Judge may not grant a voluntary departure period exceeding 120 days and may impose other conditions as deemed necessary to ensure the alien's departure, including the posting of a voluntary departure bond to be canceled upon proof that the alien has departed the United States within the time specified. INA §§ 240B(a)(2), (3). * * *

> Finally, neither the Act nor the regulations require that the alien show good moral character under INA § 240B(a), although the alien must merit a favorable exercise of discretion. * * *

> Different requirements and conditions arise if an alien applies for voluntary departure at the conclusion of removal proceedings under INA § 240B(b). First, the alien must have

been physically present in the United States for at least 1 year immediately preceding the date the Notice to Appear was served * * *. Second, the alien must show that he is, and has been, a person of good moral character for at least 5 years immediately preceding the application for voluntary departure. * * * The alien must also show by clear and convincing evidence that he has the means to depart the United States and intends to do so.

* * * [U]nlike section 240B(a), under section 240B(b) the alien must also pay a mandatory voluntary departure bond of an amount sufficient to ensure the alien's departure, in no case less than $500. * * * The alien must also merit a favorable exercise of discretion. Finally, the Immigration Judge may impose other conditions as deemed necessary to ensure the alien's departure and may not grant a voluntary departure period exceeding 60 days.

* * *

Further restrictions and penalties also exist under both parts of INA § 240B. First, an alien is ineligible for voluntary departure under section 240B if the alien was previously permitted to so depart after having been found inadmissible under section 212(a)(6)(A). * * *

Also, if an alien is permitted to depart voluntarily under section 240B and fails to depart the United States within the time period specified, the alien shall be subject to a civil penalty of $1,000 to $5,000 and be ineligible for relief of cancellation of removal, voluntary departure, adjustment of status, change of nonimmigrant classification, and registry for a 10-year period. INA § 240B(d).* * *

Id. at 814-18.

The BIA also explained how the eligibility requirements for voluntary departure operate as a docket management tool:

It is clear from the significant differences between voluntary departure under INA §§ 240B(a) and 240B(b) that Congress intended the two provisions to be used for different purposes. * * * [S]ection 240B(a) requires much less from the alien. Under section 240B(a), an alien need not show that he has good moral character or that he has the financial means to depart the United States. An alien must request section 240B(a) relief either in lieu of being subject to proceedings, or early in removal proceedings. He must also voluntarily forego all other forms of relief. Thus, Immigration Judges can use section 240B(a) relief to quickly and efficiently dispose of numerous cases on their docket, where appropriate. We accept the need for such a tool and support its purpose.

Id. at 817.

EXERCISE

Carolina entered the United States without inspection five months before receiving a Notice to Appear for a removal proceeding, charging her with being inadmissible under INA § 212(a)(6)(A)(i). At her first court appearance, she conceded she was inadmissible as charged, and applied for cancellation of removal under INA § 240A(b). She has never been convicted of a crime. Her husband is a lawful permanent resident of the United States.

A second court appearance is imminent, and you must decide whether to apply for voluntary departure. Does Carolina meet the threshold eligibility requirements for voluntary departure? Does it matter when you seek it?

[Handwritten margin notes: "5 months · NTA · applies for cancell. of removal. · husband LPR" ; "· apply under 240 B(a) · apply at beginning (arraignment)"]

b. Discretion in Voluntary Departure Applications

In *Matter of Arguelles-Campos,* 22 I & N 811 (1999), the Board summarized the discretionary factors to be considered once the eligibility requirements for voluntary departure are met:

> [M]any factors may be weighed in exercising discretion with voluntary departure applications, including the nature and underlying circumstances of the deportation ground at issue; additional violations of the immigration laws; the existence, seriousness, and recency of any criminal record; and other evidence of bad character or the undesirability of the applicant as a permanent resident. We further stated that discretion may be favorably exercised in the face of adverse factors where there are compensating elements such as long residence here, close family ties in the United States, or humanitarian needs. We find that these factors, which we have enunciated as pertinent to the exercise of discretion under [pre-1996 law], are equally relevant to the exercise of discretion under section 240B of the Act in removal proceedings. However, an Immigration Judge has broader authority to grant voluntary departure in discretion under section 240B(a) than under section 240B(b) or [under pre-1996 law].

[Handwritten margin notes: "Discretionary factors to consider ← factors" ; "← competing elements"]

Id. at 817.

5. RELIEF FOR VICTIMS

Congress has established several forms of relief for noncitizen victims of violence or crime. Cancellation of removal for battered spouses and children provides an immediate pathway to permanent residence. The T and U visas, despite their designation as nonimmigrant visas, function as forms of relief and similarly provide a pathway to permanent residence.

a. Cancellation for Battered Spouses or Children

The Violence Against Women Act of 1994 (VAWA), Pub. L. 103–322, § 40703, 108 Stat. 1796, 1955, added a special form of relief for battered spouses and children in INA § 240A(b)(2). However, VAWA cancellation applies only if the batterer is a U.S. citizen or lawful permanent resident. VAWA cancellation parallels cancellation of removal for nonpermanent residents, with relaxed requirements.

These requirements deserve special focus. First, the continuous physical presence requirement is only three years, which can accrue after the noncitizen has received a notice to appear, despite the general stop-time rule. Absences from the United States that are connected to the abuse do not count toward the 90/180-day periods that interrupt continuous physical presence.

To see how threshold eligibility works, try the following problem:

PROBLEM

N lawfully entered the United States as the spouse of a U.S. citizen. Exactly 33 months after she entered, she received a notice to appear in a removal proceeding based on termination of her conditional LPR status. (Assume that she committed no offense that under INA § 240A(d)(1)(B) would stop the accrual of qualifying time.) K has been battered by her U.S. citizen spouse. Six months have passed since she received the notice to appear. Is N eligible to apply for cancellation?

Second, the hardship standard is "extreme," not "exceptional and extremely unusual," and it may be hardship to the applicant, not just to the applicant's parent or child. Third, to establish good moral character, a waiver is available for any otherwise disqualifying conduct or conviction connected to the abuse.

Two VAWA cancellation cases follow. The first interprets some of the statutory elements, and the second illustrates the exercise of discretion.

LOPEZ-BIRRUETA V. HOLDER   *Interpretation of statutory element*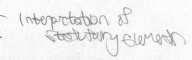

United States Court of Appeals, Ninth Circuit, 2011.
633 F.3d 1211.

GRABER, CIRCUIT JUDGE:

Petitioner Maria Lopez-Birrueta petitions for review of the Board of ← BIA
Immigration Appeals' ("BIA") denial of special-rule cancellation of
removal under the Violence Against Women Act of 1994 ("VAWA"). The
BIA held that, although Petitioner's children were mistreated by their
lawful-permanent-resident father, that mistreatment did not rise to the
level of "battery" under INA § 240A(b)(2)(A). We disagree. * * *

FACTUAL AND PROCEDURAL HISTORY

Petitioner is a native and citizen of Mexico. She entered the United
States without inspection in 1994 at the age of 14. In 2002, the
government served her with a notice to appear. She conceded
removability but applied for special-rule cancellation of removal under
INA § 240A(b)(2)(A). To qualify, an alien must demonstrate (1) the   *Elements for relief under 240A(b)(2)(A)*
existence of battery or extreme cruelty, (2) physical presence, (3) good
moral character, (4) not being inadmissible for certain specified reasons,
and (5) extreme hardship. Regarding the first requirement, Petitioner
sought to demonstrate that she "is the parent of a child of an alien who is
. . . a lawful permanent resident and the child has been battered or
subjected to extreme cruelty by such permanent resident parent."

At a merits hearing in 2008, Petitioner testified as follows. After
arriving in the United States, and still at the age of 14, Petitioner began a
sexual relationship with Gill Campos, who was then 36 years old. Campos
is a legal permanent resident of the United States.

Petitioner and Campos had two children together. At age 16,
Petitioner gave birth to E—. At age 18, she gave birth to G—. Petitioner
and Campos lived together while the children were very young.

During that time, Campos repeatedly threatened Petitioner, insulted
her, prohibited her from talking with others, acted aggressively toward
her, and threatened to alert immigration officials if Petitioner disobeyed
his orders. While they lived together, Campos was not a loving father. He
was violent toward his children, yelled at them, and often took them for
rides in his car when he was drunk.

Petitioner described one incident in detail. In front of his "drunken
friends," Campos struck E—, then 3 years old, three times on the legs
with a stick that was 24 inches long and one-half inch in diameter. The
strikes caused red welts to appear on E—'s legs, which Petitioner treated
with ointment and ice. That same form of beating occurred two to three
times a week. Campos subjected G—to the same mistreatment. Asked

why, Petitioner responded that Campos "probably want[ed] to control me through the children."

Twice, Petitioner left Campos but, both times, she returned after Campos convinced her that he had changed. Petitioner left for good in 1999 and moved to Yakima, Washington, with her children. Since Petitioner left, the children have visited Campos for one or two months at a time, and once for almost a year. Campos no longer strikes the children.

Both children testified at the hearing. At the time, E—was 12 years old, and G—was 11 years old. E—testified that he has not had any problems with his father in the past few years and that, although he did not love his father when he was younger, he loves him now. He remembers his father striking him, "for no reason," with a tree branch and with his hand. G—testified that he remembers that his father would beat him and E—with a stick, on the legs. When his father came home, G—was scared and hid to "try[ ] to get away." But he no longer feels that way about his father.

In a written decision, an immigration judge ("IJ") denied cancellation of removal. The IJ expressly found Petitioner credible but found that she failed to establish that the children had been "battered" or subjected to "extreme cruelty" under the statute. Because the IJ held that Petitioner did not meet the statutory requirement of battery or extreme cruelty, he did not reach any of the other statutory requirements for relief.

* * * [T]he BIA adopted and affirmed the IJ's decision. * * *

* * *

DISCUSSION

A. *Sources of Law*

* * *

Because Petitioner and Campos never married (legally or bigamously), Petitioner cannot claim protection under VAWA for Campos' mistreatment *of her*. Instead, Petitioner sought to demonstrate that she fell within the category protected by the parenthetical in subsection (II), that she "is the parent of a child of an alien who is . . . a lawful permanent resident and the child has been battered or subjected to extreme cruelty by such permanent resident parent." None of the other categories applies.

The statute does not define the phrase "has been battered or subjected to extreme cruelty." But the agency has promulgated a regulation at 8 C.F.R. § 204.2 that pertains to the topic. Although we ultimately agree with the BIA and the parties that the regulation's definitions of "battery or extreme cruelty" apply, some explanation is required.

* * * Relevant here, subsection (c) [of the regulation] is entitled "Self-petition by spouse of abusive citizen or lawful permanent resident," and subsection (e) is entitled "Self-petition by child of abusive citizen or lawful permanent resident." Both subsections (c) and (e) describe the requirements for special-rule cancellation of removal under VAWA, and both subsections contain a definition of "battery or extreme cruelty." Except for their respective final sentences, the two definitions are identical:

> Battery or extreme cruelty. For the purpose of this chapter, the phrase "was battered by or was the subject of extreme cruelty" includes, but is not limited to, being the victim of any act or threatened act of violence, including any forceful detention, which results or threatens to result in physical or mental injury. Psychological or sexual abuse or exploitation, including rape, molestation, incest (if the victim is a minor), or forced prostitution shall be considered acts of violence. Other abusive actions may also be acts of violence under certain circumstances, including acts that, in and of themselves, may not initially appear violent but that are a part of an overall pattern of violence. *Pattern of violence*

The final sentence in the two definitions varies depending on whether the petitioner is a spouse or child. The subsection concerning a petition for a spouse states: "The qualifying abuse must have been committed by the citizen or lawful permanent resident spouse, must have been perpetrated against the self-petitioner or the self-petitioner's child, and must have taken place during the self-petitioner's marriage to the abuser." The subsection concerning a petition for a child states: "The qualifying abuse must have been committed by the citizen or lawful permanent resident parent, must have been perpetrated against the self-petitioner, and must have taken place while the self-petitioner was residing with the abuser."

* * *

* * * [T]he definitions do not cover Petitioner's situation. Petitioner filed neither a petition from an abusive *spouse,* covered by the definition at § 204.2(c)(1)(vi), nor a petition from a *child,* covered by the definition at § 204.2(e)(1)(vi). Petitioner is the non-married parent of a child abused by the other parent. Even though the *statute* covers Petitioner's situation, it appears that the agency failed to promulgate regulations specifically covering that situation. * * * We agree that the BIA permissibly extended the use of the definitions here. There is no indication in the statute or elsewhere that a different definition of battery or extreme cruelty should apply depending on the marital status of the petitioner.

B. Battery Under VAWA

"Congress's goal in enacting VAWA was to eliminate barriers to women leaving abusive relationships." *Hernandez v. Ashcroft,* 345 F.3d 824, 841 (9th Cir. 2003). * * * [W]hen interpreting this statute, we have "adhere[d] to the general rule of construction that when the legislature enacts an ameliorative rule designed to forestall harsh results, the rule will be interpreted and applied in an ameliorative fashion." *Id.* [at 840].

"The text of the statute reveals that Congress distinguished between 'battery' and 'extreme cruelty,' reserving the term extreme cruelty for something other than physical assault, presumably actions in some way involving mental or psychological cruelty." *Id.* at 838. * * * Relevant here, the regulation states that battery "includes, but is not limited to, . . . any act or threatened act of violence, including any forceful detention, which results or threatens to result in physical or mental injury." 8 C.F.R. § 204.2(c)(1)(vi), (e)(1)(vi).

* * *

Campos struck his children with a stick two or three times a week, when they were 2 and 3 years old, in front of his "drunken friends," for no reason at all (that is, not as punishment), causing red welts that required home medical treatment of ointment and ice and causing his children to fear him. We are compelled to conclude that those regular, arbitrary beatings causing injury constituted an "act of physical abuse," *Hernandez,* 345 F.3d at 840, or an "act of violence . . . which results . . . in physical . . . injury," 8 C.F.R. § 204.2(c)(1)(vi), (e)(1)(vi). We therefore hold that the BIA erred in concluding otherwise.

* * *

C. The BIA's Legal Errors

[Because the BIA adopted the immigration judge's reasoning, the court reviewed the immigration judge's decision as if it were the BIA's.]

First, the IJ held that "[t]he regulatory definition of 'battery or extreme cruelty' requires a heightened level of violence that 'results or threatens to result in physical or mental injury.'" (Quoting 8 C.F.R. § 204.2(c)(1)(vi).) But the regulation states that battery "*includes, but is not limited to*" an act of violence resulting in injury. (emphasis added). The definition does not *require* that the violence be "heightened" or result in injury, though physically injurious acts of violence qualify per se as battery.

Second, and perhaps most egregious, the IJ turned to California's criminal-law definition of "battery" and its definition of "injury" for certain sentencing purposes. From that premise, the IJ held that the term "injury" in the federal regulation "means 'any physical injury which requires professional medical treatment.' " (Quoting Cal. Penal Code § 243(f)(5)). As an initial matter, nothing in the *federal* statute suggests that the acts required to constitute battery depend on *state* law. Given the strong uniformity sought by Congress in the area of immigration law and its remedial purpose in enacting VAWA, we doubt that acts of violence would qualify (or fail to qualify) as battery depending on locale.

* * *

Finally, the BIA also suggested (as does the government on appeal) that no battery occurred for reasons that, while facially appealing, are in fact irrelevant. For example, it is true that the children now love their father and that he no longer beats them. But Congress chose to provide protection for anyone who *"has been"* battered while residing with the abuser. Petitioner and the amicus point out that, in the context of an abusive relationship, the abuser may re-start the abuse when he or she once again has that opportunity, for instance, if Petitioner is removed and the children move in with their father again and, if they wish to remain in the United States, have no choice but to remain with their father. Congress chose to prevent that opportunity by granting relief to those who *had been* subjected to battery. The BIA's suggestion that no battery occurred *in the past* because of the state of the relationship *today* is irrelevant under the plain text of the statute.

CONCLUSION

We hold that Petitioner demonstrated that her children had been battered by Campos within the meaning of INA § 240A(b)(2)(A)(i)(II). We therefore grant the petition. * * * Because we grant the petition on other grounds, we do not reach the issue of extreme cruelty.

* * *

MATTER OF A-M-

Board of Immigration Appeals, 2009.
25 I & N Dec. 66.

COLE, BOARD MEMBER:

* * *

The record reflects that the respondent, a 41-year-old native and citizen of Mexico, married her ex-husband in Oaxaca, Mexico, in 1984. They have four children together, one of whom is a United States citizen. In 1989 the respondent's ex-husband was working in the United States and arranged for the respondent, who did not have lawful status, to join him. The record contains extensive documentation that the respondent's ex-husband abused her both physically and mentally for a number of years. The couple eventually separated in 1996, and the respondent stated that she has not seen her ex-husband since 1998. After their separation, the respondent filed a self-petition to adjust her status to that of a lawful permanent resident as the battered spouse of a lawful permanent resident pursuant to INA § 204(a). The former Immigration and Naturalization Service (now the DHS) approved the respondent's self-petition on September 25, 2001. [She became a lawful permanent resident through adjustment of status.] Thereafter, the respondent and her ex-husband divorced on August 18, 2004, and she remarried in March 2006. Her current husband does not have lawful status in the United States.

The respondent was placed in removal proceedings on July 30, 2004, after she attempted to enter the United States from Mexico at the Otay Mesa port of entry in California with two minor children who were not her own. The respondent testified that she agreed to drive the children, who did not have lawful status or documentation to enter the United States, as a favor to their mother. There is no evidence in the record that she was criminally charged for this incident. The DHS issued a Notice to Appear (Form I–862), charging her as an arriving alien who is inadmissible under INA § 212(a)(6)(E)(i), for alien smuggling.

During her proceedings before the Immigration Judge, the respondent requested several forms of relief, including special rule cancellation for battered spouses under INA § 240A(b)(2). At a hearing on April 26, 2007, the parties stipulated that the respondent's ex-husband is a lawful permanent resident. The respondent also testified about the hardship that her United States citizen son, who is now 16 years old, would suffer if she were removed to Mexico. The respondent stated that he was born with a birth defect because his right ear is physically deformed, and he has hearing loss in that ear. She testified that her son is eligible for reconstructive surgery and that because of his hearing problems, he has been enrolled in special education classes since kindergarten.

* * *

[The immigration judge granted special rule cancellation, and DHS appealed. After a lengthy discussion of a complicated statutory interpretation question, the BIA held:]

[N]otwithstanding the heading of INA § 240A(b), which only refers to nonpermanent residents, we find that lawful permanent residents may be eligible to apply for special rule cancellation of removal for battered spouses under INA § 240A(b)(2). * * *

* * *

Cancellation of removal, like the relief available under former INA §§ 212(c) and 244(a), is a discretionary form of relief. In this case, the Immigration Judge found that the respondent was deserving of a discretionary grant of cancellation of removal. As previously noted, we have authority to review questions of discretion de novo.

* * *

The positive factors presented in the respondent's case include her residence in the United States since 1989, her three children with legal status living in the United States, and her gainful employment as a housekeeper. The Immigration Judge also found that her United States citizen son will suffer extreme hardship if she is removed and noted that she expressed remorse concerning the reasons for her removability. The negative factors include the circumstances underlying the respondent's removability, her failure to provide evidence that she filed income taxes, and her May 2003 conviction for driving under the influence.

Furthermore, given that the respondent is seeking relief as the battered spouse of a lawful permanent resident, we find that there are additional factors relevant to our consideration. Importantly, the Immigration Judge found that the respondent divorced her abusive ex-husband in 2004, and that she has already relied on her relationship with her ex-husband to adjust her status as a VAWA self-petitioner. Moreover, the respondent has been remarried since 2006 and is no longer in an abusive relationship with her ex-husband.

Given the underlying purpose of the battered spouse provisions of the Act, which is to enable aliens to leave their abusive citizen or lawful permanent resident spouses who may use the threat of deportation or sponsorship for an immigration benefit to maintain control over them, we find that these factors weigh heavily against granting the respondent's request for cancellation of removal under INA § 240A(b)(2). The respondent has already obtained a form of VAWA relief once, has become removable, and has not argued that she needs or is eligible for VAWA protection in her current relationship. The VAWA should not be invoked again to benefit an alien when the past abusive relationship has ended and the former abusive spouse no longer poses a threat. We recognize that the same factors, namely, the respondent's divorce, remarriage, and previous self-petition based on her abusive marriage, may not be equally relevant to other forms of discretionary relief. However, the respondent has requested cancellation of removal as a battered spouse, and such factors are significant to the nature and purpose of the relief she is seeking.

As a result, despite the respondent's equities, which are substantial, we find that on balance, given the adverse factors and the nature of the relief she is seeking, she has not shown that cancellation of removal under INA § 240A(b)(2) should be granted as a matter of discretion. Accordingly, we conclude that the Immigration Judge's grant of relief in the exercise of discretion was not appropriate.

Grant of discretion Not appropriate.

* * *

NOTES AND QUESTIONS ON *VAWA* CANCELLATION

1. Under INA § 242(a)(2)(B)(I), "any judgment regarding the granting of relief under . . . [§ 240A]" is not reviewable in federal court, with courts interpreting "judgment" to mean any discretionary decision. This provision bars judicial review of the BIA panel's ruling in *Matter of A-M-*. But if you were rearguing the discretionary aspect of VAWA cancellation on rehearing before the BIA en banc, could you argue persuasively that the panel erred by citing prior adjustment of status as a VAWA self-petitioner and the fact that her "former abusive spouse no longer poses a threat"? How might the government respond to your arguments?

PP. stay in relationships until granted VAWA relief

2. What is the smallest change in facts that would have persuaded the BIA panel in *Martinez* to affirm the immigration judge's decision?

3. The Ninth Circuit explains in *Lopez-Birrueta* that "Congress distinguished between 'battery' and 'extreme cruelty,' reserving the term extreme cruelty for something other than physical assault, presumably actions in some way involving mental or psychological cruelty." Though this alternative showing expands eligibility for VAWA cancellation, the majority of circuits have held that immigration judge and BIA determinations regarding the presence or absence of extreme cruelty are discretionary and under INA § 242(a)(2)(B)(I) are not reviewable in federal court. *Compare Johnson v. Attorney General*, 602 F.3d 508, 510–11 (3d Cir. 2010); *and Perales-Cumpean v. Gonzales*, 429 F.3d 977, 982 (10th Cir. 2005); *with Hernandez v. Ashcroft*, 345 F.3d 824, 833–35 (9th Cir. 2003).

b. Law Enforcement-Related or Victim Visas (T and U)

Immigration enforcement can impede criminal law enforcement if the threat of removal chills victims from seeking help or assisting law enforcement. In order to encourage victims to come forward and assist law enforcement, Congress created in 2000 two new nonimmigrant visa categories for certain victims of abuse or trafficking-related crimes if they are being helpful in prosecution or investigation of the perpetrators. Victims of Trafficking and Violence Protection Act of 2000 (VTVPA), Pub. L. 106–386, 114 Stat. 1464.

Advocates and lawmakers had in mind a variety of stories, among which this one was typical:

>   Various setbacks led the workers * * * to leave their homes
> and families in Mexico in 2004 and, ultimately, arrive in rural

Hudson, Colorado. * * * Yet none of the group ever imagined— much less consented to—debt bondage in a farm labor camp.

Moises Rodriguez, a labor contractor or crew boss, had purchased a farm labor camp (the Highway 52 compound) in Hudson in 2001. The Highway 52 Compound contained two two-story, barrack-style buildings with detached bathroom facilities. As the growing season began in March 2004, Rodriguez began recruiting workers in Mexico to come to Colorado to work in agriculture. * * * [D]uring the spring of 2004, Rodriguez made arrangements via various agents and *polleros* (smuggling guides) to bring groups of workers to the U.S.-Mexico border where the workers would cross the border without inspection by U.S. authorities and travel to Phoenix, Arizona where he had arranged temporary housing.

* * * Once the workers arrived in Phoenix, Rodriguez and family members then personally traveled from Hudson to Phoenix on several occasions to pay off the smugglers and pick up the groups of workers. * * * Rodriguez failed to make any of the disclosures about the terms and conditions of employment that are required under federal laws protecting migrant farm workers. For example, such laws require that migrant farm workers receive, at recruitment, written disclosures of the place of employment, the wage rates to be paid, the crops and kinds of activities in which the worker may be employed, the period of employment, the transportation, housing, and any other employee benefit to be provided, and any costs to be charged for each of them, among other details. These laws also require the payment of wages and prohibit employers from violating the terms of the working arrangement entered into with a worker.

While traveling from Phoenix to the Highway 52 compound, Rodriguez forced the workers to lie down in the back of his vehicle without seatbelts so that they could not be viewed from outside of the vehicle. * * *

Approximately forty workers lived in the compound, with four to six workers in each unit. Some people had to sleep on the floor. The water in the camp was not drinkable and had made people sick in the past. The compound contained a bathhouse with only two showers for all of the men. Usually only one toilet out of four in the bathhouse was functional. Inside the units, the beds and kitchens were infested with insects. Each night the workers were bitten by insects as they slept.

When each worker arrived at the Highway 52 compound, Rodriguez imposed a system of debt bondage that is prohibited under the TVPA and [the Trafficking Victims Protection Reauthorization Act of 2003]. Rodriguez informed the workers that they each owed him $1300 in smuggling fees. He further stated they would not be permitted to leave his employment until they paid the debt and indicated that he would track them down if they attempted to escape. The workers also understood that they would be forced to pay the debt of any coworker who fled. Rodriguez instructed the workers to behave so that the camp would not come to the attention of police.

Rodriguez served as landlord, supervisor, and coyote, and thus exercised enormous power and control over the workers. Six or seven days a week, a foreman transported the workers sixty to ninety minutes each way in a yellow school bus to work in fields in and around Wellington, Colorado. * * *

[Rodriguez] sat daily [in his vehicle] and watched the workers in the fields through binoculars to ensure they did not stray too far from the rest of the group. Because the Highway 52 compound was so far from the farm, the workers generally were away from the compound from 4:30 a.m. until 8 p.m. Thus, they had little contact with the outside world. * * *

Rodriguez further imposed a complex system of debts and other illegal deductions so that the workers were unable to earn more than a pittance and were unable to pay off their debt. For example, pay statements provided to the workers included the following deductions: rent charges of $50 twice per month, charges for rides to work of $48 twice per month, bathroom cleaning charges for filthy bathrooms, a deposit for clippers, rain gear, knives for work, illegal Social Security, and the ongoing total of smuggling fees owed. The deductions for Social Security appeared to be completely fabricated[.] * * *

* * * [T]he exploitation constituted involuntary servitude under the TVPA. On some weeks the workers were paid as little as $2.90 per hour for more than sixty hours of work. * * *

By late in the season, the Hudson workers determined that they would take a stand against this abuse. * * * However, they had no idea that to seek justice, they would undergo numerous law enforcement interviews, fingerprinting, photographing by three federal agencies, and interactions with several other federal and social service agencies between September 2004 and October 2005.

Patricia Medige, *The Labyrinth: Pursuing a Human Trafficking Case in Middle America*, 10 J. Gender Race & Just. 269, 273–78 (2007). Medige recounts the workers' interaction with the law enforcement agencies that successfully prosecuted Rodriguez for immigration violations (but not trafficking).

The workers in the above excerpt all eventually received T visas. This is a nonimmigrant category for victims of a "severe form of trafficking in persons," which includes the legal categories of forced commercial sex and forced labor. The definition generally requires the use of "force, fraud, or coercion" by the trafficker. *See* 8 C.F.R. § 214.11(a). For the grant of a T visa, the statute also requires a finding that the individual "would suffer extreme hardship involving unusual and severe harm upon removal," and that the individual (unless under 18 years of age) "has complied with any reasonable request for assistance in the Federal, State, or local investigation or prosecution of acts of trafficking or the investigation of crime where acts of trafficking are at least one central reason for the commission of that crime." *See* INA §§ 101(a)(15)(T), 214(*o*).

The U category, also created by statute in 2000, is for persons who "have suffered substantial physical or mental abuse" as victims of certain kinds of crimes—a broad and varied statutory list. *See* INA §§ 101(a)(15)(U), 214(p). Eligibility requires that the individual possesses information concerning that criminal activity, and "has been helpful, is being helpful, or is likely to be helpful" to law enforcement officials, prosecutors, judges, or other Federal, state, or local authorities.

Visas are capped at 5,000 per year for T visas and 10,000 for U. The statute imposes subtly different requirements in each category for judging the adequacy of assistance the applicant provides in the investigation and prosecution of the offender, as well as slightly variant procedures and presumptions. In U cases, for example, a law enforcement agency, prosecutor, or judge must submit a certification of assistance. For T visas, law enforcement letters or endorsements are useful evidence, but not indispensable. T and U status both result in work authorization, but only T status qualifies the individual for public benefits. VTVPA, Pub. L. 106–386, 114 Stat. 1464, § 107(b)(1)(A) (2000).

T and U visa holders can adjust to LPR status after three years' physical presence in the United States, with certain modest qualifications such as continued willingness to assist in the investigation or prosecution. INA § 245(*l*), (m). T and U nonimmigrants have real incentives to make timely application for adjustment, because T or U status is normally limited to four years' duration unless adjustment is pending. Spouses and children, and in some circumstances parents or siblings, can qualify for the initial status and also for adjustment as derivatives. Derivatives do not count against the annual ceilings on grants of the status.

We reprint as Figures 7.3 and 7.4 two tables from a DHS report that helpfully summarize and compare the requirements for the two types of visa and the two procedures, initial grant and adjustment to LPR status.

Citizenship and Immigration Services Ombudsman, *Improving the Process for Victims of Human Trafficking and Certain Criminal Activity: The T and U Visa* 16–18 (Jan. 29, 2009) [hereafter *Improving the Process for Victims*].

**Figure 7.3
Comparison of T and U Visa
Non-Immigrant Eligibility Requirements**

Eligibility	T Non-Immigrant Visa	U Non-Immigrant Visa
Type of Abuse	Victim of severe trafficking	Suffered substantial physical or mental abuse from certain criminal activity.
Where	Applicant must have been physically present in the United States or at a U.S. port of entry on account of such trafficking	Crime occurred in the United States or otherwise violated U.S. law
Helpfulness with Investigation or Prosecution	Comply with reasonable request for assistance with the investigation of trafficking act	Provide law enforcement certificate that victim has been, is likely to be or is being helpful to an investigation or prosecution of criminal activity.
Other	Applicant would suffer extreme hardship involving unusual and severe harm if removed	Victim possesses information about the criminal activity.

**Figure 7.4
Comparison of T and U Visa
Adjustment of Status Eligibility Requirements**

Eligibility	T Visa Adjustment of Status	U Visa Adjustment of Status
Lawful Admission	As T non-immigrant	As U non-immigrant
Physical Presence	Continuous period of 3 years since T non-immigrant status was granted OR a continuous period during the investigation, provided that it	Continuous period of 3 years since U non-immigrant status was granted

	has been certified [before 3 years] that the investigation is complete	
Character	Good moral character since being admitted as T non-immigrant	N/A
Helpfulness with Investigation or Prosecution	Continued compliance with reasonable requests for assistance in the investigation or prosecution OR extreme hardship involving unusual and severe harm upon removal	No unreasonable refusal to provide assistance in the criminal investigation or prosecution
Admissible	Admissible at the time of adjustment or otherwise have been granted a waiver for any ground of inadmissibility.	The only [sic] inadmissibility issue that is not waivable includes: Nazi persecution, genocide, or act of torture or extrajudicial killing. Not required to establish that they are admissible. USCIS uses discretion.

The agencies adopted T visa regulations in 2002, 8 C.F.R. §§ 212.16, 214.11, and 245.23, but U visa regulations were not finalized until 2007, *id.* §§ 212.17, 214.14, and 245.24, resulting in a significant backlog of U cases held for adjudication. T visa applications and grants have steadily increased since 2010, with almost 850 grants in 2013, and exceeding 1,000 applications in 2015, not counting derivatives. USCIS, *Number of I–914 Applications for T Nonimmigrant Status (Victims of Severe Forms of Trafficking and Family Members) by Fiscal Year, Quarter, and Case Status 2008–2015.* Because of the delayed regulations, virtually no U visas were granted before FY 2009, but over 5,800 were approved that year. The 10,000 cap on U visas has been met each year since 2010, including 2015 when the cap was met in the 1st quarter with over 63,000 applications pending. USCIS, *Number of I–918 Petitions for U Nonimmigrant Status (Victims of Certain Criminal Activities and Family Members) by Fiscal Year, Quarter, and Case Status 2009–2015.*

The Violence Against Women Reauthorization Act of 2013, Pub. L. 113–14, 127 Stat. 54, expanded modestly the range of crimes covered by the U visa provisions, the list of family members who could qualify for protection along with the principal, the applicable anti-aging-out provisions, and the possible waivers of otherwise applicable inadmissibility grounds for U and T visa applicants. *See especially* Title

VIII and §§ 1221, 1222. The final compromise legislation did not include provisions to raise the ceiling on U visas, nor to tighten eligibility and antifraud provisions, as different groups of legislators had advocated.

USCIS has reported informally that at least three-fourths of the U visa applicants have based their claims on domestic violence. Katherine Ellison, *A Special Visa Program Benefits Abused Illegal Immigrants*, N.Y. Times, Jan. 8, 2010. Perhaps this is not surprising; the caption on the U visa adjustment provision, INA § 245(m), reads "adjustment of status for victims of crimes against women," though the substance of the adjustment provision is not so limited. This odd caption also reflects the primary concerns that animated enactment of the U provision, as well as the rather limited and hasty legislative deliberation that preceded adoption.

NOTES AND QUESTIONS ON *T* AND *U* VISAS

1.   One of the fundamental questions raised by both the T and U nonimmigrant categories is implied by the title of this subsection: are these statuses intended to provide assistance to law enforcement, or are they statuses intended to provide relief to survivors and victims of criminal activity? *See generally* Jennifer M. Chacón, *Tensions and Trade-offs: Protecting Trafficking Victims in the Era of Immigration Enforcement*, 158 U. Pa. L. Rev. 1609 (2010); Dina Francesca Haynes, *(Not) Found Chained to a Bed in a Brothel: Conceptual, Legal, and Procedural Failures to Fulfill the Promise of the Trafficking Victims Protection Act*, 21 Geo. Immigr. L.J. 337 (2007). What balance should be struck when assisting survivors and victims amounts to overcoming their prior unauthorized presence in the United States? Note the strong form of assistance the statute makes available: a nonimmigrant status that is designed to lead fairly routinely to a green card. How vulnerable is this system to manipulation or collusion by smugglers? What checks, if any, exist against such possible misuse?

2.   The USCIS Ombudsman's office has described one important way in which the tension between statutory objectives works its way into practice. Discussing the certification required from a law enforcement agency for U visa applicants, it said:

> The certificate must be signed by a "certifying official," which is explicitly defined in the regulations as "[t]he head of the certifying agency or any person(s) in a supervisory role who has been specifically designated by the head of the certifying agency to issue U non-immigrant status certifications on behalf of that agency; or a Federal, State, or local judge."

> Stakeholders have reported to the Ombudsman that the requirement that the certification be signed by a supervisor or agency head is a significant administrative obstacle for applicants because the supervisor or agency head is often unavailable or not as

familiar with the case as another officer who worked on the case. Also, stakeholders have indicated that some officials are not always cooperative and are unaware of the protections afforded to victims in the [statute]. Others claim that officers are more responsive to certain types of crimes, such as sexual assault, but not other crimes, such as domestic violence.

USCIS Ombudsman, *Improving the Process for Victims, supra,* at 10. Some advocates have been urging that Congress delete the certification requirement altogether, permitting USCIS to assess helpfulness to investigation and prosecution based on the individual's own account plus any papers he or she chooses to submit. Do you agree?

3. What differentiates trafficking from smuggling? *See* 8 C.F.R. § 214.11(a). What would be the "extreme hardship involving unusual and severe harm upon removal" that the victims of Moises Rodriguez's trafficking could have asserted upon return to Mexico? How strict should these standards be?

c. Special Immigrant Juvenile Status (SIJS)

Another route to lawful permanent residence is special immigrant juvenile status (SIJS), which applies to individuals under the age of 21 who cannot be reunited with one or both of their parents due to abuse, neglect, or abandonment. They must have been placed in the custody of a state agency and there must be a determination that it would not be in the child's best interest to be returned to his or her homeland. INA § 101(a)(27)(J).

6. PROSECUTORIAL DISCRETION

a. Defining Prosecutorial Discretion

Prosecutorial discretion has been a main ingredient of the immigration system since its creation. * * * A favorable exercise of prosecutorial discretion in immigration law identifies the agency's authority to refrain from asserting the full scope of the agency's enforcement authority in a particular case. * * *

The theory behind immigration prosecutorial discretion is * * * twofold. The first part of the theory is economic. Specifically, the number of noncitizens who are technically "deportable" * * * is much larger than the number that the immigration agency can successfully handle with its available resources. * * *

The second part of the theory of prosecutorial discretion is humanitarian. Some individuals who are in technical violation of the law may nonetheless have redeeming qualities such as a loving marriage, continued valuable employment* * *

A closely tied and possible third-party theory is somewhat more political and describes the creation of prosecutorial discretion policies and statutory attempts to fixed immigration laws stall or fail.

Shoba Sivaprasad Wadhia, Beyond Deportation: The Role of Prosecutorial Discretion in Immigration Cases 8 (2015).

Exercises of "prosecutorial discretion" occur at both macro and micro levels. Macro-level decisionmaking to set enforcement priorities clearly influences which noncitizens are likely to be removed. For example, deciding to open a new ICE office in Omaha rather than Fargo will surely increase enforcement activity in Nebraska more than North Dakota. On a larger scale, DHS enforcement decisions post-September 11 emphasized national security issues (and noncitizens from particular countries). The Obama administration has continued prior administrations' emphasis on border enforcement, reinvigorated efforts to remove noncitizens with criminal convictions, and increased expedited removal of recent arrivals. We address macro-level discretion in the materials on enforcement choices in Chapter Ten. This chapter's discussion of prosecutorial discretion adopts the term's more typical usage, referring to micro-level decisions that affect particular individuals. On the micro-level, exercising prosecutorial discretion necessarily has two aspects: selecting particular individuals or members of groups for prosecution, and declining or deferring enforcement against others.

(i) Selective Prosecution

The U.S. Supreme Court briefly addressed selective prosecution in *Reno v. American-Arab Anti-Discrimination Committee*, 525 U.S. 471, 119 S.Ct. 936, 142 L.Ed.2d 940 (1999), which we encountered earlier in this chapter in the materials on deportability, p. 656 *supra*. The respondents, eight noncitizens who belonged to the Popular Front for the Liberation of Palestine, alleged that the INS selectively enforced immigration laws against them in violation of their First and Fifth Amendment rights. The district court preliminarily enjoined the deportation proceedings against some of the noncitizens as amounting to unlawful selective prosecution.

The issue that reached the Supreme Court was jurisdiction, since INA § 242(b)(9) seems to require a final removal order before decisions in proceedings may be challenged, and § 242(g) seems to eliminate federal court jurisdiction over decisions or actions "to commence proceedings, adjudicate cases, or execute removal orders." The noncitizens sought immediate review, claiming that selective prosecution would otherwise unconstitutionally chill their exercise of First Amendment rights. They argued that the Court should read the jurisdictional statute to allow immediate review to avoid serious constitutional questions concerning the First Amendment.

Holding

Finding that § 242(g) deprived the district court of jurisdiction, the Court, in a majority opinion by Justice Scalia, addressed selective prosecution:

> * * * As a general matter—and assuredly in the context of claims such as those put forward in the present case—an alien unlawfully in this country has no constitutional right to assert selective enforcement as a defense against his deportation.
>
> Even in the criminal-law field, a selective prosecution claim is a *rara avis*. Because such claims invade a special province of the Executive—its prosecutorial discretion—we have emphasized that the standard for proving them is particularly demanding, requiring a criminal defendant to introduce "clear evidence" displacing the presumption that a prosecutor has acted lawfully. *United States v. Armstrong,* 517 U.S. 456, 463–465, 116 S.Ct. 1480, 134 L.Ed.2d 687 (1996). We have said:

to prove selective prosecution need

>> This broad discretion [afforded the Executive] rests largely on the recognition that the decision to prosecute is particularly ill-suited to judicial review. Such factors as the strength of the case, the prosecution's general deterrence value, the Government's enforcement priorities, and the case's relationship to the Government's overall enforcement plan are not readily susceptible to the kind of analysis the courts are competent to undertake. Judicial supervision in this area, moreover, entails systemic costs of particular concern. Examining the basis of a prosecution delays the criminal proceeding, threatens to chill law enforcement by subjecting the prosecutor's motives and decisionmaking to outside inquiry, and may undermine prosecutorial effectiveness by revealing the Government's enforcement policy. All of these are substantial concerns that make the courts properly hesitant to examine the decision whether to prosecute.

? parts of prosec. discret.

courts cannot really evaluate that.

reasons to not evaluate

> *Wayte v. United States,* 470 U.S. 598, 607–608, 105 S.Ct. 1524, 84 L.Ed.2d 547 (1985).
>
> These concerns are greatly magnified in the deportation context. Regarding, for example, the potential for delay: Whereas in criminal proceedings the consequence of delay is merely to postpone the criminal's receipt of his just deserts, in deportation proceedings the consequence is to permit and prolong a continuing violation of United States law. Postponing justifiable deportation (in the hope that the alien's status will change—by, for example, marriage to an American citizen—or simply with the object of extending the alien's unlawful stay) is often the

principal object of resistance to a deportation proceeding, and the additional obstacle of selective-enforcement suits could leave the INS hard pressed to enforce routine status requirements. * * * The Executive should not have to disclose its "real" reasons for deeming nationals of a particular country a special threat—or indeed for simply wishing to antagonize a particular foreign country by focusing on that country's nationals—and even if it did disclose them a court would be ill equipped to determine their authenticity and utterly unable to assess their adequacy. Moreover, the consideration on the other side of the ledger in deportation cases—the interest of the target in avoiding "selective" treatment—is less compelling than in criminal prosecutions. * * * The contention that a violation must be allowed to continue because it has been improperly selected is not powerfully appealing.

To resolve the present controversy, we need not rule out the possibility of a rare case in which the alleged basis of discrimination is so outrageous that the foregoing considerations can be overcome.

525 U.S. at 489–92.

Justice Ginsburg agreed that § 242(g) deprived the court of jurisdiction notwithstanding First Amendment considerations, but on selective enforcement itself, she wrote:

It is well settled that "[f]reedom of speech and of press is accorded aliens residing in this country." *Bridges v. Wixon,* 326 U.S. 135, 148, 65 S.Ct. 1443, 89 L.Ed. 2103 (1945). Under our selective prosecution doctrine, "the decision to prosecute may not be deliberately based upon an unjustifiable standard such as race, religion, or other arbitrary classification, including the exercise of protected statutory and constitutional rights." *Wayte v. United States,* 470 U.S. 598, 608, 105 S.Ct. 1524, 84 L.Ed.2d 547 (1985). I am not persuaded that selective enforcement of deportation laws should be exempt from that prescription.

525 U.S. at 497–98, 119 S.Ct. at 950 (Ginsburg, J., concurring in part and concurring in the judgment).

(ii) Deferring Enforcement

At the individual level, the federal government may decide not to initiate removal proceedings against a noncitizen it has identified as removable, or to terminate ongoing removal proceedings. Or some noncitizens who are removable may come forward and ask that the government exercise prosecutorial discretion to refrain from enforcement.

Nonenforcement may sound counterintuitive or raise even deeper concerns. If DHS officials know that a person is unlawfully in the country, would they not as a matter of course initiate a removal proceeding and seek his or her expulsion? We know from general experience under the criminal law that authorities frequently exercise prosecutorial discretion in not bringing the force of the law against every known violator. The range of immigration law violations is similarly vast. Some are highly technical, such as a gap between two valid periods of student status, while others are more obvious, such as ignoring a final removal order.

Resource limitations are also a key part of prosecutorial discretion in immigration enforcement. In June 2010, John Morton, the director of ICE, explained that given present funding levels, the maximum capacity of the civil removal system is about 400,000 removals per year—under 4 percent of the unauthorized population. *See* Memorandum From John Morton, Assistant Sec'y, U.S. Immigration & Customs Enforcement, on Civil Immigration Enforcement (June 30, 2010). These limitations, combined with extra-statutory judgments about the seriousness of a particular offender's violation or the urgency of removing him from the United States, play a role in determining whether and which charges are actually brought.

(iii) Classifying Prosecutorial Discretion

Prosecutorial discretion ranges along a spectrum of formality, from a policy or a priority list to an informal decision, or series of them, not to act against a particular noncitizen. It can crystallize in a bureaucratic act of classifying a particular case as worthy of the exercise of discretion, taking specific form, as with deferred action. Originally known as "nonpriority enforcement status," deferred action has been in existence for many years. The initial guidelines that INS used to grant deferred action status came to light in the mid-1970s in the midst of INS attempts to remove former Beatle John Lennon for a British drug conviction.[21]

Those granted deferred action may obtain work authorization upon a showing of need, 8 C.F.R. § 274a.12(c)(14), but they receive few other benefits. They have no family reunification rights, and the status is subject to withdrawal at any time. Significantly, however, noncitizens do not accrue unlawful presence during the deferred action period for purposes of the three- and ten-year bars on future admission imposed by INA § 212(a)(9)(B). *See* Deferred Action for Childhood Arrivals:

---

[21] *See* Wildes, *The Nonpriority Program of the Immigration and Naturalization Service Goes Public: The Litigative Use of the Freedom of Information Act*, 14 San Diego L. Rev. 42, 42–49 (1976). Lennon escaped deportation (but based on judicial interpretation of the removal ground with which he was charged) and eventually became a lawful permanent resident. *Lennon v. INS*, 527 F.2d 187 (2d Cir. 1975).

Frequently Asked Questions, *https://www.dhs.gov/deferred-action-childhood-arrivals* (2015).

Stay of removal

Another form of prosecutorial discretion is a stay of removal, which can be issued at a later step in the process, after a removal order. In practical effect, it provides the same type of relief to noncitizens as deferred action. Though a discretionary stay of removal was traditionally used to give the noncitizen a reasonable amount of time to make arrangements before removal, or to forestall removal pending the outcome of a motion to reopen removal proceedings, it can be used more broadly, as a rough equivalent to deferred action for persons who already have a removal order.

NOTES AND QUESTIONS
ON DEFINING PROSECUTORIAL DISCRETION

1. Do you agree that decisions about who to select for prosecution should be immune from judicial review? Is the answer the same for decisions to defer prosecution of crimes? Or would courts be improperly inserting themselves into policy questions that are beyond their institutional competence?

2. Would broad discretion to make enforcement decisions run the risk of insulating undesirable grounds for those discretionary choices, such as justifications based on race or gender? How would a noncitizen take advantage of the exception that the Court carves out for "outrageous" discrimination in selection for enforcement?

3. Would the creation of transparent standards for exercising prosecutorial discretion ameliorate the concerns in notes 1 and 2?

b. The Regularization of Prosecutorial Discretion

The modern story of prosecutorial discretion in immigration enforcement starts with concerns that surfaced after the 1996 Act drastically limited relief from removal. Press accounts began to appear reporting on highly sympathetic cases that earlier would have generated a grant of relief but for which removal now seemed inevitable. Congress felt the pressure; in 1999, 28 members of the House wrote a letter to the Attorney General and INS Commissioner Doris Meissner calling attention to the existence of cases where removal was "unfair and resulted in unjustifiable hardship." The signatories included some of the leaders in adopting the restrictive 1996 legislation, including Congressman Lamar Smith (R-TX), chair of the House immigration subcommittee. They urged the adoption of guidelines for the use of prosecutorial discretion to avoid the hardship inflicted in such cases. 76 Interp. Rel. 1720 (1999).

In November 2000, Meissner issued a memorandum to INS field offices with guidance on prosecutorial discretion, explaining:

> Service officers are not only authorized by law but expected to exercise discretion in a judicious manner at all stages of the enforcement process—from planning investigations to enforcing final orders. * * * [Furthermore] INS officers may decline to prosecute a legally sufficient immigration case if the Federal immigration enforcement interest that would be served by prosecution is not substantial.

77 Interp. Rel. 1661 (2000). The memo identified factors to be considered in the exercise of prosecutorial discretion, including immigration history and status, length of stay in the United States, criminal history, humanitarian concerns, likelihood of ultimately removing the alien, likelihood of achieving the enforcement goal by other means, the effect on future admissibility, cooperation with law enforcement officials, community attention, U.S. military service, and available INS resources.

After the INS was abolished and immigration enforcement became the responsibility of Immigration and Customs Enforcement (ICE) within DHS, similar memos from DHS identified various enforcement priorities, leading eventually to two memos issued by ICE Director Morton in June 2011 with more refined prosecutorial discretion guidance.

One memo addressed "removal cases involving the victims and witnesses of crime, including domestic violence, and individuals involved in non-frivolous efforts related to the protection of their civil rights and liberties." It explained: "In these cases, ICE officers, special agents, and attorneys should exercise all appropriate prosecutorial discretion to minimize any effect that immigration enforcement may have on the willingness and ability of victims, witnesses, and plaintiffs to call police and pursue justice." The memo continued that absent special circumstances, it is against ICE policy "to initiate removal proceedings against an individual known to be the immediate victim or witness to a crime" or "to remove individuals in the midst of a legitimate effort to protect their civil rights or civil liberties." This would include "(for example, union organizing or complaining to authorities about employment discrimination or housing conditions) who may be in a non-frivolous dispute with an employer, landlord, or contractor." This was the first time that such civil rights-related factors appeared in official policy on prosecutorial discretion. Memorandum from John Morton, Assistant Sec'y, U.S. Immigration & Customs Enforcement, on Prosecutorial Discretion: Certain Victims, Witnesses, and Plaintiffs (June 17, 2011).

The other June 2011 memo addressed prosecutorial discretion more generally, expanding in significant respects on Morton's earlier memo on civil enforcement priorities. It greatly expanded the factors favorable to noncitizens that ICE officers, agents, and attorneys could consider in deciding whether to take a broad range of discretionary enforcement decisions. Morton clarified that "it is generally preferable to exercise such discretion as early in the case or proceeding as possible in order to preserve government resources that would otherwise be expended in pursuing the enforcement proceeding." He authorized ICE officials to exercise prosecutorial discretion without waiting for the noncitizen to request a favorable exercise of prosecutorial discretion, placing on ICE a responsibility for examining each case independently to determine whether to exercise discretion favorably. Memorandum from John Morton, Assistant Sec'y, U.S. Immigration & Customs Enforcement, on Exercising Prosecutorial Discretion Consistent With the Civil Immigration Enforcement Priorities of the Agency for the Apprehension, Detention, and Removal of Aliens (June 17, 2011).

DEVELOPMENTS AFTER THE JUNE 2011 MORTON MEMOS

Around the same time that ICE issued the June 2011 Morton memos, pressure on prosecutorial discretion came from a different direction, arising in the context of the DREAM Act, which is proposed federal legislation that would grant lawful immigration status to unauthorized migrants who were brought to the United States at a young age and who attend college or serve in the military. As part of their advocacy for the legislation, some potential DREAM Act beneficiaries deliberately made their identities known to the federal government, essentially daring ICE to arrest them and initiate removal proceedings. *See* Julia Preston, *After a False Dawn, Anxiety for Illegal Immigrant Students*, N.Y. Times, Feb. 8, 2011.

As the June 2011 Morton memo excerpted above suggests, noncitizens in this group are a low enforcement priority, and local involvement in immigration enforcement through Secure Communities and DREAM Act advocacy through self-identification as a form of advocacy raised the stakes for the federal government. Contrast the diffuse macro-decisionmaking that leads to a small likelihood that any given individual who is among the 11 million unauthorized migrants in the United States will be arrested. Those who want the federal government to pursue enforcement more vigorously will protest, but their complaints may be scattered.

In contrast, a government decision not to initiate a removal proceeding against a removable individual who not only has been identified by name, but also has been brought into custody leave the federal government much more politically exposed. The decision not to proceed—whether it reflects resource constraints or policy priorities—is much more likely to attract criticism, including the accusation that the government is disregarding the law. *See* Hiroshi Motomura, *The Discretion That Matters, Federal Immigration Enforcement, State and Local Arrests, and the Civil-Criminal Line*, 58 UCLA L. Rev. 1819, 1853–54 (2011) (explaining how this political exposure constrains the exercise of prosecutorial discretion after an individual noncitizen has been identified and arrested).

Such criticism came in the summer of 2011 from several quarters. The National ICE Council of the American Federation of Government Employees, which represents over 7,000 ICE officers, agents, and employees, sharply criticized the June 2011 Morton memos. Chris Crane, the ICE Council president, said that the memos created a "law enforcement nightmare" for ICE agents, adding: "It appears if the Obama administration doesn't like some laws, they just ignore them." *See* David Savage, *Gay Couples in Immigration Limbo*, L.A. Times, July 15, 2011.

The exercise of prosecutorial discretion in the context of immigration enforcement became front page news in June 2012 when DHS Secretary Janet Napolitano announced Deferred Action For Childhood Arrivals (DACA). The DACA guidelines provide that individuals who came to the United States as young children can seek the exercise of prosecutorial discretion to defer their removal from the United States for a renewable two-year period. Though deferred action does not convey a fully lawful status, approved DACA applicants can receive work authorization. The eligibility criteria for DACA follow:

- The applicant was under the age of 31 as of June 15, 2012

- The applicant came to the United States before the age of 16

- The applicant has continuously resided in the United States since June 15, 2007

- The applicant was physically present in the United States on June 15, 2012

- The applicant entered without inspection before June 15, 2012 or his or her lawful immigration status expired as of June 15, 2012

- The applicant is currently in school, has graduated from high school, has obtained a certificate of completion or a GED certificate, or is an honorably discharged veteran

- The applicant has not been convicted of a felony, significant misdemeanor, or three or more other misdemeanors, and does not pose a threat to public safety or national security.

As of March 31, 2016, about 820,000 of about 869,000 initial DACA applications were approved. Those with expiring initial two-year DACA periods have been able to file renewal applications. As of the same date, USCIS received about 575,000 renewal applications and approved about 539,000 of them.

Interesting data on the opportunities opened to DACA recipients, such as obtaining driver's licenses, opening bank accounts, and finding new jobs, can be found in Roberto G. Gonzales & Angie M. Bautista-Chavez, *Two Years and Counting: Assessing the Growing Power of DACA*, American Immigration Council (2014). Other useful reviews of the DACA program and those seeking relief under it can be found in Tom K. Wong, Kelly K. Richter, Ignacia Rodriguez & Philip Wolgin, *Results from a Nationwide Survey of DACA Recipients Illustrate the Program's Impact*, Center for American Progress (2015); Tom K. Wong, Angela S. Garcia, Marisa Abrajano, David FitzGerald, Karthick Ramakrishnan & Sally Le, *Undocumented No More: A Nationwide Analysis of Deferred Action for Childhood Arrivals, or DACA*, Center for American Progress (2013); Angelo Mathay & Margie McHugh, *DACA at the Three-Year Mark: High Pace of Renewals, But Processing Difficulties Evident*, Migration Policy Institute Issue Brief (2015).

The second phase of President Obama's executive actions arrived in November 2014, when he announced an expansion of the DACA program in several dimensions. One expansion was to eliminate the maximum age limit of thirty-one years. The second change was to move up from June 15, 2007, to January 1, 2010, the date by which noncitizens must have come to the United States. According to one estimate, the combination of these two changes would make approximately 290,000 additional noncitizens eligible for DACA. *See* Migration Policy Institute, *MPI: As Many as 3.7 Million Unauthorized Immigrants Could Get Relief from Deportation under Anticipated New Deferred Action Program* (press release, Nov. 19, 2014). The third change in DACA was to lengthen from two to three years the duration of a DACA grant. The expanded DACA was the same as the original version in all other respects.

At the same time that the President announced this expansion of DACA, he also launched a new deferred action program called Deferred Action for Parents of Americans and Lawful Permanent Residents (DAPA). DAPA would provide DACA-like temporary reprieves from deportation to parents of U.S. citizens and lawful permanent residents. These parents had to have been in the United States for five years before the program was announced in November 2014. Successful applicants would, as in the expanded DACA program, have a renewable but revocable reprieve for three years, and they would be eligible for employment authorization based on a showing of economic necessity. As with DACA, certain criminal convictions would be categorically disqualifying. According to one estimate, about 3.7 million people would qualify for DAPA. *See* Migration Policy Institute, *supra*.

As part of the deliberations that led to DAPA, the administration also considered deferred action for parents of noncitizens granted deferred action through DACA. On November 19, 2014, the Department of Justice Office of Legal Counsel issued an opinion explaining that a DACA-like deferred action program for parents of U.S. citizens and lawful permanent residents would be legally permissible, but that it would not be permissible for any such program to include parents of DACA recipients. OLC found that the former proposed program (which became DAPA) was permissible largely because it would be "consonant with congressional policy embodied in the INA." The opinion noted the numerous provisions of the statute that tend to favor family members of U.S. citizens and, to a lesser extent, of lawful permanent residents, but the latter program could not claim the same consonance. *See* Memorandum Opinion from Karl R. Thompson, Principal Deputy Assistant Att'y Gen., Office of Legal Counsel, to the Sec'y of Homeland Sec. and the Counsel to the President 31–33 (Nov. 19, 2014), http://www.justice.gov/sites/default/files/olc/opinions/attachments/2014/11/20/2014-11-19-auth-prioritize-removal.pdf. The government took the unusual step of releasing the OLC opinion at the time it announced its package of executive actions on November 20, 2014, in which DAPA was limited to certain parents of U.S. citizens and lawful permanent residents.

Almost immediately after the first DACA announcement in June 2012, various opponents of the program filed lawsuits to challenge the President's authority to adopt and implement it. After President Obama announced the expansion of DACA and the new DAPA program, opponents filed additional lawsuits, again arguing that the President had exceeded his authority under the U.S. Constitution and federal statutes.

Of these lawsuits, the most successful has been *Texas v. United States*, filed by 26 states in the federal district court for the Southern District of Texas. 809 F.3d 134 (5th Cir. 2015), *cert. granted*, 136 S.Ct. 906 (2016). The Fifth Circuit upheld a preliminary injunction blocking the implementation of DAPA and of the DACA expansion (though two-year DACA renewals could proceed). *See id.;* Michael D. Shear & Julia Preston, *Dealt Setback, Obama Puts Off Immigrant Plan*, N.Y. Times, Feb. 17, 2015. The court held that the state of Texas had standing to sue the federal government based on the cost of issuing state driver's licenses to noncitizens who would become eligible for licenses if the federal government approved their DAPA applications.

The Fifth Circuit then addressed District Court Judge Hanen's analysis of the merits of the plaintiffs' arguments. Judge Hanen had viewed the issue in the case as whether DAPA was within the executive authority to exercise prosecutorial discretion. On this issue, Judge Hanen's opinion reflected deep skepticism that the President has any authority to exercise prosecutorial discretion to grant anything more than a bare temporary reprieve from removal. This part of Hanen's opinion targeted the threshold eligibility that deferred action recipients gain to apply for work authorization.

The preliminary injunction that Judge Hanen issued was much narrower than his skepticism of executive authority to grant any broad form of relief from removal. He held that DAPA was a legislative rule that required the Department of Homeland Security to follow the notice and comment procedures set out in the Administrative Procedure Act, which DHS had not followed. Key to this holding was Judge Hanen's conclusion that DAPA did not truly allow DHS officers to make discretionary decisions. Rejecting the federal government's argument that DHS would exercise meaningful discretion after an applicant met threshold eligibility requirements, Hanen found that DAPA would automatically grant a reprieve to any applicant who met the threshold eligibility criteria. This meant, in turn, that DAPA represented a legislative rule that could not be adopted without notice and comment procedures.

A Fifth Circuit panel majority agreed that DAPA went beyond the nonenforcement at the core of prosecutorial discretion by conferring benefits beyond a temporary reprieve from deportation. *Texas v. United States*, 787 F.3d 733, 747–54 (5th Cir. 2015). It affirmed the basis of the district court's decision—that the APA notice-and-comment requirements applied to DAPA. The court stated that an "agency rule that modifies substantive rights and interests can only be nominally procedural, and the exemption for such rules of agency procedure cannot apply. DAPA modifies substantive rights and interests—conferring lawful presence on 500,000 illegal aliens in Texas forces the state to choose between spending millions of dollars to subsidize driver's licenses and changing its law." *Id.* at 765–66.

Judge Higginson dissented on the grounds that DAPA reflected non-justiciable agency discretion, and that the APA notice-and-comment requirements do not apply to DAPA because the program is not a legislative rule. As of this writing, this preliminary injunction against implementation remains in effect. The Supreme Court granted certiorari, directing the parties to additionally brief the issue of whether DAPA violates the Take Care Clause of the Constitution, and heard the case in May 2016. United States v. Texas, 136 S.Ct. 906 (2016).

Similar issues arose but led to a different outcome in two other court challenges to DACA and DAPA. In *Arpaio v. Obama*, 797 F.3d 11, 19–25 (D.C. Cir. 2015), the District of Columbia Circuit ruled that Maricopa County (AZ) Sheriff Joe Arpaio lacked standing to bring a legal challenge to the Obama administration's deferred action policies, including DACA and DAPA. The state of Mississippi and federal immigration enforcement personnel filed a separate lawsuit, which a federal district court dismissed for lack of standing. *Crane v. Johnson,* 783 F.3d 244, 251–55 (5th Cir. 2015).

As another part of a large package of executive reform measures announced on November 20, 2014, DHS Secretary Jeh Johnson issued a new formulation of the DHS enforcement priorities, reprinted below. Secretary Johnson's priorities memo expressly applies Department-wide, whereas Assistant Secretary Morton had authority only over ICE. (CBP failures to adhere to the priorities indicated in the Morton memorandum had been a significant point of criticism directed toward the Obama administration by immigration activists.) The Secretary also rescinded the Morton priorities memo and several other related guidance documents on prosecutorial discretion, because his directives superseded them.

POLICIES FOR THE APPREHENSION, DETENTION AND REMOVAL OF UNDOCUMENTED IMMIGRANTS

Memorandum from Jeh Charles Johnson, Secretary of Homeland Security
November 20, 2014.

* * *

In general, our enforcement and removal policies should continue to prioritize threats to national security, public safety, and border security. The intent of this new policy is to provide clearer and more effective guidance in the pursuit of those priorities. To promote public confidence in our enforcement activities, I am also directing herein greater transparency in the annual reporting of our removal statistics, to include data that tracks the priorities outlined below.

* * * Due to limited resources, DHS and its Components cannot respond to all immigration violations or remove all persons illegally in the United States. As is true of virtually every other law enforcement agency, DHS must exercise prosecutorial discretion in the enforcement of the law. And, in the exercise of that discretion, DHS can and should develop smart enforcement priorities, and ensure that use of its limited resources is devoted to the pursuit of those priorities. * * *

In the immigration context, prosecutorial discretion should apply not only to the decision to issue, serve, file, or cancel a Notice to Appear, but also to a broad range of other discretionary enforcement decisions, including deciding: whom to stop, question, and arrest; whom to detain or release; whether to settle, dismiss, appeal, or join in a motion on a case; and whether to grant deferred action, parole, or a stay of removal instead of pursuing removal in a case. While DHS may exercise prosecutorial discretion at any stage of an enforcement proceeding, it is generally preferable to exercise such discretion as early in the case or proceeding as possible in order to preserve government resources that would otherwise be expended in pursuing enforcement and removal of higher priority cases. Thus, DHS personnel are expected to exercise discretion and pursue these priorities at all stages of the enforcement process—from the earliest investigative stage to enforcing final orders of removal—subject to their chains of command and to the particular responsibilities and authorities applicable to their specific position.

* * *

A. Civil Immigration Enforcement Priorities

The following shall constitute the Department's civil immigration enforcement priorities:

> *Priority 1 (threats to national security,
> border security, and public safety)*

Aliens described in this priority represent the highest priority to which enforcement resources should be directed:

(a) aliens engaged in or suspected of terrorism or espionage, or who otherwise pose a danger to national security;

(b) aliens apprehended at the border or ports of entry while attempting to unlawfully enter the United States;

(c) aliens convicted of an offense for which an element was active participation in a criminal street gang, as defined in 18 U.S.C. § 52 l(a), or aliens not younger than 16 years of age who intentionally participated in an organized criminal gang to further the illegal activity of the gang;

(d) aliens convicted of an offense classified as a felony in the convicting jurisdiction, other than a state or local offense for which an essential element was the alien's immigration status; and

(e) aliens convicted of an "aggravated felony," as that term is defined in section 101(a)(43) of the Immigration and Nationality Act at the time of the conviction.

* * *

> *Priority 2 (misdemeanants and new
> immigration violators)*

Aliens described in this priority, who are also not described in Priority 1, represent the second-highest priority for apprehension and removal. Resources should be dedicated accordingly to the removal of the following:

(a) aliens convicted of three or more misdemeanor offenses, other than minor traffic offenses or state or local offenses for which an essential element was the alien's immigration status, provided the offenses arise out of three separate incidents;

(b) aliens convicted of a "significant misdemeanor," which for these purposes is an offense of domestic violence; sexual abuse or exploitation; burglary; unlawful possession or use of a firearm; drug distribution or trafficking; or driving under the influence; or if not an offense listed above, one for which the individual was sentenced to time in custody of 90 days or more (the sentence must involve time to be served in custody, and does not include a suspended sentence);

(c) aliens apprehended anywhere in the United States after unlawfully entering or re-entering the United States and who cannot establish to the satisfaction of an immigration officer that they have been physically present in the United States continuously since January 1, 2014; and

(d) aliens who, in the judgment of an ICE Field Office Director, USCIS District Director, or USCIS Service Center Director, have significantly abused the visa or visa waiver programs.

* * *

Priority 3 (other immigration violations)

Priority 3 aliens are those who have been issued a final order of removal on or after January 1, 2014. Aliens described in this priority, who are not also described in Priority 1 or 2, represent the third and lowest priority for apprehension and removal. Resources should be dedicated accordingly to aliens in this priority. * * *

B. Apprehension, Detention, and Removal of Other Aliens Unlawfully in the United States

Nothing in this memorandum should be construed to prohibit or discourage the apprehension, detention, or removal of aliens unlawfully in the United States who are not identified as priorities herein. However, resources should be dedicated, to the greatest degree possible, to the removal of aliens described in the priorities set forth above, commensurate with the level of prioritization identified. Immigration officers and attorneys may pursue removal of an alien not identified as a priority herein, provided, in the judgment of an ICE Field Office Director, removing such an alien would serve an important federal interest.

* * *

D. Exercising Prosecutorial Discretion

Section A, above, requires DHS personnel to exercise discretion based on individual circumstances. * * * [A]liens in Priority 1 must be prioritized for removal unless they qualify for asylum or other form of relief under our laws, or unless, in the judgment of an ICE Field Office Director, CBP Sector Chief, or CBP Director of Field Operations, there are compelling and exceptional factors that clearly indicate the alien is not a threat to national security, border security, or public safety and should not therefore be an enforcement priority. Likewise, aliens in Priority 2 should be removed unless they qualify for asylum or other forms of relief under our laws, or unless, in the judgment of an ICE Field Office Director, CBP Sector Chief, CBP Director of Field Operations, USCIS District Director, or USCIS Service Center Director, there are factors indicating the alien is not a threat to national security, border security, or public safety and should not therefore be an enforcement priority. Similarly, aliens in Priority 3 should generally be removed unless they qualify for asylum or another form of relief under our laws or, unless, in the judgment of an immigration officer, the alien is not a threat to the integrity of the immigration system or there are factors suggesting the alien should not be an enforcement priority.

In making such judgments, DHS personnel should consider factors such as: extenuating circumstances involving the offense of conviction; extended length of time since the offense of conviction; length of time in the United States; military service; family or community ties in the United States; status as a victim, witness or plaintiff in civil or criminal proceedings; or compelling humanitarian factors such as poor health, age, pregnancy, a young child, or a seriously ill relative. These factors are not intended to be dispositive nor is this list intended to be exhaustive. Decisions should be based on the totality of the circumstances.

* * *

G. No Private Right Statement

These guidelines and priorities are not intended to, do not, and may not be relied upon to create any right or benefit, substantive or procedural, enforceable at law by any party in any administrative, civil, or criminal matter.

———————

NOTES AND QUESTIONS ON THE JOHNSON PRIORITIES MEMO

1. An analysis of the Johnson memo by the Migration Policy Institute, drawing on DHS and census data, concluded that it could exempt 87 percent of the resident unauthorized population from enforcement:

[This report] estimates that about 13 percent of unauthorized immigrants currently resident in the United States (about 1.4 million out of an overall population estimated at 11 million) have previous criminal convictions or immigration histories that would make them enforcement priorities under the new policies. By comparison, about 27 percent of unauthorized immigrants (3 million people) would have been considered enforcement priorities under the 2010–11 guidelines. * * * While much of the attention to the president's executive action announcement has focused on the deferred action programs [DAPA and expanded DACA], which could grant relief from deportation to as many as 5.2 million unauthorized immigrants, implementation of the new enforcement priorities and the PEP program are likely to affect * * * about 9.6 million people.

* * * [T]he 2014 policy guidance, if strictly adhered to, is likely to reduce deportations from within the United States by about 25,000 cases annually—bringing interior removals below the 100,000 mark (as compared to the all-time high of 188,000 recorded in fiscal year 2011). Removals at the U.S.-Mexico border remain a top priority under the 2014 guidelines, so falling interior removals may be offset to some extent by increases at the border * * * .

Marc R. Rosenblum, *Understanding the Potential Impact of Executive Action on Immigration Enforcement*, 1 Migration Pol'y Inst. (2015).

What is your assessment of the priorities, in view of Rosenblum's analysis? Do they cover too little? Too much? What adjustments would you make? Would you re-order the subcategories?

2. Note that the Johnson memo, in Sections B and D, permits departure from the priorities, in either direction (for or against removal) in certain circumstances. Look carefully at the mitigating factors listed in Section D, which governs declining to enforce even though a priority applies, and also at the precise standards that apply to such a decision. The factors and standards differ for each of the three priorities, and different sets of officers or supervisors are empowered or required to make the decision to depart from the priorities. (There are still further differences in factors and procedures for Section B, which sets guidelines for when enforcement *can* occur for someone falling outside the priorities.)

Rosenblum, *supra,* at 8–9, notes that the earlier Morton memos also had a similar list of mitigating factors, but they did not provide much guidance on "how to resolve the potential tension between the DHS enforcement goals and the agency's ground for discretion." He sees the standards summarized in Section D as more effective. "Providing enforcement officials with clear direction on these ambiguous cases is important because tens, or perhaps hundreds, of thousands of unauthorized immigrants may be *both* priorities for enforcement *and* potential candidates for the favorable exercise of discretion." Does Section D provide "clear direction"? In the other direction, does Section B?

3.   Consider the treatment of Priority 3 in Section D. Note that Secretary Johnson places a relatively narrow pool of persons with final removal orders within this priority—only those with orders issued after January 1, 2014. (DHS has indicated, however, that this is a fixed date and will not be stepped up as time passes; hence this priority 3 pool will grow as persons fail to honor new removal orders. *See generally* Julia Preston, *Detention Center Presented as Deterrent to Border Crossings*, N.Y. Times, Dec. 16, 2014 (Secretary Johnson emphasized that the administration is making "a sharp distinction between past and future" with regard to enforcement). Now consider the guidance on exceptions to removal for persons within Priority 3. Can a person's willful refusal to honor a removal order duly issued after a full hearing before an immigration judge "not [be] a threat to the integrity of the immigration system"? Under what circumstances?

4.   The November 2014 executive actions touched off a firestorm of criticism and some litigation, charging that the actions were beyond the President's authority or amounted to illegal efforts to rewrite the law or abdicate enforcement of duly enacted statutes that the President had simply been unable to change through the prescribed legislative procedures. Defense of the November actions against these charges often relied heavily on the retention of officer discretion to proceed with removal even of those who fall outside the priorities or who would qualify for DACA or DAPA. (Section B preserves such discretion under the Johnson priorities memo; similar provisions exist for DACA and DAPA.) *See, e.g.,* Stephen H. Legomsky, Written Testimony Before the United States Senate Comm. on the Judiciary at 8–10 (January 28–29, 2015).

How effective is the language of Section B as a counter to complaints that the executive has simply rewritten the law? In practice, how much room does it give to an officer to decide to proceed with removal of someone otherwise outside the priorities? Despite the inclusion of the following quoted phrase in Section B, surely the priorities are meant at least to "*discourage* the apprehension, detention, or removal of aliens unlawfully in the United States who are not identified as priorities" (emphasis added). Several commentators have seen the November 2014 executive actions as primarily an effort to assure centralized control over actual street-level enforcement decisions, in service of consistency and accountability—and they therefore see such changes as a key benefit of the new directives (both the priorities memo and the deferred action programs). *See* Adam B. Cox & Cristina M. Rodríguez, *The President and Immigration Law Redux,* 125 Yale L.J. (2015); Juliet P. Stumpf, *D(e)volving Discretion: Lessons from the Life and Times of Secure Communities,* 64 Am. U. L. Rev. 1259 (2015). *See also* Hiroshi Motomura, Immigration Outside the Law 204–05 (2014) (identifying such centralization and control as a major motivating factor and benefit of DACA). For such centralized control and consistency to work, however, must Section B be largely window dressing?

CHAPTER EIGHT

ASYLUM AND THE CONVENTION AGAINST TORTURE

■ ■ ■

A. HUMANITARIAN PROTECTION

1. OVERVIEW

People are forced to leave their homelands for many reasons. They flee war, persecution, natural disaster, environmental catastrophe, severe economic privation, and other intolerable conditions. Over the decades, U.S. policymakers have responded—selectively—to the need for humanitarian action via ad hoc programs, special legislation, and flexible administrative procedures. Congress has also adopted permanent legislation that provides for more enduring and less situational protection for specified categories of forced migrants, especially through sections 208 and 241(b)(3) of the Immigration and Nationality Act.

The United States extends permanent resident status each year to refugees who are screened and selected overseas. Under the Refugee Act of 1980, Pub. L. 96–212, 94 Stat. 102 (1980), the President, in consultation with Congress, authorizes the resettlement of a specific number of refugees each year, and designates in broad terms which refugee situations will be the focus of resettlement. INA § 207. As shown in Figure 8.1, this procedure allowed more than 100,000 refugees to come to the United States annually through much of the 1990s. In the post-2001 decade the yearly quota fluctuated between 70,000 and 80,000, with heightened screening procedures sometimes resulting in fewer refugees arriving than were authorized. The outpouring of refugees from Syria into Europe in 2015 resulted in increased U.S. resettlement goals: from 70,000 in FY 2015 to 85,000 in FY 2016, with a forecast of 100,000 in FY 2017. Persons admitted as refugees can adjust status to lawful permanent resident after one year in the United States. INA § 209(a).

In addition to admitting individuals from refugee camps overseas, the Refugee Act of 1980 also authorizes individuals to apply for asylum when they arrive at the U.S. borders (or from within U.S. territory). INA § 208. There are no numerical limits on grants of asylum in the United States every year, but asylum seekers—like refugees—must demonstrate that they have a well-founded fear of persecution.

Figure 8.1
U.S. Annual Refugee Resettlement Ceilings and
Number of Refugees Admitted, 1980–Present

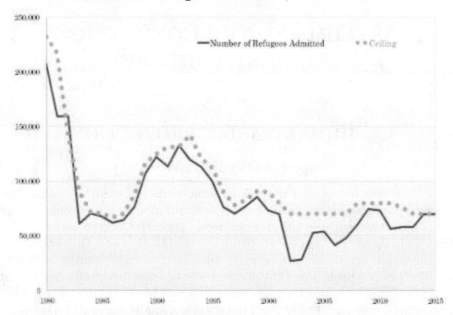

Source: Originally published on the Migration Policy Institute Data Hub,
http://www.migrationpolicy.org/programs/data-hub/us-immigration-trends.

What about those fleeing war or earthquake or a disaster at a nuclear plant? Such persons may find safe haven in the United States via temporary protected status (TPS), but only in specific situations specified by the executive branch. INA § 244. This section gives the Secretary of Homeland Security discretion to designate countries in which armed conflict, natural disaster, or other circumstances pose a serious threat to personal safety or to the ability of the home country to handle the return of its citizens. INA § 244(b)(1). TPS typically is authorized for eighteen-month renewable increments. The TPS designation protects only individuals already in the United States. INA § 244(c)(1). This substantial limitation is meant to prevent TPS from creating a magnet effect. Since the enactment of the TPS statue in 1990, TPS has been granted to hundreds of thousands of citizens from roughly 20 countries, based sometimes on the existence of armed conflict, sometimes on environmental disasters.

In addition, the Victims of Trafficking and Violence Protection Act of 2000, Pub. L. 106–386, 114 Stat. 1464 (Oct. 28, 2000), created special programs for victims of trafficking offenses and for individuals who suffered substantial physical or mental abuse. As discussed in Chapter Seven, up to 5,000 T visas are available each year to protect trafficking victims who assist in the investigation and prosecution of the traffickers. INA § 101(a)(15)(T). Separately, 10,000 U visas per year for individuals who have suffered criminal abuse and assist law enforcement officers in prosecuting the offenders. INA § 101(a)(15)(U). After three years, both the T visa holders and the U visa holders may become lawful permanent residents.

Another route to lawful permanent residence is special immigrant juvenile status (SIJS), which applies to individuals under the age of 21 who cannot be reunited with their parents due to abuse, neglect, or abandonment. As discussed in Chapter Seven, the individual must have been placed in the custody of a state agency and there must be a determination that it would not be in the child's best interest to be returned to his or her homeland. INA § 101(a)(27)(J).

This snapshot of humanitarian protection in the United States sets the context for exploring the central legal and policy issues in the core legal protections: asylum and withholding of removal. A full examination of this burgeoning area of law is beyond the scope of this chapter, but you can find a more in-depth treatment in our casebook on this subject, David A. Martin, T. Alexander Aleinikoff, Hiroshi Motomura & Maryellen Fullerton, Forced Migration: Law and Policy (2d ed. 2013).

2. THE INTERNATIONAL LEGAL FRAMEWORK FOR REFUGEES

Narratives of flight from persecution or war evoke sympathetic images of refugees. Protection, however, is usually reserved for those who meet a specific legal definition. The law of many countries, including the United States, grants refugee status only to those who arrive at the borders or who enter the country and show they satisfy the definition adopted by Article 1(A)(2) the 1951 Convention Relating to the Status of Refugees, 189 U.N.T.S. 137, signed July 28, 1951, as modified by Article I of the 1967 Protocol, 1967 Protocol Relating to the Status of Refugees, done January 31, 1967, 19 U.S.T. 6223, T.I.A.S. No. 6577, 606 U.N.T.S. 267 (both reprinted in the Statutory Supplement):

> [T]he term "refugee" shall apply to any person who * * * owing to well-founded fear of being persecuted for reasons of race, religion, nationality, membership of a particular social group or political opinion, is outside the country of his nationality and is unable or, owing to such fear, is unwilling to avail himself of the protection of that country * * * .

When governments gathered to ratify the 1951 Convention, the Second World War was a recent memory. Millions of people had been uprooted; many had not returned and were unlikely ever to go home. Given this reality, and reluctant to commit themselves to large future obligations, the governments crafted a limited definition: refugees had to have crossed an international border, to have a well-founded fear of persecution on account of one of five specified reasons, and to be unwilling to return home. Furthermore, the 1951 Convention definition limited refugees to those whose fears arose out of events prior to 1951, a temporal limitation later removed by the 1967 Protocol.

To put this definition in context, the United Nations High Commissioner for Refugees placed the world's total of refugees and asylum seekers at 20 million at the beginning of 2015, in addition to 38 million individuals living in refugee-like situations within their own countries. A great many of these people would probably not satisfy the 1951 Convention definition, for they have not fled targeted persecution. Some of the largest concentrations of refugee populations (as they are popularly understood)—for example, Afghan refugees in Pakistan and Iran, Syrian refugees in Turkey, Lebanon, and Jordan, Sudanese and Somalis in Chad and Kenya, respectively, Burmese in Thailand, or Colombians in Latin America—consist primarily of people who fled civil war and ethnic strife, or perhaps some combination of natural disasters (such as drought) and human-caused suffering. The prevailing legal definition does not include such people.

Evolving regional norms have embraced broader refugee definitions than the 1951 Convention. In Africa, the Organization of African Unity (OAU) Convention Governing the Specific Aspects of Refugee Problems in Africa, done Sept. 10, 1969, 1001 U.N.T.S. 45, (since 2002 the OAU is known as the African Union) defined its coverage to include both the 1951 Convention definition and the following:

> The term "refugee" shall also apply to every person who, owing to external aggression, occupation, foreign domination or events seriously disturbing public order in either part or the whole of his country of origin or nationality, is compelled to leave his place of habitual residence in order to seek refuge in another place outside his country of origin or nationality.

Art. I (2).

In the Americas, the Organization of American States (OAS) General Assembly endorsed the refugee definition found in the Cartagena Declaration on Refugees, but in a form that does not have the legally binding effect of a treaty:

> * * * [T]he concept of a refugee * * * [should include] persons who have fled their country because their lives, safety or freedom have been threatened by generalized violence, foreign aggression, internal conflicts, massive violation of human rights or other circumstances which have seriously disturbed public order.

Legal Status of Asylees, Refugees, and Displaced Persons in the American Hemisphere, AG/RES 774/XV–0/85 (Dec. 9, 1985).

More recently, the European Union (EU) has expanded asylum to include both refugees who satisfy the 1951 Convention definition and those who would face serious harm if returned to their homeland. EU law defines serious harm to include execution, torture, inhuman or degrading treatment, or serious threat to a civilian's life due to indiscriminate violence from armed conflict. Directive 2011/95/EU of the European Parliament and of the Council of 13 December 2011 on Standards for the Qualification of Third-country Nationals or Stateless Persons as Beneficiaries of International Protection, Art. 15.

3.   ASYLUM AND *NONREFOULEMENT*

The 1951 Convention Relating to the Status of Refugees has remained the fundamental legal framework for protecting refugees. In addition to defining those who qualify as refugees, the Convention details specific protections furnished to those who fall within its scope. Two concepts, asylum and *nonrefoulement*, are basic to understanding the legal ramifications of refugee status. Protection against *refoulement*, the French term often used to denote the return of refugees to persecution, is clearly the most basic need of a refugee. "Asylum" is subject to more varied understanding, and the treaty does not mention or define the term. Asylum usually refers to a situation wherein the refugee is not merely shielded against return but also enjoys an ample array of rights, such as the rights to work and to reunite with family, that enables him or her to rebuild a normal life in the country of refuge.

Refugees from Kosovo wait at Blace to cross into Macedonia, March 1999.
(Photo: © Roger Le Moyne, UNHCR).

The drafting history of the treaty indicates that states were not necessarily expected to grant lawful status to persons simply because they meet the definition of "refugee." Most Convention rights, including work authorization (Article 17) and access to public relief or social security (Articles 23 and 24), are restricted to refugees "lawfully in" or "lawfully staying in" the territory. Accordingly, states have discretion whether to grant these rights to refugees present without legal authority. Nonetheless, core rights, including *nonrefoulement* and access to courts (Article 16), may be claimed by refugees even if they are not lawfully present.

Article 33 of the Convention provides:

> No Contracting State shall expel or return ("*refouler*") a refugee in any manner whatsoever to the frontiers of territories where his life or freedom would be threatened on account of his race, religion, nationality, membership of a particular social group or political opinion.

This protection mandates only non-return; it does not require states to provide further rights. Indeed, it does not even require states to allow the individuals to remain—they can be sent away to any other state so long as they are not returned to a state where their life or freedom would be threatened. (Article 33(2) also allows exceptions for serious crimes and national security risks.) In practice, though, other states are unlikely to accept a person (not bearing their nationality) whom a sister state is trying to send away. Consequently, most states realize that they will not be able to expel a noncitizen who satisfies the *nonrefoulement* criteria. Many countries therefore tend to give these individuals a legal status—in many countries known as asylum—that allows them to remain and earn a living.

Most of the practice concerning *nonrefoulement* developed in the context of Article 33 of the 1951 Convention, but the *nonrefoulement* concept is not so limited. A closely related protection derives from the Convention Against Torture and Other Cruel, Inhuman, or Degrading Treatment or Punishment (CAT), adopted Dec. 10, 1984, G.A. Res. 39/46, U.N. GAOR, 39th Sess., Supp. No. 51, U.N. Doc. A/39/51 (1985), entered into force, June 26, 1987. Article 3 bars return of a person to a state "where there are substantial grounds for believing that he would be in danger of being subjected to torture." The United States became a party to the treaty in 1994 and fully implemented this specific *nonrefoulement* protection by regulations adopted in 1999. We will consider CAT protection in Section E of this chapter.

B. ASYLUM IN THE UNITED STATES

1. HISTORY AND OVERVIEW

From the very beginning of federal immigration laws, Congress has recognized that special exemptions may be necessary for otherwise inadmissible or deportable noncitizens who have become political enemies of the government in the nation to which they would be sent. In 1875, when Congress first provided that convicts would be excludable, it exempted persons who had been convicted of political offenses. Similar exemptions appeared with regularity in later laws.

There was, however, little systematic attention in the United States to providing asylum to refugees prior to the end of World War II. Indeed, much of the impetus for new American and international efforts after the war derived from a recognition that pre-war efforts, especially on behalf of Jewish refugees, had been shamefully inadequate. Although the United States did not ratify the 1951 Convention, it later became a party to the 1967 Protocol, thereby agreeing to the definition and refugee protections set forth in the 1951 treaty. *See* 1967 Protocol relating to the Status of Refugees, done January 31, 1967, 19 U.S.T. 6223, T.I.AS. No. 6577, 606 U.N.T.S. 267. For the first three decades after World War II, most legislative attention was focused on the overseas refugee situation, and statutes mainly provided for bringing forced migrants, after overseas processing and selection, from distant locations as part of a deliberate U.S. program. This included special programs to deal with displaced persons left stranded by World War II, the Displaced Persons Act of 1948, Ch. 647, 62 Stat. 1009, refugees from the Hungarian revolution in 1956, and Cubans seeking to come to the United States after Fidel Castro came to power.

Congress also began to address the situation of people who seek protection only after reaching this country. Congress enacted a statute in 1950 to exempt noncitizens from deportation "to any country in which the Attorney General shall find that such alien would be subjected to physical persecution." Internal Security Act of 1950, Ch. 1024, § 23, 64 Stat. 987, 1010. Two years later Congress rewrote this provision to authorize the Attorney General, *in his discretion*, to withhold deportation of a noncitizen who would be subject to physical persecution in his or her homeland. This *nonrefoulement* protection, which at that time appeared as § 243(h) of the INA, became known in the United States as "withholding of deportation" or, more recently, as "withholding of removal." It was administered for many years under the strong influence of Cold War assumptions. Successful claimants were, in overwhelming proportions, refugees from Communist countries, although the statute contained no such limitation.

When Congress passed the Refugee Act of 1980, five years after the Vietnam War ended, the flow of refugees from Indochina was at its peak. The Act focused primarily on reforming the overseas refugee admissions program, but also made a few important improvements respecting asylum for those who reached the United States on their own. The 1980 Refugee Act added § 208 to the INA, authorizing the government to use its discretion to grant "asylum" (or "asylee") status for individuals who meet the statutory definition of refugee—that is, who have a well-founded fear of persecution on account of one of the five specified grounds if returned to their home countries.

The Refugee Act of 1980 also amended INA § 243(h)—now INA § 241(b)(3) without significant substantive change—to make it mandatory that the Attorney General withhold deportation for noncitizens who would face persecution if returned to their homelands. This change was meant to bring the United States into line with its *nonrefoulement* obligation as a party to the 1967 Protocol relating to the Status of Refugees.

Since 1980, then, there have been two persecution-based forms of relief from removal, one discretionary and the other mandatory. Asylum, under INA § 208, requires a "well-founded fear of persecution;" the *nonrefoulement* provision, now in INA § 241(b)(3), requires that the individual's "life or freedom would be threatened." As explored below, the Supreme Court interpreted this textual variation as setting differences in the risk level that an asylum seeker must prove for the respective forms of protection.

Asylum affords more protections than withholding of removal (frequently called just "withholding" in immigration practice). Those granted asylum are allowed to work, to bring members of their immediate families to the United States, and to access some public assistance. Asylees also have a routine mechanism for adjusting to permanent resident status after one year in the United States, INA § 209(b). While those granted withholding generally receive work authorization, 8 C.F.R. § 274a.12(a)(10), and can sometimes receive public assistance, they may not bring their immediate families to the United States. In principle, they could be removed at any time to a willing third country, though such offers rarely materialize. They are likely to remain in this form of uncertain legal limbo for decades, because there is no provision for eventual adjustment of status to lawful permanent resident, although they are not precluded from adjusting their status if they otherwise qualify, such as through marriage or employment.

2. U.S. PROCEDURES FOR SEEKING
ASYLUM AND *NONREFOULEMENT*

a. Applications for Protection

Applications for protection from persecution are automatically treated as requests for both *nonrefoulement* and asylum. Asylum claims must generally be filed within one year of arrival in the United States, INA § 208(a)(2)(B), but there is no deadline for withholding applications.

The applications for protection follow three different paths, depending on whether the applicant is currently in removal proceedings, and, if so, in what type of proceeding. The two most important paths are usually called affirmative applications and defensive applications, described below. The third, triggered by the expedited removal procedure, applies to some arriving aliens and to some entrants without inspection. They must first clear the preliminary hurdle of "credible fear" screening, but if they do, their cases are thereafter handled as defensive applications. Special procedures apply to unaccompanied minors.

Under the regulations, a noncitizen applies for protection under either INA § 208 or § 241(b)(3) (as well as under the Convention Against Torture) by filing Form I–589 (available on the USCIS Forms website). This form asks why the applicant is seeking protection and what he or she thinks would happen upon return to the home country. The form requires other information that may throw further light on the claim, such as past activities and organizational affiliations, current whereabouts and condition of family members, and the circumstances of departure and travel to the United States. Many applicants provide additional material, sometimes voluminous, including affidavits, news accounts, or human rights reports, including those from nongovernmental organizations like Amnesty International or Human Rights Watch.

The statute requires that applicants be advised of the privilege of being represented by counsel, provided with a list of available pro bono representatives, and advised that knowingly filing a frivolous application makes them "permanently ineligible for any benefits under this Act." INA § 208(d)(4),   (6). The statute also sets forth a timetable: absent exceptional circumstances, the initial interview or hearing shall take place within 45 days of filing, and the final adjudication (by the immigration judge) shall be completed within 180 days. INA § 208(d)(5).

Huge backlogs in the asylum offices and the immigration courts have thoroughly undermined the statutory timeline. USCIS reported that asylum officers had interviewed 2,000 asylum applicants in December 2015, had completed 2,300 asylum cases in the same month, and had more than 128,000 pending asylum applications. USCIS Asylum Office Workload, December 2015. In January 2016 the immigration courts reported 475,000 pending cases (of all types, with a substantial percentage presenting asylum issues). Transactional Records Access Clearinghouse (TRAC), TRAC Immigration, Immigration Court January 2016: Backlog of Pending Cases. Applicants are waiting months and years for adjudication of their claims.

Applicants approved by an asylum officer or immigration judge may wait many more weeks for final documents. The statute requires that the applicant's identity must be fully checked against law enforcement and national security databases. INA § 208(d)(5)(A)(I). Accordingly, the initial grant of asylum is preliminary, subject to completion of fingerprint and name checks.

(i) Affirmative Applications

Applicants who are not currently in removal proceedings may file an affirmative application by mailing the I–589 to a regional service center (RSC), an arm of USCIS. The RSC staff checks that the application is complete and, if so, schedules the individual for an interview with an asylum officer, which is to be carried out in a "nonadversarial manner." 8 C.F.R. § 208.9. A specialized corps of full-time professional asylum officers, required by regulation to "receive special training in international human rights law, nonadversarial interview techniques, and other relevant national and international refugee laws and principles," 8 C.F.R. § 208.1(b), receives the application and interviews the applicant.

Asylum officers, also part of USCIS, are currently based in eight asylum offices located in cities throughout the country that have high concentrations of asylum applicants, and they ride circuit to hear claims at other places. Asylum officers make their decisions on the basis of the application, the interview, and possibly other information from the State Department or "other credible sources, such as international organizations, private voluntary agencies, news organizations, or academic institutions." 8 C.F.R. § 208.12(a). They are supported by their own central USCIS Resource Information Center, see id. § 208.1(b), which provides the officers with wide-ranging information about country conditions and legal developments.

Asylum officer grants of asylum in meritorious cases initially ran between 15 and 30 percent of affirmative filings, but in recent years have hovered around 40 percent. In general, asylum officers refer applicants not found to meet the standards for asylum to immigration court, rather than deny the applications. See 8 C.F.R. § 208.14(c)(1). The asylum officer does not have to explain in detail the reason for the referral. The immigration judge then considers the asylum claim further in the course of the removal proceeding. If the applicant was still in a lawful status at the time of the interview with the asylum officer, however, the officer issues a denial, stating reasons for the decision. Such applicants can renew the asylum claim later, if they are someday placed into removal proceedings.

(ii) Defensive Applications

If removal proceedings are already underway, the applicant can apply for asylum or withholding only by presenting a defensive application that is heard exclusively by the immigration judge. 8 C.F.R. § 208.2(b). Typically the noncitizen makes known at master calendar (the first appearance in immigration court) her wish to seek asylum (or withholding of removal) as a form of relief, and the judge then grants a specified period of time within which the I–589 must be completed and filed with the immigration court. The matter is then heard in the more formal setting of the immigration court, with examination and cross-examination by the noncitizen's counsel (if she has one) and the DHS trial attorney.

Sometimes, the noncitizen is ordered removed from the United States, and only then applies for asylum, perhaps because the applicant did not have counsel until after the issuance of a removal order. In such cases, the asylum claim can only be raised by means of a motion to reopen filed with the forum that last heard the matter. A motion to reopen is sometimes the first motion that a newly retained attorney files in a case.

The next set of graphs reports on affirmative asylum claims filed with INS/USCIS and claims filed with immigration judges. Figure 8.2 shows the number of asylum cases filed affirmatively and defensively between 1995 and 2014. Figure 8.3 covers the period from 1990 through 2014 and shows the number of asylum cases granted in each setting. Note that many of the claims filed with immigration judges had been preceded by affirmative asylum applications. Thus, some asylum applications appear in both portions of the asylum adjudication caseload; the sum of the two portions exceeds the total number of asylum applicants.

Figure 8.2
Asylum Cases Filed with INS/USCIS and
Immigration Judges, 1995–2014

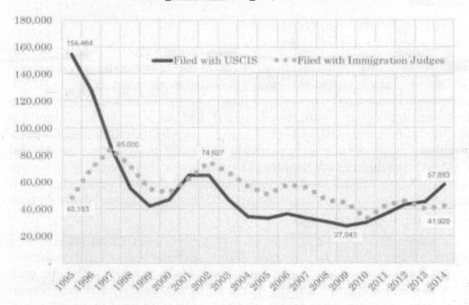

Source: USCIS Refugees, Asylum and Parole System,
Asylum Office Workload by Fiscal Year, FY 1991–2015; EOIR Statistics Yearbooks.

Figure 8.3
Asylum Cases Granted by INS/USCIS and
Immigration Judges, 1990–2014

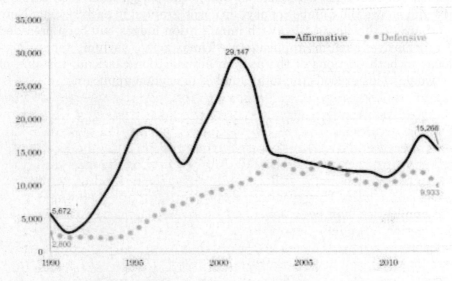

Source: USCIS Refugees, Asylum and Parole System,
Asylum Office Workload by Fiscal Year, FY 1991–2015; EOIR Statistics Yearbooks.

(iii)   Applications in Expedited Removal Proceedings

Under expedited removal, INA § 235(b)(1), described in Chapter Six, noncitizens arriving at the port of entry or brought to the United States after interdiction at sea (plus specified classes of entrants without inspection who have been in the country for less than two years) are subject to removal on the order of an immigration officer, not an immigration judge, if found inadmissible under INA § 212(a)(6)(C) or (7) (for having false or inadequate documents or for other fraud or misrepresentation, even at an unrelated time in the past). Those among this group who express a fear of return or ask for asylum are referred to an asylum officer who interviews them (no sooner than 48 hours later) to determine whether they have a "credible fear of persecution," defined in INA § 235(b)(1)(B)(v) as a "significant possibility * * * that the alien could establish eligibility for asylum." If found to have a credible fear, their claims are heard on the merits as defensive asylum claims, based upon a full hearing in immigration court.

Those not found to have a credible fear are ordered removed. They may request that an immigration judge review this negative determination in a special expedited procedure. Within seven days at the latest, and within 24 hours if practicable, an immigration judge considers the asylum officer's report and conducts a review in person, by video, or by telephone. INA § 235(b)(1)(B)(iii)(III). Judicial review of the immigration judge's decision on credible fear is available only in highly limited circumstances. INA §§ 242(a)(2)(A), 242(e). Of those who received a credible fear hearing by an asylum officer between 2006 and 2015, approximately 80% were found to have a credible fear. DHS, Briefing Paper on Expedited Removal and Credible Fear Process, Oct. 19, 2011; USCIS, Asylum Office, Credible Fear Workload Report Summary, FY 2009–2013, Summary FY 2014, Summary FY 2015.

(iv)   Work Authorization

Prior to 1995, regulations authorized work permission for all asylum seekers whose applications were not "frivolous." 8 C.F.R. § 208.7(a) (1995). Many argued that the easy acquisition of work authorization by almost every asylum seeker was an incentive to file asylum applications, whether or not they were supported. In 1995, new regulations postponed work authorization until at least 180 days elapse—unless asylum is granted before then. They also provided that no authorization would issue if the application had been denied by an immigration judge within that time period. Asylum applications decreased significantly. These constraints are now in INA § 208(d)(2). Delays requested by the asylum seeker do not count in accumulating the 180 days. Due to the enormous backlogs since about 2012, mentioned earlier, immigration judges generally cannot comply with the 180-day limit, and most asylum applicants today receive work authorization while their cases are pending. The affirmative application level, as you can see from Figure 8.4, has been increasing steadily during the current decade, exceeding 84,000 in FY 2015.

b. Immigration Court

Immigration judges provide the initial evaluation of all the defensive applications for asylum and withholding, and they provide a second consideration of the affirmative applications referred by asylum officers. In the latter case, the immigration judge receives the pre-existing I–589, with its attachments, from the asylum officer, along with copies of the charging document. Applicants of course can supplement their claims in immigration court and put on additional witnesses, but the use of the original application form in both settings is meant to enhance efficiency and save time. Immigration judges consider referred cases in much the same fashion as defensive claims, granting some asylum claims and giving rejected applicants a full statement of reasons as part of the decision in the case.

The immigration judge's decision on either a defensive asylum claim or a referred affirmative claim is appealable to the Board of Immigration Appeals (BIA). If the BIA rules against the claim for protection, judicial review may be available as part of the review of the removal order. For a more thorough discussion of judicial review and the applicable review standards, see Chapter Nine.

3. ASYLUM TRENDS AND STATISTICS

The graphs and charts in this chapter report data according to fiscal year, which the federal government defines as the 12 months ending on September 30; thus, the 2015 fiscal year ended on September 30, 2015. Figures 8.4 and 8.5 refer solely to affirmative asylum claims and do not take into account asylum decisions by immigration judges. Figure 8.4 reports the number of affirmative asylum cases filed over the past 25 years. Figure 8.5 shows the number of affirmative asylum cases filed with and approved by DHS during the past ten years.

Figure 8.4
Affirmative Asylum Applications Filed with INS/USCIS, 1991–2015

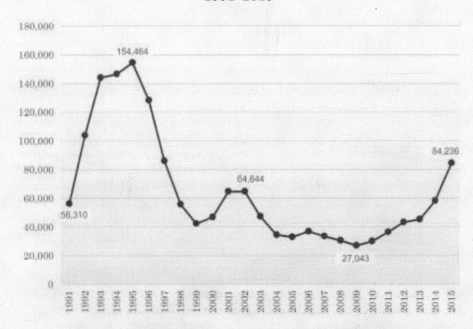

Source: USCIS Refugees, Asylum and Parole System,
Asylum Office Workload by Fiscal Year, FY 1991–2015.

Figure 8.5
Results in Affirmative Asylum Cases Filed with USCIS,
2006–2015

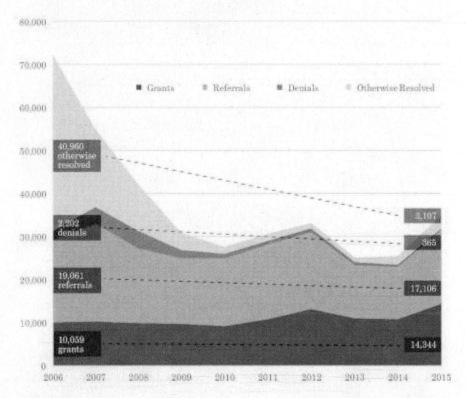

	2006	2008	2010	2012	2014
Grants	10,059	9,796	9,174	12,991	10,811
Referrals	19,061	17,374	15,784	17,948	12,034
Denials	2,202	4,188	958	922	582
Otherwise Resolved	40,960	10,780	1,677	1,318	2,008

Source: USCIS Refugees, Asylum and Parole System,
Asylum Office Workload by Fiscal Year, FY 1991–2015.

The next set of figures reports on asylum claims decided by immigration judges. Figure 8.6 shows the outcomes in cases that started with an affirmative application and then, after the Asylum Office did not grant asylum, were referred to immigration court. For 2015, for example, immigration judges granted 4,833 asylum claims and denied 1,185 claims. Looking only at the cases that were resolved by a decision to grant or to deny yields an apparent grant rate of 80 percent, but note this percentage exaggerates the rate at which the immigration court differed from the USCIS asylum officer's prior decision on the same individual's affirmative application. Figure 8.6 also shows that an additional 11,355 cases were otherwise resolved in 2015, such as by withdrawal, abandonment, the grant of some other type of relief, or change of venue. Of all asylum cases that reached a decision in 2015, 27.8 percent were grants. Over half of affirmative asylum claims referred to immigration court by asylum officers were not resolved on the merits.

Figure 8.6
Immigration Court Grants and Denials of Affirmative Asylum Claims Referred by Asylum Officers, 2011–2015

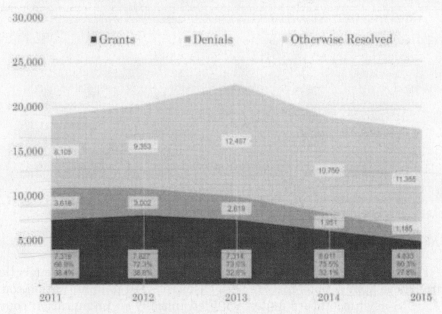

Source: Executive Office for Immigration Review,
Office of Planning, Analysis, and Statistics,
Asylum Completions by Asylum Type and Disposition, FY 2011-2015.

Figure 8.7 shows the outcomes in cases that started defensively in immigration court without a prior affirmative application to USCIS. In 2015, asylum grants in these cases numbered 3,413 and denials numbered 7,648. The grant rate was 30.9 percent of the cases that resulted in grants or denials, but an additional 13,181 cases were otherwise resolved, such as by withdrawal, abandonment, the grant of some other type of relief, or change of venue. The grant rate was 14.1 percent of all the defensive asylum claims that reached a decision in 2015.

Figure 8.7
Immigration Court Grants and Denials of Defensive
Claims First Filed in Immigration Court, 2011–2015

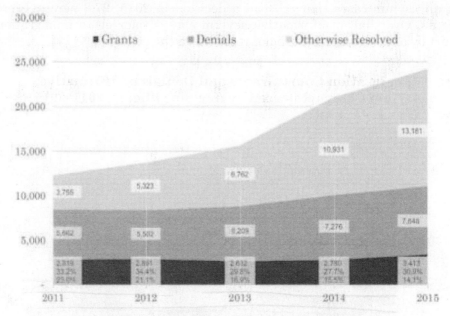

Source: Executive Office for Immigration Review,
Office of Planning, Analysis, and Statistics,
Asylum Completions by Asylum Type and Disposition, FY 2011-2015.

Figure 8.8 shows outcomes in asylum applications in immigration court. These applications include both cases referred to immigration court by USCIS asylum officers and cases filed initially in immigration court. Not included are cases in which USCIS asylum officers already granted asylum on the basis of an affirmative application.

Figure 8.8
Results in All Asylum Cases Filed with
Immigration Courts, 2006–2014

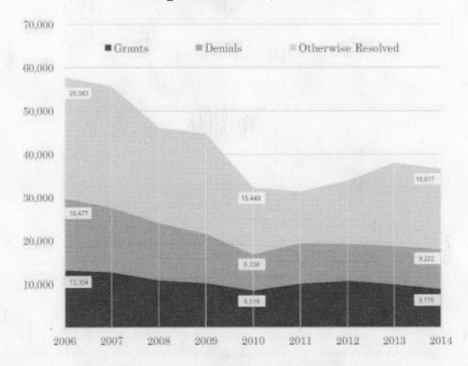

Source: EOIR FY 2014 Statistics Yearbook, Figure 19;
EOIR FY 2010 Statistical Year Book, Figure 19.

Figures 8.9 and 8.10 show the ten countries most represented among those granted asylum in the United States in 2013. Figure 8.9 shows the top ten nationalities for affirmative applications granted by USCIS. Figure 8.10 shows the top ten nationalities for asylum claims granted by immigration judges. In 2013 Chinese applicants were granted 26.7 percent of all asylum cases approved by USCIS and were granted 45.6 percent of all approvals in immigration court. The second largest group of successful applicants at USCIS came from Egypt (20.3 percent), but the second largest group of approvals in immigration court came from Ethiopia (four percent). Do any of the listed countries or any omissions surprise you?

Figure 8.9
Asylum Cases Approved by USCIS, 2013

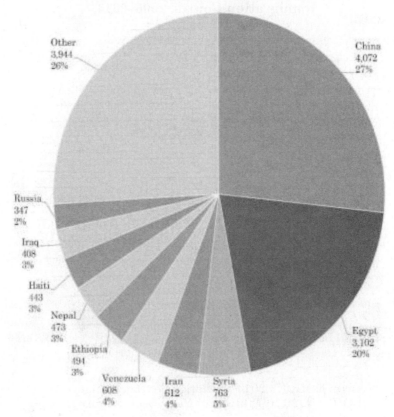

Source: Daniel C. Martin & James E. Yankay,
Refugees and Asylees: 2013, DHS Annual Flow Report, Table 7 (August 2014).

Figure 8.10
Asylum Cases Approved by Immigration Judges, 2013

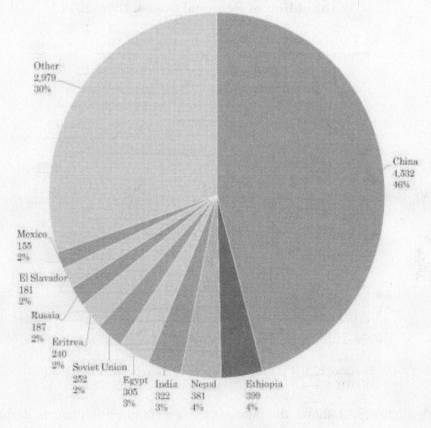

Source: Daniel C. Martin & James E. Yankay,
Refugees and Asylees: 2013, DHS Annual Flow Report, Table 8 (August 2014).

Figure 8.11 focuses on withholding of removal. Individuals seeking protection in the United States file Form I–589 to apply for asylum and withholding of removal. If an immigration judge rules against asylum, the next issue is withholding. (Immigration judges, not USCIS asylum officers, evaluate all withholding applications.) Figure 8.11 shows how many of these withholding applications—reached only after it has been established that asylum is unavailable—are granted and denied. In 2006, immigration judges granted withholding in 2,571 cases and denied in 16,778 cases. The percentage of grants was 13 percent. How had withholding decisions changed in 2014?

Figure 8.11
Immigration Courts Grants and Denials in
Withholding of Removal Cases, 2006–2014

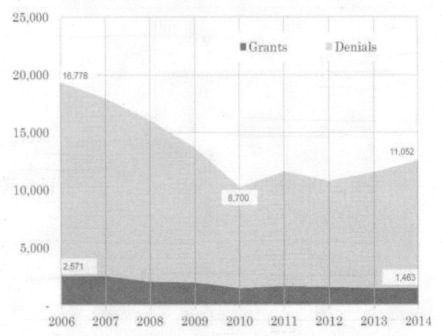

Source: EOIR FY 2014 Statistics Yearbook, Figure 20;
EOIR FY 2010 Statistical Year Book, Figure 19–A.

Figure 8.12 shows the outcomes when immigration courts decide to grant or deny a claim for protection from persecution. Counting both asylum and withholding applications together, Figure 8.12 shows that in 2014 immigration judges granted asylum in 8,775 cases and granted withholding in 1,463 cases. Thus, 48 percent of the cases resulted in grants of asylum and 8 percent of the cases granted withholding. Figure 8.12 does not reflect the substantial number of asylum grants by USCIS asylum officers based on affirmative applications without involving an immigration court. Moreover, Figure 8.12 depicts only a portion of the asylum claims raised in immigration court. Roughly one-half of asylum and withholding cases in immigration court do not reach a substantive decision to grant or deny; they are withdrawn or abandoned, or they result in another disposition, as shown earlier in this section.

Figure 8.12
Immigration Court Grants and Denials in
Asylum and Withholding Cases, 2006–2014

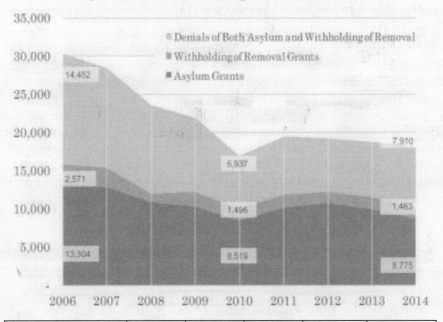

	2006	2008	2010	2012	2014
denials of both asylum & withholding	14,452	11,630	6,937	7,021	7,910
withholding grants	2,571 8%	2,055 8%	1,496 9%	1,553 8%	1,463 8%
asylum grants	13,304 44%	10,881 44%	8,519 50%	10,715 56%	8,775 48%
total grants	52%	52%	59%	64%	56%

Source: EOIR FY 2014 Statistics Yearbook, Figure 21;
EOIR FY 2010 Statistical Year Book, Figure 19–B.

C. THE SUBSTANTIVE CRITERIA FOR ASYLUM

Section 208 of the INA provides that the Attorney General may grant asylum in the United States to an applicant who satisfies the refugee definition provided in INA § 101(a)(42): an individual who has a well-founded fear of persecution on account of race, religion, nationality, membership in a particular social group, or political opinion. The *nonrefoulement* provision, § 241(b)(3), prohibits returning an individual to a country in which his or her life or freedom would be threatened on account of the individual's race, religion, nationality, membership in a particular social group, or political opinion. The concept of persecution is central to both forms of protection from removal, although the term itself does not appear in the latter statutory section.

The full framework for determining whether U.S. law will protect an individual requires not only that he or she be faced with "persecution," but also that any such persecution be "on account of race, religion, nationality, membership in a particular social group or political opinion." Each of these five grounds is a term of art, as is the phrase "on account of," which requires a certain type of nexus among the persecutor, the individual being persecuted, and the reason for the persecution. We focus first on "persecution," but the lines between these issues—(1) persecution, (2) the five grounds, and (3) nexus—are often blurred in practical application. Many cases implicate more than one of these issues, and it is not always possible to tease them neatly apart.

1.   PERSECUTION

Neither the U.S. law, nor the 1951 Convention from which it is derived, defines persecution. Several courts have offered their views. The Ninth Circuit had this to say:

> Although the term "persecution" is not defined in the Act, we have explained it as "the infliction of suffering or harm upon those who differ (in race, religion or political opinion) in a way regarded as offensive." We have cautioned that "persecution is an extreme concept that does not include every sort of treatment our society regards as offensive." Discrimination on the basis of race or religion, as morally reprehensible as it may be, does not ordinarily amount to "persecution" within the meaning of the Act. *See Bastanipour v. INS*, 980 F.2d 1129, 1133 (7th Cir. 1992) (distinguishing persecution "from mere discrimination or harassment"). The Board has held that discrimination can, in extraordinary cases, be so severe and pervasive as to constitute "persecution" within the meaning of the Act. In a case such as the one before us, however, where private discrimination is neither condoned by the state nor the prevailing social norm, it clearly does not amount to "persecution" within the meaning of the Act.

Ghaly v. INS, 58 F.3d 1425, 1431 (9th Cir. 1995).

A more succinct definition comes from Judge Posner in *Osaghae v. INS*, 942 F.2d 1160, 1163 (7th Cir. 1991): "'Persecution' means, in immigration law, punishment for political, religious, or other reasons that our country does not recognize as legitimate." The fundamental challenge in the cases in this section is to identify a workable framework for determining when this country is prepared to declare another nation's punishments (or other harms) illegitimate such that our legal system should provide protection. Some cases are easy, but a great many fall at the margin and present surprisingly difficult issues.

a. Type of Harm

As the Ninth Circuit indicated above, persecution is generally described as harmful conduct that is more severe than discrimination or harassment. Frequently, persecution takes the form of physical violence or imprisonment, but it encompasses a wide array of harm. When, for example, do economic measures rise to the level of persecution?

MIRISAWO V. HOLDER
United States Court of Appeals, Fourth Circuit, 2010.
599 F.3d 391.

NIEMEYER, CIRCUIT JUDGE:

* * *

Rosemary Mirisawo was born in Harare, Zimbabwe, in 1966 and lived there until she came to the United States in 1999. She came to the United States on a nonimmigrant G–5 visa[a] to work as a housekeeper, leaving her children with family members in Zimbabwe. Mirisawo has worked as a housekeeper, both in Zimbabwe and the United States, since she was 20 and, during this time, has lived in the homes of her employers. She has four children, as well as two brothers and eight sisters. * * * All of her children now live with family members in Harare, Zimbabwe.

Mirisawo remained in the United States, employed as a housekeeper, until August 2002, when she returned to Zimbabwe for a month to visit family and to provide better accommodations for her children and brother, Tobias. A few months prior to her visit—in March 2002—Tobias had been severely beaten by supporters of the Zimbabwean government because he was an active member of the Movement for Democratic Change ("MDC"), a political party that opposed Robert Mugabe, the leader of the ZANU-PF party and the president of Zimbabwe for the last 29 years. Tobias was hospitalized following the beating and continues to receive medical treatment for his injuries. To avoid being associated with Tobias and his political activities during her visit, Mirisawo stayed with her sister Maggie. During her stay, she purchased a home in Mabvuku, a suburb of Harare, for Tobias and her children.

---

[a] This is a type of nonimmigrant visa available for personal employees of staff members of international organizations.—eds.

While in Zimbabwe during this visit, Mirisawo did not experience any difficulties with the government—she was not stopped, questioned, harassed, or beaten. * * *

In May 2005, the Mugabe government began implementing Operation Restore Order, pursuant to which it destroyed thousands of homes and buildings in Harare for the officially stated purpose of cleaning out urban slums. It was widely believed, however, that the operation was retributive, targeting areas known by the government to have voted for the opposition in presidential and parliamentary elections. In the course of Operation Restore Order, the government bulldozed three of the four rooms in the house that Mirisawo had purchased for Tobias and her children. Tobias and Mirisawo's son continued to live in the remaining room, while her other children went to live with Mirisawo's sister, Maggie.

According to the country report prepared by the United States Department of State in 2006, the human rights record of the Zimbabwean government was "very poor." The report noted that persons perceived to be opposition supporters were tortured, raped, and abused by government-sanctioned youth militia and ruling-party supporters and that the government "routinely used selective violence to achieve its political objectives."

Despite these conditions, Tobias, Mirisawo's daughter Tsitsi, and Mirisawo's sister Maggie continue to be members of the MDC. Since his beating in 2002, Tobias has not experienced any further threats or abuses. Tsitsi has never been harmed, but she was threatened into purchasing a ZANU-PF identification card. Maggie also has never been harmed or even threatened, although she keeps her membership in the MDC secret and does not live in the area of Harare where Mirisawo claims the government presumes all residents to be MDC members.

On August 3, 2005, some three months before her G–5 visa was to expire, Mirisawo filed an application for asylum with the Department of Homeland Security. * * *

* * *

The immigration judge held that the destruction of Mirisawo's house did not amount to past persecution because Mirisawo had never lived in the house nor depended on it for her livelihood. The immigration judge also held that she was not likely to face future persecution because she had not been harassed upon her return to Zimbabwe in 2002 and because none of her family members who remained in Zimbabwe had been harmed since Tobias' beating in 2002. * * *

* * *

* * * [T]o establish eligibility for asylum, the applicant must demonstrate that she has suffered from past persecution or that she has a well-founded fear of future persecution. And to establish a well-founded fear of future persecution, the applicant must demonstrate that "(1) a reasonable person in the circumstances would fear persecution; and (2) that the fear has some basis in the reality of the circumstances and is validated with specific, concrete facts.". * * *

While "persecution" is often manifested in physical violence, "the harm or suffering [amounting to persecution] need not be physical, but may take other forms," so long as the harm is of sufficient severity. Among the forms of nonphysical harm amounting to persecution is that of "economic persecution," which includes the "deliberate deprivation of basic necessities" and the "deliberate imposition of severe economic disadvantage." Thus, to establish "economic persecution," an asylum applicant must demonstrate that, on account of one of the statutorily enumerated grounds, the applicant's life or freedom has been threatened by either (1) a deliberate and severe deprivation of basic necessities or (2) a deliberate imposition of severe financial disadvantage. It is important to emphasize that not every economic deprivation or disadvantage makes a person a "refugee." Rather, it must be a deprivation or disadvantage so severe that it threatens the person's very life or liberty.

* * *

Mirisawo contends that she is eligible for asylum and withholding of removal because she suffered past economic persecution when the government destroyed her house during Operation Restore Order. She claims that the destruction of her house constituted economic persecution either because a house is a basic necessity for survival or because its destruction caused her to suffer severe financial disadvantage. * * *

* * *

* * * At the time of the government's partial destruction of her house, Mirisawo had never lived in the house and was living and working in the United States as a live-in housekeeper. Nor is it likely that Mirisawo will ever need to live in the house, as she will likely continue to be employed as a live-in housekeeper if she returns to Zimbabwe. Mirisawo focuses on the facts that the property destroyed was a house and that the effect of Operation Restore was to deprive many Harare residents of the shelter necessary for their survival. But when evaluating the significance of the partial destruction of her house, we must focus not on the effect the government action had on the house itself or on others impacted by the government action, but on the effect the action had on *Mirisawo's* life and liberty. In this case, the record supports the conclusion that the destruction of Mirisawo's house in no way interfered with her ability to provide housing for herself, and therefore we cannot say that she was deprived of a basic necessity that threatened her "life or freedom."

With respect to Mirisawo's contention that the destruction of her house was "the deliberate imposition of severe economic disadvantage," the BIA found that the destruction of Mirisawo's house did not impose sufficiently severe financial harm to constitute economic persecution, mainly because Mirisawo did not depend on her house for her livelihood. Mirisawo spent her career employed as a housekeeper, and the destruction of her house in no way interfered with her ability to continue in this type of employment. Moreover, she never attempted to live in the house nor expressed any intention to live there. While the partial destruction of her house undoubtedly resulted in an investment loss, Mirisawo did not rely on that investment for current or future income and did not, nor does not, need a return on that investment to continue working as a housekeeper and living as she has. In these circumstances, we cannot say that the BIA erred in concluding that the harm imposed was not sufficiently severe to constitute a threat to Mirisawo's life or freedom. * * *

* * *

Mirisawo also contends that she has a well-founded fear of future persecution based on "a political opinion that may be imputed to her by virtue of her family ties or her status as an impoverished land-owner in Harare." She claims that the Zimbabwean government will believe that she is a member of the MDC because her brother Tobias, daughter Tsitsi, and sister Maggie are all members of the MDC and because it is widely believed that most of the residents of her neighborhood are members of the MDC.

While the BIA accepted Mirisawo's claim that she had a subjective fear of persecution, it rejected the notion that her fear was objectively reasonable. It reached its conclusion based in part on the fact that when Mirisawo returned to Zimbabwe in 2002, she faced no persecution of any type. It also noted that neither her oldest daughter nor her sister had ever suffered any persecution and that her brother Tobias, while having been beaten in 2002, has continued to live in Zimbabwe without further incident. We conclude that these facts provide substantial evidence to support the BIA's conclusion. The fact that family members whose political opinions Mirisawo fears will be imputed to her have not themselves faced harm fatally undermines her claim that she will suffer persecution because of her association with them. Moreover, the fact that she herself suffered no acts of persecution when she returned to Zimbabwe in 2002, shortly after her brother Tobias had been beaten, is highly probative.

For the foregoing reasons, we affirm the decision of the BIA and deny Mirisawo's petition for review.

GREGORY, CIRCUIT JUDGE, concurring in part and dissenting in part:

Petitioner Rosemary Mirisawo came to the United States in order to pursue a job; she had no illusions or desire that her residency here would become permanent. Rather, she accepted a G–5 visa and, for six years, worked as a household domestic in this country. In preparation for her eventual return to Zimbabwe, Mirisawo purchased a home in her native land. Her disabled brother and some of her children inhabited the house while she remained abroad. However, in 2005, the home, the only one she had ever owned, was destroyed by the Mugabe government in a show of force against the Movement for Democratic Change opposition. Therefore, now that Mirisawo's visa has not been renewed and she lacks status in this country, she has no shelter to which she may return. Given that destruction, Mirisawo has established past economic persecution and thus qualifies as a refugee for asylum purposes. For this reason, I dissent.

* * *

* * * Economic persecution may qualify as past persecution if it constitutes either the "deliberate deprivation of basic necessities" or the "deliberate imposition of severe economic disadvantage." Of the basic necessities of human life, shelter is certainly included. Along with food and water, housing is one of the components of fundamental human existence. Thus, its intentional deprivation constitutes past persecution.

The majority goes further, announcing for the first time that in this Circuit, for economic persecution to be shown, it must "be so severe that it threatens the life or freedom of the applicant" * * *. The majority's standard for economic persecution goes beyond our prior holding in *Li* [*v. Gonzales*, 405 F.3d 171 (4th Cir. 2005),], where we required that the economic harm "constitute a threat," not that the harm itself actually and currently threaten the individual's life or liberty. Further, the majority's requirement of a "severe" deprivation of basic necessities goes beyond any of our prior precedent which required only a "deliberate deprivation" of such essentials. * * *

* * *

There are two fundamental flaws in the majority's argument, one factual and one conceptual, both demonstrating that persecution was shown here. First, the majority unwarrantedly assumes that Mirisawo was not planning on returning to the home she purchased. Indeed, it assumes that Mirisawo was forever consigned to her role as a live-in domestic, continually inhabiting the homes and lives of other people, unable to forge her own way. Yet, there is direct evidence in the record to the contrary showing that Mirisawo was actively preparing for her return home. * * * At bottom, the majority's error is to assume that Mirisawo preferred to live in her employers' homes, when the evidence points to the fact that at the first chance she had, she purchased a home of her own that would be available for her return.

The second flaw in the majority's argument is more conceptual. It is erroneous to conclude that as a matter of law an individual who has not lived in his home cannot make out a claim of economic persecution. The logical flaw of the majority's opinion is quite clear in the following example. Imagine an alien in the United States who has secured a temporary work visa and who has no interest or reason to seek permanent resident status. As that person prepares to return home, he contacts a friend in his home country and asks him to dig a well at his house. In return, the alien will send him $1,000 via Western Union. The friend agrees, and within two weeks, the well is completed and the money transferred. Unfortunately, before the alien returns home, agents of the government come to his house and pour poison in his well, suspecting that he sympathizes with the opposition party, supporters of which live in his neighborhood. In response, the alien files an asylum claim in the United States, claiming past economic persecution which deprives him of the necessities of life: water. Confronted with that case, would this Court hold that merely because the alien had yet to drink from the well, he was not persecuted? That result is counter to logic and counter to law.

So too here the majority's decision is without basis in law or reason. Mirisawo was able to buy the house with her earnings in the United States. Like so many temporary workers, she used the money she earned abroad to provide for her future at home. Unfortunately Mirisawo was never able to enjoy the fruits of her labors because the house was bulldozed before she inhabited it. Yet, merely from her inability to occupy the house, how can we assume that Mirisawo never intended to live there in the first place? Fundamentally, it is without support in the law to hold that the destruction of the most significant investment a person has ever purchased, which is also a necessity of life, does not constitute persecution.

The majority opinion evinces some knowledge of a maid's life, but betrays no understanding of her dream. I must dissent.

NOTES AND QUESTIONS ON THE MEANING OF PERSECUTION

1.   Why is it significant to the majority that Mirisawo had not lived in the house she bought for her brother and children? Would it have mattered to the majority if the evidence had demonstrated that Mirisawo had lost her job as a housekeeper and no longer had the ability to live in the home of her employer? The dissent, in contrast, emphasized that Mirasawo had planned to return to Zimbabwe to live in her own home. Why should that matter if the government purposefully destroyed her major financial asset? On the other

hand, although destruction of her home was almost surely a human rights violation, is asylum designed to afford relocation to all who have suffered such violations? Or is it meant to protect a narrower class of persons whose life on return would be so constricted that it would amount to persecution? Since Mirisawo's children have been able to live with her sister, has Mirisawo been able to make a showing of persecution?

2.   In *Borca v. INS*, 77 F.3d 210, 215 (7th Cir. 1996), the BIA ruled that economic persecution results in refugee status only when "the persecution is so severe as to deprive an applicant of all means of earning their living." Applying this doctrine, it found that the Romanian asylum applicant was not eligible for asylum, even though she had been fired from her job as a radiologist and apparently denied a license for any other government job except farm laborer. The Seventh Circuit reversed, applying a standard derived from *Kovac v. INS*, 407 F.2d 102, 107 (9th Cir. 1969): "deliberate imposition of substantial economic disadvantage for reasons of race, religion or political opinion" would suffice to justify political asylum. More recently, the Seventh Circuit ruled that government mistreatment of a Mormon in Ukraine might compel a finding of persecution: "the government prevented her from continuing her education in the Ph.D. physics program, denied her permission to live in Kiev and reduced her to working in menial jobs that required no education, training or acuity." *Koval v. Gonzales*, 418 F.3d 798, 805–06 (7th Cir. 2005). Do the court decisions in *Borca* and *Koval* both of which ruled for the asylum applicant, go too far? Is working in a menial job really a form of persecution? If so for Koval, then why not for thousands of others who never had a shot at a Ph.D. program? At what point do economic sanctions rise to the level of persecution? In *Matter of T-Z-*, 24 I & N Dec. 163 (BIA 2007), the BIA acknowledged that there were two potentially inconsistent lines of cases dealing with economic persecution. Instead of choosing one line or the other, it sought to harmonize them by interpreting both to require "severe" and not merely "substantial" economic harm.

3.   European Union asylum law defines persecution as an act that is "sufficiently serious by its nature or repetition as to constitute a severe violation of basic human rights, . . . or an accumulation of various measures . . . sufficiently severe as to affect an individual in a similar manner as [a severe violation of basic human rights]." Directive 2011/95/EU of the European Parliament and of the Council of 13 December 2011 on Standards for the Qualification of Third-country National or Stateless Persons as Beneficiaries of International Protection, Art. 9. Torture, inhuman or degrading treatment or punishment, slavery, ex post facto criminal proceedings, and threats to life all constitute violations of basic human rights under EU law. *Id.*, art. 9(1)(a), referring to the European Convention for the Protection of Human Rights and Fundamental Freedoms, 213 U.N.T.S. 222, European T.S. No. 5, art. 15(2).

b. Uniform National Policy

As noted in the preceding case, the Zimbabwe government justified destroying private dwellings as a legitimate slum clearance project, but many characterized the actions as retribution against political opponents. What if a government applies criminal or other procedurally regular sanctions even-handedly in pursuit of a policy aim it deems legitimate, or indeed vital? If the asylum state does not share that view, it may have to pass judgment on the validity of the underlying policy. Ask yourself if it is possible to devise an approach that does not require value choices about the substantive rightness of the underlying policy—e.g., an approach that focuses only on procedural defects in implementation. Or is there anything wrong with the asylum state imposing its values, at least in this limited sense, on the policy choices of the other state?

"It Is Better to Have One Child Only." (Photo: © David Clark)

The Board of Immigration Appeals faced this issue in 1989 in deciding whether China's coercive population control policy constituted persecution. The Board's reasoning is instructive, although Congress eventually overturned the result by changing the statute.

> We do not find that the "one couple, one child" policy of the Chinese Government is on its face persecutive. China has adopted a policy whose stated objective is to discourage births through economic incentives, economic sanctions, peer pressure, education, availability of sterilization and other birth control measures, and use of propaganda. Chinese policymakers are faced with the difficulty of providing for China's vast population

in good years and in bad. The Government is concerned not only with the ability of its citizens to survive, but also with their housing, education, medical services, and the other benefits of life that persons in many other societies take for granted. For China to fail to take steps to prevent births might well mean that many millions of people would be condemned to, at best, the most marginal existence. The record reflects that China was in fact encouraged by world opinion to take measures to control its population.

There is no evidence that the goal of China's policy is other than as stated, or that it is a subterfuge for persecuting any portion of the Chinese citizenry on account of one of the reasons enumerated in section 101(a)(42)(A) of the Act. The policy does not prevent couples from having children but strives to limit the size of the family. It appears that exceptions are made so that couples facing certain hardships may have another child. The policy applies to everyone but expressly protects, and indeed is more leniently applied to, minority (non-Han) peoples within China. It appears to impose stricter requirements on Party members (state cadres) than on some non-Party members. The Chinese Government has stated that it does not condone forced sterilizations and that its policy is to take action against local officials who violate this policy.

The population problem arising in China poses a profound dilemma. We cannot find that implementation of the "one couple, one child" policy in and of itself, even to the extent that involuntary sterilizations may occur, is persecution or creates a well-founded fear of persecution "on account of race, religion, nationality, membership in a particular social group, or political opinion." This is not to say that such a policy could not be implemented in such a way as to individuals or categories of persons so as to be persecution on account of a ground protected by the Act. To the extent, however, that such a policy is solely tied to controlling population, rather than as a guise for acting against people for reasons protected by the Act, we cannot find that persons who do not wish to have the policy applied to them are victims of persecution or have a well-founded fear of persecution within the present scope of the Act.

Matter of Chang, 20 I & N Dec. 38, 44 (BIA, 1989).

NOTES AND QUESTIONS ON COERCIVE POPULATION CONTROL

1.   Although serious consequences potentially awaited the applicant in *Chang*, including his forced sterilization or his wife's forced abortion, the BIA

appeared unwilling to find that this would amount to persecution on account of one of the five reasons stated in the definition. These harms could constitute persecution in some settings, but apparently not if they are applied to virtually all in the population who fail to go along with the national policy. Persecution, in this conception, apparently requires some sort of invidious discrimination. Do you agree? Consider how the definition would apply to people who escaped Cambodia under Pol Pot, whose Khmer Rouge, in power from 1975 to 1979, attempted to purge their country of all Western influence, and who killed over a million of their countrymen in the process (often in quite indiscriminate fashion).

2.   Do you think the BIA in *Chang* considered the scope of potential immigration from the world's most populous country? Would any such attention to practical consequences and political limitations be a legitimate factor to consider in shaping the law of *nonrefoulement* and asylum?

Congress overruled the *Chang* decision in the 1996 Act by amending the statutory refugee definition, INA § 101(a)(42), to add this sentence:

> For purposes of determinations under this Act, a person who has been forced to abort a pregnancy or to undergo involuntary sterilization, or who has been persecuted for failure or refusal to undergo such a procedure or for other resistance to a coercive population control program, shall be deemed to have been persecuted on account of political opinion, and a person who has a well-founded fear that he or she will be forced to undergo such a procedure or subject to persecution for such failure, refusal, or resistance shall be deemed to have a well founded fear of persecution on account of political opinion.

In *Matter of X-P-T-*, 21 I & N Dec. 634 (BIA 1996), the BIA ruled that the 1996 amendment superseded *Chang* and applies in withholding cases as well.

Two decades later the Chinese government ended its one-child policy, announcing that all families are allowed to have two children. Chris Buckley, *China Ends One-Child Policy, Allowing Families Two Children*, N.Y. Times, Oct. 29, 2015. Would Chinese government efforts to enforce the more relaxed policy via fines or other punishments imposed on those who have more than two children constitute persecution?

c.   Persecution by Nongovernmental Actors

U.S. law has accepted that harm or threats from non-state actors can provide a basis for asylum. As the Ninth Circuit explained in *McMullen v. INS*, 658 F.2d 1312, 1315 n.2 (9th Cir. 1981), "persecution within the meaning of § 243(h) includes persecution by non-governmental groups

* * * where it is shown that the government of the proposed country of deportation is unwilling or unable to control that group." The BIA agrees. *See, e.g., Matter of O-Z- and I-Z-,* 22 I & N Dec. 23 (BIA 1998) (affirming asylum grant to a Ukrainian Jew who had been beaten and threatened by an anti-Semitic ultranationalist group).

Ascertaining when a government is unable or unwilling to control a persecuting group is a more complicated question than it might initially seem. In all countries, violent crime occurs to a greater or lesser degree, despite control efforts by the government. No one can be completely guaranteed protection against all such criminal activity. If a threatened violent crime has a political cast to it, must the potential harm be considered persecution of a kind that might give rise to a valid asylum claim? In *Matter of O-Z- and I-Z-, supra,* the BIA emphasized the fact "that the respondent reported at least three of the incidents to the police, who took no action beyond writing a report" before finding that the nongovernmental acts were sufficiently condoned by the government to justify a grant of asylum. On the other hand, in *Matter of V-T-S-,* 21 I & N Dec. 792 (BIA 1997), the Board refused to grant asylum to a person who had been threatened with kidnapping by insurgent forces in the Philippines. In dictum, the BIA noted that the applicant had failed to show a sufficient government default to make the kidnapping a sound basis for asylum, in part because the government had mounted major efforts against the perpetrators when the applicant's siblings had been kidnapped.

The infliction of harm by non-state actors also arises in many gender-related claims for asylum. For example, cases based on claims of female genital mutilation generally focus on family members who insist on compliance with the custom. Similarly, many cases raising claims of domestic violence allege that the spouse or intimate partner inflicted the harm.

d. Past Persecution

Although there is no requirement that applicants for protection under the asylum and withholding statutes have already suffered persecution, some applicants have. In U.S. practice, these applicants are the beneficiaries of an express rebuttable presumption that they have a well-founded fear of future persecution. The regulations specify that applicants who establish that they were subject to persecution on one of the protected grounds in the past will be presumed to have a well-founded fear of persecution. 8 C.F.R. § 208.13(b)(1). The government can rebut this presumption in two ways: (1) by showing that a fundamental change in circumstances has occurred that removes any well-founded fear of persecution or (2) by showing that the asylum applicant could avoid future persecution by relocating to another part of the home country and that it would be reasonable to expect the applicant to do so. 8 C.F.R. § 208.13(b)(1)(i). A similar presumption operates in the context of withholding of removal. *Id.* § 208.16(b)(1).

In addition to the explicit evidentiary presumption, the regulations allow a humanitarian grant of asylum (but not withholding) for victims of past persecution even in the absence of fears of future persecution.

> An applicant * * * may be granted asylum, in the exercise of the decision-maker's discretion, if the applicant has demonstrated compelling reasons for being unwilling * * * to return * * * arising out of the severity of the past persecution * * *.

8 C.F.R. § 208.13(b)(1)(iii)(A).

This broader form of protection is possible because Congress chose to write the INA definition of refugee in a way that departs from the Convention. The INA includes as refugees persons outside their countries of origin "because of persecution or a well-founded fear of persecution." (Compare INA § 101(a)(42)(A) to Article 1 of the Convention.) The first part of the phrase—*persecution*—has been understood to refer to persecution in the past, while *well-founded fear of persecution* has been understood to refer to future persecution. The BIA has indicated that a grant of asylum based solely on past persecution is exceptional, because refugee protection is ordinarily intended to shield against future harm. *See Matter of Chen*, 20 I & N Dec. 16 (BIA 1989) (despite absence of future persecution, discretionary grant of asylum appropriate for individual who suffered atrocious forms of persecution during Chinese Cultural Revolution).

Protection granted to individuals in the absence of threats of future persecution is generally referred to as *humanitarian asylum*. In 2014 the First Circuit ruled that genocidal actions against the Mayan Quiché community by the Guatemalan army in the civil war might entitle an individual to humanitarian asylum in the United States even though the war had ended more than a decade earlier. *Ordonez-Quino v. Holder*, 760 F.3d 80 (1st Cir. 2014).

2. DISCRETION TO GRANT OR DENY ASYLUM

Under both international and U.S. law, refugees are those who fear persecution, whose fear is well-founded, and whose threatened persecution is on account of one of the five protected grounds (the well-founded fear requirement and the protected grounds will be discussed below). Qualifying as a refugee is necessary, but not sufficient. The U.S. asylum statute provides that refugees are eligible for asylum, but the Secretary of Homeland Security and the Attorney General have discretion to decide which refugees receive asylum status. INA § 208(b)(1)(A).

The Supreme Court emphasized the discretionary nature of asylum in *INS v. Cardoza-Fonseca,* 480 U.S. 421, 107 S.Ct. 1207, 94 L.Ed.2d 434, contrasting asylum with the lesser relief offered by non-discretionary withholding of removal. The BIA has addressed factors that might warrant either a positive or negative exercise of discretion.

    * * * [T]he totality of the circumstances and actions of an alien in his flight from the country where he fears persecution should be examined in determining whether a favorable exercise of discretion is warranted. * * *

    In addition to the circumstances and actions of the alien in his flight from the country where he fears persecution, general humanitarian considerations, such as an alien's tender age or poor health, may also be relevant in a discretionary determination. A situation of particular concern involves an alien who has established his statutory eligibility for asylum but cannot meet the higher burden required for withholding of deportation. Deportation to a country where the alien may be persecuted thus becomes a strong possibility. In such a case, the discretionary factors should be carefully evaluated in light of the unusually harsh consequences which may befall an alien who has established a well-founded fear of persecution; the danger of persecution should generally outweigh all but the most egregious of adverse factors.

Matter of Pula, 19 I & N Dec. 467, 473–74 (BIA 1987).

    In a subsequent decision, *Matter of Kasinga*, 21 I & N Dec. 357, 367 (BIA 1996), the BIA noted that an asylum applicant bears the burden of proving that a favorable exercise of discretion is warranted, but stated that "[t]the danger of persecution will outweigh all but the most egregious adverse factors."

    Despite the relatively routine practice, under *Pula* and *Kasinga,* of exercising discretion in favor of granting asylum when the applicant proves a well-founded fear of persecution, there have been a few notable cases in which discretion has been used to deny asylum. One such instance involved a leader in the Islamic Salvation Front (FIS) of Algeria, which had ties to an armed group in Algeria that the U.S. Secretary of State had designated a "foreign terrorist organization." Attorney General Ashcroft personally took referral of the case from the BIA and ruled that asylum should be denied in the exercise of discretion. *Matter of A-H-,* 23 I & N Dec. 774, 782–83 (AG 2005).

NOTES AND QUESTIONS ON DISCRETION AND ASYLUM

    1.   *Matter of A-H-* was a rare instance of a "referral" from the BIA to the Attorney General. As described in Chapter Four, regulations provide

specific circumstances in which the Attorney General may personally review a BIA decision. 8 C.F.R. § 1003.1(h). Consider why Attorney General Ashcroft may have wished to use the referral procedure in this case.

2.   Over the years, Congress has modified the statutory grounds for asylum, and in doing so has converted factors that formerly were matters to be taken into account in the exercise of discretion into factors that result in a mandatory denial of asylum. These factors include firm resettlement in another country and a growing list of criminal convictions. Congress has also imposed a one-year deadline for asylum applications. Although the one-year deadline does not apply to withholding, late-filers, who are excluded from asylum by the deadline, face an added barrier. Under *INS v. Stevic,* 467 U.S. 407, 104 S.Ct. 2489, 81 L.Ed.2d 321 (1984), discussed below, they can win protection only if they show that persecution is more likely than not. We will consider the one-year deadline and mandatory bars to protection more thoroughly in Section D of this chapter.

3.   Most of the attention regarding the role of discretion in asylum cases arises in circumstances when asylum applicants have established that they have a well-founded fear of persecution in the future, but they have engaged in other conduct that this country is likely to view as objectionable. As noted above, discretion to grant asylum also plays a significant role when eligibility for protection is based on a showing of past persecution and the applicant is not able to prove future persecution.

4.   Congress wished to protect the exercise of discretion by the Secretary of Homeland Security and the Attorney General when it acted in 1996 to bar the courts from reviewing most immigration decisions that are statutorily entrusted to the discretion of these officials. Congress stated, however, that judicial review remains available for discretionary asylum decisions. INA § 242(a)(2)(B)(ii). Congress went on to specify the following standard of review in such cases: "the * * * discretionary judgment whether to grant relief under section 208(a) shall be conclusive unless manifestly contrary to the law and an abuse of discretion." *Id.* § 242(b)(4)(D). See Chapter Nine for a further discussion of judicial review.

3.   LIKELIHOOD OF HARM

In addition to exploring the meaning of persecution, many cases have examined another fundamental question: what level of risk or degree of threat or likelihood of harm in the homeland must an applicant prove to meet the threshold qualification for protection under U.S. law? The asylum provision, INA § 208, refers to a "well-founded" fear of persecution, while the withholding provision, § 241(b)(3), refers to circumstances when an individual's "life or freedom would be threatened."

A few years after the passage of the Refugee Act of 1980, the Supreme Court examined a case in which the applicant was seeking only withholding, not asylum. *INS v. Stevic,* 467 U.S. 407, 104 S.Ct. 2489, 81

L.Ed.2d 321 (1984). Justice Stevens, writing for a unanimous Court, made a sharp distinction between the two sections. He concluded that applicants for withholding must show that persecution "is more likely than not." *Id.* at 424 and n. 19, 104 S. Ct. at 2498 and n. 19. The Court rejected the "premise that every alien who qualifies as a 'refugee' under the statutory definition [referred to in § 208] is also entitled to a withholding of deportation under § 243(h)," 467 U.S. at 428, 104 S.Ct. at 2500, and left the § 208 standard for consideration on another day.

Predictably, litigation resumed over the "well-founded fear" standard in § 208. According to the BIA, applicants for asylum and withholding had to show the same likelihood that harm would occur. *Matter of Acosta*, 19 I & N Dec. 211, 219 (BIA 1985). After the courts of appeals reached disparate results, the Supreme Court returned to these questions.

INS v. CARDOZA-FONSECA
Supreme Court of the United States, 1987.
480 U.S. 421, 107 S.Ct. 1207, 94 L.Ed.2d 434.

JUSTICE STEVENS delivered the opinion of the Court.

* * *

Respondent is a 38-year-old Nicaraguan citizen who entered the United States in 1979 as a visitor. After she remained in the United States longer than permitted, and failed to take advantage of the Immigration and Naturalization Service's (INS) offer of voluntary departure, the INS commenced deportation proceedings against her. Respondent conceded that she was in the country illegally, but requested withholding of deportation pursuant to § 243(h) and asylum as a refugee pursuant to § 208(a).

To support her request under § 243(h), respondent attempted to show that if she were returned to Nicaragua her "life or freedom would be threatened" on account of her political views; to support her request under § 208(a), she attempted to show that she had a "well-founded fear of persecution" upon her return. The evidence supporting both claims related primarily to the activities of respondent's brother who had been tortured and imprisoned because of his political activities in Nicaragua. Both respondent and her brother testified that they believed the Sandinistas knew that the two of them had fled Nicaragua together and that even though she had not been active politically herself, she would be interrogated about her brother's whereabouts and activities. Respondent also testified that because of her brother's status, her own political opposition to the Sandinistas would be brought to that government's attention. Based on these facts, respondent claimed that she would be tortured if forced to return.

* * *

Under [§ 208(a)], eligibility for asylum depends entirely on the Attorney General's determination that an alien is a "refugee," as that term is defined in § 101(a)(42), which was also added to the Act in 1980. [The Court then quotes the text of INA § 101(a)(42)(A).] Thus, the "persecution or well-founded fear of persecution" standard governs the Attorney General's determination whether an alien is eligible for asylum.[5]

In addition to establishing a statutory asylum process, the 1980 Act amended the withholding of deportation provision, § 243(h). Prior to 1968, the Attorney General had discretion whether to grant withholding of deportation to aliens under § 243(h). In 1968, however, the United States agreed to comply with the substantive provisions of Articles 2 through 34 of the 1951 United Nations Convention Relating to the Status of Refugees. Article 33.1 of the Convention, which is the counterpart of § 243(h) of our statute, imposed a mandatory duty on contracting States not to return an alien to a country where his "life or freedom would be threatened" on account of one of the enumerated reasons. Thus, although § 243(h) itself did not constrain the Attorney General's discretion after 1968, presumably he honored the dictates of the United Nations Convention.[8] In any event, the 1980 Act removed the Attorney General's discretion in § 243(h) proceedings.

In *Stevic* we considered it significant that in enacting the 1980 Act Congress did not amend the standard of eligibility for relief under § 243(h). While the terms "refugee" and hence "well-founded fear" were made an integral part of the § 208(a) procedure, they continued to play no part in § 243(h).

* * *

[T]he language Congress used to describe the two standards conveys very different meanings. The "would be threatened" language of § 243(h) has no subjective component, but instead requires the alien to establish by objective evidence that it is more likely than not that he or she will be subject to persecution upon deportation.[10] *See Stevic*. In contrast, the reference to "fear" in the § 208(a) standard obviously makes the eligibility

---

[5] It is important to note that the Attorney General is *not required* to grant asylum to everyone who meets the definition of refugee. Instead, a finding that an alien is a refugee does no more than establish that "the alien *may* be granted asylum *in the discretion of the Attorney General.*" § 208(a) [1987 version](emphasis added).

[8] While the protocol constrained the Attorney General with respect to § 243(h) between 1968 and 1980, the Protocol does not require the granting of asylum to anyone, and hence does not subject the Attorney General to a similar constraint with respect to his discretion under § 208(a).

[10] "The section literally provides for withholding of deportation only if the alien's life or freedom 'would' be threatened in the country to which he would be deported; it does not require withholding if the alien 'might' or 'could' be subject to persecution." *Stevic*, 467 U.S., at 422.

determination turn to some extent on the subjective mental state of the alien. "The linguistic difference between the words 'well-founded fear' and 'clear probability' may be as striking as that between a subjective and an objective frame of reference. . . . We simply cannot conclude that the standards are identical." *Guevara Flores v. INS*, 786 F.2d 1242, 1250 (C.A.5 1986) [*cert. denied*, 480 U.S. 930, 107 S.Ct. 1565, 94 L.Ed.2d 757 (1987)].

That the fear must be "well-founded" does not alter the obvious focus on the individual's subjective beliefs, nor does it transform the standard into a "more likely than not" one. One can certainly have a well-founded fear of an event happening when there is less than a 50% chance of the occurrence taking place. As one leading authority has pointed out:

> Let us . . . presume that it is known that in the applicant's country of origin every tenth adult male person is either put to death or sent to some remote labor camp . . . In such a case it would be only too apparent that anyone who has managed to escape from the country in question will have 'well-founded fear of being persecuted' upon his eventual return.

1 A. Grahl-Madsen. The Status of Refugees in International Law 180 (1966).

This ordinary and obvious meaning of the phrase is not to be lightly discounted.

* * *

In *Stevic*, we dealt with the issue of withholding of deportation, or *nonrefoulement*, under § 243(h). This provision corresponds to Article 33.1 of the Convention. Significantly though, Article 33.1 does not extend this right to everyone who meets the definition of "refugee." Rather, it provides that "[n]o Contracting State shall expel or return ('*refouler*') a *refugee* in any manner whatsoever to the frontiers of territories *where his life or freedom would be threatened* on account of his race, religion, nationality, membership of a particular social group or political opinion." Thus, Article 33.1 requires that an applicant satisfy two burdens: first, that he or she be a "refugee," i.e., prove at least a "well-founded fear of persecution"; second, that the "refugee" show that his or her life or freedom "would be threatened" if deported. Section 243(h)'s imposition of a "would be threatened" requirement is entirely consistent with the United States' obligations under the Protocol.

Section 208(a), by contrast, is a discretionary mechanism which gives the Attorney General the *authority* to grant the broader relief of asylum to refugees. As such, it does not correspond to Article 33 of the Convention, but instead corresponds to Article 34. That Article provides that the contracting States "shall as far as possible facilitate the assimilation and naturalization of refugees. . . ." Like § 208(a), the provision is precatory; it does not require the implementing authority actually to grant asylum to all those who are eligible. Also like § 208(a), an alien must only show that he or she is a "refugee" to establish eligibility for relief. No further showing that he or she "would be" persecuted is required.

Thus, as made binding on the United States through the Protocol, Article 34 provides for a precatory, or discretionary, benefit for the entire class of persons who qualify as "refugees," whereas Article 33.1 provides an entitlement for the subcategory that "would be threatened" with persecution upon their return.

* * *

INS repeatedly argues that the structure of the Act dictates a decision in its favor, since it is anomalous for § 208(a), which affords greater benefits than § 243(h), to have a less stringent standard of eligibility. This argument sorely fails because it does not take into account the fact that an alien who satisfies the applicable standard under § 208(a) does not have a *right* to remain in the United States; he or she is simply *eligible* for asylum, if the Attorney General, in his discretion, chooses to grant it. An alien satisfying § 243(h)'s stricter standard, in contrast, is automatically entitled to withholding of deportation. In *Matter of Salim*, 18 I. & N. Dec. 311 (1982), for example, the Board held that the alien was eligible for both asylum and withholding of deportation, but granted him the more limited remedy only, exercising its discretion to deny him asylum. We do not consider it at all anomalous that out of the entire class of "refugees," those who can show a clear probability of persecution are *entitled* to mandatory suspension of deportation and *eligible* for discretionary asylum, while those who can only show a well-founded fear of persecution are not *entitled* to anything, but are *eligible* for the discretionary relief of asylum.

* * *

This vesting of discretion in the Attorney General is quite typical in the immigration area. If anything is anomalous, it is that the INS now asks us to restrict its discretion to a narrow class of aliens. Congress has assigned to the Attorney General and his delegates the task of making these hard individualized decisions; although Congress could have crafted a narrower definition, it chose to authorize the Attorney General to determine which, if any, eligible refugees should be denied asylum.

* * *

The question whether Congress intended the two standards to be identical is a pure question of statutory construction for the courts to decide. Employing traditional tools of statutory construction, we have concluded that Congress did not intend the two standards to be identical. In *Chevron U.S.A. Inc. v. Natural Resources Defense Council, Inc.*, 467 U.S. 837 (1984), we explained:

> The judiciary is the final authority on issues of statutory construction and must reject administrative constructions which are contrary to clear congressional intent. [Citing cases.] If a court, employing traditional tools of statutory construction, ascertains that Congress had an intention on the precise question at issue, that intention is the law and must be given effect.

Id. at 843, n.9, 104 S.Ct., at 2782, n.9 (citations omitted).

The narrow legal question whether the two standards are the same is, of course, quite different from the question of interpretation that arises in each case in which the agency is required to apply either or both standards to a particular set of facts. There is obviously some ambiguity in a term like "well-founded fear" which can only be given concrete meaning through a process of case-by-case adjudication. In that process of filling "'any gap left, implicitly or explicitly, by Congress,'" the courts must respect the interpretation of the agency to which Congress has delegated the responsibility for administering the statutory program. But our task today is much narrower, and is well within the province of the judiciary. We do not attempt to set forth a detailed description of how the "well-founded fear" test should be applied.[31] Instead, we merely hold that the Immigration Judge and the BIA were incorrect in holding that the two standards are identical.

* * *

Deportation is always a harsh measure; it is all the more replete with danger when the alien makes a claim that he or she will be subject to death or persecution if forced to return to his or her home country. In enacting the Refugee Act of 1980 Congress sought to "give the United States sufficient flexibility to respond to situations involving political or religious dissidents and detainees throughout the world." Our holding today increases that flexibility by rejecting the Government's contention that the Attorney General may not even consider granting asylum to one who fails to satisfy the strict § 243(h) standard. Whether or not a "refugee" is eventually granted asylum is a matter which Congress has left for the Attorney General to decide. But it is clear that Congress did not intend to restrict eligibility for that relief to those who could prove that it is more likely than not that they will be persecuted if deported.

---

[31] How "meaningful" the differences between the two standards may be is a question that cannot be fully decided in the abstract, but the fact that Congress has prescribed two different standards in the same Act certainly implies that it intended them to have significantly different meanings. * * *

The judgment of the Court of Appeals is affirmed.

[The concurring opinion of JUSTICE BLACKMUN is omitted.]

JUSTICE POWELL, with whom THE CHIEF JUSTICE and JUSTICE WHITE join, dissenting.

The Court's opinion seems to assume that the BIA has adopted a rigorous mathematical approach to asylum cases, requiring aliens to demonstrate an objectively quantifiable risk of persecution in their homeland that is more than 50%. The Court then argues that such a position is inconsistent with the language and history of the Act. But this has never been the BIA's position.

* * *

[T]he BIA does not contend that both the "well-founded fear" standard and the "clear probability" standard require proof of a 51% chance that the alien will suffer persecution if he is returned to his homeland. The BIA plainly eschews analysis resting on mathematical probabilities. Rather, the BIA has adopted a four-part test requiring proof of facts that demonstrate a realistic likelihood of persecution actually occurring. The heart of the Acosta decision is the BIA's empirical conclusion, based on its experience in adjudicating asylum applications, that if the facts establish such a basis for an alien's fear, it rarely will make a difference whether the judge asks if persecution is "likely" to occur or "more likely than not" to occur. If the alien can establish such a basis, he normally will be eligible for relief under either standard.

NOTES AND QUESTIONS ON LIKELIHOOD OF HARM

1. The *Cardoza-Fonseca* majority is convinced, *Chevron* notwithstanding, that the plain meaning of the two sections mandates a differential standard of proof for §§ 208 and 243(h). It emphasizes that the language of § 243(h) is "would," not " 'might' or 'could' be subject to persecution" (footnote 10, quoting *Stevic*). But this juxtaposition of the language is not fully responsive to the actual wording. The withholding provision extends its protection to noncitizens whose "life or freedom would be threatened" on the specified grounds, not "would be taken away." Consider the Court's own example of an individual facing return to a country where the government is killing or jailing every tenth adult male. Assuming that the asylum seeker is a male, obviously he has a well-founded fear of persecution on return. But how does the plain language apply here? Would we say that this man's life or freedom would be threatened on return?

2. Apparently the Supreme Court countenances returning a recognized "refugee" to her country of origin, provided that she falls short of the standard for § 243(h). Is this sound policy? Is it what Congress had in mind? Would the drafters of the UN treaties have intended to permit such a result? More fundamentally, does it make sense to have two different forms of

protection, with two different levels of risk required for protection under U.S. law?

3.   The BIA moved quickly in response to *Cardoza-Fonseca*. In *Matter of Mogharrabi*, 19 I & N Dec. 439 (BIA 1987), the BIA explained that the asylum applicant must show that a "reasonable person in [the asylum applicant's] circumstances would fear persecution." The current regulations, issued after the INA was amended in 1996, ask whether "there is a reasonable possibility of suffering such persecution if he or she were to return to [the home] country." 8 C.F.R. § 208.12(b)(2).

In *Mogharrabi*, the BIA also addressed the decision-making sequence.

Given that the core of evidence and testimony presented in support of the asylum and withholding applications will in almost every case be virtually the same, [they may] be presented in a single hearing. * * * We anticipate that as a general rule the asylum application, with its lower burden of proof, will be adjudicated first. If the applicant is found eligible for asylum, and worthy of the relief as a matter of discretion, there may be no need to determine * * * whether a clear probability of persecution exists.

Mogharrabi, at 447.

4.   PROTECTED GROUNDS

Both the 1951 Convention and U.S. statutes make it clear that a well-founded fear of persecution is not sufficient to trigger protection. Rather, individuals must prove that the persecution they fear is linked—in a certain way—to one of five grounds. Or, as much of the commentary frames it, there must be a connection, or a nexus, between the persecution and race, religion, nationality, membership in a particular social group, or political opinion.

On the face of it, this seems straightforward. All who fear persecution may desire protection, but under the express language of the treaty, refugee status is reserved for a subset of the persecuted. Persecution based solely on a personal grudge or persecution solely to secure financial gain will not result in refugee status. Some of this linkage between persecution and the five grounds is implicit in the very notion of "persecution." That is, harsh sanctions do not usually amount to persecution unless they are inflicted on the basis of some characteristic that is thought not to justify such a response. A person imprisoned at hard labor after a valid conviction for armed robbery is not being persecuted.

Out of this seemingly clear-cut element of the refugee definition, however, the developing law has uncovered many complex questions. What are the outer limits of each of the five specified grounds? The statute explicitly calls for attention to these linkages, and the BIA sometimes requires close connection between the allegedly persecuting act and the precise basis or motive for the oppression before the threat can serve as a valid foundation for asylum? These questions are often difficult to separate neatly.

a.   Political Opinion

For many years the majority of asylum cases filed in the United States appeared to rely on fears of persecution based on political opinion. Many of these cases involved "classic" political opinion claims: the asylum seeker was a recognizable political dissident, the asylum seeker had participated in political demonstrations, and so on. The unfortunate growth of armed insurrections and civil wars in the late twentieth century generated new legal challenges in the asylum system as they spawned many claims of politically motivated persecution that did not fit this paradigm.

Two topics—imputed political opinion and neutrality—presented special difficulties. Sometimes persecutors think individuals have opinions or beliefs that the individuals may not, in fact, hold. For example, government officials might view young men who evade military conscription as sympathetic to a local guerrilla movement and impute to the draft evaders the political opinions of the guerrillas. Other times, particularly in civil war situations, the contending factions do not tolerate neutrality and insist that the population choose sides; they essentially impute opposition to those who want to be left alone. Imputed political opinion and neutrality pose difficult questions individually, and they interact in complex ways. The Supreme Court addressed these and related issues in the following opinion.

INS v. ELIAS-ZACARIAS

Supreme Court of the United States, 1992.
502 U.S. 478, 112 S.Ct. 812, 117 L.Ed.2d 38.

JUSTICE SCALIA delivered the opinion of the Court.

The principal question presented by this case is whether a guerrilla organization's attempt to coerce a person into performing military service necessarily constitutes "persecution on account of . . . political opinion" under § 101(a)(42) of the Immigration and Nationality Act.

I

Respondent Elias-Zacarias, a native of Guatemala, was apprehended in July 1987 for entering the United States without inspection. In deportation proceedings brought by petitioner Immigration and Naturalization Service (INS), Elias-Zacarias conceded his deportability but requested asylum and withholding of deportation.

The Immigration Judge summarized Elias-Zacarias' testimony as follows:

[A]round the end of January in 1987 [when Elias-Zacarias was 18], two armed, uniformed guerrillas with handkerchiefs covering part of their faces came to his home. Only he and his parents were there. . . . [T]he guerrillas asked his parents and himself to join with them, but they all refused. The guerrillas asked them why and told them that they would be back, and that they should think it over about joining them.

[Elias-Zacarias] did not want to join the guerrillas because the guerrillas are against the government and he was afraid that the government would retaliate against him and his family if he did join the guerrillas. [H]e left Guatemala at the end of March [1987] . . . because he was afraid that the guerrillas would return.

[The Immigration Judge denied asylum and withholding of deportation. The BIA affirmed, and the Court of Appeals for the Ninth Circuit reversed the BIA.]

II

* * * The BIA's determination that Elias-Zacarias was not eligible for asylum must be upheld if "supported by reasonable, substantial, and probative evidence on the record considered as a whole." INA § 106(a)(4). It can be reversed only if the evidence presented by Elias-Zacarias was such that a reasonable factfinder would have to conclude that the requisite fear of persecution existed.[1]

The Court of Appeals found reversal warranted. In its view, a guerrilla organization's attempt to conscript a person into its military forces necessarily constitutes "persecution on account of . . . political opinion," because "the person resisting forced recruitment is expressing a political opinion hostile to the persecutor and because the persecutors' motive in carrying out the kidnapping is political." The first half of this seems to us untrue, and the second half irrelevant.

Even a person who supports a guerrilla movement might resist recruitment for a variety of reasons—fear of combat, a desire to remain with one's family and friends, a desire to earn a better living in civilian life, to mention only a few. The record in the present case not only failed

---

[1] Quite beside the point, therefore, is the dissent's assertion that "the record in this case is more than adequate to *support the conclusion* that this respondent's refusal [to join the guerrillas] was a form of expressive conduct that constituted the statement of a 'political opinion,'" (emphasis added). To reverse the BIA finding we must find that the evidence not only supports that conclusion, but *compels it*—and also compels the further conclusion that Elias-Zacarias had a well-founded fear that the guerrillas would persecute him *because of* that political opinion.

to show a political motive on Elias-Zacarias' part; it showed the opposite. He testified that he refused to join the guerrillas because he was afraid that the government would retaliate against him and his family if he did so. Nor is there any indication (assuming, *arguendo*, it would suffice) that the guerrillas erroneously *believed* that Elias-Zacarias' refusal was politically based.

As for the Court of Appeals' conclusion that the guerrillas' "motive in carrying out the kidnaping is political": It apparently meant by this that the guerrillas seek to fill their ranks in order to carry on their war against the government and pursue their political goals. But that does not render the forced recruitment "persecution on account of . . . political opinion." * * * The ordinary meaning of the phrase "persecution on account of . . . political opinion" in § 101(a)(42) is persecution on account of the victim's political opinion, not the persecutor's. If a Nazi regime persecutes Jews, it is not, within the ordinary meaning of language, engaging in persecution on account of political opinion; and if a fundamentalist Moslem regime persecutes democrats, it is not engaging in persecution on account of religion. Thus, the mere existence of a generalized "political" motive underlying the guerrillas' forced recruitment is inadequate to establish (and, indeed, goes far to refute) the proposition that Elias-Zacarias fears persecution on account of political opinion, as § 101(a)(42) requires.

Elias-Zacarias appears to argue that not taking sides with any political faction is itself the affirmative expression of a political opinion. That seems to us not ordinarily so, since we do not agree with the dissent that only a "narrow, grudging construction of the concept of 'political opinion'" would distinguish it from such quite different concepts as indifference, indecisiveness and risk-averseness. But we need not decide whether the evidence compels the conclusion that Elias-Zacarias held a political opinion. Even if it does, Elias-Zacarias still has to establish that the record also compels the conclusion that he has a "well-founded fear" that the guerrillas will persecute him because of that political opinion, rather than because of his refusal to fight with them. He has not done so with the degree of clarity necessary to permit reversal of a BIA finding to the contrary; indeed, he has not done so at all.[2]

---

[2] The dissent misdescribes the record on this point in several respects. For example, it exaggerates the "well-foundedness" of whatever fear Elias-Zacarias possesses, by progressively transforming his testimony that he was afraid the guerrillas would " 'take me or kill me,' " into, first, "the guerrillas' *implied threat* to 'take' him or to 'kill' him," (emphasis added), and, then, into the flat assertion that the guerrillas "*responded by threatening* to 'take' or to 'kill' him" (emphasis added). The dissent also erroneously describes it as "undisputed" that the cause of the harm Elias-Zacarias fears, if that harm should occur, will be "the guerrilla organization's displeasure with his refusal to join them in their armed insurrection against the government." The record shows no such concession by the INS, and all Elias-Zacarias said on the point was that he feared being taken or killed by the guerrillas. It is quite plausible, indeed likely, that the taking would be engaged in by the guerrillas in order to augment their troops rather than show

Elias-Zacarias objects that he cannot be expected to provide direct proof of his persecutors' motives. We do not require that. But since the statute makes motive critical, he must provide some evidence of it, direct or circumstantial. And if he seeks to obtain judicial reversal of the BIA's determination, he must show that the evidence he presented was so compelling that no reasonable factfinder could fail to find the requisite fear of persecution. That he has not done.

The BIA's determination should therefore have been upheld in all respects, and we reverse the Court of Appeals' judgment to the contrary.

It is so ordered.

JUSTICE STEVENS, with whom JUSTICE BLACKMUN and JUSTICE O'CONNOR join, dissenting.

Respondent refused to join a guerrilla organization that engaged in forced recruitment in Guatemala. He fled the country because he was afraid the guerrillas would return and "take me and kill me." After his departure, armed guerrillas visited his family on two occasions searching for him. In testimony that the hearing officer credited, he stated that he is still afraid to return to Guatemala because "these people" can come back to "take me or kill me."

It is undisputed that respondent has a well-founded fear that he will be harmed, if not killed, if he returns to Guatemala. It is also undisputed that the cause of that harm, if it should occur, is the guerrilla organization's displeasure with his refusal to join them in their armed insurrection against the government. The question of law that the case presents is whether respondent's well-founded fear is a "fear of persecution on account of . . . political opinion" within the meaning of § 101(a)(42) of the Immigration and Naturalization Act.

* * *

Today the Court holds that respondent's fear of persecution is not "on account of . . . political opinion" for two reasons. First, he failed to prove that his refusal to join the guerrillas was politically motivated; indeed, he testified that he was at least in part motivated by a fear that government forces would retaliate against him or his family if he joined the guerrillas. Second, he failed to prove that his persecutors' motives were political. In particular, the Court holds that the persecutors' implicit threat to retaliate against respondent "because of his refusal to fight with them," is not persecution on account of political opinion. I disagree with both parts of the Court's reasoning.

their displeasure; and the killing he feared might well be a killing in the course of resisting being taken.

I

A political opinion can be expressed negatively as well as affirmatively. A refusal to support a cause—by staying home on election day, by refusing to take an oath of allegiance, or by refusing to step forward at an induction center—can express a political opinion as effectively as an affirmative statement or affirmative conduct. Even if the refusal is motivated by nothing more than a simple desire to continue living an ordinary life with one's family, it is the kind of political expression that the asylum provisions of the statute were intended to protect.

As the Court of Appeals explained in *Bolanos-Hernandez v. INS*, 767 F.2d 1277 (9th Cir. 1985):

> Choosing to remain neutral is no less a political decision than is choosing to affiliate with a particular political faction.
> * * *

Id. at 1286.

The narrow, grudging construction of the concept of "political opinion" that the Court adopts today is inconsistent with the basic approach to this statute that the Court endorsed in *INS v. Cardoza-Fonseca*. In that case, relying heavily on the fact that an alien's status as a "refugee" merely makes him eligible for a discretionary grant of asylum—as contrasted with the entitlement to a withholding of deportation * * *—the Court held that the alien's burden of proving a well-founded fear of persecution did not require proof that persecution was more likely than not to occur. * * *

Similar reasoning should resolve any doubts concerning the political character of an alien's refusal to take arms against a legitimate government in favor of the alien. In my opinion, the record in this case is more than adequate to support the conclusion that this respondent's refusal was a form of expressive conduct that constituted the statement of a "political opinion" within the meaning of § 208(a).[5]

II

It follows as night follows day that the guerrillas' implied threat to "take" him or to "kill" him if he did not change his position constituted threatened persecution "on account of" that political opinion. As the Court of Appeals explained in *Bolanos-Hernandez, supra*:

---

[5] Here, respondent not only engaged in expressive conduct by refusing to join the guerrilla organization but also explained that he did so "[b]ecause they see very well, that if you join the guerrillas . . . then you are against the government. You are against the government and if you join them then it is to die there. And, then the government is against you and against your family." Respondent thus expressed the political view that he was for the government and against the guerrillas. The statute speaks simply in terms of a political opinion and does not require that the view be well developed or elegantly expressed.

It does not matter to the persecutors what the individual's motivation is. The guerrillas in El Salvador do not inquire into the reasoning process of those who insist on remaining neutral and refuse to join their cause. They are concerned only with an act that constitutes an overt manifestation of a political opinion. Persecution because of that overt manifestation is persecution because of a political opinion.

It is important to emphasize that the statute does not require that an applicant for asylum prove exactly why his persecutors would act against him; it only requires him to show that he has a "well-founded fear of persecution on account of . . . political opinion." As we recognized in *INS v. Cardoza Fonseca*, the applicant meets this burden if he shows that there is a " 'reasonable possibility' " that he will be persecuted on account of his political opinion (quoting *INS v. Stevic*). Because respondent expressed a political opinion by refusing to join the guerrillas, and they responded by threatening to "take" or to "kill" him if he did not change his mind, his fear that the guerrillas will persecute him on account of his political opinion is well founded.[7]

Accordingly, I would affirm the judgment of the Court of Appeals.

NOTES AND QUESTIONS ON IMPUTED POLITICAL OPINION

1.   The doctrine of imputed political opinion seemed at risk after *Elias-Zacarias*, but INS General Counsel Grover Joseph Rees issued a lengthy opinion in 1993 concluding that this doctrine was still viable. 70 Interp. Rel. 498 (1993). The BIA agreed, *see, e.g., In re T-M-B-,* 21 I & N Dec. 775 (1997), as do the courts, *see, e.g., Zhou v. Gonzales*, 437 F.3d 860, 868–70 (9th Cir. 2006); *Najjar v. Ashcroft*, 257 F.3d 1262, 1289 (11th Cir. 2001).

2.   In *Mirisawo v. Holder*, 599 F.3d 391 (4th Cir. 2010), pp. 811–816, *supra*, the asylum applicant contended that the Zimbabwean government would impute membership in a political organization to her because her brother and sister were members and because her neighborhood was known to be home to many supporters of the organization. Are these facts a more compelling depiction of imputed political opinion than those put forth by *Elias Zacarias*? Is it relevant that the Zimbabwe government had often employed violence against political opponents and disrupted electoral campaigning?

---

[7]   In response to this dissent, the Court suggests that respondent and I have exaggerated the "well-foundedness" of his fear. The Court's legal analysis, however, would produce precisely the same result no matter how unambiguous the guerrillas' threatened retaliation might have been. Moreover, any doubts concerning the sinister character of a suggestion to "think it over" delivered by two uniformed masked men carrying machine guns should be resolved in respondent's favor.

Mixed Motives

The imputed political opinion doctrine often arises in circumstances in which the persecutor may have mixed motives. In *Matter of S-P-,* 21 I & N Dec. 486 (BIA 1996), a Tamil from Sri Lanka had been beaten and detained by the Sri Lankan Army after the soldiers raided an insurgent camp where he had been conscripted to work as a welder. The BIA stated that the government may have punished the asylum applicant as a part of its intelligence gathering, for political views imputed to him, for criminal conduct, or for a mix of these and other motives. It concluded, however, that "the applicant ha[d] produced evidence from which it is reasonable to believe that those who harmed him were in part motivated by an assumption that his political views were antithetical to those of the Government," and that this was sufficient to support a well-founded fear of future persecution. *Id.* at 496.

Congress addressed persecution based on mixed motives in the REAL ID Act of 2005, Pub. L. 109–13, § 101(a), 119 Stat. 231, 303 (2005), by adding the following language to the asylum statute, INA § 208(b)(1)(B)(i):

> To establish that the applicant is a refugee * * * , the applicant must establish that race, religion, nationality, membership in a particular social group, or political opinion was or will be *at least one central reason* for persecuting the applicant.

Id. (emphasis added). The BIA's first precedent decision to consider the amendment, *Matter of J-B-N- & S-M-,* 24 I & N Dec. 208 (BIA 2007), stated:

> Having considered the conference report and the language of the REAL ID Act, we find that our standard in mixed motive cases has not been radically altered by the amendments. The prior case law requiring the applicant to present direct or circumstantial evidence of a motive that is protected under the Act still stands. As had previously been the case, the protected ground cannot play a minor role in the alien's past mistreatment or fears of future mistreatment. That is, it cannot be incidental, tangential, superficial, or subordinate to another reason for harm.

Id. at 214.

Test your understanding by applying the legal standards to the scenario below.

EXERCISE

Before coming to the United States, where he has applied for asylum, Oleg worked as a tax auditor for the government of Ruritania, part of the former Soviet Union. During an audit of the Budro Corporation, Oleg uncovered an illegal tax-evasion scheme. Oleg discovered that Budro, founded by a high-ranking government official with close ties to the former communist leaders of Ruritania during Soviet days, had evaded the payment of automobile import duties. When Oleg reported his findings to officials at Budro, they tried to bribe him to change his report. Oleg refused the bribes and referred the matter to local prosecutors.

Oleg and his wife, Nicola, soon began receiving threats. Two men forcibly removed Nicola from a bus. Three days later, she suffered a miscarriage, which she attributed to this incident. Fearing for his safety, Oleg arranged for his cousin to drive him to work. While Oleg's cousin was driving alone in his car, equipped with tinted windows, he was shot. Oleg was supposed to be in the car but had cancelled at the last minute.

After Oleg and Nicola fled Ruritania for the United States, his apartment was vandalized, and some of Nicola's relatives were hurt in a suspicious car accident that Nicola suspects was caused by Budro officials.

You are the immigration judge in Oleg's case. How would you rule on his claim that he has a well-founded fear of persecution on account of political opinion if he is returned to Ruritania?

---

b. Race, Nationality, and Religion

Although the concepts of race, nationality, and religion are familiar, the meaning of these terms in the asylum statute frequently differs from that used in general conversation. The drafters of the 1951 Convention, the model for the U.S. statute, had the suffering involved with World War II still fresh in their minds. Did they think that the Nazi persecution of the Jews was based on race? On religion? What about Nazi persecution of the Roma? Of the Poles?

The 1951 Convention did not define the term "race," and it has been used to refer to ethnic groups identifiable by their shared culture as much as by any physical distinctiveness. Absent a 1951 Convention definition of "race," many look to the International Convention on the Elimination of All Forms of Racial Discrimination, G.A. Res. 2106 (XX), Annex, 20 U.N. GAOR Supp. (No. 14) at 47, U.N. Doc. A/6014 (1966), 660 U.N.T.S. 195, *entered into force* Jan. 4, 1969, and its formulation that the term "race" includes "race, color, descent, or national or ethnic origin." Article 1(1).

The 1951 Convention's reference to persecution based on nationality takes a similarly comprehensive approach. Nationality is sometimes used to refer to those who have the same citizenship as the persecutors, but who belong to a different linguistic or ethnic community. For example, in Romania under Ceausescu, the millions of Romanian citizens of Hungarian lineage were often considered to possess Romanian citizenship but Hungarian nationality. The lines between race and nationality have also often been blurred. Infamous persecutions of the past led to the expulsion of thousands of Ugandan citizens of Indian origin in 1972; multitudes of Vietnamese citizens of ethnic Chinese origin fled in 1975; the Tamils in Sri Lanka, the Tutsi in Rwanda; the Bosnians in the Balkans, and the Black Fulanis of Mauritania have all felt the scourge of ethnic cleansing and persecution.

Religion, too, often enters into the mix of ethnic and political conflict. In Sri Lanka the conflict between the Tamil minority, largely Hindu, and the Sinhalese majority, largely Buddhist, led to years of bloodshed. A combination of ethnicity and religion have marked many asylum cases stemming from civil disturbances in Indonesia. *See, e.g., Lie v. Ashcroft*, 396 F.3d 530 (3d Cir. 2005) (attacks on ethnic Chinese Christians in Indonesia not sufficient to constitute persecution).

Other religion-based asylum claims have included challenges to Chinese laws against unregistered religious activities, *see., e.g., Chen v. INS*, 359 F.3d 121 (2d Cir. 2004) (reversing denial of asylum to lay leader of Roman Catholic Church detained for raising funds and distributing literature), and challenges to clothing requirements imposed on women in some Islamic societies. *See Matter of S-A-*, 22 I & N Dec. 1328 (BIA 2000) (Moroccan father's beating and burning of his daughter for wearing improper attire constitutes persecution based on religion).

Thorny issues arise about the extent to which decisionmakers can and should assess the sincerity of religious beliefs alleged as the basis for an asylum claim. Does it matter whether the stated beliefs are genuine if the persecutor is likely to think they are? The Ninth Circuit examined this issue in an asylum claim filed by an Iranian who alleged that he had converted to Christianity after arriving in the United States and would be persecuted as an apostate if returned to his homeland. *Toufighi v. Mukasey*, 538 F. 3d 988 (9th Cir. 2008) (upholding adverse credibility finding as to conversion and imputed religious affiliation).

The following exercise tests your understanding of the meaning of persecution, as well as the idea of persecution based on religion, and the significance of uniform national policies.

EXERCISE

Garzeh testified at his asylum hearing that he fears returning to his country of Aridonia because the government there persecutes members of his church, the Jehovah's Witnesses. Garzeh presented evidence that Jehovah's Witnesses have been denied government jobs, housing assistance, and business licenses because they refuse on religious grounds to vote or participate in national service.

Garzeh further testified that he has been a Jehovah's Witness since 1984. He stated that Jehovah's Witnesses cannot participate in national service (which in Aridonia involves military service), because they "don't intend to kill anybody because we have to love each other." According to Garzeh, Jehovah's Witnesses were denied civil service positions and travel documents because they refused to participate in national service. Garzeh also testified that the Aridonian government arrested his brother for refusing to engage in national service. After a number of severe beatings in jail, Garzeh's brother was taken to a hospital where he eventually died.

Garzeh also said that he applied to the Aridonian government for a business license, but received a letter rejecting the application:

> You have applied for a business license to open a land irrigation consulting service. We have reviewed your application and found out that you are a follower of the Jehovah's Witnesses and have not registered or participated in the national service. We are obligated to follow the guidelines given to us by the government and have denied your application for the above reasons.

Has Garzeh met his burden of establishing a well-founded fear of persecution on account of religion?

---

c. Membership in a Particular Social Group

"Membership in a particular social group" may be the most elusive of the five factors listed in the Refugee Convention and in the U.S. statute. An early decision by the Board of Immigration Appeals construed this phrase to include individuals bound together by a characteristic that is either immutable or so fundamental to their identity that they should not be required to change it. *Matter of Acosta,* 19 I & N Dec. 211 (BIA 1985).

Successful "particular social group" asylum claims have included sexual orientation, *Matter of Toboso-Alfonso,* 20 I & N Dec. 819 (BIA 1990), clan membership, *Matter of H-,* 21 I & N Dec. 337 (BIA 1996), women of the Tchamba-Kunsuntu Tribe who have not been subjected to female genital mutilation (FGM) and who oppose the practice, *Matter of Kasinga,* 21 I & N Dec. 357 (BIA 1996), former members of the Salvadoran national police, *Matter of Fuentes,* 19 I & N Dec. 658 (BIA 1988).

Recent cases have explored whether individuals connected in some way with gangs (sometimes as recruits, sometimes as former gang members, sometimes as opponents of gangs) should be viewed as particular social groups. In 2014 the BIA issued two precedent decisions that attempted to harmonize the case law and clarify the factors of "particularity" and "social visibility" or "social distinction" that had become prominent in asylum litigation.

MATTER OF M-E-V-G-

Board of Immigration Appeals, 2014
26 I. & N. Dec. 227

GUENDELSBERGER, BOARD MEMBER:

This case is before us on remand from the United States Court of Appeals for the Third Circuit for further consideration of the respondent's applications for asylum and withholding of removal. The court declined to afford deference to our conclusion that a grant of asylum or withholding of removal under the "particular social group" ground of persecution requires the applicant to establish the elements of "particularity" and "social visibility." Upon further consideration of the record and the arguments presented by the parties and amici curiae, we will clarify our interpretation of the phrase "particular social group." We adhere to our prior interpretations of the phrase but emphasize that literal or "ocular" visibility is not required, and we rename the "social visibility" element as "social distinction." * * *

* * * [T]he respondent claims that he suffered past persecution and has a well-founded fear of future persecution in his native Honduras because members of the Mara Salvatrucha gang beat him, kidnaped and assaulted him and his family while they were traveling in Guatemala, and threatened to kill him if he did not join the gang. In addition, the respondent testified that the gang members would shoot at him and throw rocks and spears at him about two to three times per week. The respondent asserts that he was persecuted "on account of his membership in a particular social group, namely Honduran youth who have been actively recruited by gangs but who have refused to join because they oppose the gangs."

* * * [The immigration judge denied asylum and withholding of removal. The BIA affirmed.] The case is now before us following a second remand from the Third Circuit. *Valdiviezo-Galdamez v. Att'y Gen. of U.S.*, 663 F.3d 582 (3d Cir. 2011). The court found that our requirement that a particular social group must possess the elements of "particularity" and "social visibility" is inconsistent with prior Board decisions, that we have not announced a "principled reason" for our adoption of that inconsistent requirement, and that our interpretation is not entitled to deference

under *Chevron, U.S.A., Inc. v. Natural Resources Defense Council, Inc.*, 467 U.S. 837 (1984). Nevertheless, the court advised that "an agency can change or adopt its policies" and recognized that the Board may add new requirements to, or even change, its definition of a "particular social group."

* * *

III. PARTICULAR SOCIAL GROUP

* * *

The phrase "membership in a particular social group," which is not defined in the Act, the Convention, or the Protocol, is ambiguous and difficult to define. * * * Congress has assigned the Attorney General the primary responsibility of construing ambiguous provisions in the immigration laws, and this responsibility has been delegated to the Board. The Board's reasonable construction of an ambiguous term in the Act, such as "membership in a particular social group," is entitled to deference. *See Nat'l Cable & Telecomms. Ass'n v. Brand X Internet Servs.*, 545 U.S. 967, 980 (2005); *Chevron.*

We first interpreted the phrase "membership in a particular social group" in *Matter of Acosta*[, 19 I & N Dec. 211 (BIA 1985)]. We found the doctrine of "ejusdem generis" helpful in defining the phrase, which we held should be interpreted on the same order as the other grounds of persecution in the Act. The phrase "persecution on account of membership in a particular social group" was interpreted to mean "persecution that is directed toward an individual who is a member of a group of persons all of whom share a common, immutable characteristic." The common characteristic that defines the group must be one "that the members of the group either cannot change, or should not be required to change because it is fundamental to their individual identities or consciences."

Matter of Acosta * * * rejected the applicant's claim that a Salvadoran cooperative organization of taxi drivers was a particular social group, because members could change jobs and working in their job of choice was not a "fundamental" characteristic. *Id.* at 234. * * *

* * *

Now, close to three decades after *Acosta*, claims based on social group membership are numerous and varied. The generality permitted by the *Acosta* standard provided flexibility in the adjudication of asylum claims. However, it also led to confusion and a lack of consistency as adjudicators struggled with various possible social groups, some of which appeared to be created exclusively for asylum purposes. * * * [We have also] cautioned that "the social group concept would virtually swallow the entire refugee definition if common characteristics, coupled with a meaningful level of harm, were all that need be shown."

* * *

In a series of cases, we applied the concepts of "social visibility" and "particularity" as important considerations in the particular social group analysis, and we ultimately deemed them to be requirements. *See Orellana-Monson v. Holder*, 685 F.3d 511, 521 (5th Cir. 2012). * * *

In *Matter of C-A-*, we recognized "particularity" as a requirement in the particular social group analysis and held that the "social visibility" of the members of a claimed social group is "an important element in identifying the existence of a particular social group." *Matter of C-A-*, 23 I & N Dec. 951, 957, 959–61 (BIA 2006) (holding that "noncriminal informants working against the Cali drug cartel" in Colombia were not a particular social group), *aff'd* 446 F.3d 1190 (11th Cir. 2006), *cert. denied*, 549 U.S. 1115 (2007). We subsequently determined that a "particular social group" cannot be defined exclusively by the claimed persecution, that it must be "recognizable" as a discrete group by others in the society, and that it must have well-defined boundaries. *Matter of A-M-E- & J-G-U-*, 24 I & N Dec. 69, 74–76 (BIA 2007) (holding that "wealthy" Guatemalans were not shown to be a particular social group within the meaning of the "refugee" description), *aff'd* 509 F.3d 70 (2d Cir. 2007).

Finally, in 2008, we issued *Matter of S-E-G-* [, 24 I & N Dec. 579 (BIA 2008),] and *Matter of E-A-G-*, [24 I & N Dec. 591 (BIA 2008),] in which we held that—in addition to the common immutable characteristic requirement set forth in *Acosta*—the previously introduced concepts of "particularity" and "social visibility" were distinct requirements for the "membership in a particular social group" ground of persecution. * * *

Our articulation of these requirements has been met with approval in the clear majority of the Federal courts of appeals [citing cases from the 1st, 2d, 4th, 6th, 8th, 10th, and 11th Circuits]. However, it has not been universally accepted [citing cases from the 3d and 7th Circuits].

* * * [T]he respondent and amici curiae [including UNHCR] argue that the Board should disavow the requirements of "social visibility" and "particularity" and should restore *Matter of Acosta* as the sole standard for determining a particular social group. The Department of Homeland Security ("DHS") argues that "social visibility" and "particularity" are valid refinements to the particular social group interpretation but that the two concepts should be clarified and streamlined into a single requirement.

IV. ANALYSIS

We take this opportunity to clarify our interpretation of the phrase "membership in a particular social group." In doing so, we adhere to the social group requirements announced in *Matter of S-E-G-* and *Matter of E-A-G-*, as further explained here and in *Matter of W-G-R-*, 26 I & N Dec. 208 (BIA 2014), a decision published as a companion to this case.[9] * * *

A. Protection Within the Refugee Context

The interpretation of the phrase "membership in a particular social group" does not occur in a contextual vacuum. * * *

The Act and the Protocol * * * identify "refugees" as only those who face persecution on account of "race, religion, nationality, membership in a particular social group, or political opinion."

The limited nature of the protection offered by refugee law is highlighted by the fact that it does not cover those fleeing from natural or economic disaster, civil strife, or war. *See Matter of Sosa Ventura*, 25 I & N Dec. 391, 394 (BIA 2010) (explaining that Congress created the alternative relief of Temporary Protected Status because individuals fleeing from life-threatening natural disasters or a generalized state of violence within a country are not entitled to asylum). Similarly, asylum and refugee laws do not protect people from general conditions of strife, such as crime and other societal afflictions.

Unless an applicant has been targeted on a protected basis, he or she cannot establish a claim for asylum. * * *

The "membership in a particular social group" ground of persecution was not initially included in the refugee definition proposed by the committee that drafted the U.N. Convention; it was added later without discussion. The guidelines to the Protocol issued by the United Nations High Commissioner for Refugees ("UNHCR") clearly state that the particular social group category was not meant to be "a 'catch all' that applies to all persons fearing persecution."

Societies use a variety of means to distinguish individuals based on race, religion, nationality, and political opinion. The distinctions may be based on characteristics that are overt and visible to the naked eye or on those that are subtle and only discernible by people familiar with the particular culture. The characteristics are sometimes not literally visible. Some distinctions are based on beliefs and characteristics that are largely internal, such as religious or political beliefs. Individuals with certain religious or political beliefs may only be treated differently within society if their beliefs were made known or acted upon by the individual. The members of these factions generally understand their own affiliation with

---

[9]   The Supreme Court has stated that administrative agencies may adopt a new or changed interpretation as long as it is based on a "reasoned explanation." *FCC v. Fox Television Stations, Inc.*, 556 U.S. 502, 515–16 (2009). Our decision in this case is not a new interpretation, but it further explains the importance of particularity and social distinction as part of the statutory definition of the phrase "particular social group."

the grouping, and other people in the particular society understand that such a distinct group exists.

Therefore these enumerated grounds of persecution have more in common than simply describing persecution aimed at an immutable characteristic. They have an external perception component within a given society, which need not involve literal or "ocular" visibility. Considering the refugee context in which they arise, we find that the enumerated grounds all describe persecution aimed at an immutable characteristic that separates various factions within a particular society.

B. Particular Social Group

Given the suggestions [in federal court opinions] that further explanation of our interpretation of the phrase "particular social group" is warranted, we now provide such clarification based on the analysis set forth above.

The primary source of disagreement with, or confusion about, our prior interpretation of the term "particular social group" relates to the social visibility requirement. Contrary to our intent, the term "social visibility" has led some to believe that literal, that is, "ocular" or "on-sight," visibility is required to make a particular social group cognizable under the Act. Because of that misconception, we now rename the "social visibility" requirement as "social distinction." This new name more accurately describes the function of the requirement.

Thus, we clarify that an applicant for asylum or withholding of removal seeking relief based on "membership in a particular social group" must establish that the group is

(1) composed of members who share a common immutable characteristic,

(2) defined with particularity, and

(3) socially distinct within the society in question.

1. Overview of Criteria

The criteria of particularity and social distinction are consistent with both the language of the Act and our earlier precedents. By defining these concepts in *Matter of C-A-* and the cases that followed it, we did not depart from or abrogate the definition of a particular social group that was set forth in *Matter of Acosta*; nor did we adopt a new approach to defining particular social groups under the Act.

Our interpretation of the phrase "membership in a particular social group" incorporates the common immutable characteristic standard set forth in *Matter of Acosta*[.] * * *

The "particularity" requirement relates to the group's boundaries or, as earlier court decisions described it, the need to put "outer limits" on the definition of a "particular social group." *See Castellano-Chacon v. INS*, 341 F.3d 533, 549 (6th Cir. 2003); *Sanchez-Trujillo v. INS*, 801 F.2d at 1576. The particular social group analysis does not occur in isolation, but rather in the context of the society out of which the claim for asylum arises. Thus, the "social distinction" requirement considers whether those with a common immutable characteristic are set apart, or distinct, from other persons within the society in some significant way. In other words, if the common immutable characteristic were known, those with the characteristic in the society in question would be meaningfully distinguished from those who do not have it. A viable particular social group should be perceived within the given society as a sufficiently distinct group. The members of a particular social group will generally understand their own affiliation with the grouping, as will other people in the particular society.[12]

* * * Our precedents have collectively focused on the extent to which the group is understood to exist as a recognized component of the society in question.

2. *"Particularity"*

While we addressed the immutability requirement in *Acosta*, the term "particularity" is included in the plain language of the Act and is consistent with the specificity by which race, religion, nationality, and political opinion are commonly defined.[13] The Tenth Circuit recently noted that "the particularity requirement flows quite naturally from the language of the statute, which, of course, specifically refers to membership in a '*particular* social group.' "

A particular social group must be defined by characteristics that provide a clear benchmark for determining who falls within the group. *Matter of A-M-E- & J-G-U-*, 24 I & N Dec. at 76 (holding that wealthy Guatemalans lack the requisite particularity to be a particular social group). It is critical that the terms used to describe the group have commonly accepted definitions in the society of which the group is a part. *Id.* (observing that the concept of wealth is too subjective to provide an adequate benchmark for defining a particular social group).

---

[12] Although members of a particular social group will generally understand their own affiliation with the group, such self-awareness is not a requirement for the group's existence. Nevertheless, as a practical matter, this point is of little import because the applicants in removal proceedings are generally professing their membership in these groups in the process of seeking asylum.

[13] However, there is a critical difference between a political opinion or religious belief, which may in theory be entirely personal and idiosyncratic, and membership in a particular social group, which requires that others in the society share the characteristics that define the group.

The group must also be discrete and have definable boundaries—it must not be amorphous, overbroad, diffuse, or subjective. The particularity requirement clarifies the point, at least implicit in earlier case law, that not every "immutable characteristic" is sufficiently precise to define a particular social group. *See, e.g., Escobar v. Gonzales*, 417 F.3d 363, 368 (3d Cir. 2005) (finding the characteristics of poverty, homelessness, and youth to be "too vague and all encompassing" to set perimeters for a protected group within the scope of the Act).

3. *"Social Distinction"*

Our definition of "social visibility" has emphasized the importance of "perception" or "recognition" in the concept of "particular social group." *See Matter of H-*, 21 I & N Dec. 337, 342 (BIA 1996) (in Somali society, clan membership is a "highly recognizable" characteristic that is "inextricably linked to family ties"). The term was never meant to be read literally. The renamed requirement "social distinction" clarifies that social visibility does not mean "ocular" visibility—either of the group as a whole or of individuals within the group—any more than a person holding a protected religious or political belief must be "ocularly" visible to others in society. Social distinction refers to social recognition, taking as its basis the plain language of the Act—in this case, the word "social." To be socially distinct, a group need not be seen by society; rather, it must be perceived as a group by society. Society can consider persons to comprise a group without being able to identify the group's members on sight.

* * * For this reason, the fact that members of a particular social group may make efforts to hide their membership in the group to avoid persecution does not deprive the group of its protected status as a particular social group.

* * * [T]here is considerable overlap between the "social distinction" and "particularity" requirements, which has resulted in confusion. * * *

The "social distinction" and "particularity" requirements each emphasize a different aspect of a particular social group. * * * While "particularity" chiefly addresses the "outer limits" of a group's boundaries and is definitional in nature, this question necessarily occurs in the context of the society in which the claim for asylum arises. Societal considerations have a significant impact on whether a proposed group describes a collection of people with appropriately defined boundaries and is sufficiently "particular." Similarly, societal considerations influence whether the people of a given society would perceive a proposed group as sufficiently separate or distinct to meet the "social distinction" test.

For example, in an underdeveloped, oligarchical society, "landowners" may be a sufficiently discrete class to meet the criterion of particularity, and the society may view landowners as a discrete group, sufficient to meet the social distinction test. However, such a group would likely be far too amorphous to meet the particularity requirement in Canada, and Canadian society may not view landowners as sufficiently distinct from the rest of society to satisfy the social distinction test. In analyzing whether either of these hypothetical claims would establish a particular social group under the Act, an Immigration Judge should make findings whether "landowners" share a common immutable characteristic, whether the group is discrete or amorphous, and whether the society in question considers "landowners" as a significantly distinct group within the society. Thus, the concepts may overlap in application, but each serves a separate purpose.

4. Society's Perception

The Ninth Circuit has recently observed that neither it nor the Board "has clearly specified whose perspectives are most indicative of society's perception of a particular social group." *Henriquez-Rivas v. Holder*, 707 F.3d at 1089). Interpreting "membership in a particular social group" consistently with the other statutory grounds within the context of refugee protection, we clarify that a group's recognition for asylum purposes is determined by the perception of the society in question, rather than by the perception of the persecutor.

Defining a social group based on the perception of the persecutor is problematic for two significant reasons. First, it is important to distinguish between the inquiry into whether a group is a "particular social group" and the question whether a person is persecuted "on account of" membership in a particular social group. In other words, we must separate the assessment whether the applicant has established the existence of one of the enumerated grounds (religion, political opinion, race, ethnicity, and particular social group) from the issue of nexus. The structure of the Act supports preserving this distinction, which should not be blurred by defining a social group based solely on the perception of the persecutor.

Second, defining a particular social group from the perspective of the persecutor is in conflict with our prior holding that "a social group cannot be defined exclusively by the fact that its members have been subjected to harm." *Matter of A-M-E- & J-G-U-*, 24 I & N Dec. at 74. The perception of the applicant's persecutors may be relevant, because it can be indicative of whether society views the group as distinct. However, the persecutors' perception is not itself enough to make a group socially distinct, and persecutory conduct alone cannot define the group.

For example, a proposed social group composed of former employees of a country's attorney general may not be valid for asylum purposes. Although such a shared past experience is immutable and the group is sufficiently discrete, the employees may not consider themselves a separate group within the society, and the society may not consider these employees to be meaningfully distinct within society in general. * * *

[If the government begins persecuting the former employees,] it is possible that these people would experience a sense of "group," and society would discern that this group of individuals, who share a common immutable characteristic, is distinct in some significant way. The act of persecution by the government may be the catalyst that causes the society to distinguish the former employees in a meaningful way and consider them a distinct group, but the immutable characteristic of their shared past experience exists independent of the persecution.

The persecutor's actions or perceptions may also be relevant in cases involving persecution on account of "imputed" grounds * * *. For example, an individual may present a valid asylum claim if he is incorrectly identified as a homosexual by a government that registers and maintains files on homosexuals—in a society that considers homosexuals a distinct group united by a common immutable characteristic. In such a case, the social group exists independent of the persecution, and the perception of the persecutor is relevant to the issue of nexus (whether the persecution was or would be on account of the applicant's imputed homosexuality).

Persecution limited to a remote region of a country may invite an inquiry into a more limited subset of the country's society * * *. However, the refugee analysis must still consider whether government protection is available, internal relocation is possible, and persecution extends countrywide. * * *

C. *Evidentiary Burdens*

* * *

[T]he applicant has the burden to establish a claim based on membership in a particular social group and will be required to present evidence that the proposed group exists in the society in question. * * * [A] successful case will require evidence that members of the proposed particular social group share a common immutable characteristic, that the group is sufficiently particular, and that it is set apart within the society in some significant way. Evidence such as country conditions reports, expert witness testimony, and press accounts of discriminatory laws and policies, historical animosities, and the like may establish that a group exists and is perceived as "distinct" or "other" in a particular society. * * *

D. *Consistency with Prior Board Precedent*

In its decision, the Third Circuit declined to afford *Chevron* deference to our prior interpretation of the requirements for a particular social group because it perceived them to be inconsistent with our past decisions, in particular *Matter of Kasinga, Matter of Toboso-Alfonso*, and *Matter of Fuentes.* * * *

* * *

[In *Matter of Toboso-Alfonso*, 20 I & N Dec. 819 (BIA 1990) the proposed group,] homosexuals in Cuba, was sufficiently particular because it was a discrete group with well-defined boundaries. The group was based on an immutable characteristic that provided an adequate benchmark for defining the members of the group, and it did not rely on a vague or subjective characteristic. The record established the existence of a Cuban governmental office that registered and maintained files on homosexuals. The applicant testified that residents threw eggs and tomatoes at him when he was being forced to leave the country because of his status as a homosexual, and he submitted evidence that suspected homosexuals were subjected to physical examinations, interrogations, and beatings. On those facts, it was clear that people in Cuban society considered homosexuals to be a discrete and distinct group within the society and that a homosexual in Cuba would have generally understood his or her affiliation with the grouping. The group was therefore particular and socially distinct within the society in question.

In *Matter of Kasinga*, [21 I & N Dec. 357 (BIA 1996), the] proposed group of young women of a certain tribe who had not been subjected to FGM and opposed the practice was sufficiently particular because it presented a group that had clear and definable boundaries. The record contained objective evidence regarding the prevalence of FGM in the society in question and the expectation that women of the tribe would undergo FGM. Based on these facts, we found that people in the Tchamba-Kunsuntu Tribe would generally consider women who had not undergone FGM and opposed the practice to be a discrete and distinct group that was set apart in a significant way from the rest of the society. Such women would clearly understand their affiliation with this grouping. Thus, the proposed group was particular and was perceived as socially distinct within the society in question.

In *Matter of Fuentes*, [19 I & N Dec. 658 (BIA 1988),] the fundamental characteristic at issue was also not visible. However, we did not hold that "former member[s] of the national police of El Salvador" necessarily constituted a viable particular social group. Rather, we merely recognized that the applicant's status as a former policeman was an immutable characteristic because it was beyond his capacity to change, and we noted that it is "*possible* that mistreatment occurring because of such a status in appropriate circumstances *could* be found to be persecution on account of political opinion or membership in a particular social group." The applicant in *Fuentes* presented some evidence of social distinction, because the national police played a high-profile role in combating guerrilla violence, and a witness testified that "guerrillas had the names of the people who had been in the service" and targeted and killed former service members. However, because we held that the applicant did not show that the harm he feared bore a nexus to his status as a former member of the national police, we did not fully assess the factors that underlie particularity and social distinction.

In Matter of C-A-, we found that "noncriminal drug informants working against the Cali drug cartel" in Colombia were not a particular social group, and we emphasized that "[s]ocial groups based on innate characteristics such as sex or family relationship are generally easily recognizable and understood by others to constitute social groups." *Matter of C-A-*, 23 I & N Dec. at 957, 959–60. * * * To the extent that *Matter of C-A-* has been interpreted as requiring literal or "ocular" visibility, we now clarify that it does not.

* * *

E. International Interpretations

Although the statutory terms "refugee" and "particular social group" occur against the backdrop of the Protocol and the Convention, international interpretations of those terms are not controlling here.

We recognize that our interpretation of the ambiguous phrase "particular social group" differs from the approach set forth in the UNHCR's social group guidelines, which sought to reconcile two international interpretations that had developed over the years. The UNHCR advocates an alternative approach, which permits an individual to establish a particular social group based on "protected characteristics" or "social perception" but does not require both. However, the European Union adopted a "particular social group" definition that departs from the UNHCR Guidelines by requiring a social group to have both an immutable/fundamental characteristic and social perception.[15]

While the views of the UNHCR are a useful interpretative aid, they are "not binding on the Attorney General, the BIA, or United States courts." *INS v. Aguirre-Aguirre*, 526 U.S. at 427. * * *

---

[15] Article 10.1(d) of the European Union's guidelines states:

[A] group shall be considered to form a particular social group where in particular:

—members of that group share an innate characteristic, or a common background that cannot be changed, or share a characteristic or belief that is so fundamental to identity or conscience that a person should not be forced to renounce it, *and*

—that group has a distinct identity in the relevant country, because it is perceived as being different by the surrounding society.

Directive 2011/95/EU, of the European Parliament and of the Council of 13 December 2011 on Standards for the Qualification of Third-Country Nationals or Stateless Persons as Beneficiaries of International Protection * * *.

We believe that our interpretation in *Matter of S-E-G-* and *Matter of E-A-G-*, as clarified, more accurately captures the concepts underlying the United States' obligations under the Protocol and will ensure greater consistency in the adjudication of asylum claims under the Act. *See Nat'l Cable & Telecomms. Ass'n v. Brand X Internet Servs.*, 545 U.S. 967; *Chevron, U.S.A., Inc. v. Natural Res. Def. Council, Inc.*, 467 U.S. 837. Unlike the UNHCR's alternative approach, we conclude that a particular social group must satisfy both the "protected characteristic" and "social perception" approaches, in addition to the particularity requirement, as described above.

V. APPLICATION TO THE RESPONDENT

In our prior decision in this case, we rejected the respondent's gang-related claim based on the reasoning set forth in *Matter of S-E-G-* and *Matter of E-A-G-*. * * *[16]

* * *

Against the backdrop of widespread gang violence affecting vast segments of the country's population [in El Salvador], the applicant in *Matter of S-E-G-* could not establish that he had been targeted on a protected basis. Although he was subjected to one of the many different criminal activities that the gang used to sustain its criminal enterprise, he did not demonstrate that he was more likely to be persecuted by the gang on account of a protected ground than was any other member of the society.

The prevalence of gang violence in many countries is a large societal problem. The gangs may target one segment of the population for recruitment, another for extortion, and yet others for kidnapping, trafficking in drugs and people, and other crimes. Although certain segments of a population may be more susceptible to one type of criminal activity than another, the residents all generally suffer from the gang's criminal efforts to sustain its enterprise in the area. A national community may struggle with significant societal problems resulting from gangs, but not all societal problems are bases for asylum. * * *

Nevertheless, we emphasize that our holdings in *Matter of S-E-G-* and *Matter of E-A-G-* should not be read as a blanket rejection of all factual scenarios involving gangs. Social group determinations are made on a case-by-case basis. For example, a factual scenario in which gangs are targeting homosexuals may support a particular social group claim.

---

[16] We also rejected the applicant's second proposed social group of "young persons who are perceived to be affiliated with gangs." We held that membership, or perceived membership, in a criminal gang cannot constitute a particular social group because "[t]reating affiliation with a criminal organization as being protected membership in a social group is inconsistent with the principles underlying the bars to asylum and withholding of removal based on criminal behavior." *Id.* at 596; *see also Arteaga v. Mukasey*, 511 F.3d 940 (9th Cir. 2007).

While persecution on account of a protected ground cannot be inferred merely from acts of random violence and the existence of civil strife, it is clear that persecution on account of a protected ground may occur during periods of civil strife if the victim is targeted on account of a protected ground.

VI. CONCLUSION

We interpret the "particular social group" ground of persecution in a manner consistent with the other enumerated grounds of persecution in the Act and clarify that our interpretation of the phrase "membership in a particular social group" requires an applicant for asylum or withholding of removal to establish that the group is (1) composed of members who share a common immutable characteristic, (2) defined with particularity, and (3) socially distinct within the society in question. Not every "immutable characteristic" is sufficiently precise to define a particular social group. The additional requirements of "particularity" and "social distinction" are necessary to ensure that the proposed social group is perceived as a distinct and discrete group by society. * * *

* * *

The clarification and guidance provided by our decision in this matter may have an impact on the validity of the respondent's proposed group, which, in turn, may affect whether any persecution would be "on account of" his membership in such group. On remand, both parties will have an opportunity to present updated country conditions evidence and arguments regarding the respondent's particular social group claim, and the Immigration Judge may conduct further proceedings as is deemed appropriate under the circumstances. Accordingly, the record will be remanded to the Immigration Judge.

In the companion case issued the same day, *Matter of W-G-R-,* 26 I & N Dec. 208 (BIA 2014), the Board rejected a protection claim from a former member of the Mara Salvatrucha gang in El Salvador who had left the gang in 2001 after less than a year's membership. He had fled to the United States "after he was targeted for retribution for leaving the group." *Id.* at 209. The decision explained (*id.* at 221–22):

> The boundaries of a group are not sufficiently definable unless the members of society generally agree on who is included in the group * * * .

> In this regard, the boundaries of the group of "former gang members who have renounced their gang membership" are not adequately defined. The group would need further specificity to meet the particularity requirement. Our analysis illustrates the

point that when a former association is the immutable characteristic that defines a proposed group, the group will often need to be further defined with respect to the duration or strength of the members' active participation in the activity and the recency of their active participation if it is to qualify as a particular social group under the Act.

The respondent also has not shown that his proposed social group meets the requirement of social distinction. The record contains scant evidence that Salvadoran society considers former gang members who have renounced their gang membership as a distinct social group. The record contains documentary evidence describing gangs, gang violence, and the treatment of gang members but very little documentation discussing the treatment or status of former gang members.

The BIA also offered an expanded discussion of when the views or perspective of the persecutor versus those of the society are relevant (*id.* at 223–24):

> While the views of the persecutor might play a role in causing members of society to view a particular group as distinct, the persecutor's views play a greater role in determining whether persecution is inflicted on account of the victim's membership in a particular social group. Whether that nexus exists depends on the views and motives of the persecutor. The respondent bears the burden of showing that his membership in a particular social group was or will be a central reason for his persecution. Section 208(b)(1)(B)(i). Thus, in this case, even if the respondent had demonstrated a cognizable particular social group, and his membership in it, he also must show that those he fears would harm him because he belongs to that social group.

> The respondent has not shown that any acts of retribution or punishment by gang members would be motivated by his status as a former gang member, rather than by the gang members' desire to enforce their code of conduct and punish infidelity to the gang. *See Matter of E-A-G-*, 24 I & N Dec. at 594 (noting that harm to a person who resisted gang recruitment "would arise from the individualized reaction of the gang to the specific behavior of the prospective recruit" and not from his general status as one who resisted recruitment). Thus, even if the respondent were a member of a cognizable particular social group, the record does not show that the retributive harm the respondent fears would bear a nexus to his status as a former gang member, as opposed to his acts in leaving the gang.

Gang-related violence has continued to generate asylum claims. One year after the BIA issued *M-E-V-G*, the Fourth Circuit considered the asylum claim of a mother threatened by gang members for her opposition to their recruitment of her son.

HERNANDEZ-AVALOS V. LYNCH
United States Court of Appeals for the Fourth Circuit, 2015.
784 F.3d 944.

SHEDD, CIRCUIT JUDGE:

[Maydai Hernandez-Avalos and her minor son, citizens of El Salvador, requested asylum in the United States. In testimony deemed credible by the Immigration Judge, Hernandez-Avalos testified that heavily armed members of the Mara 18 gang came to her house and threatened to kill her on three different occasions. Twice gang members put a gun to her head and said they would kill her if she prevented her twelve year old son from joining the gang; the evening before she fled the gang members threatened to kill her the next day if she interfered with their forced recruitment of her son. The Immigration Judge ruled that she had not shown she was likely to suffer future persecution based on membership in a particular social group, denied relief, and ordered her removed to El Salvador. The BIA affirmed.]

* * * Hernandez claims, and the government correctly acknowledges, that membership in a nuclear family qualifies as a protected ground for asylum purposes.

The government argues, however, that the BIA was correct in holding that Hernandez's persecution was not "on account of" her family ties. * * *

The BIA * * * reasoned that "[s]he was not threatened because of her relationship to her son (i.e. family), but rather because she would not consent to her son engaging in a criminal activity." The government argues that * * * the fact that the person blocking the gang members' recruitment effort was their membership target's mother was merely incidental to the recruitment aim.

We believe that this is an excessively narrow reading of the requirement that persecution be undertaken "on account of membership in a nuclear family." Hernandez's relationship to her son is why she, and not another person, was threatened with death if she did not allow him to join Mara 18, and the gang members' demands leveraged her maternal authority to control her son's activities.

The BIA's conclusion that these threats were directed at her not because she is his mother but because she exercises control over her son's activities draws a meaningless distinction under these facts. It is therefore unreasonable to assert that the fact that Hernandez is her son's mother is not *at least one* central reason for her persecution.

* * *

[I]n this case Mara 18 threatened Hernandez in order to recruit her son into their ranks, but they also threatened *Hernandez*, rather than another person, because of her family connection to her son. Thus, * * * there were multiple central reasons for the threats Hernandez received.

Because any reasonable adjudicator would be compelled to conclude that Hernandez's maternal relationship to her son is at least one central reason for two of the threats she received, we hold that the BIA's conclusion that these threats were not made "on account of" her membership in her nuclear family is manifestly contrary to law and an abuse of discretion. * * *

* * *

[The court also reviewed the evidence concerning whether the Salvadoran government was unable or unwilling to protect Hernandez-Avalos from the gang members, concluded that the evidence relied on by the immigration judge to discredit the testimony of Hernandez-Avalos was legally deficient, and held that she had established her eligibility for asylum.]

For the foregoing reasons, we grant Hernandez's petition for review and remand the case to the BIA for further proceedings consistent with this opinion.

NOTES AND QUESTIONS ON PARTICULAR SOCIAL GROUP

1.   While the BIA concluded in *Matter of M-E-V-G-* that young men who resist recruitment by Honduran gangs do not constitute a particular social group, the Fourth Circuit upheld the particular social group claim made by the mother of a youth resisting gang recruitment in El Salvador. *Hernandez-Avalos v. Lynch*, 784 F.3d 944 (2015). Can these results be reconciled? Are *mothers* (or *families*) more socially distinct than *youth*? Is it sensible to deny protection to the recruit, but to grant protection to the person who is threatened on account of the recruit?

The federal courts have split on whether persecution of a family member constitutes a particular social group claim. *Compare Hernandos-Avalos v. Lynch*, *supra*, and *Flores-Rios v. Lynch*, 807 F. 3d 1123 (9th Cir. 2015) (applicant's family constitutes particular social group when applicant's father was killed by gangs) with *Ramirez-Mejia v. Lynch*, 794 F. 3d 485 (5th Cir. 2015) (brother's murder by rival gang does not constitute persecution based on particular social group), *Lin v. Holder*, 411 F. App'x 901 (7th Cir. 2011) (persecution by father's creditors is not particular social group-based persecution), and *Malonga v. Holder*, 621 F. 3d 757 (8th Cir. 2010) (father's death during civil war does not support particular social group claim). In early 2016, the BIA invited supplemental briefing and amicus briefs on the circumstances in which persecution of a family member supports the applicant's particular social group claim. DHS filed a supplemental brief contending that it would be sufficient for an applicant to provide evidence that her membership in her immediate family was a central reason for the persecution she feared, and that the applicant would not need to furnish additional evidence that the persecutor targeted the initial family member on account of one of the five protected grounds. DHS Supplemental Brief, *In the Matter of Luis Enrique Alba*, April 21, 2016. As we go to press, the BIA has not rendered a ruling.

2.   *Matter of Acosta*, 19 I & N Dec. 211 (BIA 1985), quoted in *Matter of M-E-V-G-*, construed a *particular social group* to include individuals bound together by a characteristic that is either immutable or so fundamental to their identity that they should not be required to change it. Acosta himself was a taxi driver who helped to form a taxi cooperative that defied calls for a general strike; he received death threats afterwards. The Board rejected Acosta's assertion that members of this taxi cooperative constituted a social group, saying that driving a taxi was neither immutable nor a matter of conscience that individuals should not be forced to change. The Board also rejected Acosta's claim that the death threats were on account of his political opinion. Is the social group proffered in *Matter of M-E-V-G-* a stronger or weaker claim than the *Acosta* taxi drivers?

3.   In *M-E-V-G-* the BIA rejected the proposed social group composed of Honduran youth who refused the MS–13 recruitment efforts, because it was too amorphous and lacked social visibility. What about the converse: is a gang itself a particular social group? Gang members often can be identified by their tattoos, the color of their clothes, or other insignia. In *Arteaga v. Mukasey*, 511 F.3d 940 (9th Cir. 2007), the court affirmed a BIA conclusion that membership in a criminal gang cannot constitute membership in a particular social group. Is that outcome consistent with *M-E-V-G-?* Gangs, typically, are groups that have high social visibility and consist of a defined membership. On the other hand, the treatment that gangs receive may be prosecution, not persecution, or gang members may be ineligible for asylum because they have committed criminal offenses.

Is gang membership a changeable characteristic, as that concept is described in *Matter of Acosta*? Could such membership be fundamental to identity? Even if it is, would it be permissible for U.S. law to insist that it be changed? In any event, do *former* gang members have an immutable characteristic? *See Ramos v. Holder*, 589 F.3d 426 (7th Cir. 2009) (former members of Mara Salvatrucha may constitute a particular social group).

Unaccompanied Children and Youth at the
Southern Border

More than 47,000 children and youth traveling without their parents crossed the Mexico-United States border between October 2013 and June 2014, 92 percent more than in the same period in the prior year. Most were from Honduras, El Salvador, and Guatemala, and many said that they were fleeing gangs and gang violence. Julia Preston, *New U.S. Effort to Aid Unaccompanied Child Migrants,* N.Y. Times, June 3, 2014, at A14. President Obama ordered FEMA, the Federal Emergency Management Agency, to coordinate efforts to shelter the minors while their legal claims could be assessed and family members in the United States could be located. *Id.* By July 29, 2014, the number had increased to 57,000. Julia Preston, *Most in Poll Say Children at Border Merit Relief,* N.Y. Times, July 29, 2014, at A14. House and Senate Committees held hearings, DOJ and EOIR announced measures to redeploy resources to respond to the urgent new circumstances, and the President sought a $4.3 billion emergency supplemental appropriation to respond to the crisis, with $3.7 billion earmarked for the health and safety of the recently arrived unaccompanied children and youth. 91 Interp.Rel. 1204–1210, July 14, 2014.

Political debate became heated. Republicans proposed to amend the 2008 Trafficking Victims Protection Reauthorization Act (TVPRA), which mandates that unaccompanied children from all countries other than Mexico and Canada be placed in formal removal proceedings, rather than expedited proceedings, and be cared for by the Department of Health and Human Services while in U.S. custody.

UNHCR interviewed hundreds of unaccompanied children from Honduras, El Salvador, Guatemala, and Mexico and reported that 58 percent presented credible claims that warranted international protection. UNHCR, *Children on the Run: Unaccompanied Children Leaving Central America and Mexico and the Need for International Protection,* March 2014. Advocates for immigrants stressed the importance of thorough and deliberate hearings to ascertain whether vulnerable children are eligible for asylum, humanitarian asylum, special immigrant juvenile status (SIJS), T visas (trafficking victims), U visas (crime victims), or protection under the Convention Against Torture (CAT). *See, e.g.,* American Immigration Council, *Children in Danger: A Guide to the Humanitarian Challenge at the Border* (2014).

The Obama Administration responded to this crisis in several ways. DHS applied the expedited removal provisions, INA § 235(b), to arriving Central American children accompanied by their mothers. This led to the controversial detention of children and mothers, which, in turn, led to litigation and to subsequent revisions in detention policies. In August

2015 a federal district court in California ruled that the detention policy violated a decades-old consent decree prohibiting DHS from detaining minors in secure, unlicensed facilities. *Flores v. Lynch*, No. CV 85–04544 DMG (C.D. Cal. 2015). For a fuller discussion of the challenges and the litigation engendered by the increased arrivals of Central American youth in recent years, see Chapter Nine, Section B.

The Administration also established the Central American Minor (CAM) Refugee/Parole program in El Salvador, Guatemala, and Honduras. Designed to provide a safe alternative to long, risky journeys to the United States, the CAM program allows parents who are lawfully present in the United States to petition to bring their minor children to the United States as refugees. Faye Hipsman & Doris Meissner, *In-Country Refugee Processing in Central America: A Piece of the Puzzle*, Migration Policy Institute (August 2015). Children who have a well-founded fear of persecution and otherwise satisfy the refugee definition are eligible. Children who do not meet the statutory requirements for refugee status may be considered for humanitarian parole on a case by case basis. During the first year of the CAM program, more than 5,400 children applied. DHS interviewed 90 and approved 10 for refugee status and 75 for humanitarian parole. Michael D. Schear, *Red Tape Slows U.S. Help for Children Fleeing Central America*, N.Y. Times, Nov. 5, 2015.

Since summer 2014, the numbers of unaccompanied children arriving at the U.S. southern border have fluctuated, but they remain at historically high levels. From 24,000 in FY 2012, they increased to almost 40,000 in FY 2013, to 68,000 in FY 2014, followed by 40,000 in FY 2015. Marc R. Rosenblum, *Unaccompanied Child Migration to the United States: The Tension Between Protection and Prevention* 3, Migration Policy Institute (April 2015).

As we go to press in late spring 2016, the arrivals have begun to rise dramatically again. Jerry Markon & Joshua Partlow, *Unaccompanied Children Crossing Southern Border in Greater Numbers Again, Raising Fears of New Migrant Crisis*, Wash. Post, Dec. 16, 2015. The U.S. Border Patrol apprehended 20,000 unaccompanied children at the southwestern border during the first quarter of FY 2016, a 102 percent increase over the first quarter of FY 2015. CBP, U.S. Border Patrol Southwest Family Unit Subject and Unaccompanied Alien Children Apprehensions FY 2016. At the same time, the Border Patrol apprehended even larger numbers of families with young children there: 25,000 during the first quarter of FY 2016, a 170 percent increase over the comparable period in FY 2015. *Id.* Researchers predict continuing migration flows from Central America, in light of the high levels of violence, political instability, and food insecurity in El Salvador, Honduras, and Guatemala, as well as the Central American immigrant communities already established in the United States and the current immigration court backlogs. Marc R. Rosenblum &

Isabel Ball, *Trends in Unaccompanied Child and Family Migration from Central America,* Migration Policy Institute Fact Sheet (Jan. 2016); see also Danielle Renwick, *Central America's Violent Northern Triangle*, Council of Foreign Relations (CFR) Backgrounder (Jan. 19, 2016); Muzaffar Chishti & Faye Hipsman, *Increased Central American Migration to the United States May Prove an Enduring Phenomenon*, Migration Policy Institute (Feb. 18, 2016).

d. Gender-Related Claims

Recent years have brought increasing attention to the impact of gender on refugee and asylum issues. Neither the 1951 Convention nor the U.S. statute specifies sex or gender as one of the grounds of persecution that trigger international protection, an omission that has been criticized. Others, however, such as Rodger Haines, a longtime member of the New Zealand Refugee Status Appeals Authority and renowned refugee law scholar, assert that there is no need for an express reference to sex or gender; they argue that, so long as the Convention is interpreted without discrimination against women, the refugee definition provides ample protection:

> The failure of decision makers to recognize and respond appropriately to the experiences of women stems not from the fact that the 1951 Convention does not refer specifically to persecution on the basis of sex or gender, but rather because it has often been approached from a partial perspective and interpreted through a framework of male experiences. The main problem facing women as asylum seekers is the failure of decision makers to incorporate the gender-related claims of women into their interpretation of the existing enumerated grounds and their failure to recognize the political nature of seemingly private acts of harm to women.

Haines, *Gender-related Persecution*, in Refugee Protection in International Law 319, 327 (Erika Feller, Volker Türk & Frances Nicholson eds., 2003).

Because states are unlikely to modify the 1951 Convention to add an additional ground, the reality is that courts and agencies will grapple with gender issues within the framework of the current specified grounds of persecution: race, religion, nationality, membership in a particular social group, and political opinion.

Most, though not all, of the gender issues that arise in refugee and asylum claims concern women. Women raped on account of their perceived political loyalties have received asylum in the United States, *Matter of D-V-*, 21 I & N Dec. 77 (BIA 1993). Female genital cutting has been a basis for asylum. *Matter of Kasinga*, 21 I & N Dec. 357 (BIA 1996).

Asylum applications based on resistance to social norms regarding clothing have been less successful. *Fatin v. INS*, 12 F.3d 1233 (3rd Cir. 1993); *Fisher v. INS*, 79 F.3d 955 (9th Cir. 1996); *but see Matter of S-A-*, 22 I & N Dec. 1328 (BIA 2000). In recent years asylum officers and immigration judges have faced challenging claims involving domestic violence and forced marriage.

(i) Domestic Violence

A study conducted by the World Health Organization (WHO) and published in the medical journal *The Lancet* in October 2006 estimated the extent of physical and intimate sexual partner violence against women in 15 sites in ten countries: Bangladesh, Brazil, Ethiopia, Japan, Namibia, Peru, Samoa, Serbia and Montenegro, Thailand, and the United Republic of Tanzania. Based on interviews with nearly 25,000 women, the study found that violence against women by their live-in spouses or partners is a widespread phenomenon, in both the developed and developing world, and in both rural and urban areas. See Claudia Garcia-Moreno *et al.*, *Prevalence of Intimate Partner Violence: Findings From the WHO Multi-country Study on Women's Health and Domestic Violence*, 368 The Lancet 1260 (2006); Elizabeth Rosenthal, *Women Face Greatest Threat of Violence at Home, Study Finds*, N.Y. Times, Oct. 6, 2006.

Over the past two decades a growing number of women have filed asylum claims based on domestic violence. Typically, they fear persecution at the hands of their male partner, who may not articulate a reason for his actions and may not act in this manner toward anyone else. These cases raise multiple legal questions. Does violence by individuals, as opposed to organized groups, constitute persecution? Is the violence "on account of" one of the specified grounds? What alternatives within her home country are available to the claimant? These issues are not unique to asylum claims based on domestic violence, but they pose particularly difficult conceptual puzzles in this developing area of the law. In 2014 the BIA addressed many of these issues in an asylum case filed by a Guatemalan survivor of domestic violence.

MATTER OF A-R-C-G-

Board of Immigration Appeals, 2014.
26 I. & N. Dec. 388.

ADKINS-BLANCH, VICE CHAIRMAN:

In a decision dated October 14, 2009, an Immigration Judge found the respondents removable and denied their applications for asylum and withholding of removal under [INA] sections 208(a) and 241(b)(3). The respondents have appealed from that decision, contesting only the denial of their applications for relief from removal. We find that the lead respondent, a victim of domestic violence in her native country, is a member of a particular social group composed of "married women in Guatemala who are unable to leave their relationship." The record will be remanded to the Immigration Judge for further proceedings.

I.   FACTUAL AND PROCEDURAL HISTORY

The lead respondent is the mother of the three minor respondents. The respondents are natives and citizens of Guatemala who entered the United States without inspection on December 25, 2005. The respondent filed a timely application for asylum and withholding of removal under the Act.

The Immigration Judge found the respondent to be a credible witness, which is not contested on appeal. It is undisputed that the respondent, who married at age 17, suffered repugnant abuse by her husband. This abuse included weekly beatings after the respondent had their first child.[9] On one occasion, the respondent's husband broke her nose. Another time, he threw paint thinner on her, which burned her breast. He raped her.

The respondent contacted the police several times but was told that they would not interfere in a marital relationship. On one occasion, the police came to her home after her husband hit her on the head, but he was not arrested. Subsequently, he threatened the respondent with death if she called the police again. The respondent repeatedly tried to leave the relationship by staying with her father, but her husband found her and threatened to kill her if she did not return to him. Once she went to Guatemala City for about 3 months, but he followed her and convinced her to come home with promises that he would discontinue the abuse. The abuse continued when she returned. The respondent left Guatemala in December 2005, and she believes her husband will harm her if she returns.

The Immigration Judge found that the respondent did not demonstrate that she had suffered past persecution or has a well-founded fear of future persecution on account of a particular social group comprised of "married women in Guatemala who are unable to leave their relation- ship." The Immigration Judge determined that there was inadequate evidence that the respondent's spouse abused her "in order to overcome" the fact that she was a "married woman in Guatemala who was unable to leave the relationship." He found that the respondent's abuse was the result of "criminal acts, not persecution," which were perpetrated "arbitrarily" and "without reason." He accordingly found that the respondent did not meet her burden of demonstrating eligibility for asylum or withholding of removal under the Act.

---

[9]   This child was born in 1994 and was residing in Guatemala at the time of the proceedings.

On appeal, the respondent asserts that she has established eligibility for asylum as a victim of domestic violence. * * *

In response to our request for supplemental briefing, the DHS now concedes the respondent established that she suffered past harm rising to the level of persecution and that the persecution was on account of a particular social group comprised of "married women in Guatemala who are unable to leave their relationship." However, the DHS seeks remand, arguing that "further factual development of the record and related findings by the Immigration Judge are necessary on several issues" before the asylum claim can be properly resolved. The respondent opposes remand and maintains that she has met her burden of proof regarding all aspects of her asylum claim. We accept the parties' position on the existence of harm rising to the level of past persecution, the existence of a valid particular social group, and the issue of nexus under the particular facts of this case. We will remand the record for further proceedings.

II. ANALYSIS

A. Particular Social Group

The question whether a group is a "particular social group" within the meaning of the Act is a question of law that we review de novo. The question whether a person is a member of a particular social group is a finding of fact that we review for clear error.

* * *

B. Respondent's Claim

The DHS has conceded that the respondent established harm rising to the level of past persecution on account of a particular social group comprised of "married women in Guatemala who are unable to leave their relationship." The DHS's position regarding the existence of such a particular social group in Guatemala under the facts presented in this case comports with our recent precedents clarifying the meaning of the term "particular social group." In this regard, we point out that any claim regarding the existence of a particular social group in a country must be evaluated in the context of the evidence presented regarding the particular circumstances in the country in question.

In *Matter of W-G-R-* and *Matter of M-E-V-G-*, we held that an applicant seeking asylum based on his or her membership in a "particular social group" must establish that the group is (1) composed of members who share a common immutable characteristic, (2) defined with particularity, and (3) socially distinct within the society in question. The "common immutable characteristic" requirement incorporates the standard set forth in *Matter of Acosta*. The "particularity" requirement addresses "the question of delineation." That is, it clarifies the point that "not every 'immutable characteristic' is sufficiently precise to define a particular social group." The "social distinction" requirement renames the former concept of "social visibility" and clarifies "the importance of 'perception' or 'recognition' to the concept of the particular social group."

In this case, the group is composed of members who share the common immutable characteristic of gender. Moreover, marital status can be an immutable characteristic where the individual is unable to leave the relationship. A determination of this issue will be dependent upon the particular facts and evidence in a case. A range of factors could be relevant, including whether dissolution of a marriage could be contrary to religious or other deeply held moral beliefs or if dissolution is possible when viewed in light of religious, cultural, or legal constraints. In evaluating such a claim, adjudicators must consider a respondent's own experiences, as well as more objective evidence, such as background country information.

The DHS concedes that the group in this case is defined with particularity. The terms used to describe the group—"married," "women," and "unable to leave the relationship"—have commonly accepted definitions within Guatemalan society based on the facts in this case, including the respondent's experience with the police. In some circumstances, the terms can combine to create a group with discrete and definable boundaries. We point out that a married woman's inability to leave the relationship may be informed by societal expectations about gender and subordination, as well as legal constraints regarding divorce and separation. *See Matter of W-G-R-*, 26 I & N Dec. at 214 (observing that in evaluating a group's particularity, it may be necessary to take into account the social and cultural context of the alien's country of citizenship or nationality); Committees on Foreign Relations and Foreign Affairs, 111th Cong., 2d Sess., *Country Reports on Human Rights Practices for 2008* 2598 (Joint Comm. Print 2010) ("*Country Reports*") (discussing sexual offenses against women as a serious societal problem in Guatemala); Bureau of Human Rights, Democracy, and Labor, U.S. Dep't of State, *Guatemala Country Reports on Human Rights Practices—2008* (Feb. 25, 2009).[14] In this case, it is significant that the respondent sought protection from her spouse's abuse and that the police refused to assist her because they would not interfere in a marital relationship.

The group is also socially distinct within the society in question. To have "social distinction," there must be "evidence showing that society in general perceives, considers, or recognizes persons sharing the particular characteristic to be a group." The group's recognition is "determined by

---

[14] Notably, the group is not defined by the fact that the applicant is subject to domestic violence. See *Matter of W-G-R-,* 26 I & N Dec. at 215 (noting that circuit courts "have long recognized that a social group must have 'defined boundaries' or a 'limiting characteristic,' other than the risk of being persecuted").

the perception of the society in question, rather than by the perception of the persecutor."[15]

When evaluating the issue of social distinction, we look to the evidence to determine whether a society, such as Guatemalan society in this case, makes meaningful distinctions based on the common immutable characteristics of being a married woman in a domestic relationship that she cannot leave. Such evidence would include whether the society in question recognizes the need to offer protection to victims of domestic violence, including whether the country has criminal laws designed to protect domestic abuse victims, whether those laws are effectively enforced, and other sociopolitical factors. *Cf. Davila-Mejia v. Mukasey*, 531 F.3d 624, 629 (8th Cir. 2008) (finding that competing family business owners are not a particular social group because they are not perceived as a group by society).

Supporting the existence of social distinction, and in accord with the DHS's concession that a particular social group exists, the record in this case includes unrebutted evidence that Guatemala has a culture of "machismo and family violence." *See Guatemala Failing Its Murdered Women: Report,* Canadian Broad. Corp. (July 18, 2006). Sexual offenses, including spousal rape, remain a serious problem. *See Country Reports, supra*, at 2608. Further, although the record reflects that Guatemala has laws in place to prosecute domestic violence crimes, enforcement can be problematic because the National Civilian Police "often failed to respond to re- quests for assistance related to domestic violence." *Id*. at 2609.

We point out that cases arising in the context of domestic violence generally involve unique and discrete issues not present in other particular social group determinations, which extends to the matter of social distinction. However, even within the domestic violence context, the issue of social distinction will depend on the facts and evidence in each individual case, including documented country conditions; law enforcement statistics and expert witnesses, if proffered; the respondent's past experiences; and other reliable and credible sources of information

C. Remaining Issues

The DHS stipulates that the respondent suffered mistreatment rising to the level of past persecution. The DHS also concedes in this case that the mistreatment was, for at least one central reason, on account of her membership in a cognizable particular social group. We note that in cases where concessions are not made and accepted as binding, these issues will be decided based on the particular facts and evidence on a case-by-case basis as addressed by the Immigration Judge in the first instance. In

---

[15] The perception of the persecutor, however, is critical to the question whether a person is persecuted "on account of membership in a particular social group. *See Matter of M-E-V-G-,* 26 I & N Dec. at 242; *Matter of W-G-R-,* 26 I & N Dec. at 218.

particular, the issue of nexus will depend on the facts and circumstances of an individual claim.

We will remand the record for the Immigration Judge to address the respondent's statutory eligibility for asylum in light of this decision. Under controlling circuit law, in order for the respondent to prevail on an asylum claim based on past persecution, she must demonstrate that the Guatemalan Government was unwilling or unable to control the "private" actor.

If the respondent succeeds in establishing that the Government was unwilling or unable to control her husband, the burden shifts to the DHS to demonstrate that there has been a fundamental change in circumstances such that the respondent no longer has a well-founded fear of persecution. Alternatively, the DHS would bear the burden of showing that internal relocation is possible and is not unreasonable. The Immigration Judge may also consider, if appropriate, whether the respondent is eligible for humanitarian asylum.[b]

* * *

NOTES AND QUESTIONS ON
ASYLUM CLAIMS BASED ON DOMESTIC VIOLENCE

1.   *Matter of R-A-,* 22 I & N Dec. 906 (BIA 1999), a pathbreaking case involving an asylum claim based on domestic abuse, also involved a Honduran woman who was repeatedly beaten by her husband and whose pleas to the local police were unavailing. The BIA majority opinion concluded that the applicant had been "terribly abused and has a genuine and reasonable fear of returning to Guatemala," *id.* at 928, but concluded that she had not established membership in a particular social group nor had she demonstrated that her persecution was on account of group membership. Subsequent proceedings in *Matter of R-A-* lasted more than a decade and involved three presidential administrations. The year after *R-A-,* the Department of Justice published proposed amendments to the asylum regulations, with the intent to make the regulations more amenable to domestic violence claims. 65 Fed. Reg. 76588–98 (2000). Attorney General Janet Reno then vacated *Matter of R-A-,* thus removing its precedential value, and remanded the case to the BIA with directions to reconsider the case in the light of the new regulations. When final regulations had not appeared by 2009, DHS agreed that R-A- was eligible for asylum, and the immigration judge granted her asylum. *See* Paul Elias, *Domestic Violence Victim Granted Asylum in U.S.*, Assoc. Press, Dec. 18, 2009; Karen Musalo, *A Short History of Gender Asylum in the United States: Resistance and Ambivalence May Very Slowly Be Inching Toward Recognition of Women's Claims*, 29 Ref. Surv. Q. 46, 56–60 (2010).

---

[b]   See pp. 821–822, *supra,* for a discussion of discretionary grants of asylum based on past persecution despite the absence of threats of future persecution.—eds.

2.   Some question whether asylum and withholding claims based on domestic violence are better understood as claims involving persecution on account of religion or political opinion, rather than on account of particular social group membership. *See* Marisa Silenzi Cianciarulo, *Batterers as Agents of the State: Challenging the Public/Private Distinction in Intimate Partner Violence-Based Asylum Claims*, 35 Harv. J.L. & Gender 117 (2012). For an analysis of domestic violence asylum cases before the immigration courts and the BIA for almost two decades, see Blaine Bookey, *Domestic Violence as a Basis for Asylum: An Analysis of 206 Case Outcomes in the United States From 1994 to 2012*, 24 Hastings Women's L.F. 107 (2013) (arguing that the analyzed cases reached "contradictory and arbitrary outcomes" and that "the absence of binding norms remains a major impediment to fair and consistent outcomes").

(ii) Forced Marriage and Related Practices

Customs and practices relating to marriage can fall heavily on women in many societies. The next case analyzes whether forced marriage can constitute persecution based on membership in a particular social group. The decision was later vacated on procedural grounds, but it remains the most extensive judicial discussion of the issue.

GAO V. GONZALES

United States Court of Appeals, Second Circuit, 2006.
440 F.3d 62, vacated sub nom. Keisler v. Gao, 552 U.S. 801, 128 S.Ct. 345 (2007).

STRAUB, CIRCUIT JUDGE.

* * * Gao, who was twenty years old when she left China, grew up in a rural village in the Fujian Province. In this region of China, parents routinely sell their daughters into marriage, and this practice is sanctioned by society and by the local authorities.

When Gao was nineteen years old, her parents, through a broker, sold Gao to a man named Chen Zhi; in return for an up-front payment of 18,800 RBM [renminbi, Chinese currency—eds.], Gao's parents promised that Gao would marry Zhi when she turned twenty-one. Gao's parents used this money to pay off previous debts. At first, Gao acquiesced in the arrangement under pressure from her parents. However, because Zhi soon proved to be bad-tempered, and gambled, and beat her when she refused to give him money, Gao decided that she did not want to marry Zhi. When Gao tried to break their engagement, Zhi threatened her. He also threatened that, if she refused to marry him, his uncle, a powerful local official, would arrest her. Gao had heard that Zhi's uncle had arrested other individuals for personal reasons, and so she was afraid the same would happen to her.

To escape Zhi, Gao moved an hour away by boat and took a job in the Mawei district of Fuchou. Zhi continued to visit Gao's family and demand that she marry him, and when her parents refused to tell him where she had moved, he vandalized their home. Zhi also figured out that Gao was living in Mawei by following her to her boat one night when she was returning from a visit with her family. About half a year later, Gao fled to the United States out of fear that, if she remained in China, she would be forced to marry Zhi. Since Gao left, Zhi and his cohorts have continued to harass her family, to the point where the family has had to move repeatedly.

* * *

* * * The IJ found Gao credible, but concluded that Gao had not made out a claim for asylum or withholding of removal. Specifically, the IJ found that Gao's predicament did not arise from a protected ground such as membership in a particular social group, but was simply "a dispute between two families." * * * The BIA summarily affirmed.

* * * Of the various categories, "particular social group" is the least well-defined on its face, and the diplomatic and legislative histories shed no light on how it was understood by the parties to the Protocol or by Congress. There is, fortunately, a substantial body of case law, although its value as precedent is somewhat limited by the fact-specific nature of asylum cases.

* * *

[The] Courts of Appeals have deferred to *Matter of Acosta*'s broad interpretation of "particular social group" as encompassing any group, however populous, persecuted because of shared characteristics that are either immutable or fundamental. * * *

* * *

* * * [T]he proper balance to strike is to interpret "particular social group" broadly (requiring only one or more shared characteristics that are either immutable or fundamental) while interpreting "on account of" strictly (such that an applicant must prove that these characteristics are a central reason why she has been, or may be, targeted for persecution). As the Tenth Circuit explained in *Niang v. Gonzales*, "the focus with respect to [gender-related] claims should be not on whether either gender constitutes a social group (which both certainly do) but on whether the members of that group are sufficiently likely to be persecuted that one could say that they are persecuted 'on account of' their membership." 422 F.3d 1187, 1199–1200 (10th Cir. 2005) (quoting INA § 101(a) 42(A)).

* * *

The general law in our own Circuit on particular social groups is less clear. In *Gomez v. INS*, we denied the petition of a woman whose asylum claim was based on the fact that she had been raped and beaten by guerilla forces on five different occasions between the ages of twelve and fourteen. * * * [W]e wrote that "[p]ossession of broadly-based characteristics such as youth and gender will not by itself endow individuals with membership in a particular group."

* * *

We need not decide the exact scope of *Gomez* here because Gao belongs to a particular social group that shares more than a common gender. Gao's social group consists of women who have been sold into marriage (whether or not that marriage has yet taken place) and who live in a part of China where forced marriages are considered valid and enforceable. Clearly, these common characteristics satisfy the *Matter of Acosta* test. Moreover, Gao's testimony, which the IJ credited, also establishes that she might well be persecuted in China—in the form of lifelong, involuntary marriage—"on account of" her membership in this group.

The IJ's reasons for reaching the opposite conclusion are unclear. * * * The IJ appears to have concluded that Gao did not face persecution on account of an immutable characteristic because her situation arose from "a dispute between two families," but the logical connection between the IJ's premise and conclusion is not evident, nor is it explained in the IJ's opinion. The IJ also wrote that "[t]he other reason that [Gao] does not establish that she is a member of a particularly persecuted social group of female [sic] is because her mother violated the oral [marriage] contract that she had with this go-between, and that is what caused the anger by the boyfriend in this situation . . . ." To the extent the IJ might have reasoned that the financial arrangement between the families somehow precluded a finding that Zhi's motive in targeting Gao was discriminatory, we reject this logic as antithetical to the very notion of individual rights on which asylum law is based. While Zhi may have a legitimate financial claim against Gao's parents, the possibility remains that if they continue to be unable to repay his money, Zhi will force Gao to marry him.

* * *

For the reasons stated above, we hold that Gao has established a nexus between the persecution she fears and the "particular social group" to which she belongs. * * *

[The court also vacated the immigration judge's findings that Gao had not met her burden of establishing that the Chinese government would not protect her, and that Gao could have relocated within China.]

For the foregoing reasons the petition for review is granted, the decision of the BIA is vacated, and the case is remanded to the BIA for further proceedings consistent with this opinion.

NOTES AND QUESTIONS ON
FORCED MARRIAGE AND RELATED PRACTICES

1. The U.S. Supreme Court vacated *Gao v. Gonzales* on the procedural ground that the Second Circuit, rather than defining the particular social group to which Gao belonged, should have remanded the case to the BIA to decide that issue. *See Keisler v. Gao*, 552 U.S. 801, 128 S.Ct. 345 (2007) (relying on *Gonzales v. Thomas*, 547 U.S. 183, 126 S.Ct. 1613 (2006)). Before *Gao* was vacated, the Second Circuit cited it in several cases to overturn immigration judge and BIA decisions rejecting asylum claims based on forced marriage. *See Yi Meng Tang v. Gonzales*, 200 F. App'x 68 (2d Cir. 2006); *Himanje v. Gonzalez*, 184 F. App'x 105 (2d Cir. 2006); *Bao Yuei Chen v. Gonzalez*, 175 F. App'x 492 (2d Cir. 2006).

In sharp contrast to *Gao* is *Ying Lin v. U.S. Attorney Gen.*, 319 F. App'x 777, 779 (11th Cir. 2009), which denied an asylum claim by a woman who asserted that her parents promised her in marriage to settle a gambling debt that they owed. The court upheld the immigration judge's decision that the harm was "entirely a personal matter." The court explained: "The involuntary marriage was for no reason other than repayment of her mother's gambling debt." Other decisions are more cautious about asylum claims based on forced marriage. The court observed in *Ngengwe v. Mukasey*, 543 F.3d 1029, 1036 (8th Cir. 2008): "[t]he question of whether forced marriage constitutes persecution is an open issue."

2. The UN Convention on the Abolition of Slavery and Institutions and Practices Similar to Slavery calls on states to abolish slavery-like institutions, defined to include debt bondage, serfdom, and

(c) Any institution or practice whereby:

> (i) A woman, without the right to refuse, is promised or given in marriage on payment of a consideration in money or in kind to her parents, guardian, family or any other person or group; or

> (ii) The husband of a woman, his family, or his clan, has the right to transfer her to another person for value received or otherwise; or

> (iii) A woman on the death of her husband is liable to be inherited by another person.

Art. 1, Supplementary Convention on the Abolition of Slavery, the Slave Trade, and Institutions and Practices Similar to Slavery, 226 U.N.T.S. 3, T.I.A.S. No. 6418, signed Sept. 7, 1956. More than 120 States are parties. The

Convention entered into force with regard to the United States on Dec. 6, 1967, 18 U.S.T. 3201.

3. Courts and commentators have sometimes used the terms "forced marriage" and "arranged marriage" interchangeably. The U.K. Foreign and Commonwealth Office contrasts the two:

> In arranged marriages, the families of both spouses take a leading role in choosing the marriage partner but the choice of whether or not to accept the arrangement remains with the potential spouses. They give their full and free consent. By contrast, in a forced marriage, one or both spouses do not consent to the marriage or consent is extracted under duress. Duress includes both physical and emotional pressure.

U.K. Foreign and Commonwealth Office, *Forced Marriage: A Wrong, Not a Right* 7 (2005).

In the United States, USCIS training materials provide: "Forced marriages * * * may under some circumstances qualify, as a form of persecution. * * * The key question in determining whether a forced marriage might constitute persecution is whether the victim experienced or would experience the marriage, or events surrounding the marriage, as serious harm." Asylum Officer Basic Training Course: Female Asylum Applicants and Gender-Related Claims 15 (March 12, 2009).

D. LIMITATIONS ON ASYLUM

1. FILING DEADLINE

Asylum applicants must file their claims within one year of their arrival in the United States. INA § 208(a)(2)(B). By statute, later-filed applications may be considered only if there are changed circumstances that materially affect the asylum seeker's eligibility for asylum or if there are extraordinary circumstances that are related to the delay. INA § 208(a)(2)(D). There is no judicial review of an administrative decision that the filing fails to comply with the statutory deadline provisions, INA § 208(a)(3), but a person denied by an asylum officer because of the deadline can obtain de novo consideration of that issue before the immigration judge, and can then appeal a deadline ruling to the BIA.

The regulations spell out more detailed standards. 8 C.F.R. §§ 208.4(a)(4), (5); 1208.4(a)(5). They provide that physical and mental conditions may constitute "extraordinary circumstances" if they are "directly related to the failure to meet the 1-year deadline." Certain legal obstacles, such as ineffective assistance of counsel, or the possession of another temporary legal status until a reasonable period before filing, may also satisfy the "extraordinary circumstances" exception. *Id.* The BIA issued a precedent decision holding that the late filing by a 16-year-old unaccompanied minor satisfied the exception because the applicant was under a legal disability (minority) during the first year of his time in the United States and submitted his asylum application within five months of his release by the INS into the custody of his uncle. *Matter of Y-C-*, 23 I & N Dec. 286 (BIA 2002).

In the first few years the agencies appeared to construe the deadline in a reasonably flexible manner, finding that roughly three-quarters of asylum applications were timely. Thereafter, according to a recent study, the deadline had a more pronounced effect, disqualifying 35 percent of the affirmative asylum applicants. Philip G. Schrag, Andrew I. Schoenholtz, Jaya Ramji-Nogales & James P. Dombach, *Rejecting Refugees: Homeland Security's Administration of the One-Year Bar to Asylum*, 52 Wm & Mary L. Rev. 651 (2010). The study found that the rate of exceptions varies significantly among asylum officers and rejections based on the deadline vary significantly among asylum seekers from different countries. *Id.* at 713. It also suggested that the deadline precluded approximately 20,000 individuals from receiving asylum from DHS asylum officers, though it does not report how many ultimately received asylum or withholding of removal when their cases proceeded to immigration court. *Id.* at 704–06.

It is important to note that withholding of removal is not subject to any deadline. Because all asylum applications are simultaneously considered as requests for withholding, individuals who run afoul of the one-year deadline for asylum automatically will be screened for *nonrefoulement* protection. But because the standard of proof for withholding is higher, the impact of the asylum deadline remains significant.

2. FIRM RESETTLEMENT

The INA precludes those who have been firmly resettled in another country from asylum in the United States. INA § 208(b)(2)(A)(vi). Withholding of removal is not barred in the case of firm resettlement, but recall that withholding is country-specific. A grant of withholding would not prevent sending the asylum seeker back to the third country—if that country will still accept the asylum seeker. If not, he or she is likely to remain in the United States, with the limited protections that accompany withholding of removal status.

The concept of firm resettlement is defined in 8 C.F.R. § 208.15:

> An alien is considered to be firmly resettled if, prior to arrival in the United States, he or she entered into another nation with, or while in that nation received, an offer of permanent resident status, citizenship, or some other type of permanent resettlement * * * .

The regulation provides that a finding of firm resettlement can be overcome if the applicant shows either that "entry into that country was a necessary consequence of his or her flight from persecution, that he or she remained in that nation only as long as was necessary to arrange onward travel, and that he or she did not establish significant ties in that country" or that "the conditions of his or her residence in that country were so substantially and consciously restricted by the authority of the country of refuge that he or she was not in fact resettled." The regulation then lists factors to consider in making the second determination.

The BIA set forth a four-step analytical framework to determine whether an asylum seeker had been firmly resettled in *Matter of A-G-G-*, 25 I & N Dec. 486 (2011), a case involving a Mauritanian asylum seeker who had married a Senegalese wife and lived in Senegal for eight years without receiving permanent legal status. The Board ruled that the availability of a legal process by which an individual can obtain permanent residence may be prima facie evidence of firm resettlement, and that an individual's failure to apply for permanent residence is not dispositive. The Board then remanded the case to the immigration judge to determine whether the Senegalese law granting permanent residence to the spouses of Senegalese citizens applies to men marrying Senegalese women or only to foreign women marrying Senegalese men.

3. PERSECUTORS

Congress specified that persons who assisted in persecuting others must be excluded from asylum, INA § 208(b)(2)(A)(i), and withholding of removal. INA § 241(b)(3)(B)(i). The exclusion of persons who participated or assisted in persecution is written in very broad terms. Take a look at that statutory language. This breadth reflects the provision's provenance, for the language mirrors the language of former § 241(a)(19), now § 237(a)(4)(D), a rigorous provision originally directed at those who aided Nazi persecution in Germany. For many years the BIA interpreted these anti-Nazi provisions in a particularly strict manner, relying on a 1981 Supreme Court decision in a denaturalization case. *Fedorenko v. United States*, 449 U.S. 490, 101 S.Ct. 737, 66 L.Ed.2d 686 (1981). The BIA held that they provide for the removal of such persons, even if they assisted the persecution involuntarily or under duress. *See Matter of Fedorenko*, 19 I & N Dec. 57 (BIA 1984); *Matter of Laipenieks*, 18 I & N Dec. 433 (BIA 1983), reversed, *Laipenieks v. INS*, 750 F.2d 1427 (9th Cir.1985).

Some questioned whether the BIA's harsh construction, however appropriate it might have been for those who collaborated with the Nazis in the 1930s and 1940s, should continue to govern the persecutor exception to asylum and withholding of removal. Ultimately, the availability of a duress exception to the asylum bar for those who participated in persecution reached the Supreme Court. The Court contrasted the 1948 Displaced Persons Act at issue in *Fedorenko* with the 1980 Refugee Act provisions implicated in the case of an Ethiopian forced to work as a prison guard in Eritrea in 1998, and concluded that the BIA had mistakenly considered that the earlier cases had settled the issue in the context of INA §§ 208 and 241(b)(3). *Negusie v. Holder*, 555 U.S. 511, 129 S.Ct. 1159, 173 L.Ed. 2d 20 (2009). The Court remanded the case to the BIA so that it could properly exercise its interpretive authority and decide in the first instance whether a duress exception applies at all—and if so, to define criteria for applying it. The BIA has not yet done so. Nor, as of early 2016, have DHS and DOJ issued regulations that would resolve those issues.

Asylum claims by former child soldiers frequently involve harrowing tales of persecution and torture, including violence that the children were forced to inflict on others. The law is underdeveloped as to whether criminal and civil responsibility should be attributed to child soldiers and the significance that their coerced conduct should have on their claims for asylum and withholding. *See* Elizabeth A. Rossi, *A "Special Track" for Former Child Soldiers: Enacting a "Child Soldier" Visa as an Alternative to Asylum Protection*, 31 Berkeley J. Int'l L. 392 (2013); Kathryn White, *A Chance for Redemption: Revising the "Persecutor Bar" and the "Material Support Bar" in the Case of Child Soldiers*, 43 Vand. J. Transnat'l L. 191 (2010).

4. SECURITY DANGERS AND TERRORIST ACTIVITY

The statute prohibits asylum for those considered security dangers, INA § 208(b)(2)(A)(iv), and bars withholding when "there are reasonable grounds for regarding the alien as a danger to the security of the United States." INA § 241(b)(3)(B)(iv). The quoted language is nearly identical to Article 33(2) of the Convention, which limits the coverage of the treaty's *nonrefoulement* protection. In addition, Congress has added a provision to the withholding statute that equates engaging in terrorist activity (and certain other connections with terrorism) with posing a security danger to the United States. INA § 241(b)(3)(B) (last sentence). It also has added an explicit ban on asylum for those involved in terrorist activity, INA § 208(b)(2)(A)(v). These provisions employ intricate cross-references to various portions of a highly complex terrorist inadmissibility ground, INA § 212(a)(3)(B), which we examined earlier in Chapter Seven, at pp. 600–622.

Some of the litigation concerning bars based on terrorist activity has involved fairly well known armed groups and violence committed against political opponents. For example, a member of the Irish National Liberation Army was denied asylum and withholding based on several crimes involving firearms and a conspiracy to kill a Royal Ulster Constabulary officer, crimes for which he had been convicted and imprisoned in Northern Ireland. The BIA and the federal court concluded that he had engaged in terrorist activity, which constitutes reasonable grounds for being regarded a danger to the security of the United States. Consequently, he was ineligible for asylum and withholding, even though he had fully served out his prison sentence in the United Kingdom and there was no indication of further involvement in violent acts. *McAllister v. Attorney General*, 444 F.3d 178 (3d Cir. 2006).

Since September 11, 2001, Congress has expanded the definition of engaging in terrorist activities to a wide array of conduct, including the provision of any type of material support, "to any individual the actor knows, or reasonably should know, has committed or plans to commit a terrorist activity," or to terrorist organizations. INA § 212(a)(3)(B)(iv)(VI). The current definition of a terrorist organization includes any group of "two or more individuals, whether organized or not," INA § 212(a)(3)(B)(vi)(III), which makes the reach of the material support provision extraordinarily wide. Providing food and tents at religious meetings attended by members of militant groups can constitute material support for terrorism. *Singh-Kaur v. Ashcroft*, 385 F.3d 293 (3d Cir. 2004). As detailed in Chapter Seven, Section A, donating several hundred dollars to a group resisting the military dictatorship in Burma can constitute material support to terrorism, even though the group used armed force defensively and was allied with the U.S.-supported National League for Democracy led by Nobel Peace Prize winner Aung San Suu Kyi. *Matter of S-K-*, 23 I & N Dec. 936 (BIA 2006). Subsequent legislation specified that certain Burmese resistance groups were not terrorist organizations, Consolidated Appropriations Act, 2008, Pub. L. 110–161, 121 Stat. 1844, Div. J, § 691, but the BIA's analysis of the material support provisions remained precedential, 24 I & N Dec. 475 (BIA 2008).

DHS and the Department of Justice have construed the terrorist provisions broadly, to include even minimal support given under duress, a stance that has provoked heated debate. Critics have pointed out that the broad reach of this interpretation leads to perverse consequences. For example, refugees who had been extorted to provide food and drink to armed groups, and then fled precisely to avoid future such threats and exactions, are precluded from protection under this reading of U.S. law. The material support bar has had especially negative effects on the asylum and overseas refugee resettlement program. It has also stalled the adjustment of status to lawful permanent residence of refugees or asylees who had been admitted in earlier years before the terrorist bars were expanded.

Congress eventually addressed some of these problems caused by the breadth of the terrorism-related bars, but resisted direct amendments that would narrow the scope of those provisions. Instead it chose to give the Secretary of State or the Secretary of Homeland Security, after consulting together and with the Attorney General, the discretionary authority to exempt individuals or groups from many of the applicable bars. INA § 212(d)(3)(B). The Secretary has "sole unreviewable discretion" over such exemptions. (Consider why Congress might have chosen this type of procedure, instead of amending the bars themselves.)

Early uses of this authority by the Secretary of State facilitated the admission of specific refugee groups as part of the overseas resettlement program. Later directives by the Secretary of Homeland Security have established, for example, case-by-case procedures to exempt, with certain qualifications, persons who provided material support under duress, who extended medical care to individuals involved in terrorist activities, or who provided only minimal support. USCIS officers consider the individual case to decide whether the person fits within one of the exemption categories and also to apply the further standards set forth by the Secretary. *See, e.g.,* 72 Fed. Reg. 9954, 9958 (2007) and *id.* at 26,138 (May 8, 2007). *See also* 84 Interp. Rel. 191–192 (2007). Their waiver decisions are unreviewable by immigration judges or the courts. USCIS, *Department of Homeland Security Implements Exemption Authority for Certain Terrorist-Related Inadmissibility Grounds for Cases with Administratively Final Orders of Removal*, USCIS Fact Sheet, 23 Oct. 2008. *See also* Lisa Yu, *New Developments on the Terrorism-Related Inadmissibility Ground Exemptions*, EOIR, 2 Immigration Law Advisor 1 (Dec. 2008) Chapter Seven, Section A examines the terrorism-related inadmissibility grounds (TRIG) in more depth.

5. SERIOUS CRIMES

The asylum statute and the withholding statute both expressly prohibit relief to applicants who have been involved in certain criminal conduct:

- those who committed a serious nonpolitical crime outside the United States prior to arrival, INA §§ 208(b)(2)(A)(iii); 241(b)(3)(B)(iii) (wording slightly different in § 241); and to

- those who have been convicted of a particularly serious crime in the United States. INA §§ 208(b)(2)(A)(ii); 241(b)(3)(B)(ii).

Both of these bars are drawn from provisions of the 1951 Convention (*see* Arts. 1(F), 33(2)), but the U.S. statute applies them in somewhat different fashion from their deployment under the treaty. Focusing on when and where the criminal activity occurred helps to clarify which portion of the statute applies.

a.   Prior to Arrival in the United States

In recognition that governments frequently label their dissidents as criminals, the bar related to criminal acts outside the United States prior to arrival refers only to nonpolitical crimes. Many of the difficult challenges in analyzing this barrier to protection involve determining whether certain criminal conduct should be characterized as political or nonpolitical. For example, an asylum applicant from Guatemala had participated in political protests that involved burning buses, using force to remove passengers, breaking store windows, and attacking police cars. The Supreme Court ruled that these were serious nonpolitical crimes even though done in support of political objectives. *INS v. Aguirre-Aguirre*, 526 U.S. 415, 119 S.Ct. 1439, 143 L.Ed.2d 590 (1999). The Court approved the BIA's approach, which examined whether the political aspect of the criminal conduct outweighed its common law character, whether atrocious acts were involved, and whether there was a gross disproportion between the means and the ends.

Determining whether criminal conduct is political or nonpolitical can also arise in extradition proceedings, because most of the applicable treaties bar extradition if the crime charged is considered a "political offense" (or similar wording). A substantial case law has grown up interpreting that concept for extradition purposes, and that doctrine is sometimes consulted by courts considering what is a serious nonpolitical crime under the 1951 Convention. Extradition case law is not dispositive in the asylum context, however, as the treaty language and policy concerns are different in the two legal realms.

Even conduct determined to be nonpolitical will bar individuals from asylum and withholding only if it amounts to a "serious" crime. The UN High Commissioner for Refugees has articulated a balancing approach for determining whether a crime is serious:

> [I]t is necessary to strike a balance between the nature of the offence presumed to have been committed by the applicant and the degree of persecution feared. If a person has well-founded fear of very severe persecution, e.g. persecution endangering his life or freedom, a crime must be very grave in order to exclude him. If the persecution feared is less serious, it will be necessary to have regard to the nature of the crime * * * in order to establish whether * * * his criminal character does not outweigh his character as a *bona fide* refugee.

Office of the United Nations Commissioner of Refugees, Handbook on Procedures and Criteria for Determining Refugee Status ¶ 156 (Geneva, 1979).

The U.S. Supreme Court, however, expressly rejected the balancing approach; in the Court's view, a crime is not rendered less serious by the severity of persecution facing the applicant at home. *See Aguirre-Aguirre*, 526 U.S. at 426. Moreover, the *Aguirre-Aguirre* Court ruled that the courts owed *Chevron* deference to the BIA's determination that setting fire to busses and assaulting passengers constituted a serious nonpolitical crime. 526 U.S. at 424.

b. Within the United States

Individuals convicted of particularly serious crimes within the United States are also ineligible to apply for relief under the asylum and withholding statutes. The text of the statute, drawn directly from the UN Convention, refers not only to the seriousness of the conduct, but also to dangerousness: asylum is barred to an individual who "having been convicted by a final judgment of a particularly serious crime, constitutes a danger to the community of the United States," INA § 208(b)(2)(A)(ii). This wording has led many countries and commentators to conclude that the statute requires asylum adjudicators to make two separate findings: (1) a prior conviction of a particularly serious crime, and (2) a present danger to the community. The BIA, however, has concluded those convicted in the United States of a "particularly serious crime" are automatically deemed a danger to the community. *Matter of Carballe*, 19 I & N Dec. 357, 360 (BIA 1986).

The 1951 Convention does not define "particularly serious crime," but commentators agree that a "particularly serious crime" refers to more heinous conduct than a "serious crime." The UNHCR Handbook concludes that a "serious crime" refers to "a capital crime or a very grave punishable act." Office of the United Nations High Commissioner for Refugees, Handbook on Procedures and Criteria for Determining Refugee Status ¶ 155 (Geneva, 1979).

The BIA adopted a case-by-case approach to determining a "particularly serious crime," but Congress has expanded the criminal bars over the years and has increasingly legislated bright-line rules. The 1990 Act added language to the withholding provision to the effect that an aggravated felony, as defined in INA § 101(a)(43), is to be considered per se a "particularly serious crime." It also barred asylum for anyone convicted of an aggravated felony. The 1996 Act greatly expanded the catalog of aggravated felonies in INA § 101(a)(43) by adding new offenses to the list and by reducing the minimum sentence necessary to render many crimes aggravated felonies. For example, theft offenses formerly required a five-year sentence to be counted as an aggravated felony. Now a one-year sentence will suffice.

Congress did seem to recognize in 1996 that a complete ban for this wider class of aggravated felonies might violate the Convention—or at least that it might be overly harsh. Therefore, it added to INA

§ 241(b)(3)(B) a threshold of a five-year aggregate sentence for automatic preclusion:

> For purposes of [the clause excluding those convicted of particularly serious crimes], an alien who has been convicted of an aggravated felony (or felonies) for which the alien has been sentenced to an aggregate term of imprisonment of at least 5 years shall be considered to have committed a particularly serious crime. The previous sentence shall not preclude the Attorney General from determining that, notwithstanding the length of sentence imposed, an alien has been convicted of a particularly serious crime.

INA § 241(b)(3)(B). But asylum remains barred for all aggravated felonies. INA § 208(b)(2)(B)(i). The Attorney General is expressly authorized to consider other offenses, in addition to aggravated felonies, to be particularly serious crimes. INA § 208(b)(2)(B)(ii).

In litigation involving individuals convicted of aggravated felonies but sentenced to less than five years in prison, the BIA ruled that there is no presumption that the crime is particularly serious; instead a case-by-case inquiry is necessary. *See Matter of L-S-*, 22 I & N Dec. 645 (BIA 1999). In *Matter of Y-L-*, 23 I & N Dec. 270 (2002) Attorney General Ashcroft reviewed three applicants for withholding who had been convicted of drug trafficking offenses and had been sentenced to one or two years in prison. Modifying some of the BIA's approach, he concluded that all drug trafficking offenses should be viewed as a particularly serious crime, although he acknowledged that in a "very rare case" an individual might demonstrate "extraordinary and compelling circumstances that justify treating a particular drug trafficking crime as falling short of that standard." *Id.* at 276.

NOTES AND QUESTIONS ON PARTICULARLY SERIOUS CRIMES

1.   In *Matter of Y-L-*, Attorney General Ashcroft discussed the devastating effects of drug trafficking on the health, welfare, and security of the United States. He commented that "ruthless, sophisticated, and aggressive traffickers" use "[s]ubstantial violence * * * at all levels of the distribution chain," and "international terrorists * * * employ drug trafficking as one of their primary sources of funding." *Id.* at 276. In light of these concerns, Ashcroft asserted that it might be within the Attorney General's discretion to conclude that *all* drug trafficking offenses are particularly serious crimes. *Id.* Do you agree? Is such a conclusion consistent with the 1951 Convention?

2.   Around the same time as the *Y-L-* opinion, Attorney General Ashcroft handed down another decision greatly restricting the favorable exercise of discretion over asylum and related waivers. *Matter of Jean*, 23 I & N Dec. 373 (AG 2002). After refusing to exercise his discretion in favor of a

mother of five who had been convicted of manslaughter, the Attorney General added: "I am highly disinclined to exercise my discretion—except * * * in extraordinary circumstances, such as those involving national security or foreign policy considerations, or cases in which an alien clearly demonstrates that the denial of relief would result in exceptional and extremely unusual hardship—on behalf of dangerous or violent felons seeking asylum." *Id.* at 385.

EXERCISE

As you consider these scenarios, you should have a copy of INA §§ 208(b)(2) and 241(b)(3)(B) at hand so that you identify the specific statutory section that applies and the precise statutory language that is relevant.

A.   Crimes Outside the United States

1.   Suppose your client, an asylum seeker, was convicted of extortion and murder in Fredonia, which caused her to flee to the United States to seek protection. She has convincing proof that she is a member of an ethnic group that the Fredonian government has traditionally persecuted. Is she eligible for asylum or withholding? What additional facts would you need to learn to assess the bars to protection that she might face?

2.   Same facts as above, except your client fled as soon as she learned that criminal charges had been filed against her and she has not been convicted of any crimes.

3.   Same facts as scenario 2, and your client has proof that she is a prominent member of the pro-democracy opposition to the military government.

4.   Same facts as scenario 3, and your client says the murder charge arose when she shot her former boyfriend, a police officer, to stop him from beating her.

B.   Crimes Within the United States

1.   Suppose your client, an asylum seeker, has been convicted of extortion in the United States and sentenced to three years in prison. Nonetheless, she has strong proof that she would likely be persecuted if returned to her home country of Ruritania. She acknowledged that her erratic behavior was a result of substance abuse, and she entered a rehabilitation program. She has now been sober for two years, and her psychiatrist will testify that a relapse is extremely unlikely. Is she eligible for asylum or withholding?

2.   Same facts as scenario 1, but she was sentenced to five years in prison.

3.   Suppose your client had been charged with extortion in the United States but had been acquitted. During the trial she testified that she had been a substance abuser, but had been sober since she finished a rehabilitation program two years ago.

E. CONVENTION AGAINST TORTURE

The Convention Against Torture and Other Cruel, Inhuman, or Degrading Treatment or Punishment (CAT, reprinted in the Statutory Supplement), to which the United States became a party in 1994, provides another avenue of humanitarian protection. The centerpiece of the Convention is the agreement that torture is illegitimate. Most of the articles of the treaty impose specific obligations on state parties to prevent and punish torture committed on their territory, but the treaty also forbids governments from returning individuals to situations where they will face torture.

> No State Party shall expel, return ("*refouler*") or extradite a person to another State where there are substantial grounds for believing that he would be in danger of being subjected to torture.

Art. 3, CAT. This *nonrefoulement* provision, rather than the direct prevention and punishment provisions, has generated the greatest volume of litigation implicating the CAT.

In consenting to the ratification of the Convention Against Torture, the Senate addressed the CAT's *nonrefoulement* obligation:

> The Senate's advice and consent is subject to the following understandings, which shall apply to the obligations of the United States under this Convention:

> (2) * * * the United States understands the phrase, "where there are substantial grounds for believing that he would be in danger of being subjected to torture," as used in article 3 of the Convention, to mean "if it is more likely than not that he would be tortured."

U.S. Resolution of Advice and Consent (With Reservations, Understandings and Declarations), II (2), 136 Cong. Rec. 36198–99 (1990), reprinted in the Statutory Supplement. The implementing regulations reiterate this standard. 8 C.F.R. §§ 208.16(c)(2); 208.17(a).

Many acts that constitute torture give rise to a valid protection claim under the UN refugee treaties. Accordingly, the protection that arises under the 1951 Refugee Convention, as implemented by INA §§ 208 and 241(b)(3), substantially overlaps with the *nonrefoulement* protection afforded by the CAT. As a consequence, potential victims of torture ordinarily are granted asylum or withholding, and are thus protected from *nonrefoulement* as required by Article 3 of the CAT. But in certain circumstances the protections do not coincide. For example, torture meted out as part of the punishment of common criminals would not be inflicted on account of one of the five grounds specified in the refugee treaties, and would not trigger asylum or withholding. Moreover, as the discussion in the prior section emphasized, certain criminal and other conduct disqualifies even those with a clear probability of persecution from asylum or withholding of removal. In contrast, the CAT *nonrefoulement* provision applies to everyone—including criminals—who would face torture.

The following excerpt provides a succinct account of the relationships between CAT protection and asylum:

> * * * In an important sense * * * the [CAT's] reach is both broader and narrower than that of a claim for asylum or withholding of deportation: coverage is broader because a petitioner need not show that he or she would be tortured "on account of" a protected ground; it is narrower, however, because the petitioner must show that it is "more likely than not" that he or she will be tortured, and not simply persecuted upon removal to a given country.

Kamalthas v. INS, 251 F.3d 1279, 1283 (9th Cir. 2001).

Despite the conceptual differences, torture, in the modern world, is most commonly administered in campaigns against political opponents or against groups disfavored on account of race or religion. Therefore, potential victims of torture frequently are eligible to seek asylum. Those who qualify for both forms of protection—under the CAT and under the asylum provisions in INA § 208—clearly would prefer the latter. If they receive asylum, they will not be expelled, and compliance with the CAT will be assured. Further, they will receive a status that allows the immediate family to immigrate and also opens a direct path to LPR status. In contrast, CAT protection consists, at best, of a form of withholding of removal. Hence, as a practical matter, the Torture Convention is likely to be relied on by those excluded from the normal asylum or withholding protections by the exception clauses—primarily individuals with criminal convictions.

1. APPLICATIONS FOR PROTECTION UNDER THE TORTURE CONVENTION

In recognition of the potential overlap in eligibility for CAT protection and asylum, applicants for protection under the CAT file their claims on the I–589 form, the same form used for asylum claims. By regulation, 8 C.F.R. § 208.16, immigration judges, not asylum officers, decide applications for protection under the CAT. The immigration judge will examine all the requests for protection together and decide whether to grant asylum, withholding of removal under § 241(b)(3), or withholding of removal under the CAT. Generally, the immigration judge will determine the applicability of protection under the Torture Convention only if the person fails to qualify for asylum or regular withholding.

The expedited removal procedure, discussed in Chapter Six, also incorporates consideration of claims of torture, as well as persecution, into the credible fear determinations. A noncitizen found there to have a credible fear of torture will ordinarily be placed in full removal proceedings before an immigration judge to have the CAT claim determined. 8 C.F.R. § 235.3(b)(4).

Those denied protection under the CAT can appeal to the BIA. After receiving a final order of removal, they can file a petition of review in the federal courts of appeals. INA § 242(a)(4).

a. Withholding and Deferral of Removal

In the legislation implementing the CAT's Article 3, Congress stated that individuals barred from regular withholding under INA § 241(b)(3)(B) because of crimes, involvement in persecution of others, or other threatening behavior should be excluded from CAT protection "to the maximum extent consistent with the obligations of the United States under the Convention." Foreign Affairs Reform and Restructuring Act, § 2242, Pub. L. 105–277, Div. G., Title XXII, § 2242, 112 Stat. 2681–2822 (1998) (reprinted in the Statutory Supplement). The agency concluded that no one facing torture could be excluded from protection, however, because of the CAT's absolute *nonrefoulement* obligation. But it responded to the congressional mandate by providing two forms of CAT relief: withholding and deferral of removal.

Generally, those entitled to protection under the CAT receive withholding of removal, essentially equivalent to the protection developed in response to the persecution-based *nonrefoulement* requirement of INA § 241(b)(3). In contrast, those entitled to CAT protection who have also persecuted others, committed particularly serious crimes or serious nonpolitical crimes, or who constitute a security danger to the United States are given a lesser form of protection, "deferral of removal." 8 C.F.R. § 208.16(d). Deferral of removal allows eligibility for work authorization, but it can be terminated somewhat more easily than asylum or withholding of removal in the event that conditions change in such a way as to permit lawful deportation to the country of origin or a third country. *Compare* 8 C.F.R. § 208.17(d) *with* § 208.24(f). Furthermore, the regulations contemplate that persons granted deferral of removal might be held in detention. *Id.* at § 208.17(c). The exact authority for this potential detention is not clear, and apparently has not been exercised.

As Figure 8.13 depicts, only 536 of the 26,000 CAT applicants received protection in the United States under the Convention Against Torture in 2014. Figure 8.14 shows that of the small number of successful CAT applicants, roughly 80 percent received withholding of removal and the remaining 20 percent receiving deferral of removal.

Figure 8.13
Results in Convention Against Torture Cases, 2006–2014

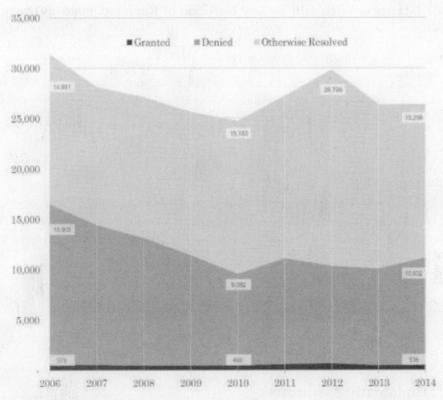

	2006	2008	2010	2012	2014
Granted	578	501	489	643	536
Denied	15,905	12,661	9,082	9,710	10,602
Otherwise Resolved	14,881	13,966	15,183	19,443	15,256

Source: EOIR FY 2006.

Figure 8.14
Convention Against Torture Cases
Grants of Withholding and Deferral of Removal, 2006–2014

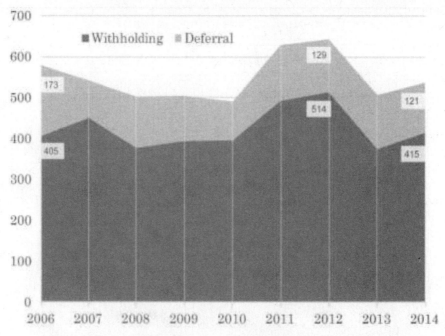

Source: EOIR FY 2006–2014 Statistics Yearbooks.

b. Diplomatic Assurances

The regulations provide that the U.S. Secretary of State may forward to the Attorney General diplomatic assurances from the government of another country that a specified individual would not be tortured if returned to that country. 8 C.F.R. § 208.18(c). The Attorney General (or a limited list of other high-level DOJ officials) must personally assess "whether the assurances are sufficiently reliable to allow the alien's removal to that country consistent with Article 3" of the CAT. Once the determination is made, the diplomatic assurances override any withholding or deferral granted by an immigration judge. The Third Circuit has ruled, however, that a noncitizen has the right to a hearing to challenge the government's reliance on diplomatic assurances as a basis for removal from the United States. *Khouzam v. Attorney General*, 549 F.3d 235 (3d Cir. 2008). DHS reported in 2011 that up to that date it had sought diplomatic assurances regarding a total of four individuals, one Egyptian and three Rwandans. Office of Inspector General, *DHS Detainee Removals and Reliance on Assurances*, OIG–11–100, Nov. 29, 2011.

Other countries have, on occasion, also relied on diplomatic assurances in returning noncitizens to their homelands. *See, e.g., Agiza v.*

Sweden, Committee Against Torture, Communication No. 233/2003, U.N. Doc. CAT/C/34/D/233/203 (May 24, 2005) (Sweden's reliance on diplomatic assurances from Egypt breached CAT); Ashley Deeks, *Promises Not To Torture: Diplomatic Assurances in U.S. Courts*, ASIL Discussion Paper Series, Dec. 2008, at 49–70 (review of European and Canadian uses of diplomatic assurances). The reliance on diplomatic assurances has been controversial. *See* Martin D. Jones, *Damned Lies and Diplomatic Assurances: The Misuse of Diplomatic Assurances in Removal Proceedings*, 8 Eur. J. Migration L. 9 (2006).

2. THE DEFINITION OF TORTURE

The Convention outlaws cruel, inhuman, or degrading treatment or punishment, in addition to torture. Nonetheless, the Convention's central focus is on preventing and punishing torture, and the *nonrefoulement* provision, Article 3, provides protection only against return to torture. Article 1 of the treaty sets forth a detailed definition of torture:

> any act by which severe pain or suffering, whether physical or mental, is intentionally inflicted on a person for such purposes as obtaining from him or a third person information or a confession, punishing him for an act he or a third person has committed or is suspected of having committed, or intimidating or coercing him or a third person, or for any reason based on discrimination of any kind when such pain and suffering is inflicted by or at the instigation of or with the consent or acquiescence of a public official or other person acting in an official capacity. It does not include pain or suffering arising only from, inherent in or incidental to lawful sanctions.

Art. 1, CAT.

a. Government Involvement or Acquiescence in Torture

Article 1 of the CAT defines torture to mean certain acts that inflict severe pain or suffering, but only "when such pain or suffering is inflicted by or at the instigation of or with the consent or acquiescence of a public official or other person acting in an official capacity." There is no similar government actor requirement in asylum, although purely private infliction of harm can raise difficult issues.

In its resolution approving ratification of the Convention Against Torture, the Senate included the following guidance for implementation of the CAT.

> The Senate's advice and consent is subject to the following understandings, which shall apply to the obligations of the United States under this Convention:

* * *

(1)(d) * * * the term "acquiescence" requires that the public official, prior to the activity constituting torture, have awareness of such activity and thereafter breach his legal responsibility to intervene to prevent such activity.

* * *

U.S. Resolution of Advice and Consent (With Reservations, Understandings and Declarations), 136 Cong. Rec. 36198–99 (1990), reprinted in the Statutory Supplement.

Interpreting "consent or acquiescence" in light of the Senate's guidance, which requires prior awareness by a public official plus breach of a duty to intervene, has yielded conflicting analyses. In 2000, the BIA confronted a CAT application filed by a citizen of Colombia, who after 17 years as a lawful permanent resident of the United States, had been convicted of grand theft, robbery, and driving with a suspended license, and was sentenced to four years in prison. He sought protection from *refoulement* because he feared that he would be a target of kidnapping by nongovernmental guerrilla, narcotrafficking, and paramilitary groups in Colombia. After ruling that his criminal conviction and sentence made him ineligible for withholding of removal, the BIA rejected his claim for relief under the CAT. It stated that "[t]o demonstrate 'acquiescence' by Colombian Government officials, the respondent must do more than show that the officials are aware of the activity constituting torture but are powerless to stop it. He must demonstrate that Colombian officials are willfully accepting of the guerrillas' torturous activities. Accordingly, we consider that a government's inability to control a group ought not lead to the conclusion that the government acquiesced to the group's activities." *Matter of S-V-,* 22 I & N Dec. 1306, 1311–13 (BIA 2000).

Several years later, Attorney General Ashcroft evaluated the acquiescence requirement of the Torture Convention with regard to several individuals who had been convicted of drug trafficking and so were precluded from withholding of removal under INA § 241(b)(3). *Matter of Y-L-,* 23 I & N Dec. 270 (AG 2002). (The prior section discussed a portion of this opinion regarding regular withholding of removal.) In essence, the applicants for CAT protection argued that they feared torture or death from their former drug-dealing associates, with the connivance of some government officials, if returned to their homelands. Ashcroft rejected their claims, stating that they had submitted no evidence that government authorities would approve or "willfully accept" torture of the applicants. He added: "[E]vidence of isolated rogue agents engaging in extrajudicial acts of brutality, which are not only in contravention of the jurisdiction's laws and policies, but are committed despite authorities' best efforts to root out such misconduct" does not constitute consent or acquiescence. *Id.* at 282.

Despite Ashcroft's designation of *Matter of Y-L-* as a precedent to guide future application of the CAT, some courts have disapproved of the "willful acceptance" interpretation and adopted a different understanding of acquiescence. The Ninth Circuit has stated: "The BIA's interpretation and application of acquiescence impermissibly requires more than awareness and instead requires that a government be willfully accepting of a third party's tortuous activities." *Zheng v. Ashcroft*, 332 F.3d 1186, 1196 (9th Cir. 2003). The standard is less stringent, according to the Ninth Circuit: does the evidence show that the government officials demonstrate "willful blindness" to torture by third parties. *Id. Accord Khouzam v. Ashcroft*, 361 F.3d 161 (2d Cir. 2004) (only knowledge or willful blindness of government officials required).

b. Burden of Proof and Level of Risk

As noted earlier, Article 3 of the Torture Convention forbids governments to return individuals if there are "substantial grounds" for believing they will face torture. The U.S. Senate's resolution of advice and consent to the Torture Convention, reprinted in the Statutory Supplement, specified that the Senate understood "substantial grounds" to mean that torture is "more likely than not" to occur. The subsequent CAT regulations reiterate this standard, set forth the burden of proof, and acknowledge the importance of uncorroborated evidence in some cases.

> The burden of proof is on the applicant for withholding of removal under this paragraph to establish that it is more likely than not that he or she would be tortured if removed to the proposed country of removal. The testimony of the applicant, if credible, may be sufficient to sustain the burden of proof without corroboration.

8 C.F.R. § 208.16(c)(2).

Many applicants for CAT relief focus on the prison conditions they may face if returned to their homelands. The BIA has established a rebuttable presumption that mistreatment in prison is not torture. *See Matter of J-E-*, 23 I & N Dec. 291 (BIA 2002). Nonetheless, the BIA continues to grapple with cases involving the likelihood that individuals removed from the United States may face torture in prison.

MATTER OF M-B-A-

Board of Immigration Appeals, 2002.
23 I & N Dec. 474.

HOLMES, BOARD MEMBER:

[A 40-year-old native and citizen of Nigeria was convicted in the United States of importing a controlled substance and of possession of heroin with intent to distribute. She presented evidence that she suffers from depression, asthma, and a chronic ulcer, and that she had no family members in Nigeria to support her. She also submitted a copy of a 1990 Nigerian government decree that criminalized Nigerians who are convicted of narcotic drug offenses in other countries or are detected carrying narcotic drugs into foreign countries on trips originating in Nigeria.]

* * *

During proceedings before the Immigration Judge on December 14, 1999, the respondent testified that she had traveled to Nigeria in 1993 to meet her then-fiancé's family and had been unwillingly involved in drug trafficking by his relatives and associates when she traveled back to the United States. She testified that because of this conviction she would be immediately turned over to drug enforcement authorities and imprisoned if she is returned to Nigeria, that she would be in jail for years before she would be able to see a judge, that she was subject to a mandatory 5-year term of imprisonment, and that she would be subjected to torture while jailed.

When asked how she knew that this would occur, the respondent referred to Decree No. 33 and also testified that some years before she had communicated with an unnamed Nigerian friend who had been convicted of a drug offense in this country and then returned to Nigeria. The respondent indicated that she spoke by telephone to her friend and her friend's parents in 1995. She was told that her friend had been detained upon her return to Nigeria in 1995, that her family had had to bring food and medication to the jail and pay money for her protection, that she slept on the floor, and that "you probably get raped and beat down" by the guards because they have authority to do "whatever they can do." Her friend remained in jail for 2 months until her family paid a bribe to get her released. The respondent did not know whether her friend had gone before a judge before being incarcerated or whether she had been raped in prison.* * *

The respondent further testified that there was no one to help her in Nigeria if she were jailed. * * *

The respondent testified, and provided supporting medical evidence, that she suffers from depression, a chronic ulcer, and asthma. She stated that she had no one to rely on to supply her with medicine if she were jailed in Nigeria. In addition, the respondent testified that she would probably be beaten and raped by prison guards. She stated that most women are subjected to such treatment in prison and that the government does not have the ability to protect them. * * *

* * *

The actual status of Decree No. 33 is not entirely clear on the record before us, but we will assume that it has not been repealed and is enforceable. However, even assuming that such is the case, there is little evidence of record on which to base any meaningful conclusion regarding the extent to which this provision is presently enforced, and how and against whom it is enforced. The fact that the decree is written in mandatory terms is not in itself determinative because it is common to couch criminal provisions in such terms. * * *

The respondent's own evidence concerning the present manner of enforcement of Decree No. 33 does not go much beyond conjecture, and her reference to the circumstances that were related to her by her friend and her friend's parents in 1995 involved one individual some 7 years ago under a different regime in Nigeria. * * *

In this regard, we do not find it sufficient for the respondent simply to cite the existence of Decree No. 33 and her unnamed friend's experiences in 1995. The respondent must provide some current evidence, or at least more meaningful historical evidence, regarding the manner of enforcement of the provisions of Decree No. 33 on individuals similarly situated to herself.

The respondent's eligibility for deferral of removal rests upon a finding that it is more likely than not that she will be identified as a convicted drug trafficker upon her return to Nigeria; that, as a result, she will be detained on arrival; that, when detained, she will be held in detention without access to bail or judicial oversight; that she will be detained for a significant period of time; and that, as a result of this detention, she will suffer mistreatment that rises to the level of torture at the hands of prison guards or authorities. Given the evidence of harsh and life-threatening prison conditions in Nigeria and the serious drug trafficking problems that Nigerian authorities are attempting to address, the respondent's fear of return to her home country is understandable. On the record before us, however, we find that the respondent's case is based on a chain of assumptions and a fear of what might happen, rather than evidence that meets her burden of demonstrating that it is *more likely than not* that she will be subjected to torture by, or with the acquiescence of, a public official or other person acting in an official capacity if she is returned to her home country.

[The BIA dismissed the appeal.]

[We have omitted the opinion of ROSENBERG, BOARD MEMBER, concurring and dissenting.]

SCHMIDT, BOARD MEMBER, dissenting [joined by four other Board Members]:

I respectfully dissent.

[T]he respondent has shown that it is more likely than not that she will be imprisoned under Decree No. 33 upon return to Nigeria.* * * I write separately to address the question the majority avoids: whether the respondent more likely than not will be tortured while in prison. I find that she will be tortured.

* * *

A.   TORTURE EXISTS IN THE NIGERIAN PRISON SYSTEM

The most recent Department of State country report on Nigeria describes the abuses that are rampant in the Nigerian prison system. Bureau of Democracy, Human Rights, and Labor, U.S. Dep't of State, *Nigeria Country Reports on Human Rights Practices—2001* (Mar. 2002). At least one aspect of that abuse, intentional withholding of needed medical treatment for improper purposes, which is relevant to this respondent's situation, constitutes "torture" under the test set forth in *Matter of J-E-,* [23 I & N Dec. 291 (BIA 2002)].

The respondent is a chronic asthmatic with no family in Nigeria who could provide food or proper medical treatment while she is in jail. The Country Reports state that "[p]rison officials, police, and security forces *often denied inmates food and medical treatment as a form of punishment or to extort money from them.*" Country Reports, *supra*, at 6 (emphasis added).

* * *

Clearly, death caused at least in part by intentional withholding of medical treatment for improper purposes is common in the Nigerian prison system. The extent of the problem probably is understated because of the difficulty in obtaining accurate documentation from the Nigerian system.

* * *

B.   RESPONDENT'S PERSONAL CHARACTERISTICS MAKE TORTURE LIKELY

The respondent is a woman, suffering from chronic asthma, without family to support and assist her in Nigeria, returning from the United States with a drug conviction. Decree No. 33, discussed by the majority, shows, at a minimum, that the Nigerian Government has a particular interest in those returning with foreign drug convictions.

The respondent's combination of personal traits places her in a particularly high-risk category to suffer torture through the intentional denial of medical treatment for her chronic asthma by Nigerian prison officials bent upon improperly punishing or extorting her.* * * Consequently, I find that the respondent more likely than not will be tortured if imprisoned in Nigeria.

NOTES AND QUESTIONS ON LEVEL OF RISK

1.　The text of Article 3 of the CAT forbids *refoulement* where there are "substantial grounds" for believing that a person would be in danger of torture. In its Understanding 2 to the resolution of advice and consent to the CAT, reprinted in the Statutory Supplement, the Senate expressly equated "substantial grounds" with "more likely than not." As discussed in Section C of this chapter, the *Stevic* standard is more difficult to satisfy than the well-founded fear standard applied in the asylum determination. Is it fair to say that by adopting a more demanding standard for assessing the threat level that triggers CAT protection, the Senate assured that fewer individuals would be protected from torture?

2.　What is the heart of the dispute between the majority and the dissent in *Matter of M-B-A-*? Does the majority believe that it is unlikely that the woman in question will be jailed in Nigeria or is the majority simply agnostic as to the likelihood of detention? What evidence could sway the majority on this point? In contrast, the dissent believes it is more likely than not that this Nigerian woman will be jailed and will have her asthma medication withheld. The Country Reports state that withholding of food or medication often occurs. Does "often" equate to "more likely than not"?

CHAPTER NINE

REMOVAL, DETENTION, AND JUDICIAL REVIEW

• • •

Removal from the United States constitutes the central and most powerful element of immigration enforcement. We consider in this chapter the administrative procedures employed in adjudicating a noncitizen's removability (Section A) and then two closely related topics. Section B examines the substantive provisions and procedures that govern detention of noncitizens, both during removal proceedings and after an order becomes final, while the Department of Homeland Security works to carry out the removal. Section C surveys the complex statutes and case law governing judicial review of removal orders and related actions.

A. REMOVAL PROCEEDINGS

The primary form of enforcement deployed against noncitizen violators of the immigration laws is physical expulsion from the United States, and the statute ordinarily requires that such a sanction be imposed as a result of a *removal proceeding*. INA § 240(a)(3). The Immigration and Nationality Act adopted this nomenclature in 1996 as an umbrella term to describe the procedure used to remove noncitizens. Until then, the INA had separately authorized *deportation proceedings* for those who had entered the United States, and *exclusion proceedings* for noncitizens whose eligibility was questioned at the border before entry (essentially the class now called by the statute "arriving aliens"). Today, charges against either category of noncitizen are to be heard in a unified form of removal proceeding. Some noncitizens in removal proceedings have been admitted but have since become deportable. Others have not been admitted to the United States at all; these noncitizens may have entered surreptitiously, or they may have been stopped at a port of entry. The removal proceeding, conducted by an immigration judge, constitutes the forum for the government to establish the basic charges of either inadmissibility or deportability and for the noncitizen to contest the charges and make any claims for relief from removal.

Each topic in this section has at least two dimensions. One is what the statute and regulations provide. The other is what constitutional due process requires at a minimum—a question typically answered by

895

applying the constitutional framework explored in Chapter Six, Section C. Recall that *Yamataya*, *Knauff*, *Chew*, *Mezei*, and *Plasencia* are key to deciding whether procedural due process applies. And that if it does, courts typically apply the three-factor analysis in *Mathews v. Eldridge*, 424 U.S. 319, 335, 96 S.Ct. 893, 47 L.Ed.2d 18 (1976), to decide whether the procedures are sufficient.

This section covers three topics. We begin with the standard removal procedures in immigration court under § 240, and then turn to the narrow avenues for a second chance when the outcome of a removal proceeding is unfavorable to the noncitizen. Finally, we consider special removal procedures for specified categories of cases.[22]

1. OVERVIEW

If the Department of Homeland Security chooses to initiate removal under § 240, it serves a charging document that commands appearance before an immigration judge for a hearing at a designated time and place. For many years, the charging document in deportation was an Order to Show Cause (you will see this term in some of the cases in this chapter), but today all removal proceedings employ a form called a Notice to Appear (NTA). The NTA is Form I–862 (in the Statutory Supplement). INA § 239 sets out the contents of the NTA and the requirements for service.

The NTA may be served in person or by mail. *See Matter of M-D-*, 23 I & N Dec. 540, 542–45 (BIA 2002) (summarizing law on mail service). In order to give the respondent a chance to obtain counsel, a hearing may not be scheduled until at least ten days after service, unless the respondent requests an earlier date in writing. (In practice, a respondent who wants to be represented by counsel can typically obtain one or more continuances to locate and engage counsel.) The NTA includes a warning that anything the respondent says may be used against her (but not that she has the right to remain silent), and a paragraph that addresses representation by counsel. Proceedings formally commence when the government files the NTA with the clerk of the immigration court.

Although many NTAs are served without the respondent being arrested, the power of arrest remains. After arrest, a DHS officer ordinarily examines the case and determines whether the noncitizen can be released on bond or on her own recognizance. Unless she is an arriving alien, she can obtain speedy review (sometimes conducted telephonically) of the release decision before an immigration judge, in what is known as a "bond redetermination" hearing.

---

[22] These summary or streamlined procedures are sometimes referred to as "removal proceedings," but we will ordinarily reserve that term in this chapter for a § 240 proceeding before an immigration judge.

INA § 236(a) governs arrest with a warrant. Under INA § 287(a), immigration officers may arrest without a warrant an alien who the officer believes (1) is entering, or attempting to enter the United States in violation of the immigration laws, or (2) is present in the United States in violation of the immigration laws and is likely to escape before an arrest warrant can be obtained. An alien arrested under § 287 must be brought before another immigration officer for examination. If the examining officer is satisfied that there is a *prima facie* case against the respondent, formal removal proceedings are initiated (unless the officer decides to permit the respondent to depart the country voluntarily). In certain circumstances, this examination may be made by the arresting officer. *See* 8 C.F.R. § 287.3(b). By regulation, the decision to begin removal proceedings must be made within 48 hours of the arrest, "except in the event of an emergency or other extraordinary circumstance in which case a determination will be made within an additional reasonable period of time." 8 C.F.R. § 287.3(d).

Many noncitizens who are apprehended are not served with NTAs, particularly those apprehended at or near the land borders who agree to a quick return to Mexico or Canada (after fingerprinting and basic paperwork). Also, those who are served may receive permission for voluntary departure, from the DHS officer or from an immigration judge. INA § 240B. By departing without a removal order, they avoid particular penalties and future disabilities associated with formal removal.

Removal proceedings are typically conducted in two stages: the master calendar hearing and the individual merits hearing. The master calendar hearing is similar to a civil calendar call or a criminal arraignment. It serves to determine whether an individual merits hearing is even required, and in many cases it is not. For example, the respondent may admit the allegations in the NTA and waive any relief, except perhaps voluntary departure, permitting the judge to issue an appropriate order and dispose of the case right at the first master calendar appearance. But if issues of fact are disputed, if inadmissibility or deportability is contested, or if the respondent seeks asylum, cancellation of removal, or other forms of relief besides voluntary departure, the immigration judge will set an individual merits hearing for a future date.

For noncitizens in removal, a very important question is whether they are released or detained while removal proceedings are pending. Besides meaning incarceration for months until a removal hearing, detention may impair a noncitizen's ability to present her case, especially if she is held far from family, friends, or counsel.

On the other hand, a significant number of noncitizens ordered removed do not voluntarily present themselves for removal (or leave the country on their own) after losing before the immigration judge or on appeal. Hence, immigration authorities use detention as a key tool in securing actual enforcement of removal orders. According to ICE, fugitive operations teams have contributed to a reduction in the total backlog of fugitive alien cases from 632,726 cases in FY 2006 to 469,157 cases in FY 2012. *See* Marc R. Rosenblum & William A. Kandel, Interior Immigration Enforcement: Programs Targeting Criminal Aliens, Cong. Res. Serv. 17 (2013). At the start of 2014, ICE reported that there were 469,151 fugitive aliens who had not been apprehended. However, "[t]he President's executive action of November 20, 2014, would no longer make such aliens enforcement priorities if they were issued final orders of removal prior to 2014 and are neither criminals nor national security concerns." William A. Kandel et. al, *President's Immigration Accountability Executive Action of November 20, 2014, Overview and Issues* 13 (Cong. Res. Serv. 2015).

2. IMMIGRATION COURT

a. The Role of Immigration Judges

For most of the twentieth century, the federal officials who conducted exclusion and deportation hearings were officers of INS or its predecessor agencies. Soon after the McCarran-Walter Act became law in 1952, the U.S. Supreme Court in *Marcello v. Bonds*, 349 U.S. 302, 311, 75 S.Ct. 757, 762, 99 L.Ed. 1107 (1955), rejected a constitutional challenge to the adjudicator's ties to INS, but criticism continued. It was not until 1983 that this arrangement ended with the creation of the Executive Office for Immigration Review (EOIR). *See* 8 C.F.R. § 1003.0. Now, immigration judges are under the general supervision of the Director of EOIR, which remains in the Department of Justice after INS functions were moved to the Department of Homeland Security.

INA § 240(b)(1) provides that an immigration judge "shall administer oaths, receive evidence, interrogate, examine, and cross-examine the alien and any witnesses." It further provides: "The immigration judge may issue subpoenas for the attendance of witnesses and presentation of evidence." While this language may suggest an inquisitorial model—conferring both prosecuting and judging functions on an immigration judge—in fact immigration court hearings generally conform to the more familiar adversarial model, with the government represented by a specialized staff of trial attorneys. But some special removal procedures, discussed later in this section, do not involve an immigration judge at all.

Within this scheme, what do constitutional due process requirements and the statute require an immigration judge to do? Consider the next case.

JACINTO V. INS

United States Court of Appeals, Ninth Circuit, 2000.
208 F.3d 725.

BRIGHT, CIRCUIT JUDGE.

Norma Antonia Jacinto Carrillo ("Jacinto") and her son, Ronald Garcia, are natives and citizens of Guatemala. On behalf of herself and her son, Jacinto petitions this court for review of the Board of Immigration Appeals' ("Board") decision denying her application for asylum and withholding of deportation. She also contests the Board's denial of voluntary departure * * *. We have jurisdiction over this petition * * *.

I

In December, 1994, Jacinto filed an affirmative asylum application with the Immigration and Naturalization Service ("INS"). Therein she alleged that members of the Guatemalan military were persecuting her and her family, including her common-law husband who is a former member of the Guatemalan military. In March, 1995, the INS issued an Order to Show Cause and Notice of Hearing.

Following two hearings, one on August 25, 1995, and the second on January 11, 1996, the immigration judge denied Jacinto's application for asylum, withholding of deportation, and voluntary departure. The immigration judge found that Jacinto did not have a well-founded fear of persecution because she could not explain why members of the military were pursuing her and her husband and had not demonstrated a subjective fear of persecution. In addition, the immigration judge found that Jacinto's testimony throughout the proceedings was not credible.

* * *

II

This court reviews claims of due process violations in deportation proceedings *de novo*.

The Fifth Amendment guarantees that individuals subject to deportation proceedings receive due process. Due process requires that an alien receive a full and fair hearing. In addition to constitutional protections, there are statutory and regulatory safeguards as well. For example, individuals in deportation proceedings are entitled to present personal testimony in their behalf. When these protections are denied and such denial results in prejudice, the constitutional guarantee of due process has been denied. Prejudice occurs when the rights of the alien have been transgressed in such a way as is likely to impact the results of the proceedings.

The case record consisted of two hearings with different immigration judges presiding at each hearing. * * *

* * *

We start with the initial hearing of August 24, 1995, concerning [Jacinto's] son Ronald Garcia. At that hearing, the immigration judge discussed her son's right to an attorney. The transcript of this matter is reproduced below:

> Q. At this hearing he has a right to an attorney at his own expense, at his family's expense. You are now being handed a Form I–618 and also a copy of the local legal aid list which contains the names of organizations and attorneys who may be able to help him for little or not [sic] fee. Do you understand all that I've said so far, Ms. Jacinto Carrillo?
>
> A. Yes.
>
> Q. All right. Do you wish the Court to give you additional time to get an attorney to speak for you, rather for your son, in these proceedings, or do you wish to speak for him?
>
> A. Yes.
>
> Q. Which one?
>
> A. The problem is—
>
> Q. Which one? I don't want to hear about the problems, I just want to know whether you want to speak for him or whether you want time to get an attorney to speak for him?
>
> A. I want to speak for him.
>
> Q. All right. At this hearing, your son has certain rights, one, to present evidence in his own behalf; two, to examine and object to evidence presented against him; and three, to question any witnesses brought into hearing. Do you understand the rights that your son enjoys?
>
> A. Yes.

The likely misunderstanding surfaces in Jacinto's answer "The problem is—" A reasonable interpretation of this colloquy is that Jacinto was given a choice: either she could get an attorney to speak for her son or she could speak for her son, but not both.

This is not the rule. She could have obtained an attorney and she also could have spoken for her son as a witness (and as an adviser to the attorney). This was never clearly explained to her. In other words, from the standpoint of this unsophisticated witness, the court gave her the choice of either being silent or getting somebody else to speak for her son.

Her general misunderstanding about the hearing process and the matters to be resolved is reflected in various places throughout the record. * * *

* * *

The manner of conducting the asylum hearing placed Jacinto at a considerable disadvantage. The asylum hearing in this case began with the immigration judge asking preliminary questions. Rather than permitting Jacinto to present her own testimony, the immigration judge then turned questioning over to the INS attorney. The questioning of Jacinto then alternated between the immigration judge and the INS attorney. At no point was she afforded the opportunity to present her own affirmative testimony, in narrative form or otherwise.

* * *

* * * During questioning of Jacinto by the INS attorney, the immigration judge would interrupt frequently and ask questions and then turn the questioning back to the government attorney. The examination of Jacinto went back and forth between the immigration judge and the government attorney with some of the questions relating to the credibility of Jacinto's statements. For example, the following colloquy occurred between the INS attorney and Jacinto:

Q. Ma'am, if they came to your house so often, and you were so afraid, why did you stay there for two years?

A. In the house?

Q. Why didn't you leave Guatemala earlier?

A. It's that we, they started, like I said, they started to bother us because he told them if they continued [to] bother him he was going to say everything he knew because he knew all the bad things that they did. That's when they started to persecute him to kill him.

Q. See, but, ma'am, please answer my question. If you were so afraid of these people and they were bothering you so often, why did you wait two years to leave Guatemala?

A. I did not wait that long. They threatened him, but they did not bother me, just at the end that they would come and bother me.

At the end of the examination on the merits, the immigration judge did not afford Jacinto any opportunity to explain her answers, but turned to the government counsel and inquired, "Anything further, counsel?"

* * * [A]t no time did the immigration judge explain that Jacinto could testify further with respect to the asylum claim, could explain or add to her previous answers, or offer additional evidence. Thus, Jacinto was never at any time given the opportunity to present directly, or fully detail, her account supporting her claim for asylum.

* * *

The immigration judge did not explain to Jacinto that she could use this opportunity to clarify any matters, dispel any conclusions, highlight certain facts, or present additional evidence supporting her right to remain in the country. For instance, Jacinto never asked Lopez[a] to further expound upon his statement that he knew of several instances of killings of Guatemalan citizens by the Guatemalan army. Jacinto failed to amplify this matter, and there is no indication that she recognized the importance of showing a political motivation for the adverse action taken against her and Lopez while in Guatemala that served as the reason to leave Guatemala.

* * *

In *Fisher* [*v. INS,* 79 F.3d 955, 972 (9th Cir. 1996) (*en banc*) (Noonan, J., dissenting)], Judge Noonan noted that the statutory and regulatory obligations required, in short, the immigration judge to fully develop the record. Reciting the statutory and regulatory mandates of the immigration judge, Judge Noonan observed that the duty of the immigration judge is analogous to that of the administrative law judge in social security disability cases. In social security disability cases, the administrative law judge has a duty to "fully and fairly develop the record. . . ." *Brown v. Heckler,* 713 F.2d 441, 443 (9th Cir. 1983). We agree.

* * *

[B]oth social security and deportation hearings are likely to be unfamiliar settings for the applicant, and, as the Supreme Court has noted, such procedures "should be understandable to the layman claimant . . . and not strict in tone and operation." *Richardson v. Perales,* 402 U.S. 389, 400, 91 S.Ct. 1420, 28 L.Ed.2d 842 (1971). When an applicant appears pro se, this rationale is all the stronger. . . . * * *

* * *

Further, aliens often lack proficiency in English, the language in which the proceedings are typically conducted. Despite the presence of a translator, the language barrier presents the potential to affect the ability of the alien to communicate and the ability of the immigration judge to understand what is being stated.

---

[a]   Francisco Javier Lopez is Jacinto's common-law husband and her only witness.—eds.

Moreover, while the proceedings are adversarial in nature, the implication of the proceedings is that an individual is required to leave this country. Thus, the petitioner could face a significant threat to his or her life, safety, and well-being. Should the immigration judge fail to fully develop the record, information crucial to the alien's future remains undisclosed.

Thus, under the statute and regulations previously cited, and for the reasons we have stated here, immigration judges are obligated to fully develop the record in those circumstances where applicants appear without counsel, as is this case.

In this case, Jacinto represented herself under circumstances in which the court did not clearly explain either that she had the right to testify even if she was represented by a lawyer or that she could present evidence, in the form of affirmative testimony, even while representing herself. Thus, not only did she not have the assistance of counsel, but she suffered because her rights were not adequately outlined for her. Her testimony was the product of an examination conducted by parties somewhat adverse to her position. Further, and perhaps most important, the immigration judge never gave her the opportunity to present her own additional narrated statement that might have added support to her claim. These combined failures resulted in a denial of a full and fair hearing.

The lack of a full and fair hearing, however, will not alone establish a due process violation. The alien must establish that she suffered prejudice. * * *

It was important for Jacinto to establish that her persecution or her well-founded fear of persecution rested on one of these factors: race, religion, nationality, membership in a particular social group or political opinion. However, this was not developed in the proceedings because the immigration judge never explained this requirement to her, and never gave her an opportunity to testify fully in her own behalf. Instead, Jacinto only was permitted to "testify" through an examination conducted by the immigration judge and the INS attorney.

Interestingly, the immigration judge observed "the Respondent herself did not know the reason why these individuals were actually after her husband." Yet it appears from the record that Jacinto's husband, Lopez, indicated they had information that members of the military were involved in murders of other persons. Had the immigration judge attempted to elicit more information from Lopez on this subject, the questions could well have led to some additional information about the relationship between military abuses and political opinions that would have lent support to Jacinto's application.

Perhaps not surprisingly, the immigration judge did not believe some of Jacinto's testimony. Yet, with further information, the credibility issue might have been resolved differently. * * * These matters might have been better resolved if Jacinto had received the necessary information about her right to present her own direct narrative testimony in explanation of her circumstances in Guatemala. * * *

We do not decide the merits of Jacinto's application for asylum. We hold only that Jacinto did not receive a full and fair hearing, that she suffered prejudice, and thus was denied due process. Accordingly, we vacate the Board's decision, and we remand the case to the Board with instructions to remand to the immigration judge for a new hearing consistent with this opinion.[6]

TROTT, CIRCUIT JUDGE, dissenting.

* * * I conclude that [Jacinto] was not denied due process.

Before the hearings, Jacinto received written notice of her rights. Then, on August 24, 1995, *after* her son's right to an attorney was explained, I.J. Martin asked, "Do you understand all that I've said so far, Ms. Jacinto Carillo?" Answer, "Yes." When she said she wished to speak for her son at the initial deportability hearing, the I.J. explained her son's rights—to present evidence in his own behalf, to examine and object to evidence, and to question any witnesses. He asked her, "Do you understand the rights that your son enjoys?" Her answer was, "Yes." At the same hearing, the I.J. told her that she had the same rights as did her son, including the rights to an attorney and to present evidence on her own behalf. He said, "The same thing applies to you. Do you understand?" Her answer was, "Yes." At the end of that hearing, the I.J. again asked, "Do you understand all that I've said?" Her answer was, "Yes, Your Honor."

* * *

NOTES AND QUESTIONS ON
DUE PROCESS AND THE IMMIGRATION JUDGE'S ROLE

1. Why isn't it enough due process for Jacinto that she received written notice of her rights, including the right to have a lawyer represent her, plus a list of attorneys available to do so at little or no cost? Shouldn't she have to live with the consequences of declining representation?

2. The government must pay for translation if the respondent is not capable of understanding the proceedings in English. Courts have held that an incompetent translation deprives a noncitizen of due process when prejudice results. *See, e.g., Amadou v. INS*, 226 F.3d 724, 726–28 (6th Cir.

---

[6] Because Jacinto received representation from counsel on this appeal, we assume on remand that she will have the assistance of an attorney.

2000) (interpreter's faulty translation likely played a significant part in the judge's credibility determination). Current practice is to provide translation only of those questions directed at those who cannot speak English. *See El Rescate Legal Services, Inc. v. EOIR*, 959 F.2d 742, 752 (9th Cir. 1991) (generally approving this practice). *Cf. United States v. Leon-Leon*, 35 F.3d 1428, 1431–32 (9th Cir. 1994) (no prejudice resulted from failure to translate other crucial parts of hearing).

3. Applying *Mathews v. Eldridge*, 424 U.S. 319 (1976), courts have developed an elaborate body of case law that defines constitutional due process in removal proceedings. Many such decisions arise, like *Jacinto*, on immediate, direct review of a removal order. Other rulings arise—as we will see later in this section—when the noncitizen seeks a second chance through a motion to reopen or to reconsider a prior removal order. Still later on, a noncitizen might raise due process as part of a collateral attack on an earlier removal order. *See, e.g., Chacon-Corral v. Weber*, 259 F.Supp.2d 1151, 1160–64 (D. Colo. 2003) (invalidating, because of multiple procedural defects, prior deportation order on which government relied in seeking removal). Also, the government may prosecute a noncitizen for the crime of illegal reentry after removal under INA § 276. One defense to that charge may be that the prior removal proceeding violated due process. The Supreme Court held in *United States v. Mendoza-Lopez*, 481 U.S. 828, 837–38, 107 S.Ct. 2148, 95 L.Ed.2d 772 (1987), that in a criminal reentry prosecution, a collateral attack on the earlier deportation order is allowed when the prior proceeding was fundamentally unfair *and* the respondent was effectively denied the opportunity for meaningful judicial review. Congress essentially codified the standards of *Mendoza-Lopez* in 1996, in INA § 276(d). The circuits apply varying standards in determining whether a flaw in the earlier proceeding (1) prejudiced the noncitizen or (2) prevented meaningful judicial review. For a survey of the case law, see Ira J. Kurzban, *Kurzban's Immigration Law Sourcebook* 310–19 (Am. Immigr. Council 2014).

4. Statutory amendments in 1996 authorized the use of video teleconferencing (VTC) to conduct removal proceedings. INA § 240(b)(2)(A). EOIR employs VTC for immigration cases in all 60 immigration court locations, with 15 jurisdictions accounting for 84% of all VTC hearings in 2012. Ingrid V. Eagly, *Remote Adjudication in Immigration*, 109 Nw. U. L. Rev. 933, 956 (2015). Either the judge and interpreter and ICE attorney are in one location with the respondent and counsel at a remote location, perhaps an ICE detention facility, or the respondent's counsel may be co-located with the immigration judge instead and thus not with her client. A 2015 study found that nearly two-thirds of all detainees attended their immigration hearings by video. *Id.* at 934. Beginning in 2014, DHS has used VTC as a matter of course in its detention of female heads of households. *See* Julia Preston, *Detention Center Presented as Deterrent to Border Crossings*, N.Y. Times, Dec. 16, 2015.

Some proponents see VTC as a welcome efficiency that can reduce immigration court backlogs (and perhaps improve the availability of counsel in remote locations). *See generally* Funmi E. Olorunnipa, Agency Use of Video Hearings: Best Practices and Possibilities for Expansion 25–38 (Administrative Conference of the United States In-House Research Report 2011). Others have identified practical and procedural problems with VTC. One study, utilizing government statistical data on VTC, in-person observation of trials, and interviews, concluded that "televideo conferences were more likely to result in deportation." *See* Eagly, *supra,* at 937. The study found no statistically significant evidence that judges adjudicated VTC cases more harshly. Instead, it attributed the discrepancy to evidence that, compared with in-person cases, detained litigants in VTC cases exhibited reduced levels of engagement in the proceeding, in that they were less likely to obtain counsel, pursue relief, or seek voluntary departure. *Id.* at 937–38 (reporting that "compared with similarly situated detained televideo respondents, detained in-person respondents were a remarkable 90% more likely to apply for relief, 35% more likely to obtain counsel, and 6% more likely to apply only for voluntary departure.").

b.   Right to Counsel

Aliens in removal proceedings "shall have the privilege of being represented, at no expense to the Government, by counsel of the alien's choosing who is authorized to practice in such proceedings." INA § 240(b)(4)(A), *see also id.* § 292. Noncitizens who cannot afford an attorney must be informed of free legal services in the area. *Id.* § 239(b)(2); 8 C.F.R. § 240.10(a)(2). Volunteer lawyers may be hard to find, however, especially for noncitizens detained in remote locations. From FY 2011 through FY 2015, 41–57 percent of noncitizens who appeared in immigration court were unrepresented. Before the BIA, representation is more common, but here too 20–24 percent are unrepresented. *See* Executive Office for Immigration Review, Department of Justice, FY 2015 Statistical Year Book, at F1, T1.

Does the Constitution require the government to provide counsel for indigent noncitizens? The Sixth Amendment's guarantee of appointed counsel explored in *Padilla v. Kentucky, see* Chapter Seven, is unavailable in removal proceedings because they are not criminal proceedings. Any right to appointed counsel in removal proceedings must be found in the Fifth Amendment's Due Process Clause.

Aguilera-Enriquez v. INS, 516 F.2d 565 (1975), decided before *Eldridge*, remains a leading discussion of the constitutional right to counsel in removal proceedings. It addressed two related doctrinal issues: whether there was a constitutional hook for a right to counsel in removal proceedings, and if so how to frame the constitutional analysis.

AGUILERA-ENRIQUEZ V. INS

United States Court of Appeals, Sixth Circuit, 1975.
516 F.2d 565, cert. denied, 423 U.S. 1050, 96 S.Ct. 776, 46 L.Ed.2d 638 (1976).

CELEBREZZE, CIRCUIT JUDGE.

Petitioner, Jesus Aguilera-Enriquez, seeks reversal of a deportation order on the ground that he was constitutionally entitled to but was not afforded the assistance of counsel during his deportation hearing. * * *

[Aguilera-Enriquez, a lawful permanent resident, pleaded guilty to a narcotics charge in April 1972, for which he received a one-year suspended sentence, probation and a fine. Neither his appointed criminal defense counsel nor the sentencing judge informed him that a narcotics conviction would almost certainly lead to his deportation.

Facing a deportability charge based on the drug conviction, he asked the immigration judge to appoint counsel for him. The judge refused on the basis that the statute explicitly precluded appointment of counsel at government expense. Aguilera-Enriquez made no defense to the deportability charge and was ordered removed. He then engaged a legal assistance attorney who argued that an indigent noncitizen has a constitutional right to appointed counsel in a deportation proceeding. He attacked the validity of the statute, which like its current version in INA § 240(b)(4)(A), conferred in deportation proceedings "the privilege of being represented (at no expense to the Government) by such counsel, authorized to practice in such proceedings, as he shall choose."]

The Supreme Court has held that once an alien has been admitted to lawful residence, "not even Congress may expel him without allowing him a fair opportunity to be heard." *Kwong Hai Chew v. Colding*, 344 U.S. 590, 598, 73 S.Ct. 472, 478, 97 L.Ed. 576 (1953). Thus, if procedures mandated by Congress do not provide an alien with procedural due process, they must yield, and the constitutional guarantee of due process must provide adequate protection during the deportation process. *Yamataya v. Fisher* (*The Japanese Immigrant Case*), 189 U.S. 86, 100, 23 S.Ct. 611, 47 L.Ed. 721 (1903).

The test for whether due process requires the appointment of counsel for an indigent alien is whether, in a given case, the assistance of counsel would be necessary to provide "fundamental fairness—the touchstone of due process." *Gagnon v. Scarpelli*, 411 U.S. 778, 790, 93 S.Ct. 1756, 1763, 36 L.Ed.2d 656 (1973).[3]

---

[3] The Supreme Court's holdings in *Gagnon*, *Morrissey v. Brewer*, 408 U.S. 471, 92 S.Ct. 2593, 33 L.Ed.2d 484 (1972), and *In re Gault*, 387 U.S. 1, 87 S.Ct. 1428, 18 L.Ed.2d 527 (1967), have undermined the position that counsel must be provided to indigents only in criminal proceedings. * * * Where an unrepresented indigent alien would require counsel to present his position adequately to an immigration judge, he must be provided with a lawyer at the Government's expense. Otherwise, "fundamental fairness" would be violated.

[Ultimately, however, the court concluded that Aguilera-Enriquez was not entitled to appointed counsel.]

[N]o defense for which a lawyer would have helped the argument was presented to the Immigration Judge for consideration. After the decision of the Immigration Judge, Petitioner moved to withdraw his guilty plea in the Texas District Court under Rule 32(d), F.R. Crim. P. He then urged before the Board of Immigration Appeals that this motion took him outside the reach of section 241(a)(11), because the likelihood of success on that motion meant that he had not been "convicted" of a narcotics offense. He was effectively represented by counsel before the Board, and his argument was considered upon briefing and oral argument. The lack of counsel before the Immigration Judge did not prevent full administrative consideration of his argument. Counsel could have obtained no different administrative result. "Fundamental fairness," therefore, was not abridged during the administrative proceedings, and the order of deportation is not subject to constitutional attack for a lack of due process.

* * *

The petition for review is denied.

DeMascio, District Judge, dissenting.

A deportation proceeding so jeopardizes a resident alien's basic and fundamental right to personal liberty that I cannot agree due process is guaranteed by a "fundamental fairness" analysis on a case-by-case basis. *Gagnon v. Scarpelli*, 411 U.S. 778, 93 S.Ct. 1756, 36 L.Ed.2d 656 (1973). I think a resident alien has an unqualified right to the appointment of counsel. *In re Gault*, 387 U.S. 1, 87 S.Ct. 1428, 18 L.Ed.2d 527 (1967). When the government, with plenary power to exclude, agrees to allow an alien lawful residence, it is unconscionable for the government to unilaterally terminate that agreement without affording an indigent resident alien assistance of appointed counsel. Expulsion is such lasting punishment that meaningful due process can require no less. Assuredly, it inflicts punishment as grave as the institutionalization which may follow an *In re Gault* finding of delinquency. A resident alien's right to due process should not be tempered by a classification of the deportation proceeding as "civil", "criminal", or "administrative." No matter the classification, deportation is punishment, pure and simple.

* * *

In my view, the absence of counsel at respondent's hearing before the immigration judge inherently denied him fundamental fairness. Moreover, I do not believe that we should make the initial determination that counsel is unnecessary; or that lack of counsel did not prevent full administrative consideration of petitioner's argument; or that counsel could not have obtained a different administrative result. We should not speculate at this stage what contentions appointed counsel could have raised before the immigration judge. For example, a lawyer may well have contended that § 241(a)(11) is an unconstitutional deprivation of the equal protection of the laws by arguing that alienage was the sole basis for the infliction of punishment, additional to that imposed by criminal law; that since the government elected to rely upon the criminal law sanctions, it may not now additionally exile petitioner without demonstrating a compelling governmental interest.

I do not intend to imply such a contention has validity. I cite this only to emphasize the danger of attempting to speculate at this stage whether counsel could have obtained a different result and to show that it is possible that the immigration judge did not fully consider all of petitioner's arguments.

Because the consequences of a deportation proceeding parallel punishment for crime, only a per se rule requiring appointment of counsel will assure a resident alien due process of law. In this case, the respondent, a resident alien for seven years, committed a criminal offense. Our laws require that he be punished and he was. Now, he must face additional punishment in the form of banishment. He will be deprived of the life, liberty, and pursuit of happiness he enjoyed by governmental consent.[6] It may be proper that he be compelled to face the consequences of such a proceeding. But, when he does, he should have a lawyer at his side and one at government expense, if necessary. * * *

Appointed Counsel in Civil Cases

Aguilera-Enriquez opened an era of active judicial exploration of the scope of a due process right to appointed counsel. In *Lassiter v. Department of Social Services*, 452 U.S. 18, 101 S.Ct. 2153, 68 L.Ed.2d 640 (1981), the Supreme Court, in a five-to-four decision, rejected the claim that indigent defendants have a right to appointed counsel in a proceeding to terminate their parental status. The Court summarized its prior right to counsel decisions as follows: "The pre-eminent generalization that emerges from this Court's precedents on an indigent's right to appointed counsel is that such a right has been recognized to exist only where the litigant may lose his physical liberty if he loses the litigation." *Lassiter*, 452 U.S. at 25, 101 S.Ct. at 2158. Is removal a loss of physical liberty, or does it simply mean that noncitizens must pursue their liberty in their home countries?

In *Turner v. Rogers*, 564 U.S. 431, 131 S.Ct. 2507, 180 L.Ed.2d 452 (2011), Turner faced imprisonment for up to one year in a civil contempt

---

6   Of course, what I have said applies only to a resident alien. I readily agree that an alien who enters illegally is entitled to less due process, if any at all. It is interesting to note that the Immigration Act seems to treat all aliens alike.

proceeding held to enforce a child support order that Turner had failed to pay. Justice Breyer's opinion for the Court (in another five-to-four decision) surveyed *Lassiter* and other Court precedents, and suggested that loss of physical liberty is a necessary condition for requiring counsel in a civil proceeding, but not always a sufficient condition. The Court vacated Turner's conviction and remanded, but held that alternative safeguards could often satisfy the due process clause in such cases without requiring paid counsel. In applying the *Eldridge* analysis here, one central factor was that the key factual determination, Turner's ability to pay, can be "sufficiently straightforward to warrant determination *prior* to providing a defendant with counsel." 131 S.Ct. at 2519 (emphasis in original). Alternative safeguards, such as explicit warnings and well-designed questioning or forms that elicit relevant financial information, might provide an appropriate substitute, though counsel could conceivably be required based on the specific circumstances.

Is *Turner*'s emphasis on loss of physical liberty and alternative safeguards relevant to the issue of appointed counsel in removal proceedings? Are the issues in typical removal cases also "straightforward" so that alternative safeguards would suffice? Did *Turner* open the door to arguments that some circumstances compelled a right to appointed counsel?

The issue of appointed counsel in removal proceedings arose anew in two class actions: one involving the mentally disabled and other involving children. The first suit was filed in 2010 on behalf of noncitizens held in DHS custody for removal proceedings who suffered from serious mental disabilities that rendered them mentally incompetent to represent themselves.)

FRANCO-GONZALEZ V. HOLDER

United States District Court for the Central District of California, 2013.
2013 WL 3674492, No. 10–02211.

GEE, U.S. DISTRICT JUDGE.

* * * On November 21, 2011, the Court issued an order granting Plaintiffs' motion for class certification * * *. The Court certified the following Class and Sub-Classes:

> All individuals who are or will be in DHS custody for removal proceedings in California, Arizona, and Washington who have been identified by or to medical personnel, DHS, or an Immigration Judge, as having a serious mental disorder or defect that may render them incompetent to represent themselves in detention or removal proceedings, and who presently lack counsel in their detention or removal proceedings.

Sub-Class 1: Individuals in the above-named Plaintiff Class who
have a serious mental disorder or defect that renders them
incompetent to represent themselves in detention or removal
proceedings.

Sub-Class 2: Individuals in the above-named Plaintiff Class who
have been detained for more than six months.

* * *

The [complaint] alleges the following causes of action: (1) right to a
competency evaluation under the INA; (2) right to a competency
evaluation under the Due Process Clause; (3) right to appointed counsel
under the INA; (4) right to appointed counsel under Section 504 of the
Rehabilitation Act, 29 U.S.C. § 794 ("Section 504"); (5) right to appointed
counsel under the Due Process Clause * * * .

* * *

Plaintiffs have distilled [the factual] background into three key facts:
(1) that the Government detains and places into removal proceedings * * *
individuals who are not competent to represent themselves by reason of a
serious mental disorder or defect; (2) the Government imposes on itself no
legal obligation to provide representation for such individuals in their
immigration proceedings; and (3) the Government detains [such
individuals] for more than six months without providing bond hearings in
which it must show by clear and convincing evidence that further
detention is justified. Defendants do not dispute these basic facts.

III.

DISCUSSION

* * *

Plaintiffs first assert that the Rehabilitation Act requires legal
representation as a reasonable accommodation for individuals who are
not competent to represent themselves by virtue of their mental
disabilities. For the reasons discussed below, the Court finds that Section
504 of the Rehabilitation Act does require the appointment of a Qualified
Representative as a reasonable accommodation * * *.

* * *

[The court first concluded that the Plaintiffs had established a *prima
facie* case under the Rehabilitation Act because they had been deprived of
a benefit, namely, "the exercise of rights to present evidence, cross-
examine witnesses, and make legal arguments against the Government's
charges" to which all individuals in immigration proceedings were
entitled. The court found that the plaintiffs were "unable to meaningfully

access the benefit offered—in this case, full participation in their removal and detention proceedings—because of their disability."]

Defendants next argue that, even if Plaintiffs are able to establish a *prima facie* case, legal representation for all mentally incompetent aliens detained for removal proceedings is far beyond a "reasonable accommodation" and amounts to a "fundamental alteration" of the immigration court system, primarily because the Executive Office of Immigration Review ("EOIR") does not have the capacity or funding to implement such a program.

Whether an accommodation is reasonable depends on the individual circumstances of each case and requires a fact-specific, individualized analysis of the individual's circumstances and the accommodations that enable meaningful access to the federal program. * * * Plaintiffs do not seek relief from removal or automatic termination of their proceedings. They seek only the ability to meaningfully participate in the immigration court process, including the rights to "examine the evidence against the alien, to present evidence on the alien's own behalf, and to cross-examine witnesses presented by the Government." INA § 240(b)(4)(B). Plaintiffs' ability to exercise these rights is hindered by their mental incompetency, and the provision of competent representation able to navigate the proceedings is the only means by which they may invoke those rights.

i. The Requested Accommodation Does Not Impose an Undue Financial Burden

* * *

The Court is wary of issuing an unfunded mandate requiring Government-paid counsel for all mentally incompetent class members. Indeed, neither this Order nor the Court's previous preliminary injunction rulings requires Defendants to provide Sub-Class One members with paid legal counsel. Defendants have in the past been able to obtain *pro bono* counsel for certain class members from various non-profit organizations and *pro bono* panels.

Nevertheless, EOIR claims that it has found "relatively scarce capacity among pro bono providers to fill very limited roles." Defendants are not required, however, to provide bar-certified attorneys, as long as the representatives they provide meet the requirements for a Qualified Representative. For example, the regulations allow for representation by law students and law graduates not admitted to the bar and "accredited representatives" who represent qualified non-profit religious, charitable, social service, or similar organizations. 8 C.F.R. §§ 1292.1, 1292.2.7 Defendants fail to address why the provision of these types of Qualified Representatives would not be feasible. * * *

ii. The Requested Accommodation Does Not Contravene the Statutory Framework Governing the Privilege of Counsel

Defendants also argue that the requirement of representation runs counter to the INA, which provides in several provisions that individuals have a "privilege" to obtain representation at no expense to the Government. INA § 240(b)(4)(A), 1362. EOIR asserts its belief that these provisions bar the use of federal funding to provide for direct representation [and] that, "[a]s a result of Section 292, the legal orientation services funded by the [Legal Orientation Program] do not include funds for direct representation * * * .

Yet, writing on behalf of the Office of the General Counsel for the DHS, David P. Martin [*sic*], Principal Deputy General Counsel, confirmed that the plain language of Section 1362 does not lend itself to the interpretation that it "prohibits the provision of counsel at government expense." "[N]othing in INA § 240, 1362] or 5 U.S.C. § 3106 prohibits the use of discretionary federal funding for representation of aliens in immigration proceedings" and "[w]hether any particular expenditure would be permissible . . . depends on a fiscal law analysis of the specific proposed funding source." The Court agrees that these statutes cannot reasonably be interpreted to forbid the appointment of a Qualified Representative to individuals who otherwise lack meaningful access to their rights in immigration proceedings as a result of mental incompetency.

Thus, the proposed accommodation would not contravene any existing statutory prohibition.

iii. The Requested Accommodation Does Not Expand the Scope of Benefits Available to Class Members

Defendants also reiterate their position that Plaintiffs' requested relief would place Sub-Class One members in a significantly better position than nondisabled, detained aliens because providing legal representation "would do much more than remove a barrier to access; it would expand the scope of benefits provided to aliens in immigration court." * * *

* * *

* * * Plaintiffs here seek only to meaningfully participate in their removal proceedings. The opportunity to "examine the evidence against the alien, to present evidence on the alien's own behalf, and to cross-examine witnesses presented by the Government" is available to all individuals in immigration proceedings, but is beyond Plaintiffs' reach as a result of their mental incompetency. INA § 240(b)(4)(B). Thus, the provision of a Qualified Representative is merely the means by which

Plaintiffs may exercise the same benefits as other non-disabled individuals, and not the benefit itself.* * *

* * *

Aspiring to a system that allows the mentally incompetent to similarly participate in the removal proceedings against them is not tantamount to "creating an entirely new system of benefits in immigration." Defendants can hardly argue that it is audacious to require a Qualified Representative for mentally incompetent individuals in immigration proceedings when the INA itself has pronounced that some form of procedural safeguards are required for those who are mentally incompetent. See INA § 240(b)(3). ("If it is impracticable by reason of an alien's mental incompetency for the alien to be present at the proceeding, the Attorney General shall prescribe safeguards to protect the rights and privileges of the alien."). By the same token, the appointment of a Qualified Representative for Sub-Class One members serves only to level the playing field by allowing them to meaningfully access the hearing process. Indeed, the accommodation is just as reasonable as and no more burdensome than EOIR's requirement that interpreters be provided to those who cannot understand English. * * *

* * * [T]he Court finds that providing Sub-Class One members with a Qualified Representative is a reasonable accommodation. Defendants have failed to raise any triable issue of fact in support of their contention that the accommodation poses a fundamental alteration of the immigration court system. * * *

c. Matter of M-A-M- Fails to Provide Sufficient Safeguards

* * *

* * * [Matter of] M-A-M- [, 25 I. & N. Dec. 474 (BIA 2011)] allows Immigration Judges to adopt certain "safeguards" where an alien has been determined incompetent to proceed with the hearing. 25 I&N Dec. at 482. For example, an Immigration Judge may refuse to accept an admission of removability from an incompetent, unrepresented alien; allow the alien's custodian to appear on his behalf; continue proceedings to allow the alien to obtain representation; aid in the development of the record, including cross-examination of witnesses; and allow representation by a family member or close friend. Id. at 483. The majority of these "safeguards," however, are left to the Immigration Judge's discretion, and none guarantee that the incompetent alien may participate in his proceedings as fully as an individual who is not disabled. Id. at 482 (noting that Immigration Judges "have discretion to determine which safeguards are appropriate").

Moreover, while both the regulations and M-A-M- allow for "representation" by a family member or close friend to "assist the respondent and provide the court with information," Defendants offer no safeguard that such individuals are qualified to provide this type of assistance for a mentally incompetent person. *See also* 8 C.F.R. § 1240.4 (allowing for representation by a "legal guardian, near relative, or friend who was served with a copy of the notice to appear," or the respondent's "custodian"). * * *

Accordingly, the Court finds that Plaintiffs are entitled to the reasonable accommodation of appointment of a Qualified Representative to assist them in their removal and detention proceedings * * *.

* * *

Having decided in favor of Plaintiffs on their Rehabilitation Act claim, * * * it is not necessary for the Court to reach the constitutional [due process] dimensions of their request for relief * * *.

Would it matter if the noncitizens in proceedings were children? In *Perez-Funez v. District Director*, 619 F.Supp. 656, 664–65 (C.D. Cal. 1985), the court struck down, on due process grounds, voluntary departure procedures as applied to unaccompanied minors. Given their "limited understanding and decision-making ability," as well as "the critical importance of the decisions, and the inherently coercive nature" of the proceedings, the court asserted that "legal counsel certainly would be the best insurance against a deprivation of rights." But the court stopped short of holding that unaccompanied minors have a right to appointed counsel, instead noting that an alternative would be "to have children contact a parent, close adult relative, or adult friend who can put the child on a more equal footing" with immigration authorities.

The volume of juvenile cases in immigration courts has expanded from 6,438 in 2011, to a peak of 56,212 in 2014, dropping to just over 30,000 in 2015. Transactional Records Access Clearinghouse (TRAC), Syracuse University, *Juveniles—Immigration Court Deportation Proceedings*, http://trac.syr.edu/phptools/immigration/juvenile.

J.E.F.M. v. HOLDER

United States District Court for the Western District of Washington, 2015.
107 F.Supp.3d 1119.

ZILLY, U.S. DISTRICT JUDGE.

* * *

In this action, nine juveniles ranging in age from 3 to 17, on behalf of themselves and others similarly situated, assert both a statutory and a constitutional claim that they are entitled to have attorneys appointed to represent them at government expense in connection with their removal proceedings. They assert the statutory claim under § 240 of the [INA] and they bring the constitutional claim under the Due Process Clause of the Fifth Amendment. As to five of the nine plaintiffs, three of whom are siblings, removal proceedings are ongoing. As to the other four plaintiffs, however, removal proceedings are not currently pending.

* * *

* * * An alien * * * has the statutory "privilege of being represented, at no expense to the Government, by counsel of the alien's choosing" in both "removal proceedings before an immigration judge" and "appeal proceedings before the Attorney General." INA §§ 240(b)(4)(A) & 292. In this case, plaintiffs contend that, because they are unable to retain counsel, for either financial or other reasons, they cannot exercise their statutory right to present evidence and cross-examine witnesses and are being denied their constitutional right to due process of law.

Discussion

Defendants move to dismiss * * * for failure to state a claim. * * *

* * *

B. Failure to State a Claim

* * *

Historically, right-to-counsel claims under the Due Process Clause of the Fifth Amendment in the immigration context were analyzed under a two-part standard: (i) whether the proceedings were rendered "fundamentally unfair," and (ii) whether the alien was thereby prejudiced. * * * The procedural postures of previous right-to-counsel cases, however, differ from that of the one before the Court. Those cases all involved either direct review of a removal or other BIA order or collateral attack of a removal order being used as evidence in a prosecution for illegal reentry.

* * * *Mathews [v. Eldridge]* sets forth the appropriate test. * * * At oral argument, counsel for defendants seemed to suggest that *Mathews* would apply with respect to "deportable" aliens, but not as to "inadmissible" aliens. Defendants, however, have cited no authority to support the proposition that such distinction can now be drawn, in the context of analyzing what process is due to such individuals, in light of IIRIRA's merger of matters involving inadmissible and deportable aliens into one proceeding known as "removal." The Court is satisfied that plaintiffs' due process right-to-counsel claim requires a weighing of the three factors articulated in *Mathews,* namely, the nature of plaintiffs' interest, the risk of erroneous deprivation, and the fiscal or administrative burdens on the government associated with additional or substitute safeguards. *See* 424 U.S. at 335, 96 S.Ct. 893; *see also Turner v. Rogers,* 564 U.S. 431, 131 S.Ct. 2507, 2517–18, 180 L.Ed.2d 452 (2011).

* * *

In *Turner,* the Supreme Court left open the issue of whether, when the government has "counsel or some other competent representative" in the proceeding, the individual involved is owed more process than the privilege of retaining an attorney. * * * The *Turner* Court similarly reserved ruling on "what due process requires in an unusually complex case" when the individual "can fairly be represented only by a trained advocate." *Id.* The right-to-counsel claim asserted by plaintiffs in this case falls squarely within the intersection of the questions unanswered in *Turner.* The removal proceedings at issue in this case pit juveniles against the full force of the federal government—the government initiates the proceedings, it is represented in them, and its discretion in executing removal orders is insulated from judicial review. Moreover, courts have repeatedly recognized "[w]ith only a small degree of hyperbole" that the immigration laws are "second only to the Internal Revenue Code in complexity." *Baltazar-Alcazar v. INS,* 386 F.3d 940, 948 (9th Cir. 2004). With this perspective in mind, the Court turns to the *Mathews* factors.

1. *First Mathews Factor: Nature of Interest*

In their motion to dismiss, defendants contend that the requisite liberty interest is not at stake, stating that "deportation is not punishment." * * *

In discounting the nature of plaintiffs' interest, defendants rely on *Turner,* in which the Supreme Court observed that, in the civil context, incarceration has been deemed a necessary, but not sufficient, prerequisite to finding a right to counsel under the Due Process Clause. Defendants, however, cite no authority for the proposition that the Court must focus on the "administrative act" of removal itself, and ignore the potential effect of removal, which might be the same or worse than incarceration for some minor aliens. Thus, for purposes of ruling on defendants' motion to dismiss, the allegations in the Second Amended Complaint, which the Court must accept as true, support the likely consequences of plaintiffs returning to their homelands.

2. *Second Mathews Factor: Risk of Erroneous Deprivation*

Defendants offer three reasons why plaintiffs cannot establish the requisite risk of erroneous deprivation: (i) the risk of error in removal decisions is the same for juveniles as it is for adults; (ii) children already receive additional process designed to reduce the risk of erroneous removal decisions; and (iii) the availability of appellate and judicial review is a sufficient substitute for the assistance of counsel in removal proceedings. The first two arguments require evidentiary support and are not properly before the Court on a Rule 12(b)(6) motion.[26] The third contention runs contrary to common sense. Under this theory, counsel would be unnecessary even in a criminal proceeding because the accused, if convicted, could always appeal. Moreover, the argument ignores the fact that review is generally limited to the administrative record, *see* INA § 242(b)(4)(A), and that the absence of counsel in the underlying proceeding is likely to affect the shape and scope of such record. The Court also observes that, despite the safeguards touted by defendants, at least one named plaintiff, J.E.V.G., was improperly ordered removed in absentia. Defendants' concession in this regard supports a "plausible" claim that the current procedures available to juveniles are not an adequate substitute for the appointment of counsel at government expense. Whether plaintiffs can ultimately prevail on this issue is a question for another day.

3. *Third Mathews Factor: Fiscal and Administrative Burdens*

Although plaintiffs' right-to-counsel claim poses significant questions about feasibility and cost, the Court cannot resolve those issues in the context of defendants' Rule 12(b)(6) motion. The parties have not indicated either the percentage of cases involving unaccompanied minors or the percentage of cases in which an attorney was retained, secured from a pro bono panel, or provided under either HHS's or the justice AmeriCorps program. Moreover, no estimates have been provided concerning either the amount of funding necessary to appoint counsel for each juvenile desiring an attorney but lacking the means to retain one[28]

---

[26] In addition, defendants' assertion of equivalent risk among minors and adults is inconsistent with their representation that special treatment is afforded to children in removal proceedings. If the risk was in fact comparable for the two populations, then presumably no additional procedural protections would exist for juveniles. Youth, however, generally correlates with a lack of proficiency in reading and comprehension, even in a native language. For those whose school-age years were stained by violence, poverty, parental neglect, or similar hardships, literacy might be an as-yet unachieved goal. * * * Moreover, even assuming children receive hearing notices and grasp their meaning, they might lack the ability to travel to and attend such hearings * * *. Finally, even when juveniles successfully navigate themselves to removal proceedings, age might still play a role in increasing their risk of receiving an erroneous ruling. The question that must be addressed in this case is whether the appointment of counsel at government expense is the only effective means of reducing the risk of erroneous removal decisions for minors. Defendants' contention that the special rules governing "juvenile dockets" serve as an effective substitute for the appointment of counsel currently lacks statistical support. In opposing plaintiffs' earlier motion for a preliminary injunction, defendants cited a report indicating that, in the first half of 2014, 42% of children having no attorney were permitted to remain in the United States. * * * The same report, however, revealed that, over the same period, juveniles having counsel received a favorable ruling 66% of the time. * * * When the statistics for the years 2005 through 2014 are considered, the gap is even wider, *i.e.,* 10% versus 47% success rates for unrepresented and represented juveniles, respectively. * * *

[28] The TVPRA requires the Secretary of HHS to "ensure, to the greatest extent practicable and consistent with" INA § 292 that all unaccompanied minors "have counsel to represent them in legal proceedings or matters and protect them from mistreatment, exploitation, and trafficking." INA § 235(c)(5). Defendants represent that $9 million has been allocated to perform this mandate and provide attorneys to 2,600 unaccompanied minors. Defendants have also indicated that, in the fall of 2014, the Department of Justice and the Corporation for National and Community Service implemented a program known as "justice AmeriCorps," which will

or the financial burden that might be associated with less expansive schemes.

Rather than attempting to quantify the financial and administrative burdens associated with plaintiffs' requested relief or possible alternatives, defendants speak broadly in "slippery slope" terms. They express concern about the wheels of removal proceedings involving minors grinding to a halt if the government is required to provide counsel for every juvenile in a removal proceeding. Defendants assert that the effect of a ruling favorable to plaintiffs would be to encourage even more youngsters to journey illegally to the United States. They also seem to fear that the Court will inadvertently create a loophole through which parents, guardians, or other adult aliens might receive the services of an appointed attorney. * * * Although the financial constraints and border-policing concerns raised by defendants must play a role in any analysis concerning plaintiffs' assertion of a right to appointed counsel under the Due Process Clause of the Fifth Amendment, at this juncture, they are not sufficiently quantified or developed to allow the Court to engage in the balancing required by *Mathews*.

NOTES AND QUESTIONS ABOUT THE RIGHT TO COUNSEL

1.   In *Franco*, in addition to the injunction, the court ordered screening and competency hearings to identify class members eligible for representation and appointed an independent monitor to oversee the implementation. *Franco-Gonzalez v. Holder,* 2014 WL 5475097, at 1 (Oct. 29, 2014). In 2015, the case settled with an agreement that permitted class members to move to reopen final removal orders. In addition to reopening the cases, the federal government agreed to "take reasonable steps to facilitate the [qualifying noncitizen's] prompt return to the United States." *See* Agreement Regarding Procedures for Notifying and Reopening Cases of *Franco* Class Members Who Have Received Final Orders of Removal, at 17, 23 (Feb. 24, 2015).

2.   Are these class actions, which require fashioning class-wide relief, consistent with *Aguilera-Enriquez*, which took a case-by-case approach to right to counsel? Some older juveniles, for example, may represent themselves as well as some adults, who will not have the benefit of appointed counsel. Also, the majority in *Aguilera-Enriquez* reasoned that some cases are straightforward, leaving little for counsel to do.

   a.   Does your analysis change when cost considerations come into play? Or the availability of sufficient qualified representatives? As discussed above, nearly 60,000 children were in immigration

---

enroll approximately 100 lawyers and paralegals to provide services to "certain children who have crossed the U.S. Border without a parent or legal guardian." * * * Defendants have offered no projections concerning the anticipated number of indigent juveniles who are not eligible for either the HHS or justice AmeriCorps program or the amount needed to provide attorneys to all such youngsters.

court in 2014 and over 30,000 more juvenile cases were filed in 2015.

b.   In light of these considerations, should the courts have deferred to the agency? The BIA issued a precedent decision in a case involving alleged mental incompetency (discussed in *Franco*). After specifically outlining the procedures and standards to be used in assessing such claims, the decision noted that safeguards are required by statute when the respondent is incompetent. INA § 240(b)(3). The ruling discussed the various safeguards available, including those specified in statute or regulation, and then remanded the case to the immigration judge for further proceedings. Among the safeguards are the appearance of a friend, custodian, or attorney on behalf of the noncitizen, but the decision does not expressly mention the possibility of appointed counsel. *Matter of M-A-M-,* 25 I & N Dec. 474 (BIA 2011).

3.   Alternative sources of representation are center stage in *Franco* and *J.E.F.M.* in determining the scope of a right to appointed counsel. Consider these factors:

a.   The statute requires that everyone placed into removal proceedings shall receive a list, updated at least quarterly, of persons in the area who are available to represent aliens on a pro bono basis. INA § 239(b)(2). This section codifies a practice developed administratively several decades ago to address the representation issue. *See also* 8 C.F.R. § 1240.10(a)(2),   (3). Immigration judges regularly grant continuances, sometimes multiple continuances, to enable a noncitizen to find pro bono counsel willing to take his or her case. The regulations also permit representation in immigration court by EOIR-accredited representatives who are not attorneys, and under certain circumstances by "reputable individuals." *Id.,* § 1292.1, 1292.2.

b.   Law students and law graduates not yet admitted to practice may represent noncitizens before federal agencies in immigration matters under certain circumstances and with permission of the official before whom they wish to appear. *See* 8 C.F.R. §§ 292.1(a)(2), 1292.1(a)(2). Law students must be directly supervised by a faculty member, attorney, or accredited representative in a legal aid program or clinic conducted by a law school or non-profit organization. Law graduates (who are not yet admitted to the bar) must appear under the supervision of an attorney or accredited representative. Law students and law graduates must appear without direct or indirect remuneration from the noncitizen whom they represent.

c.   Since 1983, the federally funded Legal Services Corporation (LSC) generally may not fund any person or entity providing legal assistance—even using non-LSC funds—to noncitizens who are not permanent residents, immediate relatives of U.S. citizens who have applied for adjustment of status, noncitizens granted refugee status or asylum, or noncitizens granted withholding of removal under INA § 241(b)(3). An exception allows entities receiving LSC funds to use non-LSC funds for legal assistance to noncitizen victims of domestic abuse. *See* 45 C.F.R. §§ 1626.4, 1626.5. Would expanded availability of LSC funds be a meaningful alternative to appointed counsel?

d. Since 2003, the Legal Orientation Program of the Executive Office for Immigration Review has funded pre-hearing "legal orientation presentations" by private non-profit agencies to all detainees in certain facilities, in cooperation with federal immigration officials. *See* Vera Institute, Improving Efficiency and Promoting Justice in the Immigration System: Lessons from the Legal Orientation Program (2008). Many detainees then choose not to contest removal, and their cases are usually completed that day at a master calendar hearing before the immigration judge. Others are then ordinarily able to meet privately after the presentation with lawyers or paralegals from the organization to discuss the case or at least provide information that may help line up appropriate pro bono representation. With this further advice, some choose not to contest, while others are given written materials and counseling that will help them to pursue their claims themselves, and still others may obtain full pro bono representation. As of October 2014, EOIR was funding LOP programs at 32 detention sites around the country,[23] servicing 60,000 detainees that year. *See* U.S. Dept. of Justice, EOIR Expands Legal Orientation Program Sites (Oct. 22, 2014), https://www.justice.gov/eoir/pr/eoir-expands-legal-orientation-program-sites.

e. Under the Equal Access to Justice Act (EAJA), 5 U.S.C. § 504, a "prevailing party" in an "adversary adjudication" against the government is entitled to recover attorneys' fees if the government's position was "not substantially justified." EAJA does not apply to deportation hearings, according to the Supreme Court in *Ardestani v. INS*, 502 U.S. 129, 112 S.Ct. 515, 116 L.Ed.2d 496 (1991). The Court reasoned that a deportation hearing is not an "adversary adjudication" for EAJA purposes, even though it is identical in key respects to administrative hearings that are. Attorneys' fees may be available under EAJA for successful review of removal orders in federal court, and for certain other sorts of

---

[23] This includes the Artesia family detention center that closed in November of 2014. *See* Dept. of Homeland Security, U.S. Immigration and Customs Enforcement, "ICE's New Family Detention Center in Dilley, Texas to Open in December," News Release (Nov. 17, 2014) (https://www.ice.gov/news/releases/ices-new-family-detention-center-dilley-texas-open-december) (". . . ICE is transitioning out of the temporary family residential facility at the Federal Law Enforcement Training Campus (FLETC) in Artesia, New Mexico, and returning this facility full time to FLETC operations during the month of December.").

court challenges to immigration decisions or practices. Would allowing EAJA fees in removal proceedings be a sound alternative to appointed counsel?

4.   A study conducted from 2007 to 2012 found that represented, non-detained noncitizens obtained relief in 60 percent of their cases, in contrast to 17 percent of non-detained noncitizens who were unrepresented. Represented detainees received relief in 21 percent of their cases, compared to 2 percent for unrepresented detainees. *Id.* at 9. *See* Ingrid V. Eagly & Steven Shafer, *A National Study of Access to Counsel in Immigration Court*, 164 U. Penn. L. Rev. 1, 9 (2015). The difference in approval rates was even greater between represented and unrepresented asylum applicants—a result echoed in several other studies over the past decade. (The disparity between represented and unrepresented cases may not be surprising, given that many respondents must rely on counsel willing to serve on a pro bono basis, and pro bono attorneys typically interview prospective clients carefully so as to focus their limited resources on cases they believe to be meritorious.) *See* U.S. Gov't Accountability Office, *U.S. Asylum System: Significant Variation Existed in Asylum Outcomes across Immigration Courts and Judges* 30 (2008). *See also* Eagly & Shafer, *supra,* at 29 (finding that only 4 percent of pro se removal respondents even applied for asylum).

Several studies have offered their own suggestions for reforms that would improve representation. *See, e.g.,* American Bar Association Commission on Immigration, Reforming the Immigration System: Proposals to Promote Independence, Fairness, Efficiency, and Professionalism in the Adjudication of Removal Cases, chap. 5 (2010); Robert A. Katzmann, *The Legal Profession and the Unmet Needs of the Immigrant Poor*, 21 Geo. J. Legal Ethics 3 (2008). The groundbreaking New York Immigrant Representation Study, launched by Judge Robert A. Katzmann of the U.S. Court of Appeals for the Second Circuit, advocated for an "integrated, citywide removal-defense system influenced by other, existing indigent defense systems (juvenile, criminal, family court)" so as to provide indigent immigrants comprehensive legal representation. *See Accessing Justice—The Availability and Adequacy of Counsel in Immigration Proceedings, New York Immigrant Representation Study* 1, 37 (2011). This resulted in the New York City Council funding the New York Immigrant Family Unity Project, the first universal, government funded public defense system that provides legal services for indigent immigrants facing deportation. *See* VERA Institute of Justice, "New York Immigrant Family Unity Project," http://www.vera.org/project/new-york-immigrant-family-unity-project. *See also* Kirk Semple, *New Help for Poor Immigrants Who Are in Custody and Facing Deportation,* N.Y. Times, Nov. 6, 2013; The Bronx Defenders, "New York Immigrant Family Unity Project," http://www.bronxdefenders.org/programs/new-york-immigrant-family-unity-project/ (announcing that the New York City Council granted funding for the project to continue for FY 2014).

5.   Today, counsel's failure to advise Aguilera of the deportation consequences of his guilty plea to the cocaine charge would raise serious

questions under *Padilla v. Kentucky,* 559 U.S. 356, 130 S.Ct. 1473, 176 L.Ed.2d 284 (2010), discussed in Chapter Seven. Those questions would be litigated initially in the context of a challenge to the criminal conviction. Does the potential *Padilla* remedy reduce or enhance the claim to counsel in a removal proceeding of this type?

EXERCISE

You work for a member of Congress who wants to make appointed counsel available in removal proceedings, but is concerned about the cost of appointing counsel for every indigent noncitizen. Your assignment is to redraft INA § 240(b)(4)(A) and § 292 to provide appointed counsel for some indigent noncitizens in some cases, and write a memorandum explaining your policy and drafting decisions. If there is additional information that you would like to have before finalizing your recommendation, describe the needed information. Would other changes to the INA be needed to implement your recommendation?

---

c.   Evidentiary Rules

As with most administrative proceedings, the formal rules of evidence do not apply in removal hearings. Hearsay and unauthenticated documents may be admitted if the immigration judge deems them material and relevant. *See* 8 C.F.R. § 1240.7(a), *N.L.A. v. Holder,* 744 F. 3d 425, 436 (7th Cir. 2014). However, courts have ordered the exclusion of evidence if its admission would be unfair, or set aside a removal order based on unauthenticated documents. *See, e.g., Pouhova v. Holder,* 726 F.3d 1007, 1012 (7th Cir. 2013) (finding due process violation where the only evidence supporting removal was statement taken in English without interpreter and report written seven years later); *Cinapian v. Holder,* 567 F.3d 1067, 1075 (9th Cir. 2009) (denial of fair hearing when government failed to disclose report in advance of hearing or make its author available for cross-examination). Why aren't removal hearings subject to the Federal Rules of Evidence? Should they be?

(i) Burden of Proof, Silence, and Adverse Inferences

In a removal proceeding, who has the burden of proof; *i.e.,* who must prove what, and to what degree of likelihood or certainty? When Congress in 1996 created a unified removal proceeding governing both allegedly inadmissible and deportable noncitizens, the statute spelled out by issue some of the allocation of the burden and also the relevant standard of proof. INA § 240(c). On certain other issues, these questions are answered by the regulations or by case law.

Because the immigration laws do not apply to citizens, the government initially bears the burden of proof on the threshold issue of whether an individual is in fact a noncitizen. The regulations provide: "In the case of a respondent charged as being in the United States without being admitted or paroled, the Service must first establish the alienage of the respondent." 8 C.F.R. § 1240.8(c). If the individual is an alien, she must establish either "by clear and convincing evidence" that she is "lawfully present in the United States pursuant to a prior admission" or that she "is clearly and beyond doubt entitled to be admitted and is not inadmissible under section 212." INA § 240(c)(2). If the noncitizen has been admitted, the government then has the burden to establish deportability "by clear and convincing evidence." INA § 240(c)(3)(A). In some cases, it can matter a great deal who has the burden of proof on key issues. But often there is no real contest over alienage or whether the person had been admitted. Moreover in the majority of contested cases, the noncitizen concedes removability, and the hearing focuses instead on relief from removal, where the noncitizen has the burden. INA § 240(c)(4).

Noncitizens have a Fifth Amendment right to refuse to provide answers in a removal hearing that could be used against them in a criminal proceeding. Note that unlawful entry is not just a ground for removal but a potential criminal offense as well, *see* INA §§ 275, 276. The Board of Immigration Appeals has held that when the government introduces no evidence at all, the noncitizen's silence is insufficient by itself to meet the government's burden to show deportability by clear, unequivocal, and convincing evidence. *See Matter of Guevara*, 20 I & N Dec. 238 (BIA 1991).

The situation is different, however, once the government introduces evidence of, for example, alienage or the circumstances of entry. Then silence may leave the noncitizen open to adverse inferences. *See United States ex rel. Bilokumsky v. Tod*, 263 U.S. 149, 153–54, 44 S.Ct. 54, 55–56, 68 L.Ed. 221 (1923): "Conduct which forms a basis for inference is evidence. Silence is often evidence of the most persuasive character. * * * [T]here is no rule of law which prohibits officers charged with the administration of the immigration law from drawing an inference from the silence of one who is called upon to speak." Similarly, the Court in *Baxter v. Palmigiano*, 425 U.S. 308, 316–20, 96 S.Ct. 1551, 1557–59, 47 L.Ed.2d 810 (1976), allowed the drawing of an adverse inference from a prisoner's silence after invocation of the Fifth Amendment in a prison disciplinary proceeding, on the basis that the privilege applies only "in a criminal case." *See also INS v. Lopez-Mendoza*, 468 U.S. 1032, 1044, 104 S.Ct. 3479, 3486, 82 L.Ed.2d 778 (1984) (holding that the exclusionary rule does not apply to civil deportation proceedings; the case is discussed in Chapter 10, Section B, *supra*). *See generally* Daniel Kanstroom, *Hello Darkness: Involuntary Testimony and Silence as Evidence in Deportation Proceedings*, 4 Geo. Immigr. L.J. 599 (1990) (analyzing "the complex relationship between the fifth amendment self-incrimination clause and civil deportation proceedings").

(ii) Standard of Proof

Under INA § 240(c)(3)(A), the government must show deportability by "clear and convincing evidence." To understand the rationale for this standard, it may be useful to consider the reasoning used by the Supreme Court in establishing the practically indistinguishable "clear, unequivocal, and convincing evidence" standard for deportability under the pre-1996 statute, which did not itself specify a standard of proof.

> The petitioners urge that the appropriate burden of proof in deportation proceedings should be that which the law imposes in criminal cases—the duty of proving the essential facts beyond a reasonable doubt. The Government, on the other hand, points out that a deportation proceeding is not a criminal case, and that the appropriate burden of proof should consequently be the one generally imposed in civil cases and administrative proceedings—the duty of prevailing by a mere preponderance of the evidence.

> To be sure, a deportation proceeding is not a criminal prosecution. *Harisiades v. Shaughnessy*, 342 U.S. 580, 72 S.Ct. 512, 96 L.Ed. 586. But it does not syllogistically follow that a person may be banished from this country upon no higher degree of proof than applies in a negligence case. This Court has not closed its eyes to the drastic deprivations that may follow when a resident of this country is compelled by our Government to forsake all the bonds formed here and go to a foreign land where he often has no contemporary identification. * * *

> In denaturalization cases the Court has required the Government to establish its allegations by clear, unequivocal, and convincing evidence. The same burden has been imposed in expatriation cases. That standard of proof is no stranger to the civil law.

> No less a burden of proof is appropriate in deportation proceedings. The immediate hardship of deportation is often greater than that inflicted by denaturalization, which does not, immediately at least, result in expulsion from our shores. And many resident aliens have lived in this country longer and established stronger family, social, and economic ties here than some who have become naturalized citizens.

> We hold that no deportation order may be entered unless it is found by clear, unequivocal, and convincing evidence that the facts alleged as grounds for deportation are true. * * *

Woodby v. INS, 385 U.S. 276, 284–86, 87 S.Ct. 483, 487–88, 17 L.Ed.2d 362 (1966).

Looking more broadly at the standard of proof, it is important to recognize that opting for a heightened standard does more than simply ensure that fewer noncitizens are wrongfully removed. It also means that more noncitizens who should be removed will not be removed, because the government will not be able to meet the higher standard. Justice Harlan, addressing the constitutionally required standard of proof in a juvenile delinquency determination, explained this trade-off as follows:

> In a lawsuit between two parties, a factual error can make a difference in one of two ways. First, it can result in a judgment in favor of the plaintiff when the true facts warrant a judgment for the defendant. The analogue in a criminal case would be the conviction of an innocent man. On the other hand, an erroneous factual determination can result in a judgment for the defendant when the true facts justify a judgment in plaintiff's favor. The criminal analogue would be the acquittal of a guilty man.

> The standard of proof influences the relative frequency of these two types of erroneous outcomes. If, for example, the standard of proof for a criminal trial were a preponderance of the evidence rather than proof beyond a reasonable doubt, there would be a smaller risk of factual errors that result in freeing guilty persons, but a far greater risk of factual errors that result in convicting the innocent. Because the standard of proof affects the comparative frequency of these two types of erroneous outcomes, the choice of the standard to be applied in a particular kind of litigation should, in a rational world, reflect an assessment of the comparative social disutility of each.

In re Winship, 397 U.S. 358, 370–71, 90 S.Ct. 1068, 1075–76, 25 L.Ed.2d 368 (1970) (Harlan, J., concurring).

NOTES AND QUESTIONS ON STANDARDS OF PROOF AND OTHER PROCEDURAL PROTECTIONS

1.   How would you allocate the risk of error in removal? Making a reasonable decision requires you to consider at least these issues:

(a)   by how much will wrongful non-removals increase by imposing a higher standard of proof on the government?

(b)   how do you (or the American public, or Congress) value a wrongful removal as compared to a wrongful non-removal?

(c)   how might other procedural protections—such as appointed counsel—affect the error rate?

Does it matter what the reason for removal is? Does it matter whether the respondent is a lawful permanent resident as opposed to a nonimmigrant or someone who was never admitted? What role do the stakes for the individual play in your determination? How should one assess those stakes?

2. How are the immigration judge's role (*see Jacinto*), the right to counsel (*see Aguilera-Enriquez*), the burden of proof, and the standard of proof all related to each other? For example, does a demanding standard of proof compensate for the absence of appointed counsel? If you were a noncitizen in removal proceedings, which procedural protections would you find more important? Which would you find less important?

3. A SECOND CHANCE?

a. Introduction

So far we have examined what happens from the NTA to a final removal order and the major procedural issues that arise along the way. Is there any chance to revisit what happened in the proceeding and correct errors? Of course, direct appeal is available, first to the Board of Immigration and Appeals and then in most circumstances to a federal court of appeals. But in a surprisingly large number of cases (though still a modest percentage), a noncitizen finds good reason to present new evidence or argument after losing on direct appeal or after the appeal time has already run. Often this new material is associated with obtaining new counsel—or obtaining counsel for the first time—perhaps shortly before the date when removal is scheduled.

Noncitizens board an ICE removal flight
from Buffalo, New York, to Liberia, Ghana, and Nigeria, August 2007.
(Photo: Department of Homeland Security)

To fill out our picture of removal proceedings, two cases from the courts of appeals, *Saakian* and *Anin*, raise three linked issues: (1) *in absentia* removal orders, (2) ineffective assistance of counsel, and (3) motions to reopen. These issues may seem analytically distinct from each other, but they often arise together, and they share this fundamental question: what is the best balance between the need for finality in immigration court decisions and the need for confidence that those decisions are accurate?

Before reading the two cases, take a look at the general statutory provisions governing motions to reopen or to reconsider, INA §§ 240(c)(6) and (7). The statute and the regulations provide the following basic framework for these motions. (There are additional and specialized rules governing several details of motions to reopen in order to challenge an *in absentia* removal order; those details are addressed in the *Saakian* and *Anin* decisions below, and in the notes following those cases.) Motions to reopen are used to offer previously unavailable, material evidence; here INA § 240(c)(7) and 8 C.F.R. § 1003.2 govern. A motion to reconsider is different; it asks for review of claimed errors in an earlier appraisal of the law or the facts. *See* INA § 240(c)(6). These motions are to be filed with either the immigration judge or the BIA—whichever adjudicating body last considered the case. Filing a motion to reopen or reconsider does not automatically stay the execution of a removal order (unless it is a motion to reopen an *in absentia* order). But immigration judges, the BIA, and certain DHS officers have discretion to stay removal pending a decision. 8 C.F.R. §§ 241.6, 1003.2(f), 1003.23(b)(1)(v).

Generally, only one motion to reopen and one motion to reconsider may be filed. A motion to reconsider must be filed within 30 days and a motion to reopen within 90 days of entry of a final removal order. The statute sets out exceptions to the 90-day deadline, primarily for battered spouses, changed circumstances affecting an asylum claim, and challenges to *in absentia* removal orders. INA § 240(c)(7)(C). Importantly, the statute's numerical and time limits apply only to motions filed by the noncitizen, not DHS. Therefore respondent's counsel seeking to file a belated motion often seeks to persuade the ICE attorney that a gross mistake was made, and that ICE should therefore agree to file a joint motion to reopen, which would obviate any late filing problem. In addition, the Board or immigration judge may at any time reopen *sua sponte,* though this power is to be used in "exceptional situations," and not "as a general cure for filing defects or to otherwise circumvent the regulations, where enforcing them might result in hardship." *Matter of J-J-,* 21 I & N Dec. 976, 984 (1997). *See* 8 C.F.R. §§ 1003.2(a), 1003.23(b)(1). Judicial review of a motion to reopen must be consolidated with review of the underlying order. INA § 242(b)(6).

In *INS v. Abudu*, 485 U.S. 94, 108 S.Ct. 904, 99 L.Ed.2d 90 (1988), the U.S. Supreme Court discussed the standards for judicial review of decisions to grant or deny a motion to reopen. *See also Reyes Mata v. Lynch*, 135 S.Ct. 2150, 192 L.Ed.2d 225 (2015) (holding that the courts of appeal retain jurisdiction to review BIA decisions to grant or deny a motion to reopen). Abudu, a citizen of Ghana, had overstayed his student visa. After he pleaded guilty to drug charges in 1981, Abudu was ordered deported in 1982, and in 1984 the BIA dismissed his appeal. In 1985, Abudu moved to reopen so that he could apply for asylum, seeking to introduce new facts that he believed would show his life and freedom would be threatened if he returned to Ghana. In upholding the BIA's denial of Abudu's motion, the Court explained:

> There are at least three independent grounds on which the BIA may deny a motion to reopen. First, it may hold that the movant has not established a *prima facie* case for the underlying substantive relief sought. * * * . Second, the BIA may hold that the movant has not introduced previously unavailable, material evidence, or, in an asylum application case, that the movant has not reasonably explained his failure to apply for asylum initially. * * * We decide today that the appropriate standard of review of such denials is abuse of discretion.[b] Third, in cases in which the ultimate grant of relief is discretionary, * * * the BIA may leap ahead, as it were, over the two threshold concerns (prima facie case and new evidence/reasonable explanation), and simply determine that even if they were met, the movant would not be entitled to the discretionary grant of relief. We have consistently held that denials on this third ground are subject to an abuse-of-discretion standard.

485 U.S. at 104–05, 108 S.Ct. at 912.

The Court also made clear that at this late stage the noncitizen did not enjoy a presumption that the facts as alleged were true:

> We have never suggested that all ambiguities in the factual averments must be resolved in the movant's favor [as the lower court had ruled], and we have never analogized such a motion to a motion for summary judgment. The appropriate analogy is a motion for a new trial in a criminal case on the basis of newly discovered evidence, as to which courts have uniformly held that the moving party bears a heavy burden.

Id. at 109–10.

---

[b] Abuse of discretion is a standard of review that is generally highly deferential to the administrative determination. We will consider standards for judicial review in Section C of this chapter.—eds.

SAAKIAN V. INS

United States Court of Appeals, First Circuit, 2001.
252 F.3d 21.

STAHL, SENIOR CIRCUIT JUDGE.

* * *

I.   BACKGROUND

Saakian, a native and citizen of Armenia, entered the United States on November 13, 1993, as a non-immigrant visitor for pleasure. He was accompanied by his father and stepmother. The family's visas authorized them to remain in the United States until May 12, 1994. On January 12, 1994, Saakian's father applied for asylum on behalf of the three of them. The record is silent as to the disposition of this application.

On June 26, 1996, Saakian filed his own individual request for asylum, about which he was interviewed by the Immigration and Naturalization Service (INS) on September 17, 1996. His request was denied on September 30, 1996, and an Order to Show Cause issued, stating that Saakian was deportable because he had stayed in the United States beyond the time allowed by his visa. This Order was served on Saakian on October 16, 1996, and it directed him to appear before an IJ on November 20, 1996. When Saakian appeared on that date, he was told to return for a full hearing on March 19, 1997.

Saakian thereafter retained Connie Frentzos, of the Khmer Humanitarian Organization in Los Angeles, to represent him in the proceeding. Frentzos is not an attorney, though Saakian alleges that he believed that she was one at the time he retained her. Despite her non-attorney status, Frentzos is authorized by the Executive Office for Immigration Review to represent aliens in deportation proceedings. On March 4, 1997, Frentzos filed a motion to change venue from Boston to Los Angeles because Saakian intended to relocate there. According to Saakian, Frentzos thereafter advised him that the motion rendered it unnecessary for him to appear at the March 19 hearing. Saakian, allegedly acting on this advice, did not appear at the hearing. The IJ subsequently ordered him deported *in absentia*.

On April 18, 1997, Saakian filed with the IJ a motion to reopen, stating that his failure to appear was caused by his belief that he did not have to show up because of the pending motion to change venue. He filed this motion *pro se*, near the beginning of the 180-day period provided by law for filing such a motion. The INS filed its opposition to this motion on April 25, 1997, arguing that the motion to change venue did not excuse Saakian's absence. On April 28, 1997, only ten days after Saakian had filed his motion, he filed a supporting affidavit, in which he stated that his erroneous belief was the result of bad advice from Frentzos, who had told him not to appear. He did not specifically allege "ineffective assistance of counsel" at this stage, but he did allege facts which, if true, could be defined as ineffective assistance.

On June 19, 1997, the IJ denied Saakian's motion to reopen. In that order, the IJ construed Saakian's claim as one of ineffective assistance of counsel, and proceeded to note that only one of the three evidentiary requirements for such claims, as set forth in *Matter of Lozada,* 19 I & N Dec. 637, 639 (BIA 1988), had been met by Saakian. Although Saakian had filed his motion *pro se,* and was well within the 180-day window for filing motions to reopen, the IJ did not give him an opportunity to satisfy the other two *Lozada* requirements. Instead, he denied the motion in language suggesting that Saakian was foreclosed from remedying the deficiencies in his motion.

Saakian timely appealed to the BIA. In his appellate papers Saakian requested, and was granted, additional time to retain an attorney before briefing the appeal. The appeal alleged, *inter alia,* that the IJ's *de facto* denial with prejudice of his motion to reopen deprived him of due process under the circumstances of this case. Along with his appellate brief, counsel submitted to the BIA the remaining documents required by *Lozada.*

On May 26, 2000, the BIA dismissed Saakian's appeal. It noted that, because Saakian had not met all three *Lozada* requirements when he initially filed his motion to reopen, the IJ had properly denied it. The BIA did not address Saakian's due process claim on the merits. Saakian now petitions us to review the BIA's decision.

II. DISCUSSION

In his petition, Saakian argues that, under the facts of this case, the IJ and BIA denied him due process by denying his motion to reopen with prejudice. In Saakian's view, due process required that he be afforded the opportunity to satisfy the *Lozada* requirements and have his ineffective assistance claim heard on the merits. We agree.

Deportation is a civil, not a criminal, proceeding; as such, there is no Sixth Amendment right to counsel. Nonetheless, "[i]t is well established that the Fifth Amendment entitles aliens to due process of law in deportation proceedings." *Reno v. Flores,* 507 U.S. 292, 306, 113 S.Ct. 1439, 123 L.Ed.2d 1 (1993) (citing *[Yamataya v. Fisher],* 189 U.S. 86, 100–101, 23 S.Ct. 611, 47 L.Ed. 721 (1903)).

In *Bridges v. Wixon,* the Supreme Court emphasized the importance of strictly protecting an alien's right to procedural due process:

> Here the liberty of an individual is at stake. . . . We are dealing here with procedural requirements prescribed for the protection of the alien. Though deportation is not technically a

criminal proceeding, it visits a great hardship on the individual and deprives him of the right to stay and live and work in this land of freedom. That deportation is a penalty—at times a most serious one—cannot be doubted. Meticulous care must be exercised lest the procedure by which he is deprived of that liberty not meet the essential standards of fairness.

326 U.S. 135, 154, 65 S.Ct. 1443, 89 L.Ed. 2103 (1945).

Aliens have a statutory right to be represented by counsel, at their own expense, in deportation proceedings. That right is "an integral part of the procedural due process to which the alien is entitled." *Batanic v. INS,* 12 F.3d 662, 667 (7th Cir. 1993). Ineffective assistance of counsel exists where, as a result of counsel's actions (or lack thereof), "the proceeding was so fundamentally unfair that the alien was prevented from reasonably presenting his case." *Bernal-Vallejo v. INS,* 195 F.3d 56, 63 (1st Cir. 1999). It is generally also expected that the alien show at least a reasonable probability of prejudice. The BIA has held, however, that the prejudice requirement does not apply in cases where an order was issued on the basis of a hearing held *in absentia.*

As a procedural matter, a claim of ineffective assistance of counsel is typically raised through a motion to reopen, which can be brought before either the BIA or the IJ directly. * * * [W]here an order has been entered against the alien *in absentia,* the alien has 180 days from that order to file any motions to reopen, assuming the alien can demonstrate that the failure to appear was caused by exceptional circumstances beyond his control. The BIA has stated that incompetent representation qualifies as an "exceptional circumstance." *In re Grijalva-Barrera,* 21 I & N Dec. 472, 473–74 (BIA 1996). Moreover, there is no numerical limit on the number of motions to reopen an alien may file pursuant to this provision. Saakian thus was entitled to file multiple motions to reopen during the 180-day period.

As to the contents of a motion to reopen, the regulation requires that the motion "state the new facts that will be proven at a hearing to be held if the motion is granted and . . . be supported by affidavits and other evidentiary material." 8 C.F.R. § 1003.23(b)(3). "Claims of ineffective assistance of counsel satisfy the general requirement that motions to reopen present 'new facts' that are 'material and [were] not available and could not have been discovered or presented at the former hearing.'" *Iavorski v. INS,* 232 F.3d 124, 129 (2d Cir. 2000) (brackets in original).

In *Matter of Lozada,* the BIA specified the documents an alien is expected to file with a motion to reopen founded upon ineffective assistance of counsel. 19 I & N Dec. 637, 639 (BIA 1988). There, the BIA stated that when an alien makes such a claim to the Board, the motion should be supported by 1) an affidavit setting forth "in detail the agreement that was entered into with former counsel with respect to the actions to be taken," as well as any representations made by counsel to the alien; 2) proof that the movant has informed former counsel of the allegations in writing, as well as any response received; and 3) a statement detailing "whether a complaint has been filed with appropriate disciplinary authorities regarding such representation, and if not, why not."

* * *

We have not had occasion to decide whether a failure to satisfy the *Lozada* requirements in an initial motion to reopen justifies a denial of the motion with prejudice to its being subsequently refiled. But the Ninth Circuit has consistently held that, "[a]lthough the BIA acts within its discretion to impose the heightened *Lozada* procedural requirements, it may not impose the *Lozada* requirements arbitrarily." *Ontiveros-Lopez v. INS,* 213 F.3d 1121, 1124–25 (9th Cir. 2000) (internal citations omitted). We agree. Furthermore, we regard this as a case involving an arbitrary application of *Lozada.*

As we have noted, Saakian filed his *Lozada*-deficient motion a mere one month into the 180-day period provided for filing a motion to reopen an *in absentia* deportation order. Despite this fact, and despite Saakian's *pro se* status, the IJ denied the motion without either inviting Saakian to remedy its deficiencies or noting Saakian's entitlement to file a second, properly supported motion. Moreover, in ruling as he did, the IJ actually used language seeming to suggest that, by filing a deficient motion, Saakian had lost his one and only opportunity to allege ineffective assistance of counsel. Elevating form over substance, the BIA then upheld this course of conduct without analysis. As a result, Saakian's ineffective assistance of counsel claim has not been examined, despite Saakian's persistent efforts to have it heard. This violates due process.

* * *

Here, the BIA did not analyze the merits of Saakian's claim based on the *Lozada* materials he had submitted, even though he was entitled, as an in absentia deportee, to more than one bite at the apple. The BIA's refusal to consider his newly formed *Lozada* claim was also despite the fact that Saakian had not been provided with an adequate opportunity to fulfill *Lozada*'s requirements with the IJ. As a result, Saakian did what he was supposed to do in order to be heard on the merits (prepared an affidavit, notified Frentzos, and filed complaints against her), but, nonetheless, his claim never was heard on the merits.

III. CONCLUSION

For the reasons stated, we grant Saakian's petition for review, and remand to the BIA for further proceedings consistent with this opinion.

ANIN V. RENO
United States Court of Appeals, Eleventh Circuit, 1999.
188 F.3d 1273.

* * *

I

Petitioner Alexis Anin, a native of Burkina-Faso, entered the United States on October 30, 1991 with a C–1 visa as an "alien in transit." The visa gave him permission to remain in the United States only until the next day. However, Anin did not depart as required and remained in the United States without seeking approval from the Immigration and Naturalization Service ("INS"). During this time he met Linda McSwain, a United States citizen, and married her on January 14, 1994. On July 26, 1994, the INS concluded that Anin had entered into a sham marriage for the purpose of obtaining immigration benefits and issued an order to show cause * * * . While in custody, pursuant to the order to show cause, Anin filed an application for asylum. His wife also filed an I–130 Visa Petition seeking permanent residence status for Anin.

On November 16, 1994, the Immigration Court scheduled a February 21, 1995 hearing on these matters, and sent notice of the hearing by certified mail to Anin's attorney of record. The notice was received and signed by someone in the office of Anin's attorney. Neither Anin nor his attorney appeared at the February hearing. At the hearing, a deportation order for Anin was entered *in absentia.* Later, after being notified of an interview for the I–130 Visa Petition, Anin and his wife appeared at the INS office in Atlanta and Anin was taken into custody. At that point, Anin's counsel of record claimed that he had not received notice of the deportation hearing. The attorney then informed Anin that he would be able to reopen the case. This conversation marked the first time that Anin learned of the deportation order entered *in absentia* against him.

A motion then was filed to reopen the deportation proceedings on account of the attorney's lack of notice. The Immigration Court denied the motion after Anin's attorney admitted that a member of his staff received and signed for the notice of the deportation hearing. Anin's lawyer never informed his client that his firm actually had received notice of the hearing. Moreover, he advised Anin that the case would be reopened as soon as his wife's I–130 Petition was approved. The BIA denied Anin's appeal on March 7, 1996. Anin was never informed of this adverse decision by his lawyer.

In December 1996, Anin learned for the first time that his appeal to the BIA had been denied by way of a "bag and baggage" letter ordering Anin to report for deportation on February 1, 1997. Anin then went to his attorney's office and examined his case file where he learned that the original notice of hearing had been received by his attorney. Anin then sought the assistance of new counsel. On February 20, 1997, almost two years after the *in absentia* deportation order was issued, Anin filed a new motion to reopen his deportation order alleging lack of notice, and for the first time, exceptional circumstances of ineffective assistance of counsel, and a denial of due process. Anin and his wife also filed affidavits which outlined his ineffective assistance of counsel claim as required by law. *See Matter of Lozada,* 19 I & N Dec. 637 (BIA 1988).

On July 16, 1998, a majority of the BIA, with four members dissenting and two members not participating, denied the motion. The BIA held that Anin was time-barred * * * from advocating an "exceptional circumstance" exception to a denial of a motion to reopen a deportation order. The court ruled that the 180 day filing deadline was unambiguous and that even an ineffective assistance of counsel claim did not justify a statutory exemption. On August 10, 1998, Anin filed a petition to this Court for review of this decision.

II

This Court reviews the BIA's denial of Anin's motion to reopen his deportation order for abuse of discretion. *See INS v. Doherty,* 502 U.S. 314, 323–24, 112 S.Ct. 719, 116 L.Ed.2d 823 (1992). In this particular area, the BIA's discretion is quite " 'broad.' " *Id.* (quoting *INS v. Rios-Pineda,* 471 U.S. 444, 449, 105 S.Ct. 2098, 85 L.Ed.2d 452 (1985)). An immigration judge may conduct a scheduled deportation hearing *in absentia* if an alien fails to appear at the appointed time. However, a deportation order entered *in absentia* may be rescinded if a petitioner proves that his failure to appear resulted from exceptional circumstances or a lack of proper notice. Under this statutory framework, we evaluate Anin's petition to reopen his deportation proceedings.

The INA's plain language clearly allows the INS to fulfill its notice requirement in deportation proceedings by notifying an alien's attorney through certified mail. Anin concedes that his attorney of record at the time received notice of the February deportation hearing by certified mail in accordance with this provision of the INA. Furthermore, no statutory provision requires an alien to receive *actual* notice of a deportation proceeding. Indeed, the Code of Federal Regulations instructs that notice be provided to the attorney of record rather than the alien.

* * * The statute unambiguously holds Anin responsible for his lawyer's actions and omissions. Therefore, despite the fact that Anin may not have received actual notice, the BIA did not abuse its discretion in denying his motion to reopen his deportation proceeding.

Additionally, the fact that Anin did not receive actual notice of the deportation hearing does not present a violation of the Due Process Clause. Although procedural due process in the deportation context requires a meaningful and fair hearing with a reasonable opportunity to be heard, *see Landon v. Plasencia,* 459 U.S. 21, 32–33, 103 S.Ct. 321, 74 L.Ed.2d 21 (1982), it does not demand that an alien receive actual notice. Due process is satisfied if notice is accorded "in a manner 'reasonably calculated' to ensure that notice reaches the alien." *Farhoud v. INS,* 122 F.3d 794, 796 (9th Cir. 1997) (quoting *United States v. Estrada-Trochez,* 66 F.3d 733, 736 & 736 n.1 (5th Cir. 1995)); *cf. Mullane v. Central Hanover Bank & Trust Co.,* 339 U.S. 306, 318, 70 S.Ct. 652, 94 L.Ed. 865 (1950) (finding that "notice must be such as is reasonably calculated to reach interested parties"). In this case, the INS simply followed the INA statute and chose a method of notice authorized by the statute—a method Congress itself determined was reasonably calculated to ensure proper notice. This method of notification does not violate an alien's due process rights. So long as the method of notification was "reasonably calculated" to procure notice, the notice requirements of due process are satisfied. *Id.* For this reason, the BIA's refusal to reopen Anin's deportation proceeding did not violate due process.

The BIA also did not err in refusing to reopen Anin's deportation order based on an ineffective assistance claim. Section [240(b)(5)(C)(i)] of the INA contains a 180 day filing deadline to contest deportation orders if "exceptional circumstances" arise such as ineffective assistance. All exceptional circumstances claims must be filed 180 days from the date of the deportation order. Notably, Anin filed his exceptional circumstances appeal almost two years after the *in absentia* deportation order was issued. As a result, Anin's appeal is statutorily time-barred. Congressional filing deadlines are given a literal reading by federal courts. * * * The provision is jurisdictional and mandatory. As a result, no exceptions have been carved into the 180 day filing deadline by federal courts. More generally, no exception to an INA deadline has been found even where an alien acts blamelessly.

* * *

Filing deadlines inherently are arbitrary and harsh. As the Supreme Court has explained, "filing deadlines, like statutes of limitations, necessarily operate harshly and arbitrarily with respect to persons who fall just on the other side of them, but if the concept is to have any content, the deadline must be enforced." [*United States v. Locke,* 471 U.S. 84, 91, 105 S.Ct. 1785, 85 L.Ed.2d 64 (1985).] Here, Anin did not even narrowly miss the filing deadline. He filed late not by a day or so but by almost two years. To allow an exception in this case would stretch the filing provisions too far. As the Supreme Court has instructed, "with respect to filing deadlines a literal reading of Congress' words is generally the only proper reading of those words." *Id.* Based on these authorities, the statute's plain language, and general principles of statutory construction, we can find no exception to the 180 day filing deadline.

Lastly, the BIA did not abuse its discretion by not [using its sua sponte authority to reopen] Anin's deportation order under 8 C.F.R. [§ 1003.2(a)]. The provision reposes very broad discretion in the BIA "to reopen or reconsider" any motion it has rendered at any time or, on the other hand, "[to] deny a motion to reopen." The discretion accorded in this provision is so wide that "even if the party moving has made out a prima facie case for relief," the BIA can deny a motion to reopen a deportation order. No language in the provision requires the BIA to reopen a deportation proceeding under any set of particular circumstances. Instead, the provision merely provides the BIA the discretion to reopen immigration proceedings as it sees fit. Federal circuit courts consistently have interpreted the provision in this way. They have read 8 C.F.R. [§ 1003.2(a)] to give the BIA the discretion to reopen immigration proceedings in situations where federal courts lack the legal authority to mandate reopening. In short, the provision gives the BIA non-reviewable discretion to dismiss Anin's claim. We can find no abuse of discretion here.

Accordingly, we affirm.

NOTES AND QUESTIONS ON THE ISSUES RAISED BY SAAKIAN AND ANIN

1. Both *Saakian* and *Anin* ask: what is the best balance between fairness and finality? On the one hand, it seems unfair—and arguably a violation of due process—to burden a noncitizen with representation that is incompetent or even deceptive. But when does the system's interest in finality justify the response that clients must live with their choice of lawyers and that at some point it is simply too late to contest removal? What is your assessment of the answers provided by each of these decisions?

One difference between the two cases is that the 180 days had run before the motion was filed in *Anin* but not in *Saakian*. Does this explain the different outcomes? Does it justify them? Or do the differences that matter run deeper?

2. Both cases discuss the constitutional underpinnings of ineffective assistance of counsel doctrine. Addressing this issue, an oft-cited decision held that a noncitizen "must show not merely ineffective assistance of counsel, but assistance which is so ineffective as to have impinged upon the fundamental fairness of the hearing in violation of the fifth amendment due process clause." *Magallanes-Damian v. INS*, 783 F.2d 931, 933 (9th Cir. 1986). *See also Dakane v. U.S. Att'y Gen.*, 399 F.3d 1269, 1273–74 (11th Cir. 2005).

b. In Absentia Orders

Statistics. In FY 2014, about 19 percent of immigration judge decisions involved noncitizens who failed to appear, which led to the issuance of an *in absentia* order in over 80 percent of these cases. This non-appearance rate has risen since FY 2011 and FY 2012 when 11 percent of immigration judge decisions involved noncitizens who failed to appear. *See* Executive Office for Immigration Review, Department of Justice, FY 2014 Statistical Year Book, at P1. FY 2014's figures are still much lower than the rates experienced a decade ago, in which both FY 2005 and FY 2006 yielded a non-appearance rate of 39 percent, with an *in absentia* order issued in over 90 percent of these cases; in FY 2006, this totaled 102,834 *in absentia* orders. *See* Executive Office for Immigration Review, Department of Justice, FY 2006 Statistical Year Book, at H1–H2.

The decline in the non-appearance rate beginning in FY 2007, from 39 percent to the current lower rates, can probably be attributed to DHS's decision in 2006 to end the "catch and release" policy. Instead, the agency provided sufficient detention space to hold virtually all persons apprehended at or near the land borders, rather than releasing many to await an immigration court hearing months later. But the lower nonappearance figures may be somewhat misleading in view of the greater use of detention. The nonappearance rate for nondetained aliens has remained at around the 30 percent level since FY 2007, after peaking at 60 percent in 2005 and 2006 and dipping slightly to 20 percent in FY 2012. *See* Executive Office for Immigration Review, Department of Justice, FY 2006 Statistical Year Book, at H3; Executive Office for Immigration Review, Department of Justice, FY 2014 Statistical Year Book, at P2.

A noncitizen ordered removed—whether *in absentia* or not—is inadmissible for ten years after removal or departure (for arriving aliens formally removed, the period is five years). *See* INA § 212(a)(9)(A). Moreover, a noncitizen ordered removed *in absentia* is ineligible for ten years for discretionary relief, *i.e.,* voluntary departure, cancellation of removal, adjustment of status, change of nonimmigrant classification, and registry. *See* INA § 240(b)(7). And under § 212(a)(6)(B), "an alien who without reasonable cause fails or refuses to attend or remain in attendance at a proceeding to determine the alien's inadmissibility or deportability" is inadmissible for five years after her departure or removal.

Rescission and equitable tolling of the deadline. INA § 240(b)(5) provides for *in absentia* orders against respondents who fail to appear at a removal hearing after receiving the notice required by statute. To rescind an *in absentia* order, the noncitizen must move to reopen by showing (1) lack of notice, (2) custody in a state or federal facility, or (3) "exceptional circumstances" (defined in INA § 240(e)(1)). A motion alleging grounds (1) or (2) can be filed at any time; for an exceptional circumstances claim, the statute requires filing within 180 days.

Anin's reading of the 180-day deadline as mandatory and jurisdictional was abrogated by *Avila-Santoyo v. Att'y Gen.*, 713 F.3d 1357, 1362 (11th Cir. 2013). *Anin's* stance against equitable tolling would appear to be bolstered by the U.S. Supreme Court's ruling in *Bowles v. Russell*, 551 U.S. 205, 127 S.Ct. 2360, 168 L.Ed.2d 96 (2007), which held that time limits *set by statute* for appealing judgments in civil cases to federal courts of appeals are jurisdictional and do not allow equitable exceptions. The Eleventh Circuit joined several other circuits that had found that the deadline is subject to equitable tolling to permit a late filing in cases where ineffective assistance of counsel is alleged, if the noncitizen moves with due diligence after learning of the entry of the order. *See, e.g., Iavorski v. INS*, 232 F.3d 124 (2d Cir. 2000); *Pervaiz v. Gonzales*, 405 F.3d 488 (7th Cir. 2005); *Aris v. Mukasey*, 517 F.3d 595, 599 (2d Cir. 2008). *Khan v. Gonzales*, 494 F.3d 255, 257–59 (2d Cir. 2007), distinguished *Bowles* in allowing an equitable exception to the 30-day deadline for appeals to the BIA, because that time limit was established in regulations. But the 180-day deadline for filing to rescind an *in absentia* order is provided by statute. Other circuit rulings after *Bowles* have similarly indicated the continued availability of equitable tolling of deadlines for motions to reopen, though often in dicta. *See, e.g., Valencia v. Holder*, 657 F.3d 745 (8th Cir. 2011).

"Exceptional circumstances." Assuming a motion to reopen is timely, what besides incompetent representation could constitute "exceptional circumstances"? Look at the statutory definition in INA § 240(e)(1), and then consider these facts:

> On January 11, de Morales left his home in Boerne, Texas at approximately 7:00 a.m. to travel sixty miles to his 8:30 a.m. deportation hearing in San Antonio. The engine of his car died on the way to the hearing. Because de Morales was unable to repair the car himself or pay to have it towed to San Antonio and fixed there, he decided to try to get a ride home so that a relative could repair the car.

> At approximately 8:00 a.m., de Morales obtained a ride from a passing driver who took him to a grocery store in Boerne. From there, he called a relative who picked him up and drove him home. De Morales arrived home at approximately 8:50 a.m.

> De Morales attempted to call the immigration court in San Antonio when he arrived home but was unable to locate the phone number in the San Antonio phone book or in his notice of hearing. De Morales did not attempt any further correspondence with the immigration court until he received notice of the order of deportation entered against him. At that time, de Morales

940 REMOVAL, DETENTION, AND JUDICIAL REVIEW CH. 9

contacted an attorney who filed a motion to reopen the proceedings on his behalf.

Are these "exceptional circumstances"? *See de Morales v. INS,* 116 F.3d 145, 146–47, 148–49 (5th Cir. 1997). Beth Werlin, *Practice Advisory: Rescinding an* In Absentia *Order of Removal,* LEGAL ACTION CENTER, AMERICAN IMMIGRATION COUNCIL 7–11 (2010).

c. Ineffective Assistance of Counsel

As *Saakian* notes, the BIA decision in *Matter of Lozada,* 19 I & N Dec. 637 (BIA 1988), sets forth procedural requirements for motions to reopen based on ineffective assistance of counsel. (Chapter Seven addressed ineffective assistance of counsel in a different setting: as the basis for withdrawing a guilty plea in a criminal proceeding. *See Padilla v. Kentucky,* 559 U.S. 356, 130 S.Ct. 1473, 176 L.Ed.2d 284 (2010).)

In *Lozada,* the Board explained the reason for imposing its threefold requirements:

> Where essential information is lacking, it is impossible to evaluate the substance of such a claim. * * * [T]he potential for abuse is apparent where no mechanism exists for allowing former counsel, whose integrity or competence is being impugned, to present his version of events if he so chooses, thereby discouraging baseless allegations. The requirement that disciplinary authorities be notified of breaches of professional conduct not only serves to deter meritless claims of ineffective representation but also highlights the standards which should be expected of attorneys who represent persons in immigration proceedings, the outcome of which may, and often does, have enormous significance for the person.

Id. at 639. Courts' insistence on compliance with the *Lozada* requirements has varied. *Compare United States v. Lopez-Chavez,* 757 F.3d 1033, 1044 (9th Cir. 2014) (*Lozada* requirements need not be applied where ineffective assistance of counsel is "clear and obvious from the record."); *and Yang v. Gonzales,* 478 F.3d 133, 142–43 (2d Cir. 2007) (only substantial compliance is necessary); *with Guzman-Rivadeneira v. Lynch,* 2016 WL 2798678, at 5 (7th Cir. 2016) (upholding denial of motion to reopen for failure to comply with *Lozada*).

In *Matter of Assaad,* 23 I & N Dec. 553 (BIA 2003), the BIA considered a challenge to *Lozada* that was based on the U.S. Supreme Court's decision in *Coleman v. Thompson,* 501 U.S. 722, 752–54, 111 S.Ct. 2546, 2566–68, 115 L.Ed.2d 640 (1991). In *Coleman,* the Court had held in a habeas case challenging a conviction for rape and capital murder that there was no right to counsel on appeal from a state habeas trial court judgment, because the defendant had had the benefit of appointed counsel for his first direct appeal from the conviction. The Court then concluded that because there was no constitutional right to appointed counsel for that appeal, there was no constitutional basis for a claim of ineffective assistance of counsel. In *Assaad*, the BIA concluded that the reasoning from *Coleman* does not apply in removal proceedings and conflicts with *Lozada*. The BIA distinguished the Fifth Amendment due process underpinnings of ineffective assistance of counsel claims in removal proceedings. 23 I & N Dec. at 557–60.

Despite the BIA's ruling, DHS and the DOJ Office of Immigration Litigation remained interested in pressing the *Coleman* issue. In 2009, these lingering questions came to a head in a case that prompted the rare intervention of two attorneys general of the United States, one of whom reversed his predecessor. The case grew out of three separate removal proceedings. All three respondents were unlawfully in the United States, but each claimed some form of relief from removal. After an adverse ruling in his removal proceeding, each respondent moved to reopen, arguing that his attorney had rendered ineffective assistance of counsel by failing to present highly relevant evidence or failing to file an appellate brief. Applying prevailing law based on *Lozada*, the three immigration judges denied these motions, and the Board of Immigration Appeals (BIA) affirmed all three.

Attorney General Michael Mukasey then ordered that the cases be referred to him for consolidated review. *Matter of Compean*, 24 I & N Dec. 710, 714 (Att'y Gen. 2009). His ultimate decision in *Compean* was handed down two weeks before President Bush left office.

Noting that several federal appeals courts in the six years since *Assaad* had found no constitutional right to effective assistance of counsel in removal proceedings, Mukasey overruled *Lozada* and *Assaad*. The core of his reasoning was that the Constitution does not guarantee counsel at all, so there is no constitutional right to effective assistance of counsel. Nonetheless, "as a matter of sound discretion," *id.* at 727, the Attorney General directed that there be remedies for noncitizens who could show egregious errors by counsel and clear prejudice. *Id.* at 714. He went on to outline procedures and requirements for such filings, tracking much of *Lozada,* but imposing more detailed and rigorous requirements.

In the fifth month of the Obama administration, Attorney General Eric Holder vacated his predecessor's decision. *Matter of Compean*, 25 I & N Dec. 1 (2009). Noting that the *Lozada* framework had "largely stood the test of time," having been expressly reaffirmed by the Board 15 years after its initial adoption, the Attorney General cast doubt on the new framework that his predecessor had initiated. He directed that the agency resolve the issue through regulation after a public notice-and-comment rulemaking process.

He added:

> Finally, prior to *Compean*, the Board itself had not resolved whether its discretion to reopen removal proceedings includes the power to consider claims of ineffective assistance of counsel based on conduct of counsel that occurred after a final order of removal had been entered. * * * I resolve the question in the interim by concluding that the Board does have this discretion, and I leave it to the Board to determine the scope of such discretion.

> Turning to the merits of the particular cases at issue, I find that * * * the orders denying reopening of the three matters reviewed in *Compean* were appropriate under the *Lozada* framework and standards as established by the Board before *Compean*. On that basis, I concur with Attorney General Mukasey's decision to affirm the Board's decisions denying reopening of these matters.

As of spring 2016, no proposed rules implementing the Holder decision had been published, but the semiannual rulemaking agenda for the Department of Justice indicates that such rules are in the works.

d.   Motions to Reopen or Reconsider

In practice, many noncitizens who may benefit from a motion to reopen have been granted voluntary departure, which allows them a stated period of time to leave the United States to avoid a formal removal and its adverse consequences. See Chapter Seven, pp. 749–753. The statute imposes disabilities, however, on persons who do not leave within the allowed period. In particular, they become ineligible for 10 years for specified forms of relief, including for adjustment of status under § 245. *See* INA § 240B(d). If such a noncitizen moves to reopen in order to apply for one of the listed forms of relief, does the pendency of the motion suspend the voluntary departure deadline? If the answer is no, can she withdraw the voluntary departure request, to avoid incurring the ineligibility (and thus wholly defeating the purpose of the desired reopening)?

Addressing the significance of motions to reopen and voluntary departure, the Supreme Court grappled with this dilemma in the following case.

DADA V. MUKASEY

Supreme Court of the United States, 2008.
554 U.S. 1, 128 S.Ct. 2307, 171 L.Ed.2d 178.

KENNEDY, J., delivered the opinion of the Court.

* * *

[Nigerian citizen Samson Taiwo Dada came to the United States in April 1998 on a nonimmigrant visa, overstayed it, and married an American citizen a year after admission. His wife filed an I–130 Petition for Alien Relative on his behalf that was denied in February 2003 due to lack of documentation.

In 2004, DHS charged Dada with being removable under § 237(a)(1)(B) for overstaying his visa. His wife then filed a second I–130 petition, but the immigration judge denied Dada's request for a continuance pending adjudication of the newly filed petition. The IJ found petitioner to be removable but granted the request for voluntary departure. The BIA affirmed and granted a voluntary departure period of 30 days.

Two days before expiration of the 30-day period, Dada sought to withdraw his request for voluntary departure and moved to reopen the removal proceedings.] He contended that his motion recited new and material evidence demonstrating a bona fide marriage and that his case should be continued until the second I–130 petition was resolved.

On February 8, 2006, more than two months after the voluntary departure period expired, the BIA denied the motion to reopen on the ground that petitioner had overstayed his voluntary departure period. * * * [T]he BIA reasoned [that] an alien who has been granted voluntary departure but fails to depart in a timely fashion is statutorily barred from applying for and receiving certain forms of discretionary relief, including adjustment of status. The BIA did not address petitioner's motion to withdraw his request for voluntary departure.

* * *

Resolution of the questions presented turns on the interaction of two statutory schemes—the statutory right to file a motion to reopen in removal proceedings; and the rules governing voluntary departure.

* * *

The Government argues that, by requesting and obtaining permission to voluntarily depart, the alien knowingly surrenders the opportunity to seek reopening. Further, according to the Government, petitioner's proposed rule for tolling the voluntary departure period would undermine the "carefully crafted rules governing voluntary departure," including the statutory directive that these aliens leave promptly.

* * *

Absent tolling or some other remedial action by the Court, then, the alien who is granted voluntary departure but whose circumstances have changed in a manner cognizable by a motion to reopen is between Scylla and Charybdis: He or she can leave the United States in accordance with the voluntary departure order; but, pursuant to regulation, the motion to reopen will be deemed withdrawn. Alternatively, if the alien wishes to pursue reopening and remains in the United States to do so, he or she risks expiration of the statutory period and ineligibility for adjustment of status, the underlying relief sought.

The purpose of a motion to reopen is to ensure a proper and lawful disposition. We must be reluctant to assume that the voluntary departure statute was designed to remove this important safeguard for the distinct class of deportable aliens most favored by the same law. * * *

It is necessary, then, to read the Act to preserve the alien's right to pursue reopening while respecting the Government's interest in the *quid pro quo* of the voluntary departure arrangement.

Some solutions, though, do not conform to the statutory design. Petitioner, as noted, proposes automatic tolling of the voluntary departure period during the pendency of the motion to reopen. We do not find statutory authority for this result. * * * If the alien is permitted to stay in the United States past the departure date to wait out the adjudication of the motion to reopen, he or she cannot then demand the full benefits of voluntary departure; for the benefit to the Government—a prompt and costless departure—would be lost. Furthermore, it would invite abuse by aliens who wish to stay in the country but whose cases are not likely to be reopened by immigration authorities.

* * *

We hold that, to safeguard the right to pursue a motion to reopen for voluntary departure recipients, the alien must be permitted to withdraw, unilaterally, a voluntary departure request before expiration of the departure period, without regard to the underlying merits of the motion to reopen. As a result, the alien has the option either to abide by the terms, and receive the agreed-upon benefits, of voluntary departure; or, alternatively, to forgo those benefits and remain in the United States to pursue an administrative motion.

If the alien selects the latter option, he or she gives up the possibility of readmission and becomes subject to the IJ's alternate order of removal. The alien may be removed by the Department of Homeland Security within 90 days, even if the motion to reopen has yet to be adjudicated. But the alien may request a stay of the order of removal and, though the BIA has discretion to deny the motion for a stay, it may constitute an abuse of discretion for the BIA to do so where the motion states nonfrivolous grounds for reopening.

* * *

A more expeditious solution to the untenable conflict between the voluntary departure scheme and the motion to reopen might be to permit an alien who has departed the United States to pursue a motion to reopen postdeparture, much as Congress has permitted with respect to judicial review of a removal order. * * *

* * *

JUSTICE SCALIA, with whom THE CHIEF JUSTICE and JUSTICE THOMAS join, dissenting.

* * *

It seems to me that the BIA proceeded just as it should have, and just as petitioner had every reason to expect. To be sure, the statute provides for the right to file (and presumably to have ruled upon in due course) a petition to reopen. But it does not forbid the relinquishment of that right in exchange for other benefits that the BIA has discretion to provide. Nor does it suggest any weird departure from the ancient rule that an offer (the offer to depart voluntarily in exchange for specified benefits, and with specified consequences for default) cannot be "withdrawn" after it has been accepted and after the *quid pro quo* promise (to depart) has been made.

* * *

The Court is quite right that the Act does not allow us to require that an alien who agrees to depart voluntarily must receive the benefits of his bargain without the costs. But why does it allow us to convert the alien's statutorily required promise to depart voluntarily into an "option either to abide by the terms, and receive the agreed-upon benefits, of voluntary departure; or, alternatively, to forgo those benefits and remain in the United States to pursue an administrative motion"? And why does it allow us to nullify the provision of § 240B(d)(1) that failure to depart within the prescribed and promised period causes the alien to be ineligible for certain relief, including adjustment of status (which is what petitioner seeks here) for 10 years?

* * *

[JUSTICE ALITO'S dissent is omitted.]

NOTES AND QUESTIONS ON DADA

1.   The majority characterizes the motion to reopen as an "important safeguard" meant "to ensure a proper and lawful disposition." And it even

suggests that denial of a related motion for a stay of removal might constitute an abuse of discretion if the movant has offered "nonfrivolous grounds for reopening." These statements stand in some tension with concerns the Court expressed in *INS v. Abudu, supra,* where Justice Stevens wrote for the Court:

> The reasons why motions to reopen are disfavored in deportation proceedings are comparable to those that apply to petitions for rehearing, and to motions for new trials on the basis of newly discovered evidence. There is a strong public interest in bringing litigation to a close as promptly as is consistent with the interest in giving the adversaries a fair opportunity to develop and present their respective cases.

INS v. Abudu, 485 U.S. 94, 107, 109–10, 108 S.Ct. 904, 913–15, 99 L.Ed.2d 90 (1988). Which is the better view of motions to reopen? Why?

2.   The *Dada* Court suggested that the executive branch should consider a "more expeditious solution" to the dilemma it faced: changing the current regulation that now forbids the consideration of a motion to reopen filed after the respondent has departed from the country (either voluntarily or pursuant to a removal order). 8 C.F.R. § 1003.2(d); *see Matter of Armendarez-Mendez,* 24 I & N Dec. 646 (BIA 2008). Since then, several courts have ruled that this regulation is in conflict with the statute or that the BIA at least retains jurisdiction to consider in its discretion motions to reopen or reconsider filed by persons who have been removed, notwithstanding the regulation. *See, e.g., Pruidze v. Holder,* 632 F.3d 234 (6th Cir. 2011); *Marin-Rodriguez v. Holder,* 612 F.3d 591 (7th Cir. 2010). Other judicial decisions have upheld the departure bar as a jurisdictional limitation on consideration of some or all such motions. *See, e.g. Zhang v. Holder,* 617 F.3d 650 (2d Cir. 2010) (collecting and discussing cases from many circuits). If that regulation is amended, or if the BIA applies these court rulings nationwide to permit consideration of motions to reopen filed from abroad, could the BIA revert to the practice of refusing permission to withdraw from a voluntary departure agreement? Should it?

4.   REMOVAL PROCEEDINGS WITHOUT IMMIGRATION COURT

For decades the immigration laws have provided for summary determinations of removability, by immigration officers rather than immigration judges, in certain classes of cases deemed especially in need of speedy resolution. In 1996, Congress significantly expanded the set of summary proceedings. Each provision has its own specific procedures and scope of application.

Consider as you read this subsection several related questions: Why was this particular abbreviated procedure adopted? What policy goals support these provisions? Which other policy goals are undercut or hampered by their operation? Could they be refined to do a better job of serving each of the counterpoised goals? What changes would you make?

a. Overview

The statute for decades has prescribed summary procedures for *stowaways and crewmen*. *See* INA §§ 235(a)(2) (stowaways); 252(b), 8 C.F.R. § 252.2 (crewmen). These procedures currently spark little controversy. Why do you think that is?

235(a)(2)
252(b)
252.2

Also, since 1986, when the visa waiver provision, INA § 217, was initially adopted, denial of admission and determination of deportability for *visa waiver travelers* have been placed within the sole authority of immigration officers. *See* 8 C.F.R. § 217.4; *Bingham v. Holder*, 637 F.3d 1040 (9th Cir. 2011) (upholding constitutional validity of such procedures). In each of these cases, more complete consideration, sometimes involving an immigration judge, is available when the individual claims asylum or protection from torture.

217.4

Five other procedures that entail little or no direct involvement by immigration judges have been adopted or else refined and greatly expanded over the last 20 years.

— 5
5 other procedures w/out judge

① One, *expedited removal*, under INA § 235(b)(1), applicable primarily to arriving aliens who lack documents or are judged to be committing or to have committed immigration fraud, was considered in some detail in Chapter Six, pp. 503–511. It has also been applied to certain entrants without inspection, primarily persons apprehended within 100 miles of the border and within 14 days of entry.

①
235(b)(1)
ⓐ
ⓑ

② A second, *judicial removal*, was initially authorized by statute in 1994. *See* INA § 238(c) (there are two subsections (c) in § 238; this is the second). It empowers federal district courts to order removal when sentencing noncitizens for conviction of a crime that makes them deportable. Judicial removal is available only when the U.S. Attorney seeks it with the concurrence of federal immigration authorities, and the court has discretion to decide whether to hear the removal case. If not, the removal charges can still be heard via the more customary removal procedures. The defendant must receive notice and be given an opportunity to establish eligibility for relief from removal. The judicial removal procedure did not meet with welcome from federal judges, who often expressed misgivings about dealing with such specialized matters, especially when the defendant made a request for relief from removal that required the exercise of discretion. *See, e.g., United States v. Qadeer*, 953 F. Supp. 1570, 1583 (S.D. Ga. 1997). The procedure is rarely used today (in part because of the growth of stipulated removals, considered below, which are sometimes negotiated as part of a plea agreement in a criminal case.) For a thoughtful discussion of judicial removal and

238(c)
ⓥ

possible reforms that could be built on that framework, see Margaret H. Taylor & Ronald F. Wright, *The Sentencing Judge as Immigration Judge*, 51 Emory L.J. 1131, 1175–76 (2002).

Third, *stipulated removals* are authorized by INA § 240(d), which permits "the entry by an immigration judge of an order of removal stipulated to by the alien * * * [and DHS]. A stipulated determination shall constitute a conclusive determination of the alien's removability from the United States." See 8 C.F.R. § 1003.25(b). As described in guidance issued by the Chief Immigration Judge, this procedure "allows interested respondents * * * to have their cases adjudicated expeditiously and without an in-person hearing. For interested respondents, stipulated removal orders reduce their time in detention and expedite their return to their homeland." Procedures for Handling Requests for a Stipulated Removal Order (OPPM 10–01, Sept. 15, 2010), http://www.justice. gov/eoir/efoia/ocij/oppm10/10–01.pdf. Critics have charged that ICE officers pressure detained noncitizens into signing such stipulations, and that those who sign are usually unrepresented by counsel. Some immigration judges have also been resistant to approving orders on the basis of the papers, voicing doubts about whether the waivers are voluntary, knowing, and intelligent. *See* Jennifer L. Koh, Jayashri Srikantiah & Karen Tumlin, *Deportation Without Due Process* (2011) http://www.nilc.org/wp-content/uploads/2016/02/Deportation-Without-Due-Process-2011-09.pdf (also reporting that over 40,000 stipulated orders were issued in FY 2008, declining to approximately 30,000 in 2010); ACLU, American Exile: Rapid Deportations That Bypass the Courtroom 1, 30 (2014) (reporting that "between 2004 and 2010, over 160,000 individuals were deported through stipulated orders of removal" and that while DHS has not made recent figures public, "it appears that reliance on those orders has declined . . . in FY 2012 approximately 15,000 non-citizens were removed through stipulated removals."). The guidance in EOIR's OPPM 10–01, quoted above, clarifies the procedures and also includes a template for an 8-page stipulation form that ICE is expected to use going forward. The questions on the template, in both English and Spanish, appear designed to help provide more information to the individual about his or her rights and the nature of the waiver, as well as more complete information to the immigration judge who must decide whether to issue the stipulated order without direct contact with the noncitizen.

We consider the remaining two summary procedures at somewhat greater length. *See also* Shoba Sivaprasad Wadhia, *The Rise of Speed Deportation and the Role of Discretion*, 5 Colum. J. Race & L. 1 (2015) (describing the common features of these procedures).

b. Administrative Removal Under INA § 238(b)

238(b)

Administrative removal under INA § 238(b) applies to certain persons convicted of an aggravated felony. Because of the caption to § 238, some reviewing courts refer to this procedure as "expedited removal." Immigration officers, however, refer to it as "administrative removal," and we follow this terminology. In any event, it is important to distinguish the § 238(b) process from expedited removal under § 235(b)(1), discussed above and in Chapter Six.

Administrative removal applies to two groups of noncitizens charged with deportability under the aggravated felony ground, INA § 237(a)(2)(A)(iii)—those who are not lawful permanent residents, and those who are conditional permanent residents under § 216 based on marriage. The statute prescribes in some detail the required procedures to be followed by the deciding immigration officer. INA § 238(b)(4). Judicial review is available in the courts of appeals, subject to the scope restrictions that apply generally to aliens with criminal convictions (considered in Section C below). So that the respondent can seek judicial review, the order cannot be executed for fourteen days from entry.

The first of the two subsections (c) of § 238 provides the substantive basis for removal: "An alien convicted of an aggravated felony shall be conclusively presumed to be deportable from the United States." The statute also provides that covered persons are not eligible for any discretionary relief from removal. § 238(b)(5). The regulations provide for an initial "reasonable fear" screening by an asylum officer for anyone in administrative removal who claims to be eligible for withholding of removal under INA § 241(b)(3) or for protection under the Convention Against Torture. Those who pass this screening are referred to immigration court for full consideration of the claim. 8 C.F.R. § 208.31.

screening for reasonable fear

Courts have uniformly rejected arguments that administrative removal violates constitutional due process. *United States v. Benitez-Villafuerte*, 186 F.3d 651, 657 (5th Cir. 1999) upheld a criminal prosecution for illegal reentry against a challenge that the prior removal under § 238(b) violated procedural due process. The court held that § 238(b) satisfies the requirements of notice of charges, a hearing before an executive or administrative tribunal, and a fair opportunity to be heard.

satisfies due process.

Statistics on the number of administrative removals are hard to find. A 2007 study found that about half of the removal orders issued on the basis of the aggravated felony charge from 2002 to 2006 were administrative removal orders issued under § 238(b), a rough average of 11,000 administrative removal orders a year. Transactional Records Access Clearinghouse (TRAC), Syracuse University, New Data on the Processing of Aggravated Felons, http://trac.syr.edu/immigration/reports/

175/. Data obtained from ICE showed that 12,758 administrative removals under § 238(b) occurred in 2010. Lenni B. Benson & Russell R. Wheeler, *Enhancing Quality and Timeliness in Immigration Removal Adjudication* 12, Chart 1, ACUS.GOV, https://www.acus.gov/sites/default/files/documents/Enhancing-Quality-and-Timeliness-in-Immigration-Removal-Adjudication-Final-June-72012.pdf (last updated June 7, 2012). It appears likely that usage has continued to increase since then.

Would it be constitutional to expand § 238(b) to include any noncitizen, including lawful permanent residents, convicted of an aggravated felony? Would it be sound policy? What about extending coverage to include conviction of any felony? Of any drug offense? Is the application of current § 238(b) to conditional permanent residents under § 216 constitutional? On the other hand, even if a permanent resident has substantial stake in the United States, why require more procedure, if the substantive law forecloses any relief from removal?

c. Reinstatement of Removal Orders

241(a)(5)
illegal re-entry.

INA § 241(a)(5) provides for the reinstatement of removal orders against noncitizens who illegally reenter the United States after having been removed or after having departed voluntarily under a removal order. As amended in 1996, the statute also provides explicitly that the original order is not subject to being reopened or reviewed, and that the noncitizen is ineligible for any discretionary relief under the INA. This procedure is highly useful from an enforcement perspective, because an individual subject to reinstatement can ordinarily be removed within a few days of apprehension. Reinstatements have accounted for a quarter to a third of all removals in recent years.

The regulations provide that an immigration officer will make the relevant determinations—prior order, identity, and unlawful reentry—without review by an immigration judge. *See* 8 C.F.R. § 241.8. If the noncitizen expresses a fear of returning to the country designated in the prior removal order, however, the case will be referred to an asylum officer to initiate a procedure for "reasonable fear" screening and possible referral to an immigration judge to consider withholding of removal. *Id.* § 208.31.

Are reinstatements consistent with the INA and with the Constitution's due process guarantee? A panel of the Ninth Circuit initially found the procedure constitutionally dubious and therefore applied the constitutional avoidance canon to interpret the INA to require a hearing before an immigration judge as part of the reinstatement process. But upon rehearing en banc, the court reversed course. *Morales-Izquierdo v. Gonzales,* 486 F.3d 484 (9th Cir. 2007) (en banc). The case involved a previously deported Mexican citizen who returned without permission, married an American citizen, and was subjected to the

reinstatement procedure when he and his wife came to an INS office to
pursue her I–130 petition on his behalf.

The majority, in an opinion by Judge Kozinski, first signaled its view
that the statute is properly construed to establish a more summary
procedure conducted by an immigration officer. The majority then turned
to consider the constitutional question:

> Morales first argues that the regulation violates due process
> because it assigns the reinstatement determination to an
> immigration officer—an official not qualified to resolve disputed
> questions as to the factual predicates for reinstatement. But
> reinstatement only requires proof that (1) petitioner is an alien,
> (2) who was subject to a prior removal order, and (3) who
> illegally reentered the United States. * * *

reqs. (3)

> We note at the outset that the regulation provides
> significant procedural safeguards against erroneous
> reinstatements. First, the immigration officer must verify the
> identity of the alien. "In disputed cases, verification of identity
> shall be accomplished by a comparison of fingerprints." If no
> fingerprints are available, the removal order cannot be
> reinstated under 8 C.F.R. § 241.8. Second, the immigration
> officer "must obtain the prior order of exclusion, deportation, or
> removal relating to the alien." Without this documentation, 8
> C.F.R. § 241.8 cannot be used and the matter is referred to an
> immigration judge. And, third, the officer must determine
> whether the alien reentered the United States illegally. "In
> making this determination, the officer shall consider all relevant
> evidence, including statements made by the alien and any
> evidence in the alien's possession. The immigration officer shall
> attempt to verify an alien's claim, if any, that he or she was
> lawfully admitted, which shall include a check of Service data
> systems available to the officer." 8 C.F.R. § 241.8(a)(3).

safeguards (3)

fingerprints

prior order

entered illegally?

> * * *

> We are satisfied, moreover, that the regulation provides
> sufficient procedural safeguards to withstand a facial challenge
> for patent procedural insufficiency. Given the narrow and
> mechanical determinations immigration officers must make and
> the procedural safeguards provided by 8 C.F.R. § 241.8, the risk
> of erroneous deprivation is extremely low. * * * [Therefore,] any
> additional or substitute procedural safeguards—including those
> Morales seeks—would produce marginal protections, if any,
> against erroneous determinations, while the cost in terms of
> resources and delay would be substantial. Due process does not

require such a poor bargain. *See Mathews v. Eldridge,* 424 U.S. 319, 335, 96 S.Ct. 893, 47 L.Ed.2d 18 (1976).

* * *

Morales also claims that a removal order may not constitutionally be reinstated if the underlying removal proceeding itself violated due process. * * *

* * * We hold that reinstatement] of a prior removal order—regardless of the process afforded in the underlying order—does not offend due process because reinstatement of a prior order does not change the alien's rights or remedies. The *only* effect of the reinstatement order is to cause Morales' removal, thus denying him any benefits from his latest violation of U.S. law, committed when he reentered the United States without the Attorney General's permission in contravention of INA § 212(a)(9). * * *

The Supreme Court noted this very point in *Fernandez-Vargas* [*v. Gonzales,* 548 U.S. 30, 126 S.Ct. 2422 (2006)]:

> While the [reinstatement] law looks back to a past act in its application to "an alien [who] has reentered . . . illegally," INA § 241(a)(5), the provision does not penalize an alien for reentry (criminal and civil penalties do that); it establishes a process to remove him "under the prior order at any time after the reentry." *Ibid.* . . . [T]he statute applies to stop an indefinitely continuing violation that the alien himself could end at any time by voluntarily leaving the country.

126 S.Ct. at 2432 (second alteration in original). While aliens have a right to fair procedures, they have no constitutional right to force the government to re-adjudicate a final removal order by unlawfully reentering the country. Nor is the government required to expend vast resources on extraneous procedures before reinstating a removal order that has already been finalized and executed.

Or, to put it differently, an alien who respects our laws and remains abroad after he has been removed should have no fewer opportunities to challenge his removal order than one who unlawfully reenters the country despite our government's concerted efforts to keep him out. If Morales has a legitimate basis for challenging his prior removal order, he will be able to pursue it after he leaves the country, just like every other alien in his position. If he has no such basis, nothing in the Due Process Clause gives him the right to manufacture for himself a new opportunity to raise such a challenge. The contrary conclusion would create a new and wholly unwarranted incentive for aliens who have previously been removed to reenter the country illegally in order to take advantage of this self-help remedy. * * * Nothing in the Constitution requires such a perverse result.

* * *

486 F.3d, at 495–98.

Judge Thomas, joined by three colleagues, said this about the due process issue in his dissent:

First, purely on a facial analysis, the reinstatement process itself approaches the "constitutional danger zone" because it does not provide any opportunity for the alien to challenge the legality of a prior removal order. * * * Thus, an alien that previously has been removed *in absentia* and without due process [as the respondent claims here] has no means of raising his due process claim.

* * * The reinstatement procedure does not provide adequate means to contest the predicates to reinstatement. * * * [The] alien has no right to introduce documents or other evidence to be considered by the officer; the officer alone determines what will constitute the administrative record. Furthermore, the alien has no right to a hearing at which he or she could call witnesses to testify, and the alien is not afforded the right to review the immigration file upon which the charges are based or to confront the evidence assembled by the government in support of reinstatement.

* * *

Because the reinstatement procedures fall within the constitutional danger zone, both facially and as applied to Morales, the doctrine of constitutional avoidance requires a presumption that Congress intended to afford Morales a full § 240 hearing before an immigration judge.

Id. at 505–08.

NOTES AND QUESTIONS ON REINSTATEMENT OF REMOVAL

1. As the Ninth Circuit notes, the U.S. Supreme Court held in *Fernandez-Vargas v. Gonzales*, 548 U.S. 30, 126 S.Ct. 2422, 165 L.Ed.2d 323 (2006), that reinstatement of removal pursuant to § 241(a)(5) applies to noncitizens who unlawfully reentered the United States before the 1997 effective date of § 241(a)(5). The Court reasoned that applying the statute in these circumstances is not retroactive because it did not attach new

consequences to past acts. Section 241(a)(5) "applies to Fernandez-Vargas today not because he reentered in 1982 or at any other particular time, but because he chose to remain after the new statute became effective." *Id.* at 2431. Moreover, according to the Court, the six-month delay between the provision's enactment date and its effective date "shows that Fernandez-Vargas had an ample warning of the coming change in the law, but chose to remain until the old regime expired and § 241(a)(5) took its place." *Id.*

2.   Section 241(a)(5) requires that the noncitizen have "reentered the United States illegally after having been removed." What if she reenters through a port of entry and her inadmissibility is not discovered there? Would reinstatement still apply? One circuit has said yes. *Cordova-Soto v. Holder,* 659 F.3d 1029 (10th Cir. 2011) (a procedurally regular entry can count as an illegal reentry for purposes of the reinstatement statute, even if it is sufficient to constitute an "admission" for purposes of INA § 101(a)(13), as construed in *Matter of Quilantan,* 25 I & N Dec. 285 (BIA 2010)).

3.   *Morales-Izquierdo* involves several interlocking issues: statutory authority for an agency regulation, *Chevron* deference, constitutional avoidance, and due process. And the court decides the case against the backdrop of *Fernandez-Vargas*, where the U.S. Supreme Court addressed another topic: retroactivity. Each of these issues—and all of them in combination—may turn on a decisionmaker's view of what it means for Morales-Izquierdo (or Fernandez-Vargas) to have returned unlawfully, lived in the United States, married a U.S. citizen, and carried on his life. How do the majority and dissent in *Morales-Izquierdo* differ in this fundamental respect? Which view is more persuasive?

5.   SECRET EVIDENCE AND EXCEPTIONAL REMOVAL PROCEEDINGS

In some removal proceedings, the government tries to limit disclosure of evidence that it regards as sensitive national security information. Here we address three situations in which the INA authorizes nondisclosure or limited disclosure.

a.   Removal Proceedings Under INA § 235(c)

In 1952, Congress provided explicit statutory authority for the kinds of secret procedures that had been employed, on the authority of regulations alone, against the two applicants for admission in the *Knauff* and *Mezei* cases (considered in detail in Chapter Six, pp. 523–536). INA § 235(c) permits the Attorney General to order removal—but of arriving aliens only—on most of the national security inadmissibility grounds without a further hearing on the basis of "confidential information," the disclosure of which "would be prejudicial to the public interest, safety, or security." Section 235(c) does not preclude an asylum claim or other possible relief.

This procedure is invoked less frequently today than it was in the 1950s, but it is still employed. *See, e.g., Avila v. Rivkind,* 724 F. Supp. 945 (S.D. Fla. 1989) (sustaining summary exclusion of Orlando Bosch, who had often been involved in violent anti-Castro activity); *Arar v. Ashcroft,* 532 F.3d 157, 162 (2d Cir. 2008) (describing the use of § 235(c) in 2002 in the internationally controversial case of Maher Arar, who was summarily removed to Jordan and later sent to Syria, where he was allegedly subjected to torture), *vacated and superseded on rehearing en banc,* 585 F.3d 559 (2d Cir. 2009), *cert. denied,* 560 U.S. 978, 130 S.Ct. 3409, 177 L.Ed.2d 349 (2010). A leading case, *Rafeedie v. INS,* 880 F.2d 506 (D.C. Cir. 1989), *on remand,* 795 F. Supp. 13, 18–20 (D.D.C. 1992)—which is sketched in the next principal case in this section—held that a returning permanent resident is entitled to more procedural due process than § 235(c) provides.

b. Removal Proceedings Under § 240

Outside the situation of arriving aliens addressed in § 235(c), INA § 240(b)(4)(B) guarantees the respondent in a removal hearing "a reasonable opportunity to examine the evidence against the alien, to present evidence on the alien's own behalf, and to cross-examine witnesses presented by the Government." But it expressly exempts national security information offered in opposition to a noncitizen's admission or to an application for discretionary relief from this guarantee. Importantly, this provision thus does not allow the use of undisclosed evidence as part of the government's case-in-chief for inadmissibility or deportability. But it is worth noting that only a very small number of noncitizens are formally charged on the terrorism grounds in removal proceedings, for a straightforward practical reason: terrorism grounds are difficult to prove. Even if the government focuses on a noncitizen because it believes he is involved in terrorist activity, if the person is removable on another ground, those charges will suffice.

In many if not most cases, moreover, relief issues take up most of the time at merits hearings, because ordinarily the government can easily prove entry without inspection, overstaying a nonimmigrant admission, or deportability based on a criminal conviction. For example, if a nonimmigrant has clearly overstayed his authorized admission period, the central issue in immigration court will be relief from removal. This is precisely when § 240(b)(4)(B) applies to limit the noncitizen's access to classified evidence. *See* David A. Martin, *Graduated Application of Constitutional Protections for Aliens: The Real Meaning of Zadvydas v. Davis,* 2001 Sup. Ct. Rev. 47, 132–33.

Is the exemption in § 240(b)(4)(B)—or its application in certain cases—unconstitutional? The next case gives one answer and a useful survey of the precedents. The district court's conclusions subsequently triggered a strong reaction from the court of appeals in related litigation. The appellate court's decision, issued shortly after the attacks of September 11, is summarized following the district court's opinion.

KIARELDEEN V. RENO

United States District Court for the District of New Jersey, 1999.
71 F.Supp.2d 402.

WALLS, DISTRICT JUDGE.

This matter is before the court on the petition for a writ of habeas corpus brought by Hany Mahmoud Kiareldeen, who, since March 1998, has been in the custody of the Immigration and Naturalization Service (INS) pending the resolution of his removal proceedings. His petition alleges [two primary] grounds for release: (1) the petitioner's detention violates the Due Process Clause because it is based on secret evidence that he has not had the opportunity to examine or confront; (2) his continued detention violates his due process rights because the government's evidence consists of uncorroborated hearsay accusations which he has rebutted[.] * * *

FACTUAL BACKGROUND

Hany Kiareldeen is a Palestinian who has resided continuously in the United States since 1990, when he entered from Israel on a student visa. In 1994, Kiareldeen married Amal Kamal, with whom he had a daughter. That marriage had ended in a bitter divorce. And in 1997, Kiareldeen married an United States citizen, Carmen Negron, who soon after submitted a relative petition to adjust his status to a conditional legal permanent resident.

In March 1998, INS and FBI agents arrested the petitioner and charged him as deportable for overstaying the time period of his student visa after his completion of his studies. He has been detained without bond pending the outcome of the deportation hearing. * * * Kiareldeen conceded that he had overstayed his visa, but sought discretionary adjustment of status and mandatory relief pursuant to the asylum provisions of the INA and the United Nations Convention Against Torture.

In opposition to the petitioner's applications for relief, the INS presented classified evidence *ex parte* and *in camera* to the Immigration Judge which allegedly demonstrated that Kiareldeen was a suspected member of a terrorist organization and a threat to the national security. Throughout the proceedings, the INS never presented any evidence in open court. According to [the immigration judge (IJ)], the INS did not call a single witness from the FBI's Joint Terrorism Task Force (the "JTTF"), which produced the unclassified documentary evidence that the petitioner has submitted to this court. * * *

On April 2, 1999, the IJ issued two opinions: the first granted the petitioner's request for adjustment of status, and the second allowed his release from custody on $1500 bond. That day, the INS appealed the decision to the Board of Immigration Appeals ("BIA"), which stayed execution of the IJ's release order. Kiareldeen moved to dissolve the stay. On June 29, 1999, a panel of BIA judges by a divided 2–1 decision denied his request for release.

* * * [T]he BIA affirmed the IJ's decision to grant the petitioner permanent resident status. Normally, this decision would moot the habeas petition because the petitioner would be released from custody upon receipt of his green card. In this case, however, the INS has applied to the BIA for a stay of execution of its order until October 29, 1999, to give the agency time to file a motion to reconsider or to request that the case be referred to the Attorney General for review. Pending the resolution of the INS' application, the petitioner still remains in custody.

The petitioner has never been charged with violation of any criminal laws. And in July 1999, the FBI closed its criminal investigation. The government has disclosed that it does not intend to reopen the investigation unless it receives new information that Kiareldeen is involved in terrorist activity.

ANALYSIS

* * *

At the threshold, the court notes that several of the decisions relied on by the respondents to demonstrate that secret evidence passes constitutional muster provide no support. *United States ex rel. Knauff v. Shaughnessy,* 338 U.S. 537, 70 S.Ct. 309, 94 L.Ed. 317 (1950), and *Shaughnessy v. U.S. ex rel. Mezei,* 345 U.S. 206, 73 S.Ct. 625, 97 L.Ed. 956 (1953), address the due process implications of secret evidence used to exclude nonresident aliens who seek admission to the country.

There is no doubt that the legislative and executive branches have plenary power to exclude nonresident aliens from the United States [citing the *Chinese Exclusion Case,* 130 U.S. 581, 9 S.Ct. 623, 32 L.Ed. 1068 (1889); and *Mezei.*] Moreover, such exclusion may employ one-sided procedures and be based on discriminatory distinctions offensive to the Constitution if applied to citizens or resident aliens. *See, e.g., Fiallo v. Bell,* 430 U.S. 787, 97 S.Ct. 1473, 52 L.Ed.2d 50 (1977); *Kleindienst v. Mandel,* 408 U.S. 753, 92 S.Ct. 2576, 33 L.Ed.2d 683 (1972). Precisely because Congressional power over alien exclusion is so broad, the respondents' reliance on exclusion cases such as *Knauff* and *Mezei* is somewhat disingenuous. The limited judicial inquiry undertaken in alien exclusion cases stands in marked contrast to the searching scrutiny required of governmental actions taken against resident aliens such as Kiareldeen, which are clearly circumscribed by the bounds of the Constitution. *See, e.g., Kwong Hai Chew v. Colding,* 344 U.S. 590, 596–97, 73 S.Ct. 472, 97 L.Ed. 576 (1953) (holding that because resident aliens are guaranteed due process rights by the Fifth Amendment, INS procedures applied to permanent residents must meet a higher standard than government actions taken to exclude nonresidents).

The respondents contend that even if the petitioner is entitled to constitutional protections, he "forfeited" his due process rights by "conceding deportability." They assert that, because the petitioner conceded that he overstayed his student visa, he has no more due process rights than an excludable alien. This argument ignores the axiomatic, constitutional premise that aliens, once legally admitted into the United States, are entitled to the shelter of the Constitution. *See, e.g., Yick Wo v. Hopkins,* 118 U.S. 356, 369, 6 S.Ct. 1064, 30 L.Ed. 220 (1886); *Landon v. Plasencia,* 459 U.S. 21, 31, 103 S.Ct. 321, 74 L.Ed.2d 21 (1982).

* * * Although Kiareldeen conceded that he had overstayed his student visa, he * * * applied for several forms of relief from deportation, including discretionary adjustment of status, and mandatory relief under the asylum provisions of the INA and the United Nations Convention Against Torture. Moreover, the IJ granted the petitioner's application for discretionary adjustment of status pursuant to INA § 245(a), and this decision was recently affirmed by the BIA.

* * *

* * * The essence of the petitioner's constitutional claim is that the INS' reliance on evidence never disclosed to the petitioner violated "every tenet of due process." The petitioner claims that the government's use of secret evidence denied him meaningful notice of the charges against him, rendered illusory any opportunity to defend himself, and carried with it a high risk of error.

* * *

[T]he court finds guidance from several recent decisions which have considered the constitutional implications of the use of confidential information in immigration proceedings. In *Rafeedie v. INS,* 688 F. Supp. 729 (D.D.C. 1988), the District Court addressed the INS' use of a special summary proceeding to exclude a permanent resident from re-entry into the United States. The underlying statute authorized the Attorney General to rely upon confidential information and to issue an order of exclusion and deportation without giving the alien an opportunity to cross-examine witnesses, to consider the government's evidence, or to appeal the decision. The INS had invoked the summary procedure because of allegations (vehemently contested) that the resident alien was a high-ranking member of a purportedly terrorist organization, the Popular Front for the Liberation of Palestine ("PFLP"). Because the circumscribed process provided no opportunity to the resident alien to confront the INS or the evidence against him directly, the District Court granted him a preliminary injunction that barred the government from employing the summary proceeding.

On appeal, the District of Columbia Circuit Court affirmed the preliminary injunction, held that "[t]here can be no doubt that, as a permanent resident alien, Rafeedie has a liberty interest in remaining in the United States, which is protected by the Due Process Clause of the Fifth Amendment," and remanded the case to the District Court for further exploration of the due process issues. *Rafeedie,* 880 F.2d 506, 524 (D.C. Cir. 1989). That Circuit Court noted that Rafeedie, like Joseph K. in Kafka's allegory *The Trial,* was in the untenable position of being forced to prove that he was not a terrorist in face of the Government's confidential information: "It is difficult to imagine how even someone innocent of all wrongdoing could meet such a burden."

On remand, the District Court ruled that * * * the summary proceedings in his case did not satisfy the "basic and fundamental standard" of due process. *Rafeedie,* 795 F. Supp. 13, 20 (D.D.C.1992).

The Ninth Circuit joined in this conclusion in *American-Arab Anti-Discrimination Committee v. Reno,* 70 F.3d 1045 (9th Cir. 1995). Two permanent resident aliens applied for adjustment of their status pursuant to a provision of the INA which the INS claimed authorized the use of secret evidence in legalization proceedings. The INS had earlier arrested the immigrants, charged them with membership in the allegedly communist PFLP, and denied the applications on the basis of undisclosed classified information. After examination of the government's evidence, the District Court had found that the government's reliance on the information would constitute a due process violation and granted the plaintiffs a permanent injunction against its use.

The Ninth Circuit affirmed. * * *

The appellate court found that after ten years' residence in the United States, the immigrants had a strong liberty interest in remaining in their homes and at their work, even though they had committed technical visa violations. Next, the Court * * * determined that because secret procedures deprive individuals of their rights of confrontation and cross-examination, the use of undisclosed information presented an "exceptionally high risk of erroneous deprivation." Finally, the Court recognized the legitimate governmental interest in removing persons deemed to be threats to the national security while protecting its confidential sources. However, it determined that the government's failure to produce evidence that the targeted individuals had personally advocated prohibited doctrines or participated in terrorist activities belied its claim that they constituted a national security threat. * * * The Court concluded: "Because of the danger of injustice when decisions lack the procedural safeguards that form the core of constitutional due process, the *Mathews* balancing suggests that use of undisclosed information in adjudications should be presumptively unconstitutional. Only the most extraordinary circumstances could support one-sided process."

* * * Review of the Service's procedures involving Kiareldeen leads the court to believe that the petitioner's case is an example of the dangers of secret evidence. The petitioner came to the United States to attend a language program at Rutgers University, and continued his studies until he married for the first time and no longer could afford to work [*sic*]. He has supported himself and his family by working at a pizzeria and an electronics store in New Jersey. He has lived in the United States for almost a decade, married an American citizen, and applied to become a permanent resident. In March 1998, INS and FBI agents arrested the petitioner without warning and placed him in indefinite detention. Kiareldeen has presented evidence on his own behalf at two separate bond hearings and a removal proceeding that spanned seven months. He has subpoenaed the only government witness that he is able to identify: his ex-wife Amal Kamal, whom he suspects may be the source of the accusations against him. The Immigration Judge who presided over his removal proceedings and second bond hearing determined that "[a]n evaluation of the evidence by a person of ordinary prudence and caution cannot sustain a finding that this respondent has engaged in terrorist activity" and ordered his release from custody * * * .

The unclassified evidence that the government made available to the petitioner to support these extraordinary measures consists of five separate "summaries" of information gathered by the FBI's Joint Terrorism Task Force, which the agency assures was "obtained from multiple reliable sources who have provided reliable information in the past." The most detailed of these identifies not a single source and is barely over two pages.

To assay the constitutionality of the INS procedures applied to the petitioner, the court considers the three factors enunciated in *Mathews v. Eldridge*. The first, the petitioner's private interest in his physical liberty, must be accorded the utmost weight. * * * The second, the risk of erroneous deprivation, also militates in the petitioner's favor. Use of secret evidence creates a one-sided process by which the protections of our adversarial system are rendered impotent. The petitioner has been compelled by the government to attempt to prove the negative in the face of anonymous "slurs of unseen and unsworn informers." *Jay [v. Boyd]*, 351 U.S. [345], 365, 76 S.Ct. 919 (1956) (Warren, J., dissenting). * * *

Finally, the court considers the government's interest in relying on secret evidence. Even if the interest is deemed to be the unarguably weighty one of national security, as the government maintains, the court must inquire "whether that interest is so all-encompassing that it requires that [the petitioner] be denied virtually every fundamental feature of due process." *Rafeedie,* 795 F. Supp. at 19.

The court does not, however, necessarily accept at face value the government's contentions that the national security is implicated by the petitioner's alleged misdeeds. The court has considered the government's unclassified "summary" evidence and finds it lacking in either detail or attribution to reliable sources which would shore up its credibility. More important, however, is the apparent conclusion that even the government does not find its own allegations sufficiently serious to commence criminal proceedings. * * *

Here, the government's reliance on secret evidence violates the due process protections that the Constitution directs must be extended to all persons within the United States, citizens and resident aliens alike. * * * [T]he court finds this failure to be sufficient basis to grant the petitioner's writ of habeas corpus and direct his release from custody.

* * *

The Court of Appeals Considers the *Kiareldeen* Issues

The federal government filed a notice of appeal and sought an emergency stay of the decision on secret evidence that you have just read. But Kiareldeen was released, and the government eventually dropped its appeal. *See Kiareldeen v. Ashcroft*, 273 F.3d 542, 547 (3d Cir. 2001). The district court later issued a separate decision awarding attorneys' fees and costs to Kiareldeen. The government appealed this second district court decision to the Court of Appeals for the Third Circuit, which vacated the award. Although the appeal was theoretically limited to the award of fees and costs, the governing standard—whether the government's position on secret evidence was "substantially justified," 28 U.S.C. § 2412(d)—allowed the appeals court to revisit the merits.

The Third Circuit, writing less than two months after the attacks of September 11, 2001, bluntly criticized the district court's analysis:

> * * * The district court * * * attacked the credibility of the
> summaries directly, describing them as "lacking in either detail
> or attribution to reliable sources." *Kiareldeen v. Reno*, 71 F.
> Supp. 2d at 414. That the FBI would be unwilling to compromise
> national security by revealing its undercover sources, is both
> understandable and comforting. That a court would then choose

to criticize the FBI for being unwilling to risk undermining its covert operations against terrorists is somewhat unnerving.

The district court also criticized the government for its apparent unwillingness to also bring criminal charges against Kiareldeen. It stated that "even the government does not find its own allegations sufficiently serious to commence criminal proceedings."

This statement illustrates both a simplistic and entirely uninformed view of the processes by which the Justice Department investigates and deals with suspected terrorists within our borders. It completely disregards the often complex determinations involved in releasing confidential counter-terrorism intelligence into the public arena through its introduction into both administrative hearings and court proceedings. Such a criticism implies that the government may only utilize information against an individual in a civil context, such as in deportation procedures, if it also intends to commence criminal proceedings against that same individual. Such a fettering of the Executive Branch has no support in either case law or statute.

* * *

We are not inclined to impede investigators in their efforts to cast out, root and branch, all vestiges of terrorism both in our homeland and in far off lands. As the Court has stated:

> Few interests can be more compelling than a nation's need to ensure its own security. It is well to remember that freedom as we know it has been suppressed in many countries. Unless a society has the capability and will to defend itself from the aggressions of others, constitutional protections of any sort have little meaning.

Wayte v. United States, 470 U.S. 598, 611–612, 105 S.Ct. 1524, 84 L.Ed.2d 547 (1985). The district court, in its fact finding process, understandably felt shackled by the government's unwillingness to provide Kiareldeen the names and addresses of its counter-terrorism personnel, both in uniform and in civilian clothes. Nonetheless, the public fisc should not lightly be exposed to financial penalties when the war on terrorism is transferred from the domestic battlefield that our country has become, to the vacuum-sealed environment of a federal courtroom, with such civilized accouterments as burdens of proof and axioms of evidence.

Kiareldeen v. Ashcroft, 273 F.3d 542, 552–53, 555–56 (3d Cir. 2001), *rev'g Kiareldeen v. Reno*, 92 F. Supp. 2d 403 (D.N.J. 2000).

NOTES AND QUESTIONS ON THE USE OF SECRET EVIDENCE

1. The district court relies heavily on *Rafeedie*. Is that reliance appropriate? Rafeedie had been admitted as a lawful permanent resident. Kiareldeen had several years of de facto residence in the United States, but most of his ties, including his employment, were acquired only after he violated the terms of his nonimmigrant admission. For an argument that immigration status should be considered in the *Eldridge* due process balance, and that the interest of LPRs should be given the greatest weight (while still affording some protections for other noncitizens), see Martin, *Graduated Application, supra,* 2001 Sup. Ct. Rev. at 84–101. *See also* Jaya Ramji-Nogales, *A Global Approach to Secret Evidence: How Human Rights Law Can Reform Our Immigration System*, 39 Colum. Hum. Rts. L. Rev. 287 (2008); Susan Akram, *Scheherezade Meets Kafka: Two Dozen Sordid Tales of Ideological Exclusion*, 14 Geo. Immigr. L.J. 51 (1999); Niels W. Frenzen, *National Security and Procedural Fairness: Secret Evidence and the Immigration Laws*, 76 Interp. Rel. 1677 (1999) (arguing against the use of secret evidence or for greater protections).

2. How do you evaluate the competing visions of the government's interest, in *Eldridge* terms, offered by the district court and the court of appeals? Which has the better view? Even if you are persuaded by the higher court's assessment of the weight of the government's interest, how should the *Eldridge* balance come out? Some of the answer to this question may depend on the possibility and nature of alternative safeguards for the individual, even if direct access to the classified information is denied. Part (iii) below explores certain possible alternatives.

3. In 2002, the regulations were amended to provide more precise procedures for the submission of evidence under seal, including in national security-related cases, and for the issuance of a protective order forbidding respondent and counsel, as well as others, from disclosing the covered information. 8 C.F.R. § 1003.46.

c. The Alien Terrorist Removal Court

The Alien Terrorist Removal Court (ATRC) represents one possible alternative framework for the use of secret evidence. *See* INA §§ 501–507. Because classified information can be withheld from the respondent under INA § 235(c) for an "arriving alien," and under § 240 to contest discretionary relief for any noncitizen, the government has no need to invoke the more complex arrangements of the ATRC unless it needs the information to prove baseline removability for an alien who is not an arriving alien.

Practically, this means that the ATRC will likely be used only to remove a permanent resident, or possibly a nonimmigrant in valid immigration status (though in the latter case the government might choose to wait until that nonimmigrant status expires before initiating removal proceedings). As of this writing no case has ever been brought in the ATRC, but the structure merits close examination, not only because the court may be convened in the future, but also because of the vision these provisions set forth of an alternative set of procedures to protect important individual interests while still meeting core government security objectives. In fact, procedures roughly along the lines set forth for the ATRC have in fact been used increasingly since 2001 in judicial settings, mentioned in the notes below, where a government seeks to shelter classified information.

The ATRC consists of five federal district judges appointed to this court by the Chief Justice of the United States for five-year terms. INA § 502(a). These judges are full life-tenured Article III judges; when not conducting ATRC business, they retain their normal district court responsibilities. The ATRC hears cases only if the Attorney General submits an application under INA § 503. The special ATRC procedures apply if the Attorney General certifies, and a single judge of the removal court determines: that the charged noncitizen is an "alien terrorist," that the person is physically present in the United States, and that his removal under normal procedures "would pose a risk to the national security of the United States." INA § 503(a), (c). An "alien terrorist" is any alien deportable under § 237(a)(4)(B), which now includes any admitted alien described in the broad terrorism inadmissibility ground, INA § 212(a)(3)(B). The Attorney General may take into custody any person who is the subject of such certification. Permanent residents are given a hearing to decide on release while the case is pending. *See* INA § 506.

A public hearing follows "as expeditiously as practicable." *See* INA § 504. The respondent must be given notice, including "a general account of the basis for the charges." He has the right to be present and to be represented by counsel, including appointed counsel for any person financially unable to obtain counsel. Information may not be disclosed "if disclosure would present a risk to the national security of the United States." Where removal is to be based on any such information, the judge must examine it *ex parte* and *in camera*. The respondent generally receives only an unclassified summary of the classified information. But he does not get even that summary if the judge finds that "(I) the continued presence of the alien in the United States would likely cause serious and irreparable harm to the national security or death or serious bodily injury to any person, and (II) the provision of the summary would likely cause serious and irreparable harm to the national security or death or serious bodily injury to any person." INA § 504(e)(3). In such cases, if the respondent is a lawful permanent resident, the judge appoints a "special attorney" to represent the individual, an attorney who has received an appropriate clearance to examine secret information. *See* § 502(e). That attorney's role is to review and challenge the classified information *in camera*. A special attorney who discloses the information "to the alien or to any other attorney representing the alien" is subject to substantial criminal penalties. INA § 504(e)(3)(F).

NOTES AND QUESTIONS ON SAFEGUARDS WHEN SECRET EVIDENCE IS USED

1.   What are the strengths and weaknesses of the ATRC? Do its procedures satisfy due process, especially as applied to lawful permanent residents? Should the statute be amended to permit using this procedure in a wider class of cases where secret evidence is involved? Which cases? Consider, for example, asylum cases where the government submits classified information for the immigration judge's *in camera* review as part of its evidence in opposition to the claim. The regulations already provide that when the government uses classified information in an asylum case, it shall provide an unclassified summary that is "as detailed as possible, in order that the applicant may have an opportunity to offer opposing evidence." 8 C.F.R. § 1240.33(c)(4). What other protections would the ATRC procedures entail?

2.   It may be useful to compare due process requirements in criminal prosecutions:

> In proceedings where the fullest measure of due process protection unmistakably applies, criminal trials, secret evidence simply cannot be used as the basis for a prosecution. The Fifth and Sixth Amendments generally require giving the defendant the details of the government's case and affording the right to cross-examine adverse witnesses. If the classified information is needed for the case in chief, the government is put to a choice whether to "burn the asset"—that is, pull in the informant and shield him in other ways after he testifies in open court, thereby losing future information—or else abandon the prosecution. Should a similar rule apply to immigration proceedings? The black-letter law holds that deportation is not punishment, thereby making criminal law protections not directly applicable. But it also provides that deportable aliens are entitled to procedural due process protection, superintended by the courts, in removal proceedings. If the potential for unfairness is so great, perhaps results similar to those in criminal proceedings should obtain. [The author goes on to explore other "middle ground" arrangements that might be more appropriate for various types of immigration proceedings.]

Martin, *Graduated Application*, *supra*, 2001 Sup. Ct. Rev. at 129–30.

For certain matters that do not go to the heart of the criminal charges, however, provision has been made for sheltering the classified information while making available to the accused unclassified summaries or other substitutes. Congress provided for such procedures, identifying the circumstances in which they would be appropriate, in the Classified Information Procedures Act (CIPA). 18 U.S.C. App. 3 §§ 1–16. In the prosecution of Zacarias Moussaoui, who was charged with conspiracy with the September 11 plotters, the court crafted procedures by analogy to CIPA that gave the accused access to unclassified summaries of classified statements by detainees at Guantánamo, as a substitute for interviewing those witnesses to seek information that might help in his defense. *United States v. Moussaoui,* 365 F.3d 292, 312–17 (4th Cir. 2004).

3.   In a related arena, the cases challenging the detention of U.S. prisoners at Guantánamo have often involved the use of classified evidence. The Supreme Court in *Boumediene v. Bush,* 553 U.S. 723, 128 S.Ct. 2229, 171 L.Ed.2d 41 (2008), held that the constitutional guarantee of habeas corpus applies at Guantánamo, but left most of the substantive and procedural details to be resolved by the district courts hearing these cases. The district court has proceeded by way of requiring the government to prepare an unclassified summary, reviewed for adequacy by the judge, who has access to the unredacted information. Moreover, the executive branch, after background checks, has granted secret-level security clearances to certain counsel for the petitioners, so that they can have access to much of the evidence and can thus challenge the validity or significance of the secret information before the judge *in camera,* even when it cannot be disclosed to the client. *See In re Guantanamo Bay Detainee Litigation*, 577 F.Supp.2d 143 (D.D.C. 2008). *See also* Daphne Barak-Erez & Matthew C. Waxman, *Secret Evidence and the Due Process of Terrorism Detentions*, 48 Colum. J. Transnat'l L. 3 (2009) (comparative study involving United Kingdom, Canadian, Israeli and U.S. procedures, finding common components, albeit with many variations: requirements that the individual receive the core or gist of the information in unclassified form, that the judge take an expanded management role *in camera,* and that some form of special advocate with security clearance have access to the information on behalf of the individual).

4.   Surprisingly, despite the various avenues available for the use of secret evidence in removal proceedings, the government has rarely even attempted to employ such information since 2001. *See* Dan Eggen, *U.S. Uses Secret Evidence in Secrecy Fight with ACLU*, Wash. Post, Aug. 20, 2004 (reporting expert views that secret evidence has been rarely used since the late 1990s). This may result from far more rigorous internal review procedures, adopted by the Justice Department in 1999 following several court setbacks, including the initial ruling in *Kiareldeen,* but no public explanation has been offered. *See* David A. Martin, *Offshore Detainees and the Role of Courts after* Rasul v. Bush, 25 Boston Coll. Third World L.J. 125, 157 (2005). Obtaining statistical information about current use of secret

evidence is difficult. *See* Ramji-Nogales, *supra,* at 306 (describing practical barriers).

d. Public Access

A related issue came to a head in 2002. The regulations give an immigration judge the discretion to limit attendance or to close a removal hearing to the public "[f]or the purpose of protecting witnesses, parties, or the public interest." 8 C.F.R. § 1003.27. Though this power has long been exercised case by case, soon after the September 11 attacks, the Department of Justice issued a directive to close off access on a blanket basis to several hundred removal proceedings involving noncitizens determined by the Department to be of "special interest," going so far as to order employees not to confirm or deny whether such cases were even on the docket. The practice was challenged, primarily by press organizations, claiming violation of a First Amendment right of access. The Court of Appeals for the Sixth Circuit held that the First Amendment provided a right of access:

> Democracies die behind closed doors. The First Amendment, through a free press, protects the people's right to know that their government acts fairly, lawfully, and accurately in deportation proceedings. When government begins closing doors, it selectively controls information rightfully belonging to the people.

* * *

> The Government's ongoing anti-terrorism investigation certainly implicates a compelling interest. However, the [closure] directive is neither narrowly tailored, nor does it require particularized findings. Therefore, it impermissibly infringes on the Newspaper Plaintiffs' First Amendment right of access.

Detroit Free Press v. Ashcroft, 303 F.3d 681, 683, 700, 705 (6th Cir. 2002).

Shortly thereafter, the Third Circuit reached the opposite result in *North Jersey Media Group v. Ashcroft*, 308 F.3d 198 (3d Cir. 2002), *cert. denied*, 538 U.S. 1056, 123 S.Ct. 2215, 155 L.Ed.2d 1106 (2003). The court found no historical right of access, [especially in light of] evidence that some deportation proceedings were, and are, explicitly closed to the public or conducted in places unlikely to allow general public access." *Id.* at 212. Considering "whether public access plays a significant positive role in the functioning of the particular process in question," the court approved the decision "to close the deportation hearings of those who may have been affiliated with the persons responsible for the events of September 11th, all of the known perpetrators of which were aliens." The court reasoned that those most directly affected by the closure directive were the media, not the noncitizens, who are "given a heavy measure of due process—the right to appeal the decision of the Immigration Judge (following the closed hearing) to the Board of Immigration Appeals (BIA) and the right to petition for review of the BIA decision" to the courts of appeals. 308 F.3d at 220.

By the time the issue was presented to the Supreme Court, nearly all the closed removal hearings had been concluded and most of the respondents deported. The Court denied certiorari. Thereafter, blanket closure ceased, and the immigration courts have returned to the practice of infrequent case-by-case closure.

B. DETENTION

Detention serves multiple purposes in a system of removal procedures. In a perfect procedural world, removal decisions are error-free and carried out immediately, and detention is unnecessary. But in reality, detention has come to provide part of the answer to several important, unavoidable questions.

First, what happens when a noncitizen arrives in the United States and her admissibility is in doubt? Should she be provisionally allowed into the country while her status is being decided? Second, what happens if a noncitizen already in the United States appears to be deportable? Should he be taken into custody while his status is being decided? Third, what if a final removal order has issued? Should the noncitizen be detained until she actually leaves the United States? Fourth, what if a noncitizen is ordered removed, but no other country will take her? Should she be detained indefinitely, released as if she had never been ordered removed, or something in between?

Each of these questions might call for a different answer, but they have much in common. Detention is an obvious restraint on personal liberty that should not be imposed without good reason. To a visitor to an immigration detention facility and especially to a detainee, detention may seem indistinguishable from a prison sentence for a criminal conviction. Especially for a detainee who has lived in the United States for a while, detention may mean separation from family and friends, and the loss of a job. Detention is costly, both to the government and to the detainee, for whom the harm is greatly magnified if he turns out not to be removable. Detention, particularly in remote locations, can severely limit a noncitizen's ability to obtain legal representation, especially if she must rely on volunteer counsel, and to present her case. *See* Anil Kalhan, *Rethinking Immigration Detention*, 110 Colum. L. Rev. Sidebar 42 (2010) (surveying detention practices and their consequences, including implications for access to legal representation).

Detention plays a prominent role in immigration enforcement initiatives. Federal policy promotes detention in each of the four situations that we have sketched to achieve particular goals. Law enforcement authorities use detention to ensure that noncitizens appear for removal hearings, and that they will actually leave the United States if ordered removed. Moreover, some noncitizens are removable because they are deemed to pose a risk to society; detaining them pending removal minimizes that risk. Detention is also seen as playing a deterrent role in any system of immigration enforcement. If arriving noncitizens are seldom detained, noncitizens who are clearly inadmissible may have a strong incentive to come to the United States to stay as long as they can before being removed. *See generally* Stephen H. Legomsky, *The Detention of Aliens: Theories, Rules, and Discretion*, 30 Univ. Miami Inter-Am. L. Rev. 531 (1999). Beyond these practical imperatives, the federal government may sometimes use detention to crack down on certain groups of violators, or to "restore credibility" to the entire immigration enforcement system. *See* Margaret H. Taylor, *Symbolic Detention*, 20 In Defense of the Alien 153 (1998) (criticizing this use of detention policy).

1. OVERVIEW

a. The Statutory Framework

Arriving aliens. The statutory provisions on detention provide different coverage and procedures for arriving aliens as distinguished from other noncitizens. Under INA § 235(b)(2), arriving aliens not in expedited removal "shall be detained," but the immigration authorities have consistently interpreted this provision to leave open a noncitizen's eligibility for release on parole under § 212(d)(5). The regulations prescribe these circumstances for such paroles: (1) serious medical conditions; (2) pregnant women; (3) certain juveniles; (4) witnesses in government proceedings in the United States; and (5) aliens "whose continued detention is not in the public interest." 8 C.F.R. § 212.5. ICE field office directors decide about release and any conditions (e.g., amount of bond, electronic monitoring, or periodic reporting requirements). Immigration judges lack jurisdiction to review bond decisions regarding arriving aliens, including lawful permanent residents who fall into that category. *See* 8 C.F.R. §§ 236.1(c)(11), 1003.19(h)(2)(i)(B).

Noncitizens within the United States. Different rules apply to noncitizens who are not arriving aliens. They may be detained or released either on their own recognizance or on bond (minimum $1500). *See* INA § 236(a); 8 C.F.R. § 236.1(c). Here, too, the ICE field office director makes the initial decision regarding any release and its terms, but then the noncitizen may ask an immigration judge for "bond redetermination"—a process that allows the judge to revise the bond or order release without bond. The judge has limited authority to change the other terms of release as well. *See Matter of Aguilar-Aquino*, 24 I & N Dec. 747 (BIA

2009); *Matter of Garcia-Garcia,* 25 I & N Dec. 93 (BIA 2009). The central criteria for release decisions, whether done by an ICE officer or an immigration judge, are flight risk and possible danger to the community. *See Matter of Guerra,* 24 I & N Dec. 37 (BIA 2006). Bond hearings should consider the noncitizen's employment history, length of residence in the community, family ties, record of appearance or nonappearance at court proceedings, and previous criminal or immigration law violations. *See id.; Matter of Sugay,* 17 I & N Dec. 637, 638–39 (BIA 1981). Both the noncitizen and DHS may appeal the judge's decision to the BIA, which may stay release until it decides. But if a field office director originally ordered detention without bond or a bond of at least $10,000, an immigration judge orders release, and the government promptly files its appeal, the order is automatically stayed until the BIA rules. *See* 8 C.F.R. §§ 236.1(d)(4), 1003.19(i).

Janet Gilboy's empirical study of the Chicago district office found that immigration judges in de novo bond redeterminations reduced the original bonds set by an INS officer by an average of over two-thirds. Gilboy suggests that at the heart of the "interinstitutional differences" lies a "value dissensus." The INS (and now ICE) focuses on immigration enforcement, in which bail is an important tool, especially in "the difficult environment in which INS investigators see themselves operating—one that contains immigration court delays and BIA appeals, extensive reliance on aliens leaving the country voluntarily on their own, and limited resources for locating abscondees." Janet A. Gilboy, *Administrative Review in a System of Conflicting Values,* 13 Law & Soc. Inquiry 515, 523–25 (1988). In contrast, immigration judges can strike a different balance between effective immigration law enforcement and protection of the liberty interests of the individual noncitizens because they "do not face the same pressures, constraints, and responsibilities." *Id.* For an analysis of "bureaucratic biases" favoring detention over release of asylum seekers, see Michele R. Pistone, *Justice Delayed Is Justice Denied: A Proposal for Ending the Unnecessary Detention of Asylum Seekers,* 12 Harv. Human Rights L.J. 197, 239–47 (1999). But consider this contrasting view: "Compared to the [immigration judges], the [field office director] almost certainly faces an array of incentives, responsibilities, and constraints * * * that are more balanced, more comprehensive, and more reflective of the full benefits and costs (social, fiscal, political, and otherwise) of detention and bonding decisions." Peter H. Schuck, *INS Detention and Removal: A White Paper,* 11 Geo. Immigr. L.J. 667, 684 (1997).

Mandatory detention. None of the foregoing possibilities for release from detention are available to noncitizens who are subject to mandatory detention while removal proceedings are pending. Under INA § 236(c), the following aliens must be detained and may not be released:

aliens covered by the terrorist grounds and aliens removable on the following criminal grounds: multiple crimes of moral turpitude, aggravated felonies, controlled substance offenses, firearms offenses, "miscellaneous crimes," or, in some cases, single crimes of moral turpitude. The only statutory exceptions are release for witness protection or cooperation, and then only if the detainee is neither a security risk nor a flight risk. We will consider court-imposed limits on mandatory detention later in this section.

A more targeted mandatory detention provision is INA § 236A, enacted in 2011 as part of the USA PATRIOT Act, which requires detention of specified noncitizens reasonably believed to be involved in terrorism or other activity, for up to seven days before placing them in removal proceedings or filing criminal charges, and then throughout proceedings. But this form of detention requires a certification, signed personally by either the Attorney General or the Deputy Attorney General, which must be reviewed every six months. As of early 2016, this power had not been used. *See Plan for Closing the Guantanamo Bay Detention Facility*, Department of Defense, at 8 n. 33 (2016), http://www.defense.gov/Portals/1/Documents/pubs/GTMO_Closure_Plan_0216.pdf.

b. ICE's Detention System

Capacities. As of 2016, immigration detainees are housed in about 250 detention facilities, including three solely for families. Twenty-one large facilities hold about 50 percent of the detained population. Of these 21, seven are ICE-owned, though generally operated under contract with private companies, seven more facilities are owned and operated by private contractors, and seven are dedicated county jail facilities with which ICE maintains intergovernmental service agreements (IGSAs). The other 50 percent are detained in state and local detention facilities also operated under IGSAs.

The number of individuals held in immigration detention over the course of a fiscal year was approximately 100,000 in FY 2001. That number rose steeply over the succeeding decade, reaching 440,600 in FY 2013. *See* U.S. Gov't Accountability Office, *Immigration Detention: Additional Actions Needed to Strengthen Management and Oversight of Facility* 1 (2014). Higher annual detention numbers are a product of both more detention beds and shorter lengths of stay. ICE's detention capacity, which was under 20,000 beds in FY 2005 and rose to 33,000 by July 2011, may increase further, based on its FY 2016 funding request for 34,040 beds. The average length of stay declined from 37.2 days in 2007 to 29.0 in 2011. ICE Total Removals Through July 31, 2011, http://www.ice.gov/doclib/about/offices/ero/pdf/ero-removals.pdf; DHS, Budget-in-Brief Fiscal Year 2016, at 54, https://www.dhs.gov/sites/default/files/publications/FY_2016_DHS_Budget_in_Brief.pdf. Within those averages, of course, there are many uncontested cases that lead to release or removal within a few days, whereas some detainees remain incarcerated for months or even years.

In FY 2005, 29 percent of completed cases in immigration court involved detained noncitizens; that number rose to 44 percent by FY 2010. *See* Executive Office for Immigration Review, Department of Justice, FY 2005 Statistical Year Book, at O1; FY 2010 Statistical Year Book, at O1. In FY 2014, 37 percent of *initial* completed cases in immigration court involved detained non-citizens, down from 53 percent in FY 2010. *See* Executive Office for Immigration Review, Department of Justice, FY 2014 Statistical Year Book, at G1. (For FY 2014 EOIR did not include data on completed cases generally.).

Reforms. Significant concerns about the immigration detention system have been heard for decades, and numerous reports and studies have documented problems and complaints. *See; e.g.,* Amnesty International, Jailed without Justice: Immigration Detention in the USA, (2009) http://www.amnestyusa.org/pdfs/JailedWithoutJustice.pdf; Mark Dow, American Gulag: Inside U.S. Immigration Prisons (2004).

Some of the concerns go to the conditions in the facilities, which have traditionally been designed based on American Correctional Association standards that were developed to cover facilities in the criminal justice system. Oversight of contract and IGSA facilities has been decentralized and inconsistent, with what critics saw as insufficient responses to poor performance or even major violations of applicable performance standards. Medical care for detainees drew many complaints, and a few notorious incidents of delayed responses to serious medical conditions over the past decades apparently contributed to detainee deaths (and ensuing litigation). *See, e.g.,* Sandra Hernandez, *Denied Medication, AIDS Patient Dies in Custody*, L.A. Daily Journal, Aug. 9, 2007; Nina Bernstein, *Before Deaths that Caught Public's Eye, Others Stayed Hidden*, N.Y. Times, Jan. 10, 2010. Critics also noted that many of the largest facilities are distant from major urban areas where legal assistance might be more readily found, and arrested noncitizens have often been transferred to one of these facilities, far from family and friends.

Systemic critiques have drawn connections between immigration detention and mass incarceration, tracing common roots to the legislative and executive initiatives underlying the War on Drugs, and highlighting the common racial impacts. *See* César Cuauhtémoc García Hernández, *Immigration Detention as Punishment*, 61 UCLA L. Rev. 1346, 1360–72 (2014) (providing a history of immigration detention); Yolanda Vazquez, *Constructing Crimmigration: Latino Subordination in a "Post-Racial" World*, 76 Ohio St. L.J. 599, 654 (2015) (reporting that by 2012, Latinos represented over 90% of those in immigration detention).

In its earliest weeks, the Obama administration initiated an internal process meant to lead to significant detention reform. DHS Secretary Janet Napolitano engaged an experienced expert on detention management, Dr. Dora Schriro, to study the detention system and suggest specific reforms. Her report, Schriro, *supra,* documented problems and urged multi-year changes to shift from the criminal model to a civil detention system, with greater outside access by family and counsel, contact visits, enhanced recreational opportunities, and permission for more detainees to wear their own clothing. The Secretary and ICE Director John Morton accepted the report and launched an ambitious reform process in 2009. *See* DHS Fact Sheet, ICE Detention Reform: Principles and Next Steps (Oct. 6, 2009).

Critics remain skeptical of the pace of progress, but ICE has made many changes. Under the lead of a new Office of Detention Policy and Planning, it began acquisition of new facilities appropriate to a civil detention model, looking especially at converted hotels (emulating a pioneering facility of this sort in Broward County, Florida), nursing homes, and other residential facilities. ICE terminated several detention contracts and consolidated existing facilities, reducing the number from 341 to 255 by 2010, while centralizing management to help assure more uniform performance. To cut down on distant transfers, it opened large new facilities in underserved areas, such as California and the northeast corridor. In the meantime, ICE developed a well-received online detainee locator system, launched in 2010, for use by family, friends and counsel.

Other changes included the development of a detainee assessment tool, to facilitate and standardize decisions on whether to detain, and if so, in what level of security. *See* Mark Noferi & Robert Koulish, *The Immigration Detention Risk Assessment*, 29 Geo. Immigr. L.J. 45 (2014) (examining the outcomes of ICE's risk assessment initiative and concluding that the tool would not reduce current over-detention trends). Supervision of medical care was overhauled, and clinical directors at the facilities received greater autonomy to approve medical requests and thus speed the provision of needed treatment. To achieve improved accountability, ICE expanded the staff of ICE officers who provide full-time on-site oversight at the largest detention facilities (covering 80 percent of detainees). It also created a centralized Office of Detention Oversight as part of the Office of Professional Responsibility, which reports directly to the head of ICE and is independent of the ICE division that manages detention. ICE has also developed, in wide consultations that included NGOs, a new set of Performance Based National Detention Standards, with clearer benchmarks for judging contractor performance and imposing sanctions for failures. *See* ICE Detention Reform Accomplishments, *supra*; Human Rights First, Jails and Jumpsuits:

Transforming the U.S. Immigration Detention System—A Two-Year Review (2011).

Juveniles. Separate standards apply to the detention of juveniles, which has been an area of special concern at least as far back as the U.S. Supreme Court decision in *Reno v. Flores*, 507 U.S. 292, 113 S.Ct. 1439, 123 L.Ed.2d 1 (1993). That case led to a settlement on detention, processing, and release of minors, which provided standards and procedures that continues to govern juvenile detention. The Homeland Security Act of 2002 transferred most responsibility for detention of unaccompanied minors to the Office of Refugee Resettlement in the Department of Health and Human Services, and the William Wilberforce Trafficking Victims Protection Reauthorization Act of 2008 strengthened the procedures and protections applicable to unaccompanied children who come into the immigration system. *See* Jacqueline Bhabha & Susan Schmidt, *From Kafka to Wilberforce: Is the U.S. Government's Approach to Child Migrants Improving?*, 11–02 Imm. Briefings (2011); William A. Kandel, *Unaccompanied Alien Children: An Overview* (Cong. Res. Serv. 2016).

Detention of female-headed families. In the spring of 2014, the Obama Administration's plans for a more generous immigration approach collided with news of the arrival of thousands of unaccompanied children and families at the southern U.S. border. Most had left Central American countries that were experiencing unprecedented levels of gang activity and violence. David Martin frames the conflict between the situation at the border and the Administration's goals in this way:

> Record numbers of child migrants began arriving from Central America—sometimes alone and sometimes accompanied by family members. Up until that point, a major selling point for some form of legalization of long-resident undocumented populations (whether done through legislation or by executive action) had been the public perception that the border was under increasingly effective control. The arrival of children in such large numbers vividly undermined that perception, because this was a flow that seemed unlikely to yield to the tools previously used to beef up the border, such as frontier fencing or massive new deployments of the Border Patrol. The children and their family members were not trying to evade *la migra*. They were actually seeking officers out, in order to turn themselves in. They apparently perceived that this would lead to haven in the United States, perhaps through political asylum or through other special measures for children. . . .

David A. Martin, *Resolute Enforcement Is Not Just for Restrictionists: Building A Stable and Efficient Immigration Enforcement System*, 30 J.L. & Pol. 411, 421 (2015).

Facing congressional pressure to act, resistance from some communities to locating shelter care for the children within their boundaries, and a drop in public support for a legalization program, the Administration took an enforcement-minded approach to the crisis. In June 2014, DHS began to apply the expedited removal provisions of INA § 235(b)(1) to arriving Central American children accompanied by their mothers. The Administration announced it would detain the mothers and children rather than releasing them while their asylum claims were processed, as had been the common practice. DHS established a temporary facility in Artesia, New Mexico and contracted with private prison contractors to build and expand additional facilities in Dilley and Karnes City, Texas, bringing the capacity for family detention from approximately 100 beds to over 3,000. High-level executive officials announced the opening of the Artesia facility, to be paired with a new policy of rapid removal processing. See Remarks to the Press with Q&A by Vice President Joe Biden in Guatemala, https://www.whitehouse.gov/the-press-office/2014/06/20/remarks-press-qa-vice-president-joe-biden-guatemala, June 21, 2014; Julia Preston & Randal C. Archibold, *U.S. Moves to Stop Surge in Illegal Immigration*, N.Y. Times, June 21, 2014.

The decision to channel the mothers and their children into expedited removal proceedings had two consequences. It triggered mandatory detention and a truncated removal process that lacks judicial review, unless the person is found to have a credible fear of persecution. See INA § 235(b)(1)(B)(iii)(IV) ("Any alien subject to the procedures under this clause shall be detained pending a final determination of credible fear of persecution and, if found not to have such a fear, until removed."). The expedited removal process requires Customs and Border Patrol agents to inquire whether apprehended noncitizens have a fear of returning to their country of origin. Expressing a fear of return leads to an interview with a USCIS asylum officer to determine whether the noncitizen has a credible fear or reasonable fear of return. INA § 235(b)(1)(A) & (B); 8 C.F.R. § 208.30(d)–(g). If the asylum officer makes a positive determination, the noncitizen exits the expedited removal process and is entitled to pursue an asylum claim in a traditional removal proceeding under INA § 240. 8 C.F.R. § 235.6(a)(2)(ii). (For a lengthier discussion of expedited removal at the border, limits on judicial review, the procedure for identifying asylum seekers, and detention, see Chapter Six, pp. 503–511.)

Litigation and controversy enshrouded the detention facilities almost immediately. The detention of asylum-seeking mothers and children, a highly sympathetic group, inspired fierce critique from immigrant and child advocates, members of Congress, and other groups that the

Administration usually counted as allies. It galvanized immigration advocates, law school clinics and law students around the country. Brigades of volunteer legal teams traveled to the remote town of Artesia to represent the detainees and, after the Artesia facility closed, to the larger contractor-run sites in Karnes City and Dilley. *See* Stephen Manning, Ending Artesia, Chap. VI, Jan. 2015, https://innovationlawlab. org/the-artesia-report.

The Administration took a hard line on efforts to release the mothers and children on bond, initially declining to set any bond for release or setting unreachably high bonds for nearly all of the detained women and children. *See R.I.L-R v. Johnson*, 80 F. Supp. 3d 164, 172–73 (D.D.C. 2015); *see also* Martin, *supra* at 424 (reflecting that the Administration's severe reaction to the migrants "is explainable largely as a White House recognition that its long-term goals for dealing with the resident undocumented population can succeed only if that population exhibits no significant or visible net growth"). The government argued that the detainees lacked constitutional due process and habeas protections, relying *on United States ex rel. Knauff v. Shaughnessy*, 338 U.S. 537, 542–44 (1950). *See M.S.P.C. v. U.S. Customs & Border Prot.*, 60 F. Supp. 3d 1156, 1167–72 (D.N.M. 2014) (also citing *Shaughnessy v. United States ex rel. Mezei*, 345 U.S. 206, 215, 73 S.Ct. 625, 97 L.Ed. 956 (1953)). DHS maintained that detention was necessary to deter other children and families from making the journey, and that preventing further mass migration was a matter of national security. *See Matter of D-J-*, 23 I & N Dec. 572 (2003).

One federal district court agreed with the government that the detainees were not covered by the Constitution's guarantee of due process. *M.S.P.C.*, 60 F. Supp. 3d at 1176. Another rejected that argument and enjoined the government from detaining the families if the basis for detention was the deterrence of others. *R.I.L-R*, 80 F. Supp. 3d at 188–90.

Underlying the decision to institute detention and speedy deportation processing was an expectation that few, if any, of the mothers and children would establish meritorious asylum cases. *See* Remarks to the Press with Q&A by Vice President Joe Biden in Guatemala, https://www. whitehouse.gov/the-press-office/2014/06/20/remarks-press-qa-vice-president-joe-biden-guatemala, June 20, 2014 (predicting that the "vast majority" of detainees would be denied asylum and removed). Aided by the BIA's issuance of *Matter of A-R-C-G-*, 26 I & N Dec. 388 (BIA 2014) recognizing domestic violence as a basis for asylum, fourteen of the fifteen families who went forward with asylum claims in the fall of 2014 prevailed on the merits. *See* Manning, *supra*, at Chap. XIV. Average bond amounts at the Texas facilities dropped as immigration judges consistently reduced ICE's initial bond determinations, and release through conditional parole became more common.

Detainees acknowledged that the new detention facilities were an improvement over the holding cells at the border, nicknamed *hieleras* (iceboxes) for their temperature settings and *perreras* (dog kennels) after their chain-link box construction. *See Flores v. Lynch*, No. CV 85–04544 DMG, at 16 (July 24, 2015). The new detention facilities featured playgrounds, a school, a basketball gym, and a medical clinic. However, evidence mounted of psychological deterioration of the detained women and children. Allegations of substandard medical care by the private contractors appeared in the media, increasing the pressure on the Administration to back away from detention as a solution to the presence of families at the border. *See* Julia Preston, *Hope and Despair as Families Languish in Texas Immigration Centers*, N.Y. Times, June 14, 2015; Karen Lucas, et al, Letter to Megan Mack re The Psychological Impact of Family Detention on Mothers and Children Seeking Asylum, https://womensrefugeecommission.org/images/zdocs/CRCL-Complaint-Psych-Impact-of-Family-Detention.pdf, June 30, 2015 (summarizing academic research on the mental health impacts of detaining asylum seekers and the psychological evaluations of nine detained women and their children).

In May and June 2015, the Administration announced a softening of its strict position on releasing the detainees, promising to review the cases of mothers and children detained for longer than 90 days and to release those who had established a credible fear or reasonable fear of return. Nevertheless, in August 2015, a federal district court in California ruled that the agency's detention policy violated the consent decree in *Flores* that prohibited DHS from detaining minors in secure, unlicensed facilities and required DHS to place children with a suitable relative—even if that meant releasing the accompanying parent. *Flores v. Lynch*, No. CV 85–04544 DMG (Aug. 21, 2015).

While the numbers of Central American children arriving at the border have abated somewhat as of early 2016, migration of children and families from Central America continues to put pressure on the Administration's immigration agenda.

Alternatives to detention. ICE has also made increasing use in recent years of what are called alternatives to detention (ATDs). These are programs that enable release of the individual, but provide enhanced supervision, periodic reporting, and usually either telephone or ankle bracelet (GPS) monitoring. These steps are meant to help assure that the noncitizen appears for proceedings and will be reachable for removal if an order becomes final, but without the need for physical incarceration. Congress has mandated a nationwide plan to expand the use of ATDs, in part because such a system can be more humane, affording greater opportunity for the individual to prepare his case and consult with counsel and others, but also because ATDs are generally less expensive. For example, the Obama Administration's FY 2016 budget request for ICE included funding for 34,040 detention beds—31,280 adult beds that run an average rate of $123.54 per day and 2,760 beds at family detention centers that run an average of $342.73 per day. Statement of Sarah Saldaña, Director ICE DHS, Regarding the President's Fiscal Year 2016 Budget Request, Before the U.S. House of Reps. Committee on Appropriations Subcommittee on Homeland Security 5 (2015).

However, ATDs, according to 2014 ICE contractor data, cost $0.17 daily per person for telephonic monitoring, $4.41 daily per person for GPS monitoring, and an average of $8.37 daily per person for "full service supervision" (supervision, electronic monitoring, and case management). DHS Office of Inspector General, U.S. Immigration and Enforcement's Alternatives to Detention (Revised) 4 (2015). Detained cases have typically been prioritized for expeditious resolution by EOIR, and ICE was concerned that the savings from ATDs would be undercut if those cases shared the the slower track that ordinary nondetained cases follow. ICE therefore negotiated arrangements with EOIR to provide a separate expedited track for ATD cases. *See generally* Schriro, *supra* at 20–21; Donald Kerwin, Testimony on "Moving Toward More Effective Immigration Detention Management," Hearing before the House Subcommittee on Border, Maritime, and Global Counterterrorism [hereafter Detention Management Hearing], Dec. 10, 2009, at 4–5; Detention Watch Network & Mills Legal Clinic, Stanford Law School, Community-Based Alternatives to Immigration Detention 7–11 (2010). Since 2003, ICE has also implemented and expanded its Intensive Supervision Appearance Program (ISAP). Now in its third programmatic version, ISAP utilizes ATDs "in conjunction with the less restrictive release conditions associated with payment of a bond, or having to report periodically to an [Enforcement and Removal Operations] field office." DHS Office of Inspector General, *supra,* at 3.

Though there is cautious support in the NGO community for increasing use of ATDs, a 2015 DHS Office of the Inspector General evaluation of the use of ATD programs, in particular ISAP, raised questions about the effectiveness of ATDs, as well as the capacity needed to expand its use given resource constraints including financial and enforcement personnel.

According to ICE, the [ISAP] is effective because . . . few program participants abscond. However, ICE has changed how it uses the program and no longer supervises some participants throughout their immigration proceedings. As a result, ICE cannot definitively determine whether [ISAP] has reduced the rate at which aliens, who were once in the program but who are no longer participating, have absconded or been arrested for criminal acts. * * *

ICE instructed field offices to consider redetaining noncompliant [ISAP] participants, but most field offices do not have sufficient funding for detention bed space to accommodate all noncompliant participants. * * *

ICE developed a Risk Classification Assessment to assist its release and custody classification decisions. However, the tool is time consuming, resource intensive, and not effective in determining which aliens to release or under what conditions.

Id. at 2.

2. LIMITS ON DETENTION

Are there constitutional or statutory limits on detention? We consider this in two settings: (1) indefinite detention when a removal order has issued but the noncitizen cannot be removed; and (2) mandatory detention pending removal proceedings. It might seem more logical to consider detention pending proceedings first, but because indefinite detention reached the Supreme Court before the other procedures were litigated there, we take them in this order.

a. Indefinite Detention After a Final Removal Order

Under INA § 241(a), removal must normally take place within the 90-day "removal period" after the order becomes final. During these 90 days, the Attorney General "shall detain the alien," and may not release those found inadmissible or deportable under the criminal or certain national security grounds. *See* INA § 241(a)(2). If removal does not occur during this period, the Attorney General has discretion to release the noncitizen under supervision. *See* INA § 241(a)(3), (6); 8 C.F.R. §§ 241.4, 241.5.

Noncitizens almost always have somewhere to be sent. Indeed, international law usually obligates countries to permit its nationals to return. The Universal Declaration of Human Rights states: "Everyone has the right to leave any country, including his own, and to return to his country." Art. 13(2), UNGA Res. 217 (III), UN Doc. A/801 (1948). But what if the noncitizen cannot be removed because no country will take him? Can the government detain him indefinitely? In *Shaughnessy v. United States ex rel. Mezei*, 345 U.S. 206, 73 S.Ct. 625, 97 L.Ed. 956 (1953), considered in Chapter Six, the Supreme Court approved indefinite detention of an excludable alien, without any judicial testing of the substantive merits or even the procedural validity of the detention order. But *Wong Wing v. United States*, 163 U.S. 228, 16 S.Ct. 977, 41 L.Ed. 140

(1896), excerpted in Chapter Three, may limit *Mezei*, if the noncitizen succeeds in characterizing his detention as criminal punishment.

Succeeding years presented few opportunities to rethink the *Mezei* approach to indefinite detention. But cases of prolonged, perhaps indefinite detention began to reach the federal courts in the 1990s because a small but significant group of countries would not take back their own citizens who received final orders for removal from the United States. Other indefinite detainees were either stateless or of uncertain citizenship, and no country would accept them. In the following case, the U.S. Supreme Court considered whether indefinite detention is lawful.

ZADVYDAS V. DAVIS

Supreme Court of the United States, 2001.
533 U.S. 678, 121 S.Ct. 2491, 150 L.Ed.2d 653.

JUSTICE BREYER delivered the opinion of the Court.

When an alien has been found to be unlawfully present in the United States and a final order of removal has been entered, the Government ordinarily secures the alien's removal during a subsequent 90-day statutory "removal period," during which time the alien normally is held in custody.

A special statute authorizes further detention if the Government fails to remove the alien during those 90 days. It says:

> An alien ordered removed [1] who is inadmissible . . . [2] [or] removable [as a result of violations of status requirements or entry conditions, violations of criminal law, or reasons of security or foreign policy] or [3] who has been determined by the Attorney General to be a risk to the community or unlikely to comply with the order of removal, may be detained beyond the removal period and, if released, shall be subject to [certain] terms of supervision. . . .

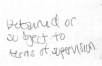 *detained or subject to terms of supervision*

INA § 241(a)(6).

In these cases, we must decide whether this post-removal-period statute authorizes the Attorney General to detain a removable alien *indefinitely* beyond the removal period or only for a period *reasonably necessary* to secure the alien's removal. We deal here with aliens who were admitted to the United States but subsequently ordered removed. Aliens who have not yet gained initial admission to this country would present a very different question. Based on our conclusion that indefinite detention of aliens in the former category would raise serious constitutional concerns, we construe the statute to contain an implicit "reasonable time" limitation, the application of which is subject to federal court review.

I

* * *

We consider two separate instances of detention. The first concerns Kestutis Zadvydas, a resident alien who was born, apparently of Lithuanian parents, in a displaced persons camp in Germany in 1948. When he was eight years old, Zadvydas immigrated to the United States with his parents and other family members, and he has lived here ever since.

Zadvydas has a long criminal record, involving drug crimes, attempted robbery, attempted burglary, and theft. He has a history of flight, from both criminal and deportation proceedings. Most recently, he was convicted of possessing, with intent to distribute, cocaine; sentenced to 16 years' imprisonment; released on parole after two years; taken into INS custody; and, in 1994, ordered deported to Germany.

In 1994, Germany told the INS that it would not accept Zadvydas because he was not a German citizen. Shortly thereafter, Lithuania refused to accept Zadvydas because he was neither a Lithuanian citizen nor a permanent resident. In 1996, the INS asked the Dominican Republic (Zadvydas' wife's country) to accept him, but this effort proved unsuccessful. In 1998, Lithuania rejected, as inadequately documented, Zadvydas' effort to obtain Lithuanian citizenship based on his parents' citizenship; Zadvydas' reapplication is apparently still pending.

* * *

The second case is that of Kim Ho Ma. Ma was born in Cambodia in 1977. When he was two, his family fled, taking him to refugee camps in Thailand and the Philippines and eventually to the United States, where he has lived as a resident alien since the age of seven. In 1995, at age 17, Ma was involved in a gang-related shooting, convicted of manslaughter, and sentenced to 38 months' imprisonment. He served two years, after which he was released into INS custody.

In light of his conviction of an "aggravated felony," Ma was ordered removed. The 90-day removal period expired in early 1999, but the INS continued to keep Ma in custody, because, in light of his former gang membership, the nature of his crime, and his planned participation in a prison hunger strike, it was "unable to conclude that Mr. Ma would remain nonviolent and not violate the conditions of release."

* * *

III

The post-removal-period detention statute applies to certain categories of aliens who have been ordered removed, namely inadmissible aliens, criminal aliens, aliens who have violated their nonimmigrant status conditions, and aliens removable for certain national security or foreign relations reasons, as well as any alien "who has been determined by the Attorney General to be a risk to the community or unlikely to comply with the order of removal." It says that an alien who falls into one of these categories "may be detained beyond the removal period and, if released, shall be subject to [certain] terms of supervision." INA § 241(a)(6).

The Government argues that the statute means what it literally says. It sets no "limit on the length of time beyond the removal period that an alien who falls within one of the Section 241(a)(6) categories may be detained." Hence, "whether to continue to detain such an alien and, if so, in what circumstances and for how long" is up to the Attorney General, not up to the courts.

"[I]t is a cardinal principle" of statutory interpretation, however, that when an Act of Congress raises "a serious doubt" as to its constitutionality, "this Court will first ascertain whether a construction of the statute is fairly possible by which the question may be avoided." *Crowell v. Benson*, 285 U.S. 22, 62 (1932). We have read significant limitations into other immigration statutes in order to avoid their constitutional invalidation. For similar reasons, we read an implicit limitation into the statute before us. In our view, the statute, read in light of the Constitution's demands, limits an alien's post-removal-period detention to a period reasonably necessary to bring about that alien's removal from the United States. It does not permit indefinite detention.

A

A statute permitting indefinite detention of an alien would raise a serious constitutional problem. The Fifth Amendment's Due Process Clause forbids the Government to "depriv[e]" any "person . . . of . . . liberty . . . without due process of law." Freedom from imprisonment—from government custody, detention, or other forms of physical restraint—lies at the heart of the liberty that Clause protects. And this Court has said that government detention violates that Clause unless the detention is ordered in a *criminal* proceeding with adequate procedural protections, *see United States v. Salerno*, 481 U.S. 739, 746 (1987), or, in certain special and "narrow" non-punitive "circumstances," *Foucha* [*v. Louisiana*, 504 U.S. 71, 80 (1992)], where a special justification, such as harm-threatening mental illness, outweighs the "individual's constitutionally protected interest in avoiding physical restraint." *Kansas v. Hendricks*, 521 U.S. 346, 356 (1997). The proceedings at issue here are civil, not criminal, and we assume that they are nonpunitive in purpose and effect. There is no sufficiently strong special justification here for indefinite civil detention—at least as administered under this statute. The statute, says the Government, has two regulatory goals: "ensuring the appearance of aliens at future immigration proceedings" and "[p]reventing danger to the community." But by definition the first justification—preventing flight—is weak or nonexistent where removal seems a remote possibility at best. * * *

The second justification—protecting the community—does not necessarily diminish in force over time. But we have upheld preventive detention based on dangerousness only when limited to specially dangerous individuals and subject to strong procedural protections. [Citing *Hendricks*, *Salerno*, and *Foucha*.] In cases in which preventive detention is of potentially *indefinite* duration, we have also demanded that the dangerousness rationale be accompanied by some other special circumstance, such as mental illness, that helps to create the danger.

* * * [O]nce the flight risk justification evaporates, the only special circumstance present is the alien's removable status itself, which bears no relation to a detainee's dangerousness.

Moreover, the sole procedural protections available to the alien are found in administrative proceedings, where the alien bears the burden of proving he is not dangerous, without (in the Government's view) significant later judicial review. * * * The serious constitutional problem arising out of a statute that, in these circumstances, permits an indefinite, perhaps permanent, deprivation of human liberty without any such protection is obvious.

The Government argues that, from a constitutional perspective, alien status itself can justify indefinite detention, and points to *Shaughnessy v. United States ex rel. Mezei*, 345 U.S. 206 (1953), as support. * * *

Although *Mezei*, like the present cases, involves indefinite detention, it differs from the present cases in a critical respect. As the Court emphasized, the alien's extended departure from the United States required him to seek entry into this country once again. His presence on Ellis Island did not count as entry into the United States. Hence, he was "treated," for constitutional purposes, "as if stopped at the border." And that made all the difference.

The distinction between an alien who has effected an entry into the United States and one who has never entered runs throughout immigration law. It is well established that certain constitutional protections available to persons inside the United States are unavailable to aliens outside of our geographic borders. But once an alien enters the country, the legal circumstance changes, for the Due Process Clause applies to all "persons" within the United States, including aliens, whether their presence here is lawful, unlawful, temporary, or permanent. *See Plyler v. Doe*, 457 U.S. 202, 210 (1982); *Mathews v. Diaz*, 426 U.S. 67, 77 (1976); *Kwong Hai Chew v. Colding*, 344 U.S. 590, 596–598, and n.5 (1953); *Yick Wo v. Hopkins*, 118 U.S. 356, 369 (1886); *cf.*

Mezei, supra, at 212 ("[A]liens who have once passed through our gates, even illegally, may be expelled only after proceedings conforming to traditional standards of fairness encompassed in due process of law"). Indeed, this Court has held that the Due Process Clause protects an alien subject to a final order of deportation, *see Wong Wing v. United States,* 163 U.S. 228, 238 (1896), though the nature of that protection may vary depending upon status and circumstance, *see Landon v. Plasencia,* 459 U.S. 21, 32–34 (1982).

In *Wong Wing, supra,* the Court held unconstitutional a statute that imposed a year of hard labor upon aliens subject to a final deportation order. That case concerned substantive protections for aliens who had been ordered removed, not procedural protections for aliens whose removability was being determined. * * * And contrary to Justice Scalia's characterization, in *Mezei* itself, both this Court's rejection of Mezei's challenge to the procedures by which he was deemed excludable and its rejection of his challenge to continued detention rested upon a basic territorial distinction.

* * *

The Government also looks for support to cases holding that Congress has "plenary power" to create immigration law, and that the judicial branch must defer to executive and legislative branch decisionmaking in that area. But that power is subject to important constitutional limitations. In these cases, we focus upon those limitations. In doing so, we nowhere deny the right of Congress to remove aliens, to subject them to supervision with conditions when released from detention, or to incarcerate them where appropriate for violations of those conditions. The question before us is not one of " 'confer[ring] on those admitted the right to remain against the national will' " or " 'sufferance of aliens' " who should be removed. Rather, the issue we address is whether aliens that the Government finds itself unable to remove are to be condemned to an indefinite term of imprisonment within the United States.

Nor do the cases before us require us to consider the political branches' authority to control entry into the United States. Hence we leave no "unprotected spot in the Nation's armor." *Kwong Hai Chew, supra,* at 602. Neither do we consider terrorism or other special circumstances where special arguments might be made for forms of preventive detention and for heightened deference to the judgments of the political branches with respect to matters of national security. The sole foreign policy consideration the Government mentions here is the concern lest courts interfere with "sensitive" repatriation negotiations. But neither the Government nor the dissents explain how a habeas court's efforts to determine the likelihood of repatriation, if handled with appropriate sensitivity, could make a significant difference in this respect.

Finally, the Government argues that, whatever liberty interest the aliens possess, it is "greatly diminished" by their lack of a legal right to "liv[e] at large in this country." The choice, however, is not between imprisonment and the alien "living at large." It is between imprisonment and supervision under release conditions that may not be violated. And, for the reasons we have set forth, we believe that an alien's liberty interest is, at the least, strong enough to raise a serious question as to whether, irrespective of the procedures used, the Constitution permits detention that is indefinite and potentially permanent.

B

Despite this constitutional problem, if "Congress has made its intent" in the statute "clear, 'we must give effect to that intent.'" *Miller v. French*, 530 U.S. 327, 336 (2000) (quoting *Sinclair Refining Co. v. Atkinson*, 370 U.S. 195, 215 (1962)). We cannot find here, however, any clear indication of congressional intent to grant the Attorney General the power to hold indefinitely in confinement an alien ordered removed. * * *

The Government points to the statute's word "may." But while "may" suggests discretion, it does not necessarily suggest unlimited discretion. In that respect the word "may" is ambiguous. Indeed, if Congress had meant to authorize long-term detention of unremovable aliens, it certainly could have spoken in clearer terms. Compare INA § 507(b)(2)(C) ("If no country is willing to receive" a terrorist alien ordered removed, "the Attorney General may, notwithstanding any other provision of law, retain the alien in custody" and must review the detention determination every six months).

* * *

We have found nothing in the history of [the] statutes [that are precursors of § 241(a)(6)] that clearly demonstrates a congressional intent to authorize indefinite, perhaps permanent, detention. Consequently, interpreting the statute to avoid a serious constitutional threat, we conclude that, once removal is no longer reasonably foreseeable, continued detention is no longer authorized by statute. *See* 1 E. Coke, Institutes *70b ("*Cessante ratione legis cessat ipse lex*") (the rationale of a legal rule no longer being applicable, that rule itself no longer applies).

IV

* * *

[A court considering a habeas corpus petition] must ask whether the detention in question exceeds a period reasonably necessary to secure removal. It should measure reasonableness primarily in terms of the statute's basic purpose, namely assuring the alien's presence at the moment of removal. Thus, if removal is not reasonably foreseeable, the court should hold continued detention unreasonable and no longer authorized by statute. In that case, of course, the alien's release may and should be conditioned on any of the various forms of supervised release that are appropriate in the circumstances, and the alien may no doubt be returned to custody upon a violation of those conditions. And if removal is reasonably foreseeable, the habeas court should consider the risk of the alien's committing further crimes as a factor potentially justifying confinement within that reasonable removal period.

* * *

Ordinary principles of judicial review in this area recognize primary Executive Branch responsibility. They counsel judges to give expert agencies decisionmaking leeway in matters that invoke their expertise. They recognize Executive Branch primacy in foreign policy matters. And they consequently require courts to listen with care when the Government's foreign policy judgments, including, for example, the status of repatriation negotiations, are at issue, and to grant the Government appropriate leeway when its judgments rest upon foreign policy expertise.

We realize that recognizing this necessary Executive leeway will often call for difficult judgments. In order to limit the occasions when courts will need to make them, we think it practically necessary to recognize some presumptively reasonable period of detention. We have adopted similar presumptions in other contexts to guide lower court determinations.

While an argument can be made for confining any presumption to 90 days, we doubt that when Congress shortened the removal period to 90 days in 1996 it believed that all reasonably foreseeable removals could be accomplished in that time. We do have reason to believe [based on the legislative history of a precursor statute], however, that Congress previously doubted the constitutionality of detention for more than six months. Consequently, for the sake of uniform administration in the federal courts, we recognize that period. After this 6-month period, once the alien provides good reason to believe that there is no significant likelihood of removal in the reasonably foreseeable future, the Government must respond with evidence sufficient to rebut that showing. And for detention to remain reasonable, as the period of prior post-removal confinement grows, what counts as the "reasonably foreseeable future" conversely would have to shrink. This 6-month presumption, of course, does not mean that every alien not removed must be released after six months. To the contrary, an alien may be held in confinement until it has been determined that there is no significant likelihood of removal in the reasonably foreseeable future.

[margin note: ② legislative history points to question of constitutionality of a 6 month hold]

* * *

JUSTICE SCALIA, with whom JUSTICE THOMAS joins, dissenting.

I join Part I of Justice Kennedy's dissent, which establishes the Attorney General's clear statutory authority to detain criminal aliens with no specified time limit. I write separately because I do not believe that, as Justice Kennedy suggests in Part II of his opinion, there may be some situations in which the courts can order release. * * * A criminal alien under final order of removal who allegedly will not be accepted by any other country in the reasonably foreseeable future claims a constitutional right of supervised release into the United States. This claim can be repackaged as freedom from "physical restraint" or freedom from "indefinite detention," but it is at bottom a claimed right of release into this country by an individual who *concededly* has no legal right to be here. There is no such constitutional right.

Like a criminal alien under final order of removal, an inadmissible alien at the border has no right to be in the United States. *The Chinese Exclusion Case*, 130 U.S. 581, 603 (1889). In *Shaughnessy v. United States ex rel. Mezei*, 345 U.S. 206 (1953), we upheld potentially indefinite detention of such an inadmissible alien whom the Government was unable to return anywhere else. We said that "we [did] not think that respondent's continued exclusion deprives him of any statutory or constitutional right." While four members of the Court thought that Mezei deserved greater procedural protections (the Attorney General had refused to divulge any information as to why Mezei was being detained), no Justice asserted that Mezei had a substantive constitutional right to release into this country. * * * Insofar as a claimed legal right to release into this country is concerned, an alien under final order of removal stands on an equal footing with an inadmissible alien at the threshold of entry: He has no such right.

The Court expressly declines to apply or overrule *Mezei*, but attempts to distinguish it—or, I should rather say, to obscure it in a legal fog. First, the Court claims that "[t]he distinction between an alien who has effected an entry into the United States and one who has never entered runs throughout immigration law." True enough, but only where that distinction makes perfect sense: with regard to the question of what *procedures* are necessary to prevent entry, as opposed to what *procedures* are necessary to eject a person already in the United States. See, *e.g., Landon v. Plasencia*, 459 U.S. 21, 32 (1982) ("Our cases have frequently suggested that a continuously present resident alien is entitled to a fair hearing *when threatened with deportation*" (emphasis added)). The Court's citation of *Wong Wing v. United States*, 163 U.S. 228 (1896), for the proposition that we have "held that the Due Process Clause protects an alien subject to a final order of deportation," is arguably relevant. That case at least involved aliens under final order of deportation.* But all it held is that they could not be subjected to the punishment of hard labor without a judicial trial. I am sure they cannot be tortured, as well—but neither prohibition has anything to do with their right to be released into the United States. Nor does *Wong Wing* show that the rights of detained aliens subject to final order of deportation are different from the rights of aliens arrested and detained at the border—unless the Court believes that the detained alien in *Mezei could* have been set to hard labor.

Mezei thus stands unexplained and undistinguished by the Court's opinion. We are offered no justification why an alien under a valid and final order of removal—which has *totally extinguished* whatever right to presence in this country he possessed—has any greater due process right to be released into the country than an alien at the border seeking entry. * * *

JUSTICE KENNEDY, with whom THE CHIEF JUSTICE joins, and with whom JUSTICE SCALIA and JUSTICE THOMAS join as to Part I, dissenting.

The Court says its duty is to avoid a constitutional question. It deems the duty performed by interpreting a statute in obvious disregard of congressional intent; curing the resulting gap by writing a statutory amendment of its own; committing its own grave constitutional error by arrogating to the Judicial Branch the power to summon high officers of the Executive to assess their progress in conducting some of the Nation's most sensitive negotiations with foreign powers; and then likely releasing into our general population at least hundreds of removable or inadmissible aliens who have been found by fair procedures to be flight risks, dangers to the community, or both. * * *

I

* * *

The Court, it is submitted, misunderstands the principle of constitutional avoidance which it seeks to invoke. The majority gives a brief bow to the rule that courts must respect the intention of Congress, but then waltzes away from any analysis of the language, structure, or purpose of the statute. Its analysis is not consistent with our precedents explaining the limits of the constitutional doubt rule. The rule allows courts to choose among constructions which are "fairly possible," *Crowell v. Benson*, 285 U.S. 22, 62 (1932), not to " 'press statutory construction to the point of disingenuous evasion even to avoid a constitutional question,' " *Salinas v. United States*, 522 U.S. 52, 60 (1997) (quoting *Seminole Tribe of Fla. v. Florida*, 517 U.S. 44, 57, n.9 (1996)). Were a court to find two interpretations of equal plausibility, it should choose the

---

* The Court also cites *Landon v. Plasencia*, 459 U.S. 21 (1982), * * * [b]ut that case is entirely inapt because it did not involve an alien subject to a final order of deportation. * * *

construction that avoids confronting a constitutional question. The majority's reading of the statutory authorization to "detai[n] beyond the removal period," however, is not plausible. * * *

Other provisions in § 241 itself do link the requirement of a reasonable time period to the removal process [citing §§ 241(c)(1)(A), § 241(c)(3)(A)(ii)(II)]. That Congress chose to impose the limitation in these sections and not in § 241(a)(6) is evidence of its intent to measure the detention period by other standards. When Congress has made express provisions for the contingency that repatriation might be difficult or prolonged in other portions of the statute, it should be presumed that its omission of the same contingency in the detention section was purposeful. * * *

The 6-month period invented by the Court, even when modified by its sliding standard of reasonableness for certain repatriation negotiations, makes the statutory purpose to protect the community ineffective. The risk to the community exists whether or not the repatriation negotiations have some end in sight; in fact, when the negotiations end, the risk may be greater. The authority to detain beyond the removal period is to protect the community, not to negotiate the aliens' return. The risk to the community survives repatriation negotiations. To a more limited, but still significant, extent, so does the concern with flight. It is a fact of international diplomacy that governments and their policies change; and if repatriation efforts can be revived, the Attorney General has an interest in ensuring the alien can report so the removal process can begin again.

* * *

The majority's unanchored interpretation ignores another indication that the Attorney General's detention discretion was not limited to this truncated period. Section 241(a)(6) permits continued detention not only of removable aliens but also of inadmissible aliens, for instance those stopped at the border before entry. Congress provides for detention of both categories within the same statutory grant of authority. Accepting the majority's interpretation, then, there are two possibilities, neither of which is sustainable. On the one hand, it may be that the majority's rule applies to both categories of aliens, in which case we are asked to assume that Congress intended to restrict the discretion it could confer upon the Attorney General so that all inadmissible aliens must be allowed into our community within six months. On the other hand, the majority's logic might be that inadmissible and removable aliens can be treated differently. Yet it is not a plausible construction of § 241(a)(6) to imply a time limit as to one class but not to another. The text does not admit of this possibility. As a result, it is difficult to see why "[a]liens who have not yet gained initial admission to this country would present a very different question."

* * * It is reasonable to assume, then, and it is the proper interpretation of the INA and § 241(a)(6), that when Congress provided for detention "beyond the removal period," it exercised its considerable power over immigration and delegated to the Attorney General the discretion to detain inadmissible and other removable aliens for as long as they are determined to be either a flight risk or a danger to the Nation.

The majority's interpretation, moreover, defeats the very repatriation goal in which it professes such interest. * * * One of the more alarming aspects of the Court's new venture into foreign affairs management is the suggestion that the district court can expand or contract the reasonable period of detention based on its own assessment of the course of negotiations with foreign powers. The Court says it will allow the Executive to perform its duties on its own for six months; after that, foreign relations go into judicially supervised receivership.

* * *

II

The aliens' claims are substantial; their plight is real. They face continued detention, perhaps for life, unless it is shown they no longer present a flight risk or a danger to the community. In a later case the specific circumstances of a detention may present a substantial constitutional question. That is not a reason, however, for framing a rule which ignores the law governing alien status.

As persons within our jurisdiction, the aliens are entitled to the protection of the Due Process Clause. Liberty under the Due Process Clause includes protection against unlawful or arbitrary personal restraint or detention. The liberty rights of the aliens before us here are subject to limitations and conditions not applicable to citizens, however. See, *e.g., Mathews v. Diaz*, 426 U.S. 67, 79–80 (1976) ("In the exercise of its broad power over naturalization and immigration, Congress regularly makes rules that would be unacceptable if applied to citizens"). No party to this proceeding contests the initial premise that the aliens have been determined to be removable after a fair hearing under lawful and proper procedures. * * *

* * *

When an alien is removable, he or she has no right under the basic immigration laws to remain in this country. The removal orders reflect the determination that the aliens' ties to this community are insufficient to justify their continued presence in the United States. An alien's admission to this country is conditioned upon compliance with our laws, and removal is the consequence of a breach of that understanding.

* * * Removable and excludable aliens are situated differently before an order of removal is entered; the removable alien, by virtue of his continued presence here, possesses an interest in remaining, while the excludable alien seeks only the privilege of entry.

Still, both removable and inadmissible aliens are entitled to be free from detention that is arbitrary or capricious. Where detention is incident to removal, the detention cannot be justified as punishment nor can the confinement or its conditions be designed in order to punish. *See Wong Wing v. United States*, 163 U.S. 228 (1896). * * * It is neither arbitrary nor capricious to detain the aliens when necessary to avoid the risk of flight or danger to the community.

Whether a due process right is denied when removable aliens who are flight risks or dangers to the community are detained turns, then, not on the substantive right to be free, but on whether there are adequate procedures to review their cases, allowing persons once subject to detention to show that through rehabilitation, new appreciation of their responsibilities, or under other standards, they no longer present special risks or danger if put at large. The procedures to determine and to review the status-required detention go far toward this objective.

By regulations, promulgated after notice and comment, the Attorney General has given structure to the discretion delegated by the INA in order to ensure fairness and regularity in INS detention decisions. First, the INS provides for an initial postcustody review, before the expiration of the 90-day removal period, at which a district director conducts a record review. 8 CFR § 241.4 (2001). The alien is entitled to present any relevant information in support of release, and the district director has the discretion to interview the alien for a personal evaluation. § 241.4(h)(1). At the end of the 90-day period, the alien, if held in custody, is transferred to a postorder detention unit at INS headquarters, which in the ordinary course will conduct an initial custody review within three months of the transfer. § 241.4(k)(2)(ii). If the INS determines the alien should remain in detention, a two-member panel of INS officers interviews the alien and makes a recommendation to INS headquarters. §§ 241.4(i)(1)–(3). The regulations provide an extensive, nonexhaustive list of factors that should be considered in the recommendation to release or further detain. Those include: "[t]he nature and number of disciplinary infractions"; "the detainee's criminal conduct and criminal convictions, including consideration of the nature and severity of the alien's convictions, sentences imposed and time actually served, probation and criminal parole history, evidence of recidivism, and other criminal history"; "psychiatric and psychological reports pertaining to the detainee's mental health"; "[e]vidence of rehabilitation"; "[f]avorable factors, including ties to the United States such as the number of close relatives"; "[p]rior immigration violations and history"; "[t]he likelihood that the alien is a significant flight risk or may abscond to avoid removal, including history of escapes"; and any other probative information. § 241.4(f). Another review must occur within one year, with mandatory evaluations each year thereafter; if the alien requests, the INS has the discretion to grant more frequent reviews. § 241.4(k)(2)(iii). The INS must provide the alien 30-days advance, written notice of custody reviews; and it must afford the alien an opportunity to submit any relevant materials for consideration. § 241.4(i)(3)(ii). The alien may be assisted by a representative of his choice during the review, §§ 241.4(i)(3)(i), (ii), and the INS must provide the alien with a copy of its decision, including a brief statement of the reasons for any continued detention, § 241.4(d).

* * *

* * * [T]he procedural protection here is real, not illusory; and the criteria for obtaining release are far from insurmountable. Statistics show that between February 1999 and mid-November 2000 some 6,200 aliens were provided custody reviews before expiration of the 90-day removal period, and of those aliens about 3,380 were released. As a result, although the alien carries the burden to prove detention is no longer justified, there is no showing this is an unreasonable burden.

* * *

* * * The majority instead would have the Judiciary review the status of repatriation negotiations, which, one would have thought, are the paradigmatic examples of nonjusticiable inquiry. * * * The Court's rule is a serious misconception of the proper judicial function, and it is not what Congress enacted.

* * *

NOTES AND QUESTIONS ON ZADVYDAS V. DAVIS

1.   Justice Scalia not only endorses *Mezei*; he believes it should control the result in *Zadvydas*, because both detainees had final removal orders that ended their permanent resident status:

> We are offered no justification why an alien under a valid and final order of removal—which has *totally extinguished* whatever right to presence in this country he possessed—has any greater due process right to be released into the country than an alien at the border seeking entry.

> Is there a good response to this argument?

2.   How persuasive is the Court's reading of the statute? If it is unconvincing, why did the Court adopt it? Consider the view that "[t]he principal decisions that have contributed to [the] expansion of judicial review in immigration cases have not been decisions of constitutional immigration

law. Instead, they reached results favorable to noncitizens by interpreting statutes, regulations, or other forms of subconstitutional immigration law." Hiroshi Motomura, *Immigration Law After a Century of Plenary Power: Phantom Constitutional Norms and Statutory Interpretation*, 100 Yale L.J. 545, 560 (1990). Motomura continues:

> In immigration law, the "constitutional" norms that actually inform statutory interpretation—which are norms borrowed from public norms generally—conflict with the expressly articulated constitutional norm—unreviewable plenary power. The former are "phantom" rather than "real" constitutional norms in the sense that they do not serve the first function of "constitutional" norms— namely, direct application to constitutional issues raised in immigration cases. * * * But "phantom constitutional norms" are "constitutional" in the sense that they, having been at least seriously entertained as a constitutional argument and in many cases actually adopted as an expressly constitutional decision in other areas of law, then carry over to immigration cases, where they are substantial enough to serve the limited function of informing interpretation of immigration statutes and other subconstitutional texts. Or, to use an image from the physical sciences, they have enough gravitational force to exercise a pull on these other sources of law. In this context, phantom norms produce results that are much more sympathetic to aliens than the results that would follow from the interpretation of statutes in light of * * * plenary power.

Id. at 564–65. *Cf.* T. Alexander Aleinikoff, *Detaining Plenary Power: The Meaning and Impact of Zadvydas v. Davis*, 16 Geo. Immigr. L.J. 365, 369 (2002) ("the Court has moved beyond invoking a 'phantom' constitutional norm"; characterizing *Zadvydas* as a decision of constitutional law).

3. The Court wants to distinguish noncitizens in the United States from those who are not here, and it cites *Mezei* as a prime example of a case involving a noncitizen on the wrong side of the constitutional borderline. But what line does *Zadvydas* draw? Is it based on physical presence in the United States, on having been admitted, or having entered? (Recall from Chapter Six that entry marked the pre-1996 line between exclusion and deportation proceedings, and that entry generally included physically present noncitizens who had crossed the border surreptitiously.) All three lines appear in *Zadvydas*, though they did not matter on the facts, because both Zadvydas and Ma were physically present, had been admitted, and had entered the United States. *See* Linda Bosniak, *A Basic Territorial Distinction*, 16 Geo. Immigr. L.J. 407 (2002).

Although many immigrants' rights groups hailed *Zadvydas* as a victory, the Court reaffirmed the vitality of their old nemesis, *Mezei*. "In an odd and unfortunate way, the case reaffirms what most scholars thought constitutional law was moving beyond: a distinction between the constitutional rights of non-citizens at the U.S border and those located inside the country." Aleinikoff, *Detaining Plenary Power*, *supra*, 16 Geo. Immigr. L.J. at 366. Ironically, the dissenters Kennedy and Rehnquist "would not let the substantive liberty decision turn on the exclusion-deportation line" and thus implied their disagreement with *Mezei's* approval of indefinite detention of a returning permanent resident. *See* David A. Martin, *Graduated Application of Constitutional Protections for Aliens: The Real Meaning of* Zadvydas v. Davis, 2001 Sup. Ct. Rev. 47, 78.

4.   Is *Zadvydas* best understood (and defended) as a decision distinguishing once-permanent residents from other noncitizens?

> If we focus on LPRs, we can perhaps recast the majority as saying something important about the deep structure or the trans-statutory understanding of just what lawful permanent residence really means. Historically and psychologically, admission in this category amounts to an invitation to full membership in the society and eventually the polity. Immigrants—that is, aliens selected for lawful permanent resident status—pass through the most rigorous screening our immigration system imposes. But having done so, they are then invited to become part of our community, to sink roots—permanent roots—and to chart out life plans in reliance on enduring rights to remain. With minimal additional effort, an LPR can also graduate to the highest level of membership, by becoming a naturalized citizen after five years residence. And in general it is fair to say that our reigning national mythology, bolstered by certain practical inducements, reflects an expectation that immigrants should and will naturalize. The exact holding in *Zadvydas*, which involved only LPRs, could be understood as saying that roots or connections established in that fashion, on the basis of such an invitation, simply count for more when calculating the constitutional limits on future treatment—even if the initially favorable legal status, for valid reasons, has been terminated. The historical paths these two aliens followed to a removal order leave them in a genuinely different constitutional position from [someone detained at the time of initial entry].

Martin, *Graduated Application*, *supra*, 2001 Sup. Ct. Rev. at 101–02.

5.   Detention and release issues related to *Mezei* arose in one branch of the judicial battles over the detention at Guantánamo of prisoners apprehended by the United States during its military operations in Afghanistan. After early rounds of litigation, the U.S. government conceded that 17 ethnic Uighur detainees from China, captured in late 2001, were not enemy combatants and so had to be released. But because the government agreed not to send them to China, where they were at risk of torture, they remained at Guantánamo, under slightly better conditions of detention, for a lengthy period thereafter, while the U.S. government sought to resettle them in other countries. In late 2008 the district court, frustrated at the slow pace, ordered that they be released into the United States, in view of the

"exceptional" circumstances of the case and the need to safeguard "an individual's liberty from unbridled executive fiat." The D.C. Circuit reversed, holding that no law authorized the release of these detainees into the United States. The dissent suggested that the habeas corpus statute, as construed by the Supreme Court in *Boumediene v. Bush,* 553 U.S. 723, 128 S.Ct. 2229, 171 L.Ed.2d 41 (2008), justified such a step. But the majority disagreed. The issue was not whether they should be released—the issue that habeas opens up—but where. Under *Knauff* and *Mezei,* the political branches retain authority over any entry into the United States. *Kiyemba v. Obama,* 555 F.3d 1022 (D.C. Cir. 2009), *opinion reinstated as amended, after remand from Supreme Court,* 605 F.3d 1046 (D.C. Cir. 2010).

The D.C. Circuit ruling carries echoes of Justice Scalia's comment in *Zadvydas.* "I am sure they cannot be tortured, as well—but neither prohibition has anything to do with their right to be released into the United States." Scalia was in dissent. Under the *Zadvydas* majority's approach, how should the Uighur's claims have been treated? Are there relevant differences between those detainees and Zadvydas or Ma?

As the Uighur case unfolded, the Supreme Court granted certiorari to review the D.C. Circuit's ruling described above, but the U.S. government's efforts to find resettlement offers in third countries then found success for all 17. Twelve of the Uighurs accepted the offers and are now living in Palau or Switzerland. When the Supreme Court remanded the case for reconsideration of the five remaining petitions in light of the resettlement offers, the D.C. Circuit reinstated its earlier ruling, and the Supreme Court then denied certiorari. *Kiyemba v. Obama,* 605 F.3d 1046 (D.C. Cir. 2010), *cert. denied,* 563 U.S. 954, 131 S.Ct. 1631, 179 L.Ed.2d 925 (2011).

b. Detention Pending Removal Proceedings

Much more common than lengthy detention after a final removal order is detention during removal proceedings. INA § 236(c) requires detention of certain categories of aliens in removal proceedings, not excluding lawful permanent residents. There is no individual bond hearing. Is this constitutional? The U.S. Supreme Court addressed this question two years after *Zadvydas.*

DEMORE V. KIM

Supreme Court of the United States, 2003.
538 U.S. 510, 123 S.Ct. 1708, 155 L.Ed.2d 724.

CHIEF JUSTICE REHNQUIST delivered the opinion of the Court.

LPR for 10yrs

* * * Respondent is a citizen of the Republic of South Korea. He entered the United States in 1984, at the age of six, and became a lawful permanent resident of the United States two years later. In July 1996, he was convicted of first-degree burglary in state court in California and, in April 1997, he was convicted of a second crime, "petty theft with priors."

The Immigration and Naturalization Service (INS) charged respondent with being deportable from the United States in light of these convictions, and detained him pending his removal hearing. We hold that Congress, justifiably concerned that deportable criminal aliens who are not detained continue to engage in crime and fail to appear for their removal hearings in large numbers, may require that persons such as respondent be detained for the brief period necessary for their removal proceedings.

* * * In conceding that he was deportable, respondent forwent a hearing at which he would have been entitled to raise any nonfrivolous argument available to demonstrate that he was not properly included in a mandatory detention category. See 8 CFR [§ 1003.19(h)(2)(ii)] (2002); *Matter of Joseph,* 22 I & N Dec. 799 (1999).[3] Respondent instead filed a habeas corpus action pursuant to 28 U.S.C. § 2241 in the United States District Court for the Northern District of California challenging the constitutionality of § 236(c) itself. He argued that his detention under § 236(c) violated due process because the INS had made no determination that he posed either a danger to society or a flight risk.

* * *

II

* * * Section 236(c) mandates detention during removal proceedings for a limited class of deportable aliens—including those convicted of an aggravated felony. Congress adopted this provision against a backdrop of wholesale failure by the INS to deal with increasing rates of criminal activity by aliens. Criminal aliens were the fastest growing segment of the federal prison population, already constituting roughly 25% of all federal prisoners, and they formed a rapidly rising share of state prison populations as well. Congress' investigations showed, however, that the INS could not even *identify* most deportable aliens, much less locate them and remove them from the country. One study showed that, at the then-current rate of deportation, it would take 23 years to remove every criminal alien already subject to deportation. Making matters worse, criminal aliens who were deported swiftly reentered the country illegally in great numbers.

The agency's near-total inability to remove deportable criminal aliens imposed more than a monetary cost on the Nation. First, as Congress explained, "[a]liens who enter or remain in the United States in violation of our law are effectively taking immigration opportunities that might

---

[3] This *"Joseph* hearing" is immediately provided to a detainee who claims that he is not covered by § 236(c). At the hearing, the detainee may avoid mandatory detention by demonstrating that he is not an alien, was not convicted of the predicate crime, or that the INS is otherwise substantially unlikely to establish that he is in fact subject to mandatory detention. Because respondent conceded that he was deportable because of a conviction that triggers § 236(c) and thus sought no *Joseph* hearing, we have no occasion to review the adequacy of *Joseph* hearings generally in screening out those who are improperly detained * * * .

otherwise be extended to others." Second, deportable criminal aliens who remained in the United States often committed more crimes before being removed. One 1986 study showed that, after criminal aliens were identified as deportable, 77% were arrested at least once more and 45%— nearly half—were arrested multiple times before their deportation proceedings even began. Hearing on H.R. 3333 before the Subcommittee on Immigration, Refugees, and International Law of the House Committee on the Judiciary, 101st Cong., 1st Sess., 54, 52 (1989) (hereinafter 1989 House Hearing).

Congress also had before it evidence that one of the major causes of the INS' failure to remove deportable criminal aliens was the agency's failure to detain those aliens during their deportation proceedings. * * *

Once released, more than 20% of deportable criminal aliens failed to appear for their removal hearings. * * *

* * *

As a response, congress reenacted § 236.

* * * Some studies presented to Congress suggested that detention of criminal aliens during their removal proceedings might be the best way to ensure their successful removal from this country. It was following those Reports that Congress enacted INA § 236, requiring the Attorney General to detain a subset of deportable criminal aliens pending a determination of their removability.

requiring

"In the exercise of its broad power over naturalization and immigration, Congress regularly makes rules that would be unacceptable if applied to citizens." *Mathews v. Diaz,* 426 U.S. 67, 79–80, 96 S.Ct. 1883, 48 L.Ed.2d 478 (1976). * * *

unacceptable if we did this to citizens

In his habeas corpus challenge, respondent did not contest Congress' general authority to remove criminal aliens from the United States. Nor did he argue that he himself was not "deportable" within the meaning of § 236(c).[6] Rather, respondent argued that the Government may not, consistent with the Due Process Clause of the Fifth Amendment, detain him for the brief period necessary for his removal proceedings. The dissent, after an initial detour on the issue of respondent's concession, ultimately acknowledges the real issue in this case.

p's arg

"It is well established that the Fifth Amendment entitles aliens to due process of law in deportation proceedings." *Reno v. Flores,* 507 U.S. 292, 306, 113 S.Ct. 1439, 123 L.Ed.2d 1 (1993). At the same time, however, this Court has recognized detention during deportation proceedings as a constitutionally valid aspect of the deportation process. As we said more than a century ago, deportation proceedings "would be

okay to detain for deport.

---

[6]   * * * Lest there be any confusion, we emphasize that by conceding he is "*deportable*" and, hence, subject to mandatory detention under § 236(c), respondent did not concede that he *will ultimately be deported.* As the dissent notes, respondent has applied for withholding of removal.

vain if those accused could not be held in custody pending the inquiry into their true character." *Wong Wing v. United States,* 163 U.S. 228, 235, 16 S.Ct. 977, 41 L.Ed. 140 (1896).

In *Carlson v. Landon,* 342 U.S. 524, 72 S.Ct. 525, 96 L.Ed. 547 (1952), the Court considered a challenge to the detention of aliens who were deportable because of their participation in Communist activities. The detained aliens did not deny that they were members of the Communist Party or that they were therefore deportable. Instead, like respondent in the present case, they challenged their detention on the grounds that there had been no finding that they were unlikely to appear for their deportation proceedings when ordered to do so. Although the Attorney General ostensibly had discretion to release detained Communist aliens on bond, the INS had adopted a policy of refusing to grant bail to [them]. * * *

* * * The Court noted that Congress had chosen to make such aliens deportable based on its "understanding of [Communists'] attitude toward the use of force and violence . . . to accomplish their political aims." And it concluded that the INS could deny bail to the detainees "by reference to the legislative scheme" even without any finding of flight risk. * * *

* * *

Despite this Court's longstanding view that the Government may constitutionally detain deportable aliens during the limited period necessary for their removal proceedings, respondent argues that the narrow detention policy reflected in § 236(c) violates due process. Respondent, like the four Courts of Appeals that have held § 236(c) to be unconstitutional, relies heavily upon our recent opinion in *Zadvydas v. Davis,* 533 U.S. 678, 121 S.Ct. 2491, 150 L.Ed.2d 653 (2001).

* * *

But *Zadvydas* is materially different from the present case in two respects.

First, in *Zadvydas,* the aliens challenging their detention following final orders of deportation were ones for whom removal was "no longer practically attainable." * * *

In the present case, the statutory provision at issue governs detention of deportable criminal aliens *pending their removal proceedings.* Such detention necessarily serves the purpose of preventing deportable criminal aliens from fleeing prior to or during their removal proceedings, thus increasing the chance that, if ordered removed, the aliens will be successfully removed. Respondent disagrees, arguing that there is no evidence that mandatory detention is necessary because the Government has never shown that individualized bond hearings would be ineffective. But as discussed above, in adopting § 236(c), Congress had before it evidence suggesting that permitting discretionary release of aliens pending their removal hearings would lead to large numbers of deportable criminal aliens skipping their hearings and remaining at large in the United States unlawfully.

Respondent argues that these statistics are irrelevant and do not demonstrate that individualized bond hearings "are ineffective or burdensome." It is of course true that when Congress enacted § 236, individualized bail determinations had not been tested under optimal conditions, or tested in all their possible permutations. But when the Government deals with deportable aliens, the Due Process Clause does not require it to employ the least burdensome means to accomplish its goal. The evidence Congress had before it certainly supports the approach it selected even if other, hypothetical studies might have suggested different courses of action.

Zadvydas is materially different from the present case in a second respect as well. While the period of detention at issue in *Zadvydas* was "indefinite" and "potentially permanent," the detention here is of a much shorter duration.

Zadvydas distinguished the statutory provision it was there considering from § 236 on these very grounds, noting that "post-removal-period detention, *unlike detention pending a determination of removability* . . . , has no obvious termination point." *Id.,* at 697, 121 S.Ct. 2491 (emphasis added). Under § 236(c), not only does detention have a definite termination point, in the majority of cases it lasts for less than the 90 days we considered presumptively valid in *Zadvydas.* The Executive Office for Immigration Review has calculated that, in 85% of the cases in which aliens are detained pursuant to § 236(c), removal proceedings are completed in an average time of 47 days and a median of 30 days. In the remaining 15% of cases, in which the alien appeals the decision of the Immigration Judge to the Board of Immigration Appeals, appeal takes an average of four months, with a median time that is slightly shorter.

These statistics do not include the many cases in which removal proceedings are completed while the alien is still serving time for the underlying conviction. In those cases, the aliens involved are never subjected to mandatory detention at all. In sum, the detention at stake under § 236(c) lasts roughly a month and a half in the vast majority of cases in which it is invoked, and about five months in the minority of cases in which the alien chooses to appeal. Respondent was detained for somewhat longer than the average—spending six months in INS custody prior to the District Court's order granting habeas relief, but respondent himself had requested a continuance of his removal hearing.

For the reasons set forth above, respondent's claim must fail. * * *

JUSTICE KENNEDY, concurring.

While the justification for INA § 236(c) is based upon the Government's concerns over the risks of flight and danger to the community, the ultimate purpose behind the detention is premised upon the alien's deportability. As a consequence, due process requires individualized procedures to ensure there is at least some merit to the Immigration and Naturalization Service's (INS) charge and, therefore, sufficient justification to detain a lawful permanent resident alien pending a more formal hearing. * * *

As the Court notes, these procedures were apparently available to respondent in this case. Respondent was entitled to a [*Joseph*] hearing in which he could have "raise[d] any nonfrivolous argument available to demonstrate that he was not properly included in a mandatory detention category." * * * Respondent, however, did not seek relief under these procedures, and the Court had no occasion here to determine their adequacy.

For similar reasons, since the Due Process Clause prohibits arbitrary deprivations of liberty, a lawful permanent resident alien such as respondent could be entitled to an individualized determination as to his risk of flight and dangerousness if the continued detention became unreasonable or unjustified. *Zadvydas,* 533 U.S., at 684–686, 121 S.Ct. 2491; *id.,* at 721, 121 S.Ct. 2491 (Kennedy, J., dissenting) ("[A]liens are entitled to be free from detention that is arbitrary or capricious"). Were there an unreasonable delay by the INS in pursuing and completing deportation proceedings, it could become necessary then to inquire whether the detention is not to facilitate deportation, or to protect against risk of flight or dangerousness, but to incarcerate for other reasons. That is not a proper inference, however, either from the statutory scheme itself or from the circumstances of this case. The Court's careful opinion is consistent with these premises, and I join it in full.

[JUSTICE O'CONNOR, with JUSTICE SCALIA and JUSTICE THOMAS, joined the Court's opinion on the merits but would have found that the federal courts lacked jurisdiction to hear the case.]

* * *

JUSTICE SOUTER, with whom JUSTICE STEVENS and JUSTICE GINSBURG join, concurring in part and dissenting in part.

* * *

* * * The Court's holding that the Constitution permits the Government to lock up a lawful permanent resident of this country when there is concededly no reason to do so forgets over a century of precedent acknowledging the rights of permanent residents, including the basic liberty from physical confinement lying at the heart of due process. The

INS has never argued that detaining Kim is necessary to guarantee his appearance for removal proceedings or to protect anyone from danger in the meantime. Instead, shortly after the District Court issued its order in this case, the INS, *sua sponte* and without even holding a custody hearing, concluded that Kim "would not be considered a threat" and that any risk of flight could be met by a bond of $5,000. He was released soon thereafter, and there is no indication that he is not complying with the terms of his release.

* * *

At the outset, there is the Court's mistaken suggestion that Kim "conceded" his removability. The Court cites no statement before any court conceding removability, and I can find none. At the first opportunity, Kim applied to the Immigration Court for withholding of removal, and he represents that he intends to assert that his criminal convictions are not for removable offenses and that he is independently eligible for statutory relief from removal. * * *

* * *

II

A

It has been settled for over a century that all aliens within our territory are "persons" entitled to the protection of the Due Process Clause. Aliens "residing in the United States for a shorter or longer time, are entitled, so long as they are permitted by the government of the United States to remain in the country, to the safeguards of the Constitution, and to the protection of the laws, in regard to their rights of person and of property, and to their civil and criminal responsibility." *Fong Yue Ting v. United States,* 149 U.S. 698, 724, 13 S.Ct. 1016, 37 L.Ed. 905 (1893). *The Japanese Immigrant Case* [*Yamataya v. Fisher*], 189 U.S. 86, 100–101, 23 S.Ct. 611, 47 L.Ed. 721 (1903), settled any lingering doubt that the Fifth Amendment's Due Process Clause gives aliens a right to challenge mistreatment of their person or property.

The constitutional protection of an alien's person and property is particularly strong in the case of aliens lawfully admitted to permanent residence (LPRs). The immigration laws give LPRs the opportunity to establish a life permanently in this country by developing economic, familial, and social ties indistinguishable from those of a citizen. In fact, the law of the United States goes out of its way to encourage just such attachments by creating immigration preferences for those with a citizen as a close relation, and those with valuable professional skills or other assets promising benefits to the United States.

Once they are admitted to permanent residence, LPRs share in the economic freedom enjoyed by citizens: they may compete for most jobs in the private and public sectors without obtaining job-specific authorization, and apart from the franchise, jury duty, and certain forms of public assistance, their lives are generally indistinguishable from those of United States citizens. That goes for obligations as well as opportunities. Unlike temporary, nonimmigrant aliens, who are generally taxed only on income from domestic sources or connected with a domestic business, LPRs, like citizens, are taxed on their worldwide income. Male LPRs between the ages of 18 and 26 must register under the Selective Service Act of 1948. "Resident aliens, like citizens, pay taxes, support the economy, serve in the Armed Forces, and contribute in myriad other ways to our society." *In re Griffiths,* 413 U.S. 717, 722, 93 S.Ct. 2851, 37 L.Ed.2d 910 (1973). And if they choose, they may apply for full membership in the national polity through naturalization.

The attachments fostered through these legal mechanisms are all the more intense for LPRs brought to the United States as children. They grow up here as members of the society around them, probably without much touch with their country of citizenship, probably considering the United States as home just as much as a native-born, younger brother or sister entitled to United States citizenship. * * * Kim is an example. He moved to the United States at the age of six and was lawfully admitted to permanent residence when he was eight. His mother is a citizen, and his father and brother are LPRs. LPRs in Kim's situation have little or no reason to feel or to establish firm ties with any place besides the United States.

* * * [I]n *Kwong Hai Chew v. Colding,* 344 U.S. 590, 73 S.Ct. 472, 97 L.Ed. 576 (1953), we read the word "excludable" in a regulation as having no application to LPRs, since such a reading would have been questionable given "a resident alien's constitutional right to due process." *Id.,* at 598–599, 73 S.Ct. 472. *Kwong Hai Chew* adopted the statement of Justice Murphy, concurring in *Bridges* [*v. Wixon,* 326 U.S. 135, 65 S.Ct. 1443, 89 L.Ed. 2103 (1945)], that " 'once an alien lawfully enters and resides in this country he becomes invested with the rights guaranteed by the Constitution to all people within our borders. Such rights include those protected by the First and the Fifth Amendments and by the due process clause of the Fourteenth Amendment. None of these provisions acknowledges any distinction between citizens and resident aliens. They extend their inalienable privileges to all "persons" and guard against any encroachment on those rights by federal or state authority.' " 344 U.S., at 596–597, n.5, 73 S.Ct. 472 (quoting *Bridges, supra,* at 161, 65 S.Ct. 1443).

The law therefore considers an LPR to be at home in the United States, and even when the Government seeks removal, we have accorded LPRs greater protections than other aliens under the Due Process Clause [citing *Landon v. Plasencia,* 459 U.S. 21, 103 S.Ct. 321, 74 L.Ed.2d 21 (1982).]

Although LPRs remain subject to the federal removal power, that power may not be exercised without due process, and any decision about the requirements of due process for an LPR must account for the difficulty of distinguishing in practical as well as doctrinal terms between the liberty interest of an LPR and that of a citizen. In evaluating Kim's challenge to his mandatory detention under INA § 236(c), the only reasonable starting point is the traditional doctrine concerning the Government's physical confinement of individuals.

B

Kim's claim is a limited one: not that the Government may not detain LPRs to ensure their appearance at removal hearings, but that due process under the Fifth Amendment conditions a potentially lengthy detention on a hearing and an impartial decisionmaker's finding that detention is necessary to a governmental purpose. He thus invokes our repeated decisions that the claim of liberty protected by the Fifth Amendment is at its strongest when government seeks to detain an individual. The Chief Justice wrote in 1987 that "[i]n our society liberty is the norm, and detention prior to trial or without trial is the carefully limited exception." *United States v. Salerno,* 481 U.S. 739, 755, 107 S.Ct. 2095, 95 L.Ed.2d 697.

* * *

[Our prior cases on physical confinement, *Salerno, supra*; *Foucha v. Louisiana*, 504 U.S. 71, 112 S.Ct. 1780, 118 L.Ed.2d 437 (1992); *Addington v. Texas*, 441 U.S. 418, 99 S.Ct. 1804, 60 L.Ed.2d 323 (1979); *Kansas v. Hendricks*, 521 U.S. 346, 117 S.Ct. 2072, 138 L.Ed.2d 501 (1997); *Jackson v. Indiana*, 406 U.S. 715, 92 S.Ct. 1845, 32 L.Ed.2d 435 (1972)] yield a simple distillate that should govern the result here. Due process calls for an individual determination before someone is locked away. In none of the cases cited did we ever suggest that the government could avoid the Due Process Clause by doing what § 236(c) does, by selecting a class of people for confinement on a categorical basis and denying members of that class any chance to dispute the necessity of putting them away. The cases, of course, would mean nothing if citizens and comparable residents could be shorn of due process by this sort of categorical sleight of hand. Without any "full-blown adversary hearing" before detention, *Salerno, supra,* at 750, 107 S.Ct. 2095, or heightened burden of proof, *Addington, supra,* or other procedures to show the government's interest in committing an individual, *Foucha, supra*; *Jackson, supra*, procedural rights would amount to nothing but mechanisms for testing group membership. And if procedure could be dispensed with so expediently, so presumably could the substantive requirements that the class of detainees be narrow and the detention period strictly limited.

C

We held as much just two Terms ago in *Zadvydas v. Davis,* which stands for the proposition that detaining an alien requires more than the rationality of a general detention statute; any justification must go to the alien himself. * * *

The *Zadvydas* opinion opened by noting the clear applicability of general due process standards: physical detention requires both a "special justification" that "outweighs the 'individual's constitutionally protected interest in avoiding physical restraint'" and "adequate procedural protections." 533 U.S., at 690, 121 S.Ct. 2491 (quoting *Hendricks,* 521 U.S. at 356, 117 S.Ct. 2072). Nowhere did we suggest that the "constitutionally protected liberty interest" in avoiding physical confinement, even for aliens already ordered removed, was conceptually different from the liberty interest of citizens considered in *Jackson, Salerno, Foucha,* and *Hendricks.* On the contrary, we cited those cases and expressly adopted their reasoning, even as applied to aliens whose right to remain in the United States had already been declared forfeited.

* * *

Our individualized analysis and disposition in *Zadvydas* support Kim's claim for an individualized review of his challenge to the reasons that are supposed to justify confining him prior to any determination of removability. In fact, aliens in removal proceedings have an additional interest in avoiding confinement, beyond anything considered in *Zadvydas:* detention prior to entry of a removal order may well impede the alien's ability to develop and present his case on the very issue of removability * * * [because they could be transferred and isolated] away from their lawyers, witnesses, and evidence. * * *

In fact, the principal dissenters in *Zadvydas,* as well as the majority, accepted a theory that would compel success for Kim in this case. The dissent relied on the fact that Zadvydas and Ma were subject to a "final order of removal" and had "no right under the basic immigration laws to remain in this country," 533 U.S., at 720, 121 S.Ct. 2491 (opinion of KENNEDY, J.), in distinguishing them "from aliens with a lawful right to remain here," which is Kim's position. The dissent recognized the right of all aliens, even "removable and inadmissible" ones, to be "free from detention that is arbitrary or capricious," and the opinion explained that detention would pass the "arbitrary or capricious" test "when necessary to avoid the risk of flight or danger to the community."

* * * The references to the "necessity" of an individual's detention and the discussion of the procedural requirements show that the principal *Zadvydas* dissenters envisioned due process as individualized review, and the Court of Appeals in this case correctly held that Kim's mandatory

detention without benefit of individualized enquiry violated due process as understood by both the *Zadvydas* majority and Justice Kennedy in dissent.

D

* * *

By these standards, Kim's case is an easy one. * * * Detention is not limited to dangerous criminal aliens or those found likely to flee, but applies to all aliens claimed to be deportable for criminal convictions, even where the underlying offenses are minor. *E.g., Michel v. INS,* 206 F.3d 253, 256 (C.A.2 2000) (possession of stolen bus transfers); *Matter of Bart,* 20 I & N Dec. 436 (BIA 1992) (issuance of a bad check). Detention under § 236(c) is not limited by the kind of time limit imposed by the Speedy Trial Act, and while it lasts only as long as the removal proceedings, those proceedings have no deadline and may last over a year. * * *

Kim's detention without particular justification in these respects, or the opportunity to enquire into it, violates both components of due process, and I would accordingly affirm the judgment of the Court of Appeals requiring the INS to hold a bail hearing to see whether detention is needed to avoid a risk of flight or a danger to the community. This is surely little enough, given the fact that INA § 506 gives an LPR charged with being a foreign terrorist the right to a release hearing pending a determination that he be removed.

III

* * *

A

The Court spends much effort trying to distinguish *Zadvydas,* but even if the Court succeeded, success would not avail it much. *Zadvydas* was an application of principles developed in over a century of cases on the rights of aliens and the limits on the government's power to confine individuals. While there are differences between detention pending removal proceedings (this case) and detention after entry of a removal order *(Zadvydas),* the differences merely point up that Kim's is the stronger claim. In any case, the analytical framework set forth in *Salerno, Foucha, Hendricks, Jackson*, and other physical confinement cases applies to both, and the two differences the Court relies upon fail to remove Kim's challenge from the ambit of either the earlier cases or *Zadvydas* itself.[16]

* * *

---

[16] The Court tellingly does not even mention *Salerno, Foucha, Hendricks,* or *Jackson.*

The Court's closest approach to a reason justifying class-wide detention without exception here is a Senate Report stating that over 20% of nondetained criminal aliens failed to appear for removal hearings. To begin with, the Senate Report's statistic treats all criminal aliens alike and does not distinguish between LPRs like Kim, who are likely to have developed strong ties within the United States, and temporary visitors or illegal entrants. Even more importantly, the statistic tells us nothing about flight risk at all because, as both the Court and the Senate Report recognize, the INS was making its custody determinations not on the ground of likelihood of flight or dangerousness, but "in large part, according to the number of beds available in a particular region." Senate Report, at 23. * * * Four former high-ranking INS officials explained the Court's statistics as follows: "Flight rates were so high in the early 1990s not as a result of chronic discretionary judgment failures by [the] INS in assessing which aliens might pose a flight risk. Rather, the rates were alarmingly high because decisions to release aliens in proceedings were driven overwhelmingly by a lack of detention facilities." Brief for T. Alexander Aleinikoff et al. as *Amici Curiae* 19.

* * *

The Court's second effort is its claim that mandatory detention under § 236(c) is generally of a "much shorter duration" than the incarceration at issue in *Zadvydas*. While it is true that removal proceedings are unlikely to prove "indefinite and potentially permanent," they are not formally limited to any period, and often extend beyond the time suggested by the Court[.] * * *

* * * As the Solicitor General conceded, the length of the average detention period in great part reflects the fact that the vast majority of cases involve aliens who raise no challenge to removability at all. LPRs like Kim, however, will hardly fit that pattern. Unlike many illegal entrants and temporary nonimmigrants, LPRs are the aliens most likely to press substantial challenges to removability requiring lengthy proceedings. Successful challenges often require several months of proceedings; detention for an open-ended period like this falls far short of the "stringent time limitations" held to be significant in *Salerno*. The potential for several months of confinement requires an individualized finding of necessity under *Zadvydas*.

* * *

IV

This case is not about the National Government's undisputed power to detain aliens in order to avoid flight or prevent danger to the community. The issue is whether that power may be exercised by detaining a still lawful permanent resident alien when there is no reason for it and no way to challenge it. The Court's holding that the Due Process Clause allows this under a blanket rule is devoid of even ostensible justification in fact and at odds with the settled standard of liberty. I respectfully dissent.

JUSTICE BREYER, concurring in part and dissenting in part.

* * *

This case * * * is not one in which an alien concedes deportability. As Justice Souter points out, Kim argues to the contrary. Kim claims that his earlier convictions were neither for an " 'aggravated felony,' " nor for two crimes of " 'moral turpitude.' " And given shifting lower court views on such matters, I cannot say that his arguments are insubstantial or interposed solely for purposes of delay.

That being so—as long as Kim's legal arguments are neither insubstantial nor interposed solely for purposes of delay—then the immigration statutes, interpreted in light of the Constitution, permit Kim (if neither dangerous nor a flight risk) to obtain bail. For one thing, Kim's constitutional claims to bail in these circumstances are strong. Indeed, they are strong enough to require us to "ascertain whether a construction of the statute is fairly possible by which the [constitutional] question may be avoided." *Crowell v. Benson,* 285 U.S. 22, 62, 52 S.Ct. 285, 76 L.Ed. 598 (1932); accord, *Zadvydas, supra,* at 689, 121 S.Ct. 2491.

For another, the relevant statutes literally say nothing about an individual who, armed with a strong argument against deportability, might, or might not, fall within their terms. INA § 236(c) tells the Attorney General to "take into custody any alien who . . . *is* deportable" (emphasis added), not one who may, or may not, fall into that category. Indeed, the Government now permits such an alien to obtain bail if his argument against deportability is significantly *stronger* than substantial, *i.e.,* strong enough to make it "substantially unlikely" that the Government will win. *In re Joseph,* 22 I & N Dec. 799 (1999).

Finally, bail standards drawn from the criminal justice system are available to fill this statutory gap. Federal law makes bail available to a criminal defendant after conviction and pending appeal provided (1) the appeal is "not for the purpose of delay," (2) the appeal "raises a substantial question of law or fact," and (3) the defendant shows by "clear and convincing evidence" that, if released, he "is not likely to flee or pose a danger to the safety" of the community. 18 U.S.C. § 3143(b). These standards give considerable weight to any special governmental interest in detention (*e.g.,* process-related concerns or class-related flight risks). The standards are more protective of a detained alien's liberty interest than those currently administered in the INS' *Joseph* hearings. And they have proved workable in practice in the criminal justice system. Nothing in the statute forbids their use when § 236(c) deportability is in doubt.

I would interpret the (silent) statute as imposing these bail standards. So interpreted, the statute would require the Government to permit a detained alien to seek an individualized assessment of flight risk and dangerousness as long as the alien's claim that he is not deportable is (1) not interposed solely for purposes of delay and (2) raises a question of "law or fact" that is not insubstantial. And that interpretation, in my view, is consistent with what the Constitution demands. * * *

NOTES AND QUESTIONS ON DEMORE V. KIM

1. Chief Justice Rehnquist and Justice Souter clearly disagree on the significance of a noncitizen's concession that he is "deportable." Rehnquist places great weight on deportability, while Souter regards it as much less significant than Kim's application for discretionary relief. Who is right on this point? *See* Margaret H. Taylor, *Judicial Deference to Congressional Folly*: *The Story of* Demore v. Kim, in Immigration Stories 343, 357 (David A. Martin & Peter H. Schuck eds., 2005) ("the *Demore* majority equated an apparent concession of baseline deportability—an admission that Kim's convictions fit within some deportation ground—with a concession that the government had properly classified him as an aggravated felon, rendering him ineligible for discretionary relief from removal").

If you agree with Justice Souter, how likely must it be that a noncitizen will be granted discretionary relief before mandatory detention is unconstitutional? How does Justice Breyer's approach differ on this point? After *Demore*, can a noncitizen avoid mandatory detention under § 236(c) simply by contesting deportability?

2. As between the majority and Justice Souter's dissent, which analysis is more faithful to *Zadvydas*? How can Justice O'Connor be consistent and join the majority in both *Zadvydas* and *Demore*? In particular, how can she rely on the *Salerno-Foucha* line of cases in *Zadvydas*, but agree to an opinion that does not even mention them in *Demore*?

3. Why isn't Chief Justice Rehnquist correct in noting that Kim did get an individualized hearing, namely to determine whether he falls within the category of noncitizens subject to mandatory detention? Justice Souter seems to reply that this is not a truly individualized determination. But doesn't *all* decisionmaking, even decisions that seem to focus on an individual, ultimately depend on generalizations based on categories? If so, what is Justice Souter's basis for believing that the Congress overstepped its authority in enacting § 236(c)?

4. What does Justice Kennedy, writing separately, have in mind when he suggests that he might differently approach detention in another case, if intended "not to facilitate deportation, or to protect against risk of flight or dangerousness, but to incarcerate for other reasons"? Does he cast

constitutional doubt on mandatory detention that lasts much longer than the usual period of removal proceedings? How much longer?

5.   How plausible is the reading of INA § 236 that Justice Breyer proposes? Is it as plausible as the Court's reading of § 241(a)(6) in *Zadvydas*?

6.   How would the dissenters rule on a constitutional challenge to mandatory detention of a noncitizen who is *not* a permanent resident?

c.   Defining the Scope of *Zadvydas*

Zadvydas left undefined its implications for detained noncitizens who had never been admitted. DHS regulations adopted the view that *Zadvydas* applied only to noncitizens who had been admitted or were in the United States after having entered without inspection. *See* 8 C.F.R. § 241.13(b). This meant that it would not require release of excludable aliens (as they were called before 1996) or arriving aliens (as they are now known) who faced indefinite detention because they could not be readily removed. As of mid-2002, about 2000 such noncitizens were believed to be in federal custody, of which about 1700 were Mariel Cubans, and the rest arriving aliens. *See* Laurie Joyce, *INS Detention Practices Post-Zadvydas v. Davis*, 79 Interp. Rel. 809, 813 (2002).

The Mariel Cubans (or "Marielitos") arrived in 1980 from the port of Mariel, opened by the Cuban government with an invitation to relatives in the United States to come pick up their family members. In this sudden and chaotic process, Cuban officials also forced returning boats to carry thousands of others whom the Cuban government wished to remove, including hundreds escorted from prisons or mental hospitals to the docks. The 125,000 Marielitos were undocumented, but the vast majority were paroled into the United States shortly after arrival. Most eventually obtained LPR status under special legislation.

But a different outcome ensued if the person committed a crime in the United States while released. INS then revoked parole and took the person back into custody. These detainees were nearly all found excludable, but Cuba generally refused to take them back. The pattern of Cuban acceptance was erratic, however, and Washington continued trying to negotiate conditions for their return. Meanwhile, wishing to avoid the expense of lengthy detentions, but also not wanting to release dangerous criminals, the U.S. government undertook various screening measures to decide who would be released while the diplomacy continued. Some who were released in this fashion committed new offenses and found themselves back in custody. Over the course of 20-plus years, thousands of Cubans encountered lengthy incarceration—physically in the United States, inadmissible because of criminal convictions, and detained indefinitely because they failed to secure release through the review process and because Cuba would not take them back.

Many Marielitos brought statutory and constitutional challenges to their detention, but their claims were rejected by most of the federal appeals courts that heard them. *See, e.g., Carrera-Valdez v. Perryman,* 211 F.3d 1046, 1048 (7th Cir. 2000); *Barrera-Echavarria v. Rison,* 44 F.3d 1441 (9th Cir.) (en banc), *cert. denied,* 516 U.S. 976, 116 S.Ct. 479, 133 L.Ed.2d 407 (1995); *but see Rosales-Garcia v. Holland,* 238 F.3d 704, 725–27 (6th Cir.), *vacated,* 534 U.S. 1063, 122 S.Ct. 662, 151 L.Ed.2d 577 (2001), *on remand, Rosales-Garcia v. Holland,* 322 F.3d 386 (6th Cir.), *cert. denied,* 539 U.S. 941, 123 S.Ct. 2607, 156 L.Ed.2d 627 (2003).

Then came the U.S. Supreme Court decision in *Zadvydas.* Did that case—which involved detainees who had been admitted to the United States as lawful permanent residents—have implications for the indefinite detention of arriving aliens and parolees?

In *Clark v. Martinez,* 543 U.S. 371, 125 S.Ct. 716 (2005), the petitioners, Sergio Suarez Martinez and Daniel Benitez, had arrived in the United States from Cuba as part of the Mariel boatlift in June 1980, and were paroled into the United States under INA § 212(d)(5). Because of criminal convictions that made them inadmissible, they never became permanent residents. Their convictions also led to the revocation of their parole and ultimately to final removal orders. Now ordered removed and inadmissible under § 212, petitioners fell under the first category of aliens under INA § 241(a)(6), "(1) those ordered removed who are inadmissible under § 212"—in other words, non-admitted aliens. Thus, the question arose as to whether the Court's interpretation of § 241 in *Zadvydas,* that the government can detain admitted aliens in the second category of § 241 ("those ordered removed who are removable under § 237(a)(1)(C), 237(a)(2), or 237(a)(4)") for "only as long as 'reasonably necessary' to remove them from the country," applied to the § 241 category for non-admitted aliens.

According to the Supreme Court:

> [T]he answer must be yes. The operative language of § 241(a)(6), 'may be detained beyond the removal period,' applies without differentiation to all three categories of aliens that are its subject. To give these same words a different meaning for each category would be to invent a statute rather than interpret one."

543 U.S. at 378. Moreover, the Court found that a differing construction of the statute for each category of § 241 aliens would run counter to the canon of constitutional avoidance. As the Court stated:

> The Government, joined by the dissent, argues that the statutory purpose and the constitutional concerns that influenced our statutory construction in *Zadvydas* are not present for aliens, such as Martinez and Benitez, who have not been admitted to the United States. Be that as it may, it cannot

justify giving the *same* detention provision a different meaning when such aliens are involved. It is not at all unusual to give a statute's ambiguous language a limiting construction called for by one of the statute's applications, even though other of the statute's applications, standing alone, would not support the same limitation. The lowest common denominator, as it were, must govern. In other words, when deciding which of two plausible statutory constructions to adopt, a court must consider the necessary consequences of its choice. If one of them would raise a multitude of constitutional problems, the other should prevail—whether or not those constitutional problems pertain to the particular litigant before the Court.

The dissent takes issue with this maxim of statutory construction on the ground that it allows litigants to "attack statutes as constitutionally invalid based on constitutional doubts concerning other litigants or factual circumstances" and thereby to effect an "end run around black-letter constitutional doctrine governing facial and as-applied constitutional challenges." This accusation misconceives—and fundamentally so—the role played by the canon of constitutional avoidance in statutory interpretation. The canon is not a method of adjudicating constitutional questions by other means. Indeed, one of the canon's chief justifications is that it allows courts to *avoid* the decision of constitutional questions. It is a tool for choosing between competing plausible interpretations of a statutory text, resting on the reasonable presumption that Congress did not intend the alternative which raises serious constitutional doubts. The canon is thus a means of giving effect to congressional intent, not of subverting it. And when a litigant invokes the canon of avoidance, he is not attempting to vindicate the constitutional rights of others, as the dissent believes; he seeks to vindicate his own *statutory* rights. We find little to recommend the novel interpretive approach advocated by the dissent, which would render every statute a chameleon, its meaning subject to change depending on the presence or absence of constitutional concerns in each individual case.

Id. at 380–82.

d. Detention After *Zadvydas, Demore,* and *Clark*

(i) *Repatriation*

Repatriation agreements are useful in setting the framework for return of the nationals of the contracting state (in both directions) when a person is ruled removable by the authorities. But such agreements are not indispensable; arrangements can be made ad hoc with a focus on a particular case. *See Kassama v. DHS*, 553 F. Supp. 2d 301, 305 (W.D.N.Y. 2008). With or without a broad or formal repatriation agreement, ICE removal officers frequently deal with consular officers from the country of nationality at the retail level to overcome specific problems, supply or obtain necessary documents, or make precise travel arrangements. Shortly after the Supreme Court's ruling in *Zadvydas,* the U.S. government concluded a long-sought repatriation agreement with Cambodia, signed in March 2002, and soon thereafter the Cambodian government accepted the return of Kim Ho Ma. *See* Jay Stansell, *The Deportation of Kim Ho Ma*, 7 Bender's Immigr. Bull. 1500 (2002).

But repatriation can face a variety of barriers beyond a foreign government's refusal to accept its own citizens. Sometimes, the citizenship of a removable noncitizen is not clear. And what if the country has no functioning government? This question reached the U.S. Supreme Court in *Jama v. Immigration & Customs Enforcement*, 543 U.S. 335, 125 S.Ct. 694, 160 L.Ed.2d 708 (2005). Justice Scalia, writing for a five-to-four majority, rejected Keyse Jama's statute-based argument that he could not be removed to Somalia, where he remained a citizen, on the grounds that "Somalia has no functioning government, that Somalia therefore could not consent in advance to his removal, and that the Government was barred from removing him to Somalia absent such advance consent." Justice Scalia reasoned that in view of the limits on detention and removal in *Clark* and *Zadvydas*, "there is every reason to refrain from reading restrictions into that process that do not clearly appear." He also observed: "To infer an absolute rule [requiring explicit governmental] acceptance where Congress has not clearly set it forth would run counter to our customary policy of deference to the President in matters of foreign affairs." 543 U.S. at 348, 125 S.Ct. at 704.

After the Supreme Court's decision, the U.S. government tried to remove Jama to Somalia in 2005 by flying him first to Kenya, where he was turned over to a private security company that then flew him to the city of Bosasso in Puntland, a self-declared autonomous region of Somalia. There, however, local officials refused to accept Jama, and he was flown back to Kenya and then back to the United States. A federal district court ordered his release, but that order was stayed pending the government's appeal, which the Eighth Circuit rejected. The government then released Jama under supervision while it continued in its efforts to remove him to Somalia. *See* Kristin Tillotson, *A free man, at least for now*, Minneapolis Star Tribune, July 17, 2005, at 3B. Soon thereafter, Jama moved to Canada. He was later convicted in Winnipeg of aggravated assault and robbery for an armed home invasion where he stabbed a man. Canada eventually deported him to Somalia based on his long criminal record. Jama reported that he was trapped on the plane when it landed in

Somalia by armed men who threatened to kill him. *Deported Somali Says "Extremists" Shot at Plane,* CBC News, Sept. 15, 2010. Later reporting discredited that claim. Tom Brodbeck, *Refugee's Safety Not Our Problem,* Winnipeg Sun, Sept. 18, 2010.

(ii) Post-Order Custody Review

According to a February 2007 report by the Office of Inspector General of the Department of Homeland Security, approximately 80 percent of those detained following a final order are either removed or released within the 90-day removal period. DHS Office of Inspector General, ICE's Compliance with Detention Limits for Aliens with a Final Order of Removal from the United States 10 (2007). The remainder are entitled to prompt review of their situation to determine whether removal can be effectuated within the time frame set out by the Supreme Court or whether continued detention is justified, in accordance with a post-order custody review (POCR) process set forth in regulations adopted shortly after *Zadvydas.* 8 C.F.R. §§ 241.4, 241.13, 241.14. *See* 66 Fed. Reg. 38433 (2001).

The detainee must first show that he has cooperated in trying to obtain travel documents and that there is no significant likelihood of removal in the reasonably foreseeable future. *See* 8 C.F.R. § 241.4(g). If the detainee makes these showings, he is generally to be released under conditions designed "to protect the public safety and to promote the ability of the Service to effect the alien's removal as ordered." 8 C.F.R. § 241.13(h). He may still be detained, however, subject to stated procedures and review, if he falls into any of four categories: (1) aliens with a highly contagious disease that is a threat to public safety; (2) aliens detained on account of serious adverse foreign policy consequences if they are released; (3) aliens detained on account of security and terrorism concerns; and (4) aliens determined to be specially dangerous because they have been convicted of a crime of violence and have a mental condition or personality disorder indicating that they are likely to commit acts of violence in the future. *See* 8 C.F.R. §§ 241.13(e)(6), 241.14. The overwhelming majority of this remaining population is then either removed or released, subject to supervision, before the 180-day mark. Courts have divided on whether these regulations permitting extended detention in the four specific circumstances are consistent with the statute. *Compare Tran v. Mukasey,* 515 F.3d 478 (5th Cir. 2008), *and Tuan Thai v. Ashcroft,* 366 F.3d 790 (9th Cir. 2004) (finding regulation invalid), *with Hernandez-Carrera v. Carlson,* 547 F.3d 1237 (10th Cir. 2008) (upholding regulation).

In testimony given in 2011, the head of ICE's Office of Enforcement and Removal Operations singled out four countries for being "very slow to issue travel documents to ICE"—the main reason for lengthy post-order detention: China, India, Iran, and Laos. He also listed 19 other countries that are "recalcitrant" in accepting return of their nationals, setting forth the average time required to obtain travel documents from each, ranging from 52 days to 344 days. ICE is working with the Department of State to work out better arrangements with each such country to facilitate return. Gary Mead, Testimony at Hearing on H.R. 1932, The Keep Our Communities Safe Act, before the Subcomm. on Immigration and Border Security of the House Comm. on the Judiciary, 112th Cong., 1st Sess. 36–40 (2011).

A number of court decisions since *Zadvydas* have addressed the question whether removal in an individual case is "reasonably foreseeable," in which case continued detention would be authorized by INA § 241(a)(6). *Compare Beckford v. Smith,* No. 15–CV–1020–JTC, 2016 WL 827389, at 6 (W.D.N.Y. Mar. 3, 2016) (burden of showing no significant likelihood of removal not met where DHS had repatriated many aliens to Jamaica in recent years, and request from consulate for travel document remained pending); *with Poeuv v. Smith,* No. 15–cv–14220–ADB, 2016 WL 953223, at 2 (D. Mass. Mar. 11, 2016) (no significant likelihood of removal where U.S. had not pursued required procedures set forth in agreement between U.S. and Cambodia). *Diouf v. Napolitano,* 634 F.3d 1081 (9th Cir. 2011) also found the regulations deficient for failing to provide a hearing before an immigration judge on the issue of whether removal is reasonably foreseeable.

Another post-*Zadvydas* issue concerns the conditions placed upon release under § 241(a)(3), which lists specific forms of allowed supervision. According to the Ninth Circuit, the government may also require a bond even though that is not listed in § 241(a)(3), but it stated that "serious questions may arise concerning the reasonableness of the amount of the bond if it has the effect of preventing an alien's release." *Doan v. INS,* 311 F.3d 1160, 1162 (9th Cir. 2002).

Would the same "serious questions" arise in the case of bond that was set under § 236(a), which governs pre-final-order detention pending a hearing or an appeal? Decisions point in different directions. The Ninth Circuit has suggested that they do not. In *Prieto-Romero v. Clark,* 534 F.3d 1053 (9th Cir. 2008), three bond hearings before immigration judges had not resulted in the release of the respondent, a lawful permanent resident, while he awaited the court's decision on his petition for review of his removal order. At the third, the IJ set a $15,000 bond, which the respondent said he could not pay. The court ruled that "*Doan* does not license us to review the reasonableness of the amount of bond, even if Prieto-Romero cannot afford to post it," citing the tight limits on judicial review of pre-order release decisions in INA § 236(e) (the discretionary judgment regarding application of § 236 "shall not be subject to review"). More recently, however, a district court enjoined a no-release policy applied to Central American asylum seekers, reasoning that deterrence of mass migration could not sustain a practice of denying bond or setting unattainably high bonds. *R.I.L-R v. Johnson*, 80 F. Supp. 3d 164, 189 (D.D.C. 2015) ("Even assuming that general deterrence could, under certain circumstances, constitute a permissible justification for such detention, the Court finds the Government's interest here particularly insubstantial").

e. Limits on Government Authority to Detain

Though details are still contested, *Zadvydas* establishes a reasonably clear framework for deciding on the validity of lengthy detention after the removal period has begun and INA § 241(a)(6) comes into play. But under what circumstances is detention before that point subject to challenge? Somewhat surprisingly, the lower courts have found significant constraints on lengthy detention under the mandatory detention provision in INA § 236(c), despite the Supreme Court's apparent endorsement of that provision in *Demore*. The key to the cases has been the meaning of *Demore*'s observations that detention under INA § 236(c) without an individualized determination as to dangerousness and flight risk was constitutionally permissible because it lasted for only a "brief period" and had "a definite termination point." *See Demore,* 538 U.S. at 529. A series of incremental decisions in the Ninth Circuit—examining when the limits of *Zadvydas* take effect, what the government must do once a limit is reached, and what precise statutory authority provides the basis for these conclusions—culminated in 2015 in a class action appeal.

The next case addresses three different statutory provisions authorizing detention. Reading the case will be easier if you first review INA §§ 236(a), 236(c), and 235(b).

RODRIGUEZ V. ROBBINS

United States Court of Appeals, Ninth Circuit, 2015.
804 F.3d 1060,
petition for cert. filed, sub nom Jennings v. Rodriguez, 84 U.S.L.W. 3562 (Mar 25, 2016).

WARDLAW, CIRCUIT JUDGE:

This is the latest decision in our decade-long examination of civil, i.e. non-punitive and merely preventative, detention in the immigration context. As we noted in our prior decision in this case, *Rodriguez v. Robbins* (*Rodriguez II*), 715 F.3d 1127 (9th Cir. 2013), thousands of immigrants to the United States are locked up at any given time, awaiting the conclusion of administrative and judicial proceedings that will determine whether they may remain in this country. In 2014, U.S. Immigration and Customs Enforcement ("ICE") removed 315,943 individuals, many of whom were detained during the removal process.

According to the most recently available statistics, ICE detains more than 429,000 individuals over the course of a year, with roughly 33,000 individuals in detention on any given day.

Alejandro Rodriguez, Abdirizak Aden Farah, Jose Farias Cornejo, Yussuf Abdikadir, Abel Perez Ruelas, and Efren Orozco ("petitioners") represent a certified class of noncitizens who challenge their prolonged detention pursuant to INA §§ 235(b), 236(a), [and] 236(c) * * * without individualized bond hearings and determinations to justify their continued detention. * * * [T]he district court granted summary judgment to the class and entered a permanent injunction. Under the permanent injunction, the government must provide any class member who is subject to "prolonged detention"—six months or more—with a bond hearing before an Immigration Judge ("IJ"). At that hearing, the government must prove by clear and convincing evidence that the detainee is a flight risk or a danger to the community to justify the denial of bond. * * *

* * *

II. NATURE OF CIVIL IMMIGRATION DETENTION

Class members spend, on average, 404 days in immigration detention. Nearly half are detained for more than one year, one in five for more than eighteen months, and one in ten for more than two years. In some cases, detention has lasted much longer: As of April 28, 2012, when the government generated data to produce to the petitioners, one class member had been detained for 1,585 days, approaching four and a half years of civil confinement.[4]

Non-citizens who vigorously pursue claims for relief from removal face substantially longer detention periods than those who concede removability. Requesting relief from an IJ increases the duration of class members' detention by an average of two months; appealing a claim to the BIA adds, on average, another four months; and appealing a BIA decision to the Ninth Circuit typically leads to an additional eleven months of confinement. Class members who persevere through this lengthy process are often successful: About 71% of class members have sought relief from removal, and roughly one-third of those individuals prevailed. However, many detainees choose to give up meritorious claims and voluntarily leave the country instead of enduring years of immigration detention awaiting a judicial finding of their lawful status.

---

[4] The government challenges the accuracy of these figures, which are drawn from petitioners' expert report, based on disagreements with that expert's methodology. Using the government's preferred data set and process generates an average detention length of 347 days and a range of 180 to 1,037 days of civil detention for each non-citizen. Under either set of figures, typical class members are detained for well over 180 days. The differences in precise numbers are not material to our decision.

Class members frequently have strong ties to this country: Many immigrated to the United States as children, obtained legal permanent resident status, and lived in this country for as long as twenty years before ICE initiated removal proceedings. As a result, hundreds of class members are married to U.S. citizens or lawful permanent residents, and have children who were born in this country. Further, many class members hold steady jobs—including as electricians, auto mechanics, and roofers—to provide for themselves and their families. At home, they are caregivers for young children, aging parents, and sick or disabled relatives. To the extent class members have any criminal record—and many have no criminal history whatsoever—it is often limited to minor controlled substances offenses. Accordingly, when class members do receive bond hearings, they often produce glowing letters of support from relatives, friends, employers, and clergy attesting to their character and contributions to their communities.

Prolonged detention imposes severe hardship on class members and their families. Civil immigration detainees are treated much like criminals serving time: They are typically housed in shared jail cells with no privacy and limited access to larger spaces or the outdoors. Confinement makes it more difficult to retain or meet with legal counsel, and the resources in detention facility law libraries are minimal at best, thereby compounding the challenges of navigating the complexities of immigration law and proceedings. In addition, visitation is restricted and is often no-contact, dramatically disrupting family relationships. While in detention, class members have missed their children's births and their parents' funerals. After losing a vital source of income, class members' spouses have sought government assistance, and their children have dropped out of college. * * *

* * *

IV. DISCUSSION

* * * Based on our precedents, we hold that the canon of constitutional avoidance requires us to construe the statutory scheme to provide all class members who are in prolonged detention with bond hearings at which the government bears the burden of proving by clear and convincing evidence that the class member is a danger to the community or a flight risk. * * * We affirm the district court's order insofar as it requires automatic bond hearings and requires IJs to consider alternatives to detention because we presume, like the district court, that IJs are already doing so when determining whether to release a non-citizen on bond.[5] Because the same constitutional concerns arise

---

[5]   *See* 8 C.F.R. § 241.4(f) (listing factors that Department of Homeland Security ("DHS") must "weigh[ ] in considering whether to recommend further detention or release of a detainee," including the detainee's criminal history, evidence of recidivism or rehabilitation, ties to the

when detention approaches another prolonged period, we hold that IJs must provide bond hearings periodically at six month intervals for class members detained for more than twelve months. However, we reject the class's suggestion that we mandate additional procedural requirements.

A. Civil Detention

"In our society liberty is the norm, and detention prior to trial or without trial is the carefully limited exception." *United States v. Salerno,* 481 U.S. 739 (1987). Civil detention violates the Due Process Clause except "in certain special and narrow nonpunitive circumstances, where a special justification, such as harm-threatening mental illness, outweighs the individual's constitutionally protected interest in avoiding physical restraint." *Zadvydas,* 533 U.S. at 690. Consistent with these principles, the Supreme Court has—outside of the immigration context—found civil detention constitutional without any individualized showing of need only when faced with the unique exigencies of global war or domestic insurrection. *See Ludecke v. Watkins,* 335 U.S. 160 (1948); *Korematsu v. United States,* 323 U.S. 214 (1944); *Moyer v. Peabody,* 212 U.S. 78 (1909). And even in those extreme circumstances, the Court's decisions have been widely criticized. *See, e.g.,* Eugene V. Rostow, *The Japanese American Cases—A Disaster,* 54 Yale L.J. 489 (1945). In all contexts apart from immigration and military detention, the Court has found that the Constitution requires some individualized process and a judicial or administrative finding that a legitimate governmental interest justifies detention of the person in question.

* * *

Early cases upholding immigration detention policies were a product of their time. *See Carlson v. Landon,* 342 U.S. 524 (1952) (McCarthy Era deportation of communists); *Ludecke v. Watkins,* 335 U.S. 160, (1948) (removal of German enemy aliens during World War II); *Wong Wing v. United States,* 163 U.S. 228, (1896) (Chinese exclusion). Yet even these cases recognized some limits on detention of non-citizens pending removal. Such detention may not be punitive—Congress may not, for example, impose sentences of "imprisonment at hard labor" on non-citizens awaiting deportation, *Wong Wing*—and it must be supported by a legitimate regulatory purpose. Under these principles, the Court authorized the "detention or temporary confinement" of Chinese-born non-citizens "pending the inquiry into their true character, and while arrangements were being made for their deportation." *Id.* The Court also upheld executive detention of enemy aliens after the cessation of active hostilities because deportation is "hardly practicable" in the midst of war, and enemy aliens' "potency for mischief" continues "even when the guns

---

United States, history of absconding or failing to appear for immigration or other proceedings, and the likelihood that the detainee will violate the conditions of release) * * *.

are silent." *Ludecke,* 335 U.S. at 166. Similarly, the Court approved detention of communists to limit their "opportunities to hurt the United States during the pendency of deportation proceedings." *Carlson,* 342 U.S. at 538. The Court recognized, however, that "purpose to injure could not be imputed generally to all aliens subject to deportation." *Id.* Rather, if the Attorney General wished to exercise his discretion to deny bail, he was required to do so at a hearing, the results of which were subject to judicial review. *Id.* at 543.

More recently, the Supreme Court has drawn on decades of civil detention jurisprudence to hold that "[a] statute permitting indefinite detention of an alien would raise a serious constitutional problem." *Zadvydas,* 533 U.S. at 690. * * *

Soon after *Zadvydas,* the Court rejected a due process challenge to mandatory detention under INA § 236(c), which applies to non-citizens convicted of certain crimes. *Demore v. Kim,* 538 U.S. at 517–18. While affirming its "longstanding view that the Government may constitutionally detain deportable aliens during the limited period necessary for their removal proceedings," *id.* at 526, the Court emphasized that detention under INA § 236(c) was constitutionally permissible because it has "a definite termination point" and typically "lasts for less than . . . 90 days," *id.* at 529.

Since *Zadvydas* and *Demore,* our court has "grappled in piece-meal fashion with whether the various immigration detention statutes may authorize indefinite or prolonged detention of detainees and, if so, may do so without providing a bond hearing." *Rodriguez II,* 715 F.3d at 1134. As we recognized in *Casas,* "prolonged detention without adequate procedural protections would raise serious constitutional concerns." *Casas,* 535 F.3d at 950 * * * . We have therefore held that non-citizens detained pursuant to INA § 236(a) * * * are entitled to bond hearings before an IJ when detention becomes prolonged. *See Casas,* 535 F.3d at 949 (requiring bond hearings for individuals detained under § 236(a)) * * *.

* * *

Prior decisions have also clarified that detention becomes "prolonged" at the six-month mark. In *Zadvydas,* the Supreme Court recognized six months as a "presumptively reasonable period of detention." 533 U.S. at 701 * * * . Following *Zadvydas,* we have defined detention as "prolonged" when "it has lasted six months and is expected to continue more than minimally beyond six months." *Diouf II,* 634 F.3d at 1092 n. 13. At that point, we have explained, "the private interests at stake are profound," and "the risk of an erroneous deprivation of liberty in the absence of a hearing before a neutral decisionmaker is substantial." *Id.* at 1092.

B. Entitlement to a Bond Hearing

With this well-established precedent of the Supreme Court and our Court in mind, we review the district court's grant of summary judgment and entry of a permanent injunction. We consider, in turn, whether individuals detained under INA §§ 236(c), 235(b), [and] 236(a) * * * are entitled to bond hearings after they have been detained for six months.

1. The INA § 236(c) Subclass

Section 236(c) requires that the Attorney General detain any non-citizen who is inadmissible or deportable because of his criminal history upon that person's release from imprisonment, pending proceedings to remove him from the United States.[8] Detention under INA § 236(c) is mandatory. Individuals detained under that section are not eligible for release on bond or parole, *see* INA § 236(a); they may be released only if the Attorney General deems it "necessary" for witness protection purposes, *id.* § 236(c)(2).

An individual detained under § 236(c) may ask an IJ to reconsider whether the mandatory detention provision applies to him, *see* 8 C.F.R. § 1003.19(h)(2)(ii), but such review is limited in scope and addresses only whether the individual is properly included in a category of non-citizens subject to mandatory detention based on his criminal history. *See generally In re Joseph,* 22 I. & N. Dec. 799 (BIA 1999). At a "*Joseph* hearing," a detainee "may avoid mandatory detention by demonstrating that he is not an alien, was not convicted of the predicate crime, or that the [DHS] is otherwise substantially unlikely to establish that he is in fact subject to mandatory detention." *Demore,* 538 U.S. at 514 n. 3. "A determination in favor of an alien" at a *Joseph* hearing "does not lead to automatic release," *Joseph,* 22 I. & N. Dec. at 806, because the government retains discretionary authority to detain the individual under § 236(a). Instead, such a determination allows the IJ to consider granting bond under the § 236(a) standards, namely, whether the detainee would pose a danger or flight risk if released. * * *

---

[8] Mandatory detention under § 236(c) applies to non-citizens who are inadmissible on account of having committed a crime involving moral turpitude or a controlled substance offense; having multiple criminal convictions with an aggregate sentence of five years or more of confinement; having connections to drug trafficking, prostitution, commercialized vice, money laundering, human trafficking, or terrorism; having carried out severe violations of religious freedom while serving as a foreign government official; or having been involved in serious criminal activity and asserting immunity from prosecution. It also applies to noncitizens who are deportable on account of having been convicted of two or more crimes involving moral turpitude, an aggravated felony, a controlled substance offense, certain firearm-related offenses, or certain other miscellaneous crimes; having committed a crime of moral turpitude within a certain period of time since their date of admission for which a sentence of one year or longer has been imposed; or having connections to terrorism. *See* INA § 236(c) (cross-referencing INA §§ 212(a)(2), 237(a)(2)(A)(ii), 237(a)(2)(A)(iii), 237(a)(2)(B), 237(a)(2)(C), 237(a)(2)(D), 237(a)(2)(A)(i), 212(a)(3)(B), 237(a)(4)(B)).

As a result of § 236(c)'s mandatory language and the limited review available through a *Joseph* hearing, individuals are often detained for years without adequate process. * * * Members of the § 236(c) subclass also tend to be detained for longer periods than other class members: The longest-detained class member was confined for 1,585 days and counting as of April 28, 2012, and the average subclass member faces detention for 427 days. These lengthy detention times bear no relationship to the seriousness of class members' criminal history or the lengths of their previously served criminal sentences. In several instances identified by class counsel, a class member was sentenced to one to three months in prison for a minor controlled substances offense, then endured one or two *years* in immigration detention. Nor do these detention durations bear any relation to the merits of the subclass members' claims: Of the § 236(c) subclass members who apply for relief from removal, roughly 40% are granted such relief, a rate even higher than that of the overall class.

In *Rodriguez II*, we held that "the prolonged detention of an alien [under § 236(c)] without an individualized determination of his dangerousness or flight risk would be constitutionally doubtful." 715 F.3d at 1137–38 (quoting *Casas,* 535 F.3d at 951). To avoid these "constitutional concerns, § 236(c)'s mandatory language must be construed 'to contain an implicit reasonable time limitation.' " *Id.* at 1138 (quoting *Zadvydas,* 533 U.S. at 682). Accordingly, at the six-month mark, "when detention becomes prolonged, § 236(c) becomes inapplicable," and "the Attorney General's detention authority rests with § 236(a)." *Id.* Under *Casas,* those detainees are then entitled to a bond hearing. * * *

Contrary to the government's argument, this holding is consistent with the text of § 236(c), which requires that the government detain certain non-citizens but does not mandate such detention for any particular length of time. * * * Our holding is also consistent with the Supreme Court's decision in *Demore,* which turned on the brevity of the detention at issue. *See Demore,* 538 U.S. at 513, (holding that Congress may require detention "for the brief period necessary for [a non-citizen's] removal proceedings"); *id.* at 526 * * * (discussing the "longstanding view that the Government may constitutionally detain deportable aliens during the limited period necessary for their removal proceedings"); *id.* at 530 n. 12 * * * (emphasizing the "very limited time of the detention at stake under § 236(c)").

* * *

2. The § 235(b) Subclass

Section 235(b) applies to "applicants for admission" who are stopped at the border or a port of entry, or who are "present in the United States" but "ha[ve] not been admitted." INA § 235(a)(1). The statute provides that asylum seekers "shall be detained pending a final determination of credible fear of persecution and, if found not to have such a fear, until removed." *Id.* § 235(b)(1)(B)(iii)(IV). As to all other applicants for admission, the statute provides that "if the examining immigration officer determines that an alien seeking admission is not clearly and beyond a doubt entitled to be admitted, the alien shall be detained" for removal proceedings. *Id.* § 235(b)(2)(A).

Under DHS regulations, non-citizens detained pursuant to § 235(b) are generally not eligible for release on bond. 8 C.F.R. § 236.1(c)(2). If there are "urgent humanitarian reasons or significant public benefit[s]" at stake, however, the Attorney General has discretion to temporarily parole such an individual into the United States, provided that the individual presents neither a danger nor a risk of flight. INA § 212(d)(5)(A). Because parole decisions under § 212 are purely discretionary, they cannot be appealed to IJs or courts. This lack of review has proven especially problematic when immigration officers have denied parole based on blatant errors: In two separate cases identified by the petitioners, for example, officers apparently denied parole because they had confused Ethiopia with Somalia. And in a third case, an officer denied parole because he had mixed up two detainees' files.

As with § 236(c), the government often cites § 235(b)'s mandatory language to justify indefinite civil detention without an individualized determination as to whether the detainee would pose a danger or flight risk if released. *See, e.g., Nadarajah,* 443 F.3d at 1071, 1076 (asylum seeker detained for nearly five years). Section 235(b) subclass members have been detained for as long as 831 days, and for an average of 346 days each. These individuals apply for and receive relief from removal at very high rates: 94% apply, and of those who apply, 64% are granted relief. In illustrative cases identified by the petitioners, non-citizens fled to the United States after surviving kidnapping, torture, and murder of their family members in their home countries. Upon arrival, these individuals were detained under § 235(b), and they remained in detention until the government granted their asylum applications hundreds of days later.

* * * [T]o avoid serious constitutional concerns, mandatory detention under § 235(b), like mandatory detention under § 236(c), must be construed as implicitly time-limited. *Rodriguez II,* 715 F.3d at 1144. Accordingly, "the mandatory provisions of [INA § 235(b)] simply expire at six months, at which point the government's authority to detain the alien shifts to § 236(a), which is discretionary and which we have already held requires a bond hearing." *Id.* * * *

* * * [M]any members of the § 235(b) subclass are subject to the "entry fiction" doctrine, under which non-citizens seeking admission to the United States "may physically be allowed within its borders pending a

determination of admissibility," but "are legally considered to be detained at the border and hence as never having effected entry into this country." *Id.* at 1140 (quoting *Barrera-Echavarria,* 44 F.3d at 1450). Such non-citizens therefore "enjoy very limited protections under the United States constitution." *Id.* (quoting *Barrera-Echavarria,* 44 F.3d at 1450). However, even if the majority of prolonged detentions under § 235(b) are constitutionally permissible, "the Supreme Court has instructed that, where one possible application of a statute raises constitutional concerns, the statute as a whole should be construed through the prism of constitutional avoidance." *Id.* at 1141 (citing *Clark,* 543 U.S. at 380, 125 S.Ct. 716). Section 235(b) applies to several categories of lawful permanent residents who are not subject to the entry fiction doctrine but may be treated as seeking admission under § 101(a)(13)(C). * * *

* * * Because the government concedes that detention of lawful permanent residents under § 235(b) is possible under § 101(a)(13)(C), "the statute as a whole should be construed through the prism of constitutional avoidance." *Rodriguez II,* 715 F.3d at 1141. * * *

* * *

3. The § 236(a) Subclass

Section 236(a) authorizes detention "pending a decision on whether the alien is to be removed from the United States." * * * The statute expressly authorizes release on "bond of at least $1,500" or "conditional parole."[13] *Id.* § 236(a)(2). Following an initial custody determination by DHS, a non-citizen may apply for a review or redetermination by an IJ, and that decision may be appealed to the BIA. * * * At these hearings, the detainee bears the burden of establishing "that he or she does not present a danger to persons or property, is not a threat to the national security, and does not pose a risk of flight." *Guerra,* 24 I. & N. Dec. at 38. "After an initial bond redetermination," a request for another review "shall be considered only upon a showing that the alien's circumstances have changed materially since the prior bond redetermination." 8 C.F.R. § 1003.19(e). The government has taken the position that additional time spent in detention is not a "changed circumstance" that entitles a detainee to a new bond hearing.

* * *

---

[13] " '[C]onditional parole' under [INA § 236(a)(2)(B)] is a 'distinct and different procedure' from 'parole' under [INA § 212(d)(5)(A)]." *Garcia v. Holder,* 659 F.3d 1261, 1268 (9th Cir.2011) (quoting *In re Castillo-Padilla,* 25 I. & N. Dec. 257, 258 (BIA 2010)). As discussed above, [INA § 212(d)(5)(A)] authorizes the Attorney General to temporarily release non-citizens detained under [INA § 235(b)] "for urgent humanitarian reasons or significant public benefit." Conditional parole under [INA § 236(a)], by contrast, provides for release from detention if the non-citizen "would not pose a danger to property or persons" and "is likely to appear for any further proceeding." 8 C.F.R. § 236.1(c)(8).

Although § 236(a) provides for discretionary, rather than mandatory, detention and establishes a mechanism for detainees to seek release on bond, non-citizens often face prolonged detention under that section.

* * *

[The] government argues that § 236(a) affords detainees the right to request bond hearings, *see* 8 C.F.R. § 236.1, so there is no basis for requiring the government to automatically provide bond hearings after six months of detention. * * * Detainees, who typically have no choice but to proceed *pro se,* have limited access to legal resources, often lack English-language proficiency, and are sometimes illiterate. As a result, many class members are not aware of their right to a bond hearing and are poorly equipped to request one. Accordingly, we conclude that class members are entitled to automatic bond hearings after six months of detention. We address the other procedural requirements for these hearings in Section IV.B, *infra.*

* * *

C. Procedural Requirements

* * *

In their cross-appeal, petitioners argue that the district court erred in failing to require IJs to consider the length of a non-citizen's past and likely future detention and, relatedly, the likelihood of eventual removal from the United States * * * . As to the likely duration of future detention and the likelihood of eventual removal, however, those factors are too speculative and too dependent upon the merits of the detainee's claims for us to require IJs to consider during a bond hearing. We therefore affirm the district court's ruling that consideration of those factors "would require legal and political analyses beyond what would otherwise be considered at a bond hearing" and is therefore not appropriate. We note that *Zadvydas* and its progeny require consideration of the likelihood of removal in particular circumstances,[18] but we decline to require such analysis as a threshold inquiry in all bond hearings.

* * *

For the same reasons the IJ must consider the length of past detention, we hold that the government must provide periodic bond hearings every six months so that noncitizens may challenge their

---

[18] Several of our cases have addressed petitions for habeas relief under *Zadvydas*, which requires a detainee to prove that he "is not significantly likely to be removed." *Owino*, 575 F.3d at 955; *see also Diouf v. Mukasey* (*Diouf I*), 542 F.3d 1222, 1233 (9th Cir.2008); *Prieto-Romero*, 534 F.3d at 1065; *Nadarajah*, 443 F.3d at 1080. Those decisions instruct IJs to consider the likelihood of removal when, for instance, a detainee is stateless. *See Owino, 575 F.3d at 955–56.* However, petitioners have not identified, and we have not found, authority that supports requiring this inquiry in all bond hearings.

continued detention as "the period of . . . confinement grows." *Diouf II,* 634 F.3d at 1091 (quoting *Zadvydas,* 533 U.S. at 701, 121 S.Ct. 2491).

V. CONCLUSION

* * * By upholding the district court's order that Immigration Judges must hold bond hearings for certain detained individuals, we are not ordering Immigration Judges to release any single individual; rather we are affirming a minimal procedural safeguard—a hearing at which the government bears only an intermediate burden of proof in demonstrating danger to the community or risk of flight—to ensure that after a lengthy period of detention, the government continues to have a legitimate interest in the further deprivation of an individual's liberty. Immigration Judges, a specialized and experienced group within the Department of Justice, are already entrusted to make these determinations, and need not release any individual they find presents a danger to the community or a flight risk after hearing and weighing the evidence. * * * We hereby remand to the district court to enter a revised injunction consistent with our instructions.

NOTES AND QUESTIONS ON
THE JUDICIAL NARROWING OF MANDATORY DETENTION

1. Early on, *Demore* was viewed as a severe limitation on the due process rights of detainees and an augmentation of the role of detention in immigration enforcement. What role does *Demore* play in reaching the result in *Rodriguez*?

2. *Rodriguez* finds that noncitizens subject to mandatory detention under § 236(c) and § 235(b) revert to the discretionary detention regime of § 236(a) after the presumptively constitutional six-month detention period has passed. Can that reading of § 236(c) be squared with the policy reasons cited by the *Demore* majority in explaining why Congress adopted mandatory detention in the first place (e.g., "detention of criminal aliens * * * might be the best way to ensure their successful removal from the country")? Wasn't the elimination of bond hearings for noncitizens with certain criminal convictions Congress's precise purpose in enacting § 236(c) in 1996? Similarly, isn't the purpose of § 235(b) to prevent the presence in the United States of arriving aliens without authorization to enter?

3. After the 1996 Immigration Reform Act, removed noncitizens can still pursue their judicial appeal from abroad. Should that have been seen as a sufficient answer to the class members' argument for release from detention, at least after the BIA had ruled? Each could apparently have ended his detention by accepting removal in the interim, without jeopardizing his right to judicial review of the issues raised on appeal.

4. Surveying cases, one district court compiled a non-exclusive list of factors that go into determining whether the length of detention is reasonable

(and hence whether an individualized bond hearing is required): (1) whether detention has extended beyond the average time ordinarily necessary for completion of removal proceedings; (2) the probable extent of future removal proceedings; (3) the likelihood that removal proceedings will actually result in removal; and (4) the conduct of both the alien and the government— essentially, who bears the primary responsibility for any delays. *Alli v. Decker,* 644 F.Supp.2d 535, 543–45 (M.D. Pa. 2009), *rev'd in part on other grounds,* 650 F.3d 1007 (3d Cir. 2011). Would this factor approach produce more accurate results than the bright-line six-month rule that *Rodriguez* adopts?

5.   Does *Padilla* shed any light here? On the one hand, *Padilla* declares that deportation is a penalty, even if it is distinct from criminal punishment. Does *Padilla* similarly support an argument that detention is enough like incarceration so that constitutional protections for detainees should thicken? *See* César Cuauhtémoc García Hernández, *Immigration Detention As Punishment,* 61 UCLA L. Rev. 1346, 1379 (2014). Or alternatively, since *Padilla* provides a right to defense counsel's advice about the immigration consequences of a conviction, isn't it more likely that those in mandatory detention under § 236(c) are removable, therefore providing greater justification for detention?

6.   In view of the widespread judicial resistance to mandatory detention, basically giving *Demore* its narrowest possible application, should the detention statutes be changed? Would it be simpler and more efficient just to provide for an individualized release procedure in each case, in which a past criminal record would of course be given weight in assessing flight risk and dangerousness? On the other hand, are the courts placing too much faith in the capacity for individualized assessment of flight risk, given the serious problem of noncompliance on the part of people once deemed appropriate for release?

7.   There have been several legislative efforts, so far unsuccessful, to revise the statutes construed in *Demore* and *Zadvydas* to clarify the authorization for wider use of detention. Some would overrule *Clark v. Martinez* to permit indefinite detention of arriving aliens. Other proposed legislation would amend INA § 241(a)(6) to authorize indefinite detention for certain admitted aliens, based on a wider set of factors such as past convictions for crimes of violence or aggravated felonies. Additional proposed changes would specify that mandatory detention under § 236(c) applies from initial ICE arrest to either removal or a ruling that the individual is not removable. *See, e.g.,* S. 1984, 110th Cong., § 202 (2007); H.R.1932, 112th Cong. (2011). For a description of the latter bill, the "Keep Our Communities Safe Act," as approved by the House Judiciary Committee, see 88 Interp.Rel. 1680 (2011).

ATD = alt. to detention

- *release more*
  - *lower bonds*
- *ATDs — yes*
- *more supervision — ok*

- *consider ability to pay.*

EXERCISE

If you were a member of Congress, how would you vote to alter the provisions governing decisions on release? Should the system release more or fewer respondents? Set higher bonds? Make more use of ATDs? Deploy more intensive supervision, perhaps including GPS ankle bracelets? Specify the categories to which your changes would apply, or at least identify factors that could give more precise guidance to the DHS officers and immigration judges who have to make release decisions and stand accountable for each such release.

C. JUDICIAL REVIEW

Decisions under the immigration laws can carry the most telling personal consequences known to the federal administrative process. To be sure, a ratemaking order or a broadcast licensing proceeding might mean millions of dollars in profit or loss to the contending parties—sums far beyond what one encounters in the immigration field. But those on the losing side, even in such titanic administrative battles, can go home and relieve their disappointment among family and friends. Immigration decisions, in contrast, often bear directly on just where home will be, and on which relatives and friends will share in life's triumphs and defeats.

Given the potential stakes, both the noncitizen and the government have the strongest reasons for wanting to be sure that such decisions are reached correctly. To this end, complex mechanisms for administrative review have evolved, as we have seen, that vary considerably depending on the precise application or decision at issue. But Americans have probably always harbored a measure of distrust for bureaucrats, even those who serve in purely corrective or appellate roles. With the growth of the modern administrative state, the federal courts, staffed with life-tenured judges, have come to be seen as the ultimate guarantors of administrative reliability. Whether or not this great faith in the bench is always well-placed, this judicial role is a well-entrenched feature of modern life. Under doctrines worked out over the last fifty years or so, federal agency actions—not just agencies concerned with immigration—are now presumptively subject to review in the courts, *Abbott Laboratories v. Gardner*, 387 U.S. 136, 140–41, 87 S.Ct. 1507, 1510, 1511, 18 L.Ed.2d 681 (1967). The Supreme Court has emphasized, however, that this is "just a presumption" that can be overcome if Congress has foreclosed review in a given category of cases. *See Lincoln v. Vigil*, 508 U.S. 182, 190, 113 S.Ct. 2024, 2030, 124 L.Ed.2d 101 (1993).

The immigration caseload in the federal courts grew dramatically over the past decade. In 2001, such cases constituted only three percent of the caseload in the courts of appeals. By 2006, they accounted for nearly

18 percent, slowly declined to 12 percent in 2010, and leveled off to 11 percent in 2014. The volume varies considerably by circuit. Over the past decade, roughly two-thirds of appeals from the BIA went to the Second and Ninth Circuits. In FY 2014, the Ninth Circuit received 3,419 cases, and the Second reviewed 837. Together this equaled more than 70 percent of the total immigration caseload in the federal courts of appeal. The Fifth Circuit ranked third with 416, followed by the Eleventh and Sixth Circuits with 253 and 236 cases, respectively. The Tenth Circuit had the lightest load with 89 cases. *See* Judicial Business of the United States Courts, Table B–3 (2014 Annual Report of the Director, Administrative Office of the United States Courts); Stacy Caplow, *After the Flood: The Legacy of the "Surge" of Federal Immigration Appeals,* 7 Nw. J. L. & Soc. Pol'y 1 (2012) (discussing the causes and effects of the surge of immigration cases in appellate courts).

In considering judicial review, we encounter a familiar tension. We do not want to foster manipulation by noncitizens who might use judicial review only to prolong a stay to which they are not entitled. At the same time, we do not want to stint on measures to assure accurate and humane application of the laws. What is the right balance?

1.   A BRIEF HISTORY

At least since 1891, federal statutes have regularly provided that orders of executive branch officers in deportation and exclusion cases are "final." Some early Supreme Court decisions seemed to read this in its harshest literal sense, as precluding any possible judicial role. But that phase did not last long. Soon the courts began to entertain cases challenging the decisions of the administrators in exclusion and deportation cases. Often the substantive standard for review was extraordinarily deferential to the administrators, when viewed from a modern perspective, but the immigration authorities did not always prevail. In any event, the mere fact of judicial consideration was significant, in the face of the statute's command of finality. Many of the cases that you have read throughout this book—the *Chae Chan Ping, Fong Yue Ting, Yamataya, Knauff,* and *Mezei,* to mention just a few—reached the courts, even if the outcome on the merits was to uphold the government decision in question.

These cases present an apparent puzzle. Federal courts are courts of limited jurisdiction, and they must ordinarily trace their power to hear a case to a specific congressional authorization. The early immigration statutes merely set forth the administrative arrangements and purported to make the resulting orders final. Clearly *they* bestowed no review authority on the courts. Indeed, it was not until 1961 that any general provisions for judicial review appeared in our immigration laws. Just how did the courts manage to assume jurisdiction?

The answer derives from the brute requirements of the removal process. No unwilling noncitizen can be removed without being physically restrained at some point. Classically, such physical restraint—custody—is the foundation for issuance of the Great Writ, the writ of habeas corpus, a remedy guaranteed in the text of the Constitution. Article I, section 9, clause 2 states: "The privilege of the Writ of Habeas Corpus shall not be suspended, unless when in Cases of Rebellion or Invasion the public Safety may require it." Federal statutes also provided a habeas corpus remedy well before the first immigration acts were passed, and sometimes it is not clear whether particular features of habeas practice derived from constitutional command or from statutory refinement.

Until 1955, habeas review was the standard basis of court jurisdiction to review agency immigration decisions. However, as habeas was understood until recent decades, the noncitizen could not petition for the writ until he was actually in physical custody. By then he may have had to sell his belongings, bid farewell to family and friends, and wait from his jail cell for the court's decision.

Could noncitizens get to court without using habeas, and thus obtain review without having to undergo physical custody? Noncitizens tried different statutes for this purpose without success until 1955, when the Supreme Court held that under the 1946 Administrative Procedure Act (APA), combined with the then-new INA, declaratory and injunctive relief was available to test deportation and exclusion orders. *Shaughnessy v. Pedreiro*, 349 U.S. 48, 75 S.Ct. 591, 99 L.Ed. 868 (1955); *Brownell v. Shung*, 352 U.S. 180, 77 S.Ct. 252, 1 L.Ed.2d 225 (1956). Noncitizens could at last contest exclusion and deportation orders without having to wait until they were detained. But Congress grew concerned that the court access opened up by *Pedreiro* and *Brownell* would be abused to string out review beyond reasonable bounds. *See, e.g.,* H.R. Rep. No. 1086, 87th Cong., 1st Sess. 28–32 (1961).

In 1961, Congress separated review of exclusion and deportation with the passage of INA § 106, the first statute specifically governing review of exclusion and deportation orders. For exclusion cases, § 106(b) reestablished habeas corpus as the exclusive means for review. Habeas petitions were almost invariably filed in the federal district courts, with appeal available in the court of appeals and certiorari in the Supreme Court. For deportation, § 106(a) took a wholly new approach, taking review out of the district courts and making a petition for review in the courts of appeals the "sole and exclusive" procedure for judicial review of final deportation orders under the Hobbs Act. *See* 28 U.S.C. §§ 2341–2351. Habeas review of deportation was available only under specific circumstances.

Since 1996, Congress has worked to channel, limit, or expedite review of removal orders, beginning with a pair of statutes. The Antiterrorism and Effective Death Penalty Act of 1996 (AEDPA), Pub. L. 104–132, 110 Stat. 1214, significantly amended the 1961 scheme, and the 1996 Illegal Immigration Reform and Immigrant Responsibility Act (IIRIRA) adopted an entirely new judicial review scheme that appears in the current INA § 242.

Now there is a single scheme for removal orders. Under § 242(b), review of both exclusion and deportation orders is exclusively in the court of appeals and is obtained by filing a petition for review with the court for the circuit in which the immigration court proceedings were completed. This petition for review is the "sole and exclusive means for judicial review of an order of removal," *see* § 242(a)(5)—namely the Hobbs Act procedure that the 1961 Act had applied to deportation orders. *See* INA § 242(a)(1). Section 242(b) also sets out rules for service and a filing deadline of 30 days after the date of the final order.

Under § 242(b)(3)(B), removal orders are no longer stayed automatically pending court review, as they had been before 1996, but noncitizens may apply for a discretionary stay. They may also initiate or continue court review even after leaving the United States, in contrast with pre-1996 law, which barred review after the noncitizen's departure from the United States.

What about judicial review of agency decisions or actions other than removal orders? Here the path for review, when it exists, has been guided by the Administrative Procedure Act, which provides: "A person suffering a legal wrong because of agency action, or adversely affected or aggrieved by agency action within the meaning of a relevant statute, is entitled to judicial review thereof." 5 U.S.C. § 702. A noncitizen may pursue "any applicable form of legal action," including injunctions, declaratory judgments, and habeas corpus. Id. § 703. This entitlement, however, is qualified: the general judicial review provisions of the APA apply "except to the extent that * * * statutes preclude judicial review." *Id.* § 701(a). Review is to be had through any special statutory review proceeding, if one is provided. (That is why review of removal orders must follow § 242.) The APA is not a jurisdictional statute, but 28 U.S.C. § 1331 would provide federal subject matter jurisdiction based on a federal question.

APA review, typically an action for injunctive or declaratory relief in federal district court, would be the avenue to challenge, for example, a denial of a visa petition, *see Soltane v. USDOJ*, 381 F.3d 143, 148 (3d Cir. 2004); *Fred 26 Importers v. U.S. DHS*, 445 F. Supp. 2d 1174, 1178–79

(C.D. Cal. 2006), or a denial by USCIS of an application for adjustment of status, *see Pinho v. Gonzales*, 432 F.3d 193 (3d Cir. 2005).[24]

One further wrinkle must be kept in mind. Many applications denied by USCIS (primarily adjustment of status or asylum) can be renewed in removal proceedings for de novo consideration by an immigration judge. If such a removal process is underway for, say, a denied adjustment applicant, a district court would ordinarily dismiss APA review of the USCIS denial, leaving review to the court of appeals if the IJ does not provide the relief. *See Ibarra v. Swacina,* 628 F.3d 1269 (11th Cir. 2010). Denial of an application for relief from removal by an immigration judge in the course of a removal proceeding is reviewable only on petition for review in the court of appeals.

This Section will focus on a few key issues of judicial review. First, under what circumstances must noncitizens wait until the end of agency decisionmaking before going to court? Second, § 242(a)(2) limits or eliminates review in certain categories of cases. When and how does it do so? Third, when is a stay of removal appropriate while judicial review proceeds? And finally, when may multiple litigants combine their cases to challenge a government practice or policy?

2. LIMITING JUDICIAL REVIEW

Section 242 of the INA significantly curtails judicial review in a variety of ways, of which the most important are treated below. (There are also other jurisdiction-limiting provisions sprinkled elsewhere within the INA. *See, e.g.,* INA § 208(a)(3), (b)(2)(D). We touch upon only a few of them in this chapter.)

a. Exhaustion of Administrative Remedies

INA § 242(d)(1) provides: "A court may review a final order of removal only if * * * the alien has exhausted all administrative remedies available to the alien as of right." The exhaustion rule, a traditional prerequisite to judicial review, "is based on the need to allow agencies to develop the facts, to apply the law in which they are particularly expert, and to correct their own errors. The rule ensures that whatever judicial review is available will be informed and narrowed by the agencies' own decisions. It also avoids duplicative proceedings, and often the agency's ultimate decision will obviate the need for judicial intervention." *Schlesinger v. Councilman,* 420 U.S. 738, 756–57, 95 S.Ct. 1300, 1312–13, 43 L.Ed.2d 591 (1975). Courts have found limited exceptions to the

---

[24] There are conflicting court rulings, however, as to whether INA § 242(b)(2)(B), discussed below, may apply to bar review of such USCIS decisions in visa petition and adjustment of status cases, because they are seen—by the courts that restrict review—as discretionary. *See* Gerald Seipp, Federal Court Jurisdiction to Review Immigration Decisions: A Tug of War Between the Three Branches, 07–04 Imm. Briefings 6–7, 9–10 (2007).

statutory requirement, such as when a particular available procedure cannot be considered a remedy, *see Castro-Cortez v. INS*, 239 F.3d 1037, 1044–45 (9th Cir. 2001), *overruled on other grounds by Fernandez-Vargas v. Gonzales*, 548 U.S. 30, 126 S.Ct. 2422, 165 L.Ed.2d 323 (2006), but exceptions to a statutory exhaustion requirement are infrequent.

If the noncitizen is not challenging a final removal order, however, the § 242(d)(1) restriction is usually considered not to apply. Courts still impose a prudential exhaustion requirement, but a wider range of traditional exceptions may be available, such as a showing that pursuing an administrative remedy would be futile. *See Gonzalez v. O'Connell*, 355 F.3d 1010, 1015–18 (7th Cir. 2004).

b. Discretionary Relief

Section 242(a)(2)(B)(i) bars judicial review of "any judgment regarding the granting of relief" under the waiver provisions in § 212(h) and § 212(i), cancellation of removal, voluntary departure, and adjustment of status. INA § 242(a)(2)(B)(ii) bars judicial review of any other "decision or action" that is specified under Title II of the INA (therefore not applicable to Title III, which concerns Nationality and Naturalization) to be in the discretion of the Attorney General or Secretary of Homeland Security. An exception leaves judicial review available for asylum decisions, but the statute specifies a highly deferential standard of review, *see* INA § 242(b)(4)(D). This scheme raises questions about what review is precluded, who decides whether a decision is discretionary, and how to distinguish decisions that are discretionary from those that are not and therefore subject to judicial review.

What review is precluded? Suppose a noncitizen seeks review of a decision denying discretionary relief. Does § 242(a)(2)(B)(i) bar review only of the decision's discretionary elements, or also of the decision's nondiscretionary elements, such as whether he meets threshold eligibility requirements for the relief sought? One might have thought that the Congress that passed the highly restrictive IIRIRA in 1996 intended to bar all such review, and the government so argued. But most courts have construed the bar narrowly. In *Montero-Martinez v. Ashcroft*, 277 F.3d 1137, 1141–44 (9th Cir. 2002), the Ninth Circuit held that under § 242(a)(2)(B)(i) it still could review nondiscretionary eligibility issues—in particular, whether Montero-Martinez was ineligible for cancellation of removal because his adult daughter was no longer a "child." *See also Morales-Morales v. Ashcroft*, 384 F.3d 418, 423 (7th Cir. 2004) (jurisdiction exists to review legal standards applied in determining whether an applicant for cancellation had been continuously physically present). On the other hand, whether "exceptional and extremely unusual hardship" exists for purposes of cancellation of removal is a discretionary determination beyond judicial review. *See Romero-Torres v. Ashcroft*, 327 F.3d 887, 889–92 (9th Cir. 2003).

Some circuits also consider "good moral character" to be a discretionary determination, as discussed in Chapter 7, *supra*, at 735–736. *Portillo-Rendon v. Holder*, 662 F.3d 815, 817 (7th Cir. 2011). *Portillo-Rendon* explained that, while good moral character is a statutory condition of eligibility for cancellation of removal, "the decision *whether* an alien has the required character reflects an exercise of administrative discretion." *Id.* The court expanded on this distinction:

> For the purpose of § 242(a)(2)(D), "law" means a dispute about the meaning of a legal text, so that the alien wins if the text means one thing and loses if it means something else." * * * There is no dispute about a controlling text here; there is only a (potential) dispute about whether Portillo-Rendon's driving infractions are serious and frequent enough to show that he lacks good moral character, as opposed to making isolated mistakes. The IJ and BIA thought that this record shows poor moral fiber; that is a discretionary call and thus is not subject to judicial review.

Id.

Essentially the early judicial readings of § 242(a)(2)(B) marked out this rough dividing line: legal determinations are subject to review, while factual findings and discretionary decisions are not. *See, e.g., Pareja v. Attorney General*, 615 F.3d 180, 187–88 (3d Cir. 2010) (though "exceptional and extremely unusual hardship" is a discretionary determination, jurisdiction exists to review the legal standard the BIA employs in making that decision). After the enactment of INA § 242(a)(2)(D) in the REAL ID Act of 2005, which expressly preserved judicial review over "constitutional claims and questions of law" (discussed in Section C.3 below), the statute now provides more directly for using this same general line to differentiate reviewable from nonreviewable issues.

Who defines what is discretionary? What if a decision is made discretionary by agency regulation, not by statute? Does INA § 242(a)(2)(B) bar judicial review? The Supreme Court said no, in *Kucana v. Holder*, 558 U.S. 233, 130 S.Ct. 827, 175 L.Ed.2d 694 (2010). At issue in *Kucana* was denial of a motion to reopen an asylum proceeding. The relevant regulation places a decision to grant or deny a motion to reopen "within the discretion of the Board." 8 C.F.R. § 1003.2(a). The core of the Supreme Court's reasoning follows:

> To the clause (i) enumeration of administrative judgments that are insulated from judicial review under § 242(a)(2)(B), Congress added in clause (ii) a catchall provision covering "any

other decision . . . the authority for which is specified under this subchapter [to be within administrative discretion]." * * * Read harmoniously, both clauses convey that Congress barred court review of discretionary decisions only when Congress itself set out the Attorney General's discretionary authority in the statute.

* * *

Any lingering doubt about the proper interpretation of § 242(a)(2)(B)(ii) would be dispelled by a familiar principle of statutory construction: the presumption favoring judicial review of administrative action. When a statute is "reasonably susceptible to divergent interpretation, we adopt the reading that accords with traditional understandings and basic principles: that executive determinations generally are subject to judicial review." * * * It therefore takes "clear and convincing evidence" to dislodge the presumption. There is no such evidence here.

Finally, we stress a paramount factor in the decision we render today. By defining the various jurisdictional bars by reference to other provisions in the INA itself, Congress ensured that it, and only it, would limit the federal courts' jurisdiction. To read § 242(a)(2)(B)(ii) to apply to matters where discretion is conferred on the Board by regulation, rather than on the Attorney General by statute, would ignore that congressional design. If the [contrary] construction * * * were to prevail, the Executive would have a free hand to shelter its own decisions from abuse-of-discretion appellate court review simply by issuing a regulation declaring those decisions "discretionary." Such an extraordinary delegation of authority cannot be extracted from the statute Congress enacted.

Id. at 246–53.

Which decisions are discretionary? In 2015, in *Reyes Mata v. Lynch,* 135 S.Ct. 2150, 192 L.Ed.2d 225 (2015), the Supreme Court again addressed judicial review and discretionary agency decisions. After an immigration judge ordered Noel Reyes Mata removed based on an assault conviction, his attorney filed an appeal with the BIA but failed to file a brief or any other written materials in support of the appeal. The BIA dismissed the appeal. Reyes Mata's new lawyer filed a motion to reopen, arguing that the first lawyer's ineffective assistance should equitably toll the statutory time limit for motions to reopen. The BIA refused to extend this relief to Reyes Mata, despite acknowledging its reliance on the equitable tolling doctrine in other ineffective representation situations. The BIA also declined to exercise its discretion to open the removal proceeding *sua sponte.*

The Fifth Circuit dismissed Reyes Mata's appeal for lack of jurisdiction. The court characterized his equitable tolling request as a petition for *sua sponte* discretionary relief from the BIA and ruled that courts have no power to review the BIA's refusal to *sua sponte* reopen cases. The Supreme Court reversed, in an 8–1 decision. (Though he dissented, Justice Thomas agreed that the Fifth Circuit's reasoning was erroneous; he would have remanded for consideration in light of the correct legal standard.) The Court chastised the Fifth Circuit for refusing to hear the case despite the duty of the federal courts to exercise their jurisdiction. The Court cautioned that the Fifth Circuit's approach could effectively insulate certain federal appellate decisions from Supreme Court review.

> As we held in *Kucana v. Holder*, circuit courts have jurisdiction when an alien appeals from the Board's denial of a motion to reopen a removal proceeding. The INA * * * gives the courts of appeals jurisdiction to review "final order[s] of removal." That jurisdiction, as the INA expressly contemplates, encompasses review of decisions refusing to reopen or reconsider such orders. * * * [E]ven as Congress curtailed other aspects of courts' jurisdiction over BIA rulings, it left that authority in place.

> Nothing changes when the Board denies a motion to reopen because it is untimely—nor when, in doing so, the Board rejects a request for equitable tolling. Under the INA, as under our century-old practice, the reason for the BIA's denial makes no difference to the jurisdictional issue. Whether the BIA rejects the alien's motion to reopen because it comes too late or because it falls short in some other respect, the courts have jurisdiction to review that decision.

> Similarly, that jurisdiction remains unchanged if the Board, in addition to denying the alien's statutorily authorized motion, states that it will not exercise its separate *sua sponte* authority to reopen the case. [Even assuming the courts cannot review the BIA's exercise of *sua sponte* authority], it means only that judicial review ends after the court has evaluated the Board's ruling on the alien's motion. That courts lack jurisdiction over one matter (the *sua sponte* decision) does not affect their jurisdiction over another (the decision on the alien's request).

> * * *

> [If construing Reyes Mata's request as a motion for *sua sponte* relief from the BIA] rests on an underlying merits decision—that the INA precludes any equitable tolling—then the Court of Appeals has effectively insulated a circuit split from our

review. Putting the Fifth Circuit to the side, all appellate courts to have addressed the matter have held that the Board may sometimes equitably toll the time limit for an alien's motion to reopen. Assuming the Fifth Circuit thinks otherwise, that creates the kind of split of authority we typically think we need to resolve. * * * But the Fifth Circuit's practice of recharacterizing appeals like Mata's as challenges to the Board's *sua sponte* decisions and then declining to exercise jurisdiction over them prevents that split from coming to light. Of course, the Court of Appeals may reach whatever conclusion it thinks best as to the availability of equitable tolling; we express no opinion on that matter. What the Fifth Circuit may not do is to wrap such a merits decision in jurisdictional garb so that we cannot address a possible division between that court and every other. * * *

135 S.Ct. at 2154–56.

c. Review Standards

Statutes and case law prescribe the scope and standard of review of various kinds of decisions taken by administrative agencies. The standard ranges from the most intrusive form of appellate review, *de novo* consideration of findings of fact and rulings of law (which applies, for example, to a denial of naturalization, INA § 310(c)), to others that are far more deferential. Examples of the latter include standards that permit the setting aside of agency decisions only on a judicial determination that they were "arbitrary and capricious" or amounted to an "abuse of discretion." *See generally* Charles H. Koch & Richard W. Murphy, 3 Admin. L. & Prac. § 9:21 (3d ed. 2010).

Section 242(b)(4) sets the general judicial review standards governing orders of removal, formulations clearly designed to elicit deference to the administrative agency. For example, "administrative findings of fact are conclusive unless any reasonable adjudicator would be compelled to conclude the contrary," and "a decision that an alien is not eligible for admission to the United States is conclusive unless manifestly contrary to law." Asylum, as noted above, is one of the few discretionary decisions that remains subject to judicial review after the 1996 Act. For asylum decisions, however, the "discretionary judgment whether" to grant asylum "shall be conclusive unless manifestly contrary to the law and an abuse of discretion." INA § 242(b)(4).

d. Removal Based on Criminal Convictions

Among the most far-reaching limits on court review are those that purport to bar judicial review completely in certain cases, based not on the issues raised but the characteristics of the person raising them. The

central example is INA § 242(a)(2)(C), which, as originally enacted in
IIRIRA in 1996, provided:

> Notwithstanding any other provision of law, no court shall have
> jurisdiction to review any final order of removal against an alien
> who is removable by reason of having committed a criminal
> offense covered in [the subsections dealing with criminal grounds
> of inadmissibility or deportability, with a limited exception for a
> person convicted only of a single crime involving moral
> turpitude].

This provision, along with a similar provision in the Antiterrorism
and Effective Death Penalty Act (AEDPA), § 440(a), enacted earlier that
same year, triggered a massive round of constitutional challenges. The
litigants claimed that such a broad bar to judicial review violates the due
process clause, the principle of separation of powers, or the clause
generally forbidding suspension of the privilege of habeas corpus (Art. I,
§ 9, cl. 2).

The 1996 jurisdiction-stripping provision fit into a long line of
congressional attempts over the preceding decades to restrict federal
court jurisdiction in response to judicial decisions Congress found
objectionable. All such attempts raise a classic question of constitutional
law and the law of federal courts: what are the limits, if any, on
Congress's power under the Constitution (U.S. Const. Art. III, § 1, and
§ 2, cl. 2) to restrict the jurisdiction of the federal courts? *See* Henry M.
Hart, *The Power of Congress to Limit the Jurisdiction of Federal Courts:
An Exercise in Dialectic*, 66 Harv. L. Rev. 1362, 1395–97 (1953).

Earlier attempts of this sort have included proposals to strip the
courts of jurisdiction over cases involving school prayer, abortions, prison
litigation and, more recently, challenges to the Pledge of Allegiance or to
the Defense of Marriage Act. *See* Erwin Chemerinsky, Federal
Jurisdiction 174–77 (6th ed. 2012). Erwin Chemerinsky commented on
those earlier efforts: "The obvious purpose of these jurisdiction stripping
bills is to achieve a change in the substantive law by a procedural device."
Id. at 177. Congress has only rarely managed to enact jurisdiction-
stripping provisions, leaving little case law and considerable room for rich
debate over the constitutional issues presented by the 1996 restrictions
on judicial review of removal orders.

What is the relationship between constitutional challenges based on
due process and separation of powers? Are they identical, overlapping, or
distinct? Can the government respond in the same way to both? Or are
there responses that rebut only one type of challenge or the other? For
discussions of due process, separation of powers, and habeas corpus as
constitutional sources of court review of immigration decisions, see
Gerald L. Neuman, *Jurisdiction and the Rule of Law After the 1996*

Immigration Act, 113 Harv. L. Rev. 1963, 1969–75 (2000); David Cole, *Jurisdiction and Liberty: Habeas Corpus and Due Process as Limits on Congress's Control of Federal Jurisdiction*, 86 Geo. L.J. 2481, 2489–2506 (1998); Richard H. Fallon, Jr., *Applying the Suspension Clause to Immigration Cases*, 98 Colum. L. Rev. 1068, 1077–91 (1998). *See also* David S. Rubenstein, *Immigration Structuralism: A Return to Form*, 8 Duke J. Const. L. & Pub. Pol'y 81 (2013) (offering an account of how separation of powers norms are seriously threatened in immigration law).

Why is judicial review important in the first place? For answers to this question, a discussion of the costs of judicial review, and analysis of congressional skepticism of judicial review, see Stephen H. Legomsky, *Fear and Loathing in Congress and the Courts*, 78 Tex. L. Rev. 1615 (2001). For a discussion of the general objectives that Congress and the administration had in mind in channeling and recasting court review in the 1996 Act, and an assessment of their legitimacy, see David A. Martin, *Behind the Scenes on A Different Set: What Congress Needs to Do in the Aftermath of* St. Cyr *and* Nguyen, 16 Geo. Immigr. L.J. 313, 314–32 (2002).

Most of the early decisions on INA § 242(a)(2)(C) or its statutory predecessor in AEDPA upheld the restrictions, but on the basis that an individual thus barred from the ordinary petition for review in the court of appeals could still obtain judicial consideration under the general habeas corpus statute, 28 U.S.C. § 2241. *See, e.g., Kolster v. INS,* 101 F.3d 785 (1st Cir. 1996); *Duldulao v. INS,* 90 F.3d 396 (9th Cir. 1996). That statute gives federal courts jurisdiction to hear petitions for habeas corpus filed by persons "in custody * * * under the authority of the United States," and the writ may issue if the petitioner is "in custody in violation of the Constitution or laws or treaties of the United States." The government fought this conclusion, in part because it would mean that persons with criminal convictions who are barred from the normal petition for review process would have more rounds of judicial access than other respondents; habeas petitions are typically heard in district court and the decision can then be appealed to the court of appeals. The government urged that the preclusion of review be read to apply as well to habeas, but it did concede that the statute would have to be read to permit barred individuals to use the petition for review process if they presented "substantial" constitutional claims.

The issue ultimately came to the Supreme Court in the following case.

INS v. ST. CYR

Supreme Court of the United States, 2001.
533 U.S. 289, 121 S.Ct. 2271, 150 L.Ed.2d 347.

JUSTICE STEVENS delivered the opinion of the Court.

* * *

Respondent, Enrico St. Cyr, is a citizen of Haiti who was admitted to the United States as a lawful permanent resident in 1986. Ten years later, on March 8, 1996, he pled guilty in a state court to a charge of selling a controlled substance in violation of Connecticut law. That conviction made him deportable. Under pre-AEDPA law applicable at the time of his conviction, St. Cyr would have been eligible for a waiver of deportation at the discretion of the Attorney General [under former INA § 212(c)].[c.] However, removal proceedings against him were not commenced until April 10, 1997, after both AEDPA and IIRIRA became effective, and, as the Attorney General interprets those statutes, he no longer has discretion to grant such a waiver.

* * *

The first question we must consider is whether the District Court retains jurisdiction under the general habeas corpus statute, 28 U.S.C. § 2241, to entertain St. Cyr's challenge. His application for a writ raises a pure question of law. He does not dispute any of the facts that establish his deportability or the conclusion that he is deportable. Nor does he contend that he would have any right to have an unfavorable exercise of the Attorney General's discretion reviewed in a judicial forum. Rather, he contests the Attorney General's conclusion that, as a matter of statutory interpretation, he is not eligible for discretionary relief.

The District Court held, and the Court of Appeals agreed, that it had jurisdiction to answer that question in a habeas corpus proceeding. The INS argues, however, that four sections of the 1996 statutes * * * stripped the courts of jurisdiction to decide the question of law presented by respondent's habeas corpus application.

For the INS to prevail it must overcome both the strong presumption in favor of judicial review of administrative action and the longstanding rule requiring a clear statement of congressional intent to repeal habeas jurisdiction. *See Ex parte Yerger*, 8 Wall. 85, 102 (1869) ("We are not at liberty to except from [habeas corpus jurisdiction] any cases not plainly excepted by law"); *Felker v. Turpin*, 518 U.S. 651, 660–661 (1996). Implications from statutory text or legislative history are not sufficient to repeal habeas jurisdiction; instead, Congress must articulate specific and unambiguous statutory directives to effect a repeal.

---

c. Discretionary relief under former § 212(c) is discussed in Chapter Seven.—eds.

In this case, the plain statement rule draws additional reinforcement from other canons of statutory construction. First, as a general matter, when a particular interpretation of a statute invokes the outer limits of Congress' power, we expect a clear indication that Congress intended that result. Second, if an otherwise acceptable construction of a statute would raise serious constitutional problems, and where an alternative interpretation of the statute is "fairly possible," *see Crowell v. Benson*, 285 U.S. 22, 62 (1932), we are obligated to construe the statute to avoid such problems.

A construction of the amendments at issue that would entirely preclude review of a pure question of law by any court would give rise to substantial constitutional questions. Article I, § 9, cl. 2, of the Constitution provides: "The Privilege of the Writ of Habeas Corpus shall not be suspended, unless when in Cases of Rebellion or Invasion the public Safety may require it." Because of that Clause, some "judicial intervention in deportation cases" is unquestionably "required by the Constitution." *Heikkila v. Barber*, 345 U.S. 229, 235 (1953).

* * *

At its historical core, the writ of habeas corpus has served as a means of reviewing the legality of executive detention, and it is in that context that its protections have been strongest. In England prior to 1789, in the Colonies, and in this Nation during the formative years of our Government, the writ of habeas corpus was available to nonenemy aliens as well as to citizens. It enabled them to challenge executive and private detention in civil cases as well as criminal. Moreover, the issuance of the writ was not limited to challenges to the jurisdiction of the custodian, but encompassed detentions based on errors of law, including the erroneous application or interpretation of statutes. It was used to command the discharge of seamen who had a statutory exemption from impressment into the British Navy, to emancipate slaves, and to obtain the freedom of apprentices and asylum inmates. Most important, for our purposes, those early cases contain no suggestion that habeas relief in cases involving executive detention was only available for constitutional error.

* * *

[E]ven assuming that the Suspension Clause protects only the writ as it existed in 1789, there is substantial evidence to support the proposition that pure questions of law like the one raised by the respondent in this case could have been answered in 1789 by a common law judge with power to issue the writ of habeas corpus. It necessarily follows that a serious Suspension Clause issue would be presented if we were to accept the INS's submission that the 1996 statutes have withdrawn that power from federal judges and provided no adequate substitute for its exercise. * * *

* * *

Until the enactment of the 1952 Immigration and Nationality Act, the sole means by which an alien could test the legality of his or her deportation order was by bringing a habeas corpus action in district court. In such cases, other than the question whether there was some evidence to support the order, the courts generally did not review factual determinations made by the Executive. *See Ekiu v. United States*, 142 U.S. 651, 659 (1892). However, they did review the Executive's legal determinations. * * * In case after case, courts answered questions of law in habeas corpus proceedings brought by aliens challenging Executive interpretations of the immigration laws.

Habeas courts also regularly answered questions of law that arose in the context of discretionary relief. *See, e.g., United States ex rel. Accardi v. Shaughnessy*, 347 U.S. 260 (1954); *United States ex rel. Hintopoulos v. Shaughnessy*, 353 U.S. 72, 77 (1957). Traditionally, courts recognized a distinction between eligibility for discretionary relief, on the one hand, and the favorable exercise of discretion, on the other hand. *See* Neuman, 113 Harv. L. Rev., at 1991 (noting the "strong tradition in habeas corpus law . . . that subjects the legally erroneous failure to exercise discretion, unlike a substantively unwise exercise of discretion, to inquiry on the writ"). Eligibility that was "governed by specific statutory standards" provided "a right to a ruling on an applicant's eligibility," even though the actual granting of relief was "not a matter of right under any circumstances, but rather is in all cases a matter of grace." *Jay v. Boyd*, 351 U.S. 345, 353–354 (1956). Thus, even though the actual suspension of deportation authorized by § 19(c) of the Immigration Act of 1917 was a matter of grace, in *United States ex rel. Accardi v. Shaughnessy*, 347 U.S. 260 (1954), we held that a deportable alien had a right to challenge the Executive's failure to exercise the discretion authorized by the law. The exercise of the District Court's habeas corpus jurisdiction to answer a pure question of law in this case is entirely consistent with the exercise of such jurisdiction in *Accardi*.

Thus, under the pre-1996 statutory scheme—and consistent with its common-law antecedents—it is clear that St. Cyr could have brought his challenge to the Board of Immigration Appeals' legal determination in a habeas corpus petition under 28 U.S.C. § 2241. The INS argues, however, that AEDPA and IIRIRA contain four provisions that express a clear and unambiguous statement of Congress' intent to bar petitions brought under § 2241, despite the fact that none of them mention that section. [The Court then examines those four sections in detail and concludes that none provides a sufficiently clear statement of Congress' intent to bar habeas corpus relief.]

* * *

If it were clear that the question of law [presented by the petitioner regarding the availability of § 212(c) relief] could be answered in another judicial forum, it might be permissible to accept the INS' reading of § 242. But the absence of such a forum, coupled with the lack of a clear, unambiguous, and express statement of congressional intent to preclude judicial consideration on habeas of such an important question of law, strongly counsels against adopting a construction that would raise serious constitutional questions. Accordingly, we conclude that habeas jurisdiction under § 2241 was not repealed by AEDPA and IIRIRA.

[On the substantive legal issue, the Court concluded: "§ 212(c) relief remains available for aliens, like respondent, whose convictions were obtained through plea agreements and who, notwithstanding those convictions, would have been eligible for § 212(c) relief at the time of their plea under the law then in effect." For more on § 212(c) relief, see Chapter Seven.]

[The dissenting opinion of JUSTICE O'CONNOR is omitted.]

JUSTICE SCALIA, with whom THE CHIEF JUSTICE and JUSTICE THOMAS join, and with whom JUSTICE O'CONNOR joins [in part], dissenting.

* * *

In categorical terms that admit of no exception, the Illegal Immigration Reform and Immigrant Responsibility Act of 1996 (IIRIRA), unambiguously repeals the application of 28 U.S.C. § 2241 (the general habeas corpus provision), and of all other provisions for judicial review, to deportation challenges brought by certain kinds of criminal aliens. * * * I will begin by * * * explaining IIRIRA's jurisdictional scheme. It begins with what we have called a channeling or " 'zipper' clause," *Reno v. American-Arab Anti-Discrimination Comm.*, 525 U.S. 471, 483 (1999)— namely, § 242(b)(9). This provision, entitled "Consolidation of questions for judicial review," provides as follows:

> Judicial review of *all* questions of law and fact, including interpretation and application of constitutional and statutory provisions, arising from *any action taken or proceeding brought to remove an alien* from the United States under this subchapter shall be available *only* in judicial review of a final order under this section.

(Emphases added.)

In other words, *if* any review is available of any "questio[n] of law . . . arising from any action taken or proceeding brought to remove an alien from the United States under this subchapter," it is available "only in judicial review of a final order under this section [§ 242]." What kind of review does that section provide? That is set forth in § 242(a)(1) * * * . In other words, *if* judicial review is available, it consists *only* of the modified Hobbs Act review specified in § 242(a)(1).

In some cases (including, as it happens, the one before us), there can be no review at all, because IIRIRA categorically and unequivocally rules out judicial review of challenges to deportation brought by certain kinds of criminal aliens. Section 242(a)(2)(C) provides:

> Notwithstanding *any* other provision of law, *no court* shall have jurisdiction to review any final order of removal against an alien who is removable by reason of having committed [one or more enumerated] criminal offense[s] [including drug-trafficking offenses of the sort of which respondent had been convicted].

(Emphases added.)

* * *

Unquestionably, unambiguously, and unmistakably, IIRIRA expressly supersedes § 2241's general provision for habeas jurisdiction. * * * In the present case, unlike in *Felker* and *Yerger*, none of the statutory provisions relied upon * * * requires us to imply from one statutory provision the repeal of another. All *by their terms* prohibit the judicial review at issue in this case.

* * *

* * * By authorizing § 2241 habeas review in the district court but foreclosing review in the court of appeals, the Court's interpretation routes all legal challenges to removal orders brought by criminal aliens to the district court, to be adjudicated under that court's § 2241 habeas authority, which specifies no time limits. After review by that court, criminal aliens will presumably have an appeal as of right to the court of appeals, and can then petition this Court for a writ of certiorari. In contrast, noncriminal aliens seeking to challenge their removal orders— for example, those charged with having been inadmissible at the time of entry, with having failed to maintain their nonimmigrant status, with having procured a visa through a marriage that was not bona fide, or with having become, within five years after the date of entry, a public charge, will still presumably be required to proceed directly to the court of appeals by way of petition for review, under the restrictive modified Hobbs Act review provisions set forth in § 242(a)(1), including the 30-day filing deadline, *see* § 242(b)(1). * * * The Court has therefore succeeded in perverting a statutory scheme designed to *expedite* the removal of criminal aliens into one that now affords them *more* opportunities for (and layers of) judicial review (and hence more opportunities for delay) than are afforded *non*-criminal aliens—and more than were afforded criminal aliens prior to the enactment of IIRIRA. This outcome speaks for itself; no Congress ever imagined it.

* * *

In the remainder of this opinion I address the question the Court *should* have addressed: Whether these provisions of IIRIRA are unconstitutional.

* * *

Even if one were to assume that the Suspension Clause, despite its text * * *, guarantees some constitutional minimum of habeas relief, that minimum would assuredly not embrace the rarified right asserted here: the right to judicial compulsion of the exercise of Executive *discretion* (which may be exercised favorably or unfavorably) regarding a prisoner's release.

* * *

All the other Framing-era or earlier cases cited in the Court's opinion—indeed, *all the later Supreme Court cases until United States ex rel. Accardi v. Shaughnessy*, 347 U.S. 260, *in 1954*—provide habeas relief from executive detention only when the custodian had no legal authority to detain. * * * [C]ourts understood executive discretion as lying entirely beyond the judicial ken. * * *

* * *

The Due Process Clause does not "[r]equir[e] [j]udicial [d]etermination [o]f" respondent's claim. Respondent has no legal entitlement to suspension of deportation, no matter how appealing his case. "[T]he Attorney General's suspension of deportation [is] 'an act of grace' which is accorded pursuant to her 'unfettered discretion,' *Jay v. Boyd*, 351 U.S. 345, 354 (1956) . . . , and [can be likened, as Judge Learned Hand observed,] to 'a judge's power to suspend the execution of a sentence, or the President's to pardon a convict,' " *INS v. Yueh-Shaio Yang*, 519 U.S. 26, 30 (1996). * * *

* * * The notion that Article III requires every Executive determination, on a question of law or of fact, to be subject to judicial review has no support in our jurisprudence. Were it correct, the doctrine of sovereign immunity would not exist, and the APA's general permission of suits challenging administrative action, *see* 5 U.S.C. § 702, would have been superfluous. * * *

* * *

The Court has created a version of IIRIRA that is not only unrecognizable to its framers (or to anyone who can read) but gives the statutory scheme precisely the *opposite* of its intended effect, affording criminal aliens *more* opportunities for delay-inducing judicial review than others have, or even than criminal aliens had prior to the enactment of this legislation. Because § 2241's exclusion of judicial review is unmistakably clear, and unquestionably constitutional, both this Court and the courts below were without power to entertain respondent's claims. * * *

On the same day the Supreme Court issued the *St. Cyr* opinion, it also decided *Calcano-Martinez v. INS,* 533 U.S. 348, 121 S.Ct. 2268, 150 L.Ed.2d 392 (2001), upholding the constitutionality of INA § 242(a)(2)(C). That section's restrictions on judicial review, the court held, were permissible because any constitutionally required court scrutiny remained available through habeas corpus, as described in *St. Cyr.*

3. THE REAL ID ACT

The REAL ID Act of 2005, Pub. L. No. 109–13, Div. B, § 106, 119 Stat. 231, 310–11, responded to *St. Cyr* and revised the system for court review of immigration decisions. In the legislative history, Congress focused on the problem that Justice Scalia identified: that noncitizens with criminal convictions would have more layers of review than others involved in removal proceedings. Even for respondents with no criminal records, the system was deeply confusing, with some issues including denials of relief from removal going to the district court on habeas because of § 242(a)(2)(B) and challenges to baseline deportability by the same respondent going to the court of appeals directly on a petition for review. *See* H.R. Rep. No. 109–72, at 173–74 (2005), reprinted in 2005 U.S.C.C.A.N. 240 (Conference Report).

The REAL ID Act re-established petitions for review in the courts of appeals as the principal vehicle for court review of final removal orders and certain other immigration decisions by the government. The Act did this by making it clear that the various provisions that had previously eliminated judicial review also eliminated habeas corpus jurisdiction, mandamus jurisdiction, and jurisdiction under the All Writs Act, 28 U.S.C. § 1651. The amendments made by the REAL ID Act expressly provided that these forms of jurisdiction no longer exist for review of removal orders. *See, e.g.,* the current version of INA § 242(a)(2)(A)–(C), and (a)(5).

At the same time, Congress minimized possible constitutional confrontation by adding a provision that preserves judicial review, in the courts of appeals, of the major immigration issues that had been considered via habeas corpus in federal district courts since 1996. The REAL ID Act did this by adding section 242(a)(2)(D) to the INA:

> Nothing in subparagraph (B) or (C), or in any other provision of
> this Act (other than this section) which limits or eliminates

judicial review, shall be construed as precluding review of constitutional claims or questions of law raised upon a petition for review filed with an appropriate court of appeals in accordance with this section.

The REAL ID Act inspired two broad areas of inquiry: (1) what sort of review is available in the courts of appeals, and (2) whether habeas corpus jurisdiction remains, and if so, what sort? *See generally* Hiroshi Motomura, *Immigration Law and Federal Court Jurisdiction Through the Lens of Habeas Corpus*, 91 Corn. L. Rev. 459 (2006). The next decision grapples with these questions.

a.   "Questions of Law"

CHEN V. GONZALES
United States Court of Appeals, Second Circuit, 2006.
471 F.3d 315.

JOSÉ A. CABRANES, CIRCUIT JUDGE.

* * *

Petitioner Xiao Ji Chen, a native and citizen of China, seeks review of a September 25, 2002 order of the Board of Immigration Appeals ("BIA") affirming the November 17, 2000 decision of Immigration Judge ("IJ")[.] * * *

* * *

In her removal hearing before the IJ, petitioner alleged past and future persecution based on her opposition to the Chinese family planning policy, testifying that she had been forced to undergo an abortion in October 1997 and that she would be sterilized were she to return to China.

* * *

Rather than [report to a doctor] for sterilization, as she had been instructed [by local birth control officials], petitioner states that she made arrangements to flee to the United States, where she arrived on or about May 21, 1998. Petitioner gave birth in the United States to a second child in April 2000.

On April 27, 1999, approximately eleven months after her arrival in the United States, petitioner was detained for approximately 5–6 hours by INS officials and was ordered to appear at a removal hearing in August 1999. Petitioner filed her written application for asylum with the immigration court on October 13, 1999, nearly fifteen months after her arrival in the United States, and a merits hearing was held before the IJ on November 17, 2000.

In a decision issued at the conclusion of petitioner's hearing, the IJ rejected petitioner's application for asylum on the grounds that she had failed to file her application within one year of her arrival in the United States, as required by INA § 208(a)(2)(B), and that she had failed to establish either "changed circumstances" materially affecting her eligibility for asylum or "extraordinary circumstances" excusing her untimely filing. The IJ then concluded that, even if petitioner's asylum application was not in fact time-barred, she had failed to establish a credible case of past or future persecution entitling her either to asylum or withholding of removal under the INA or the CAT [Convention Against Torture]. * * *

* * *

In this case, we consider first whether we have jurisdiction to review the IJ's discretionary and factual determination, with respect to petitioner's asylum claim, that petitioner failed to establish either changed or extraordinary circumstances under INA § 208(a)(2)(D). We then evaluate petitioner's claim that the IJ improperly rejected her request for withholding of removal under both the INA and the CAT.

I.   Asylum

[The statutory entitlement to apply for asylum] is limited by § 208(a)(2)(B), which states that § 208(a)(1) "shall not apply to an alien unless the alien demonstrates by clear and convincing evidence that the application [for asylum] has been filed within 1 year after the date of the alien's arrival in the United States." A discretionary exception to § 208(a)(2)(B)'s one-year bar is created by § 208(a)(2)(D), which provides that

> [a]n application for asylum of an alien *may be considered,* notwithstanding [an alien's failure to apply for asylum within one year of the alien's arrival or the denial of a prior asylum application], if the alien demonstrates *to the satisfaction of the Attorney General* either the existence of changed circumstances which materially affect the applicant's eligibility for asylum or extraordinary circumstances relating to the delay in filing an application within the [one-year] period[.]

§ 208(a)(2)(D) (emphases added). Finally, § 208(a)(3) provides that "[n]o court shall have jurisdiction to review any determination of the Attorney General under [§ 208(a)(2)]."

* * *

* * * [INA § 242(a)(2)(D), as added by section 106 of the REAL ID Act,] restored the jurisdiction of courts to review even factual and discretionary decisions of the Attorney General (and his representatives)

under the INA, but only to the limited extent that the petition for review of such decisions raises a constitutional claim or a question of law. * * *

The term "constitutional claims" clearly relates to claims brought pursuant to provisions of the Constitution of the United States. By contrast, "questions of law" does not have a similarly clear meaning, and the terms of the REAL ID Act provide no guidance as to the precise content of that phrase, which is subject to countless interpretations. * * *

We find ambiguity in the meaning of this term. First, "questions of law" would include all constitutional claims, which by definition raise legal questions. Yet the statute refers to two separate categories: "constitutional claims or questions of law." * * *

Second, the broadest meaning of "questions of law" would bring within our jurisdiction certain kinds of claims that the INA otherwise removes from our jurisdiction. See, e.g., § 242(a)(2)(B)(i) (depriving courts of jurisdiction to review "any judgment regarding the granting of relief under section 212(h), 212(i), 240A, 240B, or 245 of this title") (emphasis added); id. § 242(a)(2)(B)(ii) (depriving courts of jurisdiction to review "any other decision or action of the Attorney General . . . the authority for which is specified under this subchapter to be in the discretion of the Attorney General") (emphases added); § 208(a)(3) ("No court shall have jurisdiction to review any determination of the Attorney General under [§ 208(a)(2)].") (emphasis added). * * * Although it is clear that Congress has expressly limited the effect of the jurisdiction-denying provisions of the INA by restoring our jurisdiction to review "questions of law," * * * nothing in the text of [INA § 242(a)(2)(D)] suggests that Congress intended to engage effectively in a wholesale repeal of these jurisdiction-denying provisions by adopting the broadest meaning of "questions of law." As a result, we are left with uncertainty as to the meaning of the phrase.

Third, * * * the title of the subsection containing the phrase "questions of law" is "JUDICIAL REVIEW OF *CERTAIN* LEGAL CLAIMS," thereby suggesting that not all legal claims are included within the phrase "questions of law." * * *

* * *

The [House Conference Committee Report on the REAL ID Act] makes clear that Congress, in enacting the REAL ID Act, sought to avoid the constitutional concerns outlined by the Supreme Court in *St. Cyr,* which stated that as a result of the Suspension Clause, *"some* judicial intervention in deportation cases is unquestionably required by the Constitution."

* * *

* * * We construe the intent of Congress's restoration under the REAL ID Act rubric of "constitutional claims or questions of law" to encompass the same types of issues that courts traditionally exercised in habeas review over Executive detentions. * * *

Traditionally, habeas review for Executive detention had encompassed both constitutional claims and questions of law. In *St. Cyr,* the Supreme Court noted that historically, habeas review of Executive detentions was broader than habeas review over other types of detentions resulting from judicial determinations. "While habeas review of a court judgment was limited to the issue of the sentencing court's jurisdictional competency, an attack on an executive order could raise *all issues* relating to the legality of detention." (emphasis added). This was because "[a]t its historical core, the writ of habeas corpus has served as a means of reviewing the legality of Executive detention, and it is in that context that its protections have been strongest."

As part of its historical review of the scope of habeas jurisdiction, the Supreme Court did not expressly limit its analysis to issues of "statutory construction," but instead stated that such review traditionally had "encompassed detentions based on *errors of law,* including the erroneous *application or interpretation* of statutes," (emphases added), as well as challenges to "Executive interpretations of the immigration laws," and determinations regarding an alien's "statutory eligibility for discretionary relief." Furthermore, one of the habeas corpus cases on which *St. Cyr* relied—*United States ex rel. Accardi v. Shaughnessy,* 347 U.S. 260, 74 S.Ct. 499, 98 L.Ed. 681 (1954)—involved the application and interpretation of a *regulation,* not a statute.

With respect to determinations committed to the discretion of the Attorney General, the Supreme Court found that "[h]abeas courts also regularly answered *questions of law* that arose in the context of discretionary relief." *St. Cyr,* 533 U.S. at 307, 121 S.Ct. 2271 (emphasis added). At the same time, the Supreme Court emphasized in both *St. Cyr* and *Accardi* that habeas jurisdiction is not without limits. In *St. Cyr,* the Court wrote:

> [St. Cyr] does not dispute any of the *facts* that establish his deportability or the conclusion that he is deportable. Nor does he contend that he would have any right to have an unfavorable *exercise* of the Attorney General's discretion reviewed in a judicial forum. Rather, he contests the Attorney General's conclusion that, *as a matter of statutory interpretation,* he is not *eligible* for discretionary relief.

Id. at 298, 121 S.Ct. 2271 (emphases added). [The applicant in *Accardi*] raised a reviewable claim because he had challenged the BIA's "alleged *failure to exercise* its own discretion, contrary to existing valid regulations." (emphasis added).

* * *

In deciding this case, we need not determine the precise outer limits of the term "questions of law" under the REAL ID Act, nor need we define the full extent of "those issues that were historically reviewable on habeas," or what the Suspension Clause itself requires on direct, non-habeas review of a removal order. * * * To determine whether a reviewing court has jurisdiction under Section 106 to consider a petition for review, especially one challenging the agency's fact-finding or its exercise of discretion, the court would need to study the arguments asserted. The court would need to determine, regardless of the rhetoric employed in the petition, whether it merely quarrels over the correctness of the factual findings or justification for the discretionary choices, in which case the court would lack jurisdiction, or whether it instead raises a "constitutional claim" or "question of law," in which case the court could exercise jurisdiction to review those particular issues. Such an issue would arise for example in fact-finding which is flawed by an error of law, such as might arise where the IJ states that his decision was based on petitioner's failure to testify to some pertinent fact when the record of the hearing reveals unambiguously that the petitioner *did* testify to that fact. Such an issue would also arise where a discretionary decision is argued to be an abuse of discretion because it was made without rational justification or based on a legally erroneous standard. But when analysis of the arguments raised by the petition for judicial review reveals that they do not in fact raise any reviewable issues, the petitioner cannot overcome this deficiency and secure review by using the rhetoric of a "constitutional claim" or "question of law" to disguise what is essentially a quarrel about fact-finding or the exercise of discretion.[8]

Petitioner here argues that the IJ erred in either his fact-finding or in his exercise of discretion in rejecting petitioner's contention that changed or extraordinary circumstances excused the untimeliness of her petition for asylum. In her effort to establish such changed or extraordinary circumstances, petitioner argued changed circumstances because the government of China had recently cracked down on political dissidents and extraordinary circumstances because petitioner made an

---

[8] In so holding, we emphasize the particular role played by Section 106 of the REAL ID Act—namely, to *restore* some of the jurisdiction that is otherwise *denied* by another provision of the INA. *See* § 242(a)(2)(D) ("Nothing in subparagraph (B) or (C), or in any other provision of this chapter (other than this section) *which limits or eliminates judicial review,* shall be construed as precluding review of constitutional claims or questions of law raised upon a petition for *review. . . .*") (emphasis added). By contrast, where no jurisdiction-denying provision of the INA is implicated, a reviewing court need not resort to the jurisdictional terms of Section 106, but is instead presumed to have the authority to consider *"all* questions of law and fact, including interpretation and application of constitutional and statutory provisions" in reviewing a final order of removal. *See* INA § 242(b)(9) (emphasis added).

oral request to file for asylum when she was detained by the INS. The IJ rejected these contentions, finding that "nothing had changed" in China's family planning policies that would have affected her eligibility for asylum, and that she had "ample opportunity" to file her asylum application within one year as required, notwithstanding her "very brief" detention in April 1999. Petitioner's challenge to the IJ's rulings are just the kind of quarrels with fact-finding determinations and with exercises of discretion that courts continue to have no jurisdiction to review, notwithstanding the REAL ID Act's restoration of jurisdiction over constitutional claims and questions of law.

In an effort to come within the restored jurisdiction for constitutional claims and questions of law, petitioner asserts that the IJ "fail[ed] to apply the law," and argues that a claim of failure to apply the law raises a question of law, if not also a constitutional claim of violation of due process. A petitioner cannot overcome the lack of jurisdiction to review by invocation of such rhetoric.

* * * [P]etitioner's mere assertion that the IJ and the BIA "fail[ed] to apply the law" does not convert a mere disagreement with the IJ's factual findings and exercise of discretion into a constitutional claim or a question of law.

Moreover, we emphasize that our jurisdiction in this case is not restored by the REAL ID Act on the ground that the IJ's decision involved the allegedly erroneous "application" of a statute—here, INA § 208(a)(2)(B) and (D). While the term "questions of law" undeniably can encompass claims of "erroneous *application* or interpretation of statutes," *St. Cyr,* 533 U.S. at 302, 121 S.Ct. 2271 (emphasis added), every discretionary determination under the INA can in some sense be said to reflect an "application" of a statute to the facts presented. The mere use of the term "erroneous application" of a statute will not, however, convert a quarrel over an exercise of discretion into a question of law.[11] We must look to the *nature of the argument* being advanced in the petition and

---

[11] We emphasize, however, that our analysis above does not foreclose the possibility of a case in which the "application" of a statute actually presents a "question of law" within the meaning of the REAL ID Act. Although we need not specify here any precise dividing line between the "application or interpretation" of a statute, on the one hand, and the "exercise of discretion," on the other, we note that the Fourth Circuit's analysis in *Jean v. Gonzales,* 435 F.3d 475 (4th Cir. 2006), is instructive on this score. In that case, the Court held that the BIA's decision that the petitioner was *"statutorily precluded* from demonstrating good moral character" was "not a discretionary decision," but rather, was "essentially a legal determination involving the application of law to factual findings."

At the same time, however, the Fourth Circuit declined to review the BIA's discretionary denial of a waiver of inadmissibility under INA § 212(h), noting that the petitioner "argue[d] only that the immigration judge drew the wrong *factual* conclusions from the evidence and then determined these conclusions outweighed any factors supporting a favorable exercise of *discretion." Id.* at 480 (emphases added). Because the petitioner had in that respect failed to present a "question of law" under the REAL ID Act, the Court lacked jurisdiction to review the claim.

determine whether the petition raises "constitutional claims or questions of law" or merely objects to the IJ's fact-finding or exercise of discretion. This petitioner's challenge is merely an objection to the IJ's factual findings and the balancing of factors in which discretion was exercised. Accordingly, for the reasons stated above, we dismiss the petition for review of the denial of asylum because we lack jurisdiction to hear it.

[The court also denied the petition for review of the immigration judge's denial of withholding of removal.]

* * *

NOTES AND QUESTIONS ON
THE SCOPE OF REVIEW AFTER THE REAL ID ACT

1.   With regard to the one-year deadline on applying for asylum, most other circuits have agreed with the general approach in *Chen* and have concluded that the timeliness of an asylum application and the decision whether the lateness is excused by "changed circumstances" or "extraordinary circumstances" are factual or discretionary decisions over which review is barred. *See, e.g., Gomis v. Holder*, 571 F.3d 353, 358–359 (4th Cir. 2009) (collecting cases), *rehearing and rehearing en banc denied,* 585 F.3d 197 (4th Cir. 2009), *cert. denied,* 558 U.S. 1110, 130 S.Ct. 1048, 175 L.Ed.2d 881 (2010).

2.   In another case involving a question of late filing for asylum, the Ninth Circuit announced a more expansive understanding of what is open to review under INA § 242(a)(2)(D):

> * * * [T]he phrase "questions of law" as it is used in section 106 of the Real ID Act includes review of the application of statutes and regulations to undisputed historical facts. This construction is amply supported by the statute and legislative history, and a narrower interpretation would pose a serious Suspension Clause issue.
>
> * * *
>
> * * * [W]e dispute the government's characterization of the changed circumstances determination as "not only a 'predominately factual' inquiry, but also a discretionary determination," relying on the statutory requirement that changed circumstances be established "to the satisfaction of the Attorney General."

The words "to the satisfaction of the Attorney General" do not render the changed circumstances determination discretionary. Instead, this phrase is a specification of *who* is to make the decision, rather than a characterization of that decision itself. * * * We have explicitly held that "to the satisfaction of the Attorney General" does *not* render a determination discretionary.

* * *

We now turn to Ramadan's claims. Ramadan's challenge to the IJ's determination that Ramadan failed to show changed circumstances is a reviewable mixed question of law and fact. The Supreme Court has defined such questions as those in which "the historical facts are admitted or established, the rule of law is undisputed, and the issue is whether the facts satisfy the statutory standard." Here, the factual basis of Ramadan's petition is undisputed; we only review whether the IJ appropriately determined that the facts did not constitute "changed circumstances" as defined by immigration law. * * * [W]e have jurisdiction to hear Ramadan's petition * * * .

Ramadan v. Gonzales, 479 F.3d 646, 654–57 (9th Cir. 2007).

The Seventh Circuit, however, announced its strong disagreement with the approach in *Ramadan*:

The panel in *Ramadan* held that § 242(a)(2)(D) authorizes judicial review of all "mixed questions of law and fact," including all applications of law to fact. Only pure findings of fact are outside the scope of subsection (D), the panel concluded. Because no administrative case can be decided without applying some law to some facts, that understanding of § 242(a)(2)(D) vitiates all clauses in the statute, including § 208(a)(3), that limit judicial review of particular classes of decisions. * * * The panel in *Ramadan* conceded that § 242(a)(2)(D) does not say that "mixed" or "ultimate" questions are reviewable—and * * * the legislative history of § 242(a)(2)(D) is incompatible with extending that proviso beyond pure questions of law—but adopted its interpretation to avoid any need to consider constitutional objections to § 242(a)(2)(D).

It is hard to appreciate what those objections might be; the Constitution itself allows Congress to create exceptions to the jurisdiction of the federal courts. Provisions foreclosing judicial review of particular administrative decisions are common. The most famous such exclusion is in the Administrative Procedure Act of 1946, 5 U.S.C. § 701(a)(2) (decisions "committed to agency discretion by law" are not judicially reviewable), and to our knowledge no serious argument has ever been made that § 701(a)(2) is unconstitutional. * * *

Nine judges dissented from the denial of rehearing en banc in *Ramadan*. * * * [T]he ninth circuit stands alone: at least eight circuits read § 242(a)(2)(D) as limited to pure questions of law. * * *

Viracacha v. Mukasey, 518 F.3d 511, 515–16 (7th Cir.), *cert. denied,* 129 S.Ct. 451, 172 L.Ed.2d 326 (2008).

3.   In confronting the issues with which *Chen* grapples, patterns vary among circuits (and sometimes within circuits) regarding when § 242(a)(2)(D) is judged to preserve review. Those courts that are inclined to preserve as much review as possible tend to find ways to subdivide the questions presented and locate a separately identifiable question of law, or possibly a due process issue. Other courts are more resistant to such arguments by the petitioner. Here are some examples in which the court found jurisdiction—or not—under § 242(a)(2)(D) based on an asserted constitutional claim or question of law:

a.   A claim that a statute that gives the Attorney General the discretion to remove an aggravated felon under either the administrative removal procedure in INA § 238 or standard removal proceeding under INA § 240 violates equal protection?

Held: jurisdiction. *Flores-Ledezma v. Gonzales*, 415 F.3d 375, 380 (5th Cir. 2005) (statute upheld).

b.   A claim that the immigration judge failed to consider adequately a waiver applicant's daughter's U.S. citizenship in making the factual determination that she would not suffer hardship?

Held: no jurisdiction. *Rodrigues-Nascimento v. Gonzales*, 485 F.3d 60, 62 (1st Cir. 2007).

c.   A claim that the Board of Immigration Appeals violated the noncitizen's right to due process when it (1) overturned the immigration judge's finding that the asylum applicant was a "persecutor" but (2) did not overturn the immigration judge's denial of voluntary departure that had been based solely on the "persecutor" finding.

Held: jurisdiction. *Patel v. Gonzales*, 470 F.3d 216, 219–20 (6th Cir. 2006) (remanded to BIA so that it can exercise discretion on voluntary departure).

d.   A claim that the BIA improperly denied cancellation of removal when it found that petitioner had not established "exceptional and extremely unusual hardship."

Held: no jurisdiction to consider claim that BIA improperly assumed that the U.S. citizen child would return to Mexico with petitioner (because not a colorable claim in light of the record), but jurisdiction exists to consider whether the legal interpretation in the controlling BIA precedent was valid, and whether the BIA improperly attached weight to the number of qualifying relatives in its hardship determination. *Pareja v. Attorney General,* 615 F.3d 180, 188 (3d Cir. 2010) (sustaining BIA legal interpretation under *Chevron*; but remanding for BIA to clarify its decision in light of court's holding on weight to be given the number of qualifying relatives).

4. For a thorough discussion of what it means for an immigration decision to be "discretionary," see Daniel Kanstroom, Deportation Nation: Outsiders in American History 228–40 (2007).

b. Immigration Habeas After the REAL ID Act

Most of the review that would have been available via habeas corpus before the REAL ID Act can and must take place now through petitions for review in the courts of appeals. This is because the REAL ID Act both significantly expanded court of appeals jurisdiction and made habeas corpus jurisdiction under 28 U.S.C. § 2241 unavailable for review of removal orders, *see* INA § 242(a), or for consideration of certain other specified issues, *see, e.g.,* INA § 208(a)(3), (b)(2)(D). After the REAL ID Act, what habeas corpus jurisdiction remains?

It is now well-settled that habeas corpus is available to consider challenges to detention before, during or after removal proceedings. *See, e.g., Kellici v. Gonzales,* 472 F.3d 416, 419–20 (6th Cir. 2006); *Hernandez v. Gonzales*, 424 F.3d 42, 42 (1st Cir. 2005). Thus *Zadvydas* and *Demore,* were they to arise today, would still be habeas actions, because they challenge the validity of pre-hearing or post-order detention, and the issues are independent of the validity of the removal charges. Although this conclusion sits somewhat uneasily with the actual text of INA § 242 as amended, especially in view of § 242(b)(9) (a consolidation provision discussed later in this chapter), it is consistent with the legislative history. The Conference Report stated that the Act's changes to the INA's jurisdictional provisions were not intended to "preclude habeas review over challenges to detention that are independent of challenges to removal orders." H.R. Conf. Rep. No. 109–72, at 175 (2005).

What, if any, habeas jurisdiction remains to review final removal orders? When might petitions for review in the courts of appeals fail to provide the "adequate substitute" for habeas corpus that *St. Cyr* said would be necessary to avoid Suspension Clause problems? Consider two situations.

(i) Missing the 30-Day Deadline for Filing a Petition for Review

Assume that a noncitizen who has a final removal order misses the 30-day deadline for filing a petition for review in the courts of appeals. He asserts that this default occurred because of ineffective assistance of counsel or government interference, and argues that the law should be read to permit a late filing or some other remedy. The REAL ID Act would seem to repeal habeas and thus leave him with no court review at all.

In *Singh v. Gonzales*, 499 F.3d 969 (9th Cir. 2007), the Ninth Circuit held that habeas jurisdiction remained available for a claim that ineffective assistance of counsel had prevented timely filing of the petition for review, because the ineffective assistance occurred after the issuance of the final order of removal and therefore was not a review of a removal order under the REAL ID Act. The Court noted that "a successful habeas petition in this case will lead to nothing more than 'a day in court' for Singh, which is consistent with Congressional intent underlying the REAL ID Act." *Id.* at 979.

Four years later, the Second Circuit held that the statutory procedure permitting a motion to reopen before the BIA was an adequate and effective substitute for habeas jurisdiction. *Luna v. Holder,* 637 F.3d 85, 95–97 (2d Cir. 2011). Key to its conclusion that the petition for review was a sufficient substitute for habeas review was the Attorney General's decision in *Matter of Compean,* (discussed earlier in this chapter, *supra* at pp. 941–942) decided after *Singh*, that the motion to reopen allowed consideration of a noncitizen's claim that ineffective assistance of counsel had prevented timely filing of a petition for review. The court warned, however, that "the statutory motion to reopen process would not be an adequate substitute for habeas if our review of BIA decisions was meaningfully 'more limited' than it would be on habeas." Moreover, for "a statutory motion to reopen to be a constitutionally adequate substitute for habeas, * * * an alien who was prevented by ineffective assistance of counsel or governmental interference from filing a timely petition for review cannot also be prevented by the same circumstances from filing a statutory motion to reopen." *Id.* at 98, 99.

(ii) Inadequate Factual Record

What about cases in which effective review requires the development of a factual record? According to INA § 242(a)(1), "the court may not order the taking of additional evidence under 28 U.S.C. § 2347(c)," and according to INA § 242(b)(4)(A), "the court of appeals shall decide the petition only on the administrative record on which the order of removal is based." The only exception permitting further factual development in district court (upon transfer from the court of appeals) is found in INA § 242(b)(5)(B), applicable only to claims that the respondent is a U.S. national.

In *Rafaelano v. Wilson*, 471 F.3d 1091 (9th Cir. 2006), the Ninth Circuit had before it a petition for review that turned on whether the noncitizen had voluntarily departed the country under a previously unappealed 1995 alternate order, which, by its terms, became an enforceable deportation order if she did not timely depart. She said she had complied. DHS, which had discovered her in this country in 2003, claimed she had not, and it was now acting to remove her summarily based on the 1995 order. The court described its factfinding dilemma:

> [W]e are left in a situation where we cannot review the decision of the district court [owing to the REAL ID Act's transitional rules] and yet have no BIA decision to review nor any administrative record regarding the relevant factual issue * * * . Further, we cannot adjudicate Rafaelano's claims in the first instance, as our review is generally limited to what is contained in the administrative record.

Id. at 1097.

The court chose this solution: "In light of these unusual circumstances, we find it necessary and appropriate to transfer this matter to the BIA to permit the executive agency to consider the contested issues and conduct any necessary fact-finding." 471 F.3d at 1097–98. (The matter was sent to the BIA even though it had apparently never heard the case before.) Judge Rawlinson, dissenting, would have appointed a special master "to recommend factual findings and disposition" as authorized by Rule 48 of the Federal Rules of Appellate Procedure. 471 F.3d at 1099 (Rawlinson, J., dissenting). *See also Florida Power & Light Co. v. Lorion*, 470 U.S. 729, 743–44, 105 S.Ct. 1598, 1606–07, 84 L.Ed.2d 643 (1985) (in a non-immigration case, requiring "remand to the agency for additional investigation or explanation" of an agency decision made without a hearing; expressing concern that the court of appeals approach—sending the case to the district court for an evidentiary hearing—would result in a counterproductive bifurcation of review). *Cf. Mohamed v. Gonzales*, 477 F.3d 522, 526 (8th Cir. 2007) (rejecting a constitutional challenge based on an allegedly inadequate factual record for petition for review, because the noncitizen could have introduced the missing evidence before the BIA); *Aguilar v. U.S. ICE*, 510 F.3d 1, 15–16 (1st Cir. 2007) ("immigration judges possess ample fact-gathering faculties"; habeas not needed to develop sufficient record of claim of inadequate access to counsel).

4. THE STANDARDS FOR A STAY PENDING JUDICIAL REVIEW

INA § 242(f)(2) provides that "no court shall enjoin the removal of any alien pursuant to a final order * * * unless the alien shows by clear and convincing evidence that the entry or execution of such order is prohibited as a matter of law." Is this also the standard that must be met to obtain a stay of a final removal order pending appeal? The courts of appeals divided on this question, until the Supreme Court resolved the issue in *Nken v. Holder*, 556 U.S. 418, 129 S.Ct. 1749, 173 L.Ed.2d 550 (2009). Nken had been unsuccessful on his asylum and withholding of removal claims before the immigration judge and the BIA. He sought a stay of the order while the court of appeals considered his petition for review. The Fourth Circuit denied a stay, applying § 242(f)(2). The U.S. Supreme Court reversed, 7–2, in an opinion by Chief Justice Roberts:

> * * * Nken argues that the "traditional" standard for a stay applies. Under that standard, a court considers four factors: "(1) whether the stay applicant has made a strong showing that he is likely to succeed on the merits; (2) whether the applicant will be irreparably injured absent a stay; (3) whether issuance of the stay will substantially injure the other parties interested in the proceeding; and (4) where the public interest lies." *Hilton v. Braunskill,* 481 U.S. 770, 776 (1987).

> The Government disagrees, arguing that a stay is simply a form of injunction * * * and therefore that the limits on injunctive relief set forth in subsection (f)(2) apply.

> * * *

> An injunction and a stay have typically been understood to serve different purposes. The former is a means by which a court tells someone what to do or not to do. When a court employs "the extraordinary remedy of injunction," it directs the conduct of a party, and does so with the backing of its full coercive powers.

> * * *

> By contrast, instead of directing the conduct of a particular actor, a stay operates upon the judicial proceeding itself. It does so either by halting or postponing some portion of the proceeding, or by temporarily divesting an order of enforceability.

> * * *

> Applying the subsection (f)(2) standard to stays pending appeal would not fulfill the historic office of such a stay. The whole idea is to hold the matter under review in abeyance because the appellate court lacks sufficient time to decide the merits. Under the subsection (f)(2) standard, however, a stay would only be granted after the court in effect *decides* the merits, in an expedited manner. * * * Subsection (f)(2), in short, would invert the customary role of a stay, requiring a definitive merits decision earlier rather than later.

556 U.S. at 425–32. The Court went on to provide further guidance on the appropriate stay standards, including a critical review of the standards used by some of the lower courts that had earlier been applying the traditional four-part test:

"A stay is not a matter of right, even if irreparable injury might otherwise result." * * * The party requesting a stay bears the burden of showing that the circumstances justify an exercise of that discretion.

The fact that the issuance of a stay is left to the court's discretion "does not mean that no legal standard governs that discretion. . . ." * * *

The first two factors of the traditional standard are the most critical. It is not enough that the chance of success on the merits be "better than negligible." *Sofinet v. INS*, 188 F.3d 703, 707 (C.A.7 1999). Even petitioner acknowledges that "[m]ore than a mere 'possibility' of relief is required." By the same token, simply showing some "possibility of irreparable injury," *Abbassi v. INS*, 143 F.3d 513, 514 (C.A.9 1998), fails to satisfy the second factor. As the Court pointed out earlier this Term, the " 'possibility' standard is too lenient."

Although removal is a serious burden for many aliens, it is not categorically irreparable, as some courts have said. * * *

The automatic stay prior to IIRIRA reflected a recognition of the irreparable nature of harm from removal before decision on a petition for review, given that the petition abated upon removal. Congress's decision in IIRIRA to allow continued prosecution of a petition after removal eliminated the reason for categorical stays * * * . It is accordingly plain that the burden of removal alone cannot constitute the requisite irreparable injury. Aliens who are removed may continue to pursue their petitions for review, and those who prevail can be afforded effective relief by facilitation of their return, along with restoration of the immigration status they had upon removal.

Once an applicant satisfies the first two factors, the traditional stay inquiry calls for assessing the harm to the opposing party and weighing the public interest. These factors merge when the Government is the opposing party. In considering them, courts must be mindful that the Government's role as the respondent in every removal proceeding does not make the public interest in each individual one negligible, as some courts have concluded.

Of course there is a public interest in preventing aliens from being wrongfully removed, particularly to countries where they are likely to face substantial harm. But that is no basis for the blithe assertion of an "absence of any injury to the public interest" when a stay is granted. There is always a public interest in prompt execution of removal orders: The continued presence of an alien lawfully deemed removable undermines the streamlined removal proceedings IIRIRA established, and "permit[s] and prolong[s] a continuing violation of United States law." [*Reno v. American-Arab Anti-Discrimination Committee*], 525 U.S. [471], at 490, 119 S.Ct. 936. The interest in prompt removal may be heightened by the circumstances as well—if, for example, the alien is particularly dangerous, or has substantially prolonged his stay by abusing the processes provided to him. *See ibid.* ("Postponing justifiable deportation (in the hope that the alien's status will change—by, for example, marriage to an American citizen—or simply with the object of extending the alien's unlawful stay) is often the principal object of resistance to a deportation proceeding"). A court asked to stay removal cannot simply assume that "[o]rdinarily, the balance of hardships will weigh heavily in the applicant's favor."

Id. at 433–36.

PROBLEMS ON STAYS PENDING APPEAL

Applying these standards from *Nken*, how would you, as a judge, assess a request for a stay pending appeal in each of the following cases? (Consider each of the lettered scenarios separately.) Your answers may require addressing whether the substantive issue being raised is reviewable at all. Identify what additional information you would find useful or indispensable in order to reach a final conclusion.

1. A lawful permanent resident found removable on the basis of convictions for a crime involving moral turpitude; the LPR contends that his convictions were not properly considered to be a CIMT.

2. A visa overstayer who sought cancellation of removal, which was denied: (a) on a finding that she lacked good moral character; (b) on a finding that she had not shown exceptional and extremely unusual hardship; or (c) in the exercise of discretion, based on a judgment that the negative factors outweighed the positive factors in her case, even though she was statutorily eligible.

3. An entrant without inspection whose asylum claim was denied: (a) on a finding that the noncitizen lacked credibility; (b) on the basis of nexus—a ruling that the claimed persecution would not be on one of the five prescribed statutory grounds; (c) on a finding that the person had shown past persecution but that conditions have changed in the country of origin; or (d) on the ground that the claim was filed more than one year after arrival and that no exceptions to the deadline apply.

5. CONSOLIDATING ISSUES FOR REVIEW

Beyond the questions of whether a court may review, which court may review, what issues it may review and by what procedural vehicle, and when a stay of removal is appropriate pending review, further questions address how review is packaged. There are two general types of such consolidation issues. One concerns timing: for example, does court review take place only after all issues relating to a single removal proceeding are reduced to a final removal order, or are issues reviewable as they arise along the way? The other type of consolidation issue concerns multiple parties. When a noncitizen goes to court to challenge a government immigration decision, must she limit her suit to her own case, or may she join forces with others to challenge a pattern or practice of government decisionmaking? We will take these two areas in turn.

a. Timing of Review in an Individual Case

Should a reviewing court take up issues individually or consolidate them after a final order? And once a court undertakes review of a final removal order, exactly what issues are reviewable? Just the removal order? All decisions on potential relief from removal, or only those decided by an immigration judge? Should the court resolve all complaints the removable noncitizen might have about decisions under the immigration laws that at any time have gone against him—such as a denial of an extension of a nonimmigrant stay (leaving him in violation of status and thus deportable), or a visa petition denial that prevents his filing for adjustment? Or should the court limit review to those matters that arose before or during the immigration court hearing, leaving resolution of other issues to another forum?

Section 242(a)(1) makes the petition for review in the courts of appeals the "sole and exclusive" procedure for reviewing removal orders. Section 242 contains two other provisions that look toward consolidating issues for judicial consideration on a petition for review in the court of appeals. INA § 242(g) forbids review, "[e]xcept as provided in this section," of "any cause or claim * * * arising from the decision or action * * * to commence proceedings, adjudicate cases, or execute removal orders." INA § 242(b)(9) consolidates all questions of law or fact "arising from any action taken or proceeding brought to remove an alien from the United States" for review in the court of appeals when it considers a final order of removal.

The first of these provisions was construed by the Supreme Court in *Reno v. American-Arab Anti-Discrimination Committee*, 525 U.S. 471, 119 S.Ct. 936, 142 L.Ed.2d 940 (1999). That case involved a collateral attack on deportation proceedings that had not yet been completed by the immigration judge. The respondents alleged that the immigration authorities had selectively targeted them for removal in violation of their First and Fifth Amendment rights. See Chapter Seven, pp. 656–658 (considering this element of the *AADC* litigation). This separate litigation had begun well before enactment of the 1996 amendments. The Supreme Court ruled that the lower courts lacked jurisdiction because of § 242(g). It explained that Congress had enacted § 242(g) partly to bar judicial review of certain matters, and partly to require consolidation of court challenges. As to the latter purpose, Justice Scalia's opinion for the Court said this:

> There was good reason for Congress to focus special attention upon, and make special provision for, judicial review of the Attorney General's discrete acts of "commenc[ing] proceedings, adjudicat[ing] cases, [and] execut[ing] removal orders"—which represent the initiation or prosecution of various stages in the deportation process. At each stage the Executive has discretion to abandon the endeavor, and at the time IIRIRA was enacted the INS had been engaging in a regular practice (which had come to be known as "deferred action") of exercising that discretion for humanitarian reasons or simply for its own convenience. * * * Since no generous act goes unpunished, however, the INS's exercise of this discretion opened the door to litigation in instances where the INS chose *not* to exercise it. * * * Such litigation was possible because courts read [the former INA] § 106's prescription that the Hobbs Act shall be "the sole and exclusive procedure for the judicial review of all final orders of deportation" to be inapplicable to various decisions and actions leading up to or consequent upon final orders of deportation, and relied on other jurisdictional statutes to permit review. Section 242(g) seems clearly designed to give some measure of protection to "no deferred action" decisions and similar discretionary determinations, providing that if they are reviewable at all, they at least will not be made the bases for separate rounds of judicial intervention outside the streamlined process that Congress has designed.

> Of course *many* provisions of IIRIRA are aimed at protecting the Executive's discretion from the courts—indeed, that can fairly be said to be the theme of the legislation. It is entirely understandable, however, why Congress would want only the discretion-protecting provision of § 242(g) applied even to pending cases: because that provision is specifically directed at the deconstruction, fragmentation, and hence prolongation of removal proceedings.

525 U.S. at 483–87, 119 S.Ct. at 943–45.

Justice Ginsburg, concurring along with Justice Breyer, agreed with the majority's reading of § 242(g):

Here, Congress has established an integrated scheme for deportation proceedings, channeling judicial review to the final order, and deferring issues outside the agency's authority until that point. Given Congress' strong interest in avoiding delay of deportation proceedings, I find the opportunity to raise a claim during the judicial review phase sufficient.

525 U.S. at 495, 119 S.Ct. at 949 (Ginsburg, J., concurring).

For illustrative applications of § 242(g), see *Elgharib v. Napolitano,* 600 F.3d 597 (6th Cir. 2010) (no jurisdiction to consider application for writ of prohibition to bar removal based on *in absentia* order); *Chapinski v. Ziglar,* 278 F.3d 718, 720–21 (7th Cir. 2002) (no jurisdiction to hear a class action to compel government to commence removal proceedings so that noncitizens could have immigration judges adjudicate their applications for relief).

The Court in *American-Arab Anti-Discrimination Committee* briefly addressed § 242(b)(9), calling it an "unmistakable 'zipper' clause"—that is, a more far-reaching consolidation provision that would apply once the IIRIRA judicial review scheme became fully effective. 525 U.S. at 482–83, 119 S.Ct. at 943. INA § 242(b)(9) seems to defer review until a final removal order has issued, but what does it mean when it refers to questions of law or fact "arising from any action taken or proceeding brought to remove an alien"? Courts have often found quite perplexing the task of distinguishing between issues that have to be consolidated and those which are not covered by § 242(b)(9) and therefore could be raised on a separate habeas petition. *See, e.g., Luna v. Holder,* 637 F.3d 85, 87 (2d Cir. 2011). Their results and applicable tests cover a spectrum.

The Ninth Circuit takes a narrow view of the issues covered by the zipper clause, permitting separate review (often by habeas) if the issue being raised is characterized as independent of a challenge to the removal order. It has included in that category challenges claiming that no enforceable removal order exists, that the noncitizen did not receive notice of a removal order, that he could not be sent to a particular country because it lacked a functioning government, and that ineffective assistance of counsel led to late filing of a petition for review with the court of appeals. *See Singh v. Gonzales,* 499 F.3d 969, 978–79 (9th Cir. 2007).

The First Circuit takes a more stringent approach toward requiring consolidation:

In enacting section 242(b)(9) Congress plainly intended to put an end to the scattershot and piecemeal nature of the review process that previously had held sway in regard to removal proceedings. * * * [N]othing in the statute limits its reach to claims arising from extant removal proceedings.

[But we do not] imply that section 242(b)(9) is limitless in its scope. * * * [T]hese words cannot be read to swallow all claims that might somehow touch upon, or be traced to, the government's efforts to remove an alien. * * * Congress's choice of phrase suggests that it did not intend section 242(b)(9) to sweep within its scope claims with only a remote or attenuated connection to the removal of an alien. * * *

We thus read the words "arising from" in section 242(b)(9) to exclude claims that are independent of, or wholly collateral to, the removal process. Among others, claims that cannot effectively be handled through the available administrative process fall within that purview.

Aguilar v. U.S. ICE, 510 F.3d 1, 9–11 (1st Cir. 2007) (paragraphing altered). *See generally* Hiroshi Motomura, *Judicial Review in Immigration Cases After AADC: Lessons From Civil Procedure*, 14 Geo. Immigr. L.J. 385, 409–30 (2000) (urging a narrow reading of (b)(9) that allows review of significant independent matters). *But cf.* David A. Martin, *Behind the Scenes on a Different Set: What Congress Needs to Do in the Aftermath of* St. Cyr *and* Nguyen, 16 Geo. Immigr. L.J. 313, 321, 327 (2002) (arguing for strong consolidation provisions that are nonetheless designed to "keep open a real and meaningful chance for judicial consideration of all issues").

Use the following exercise to test your overall understanding of consolidation issues and also the preceding material on judicial review under INA § 242. You may also want to draw upon Section A above, which covered the removal hearing itself and various motions and procedures available there.

EXERCISE

Sakha Mamadou has been a lawful permanent resident of the United States since immigrating with his parents in 1980, when he was six years old. Mamadou was convicted in early 2002 for a theft that he admitted to committing in October 2001 in Pueblo, Colorado. After spending thirty days in jail and having the remaining months of his sentence suspended, he was served with a Notice to Appear.

At a removal proceeding in Denver in which Mamadou was unrepresented (because he could not afford an attorney and could not find pro bono counsel), the judge ruled that the conviction made Mamadou deportable and ineligible for discretionary relief, and in any event that his equities were insufficient to warrant the favorable exercise of discretion. The judge ordered Mamadou removed. Mamadou then paid a lawyer recommended by a friend. The lawyer told him that he had filed an appeal to the BIA. Mamadou has heard almost nothing from his attorney about the progress of the case thereafter. He is now in custody in a detention facility in Florence, Arizona, and has just learned that the BIA ruled against him summarily. You work with an Arizona pro bono organization, which has just asked you to represent Mamadou to ask a court to review the immigration judge's rulings.

(a)   On what issues could you expect to get court review?

(b)   What procedural vehicle (petition for review or petition for a writ of habeas corpus) would you use to seek review?

(c)   In what court (court of appeals or district court, and where) would you seek review of the BIA decision?

Now assume that before your first interview with Mamadou the time for motions to reopen and reconsider had already expired. Answer each of the three questions above in light of this changed assumption. (You may need to give consideration to new administrative filings, in addition to any judicial options).

b.   Multi-Party Litigation

One final aspect of judicial review deserves analysis. What if a group of plaintiffs allege that the government has adopted a practice in its enforcement or administration of immigration law that violates a statute or is unconstitutional? This happened in *McNary v. Haitian Refugee Center, Inc.*, 498 U.S. 479, 111 S.Ct. 888, 112 L.Ed.2d 1005 (1991), a class action in which the plaintiffs alleged a pattern or practice of procedural due process violations in INS administration of the special agricultural worker (SAW) legalization program in the Immigration Reform and Control Act of 1986, INA § 210. The plaintiffs argued that the interview process implemented by the INS deprived them of due process because they were not allowed to present witnesses on their behalf, competent interpreters were not provided, and no verbatim recordings of the interviews were made. The plaintiffs sought injunctive relief in the district court.

INA § 210(e), governing court jurisdiction over SAW denials, provided in relevant part: "There shall be no administrative or judicial review of a determination respecting an application for [legalization] under this section except in accordance with this subsection," and "There shall be judicial review of such a denial only in the judicial review of an order of exclusion or deportation under [the former] section 106."

The U.S. Supreme Court read this language to constrain only direct review of individual denials of SAW status, not general challenges to agency practices and policies used in processing applications. The Court's explanation included reference to language that Congress might have adopted to foreclose jurisdiction more sweepingly:

> [H]ad Congress intended the limited review provisions of § 210(e) of the INA to encompass challenges to INS procedures and practices, it could easily have used broader statutory language. Congress could, for example, have modeled § 210(e) on the more expansive language in the general grant of district court jurisdiction under Title II of the INA by channeling into the Reform Act's special review procedures "all causes . . . arising under any of the provisions" of the legalization program. It moreover could have modeled § 210(e) on 38 U.S.C. § 211(a), which governs review of veterans' benefits claims, by referring to review "on all questions of law and fact" under the SAW legalization program.

498 U.S. at 494.

The Court was also troubled by the consequences of reading the statute to preclude jurisdiction to hear the challenge:

> Several aspects of this statutory scheme would preclude review of respondents' application denials if we were to hold that the District Court lacked jurisdiction to hear this challenge. Initially, administrative or judicial review of an agency decision is almost always confined to the record made in the proceeding at the initial decisionmaking level, and one of the central attacks on INS procedures in this litigation is based on the claim that such procedures do not allow applicants to assemble adequate records. As the District Court found, because of the lack of recordings or transcripts of LO [Legalization Office] interviews and the inadequate opportunity for SAW applicants to call witnesses or present other evidence on their behalf, the administrative appeals unit of the INS, in reviewing the decisions of LOs and regional processing facilities, and the courts of appeals, in reviewing SAW denials in the context of deportation proceedings, have no complete or meaningful basis upon which to review application determinations.

> Additionally, because there is no provision for direct judicial review of the denial of SAW status unless the alien is later apprehended and deportation proceedings are initiated, most aliens denied SAW status can ensure themselves review in courts of appeals only if they voluntarily surrender themselves

for deportation. Quite obviously, that price is tantamount to a complete denial of judicial review for most undocumented aliens.

Finally, even in the context of a deportation proceeding, it is unlikely that a court of appeals would be in a position to provide meaningful review of the type of claims raised in this litigation. To establish the unfairness of the INS practices, respondents in this case adduced a substantial amount of evidence, most of which would have been irrelevant in the processing of a particular individual application. Not only would a court of appeals reviewing an individual SAW determination therefore most likely not have an adequate record as to the pattern of INS' allegedly unconstitutional practices, but it also would lack the factfinding and record-developing capabilities of a federal district court. * * * It therefore seems plain to us, as it did to the District Court and the Court of Appeals, that restricting judicial review to the courts of appeals as a component of the review of an individual deportation order is the practical equivalent of a total denial of judicial review of generic constitutional and statutory claims.

498 U.S. at 496–97.

The key question under new § 242 is how much of the *McNary* reasoning survives. One potential limit on multi-party litigation is § 242(b)(9), which we have already considered. Compare the language of § 242(b)(9) with the models the *McNary* majority noted that Congress could have followed if it really wanted to block all review outside the one designated channel. Does (b)(9) deprive a federal court of jurisdiction to hear multi-party litigation against the government until after final removal orders have issued in those cases? For analysis suggesting that (b)(9) does not erect such a bar and therefore does not supersede *McNary*, see Motomura, *Judicial Review, supra*, 14 Geo. Immigr. L.J. 385, at 434–38 (2000); *id.* at 440 (characterizing (b)(9) as an exhaustion requirement). *But cf.* Martin, *Behind the Scenes, supra*, 16 Geo. Immigr. L.J., at 321.

Another part of INA § 242 that may affect multi-party litigation is subsection (f)(1), which provides:

Regardless of the nature of the action or claim or of the identity of the party or parties bringing the action, no court (other than the Supreme Court) shall have jurisdiction or authority to enjoin or restrain the operation of the provisions of chapter 4 of title II [INA §§ 231–244], as amended by the Illegal Immigration Reform and Immigrant Responsibility Act of 1996, other than with respect to the application of such provisions to an individual alien against whom proceedings under such chapter have been initiated.

Does (f)(1) also bar a declaratory judgment against the government with regard to a particular policy or practice? The district court in *Alli v. Decker,* 644 F.Supp.2d 535 (M.D. Pa. 2009) held that it does. "The practical effect of the class-based declaration that the petitioners seek would be indistinguishable from the effect of a class-based injunction." 457 U.S., at 408–09. A divided Third Circuit reversed. *Alli v. Decker,* 650 F.3d 1007 (3d Cir. 2011). Relying on the principle that "statutes limiting equitable relief are to be construed narrowly," the court held that "restrain" in § 242(f)(1) does not cover declaratory relief. *Id.*

Why would Congress forbid class-wide injunctions but permit class-wide declaratory relief? In *Reno v. American-Arab Anti-Discrimination Committee, supra,* the Supreme Court said of the 1996 IIRIRA, which created § 242: "protecting the Executive's discretion from the courts * * * can fairly be said to be the theme of the legislation." 525 U.S. at 487, 119 S.Ct. at 945. For general discussions favorable to finding that declaratory relief is not barred by § 242(f)(1), see Gerald L. Neuman, *Federal Courts Issues in Immigration Law,* 78 Tex. L. Rev. 1661, 1684–87 (2001); Motomura, *Judicial Review, supra,* 14 Geo. Immigr. L.J. at 438–39.

In broader perspective, what are the advantages of multi-party litigation, including class actions, for those who wish to challenge the government on immigration matters? What are the disadvantages, particularly with regard to the values traditionally served by the exhaustion of remedies requirement? What kinds of problems does such a ruling pose to an efficient legalization or general enforcement system? *See* Martin, *Behind the Scenes, supra,* 16 Geo. Immigr. L.J. at 320–23 (interlocutory orders in some post-IRCA class actions stayed in effect for seven years and probably provided benefits to large numbers who did not qualify under IRCA). Consider the impact of decisions like *McNary* on the work of pro bono lawyers who wish to challenge government policies. One factor is finding a more sympathetic judge: "The availability of class actions creates opportunities for forum shopping. A class action may, at least provisionally, project the legal views of a sympathetic district judge beyond the district, and a nationwide class action may project favorable circuit precedent beyond the circuit." Neuman, *Federal Courts Issues, supra,* 78 Tex. L. Rev. at 1681. *See also Naranjo-Aguilera v. INS,* 30 F.3d 1106, 1114 (9th Cir. 1994) (commenting on impact on counsel of disallowing class action challenge to SAW regulations). And yet, why is forum shopping—by either side—something that any system of judicial review should tolerate, let alone foster?

Other factors are financial. Recall that appointed counsel is unavailable in individual deportation proceedings, and that even if the noncitizen prevails in that forum, she cannot, unlike most other litigants against the government, obtain government reimbursement of attorney's fees under the Equal Access to Justice Act, 28 U.S.C. § 2412. *See*

Ardestani v. INS, 502 U.S. 129, 112 S.Ct. 515, 116 L.Ed.2d 496 (1991). EAJA has been available in class action challenges, however, sometimes leading to awards of several hundred thousand dollars. In fact, plaintiffs in the original *HRC v. McNary* litigation were later awarded fees amounting to $441,000 plus interest. *See Haitian Refugee Center v. Meese,* 791 F.2d 1489, 1501 (11th Cir. 1986), *opinion amended,* 804 F.2d 1573 (11th Cir. 1986).

What would you think of a bill in Congress to amend the statutes to adopt this trade-off: curtail immigration class actions, but (a) allow EAJA awards to noncitizens who prevail in deportation cases, or (b) provide the funding for appointed counsel, as needed, in removal proceedings?

Finally, consider three aspects of the reasoning in *McNary.* First, is it true that without jurisdiction over the class action that there would be no meaningful review of due process claims, because no adequate record could be created? Suppose you had represented a SAW applicant during the legalization process. At the time of application you of course could not be certain whether class actions in the district court would ultimately be allowed (because the Supreme Court did not issue its decision in *McNary* until after the application period had closed). If you believed that your client was being denied the statutory and constitutional rights at issue, could you have created some basis for later pursuit of those claims? What steps could you take?

This might prompt a second question: how sound is the assumption that adequate administrative records will be available only when factual issues were first aired in the quasi-judicial forum of the immigration court or the BIA, or else before a district court? Factual issues are routinely resolved in a variety of administrative settings that do not conform to classic trial-type procedures, and the APA certainly contemplates judicial review, on the available administrative record, of most such "informal" decisionmaking. *See Florida Power & Light Co. v. Lorion,* 470 U.S. 729, 743–44, 105 S.Ct. 1598, 84 L.Ed.2d 643 (1985), cited p. 1057 *supra;* David A. Martin, *Mandel, Cheng Fan Kwok and Other Unappealing Cases: The Next Frontier of Immigration Reform,* 27 Va. J. Int'l L. 803, 809 (1987).

Third, is it true that the statute permitting judicial review of a SAW denial only upon review of a later removal order is "tantamount to a complete denial of judicial review for most undocumented aliens"? Consider a perspective that may underpin the particular structure for judicial review in IRCA (*see generally* David A. Martin, *Judicial Review of Legalization Denials,* 65 Interp. Rel. 757, 760 (1988)): IRCA (which enacted the SAW program) was intended to end the presence of undocumented workers, both through two legalization programs and through enhanced enforcement. Bluntly stated, Congress wanted people unlawfully present either to legalize or to leave. Channeling access to judicial review through removal proceedings is precisely adapted to this two-pronged objective. Someone who believes he was wrongfully denied legalization has a genuine, even if potentially costly, avenue to correction by the courts. If he wins, Congress is fine with his remaining here. If he is wrong on the law, the removal order facilitates what the law requires— his departure.

EXERCISE

Hundreds of ICE agents took part in "Operation United Front" in New Bedford, Massachusetts. About 360 employees of Bianco, a Department of Defense subcontractor, were taken into custody. Most were taken to a holding facility at Ft. Devens in Ayer, Massachusetts. Within forty-eight hours, 210 of the detainees were flown to detention centers in Harlingen and El Paso, Texas.

In planning the sweep, ICE had taken steps to determine whether arrestees had minor dependents and had asked the Massachusetts Department of Social Services (DSS) to help address any issues of unattended children. The coordination with DSS, however, proved inadequate. Logistical difficulties and failed communications resulted in minor children being stranded without adult supervision.

The detained employees have sued ICE in federal district court, asking the court to order ICE to transfer them back to Massachusetts for removal proceedings. They allege: that ICE seized them with the intention of promptly transferring them to isolated locations where ICE knew, or should have known, that they could not effectively exercise their rights, that ICE restricted access to counsel during their detention in Fort Devens, that ICE did not coordinate with the DSS to address issues concerning the welfare of their children and families and allow the employees to make meaningful decisions concerning the care of their children, that their transfer to remote locations in Texas resulted in their inability to retain counsel of their choice or any counsel at all, that restricted access to counsel has prevented them from obtaining advice concerning potential grounds for asylum or other forms of relief, and that their transfer to Texas has severely prejudiced their ability to demonstrate ties to the community and otherwise present evidence on their behalf in bond hearings.

ICE has responded that it transferred the detainees from Massachusetts because of a shortage of bed space. ICE also contends that the detainees would receive the same procedural protections in immigration proceedings in Texas as they would in Massachusetts.

Does the court have jurisdiction to hear the employees' class-wide claims and grant the relief that they seek? If not, what avenues do they have to seek redress?

6. CONCLUDING QUESTIONS ON JUDICIAL REVIEW

In the 1996 Act, Congress responded to a judicial review scheme that it perceived as too elaborate or time-consuming with measures intended to consolidate review in many situations and to bar review altogether in others.

After a series of judicial correctives—most prominently the U.S. Supreme Court decision in *INS v. St. Cyr*—INA § 242 now sets out (1) a general scheme for judicial review via petitions for review in the federal courts of appeals, (2) a repeal of habeas corpus for most challenges that noncitizens might raise in immigration cases, (3) ostensible bars to judicial review for certain categories of persons or issues, but (4) exceptions to those bars for constitutional claims and questions of law.

Are there elements of this scheme that trouble you? If so, how would you change them? What consequences would your proposed changes have? In what ways do you think your proposed changes and their consequences would result in a more effective, efficient, and fair immigration management system?

CHAPTER TEN

ENFORCEMENT AND PROPOSED REFORMS

■ ■ ■

The last few decades have witnessed polarized and often shrill debate over immigration enforcement. Proponents on one side point to the presence of 10 to 11 million unauthorized migrants as proof that the laws are badly underenforced. They call for the agencies to toughen their stands and expand their efforts, and for Congress to provide greater resources. Others contend that there is too much immigration enforcement, emphasizing that removal often splits families that include U.S. citizen children, or at least results in the deportation of otherwise law-abiding and hard-working people who had become well-established in their local communities. Several states and cities have stepped into this arena, with measures that span a wide spectrum. Some have adopted their own immigration crackdown laws meant to involve their personnel in direct immigration enforcement or to deny work or housing to the undocumented. At the opposite pole, other municipalities and a few states have restricted cooperation with federal immigration agencies, even to the point where some localities declare themselves "sanctuary cities."

Congress's primary response through much of this period has been a substantial expansion in the funding for immigration enforcement, but it has tended to favor border enforcement (in general, the domain of CBP) over enhancements directed toward interior enforcement (roughly speaking, the domain of ICE), for reasons we will explore. And it has provided an array of new statutory tools and programs that can expedite or streamline removal for certain categories of violators, or improve the effectiveness of other control measures, such as visa screening or the verification of work authorization. Meantime, DHS has experimented with its own administrative initiatives to improve enforcement. Sometimes these changes expand the reach of enforcement or make certain procedures more efficient. Other changes emphasize a smarter use of prosecutorial discretion in an effort to narrow the focus, using limited resources to target more effectively the more dangerous or egregious violators of the immigration laws, while making sure that they not only receive a removal order but actually leave the country.

This chapter will first survey, in Section A, the array of federal tools and programs used by DHS and the Department of State in accomplishing immigration enforcement. Section B explores constitutional limitations on searches, arrests, interrogation and prosecutions, including whether or when ethnicity may be used in making enforcement choices. It also addresses issues raised by the use of immigration enforcement in the struggle against terrorism. Section C then considers the state and local role, both direct and indirect, in immigration enforcement. Section D concludes the chapter with a broad look at immigration reform proposals. We place the reform proposals in this chapter, although they range well beyond strict enforcement measures, because in our view reform is inextricably linked with enforcement. The desire to transition to an immigration regime that can be—and deserves to be—enforced effectively is central to much of the reform effort in recent years.

A. CONTROLLING ILLEGAL MIGRATION

1. INTRODUCTION AND AN OVERVIEW

The Immigration Reform and Control Act of 1986 (IRCA) announced a national policy dedicated to staunching the flow of undocumented immigration. According to the House Report:

> While there is no doubt that many who enter illegally do so for the best of motives—to seek a better life for themselves and their families—immigration must proceed in a legal, orderly, and regulated fashion. As a sovereign nation, we must secure our borders.

H.R. Rep. No. 682(I), 99th Cong., 2d Sess. 46 (1986).

How were we to gain control of our borders? IRCA adopted a multi-prong strategy, including legalization of most of the undocumented aliens then resident in the United States and a limited program for admitting temporary agricultural workers legally in the future. On the enforcement side, IRCA's main innovation focused on *private* enforcement: it required employers to verify whether new hires were authorized to work in the United States. The basic reasoning was that jobs are what attract most migrants to the United States; if their access to the labor market could be blocked up front, it would deter the attempt to migrate unlawfully.

By the early 1990s it became apparent that IRCA had not succeeded in controlling illegal migration (though its legalization programs did produce legal status for nearly 2.7 million people who had been unlawfully present in 1986). Employer verification, it turned out, could be easily defeated by the use of false documents. Since then, the nation has engaged in sporadic rounds of new initiatives and increased funding meant to bring us closer to IRCA's enforcement promise. Initially the lawmakers' attention focused primarily on the objective highlighted in the quote above: reining in large-scale illegal movement of those who are mainly economic migrants. After September 11, 2001, a great deal of additional funding and innovation was fueled by a second and more targeted objective: improving security screening and enhancing the ability to exclude or remove persons involved in terrorism. Nonetheless, many of the new post-9/11 programs, especially those that enable improved identity checks and provide for durable electronic records linked to biometrics (at present, this means fingerprints), have also contributed to improved capabilities for enforcement against violators who are not in any way security threats.

The Illegal Immigration Reform and Immigrant Responsibility Act of 1996 (IIRIRA), along with related measures also adopted that year, represented the first major post-IRCA round of statutory changes meant to toughen enforcement. For example, IIRIRA substantially restricted the availability of discretionary relief (reflected in the current provisions for cancellation of removal) and added the three- and ten-year bars to the inadmissibility grounds, applicable to noncitizens who had been unlawfully present for six months or more. These changes were covered in Chapter Seven.

IIRIRA also enacted streamlined removal procedures applicable to specified categories of persons at the border or unlawfully present in the interior. These procedures can result in a removal order issued by an immigration officer rather than an immigration judge, or allow an officer to determine that an earlier order remains in effect, permitting removal of the noncitizen without a new appearance before a judge. The primary procedures introduced by IIRIRA are: expedited removal for inadmissible aliens who lack documents or present fraudulent documents, INA § 235(b)(1); a speedy procedure to remove noncitizens who return without permission following an earlier order of removal or voluntary departure, known as reinstatement of removal, INA § 241(a)(5); and "administrative removal" for non-LPRs who have been convicted of an aggravated felony, INA § 238(b). Because these procedures are discussed in detail in Chapters Six and Nine, we do not further describe them here, but their growing importance to enforcement is reflected in Figures 10.1 and 10.2, which are based on a DHS publication. By 2010, over 62 percent of removals resulted from expedited removal or reinstatement. By 2013 that reliance had grown to 82.8 percent. (The DHS publication did not provide data on administrative removals.)

Figure 10.1
Trends in Total Removals, Expedited Removals, and Reinstatements, FY 2001–2013

Fiscal Year	Total removals	Expedited removals	Reinstatements	All other removals
2001	189,026	69,923	38,943	80,160
2002	165,168	34,624	46,436	84,108
2003	211,098	43,920	66,713	100,465
2004	240,665	51,014	84,347	105,304
2005	246,431	87,888	43,137	115,406
2006	280,974	110,663	49,539	120,772
2007	319,382	106,196	77,696	135,490
2008	359,795	112,716	91,318	155,761
2009	395,165	106,025	116,903	172,237
2010	387,242	111,116	130,840	145,286
2011	387,134	122,236	124,784	140,114
2012	418,397	163,308	146,044	109,045
2013	438,421	193,032	170,247	75,142

Source for Figures 10.1 and 10.2: DHS Office of Immigration Statistics, Immigration Enforcement Actions: 2013, table 7 (September 2014).

Figure 10.2
Removal Trends, FY 2001–2013

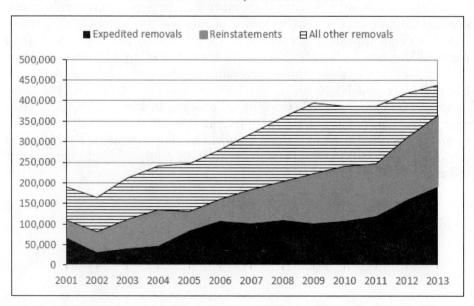

These Figures show that total removals increased fairly steadily between 2002 and 2013. Comparable official statistics are not yet available for 2014 and 2015, but less formal information signals a noticeable decline in those two years. *See DHS releases end of fiscal year 2015 statistics* (DHS Press Release Dec. 22, 2015), https://www.ice.gov/news/releases/dhs-releases-end-fiscal-year-2015-statistics. The decline probably resulted primarily from the Obama administration's narrowing of enforcement priorities and wider use of deferred action, as discussed in Chapter Seven, Section C5b supra, pp. 774–786. The demographic profile of violators has also changed significantly as unauthorized migration from Mexico has held at far lower levels than a decade ago. See the portrait of today's unauthorized population in Chapter Five, Section C pp. 444–477. A higher percentage of unauthorized migration now comes from Central America and other distant countries; each removal is therefore more time-consuming and costly for the agency than the removal of Mexican nationals.

But removals—the compulsory departure of a noncitizen on the basis of a removal order—tell only part of the enforcement story. Many apprehended individuals wind up leaving the country as a result of governmental action, usually under some type of DHS supervision or oversight, but without waiting for a formal order. (This kind of action requires the individual's consent, but it also requires DHS agreement. There are times when DHS would prefer a formal order, for example because it permits the application of more serious sanctions if the person later returns without permission.) Therefore, DHS now reports overall totals of "removals and returns" as one metric indicating its enforcement performance. *See* Figures 10.3 and 10.4.

Figure 10.3
Removals and Returns, FY 1990–2013

Fiscal year	Removals	Returns	Total
1990	30,039	1,022,533	1,054,562
1991	33,189	1,061,105	1,096,285
1992	43,671	1,105,829	1,151,492
1993	42,542	1,243,410	1,287,945
1994	45,674	1,029,107	1,076,775
1995	50,924	1,313,764	1,366,683
1996	69,680	1,573,428	1,645,104
1997	114,432	1,440,684	1,557,113
1998	174,813	1,570,127	1,746,938
1999	183,114	1,574,863	1,759,976
2000	188,467	1,675,876	1,866,343
2001	189,026	1,349,371	1,540,398
2002	165,168	1,012,116	1,179,286
2003	211,098	945,294	1,158,395
2004	240,665	1,166,576	1,409,245
2005	246,431	1,096,920	1,345,356
2006	280,974	1,043,381	1,326,361
2007	319,382	891,390	1,212,779
2008	359,795	811,263	1,173,066
2009	395,165	580,107	977,281
2010	387,242	476,405	865,657
2011	387,134	322,124	709,258
2012	418,397	230,386	648,783
2013	438,421	178,371	616,792

Source for Figures 10.3 and 10.4: DHS Office of Immigration Statistics, 2013 Yearbook of Immigration Statistics 103, table 39.

Figure 10.4
Removals and Returns, FY 1990–2013

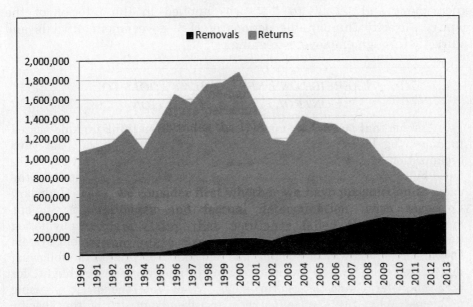

In reporting these statistics, DHS uses the following distinctions: Removals are "the compulsory and confirmed movement of an inadmissible or deportable alien out of the United States based on an order of removal." Returns are "the confirmed movement of an inadmissible or deportable alien out of the United States not based on an order of removal." 2009 DHS Statistical Yearbook 95, table 36 nn.1 & 2. Because a majority of returns in these figures are accomplished by the Border Patrol shortly after apprehending an individual at or near the border, most returnees have not spent much time on U.S. territory, at least not on this particular attempt at entry. (Border Patrol apprehension totals are summarized in Figure 10.5 below.) Since about 2004, the combined number of removals and returns has generally declined, primarily reflecting a noticeable drop in the number of returns, especially since 2008. According to DHS, these declines result primarily from decreases in entry attempts along the Southwest border. This pattern calls attention to a further element in controlling unauthorized immigration—deterrence, whether it comes from a tipping point in the impact of compulsory enforcement measures that the country has deployed along the border or instead via employer screening, increased smuggler fees, or, as in 2008 to roughly 2011, a distressed U.S. economy with high unemployment.

The materials that follow survey the various enforcement tools and initiatives now available to the immigration agencies (primarily the Departments of State and Homeland Security). We begin with a look at tools applied beyond U.S. territory, which received a major upgrade and revision since the September 11 attacks, and then move to border enforcement and finally to measures applied in the interior of the country, directly through the actions of U.S. government officials and indirectly through employer screening.

EXERCISE ON ENFORCEMENT TOOLS TO
CONTROL ILLEGAL MIGRATION

Assume that you are an intern for a Washington think tank dedicated to improving law enforcement in the United States. In the past your organization has primarily focused its research and advocacy on issues faced by police departments, but because of its expertise in that field, the executive director has been asked to testify before the Senate Judiciary Committee at a hearing on Enhancing Immigration Enforcement. She has asked you to help prepare that testimony and wants you to begin by listing the principal goals or objectives that an immigration enforcement system should serve, as a way of framing her remarks. Drawing on the following materials, outline what you believe the testimony should highlight, for both short-term and long-term steps. What are the most pressing problems? What are the advantages and disadvantages of the specific measures you might list? What tools or methods show greatest promise for overall impact—and for minimizing the disadvantages or undesirable collateral effects—even if they would not necessarily meet the most immediate problems? Which arena or arenas of enforcement deserve primary attention? What are the primary financial, logistical, or political obstacles to success? What, if any, features of the current situation present favorable opportunities for change?

---

2. "PUSHING OUT THE BORDER," INCLUDING MORE EFFECTIVE IDENTITY CHECKS

DAVID A. MARTIN, REFINING IMMIGRATION LAW'S ROLE IN COUNTERTERRORISM

Legislating the War on Terror: An Agenda for Reform,
Chap. 6, pp. 185–90 (Benjamin Wittes ed. 2009).

The U.S. admissions system historically has deployed a double layer of screening: scrutiny by a consular officer overseas of a person's eligibility for admission before a visa is issued and a second and potentially equally demanding review by an immigration inspector at the port of entry, even if the person holds a duly issued visa. One of the major responses to September 11 has been to "push out the borders"—that is, to try to maximize successful and rigorous screening well before a person embarks on a trip or shows up at the port of entry. That means designing systems to support more effective consular work or, for persons allowed to travel without a visa, to maximize the data available to U.S. officials well before the individual arrives on U.S. soil—ideally, before he or she even boards the plane. * * *

Some of the September 11 hijackers had obtained temporary visas, known as nonimmigrant visas, for travel to the United States without undergoing a face-to-face interview before a U.S. consular officer. In response, in May 2003, the State Department issued a new policy requiring a personal interview for nearly all categories of applicants for nonimmigrant or immigrant visas. Congress tightened that requirement and wrote it into the statute in the 2004 Intelligence Reform Act. * * *

More important to successful screening than face-to-face interviews is enhancing the timely availability to consular officers and immigration inspectors at the border of the best intelligence possible. That is, policymakers should not expect consular officers and immigration inspectors to play more than an occasional and adventitious role in actually detecting or unearthing terrorist plots through their questioning of applicants. What they should expect, however, is that those officers will have the best possible intelligence and law enforcement information about the people before them. * * *

Linking databases and providing user-friendly and comprehensive systems to frontline decisionmakers has been a significant focus of both statutory changes and administrative adjustments since September 11—a daunting task because the databases had developed in a haphazard and disconnected fashion. * * * Reforms have made considerable headway * * * in improving the situation, [largely through] administrative innovation in centralizing key processes and efficiently allocating the time of skilled analysts through an automated targeting system. * * *

DETECTING FRAUD AND COLLECTING BIOMETRIC IDENTIFYING INFORMATION

If a terrorist can successfully use another person's identity, then he or she can obviously defeat even the best systems for prompt checking of available intelligence and law enforcement information. * * * [T]he increasing use of biometric identifiers, as required in many pieces of immigration-related legislation since September 11, helps guard against such fraud, as does increasing international standardization of identity documents with counterfeit-resistant features and embedded machine-readable biometric data.

One element of the U.S. Visitor and Immigrant Status Indicator Technology (US-VISIT) screening system—planned to become eventually a comprehensive DHS system monitoring aliens' entry and exit—provides an important protection against a specific kind of fraud. Under the earliest system component widely deployed (beginning in 2004), aliens arriving at a port of entry have had to submit to facial photographing and the electronic capture of two fingerprints (of the right and left index fingers), conducted right at the primary inspection booth—a procedure that added about 15 seconds to each inspection. At about that time, consular officers began to capture the same two fingerprints (photos having long been required) at the time of visa issuance. The system thus permits prompt comparison of the two sets of fingerprints, to ensure that the person applying for admission is the same person cleared to receive a visa.

The database that provides the foundation for US-VISIT, known as IDENT, also affords swift access to key watchlist information on possible terrorists and increasingly to the FBI's comprehensive fingerprint system, known as the Integrated Automated Fingerprint Identification System (IAFIS). * * * The decision of former DHS secretary Michael Chertoff in 2005 to alter US-VISIT so that the fingerprint readers [at ports of entry] will capture all ten fingerprints, rather than just the index fingers, also represents a significant security gain. That change will increase the chances of detecting terrorists [and criminals] by comparing the full fingerprint set against latent prints * * * collected by [the FBI or] the Department of Defense. Though challenges remain, US-VISIT has generally proven itself to be a gratifyingly successful technological venture.

THE VISA WAIVER PROGRAM

Some critics have urged an end to the statutorily authorized visa waiver program—which allows short-term visa-free travel (lasting no more than ninety days) to citizens of selected countries—seeing it as an especially vulnerable entry point for dangerous individuals. As of December 31, 2008, thirty-five countries were on the visa waiver list, most of them European democracies that accord a reciprocal privilege to U.S. citizens. But critics point out that some noted terrorists * * * were nationals of visa waiver countries. They allege that a border inspector's quick query of the databases in the primary inspection line at an airport affords an insufficient opportunity to detect dangerous travelers. * * *

Although those concerns have some merit, * * * [r]equiring all nationals from the 35 high-volume countries involved to obtain visas, even for short trips, would deter some travel, sow ill will, probably reduce U.S. travel opportunities, and create a monumental additional workload on an already taxed consular corps. Nonetheless, Congress [has enacted changes] * * * that can reduce the vulnerabilities inherent in the visa waiver system. * * * [A]irlines are now required to send data on all passengers to U.S. border authorities well before a plane arrives from an overseas location. This Advance Passenger Information System (APIS) affords Customs and Border Protection (CBP) officers additional time before landing for checking passenger names [and other identifying information, such as Passenger Name Record (PNR) information received from airlines] against databases in order to identify those whom CBP should either reject or at least subject to more intensive review at the border. * * * [Furthermore, the prospect of inclusion in the visa waiver program has proven to be a major inducement the United States can deploy to persuade other countries to share critical information usable in the screening and selection of persons for closer scrutiny, whether they are traveling with or without a visa. In] order to join the visa waiver program, countries must agree to cooperate fully in sharing terrorist-related intelligence and also in following other security-enhancing practices.

* * * [Since 2009, visa waiver passengers are also required to obtain advance clearance through an automated electronic system for travel authorization (ESTA).] Under ESTA, a prospective traveler from a visa waiver country must apply, ordinarily through the Internet many days or weeks before the flight, for travel authorization, providing at that time specified biographical information that allows DHS to check for "law enforcement or security risk." If none is found, the person will receive a code indicating eligibility for travel to the United States without a visa. * * * [Airlines are required] to check the code through an automated system before permitting the individual to board the aircraft for the United States. All such persons will still be subject to inspection and a new database check at the port of entry.

NOTES AND QUESTIONS ON ENHANCED ADMISSION SCREENING AND IDENTITY CHECKS

1.   **More about IDENT.** DHS's IDENT database stores the biometric, biographic, and photo information obtained not only from persons applying for visas at a consulate or for admission at a port of entry but also from nearly all noncitizens encountered by any part of DHS. For example, persons apprehended by ICE or the Border Patrol (and in some circumstances the Coast Guard) are interviewed, fingerprinted, and photographed even if they are likely to be bused back to Mexico or returned to Haiti within a few hours. This information, along with whatever name and other biographical information the person provides, is shared with IDENT, matched against its extensive records, and stored for future use. (For a glimpse of the primitive record-keeping employed three decades ago by the Border Patrol, which relied on the name given by the apprehended noncitizen as well as paper storage, see the first edition of this casebook, T. Alexander Aleinikoff & David A. Martin, Immigration: Process and Policy 466 (1985).)

Using IDENT, the relevant officer can identify whether the person may be more dangerous or have additional immigration violations, thus perhaps meriting criminal prosecution or removal under a formal order, which would make future U.S. entry a felony. The sharing also generates a readily retrievable record to be consulted if the person either applies for a benefit in later years or is picked up in further enforcement actions, including enforcement actions by state and local law enforcement agencies. Applicants to USCIS for immigration benefits are also fingerprinted and checked against IDENT, as a safeguard against identity fraud or misrepresentation of previous immigration history. IDENT has become a central resource giving speedy access to all DHS information on the person, including any aliases the person may have used.

2. **Tracking overstayers: a biometric exit tracking system?** US-VISIT provides a thorough biometric check of persons who *enter* the United States. It covers nearly all arriving air and sea passengers, with very limited exceptions, mainly those under 14 or over 80 years of age. At land border ports, where high volumes and physical logistics complicate the use of biometric checks in primary inspection, the coverage is more selective, but nonetheless widely used in secondary inspection (the area to which cases are referred if they appear to merit further inquiry or if admissibility cannot be resolved at the primary inspection lane).

What about checks at time of *exit*? The 9/11 Commission recommended the creation of comprehensive biometric exit screening system as well, primarily to provide better information about overstayers—nonimmigrants who fail to depart by the end of their admission period. Congress has supported this aim in authorizing legislation since at least 1996, but has not provided the extensive funding that a comprehensive system would demand. That is, in order to be truly useful in determining who did *not* depart, the system would have to cover every departure, whether by air, land or sea. DHS estimated in July 2011 that the infrastructure to permit such checks on departing passengers would cost $3.5 billion over 10 years. *See US-VISIT backlog reduced by more than half, says Beers,* http://www.fierce governmentit.com/story/us-visit-backlog-reduced-more-half-says-beers/2011-07-13. Airlines and other carriers have also resisted cooperation, even in preliminary testing of biometric exit checks.

In 2011 DHS undertook a closer review of exit screening, especially to compare the expected benefits of a biometric exit system against the costs. In September 2011, in congressional testimony, DHS signaled that it would concentrate on using already collected biographical information (i.e., name-based rather than fingerprint-based) to expand its identification of suspected overstayers. It promised to refer all identified overstayers for some sort of action, most to the State Department to cancel the current visa (a consequence mandated by INA § 222(g)). In such a case, the person remains eligible to apply for a new visa, but only after a new review and consular interview. DHS also pledged to refer a growing percentage of overstayers identified in this fashion to ICE officers for follow-up enforcement action, according to a priority system that emphasizes criminal or security risks. *See* Testimony of John D. Cohen, DHS Principal Deputy Counterterrorism Coordinator, before the House Committee on Homeland Security,

Subcommittee on Border and Maritime Security, Sept. 13, 2011. This biographic-based exit monitoring system relies primarily on creative use of existing processes, particularly the regular collection and analysis of detailed passenger manifests from all carriers involved in international travel (APIS), rather than costly new investments. *See generally* Entry/Exit Overstay Report: Fiscal Year 2015 (Dept. of Homeland Security 2016).

For critiques of the biometric exit proposals, see *Entry-Exit System: Progress, Challenges, and Outlook*, Bipartisan Policy Ctr. 3–4 (May 2014), http://bipartisanpolicy.org/library/immigration-entry-exit-system/; David A. Martin, *Resolute Enforcement is Not Just for Restrictionists: Building a Stable and Efficient Immigration Enforcement System*, 30 J.L. & Pol'y 411, 432–37 (2015). Martin favors stronger enforcement against overstays, but argues that the government should first make systematic use of the existing biographic information systems—already capable of identifying most overstay violators—to test whether there will be sufficient political and financial commitment to finding and removing them, before spending billions on biometric exit infrastructure.

3.   **REAL ID and WHTI.** Since September 11, 2001, Congress has also pressed hard for other improvements in identification systems. The REAL ID Act of 2005, Pub. L. No. 109–13, 119 Stat. 231 (2005), established detailed minimum requirements for states to meet in improving the issuance and quality of driver's licenses and other identity documents. The statute also provided that states would have to check immigration status as part of the process of issuing new secure documents. (States could still issue driver's licenses to unauthorized immigrants, but such documents would have to be clearly marked to indicate that they are not REAL-ID compliant.) Because Congress cannot directly command these kinds of actions by states, the Act instead imposes strict limits on the use of noncompliant documents for federal purposes such as entering a federal building or, most importantly, passing federal screening to board an airplane anywhere in the United States.

Complaints based on civil liberties concerns or objections to federal mandates eventually erupted in stronger resistance from some state governors and legislatures, Some states passed laws essentially daring DHS to pull the REAL ID Act's main enforcement trigger by denying access to air travel—a sanction that would fall on all of a state's driver's license holders, clearly including citizens. For many years this defiance resulted in DHS decisions to soften or postpone deadlines, But in January 2016 the Secretary announced a full schedule for publicizing and phasing in the access bars, with most airport access blocked by January 2018 and all deadlines fully operative no later than October 1, 2020. At the time of the announcement, DHS stated that 23 states were in full compliance with REAL ID, six states were noncompliant, and the rest had received limited extensions while making progress toward meeting the Act's system requirements. *See* Statement by Secretary Jeh C. Johnson On The Final Phase Of REAL ID Act Implementation (DHS Press Release, Jan. 8, 2016).

Despite the state-level grumbling, all states have made quite substantial improvements to their ID issuance systems since 9/11, and they more readily share information among themselves. These steps have made it significantly harder to produce counterfeit IDs or to obtain genuine state identification documents through fraud. *See* Janice Kephart, REAL ID Implementation: Less Expensive, Doable, and Helpful in Reducing Fraud (Center for Immigr. Studies Backgrounder, Jan. 2011). *But see* Ashley Halsey III, *Latest Counterfeit IDs Are So Good They're Dangerous,* Wash. Post, July 30, 2011 (reporting on ability to overcome some of these measures through sophisticated fraudulent cards, many of them purchased from a purveyor in China).

Congress also acted to guard against ID fraud that could result in unauthorized access to the United States, when it enacted the Western Hemisphere Travel Initiative (WHTI) in 2004. Before WHTI, persons entering from Canada and some nearby islands could enter the United States by presenting a birth certificate or other non-secure documents. Under WHTI, which took full effect in 2009, all arriving passengers, both U.S. citizens and foreigners, must show a passport or a limited list of other secure documents, including driver's licenses from a few states that have agreed to especially rigorous anti-fraud controls. Intelligence Reform and Terrorism Prevention Act of 2004 (IRTPA), Pub. L. 108–458, § 7209, 118 Stat. 3638.

3. BORDER ENFORCEMENT

Increased border enforcement has drawn solid support from both political parties and from successive Presidential administrations. In recent decades, Congress has rapidly increased funding for the Border Patrol, so that its ranks grew to over 20,000 officers by 2010 before stabilizing there—more than double the total in 2004. About 85 percent of those officers are deployed along the southwest border. This section recounts the history of this buildup and of border control efforts generally. It also summarizes various critiques and defenses of the expansion.

PETER ANDREAS, BORDER GAMES: POLICING THE U.S.-MEXICO DIVIDE
85–86, 89–90, 92–93, 95, 111–12 (2000).

During much of the twentieth century, the United States and Mexico not only quietly tolerated but actively facilitated and encouraged the influx of cheap labor across the border; until recent decades the rising level of illegal immigration commanded little national political attention. For example, the platform of the Republican Party did not even mention immigration control until 1980, and only four years later did it affirm the country's right to control its borders and express concern about illegal immigration.

Congressional debate over how to deal with illegal immigration culminated in the passage of the Immigration Reform and Control Act of 1986, which introduced employer sanctions for the first time, as well as a limited legalization program. But although IRCA provided a temporary sedative, the law exacerbated the very problem it purported to remedy. Rather than discouraging illegal immigration, the main impact of legalization under IRCA was to reinforce and expand already well-established cross-border migration networks. * * * Meanwhile, the primary impact of the poorly designed and minimally enforced employer sanctions was to create a booming business in fraudulent documents.

IRCA's perverse consequences helped set the stage for a powerful backlash against illegal immigration in the 1990s, most acute in California, which was home to nearly half of the unauthorized immigrants estimated to be in the country. * * * The new restrictionist mood was embodied in the passage of Proposition 187 by California voters in 1994, which sought to bar illegal immigrants from receiving social services. Proposition 187 was self-consciously designed and promoted as a symbolic gesture to express frustration and "send a message" to the federal government. Even though it was subsequently declared unconstitutional (as its proponents expected), its passage [with nearly 60 percent of the vote in the referendum] sent shock waves across the country and through the halls of Congress.

* * *

Although border control was a low priority for President Clinton when he first took office, he soon became an enthusiastic proponent of tighter controls in order keep up with Republican initiatives in Congress. * * *

* * * [His] border control offensive [was] based on a strategy developed by the INS in 1993–94 called "prevention through deterrence." The objective * * * [was to use visible and extensive forward deployment of Border Patrol officers to discourage or] inhibit illegal entry and thus avoid having to apprehend entrants after they've crossed the border. * * *

Such a strategy was first tested with the launching of Operation Blockade (later given the more diplomatic name of Hold-the-Line) in El Paso in September 1993[, but it] * * * faced initial resistance * * * at INS headquarters. * * * Moreover, the emphasis on deterring entry rather than apprehending migrants as they crossed contradicted the Border Patrol's traditional reliance on high apprehension numbers to justify budget requests. * * *

[Nevertheless, as hoped, the] high profile show of force quickly reduced [the El Paso cross-border] flow to a trickle, drawing the immediate attention of Washington, the media, and California politicians eager to replicate the El Paso experience. * * * One consequence was that the rewards system within the Border Patrol was suddenly turned upside down, prevention rather than number of apprehensions becoming the new enforcement goal. [INS proceeded to expand the use of this strategy, first to high-traffic points of illegal entry, and eventually across much of the border.]

* * *

The expanding Border Patrol presence in areas between the ports of entry, meanwhile, has sparked a surge in attempted illegal entries through the ports of entry themselves, and the INS has responded with an infusion of new port inspectors. * * * The increase in staffing has been matched by stiffer penalties: those who attempt entry through the fraudulent use of documents are being prosecuted for repeat violations, and vehicles may also be confiscated. In addition, to inhibit the use of forged documents, officials are moving to replace the old border-crossing cards with high-tech visas containing a digital fingerprint.

* * *

High-profile immigration control initiatives * * * have transformed the landscape of the southwestern border. * * * [T]he most visible form of clandestine entry—groups of illegal migrants openly crossing the border near urban areas—is no longer politically tolerable. Thus, for the border crossers, evading apprehension has become a longer and more complex game requiring greater patience and stealth. * * * In other words, the old game between border enforcers and clandestine border crossers persists, but the game strategy of the enforcers has changed to maximize the appearance of control. Projecting a "winning image," it seems, has so far provided a politically viable alternative to actually winning the game.

That image has come at an enormous cost: more intensive border policing has brought with it more (and more organized) professional smuggling, greater corruption, and many border deaths. But at least for now, these negative consequences have been obscured by the powerful political and symbolic appeal of a border that appears more orderly and secure. At the same time, however, it should be emphasized that the deterrence effort has created the conditions for its own expansion, since the shifts in the methods and location of illegal border crossings have in turn placed new demands on the law enforcement system to adjust and keep up. Indeed, as envisioned by the Border Patrol, current enforcement levels are just the beginning of a long-term buildup. * * * As one agent put it, "We are taking back the border, piece by piece."

Further Evolution of Border Controls—
and the Views of Critics

The dramatic buildup of the Border Patrol continued over the succeeding years after Andreas wrote, along with less robust growth in the enforcement effort in the interior (discussed below). David Martin summarizes the practical and political considerations that help account for the choices that Congress and the executive branch have made which have generally resulted in strong support for CBP, but far more controversy over other uses of enforcement resources:

> Interior enforcement, through sending investigators out to track down and remove persons already illegally present, is costly and inefficient. It is also unglamorous and unpopular work in the eyes of most of Homeland Security's enforcement personnel; those officers who are successful at it regularly gain less administrative credit and prestige than others who are involved in criminal alien apprehension or participation in antiterrorist initiatives.

> A different specialty within internal enforcement focuses on employer compliance with the law's workplace screening requirements. Enhancing this type of enforcement should be far more efficient than one-by-one apprehensions at deterring illegal migration, but ramping up worksite enforcement carries other salient disadvantages. Primarily, it imposes visible burdens on business. As a result, significant interest group pressure quietly helps push Congress toward under-funding these enforcement endeavors, and there has been no equivalently organized constituency pushing back. Moreover, though employers may not like the current I–9 verification process, involving the examination of work authorization documents of all new hires (albeit according to a very lax standard of scrutiny), they have become accustomed to it. Proposed revisions in the employers' obligations generate determined resistance among a highly influential interest group. Border measures, in contrast, step on almost no influential toes. Border crackdowns are therefore used to demonstrate enforcement seriousness, alienating few and placating many.

David A. Martin, *Eight Myths About Immigration Enforcement*, 10 N.Y.U. J. Legis. & Pub. Pol'y 525, 544–45 (2007).

Through the first decade or so of this buildup, from the early 1990s to the mid-2000s, the flow of illegal migration continued a general and sometimes dramatic rise, as measured by Border Patrol apprehension numbers (an imperfect metric for these purposes, but conventionally relied upon, in the absence of better measures). Moreover, estimates of the resident unauthorized population rose significantly during this period. *See* Figure 10.5 below (Pew Research Center estimates of the undocumented population showing growth from approximately 4 million in 1994 to 12.2 million in 2007). Noting these statistics, some critics joined Andreas in assailing the border buildup as a political gesture that could not succeed against the economic realities that account for illegal migration. Writing in 2005, sociologist Douglas Massey leveled the following critique:

> Not only have U.S. policies failed to reduce the inflow of people from Mexico, they have perversely reduced the outflow to produce an unprecedented increase in the undocumented population of the United States. America's unilateral effort to prevent a decades-old flow from continuing has paradoxically transformed a circular flow of Mexican workers into a settled population of families and dependents.
>
> * * * Rather than choosing not to enter the United States illegally, undocumented migrants quite rationally invested more money to minimize the risks and maximize the odds of a successful border crossing. * * * [S]mugglers on the Mexican side upgraded the package of services they offered. Instead of simply accompanying small parties of undocumented migrants on foot across well-trod pathways from Tijuana to San Diego and delivering them to an anonymous urban setting, smugglers now had to transport people to remote sectors of the border, guide them across, and have them met on the other side by personnel who would arrange transport to destinations throughout the United States.
>
> The net effect of U.S. policies, in other words, was to increase the quality but also the price of border-smuggling services. * * *
>
> If the first order of business on any trip to the United States is to recover that cost, then holding constant the rate of remuneration and hours worked per week, the stay would have to be three times as long.

Douglas S. Massey, Backfire at the Border: Why Enforcement without Legalization Cannot Stop Illegal Immigration 6–8 (Cato Institute Policy Analysis, 2005).

Figure 10.5
Estimates of the U.S. Unauthorized Immigrant Population
1990–2014

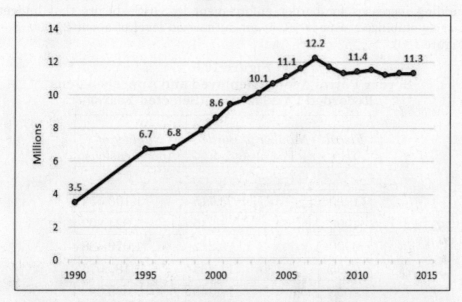

Source: Pew Research Center, U.S. Unauthorized Immigrant Population Levels Off
(July 21, 2015), http://www.pewresearch.org/fact-tank/2015/07/22/unauthorized-
immigrant-population-stable-for-half-a-decade/ft_15-07-23_unauthimmigrants/;
supplemented by earlier Pew data, available on the Pew website: http://www.pew
research.org/data-trend/society-and-demographics/immigrants/.

Other critics focused on the increased dangers to the migrants. The
Border Patrol strategy of closing traditional entry routes near major U.S.
cities such as San Diego and El Paso, plus later deployments along other
main routes in Texas, pushed unauthorized migrants to more dangerous
paths through deserts and mountains, particularly in Arizona, and
produced a significant increase in migrant deaths from exposure. As of
2015, according to Border Patrol estimates, total migrant deaths had
reached 6,571 since 1998, but 2015 saw the lowest number of deaths (280)
since that initial year. (The Patrol has expanded its capacities for search
and rescue over recent decades.) *See* Maria Jimenez, Humanitarian
Crisis: Migrant Deaths at the U.S.-Mexico Border (ACLU and Mexico's
National Comm'n of Human Rights 2009); *Fatal Journeys: Tracking Lives
Lost during Migration*, Int'l Org. for Migration 2014 (Tara Brian & Frank
Laczko eds., 2009).

Later Changes in Border Flows: Successful Control?

Supporters of the border buildup, in response to the critics, pointed
out that 1994–2007 had been a period of economic boom and record low
unemployment. Continued increases in migration proved nothing; the

question was whether, under such circumstances, migration was lower than it would have been without the expanded enforcement. Congress sided with this camp and sustained the momentum of major annual funding increases for border enforcement by DHS—before that budget largely stabilized after 2010, at an authorized level of about 21,000. See Figure 10.6.

Figure 10.6
Border Patrol Agents Deployed and Apprehensions
Recorded FY 1990–2015 (Selected Years)

Fiscal Year	Number of Border Patrol Agents	Number of Apprehensions
1990	3,715	1,103,353
1995	4,945	1,324,202
2000	9,212	1,676,438
2005	11,264	1,189,075
2006	12,349	1,089,092
2007	14,923	876,704
2008	17,499	723,825
2009	20,119	556,041
2010	20,558	463,382
2011	21,444	340,252
2012	21,394	364,768
2013	21,391	420,789
2014	20,863	486,651
2015	20,273	337,117

Sources: U.S. Border Patrol Fiscal Year Staffing Statistics (FY 1992–FY 2015), Sep. 19, 2015, http://www.cbp.gov/sites/default/files/documents/BP%20Staffing%20FY1992-FY2015.pdf; TRAC, Syracuse University, National Trends in Apprehensions and Staffing (2006), http://trac.syr.edu (for 1990 staffing figure); U.S. Border Patrol Total Apprehensions (FY 1925–FY 2015), http://www.cbp.gov/sites/default/files/documents/BP%20Total%20Apps%20FY1925-FY2015.pdf.

Congress also supported the addition of sophisticated technology, including seismic sensors, thermal imaging systems, remote video surveillance equipment, and even a fleet of Predator drone aircraft, which provide coverage from California to Texas. Further, DHS found ways to coordinate more closely with Mexican authorities to disrupt human and drug smuggling operations And Congress passed the Secure Fence Act of 2006, Pub. L. 109–367, 120 Stat. 2368, calling for approximately 700 miles of additional fencing on the southern border.

Of perhaps greater impact, Congress and DHS made far more detention spaces available to DHS during this period, so that it could end (as of 2006) an earlier policy known derisively as "catch and release." That is, in earlier years many border-crossers (especially those from countries other than Mexico) who contested return were released pending their immigration court hearings, owing to limited detention space. Many had failed to show up in court. By keeping such persons in detention, DHS obviously was able to ensure the execution of any removal orders issued in these cases. The new policy also rested on the belief that the prospect of sustained detention would help deter new migrants.

DHS also has sought to thwart return migration attempts following successful enforcement action, through what CBP sometimes calls "consequence delivery." One strand of this effort is Operation Streamline, discussed in Section A4b, pp. 1101–1106 below. In the districts where this Operation has been employed, U.S. Attorneys' offices prosecute a high percentage of apprehended noncitizens, even for the misdemeanor of simple illegal entry. INA § 275(a). Alternatively, CBP may make more extensive use of formal appearances before an immigration judge, with entry of a removal order, to impress upon the individual the gravity of the situation and thereby try to deter recidivism. Two other important strands, applied to migrants from Mexico, are the Alien Transfer Exit Program (ATEP). ATEP returns noncitizens to points distant from where they entered, in an effort to prevent them from reconnecting with their smugglers for another try. The Interior Repatriation Initiative (IRI) flies persons to the interior of Mexico near their home regions, rather than simply busing them to a town near the border.

The picture of relentlessly rising illegal migration despite border buildups, however, which had fueled the early criticism of enforcement from scholars like Andreas and Massey, eventually changed. In 2007 Border Patrol apprehensions fell by 20 percent from the 2006 total of just over one million. At first many observers attributed the decline to the severe economic recession and high U.S. unemployment. But the trend of diminished apprehensions continued (with some bumps on the curve), even as the economy improved. In fiscal year 2015, there were only 337,117 apprehensions, a 40-year low. Also, the leading estimates of the total population of unauthorized residents in the United States showed a decline in 2008 for the first time since 1988, and that general pattern has continued. *See* Figure 10.5 *supra*.

A 2016 report from the Center for Migration Studies provided more detail on the continuing decline in the unauthorized population. Robert

Warren, *US Undocumented Population Drops Below 11 Million in 2014, with Continued Declines in the Mexican Undocumented Population.*, 4 J. Migration & Human Security 1 (2016). After topping out just above 12 million in 2007, that population has dropped consistently since then, to fall below 11 million in 2014. See Figure 10.7.

Figure 10.7
Total Undocumented Population: 2008 to 2014

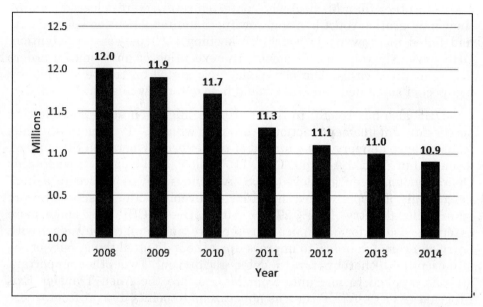

Source: Robert Warren, US Undocumented Population Drops Below 11 Million in
2014, with Continued Declines in the Mexican Undocumented Population, 4 J.
Migration & Hum. Security 1, 3 (2016).

The decline is particularly noteworthy from Mexico, for many decades the overwhelmingly dominant source country for unauthorized migration into the United States. Warren, *supra*, at 8. Significant reductions in the birthrate in Mexico, combined with a generally improving economy and expanded educational opportunities, as well as the persistence of better-resourced U.S. border controls, will probably mean that the decline continues. *See id.* at 8–9; Muzaffar Chishti & Faye Hipsman, *In Historic Shift, New Migration Flows from Mexico Fall Below Those from China and India,* Migration Information Source (Migration Policy Inst., May 21, 2015). Even Douglas Massey, an influential critic of the border buildup (quoted above), now states that "the boom in Mexican undocumented migration is likely over." Douglas S. Massey, Jorge Durand & Karen A. Pren, *Explaining Undocumented Migration to the U.S.,* 48 Int'l Migr. Rev. 1028, 1055–56 (2014). *See also* Damien Cave, *Better Lives for Mexicans Cut Allure of Going North*, N.Y. Times, July 6,

2011 (reduced population growth and improved economic opportunities in Mexico suggest long-term reductions in migration).

Against this backdrop, the Senate passed a comprehensive immigration reform measure with a heavy bipartisan majority of 68–32 in June 2013 (discussed in Section D below), which included new enforcement measures but also an expansive program to legalize those who had been unlawfully present since December 31, 2011. But the House leadership did not bring the bill to a vote in that chamber. The main opposition pointed to the fact that unauthorized migration flows persist at a level of several hundred thousand per year (even if offset by departures, deaths, and other factors that diminish the total). They called for steps that would "secure the border" first and only then consider other parts of comprehensive reform—especially legalization. This line of critique, painting a picture of a border out of control, was amplified in the 2016 Republican primaries.

4. INTERIOR ENFORCEMENT

Even with the decades-long growth in resources for CBP, border enforcement has to be supplemented or backstopped by interior enforcement. Border barriers may be more daunting now, but if it appears that anyone who once makes it past the Border Patrol has little further risk of being caught and will enjoy good access to the U.S. job market, a substantial incentive exists to keep attempting clandestine entry. Further, visa overstayers by definition cross the border legally and are essentially unaffected by enhanced border controls; they constitute an estimated 40 percent of the unauthorized population. Interior enforcement is also needed to address other violations of the terms of entry, and to remove those who commit crimes that make them deportable. Interior enforcement addresses all these groups of noncitizens, as well as smugglers and traffickers who facilitate illegal entry or illegal travel to the final destination, or who extort additional fees and payments from migrants and family members.

Interior enforcement, which is largely the domain of ICE, comprises direct apprehension, removal, and possible prosecution of persons who are unlawfully present as well as efforts to prevent unauthorized noncitizens from accessing U.S. employment. This subsection addresses both aspects.

a. Apprehension and Removal of Unauthorized Migrants

(i) Background and Overview: Area Control and Worksite Operations

With 10 to 11 million unauthorized residents in the United States, DHS would seem to have plenty of scope for interior enforcement, particularly because the statute gives immigration officers the authority, without a warrant, "to interrogate any alien or person believed to be an alien as to his right to be or to remain in the United States." INA § 287(a)(1). But such a framework raises immediate questions. How should enforcement be shaped to minimize adverse impact on other policy objectives, either those of DHS (such as facilitating legal migration) or those of other agencies (such as promoting international business and tourism, or encouraging community-based policing by state and local law enforcement)? For example, using the interrogation power delegated by § 287(a) to its maximum would surely antagonize and alienate many citizens as well as lawfully present visitors. Further, given that ICE resources permit successful enforcement against only a modest percentage of the violator population, how should DHS focus its efforts to optimize its overall effectiveness? What are the benchmarks of effectiveness? What strategies would maximize deterrence or self-imposed compliance (such as timely departure by nonimmigrants) so as to reduce the burdens of direct enforcement?

For much of federal immigration control history, there was little central attention to these questions, because key decisions were left largely to the discretion of the roughly 30 INS district directors around the country. Some INS offices employed street sweeps, known formally as "area control operations," to identify, arrest, and charge any immigration violators they encountered. *See* Edwin Harwood, In Liberty's Shadow: Illegal Aliens and Immigration Law Enforcement 96–124 (1986). Because such tactics often prompted local criticism and community opposition, by the 1980s and 1990s INS was focusing its apprehension efforts on the workplace—at farms, factories, construction sites, restaurants and hotels. This approach, with increasing efforts at centralized direction, continued through much of the Clinton administration, which reported a high of 17,500 workplace arrests in 1997—still a tiny number compared to the Border Patrol's million-plus apprehensions that year. Most of those apprehended were put into removal proceedings, though a small percentage was prosecuted for crimes. But in the later Clinton years, and continuing into the George W. Bush administration, such enforcement actions dropped off considerably. Worksite apprehensions during the first four years of the Bush administration averaged about 500 annually. They surged again in the late Bush administration, as part of a strategy to persuade Congress to pass comprehensive immigration reform.

These worksite enforcement operations, as DHS calls them—raids in the parlance of their critics—generated substantial criticism, and the Obama administration embarked on a different course. Under a policy adopted in April 2009, the new focus was to be on employer violators, as well as employment sites deemed to be critical infrastructure (such as military bases or chemical plants). ICE shifted to focusing on both criminal and civil charges against egregious employers, rather than on widespread civil arrests of workers. ICE's use of I–9 audits, discussed below, may result indirectly in the firing of unauthorized employees but usually not their placement into removal proceedings. The policy change resulted in record numbers of employer prosecutions, fines, forfeitures and restitutions, as well as debarments of violator companies from federal contracts beginning in FY 2010. *See* Andorra Bruno, *Immigration-Related Worksite Enforcement: Performance Measures*, Cong. Res. Serv. (2015).

(ii) Focus on Noncitizens Involved in Crime

Under the Obama administration, DHS has also become more systematic in focusing interior enforcement on the removal of noncitizens with criminal convictions. This does not necessarily mean that the criminal grounds of removal (INA §§ 212(a)(2) and 237(a)(2)) are invoked in the charging documents. Those grounds are ordinarily relied on only with regard to lawful permanent residents—for the obvious reason that LPRs are essentially not otherwise deportable. In the majority of the cases ICE counts as criminal removals, it can charge entrance without inspection or overstay, which is less cumbersome to prove in immigration court than a criminal conviction. The conviction is relevant primarily to mark the individual as a higher enforcement priority. Further, ICE relies in many circumstances on noncitizen encounters with the criminal justice system as a way to identify persons who are a priority for removal and to take them into custody. Figure 10.8 shows the trends in ICE removals and the increasing percentage of removals of persons who have a criminal conviction.

Table 10.8
Criminal and Noncriminal Removals and
Returns by ICE, FY 2008–2015

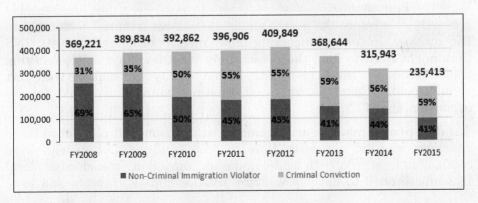

Source: FY 2015 ICE Immigration Removals, https://www.ice.gov/ removal-statistics.

We explored in Chapter Seven, Section C5b, pp. 774–776 *supra,* the priority-setting process that DHS has used to direct this change in focus, along with a variety of issues it presents. This section considers the history behind this evolution, in order to understand the situation driving much of today's effort to apprehend and remove unauthorized migrants through interior enforcement, and also to summarize the specific programs ICE uses to achieve these ends.

CAP and IRP. For decades, the immigration agencies' ability to initiate removal of noncitizens convicted of crimes rested almost entirely on informal cooperative relations with state, local, and federal law enforcement agencies (LEAs), which varied greatly among cities or regions. As a result, in the 1980s and 1990s even some persons convicted of serious crimes might not come to the attention of INS before release. But for those who were identified and placed into removal proceedings, INS would typically take custody at the end of the person's criminal sentence and start the immigration court process at that time.[25] The resulting costs, plus the unsystematic character of the enforcement efforts directed at noncitizens convicted of crimes, attracted the criticism of Congress and stimulated legal and administrative reforms in the 1980s and 1990s.

Early reforms focused on persons confined in state and federal prison—the more serious offenders, serving lengthy sentences. INS began to develop more systematic relationships with prisons (under what later became known as the Criminal Alien Program, CAP) that would allow the timely identification and charging of those inmates who were noncitizens and therefore might be removable. It also worked to make arrangements with such facilities to hold removal proceedings for such persons while they were still confined in state or federal criminal custody. Some states even made room for (or constructed) immigration courtrooms in their prisons. This Institutional Hearing Program, later called the Institutional Removal Program (IRP), was designed to produce a final enforceable removal order before the person's release from his criminal sentence into INS custody. Instead of incurring many months of detention costs, INS thus might need to hold the person only for a few days while securing travel documents from the country of nationality and making transport arrangements. Congress approved this procedure and called for its expansion. INA § 238(a).

Jail programs. The arrangements with prisons left untouched those offenders who did not serve time in such facilities, but instead were confined in local jails, both before and after conviction. In such cases, local INS offices tried to develop working relationships with state and local

---

[25] The statute generally provides that DHS shall not remove someone sentenced to prison until he or she has finished the sentence of imprisonment, not counting any term of parole or probation. INA §§ 236(c), 241(a)(4). The latter section permits an exception when the noncitizen has committed only a nonviolent offense and the relevant state or federal official determines that earlier removal is "in the best interest" of the government concerned.

LEAs, but the pattern was quite uneven throughout the country, in part because INS did not even have offices in some states until the late 1990s. INS therefore often relied on receiving a call from the local law enforcement agency when it had apprehended a person believed to be illegally present, requesting that INS pick up the individual and place him into removal proceedings. INS's ability to respond was constrained by limited resources or as the distance from the jail to the nearest INS officer or facility. Consequently INS often had to decline such requests to take custody—to the consternation of the LEA, which was convinced it had a criminal violator who was also present in the country unlawfully. Reliance on this patchwork of informal relations also meant that many noncitizens would escape INS's attention, even though they might have been a high priority for removal owing to the nature or number of their offenses.

In the 1990s and 2000s, with enhanced appropriations and various congressional urgings or mandates focused on removing criminal aliens, the immigration enforcement agencies worked to expand and systematize cooperation with local jails. Some jail initiatives involved stationing federal officers at high-volume booking locations in cities like Los Angeles or New York, to determine alienage and deportability via regular federal database checks and, as necessary, to conduct an interview of persons believed to be foreign born (information on place of birth is routinely collected as part of the booking process).

The focus of these jail programs has been intake or booking, not the far end of the process following disposition of the criminal charge, for several reasons. First, most persons thus identified could be charged as removable (as an EWI or overstayer) without relying on the current criminal charge or conviction. Second, a high percentage of the in-processed jail population, in contrast to those serving long sentences in state prisons, might be released shortly after arrest or their initial appearance in court. The prosecutor might choose to drop the charges or the judge might impose a sentence that amounted to time already served. If identification and preliminary immigration enforcement decisions, including the issuance of a detainer, were not done at the booking stage, the noncitizen could easily be freed before immigration enforcement action could occur. Some of these might be individuals with serious earlier convictions, issued at a time when DHS was not equipped to seek custody, or they could be persons with a history of more serious immigration violations, such as returning without permission to the United States after an earlier deportation. Such a return could be charged as a federal felony (INA § 276(a)), but more often simply results in the noncitizen being treated as a higher priority for removal.

When DHS does seek a particular person in a local jail for removal (even if identified separately by federal officials without the LEA's involvement), it would, until 2014, typically send an ICE detainer to the current custodian—in line with a practice common among law enforcement agencies. A detainer is a formal request that the receiving law enforcement agency notify the requesting LEA when the individual is about to be released from custody. Historically ICE detainers also asked that he or she be held for an additional period of 48 hours, not counting weekends and holidays, to permit travel and transfer arrangements. In the jail setting, the time taken to complete state or local confinement on the criminal charge could range from a few hours to months, years, or decades, depending on the length of any trial proceedings and the duration of the sentence, should the person be convicted.

Over time INS and ICE introduced further efficiencies, for example through LEA agreement to install and maintain computer and video equipment that would permit a centrally located federal staff to perform these checking and interview functions in connection with several jail facilities. The federal agencies continued to seek improvements, in part to reduce training and operational burdens on LEAs and also (out of concern to minimize the chances for racial or ethnic profiling) to make the process less dependent on subjective local decisions to choose particular inmates for a closer look by federal officers.

Section 287(g). The 287(g) program offered one possibility. As discussed in more detail in Section C3a, pp. 1215–1216 below, INA § 287(g), enacted in 1996, permits ICE to delegate certain immigration officer functions "in relation to the investigation, apprehension, or detention" of noncitizens to state and local officers, pursuant to a detailed agreement with the state or local LEA. The statute requires specific training and ongoing supervision of the participating officers by the federal agency. State and local officers could be given wide authority to arrest and detain suspected immigration violators encountered anywhere; under what came to be known as the task force model., But a majority of § 287(g) agreements focused instead on jails, training local officers to do the interview and database-checking functions described above, which could lead to the lodging of immigration charges and the eventual transfer of custody to federal officers for removal proceedings.

Secure Communities. In part because 287(g) agreements cover only a small fraction of the nearly 18,000 state and local law enforcement agencies nationwide, Congress pressed for still more systematic action against noncitizens convicted of crimes. Under specific directives contained in appropriations bills enacted from 2007 onward, ICE developed the Secure Communities program. Secure Communities at its core was a data-sharing process between the FBI and DHS. A computer interface took information submitted to the FBI as part of an LEA's routine and familiar transmission of the fingerprints of arrested individuals and sent it on to be checked against information in IDENT,

DHS's biometrics-based immigration database. For most arrestees, not surprisingly, there was no match with any IDENT record. When there was a match—for example revealing that the person just arrested had been encountered two earlier times near the border and returned by CBP to Mexico, or had been previously deported by ICE, or had once applied for a visa—the information was sent on to ICE officials for a decision on further action. Typically the ICE field office near the booking facility decided whether to proceed with enforcement action. If so, it normally sent a detainer to the LEA.

Once a jurisdiction was activated for Secure Communities, all fingerprints transmitted to the FBI were checked against IDENT; no state or local officer had any role in deciding whether the person was a noncitizen subject to DHS jurisdiction. Moreover, only the fingerprints of persons who had been arrested and booked were transmitted. Requiring the check of all fingerprints was intended to minimize any risk of selective or discriminatory referrals to ICE. Limiting checks to arrested persons was also one way of assuring that victims and witnesses would not be identified to ICE through the Secure Communities links. Only persons actually arrested and fingerprinted were checked against IDENT.

For reasons explored in detail in Section C of this chapter, pp. 1217–1223 below, Secure Communities stirred major controversy in many jurisdictions, to the point that many police executives announced that they were ceasing or greatly curtailing cooperation with ICE. During this period as well, some court cases suggested that LEAs might be found liable in damages for holding persons on the basis of certain types of ICE detainers. LEA resistance expanded. As a result, DHS Secretary Jeh Johnson decided in November 2014 to terminate Secure Communities and replace it with a far more focused Priority Enforcement Program (PEP). PEP continues the practice of checking LEA-submitted fingerprints against IDENT at the time of initial arrest, but it essentially limits ICE use of that information to persons convicted of more serious offenses. Some jurisdictions have restored cooperation with ICE, but others remain resistant.

b.   Prosecuting Immigration Violations as Crimes

One of the most significant recent enforcement trends has been a sharp increase in the number of federal criminal prosecutions for immigration law violations. No longer can a discussion of immigration enforcement confine itself to the process that may lead to a noncitizen's removal from the United States. The trend toward prosecuting immigration law violators has several major components, as sketched in the following excerpt.

INGRID V. EAGLY, PROSECUTING IMMIGRATION

104 Nw. U. L. Rev. 1281, 1301–04, 1326–30 (2010).

A roadmap to the criminal-immigration system emerges from the exploration of a 2008 prosecution that took place in Postville, Iowa. In one of the largest immigration crime prosecutions in history, immigration officers raided a meatpacking plant and arrested hundreds of factory workers. Immigration authorities then brought these workers to an enclosed cattle fairground set up as a makeshift courtroom. There, the arrestees were assigned to counsel in groups of ten or more. Within four days, 270 workers had signed "exploding" plea agreements, entered binding felony guilty pleas in court, and received criminal sentences.

Postville's large-scale prosecution received enormous media attention, far overshadowing the broader story of immigration crime prosecutions dominating the federal docket. Criminal defense attorneys called into question whether the compressed time period to accept the pleas violated due process. Immigration lawyers, who were denied access to the fairground while the workers were being interrogated, charged that the defendants had been placed on a "new high-speed judicial railroad," where they were not advised of their immigration rights prior to signing the speedy plea agreements. A federal Spanish language interpreter assigned to the Postville hearings came forward, bringing national attention to a day he critiqued as "the saddest procession [he had] ever witnessed, which the public would never see." Two months later, Congressional hearings were held to examine the propriety of the criminal proceedings.

A close analysis of the Postville prosecution reveals many aspects of the interaction between the criminal prosecutor and the administrative apparatus of immigration. First, the Postville defendants were informed that they were ineligible for bail—not because of the formal criminal bail rules, but instead because the immigration agency had lodged an immigration detainer. Despite the fact that many defendants had bail equities—including long-term residence in the United States, dependent children, friends, and family in the community, and no criminal record—not a single defendant had a bail hearing. Even if hearings had been held and bond granted, the immigration detainers would have resulted in transfer into ICE custody rather than release to the community. This functional denial of bail is consequential because of how it impacted plea-bargain dynamics. The Postville defendants would have spent a longer time in pretrial detention awaiting a trial (six to eight months) than they would serve in prison by convicting themselves (most were offered a binding sentence of five months).

Prosecutors also threatened the slaughterhouse workers with aggravated identity theft charges (carrying a mandatory two-year sentence) unless they accepted the government's "fast-track" plea. Although the exact terms of specific pleas varied, most defendants pleaded guilty to false use of a document as evidence of authorized employment. * * * [Prosecutors also] drastically abbreviated the normal time between the plea and sentencing. The standard sentencing process can take months, but the Postville defendants pleaded guilty and were sentenced on the same day. * * *

Postville prosecutors also insisted on a "stipulated removal order" as a mandatory term of the plea agreements. Although the slaughterhouse workers were alleged to be undocumented, any individual defendant might have been eligible to remain legally in the United States under established immigration law. * * * However, as a practical matter, the short-fuse exploding plea offer precluded meaningful evaluation by defense attorneys of whether such immigration relief might be possible. And with stipulated orders of removal, the defendants abandoned any and all immigration claims in the criminal plea.

Looking back at Postville, two stories emerge. The simple story tells of overcharging and overzealous prosecution. That story may well be true. A less obvious, but equally important, story contemplates the Postville prosecution as emblematic of the blending of our criminal and immigration systems. * * *

* * *

* * * After a surge in immigration prosecution in the 1950s, the immigration agency lobbied Congress to establish a misdemeanor court that would allow for criminal immigration enforcement "at less expense and with a greater amount of effectiveness" than was possible with Article III courts. Foreshadowing the anticipated creation of such a court, immigration authorities convinced Congress in 1952 to amend the Immigration and Nationality Act to reduce the penalty for the crime of simple illegal entry from one year to six months. With this change in place, illegal entry met the federal definition of "petty offense." This reduction in maximum sentence was critical because it meant that illegal entry cases could proceed before magistrate judges without the right to trial by jury or grand jury indictment.

* * * Removal of the jury screen disconnected immigration crime from the traditional system of checks and balances on prosecutorial overreaching. * * * For example, in El Paso, Texas in the late 1940s, over 90% of immigration crime cases sent to the grand jury were returned as "no bills." After the implementation of the magistrate court in 1971, petty illegal entry cases soon accounted for nearly 90% of federal criminal enforcement of immigration, virtually eliminating any form of jury screen * * *. Nationwide, criminal immigration prosecutions increased by over

700%, from 2536 in the year that the Federal Magistrate Act was passed to 17,858 in 1974.

More recently, a border prosecution program known as Operation Streamline, or simply "Streamline," has exclusively used the magistrate courts. Under Streamline, the government has adopted a zero-tolerance stance, prosecuting every noncitizen arrested sneaking across certain portions of the Mexican border, primarily with the crime of entry without inspection. Defendants in Streamline waive rights, enter guilty pleas, and are sentenced in proceedings that may last only minutes [and frequently] include multiple defendants in the same hearing. * * *

The Ninth Circuit recently considered whether the en masse plea hearings that typify Streamline violate federal law and found that they do. * * * No judge overseeing such mass proceedings could possibly determine that each defendant in the packed courtroom voluntarily and knowingly pleaded guilty, as required under federal law.

The guilty plea rate for immigration crime in magistrate court has increased significantly under the Streamline program—from 63% in 2004 to 97% in 2009. With sentences as short as time served and trials not likely to be held for months, defendants would spend more time in custody by demanding a trial than by simply pleading guilty. The logical result is an almost perfect guilty plea rate.

Under Streamline, not only are first-time entrants processed through the magistrate court, but more serious offenders are "flopped" into magistrate proceedings. With the "flip-flop" plea agreement, smugglers or illegal entrants with prior removal orders are charged with both unlawful reentry (a felony) and unlawful entry (a misdemeanor). If the defendant pleads guilty to the lesser charge within an expedited time period, the case is resolved as a misdemeanor before an Article I magistrate judge.

Between 1992 and 2009, * * * within the magistrate caseload, the percentage of immigration-related matters rose * * * from 24% to 82%. In other words, immigration prosecution has shifted much of the work of the federal criminal system into a separate system that is governed by distinct procedural rules. In the process, the magistrate criminal court has been defined, especially in the Southwest, as a separate adjudicatory system reserved almost exclusively for immigration crime.

NOTES AND QUESTIONS ON CRIMINAL PROSECUTION OF IMMIGRATION VIOLATIONS

1.   *United States v. Roblero-Solis*, 588 F.3d 692, 693 (9th Cir. 2009), is the Ninth Circuit decision mentioned by Eagly that found en masse pleas to violate federal law, specifically that they are inconsistent with Federal Rule of Criminal Procedure 11, which governs the taking of pleas from criminal defendants in federal court. In practice, the response to *Roblero-Solis* has

been to take pleas in smaller groups, to permit more individual attention by the judge to each defendant's responses. The decision has modestly altered the pace and processing in Operation Streamline, but the basic program continues in many border areas.

2.   Addressing evolving practices of obtaining guilty pleas to criminal violations of immigration laws, Jennifer Chacón offers this critique:

> The ongoing erosion of the procedural rights of these criminal defendants thus far has been effectively normalized. Such procedural moves can be framed as nothing more than an extension of longstanding limitations on the due process rights of noncitizens in immigration proceedings. However, it is important not to lose sight of the legal distinctions that separate the criminal from the civil realm. The prosecution of these offenses should not be allowed to reshape the criminal sphere to look more like the less rights-protective civil system where immigration enforcement has typically been centered. Unfortunately, at the moment, this is exactly what is happening.

Jennifer Chacón, *Managing Migration Through Crime*, 109 Colum. L. Rev. Sidebar 135 (2009).

3.   But consider this possible response: what is wrong with a special streamlined criminal justice system for criminal violations of immigration law, where penalties are less severe than in much of federal criminal law, and where defendants by definition are not citizens of the United States?

Or consider a different possible response, coming from the perspective of the enforcing agencies. Congress has greatly increased the resources for enforcement over the last two decades and has been loudly demanding meaningful results—not just tally sheets with increased numbers of removal orders or deportations, but a real impact in shrinking the unauthorized population. A classic law enforcement method applied in any regulatory field when compliance is low is to increase the de facto sanctions experienced by violators. Hence the decision to add criminal prosecution to the normal response of a simple civil deportation. These changes in the use of criminal prosecution also were seen to fit well with CBP's "consequence delivery" approach toward deterring recidivism, described in Section A3, p. 1093 above.

4.   Alan Bersin, U.S. Attorney for the Southern District of California (San Diego) during the Clinton administration and later the Acting Commissioner of CBP under Obama, co-authored an article discussing an early initiative to bring criminal charges for more serious immigration-related offenses, see Alan D. Bersin & Judith S. Feigin, *The Rule of Law at the Margin: Reinventing Prosecution Policy in the Southern District of California*, 12 Geo. Immigr. L.J. 285 (1998). For further analysis of Operation Streamline, see Joanna Jacobbi Lydgate, Comment, *Assembly-Line Justice: A Review of Operation Streamline*, 98 Calif. L. Rev. 481, 511 (2010).

5.   A proliferating literature explores and critiques the expanded linkage between criminal law and the immigration enforcement system. *See, e.g.,* Kevin R. Johnson, *Race-Based Law Enforcement: The Racially Disparate Impacts of Crimmigration Law,* Case W. Res. L. Rev. (forthcoming 2016); Walter A. Ewing, Daniel E. Martinez & Rubén G. Rumbaut, The Criminalization of Immigration in the United States (American Immigration Council Special Report, July 2015); Yolanda Vázquez, *Constructing Crimmigration: Latino Subordination in a "Post-Racial" World,* 76 Ohio St. L.J. 599 (2015); Mary Fan, *The Case for Crimmigration Reform,* 92 N.C. L. Rev. 75 (2013); Allegra M. McLeod, *The U.S. Criminal-Immigration Convergence and Its Possible Undoing,* 49 Am. Crim. L. Rev. 105 (2012); Marjorie S. Zatz & Hilary Smith, *Immigration, Crime and Victimization: Rhetoric and Reality,* 8 Ann. Rev. of L. & Social Sci. 141 (2012) ; Jennifer M. Chacón, *Overcriminalizing Immigration,* 102 J. Crim. L. & Criminology 613 (2012); Juliet P. Stumpf, *Doing Time: Crimmigration Law and the Perils of Haste,* 58 UCLA L. Rev. 1705 (2011); Stephen H. Legomsky, *The New Path Of Immigration Law: Asymmetric Incorporation Of Criminal Justice Norms,* 64 Wash. & Lee L. Rev. 469 (2007); Juliet P. Stumpf, *The Crimmigration Crisis: Immigrants, Crime, and Sovereign Power,* 56 Am. U.L. Rev. 367 (2006).

c.   Employer Sanctions and Antidiscrimination Provisions

(i)   *Employer Sanctions and the Verification Process*

Interior enforcement—at least in theory—seeks to counteract unauthorized migration not only by removing persons unlawfully in the country but also by deterring illegal entry in the first place. One major tool of deterrence is the employer sanctions regime, added to the INA by IRCA in 1986.

Take a careful look at INA § 274A, which (1) prohibits the hiring of "unauthorized aliens" (the categories of aliens authorized to work, either incident to status or by specific permission, are listed in 8 C.F.R. § 274a.12); and (2) requires that employers use form I–9, the employment eligibility verification form (available on the USCIS website) to verify the lawful status of all new hires. Good faith compliance with the I–9 procedure provides the employer an affirmative defense against a charge that it knowingly hired unauthorized workers. DHS may initiate a proceeding on either type of violation before an administrative law judge (ALJ) within the Office of the Chief Administrative Hearing Officer (OCAHO), which is part of the Executive Office for Immigration Review (EOIR). An employer who loses before the ALJ may seek a limited form of discretionary review by the Chief Administrative Hearing Officer; judicial review lies in the federal courts of appeals. *See generally* INA § 274A(e); 28 C.F.R. ch.1, part 68.

The debate over employer sanctions in the early 1980s was long and intense. Some members of Congress argued that the program might place an undue burden on employers. Not only would all employers be subject to new paperwork obligations, but a regime of employer sanctions also raised the specter that employers would have to become experts in immigration law in order to identify which categories of aliens were authorized to work. Another area of special concern was the question of what kind of documentation would suffice to establish eligibility for employment. Congress was aware of the market in fraudulent documents, and some proponents argued that a form of counterfeit-proof documentation ought to be devised to ensure the effectiveness of the program. The risk that this might lead to a "national identity card," however, caused many members of Congress to shy away from such a requirement. Those opposed to an identity card won. See INA § 274A(c).

Section A4a(i), pp. 1095–1097 above, describes changes in worksite enforcement strategies and patterns through recent presidential administrations—varying combinations of employer penalties and arrests of unauthorized workers themselves. Early in its tenure, the Obama administration reoriented the focus toward prosecuting or fining violator employers and away from the large-scale arrests of unauthorized workers that marked the last three years of the George W. Bush administration, which was itself a shift from the very limited worksite enforcement activity in President Bush's first term. Criminal arrests of employers for worksite-related violations grew from 135 in 2008 to 240 in 2012, and ICE collected over $8.5 million in administrative fines in the latter year. This does not count judicially imposed forfeitures and penalties. Such enforcement activity did decline after 2013. *See* Jessica Vaughan, *ICE Records Reveal Steep Drop in Worksite Enforcement Since 2013*, Center for Immigration Studies Backgrounder, June 2015.

(ii) Antidiscrimination Provisions

One major concern during the 1986 debate over IRCA was that employer sanctions would lead to employment discrimination against Hispanic-Americans, Asian-Americans, or others who "looked foreign," and that existing fair employment laws would provide no remedy. For example, Title VII of the Civil Rights Act of 1964, 42 U.S.C.A. § 2000e–2, applied only to employers with fifteen or more full-time employees; and it barred national origin discrimination but not discrimination based solely on alienage. *See Espinoza v. Farah Manufacturing Co.*, 414 U.S. 86, 94 S.Ct. 334, 38 L.Ed.2d 287 (1973).

As a result, Congress enacted INA § 274B as part of IRCA. That section established a Special Counsel for Immigration-Related Unfair Employment Practices in the Department of Justice to investigate and pursue charges of employment discrimination based on national origin or citizenship status. As to the latter, § 274B covers citizenship status discrimination only against citizens and certain classes of aliens—that is, lawful permanent resident aliens, newly legalized aliens, refugees, and asylees. Lawful permanent residents are not covered if they fail to initiate the naturalization process within six months after satisfying the residency requirement for citizenship. INA § 274B(a). Nonimmigrants (even those authorized to work) and parolees are not covered. Congress also supplemented Title VII protections by applying to employers with four or more employees the prohibitions of § 274B against national origin discrimination in hiring.

IRCA permits discrimination based on citizenship status when lawfully required under federal, state, or local governmental authority. And an employer may hire a U.S. citizen in preference to an alien if the two are "equally qualified." INA § 274B(a)(2), (4). Also, IRCA, unlike Title VII, applies only to hiring, referral for a fee, and firing, and thus offers no remedy for discrimination on the job. *See Ortega v. Vermont Bread*, 3 O.C.A.H.O. 475 (1992).

A sharp dispute over the coverage of the new § 274B surfaced shortly after the enactment of IRCA. Did the provision bar practices having a disparate impact on different groups or only actions motivated by discriminatory intent? Congress resolved the controversy by amending the INA in 1996 to supply an explicit intent test for discrimination claims arising out of employer verification practices. Section 274B(a)(6) now provides that requiring more or different documents in order to establish authorization to work or refusing to honor facially valid documents constitutes "an unfair immigration-related employment practice" only "if made for the purpose or with the intent of discriminating against an individual." What does this amendment mean? (Consider this provision in connection with Question 5 below.)

If the Special Counsel has not filed a complaint within 120 days after receiving an allegation of unlawful discrimination, a private party may also initiate an enforcement action. INA § 274B(d)(2). Administrative law judges hear complaints and may impose civil penalties, order equitable relief, and award attorney fees. *See* § 274B(e)–(h), 28 C.F.R. Part 44. An order of the ALJ is reviewable by the Chief Administrative Hearing Officer, and may be appealed to a federal court of appeals. *See* INA § 274B(i), 28 C.F.R. § 68.53.

QUESTIONS ON EMPLOYER SANCTIONS AND DISCRIMINATION

You have XYZ Widget Co. as a client. The President of XYZ has come to you for advice. How would you answer the following questions? (You may need to consult §§ 274A and 274B, the implementing regulations in 8 C.F.R. Part 274a, and the following parts of this Section.)

1.   "I think that illegal aliens are harder workers and more reliable than U.S. citizens. May I restrict hiring to noncitizens? Even if I can't, I intend to do so; and if I get caught I'll treat the penalty as a tax. How much could it cost me?" (What ethical problems do you confront as you contemplate answering this question?)

2.   "I have recently received a letter from the Social Security Administration informing me that the social security number that one of my employees gave me when I hired her does not match SSA's records. I am worried that she is an unauthorized worker. May I ask her for additional documentation at this point to make sure she is eligible for work in the United States?"

3.   "Do I have to ask you for identification before hiring you as my lawyer?"

4.   "I want to make sure my employees can communicate with my customers. Can I refuse to hire anyone who doesn't speak English?"

5.   "I have an employee who says he is a U.S. citizen but he speaks with an accent, so I really want to see a birth certificate before hiring him." Is that unlawful discrimination?

(iii)   The Doctrine of Constructive Knowledge and Its Role in Enforcement Strategies

The employer sanctions provisions of the INA prohibit the knowing hire of a noncitizen unauthorized to work in the United States. INA § 274A. Most employers comply with the prescribed verification process, examining documents supplied by employees and recording information on the I–9 form. Because of the widespread existence of fraudulent documents that pass as genuine—at least to employers not trained as immigration officers—the verification process, as presently constructed, does little to deter the hiring of unauthorized workers. Indeed, the statutory provisions were written expressly to establish a largely ministerial, form-filling role for employers, so as not to unduly burden them with immigration enforcement tasks and to protect against discrimination that might be occasioned by a more active employer role. The statute requires the employer to accept a document tendered by the employee if it "reasonably appears on its face to be genuine." INA § 274A(b)(1)(A). Rather than serving as an effective deterrent against the hiring of unauthorized workers, the I–9 process is more likely to serve the role of protecting the employer against charges of unlawful hiring: the employer points to the completed form as evidence that he or she has met statutory responsibilities. *See* Kitty Calavita, *Employer Sanctions Violations: Toward a Dialectical Model of White-Collar Crime*, 24 Law & Soc'y Rev. 1041, 1057, 1060 (1990).

But what if facts surrounding the employment situation would have led a reasonably alert employer to believe that the papers proffered by an employee were in fact fraudulent? Or suppose an employer has heard a rumor at the workplace that an employee is an unauthorized employee. May an employer be deemed to have *constructive knowledge* of the employment of an authorized worker and thereby be subject to sanctions?

In 1990, the INS adopted by regulation a definition of "knowing" that included "constructive knowledge":

> The term "knowing" includes not only actual knowledge but also knowledge which may fairly be inferred through notice of certain facts and circumstances which would lead a person, through the exercise of reasonable care, to know about a certain condition.

55 Fed. Reg. 25928 (1990) (amending 8 C.F.R. 274a).

The following case examines a situation in which the INS claimed that an employer had constructive knowledge that one of its employers was an unauthorized worker.

COLLINS FOODS INTERNATIONAL, INC. v. INS
United States Court of Appeals, Ninth Circuit, 1991.
948 F.2d 549.

CANBY, CIRCUIT JUDGE:

* * *

Ricardo Soto Gomez (Soto), an employee at a Phoenix Sizzler Restaurant,[a] is authorized to hire other Sizzler employees for that location. Soto extended a job offer to Armando Rodriguez in a long-distance telephone conversation; Soto was in Phoenix and Rodriguez was in California. Rodriguez said nothing in the telephone conversation to indicate that he was not authorized to work in the United States. Rodriguez was working for Sizzler in California at the time Soto extended the offer of employment in Phoenix.

When Rodriguez came to Phoenix, he reported to Sizzler for work. Before allowing Rodriguez to begin work, Soto asked Rodriguez for evidence of his authorization to work in the United States. Rodriguez informed Soto that he did not have the necessary identification with him. At that point, Soto did not let Rodriguez begin work, but sent him away with the understanding that he would return with his qualifying documents.

Rodriguez returned with a driver's license and what appeared to be a Social Security card. Soto looked at the face of the documents and copied

---

[a]   Collins Foods operates retail establishments under the name of Sizzler Restaurant—eds.

information from them onto a Form I–9. Soto did not look at the back of the Social Security card, nor did he compare it with the example in the INS handbook. After Soto completed the necessary paperwork, Rodriguez began work at the Sizzler in Phoenix. Rodriguez, it turned out, was an alien not authorized to work in the United States, and his "Social Security card" was a forgery.

DISCUSSION

The INS charged Collins Foods with one count of hiring an alien, knowing him to be unauthorized to work in the United States, in violation of INA § 274A(a)(1)(A). * * * [The] only issue to be decided at the hearing was whether Collins Foods knew that Rodriguez was unauthorized at the time of hire. The ALJ declined to decide that Collins Foods had actual knowledge of the fact that Rodriguez was an illegal alien, but decided instead that it had "constructive knowledge." The ALJ based his "constructive knowledge" conclusion on two facts: first, that Soto offered the job to Rodriguez over the telephone without having seen Rodriguez' documentation; and, second, that Soto failed to compare the back of the Social Security card with the example in the INS manual. While we do not disturb the factual determinations made by the ALJ, we hold that these two facts cannot, as a matter of law, establish constructive knowledge under INA § 274A(a)(1)(A).

I.   Job Offer Prior to Verification of Documents

The first of these facts, as a matter of law, cannot support a finding of constructive knowledge. Nothing in the statute prohibits the offering of a job prior to checking the documents; indeed, the regulations contemplate just such a course of action.

The statute that Collins Foods is charged with violating prohibits "a person or other entity [from] hir[ing] for employment" an alien not authorized to work. INA § 274A(a)(1)(A). The Regulations define "hiring" as "the actual commencement of employment of an employee for wages or other remuneration." 8 C.F.R. § 274a.1(c). As Rodriguez had not commenced employment for wages at the time Soto extended a job offer to him over the telephone, Rodriguez was not yet "hired" for purposes of section 274A. Soto was therefore not required to verify Rodriguez' documentation at that time.

Another regulation addresses the issue of the timeliness of verification, and it suggests the same result. Under 8 C.F.R. § 274a.2(b)(1)(ii), employers are required to examine an employee's documentation and complete Form I–9 "within three business days of the hire." Because Soto had examined Rodriguez' documents and completed the necessary paperwork by the time Rodriguez began work for wages, Soto was not delinquent in verifying Rodriguez' documentation.

There are additional, highly cogent reasons for rejecting the ALJ's reliance on the fact that Soto "told Rodriguez he would be hired long before Soto ever saw, or had any opportunity to verify, *any* evidence of Rodriguez' work authorization." To hold such a failure of early verification against the employer, as the ALJ did, places the employer in an impossible position. Pre-employment questioning concerning the applicant's national origin, race or citizenship exposes the employer to charges of discrimination if he does not hire that applicant. The Equal Employment Opportunity Commission has held that pre-employment inquiries concerning a job applicant's race, color, religion, national origin, or citizenship status "may constitute evidence of discrimination prohibited by Title VII." An employer who makes such inquiries will have the burden of proving that the answers to such inquiries "are not used in making hiring and placement decisions in a discriminatory manner prohibited by law." For that reason, employers attempting to comply with the Immigration Reform and Control Act of 1986 ("IRCA"), are well advised not to examine documents until after an offer of employment is made * * * .

The ultimate danger, of course, is that many employers, faced with conflicting commands from the EEOC and the INS, would simply avoid interviewing any applicant whose appearance suggests alienage. The resulting discrimination against citizens and authorized aliens would frustrate the intent of Congress embodied in both Title VII of the Civil Rights Act of 1964, and the 1986 Immigration Reform Act itself.

* * *

II.   Verification of Documents

The portion of the statute that Collins Foods allegedly violated prohibits the hiring of an alien while "knowing" the alien is not authorized to work. The statute also prohibits the hiring of an individual without complying with the verification requirements outlined in the statute at INA § 274A(b)(1)(A). These two actions, failing properly to verify an employee's work-authorization documents, and hiring an alien knowing him to be unauthorized to work, constitute separate offenses under the IRCA. Nevertheless, the INS argues, and the ALJ held, that Collins Foods' failure to comply with the verification provisions of the statute establishes the knowledge element of subsection (a)(1)(A), hiring an alien knowing him to be unauthorized. We need not decide, however, whether a violation of the verification requirement establishes the knowledge element of section (a)(1)(A); Collins Foods complied with the verification requirement.

The statute, at INA § 274A(b)(1)(A), provides that an employer will have satisfied its verification obligation by examining a document which "reasonably appears on its face to be genuine." Soto examined the face of both Rodriguez' false Social Security card and his genuine driver's license, but failed to detect that the Social Security card was invalid. But as the ALJ acknowledged, even though Rodriguez was spelled "Rodriquez" on the front of the social security card, at a glance the card on its face did not appear to be false.

* * * [T]he ALJ held that Collins Foods did not satisfy its verification obligation because Soto did not compare the back of Rodriguez' social security card with the example in the INS handbook. We can find nothing in the statute that requires such a comparison. Moreover, even if Soto had compared the card with the example, he still may not have been able to discern that the card was not genuine. The handbook contains but one example of a Social Security card, when numerous versions exist. The card Rodriguez presented was not so different from the example that it necessarily would have alerted a reasonable person to its falsity. * * *

* * *

Congress carefully crafted INA § 274A to limit the burden and the risk placed on employers. The ALJ's holding in this case places on employers a verification obligation greater than that intended by Congress and beyond that outlined in the narrowly-drawn statute.

* * * IRCA, as we have pointed out, is delicately balanced to serve the goal of preventing unauthorized alien employment while avoiding discrimination against citizens and authorized aliens. The doctrine of constructive knowledge has great potential to upset that balance, and it should not be expansively applied. * * * Indeed, the only federal cases we have found that have allowed constructive knowledge to satisfy the knowledge element of section 1324a(a)(1)(A) are two recent decisions of this court. A comparison of those cases with the one before us illustrates why constructive knowledge cannot be found here.

In *Mester Mfg. Co. v. INS*, 879 F.2d 561 (9th Cir.1989), the INS had visited the employer's plant and obtained a list of employees. It then notified the employer that certain employees were suspected unlawful aliens, and if their green cards matched the numbers listed in the INS' letter to the employer, then they were using false cards or cards belonging to someone else. The employer did not take any corrective action, and continued to employ the unlawful aliens. We found constructive knowledge.

New El Rey Sausage Co. v. INS, 925 F.2d 1153 (9th Cir.1991), is essentially the same case. The INS visited the employer to inspect paperwork. After running checks on the alien registration numbers of the workers, the INS found several using improper or borrowed numbers. The INS then hand-delivered a letter to the employer reciting the results of its investigation and saying: "Unless these individuals can provide valid employment authorization from the United States Immigration and Naturalization Service, they are to be considered unauthorized aliens, and are therefore not authorized to be employed in the United States. Their continued employment could result in fine proceedings. . . ." The employer simply accepted the word of the aliens as to their legal status, and continued to employ them. We found constructive knowledge.

These cases lead us to conclude that a finding of constructive knowledge under the hiring violation statute requires more than the ALJ found to exist here. Failure to compare the back of a Social Security card with the example in the INS handbook, when neither statute nor regulation requires the employer to do so, falls far short of the "willful blindness" found in *Mester* and *New El Rey Sausage*.[17] * * *

CONCLUSION

Collins Foods did not have the kind of positive information that the INS had provided in *Mester* and *New El Rey Sausage* to support a finding of constructive knowledge. Neither the failure to verify documentation before offering employment, nor the failure to compare the back of the applicant's Social Security card with the example in the INS manual, justifies such a finding. There is no support in the employer sanctions provisions of IRCA or in their legislative history to charge Collins Foods, on the basis of the facts relied on by the ALJ here, with constructive knowledge of Rodriguez' unauthorized status. Accordingly, we reverse.

NOTES AND QUESTIONS ON CONSTRUCTIVE KNOWLEDGE

1. The court states that, in order to maintain the balance adopted by Congress, the doctrine of constructive knowledge "should not be expansively applied." It contrasts the facts in the case with those in *Mester Manufacturing Co. v. INS* and *New El Rey Sausage Co. v. INS*. Can you derive a legal standard for what constitutes constructive knowledge from the facts in these cases?

2. Between the time *Collins* was argued and decided, the INS amended the regulation to provide several examples of what circumstances might constitute constructive knowledge:

Constructive knowledge may include, but is not limited to, situations where an employer:

(i) Fails to complete or improperly completes the Employment Eligibility Verification Form, I–9;

---

[17] Both *Mester* and *New El Rey Sausage* relied on *United States v. Jewell*, 532 F.2d 697, 698 (9th Cir.), *cert. denied*, 426 U.S. 951, 96 S.Ct. 3173, 49 L.Ed.2d 1188 (1976), for its application of the constructive knowledge standard. In *Jewell*, the constructive knowledge finding was based upon "a mental state in which the defendant is aware that the fact in question is highly probable but consciously avoids enlightenment," *id.* at 704, or the defendant evidenced willful blindness.

(ii) Has information available to it that would indicate that the alien is not authorized to work, such as Labor Certification and/or an Application for Prospective Employer; or

(iii) Acts with reckless and wanton disregard for the legal consequences of permitting another individual to introduce an unauthorized alien into its work force or to act on its behalf.

8 C.F.R. § 274a.1(*l*)(1). Had the court in *Collins* applied this regulation, would it have affected the result?

3. Suppose an employer is suspicious of the documents presented to him. May he ask for more? The Office of Special Counsel (which is responsible for enforcing the anti-discrimination provisions) has advised that an employer with "constructive knowledge" that an alien lacks work authorization must inquire further, notwithstanding the antidiscrimination provisions. *See* 70 Interp. Rel. 906 (1993).

I–9 Audits

The immigration enforcement agencies have relied on the lessons of *Mester Manufacturing* and *New El Rey Sausage*, discussed in *Collins* above, in designing the central elements of their approach to worksite enforcement. Those cases indicated that an employer might readily be found to have constructive knowledge when it has notification about specific employees whose work authorization appears questionable. Such a notification, standing alone should not provoke termination, DHS has indicated. But if the employer does not take reasonable steps to ask the employee about the issue or otherwise investigate, it may be found to have constructive knowledge that the employee's work is unauthorized.

The main current technique for identifying questionable work authorization is known as an I–9 audit. Over the past decade, ICE has made increasing use of such audits—an approach seen to fit well with the Obama administration's focus on addressing employer violations rather than seeking to arrest unauthorized workers. I–9 audits increased from 503 in FY 2008 to 3,127 in FY 2013, though the number fell off sharply thereafter. *See* Jessica Vaughan, *ICE Records Reveal Steep Drop in Worksite Enforcement Since 2013,* Center for Immigration Studies Backgrounder, June 2015, at 1 (reporting ICE data). To conduct an audit, ICE uses authority provided in IRCA to issue a notice of inspection to an employer, which must then produce its I–9 records within three days. ICE typically assesses fines if it finds paperwork violations or sloppy compliance with the verification requirements. But more importantly, it also communicates to the employer the names of workers it suspects are not authorized to work, even if the paperwork was properly filled out by the employer based on the documents the employee presented. Employers then basically must ask the named employees for an explanation of their status and fire them if no satisfactory explanation is provided. Otherwise the employer will almost certainly be subject to the more serious sanctions that apply to those who continue employing a noncitizen despite constructive knowledge of the worker's unauthorized status.

Some have criticized the extensive use of I–9 audits by ICE, calling them "paper raids" or "silent raids" that are just as damaging and unfair, they maintain, as the highly publicized worksite operations of the Bush administration, which resulted in the arrest and deportation of hundreds of workers. *See, e.g.,* Rose Arrieta, *'Silent Raids': ICE's New Tactic Quietly Wreaks Havoc on Immigrant Workers,* In These Times, Jan. 27, 2011. Other critics, including Vaughan, *supra,* contend that ICE makes insufficient use of this tool, and still others deem the audits insufficient, arguing that without arrest and deportation, the workers will simply go out and take up other unauthorized employment. *See House Judiciary Subcommittee on Immigration Policy and Enforcement Holds Hearing on ICE Worksite Enforcement,* 88 Interp. Rel. 556 (2011). ICE has defended the audits as a prudent use of the resources Congress directs toward worksite enforcement, and a strategy that is consistent with the administration's emphasis on employer violations as the root cause of the problem. *Id.*

(iv) E–Verify and the Ongoing Verification Debate

The preceding materials suggest the following paradox: the employer sanctions provisions have produced a fairly high degree of formal compliance but only minimal deterrence of actual unauthorized employment. The main cause is the ready availability of fraudulent papers and the minimal steps employers are required (or even permitted) to take to check identity or verify the authenticity of documents presented to them. Nonetheless, employer checking of work authorization enjoys wide support across the political spectrum as a key component of reform proposals—but with additional steps meant to overcome current limitations in a balanced fashion.

Most of the attention for improvements has focused on an electronic verification system that would check against government databases the documents an employee presents. The idea is that a verification program, applied consistently to all new hires, could defeat unauthorized hiring by detecting fraudulent documents and also decrease discrimination (by providing more reliable assurance to employers that the persons they have hired are in fact authorized to work in the United States). In the mid-1990s, the statutorily chartered Commission on Immigration Reform was a leading proponent of testing such an approach. *See* U.S. Commission on Immigration Reform, U.S. Immigration Policy: Restoring Credibility 52–63 (1994).

The 1996 immigration legislation (IIRIRA § 403(b)) planted the seeds for today's electronic verification system by requiring the Attorney

General to establish a verification pilot program by September 30, 1997. Employer participants in the program, initially known as the "Basic Pilot," were to obtain confirmation of work authorization through means that would check the name and number shown on the documents presented by the employee against Social Security Administration and INS databases. (The most heavily used documents to establish work authorization have been either a Social Security card or an immigration document.)

The Basic Pilot program was set to last four years, but Congress has regularly extended and expanded it, and has provided considerable funding for the operation and improvement of the system. It is now open to all employers, but the statute states that the Secretary of Homeland Security may not require any employer to participate (with very limited exceptions, primarily for employers found guilty of earlier illegal hiring). In August 2007, DHS renamed the Basic Pilot "E–Verify," as part of a major campaign to encourage employers to join.

Here is how the E–Verify system operates. An employer's online query usually generates a response within a matter of seconds. E–Verify will either confirm that the document matches the appropriate records or else state that further action is needed—a response known as a tentative nonconfirmation (TNC). The system does not generate an immediate negative response because the match failure could result from a host of other reasons besides lack of work authorization, such as clerical error in entering the data on the query screen, or a name or status change for the employee that has not yet been recorded in Social Security records. The employer is not authorized to fire the new employee based on a TNC; such an action could be an unfair employment practice actionable by the Special Counsel's office under the antidiscrimination provisions of INA § 274B. Instead, the employer is supposed to give the employee notice of the TNC along with instructions referring her to the appropriate agency (either SSA or USCIS, depending on the type of document involved), in order to correct any problems. The employee must contact the agency within eight days from the referral. If the employee tells the employer that she will not contest the TNC or does not document timely resolution of the issue, the TNC becomes a final nonconfirmation. The employer then is supposed to terminate employment, upon pain of being found to have knowingly continued the employment of an unauthorized worker. See Immigration and America's Future: A New Chapter, Report of the Independent Task Force on Immigration and America's Future 48, 49 (Migration Policy Inst. 2006).

Electronic verification has been subject to persistent criticism, in part because of the way it places a key enforcement responsibility on private actors and in part because it failed in its early years to provide prompt verification of a high percentage of persons who were in fact fully authorized to work. *See, e.g.,* Juliet P. Stumpf, *Getting to Work: Why Nobody Cares About E–Verify (And Why They Should),* 2 UC Irvine L. Rev. 381 (2012); Marc R. Rosenblum, E–Verify: Strengths, Weaknesses, and Proposals for Reform (Migration Policy Inst. Insight, Feb. 2011). Nonetheless it retains strong support across a wide range of the political spectrum. The effort to expand employer participation in E–Verify received a significant boost from a series of state laws, beginning in about 2005, that required such participation on the part of governmental agencies or of state contractors—and in some cases, of all employers in the state. *Id.* at 3–4. (The U.S. Supreme Court's decision in *Chamber of Commerce v. Whiting,* upholding the broad Arizona E–Verify law, is considered in Section C, p. 1207 below.) At the federal level, a 2008 executive order required U.S. government contractors (with limited exceptions) to use E–Verify to check both their new hires and all of their existing employees. The courts have rejected challenges to the validity of that order. *See Chamber of Commerce v. Napolitano,* 648 F. Supp.2d 726 (D. Md. 2009).

Since 2005, successive Congresses have given serious consideration to proposed bills that would make E–Verify a mandatory national program. Such a system was a central component in the major comprehensive immigration reform bills that stalled in 2006, 2007, and 2013, and it remains a key element of most discussions of comprehensive reform today. But there have also been repeated efforts to expand E–Verify to a mandatory national program as stand-alone legislation, without the provisions for legalizing much of the current undocumented workforce that balanced out the aforementioned bills.

In the following excerpt, David Martin assesses the status of E–Verify as of 2015, its promise as part of an effective overall enforcement regime, weaknesses that need to be addressed before full deployment nationwide, and steps that could overcome those problems.

> Drying up easy access to unauthorized employment would provide the most efficient possible way to induce voluntary or acquiescent compliance with the immigration laws. * * * No law enforcement regime is healthy if it must rely primarily on directly coercive "boots on the ground" enforcement. Fewer people would attempt illegal border crossing or pay expensive smugglers' fees if they knew that all they could find after a successful border crossing would be tenuous work in underground or off-the-books businesses, rather than ready access to wide segments of the job market. Similarly, fewer would overstay nonimmigrant admission periods.

* * *

This [diagnosis] is widely recognized, contributing to broad acceptance that immigration reform today must include an electronic verification system made mandatory (in phases) for virtually all U.S. hiring. * * * Much of the earlier resistance to E–Verify has dissipated, as employers have found the internet-based system to be quite user-friendly. Over half a million employers are now participating, covering 1.4 million hiring sites and an estimated 40% of new hires; on average 1400 newly participating employers join the system each week. Though there are challenges in applying E–Verify in agriculture and in certain small-business settings, most current employer users find the system easy to use. False negatives (in which authorized workers—both U.S. citizens and authorized aliens—do not receive prompt verification) were once a major issue, producing loud resistance from some quarters. But [USCIS] has made significant improvements in accuracy, muting though not altogether silencing those complaints.

* * *

E–Verify marks a highly significant advance over the employer-operated paper-based verification system adopted in IRCA, and it holds considerable promise. Nonetheless, the current consensus supporting mandatory E–Verify is much too complacent. It masks a serious issue: E–Verify remains significantly vulnerable to identity fraud. If this vulnerability is not addressed in a systematic fashion, mandatory E–Verify may prove as deeply disappointing, a few years down the road, as IRCA's I–9 system.

It is important to understand the exact contours of this vulnerability. E–Verify can quickly and accurately detect whether the name and Social Security number (or other identifier) presented by a new employee match government records of someone actually authorized to work in the United States. It can thus defeat the simple forms of fraud that rendered the 1986 law's employer verification system ineffective. Under IRCA an employer basically has to accept an identity document or work authorization card that "reasonably appears on its face to be genuine." It can certainly appear genuine even with a made-up name or ID number. * * * E–Verify, however, [can readily expose] a mismatched name and number. But what E–Verify cannot reliably do, across the full range of checked documents, is to reveal whether the person presenting the information is actually the person whose name appears on the card. Fake-ID entrepreneurs are adapting. They are acquiring actual Social Security numbers along with the associated name, either through theft or through borrowing or buying from willing citizens. Monitoring reports have spoken of this vulnerability for some time, but it has not sparked nearly enough attention or corrective action to date.

The most reliable way to verify identity, of course, would be through biometrics. Senators Charles Schumer [D-NY] and Lindsey Graham [R-SC], who since 2009 have played key roles in the Senate effort to accomplish immigration reform, strongly championed for a couple of years a system that would equip each authorized worker, citizen or foreigner, with a government-issued swipe card bearing that person's coded fingerprint data. Each employer would have access to a device that could quickly capture a fingerprint image from the worker there in the hiring office and compare it against the coded data shown through the card swipe. A no-match result would mean no job.

Schumer and Graham quietly backed off this proposal early in the 2013 reform debate—perhaps because of its high cost. Building such a system and distributing fingerprint readers to millions of employers is doable, but it would cost several billion dollars and would present significant logistical difficulties, especially to implement a reliable upfront registration system as people acquire their swipe cards. A biometric system is only as good as its initial registration procedures; scrupulously careful and potentially labor-intensive validation of identity during enrollment is crucial before a biometrically encoded ID document is issued. Rushing the enrollment process would degrade the quality and reliability of the whole system. Also, although the Schumer-Graham plan was carefully designed to avoid creation of a centralized fingerprint database, it would doubtless encounter major political resistance. At the present time, it is therefore more fruitful for E–Verify to address identity fraud through other means, although biometric identifier systems should be kept under consideration for possible adoption as technology improves in the future.

* * *

The most promising medium-term path is to build on a capability that already exists. E–Verify has a "photo tool" that can immediately show on the employer's computer screen the exact photographic image that should appear on the ID document being presented by a new employee. Impostors are thus exposed. The problem is that E–Verify now has access to database photos only for a limited range of documents: U.S. passports, U.S. permanent resident cards (green cards) and

DHS-issued employment authorization documents. The majority of new employees undergoing immigration screening, however, present state-issued driver's licenses to the employer to establish identity.

Giving the E–Verify system access to digital versions of state driver's license photos, in order to display them to employers through the photo tool, thus would provide a major new barrier to identity fraud. (The system of course requires careful privacy protections limiting the use of the database photos to the stated purposes, but models for such controls are available.) Though it is not widely appreciated, state identity card systems have greatly improved over the past dozen years. Initial improvements were driven by state officials' chagrin over the 9/11 hijackers' easy access to driver's licenses that they used to facilitate their travel. The federal REAL ID Act of 2005 also mandated extensive further improvements to state driver's license systems and better sharing of information to defeat fraud. Although several states have resisted full certification of compliance with REAL ID (because they see the Act as unwarranted federal intrusion), and though DHS has extended the Act's deadlines, in fact many of the mandated improvements have taken place, even in resisting states. Driver's license systems now provide a solid foundation for secure identification and enhanced detection of fraud.

To date, however, despite DHS requests and efforts to resolve issues, no state has agreed to share drivers' license photos digitally with USCIS for use in E–Verify. Congress could change that situation by providing serious financial incentives for states that share photo access, or, more powerfully, by conditioning related grant programs (such as federal highway funding) on agreement by recipient states to share state ID photos for these purposes.

David A. Martin, *Resolute Enforcement is Not Just for Restrictionists: Building a Stable and Efficient Immigration Enforcement System*, 30 J.L. & Politics 411, 427–32 (2015).

NOTES AND QUESTIONS ON ELECTRONIC VERIFICATION

1.   Given the various considerations discussed above, should Congress adopt a nationwide mandate that all new hires be checked against E–Verify? What are the primary arguments for and against such a change? What modifications would you seek or require for such a nationwide system? What are the advantages and disadvantages of enacting mandatory E–Verify separately, as compared to including it in a comprehensive reform bill? Consider the following:

[T]he most promising strategy for expanding E–Verify is to link new mandates to a targeted or general legalization program for unauthorized workers and/or to employment-based visa reform. While a mandatory E–Verify requirement without such reforms would create incentives for employers and workers to look for work-arounds that undermine effective verification, linking E–Verify mandates to legalization and visa reform would have the opposite effect: encouraging the most problematic workers and employers to opt in to the system and to scrupulously comply with its requirements as a condition for earning legal status (in the case of workers) and for access to employment-based visa programs (in the case of employers).

Marc Rosenblum, E–Verify: Strengths, Weaknesses, and Proposals for Reform 12–13, 15 (Migration Policy Inst. Insight, Feb. 2011).

2.   Should Congress require a federal biometric identifier as part of the E–Verify system? If adopted, how should such a system be phased in? What are the obstacles you foresee in getting the full U.S. workforce (over 150 million people) properly enrolled? Who would perform the initial authentication? On what information or documentation regarding identity (what some observers call "breeder documents") should such enrolling officers rely?

5.   EMPLOYER SANCTIONS AND WORKPLACE LAWS

How do employer sanctions affect the workplace rights and protections of workers who managed to secure employment but who are in fact not authorized to work? Suppose, for example, they present false documents, or an employer fails to ask for proof of identity and work authorization. If they are discharged for union organizing, or allege unlawful discrimination, does their unauthorized employment diminish their rights or remedies? The U.S. Supreme Court addressed this question in the following case.

HOFFMAN PLASTIC COMPOUNDS, INC. v. NLRB

Supreme Court of the United States, 2002.
535 U.S. 137, 122 S.Ct. 1275, 152 L.Ed.2d 271.

CHIEF JUSTICE REHNQUIST delivered the opinion of the Court.

The National Labor Relations Board (Board) awarded backpay to an undocumented alien who has never been legally authorized to work in the United States. We hold that such relief is foreclosed by federal immigration policy, as expressed by Congress in the Immigration Reform and Control Act of 1986 (IRCA).

Petitioner Hoffman Plastic Compounds, Inc. * * * hired Jose Castro [in 1988 after he] * * * presented documents that appeared to verify his authorization to work in the United States. In December 1988, the United Rubber, Cork, Linoleum, and Plastic Workers of America, AFL-CIO, began a union-organizing campaign at petitioner's production plant. * * * In January 1989, Hoffman laid off Castro and other employees engaged in these organizing activities.

Three years later, in January 1992, respondent Board found that Hoffman unlawfully selected four employees, including Castro, for layoff "in order to rid itself of known union supporters" in violation of * * * the National Labor Relations Act (NLRA).[Among other remedies, the Board ordered Hoffman Plastics to offer reinstatement and backpay to the four employees. At a later compliance hearing called to determine the amount of backpay,] Castro testified that he was born in Mexico and that he had never been legally admitted to, or authorized to work in, the United States. He admitted gaining employment with Hoffman only after tendering a birth certificate belonging to a friend who was born in Texas. He also admitted that he used this birth certificate to fraudulently obtain a California driver's license and a Social Security card, and to fraudulently obtain employment following his layoff by Hoffman. * * * Based on this testimony, the ALJ found the Board precluded from awarding Castro backpay or reinstatement as such relief would be contrary to *Sure-Tan, Inc. v. NLRB*, 467 U.S. 883, 104 S.Ct. 2803, 81 L.Ed.2d 732 (1984), and in conflict with IRCA, which makes it unlawful for employers knowingly to hire undocumented workers or for employees to use fraudulent documents to establish employment eligibility.

In September 1998, four years after the ALJ's decision, and nine years after Castro was fired, the Board reversed with respect to backpay. Citing its earlier decision in *A.P.R.A. Fuel Oil Buyers Group, Inc.*, 320 N.L.R.B. 408 (1995), the Board determined that "the most effective way to accommodate and further the immigration policies embodied in [IRCA] is to provide the protections and remedies of the [NLRA] to undocumented workers in the same manner as to other employees." The Board thus found that Castro was entitled to $66,951 of backpay, plus interest. It calculated this backpay award from the date of Castro's termination to the date Hoffman first learned of Castro's undocumented status, a period of 4 1/2 years. * * *

* * * [T]he Court of Appeals denied [Hoffman's] petition for review.

* * *

* * * Since the Board's inception, we have consistently set aside awards of reinstatement or backpay to employees found guilty of serious illegal conduct in connection with their employment. [For example, in *NLRB v. Fansteel Metallurgical Corp.*, 306 U.S. 240, 255 (1939)], the Board awarded reinstatement with backpay to employees who engaged in

a "sit down strike" that led to confrontation with local law enforcement officials. We set aside the award, saying:

> We are unable to conclude that Congress intended to compel employers to retain persons in their employ regardless of their unlawful conduct, to invest those who go on strike with an immunity from discharge for acts of trespass or violence against the employer's property, which they would not have enjoyed had they remained at work.

> Though we found that the employer had committed serious violations of the NLRA, the Board had no discretion to remedy those violations by awarding reinstatement with backpay to employees who themselves had committed serious criminal acts.

* * *

[W]e have accordingly never deferred to the Board's remedial preferences where such preferences potentially trench upon federal statutes and policies unrelated to the NLRA. * * *

Our decision in *Sure-Tan* followed this line of cases and set aside an award closely analogous to the award challenged here. There we confronted for the first time a potential conflict between the NLRA and federal immigration policy, as then expressed in the Immigration and Nationality Act (INA). Two companies had unlawfully reported alien-employees to the Immigration and Naturalization Service (INS) in retaliation for union activity. Rather than face INS sanction, the employees voluntarily departed to Mexico. The Board * * * directed the companies to reinstate the affected workers and pay them six months' backpay.

We affirmed the Board's determination that the NLRA applied to undocumented workers, reasoning that the immigration laws "as presently written" expressed only a " 'peripheral concern' " with the employment of illegal aliens. "For whatever reason," Congress had not "made it a separate criminal offense" for employers to hire an illegal alien, or for an illegal alien "to accept employment after entering this country illegally." Therefore, we found "no reason to conclude that application of the NLRA to employment practices affecting such aliens would necessarily conflict with the terms of the INA."

With respect to the Board's selection of remedies, however, we found its authority limited by federal immigration policy. * * * [T]o avoid "a potential conflict with the INA," the Board's reinstatement order had to be conditioned upon proof of "the employees' legal reentry." *Ibid.* "Similarly," with respect to backpay, we stated: "[T]he employees must be deemed 'unavailable' for work (and the accrual of backpay therefore tolled) during any period when they were not lawfully entitled to be present and employed in the United States." * * * [S]uch remedial limitations were appropriate even if they led to "[t]he probable unavailability of the [NLRA's] more effective remedies."

* * *

* * * Castro was never lawfully entitled to be present or employed in the United States, and thus, under the plain language of *Sure-Tan,* he has no right to claim backpay. The Board takes the view, however, that read in context, this limitation applies only to aliens who left the United States and thus cannot claim backpay without lawful reentry. * * * We need not resolve this controversy. For whether isolated sentences from *Sure-Tan* definitively control, or count merely as persuasive dicta in support of petitioner, we think the question presented here better analyzed through a wider lens, focused as it must be on a legal landscape now significantly changed.

* * * [Our cases have] established that where the Board's chosen remedy trenches upon a federal statute or policy outside the Board's competence to administer, the Board's remedy may be required to yield. Whether or not this was the situation at the time of *Sure-Tan,* it is precisely the situation today. In 1986, two years after *Sure-Tan,* Congress enacted IRCA, a comprehensive scheme prohibiting the employment of illegal aliens in the United States. * * * IRCA mandates that employers verify the identity and eligibility of all new hires by examining specified documents before they begin work. If an alien applicant is unable to present the required documentation, the unauthorized alien cannot be hired.

Similarly, if an employer unknowingly hires an unauthorized alien, or if the alien becomes unauthorized while employed, the employer is compelled to discharge the worker upon discovery of the worker's undocumented status. * * * IRCA also makes it a crime for an unauthorized alien to subvert the employer verification system by tendering fraudulent documents. It thus prohibits aliens from using or attempting to use "any forged, counterfeit, altered, or falsely made document" or "any document lawfully issued to or with respect to a person other than the possessor" for purposes of obtaining employment in the United States. INA §§ 274C(a)(1)–(3). Aliens who use or attempt to use such documents are subject to fines and criminal prosecution. There is no dispute that Castro's use of false documents to obtain employment with Hoffman violated these provisions.

Under the IRCA regime, it is impossible for an undocumented alien to obtain employment in the United States without some party directly contravening explicit congressional policies. * * * The Board asks that we overlook this fact and allow it to award backpay to an illegal alien for years of work not performed, for wages that could not lawfully have been earned, and for a job obtained in the first instance by a criminal fraud. We find, however, that awarding backpay to illegal aliens runs counter to policies underlying IRCA, policies the Board has no authority to enforce or administer. * * *

The Board contends that awarding limited backpay to Castro "reasonably accommodates" IRCA, because, in the Board's view, such an award is not "inconsistent" with IRCA. The Board argues that because the backpay period was closed as of the date Hoffman learned of Castro's illegal status, Hoffman could have employed Castro during the backpay period without violating IRCA. * * * [But there] is no reason to think that Congress nonetheless intended to permit backpay where but for an employer's unfair labor practices, an alien-employee would have remained in the United States illegally, and continued to work illegally, all the while successfully evading apprehension by immigration authorities. Far from "accommodating" IRCA, the Board's position, recognizing employer misconduct but discounting the misconduct of illegal alien employees, subverts it.

Indeed, awarding backpay in a case like this not only trivializes the immigration laws, it also condones and encourages future violations. * * *

We therefore conclude that allowing the Board to award backpay to illegal aliens would unduly trench upon explicit statutory prohibitions critical to federal immigration policy, as expressed in IRCA. * * *

Lack of authority to award backpay does not mean that the employer gets off scot-free. The Board here has already imposed other significant sanctions against Hoffman—sanctions Hoffman does not challenge. These include orders that Hoffman cease and desist its violations of the NLRA, and that it conspicuously post a notice to employees setting forth their rights under the NLRA and detailing its prior unfair practices. Hoffman will be subject to contempt proceedings should it fail to comply with these orders. We have deemed such "traditional remedies" sufficient to effectuate national labor policy regardless of whether the "spur and catalyst" of backpay accompanies them. * * * [A]ny "perceived deficienc[y] in the NLRA's existing remedial arsenal" must be "addressed by congressional action," not the courts. The judgment of the Court of Appeals is reversed.

JUSTICE BREYER, with whom JUSTICE STEVENS, JUSTICE SOUTER, and JUSTICE GINSBURG join, dissenting.

I cannot agree that the backpay award before us "runs counter to," or "trenches upon," national immigration policy. As *all* the relevant agencies (including the Department of Justice) have told us, the National Labor Relations Board's limited backpay order will *not* interfere with the implementation of immigration policy. Rather, it reasonably helps to deter unlawful activity that *both* labor laws *and* immigration laws seek to prevent. Consequently, the order is lawful.

* * *

The Court does not deny that the employer in this case dismissed an employee for trying to organize a union—a crude and obvious violation of the labor laws. And it cannot deny that the Board has especially broad discretion in choosing an appropriate remedy for addressing such violations. Nor can it deny that in such circumstances backpay awards serve critically important remedial purposes. Those purposes involve more than victim compensation; they also include deterrence, *i.e.,* discouraging employers from violating the Nation's labor laws.

Without the possibility of the deterrence that backpay provides, the Board can impose only future-oriented obligations upon law-violating employers—for it has no other weapons in its remedial arsenal. And in the absence of the backpay weapon, employers could conclude that they can violate the labor laws at least once with impunity. Hence the backpay remedy is necessary; it helps make labor law enforcement credible; it makes clear that violating the labor laws will not pay.

Where in the immigration laws can the Court find a "policy" that might warrant taking from the Board this critically important remedial power? Certainly not in any statutory language. The immigration statutes say that an employer may not knowingly employ an illegal alien, that an alien may not submit false documents, and that the employer must verify documentation. They provide specific penalties, including criminal penalties, for violations. But the statutes' language itself does not explicitly state how a violation is to effect the enforcement of other laws, such as the labor laws. What is to happen, for example, when an employer hires, or an alien works, in violation of these provisions? Must the alien forfeit all pay earned? May the employer ignore the labor laws? More to the point, may the employer violate those laws with impunity, at least once—secure in the knowledge that the Board cannot assess a monetary penalty? The immigration statutes' language simply does not say.

Nor can the Court comfortably rest its conclusion upon the immigration laws' purposes. For one thing, the general purpose of the immigration statute's employment prohibition is to diminish the attractive force of employment, which like a "magnet" pulls illegal immigrants toward the United States. H.R. Rep. No. 99–682, pt. 1, p. 45 (1986), U.S. Code Cong. & Admin. News 1986, p. 5649. To permit the Board to award backpay could not significantly increase the strength of this magnetic force, for so speculative a future possibility could not realistically influence an individual's decision to migrate illegally.

To *deny* the Board the power to award backpay, however, might very well increase the strength of this magnetic force. That denial lowers the cost to the employer of an initial labor law violation (provided, of course, that the only victims are illegal aliens). It thereby increases the employer's incentive to find and to hire illegal-alien employees. Were the Board forbidden to assess backpay against a *knowing* employer—a circumstance not before us today—this perverse economic incentive, which runs directly contrary to the immigration statute's basic objective, would be obvious and serious. But even if limited to cases where the employer did not know of the employee's status, the incentive may prove significant—for, as the Board has told us, the Court's rule offers employers immunity in borderline cases, thereby encouraging them to take risks, *i.e.,* to hire with a wink and a nod those potentially unlawful aliens whose unlawful employment (given the Court's views) ultimately will lower the costs of labor law violations. The Court has recognized these considerations in stating that the labor laws must apply to illegal aliens in order to ensure that "there will be no advantage under the NLRA in preferring illegal aliens" and therefore there will be "fewer incentives for aliens themselves to enter." *Sure-Tan.* The Court today accomplishes the precise opposite.

* * *

The Court also refers to the statement in *Sure-Tan* that "employees must be deemed 'unavailable' for work (and the accrual of backpay therefore tolled) during any period when they were not lawfully entitled to be present and employed in the United States." The Court, however, does not rely upon this statement as determining its conclusion. And it is right not to do so. *Sure-Tan* involved an order reinstating (with backpay) illegal aliens who had left the country and returned to Mexico. In order to collect the backpay to which the order entitled them, the aliens would have had to reenter the country illegally. Consequently, the order itself could not have been enforced without leading to a violation of criminal law. Nothing in the Court's opinion suggests that the Court intended its statement to reach to circumstances different from and not at issue in *Sure-Tan,* where an order, such as the order before us, does not require the alien to engage in further illegal behavior.

* * *

[Finally, the Court's focus on the employee's] unlawfully earned wages and criminal fraud * * * tell[s] us only a small portion of the relevant story. After all, the same backpay award that compensates an employee in the circumstances the Court describes *also* requires an employer who has violated the labor laws to make a meaningful monetary payment. Considered from this equally important perspective, the award simply requires that employer to pay an employee whom the employer believed could lawfully have worked in the United States, (1) for years of work that he would have performed, (2) for a portion of the wages that he would have earned, and (3) for a job that the employee would have held— had that employer not unlawfully dismissed the employee for union organizing. In ignoring these latter features of the award, the Court undermines the public policies that underlie the Nation's labor laws.

* * * The Board reached its conclusion after carefully considering both labor law and immigration law. In doing so the Board has acted "with a discriminating awareness of the consequences of its action" on the immigration laws. The Attorney General, charged with immigration law enforcement, has told us that the Board is right. And the Board's position is, at the least, a reasonable one. Consequently, it is lawful. *Chevron U.S.A. Inc. v. Natural Resources Defense Council, Inc.,* 467 U.S. 837, 842– 843, 104 S.Ct. 2778, 81 L.Ed.2d 694 (1984) (requiring courts to uphold reasonable agency position).

For these reasons, I respectfully dissent.

NOTES AND QUESTIONS ON HOFFMAN PLASTIC COMPOUNDS

1.   The majority concludes that the NLRB's reading of the statutes encourages unlawful behavior. But doesn't the majority's interpretation also encourage illegality by providing incentives to employers both to hire unauthorized migrants and to violate federal labor law? What other approaches might provide a more appropriate balance or maximize the incentives for the relevant persons to comply with both IRCA and the labor laws?

Perhaps the core underlying problem is the artificially limited remedial arsenal that the NLRA gives to the NLRB. Except for backpay, the NLRB can impose only future-oriented remedies, such as required posting of notices and a cease-and-desist order—steps that the dissenters do not regard as meaningful deterrents against employer violators. Consider this proposal: Congress should provide that employers who violate NLRA-based rights of undocumented workers pay out the full amount of a backpay award, but that the funds would go to the U.S. treasury, not the unauthorized worker. What would be the advantages and disadvantages of such an amendment? Why do you think that such an idea has not gained serious consideration in the years since the Supreme Court's decision? How would such a change affect incentives for unauthorized workers to initiate or participate in NLRA-based cases?

2.   Compare *Hoffman Plastic* with *Agri Processor Co. v. NLRB,* 514 F.3d 1 (D.C. Cir.), *cert. denied,* 129 S.Ct. 594, 555 U.S. 1031, 172 L.Ed.2d 455 (2008). In *Agri Processor,* employees had voted to join the United Food and Commercial Workers Union, but the company refused recognition on the ground that most of those who voted were not authorized to work. Are unauthorized workers "employees" for purposes of establishing an employer's

duty to bargain under the NLRA? The court held that unauthorized workers must be included in the NLRA and that the same bargaining unit may include both authorized and unauthorized workers:

> * * * [W]e think the company's reliance on *Hoffman Plastic* is entirely misplaced. In that case, the Supreme Court addressed only what remedies the Board may grant undocumented aliens when employers violate their rights under the NLRA. Nowhere in *Hoffman Plastic* did the Court hold that IRCA leaves undocumented aliens altogether unprotected by the NLRA. * * *

> * * * Leaving undocumented workers without the NLRA's protections would "create[ ] a subclass of workers without a comparable stake in the collective goals of their legally resident co-workers, thereby eroding the unity of all the employees and impeding effective collective bargaining." [*Sure-Tan, Inc. v. NLRB*, 467 U.S. 883, 892 (1984)].

* * *

> "[I]n defining bargaining units, [the Board's] focus is on whether the employees share a 'community of interest.' " The community of interests test turns "on the interests of employees *as employees,* not their interests more generally."

* * *

> * * * "[T]o determine if a community of interest exists," the Board typically looks at "the similarity of wages, benefits, skills, duties, working conditions, and supervision of the employee." With regard to each of these factors, undocumented workers and legal workers in a bargaining unit are identical. While undocumented aliens may face penalties for violating immigration laws, they receive the same wages and benefits as legal workers, face the same working conditions, answer to the same supervisors, and possess the same skills and duties.

514 F.3d at 7–9. Note that the remedy in this case involved recognition of the union rather than monetary compensation to the workers.

3.   The majority in *Hoffman Plastic* states that unauthorized work in the United States is impossible without either the employee or the employer directly contravening congressional policies, and that the Board's opinion "asks us to overlook this fact and allow it to award backpay to an illegal alien for years of work not performed, for wages that could not lawfully have been earned, and for a job obtained in the first instance by a criminal fraud." Are all three of these elements crucial to the Court's conclusion? Note how the various court decisions or administrative actions summarized in the following notes either rely upon or ignore each such factor.

4.   For a detailed discussion of the background, reasoning and impact of *Hoffman Plastic*, see Catherine L. Fisk & Michael J. Wishnie, Hoffman

Plastic Compounds, Inc. v. NLRB: *The Rules of the Workplace for Undocumented Immigrants,* in Immigration Stories (David A. Martin & Peter H. Schuck eds. 2005).

5. **FLSA.** Suppose an unauthorized migrant seeks enforcement of minimum wages or proper pay for overtime under the federal Fair Labor Standards Act (FLSA) for work she has done. Should she be able to recover— though she seeks wages that "could not lawfully have been earned"? Following *Hoffman Plastic,* the Solicitor of Labor, Eugene Scalia, stated that the Labor Department would continue to enforce the FLSA minimum wage and overtime rules irrespective of a worker's immigration status. He offered these reasons:

> A first important difference between *Hoffman Plastic* and the FLSA is the nature of the statute at issue. The National Labor Relations Act permits back pay as a remedy, but does not expressly require it. This prompted the Supreme Court in *Hoffman* to look to congressional policies external to the NLRA to identify limits on the Board's discretion to award back pay. The FLSA, by contrast, exists for the very purpose of ensuring payment of wages. The immigration laws should not trump the plain text and command of the FLSA in the way they limited NLRA remedies in *Hoffman Plastic.*
>
> A second important distinction * * * is that *Hoffman* was about hours the employee did not work, whereas FLSA by definition is about hours that were worked. One of the factors the Supreme Court emphasized in its decision was that the NLRB was seeking pay for "years of work not performed." * * * [A]warding back wages for work performed by an undocumented alien is analogous to allowing recovery in *quantum meruit* as courts have done for years for services rendered under an unenforceable contract.

Speech before the Industrial Relations Research Association, June 20, 2002. Courts have been overwhelmingly supportive of recovery under FLSA for hours actually worked. *See, e.g., Lucas v. Jerusalem Cafe, LLC,* 721 F.3d 927, 935 (8th Cir. 2013), *cert. denied,* 134 S.Ct. 1515 (2014) ("Not only is our reading of *Hoffman* consistent with the overwhelming majority of post-*Hoffman* decisions by courts at every level, but '[n]o circuit court has reached a contrary conclusion').

6. **Discrimination claims.** After *Hoffman Plastic,* the U.S. Equal Employment Opportunity Commission announced that it would continue to protect immigrant workers from prohibited workplace discrimination—on such grounds as race, national origin, gender and religion—without inquiring into a worker's immigration status. At the same time, however, it rescinded 1999 guidance that had permitted awards of post-termination backpay to unauthorized migrants for federal antidiscrimination law violations. *EEOC Reaffirms Commitment to Protecting Undocumented Workers from Discrimination,* EEOC Press Release, June 28, 2002.

In *Rivera v. NIBCO, Inc.*, 364 F.3d 1057, *reh'g en banc denied*, 384 F.3d 822 (9th Cir. 2004), *cert. denied*, 544 U.S. 905, 125 S.Ct. 1603, 161 L.Ed.2d 279 (2005), the plaintiffs asserted national-origin discrimination claims under federal law (Title VII of the 1964 Civil Rights Act) and state law (the California Fair Employment and Housing Act). During discovery, the defendant sought information from the plaintiffs regarding their immigration status and their eligibility for employment; it asserted that such information, after *Hoffman Plastic*, could be relevant to potential remedies. The plaintiffs sought a protective order, which the federal magistrate granted and the courts affirmed:

> * * * While documented workers face the possibility of retaliatory discharge for an assertion of their labor and civil rights, undocumented workers confront the harsher reality that, in addition to possible discharge, their employer will likely report them to [DHS] and they will be subjected to deportation proceedings or criminal prosecution.

> As a result, most undocumented workers are reluctant to report abusive or discriminatory employment practices. Granting employers the right to inquire into workers' immigration status in cases like this would allow them to raise implicitly the threat of deportation and criminal prosecution every time a worker, documented or undocumented, reports illegal practice or files a Title VII action. * * *

Id. at 1064–65.

The defendant argued that *Hoffman Plastic* foreclosed any backpay award to the plaintiffs and therefore discovery of immigration status and employment authorization was crucial to its defense. The Court of Appeals concluded that it was "unlikely" the case applied to Title VII cases because (1) Title VII, unlike the NLRA, relies primarily upon private causes of action for enforcement; (2) Title VII plaintiffs have a wide range of available remedies, evidencing Congress' intent that the law be strongly enforced; and (3) in *Hoffman Plastic*, the Supreme Court noted that the NLRB could enforce only the NLRA and had limited power to interpret other federal statutes; courts, however, had authority to balance Title VII against IRCA if the two are found to conflict. (The court stated that it need not issue a definitive ruling on the issue because no backpay award had yet been authorized in the case and other remedies, should a violation be found, were available.) Are you persuaded? Why wouldn't the considerations quoted above regarding Title VII apply with equal force to enforcement of the federal labor laws?

The Fourth Circuit, however, reached the opposite conclusion:

> [A job applicant is entitled to Title VII remedies] *only* upon a successful showing that the applicant was qualified for employment. When the applicant is an alien, being "qualified" for the position is not determined by the applicant's capacity to perform the job—

rather, it is determined by whether the applicant was an alien authorized for employment in the United States at the time in question.

Egbuna v. Time-Life Libraries, Inc., 153 F.3d 184, 187 (4th Cir. 1998) (en banc, per curiam), *cert. denied,* 525 U.S. 1142 (1999).

7. **Compensation for tortious injury at the workplace**. Assume an unauthorized worker is injured on the job and sues the employer for lost future wages. Would *Hoffman Plastic* limit the employee's right to recover? *Compare Balbuena v. IDR Realty LLC,* 6 N.Y.3d 338, 812 N.Y.S.2d 416, 845 N.E.2d 1246 (2006) (recovery allowed; no evidence that plaintiffs produced false work documents in violation of IRCA) and *Madeira v. Affordable Housing Foundation. Inc.,* 469 F.3d 219 (2d Cir. 2006) (same) *with Ambrosi v. 1085 Park Avenue LLC,* 2008 WL 4386751 (S.D.N.Y. 2008) ("Plaintiff's claim for lost wages must be dismissed because Plaintiff is an undocumented alien who knowingly used fraudulent documentation to obtain employment . . . in violation of IRCA.").

8. What legal rules are optimal in each of the settings discussed in notes 5 through 7? Should courts strive for a uniform approach, or should remedies be tailored for each regulatory realm? *See generally* Ellen Dewhurst, *Models of Protection of the Right of Irregular Migrants to Back Pay: The Impact of the Interconnection between Immigration Law and Labor Law,* 35 Comp. Lab. L. & Pol'y J. 217 (2014); Craig Robert Senn, *Proposing a Uniform Remedial Approach for Undocumented Workers under Federal Employment Discrimination Law,* 77 Fordham L. Rev. 113 (2008). On the general idea that unauthorized workers can successfully assert workplace rights by showing that harming them can harm coworkers who are U.S. citizens or lawful permanent residents, or who are otherwise working lawfully, see Hiroshi Motomura, *The Rights of Others: Legal Claims and Immigration Outside the Law,* 59 Duke L.J. 1723, 1751–56 (2010). Motomura also suggests that unauthorized workers can successfully assert workplace rights against more culpable employers, *id.* at 1749–51.

B. ENFORCEMENT CHOICES

Immigration law is not self-executing. Every removal of a noncitizen from the United States reflects complex choices resulting in the enforcement of immigration law. Every removal also is the product of an intricate procedural system with multiple opportunities for accuracy or error. In Chapter Seven, Section C on Relief From Removal, we looked at enforcement choices concerning specific individuals, for example when the federal government exercises prosecutorial discretion by deciding not to place someone in removal proceedings. This chapter studies enforcement choices that are more macro-level or systemic, such as whether to enforce at the border or in the interior, to conduct searches in certain patterns, to base enforcement priorities in part on nationality, or to involve state and local governments in federal immigration enforcement.

1. PERSPECTIVES ON ENFORCEMENT AND ENFORCEMENT DISCRETION

Any examination of enforcement must start by recognizing how immigration law is underenforced. Recall from Chapter Seven that John Morton, then-director of the Bureau of Immigration and Customs Enforcement (ICE) in the Department of Homeland Security, explained in June 2010 that given present funding levels, the maximum capacity of the civil removal system is about 400,000 removals per year—under 4 percent of the unauthorized population. There are many ways of understanding how this state of affairs came to be. Here is one perspective on developments starting in the first half of the twentieth century:

> * * * [R]egardless of whether immigrants from Asia or Latin America had formal permanent resident status, what mattered more was what they were expected to do in the United States. No matter if they came as permanent residents or as temporary workers, or came outside the law, the more basic fact was that they were needed as workers.

> An emerging pattern brought Mexicans as migrant workers or commuters, though many eventually stayed indefinitely. * * * The most prominent lawful path for [Mexican] workers was the Bracero program, which operated from 1942 until it formally ended in 1964 and finally was phased out in 1967. The program institutionalized the expectation that the vast majority of Mexicans who came to the United States did so temporarily to work.

> * * * Many employers of that era—like many today—also understood that unauthorized workers were easier to control and exploit than lawful temporary workers or permanent residents. Many Mexicans came without papers and readily found work in the United States. A vast border and minimal available resources limited what the US government could do to control crossings, but it could choose to tolerate unauthorized migration or sometimes move vigorously to control it, depending on what economic conditions and politics dictated. Enforcement was highly discretionary, and its intensity ebbed and flowed. * * *

> * * *

> * * * [T]he current mix of lawful and unauthorized migration began to evolve in the 1960s, with drastic changes to

the legal framework that had shaped Mexican migration up to that time. The Bracero program * * * ended in 1964, largely because of conspicuous employer exploitation and abuse of the migrant workers that seemed intolerable in a political climate that would soon produce significant domestic civil rights legislation. * * *

The coalitions that won repeal of the national origins system also secured other important civil rights legislation, most prominently the Civil Rights Act of 1964 and the Voting Rights Act of 1965. For Latin America, however, the repeal of the national origins system came at significant cost, by introducing numerical limits. Previously, the national origins system had set a numerical limit for overall immigration from the Eastern Hemisphere. The number of immigrants from the Western Hemisphere was not capped, even if individuals could be barred if they fell within certain exclusion grounds, such as those for immigrants without sufficient financial means.

The 1965 amendments changed this. * * * Congress decided to limit Western Hemisphere immigration to 120,000 per year starting in 1968. Similar pressures led in 1976 to a new annual limit of 20,000 per year on immigration from any single country [in the family and employment preferences]. * * * Long lines soon formed for populous countries where the desire to go to the United States was strong due to geographical, historical, or economic ties.

The post-1965 per-country and overall caps on the number of immigrants only partly explain the growth of the unauthorized population to over 11 million today. Another crucial contributing factor has been that the qualifying categories for admission as a lawful immigrant have been defined narrowly and limited in number. The admissions system forces many qualifying immigrants to wait years or even decades. The system completely shuts out many other immigrants who have neither qualifying family ties nor a high level of formal education. * * *

* * *

Even after the Bracero program ended and new restrictions were in place, migrants were able to come illegally with relative ease. A migration industry emerged to help them cross the border and reach locations in the US interior for work and housing. Employers continued to depend on a steady supply of inexpensive labor. Stagnation in the Mexican economy made northward emigration attractive to many Mexicans, no matter what U.S. immigration law said. * * *

Around the same time, Central America was destabilized by coups, civil wars, and other political upheavals in El Salvador, Honduras, Guatemala, and Nicaragua, accompanied by economic instability—all powerful forces that pushed people to emigrate. * * *

A combination of historical migration patterns, strong transnational networks, and robust demand for foreign workers has sustained patterns of immigration to the United States, much of it unauthorized, and all in spite of restrictions on lawful immigration. With the unauthorized population far exceeding federal enforcement capacity, enforcement must also be selective, both in the interior and at the border.

Hiroshi Motomura, Immigration Outside the Law 38–46 (2014).* *See also* the materials on unauthorized migration as a historical and social process in Chapter Five, pp. 464–477 *supra*.

In turn, underenforcement combined with limited removal capacity means that government discretion in immigration law enforcement matters a great deal. Where, when, and how will enforcement resources be brought to bear on immigration law violators?

2.   LIMITS ON GOVERNMENT ENFORCEMENT ACTIVITIES

a.   Searches and Seizures

No matter whether enforcement involves civil immigration proceedings or criminal prosecution, the question arises of when and how the law limits what federal, state, or local law enforcement officers may do by way of searches, seizures, stops, or arrests. Each of these four words is a term of art that has generated controversy and case law.

Suppose that ICE agents want to arrest unauthorized migrants suspected of working at a local factory? Or suppose they believe that other unauthorized migrants are living in a certain house? Or suppose Border Patrol agents spot a car heading north on a dirt road in southern Arizona and think that the occupants have just crossed the border surreptitiously?

The most basic sources of limits are the Fourth and Fifth Amendments to the U.S. Constitution. Because they apply to both criminal procedure and civil immigration enforcement, the substantive

---

limits on law enforcement that have developed in one area governs the other as well. But as we shall see, remedies may be more limited in civil removal proceedings than in criminal prosecution. Government officers and employees are also constrained by statutes and regulations, which may mirror constitutional commands or set more stringent limits. Even when statutes and regulations are substantively identical to what the Constitution requires, individuals harmed by the government may get remedies for statutory or regulatory violations that would not be available for constitutional violations alone.

(i) When Do Fourth Amendment Protections Apply?

Immigration enforcement typically involves a physical encounter between a government official and an individual—at a land border or other port of entry, at a traffic stop or some other highway encounter, or perhaps in a raid at a workplace or home. In these encounters, immigration officers often stop and question persons suspected of being in the country unlawfully. Under INA § 287(a)(1) and (2), respectively, officers may "interrogate any alien or person believed to be an alien as to his right to be or remain in the United States," and arrest aliens unlawfully entering, attempting to enter, or already in the United States.

Does the Fourth Amendment limit this authority? Yes, but only if the encounter amounts to a search or seizure. The first question, then, is how are these terms defined.

INS v. DELGADO
Supreme Court of the United States, 1984.
466 U.S. 210, 104 S.Ct. 1758, 80 L.Ed.2d 247.

JUSTICE REHNQUIST delivered the opinion of the Court.

* * *

Acting pursuant to two warrants, in January and September, 1977 the INS conducted a survey of the work force at Southern California Davis Pleating Co. (Davis Pleating) in search of illegal aliens. The warrants were issued on a showing of probable cause by the INS that numerous illegal aliens were employed at Davis Pleating, although neither of the search warrants identified any particular illegal aliens by name. A third factory survey was conducted with the employer's consent in October, 1977, at Mr. Pleat, another garment factory.

At the beginning of the surveys several agents positioned themselves near the buildings' exits, while other agents dispersed throughout the factory to question most, but not all, employees at their work stations. The agents displayed badges, carried walkie-talkies, and were armed, although at no point during any of the surveys was a weapon ever drawn.

Moving systematically through the factory, the agents approached employees and, after identifying themselves, asked them from one to three questions relating to their citizenship. If the employee gave a credible reply that he was a United States citizen, the questioning ended, and the agent moved on to another employee. If the employee gave an unsatisfactory response or admitted that he was an alien, the employee was asked to produce his immigration papers. During the survey, employees continued with their work and were free to walk around within the factory.

Respondents are [two U.S. citizen and two lawful permanent resident] employees questioned in one of the three surveys. In 1978 respondents and their union representative, the International Ladies Garment Workers' Union, filed two actions * * * challenging the constitutionality of INS factory surveys and seeking declaratory and injunctive relief. * * *

* * *

The Fourth Amendment does not proscribe all contact between the police and citizens, but is designed "to prevent arbitrary and oppressive interference by enforcement officials with the privacy and personal security of individuals." *United States v. Martinez-Fuerte*, 428 U.S. 543, 554, 96 S.Ct. 3074, 3081, 49 L.Ed.2d 1116 (1976). Given the diversity of encounters between police officers and citizens, however, the Court has been cautious in defining the limits imposed by the Fourth Amendment on encounters between the police and citizens. As we have noted elsewhere: "Obviously, not all personal intercourse between policemen and citizens involves 'seizures' of persons. Only when the officer, by means of physical force or show of authority, has restrained the liberty of a citizen may we conclude that a 'seizure' has occurred." *Terry v. Ohio*, [392 U.S. 1, 19, n.16, 88 S.Ct. 1868, 1879 n.16, 20 L.Ed.2d 889 (1968)]. While applying such a test is relatively straightforward in a situation resembling a traditional arrest, the protection against unreasonable seizures also extends to "seizures that involve only a brief detention short of traditional arrest." *United States v. Brignoni-Ponce*, 422 U.S. 873, 878, 95 S.Ct. 2574, 2578, 45 L.Ed.2d 607 (1975). What has evolved from our cases is a determination that an initially consensual encounter between a police officer and a citizen can be transformed into a seizure or detention within the meaning of the Fourth Amendment, "if, in view of all the circumstances surrounding the incident, a reasonable person would have believed that he was not free to leave." [*United States v. Mendenhall*, 446 U.S. 544, 554, 100 S.Ct. 1870, 1877, 64 L.Ed.2d 497 (1980)].

* * *

* * * [P]olice questioning, by itself, is unlikely to result in a Fourth Amendment violation. While most citizens will respond to a police

request, the fact that people do so, and do so without being told they are free not to respond, hardly eliminates the consensual nature of the response. Unless the circumstances of the encounter are so intimidating as to demonstrate that a reasonable person would have believed he was not free to leave if he had not responded, one cannot say that the questioning resulted in a detention under the Fourth Amendment. But if the persons refuses to answer and the police take additional steps * * * to obtain an answer, then the Fourth Amendment imposes some minimal level of objective justification to validate the detention or seizure.

* * * In support of the decision below, respondents argue that the INS created an intimidating psychological environment when it intruded unexpectedly into the workplace with such a show of officers. Besides the stationing of agents near the exits, respondents add that the length of the survey and the failure to inform workers they were free to leave resulted in a Fourth Amendment seizure of the entire work force.

We reject the claim that the entire work forces of the two factories were seized for the duration of the surveys when the INS placed agents near the exits of the factory sites. Ordinarily, when people are at work their freedom to move about has been meaningfully restricted, not by the actions of law enforcement officials, but by the workers' voluntary obligations to their employers. The record indicates that when these surveys were initiated, the employees were about their ordinary business, operating machinery and performing other job assignments. While the surveys did cause some disruption, including the efforts of some workers to hide, the record also indicates that workers were not prevented by the agents from moving about the factories.

Respondents argue, however, that the stationing of agents near the factory doors showed the INS's intent to prevent people from leaving. But there is nothing in the record indicating that this is what the agents at the doors actually did. The obvious purpose of the agents' presence at the factory doors was to insure that all persons in the factories were questioned. The record indicates that the INS agents' conduct in this case consisted simply of questioning employees and arresting those they had probable cause to believe were unlawfully present in the factory. This conduct should have given respondents no reason to believe that they would be detained if they gave truthful answers to the questions put to them or if they simply refused to answer. If mere questioning does not constitute a seizure when it occurs inside the factory, it is no more a seizure when it occurs at the exits.

A similar conclusion holds true for all other citizens or aliens lawfully present inside the factory buildings during the surveys. The presence of agents by the exits posed no reasonable threat of detention to these workers while they walked throughout the factories on job assignments.

Likewise, the mere possibility that they would be questioned if they sought to leave the buildings should not have resulted in any reasonable apprehension by any of them that they would be seized or detained in any meaningful way. Since most workers could have had no reasonable fear that they would be detained upon leaving, we conclude that the work forces as a whole were not seized.

* * * [S]ince there was no seizure of the work forces by virtue of the method of conducting the factory surveys, the only way the issue of individual questioning could be presented would be if one of the named respondents had in fact been seized or detained. Reviewing the deposition testimony of respondents, we conclude that none were.

The questioning of each respondent by INS agents seems to have been nothing more than a brief encounter. None of the three Davis Pleating employees were questioned during the January survey. During the September survey at Davis Pleating, respondent Delgado was discussing the survey with another employee when two INS agents approached him and asked him where he was from and from what city. When Delgado informed them that he came from Mayaguez, Puerto Rico, the agent made an innocuous observation to his partner and left. Respondent Correa's experience in the September survey was similar. Walking from one part of the factory to another, Correa was stopped by an INS agent and asked where she was born. When she replied "Huntington Park, [California]," the agent walked away and Correa continued about her business. Respondent Labonte, the third Davis Pleating employee, was tapped on the shoulder and asked in Spanish, "Where are your papers?". Labonte responded that she had her papers and without any further request from the INS agents, showed the papers to the agents, who then left. Finally, respondent Miramontes, the sole Mr. Pleat employee involved in this case, encountered an agent en route from an office to her worksite. Questioned concerning her citizenship, Miramontes replied that she was a resident alien, and on the agent's request, produced her work permit. The agent then left.

Respondents argue that the manner in which the surveys were conducted and the attendant disruption caused by the surveys created a psychological environment which made them reasonably afraid they were not free to leave. Consequently, when respondents were approached by INS agents and questioned concerning their citizenship and right to work, they were effectively detained under the Fourth Amendment, since they reasonably feared that refusing to answer would have resulted in their arrest. But it was obvious from the beginning of the surveys that the INS agents were only questioning people. Persons such as respondents who simply went about their business in the workplace were not detained in any way; nothing more occurred than that a question was put to them. While persons who attempted to flee or evade the agents may eventually have been detained for questioning, respondents did not do so and were not in fact detained. The manner in which respondents were questioned, given its obvious purpose, could hardly result in a reasonable fear that respondents were not free to continue working or to move about the factory. Respondents may only litigate what happened to them, and our review of their description of the encounters with the INS agents satisfies us that the encounters were classic consensual encounters rather than Fourth Amendment seizures.

* * *

[The concurring opinions of JUSTICES STEVENS AND POWELL are omitted.]

JUSTICE BRENNAN, with whom JUSTICE MARSHALL joins, concurring in part and dissenting in part.

* * *

At first blush, the Court's opinion appears unremarkable. But what is striking about today's decision is its studied air of unreality. Indeed, it is only through a considerable feat of legerdemain that the Court is able to arrive at the conclusion that the respondents were not seized. The success of the Court's sleight of hand turns on the proposition that the interrogations of respondents by the INS were merely brief, "consensual encounters," that posed no threat to respondents' personal security and freedom. The record, however, tells a far different story.

* * *

* * * I have no difficulty concluding that respondents were seized within the meaning of the Fourth Amendment when they were accosted by the INS agents and questioned concerning their right to remain in the United States. Although none of the respondents was physically restrained by the INS agents during the questioning, it is nonetheless plain beyond cavil that the manner in which the INS conducted these surveys demonstrated a "show of authority" of sufficient size and force to overbear the will of any reasonable person. Faced with such tactics, a reasonable person could not help but feel compelled to stop and provide answers to the INS agents' questions. The Court's efforts to avoid this conclusion are rooted more in fantasy than in the record of this case. The Court goes astray, in my view, chiefly because it insists upon considering each interrogation in isolation as if respondents had been questioned by the INS in a setting similar to an encounter between a single police officer and a lone passerby that might occur on a street corner. * * *

The surrounding circumstances in this case are far different from an isolated encounter between the police and a passerby on the street. Each of the respondents testified at length about the widespread disturbance among the workers that was sparked by the INS surveys and the intimidating atmosphere created by the INS's investigative tactics. First, as the respondents explained, the surveys were carried out by surprise by relatively large numbers of agents, generally from 15 to 25, who moved systematically through the rows of workers who were seated at their work stations. Second, as the INS agents discovered persons whom they suspected of being illegal aliens, they would handcuff these persons and lead them away to waiting vans outside the factory. Third, all of the factory exits were conspicuously guarded by INS agents, stationed there to prevent anyone from leaving while the survey was being conducted. Finally, as the INS agents moved through the rows of workers, they would show their badges and direct pointed questions at the workers. In light of these circumstances, it is simply fantastic to conclude that a reasonable person could ignore all that was occurring throughout the factory and, when the INS agents reached him, have the temerity to believe that he was at liberty to refuse to answer their questions and walk away.

* * *

* * * [T]he respondents' testimony paints a frightening picture of people subjected to wholesale interrogation under conditions designed not to respect personal security and privacy, but rather to elicit prompt answers from completely intimidated workers. Nothing could be clearer than that these tactics amounted to seizures of respondents under the Fourth Amendment.

* * *

* * * [W]e have explained that brief detentions may be justified on "facts that do not amount to the probable cause required for an arrest." *United States v. Brignoni-Ponce*, 422 U.S. 873, 880, 95 S.Ct. 2574, 2580, 45 L.Ed.2d 607 (1975). Nevertheless, * * * we have insisted that police may not detain and interrogate an individual unless they have reasonable grounds for suspecting that the person is involved in some unlawful activity. In *United States v. Brignoni-Ponce*, for instance, the Court held that "[Border Patrol] officers on roving patrol may stop vehicles only if they are aware of specific articulable facts, together with rational inferences from those facts, that reasonably warrant suspicion that the vehicles contain aliens who may be illegally in the country." 422 U.S., at 884, 95 S.Ct., at 2581.

* * * [A]ll workers, irrespective of whether they were American citizens, permanent resident aliens, or deportable aliens, were subjected to questioning by INS agents concerning their right to remain in the country. By their own admission, the INS agents did not selectively question persons in these surveys on the basis of any reasonable suspicion that the persons were illegal aliens. That the INS policy is so indiscriminate should not be surprising, however, since many of the employees in the surveyed factories who are lawful residents of the United States may have been born in Mexico, have a Latin appearance, or speak Spanish while at work. What this means, of course, is that the many lawful workers who constitute the clear majority at the surveyed workplaces are subjected to surprise questioning under intimidating circumstances by INS agents who have no reasonable basis for suspecting that they have done anything wrong. To say that such an indiscriminate policy of mass interrogation is constitutional makes a mockery of the words of the Fourth Amendment.

* * *

Furthermore, even if the INS agents had pursued a firm policy of stopping and interrogating only those persons whom they reasonably suspected of being aliens, they would still have failed, given the particular circumstances of this case, to safeguard adequately the rights secured by the Fourth Amendment. The first and in my view insurmountable problem with such a policy is that, viewed realistically, it poses such grave problems of execution that in practice it affords virtually no protection to lawful American citizens working in these factories. This is so because, as the Court recognized in *Brignoni-Ponce*, 422 U.S., at 886, 95 S.Ct., at 2582, there is no reliable way to distinguish with a reasonable degree of accuracy between native-born and naturalized citizens of Mexican ancestry on the one hand, and aliens of Mexican ancestry on the other. Indeed, the record in this case clearly demonstrates this danger, since respondents Correa and Delgado, although both American citizens, were subjected to questioning during the INS surveys.

Moreover, the mere fact that a person is believed to be an alien provides no immediate grounds for suspecting any illegal activity. * * *In contexts such as these factory surveys, where it is virtually impossible to distinguish fairly between citizens and aliens, the threat to vital civil rights of American citizens would soon become intolerable if we simply permitted the INS to question persons solely on account of suspected alienage. Therefore, in order to protect both American citizens and lawful resident aliens, who are also protected by the Fourth Amendment, the INS must tailor its enforcement efforts to focus only on those workers who are reasonably suspected of being illegal aliens.

Relying upon *United States v. Martinez-Fuerte*, 428 U.S. 543, 96 S.Ct. 3074, 49 L.Ed.2d 1116 (1976), however, Justice POWELL would hold that the interrogation of respondents represented a "reasonable" seizure under the Fourth Amendment, even though the INS agents lacked any particularized suspicion of illegal alienage to support the questioning. In my view, reliance on that decision is misplaced. In *Martinez-Fuerte*, the Court held that when the intrusion upon protected privacy interests is extremely limited, the INS, in order to serve the pressing governmental interest in immigration enforcement, may briefly detain travelers at fixed checkpoints for questioning solely on the basis of "apparent Mexican ancestry." 428 U.S., at 563, 96 S.Ct., at 3085. In so holding, the Court was careful to distinguish its earlier decision in *Brignoni-Ponce*, which held that Border Patrol agents conducting roving patrols may not stop and question motorists solely on the basis of apparent Mexican ancestry, and may instead make such stops only when their observations lead them "reasonably to suspect that a particular vehicle may contain aliens who are illegally in the country." *Id.*, 422 U.S., at 881, 95 S.Ct., at 2580. The "crucial distinction" between the roving patrols and the fixed checkpoints * * * was "the lesser intrusion upon the motorist's Fourth Amendment interests" caused by the checkpoint operations. * * *

* * *

In my view, therefore, the only acceptable alternatives that would adequately safeguard Fourth Amendment values in this context are for the INS either (a) to adopt a firm policy of stopping and questioning only those workers who are reasonably suspected of being illegal aliens, or (b) to develop a factory survey program that is predictably and reliably less intrusive than the current scheme under review. The first alternative would satisfy the requirement of particularized suspicion enunciated in *Terry*—a principle that must control here because the specific conditions that permitted exception to that requirement in *Martinez-Fuerte* are simply not present. The second alternative would seek to redesign the factory survey techniques used by the INS in order to bring them more closely into line with the characteristics found in *Martinez-Fuerte*. * * *

* * *

NOTES AND QUESTIONS ON SEARCHES AND SEIZURES

1.   Part of the reasoning in *Delgado* is that neither asking an individual for identification, nor its production in response, are sufficient to turn an encounter into a seizure to which the Fourth Amendment would apply. *See also Muehler v. Mena*, 544 U.S. 93, 100–01, 125 S.Ct. 1465, 1471, 161 L.Ed.2d 299 (2005) (holding that questioning a lawfully detained individual about her name, date and place of birth, or immigration status is not a discrete seizure that must independently satisfy the Fourth Amendment); *Hiibel v. Sixth Judicial District Court of Nevada*, 542 U.S. 177, 185–89, 124 S.Ct. 2451, 2458–60, 159 L.Ed.2d 292 (2004) (holding constitutional a Nevada statute requiring an individual, once stopped by a police officer based on reasonable suspicion, to disclose his name).

2.   Compare the facts in *Delgado* with *LaDuke v. Nelson*, 762 F.2d 1318 (9th Cir. 1985):

The armed Border Patrol agents periodically cordoned off migrant housing during early morning or late evening hours, surrounded the residences in emergency vehicles with flashing lights, approached the homes with flashlights, and stationed officers at all doors and windows. The agents would then conduct house-to-house searches either without consent or with the alleged "knowing" consent of the occupants.

762 F.2d at 1321.

Distinguishing *Delgado*, the Ninth Circuit found a "seizure":

* * * First, unlike *Delgado,* the INS agents do not obtain any form of warrant for ranch and farm checks. As the district court found, the INS agents base their decision to check on a random basis without any current articulable suspicion that particular units will contain illegal aliens. Also unlike *Delgado,* the INS systematically fails to obtain the consent of the owner of the farm housing. A second distinction between the factory surveys in *Delgado* and farm checks is the materially different forum in which these searches take place—the workplace versus the home. Although the INS persists in contending that farm housing is part and parcel of the workplace and should be treated similarly, the simple truth is that the INS itself has recognized that they are dissimilar. If the INS truly thought that the occupants of farm housing were living at the workplace then the INS would be obliged to seek the consent of the employer—not the occupant—to obtain access. The measure of protection accorded the home under the Fourth Amendment is qualitatively different from that afforded the workplace under *Delgado.* * * * Significantly, the *Delgado* opinion's reliance on the permissibility of questioning within the open interior of the workplace to justify questioning at the workplace exits is clearly inapplicable to the home setting.

Id. at 1328–29.

3. In addition to defining "seizure" over vigorous dissent, *Delgado* surveys several concepts and doctrines that figure prominently in setting Fourth Amendment limits on immigration enforcement. The basic idea is that searches and seizures must be reasonable, and that the definition of "reasonable" is subdivided into two scenarios.

A search or seizure pursuant to a judicial warrant (not an administrative warrant) is presumed to be reasonable, whereas a warrantless search or seizure is presumed not to be reasonable. But a warrantless search or seizure may be consistent with the Fourth Amendment if any one of several conditions is met, including several that are especially relevant to immigration law enforcement:

a. the officer making an arrest has "probable cause" to believe that the individual has violated the law, *see United States v.*

Watson, 423 U.S. 411, 417, 96 S.Ct. 820, 824–25, 46 L.Ed.2d 598 (1976).

    b.   short of a traditional arrest, the officer may engage in a brief investigatory stop of an individual or a vehicle based on "reasonable suspicion" (which is less than "probable cause") that unlawful activity "may be afoot" based on whether the officer has a particularized and objective basis for suspecting wrongdoing based on the totality of circumstances, including reasonable suspicion that the individual is in the United States unlawfully, *see Terry v. Ohio*, cited in *Delgado*; *see also United States v. Arvizu*, 534 U.S. 266, 273, 122 S.Ct. 744, 750, 151 L.Ed.2d 740 (2002);

    c.   incident to a lawful arrest, a search of the individual's person and immediate surrounding area, *see Chimel v. California*, 395 U.S. 752, 762–63, 89 S.Ct. 2034, 2040, 23 L.Ed.2d 685 (1969);

    d.   a search is based on consent given freely and voluntarily. *see Schneckloth v. Bustamonte,* 412 U.S. 218, 222, 93 S.Ct. 2041, 2045, 36 L.Ed.2d 854 (1973);

    e.   exigent circumstances, such as intervening in a fight to prevent serious injury, see *Brigham City v. Stuart*, 547 U.S. 398, 406, 126 S.Ct. 1943, 1949, 164 L.Ed.2d 650 (2006); or

    f.   a search or seizure at or near the border, where law enforcement activity is less constrained, *see Brignoni-Ponce* and *Martinez-Fuerte*, both cited in *Delgado*, and note 4 *infra*.

Each of these exceptions has been a core area of controversy in judicial decisions involving Fourth Amendment limits on immigration law enforcement. These and other judicial decisions address analogous limits based on federal statutes and regulations.

    4.   Assume that a stop is constitutionally permissible. When does the detention that is inherent in any stop become unduly prolonged as a constitutional matter? According to the U.S. Supreme Court in *Arizona v. United States*, 132 S.Ct. 2492, 2509 (2012), discussed in Section C of this chapter, p. 1229, "[d]etaining individuals solely to verify immigration status would raise constitutional concerns." On this question, see *Rodriguez v. United States*, 135 S.Ct. 1609, 191 L.Ed. 2d 492 (2015), which involved a traffic stop for a moving violation. Without reasonable suspicion of further wrongdoing, the police extended the stop by seven or eight minutes beyond the time required to issue a ticket, in order to conduct a dog sniff of the vehicle. The U.S. Supreme Court held that extending the stop under these circumstances was a violation of the Fourth Amendment. *See also Arizona v. Johnson*, 555 U.S. 323, 333, 129 S.Ct. 781, 172 L.Ed.2d 694 (2009); *Illinois v. Caballes*, 543 U.S. 405, 407, 125 S.Ct. 834, 160 L.Ed.2d 842 (2005).

    5.   In keeping with the traditional border-interior distinction in due process analysis (compare *Mezei* with *Plasencia* in the materials on constitutional due process in Chapter Six), the U.S. Supreme Court has

recognized that law enforcement officials have far greater power to search persons and property at the border than inside the country. Thus, a routine search at an official border inspection post may occur without probable cause or reasonable suspicion. *See United States v. Ramsey*, 431 U.S. 606, 619, 97 S.Ct. 1972, 52 L.Ed.2d 617 (1977). Intrusive searches that go beyond a normal border search require some degree of reasonable belief that illegal activity is occurring. In *United States v. Montoya de Hernandez*, 473 U.S. 531, 105 S.Ct. 3304, 87 L.Ed.2d 381 (1985), the Court upheld the sixteen-hour detention of a traveler seeking to enter the United States based on customs officials' "reasonable suspicion" that she was smuggling swallowed contraband.

Near (but not at) the border, the Fourth Amendment limits law enforcement more than at the border itself, but less than in the interior. In this intermediate zone, the Court has distinguished between stops made at "fixed checkpoints" and those made by "roving patrols" (that is, officers traveling in cars).

At fixed checkpoints, brief stops are allowed even without reasonable suspicion, *United States v. Martinez-Fuerte*, 428 U.S. 543, 561–62, 96 S.Ct. 3074, 49 L.Ed.2d 1116 (1976). But once a car and its riders have been held for secondary inspection at a fixed check point, a search requires probable cause or consent. *United States v. Ortiz*, 422 U.S. 891, 896–97, 95 S.Ct. 2585, 45 L.Ed.2d 623 (1975). Roving patrols may conduct brief stops and questioning only if an officer has a reasonable suspicion (the *Terry* standard) that the vehicle is involved in unlawful activity. *See United States v. Brignoni-Ponce*, 422 U.S. 873, 881–82, 95 S.Ct. 2574, 45 L.Ed.2d 607 (1975). Roving patrols may conduct arrests and full-scale searches only based on probable cause. *See Almeida-Sanchez v. United States*, 413 U.S. 266, 273, 93 S.Ct. 2535, 2539–40, 37 L. Ed. 2d 596 (1973).

6. Critiquing the majority opinion in *Delgado*, Devon Carbado and Cheryl Harris observe that "at no point in Justice Rehnquist's opinion does he engage race" even though respondent Herman Delgado, a U.S. citizen, argued in his brief that "innocuous conduct does not become suspect merely because the person observed is non-white. Yet that is precisely what occurs during these raids. Every Latin [*sic*] is suspected of being an undocumented alien due to his or her race." Devon W. Carbado & Cheryl I. Harris, *Undocumented Criminal Procedure*, 58 UCLA L. Rev. 1543, 1559 (2011).

Why should the omission of race from the Court's analysis in *Delgado* be troubling? What would be a sound basis for the plaintiff's assertion that every Latino is "suspected of being an undocumented alien"? How can the use of apparent race or ethnicity in enforcement decisions be monitored and controlled, perhaps through mechanisms within the executive branch, or by means of legal standards applied by courts? The next subsection continues this line of inquiry.

(ii) Enforcement and Ethnicity

In determining what the Fourth Amendment requires, a topic that sometimes arises is ethnicity. Should courts craft standards to protect noncitizens—and citizens—who may appear "foreign" to some law enforcement officers, leading them to believe they have reasonable suspicion or probable cause? Or given enforcement imperatives, should officials have some authority to consider ethnicity in carrying out their functions?

Besides addressing the general standard for roving patrols near the border, the U.S. Supreme Court's 1975 decision in *Brignoni-Ponce* also held that "apparent Mexican ancestry" plus presence in an area where undocumented migrants frequently travel are not enough to justify a vehicle stop. The next year, the Court held in *Martinez-Fuerte* that motorists at a fixed checkpoint may be referred to secondary inspection (where they will be questioned at greater length) "largely on the basis of apparent Mexican ancestry." But *Martinez-Fuerte* also seemed to reconfirm the Court's holding in *Ortiz* that a search during secondary inspection at a fixed check point requires probable cause or consent.

In the next case, the Ninth Circuit considered whether the Fourth Amendment allows "Hispanic appearance" to play *any* role in enforcement near the border.

UNITED STATES V. MONTERO-CAMARGO

United States Court of Appeals, Ninth Circuit, en banc, 2000.
208 F.3d 1122, cert. denied, 531 U.S. 889, 121 S.Ct. 211, 148 L.Ed.2d 148.

REINHARDT, CIRCUIT JUDGE.

* * *

On the afternoon of October 15, 1996, a passing driver told border patrol agents at the Highway 86 permanent stationary checkpoint in El Centro, California, that two cars heading north, with Mexicali license plates, had just made U-turns on the highway shortly before the checkpoint. Upon receiving the tip, two Border Patrol Agents, Brian Johnson and Carl Fisher, got into separate marked patrol cars and headed south to investigate. Approximately one minute later (and about one mile from the checkpoint), the two agents saw a blue Chevrolet Blazer and a red Nissan sedan, both with Mexicali plates, pull off the shoulder and re-enter the highway heading south.

According to the agents, the area where they first observed the cars is used by lawbreakers to drop off and pick up undocumented aliens and illegal drugs, while evading inspection. Its use for such purposes is due in part to the fact that the view of that part of the highway area from the Border Patrol checkpoint is blocked. * * *

Both agents testified that almost all of the stops made by the Border Patrol at the turnaround site resulted in the discovery of "a violation of some sort . . ." involving either illegal aliens or narcotics. * * *

The place where the agents saw that the vehicles had stopped following the U-turn was a deserted area on the side of the southbound highway located opposite the large sign on the northbound side advising drivers that the checkpoint was open. As Agent Johnson testified, the sign was the first indication to northbound drivers that the Border Patrol's facility was operational. The checkpoint in question had been closed for some time and had reopened only a day or two earlier.

* * * Agent Johnson * * * testified that as he pulled behind the Blazer, he noted that both the driver and the passenger appeared to be Hispanic. Johnson stated that when the driver and passenger noticed him behind them, the passenger picked up a newspaper and began reading. This, according to Agent Johnson, further aroused his suspicions. Johnson then stopped the Blazer, identified himself as a Border Patrol agent, and asked about the citizenship of the two occupants. In response to Johnson's inquiries, the driver, Lorenzo Sanchez-Guillen, and his passenger, Sylvia Renteria-Wolff, showed Agent Johnson [their border crossing] cards, which allow Mexican citizens to travel up to 25 miles inside the United States for no longer than 72 hours at a time. As the Blazer had been stopped approximately 50 miles from the border, Johnson then brought the two occupants to the checkpoint for processing.

In the meantime, Agent Fisher continued to follow the second car, a red Nissan sedan. According to Fisher, when he and Agent Johnson first drew near the two cars, the Nissan began to accelerate. As Fisher caught up with the vehicle, he could see that the second driver also appeared to be Hispanic. Fisher ultimately pulled the Nissan over after following it for approximately four miles. Appellant German Espinoza Montero-Camargo was the driver. After stopping the car, Agent Fisher, with the aid of Agent Johnson, who had returned to help him, searched the trunk and found two large bags of marijuana. A subsequent search of the Blazer back at the checkpoint turned up a loaded .32 caliber pistol in the glove compartment and an ammunition clip that fit the pistol in the passenger's purse.

* * *

* * * Although the level of suspicion required for a brief investigatory stop is less demanding than that for probable cause, the Fourth Amendment nevertheless requires an objective justification for such a stop. As a result, the officer in question "must be able to articulate more than an 'inchoate and unparticularized suspicion' or 'hunch' of criminal activity." *Illinois v. Wardlow,* 528 U.S. 119, 120 S.Ct. 673, 676, 145 L.Ed.2d 570 (2000). Rather, reasonable suspicion exists when an officer is

aware of specific, articulable facts which, when considered with objective and reasonable inferences, form a basis for *particularized* suspicion.

The requirement of *particularized* suspicion encompasses two elements. First, the assessment must be based upon the totality of the circumstances. Second, that assessment must arouse a reasonable suspicion that *the particular person being stopped* has committed or is about to commit a crime. Accordingly, we have rejected profiles that are "likely to sweep many ordinary citizens into a generality of suspicious appearance. . . ." *United States v. Rodriguez,* 976 F.2d 592, 595–96 (9th Cir. 1992) (concluding that the factors cited in the case—namely, a Hispanic man carefully driving an old Ford with a worn suspension who looked in his rear view mirror while being followed by agents in a marked car—described "too many individuals to create a reasonable suspicion that this particular defendant was engaged in criminal activity").

* * *

As noted above, the district court based its determination that reasonable suspicion existed on a series of factors: 1) the U-turn made before the checkpoint by the two cars; 2) the driving in tandem and the Mexicali license plates; 3) the area at which the U-turn occurred included a well-known drop-off point for smugglers; 4) the Hispanic appearance of the three defendants; and 5) Renteria-Wolff's picking up the newspaper after glancing back at the patrol cars. Although we agree with the district court that reasonable suspicion did exist to justify an investigatory stop, we conclude that some of the factors on which the district court relied are not relevant or appropriate to the reasonable suspicion analysis. We begin by considering the factors in that category, before turning to address those which the district court properly considered.

In concluding that reasonable suspicion existed, both the district court and the panel majority relied in part upon the Hispanic appearance of the three defendants. We hold that they erred in doing so. We first note that Agent Johnston testified at the suppression hearing that the majority of people who pass through the El Centro checkpoints are Hispanic, and thus, presumably have a Hispanic appearance.

As we stressed earlier, reasonable suspicion requires *particularized* suspicion. Where, as here, the majority (or any substantial number) of people share a specific characteristic, that characteristic is of little or no probative value in such a particularized and context-specific analysis. * * *

The likelihood that in an area in which the majority—or even a substantial part—of the population is Hispanic, any given person of Hispanic ancestry is in fact an alien, let alone an illegal alien, is not high enough to make Hispanic appearance a relevant factor in the reasonable suspicion calculus. As we have previously held, factors that have such a low probative value that no reasonable officer would have relied on them to make an investigative stop must be disregarded as a matter of law. Moreover, as we explain below, Hispanic appearance is not, in general, an appropriate factor.

* * *

In arriving at the dictum suggesting that ethnic appearance could be relevant, the Court [in *Brignoni-Ponce*] relied heavily on now-outdated demographic information. * * * *Brignoni-Ponce* was handed down in 1975, some twenty-five years ago. Current demographic data demonstrate that the statistical premises on which its dictum relies are no longer applicable. The Hispanic population of this nation, and of the Southwest and Far West in particular, has grown enormously—at least five-fold in the four states referred to in the Supreme Court's decision. * * *

One area where Hispanics are heavily in the majority is El Centro, the site of the vehicle stop. As Agent Johnson acknowledged, the majority of the people who pass through the El Centro checkpoint are Hispanic. His testimony is in turn corroborated by more general demographic data from that area. * * * [A]ccording to census data, five Southern California counties are home to more than a fifth of the nation's Hispanic population. * * * Accordingly, Hispanic appearance is of little or no use in determining which particular individuals among the vast Hispanic populace should be stopped by law enforcement officials on the lookout for illegal aliens. * * *[22]

Moreover, the demographic changes we describe have been accompanied by significant changes in the law restricting the use of race as a criterion in government decision-making. The use of race and ethnicity for such purposes has been severely limited. Relying on the principle that " '[o]ur Constitution is color-blind, and neither knows nor tolerates classes among citizens,' " *City of Richmond v. J.A. Croson Co.,* 488 U.S. 469, 521, 109 S.Ct. 706, 102 L.Ed.2d 854 (1989) (Scalia, J., concurring) (quoting *Plessy v. Ferguson,* 163 U.S. 537, 559, 16 S.Ct. 1138, 41 L.Ed. 256 (1896) (Harlan, J., dissenting)), the Supreme Court has repeatedly held that reliance "on racial or ethnic criteria must necessarily receive a most searching examination to make sure that it does not conflict with constitutional guarantees." *Wygant v. Jackson Bd. of Ed.,* 476 U.S. 267, 273, 106 S.Ct. 1842, 90 L.Ed.2d 260 (1986). In invalidating

---

[22] * * * Hispanic appearance, or any other racial or ethnic appearance, including Caucasian, may be considered when the suspected perpetrator of a specific offense has been identified as having such an appearance. Even in such circumstances, however, persons of a particular racial or ethnic group may not be stopped and questioned because of such appearance, unless there are other individualized or particularized factors which, together with the racial or ethnic appearance identified, rise to the level of reasonable suspicion or probable cause. To the extent that our prior cases have approved the use of Hispanic appearance as a factor where there was no particularized, individual suspicion, they are overruled. * * *

the use of racial classifications used to remedy past discrimination in *Croson*, the Court applied strict scrutiny, stating that its rigorousness would ensure that:

> the means chosen "fit" this compelling goal so closely that there is little or no possibility that the motive for the classification was illegitimate racial prejudice or stereotype. Classifications based on race carry a danger of stigmatic harm. Unless they are strictly reserved for remedial settings, they may in fact promote notions of racial inferiority and lead to a politics of racial hostility.

Croson, 488 U.S. at 493, 109 S.Ct. 706. The danger of stigmatic harm of the type that the Court feared overbroad affirmative action programs would pose is far more pronounced in the context of police stops in which race or ethnic appearance is a factor. So, too, are the consequences of "notions of racial inferiority" and the "politics of racial hostility" that the Court pointed to. Stops based on race or ethnic appearance send the underlying message to all our citizens that those who are not white are judged by the color of their skin alone. Such stops also send a clear message that those who are not white enjoy a lesser degree of constitutional protection—that they are in effect assumed to be potential criminals first and individuals second. It would be an anomalous result to hold that race may be considered when it harms people, but not when it helps them.

We decide no broad constitutional questions here. Rather, we are confronted with the narrow question of how to square the Fourth Amendment's requirement of individualized reasonable suspicion with the fact that the majority of the people who pass through the checkpoint in question are Hispanic. In order to answer that question, we conclude that, at this point in our nation's history, and given the continuing changes in our ethnic and racial composition, Hispanic appearance is, in general, of such little probative value that it may not be considered as a relevant factor where particularized or individualized suspicion is required. Moreover, we conclude, for the reasons we have indicated, that it is also not an appropriate factor.

* * *

In this case, the two cars driven in tandem by Montero-Camargo and Sanchez-Guillen made U-turns on a highway, at a place where the view of the border officials was obstructed, and stopped briefly at a locale historically used for illegal activities, before proceeding back in the direction from which they had come. The U-turn occurred at a location where it was unlikely that the cars would have reversed directions because they had missed an exit. Moreover, the vehicles in question bore Mexicali license plates and the U-turn occurred just after a sign indicating that a Border Patrol checkpoint that had been closed for some time was now open. We conclude that these factors, although not overwhelming, are sufficient to constitute reasonable suspicion for the stop. In reaching that result, however, we firmly reject any reliance upon the Hispanic appearance or ethnicity of the defendants. * * *

* * *

[The concurring opinion of KOZINSKI, CIRCUIT JUDGE, joined by JUDGES T.G. NELSON, KLEINFELD and SILVERMAN, is omitted.]

NOTES AND QUESTIONS ON ENFORCEMENT AND ETHNICITY

1. Why does Judge Reinhardt conclude in *Montero-Camargo* that "Hispanic appearance" is not a relevant factor in "reasonable suspicion"? Would he have reached the same result in a border area sparsely populated by Latinos? In *United States v. Manzo-Jurado*, 457 F.3d 928, 935 n.6 (9th Cir. 2006), the court noted that *Montero-Camargo* did not apply "because Havre, Montana, is sparsely populated with Hispanics" and "Hispanics comprise 1.5 percent of the Havre population." But the court concluded that even considering factors that *Montero-Camargo* disallows, Border Patrol agents had no reasonable basis for a particularized suspicion that the arrestees were in the United States unlawfully. Conversely, in *Montero-Camargo*, other factors made the stop lawful, in spite of impermissible reliance on "Hispanic appearance."

2. Writing broadly about profiling in law enforcement generally, Frank Wu has outlined a useful framework. The first question, he suggests, is whether law enforcement uses profiling based on race, ethnicity, or other factors. The second question is whether it is rational, *e.g.,* whether persons of Asian ancestry are more likely than Caucasians to be foreign-born. And the third is whether profiling, even if rational, is morally right. Wu emphasizes that the second and third questions are quite separate, so that racial profiling might be rational and yet wrong. *See generally* Frank H. Wu, Yellow: Race in America Beyond Black and White 173–213 (2002). *Cf.* Kevin R. Johnson, *The Case Against Racial Profiling in Immigration Enforcement*, 78 Wash. U.L.Q. 675, 728–29 (2000) (arguing that racial profiling in immigration enforcement and immigration admissions combine to "contribute to less than full membership in U.S. society for persons of Latin American ancestry").

3. In 2014, the Department of Justice issued guidance on the use of race, ethnicity, and other factors by federal law enforcement officers performing federal law enforcement activities, and by state and local law enforcement officers while participating in federal law enforcement task forces. It provides in part:

> In making routine or spontaneous law enforcement decisions, such as ordinary traffic stops, Federal law enforcement officers may not use race, ethnicity, gender, national origin, religion, sexual orientation, or gender identity to any degree, except that officers

may rely on the listed characteristics in a specific suspect description. This prohibition applies even where the use of a listed characteristic might otherwise be lawful.

In conducting all activities other than routine or spontaneous law enforcement activities, Federal law enforcement officers may consider race, ethnicity, gender, national origin, religion, sexual orientation, or gender identity only to the extent that there is trustworthy information, relevant to the locality or time frame, that links persons possessing a particular listed characteristic to an identified criminal incident, scheme, or organization, a threat to national or homeland security, a violation of Federal immigration law, or an authorized intelligence activity.

Department of Justice, *Guidance for Federal Law Enforcement Agencies Regarding the Use of Race, Ethnicity, Gender, National Origin, Religion, Sexual Orientation, or Gender Identity* 1–2 (2014). A footnote clarified:

* * * This Guidance does not apply to Federal non-law enforcement personnel, including U.S. military, intelligence, or diplomatic personnel, and their activities. In addition, this Guidance does not apply to interdiction activities in the vicinity of the border, or to protective, inspection, or screening activities. All such activities must be conducted consistent with the Constitution and applicable Federal law and policy, in a manner that respects privacy, civil rights and civil liberties, and subject to appropriate oversight.

Id. at 2 n.2.

(iii)   Remedies for Fourth Amendment Violations

Is evidence admissible in removal proceedings even if the government obtained it in violation of the Fourth Amendment? Generally yes, said the U.S. Supreme Court in *INS v. Lopez-Mendoza*, 468 U.S. 1032, 1043–50, 104 S.Ct. 3479, 82 L.Ed.2d 778 (1984). Distinguishing criminal prosecution, Justice O'Connor's majority opinion weighed "the likely social benefits of excluding unlawfully seized evidence against the likely costs." She was skeptical about the benefits of an exclusionary rule. She explained that deportation would still be possible in many cases without evidence derived from the arrest, that few officers would expect challenges to the circumstances of the arrest, that the government has its own scheme to deter Fourth Amendment violations, and that alternative private remedies are available. O'Connor noted that excluding evidence would have "unusual and significant" costs, including that it would "require the courts to close their eyes to ongoing violations of the law" and complicate the system of immigration proceedings.

Four Justices dissented. Justices Brennan and Marshall rejected the majority's balancing approach, arguing that "the basis of the exclusionary rule does not derive from its effectiveness as a deterrent, but is instead found in the requirements of the Fourth Amendment itself." Justice White, joined in substantial part by Justice Stevens, argued that "the costs and benefits of applying the exclusionary rule in civil deportation proceedings do not differ in any significant way from the costs and benefits of applying the rule in ordinary criminal proceedings."

In a part of the opinion joined by three other Justices, Justice O'Connor added:

> Our conclusions concerning the exclusionary rule's value might change, if there developed good reason to believe that Fourth Amendment violations by INS officers were widespread. Finally, we do not deal here with egregious violations of Fourth Amendment or other liberties that might transgress notions of fundamental fairness and undermine the probative value of the evidence obtained.

Id. at 1050–51, 104 S.Ct. at 3490.

Counting the four dissenters, eight justices seemed to recognize an egregious violation exception. In a removal proceeding, when might this exception support a motion to suppress unlawfully obtained evidence?

LOPEZ-RODRIGUEZ V. MUKASEY

United States Court of Appeals, Ninth Circuit, 2008.
536 F.3d 1012.

CANBY, CIRCUIT JUDGE.

* * *

In October 2000, the Immigration and Naturalization Service ("INS") received a tip that a female by the name of Fabiola was fraudulently using a birth certificate belonging to Sugeyra Torres-Carillo, a citizen of the United States, to obtain employment. The tip also indicated that the suspect lived at a specified address in Fresno, California. [Fabiola Gastelum-Lopez ("Gastelum") and Luz Lopez-Rodriguez ("Lopez")], niece and aunt, resided at that address. Gastelum was seventeen years old at the time.

Three INS agents decided to act on the tip and visit the residence to investigate the matter. They did not obtain an arrest or search warrant prior to conducting their visit. * * * Once inside, the three INS agents questioned Gastelum. They asked her whether she was "Sugeyra." She answered that she was. They asked her to provide the names of her parents. She complied. They asked her where she had been born, and she responded that she was born in Texas. They asked where in Texas she was born, and she did not reply. They asked, "Who is Fabiola?" She said she was Fabiola. They immediately handcuffed her. The agents also arrested Lopez on suspicion of being an alien unlawfully present in the United States.

While in INS custody, Gastelum and Lopez were questioned about, among other things, their country of origin and immigration status in the United States. On the basis of the information they obtained, the INS agents prepared individual Forms I–213, Record of Deportable/ Inadmissible Aliens, for Gastelum and Lopez. * * * According to the forms, both Gastelum and Lopez are natives and citizens of Mexico not authorized to be in the United States. The forms also show that neither Gastelum nor Lopez had a criminal record.

The INS agents also produced a Record of Sworn Statement by Gastelum. In her sworn statement, Gastelum acknowledged that she was a native and citizen of Mexico. She also admitted that she had received a birth certificate in the name of Sugeyra from a 43-year-old foreman, Francisco Lopez-Fuentes (Fuentes), who had supervised her when she worked in the fields. Fuentes did not ask Gastelum for any money in exchange for the birth certificate.

The government issued Notices to Appear in removal proceedings to both Gastelum and Lopez. In joint proceedings, Gastelum and Lopez moved to suppress the Forms I–213 as well as Gastelum's sworn statement. They submitted an affidavit by Gastelum asserting that she did not consent to the INS agents' entry into their home. In the Forms I– 213, the INS agents asserted that she had in fact consented. The IJ required Gastelum to testify at the removal hearing in support of her motion to suppress. She testified that, when the agents arrived, she was asleep in her bedroom. Her aunt Lopez woke her up to let her know that some individuals were calling her. Gastelum went to the door, which was "slightly open and not locked," "opened it a little more and . . . peeked outside." She saw two men standing outside the door. They asked her if her name was "Sugeyra." She did not open the door for them and did not allow them to enter. She testified that the two men pushed the door and entered, accompanied by a third, female agent. Once inside, the agents proceeded to interrogate her as described above. After Gastelum answered several questions and was being handcuffed, the INS agents finally identified themselves.

* * *

* * * We conclude that, on the facts developed before the IJ, the evidence of alienage[5] contained in these documents was obtained in

---

[5] "[T]he INS must show only identity and alienage; the burden then shifts to the respondent to prove the time, place, and manner of his entry." *INS v. Lopez-Mendoza,* 468 U.S. 1032, 1039, 104 S.Ct. 3479, 82 L.Ed.2d 778 (1984). Because the identity of an alien in removal proceedings is "never itself suppressible as a fruit of an unlawful arrest, even if it is conceded

violation of Gastelum's and Lopez's Fourth Amendment rights and that the violation was "egregious." Because the government did not produce any other evidence tending to show the petitioners' alienage in the proceedings before the IJ, we grant their petition for review and reverse the order of removal.

* * * The presumption of unconstitutionality that accompanies "the [warrantless] entry into a home to conduct a search or make an arrest" may be overcome only by showing "consent or exigent circumstances." *Steagald v. United States,* 451 U.S. 204, 211, 101 S.Ct. 1642, 68 L.Ed.2d 38 (1981).

The government does not dispute that the INS agents entered the residence of Gastelum and Lopez and, after briefly questioning Gastelum, arrested both in their home. It is also evident that, prior to entering the premises, the INS agents did not obtain a warrant to arrest either Gastelum or Lopez or, for that matter, to conduct a search of their residence. The government makes no claim of exigent circumstances. Thus, in order to overcome the presumption of unconstitutionality attaching to the agents' entry, the government must show that the petitioners gave legally sufficient consent.

* * *

* * * As we have made clear, "the government may not show consent to enter from the defendant's failure to object to the entry." *United States v. Shaibu,* 920 F.2d 1423, 1427 (9th Cir. 1990). We have sustained an *inference* of consent to enter a residence only under very limited circumstances—i.e., where the officers have verbally requested permission to enter and the occupant's action suggests assent, or where prior collaborative interactions between the suspect and the officers make the inference of consent unequivocal. Here, there is no indication that the officers made any request to enter or that Gastelum collaborated with the INS officers in any way when they were at the door. Accordingly, the bare fact that Gastelum neither refused to speak to them nor ordered them to leave after they pushed the door open and entered her home is insufficient to establish consent. As a consequence, the arrest of the petitioners in their home violated their Fourth Amendment rights.

* * *

The statements sought to be suppressed were obtained from Gastelum and Lopez in the custody immediately following the unconstitutional entry of their residence. The government has made no attempt to bear its burden of showing any change in circumstances or attenuation that would prevent the statements from qualifying as fruits

---

that an unlawful arrest, search, or interrogation occurred," *id.,* the only suppressible evidence at issue here is that pertaining to alienage.

of the Fourth Amendment violation. The statements would therefore be excludible in a criminal case. In the present proceeding, however, we must next consider whether "the violations were sufficiently egregious to warrant the application of the exclusionary rule in these civil deportation proceedings." *Orhorhaghe* [*v. INS*, 38 F.3d 488, 501 (9th Cir. 1994).] A Fourth Amendment violation is "egregious" if "evidence is obtained by deliberate violations of the [F]ourth [A]mendment, or by conduct a *reasonable officer should [have known]* is in violation of the Constitution." *Gonzalez-Rivera v. INS,* 22 F.3d 1441, 1449 (9th Cir. 1994) * * *

Few principles in criminal procedure are as well established as the maxim that "the Fourth Amendment has drawn a firm line at the entrance to the house. * * * As we have already noted, in keeping with the narrow scope of the consent exception, we "ha[ve] never sanctioned entry to the home based on inferred consent" in the absence of a request by the officers or ongoing, affirmative cooperation by the suspect. *Shaibu,* 920 F.2d at 1426. * * *

Against this unequivocal doctrinal backdrop, reasonable officers would not have thought it lawful to push open the door to petitioners' home simply because Gastelum did not "tell them to leave or [that] she did not want to talk to them." * * * Nor has the government pointed to any authority in our Fourth Amendment jurisprudence suggesting that the warrant requirement applies with any less force in the administrative context. We conclude that reasonable INS agents should have known that they were violating the Fourth Amendment when they entered Gastelum's and Lopez's residence. * * * Thus, the INS agents' Fourth Amendment violation was "egregious" under this Circuit's controlling interpretation of the term. The fruits of the constitutional violation accordingly should have been suppressed.

* * *

BYBEE, CIRCUIT JUDGE, concurring:

I concur fully in the majority opinion. I write separately to caution that our precedent has set us on a collision course with the Supreme Court.

* * *

* * * In our circuit, the exclusionary rule must be applied in a deportation proceeding if the agents violated the Fourth Amendment and "the agents committed the violations deliberately or by conduct a reasonable officer should have known would violate the Constitution." *Orhorhaghe,* 38 F.3d at 493. If I am reading our decisions correctly, we have linked the exclusionary rule in civil cases to the qualified immunity standard: any constitutional violation for which an officer would lose immunity from suit is sufficient to trigger the exclusionary rule in a civil

deportation proceeding. Regardless of how we arrived at this definition of "egregious," it is a definition of an exception that is almost certain, over time, to swallow up the rule. Moreover, I suspect it is a definition which might even include the unseemly conduct of the INS agents in *Lopez-Mendoza,* which the Court held did *not* warrant applying the exclusionary rule in that petitioner's immigration proceedings.

* * * Our case law appears destined to import the exclusionary rule, with all of its attendant costs, back into immigration proceedings, after the Court has taken it out. * * *

NOTES AND QUESTIONS ON REMEDIES FOR FOURTH AMENDMENT VIOLATIONS

1.   As the court observes in its footnote 5, *Lopez-Mendoza* made clear that motions to suppress cannot be used to exclude the identity of the respondent in a removal proceeding, but rather must seek to exclude or suppress specific evidence, such as evidence of alienage, which is essential to establishing removability.

2.   Some Ninth Circuit decisions have granted suppression motions based on egregious violations when the enforcement was based on apparent ethnicity. For example, *Gonzalez-Rivera v. INS*, 22 F.3d 1441, 1449 (9th Cir. 1994), suppressed evidence from a vehicle stop based *solely* on the passengers' Hispanic appearance. The court held that this was an egregious Fourth Amendment violation because it was committed in bad faith when the law enforcement officer knew or reasonably should have known that his conduct would violate the Constitution. Another Ninth Circuit decision, *Orhorhaghe v. INS*, 38 F.3d 488, 501–04 (9th Cir. 1994), found it egregious to investigate a noncitizen because of his "Nigerian-sounding name" and then seize him outside of his apartment and conduct a nonconsensual, warrantless entry. Second Circuit decisions have indicated that race-based violations would be considered egregious. *See, e.g., Pinto-Montoya v. Mukasey*, 540 F.3d 126, 131 (2d Cir. 2008).

3.   In a footnote to his concurrence in *Lopez-Rodriguez*, Judge Bybee observed that other circuits recognizing the egregious violation exception read it more narrowly. Consider this critique from the Fourth Circuit, which joined the Second, Third, and Eighth Circuits in rejecting the approach in *Lopez-Rodriguez*:

> The Ninth Circuit's approach requires a suppression hearing any time an alien alleges that the law enforcement officers acted in bad faith. This sets the evidentiary proffer bar too low. * * * It is easy to see how the bad faith standard can be manipulated by clever lawyers and encourages aliens to file frivolous improper motivation claims. Thus, we see the Ninth Circuit's standard as stymieing, rather than promoting, the streamlined nature of the removal hearing process as recognized by the Court in *Lopez-Mendoza*.

Relatedly, the Ninth Circuit's standard runs the risk of routinely requiring the arresting law enforcement officer to appear at a suppression hearing to testify concerning motivation, which the Court noted in *Lopez-Mendoza* would unacceptably burden the administration of the immigration laws.

The Ninth Circuit's standard is inconsistent with *Lopez-Mendoza* on another front. The cases cited by the *Lopez-Mendoza* Court in support of the egregiousness exception * * * turned on the *conduct* of the law enforcement officers not on the *knowledge* or *intent* of the law enforcement officers. * * * Yet, the Ninth Circuit's standard permits the application of the exclusionary rule in a removal proceeding any time law enforcement officers knowingly or intend to violate the Fourth Amendment regardless of the severity of their conduct. Eliminating the severity of the law enforcement officers' conduct essentially guts the definition of egregiousness envisioned by the Court in *Lopez-Mendoza*.

The Ninth Circuit's approach faces another obstacle as well. * * * [It] allows law enforcement officers a free pass any time they unconstitutionally act pursuant to an agency regulation. * * *

In our view, the sounder egregiousness approach is the totality of the circumstances standard * * *. * * * Factors a court may consider include: (1) whether the Fourth Amendment violation was intentional; (2) whether the violation was unreasonable in addition to being illegal; (3) whether there were threats, coercion, physical abuse, promises, or an unreasonable show of force by the law enforcement officers; (4) whether there was no articulable suspicion for the search or seizure whatsoever; (5) where, when, and how the search, seizure or questioning took place; (6) whether the search, seizure, or questioning was particularly lengthy; (7) whether the law enforcement officers procured an arrest or search warrant; (8) any unique characteristics of the alien involved; and (9) whether the violation was based on racial considerations. * * * Suppression hearings should be the exception, not the rule in removal proceedings * * *.

Yanez-Marquez v. Lynch, 789 F.3d 434, 459–61 (4th Cir. 2015). *See also Maldonado v. Holder*, 763 F.3d 155, 160 (2d Cir. 2014); *Lopez-Fernandez v. Holder*, 735 F.3d 1043, 1046–48 (8th Cir. 2013); *Cotzojay v. Holder*, 725 F.3d 172, 180–83 (2d Cir. 2013); *Oliva-Ramos v. Att'y Gen.*, 694 F.3d 259, 279 (3d Cir. 2012). *Cf. Almeida-Amaral v. Gonzales*, 461 F.3d 231, 237 (2d Cir. 2006) ("Because of the absence of evidence that the stop was race-based, we conclude that Almeida-Amaral has not established that the Fourth Amendment violation was an egregious one.").

Was there an egregious violation on the facts in *Lopez-Rodriguez* under the Fourth Circuit's approach? Which is a better approach to the egregious violation exception? Which is more faithful to *Lopez-Mendoza*?

4. Justice O'Connor wrote in *Lopez-Mendoza*: "Our conclusions concerning the exclusionary rule's value might change, if there developed good reason to believe that Fourth Amendment violations by INS officers were widespread." For an argument based on this statement for applying the exclusionary rule to removal proceedings, see Stella Burch Elias, *"Good Reason to Believe": Widespread Constitutional Violations in the Course of Immigration Enforcement and the Case for Revisiting* Lopez-Mendoza, 2008 Wis. L. Rev. 1109. *See Oliva-Ramos*, at 279–82 ("most constitutional violations that are part of a pattern of widespread violations of the Fourth Amendment would also satisfy the test for an egregious violation"; remanding to decide if violations were widespread).

5. DHS regulations provide as follows:

(1) Interrogation is questioning designed to elicit specific information. An immigration officer, like any other person, has the right to ask questions of anyone as long as the immigration officer does not restrain the freedom of an individual, not under arrest, to walk away.

(2) If the immigration officer has a reasonable suspicion, based on specific articulable facts, that the person being questioned is, or is attempting to be, engaged in an offense against the United States or is an alien illegally in the United States, the immigration officer may briefly detain the person for questioning.

(3) Information obtained from this questioning may provide the basis for a subsequent arrest * * * .

8 C.F.R. § 287.8(b).

Evidence obtained in violation of this regulation or others can be suppressed, according to the BIA in *Matter of Garcia-Flores*, 17 I & N Dec. 325, 327 (BIA 1980), if the regulation was promulgated to benefit the alien and the violation resulted in prejudice.

6. For a discussion of the exercise of prosecutorial discretion to administratively close removal cases in which Fourth Amendment violations occurred but suppression of unlawfully obtained evidence is unavailable, see Jason A. Cade, *Policing the Immigration Police: ICE Prosecutorial Discretion and the Fourth Amendment*, 113 Colum. L. Rev. Sidebar 180 (2013).

7. Suppose federal immigration officers raid a workplace after receiving a tip about unauthorized workers from the employer, who wanted to disrupt union organizing, in clear violation of federal labor law. Should the evidence obtained in the raid be suppressed when the apprehended workers are put in removal hearings? Here is one answer:

Beyond violations of the Fourth Amendment, it is clear from *Lopez-Mendoza* that the exclusionary rule is applicable, if at all, only to deprivations that affect the fairness or reliability of the deportation proceeding. However, there is nothing inherently unfair about utilizing evidence obtained during a labor dispute, nor does the existence of a labor dispute make that evidence any less reliable. Thus, this case does not present us with the type of situation to which the exclusionary rule even arguably is applicable.

Montero v. INS, 124 F.3d 381, 386 (2d Cir. 1997).

The federal government apparently did not know of the labor dispute when it began to investigate unauthorized workers at the worksite, but then learned before the raid that the tip came from the employer. What if the government had known this from the start? Or should immigration officers stay away from worksites with labor disputes altogether?

In 2014, the Interagency Working Group for the Consistent Enforcement of Federal Labor, Employment and Immigration Laws, composed of DOL, DHS, Department of Justice, Equal Employment Opportunity Commission and the National Labor Relations Board, was formed with these goals:

> to ensure that workers who cooperate with labor and employment enforcement may continue to do so without fear of retaliation, to ensure that unscrupulous parties do not attempt to misuse immigration enforcement or labor laws to thwart or manipulate worker protections or labor and immigration enforcement, and to ensure the effective enforcement of these laws.

See Interagency Working Group for the Consistent Enforcement of Federal Labor, Employment and Immigration Laws Outlines Progress, 92 Interp. Rel. 2270 (2015).

Compare article 36 of the Vienna Convention on Consular Relations, April 24, 1963, 21 U.S.T. 77, 5596 U.N.T.S. 261, which requires notification of an arrest to consular officials of the arrested noncitizen's home country. The U.S. Supreme Court declined to adopt suppression of evidence as a remedy for a violation in *Sanchez-Llamas v. Oregon*, 548 U.S. 331, 343–50, 126 S.Ct. 2669, 2677–82, 165 L.Ed.2d 557 (2006).

b. Interrogations

Under the famous case of *Miranda v. Arizona*, 384 U.S. 436, 86 S.Ct. 1602, 16 L.Ed.2d 694 (1966), the government's failure to inform an individual who is in custody of her rights to remain silent and to have a lawyer renders any statements she makes during a custodial interrogation inadmissible in her criminal trial. The courts have not read the Constitution to require such warnings in the removal context. Under current law, failure to give warnings means that any admissions by the noncitizen could be excluded from subsequent criminal proceedings, but the admissions would not be excluded automatically from the removal proceeding itself. *See, e.g., Bustos-Torres v. INS*, 898 F.2d 1053, 1056–57 (5th Cir. 1990).

This conclusion, like *Lopez-Mendoza*, relies heavily on the characterization of removal proceedings as civil rather than criminal, as well as on the following considerations:

> A principal purpose of the *Miranda* warnings is to permit the suspect to make an intelligent decision as to whether to answer the government agent's questions. In deportation proceedings, however—in light of the alien's burden of proof, the requirement that the alien answer non-incriminating questions, the potential adverse consequences to the alien of remaining silent, and the fact that an alien's statement is admissible in the deportation hearing despite his lack of counsel at the preliminary interrogation—*Miranda* warnings would be not only inappropriate but could also serve to mislead the alien.

Chavez-Raya v. INS, 519 F.2d 397, 402 (7th Cir. 1975).

The current regulations provide:

> Except in the case of an alien subject to the expedited removal provisions of section 235(b)(1)(A) of the Act, an alien arrested without warrant and placed in formal proceedings under section 238 or 240 of the Act will be advised of the reasons for his or her arrest and the right to be represented at no expense to the Government. The examining officer will provide the alien with a list of the available free legal services provided by organizations and attorneys qualified under 8 CFR part 1003 and organizations recognized under § 292.2 of this chapter or 8 CFR 1292.2 that are located in the district where the hearing will be held. The examining officer shall note on Form I–862 [Notice to Appear] that such a list was provided to the alien. The officer will also advise the alien that any statement made may be used against him or her in a subsequent proceeding.

8 C.F.R. § 287.3(c). Interestingly, however, the regulation also requires a notation on the Notice to Appear [NTA] that a list of free legal services was provided to the alien. This seems to presuppose that the list is provided before the NTA is filed. However, to the extent that "formal proceedings" commence with the filing of the NTA in immigration court, this regulation suggests that notifications are required only after the NTA is filed, and the BIA so held in *Matter of E-R-M-F- & A-S-M-*, 25 I & N Dec. 580, 582 (BIA 2011).

Whether warnings are given or not, the courts and the BIA will sometimes order the exclusion of prior statements on due process grounds in several types of situations: (1) where the government's behavior violated fundamental fairness, (2) the circumstances of the interrogation rendered the statements involuntary, or (3) the noncitizen was prejudiced by the government's violation of regulations promulgated for his benefit.

See Singh v. Mukasey, 553 F.3d 207, 214–16 (2d Cir. 2009) (excluding a statement signed after a four-hour interrogation in the middle of the night, under repeated threats of imprisonment and without an opportunity to read the statement before signing); *Navia-Duran v. INS*, 568 F.2d 803, 805 (1st Cir. 1977); *Matter of Garcia*, 17 I & N Dec. 319, 321 (BIA 1980).

For suppression motions, does the inquiry into fundamental fairness, by being more flexible, provide a better accommodation between law enforcement needs and the rights of noncitizens than application of a strict *Miranda* rule?

c. Other Constitutional Violations and Remedies

Enforcement efforts must not violate equal protection. This is the key issue in the next case, which does not involve suppression of evidence but instead is a civil suit under 42 U.S.C. § 1983 seeking damages from government officials for violating an individual's constitutional rights.

FARM LABOR ORGANIZING COMMITTEE V. OHIO STATE HIGHWAY PATROL

United States Court of Appeals, Sixth Circuit, 2002.
308 F.3d 523.

MOORE, CIRCUIT JUDGE.

* * *

Plaintiffs Jose Aguilar and Irma Esparza ("plaintiffs") are lawfully admitted permanent resident aliens. On Sunday, March 26, 1995, Aguilar and Esparza were driving from their home in Chicago, Illinois, to Toledo, Ohio, to visit family members. During this trip, an Ohio State Highway Patrol ("OSHP") trooper, Kevin Kiefer, stopped Aguilar and Esparza for driving with a faulty headlight. After the plaintiffs pulled over, Trooper Kiefer approached the plaintiffs' car and asked to see Aguilar's driver's license. Aguilar provided Trooper Kiefer with a valid Illinois driver's license. Trooper Kiefer then ordered Aguilar out of the car and placed him in the back of his cruiser.

Almost immediately thereafter, a second OSHP cruiser arrived. A trooper from the second cruiser walked a drug-sniffing dog around the outside of the plaintiffs' vehicle. The dog "alerted," indicating that the vehicle contained narcotics.[2]

The second trooper then asked Esparza for identification. She offered the trooper an Illinois identification card, but the trooper reportedly grabbed her wallet and removed her green card. The trooper then

---

[2] It was later determined that the dog had alerted in error, and that neither of the plaintiffs were carrying drugs.

instructed Esparza to step out of the vehicle. She was locked in the back of Trooper Kiefer's cruiser next to Aguilar. Trooper Kiefer then demanded to see Aguilar's green card. The green cards of both Aguilar and Esparza were valid and in force at the time of this encounter.

After examining the green cards, the troopers asked Aguilar and Esparza where they had obtained their green cards and whether they had paid for them. The troopers were attempting to inquire whether the documents were forged, since green cards are not offered for sale. Aguilar and Esparza speak limited English, however, and believed that the troopers were asking whether they had paid the required processing fees. They responded that they had paid for the cards, meaning that they had paid all required fees. Trooper Kiefer interpreted the plaintiffs' response as an indication that the cards were likely forged, and retained the green cards for authentication.

Trooper Kiefer was unable to contact the INS to verify the authenticity of plaintiffs' green cards at the time of the encounter, because it was a Sunday, so he took the green cards and let the plaintiffs go. * * *

The next day (Monday), the plaintiffs retained an attorney. That day, paralegal Arturo Ortiz contacted the OSHP on behalf of Aguilar and Esparza, but was unable to obtain assistance because he lacked information regarding the incident. On Thursday, Ortiz again contacted OSHP and spoke to Trooper Kiefer. Kiefer returned the green cards personally that same day, four days after the initial seizure. When asked in his deposition why it took so long to verify the green cards, Trooper Kiefer explained that he had taken a few days off from work and was unable to reach the INS during that time.

The plaintiffs contend that Trooper Kiefer's actions were, in part, the product of a pattern and practice by the OSHP of questioning motorists about their immigration status on the basis of their Hispanic appearance. From the record, it appears that the OSHP—particularly its Traffic and Drug Interdiction Team (TDIT)—began taking a more active role in immigration enforcement in 1995. Pursuant to this role, OSHP troopers have been known to inquire into motorists' immigration status during routine traffic stops. When these inquiries lead an OSHP trooper to conclude that an individual may be an illegal immigrant, the trooper will contact the Border Patrol and detain the suspect until the Border Patrol arrives. * * * Although the OSHP maintains that it does not do so frequently, troopers sometimes seize alien registration cards of suspected illegal immigrants and deliver them to federal authorities.

* * *

Plaintiffs allege that Trooper Kiefer violated their rights under the Equal Protection Clause of the Fourteenth Amendment by targeting them for investigation concerning immigration status and seizing their green cards because of their Hispanic appearance. * * * Trooper Kiefer contends that he is entitled to qualified immunity because the undisputed facts show that his inquiries into the plaintiffs' immigration status were motivated by the plaintiffs' difficulties speaking and understanding English, which he contends is a legitimate race-neutral reason for the investigative steps taken.

* * * The plaintiffs allege that Trooper Kiefer singled them out for inquiry into their immigration status on the basis of their Hispanic appearance during the course of a lawful traffic stop. The plaintiffs do not challenge the validity of their initial stop for a faulty headlight. Nor do they assert that the questioning exceeded the permissible scope of the stop under the Fourth Amendment. Nevertheless, as this court has recognized, "[t]he Equal Protection Clause of the Fourteenth Amendment provides citizens a degree of protection independent of the Fourth Amendment protection against unreasonable searches and seizures." *United States v. Avery,* 137 F.3d 343, 352 (6th Cir. 1997). Similarly, the Supreme Court, in *Whren v. United States,* confirmed that an officer's discriminatory motivations for pursuing a course of action can give rise to an Equal Protection claim, even where there are sufficient objective indicia of suspicion to justify the officer's actions under the Fourth Amendment * * * . 517 U.S. 806, 813, 116 S.Ct. 1769, 135 L.Ed.2d 89 (1996). Therefore, if the plaintiffs can show that they were subjected to unequal treatment based upon their race or ethnicity during the course of an otherwise lawful traffic stop, that would be sufficient to demonstrate a violation of the Equal Protection Clause. *Cf. United States v. Montero-Camargo,* 208 F.3d 1122, 1135 (9th Cir.) (*en banc*) (holding that equal protection principles precluded use of Hispanic appearance as a relevant factor for Fourth Amendment individualized suspicion requirement), *cert. denied,* 531 U.S. 889, 121 S.Ct. 211, 148 L.Ed.2d 148 (2000).

The Supreme Court has explained that a claimant alleging selective enforcement of facially neutral criminal laws must demonstrate that the challenged law enforcement practice "had a discriminatory effect and that it was motivated by a discriminatory purpose." *Wayte v. United States,* 470 U.S. 598, 608, 105 S.Ct. 1524, 84 L.Ed.2d 547 (1985). "To establish discriminatory effect in a race case, the claimant must show that similarly situated individuals of a different race were not prosecuted." *United States v. Armstrong,* 517 U.S. 456, 465, 116 S.Ct. 1480, 134 L.Ed.2d 687 (1996). * * * Determining whether official action was motivated by intentional discrimination "demands a sensitive inquiry into such circumstantial and direct evidence of intent as may be available." *Village of Arlington Heights v. Metro. Hous. Dev. Corp.,* 429 U.S. 252, 266,

97 S.Ct. 555, 50 L.Ed.2d 450 (1977). "[A]n invidious discriminatory purpose may often be inferred from the totality of the relevant facts, including the fact, if it is true, that the [practice] bears more heavily on one race than another." *Washington v. Davis,* 426 U.S. 229, 242, 96 S.Ct. 2040, 48 L.Ed.2d 597 (1976).

* * *

In its April 20, 2000, order, the district court determined that the plaintiffs had presented sufficient evidence to prove the requisite facts for a prima facie case of intentional discrimination under the selective prosecution framework. * * * The court noted that the record contained a range of circumstantial evidence supporting such a finding of intent. Perhaps most significantly, the court cited the deposition testimony of Kiefer and other OSHP officials:

> Trooper Kiefer . . . testified that when he found Hispanic passengers hiding under a blanket, he called the Border Patrol, but that if he found white people hiding under a blanket, he would not. Sgt. Elling likewise testified that he would not call the Border Patrol regarding a motorist . . . unless ["he] would think that they would probably be Hispanic in nature." And Trooper Pahl admitted that she once had contacted the Border Patrol after coming across two Hispanic men whose car had broken down, but that she wouldn't do the same for a white man.

The court also cited additional circumstantial evidence of discriminatory intent. The court noted that over ninety percent of OSHP's immigration inquiries concerned Hispanic motorists. The court also appears to have credited plaintiffs' argument that "[g]iven defendants' admitted lack of training in the identification of illegal immigrants, the only reasoned basis on which to question a motorist about immigration status . . . is the motorist's Hispanic appearance coupled with indicators of Hispanic ethnicity." * * *

As to the discriminatory effect prong, the district court observed that "[t]he burden rests on plaintiffs to show, by a preponderance of the evidence, that they were treated differently than similarly situated non-minorities." The court considered, and rejected, defendants' argument that "no evidence presented thus far indicates that Hispanic motorists are treated differently than non-Hispanic motorists." * * * The district court noted that "most motorists . . . [who were] asked about their green cards were Hispanic-looking" and defendants' misinformation and lack of training concerning what facts give rise to reasonable suspicion of immigration violations.

* * *

* * * The selective enforcement framework does not require a plaintiff to show that the defendant had *no* race-neutral reasons for the challenged enforcement decision. Instead, it is enough to show that the challenged action was taken "at least *in part* 'because of' . . . its adverse effects upon an identifiable group." *Wayte,* 470 U.S. at 610, 105 S.Ct. 1524 (quoting *Feeney,* 442 U.S. at 279, 99 S.Ct. 2282).

* * *

[W]e disagree with Trooper Kiefer's contention that the plaintiffs' difficulty speaking English necessarily establishes a valid race-neutral basis for initiating an immigration investigation. Kiefer relies on *United States v. Ortiz,* 422 U.S. 891, 897, 95 S.Ct. 2585, 45 L.Ed.2d 623 (1975), in which Supreme Court identified one's "inability to speak English" as one of many factors that may be taken into account in deciding whether there is probable cause to search a private vehicle for illegal aliens. * * *

We think *Ortiz* provides little guidance in the instant case. *Ortiz* was a Fourth Amendment case involving automobile searches at a Border Patrol checkpoint less than 100 miles from the U.S.-Mexican border. The respondent in *Ortiz* did not raise a Fourteenth Amendment claim and the Court mentioned the use of one's English-speaking ability as a basis for selection only once in a laundry list of factors that might be used in deciding whether there is probable cause to refer an automobile for further inspection. * * * Moreover, the Supreme Court has cautioned against extending the logic of border enforcement cases to situations remote from the border, where the government interest in immigration policing may be less compelling. *See United States v. Martinez-Fuerte,* 428 U.S. 543, 564 n.17, 96 S.Ct. 3074, 49 L.Ed.2d 1116 (1976); *accord United States v. Brignoni-Ponce,* 422 U.S. 873, 881, 95 S.Ct. 2574, 45 L.Ed.2d 607 (1975).

The Supreme Court did consider the equal protection implications of using language as a basis for selection in *Hernandez v. New York,* 500 U.S. 352, 111 S.Ct. 1859, 114 L.Ed.2d 395 (1991). In *Hernandez,* the Court cautioned that when a government official uses as a criterion for decision a person's ability to speak a *particular* language that is closely associated with a specific ethnic group, that fact may "raise . . . a plausible, though not a necessary, inference that language might be a pretext for what in fact were race-based" actions. *Id.* at 363, 111 S.Ct. 1859. * * *

Considering *Ortiz* in light of *Hernandez,* we think that an officer's reliance upon a suspect's *inability to speak English* may be a proper race-neutral factor, but that fact questions as to pretext are necessarily present where an officer acts based upon the fact that a suspect speaks *Spanish* due to the close connection between the Spanish language and a specific ethnic community, such as the large migrant labor community in

Northwest Ohio. In light of this principle, it may be that genuine issues of material fact exist as to whether Trooper Kiefer's reliance on plaintiffs' inability to speak English was a legitimate race-neutral reason or a mere pretext for discrimination. * * *

[The court found that the relevant law was clearly established at the time of the encounter, and that therefore the district court correctly denied Kiefer's motion for summary judgment on his qualified immunity defense to the plaintiffs' equal protection claims. The court then found that Kiefer violated the plaintiffs' Fourth Amendment rights by detaining their green cards for four days without probable cause, that this law was clearly established, and that therefore the district court properly denied his summary judgment motion on qualified immunity as to these claims.]

* * *

KENNEDY, CIRCUIT JUDGE, dissenting.

* * *

[T]he majority would adopt a standard shifting to the defendant the burden of establishing that the same decision would have resulted even if the impermissible purpose had not been considered, relying on *Wayte* and *Armstrong*. The effect of the majority's holding would greatly diminish the protection of qualified immunity in equal protection claims. It would be a rare case involving a minority where plaintiff could not assert an issue of fact as to an officer's intent no matter how strong the non-discriminatory motive may be. * * *

* * *

NOTES AND QUESTIONS ON OTHER CONSTITUTIONAL VIOLATIONS

1.　As the Sixth Circuit notes in *Farm Labor Organizing Committee*, asserting an equal protection violation allowed plaintiffs to rely on evidence of an officer's subjective intent that would not support a Fourth Amendment claim.

2.　Suppression of evidence would have been no remedy at all in *Farm Labor Organizing Committee*, so plaintiffs pursued another remedy, seeking an award of damages for the constitutional violation. Other remedies include *Bivens* suits directly against a federal officer in his private capacity for the violation of an individual's constitutional rights, also resulting in a damages award if successful. *See Bivens v. Six Unknown Agents of the Federal Bureau of Narcotics*, 403 U.S. 388, 91 S.Ct. 1999, 29 L.Ed.2d 619 (1971). Another potential remedy is an action under the Federal Tort Claims Act, 28 U.S.C. §§ 1346(b), 2671–2680. Attorneys' fees may be available in lawsuits successfully seeking some of these remedies.

3. Another possible remedy is injunctive relief. For example, a class action against the Sheriff Joe Arpaio and his office in Maricopa County, Arizona, resulted in a permanent injunction against defendants, based on Fourth Amendment and equal protection violations. The key findings supporting the injunction were various types and instances of intentional discrimination in investigating and detaining Latino motor vehicle occupants, when they were suspected of being in the United States unlawfully. *See Melendres v. Arpaio*, 989 F. Supp. 2d 822, 891–910 (D. Ariz. 2013), *aff'd in part, vacated in part*, 784 F.3d 1254 (9th Cir. 2015). *See also DOJ Civil Rights Division Settles Several Claims Against Maricopa County, Arizona and Sheriff Joseph Arpaio; Negotiations Continue*, 92 Interp. Rel. 1351 (2015).

3.   IMMIGRATION LAW AS ANTI-TERRORISM LAW

a.   Responses to September 11

Starting right after the attacks of September 11, 2001, the U.S. government adopted a variety of anti-terrorism initiatives. For example, the Department of Justice set out to interview about 7,600 nonimmigrants, focusing on Middle Eastern men ages 18 to 46, to discover what knowledge these interviewees had of terrorists and planned terrorist activities.

Other initiatives reflected the exercise of government discretion in immigration law enforcement. In October 2001 Attorney General Ashcroft announced that the Department of Justice would, as an antiterrorism strategy, detain and remove noncitizens for minor immigration violations. Several measures included a focus on noncitizens from predominantly Arab or Muslim countries. For example, the DHS announced in May 2003 that it would search for noncitizens who had violated the terms of their student visas, concentrating on potential national security risks, defined partly by nationality. Many hundreds of noncitizens were arrested and detained on the basis of generally minor crimes and immigration violations, but with the apparent purpose of preventing further acts of terrorism and aiding in the investigation of acts of terrorism that had already occurred. Many of these detainees were held for long periods, even exceeding one year.

Starting in September 2002, the National Security Entry-Exit Registration System (NSEERS) required certain nonimmigrants from listed countries (and some nonimmigrants from other countries as well, identified by individual characteristics deemed to signal risk) who arrive at U.S. ports of entry to undergo "special registration." As outlined in Chapter Six, special registration was designed to subject their stay in the United States to greater scrutiny than normal. In November 2002, NSEERS expanded to include individuals already in the United States through "call-in registration." This part of NSEERS was limited to certain nonimmigrant males at least 16 years of age who were nationals of 25 listed countries—all predominantly Arab or Muslim, plus North Korea. Registrants were photographed, fingerprinted, interviewed under oath, and sometimes asked for credit card and banking information, and personal information, for example about political groups, places of worship, and roommates. Noncompliance with the call-in was deemed a deportable failure to maintain nonimmigrant status under INA § 237(a)(1)(C)(i), as well as a criminal violation under § 266.

Of about 84,000 noncitizens who complied with call-in registration, almost 14,000 were unlawfully present and faced removal proceedings as a result of the program. *See* U.S. Immigration and Customs Enforcement, Changes to National Security Entry/Exit Registration System (NSEERS) (2006). Implementation appeared to be uneven, especially for registrants with minor violations or approvable pending applications for lawful status. In some districts, these individuals were free to go, but about 2900 of them were detained, sometimes for long periods in squalid isolation. *See* Dan Eggen & Nurith C. Aizenman, *Registration Stirs Panic, Worry*, Washington Post, Jan. 10, 2003. The government reported that call-in registration identified 11 noncitizens with links to terrorism, plus about 400 persons sought on criminal charges or barred from the United States. *See* Rachel L. Swarns, *More Than 13,000 May Face Deportation*, N.Y. Times, June 7, 2003. Call-in registration was terminated in December 2003, and the other reporting and review requirements were greatly scaled back at that time. The entire NSEERS program was ended in April 2011.

Very soon after the post-September 11 detentions began, allegations surfaced that the detainees were being mistreated. Two reports by the Office of the Inspector General of the Department of Justice on the treatment of detainees at the special high-security unit, known as the ADMAX SHU, at the Metropolitan Detention Center in Brooklyn detailed prolonged detention as well as patterns of physical and verbal abuse by guards that included: (1) slamming detainees against walls; (2) bending or twisting detainees' arms, hands, wrists, and fingers; (3) lifting restrained detainees off the ground by their arms, and pulling their arms and handcuffs; (4) stepping on detainees' leg restraint chains; and (5) using restraints improperly. Office of the Inspector General, Department of Justice, Supplemental Report on September 11 Detainees' Allegations of Abuse at the Metropolitan Detention Center in Brooklyn, NY 6 (2003); *see also* Office of the Inspector General, Department of Justice, The September 11 Detainees: A Review of the Treatment of Aliens Held on Immigration Charges in Connection with the Investigation of the September 11 Attacks (2003).

Some of the abused detainees sued the federal government and numerous federal officials, seeking damages for violations of rights under the First (freedom of speech and free exercise of religion), Fourth, Fifth (due process), and Fourteenth (equal protection) Amendments and claims under the Federal Tort Claims Act. In 2009, five of the plaintiffs agreed to a $1.26 million settlement against the federal government. *See* Nina Bernstein, *U.S. to Pay $1.2 Million to 5 Detainees Over Abuse Lawsuit*, N.Y. Times, Nov. 3, 2009, at A22. As we go to press in late spring 2016, litigation by other plaintiffs suing for damages is continuing, *see Turkmen v. Hasty*, 789 F.3d 218 (2d Cir.), *rehearing en banc denied*, 808 F.3d 197 (2d Cir. 2015).

b. Historical Background

U.S. history includes precedents for focusing immigration law enforcement on noncitizens from certain countries. In November 1979, a crowd of militant student followers of the Ayatollah Khomeini stormed the U.S. Embassy in Tehran, Iran. They took hostage over 60 Americans and held over 50 of them for 444 days, with backing from the government of Iran. Attorney General Benjamin Civiletti ordered all Iranians admitted as nonimmigrant students to report to INS district offices to demonstrate that they were in a lawful status (*e.g.,* still in the school they were authorized to attend). 44 Fed. Reg. 65728 (1979), *amended,* 44 Fed. Reg. 75165 (1979), *rescinded,* 46 Fed. Reg. 25599 (1981). More than 50,000 Iranian students reported. Although the vast majority were found to be lawfully in the country, those who were out of status were placed into deportation proceedings. This regulation of nonimmigrants was challenged as beyond the Attorney General's authority and a violation of equal protection.

NARENJI v. CIVILETTI

United States Court of Appeals, District of Columbia Circuit, 1979.
617 F.2d 745, cert. denied, 446 U.S. 957, 100 S.Ct. 2928, 64 L.Ed.2d 815 (1980).

ROBB, CIRCUIT JUDGE.

* * *

Regulation 214.5 requires all nonimmigrant alien post-secondary school students who are natives or citizens of Iran to report to a local INS office or campus representative to "provide information as to residence and maintenance of nonimmigrant status." * * * The regulation provides that failure to comply with the reporting requirement will be considered a violation of the conditions of the nonimmigrant's stay in the United States and will subject him to deportation proceedings * * * .

The regulation is within the authority delegated by Congress to the Attorney General under the Immigration and Nationality Act. That statute charges the Attorney General with "the administration and enforcement" of the Act, INA § 103(a), and directs him to "establish such regulations . . . and perform such other acts as he deems necessary for carrying out his authority under the provisions of" the Act. * * *

* * *

The District Court concluded that even if authorized by statute regulation 214.5 is unconstitutional because it violates the Iranian students' right to equal protection of the laws. The court found no basis for the "discriminatory classification" of the students established by the regulation. Here again we must differ. Distinctions on the basis of nationality may be drawn in the immigration field by the Congress or the Executive. *See Mathews v. Diaz*, 426 U.S. 67, 81–82, 96 S.Ct. 1883, 48 L.Ed.2d 478 (1976); *Fiallo v. Bell*, 430 U.S. 787, 97 S.Ct. 1473, 52 L.Ed.2d 50 (1977). So long as such distinctions are not wholly irrational they must be sustained.

By way of an affidavit from the Attorney General we are informed that his regulation was issued "as an element of the language of diplomacy by which international courtesies are granted or withdrawn in response to actions by foreign countries. The action implemented by these regulations is therefore a fundamental element of the President's efforts to resolve the Iranian crisis and to maintain the safety of the American hostages in Tehran." The Attorney General refers of course to the lawless seizure of the United States Embassy in Tehran and the imprisonment of the embassy personnel as hostages. * * * The lawlessness of this conduct of the Iranian government was recognized by the decision of the World Court on December 15, 1979. *United States v. Iran*, General List No. 64 (Int'l Ct. Justice, Dec. 15, 1979). Thus the present controversy involving Iranian students in the United States lies in the field of our country's foreign affairs and implicates matters over which the President has direct constitutional authority.

The District Court perceived no "overriding national interest" justifying the Attorney General's regulation: it found that "although defendants' regulation is an understandable effort designed to somehow reply to the Iranian attack upon this nation's sovereignty and the seizure of its citizens, it is one that does not support a legitimate national interest." In this we think the District Court erred.

As we have said, classifications among aliens based upon nationality are consistent with due process and equal protection if supported by a rational basis. The Attorney General's regulation 214.5 meets that test; it has a rational basis. To reach a contrary conclusion the District Court undertook to evaluate the policy reasons upon which the regulation is based. In doing this the court went beyond an acceptable judicial role. Certainly in a case such as the one presented here it is not the business of courts to pass judgment on the decisions of the President in the field of foreign policy. Judges are not expert in that field and they lack the information necessary for the formation of an opinion. The President on the other hand has the opportunity of knowing the conditions which prevail in foreign countries, he has his confidential sources of information and his agents in the form of diplomatic, consular and other officials. *United States v. Curtiss-Wright Export Corp.*, 299 U.S. 304, 320, 57 S.Ct. 216, 81 L.Ed. 255 (1936). As the Supreme Court said in *Mathews v. Diaz*, *supra*, 426 U.S. at 81, 82, 96 S.Ct. at 1892:

> * * * [T]he responsibility for regulating the relationship between the United States and our alien visitors has been committed to the political branches of the Federal Government. Since decisions in these matters may implicate our relations with foreign powers, and since a wide variety of classifications must be defined in the light of changing political and economic circumstances, such decisions are frequently of a character more appropriate to either the Legislature or the Executive than to the Judiciary. * * *

And in *Harisiades v. Shaughnessy*, 342 U.S. 580, 588–89, 72 S.Ct. 512, 519, 96 L.Ed. 586 (1952), Mr. Justice Jackson wrote for the Court:

> * * * [A]ny policy toward aliens is vitally and intricately interwoven with contemporaneous policies in regard to the conduct of foreign relations, the war power, and the maintenance of a republican form of government. Such matters are so exclusively entrusted to the political branches of government as to be largely immune from judicial inquiry or interference.

This court is not in a position to say what effect the required reporting by several thousand Iranian students, who may be in this country illegally, will have on the attitude and conduct of the Iranian government. That is a judgment to be made by the President and it is not for us to overrule him, in the absence of acts that are clearly in excess of his authority.

* * *

MacKinnon, Circuit Judge concurring.

I concur completely in the court's opinion but write separately to add additional support for its ruling.

First, to indicate that this is not an isolated act of diplomacy in the international crisis that faces the United States I would stress that the record also reflects that, as part of the same diplomatic effort, the President by order prohibited "crude oil produced in Iran (from entering) the . . . United States" and blocked all property and interests of the Government of Iran subject to United States jurisdiction. I also take judicial notice of the reports that substantial forces of the United States Navy have been moved to the Indian Ocean and the President has ordered the Iranian Embassy and consulate to return approximately 85% of its diplomatic staff to Iran.

* * *

The disparity in treatment afforded the appellee nonimmigrant alien students who are in violation of our immigration laws is based upon the fact that the Government of their home country has committed, and is committing, a number of violent lawless acts against the United States and its citizens. That unlawful conduct against the United States places appellees, and others similarly situated who owe their allegiance to that country, in a different class for immigration purposes from the nonimmigrants of any other country. Therefore, since their government has made appellees part of a distinctly separate class, the United States under our Constitution may treat them differently because of the reasons that separate them from other aliens in the United States. The different treatment they may receive under subject regulation is directly related to the reasons for their different classification.

The status of Iranian aliens cannot be disassociated from their connection with their mother country since the alien "leaves outstanding a foreign call on his loyalties which international law not only permits our Government to recognize but commands it to respect." *Harisiades v. Shaughnessy*, 342 U.S. 580, 585–586, 72 S.Ct. 512, 517, 96 L.Ed. 586 (1951). * * *

* * *

NOTES AND QUESTIONS ON NARENJI

1.   For an argument that race or ethnicity-based enforcement targeting Arabs and Muslims are not as narrowly tailored and are more subject to abuse—and therefore are even more troubling than the nationality-based rule in *Narenji*—see Susan M. Akram & Kevin R. Johnson, *Race, Civil Rights, and Immigration After September 11, 2001: The Targeting of Arabs and Muslims*, 58 N.Y.U. Ann. Surv. Am. L. 295, 338 (2002). Do you agree?

2.   Do some or all of the government's post-September 11 immigration enforcement initiatives constitute profiling by ethnicity, religion, or race? More fundamentally, what, if anything, is objectionable about any of them? Consider the following framework for analysis.

c. Profiling and Immigration Law as Anti-Terrorism Law

SAMUEL R. GROSS & DEBRA LIVINGSTON, RACIAL PROFILING UNDER ATTACK

102 Colum. L. Rev. 1413, 1413, 1415, 1417–18, 1420–25, 1427, 1429–30 (2002).

We had just reached a consensus on racial profiling. By September 10, 2001, virtually everyone, from Jesse Jackson to Al Gore to George W. Bush to John Ashcroft, agreed that racial profiling was very bad. We also knew what racial profiling was: Police officers would stop, question, and search African American and Hispanic citizens disproportionately, because of their race or ethnicity, in order to try to catch common criminals. All this has changed in the wake of the September 11 attacks on the World Trade Center and the Pentagon. Now racial profiling is more likely to mean security checks or federal investigations that target Muslim men from Middle Eastern countries, in order to try to catch terrorists. And now lots of people are for it. In the fall of 1999, 81% of respondents in a national poll said they disapproved of "racial profiling," which was defined as the practice by some police officers of stopping "motorists of certain racial or ethnic groups because the officers believe that these groups are more likely than others to commit certain types of crimes." Two years later, 58% said they favored "requiring Arabs, including those who are U.S. citizens, to undergo special, more intensive security checks before boarding airplanes in the U.S." This new attitude has emerged across the political spectrum. Even as stalwart a civil libertarian as Floyd Abrams, the celebrated First Amendment lawyer, has said that under the circumstances we now face, "it seems entirely appropriate to look harder at such people. Remember, Justice [Robert] Jackson said 'the Constitution is not a suicide pact.'"

* * *

As we use the term, "racial profiling" occurs whenever a law enforcement officer questions, stops, arrests, searches, or otherwise investigates a person because the officer believes that members of that person's racial or ethnic group are more likely than the population at large to commit the sort of crime the officer is investigating. The essence of racial profiling is a global judgment that the targeted group—before September 11, usually African Americans or Hispanics—is more prone to commit crime in general, or to commit a particular type of crime, than other racial or ethnic groups. If the officer's conduct is based at least in part on such a general racial or ethnic judgment, it does not matter if she uses other criteria as well in deciding on her course of action. It is racial profiling to target young black men on the basis of a belief that they are more likely than others to commit crimes, even though black women and older black men are not directly affected.

It is not racial profiling for an officer to question, stop, search, arrest, or otherwise investigate a person because his race or ethnicity matches information about a perpetrator of a specific crime that the officer is investigating. That use of race—which usually occurs when there is a racially specific description of the criminal—does not entail a global judgment about a racial or ethnic group as a whole. Likewise, a deliberate practice of discrimination between known suspects of different races—stopping all speeders but giving tickets to black drivers only, and warnings to whites—is a violation of the Equal Protection Clause of the Fourteenth Amendment, but it is not racial profiling. Racial profiling can occur in almost any type of criminal investigation. It has received particular attention in the context of highway drug interdiction, and more recently, of course, in investigations of terrorism.

* * *

We will focus our discussion of racial and ethnic profiling on a concrete example. In November 2001, the Department of Justice began efforts to interview "more than 5,000 people nationwide—the majority Middle Eastern men ages eighteen to thirty-three who came here within the last two years on nonimmigrant visas—in search of information on terrorist organizations such as al Qaeda."[14] Four months later, the Justice Department announced that it would seek to interview 3,000 additional men, ages eighteen to forty-six, who entered the United States on nonimmigrant visas, between October 2001 and February 2002, from countries with an al Qaeda presence. The Department said that these men are not suspected of crimes but "might, either wittingly or unwittingly, be in the same circles, communities, or social groups as those engaged in terrorist activities."

Is the Justice Department's interview campaign an ethnic profiling program? Some civil libertarians, Arab American organizations, and local police departments say it is; the Department of Justice says it is not. Who is right? And would answering this question tell us whether the Justice Department's program is appropriate? We will discuss these questions in the context of five factors. * * * In actual cases * * * these factors are often inextricably intertwined.

A.   IS THE INVESTIGATION BASED ON RACE OR ETHNICITY?

* * *

[I]s the Justice Department's interview program ethnic profiling? The answer is not clear even assuming that ethnicity was a central factor in the selection of subjects. By our definition, it is not ethnic profiling for

---

14   * * * See Memorandum from the Deputy Attorney General, to All United States Attorneys and All Members of the Anti-Terrorism Task Forces (Nov. 9, 2001) (describing the manner of conducting interviews and topics to be covered).

officers to focus their attention on people of a given ethnicity because the police have information that the specific crime they are investigating was committed by someone of that ethnic group. There is plenty of information that Middle Eastern men, some of whom remain at large, engaged in a conspiracy to commit acts of mass terror in the United States on September 11, 2001. Granted, the concept of a "specific crime" grows somewhat hazy when the crime at issue is an ongoing conspiracy of indeterminate size—and one that potentially involves not just Middle Eastern men, but also others, from different racial or ethnic groups. Nevertheless, if the sole purpose for this interview program was to determine whether any of the thousands to be interviewed was involved in this conspiracy, or had information that might lead to those who were, this would not be ethnic profiling. (Which is not to say that such a broad brush investigation would be unproblematic; that's a different question, as we will see). On the other hand, the Justice Department's program would involve ethnic profiling if it was undertaken even in part based upon a general belief that Middle Eastern men are more likely to commit acts of terrorism than people of other ethnic groups—if it was based upon a global assumption about the criminal propensities of people of Middle Eastern descent. In practice, it is probably impossible to make that distinction in a case like this, involving the protracted investigation of a far-flung conspiracy.

B.   IS RACE (OR ETHNICITY) A STRONG PREDICTOR OF CRIMINAL BEHAVIOR?

* * *

Before September 11, 2001, a few conservative commentators were the only people who publicly defended racial profiling on practical grounds. That has changed. Journalists, politicians, and pollsters have all expressed and documented a widespread sentiment that in order to win the "war on terrorism" we must focus our scrutiny on Middle Eastern Muslim men. The Justice Department's interview program may not be expressly aimed at such individuals, but it has this effect. It is explicitly aimed at individuals from Middle Eastern countries and other countries with an al Qaeda presence—and for good reason. Although other groups and individuals have committed terrorist acts in the United States, before September 11 and probably after, it is very likely true that al Qaeda, an organization that consists entirely of Muslim men, primarily from the Middle East, poses the greatest immediate threat of mass terrorist killings.

Fortunately, it is also no doubt true that only a tiny proportion of Middle Eastern men are affiliated with al Qaeda. A similar pattern can occur in other settings: Even if race or ethnicity is a strong predictor of criminal behavior, an individual member of the relevant groups is very unlikely to be a criminal. For example, it could simultaneously be true that 90% of major cocaine traffickers on I–95 are black and Hispanic, and that 99.9% of black and Hispanic motorists on that highway are not drug traffickers of any description. When this type of juxtaposition does occur—and we rarely, if ever, have information this definitive—choosing suspects by race will increase the efficiency of the police. But the benefit to law enforcement may be slight, and it will come at a price that may be very steep, depending on the other factors we consider.

C. WHAT DOES THE GOVERNMENT DO BASED ON RACE OR ETHNICITY?

Southeastern Michigan has the largest concentration of Arab Americans and Near Eastern visitors in the country, perhaps 300,000 or more, including 521 of the 600 or so Michigan residents on the Justice Department's initial interview list. These subjects were contacted by letters from the local United States Attorney that said:

> Your name was brought to our attention because, among other things, you came to Michigan on a visa from a country where there are groups that support, advocate, or finance international terrorism. We have no reason to believe that you are, in any way, associated with terrorist activities. Nevertheless, you may know something that could be helpful in our efforts.

They were then asked to call the United States Attorney's office by a given date to set up an appointment for an interview.

* * *

Perhaps the worst instance of ethnic profiling in American history began on February 19, 1942, when President Franklin Delano Roosevelt signed Executive Order 9066, giving the Secretary of War the power to order over 110,000 Japanese Americans on the west coast to be "resettle[d]" in "relocation centers" for the duration of the war. The Japanese internment was a disgraceful episode in American history. It is frequently cited as the prime example of the evil things we might do if we pursue racial profiling in response to the attacks of September 11. But what if, instead of being forced to sell their property for pennies on the dollar, to leave their homes, schools, farms, jobs, and communities, and to spend three and a half years behind barbed wire, Japanese Americans had been asked to report for interviews with the FBI? What if in addition they were required—because of their ethnicity—to report their whereabouts to the police periodically, but were otherwise allowed to lead their lives as they wished? Perhaps these policies, especially the second, would also have been unjustified, even during an all out war. Certainly both programs—like the actual internment program—would have involved ethnic profiling. Under any name, however, these sorts of ethnic profiling would have been far preferable to the relocation and imprisonment that were in fact ordered.

* * *

D. HOW STRONG IS THE EVIDENCE OF A RACIALLY IDENTIFIED SUSPECT'S GUILT OR INNOCENCE?

Our normal operating assumption about racial profiling is that the typical individual who is profiled is very unlikely to be guilty. (Certainly no more than a tiny proportion of the men interviewed by the FBI are members of al Qaeda, if any.) The less likely the guilt of any individual, the higher the proportion of innocent people among those affected, and the higher the social cost of the practice. But what if the evidence of individual guilt becomes much stronger? Would this change our view on the use of profiling? The New York City Police Department's anti-gun campaign is a good illustration. From January 1998 through March 1999, guns were found on only 2.5% of the nearly 60,000 people who were stopped for suspected gun possession—one person in 40. Assuming the police did use race to decide whom to stop and frisk, would we feel differently about the practice if they had found weapons on 90% of those they searched? How about 30%?

* * *

E. WHAT ARE THE LIKELY BENEFITS OF RACIAL PROFILING?

* * *

* * * If we thought we could reduce the risk of hijacking by 15%, would that justify searching every Middle Eastern man who boards a plane? This may well be within the current national consensus that we must take strong measures to protect ourselves. On the other hand, the same people who would accept severe measures (including ones based on race) that offered any promise of reducing a genuine threat of nuclear terrorism, might still readily condemn a racial profiling program that efficiently combats the threat of marijuana possession or ticket scalping. And even people who favor the Justice Department's post-September 11 interview program might be angry if the Department sent out letters to 5000 Mexican nationals, almost all of them law abiding, asking them to come in for interviews because:

> Your name was brought to our attention because, among other things, you came to the United States on a visa from a country where there are groups that engage in or finance international drug trafficking. We have no reason to believe that you are, in any way, associated with drug trafficking.

Nevertheless, you may know something that could be helpful in our efforts.

There are two parts to this calculation: How great is the harm we are fighting? And how likely is our conduct to be useful? When the danger is extreme, we may accept unpleasant methods that have only a slight chance of success. But it is one thing to sketch out these calculations on paper, and quite another to do so in a real emergency. We never actually know either the magnitude of the danger or the effectiveness of possible countermeasures. Urgency and fear do not improve our judgment. They may lead us to overestimate the danger, or the value of preventive steps, or both. Racism and ethnic prejudice may color every step of the process. Most Americans probably feel particularly threatened because the September 11 suicide hijackers were foreign, and some may be especially fearful because they were Arabs. This fear may cause us to exaggerate the danger of future attacks in general, and of attacks by Middle Eastern terrorists in particular. As a result, we may overestimate the effect of racially specific security measures. And unfortunately, we are more willing to accept aggressive measures when they target small and politically disempowered groups, specifically racial and ethnic minorities, and foreign nationals.

* * *

Additional Perspectives on
Profiling and Anti-Terrorism Law

1.   When the Department of Justice published the final NSEERS rule in 2002, it responded to the charge that NSEERS targets specific minority ethnic groups and members of a specific religion:

> The Department strongly disagrees with the premise of the comments that the rule is invidiously discriminatory. Congressional enactments and regulations concerning immigration have historically drawn distinctions on the basis of nationality and related criteria. The political branches of the government have plenary authority in the immigration area. * * * The substantive decision to relax requirements for only specified nationals, while excluding all others, is among those political decisions that are "wholly outside the concern and competence of the Judiciary," *Harisiades v. Shaughnessy*, 342 U.S. 580, 596 (1952) (Frankfurter, J., concurring). * * * The distinctions drawn by the rule are appropriate in the context of immigration law and national security.

> The Department recognizes that a few individuals in the United States have questioned the loyalty of some Muslim Americans to the United States. The Department also recognizes

that some American Muslims have been targets of discrimination. Some mosques have been damaged and desecrated. A number of Muslim Americans—and others wrongly believed to be Muslims—have been threatened or attacked. These attacks against Muslim Americans and the Muslim communities are not only reprehensible; like terrorism, they are also attacks against the United States and humanity. The Federal Bureau of Investigation (FBI) has investigated such attacks and threats against Arab, Muslim, and Sikh Americans. * * * The Department continues to treat such crimes as civil rights violations and will vigorously prosecute these violations.

67 Fed. Reg. 52585 (2002).

2. Leti Volpp has argued that the post-September 11 focus on Arabs and Muslims had precursor episodes in which other racial groups were similarly targeted as foreign threats, often regardless of citizenship status:

There are obviously enormous resonances in what has been happening to the treatment of Japanese Americans during World War II, whereby the fungibility of members of a racially defined community was considered to make it impossible to screen individually loyal citizens from enemy aliens. Recently, the publisher of the Sacramento Bee attempted to deliver a graduation speech at Cal State Sacramento. Booed and heckled, she was unable to finish her speech about the need for the protection of civil liberties; when she wondered what would happen if racial profiling became routine, the audience cheered. Witnesses described the event as terrifying; the president of the faculty senate was quoted in the New York Times as stating, " 'For the first time in my life, I can see how something like the Japanese internment camps could happen in our country.' "[67]

And, in fact, a Gallup poll found that one-third of the American public surveyed thought that we should intern Arab Americans. Motivation for the internment of over 120,000 Japanese Americans was fear of what we today might call sleeper cells. The fact that the Japanese Americans did not attack after Pearl Harbor was understood to mean that they were patiently waiting to strike and therefore must be interned. Japanese American internment constituted a pivotal moment in American Orientalism; the present moment is another.

* * *

---

[67] Timothy Egan, *In Sacramento, a Publisher's Questions Draw the Wrath of the Crowd*, N.Y. Times, Dec. 21, 2001, at B1 (quoting Bob Buckley, computer science professor at California State University, Sacramento).

In the American imagination, those who appear "Middle Eastern, Arab, or Muslim" may be theoretically entitled to formal rights, but they do not stand in for or represent the nation. Instead, they are interpellated as antithetical to the citizen's sense of identity. Citizenship in the form of legal status does not guarantee that they will be constitutive of the American body politic. In fact, quite the opposite: The consolidation of American identity takes place against them.

* * *

Thus, the boundaries of the nation continue to be constructed through excluding certain groups. The "imagined community"[79] of the American nation, constituted by loyal citizens, is relying on difference from the "Middle Eastern terrorist" to fuse its identity at a moment of crisis. Discourses of democracy used to support the U.S. war effort rest on an image of anti-democracy, in the form of those who seek to destroy the "American way of life." The idea that there are norms that are antithetical to "Western values" of liberty and equality helps solidify this conclusion.

Leti Volpp, *The Citizen and the Terrorist*, 49 UCLA L. Rev. 1575, 1591–95 (2002). *See also* Leti Volpp, *The Boston Bombers*, 82 Fordham L. Rev. 2209 (2014).

Relatedly, consider this critique of "radicalization theory," that is, the idea that increased religiosity and politicization among Muslims represents an increased threat of terrorism:

Under the guise of predicting future terrorism, radicalization provides a guide for government activity. In so doing, it redefines and expands the relevant field of state concern: from terrorism to radicalization in Muslim communities. Marking religious and political activities as the indicators of radicalization, the discourse links religious and political practices in Muslim communities with the likelihood of terrorism—inviting state scrutiny into the halls of Muslim communities, and changing the terms of engagement with the state for Muslims.

Amna Akbar, *National Security's Broken Windows*, 62 UCLA L. Rev. 834. 879 (2015).

---

[79] *See* Benedict Anderson, Imagined Communities 7 (1991) (writing that the nation is "an imagined political community"). * * *

3.   Compare these comments from Eric Muller:

We might roll our eyes when our government today defends its interrogation program as ethnicity-neutral. After all, while the five thousand young men may not have been selected because they are Arab, we do know that they were selected because they arrived recently from countries where al Qaeda operates, and that certainly sounds like a pretext for anti-Arab discrimination. But on closer examination, especially in the comparative light of the interrogation of the ethnically Japanese during World War II, the government's defense of its program is plausible. The 1990 census counted about 940,000 people of Arab ancestry in the United States, about eighteen percent of whom were non-citizens. This made for a total of about 170,000 aliens of Arab ancestry living in the United States in 1990. * * * Still, 5,000 is just under three percent of 170,000, a number so small as to suggest that the government did in fact target people for questioning on the basis of criteria other than the raw fact of their origin in an Arab country. The additional criteria that the government announced—age of between eighteen and thirty-three years and recent arrival from a country believed to have been a way-station for members of al Qaeda—certainly seem to describe a major subset of those who might have some information, perhaps to them entirely innocent-seeming, that would help the government fend off future al Qaeda attacks.

Most importantly, despite dire predictions that the supposedly information-gathering interviews would be mere pretext for coercive criminal interrogations, this turned out not to be so. After a somewhat clumsy start, the FBI quickly responded to suggestions and complaints from the Arab American community and ran interviews that lawyers in attendance called "polite, even solicitous." * * * In the meantime, the response rate from those the government asked to interview was around ninety percent, and the Attorney General reported when the interviews were through that they had produced "several leads." Of course, the government now also has a list of those who declined to be interviewed, and it remains to be seen what use the government will make of that information. On the whole, though, the program of interrogation, if it was ethnic profiling at all, was ethnic profiling with a decidedly light touch.

Eric L. Muller, *12/7 and 9/11: War, Liberties, and the Lessons of History*, 104 W. Va. L. Rev. 571, 575–77 (2002). Does Muller's view apply more to some aspects of the government's antiterrorism campaign than to others?

4.   A key question in assessing the uses of immigration law as anti-terrorism law is to ask how citizenship matters. David Cole has argued that while noncitizen status accounts for the harshness of many of the recent measures taken in the struggle against terrorism, how we treat nonmembers may ultimately have an impact on rights of full members:

> Some argue that a "double standard" for citizens and noncitizens is perfectly justified. The attacks of September 11 were perpetrated by 19 Arab noncitizens, and we have reason to believe that other Arab noncitizens are associated with the attackers and will seek to attack again. Citizens, it is said, are presumptively loyal; noncitizens are not. * * *
>
> * * *
>
> [W]hat we are willing to allow our government to do to immigrants creates precedents for how it treats citizens. In 1798, for example, Congress enacted the Enemy Alien Act, which remains on the books to this day and authorizes the President during wartime to detain, deport, or otherwise restrict the liberties of any citizen over 14 years of age of a country with which we are at war, without any individualized showing of disloyalty, criminal conduct, or even suspicion. In World War II, the government extended that logic to intern 110,000 persons of Japanese ancestry, about two-thirds of whom were U.S. citizens. Similarly, while we think of the McCarthy era as beginning in the 1940s, it was in fact preceded by several decades of targeting immigrants for their purportedly subversive political associations using immigration law. Joe McCarthy simply applied to citizens techniques developed in the 1910s under the leadership of a young J. Edgar Hoover, head of the Justice Department's "Alien Radical" division. Measures initially targeted at noncitizens may well come back to haunt us all.

David Cole, *Enemy Aliens*, 54 Stan. L. Rev. 953, 957–59 (2002).

Cole focuses on future consequences, but consider this 2003 comment on the present-day link between the treatment of citizens and noncitizens:

> [M]any noncitizens caught up in today's dragnets are * * * the mothers and fathers and husbands and wives of U.S. citizens. These noncitizens are vital members of ethnic communities composed of citizens and noncitizens, and these noncitizens were targeted because of their race, ethnicity, or nationality. The administration acts as if it is possible to affect noncitizens without also affecting U.S. citizens and communities,

when in fact, U.S. citizens and communities have been devastated. * * *

In the time since the September 11 attacks, the government has tightened the circle in ways that leave many U.S. citizens and communities on the outside if they are the wrong race, ethnicity, or nationality. When enforcement measures are based on these factors, it is only natural for U.S. citizens and noncitizens in Arab and South Asian communities in the United States to feel real fear in these terms. To identify U.S. citizens by race, ethnicity, or nationality has taken away a vital part of what these citizens thought it meant to be a U.S. citizen in the first place. Profiling by race begets fear by race—fear on the part of citizens and noncitizens alike.

Hiroshi Motomura, *Immigration and We the People After September 11*, 66 Albany L. Rev. 413, 422–24 (2003).

C. STATE AND LOCAL GOVERNMENTS

We now expand our inquiry to immigration federalism—that is, state and local measures relating to immigration and immigrants. Some state and local activity reflects an effort to be involved indirectly in immigration law enforcement by limiting unauthorized migrants' access to education, jobs, or housing, and thus minimizing the fiscal burdens that they might impose and encouraging them to "self-deport." Other states and localities have become more directly involved in immigration enforcement, with or without express federal authorization. At the same time, other state and local governments have taken actions that tend to neutralize some aspects of federal immigration enforcement. In considering whether these state and local measures are constitutional, we start with excerpts from three U.S. Supreme Court decisions from the 1970s that are foundational to modern immigration federalism.

1. THE FOUNDATION CASES

a. *Graham v. Richardson*

The plaintiffs in *Graham v. Richardson*, 403 U.S. 365, 91 S.Ct. 1848, 29 L.Ed.2d 534 (1971), were lawful permanent residents who objected to laws that limited eligibility for state welfare programs. Pennsylvania required U.S. citizenship, and Arizona limited eligibility to citizens and noncitizens who had lived in the United States for fifteen years. The Court found these laws unconstitutional. Part of its analysis explained:

> Under traditional equal protection principles, a State retains broad discretion to classify as long as its classification has a reasonable basis. * * * But the Court's decisions have

established that classifications based on alienage, like those based on nationality or race, are inherently suspect and subject to close judicial scrutiny. Aliens as a class are a prime example of a "discrete and insular" minority (*see United States v. Carolene Products Co.*, 304 U.S. 144, 152–153, n.4, 58 S.Ct. 778, 783–784, 82 L.Ed. 1234 (1938)) for whom such heightened judicial solicitude is appropriate. * * *

403 U.S. at 371–72, 91 S.Ct. 1852.

Besides equal protection, the Court cited preemption as an "additional reason" to strike down the statutes:

Congress has broadly declared as federal policy that lawfully admitted resident aliens who become public charges for causes arising after their entry are not subject to deportation, and that as long as they are here they are entitled to the full and equal benefit of all state laws for the security of persons and property. * * *

In *Truax* [*v. Raich*, 239 U.S. 33, 36 S.Ct. 7, 60 L.Ed. 131 (1915)], the Court considered the "reasonableness" of a state restriction on the employment of aliens in terms of its effect on the right of a lawfully admitted alien to live where he chooses:

* * * The authority to control immigration—to admit or exclude aliens—is vested solely in the Federal Government. * * * The assertion of an authority to deny to aliens the opportunity of earning a livelihood when lawfully admitted to the state would be tantamount to the assertion of the right to deny them entrance and abode, for in ordinary cases they cannot live where they cannot work. And, if such a policy were permissible, the practical result would be that those lawfully admitted to the country under the authority of the acts of Congress, instead of enjoying in a substantial sense and in their full scope the privileges conferred by the admission, would be segregated in such of the states as chose to offer hospitality.

[*Truax*], 239 U.S., at 42, 36 S.Ct., at 11.

The same is true here, for in the ordinary case an alien, becoming indigent and unable to work, will be unable to live where, because of discriminatory denial of public assistance, he cannot "secure the necessities of life, including food, clothing and shelter." State alien residency requirements that either deny welfare benefits to noncitizens or condition them on longtime residency [shorter than applicable federal requirements], equate with the assertion of a right, inconsistent with federal policy, to deny entrance and abode. Since such laws encroach upon exclusive federal power, they are constitutionally impermissible.

Graham, 403 U.S. at 378–80, 91 S.Ct. 1856.

b.   *De Canas v. Bica*

The noncitizens in *Graham* were lawful permanent residents. What if noncitizens are in the United States unlawfully? Does equal protection or preemption limit state or local laws that treat them differently on account of their unlawful status? This question arose in *De Canas v. Bica*, 424 U.S. 351, 96 S.Ct. 933, 47 L.Ed.2d 43 (1976). The plaintiffs were migrant farmworkers who alleged they had lost their jobs because the defendant farm labor contractors hired unauthorized migrants. The plaintiffs sought reinstatement and a permanent injunction against the hiring practices based on this language in California Labor Code § 2805(a): "(n)o employer shall knowingly employ an alien who is not entitled to lawful residence in the United States if such employment would have an adverse effect on lawful resident workers."

This was a decade before federal employer sanctions became law in 1986. Did federal law preempt the California statute? No, said the Court in a unanimous decision that established several propositions still central to immigration federalism. The Court emphasized limits on preemption:

> Power to regulate immigration is unquestionably exclusively a federal power. But the Court has never held that every state enactment which in any way deals with aliens is a regulation of immigration and thus per se pre-empted by this constitutional power, whether latent or exercised. * * * [S]tanding alone, the fact that aliens are the subject of a state statute does not render it a regulation of immigration, which is essentially a determination of who should or should not be admitted into the country, and the conditions under which a legal entrant may remain. * * *

424 U.S. at 354–55, 96 S.Ct. 936.

The Court noted that "States possess broad authority under their police powers to regulate the employment relationship to protect workers within the State." 424 U.S. at 356, 96 S.Ct. 937. It added:

> Of course, even state regulation designed to protect vital state interests must give way to paramount federal legislation. But we will not presume that Congress, in enacting the INA, intended to oust state authority to regulate the employment relationship * * * in a manner consistent with pertinent federal laws. Only a demonstration that complete ouster of state power including state power to promulgate laws not in conflict with

federal laws was " 'the clear and manifest purpose of Congress' " would justify that conclusion. *Florida Lime & Avocado Growers v. Paul, supra,* at 146, 83 S.Ct., at 1219, quoting *Rice v. Santa Fe Elevator Corp.,* 331 U.S. 218, 230, 67 S.Ct. 1146, 1152, 91 L.Ed. 1447 (1947). Respondents have not made that demonstration. They fail to point out, and an independent review does not reveal, any specific indication in either the wording or the legislative history of the INA that Congress intended to preclude even harmonious state regulation touching on aliens in general, or the employment of illegal aliens in particular.

>   Nor can such intent be derived from the scope and detail of the INA. The central concern of the INA is with the terms and conditions of admission to the country and the subsequent treatment of aliens lawfully in the country. The comprehensiveness of the INA scheme for regulation of immigration and naturalization, without more, cannot be said to draw in the employment of illegal aliens as "plainly within . . . (that) central aim of federal regulation." *San Diego Unions v. Garmon,* 359 U.S. 236, 244, 79 S.Ct. 773, 779, 3 L.Ed.2d 775 (1959).

424 U.S. at 357–59, 96 S.Ct. 937–38.

De Canas is often cited for three ways that state and local laws relating to immigration and immigrants may be preempted. The first is "express preemption": a federal law expressly preempts state laws of a certain type. The other two types of preemption are implied. "Field preemption" occurs when the federal government occupies a field pervasively and exclusively, leaving no room for state laws. "Conflict preemption" occurs if complying with both federal and state law is impossible, or the state law stands as an obstacle to accomplishing the purposes of federal law.

In *De Canas*, the Court found neither express preemption nor field preemption of the California statute. It next asked whether the California statute was unconstitutional because it "stands as an obstacle to the accomplishment and execution of the full purposes and objectives of Congress in enacting the INA." Concluding that it should let California courts interpret the statute before assessing any conflict with federal law, the Court remanded the case.

c. *Mathews v. Diaz*

The plaintiffs in *Mathews v. Diaz,* 426 U.S. 67, 96 S.Ct. 1883, 48 L.Ed.2d 478 (1976), decided three months after *De Canas*, were three Cuban refugees. All were lawfully present, one as a permanent resident and two after being been paroled into the country. But they did not qualify for federal Medicare, which required that any noncitizen be a permanent resident who has lived in the United States for five years. They argued that the requirement violated equal protection. In rejecting this challenge, the Court first addressed constitutional protections for noncitizens generally:

> In the exercise of its broad power over naturalization and immigration, Congress regularly makes rules that would be unacceptable if applied to citizens. The exclusion of aliens and the reservation of the power to deport have no permissible counterpart in the Federal Government's power to regulate the conduct of its own citizenry. The fact that an Act of Congress treats aliens differently from citizens does not in itself imply that such disparate treatment is "invidious."

> In particular, the fact that Congress has provided some welfare benefits for citizens does not require it to provide like benefits for all aliens. Neither the overnight visitor, the unfriendly agent of a hostile foreign power, the resident diplomat, nor the illegal entrant, can advance even a colorable constitutional claim to a share in the bounty that a conscientious sovereign makes available to its own citizens and some of its guests. The decision to share that bounty with our guests may take into account the character of the relationship between the alien and this country: Congress may decide that as the alien's tie grows stronger, so does the strength of his claim to an equal share of that munificence.

426 U.S. at 79–80, 96 S.Ct. 1891–92.

The Court distinguished *Graham*:

> Of course, the latter ground of decision [federal preemption] actually supports our holding today that it is the business of the political branches of the Federal Government, rather than that of either the States or the Federal Judiciary, to regulate the conditions of entry and residence of aliens. The equal protection analysis also involves significantly different considerations because it concerns the relationship between aliens and the States rather than between aliens and the Federal Government.

426 U.S. at 84–85, 96 S.Ct. 1893–94.

Diaz makes clear that the federal government may treat noncitizens less favorably than it treats citizens, but that under *Graham* the states' constitutional authority to do so is far more constricted. Why the difference? Some have argued that it reflects preemption, *see* Michael J. Perry, *Modern Equal Protection: A Conceptualization and Appraisal*, 79 Colum. L. Rev. 1023, 1061–63 (1979). According to others, federal government interests are stronger than state or local government interests in an equal protection analysis, *see* Harold Hongju Koh, *Equality With a Human Face: Justice Blackmun and the Equal Protection of Aliens*, 8 Hamline L. Rev. 51, 98–102 (1985).

2.   INDIRECT STATE AND LOCAL ENFORCEMENT

State and local involvement in immigration enforcement can take different forms that might be arrayed on a spectrum from indirect to direct involvement. By "indirect," we refer to state or local measures to make life hard or costly enough for unauthorized migrants to induce them to leave or to mitigate any state or local fiscal burdens if they stay. We will use "direct" involvement in enforcement to mean some state and local role in arrest, detention, or removal based on a federal immigration violation. One can debate where a given state and local law fits, but this direct/indirect spectrum may help understand how the law has evolved and been applied.

When, if ever, is it constitutional for a state or local government to make it difficult or impossible for unauthorized migrants to rent housing, find work, or go to school? In such a situation, the three foundation cases suggest that two types of facts might make a constitutional difference: (1) the source of regulation—federal versus state or local; and (2) the noncitizen's status—lawfully in the United States or not. Consider how these facts mattered to the Supreme Court in the next case.

PLYLER V. DOE
Supreme Court of the United States, 1982.
457 U.S. 202, 102 S.Ct. 2382, 72 L.Ed.2d 786.

JUSTICE BRENNAN delivered the opinion of the Court.

* * *

In May 1975, the Texas Legislature * * * authorized local school districts to deny enrollment in their public schools to children not "legally admitted" to the country. Tex. Educ. Code Ann. § 21.031. These cases involve constitutional challenges to those provisions.

* * *8

* * * Appellants argue at the outset that undocumented aliens, because of their immigration status, are not "persons within the jurisdiction" of the State of Texas, and that they therefore have no right to the equal protection of Texas law. We reject this argument. Whatever his status under the immigration laws, an alien is surely a "person" in

---

8   Appellees * * * continue to press the argument that § 21.031 is pre-empted by federal law and policy. In light of our disposition of the Fourteenth Amendment issue, we have no occasion to reach this claim.

any ordinary sense of that term. Aliens, even aliens whose presence in this country is unlawful, have long been recognized as "persons" guaranteed due process of law by the Fifth and Fourteenth Amendments. *Shaughnessy v. Mezei*, 345 U.S. 206, 212, 73 S.Ct. 625, 629, 97 L.Ed. 956 (1953); *Wong Wing v. United States*, 163 U.S. 228, 238, 16 S.Ct. 977, 981, 41 L.Ed. 140 (1896); *Yick Wo v. Hopkins*, 118 U.S. 356, 369, 6 S.Ct. 1064, 1070, 30 L.Ed. 220 (1886). Indeed, we have clearly held that the Fifth Amendment protects aliens whose presence in this country is unlawful from invidious discrimination by the Federal Government. *Mathews v. Diaz*, 426 U.S. 67, 77, 96 S.Ct. 1883, 1890, 48 L.Ed.2d 478 (1976).

* * *

* * * In applying the Equal Protection Clause to most forms of state action, we * * * seek only the assurance that the classification at issue bears some fair relationship to a legitimate public purpose.

But we would not be faithful to our obligations under the Fourteenth Amendment if we applied so deferential a standard to every classification. The Equal Protection Clause was intended as a restriction on state legislative action inconsistent with elemental constitutional premises. Thus we have treated as presumptively invidious those classifications that disadvantage a "suspect class," or that impinge upon the exercise of a "fundamental right." With respect to such classifications, it is appropriate to enforce the mandate of equal protection by requiring the State to demonstrate that its classification has been precisely tailored to serve a compelling governmental interest. In addition, we have recognized that certain forms of legislative classification, while not facially invidious, nonetheless give rise to recurring constitutional difficulties; in these limited circumstances we have sought the assurance that the classification reflects a reasoned judgment consistent with the ideal of equal protection by inquiring whether it may fairly be viewed as furthering a substantial interest of the State. * * *

Sheer incapability or lax enforcement of the laws barring entry into this country, coupled with the failure to establish an effective bar to the employment of undocumented aliens, has resulted in the creation of a substantial "shadow population" of illegal migrants—numbering in the millions—within our borders. This situation raises the specter of a permanent caste of undocumented resident aliens, encouraged by some to remain here as a source of cheap labor, but nevertheless denied the benefits that our society makes available to citizens and lawful residents. The existence of such an underclass presents most difficult problems for a Nation that prides itself on adherence to principles of equality under law.

The children who are plaintiffs in these cases are special members of this underclass. Persuasive arguments support the view that a State may withhold its beneficence from those whose very presence within the

United States is the product of their own unlawful conduct. These arguments do not apply with the same force to classifications imposing disabilities on the minor *children* of such illegal entrants. At the least, those who elect to enter our territory by stealth and in violation of our law should be prepared to bear the consequences, including, but not limited to, deportation. But the children of those illegal entrants are not comparably situated. Their "parents have the ability to conform their conduct to societal norms," and presumably the ability to remove themselves from the State's jurisdiction; but the children who are plaintiffs in these cases "can affect neither their parents' conduct nor their own status." *Trimble v. Gordon*, 430 U.S. 762, 770, 97 S.Ct. 1459, 1465, 52 L.Ed.2d 31 (1977). Even if the State found it expedient to control the conduct of adults by acting against their children, legislation directing the onus of a parent's misconduct against his children does not comport with fundamental conceptions of justice. * * *

Of course, undocumented status is not irrelevant to any proper legislative goal. Nor is undocumented status an absolutely immutable characteristic since it is the product of conscious, indeed unlawful, action. But § 21.031 is directed against children, and imposes its discriminatory burden on the basis of a legal characteristic over which children can have little control. It is thus difficult to conceive of a rational justification for penalizing these children for their presence within the United States. Yet that appears to be precisely the effect of § 21.031.

Public education is not a "right" granted to individuals by the Constitution. But neither is it merely some governmental "benefit" indistinguishable from other forms of social welfare legislation. Both the importance of education in maintaining our basic institutions, and the lasting impact of its deprivation on the life of the child, mark the distinction. * * * [E]ducation provides the basic tools by which individuals might lead economically productive lives to the benefit of us all. In sum, education has a fundamental role in maintaining the fabric of our society. We cannot ignore the significant social costs borne by our Nation when select groups are denied the means to absorb the values and skills upon which our social order rests.

In addition to the pivotal role of education in sustaining our political and cultural heritage, denial of education to some isolated group of children poses an affront to one of the goals of the Equal Protection Clause: the abolition of governmental barriers presenting unreasonable obstacles to advancement on the basis of individual merit. * * * What we said 28 years ago in *Brown v. Board of Education*, 347 U.S. 483, 74 S.Ct. 686, 98 L.Ed. 873 (1954), still holds true:

> * * * In these days, it is doubtful that any child may reasonably be expected to succeed in life if he is denied the opportunity of an

education. Such an opportunity, where the state has undertaken to provide it, is a right which must be made available to all on equal terms.

These well-settled principles allow us to determine the proper level of deference to be afforded § 21.031. Undocumented aliens cannot be treated as a suspect class because their presence in this country in violation of federal law is not a "constitutional irrelevancy." Nor is education a fundamental right; a State need not justify by compelling necessity every variation in the manner in which education is provided to its population. But more is involved in these cases than the abstract question whether § 21.031 discriminates against a suspect class, or whether education is a fundamental right. * * * By denying these children a basic education, we deny them the ability to live within the structure of our civic institutions, and foreclose any realistic possibility that they will contribute in even the smallest way to the progress of our Nation. In determining the rationality of § 21.031, we may appropriately take into account its costs to the Nation and to the innocent children who are its victims. In light of these countervailing costs, the discrimination contained in § 21.031 can hardly be considered rational unless it furthers some substantial goal of the State.

* * * [I]n the State's view, Congress' apparent disapproval of the presence of these children within the United States, and the evasion of the federal regulatory program that is the mark of undocumented status, provides authority for its decision to impose upon them special disabilities. Faced with an equal protection challenge respecting the treatment of aliens, we agree that the courts must be attentive to congressional policy; the exercise of congressional power might well affect the State's prerogatives to afford differential treatment to a particular class of aliens. But we are unable to find in the congressional immigration scheme any statement of policy that might weigh significantly in arriving at an equal protection balance concerning the State's authority to deprive these children of an education.

The Constitution grants Congress the power to "establish an uniform Rule of Naturalization." Art. I., § 8, cl. 4. Drawing upon this power, upon its plenary authority with respect to foreign relations and international commerce, and upon the inherent power of a sovereign to close its borders, Congress has developed a complex scheme governing admission to our Nation and status within our borders. The obvious need for delicate policy judgments has counseled the Judicial Branch to avoid intrusion into this field. But this traditional caution does not persuade us that unusual deference must be shown the classification embodied in § 21.031. The States enjoy no power with respect to the classification of aliens. This power is "committed to the political branches of the Federal Government." *Mathews*, 426 U.S., at 81, 96 S.Ct., at 1892. Although it is "a routine and normally legitimate part" of the business of the Federal Government to classify on the basis of alien status, *id.*, at 85, 96 S.Ct., at 1894, and to "take into account the character of the relationship between the alien and this country," *id.*, at 80, 96 S.Ct., at 1891, only rarely are such matters relevant to legislation by a State.

As we recognized in *De Canas v. Bica*, 424 U.S. 351, 96 S.Ct. 933, 47 L.Ed.2d 43 (1976), the States do have some authority to act with respect to illegal aliens, at least where such action mirrors federal objectives and furthers a legitimate state goal. In *De Canas*, the State's program reflected Congress' intention to bar from employment all aliens except those possessing a grant of permission to work in this country. In contrast, there is no indication that the disability imposed by § 21.031 corresponds to any identifiable congressional policy. The State does not claim that the conservation of state educational resources was ever a congressional concern in restricting immigration. More importantly, the classification reflected in § 21.031 does not operate harmoniously within the federal program.

To be sure, like all persons who have entered the United States unlawfully, these children are subject to deportation. But there is no assurance that a child subject to deportation will ever be deported. An illegal entrant might be granted federal permission to continue to reside in this country, or even to become a citizen. In light of the discretionary federal power to grant relief from deportation, a State cannot realistically determine that any particular undocumented child will in fact be deported until after deportation proceedings have been completed. It would of course be most difficult for the State to justify a denial of education to a child enjoying an inchoate federal permission to remain.

We are reluctant to impute to Congress the intention to withhold from these children, for so long as they are present in this country through no fault of their own, access to a basic education. In other contexts, undocumented status, coupled with some articulable federal policy, might enhance state authority with respect to the treatment of undocumented aliens. But in the area of special constitutional sensitivity presented by these cases, and in the absence of any contrary indication fairly discernible in the present legislative record, we perceive no national policy that supports the State in denying these children an elementary education. * * * We therefore turn to the state objectives that are said to support § 21.031.

* * *

First, appellants appear to suggest that the State may seek to protect itself from an influx of illegal immigrants. While a State might have an interest in mitigating the potentially harsh economic effects of sudden shifts in population, § 21.031 hardly offers an effective method of dealing with an urgent demographic or economic problem. There is no evidence in the record suggesting that illegal entrants impose any significant burden on the State's economy. To the contrary, the available evidence suggests that illegal aliens underutilize public services, while contributing their labor to the local economy and tax money to the state fisc. The dominant incentive for illegal entry into the State of Texas is the availability of employment; few if any illegal immigrants come to this country, or presumably to the State of Texas, in order to avail themselves of a free education. * * * [W]e think it clear that "[c]harging tuition to undocumented children constitutes a ludicrously ineffectual attempt to stem the tide of illegal immigration," [citing the district court decision], at least when compared with the alternative of prohibiting the employment of illegal aliens.

Second, * * * appellants suggest that undocumented children are appropriately singled out for exclusion because of the special burdens they impose on the State's ability to provide high-quality public education. But the record in no way supports the claim that exclusion of undocumented children is likely to improve the overall quality of education in the State. * * * Of course, even if improvement in the quality of education were a likely result of barring some *number* of children from the schools of the State, the State must support its selection of *this* group as the appropriate target for exclusion. * * *

Finally, appellants suggest that undocumented children are appropriately singled out because their unlawful presence within the United States renders them less likely than other children to remain within the boundaries of the State, and to put their education to productive social or political use within the State. Even assuming that such an interest is legitimate, it is an interest that is most difficult to quantify. The State has no assurance that any child, citizen or not, will employ the education provided by the State within the confines of the State's borders. In any event, the record is clear that many of the undocumented children disabled by this classification will remain in this country indefinitely, and that some will become lawful residents or citizens of the United States. * * *

* * *

JUSTICE MARSHALL, concurring.

While I join the Court's opinion, I do so without in any way retreating from my opinion in *San Antonio Independent School District v. Rodriguez*, 411 U.S. 1, 70–133, 93 S.Ct. 1278, 1315–1348, 36 L.Ed.2d 16 (1973) (dissenting opinion). I continue to believe that an individual's interest in education is fundamental, and that this view is amply supported "by the unique status accorded public education by our society, and by the close relationship between education and some of our most basic constitutional values." *Id.*, at 111, 93 S.Ct., at 1336. * * * It continues to be my view that a class-based denial of public education is utterly incompatible with the Equal Protection Clause of the Fourteenth Amendment.

JUSTICE BLACKMUN, concurring.

* * *

* * * Children denied an education are placed at a permanent and insurmountable competitive disadvantage, for an uneducated child is denied even the opportunity to achieve. * * * Other benefits provided by the State, such as housing and public assistance, are of course important; to an individual in immediate need, they may be more desirable than the right to be educated. But classifications involving the complete denial of education are in a sense unique, for they strike at the heart of equal protection values by involving the State in the creation of permanent class distinctions. In a sense, then, denial of an education is the analogue of denial of the right to vote: the former relegates the individual to second-class social status; the latter places him at a permanent political disadvantage.

* * *

JUSTICE POWELL, concurring.

* * *

Our review in a case such as these is properly heightened. The classification at issue deprives a group of children of the opportunity for education afforded all other children simply because they have been assigned a legal status due to a violation of law by their parents. These children thus have been singled out for a lifelong penalty and stigma. A legislative classification that threatens the creation of an underclass of future citizens and residents cannot be reconciled with one of the fundamental purposes of the Fourteenth Amendment. In these unique circumstances, the Court properly may require that the State's interests be substantial and that the means bear a "fair and substantial relation" to these interests.

* * * [T]he interests relied upon by the State would seem to be insubstantial in view of the consequences to the State itself of wholly uneducated persons living indefinitely within its borders. * * * [T]he exclusion of appellees' class of children from state-provided education is a type of punitive discrimination based on status that is impermissible under the Equal Protection Clause.

In reaching this conclusion, I am not unmindful of what must be the exasperation of responsible citizens and government authorities in Texas and other States similarly situated. Their responsibility, if any, for the influx of aliens is slight compared to that imposed by the Constitution on the Federal Government. So long as the ease of entry remains inviting, and the power to deport is exercised infrequently by the Federal Government, the additional expense of admitting these children to public schools might fairly be shared by the Federal and State Governments. But it hardly can be argued rationally that anyone benefits from the creation within our borders of a subclass of illiterate persons many of whom will remain in the State, adding to the problems and costs of both State and National Governments attendant upon unemployment, welfare, and crime.

CHIEF JUSTICE BURGER, with whom JUSTICE WHITE, JUSTICE REHNQUIST, and JUSTICE O'CONNOR join, dissenting.

* * * I fully agree that it would be folly—and wrong—to tolerate creation of a segment of society made up of illiterate persons, many having a limited or no command of our language. However, the Constitution does not constitute us as "Platonic Guardians" nor does it vest in this Court the authority to strike down laws because they do not meet our standards of desirable social policy, "wisdom," or "common sense." * * *

* * *

The Court acknowledges that, except in those cases when state classifications disadvantage a "suspect class" or impinge upon a "fundamental right," the Equal Protection Clause permits a state "substantial latitude" in distinguishing between different groups of persons. Moreover, the Court expressly—and correctly—rejects any suggestion that illegal aliens are a suspect class, or that education is a fundamental right. Yet by patching together bits and pieces of what might be termed quasi-suspect-class and quasi-fundamental-rights analysis, the Court spins out a theory custom-tailored to the facts of these cases.

* * *

The Court does not presume to suggest that appellees' purported lack of culpability for their illegal status prevents them from being deported or otherwise "penalized" under federal law. Yet would deportation be any less a "penalty" than denial of privileges provided to legal residents? Illegality of presence in the United States does not—and need not—depend on some amorphous concept of "guilt" or "innocence" concerning an alien's entry. Similarly, a state's use of federal immigration status as a basis for legislative classification is not necessarily rendered suspect for its failure to take such factors into account.

* * * This Court has recognized that in allocating governmental benefits to a given class of aliens, one "may take into account the character of the relationship between the alien and this country."

Mathews v. Diaz, 426 U.S. 67, 80, 96 S.Ct. 1883, 1891, 48 L.Ed.2d 478 (1976). When that "relationship" is a federally prohibited one, there can, of course, be no presumption that a state has a constitutional duty to include illegal aliens among the recipients of its governmental benefits.

* * *

The central question in these cases, as in every equal protection case not involving truly fundamental rights "explicitly or implicitly guaranteed by the Constitution," *San Antonio Independent School Dist., supra,* 411 U.S., at 33–34, 93 S.Ct., at 1296–1297, is whether there is some legitimate basis for a legislative distinction between different classes of persons. The fact that the distinction is drawn in legislation affecting access to public education—as opposed to legislation allocating other important governmental benefits, such as public assistance, health care, or housing—cannot make a difference in the level of scrutiny applied.

Once it is conceded—as the Court does—that illegal aliens are not a suspect class, and that education is not a fundamental right, our inquiry should focus on and be limited to whether the legislative classification at issue bears a rational relationship to a legitimate state purpose.

* * *

Without laboring what will undoubtedly seem obvious to many, it simply is not "irrational" for a state to conclude that it does not have the same responsibility to provide benefits for persons whose very presence in the state and this country is illegal as it does to provide for persons lawfully present. By definition, illegal aliens have no right whatever to be here, and the state may reasonably, and constitutionally, elect not to provide them with governmental services at the expense of those who are lawfully in the state. In *De Canas v. Bica*, 424 U.S. 351, 357, 96 S.Ct. 933, 937, 47 L.Ed.2d 43 (1976), we held that a State may protect its "fiscal interests and lawfully resident labor force from the deleterious effects on its economy resulting from the employment of illegal aliens." * * *

And yet they still pay taxes.

It is significant that the Federal Government has seen fit to exclude illegal aliens from numerous social welfare programs, such as the food stamp program, the old-age assistance, aid to families with dependent children, aid to the blind, aid to the permanently and totally disabled, and supplemental security income programs, the Medicare hospital insurance benefits program, and the Medicaid hospital insurance benefits for the aged and disabled program. Although these exclusions do not conclusively demonstrate the constitutionality of the State's use of the same classification for comparable purposes, at the very least they tend to support the rationality of excluding illegal alien residents of a state from such programs so as to preserve the state's finite revenues for the benefit of lawful residents.

* * *

NOTES AND QUESTIONS ON PLYLER V. DOE

1.   Several sources richly tell of the origins, backstory, and aftermath of *Plyler*. For a perceptive analysis of the role of the Mexican-American Legal Defense and Educational Fund (MALDEF) and the myriad lawyering choices, see Michael A. Olivas, *Plyler v. Doe, the Education of Undocumented Children, and the Polity*, in Immigration Stories 197–220 (David A. Martin & Peter H. Schuck eds., 2005). Looking at the families and offering a fascinating glimpse of the justices' deliberations, journalist Barbara Belejack unearthed this intriguing fact:

> The day the opinion was issued, a little-known Department of Justice lawyer co-wrote a memo chastising the U.S. solicitor general for not filing a brief taking Texas' side. Had such a brief been filed, future Supreme Court Chief Justice John Roberts suggested, Powell might have voted differently.

Barbara Belejack, *A Lesson in Equal Protection: The Texas cases that opened the schoolhouse door to undocumented immigrant children*, 99 Texas Observer no. 14 (July 13, 2007).

2.   Is *Plyler* consistent with *De Canas*, which figures prominently in both majority and dissent in *Plyler*? Why does depriving undocumented children of an education differ from depriving their parents of a job?

3.   In *De Canas*, the argument for federal preemption of California's employer sanctions was made by employers who, the plaintiffs contended, were maintaining an illegal workforce that excluded authorized workers. In *Plyler*, the federal preemption argument was made by migrant children. Did this difference affect the outcomes?

4.   Justice Brennan relies in part on the "[s]heer incapability or lax enforcement of the laws barring entry into this country, coupled with the failure to establish an effective bar to the employment of undocumented aliens." Quoting the district court, Brennan adds that "[c]harging tuition to undocumented children constitutes a ludicrously ineffectual attempt to stem the tide of illegal immigration," at least when compared with the alternative of prohibiting the employment of illegal aliens. And he notes "[t]here is no evidence in the record suggesting that illegal entrants impose any significant burden on the State's economy." Do these observations remain valid today? If not, what follows?

5.   The majority and dissent reflect remarkably different views of societal membership. Justice Brennan seems to see the children as members and reasons that denying education would "foreclose any realistic possibility that they will contribute in even the smallest way to the progress of our Nation." Contrast Chief Justice Burger: "By definition, illegal aliens have no right whatever to be here, and the state may reasonably, constitutionally, elect not to provide them with governmental services." Which account is more

persuasive? For thoughtful arguments in favor of recognizing unauthorized residents as members of the U.S. community, see Linda S. Bosniak, *Exclusion and Membership: The Dual Identity of the Undocumented Worker under United States Law,* 1988 Wis. L. Rev. 955; Gerald P. López, *Undocumented Mexican Migration: In Search of a Just Immigration Law and Policy,* 28 UCLA L. Rev. 615 (1981).

6.   Despite the significance of *Plyler* for education, Michael Olivas has commented on the decision's limited doctrinal reach outside this realm: "*Plyler*'s incontestably bold reasoning has not substantially influenced subsequent Supreme Court immigration jurisprudence in the twenty-plus years since it was decided." Olivas, *supra,* at 210–11. Moreover, no court has ever applied *Plyler* to require access to public colleges and universities. Some states have expressly barred persons who are unlawfully present in the United States from admission, public financial aid, or both.

7.   Does *Diaz* say that a *federal* law could constitutionally bar unauthorized children from public K–12 education? During debate on the 1996 Immigration Act, Congress considered an amendment by Congressman Elton Gallegly (R-CA) to let states bar unauthorized children from public education. After strong opposition from the Clinton administration, the proposal was removed from the final version of the 1996 Act. Though passed by the House 254–175 as a separate bill, it never came up for a Senate vote. What if the Gallegly amendment had been enacted and Texas re-adopted the statute invalidated in *Plyler*?

In answering this question, consider this passage in *Graham*: "Although the Federal Government admittedly has broad constitutional power to determine what aliens shall be admitted to the United States, the period they may remain, and the terms and conditions of their naturalization, Congress does not have the power to authorize the individual States to violate the Equal Protection Clause." 403 U.S. at 382, 91 S.Ct. 1857.

8.   Issues concerning the enforcement of *Plyler*'s doctrine persist where public school districts make it difficult for unauthorized children to enroll in K–12 public schools. *See, e.g.,* Benjamin Mueller, *New York Compels 20 School Districts to Lower Barriers to Immigrants,* N.Y. Times, Feb. 19, 2015, at A20; *Departments of Justice and Education Reach Settlement Agreement with Louisiana School System,* 91 Interp. Rel. 1225 (2014). A 2011 Alabama law required that parents provide immigration status information on their children before enrolling them in public schools. The Eleventh Circuit struck down this provision as a violation of equal protection and inconsistent with *Plyler. See Hispanic Interest Coalition of Alabama v. Governor of Alabama,* 691 F.3d 1236, 1244–49 (11th Cir. 2012).

Proposition 187

In November 1994, California voters approved Proposition 187, reprinted in the Statutory Supplement. This "Save Our State" initiative was intended to "provide for cooperation between [the] agencies of state and local government with the federal government, and to establish a system of required notification by and between such agencies to prevent illegal aliens in the United States from receiving benefits or public services in the State of California." As Republican Governor Pete Wilson, one of its most prominent champions, put it, illegal aliens would "self-deport."

As drafted, Proposition 187 restricted unauthorized migrants' access to public services, including education and non-emergency health care. It required state and local law enforcement, social services, health care and education officials to verify the immigration status of persons with whom they came in contact and to report to the INS anyone suspected of being unlawfully in the United States. It also imposed criminal penalties for the manufacture, distribution, sale, or use of false citizenship or permanent residence documents.

Lawsuits immediately challenged Proposition 187, and a federal district court held that federal immigration law preempted the requirements that state officials ascertain immigration status and report suspected unauthorized migrants to federal authorities. *League of United Latin American Citizens v. Wilson*, 908 F. Supp. 755 (C.D. Cal. 1995). Applying *Plyler*, the court also found it unconstitutional to deny public education to children without lawful immigration status, but it upheld the new criminal provisions relating to false documents.

Did federal law preempt California's denial of state benefits to unauthorized migrants? This aspect of Proposition 187 remained unresolved until the federal 1996 Welfare Act pervasively regulated noncitizen eligibility for state and federal benefits. The district court then ruled that this federal law preempted Proposition 187's public benefits provisions. *League of United Latin American Citizens v. Wilson*, 997 F. Supp. 1244, 1261 (C.D. Cal.1997).

The Proposition 187 litigation was ultimately settled after Democratic Governor Gray Davis took office. The state dropped its appeal. The public school access bar, the public benefits restrictions, and the requirements that state employees check status and report suspected unauthorized migrants never took effect, though the false documents provisions did. With the settlement, Proposition 187 never gave the U.S. Supreme Court a chance to revisit *Plyler*.

The supporters of Proposition 187 may have lost the battle but won the war. Though the Proposition was almost entirely invalidated as preempted by federal welfare legislation, congressional amendments two years later accomplished much of the supporters' original goal of excluding unauthorized migrants from benefit programs. This may remind you of another link between state and federal lawmaking over a century before—the enactment of the federal Chinese exclusion laws after similar state laws had been found unconstitutional as beyond state authority. Similarly, the popularity of Proposition 187 with California's voters in 1994 produced strong political incentives to change federal law and to toughen up enforcement practices before the 1996 Presidential election. Both political branches responded, leading to adoption of the restrictive 1996 Act.

Support for Proposition 187 reflected concern over the fiscal and social consequences of unauthorized migration, fear among some voters of a loss of control over culture and language, and anger at the federal government for failure to enforce immigration laws effectively. Kevin Johnson added: "it is difficult to refute the claim that the ethnicity of the stereotypical undocumented immigrant played at least *some* role in the passage of Proposition 187." Kevin R. Johnson, *An Essay on Immigration Politics, Popular Democracy, and California's Proposition 187: The Political Relevance and Legal Irrelevance of Race*, 70 Wash. L. Rev. 629, 651 (1995). What would it take to persuade you that Proposition 187—or any similar measure—does or does not reflect racial or ethnic animus?

The opposition to Proposition 187 also deserves comment. "What is striking," writes Linda Bosniak, "is the relatively narrow range of arguments that were made against Prop. 187." She continues:

> Especially notable was the near-complete omission from the public debate of one particular opposing argument which might have seemed, in theory, an obvious one to make: * * * that Prop. 187 should be rejected on grounds that its treatment of undocumented immigrants is unjust. * * *
>
> * * *
>
> * * * [W]hat the public mainly heard—in addition to charges of racism—were empirically-based predictions that the proposed policy provisions would fail to achieve their stated goal, and arguments highlighting the deleterious effects of the law on Americans (or Californians). The former arguments, of course, are not, by their terms, concerned with matters of justice at all, and although the latter arguments address human interests by addressing the law's social consequences, their concern is the law's effect on *American* well-being, and *American* interests. Even the racism argument * * * most often characterized the problem as one in which United States citizens or lawful permanent residents of color would be either maliciously or mistakenly ensnared by the initiative's provisions.
>
> * * *
>
> Here is the problem: Despite progressives' commitment to challenging   systemic   forms   of   subordination   and

marginalization, the political and legal landscape they are concerned with is most often a national landscape, and the boundaries they seek to dismantle are, most often, political and legal boundaries that exist within the already bounded community of the nation-state.

Linda S. Bosniak, *Opposing Prop. 187: Undocumented Immigrants and the National Imagination*, 28 Conn. L. Rev. 555, 567, 568, 580 (1996).

Starting in earnest about ten years after Proposition 187, a new wave of state and local laws limited unauthorized migrants' access to housing and work—and prompted court challenges. A prominent early example is an ordinance in Hazleton, Pennsylvania. According to its Findings and Declaration of Purpose:

> D. * * * [T]he City of Hazleton is authorized to abate public nuisances and empowered and mandated by the people of Hazleton to abate the nuisance of illegal immigration by diligently prohibiting the acts and policies that facilitate illegal immigration in a manner consistent with federal law and the objectives of Congress.
>
> * * *
>
> F. This ordinance seeks to secure to those lawfully present in the United States and this City, whether or not they are citizens of the United States, the right to live in peace free of the threat crime [*sic*], to enjoy the public services provided by this city without being burdened by the cost of providing goods, support and services to aliens unlawfully present in the United States, and to be free of the debilitating effects on their economic and social well being imposed by the influx of illegal aliens to the fullest extent that these goals can be achieved consistent with the Constitution and Laws of the United States and the Commonwealth of Pennsylvania.

Illegal Immigration Relief Act Ordinance (IIRAO) §§ 2D, 2F.

The City of Hazleton then addressed two main issues: employment and housing:

- **Employment:** Section 4 of the ordinance made it unlawful "for any business entity" to "recruit, hire for employment, or continue to employ" *or* "permit, dispatch, or instruct any person" who is an "unlawful worker" to work in Hazleton. "Unlawful worker" was defined to include any noncitizen not authorized to work under federal immigration law. Employers could protect themselves from liability by checking an employee's work authorization through the federal E–Verify system.

- **Housing:** Section 5 of the ordinance made it "unlawful for any person or business entity that owns a dwelling unit in the City to harbor an illegal alien in the dwelling unit, knowing or in reckless disregard of the fact that an alien has come to, entered, or remains in the United States in violation of law." § 5. To "harbor" meant "to let, lease, or rent a dwelling unit to an illegal alien." Section 7 required lawful immigration status to enter into a lease. A related Rental Registration Ordinance required any adult occupant of rental housing to have an occupancy permit, which could be obtained only with "[p]roper identification showing proof of legal citizenship and/or residency."

The district court held that federal law preempted these employment and housing provisions, and the Third Circuit affirmed.

Employment: The Third Circuit found that federal law did not preempt the field of employment of noncitizens not authorized to work, citing *De Canas*. The court then concluded that the employer sanctions in the Immigration Reform and Control Act (IRCA) of 1986 did not expressly preempt the employment sections of the Hazleton ordinance. The court reasoned that though part of IRCA expressly preempts state and local employer sanctions, IRCA exempts from express preemption any licensing laws, which it found the IIRAO to be.

The court next explained that a law that is not expressly preempted may still be preempted because it conflicts with federal law. The court found four types of conflict, in that the IIRAO:

(1) created a separate system for employer sanctions with increased burdens on employers;

(2) altered IRCA's employment verification scheme;

(3) included independent contractors, which IRCA excludes from coverage; and

(4) failed to balance employer sanctions with provisions to remedy discrimination that may be a consequence of employer sanctions.

See Lozano v. City of Hazleton, 620 F.3d 170, 209, 212–19 (3d Cir. 2010).

Housing: The Third Circuit found field preemption of the Hazleton housing provisions. It held that regulating who may be admitted to the United States and who may remain is a federal power "even if Congress had never acted in the field." According to the court, the INA comprehensively regulates immigration and naturalization, further strengthening the case for preemption. *Id.* at 220. The court also found conflict preemption: "these provisions attempt to effectively 'remove' persons from Hazleton based on a snapshot of their current immigration status, rather than based on a federal order of removal. This is fundamentally inconsistent with the INA." *Id.* at 221.

> Hazleton would effectively remove from its City an alien college student the federal government has purposefully declined to initiate removal proceedings against. So too would Hazleton remove an alien battered spouse, currently unlawfully present, but eligible for adjustment of status to lawful permanent resident under the special protections Congress has afforded to battered spouses and children. In each of these instances, as in every single instance in which Hazleton would deny residence to an alien based on immigration status rather than on a federal order of removal, Hazleton would act directly in opposition to federal law. * * * Hazleton is also plainly incorrect in claiming that its housing provisions "mirror" federal law.

Id. at 222–23.

A few localities in several other states enacted laws that similarly limited housing or employment for unauthorized migrants. In 2006, for example, Escondido, California, adopted housing restrictions similar to those in Hazleton. Valley Park, Missouri, adopted ordinances in 2006 and 2007 that made it unlawful to provide housing or employment to unauthorized migrants. In Farmers Branch, Texas, a series of city ordinances starting in 2006 required landlords to have "evidence of citizenship or eligible immigration status for each tenant family." Other localities enacted laws targeting day laborers, or they used existing trespassing, anti-solicitation, and similar ordinances to keep day laborers from gathering or seeking work. Several states moved to restrict unauthorized employment, some by going beyond federal law by requiring all employers to verify work authorization or by imposing extra penalties. On another front, Alabama, Georgia, and South Carolina banned unauthorized migrants from public colleges and universities. *See Hispanic Interest Coalition of Alabama v. Governor of Alabama*, 691 F.3d 1236, 1242 (11th Cir. 2012) (HB 56, § 8); Hiroshi Motomura, Immigration Outside the Law 73–75 (2014). Many of these efforts reflected coordinated advocacy, with one local or state law being used as a model for others. *See id.*; Julia Preston, *Lawyer Leads an Immigration Fight*, N.Y. Times, July 20, 2009, at A10.

———————

Soon after the Third Circuit's decision on Hazleton's housing employment restrictions, the U.S. Supreme Court issued the following decision.

CHAMBER OF COMMERCE V. WHITING

Supreme Court of the United States, 2011.
563 U.S. 582, 131 S.Ct. 1968, 179 L.Ed.2d 1031.

ROBERTS, C. J., delivered the opinion of the Court, except as to Parts II–B and III–B. SCALIA, KENNEDY, and ALITO, JJ., joined that opinion in full, and THOMAS, J., joined as to Parts I, II–A, and III–A and concurred in the judgment.

Federal immigration law expressly preempts "any State or local law imposing civil or criminal sanctions (other than through licensing and similar laws) upon those who employ . . . unauthorized aliens." INA § 274A(h)(2). A recently enacted Arizona statute—the Legal Arizona Workers Act—provides that the licenses of state employers that knowingly or intentionally employ unauthorized aliens may be, and in certain circumstances must be, suspended or revoked. The law also requires that all Arizona employers use a federal electronic verification system [E–Verify] to confirm that the workers they employ are legally authorized workers. The question presented is whether federal immigration law preempts those provisions of Arizona law. * * *

* * *

The Arizona law * * *requires that "every employer, after hiring an employee, shall verify the employment eligibility of the employee" by using E–Verify. "[P]roof of verifying the employment authorization of an employee through the E–verify program creates a rebuttable presumption that an employer did not knowingly employ an unauthorized alien."

* * *

IRCA expressly preempts States from imposing "civil or criminal sanctions" on those who employ unauthorized aliens, "other than through licensing and similar laws." INA 274A(h)(2). The Arizona law, on its face, purports to impose sanctions through licensing laws. The state law authorizes state courts to suspend or revoke an employer's business licenses if that employer knowingly or intentionally employs an unauthorized alien. * * *

* * *

A license is "a right or permission granted in accordance with law . . . to engage in some business or occupation, to do some act, or to engage in some transaction which but for such license would be unlawful." Webster's Third New International Dictionary 1304 (2002). Articles of incorporation and certificates of partnership allow the formation of legal entities and permit them as such to engage in business and transactions "which but for such" authorization "would be unlawful." *Ibid*. * * * Moreover, even if a law regulating articles of incorporation, partnership certificates, and the like is not itself a "licensing law," it is at the very least "similar" to a licensing law, and therefore comfortably within the savings clause.

* * *

IRCA expressly preempts some state powers dealing with the employment of unauthorized aliens and it expressly preserves others. We hold that Arizona's licensing law falls well within the confines of the authority Congress chose to leave to the States and therefore is not expressly preempted.

As an alternative to its express preemption argument, the Chamber contends that Arizona's law is impliedly preempted because it conflicts with federal law. At its broadest level, the Chamber's argument is that Congress "intended the federal system to be exclusive," and that any state system therefore necessarily conflicts with federal law. But Arizona's procedures simply implement the sanctions that Congress expressly allowed Arizona to pursue through licensing laws. Given that Congress specifically preserved such authority for the States, it stands to reason that Congress did not intend to prevent the States from using appropriate tools to exercise that authority.

And here Arizona went the extra mile in ensuring that its law closely tracks IRCA's provisions in all material respects. The Arizona law begins by adopting the federal definition of who qualifies as an "unauthorized alien."

Not only that, the Arizona law expressly provides that state investigators must verify the work authorization of an allegedly unauthorized alien with the Federal Government, and "shall not attempt to independently make a final determination on whether an alien is authorized to work in the United States." * * *

The federal determination on which the State must rely is provided under 8 U.S.C. § 1373(c). That provision requires the Federal Government to "verify or ascertain" an individual's "citizenship or immigration status" in response to a state request. Justice BREYER is concerned that this information "says nothing about work authorization." Justice SOTOMAYOR shares that concern. But if a § 1373(c) inquiry reveals that someone is a United States citizen, that certainly answers the question whether that individual is authorized to work. The same would be true if the response to a § 1373(c) query disclosed that the individual was a lawful permanent resident alien or, on the other hand, had been ordered removed. In any event, if the information provided under § 1373(c) does not confirm that an employee is an unauthorized alien, then the State cannot prove its case.

From this basic starting point, the Arizona law continues to trace the federal law. Both the state and federal law prohibit "knowingly" employing an unauthorized alien. * * *

The Arizona law provides employers with the same affirmative defense for good-faith compliance with the I–9 process as does the federal law. And both the federal and Arizona law accord employers a rebuttable presumption of compliance with the law when they use E–Verify to validate a finding of employment eligibility.

* * *

All that is required to avoid sanctions under the Legal Arizona Workers Act is to refrain from knowingly or intentionally violating the employment law. Employers enjoy safe harbors from liability when they use the I–9 system and E–Verify—as Arizona law requires them to do. The most rational path for employers is to obey the law—both the law barring the employment of unauthorized aliens and the law prohibiting discrimination [against U.S. citizens and some lawful permanent residents, which some Congress feared would be a result of employer sanctions]—and there is no reason to suppose that Arizona employers will choose not to do so.

As with any piece of legislation, Congress did indeed seek to strike a balance among a variety of interests when it enacted IRCA. Part of that balance, however, involved allocating authority between the Federal Government and the States. The principle that Congress adopted in doing so was not that the Federal Government can impose large sanctions, and the States only small ones. IRCA instead preserved state authority over a particular category of sanctions—those imposed "through licensing and similar laws."

Of course Arizona hopes that its law will result in more effective enforcement of the prohibition on employing unauthorized aliens. But in preserving to the States the authority to impose sanctions through licensing laws, Congress did not intend to preserve only those state laws that would have no effect. The balancing process that culminated in IRCA resulted in a ban on hiring unauthorized aliens, and the state law here simply seeks to enforce that ban.

* * *

The Chamber also argues that Arizona's requirement that employers use the federal E–Verify system to determine whether an employee is authorized to work is impliedly preempted. * * *

* * * The provision of IIRIRA setting up the program that includes E–Verify contains no language circumscribing state action. * * * [A]bsent a prior violation of federal law, "the Secretary of Homeland Security may not require any person or other entity [outside of the Federal

Government] to participate in a pilot program" such as E–Verify. That provision limits what the Secretary of Homeland Security may do—nothing more.

* * *

Arizona's use of E–Verify does not conflict with the federal scheme. The Arizona law requires that "every employer, after hiring an employee, shall verify the employment eligibility of the employee" through E–Verify. That requirement is entirely consistent with the federal law. And the consequences of not using E–Verify under the Arizona law are the same as the consequences of not using the system under federal law. In both instances, the only result is that the employer forfeits the otherwise available rebuttable presumption that it complied with the law.

Congress's objective in authorizing the development of E–Verify was to ensure reliability in employment authorization verification, combat counterfeiting of identity documents, and protect employee privacy. Arizona's requirement that employers operating within its borders use E–Verify in no way obstructs achieving those aims.

In fact, the Federal Government has consistently expanded and encouraged the use of E–Verify. When E–Verify was created in 1996, it was meant to last just four years and it was made available in only six States. Congress since has acted to extend the E–Verify program's existence on four separate occasions, the most recent of which ensures the program's vitality through 2012. And in 2003 Congress directed the Secretary of Homeland Security to make E–Verify available in all 50 States. * * *

* * *

IRCA expressly reserves to the States the authority to impose sanctions on employers hiring unauthorized workers, through licensing and similar laws. In exercising that authority, Arizona has taken the route least likely to cause tension with federal law. It uses the Federal Government's own definition of "unauthorized alien," it relies solely on the Federal Government's own determination of who is an unauthorized alien, and it requires Arizona employers to use the Federal Government's own system for checking employee status. If even this gives rise to impermissible conflicts with federal law, then there really is no way for the State to implement licensing sanctions, contrary to the express terms of the savings clause.

Because Arizona's unauthorized alien employment law fits within the confines of IRCA's savings clause and does not conflict with federal immigration law, the judgment of the United States Court of Appeals for the Ninth Circuit is affirmed.

JUSTICE KAGAN took no part in the consideration or decision of this case.

JUSTICE BREYER, with whom JUSTICE GINSBURG joins, dissenting.

* * *

* * * [T]he state law falls within [IRCA's] general pre-emption rule and is pre-empted—unless it also falls within that rule's exception for "licensing and similar laws." Unlike the Court, I do not believe the state law falls within this exception, and I consequently would hold it pre-empted.

* * *

Essentially, the federal Act requires employers to verify the work eligibility of their employees. And in doing so, the Act balances three competing goals. First, it seeks to discourage American employers from hiring aliens not authorized to work in the United States.

Second, Congress wished to avoid "placing an undue burden on employers," *id.*, at 90, and the Act seeks to prevent the "harassment" of "innocent employers," S. Rep. No. 99–132, p. 35 (1985).

Third, the Act seeks to prevent employers from disfavoring job applicants who appear foreign. * * *

The Act reconciles these competing objectives in several ways:

First, the Act prohibits employers from hiring an alien knowing that the alien is unauthorized to work in the United States. INA § 274A(a)(1)(A).

Second, the Act provides an easy-to-use mechanism that will allow employers to determine legality: the I–9 form. * * *

* * *

Third, the Act creates a central enforcement mechanism. The Act directs the Attorney General to establish a single set of procedures for receiving complaints, investigating those complaints that "have a substantial probability of validity," and prosecuting violations. INA § 274A(e)(1). * * *

Fourth, the Act makes it "an unfair immigration-related employment practice ... to discriminate against any individual" in respect to employment "because of such individual's national origin." INA § 274B(a).

Fifth, the Act sets forth a carefully calibrated sanction system. * * *

* * *

Why would Congress, after deliberately limiting ordinary penalties to the range of a few thousand dollars per illegal worker, want to permit far more drastic state penalties that would directly and mandatorily destroy entire businesses? Why would Congress, after carefully balancing sanctions to avoid encouraging discrimination, want to allow States to destroy that balance? Why would Congress, after creating detailed procedural protections for employers, want to allow States to undermine them? Why would Congress want to write into an express pre-emption provision—a provision designed to prevent States from undercutting federal statutory objectives—an exception that could so easily destabilize its efforts? The answer to these questions is that Congress would not have wanted to do any of these things. And that fact indicates that the majority's reading of the licensing exception—a reading that would allow what Congress sought to forbid—is wrong.

* * *

I would therefore read the words "licensing and similar laws" as covering state licensing systems applicable primarily to the licensing of firms in the business of recruiting or referring workers for employment, such as the state agricultural labor contractor licensing schemes in existence when the federal Act was created. This reading is consistent with the provision's history and language, and it minimizes the risk of harm of the kind just described.

* * *

Congress had strong reasons for insisting on the voluntary nature of the program. E–Verify was conceived as, and remains, a pilot program. Its database consists of tens of millions of Social Security and immigration records kept by the Federal Government. These records are prone to error. And making the program mandatory would have been hugely expensive.

* * *

In co-opting a federal program and changing the key terms under which Congress created that program, Arizona's mandatory state law simply ignores both the federal language and the reasoning it reflects, thereby posing an " 'obstacle to the accomplishment' " of the objectives Congress' statute evinces. *Crosby [v. National Foreign Trade Council,* 530 U.S. 363, 373, 120 S.Ct. 2288, 147 L.Ed.2d 352 (2000) (quoting *Hines v. Davidowitz,* 312 U.S. 52, 67, 61 S.Ct. 399, 85 L.Ed. 581 (1941))].

* * *

JUSTICE SOTOMAYOR, dissenting.

* * *

The Act * * * escapes express pre-emption only if it falls within IRCA's parenthetical saving clause for "licensing and similar laws."

* * *

* * * Putting aside the question whether § 1373(c) actually provides access to work authorization information, § 1373(c) did not exist when IRCA was enacted in 1986. Arizona has not identified any avenue by which States could have accessed work authorization information in the first decade of IRCA's existence. The absence of any such avenue at the time of IRCA's enactment speaks volumes as to how Congress would have understood the saving clause to operate: If States had no access to information regarding the work authorization status of aliens, how could state courts have accurately adjudicated the question whether an employer had employed an unauthorized alien?

* * *

* * * [G]iven Congress' express goal of "unifor[m]" enforcement of "the immigration laws of the United States," IRCA § 115, I cannot believe that Congress intended for the 50 States and countless localities to implement their own distinct enforcement and adjudication procedures for deciding whether employers have employed unauthorized aliens. * * *

In sum, the statutory scheme as a whole defeats Arizona's and the majority's reading of the saving clause. Congress would not sensibly have permitted States to determine for themselves whether a person has employed an unauthorized alien, while at the same time creating a specialized federal procedure for making such a determination, withholding from the States the information necessary to make such a determination, and precluding use of the I–9 forms in nonfederal proceedings.

To render IRCA's saving clause consistent with the statutory scheme, I read the saving clause to permit States to impose licensing sanctions following a final federal determination that a person has violated § 274A(a)(1)(A) by knowingly hiring, recruiting, or referring for a fee an unauthorized alien. This interpretation both is faithful to the saving clause's text, and best reconciles the saving clause with IRCA's "careful regulatory scheme," [*United States v. Locke,* 529 U.S. 89, 106, 120 S.Ct. 1135, 146 L.Ed.2d 69 (2000)]. It also makes sense as a practical matter. In enacting IRCA's pre-emption clause, Congress vested in the Federal Government the authority to impose civil and criminal sanctions on persons who employ unauthorized aliens. Licensing and other types of business-related permissions are typically a matter of state law, however. * * *

* * *

NOTES AND QUESTIONS ON
CHAMBER OF COMMERCE V. WHITING

1.   Assume that you are advising a councilmember in your city who asks: Does *Chamber of Commerce v. Whiting* foreclose any preemption challenge, as long as the city enacts an ordinance that "mirrors" federal immigration law by prohibiting employment for only noncitizens who are not authorized to work under federal law? Or did the Court's holding turn on the specifics of the Arizona law? Suppose the same councilmember also asks: What are the implications of *Chamber of Commerce v. Whiting* for preemption of state and local restrictions on *housing* for unauthorized migrants?

2.   What does it mean for state or local activity to be consistent with federal immigration law? Why isn't Hazleton's housing ordinance consistent with federal immigration law? When the federal government makes immigration-related decisions, must it do so in certain ways so that it is federal "law" for preemption purposes? *Compare Erie RR. v. Tompkins*, 304 U.S. 64, 58 S.Ct. 817, 82 L.Ed. 1188 (1938), *with Swift v. Tyson*, 41 U.S. 1, 10 L.Ed. 865 (1842).

3.   Another way to view the effect of state and local immigration activity is to assess its relationship to immigration law and policy at the national level through some combination of experimentation and political influence. According to one interpretation, "state involvement in the immigration context has long been driven by political actors seeking to reshape the federal policy-making process." Rick Su, *The States of Immigration*, 45 Wm. & Mary L. Rev. 1339, 1357 (2013). Another view is the practical effect of state and local activity is to keep some perspectives from becoming nationwide policy, if states or localities are allowed to vent on immigration issues through their own decisionmaking as an exercise of "steam-valve federalism." Peter J. *Spiro, Learning to Live With Immigration Federalism*, 29 Conn. L. Rev. 1627, 1630 (1997). *See also* Hiroshi Motomura, Immigration Outside the Law 71–73, 138–41 (2014). On the political contexts in which state and local measures on immigration and immigrants arise, see Pratheepan Gulasekaram & Karthick Ramakrishnan, The New Immigration Federalism 57–118 (2015).

4.   When states and localities take steps to reinforce immigration law enforcement in their jurisdictions, is the conflict not principally between federal and state/local government, but between two groups of states—those that act against unauthorized migration, and those that do not? Consider this comment, originally about Proposition 187, but applicable to any state effort to diminish the perceived costs of unauthorized migration, either by securing federal reimbursement or more directly by reducing the unauthorized population itself:

> If California and similar states secure increased federal
> reimbursement, they will have succeeded in harnessing the power of
> the federal budget to shift immigration-related costs to the other

group of states. Proposition 187 is a more direct means to the same end. If it works as intended and reduces the undocumented population in California, it will likely do so as much by shifting the undocumented population to other states as by deterring its entry into the United States as a whole.

Hiroshi Motomura, *Immigration and Alienage, Federalism and Proposition 187*, 35 Va. J. Int'l L. 201 (1994). In striking down a local ordinance in Farmers Branch, Texas, that restricted rental housing based on lawful immigration status, Judge Higginson wrote for the majority but also wrote separately in a special concurring opinion:

> the Ordinance, inasmuch as it attempts to isolate Farmers Branch from a problem common to other states by burdening other localities with non-citizens illegally in the United States, may be invalid under the dormant Commerce Clause. As Justice Cardozo wrote in *Baldwin v. G.A.F. Seelig, Inc.*, "the peoples of the several states must sink or swim together." 294 U.S. 511, 523, 55 S.Ct. 497, 79 L.Ed. 1032 (1935).

See also Erin F. Delaney, Note, *In the Shadow of Article I: Applying a Dormant Commerce Clause Analysis to State Laws Regulating Aliens*, 82 NYU L. Rev. 1821 (2007). If this is true, should the federal government equalize the fiscal effects of unauthorized migration among the several states? How could a fair accounting of the benefits and costs be reached?

3. DIRECT STATE AND LOCAL ENFORCEMENT

State and local officers may be active in direct immigration law enforcement by involving themselves in identification, arrest, or detention of individuals who are believed to be violating federal immigration law. We will first examine federal statutes or programs that clearly and expressly authorize state or local involvement. We will then turn to state and local involvement in direct enforcement that may go beyond what the federal government has authorized.

a. With Federal Authorization

Federal law and practice provide an array of programs that expressly authorize state and local direct involvement in immigration law enforcement. We sketch some of the major programs here. For a fuller account, see Jennifer M. Chacón, *A Diversion of Attention: Immigration Courts and the Adjudication of Fourth and Fifth Amendment Rights*, 58 Duke L.J. 1563, 1586–98 (2010).

Section 287(g) agreements. Under INA § 287(g), enacted in 1996 and first implemented in 2002, the federal government may authorize state and local law enforcement officials to carry out immigration law enforcement functions "in relation to the investigation, apprehension, or detention of aliens in the United States (including the transportation of such aliens * * * to detention centers)," under an agreement with DHS that provides for training and ongoing federal supervision of the state and local officers involved (though the cost is usually borne by the nonfederal agency). The agreement spells out the specific functions expected of the cooperating state or local agency; it is not a blanket deputization of state and local officers to act as federal immigration enforcers.

Agreements follow two basic models, with some agreements combining the two. The "jail model" authorizes trained state officers to carry out immigration enforcement only in local jails, affecting persons already arrested on a criminal charge under state or local law. These officers interview detainees and query immigration databases to determine removability, issue charging documents if appropriate, and then possibly transport the person to ICE custody. The "task force model" authorizes immigrant status determination as part of a wider range of state or local policing activities that involve contact with the general public.

The number of § 287(g) agreements grew to about 70 in 2010, but since that time the program has been scaled back. ICE announced in 2012 that it would not renew existing agreements following the task force model, stating that other programs, notably Secure Communities (discussed below) "are a more efficient use of resources." U.S. Immigr. & Customs Enforcement, *FY 2012: ICE Announces Year-End Removal Numbers, Highlights Focus on Key Priorities and Issues New National Detainer Guidance to Further Focus Resources* (Dec. 20, 2012. By early 2016, only 32 jurisdictions in 16 states had § 287(g) agreements with ICE. *See Fact Sheet: Delegation of Immigration Authority Section 287(g) Immigration and Nationality Act*, U.S. Immigr. & Customs Enforcement, https://www.ice.gov/287g. *See generally* Doris Meissner, Donald M. Kerwin, Muzaffar Chishti & Claire Bergeron, Immigration Enforcement in the United States: The Rise of a Formidable Machinery 103–07 (Migration Policy Inst. 2013).

The Criminal Alien Program (CAP). Under this program, ICE officers screen arrestees in local jails—sometimes in-person and sometimes through remote electronic means—to identify and issue detainers against noncitizens in local custody who lack authorization to be in the United States. CAP also operates in state and federal prisons, where longer sentences often permit the completion of removal proceedings (rather than the simple issuance of a detainer) while the person is incarcerated. If the person is ruled removable, ICE will then have an enforceable final order at the point of release and will incur only limited detention expenses before removal. *See generally* Meissner, et al., Immigration Enforcement in the United States, *supra*, at 100–02. For a critical examination of CAP's operation in one Texas city, see Trevor Gardner II & Aarti Kohli, The C.A.P. Effect: Racial Profiling in the ICE

Criminal Alien Program (2009), http://www.law.berkeley.edu/files/policy brief_irving_0909_v9.pdf.

Secure Communities. Under DHS' Secure Communities initiative, now discontinued, the fingerprints sent by the local law enforcement agency to the FBI as part of the ordinary criminal arrest and booking process were also checked automatically against IDENT, the DHS biometrics-based immigration database, to determine any previous encounters with immigration agencies or consular officers. No state or local officer made a preliminary decision whether the person was a noncitizen subject to DHS jurisdiction, and only persons actually arrested and fingerprinted were checked against IDENT. The stated purpose was to facilitate the removal of aliens with criminal convictions, with more serious crimes as the priority.

Compared to § 287(g) agreements, Secure Communities was much broader, with nationwide coverage as of 2013. But as Secure Communities brought more noncitizens into contact with federal immigration enforcement, the initiative came under heavy criticism that it targeted noncitizens who were not serious criminal offenders at all, and that it undermined immigrants' trust in local law enforcement. *But see* Adam B. Cox & Thomas J. Miles, *Legitimacy and Cooperation: Will Immigrants Cooperate with Local Police Who Enforce Federal Immigration Law?*, http://papers.ssrn.com/sol3/papers.cfm?abstract_id= 2658265 (citing sources for the concern that Secure Communities interfered with policing in immigrant communities, but casting doubt on that view).

Partly in response to criticism of Secure Communities, ICE director John Morton issued memoranda in June 2010 and June 2011 to regularize the exercise of prosecutorial discretion as to individuals identified through Secure Communities and other ICE enforcement programs. These memos are available at http://www.ice.gov/doclib/secure-communities/pdf/prosecutorial-discretion-memo.pdf, and discussed in Chapter Seven, p. 775. The next reading analyzes the evolution of Secure Communities from that point onward.

DAVID A. MARTIN, RESOLUTE ENFORCEMENT IS NOT JUST FOR RESTRICTIONISTS: BUILDING A STABLE AND EFFICIENT IMMIGRATION ENFORCEMENT SYSTEM

30 J. L. & Politics 401, 443–45, 449–54 (2015).

* * * [Secure Communities (SC)] was planned and initially launched during a period in 2007 and 2008, when the undocumented population still showed substantial annual growth, and when a great many state and local governments were clamoring for a role in tougher immigration enforcement. The main pressures on DHS were for *more* cooperation,

more sharing of information, and more vigor in removing immigration violators who had been arrested by local authorities. In that environment, key federal officials viewed SC as presenting fewer risks of inappropriate LEA [law enforcement agency] behavior than, for example, Section 287(g) task force agreements, because local officers have no occasion to make immigration status decisions as part of the SC process; they were expected simply to continue making arrests for crimes within their own clear jurisdiction.

* * *

Nonetheless, SC became controversial because of missteps in its early implementation and in the explanations and defenses offered by DHS, and—perhaps most importantly—because its primary deployments came at a time when a solid majority of the unauthorized population had lived in the United States for a decade or more and thus enjoyed substantial community ties. Initiating removal of undocumented arrestees charged with minor offenses or whose criminal charges were dropped before conviction—even if fully justified under the immigration laws—therefore clashed with expectations held by a growing portion of the politically active U.S. population for the legalization of much of the long-resident undocumented population.

Again, the timing is important in understanding how the controversy unfolded. The enforcement fervor of 2007 through 2009—the climate in which certain key design decisions about the program were made—had abated considerably by 2011 through 2013, the period when Secure Communities was activated in most jurisdictions. * * * [T]he fervor cooled largely because recession and border deployments had actually ended the net growth of the unauthorized population. In response, many communities were increasingly coming to terms with the migrants already in their midst.

Immigrant advocates adapted skillfully to the changed public climate, while also widely publicizing DHS's mistakes and course changes.

* * *

Faced with mounting [political] opposition, some [state and local] jurisdictions, starting in 2010, began telling ICE that they did not want to participate in Secure Communities. ICE's initial manner of handling local relations in communities where it was planning to activate SC had led localities to believe that they had a choice in whether or not to participate, because participation in the early stages commenced only with a Memorandum of Agreement (MOA) worked out with the local authorities. The exact reason for ICE's initial reliance on jointly signed MOAs appears obscure, but it was in any event legally erroneous. Secure

Communities was fundamentally an arrangement between two federal agencies to share information voluntarily supplied to one of them. A locality could opt out of the data-sharing with ICE only by declining to provide the fingerprint images to the FBI—a wholly unlikely outcome, because obtaining the criminal history information from the FBI remains highly important to all LEAs.

As ICE encountered this kind of local resistance, it dropped the use of MOAs and announced that opting out was not possible. This sharp change of signals, though legally correct, further angered some state and local officials and many activists. Pressure at the local level then shifted, as SC opponents worked to cultivate different forms of LEA opt-outs. If the fingerprints were going to reach ICE in any event, the main avenue for disaffected LEAs was to decline to cooperate in transfers requested by ICE—that is, to refuse to honor ICE detainers. This step is potentially much more damaging to immigration enforcement, at least in blanket form, for it greatly complicates ICE's process for taking custody, even of deportable noncitizens with serious criminal records—whether ICE learned of their local detention through SC or through any other source. Some jurisdictions adopted blanket noncompliance. Most resisting jurisdictions took a more measured step, however, announcing that they would not honor detainers in the absence of a serious criminal charge— or, for some, in the absence of an actual conviction for a serious crime. Covered crimes varied widely. California's adoption of the TRUST Act [reprinted in the Statutory Supplement] in October 2013, which limited cooperation to cases where the person has been convicted of a serious or violent felony or certain other designated crimes, or has been arrested for such an offense and a magistrate has found that the arrest is supported by probable cause, proved influential in leading to wider adoption of similar policies by other state and local legislatures and enforcement agencies.

But the detainer-resistance snowball truly gained momentum with the issuance of several court decisions, beginning in 2013, which held out the prospect that municipalities could face significant damages liability for prolonging an individual's period of detention or tightening custody conditions based only on the issuance of an ICE detainer. The core problem was that ICE detainers at that time did not necessarily represent a finding that probable cause existed to justify detention for an immigration violation, because issuing officers often checked only that box on the detainer form stating that ICE had "initiated an investigation to determine" whether the person is removable. Courts held this insufficient to meet Fourth Amendment requirements. * * * These decisions, though many of them ruled merely on preliminary issues, tipped dozens of new jurisdictions toward limiting or rejecting cooperation with ICE detainers.

As public objections and LEA defections from at least some forms of ICE cooperation mounted, advocates proposed major changes to Secure Communities. The proposals ranged from termination of the program altogether to more focused operational changes, such as postponing checks against the DHS fingerprint database until a criminal conviction (or for some advocates, a felony conviction) was final. Termination was not a realistic outcome, given SC's strong congressional support, manifested in generous appropriations statutes. Checking fingerprints only *after* conviction was equally unrealistic. Such a requirement would add expensive logistical complexity, necessitating either a cumbersome second taking and transmitting of prints by the LEA or the deployment of a brand new system that would notify ICE upon conviction and somehow pull up just the newly-convicted person's long-stored fingerprints for checking against IDENT. It would also disable one of the cardinal efficiencies of SC, because the early check helped assure ICE action against high-priority violators even if the criminal process terminated abruptly.

* * *

By late 2014, it was apparent that DHS would probably need significant changes to regain the willing trust and cooperation of LEAs— and to ameliorate their litigation exposure deriving from DHS's former detainer practices. The challenge, however, was to figure out how to make prudent cutbacks while still preserving the core immigration enforcement advantages possible from efficient IDENT checks of fingerprints sent to the FBI—and to do so in a way that might foster gradual restoration of wider cooperation, if the background conditions someday become more favorable (particularly in a post-legalization world).

[DHS] Secretary [Jeh] Johnson issued a memorandum on Secure Communities on November 20, 2014, directing significant modifications [hereafter referred to as the "PEP Memorandum"]. As usual, much will depend on the details of implementation. But the reforms, in my view, are reasonably well-designed to meet the objectives just mentioned.

Johnson's memo begins by announcing that "[t]he Secure Communities program, as we know it, will be discontinued." Stating that the overarching goal of Secure Communities remains valid, the Secretary directed that "a fresh start and a new program are necessary," the latter to be known as the Priority Enforcement Program (PEP). Importantly, the new program will "continue to rely on fingerprint-based biometric data submitted during bookings" by LEAs, to be immediately checked against IDENT. The key operational change comes at the next step in the process. Johnson directed that ICE henceforth will seek the transfer of a noncitizen from the LEA after an IDENT hit only when the person fits a limited subset of the new and narrower enforcement priorities also promulgated the same day in another memo from the Secretary. In essence, the applicable priorities require *conviction* of a specifically described set of crimes, which excludes misdemeanors not deemed "significant" according to a definition spelled out in the priorities memo. * * *

Of perhaps greater long-term importance, Secretary Johnson's PEP Memorandum also entrenches significant changes to the ICE detainer practices that had been primarily responsible for most of the damages litigation directed at LEAs. Johnson directed that ICE replace requests for detention with simple requests for timely notification of when the LEA would release an individual falling within the PEP priorities. ICE then bears the responsibility to assure that it arrives in time to take custody; it cannot rely on or expect a 48-hour extension of detention, as had been the customary request in the previous versions of ICE detainers. Presumably no detainee will be subjected to a lengthened period of detention based on the ICE request for information—thus apparently avoiding one of the main triggers for Fourth Amendment litigation.

The PEP Memorandum also countenances the use of a stronger ICE action, an actual request for detention leading to transfer, "in special circumstances," which will apparently be defined in later guidance. The Memo directs that any such request must state that the person is subject to a final order of removal or else specify other reasons why "there is . . . sufficient probable cause to find that the person is a removable alien, thereby addressing the Fourth Amendment concerns raised in recent federal court decisions."

NOTES AND QUESTIONS ON
PEP, DETAINERS, AND "SANCTUARY CITIES"

1.   For other accounts and evaluations of the growing resistance to Secure Communities and the evolution to PEP, see, *e.g.,* Juliet P. Stumpf, *D(e)volving Discretion: Lessons from the Life and Times of Secure Communities,* 64 Am. U.L. Rev. 1259 (2015) ; Cristina M. Rodríguez, *Toward Détente in Immigration Federalism*, 30 J.L. & Politics 505, 512–20 (2015); Ming Hsu Chen, *Trust in Immigration Enforcement: State Noncooperation and Sanctuary Cities after Secure Communities*, 91 Chicago-Kent L. Rev. 13 (2016); Eisha Jain, *Arrests as Regulation*, 67 Stan. L. Rev. 809 (2015); Christopher N. Lasch, *Rendition Resistance,* 92 N.C.L. Rev. 149 (2014).

2.   **PEP's shorter list of priorities.** In November 2014, DHS Secretary Johnson issued the Priorities Memorandum, described and excerpted in Chapter 7, pp. 781–786, on the same day that he issued the separate PEP Memo terminating Secure Communities. The Priorities Memo essentially exempts an estimated 87 percent of the resident undocumented population from enforcement. The PEP Memorandum mandates enforcement through PEP against an even narrower population; it authorizes "requests for

notification" only when the person falls into the following *subset* of the new priorities:

> 1(a)—aliens engaged in or suspected of terrorism or espionage, or who otherwise pose a danger to national security

> 1(c)—aliens convicted of an offense for which an element was active participation in a criminal street gang, as defined in 18 U.S.C. § 521(a), or aliens not younger than 16 years of age who intentionally participated in an organized criminal gang to further the illegal activity of the gang

> 1(d)—aliens convicted of an offense classified as a felony in the convicting jurisdiction, other than a state or local offense for which an essential element was the alien's immigration status

> 1(e)—aliens convicted of an "aggravated felony," as that term is defined in section 101(a)(43) of the Immigration and Nationality Act at the time of the conviction

> 2(a)—aliens convicted of three or more misdemeanor offenses, other than minor traffic offenses or state or local offenses for which an essential element was the alien's immigration status, provided the offenses arise out of three separate incidents

> 2(b)—aliens convicted of a "significant misdemeanor," which for these purposes is an offense of domestic violence; sexual abuse or exploitation; burglary; unlawful possession or use of a firearm; drug distribution or trafficking; or driving under the influence; or if not an offense listed above, one for which the individual was sentenced to time in custody of 90 days or more (the sentence must involve time to be served in custody, and does not include a suspended sentence)

See Memorandum from Jeh Charles Johnson, Secretary of Homeland Security, on Policies for the Apprehension, Detention and Removal of Undocumented Immigrants, Nov. 20, 2014 [the Priorities Memo]; Memorandum from Jeh Charles Johnson, Secretary of Homeland Security, on Secure Communities, Nov. 20, 2014 [the PEP Memo].

PEP will *not* ordinarily be used for the following categories listed in the Priorities Memorandum, even though such persons remain subject to DHS enforcement if located in some other fashion:

> 1(b)—"aliens apprehended at the border or ports of entry while attempting to unlawfully enter the United States";

> 2(c)—"aliens apprehended anywhere in the United States after unlawfully entering or re-entering the United States * * * [after] January 1, 2014";

2(d)—"aliens who * * * have significantly abused the visa or visa waiver programs";

3—"those who have been issued a final order of removal on or after January 1, 2014."

Be sure you understand when ICE will issue a PEP request for notification. On what grounds, if any, can a state or local LEA still legitimately resist cooperation with a PEP request?

3. **Detainers.** The detainers that play a key role in the events discussed in the Martin excerpt are by no means unique to the immigration field. In other parts of the criminal justice system their use is routine and usually not controversial; they represent a common form of cooperation among law enforcement agencies. For example, a Virginia county that has issued an arrest warrant may learn that the subject has been arrested for a different offense by a sheriff in Maryland. The Virginia county may issue a detainer addressed to the Maryland sheriff, asking the sheriff to notify it when the person is about to be released, and to hold him for a short additional period in order to permit the Virginia county to arrange for his pickup or transfer. That Maryland release may not occur for many years (if the accused is convicted and sentenced to prison), or it could happen quickly, for example if the Maryland prosecutor decides not to pursue the case. Such cooperation among LEAs is partially structured under a federal statute, the Interstate Agreement on Detainers Act, codified at 18 U.S.C.A. app. 2 § 2 (2012), which contains safeguards for an individual who wants a speedy trial in the jurisdiction that filed the detainer.

Immigration detainers, sometimes called "immigration holds," have been in use for decades, developed as a kind of administrative analogy to the criminal-justice practice. But they have never had a clear and general statutory foundation. The traditional detainer form (now discontinued) indicated the federal immigration agency's interest in the individual, asked for notification before the named person would be released, and also requested that the person be held for up to an additional 48 hours (not counting weekends or holidays), to provide time for INS or ICE to send an officer to pick him or her up. Some language in that traditional detainer form suggested that LEA cooperation was mandatory. But when that issue came into clear focus (a byproduct of the Secure Communities controversy), DHS clarified internally that ICE detainers serve only as requests.

As the Martin excerpt explains, it was not widely understood that detainers are simply requests until numerous damages lawsuits were filed in the years 2012–14 against LEAs or officers who had extended confinement or made it more restrictive based on an ICE detainer. In preliminary rulings, several courts rejected the LEA defense that detention pursuant to an ICE detainer was mandatory. These decisions received wide publicity among state and local officials, because they suggested significant monetary liability if an LEA or local officer enforced an ICE detainer. *Miranda-Olivares v. Clackamas County*, 2014 WL 1414305 (D. Ore. Apr. 11, 2014), probably drew the most attention, because the court found possible liability in the very common scenario of extended detention for a noncitizen arrestee. Other cases involved ICE detainers mistakenly placed on U.S. citizens, a far less frequent occurrence. *See Morales v. Chadbourne,* 793 F.3d 208 (1st Cir. 2015); *Galarza v. Szalczyk,* 745 F.3d 634 (3d Cir. 2014). On the LEA reaction, see Jennifer Medina, *Fearing Lawsuits, Sheriffs Balk at U.S. Request to Hold Noncitizens for Extra Time,* N.Y. Times, July 6, 2014, at A10; Julia Preston, *Sheriffs Limit Detention of Immigrants,* N.Y. Times, Apr. 19, 2014, at A11.

A significant number of jurisdictions throughout the United States curtailed their compliance with federal detainers—at least 134 jurisdictions nationwide as of mid-2014, including localities in Colorado, Florida, Kansas, Maryland, Massachusetts, Minnesota, New Mexico, Oregon, Pennsylvania, and Washington. In California, Attorney General Kamala Harris advised local law enforcement agencies that complying with federal detainer requests could expose them to civil liability, even in cases listed in the California TRUST Act as appropriate for transfer to ICE.

The PEP reforms attempt in two ways to reassure LEAs that the limited form of cooperation now being sought will not expose them to liability. First, as discussed above, DHS will shift in most cases to issuing "requests for notification" that explicitly do not request or authorize detention beyond the ordinary time of release based on the local charge or conviction. *See* Martin, *supra,* at 454. To minimize other possible grounds of resistance to cooperation with DHS, the request form also specifically calls for ICE to identify the grounds for believing that the person fits one of the DHS high-priority categories included within PEP. This would involve either prior convictions of the more serious offenses identified in Secretary Johnson's memo, or grounds for believing the person to be a national security threat.

The new request for notification, Form I–247N, issued in mid-2015 to implement the PEP reforms, can be found in the Statutory Supplement, along with two related forms, the I–247D and I–247X. The latter two are more clearly in the nature of detainers, to be used only with voluntarily cooperating LEAs. For more on these forms and the circumstances of their use, see https://www.ice.gov/pep.

4. **"Sanctuary cities" and the *Steinle* case.** Some critics assert that PEP has many of the same flaws as Secure Communities, especially by impeding the reporting of ordinary crime to local LEAs (especially within communities with a high concentration of immigrants) and thus undercutting community policing. *See, e.g.,* National Immigration Law Center, Priority Enforcement Program: Why 'PEP' Doesn't Fix S-Comm's Failings (2015). Other critics reach the opposite conclusion, finding that PEP cuts back too far on efforts against noncitizens involved in crime. *See, e.g.,* Jessica Vaughan, *Sanctuary Cities: A Threat to Public Safety,* Testimony before the U.S. House Judiciary Subcommittee on Immigration and Border Security, July 23, 2015, http://cis.org/Testimony/Vaughan-Sanctuary-Cities--072315 (compiling data on detainer refusals by LEAs). It has been a slow process for DHS to restore

cooperation (on these more limited terms) with previously resistant LEAs. Many jurisdictions—sometimes called (with some imprecision) "sanctuary cities"—still hold out against honoring even requests for notification.

Local skepticism or resistance to federal immigration law enforcement is not new. In the 1996 Act, Congress took aim at local regulations that prohibited officials from communicating with federal authorities about the immigration status of persons with whom they came in contact, by providing in 8 U.S.C.A. § 1373(a):

> Notwithstanding any other provision of Federal, State, or local law, a Federal, State, or local government entity or official may not prohibit, or in any way restrict, any government entity or official from sending to, or receiving from, the Immigration and Naturalization Service information regarding the citizenship or immigration status, lawful or unlawful, of any individual.

See also 8 U.S.C.A. § 1644 (setting out the same prohibition).).

Working within the constraints of 8 U.S.C.A. § 1373, the City of Seattle adopted an ordinance in 2003, still in effect, that bars city employees from "inquir[ing] into the immigration status of any person, or engag[ing] in activities designed to ascertain the immigration status of any person." Police officers are exempted from the prohibition with respect to a person who the officer has a "reasonable suspicion" has previously been removed from the U.S. and is committing or has committed a felony. The ordinance also states that it shall not be construed to prohibit any city employee from cooperating with federal immigration authorities as required by law. *See* Seattle Municipal Code, 4.18.015.

Though such measures are sometimes referred to as "sanctuary" policies, they generally do not inhibit cooperation with federal immigration authorities in enforcement priority cases, especially those involving noncitizens arrested for crimes. Many policies are limited to assurances that government officials will not as a general matter ask about an individual's immigration status nor report any such information to the federal government absent an affirmative federal request. In Los Angeles, for example, Special Order 40, issued by police chief Daryl Gates in 1979 and still in effect, provides that "officers shall not initiate police action with the objective of discovering the alien status of a person," but it does not keep officers from turning over arrested individuals to federal authorities.

As part of a strong noncooperation policy, San Francisco requires prior convictions of violent offenses before it will turn over a detainee to ICE—even if the person has other prior offenses that would make transfer appropriate under California's TRUST Act. This policy was linked to tragic consequences in summer 2015, when a woman named Kathryn Steinle was shot while walking with her family on a public pier. The man charged with her murder, Juan Francisco Lopez-Sanchez, is an unauthorized migrant with several prior felony convictions, mostly drug offenses. He had been in federal prison earlier that year, serving a sentence based on his unauthorized return to the country after his fifth deportation. When that sentence ended, instead of deporting him, federal authorities honored a San Francisco warrant and transferred him to the sheriff for prosecution on long-standing drug charges. ICE specifically requested notification before he was released, but the San Francisco sheriff refused to honor that request when the prosecutor dropped the drug charges in April. Hence Lopez-Sanchez was at large when the crime occurred. *See* Christina Littlefield, *Sanctuary cities: How Kathryn Steinle's death intensified the immigration debate*, L.A. Times, July 24, 2015.

Outcry over the Steinle murder (and similar cases in other states) brought strong calls for legislative changes at the local, state and federal levels. Several bills to stiffen the federal requirement of cooperation with ICE detainers were quickly introduced in Congress. The U.S. House of Representatives passed a bill in July 2015 to cut off several types of federal law-enforcement funding to localities that do not honor ICE requests or detainers. But critics of ICE enforcement renewed their defense of the noncooperation policies, and President Obama indicated he would veto funding cut-offs. The San Francisco Board of Supervisors voted in October 2015 not to rescind its noncooperation policy. *See San Francisco Votes to Keep Shielding Immigrants From Deportation Officials*, N.Y. Times, Oct. 20, 2015. In the Senate, the "Stop Sanctuary Policies and Protect Americans Act," S. 2145, failed in October 2015 to secure the 60 votes required to proceed. As we go to press in late spring 2016, renewed proposals along these lines can be expected in the future.

Directly mandating that a state or local agency detain a person on the basis of a federal detainer would probably run afoul of the Tenth Amendment, which the Supreme Court has read to bar the federal "commandeering" of state or local resources to administer or enforce a federal regulatory program. *See Printz v. United States*, 521 U.S. 898 (1997); *New York v. United States*, 505 U.S. 144 (1992). But dictum in *Printz*, 521 U.S. at 917–18, may allow federal information-reporting mandates, and thus perhaps a mandate governing PEP requests for notification. In any event, the Supreme Court has not read the Tenth Amendment to keep the federal government from imposing conditions on federal grants that require local implementation of federal programs. See *New York*, 505 U.S., at 167; *South Dakota v. Dole*, 483 U.S. 203, 206 (1987). The bill passed by the House in July 2015 essentially relied on that funding leverage.

EXERCISE

You are the mayor of a large city where a significant part of the voting population seems skeptical of cooperation with federal agencies involved in immigration enforcement. How would you structure your relationship with the federal government to reflect this skepticism, while also minimizing the chances that an incident like the Steinle case will occur?

---

b. Without Federal Authorization?

Now we examine state and local direct involvement in federal immigration law enforcement *outside* the express and clear federal authorization embodied in § 287 agreements and programs like Secure Communities and PEP. When may state and local officials enforce federal immigration laws without express federal authorization? Under INA § 103(a)(10), the federal government may authorize state or local law enforcement officers to perform the duties of federal immigration officers or employees if "an actual or imminent influx" of aliens off the coast or near a land border presents "urgent circumstances requiring an immediate Federal response." (This authority has not yet been used.) What about in less extraordinary circumstances?

Analysis has traditionally started with the view that state and local law enforcement officers do not require express federal authorization to make arrests for criminal violations of federal immigration law. *See Gonzales v. City of Peoria*, 722 F.2d 468, 474–75 (9th Cir. 1983). This conclusion is consistent with a long-standing recognition, manifest in numerous nonimmigration cases, that state government have inherent authority to arrest persons for violation of federal criminal law. State and local police thus could arrest any unauthorized migrant who entered without inspection—a misdemeanor criminal offense under INA § 275. In contrast, unauthorized migrants who overstay or otherwise violate a condition of admission have committed no federal crime, even if they are removable.

Do state and local police have inherent arrest authority for *civil* immigration violations ? Under President Bill Clinton in 1996, the Office of Legal Counsel (OLC) of the Department of Justice gave one answer. After acknowledging authority under *Gonzales* to arrest for criminal immigration violations, OLC opined:

> Whether state officers may assist in enforcing the *civil* component of federal immigration law raises a separate issue. Deportation of aliens under the INA is a civil proceeding.

> In *Gonzales*, the Ninth Circuit held that the authority of state officials to enforce the provisions of the INA "is limited to criminal violations." The court based this distinction between the

civil and criminal provisions of the INA on the theory that the former constitute a pervasive and preemptive regulatory scheme, whereas the latter do not. Application of this rule would seem to preclude detentions by state officers based solely on suspicion of deportability (as opposed to *criminal* violations of the INA).

Teresa Wynn Roseborough, Deputy Assistant Attorney General, Office of Legal Counsel, Memorandum Opinion for the United States Attorney, Southern District of California, *Assistance by State and Local Police in Apprehending Illegal Aliens* (Feb. 5, 1996) (emphasis in original).

In 2002, an OLC opinion issued under President George W. Bush took a very different view. It first articulated this view of state authority:

> We * * * do not believe that the authority of state police to make arrests for violation of federal law is limited to those instances in which they are exercising delegated federal power. We instead believe that such arrest authority inheres in the States' status as sovereign entities. In the same way that police in Canada do not exercise delegated Article II power when they arrest someone who has violated U.S. law and turn him over to U.S. authorities, state police, too, need not be exercising such federal power when they make arrests for violation of federal law. Instead, the power to make such arrests inheres in the ability of one sovereign to accommodate the interests of another sovereign.

This opinion then withdrew the key part of the 1996 opinion, explaining:

> Unlike the typical preemption scenario, this question does not involve an attempt by States to enact *state* laws, or to promulgate regulations pursuant to state laws, that arguably conflict with federal law or intrude into a field that is reserved to Congress or that federal law has occupied. What this question instead presents is whether States can assist the federal government by arresting aliens who have violated *federal* law and by turning them over to federal authorities.

Jay S. Bybee, Assistant Attorney General, Office of Legal Counsel, *Memorandum for the Attorney General, Non-Preemption of the Authority of State and Local Law Enforcement Officials to Arrest Aliens for Immigration Violations* (Apr. 3, 2002).

The question of how far state (and local) governments may go in directly enforcing federal immigration law drew intensive public and judicial attention after Arizona Governor Janice Brewer signed Senate Bill 1070 into law in April 2010. (SB 1070, as amended one week later by House Bill 2162, is in the Statutory Supplement.) In contrast to the emphases on employment and housing in the Hazelton ordinances and the Arizona employment statute in *Chamber of Commerce v. Whiting*, SB 1070 authorized state and local activity that would more directly—or at least less indirectly—enforce federal immigration laws. Several other states—Utah, Georgia, South Carolina, Alabama, and Indiana—soon enacted similar statutes.

Soon after enactment of these state laws, individual and organizational plaintiffs filed lawsuits to invalidate each of them as unconstitutional and to seek preliminary injunctions to keep each from taking effect. The federal government then took the highly unusual step of filing its own lawsuits to invalidate the laws and block their implementation in Arizona, Alabama, South Carolina, and Utah. The federal government asserted preemption of these state laws. However, the federal government left it to private party lawsuits to bring the individual rights challenges, for example based on equal protection, that featured prominently in those cases.

One day before SB 1070 was to take effect, District Judge Susan Bolton issued a preliminary injunction, and Arizona appealed. The case reached the U.S. Supreme Court as a constitutional challenge to several of the law's key provisions.

ARIZONA V. UNITED STATES

Supreme Court of the United States, 2012.
567 U.S. ___, 132 S.Ct. 2492, 183 L.Ed.2d 351.

JUSTICE KENNEDY delivered the opinion of the Court.

* * *

The Government of the United States has broad, undoubted power over the subject of immigration and the status of aliens. This authority rests, in part, on the National Government's constitutional power to "establish an uniform Rule of Naturalization," U.S. Const., Art. I, § 8, cl. 4, and its inherent power as sovereign to control and conduct relations with foreign nations.

The federal power to determine immigration policy is well settled. Immigration policy can affect trade, investment, tourism, and diplomatic relations for the entire Nation, as well as the perceptions and expectations of aliens in this country who seek the full protection of its laws. Perceived mistreatment of aliens in the United States may lead to harmful reciprocal treatment of American citizens abroad.

It is fundamental that foreign countries concerned about the status, safety, and security of their nationals in the United States must be able to confer and communicate on this subject with one national sovereign, not the 50 separate States. See *Chy Lung v. Freeman*, 92 U.S. 275, 279–280, 23 L.Ed. 550 (1876). * * *

Federal governance of immigration and alien status is extensive and complex. Congress has specified categories of aliens who may not be admitted to the United States. Unlawful entry and unlawful reentry into the country are federal offenses. Once here, aliens are required to register with the Federal Government and to carry proof of status on their person. Failure to do so is a federal misdemeanor. Federal law also authorizes States to deny noncitizens a range of public benefits; and it imposes sanctions on employers who hire unauthorized workers.

Congress has specified which aliens may be removed from the United States and the procedures for doing so. * * * Removal is a civil, not criminal, matter. A principal feature of the removal system is the broad discretion exercised by immigration officials. Federal officials, as an initial matter, must decide whether it makes sense to pursue removal at all. If removal proceedings commence, aliens may seek asylum and other discretionary relief allowing them to remain in the country or at least to leave without formal removal.

Discretion in the enforcement of immigration law embraces immediate human concerns. Unauthorized workers trying to support their families, for example, likely pose less danger than alien smugglers or aliens who commit a serious crime. The equities of an individual case may turn on many factors, including whether the alien has children born in the United States, long ties to the community, or a record of distinguished military service. Some discretionary decisions involve policy choices that bear on this Nation's international relations. Returning an alien to his own country may be deemed inappropriate even where he has committed a removable offense or fails to meet the criteria for admission. The foreign state may be mired in civil war, complicit in political persecution, or enduring conditions that create a real risk that the alien or his family will be harmed upon return. The dynamic nature of relations with other countries requires the Executive Branch to ensure that enforcement policies are consistent with this Nation's foreign policy with respect to these and other realities.

* * *

The pervasiveness of federal regulation does not diminish the importance of immigration policy to the States. Arizona bears many of the consequences of unlawful immigration. Hundreds of thousands of deportable aliens are apprehended in Arizona each year. Unauthorized aliens who remain in the State comprise, by one estimate, almost six percent of the population. And in the State's most populous county, these aliens are reported to be responsible for a disproportionate share of serious crime.

* * *

STATE AND LOCAL GOVERNMENTS

These concerns are the background for the formal legal analysis that follows. The issue is whether, under preemption principles, federal law permits Arizona to implement the state-law provisions in dispute.

* * *

* * * First, the States are precluded from regulating conduct in a field that Congress, acting within its proper authority, has determined must be regulated by its exclusive governance. The intent to displace state law altogether can be inferred from a framework of regulation "so pervasive . . . that Congress left no room for the States to supplement it" or where there is a "federal interest . . . so dominant that the federal system will be assumed to preclude enforcement of state laws on the same subject." *Rice v. Santa Fe Elevator Corp.,* 331 U.S. 218, 230, 67 S.Ct. 1146, 91 L.Ed. 1447 (1947).

Second, state laws are preempted when they conflict with federal law. This includes cases where "compliance with both federal and state regulations is a physical impossibility," *Florida Lime & Avocado Growers, Inc. v. Paul,* 373 U.S. 132, 142–143, 83 S.Ct. 1210, 10 L.Ed.2d 248 (1963), and those instances where the challenged state law "stands as an obstacle to the accomplishment and execution of the full purposes and objectives of Congress," *Hines [v. Davidowitz,* 312 U.S. 52, 67, 61 S.Ct. 399, 85 L.Ed. 581]. In preemption analysis, courts should assume that "the historic police powers of the States" are not superseded "unless that was the clear and manifest purpose of Congress." *Rice, supra,* at 230, 67 S.Ct. 1146.

The four challenged provisions of the state law each must be examined under these preemption principles.

Section 3

Section 3 of S.B. 1070 creates a new state misdemeanor. It forbids the "willful failure to complete or carry an alien registration document . . . in violation of 8 United States Code section 1304(e) or 1306(a)." In effect, § 3 adds a state-law penalty for conduct proscribed by federal law. * * *

The Court discussed federal alien-registration requirements in *Hines v. Davidowitz,* 312 U.S. 52, 61 S.Ct. 399, 85 L.Ed. 581. In 1940, as international conflict spread, Congress added to federal immigration law a "complete system for alien registration." *Id.,* at 70, 61 S.Ct. 399. * * * As a consequence, the Court ruled that Pennsylvania could not enforce its own alien-registration program.

The present regime of federal regulation is not identical to the statutory framework considered in *Hines,* but it remains comprehensive. Federal law now includes a requirement that aliens carry proof of registration. INA § 264(e). Other aspects, however, have stayed the same. * * *

The framework enacted by Congress leads to the conclusion here, as it did in *Hines,* that the Federal Government has occupied the field of alien registration. The federal statutory directives provide a full set of standards governing alien registration, including the punishment for noncompliance. * * * Field preemption reflects a congressional decision to foreclose any state regulation in the area, even if it is parallel to federal standards.

* * *

Arizona contends that § 3 can survive preemption because the provision has the same aim as federal law and adopts its substantive standards. This argument not only ignores the basic premise of field preemption—that States may not enter, in any respect, an area the Federal Government has reserved for itself—but also is unpersuasive on its own terms. Permitting the State to impose its own penalties for the federal offenses here would conflict with the careful framework Congress adopted. Were § 3 to come into force, the State would have the power to bring criminal charges against individuals for violating a federal law even in circumstances where federal officials in charge of the comprehensive scheme determine that prosecution would frustrate federal policies.

There is a further intrusion upon the federal scheme. * * * Under federal law, the failure to carry registration papers is a misdemeanor that may be punished by a fine, imprisonment, or a term of probation. State law, by contrast, rules out probation as a possible sentence (and also eliminates the possibility of a pardon). This state framework of sanctions creates a conflict with the plan Congress put in place.

* * *

Section 5(C)

Unlike § 3, which replicates federal statutory requirements, § 5(C) enacts a state criminal prohibition where no federal counterpart exists. The provision makes it a state misdemeanor for "an unauthorized alien to knowingly apply for work, solicit work in a public place or perform work as an employee or independent contractor" in Arizona. Violations can be punished by a $2,500 fine and incarceration for up to six months. * * *

When there was no comprehensive federal program regulating the employment of unauthorized aliens, this Court found that a State had authority to pass its own laws on the subject. In 1971, for example, California passed a law imposing civil penalties on the employment of aliens who were "not entitled to lawful residence in the United States if such employment would have an adverse effect on lawful resident workers." 1971 Cal. Stats. ch. 1442, § 1(a). The law was upheld against a preemption challenge in *De Canas v. Bica,* 424 U.S. 351, 96 S.Ct. 933, 47 L.Ed.2d 43 (1976). * * *

Current federal law is substantially different from the regime that prevailed when *De Canas* was decided. * * * The law makes it illegal for employers to knowingly hire, recruit, refer, or continue to employ unauthorized workers. It also requires every employer to verify the employment authorization status of prospective employees. These requirements are enforced through criminal penalties and an escalating series of civil penalties tied to the number of times an employer has violated the provisions.

* * *

The legislative background of IRCA underscores the fact that Congress made a deliberate choice not to impose criminal penalties on aliens who seek, or engage in, unauthorized employment. * * * In the end, IRCA's framework reflects a considered judgment that making criminals out of aliens engaged in unauthorized work—aliens who already face the possibility of employer exploitation because of their removable status— would be inconsistent with federal policy and objectives.

* * *

* * * It follows that a state law to the contrary is an obstacle to the regulatory system Congress chose. Section 5(C) is preempted by federal law.

Section 6

Section 6 of S.B. 1070 provides that a state officer, "without a warrant, may arrest a person if the officer has probable cause to believe . . . [the person] has committed any public offense that makes [him] removable from the United States." * * *

* * *

The federal statutory structure instructs when it is appropriate to arrest an alien during the removal process. For example, the Attorney General can exercise discretion to issue a warrant for an alien's arrest and detention "pending a decision on whether the alien is to be removed from the United States." INA § 236(a). And if an alien is ordered removed after a hearing, the Attorney General will issue a warrant. In both instances, the warrants are executed by federal officers who have received training in the enforcement of immigration law. If no federal warrant has been issued, those officers have more limited authority. They may arrest an alien for being "in the United States in violation of any [immigration] law or regulation," for example, but only where the alien "is likely to escape before a warrant can be obtained." INA § 287(a)(2).

Section 6 attempts to provide state officers even greater authority to arrest aliens on the basis of possible removability than Congress has given to trained federal immigration officers. Under state law, officers who believe an alien is removable by reason of some "public offense" would have the power to conduct an arrest on that basis regardless of whether a federal warrant has issued or the alien is likely to escape. This state authority could be exercised without any input from the Federal Government about whether an arrest is warranted in a particular case. This would allow the State to achieve its own immigration policy. The result could be unnecessary harassment of some aliens (for instance, a veteran, college student, or someone assisting with a criminal investigation) whom federal officials determine should not be removed.

This is not the system Congress created. Federal law specifies limited circumstances in which state officers may perform the functions of an immigration officer. A principal example is when the Attorney General has granted that authority to specific officers in a formal agreement with a state or local government. See INA § 287(g)(1). Officers covered by these agreements are subject to the Attorney General's direction and supervision. * * *

By authorizing state officers to decide whether an alien should be detained for being removable, § 6 violates the principle that the removal process is entrusted to the discretion of the Federal Government. A decision on removability requires a determination whether it is appropriate to allow a foreign national to continue living in the United States. Decisions of this nature touch on foreign relations and must be made with one voice.

In defense of § 6, Arizona notes a federal statute permitting state officers to "cooperate with the Attorney General in the identification, apprehension, detention, or removal of aliens not lawfully present in the United States." INA § 287(g)(10)(B). There may be some ambiguity as to what constitutes cooperation under the federal law; but no coherent understanding of the term would incorporate the unilateral decision of state officers to arrest an alien for being removable absent any request, approval, or other instruction from the Federal Government. * * *

Congress has put in place a system in which state officers may not make warrantless arrests of aliens based on possible removability except in specific, limited circumstances. By nonetheless authorizing state and local officers to engage in these enforcement activities as a general matter, § 6 creates an obstacle to the full purposes and objectives of Congress.

Section 2(B)

Section 2(B) of S.B. 1070 requires state officers to make a "reasonable attempt . . . to determine the immigration status" of any person they stop, detain, or arrest on some other legitimate basis if "reasonable suspicion exists that the person is an alien and is unlawfully present in the United States." The law also provides that "[a]ny person who is arrested shall have the person's immigration status determined before the person is released." The accepted way to perform these status checks is to contact ICE, which maintains a database of immigration records.

Three limits are built into the state provision. First, a detainee is presumed not to be an alien unlawfully present in the United States if he or she provides a valid Arizona driver's license or similar identification. Second, officers "may not consider race, color or national origin . . . except to the extent permitted by the United States [and] Arizona Constitution[s]." Third, the provisions must be "implemented in a manner consistent with federal law regulating immigration, protecting the civil rights of all persons and respecting the privileges and immunities of United States citizens."

* * *

Consultation between federal and state officials is an important feature of the immigration system. Congress has made clear that no formal agreement or special training needs to be in place for state officers to "communicate with the [Federal Government] regarding the immigration status of any individual, including reporting knowledge that a particular alien is not lawfully present in the United States." INA § 287(g)(10)(A). And Congress has obligated ICE to respond to any request made by state officials for verification of a person's citizenship or immigration status. *See* 8 U.S.C. § 1373(c). * * *

The United States argues that making status verification mandatory interferes with the federal immigration scheme. It is true that § 2(B) does not allow state officers to consider federal enforcement priorities in deciding whether to contact ICE about someone they have detained. In other words, the officers must make an inquiry even in cases where it seems unlikely that the Attorney General would have the alien removed. This might be the case, for example, when an alien is an elderly veteran with significant and longstanding ties to the community.

Congress has done nothing to suggest it is inappropriate to communicate with ICE in these situations, however. Indeed, it has encouraged the sharing of information about possible immigration violations. A federal statute regulating the public benefits provided to qualified aliens in fact instructs that "no State or local government entity may be prohibited, or in any way restricted, from sending to or receiving from [ICE] information regarding the immigration status, lawful or unlawful, of an alien in the United States." 8 U.S.C. § 1644. The federal scheme thus leaves room for a policy requiring state officials to contact ICE as a routine matter.

Some who support the challenge to § 2(B) argue that, in practice, state officers will be required to delay the release of some detainees for no reason other than to verify their immigration status. Detaining individuals solely to verify their immigration status would raise constitutional concerns. And it would disrupt the federal framework to put state officers in the position of holding aliens in custody for possible unlawful presence without federal direction and supervision. The program put in place by Congress does not allow state or local officers to adopt this enforcement mechanism.

But § 2(B) could be read to avoid these concerns. To take one example, a person might be stopped for jaywalking in Tucson and be unable to produce identification. The first sentence of § 2(B) instructs officers to make a "reasonable" attempt to verify his immigration status with ICE if there is reasonable suspicion that his presence in the United States is unlawful. The state courts may conclude that, unless the person continues to be suspected of some crime for which he may be detained by state officers, it would not be reasonable to prolong the stop for the immigration inquiry.

To take another example, a person might be held pending release on a charge of driving under the influence of alcohol. As this goes beyond a mere stop, the arrestee (unlike the jaywalker) would appear to be subject to the categorical requirement in the second sentence of § 2(B) that "[a]ny person who is arrested shall have the person's immigration status determined before [he] is released." State courts may read this as an instruction to initiate a status check every time someone is arrested, or in some subset of those cases, rather than as a command to hold the person until the check is complete no matter the circumstances. Even if the law is read as an instruction to complete a check while the person is in custody, moreover, it is not clear at this stage and on this record that the verification process would result in prolonged detention.

However the law is interpreted, if § 2(B) only requires state officers to conduct a status check during the course of an authorized, lawful detention or after a detainee has been released, the provision likely would survive preemption—at least absent some showing that it has other consequences that are adverse to federal law and its objectives. There is no need in this case to address whether reasonable suspicion of illegal entry or another immigration crime would be a legitimate basis for prolonging a detention, or whether this too would be preempted by federal law.

The nature and timing of this case counsel caution in evaluating the validity of § 2(B). The Federal Government has brought suit against a sovereign State to challenge the provision even before the law has gone into effect. There is a basic uncertainty about what the law means and how it will be enforced. At this stage, without the benefit of a definitive interpretation from the state courts, it would be inappropriate to assume

§ 2(B) will be construed in a way that creates a conflict with federal law. As a result, the United States cannot prevail in its current challenge. This opinion does not foreclose other preemption and constitutional challenges to the law as interpreted and applied after it goes into effect.

* * *

The National Government has significant power to regulate immigration. With power comes responsibility, and the sound exercise of national power over immigration depends on the Nation's meeting its responsibility to base its laws on a political will informed by searching, thoughtful, rational civic discourse. Arizona may have understandable frustrations with the problems caused by illegal immigration while that process continues, but the State may not pursue policies that undermine federal law.

* * *

JUSTICE KAGAN took no part in the consideration or decision of this case.

JUSTICE SCALIA, concurring in part and dissenting in part.

The United States is an indivisible "Union of sovereign States." *Hinderlider v. La Plata River & Cherry Creek Ditch Co.,* 304 U.S. 92, 104, 58 S.Ct. 803, 82 L.Ed. 1202 (1938). * * *

As a sovereign, Arizona has the inherent power to exclude persons from its territory, subject only to those limitations expressed in the Constitution or constitutionally imposed by Congress. That power to exclude has long been recognized as inherent in sovereignty. * * *

* * *

Notwithstanding "[t]he myth of an era of unrestricted immigration" in the first 100 years of the Republic, the States enacted numerous laws restricting the immigration of certain classes of aliens, including convicted criminals, indigents, persons with contagious diseases, and (in Southern States) freed blacks. Neuman, The Lost Century of American Immigration (1776–1875), 93 Colum. L. Rev. 1833, 1835, 1841–1880 (1993). * * *

* * *

* * * [T]here is no federal law prohibiting the States' sovereign power to exclude (assuming federal authority to enact such a law). The mere existence of federal action in the immigration area—and the so-called field preemption arising from that action, upon which the Court's opinion so heavily relies—cannot be regarded as such a prohibition. * * *

Nor can federal power over illegal immigration be deemed exclusive because of what the Court's opinion solicitously calls "foreign countries[']

concern[s] about the status, safety, and security of their nationals in the United States". * * *

What this case comes down to, then, is whether the Arizona law conflicts with federal immigration law—whether it excludes those whom federal law would admit, or admits those whom federal law would exclude. It does not purport to do so. It applies only to aliens who neither possess a privilege to be present under federal law nor have been removed pursuant to the Federal Government's inherent authority. * * *

§ 2(B)

* * *

The Government has conceded that "even before Section 2 was enacted, state and local officers had state-law authority to inquire of DHS [the Department of Homeland Security] about a suspect's unlawful status and otherwise cooperate with federal immigration officers." That concession, in my view, obviates the need for further inquiry. The Government's conflict-pre-emption claim calls on us "to determine whether, *under the circumstances of this particular case,* [the State's] law stands as an obstacle to the accomplishment and execution of the full purposes and objectives of Congress." *Hines v. Davidowitz,* 312 U.S. 52, 67, 61 S.Ct. 399, 85 L.Ed. 581 (1941) (emphasis added). It is impossible to make such a finding without a factual record concerning the manner in which Arizona is implementing these provisions—something the Government's pre-enforcement challenge has pretermitted. * * *

* * *

§ 6

* * *

Of course on this pre-enforcement record there is no reason to assume that Arizona officials will ignore federal immigration policy (unless it be the questionable policy of not wanting to identify illegal aliens who have committed offenses that make them removable). * * * It is consistent with the Arizona statute, and with the "cooperat[ive]" system that Congress has created, for state officials to arrest a removable alien, contact federal immigration authorities, and follow their lead on what to do next. * * *

But that is not the most important point. The most important point is that, as we have discussed, Arizona is *entitled* to have "its own immigration policy"—including a more rigorous enforcement policy—so long as that does not conflict with federal law. * * *

* * *

SEC. C STATE AND LOCAL GOVERNMENTS 1239

* * * And it makes no difference that federal officials might "determine [that some unlawfully present aliens] should not be removed." They may well determine not to remove from the United States aliens who have no right to be here; but unless and until these aliens have been given the right to remain, Arizona is entitled to arrest them and *at least* bring them to federal officials' attention, which is all that § 6 necessarily entails. (In my view, the State can go further than this, and punish them for their unlawful entry and presence in Arizona.)

* * *

§ 3

* * *

It is beyond question that a State may make violation of federal law a violation of state law as well. We have held that to be so even when the interest protected is a distinctively federal interest, such as protection of the dignity of the national flag. Much more is that so when, as here, the State is protecting its *own* interest, the integrity of its borders. * * *

The Court's opinion relies upon *Hines v. Davidowitz*. But that case did not, as the Court believes, establish a "field preemption" that implicitly eliminates the States' sovereign power to exclude those whom federal law excludes. It held that the States are not permitted to establish "additional or auxiliary" registration requirements for aliens. But § 3 does not establish additional or auxiliary registration requirements. It merely makes a violation of state law the *very same* failure to register and failure to carry evidence of registration that are violations of federal law. * * *

* * *

§ 5(C)

* * *

[In] *De Canas v. Bica,* 424 U.S. 351, 96 S.Ct. 933, 47 L.Ed.2d 43 (1976), * * * [t]his Court concluded that the California [employer sanctions] law was not pre-empted, as Congress had neither occupied the field of "regulation of employment of illegal aliens" nor expressed "the clear and manifest purpose" of displacing such state regulation. * * *

The only relevant change is that Congress has since enacted its own restrictions on employers who hire illegal aliens, in legislation that also includes some civil (but no criminal) penalties on illegal aliens who accept unlawful employment. The Court concludes from this (reasonably enough) "that Congress made a deliberate choice not to impose criminal penalties on aliens who seek, or engage in, unauthorized employment." But that is not the same as a deliberate choice to prohibit the States from imposing criminal penalties. * * *

* * *

The brief for the Government in this case asserted that "the Executive Branch's ability to exercise discretion and set priorities is particularly important because of the need to allocate scarce enforcement resources wisely." Of course there is no reason why the Federal Executive's need to allocate *its* scarce enforcement resources should disable Arizona from devoting *its* resources to illegal immigration in Arizona that in its view the Federal Executive has given short shrift. * * *

But leave that aside. It has become clear that federal enforcement priorities—in the sense of priorities based on the need to allocate "scarce enforcement resources"—is not the problem here. After this case was argued and while it was under consideration, the Secretary of Homeland Security announced a program exempting from immigration enforcement some 1.4 million illegal immigrants under the age of 30. * * * U.S. immigration officials have been directed to "defe[r] action" against such individual "for a period of two years, subject to renewal." The husbanding of scarce enforcement resources can hardly be the justification for this, since the considerable administrative cost of conducting as many as 1.4 million background checks, and ruling on the biennial requests for dispensation that the nonenforcement program envisions, will necessarily be *deducted* from immigration enforcement.[a] The President said at a news conference that the new program is "the right thing to do" in light of Congress's failure to pass the Administration's proposed revision of the Immigration Act. Perhaps it is, though Arizona may not think so. But to say, as the Court does, that Arizona *contradicts federal law* by enforcing applications of the Immigration Act that the President declines to enforce boggles the mind.

The Court opinion's looming specter of inutterable horror—"[i]f § 3 of the Arizona statute were valid, every State could give itself independent authority to prosecute federal registration violations"—seems to me not so horrible and even less looming. But there has come to pass, and is with us today, the specter that Arizona and the States that support it predicted: A Federal Government that does not want to enforce the immigration laws as written, and leaves the States' borders unprotected against immigrants whom those laws would exclude. So the issue is a stark one. Are the sovereign States at the mercy of the Federal Executive's refusal to enforce the Nation's immigration laws?

A good way of answering that question is to ask: Would the States conceivably have entered into the Union if the Constitution itself contained the Court's holding? Today's judgment surely fails that test.

---

[a] In fact, DACA, as a USCIS program, is funded by the fees charged for the work authorization that most DACA recipients obtain along with deferred action; therefore the administrative cost is not deducted from enforcement funds.—eds.

* * * [I]magine a provision—perhaps inserted right after Art. I, § 8, cl. 4, the Naturalization Clause—which included among the enumerated powers of Congress "To establish Limitations upon Immigration that will be exclusive and that will be enforced only to the extent the President deems appropriate." The delegates to the Grand Convention would have rushed to the exits.

* * *

JUSTICE THOMAS, concurring in part and dissenting in part.

* * *

* * * States, as sovereigns, have inherent authority to conduct arrests for violations of federal law, unless and until Congress removes that authority. Here, no federal statute purports to withdraw that authority. * * *

* * *

* * * Under the Supremacy Clause, pre-emptive effect is to be given to congressionally enacted laws, not to judicially divined legislative purposes. Thus, even assuming the existence of some tension between Arizona's law and the supposed "purposes and objectives" of Congress, I would not hold that any of the provisions of the Arizona law at issue here are pre-empted on that basis.

JUSTICE ALITO, concurring in part and dissenting in part.

* * *

Section 2(B)

* * *

Section 2(B) quite clearly does not expand the authority of Arizona officers to make stops or arrests. It is triggered only when a "lawful stop, detention or arrest [is] made . . . in the enforcement of *any other [state or local] law or ordinance.*" Section 2(B) thus comes into play only when an officer has reasonable suspicion or probable cause to believe that a person has committed a nonimmigration offense. Arizona officers plainly possessed this authority before § 2(B) took effect.

Section 2(B) also does not expand the authority of Arizona officers to inquire about the immigration status of persons who are lawfully detained. When a person is stopped or arrested and "reasonable suspicion exists that the person is an alien and is unlawfully present in the United States," § 2(B) instructs Arizona officers to make a "reasonable attempt," "when practicable," to ascertain that person's immigration status. Even before the Arizona Legislature enacted § 2(B), federal law permitted state and local officers to make such inquiries. * * *

* * *

* * * At bottom, the discretion that ultimately matters is not whether to verify a person's immigration status but whether to act once the person's status is known. For that reason, § 2(B)'s verification requirement is not contrary to federal law because the Federal Government retains the discretion that matters most—that is, the discretion to enforce the law in particular cases. * * *

The United States' attack on § 2(B) is quite remarkable. The United States suggests that a state law may be pre-empted, not because it conflicts with a federal statute or regulation, but because it is inconsistent with a federal agency's current enforcement priorities. Those priorities, however, are not law. They are nothing more than agency policy. I am aware of no decision of this Court recognizing that mere policy can have pre-emptive force. If § 2(B) were pre-empted at the present time because it is out of sync with the Federal Government's current priorities, would it be unpre-empted at some time in the future if the agency's priorities changed?

* * *

It has been suggested that § 2(B) will cause some persons who are lawfully stopped to be detained in violation of their constitutional rights while a prolonged investigation of their immigration status is undertaken. But nothing on the face of the law suggests that it will be enforced in a way that violates the Fourth Amendment or any other provision of the Constitution. * * *

* * *

Section 3

I agree that § 3 is pre-empted because, like the Court, I read the opinion in *Hines* to require that result. * * *

Section 5(C)

* * *

The one thing that is clear from the federal scheme is that Congress chose not to impose *federal* criminal penalties on aliens who seek or obtain unauthorized work. But that does not mean that Congress also chose to pre-empt *state* criminal penalties. The inference is plausible, but far from necessary. * * * With any statutory scheme, Congress chooses to do some things and not others. If that alone were enough to demonstrate pre-emptive intent, there would be little left over for the States to regulate, especially now that federal authority reaches so far and wide. States would occupy tiny islands in a sea of federal power. This explains why state laws implicating traditional state powers are not pre-empted unless there is a "clear and manifest" congressional intention to do so.

* * *

Section 6

* * *

The idea that state and local officers may carry out arrests in the service of federal law is not unprecedented. * * * Therefore, given the premise, which I understand both the United States and the Court to accept, that state and local officers do have inherent authority to make arrests in aid of federal law, we must ask whether Congress has done anything to curtail or pre-empt that authority in this particular case.

* * *

* * * State and local officers do not frustrate the removal process by arresting criminal aliens. The Executive retains complete discretion over whether those aliens are ultimately removed. And once the Federal Government makes a determination that a particular criminal alien will not be removed, then Arizona officers are presumably no longer authorized under § 6 to arrest the alien.

* * *

Finally, * * * § 6 is an obstacle only to the extent it conflicts with Congress' clear and manifest intent to preclude state and local officers from making arrests except where a federal warrant has issued or the arrestee is likely to escape. By granting warrantless arrest authority to *federal officers,* Congress has not manifested an unmistakable intent to strip *state and local officers* of their warrantless arrest authority under state law.

* * *

NOTES AND QUESTIONS ON ARIZONA V. UNITED STATES

1.   What exactly is involved in state or local authority to enforce civil or criminal immigration laws directly? No state has gone so far as to contemplate full operation of a state-run deportation or criminal punishment system. Dissenting in *Arizona,* Justice Alito observed that the federal government "retains the discretion that matters most—that is, the discretion to enforce the law in particular case." This means that federal immigration authorities—like any federal prosecutor in a criminal case—decide whether to proceed based on an independent assessment of the facts and law, and on exercising its own prosecutorial discretion. Declining to proceed results in the person's release—and thus exerts pressure on state and local officers not to persist in presenting cases that federal authorities will not pursue. Do these

limits make state or local involvement in direct immigration enforcement more acceptable?

But consider this argument: arrests are highly unlikely, but if arrested, unauthorized migrants are much more likely to end up in removal proceedings, so the discretion to arrest is the "discretion that matters":

> The core problem is that state and local decisionmakers will act as gatekeepers, filling the enforcement pipeline with cases of their choice for civil removal and possibly criminal prosecution as well. Even assuming that more federal post-arrest discretion becomes available and actually offsets the state and local choices made by exercising arrest discretion, any such federal discretion is fundamentally reactive.

Hiroshi Motomura, *The Discretion That Matters: Federal Immigration Enforcement, State and Local Arrests, and the Civil-Criminal Line*, 58 UCLA L. Rev. 1819, 1856 (2011). *See also* Eisha Jain, *Arrests as Regulation*, 67 Stan. L. Rev. 809 (2015).

2.   An important aspect of the background of SB 1070 is Arizona's use of state law before SB 1070 to impose state criminal penalties on persons who commit acts that violate federal immigration law. *See* Ingrid V. Eagly, *A Study of Arizona Before SB 1070*, 58 UCLA L. Rev. 1749 (2011) (analyzing how the implementation of a 2005 Arizona alien smuggling law influenced federal practices for punishing immigration crimes).

3.   Writing in the context of an earlier group of state and local enforcement laws, Michael Wishnie argued that "the permanent involvement of state and local police in routine immigration enforcement raises the further risk of racial profiling and selective immigration enforcement beyond moments of real or perceived national threat." Michael J. Wishnie, *State and Local Police Enforcement of Immigration Laws*, 6 U. Pa. J. Const. L. 1084, 1104 (2004). Huyen Pham offered a different criticism: "local enforcement will result in a "thousand borders" problem, violating the constitutional mandate for uniform immigration laws as local authorities will enforce federal immigration laws differently, creating, in effect, different immigration laws." Huyen Pham, *The Inherent Flaws in the Inherent Authority Position: Why Inviting Local Enforcement of Immigration Laws Violates the Constitution*, 31 Fla. St. U. L. Rev. 965, 995 (2004). For an opposing view, see Kris W. Kobach, *The Quintessential Force Multiplier: The Inherent Authority of Local Police to Make Immigration Arrests*, 69 Alb. L. Rev. 179, 183 (2005–06). Kobach served as Counsel to Attorney General Ashcroft when the OLC issued its 2002 opinion finding inherent state and local arrest authority for civil immigration law violations.

4.   One of the most prominent figures in state and local efforts to be directly involved in federal immigration law enforcement is Sheriff Joe Arpaio of Maricopa County, Arizona, which is home to over 4 million people, over 60 percent of Arizona's total population. While the lawsuits challenging

SB 1070 were in their early stages, a three-year U.S. Department of Justice investigation concluded in 2011 that Arpaio had violated the constitutional rights of Latinos by habitually targeting them for discriminatory arrest and detention for immigration violations and other charges. Federal investigators also looked into Arpaio's apparent practice of retaliating against critics. *See* Marc Lacey, *U.S. Says Arizona Sheriff Shows Pervasive Bias Against Latinos*, N.Y. Times, Dec. 16, 2011, at A1.

After fruitless negotiations with Arpaio to address the Justice Department's findings, the federal government revoked its § 287(g) agreement with the Maricopa County Sheriff's Office. *See* Statement by Secretary Napolitano on DOJ's Findings of Discriminatory Policing in Maricopa County, Department of Homeland Security Press Release, Dec. 15, 2011. In May 2012, DOJ filed a civil lawsuit against Arpaio and his department. A separate class action lawsuit against Arpaio alleged racial discrimination and unlawful detention in violation of the Fourth Amendment's protection against unreasonable searches and seizures. In May 2013, federal district judge Murray Snow ruled in the private lawsuit that Arpaio and his deputies had engaged in racial discrimination and related wrongdoing. *See* Melendres v. Arpaio, 989 F. Supp. 2d 822 (D. Ariz. 2013), *aff'd in part, vacated in part,* 784 F.3d 1254 (9th Cir. 2015); Fernanda Santos, *Judge Finds Violations of Rights by Sheriff*, N.Y. Times, May 24, 2013, at A14. In July 2015, DOJ and Sheriff Arpaio settled the federal government's lawsuit, with the Maricopa County Sheriff's Office agreeing to various measures to safeguard against future constitutional violations. *See DOJ Civil Rights Division Settles Several Claims Against Maricopa County, Arizona and Sheriff Joseph Arpaio; Negotiations Continue*, 92 Interp. Rel. 1351 (2015).

5. On one view, *Arizona v. United States* is best explained as rejecting the approach, typical in many areas of law, that state and federal governments simultaneously impose penalties on the same behavior. The Court's rejection of this enforcement redundancy makes sense only if federal law for preemption purposes is not a set of obligations in immigration statutes, but rather a set of consequences for immigration law violations.

> First, this approach leads inevitably to the conclusion that any action by state officials to assist in the enforcement of federal law is impermissible: * * * law is nothing more than the expected sanction associated with particular conduct, and anything a state actor does to enforce federal law will alter either the chance of getting caught or the severity of punishment. Second, the approach elevates every act of prosecutorial discretion by an executive branch official to the status of supreme federal law for purposes of preemption analysis. * * *

> The Court's approach makes *Arizona* as much a case about separation of powers as about federalism. It consolidates tremendous immigration policymaking power in the executive

branch, endorsing the idea that immigration law is centrally the product of executive "lawmaking" that bears little relation to immigration law on the books.

Adam B. Cox, *Enforcement Redundancy and the Future of Immigration Law*, 2012 Sup. Ct. Rev. 31, 32–33. *See also* Kerry Abrams, *Plenary Power Preemption*, 99 Va. L. Rev. 601, 635–37 (2013).

6.   Though much of the legal debate over SB 1070 has concerned federal-state relations, Rick Su has written that a central but often overlooked objective of SB 1070 is "to eliminate local discretion with respect to immigration enforcement." He explains:

> [T]he purpose of S.B. 1070 is not to *allow* state and local law enforcement officials to enforce federal immigration laws. Rather it *requires* such officials and their departments to do so, even if— perhaps especially if—they would ordinarily refrain out of concerns about relations with immigrant neighborhoods, competing local priorities, or lack of fiscal resources. Thus, S.B. 1070 not only targets undocumented immigrants and those who may be suspected of being such, but also local law enforcement agencies and the counties, cities, and towns that they serve.

Rick Su, *The Overlooked Significance of Arizona's New Immigration Law*, 108 Mich. L. Rev. First Impressions 76 (2010).

7.   Consider also this reading of *Arizona v. United States*: "while the Court brushed back the state's unilateral attempts to regulate and enforce immigration law, it simultaneously gave a boost to state and local immigration policing under the aegis of federal initiatives that enlist state and local cooperation." Anil Kalhan, *Immigration Policing and Federalism Through the Lens of Technology, Surveillance, and Privacy*, 74 Ohio St. L.J. 1105, 1107 (2013). Does this help explain why the federal government relied entirely on preemption, rather than assert the individual rights claims that private plaintiffs raised to challenge SB 1070?

4. STATE AND LOCAL ENFORCEMENT AFTER *ARIZONA*

a. Applying *Arizona* to Other State or Local Direct Enforcement

The Supreme Court decision in *United States v. Arizona* strongly influenced the challenges that were pending in the federal courts against laws in Alabama, Georgia, Indiana, South Carolina, and Utah, with provisions similar to SB 1070. For example, courts found that federal law preempts Alabama and South Carolina state registration provisions that resemble § 3 of SB 1070. *See United States v. South Carolina*, 720 F.3d 518, 532 (4th Cir. 2013) (Act 69, §§ 5, 6(B)(2)); *United States v. Alabama*, 691 F.3d 1269, 1282 (11th Cir. 2012) (HB 56, § 10), *cert. denied*, 133 S.Ct.

2022 (2013). *Cf. Utah Coalition of La Raza v. Herbert*, 26 F. Supp. 3d 1125, 1138–40 (D. Utah 2014) (HB 497, § 4, is not a *de facto* registration law and is not preempted).

A section of the Alabama law that criminalized unauthorized work in ways similar to § 5(C) of SB 1070 was struck down as preempted. *See United States v. Alabama*, 691 F.3d 1269, 1282–83 (11th Cir. 2012) (HB 56, § 11), *cert. denied*, 133 S.Ct. 2022 (2013). Courts found that federal law preempts parts of the Indiana and Utah laws that, like § 6 of SB 1070, would expand state arrest authority based on violations or removability based on federal immigration laws. *See Buquer v. City of Indianapolis*, 2013 WL 1332158, at 7–11 (S.D. Ind. 2013) (SEA 590, § 20); *Utah Coalition of La Raza v. Herbert*, 26 F. Supp. 3d 1125, 1145–47 (D. Utah 2014) (HB 497, § 11) (also unconstitutional under Fourth Amendment).

The Alabama, Georgia, and Utah laws included provisions resembling section 2(B) of Arizona SB 1070. Federal courts applied the Supreme Court's reasoning in *United States v. Arizona* to let these provisions take effect. *See United States v. Alabama*, 691 F.3d 1269, 1283–85 (11th Cir. 2012) (HB 56, §§ 12, 18), *cert. denied*, 133 S.Ct. 2022 (2013); *Georgia Latino Alliance of Human Rights v. Governor of Georgia*, 691 F.3d 1250, 1267–68 (11th Cir. 2012) (HB 87, § 8); *Utah Coalition of La Raza v. Herbert*, 26 F. Supp. 3d 1125, 1135–38 (D. Utah 2014) (HB 497, § 3). Recall that according to the U.S. Supreme Court in *Arizona v. United States*, 132 S.Ct. 2492, 2509 (2012), "[d]etaining individuals solely to verify immigration status would raise constitutional concerns." The 2015 Supreme Court decision in *Rodriguez v. United States*, 135 S.Ct. 1609, 191 L.Ed. 2d 492 (2015), which addressed the permissible duration of traffic stops in general, may be crucial in determining the extent of any such concerns.

Also challenged were new state criminal penalties on various types of involvement in the transportation of persons unlawfully present, or in the aiding or concealing of unlawful presence (including one's own presence). Arizona's SB 1070 includes such a harboring prohibition. The Supreme Court did not consider its validity in *United States v. Arizona*, but federal courts held that federal law preempts such "harboring" or "self-harboring" prohibitions in the Alabama, Georgia, and South Carolina laws. *See United States v. South Carolina*, 720 F.3d 518, 529–32 (4th Cir. 2013) (Act 69, § 4); *United States v. Alabama*, 691 F.3d 1269, 1285–88 (11th Cir. 2012) (HB 56, § 13), *cert. denied*, 133 S.Ct. 2022 (2013); *Georgia Latino Alliance of Human Rights v. Governor of Georgia*, 691 F.3d 1250, 1263–67 (11th Cir. 2012) (HB 87, § 7); *Utah Coalition of La Raza v. Herbert*, 26 F. Supp. 3d 1125, 1144–45 (D. Utah 2014) (HB 497, § 10).

Other lawsuits challenged state provisions with no counterpart in SB 1070. For example, Alabama's law would require public schools to report on the immigration law status of new students. The Eleventh Circuit relied on *Plyler v. Doe, supra,* to find that this requirement violates equal protection. *See Hispanic Interest Coalition of Alabama v. Governor of Alabama,* 691 F.3d 1236, 1244–49 (11th Cir. 2012) (HB 56, § 28), *cert. denied,* 133 S.Ct. 2022 (2013). A federal district court found that Indiana's prohibition on the use of foreign government consular identification cards is preempted by federal law and violates substantive due process. *See Buquer v. City of Indianapolis,* 2013 WL 1332158, at 11–14 (S.D. Ind. 2013) (SEA 590, § 18). *But cf. Georgia Latino Alliance for Human Rights v. Deal,* 793 F. Supp. 2d 1317 (N.D. Ga. 2011) (rejecting a challenge to a similar provision on consular identification cards). An unusual provision in the series of Utah laws that expanded state involvement in enforcement also established a state guest worker program contingent on federal government approval. *See Utah Coalition of La Raza v. Herbert,* 26 F. Supp. 3d 1125, 1130 n.1 (D. Utah 2014) (HB 116).

The Eleventh Circuit found that federal law preempts another part of the Alabama law, which would make contracts with unauthorized migrants unenforceable in Alabama state courts, with some exceptions. *See United States v. Alabama,* 691 F.3d 1269, 1292–97 (11th Cir. 2012) (HB 56, § 27), *cert. denied,* 133 S.Ct. 2022 (2013). The same Eleventh Circuit decision held, however, that federal law does not preempt, on its face, a provision of Alabama law making it a felony for an "alien not lawfully present in the United States" to conduct a business transaction with the state of Alabama or any political subdivision thereof. *United States v. Alabama,* 691 F.3d 1269, 1297–30 (11th Cir. 2012) (HB 56, § 30), *cert. denied,* 133 S.Ct. 2022 (2013).

After this series of court decisions settled the validity of key parts of these state laws, the opposing parties agreed to several settlements. In Alabama, litigation ended in November 2013 when the state, the federal government, and private plaintiffs entered into a settlement that permanently blocked the law's major provisions, including the requirement to provide immigration status information for public school enrollment, the ban on contracts with unauthorized migrants, and criminal penalties on seeking work. Significantly limiting the Alabama analog to section 2(B) of SB 1070, the settlement prohibited state and local police from detaining anyone based on immigration status alone. Under the settlement, Alabama also paid $580,000 in attorneys' fees to the private plaintiffs.

The South Carolina litigation was settled in March 2014 under an agreement between the state, the federal government, and private plaintiffs that permanently blocked the state law's major provisions. As in Alabama, the settlement limited the South Carolina analog to section

2(B) of SB 1070, by barring local and state law enforcement officers from detaining individuals on the basis of immigration status alone. In December 2014, the district court approved a settlement of the Utah litigation providing, among other things, that the police officers may not stop or detain an individual simply to verify his or her immigration status or to transport the individual to federal officials based on a suspicion of unlawful presence. *See Texas Governor Orders Use of E–Verify; Utah Settles Lawsuit Challenging H.B. 497*, 91 Interp. Rel. 2207 (2014).

Under a settlement in May 2014, the federal government abandoned its challenge to section 2(B) of Arizona's SB 1070, and Arizona abandoned its defense of SB 1070's harboring provision. *See* Fernanda Santos, *U.S. and Arizona Yield on Immigration*, N.Y. Times, May 31, 2014, at A13. As of early 2016, private party lawsuits continue against various parts of SB 1070, as left open in *United States v. Arizona*. No other states have enacted legislation with the broad array of immigration enforcement provisions in the Alabama, Georgia, Indiana, South Carolina, or Utah laws.

b. Hazleton: The Rest of the Story

As explained earlier in this Section, the Third Circuit in *Lozano v. Hazleton* held in 2010 that federal law preempts the employment and housing provisions in the Hazleton ordinances. In 2011, the U.S. Supreme Court vacated that decision, remanding for further consideration in light of *Chamber of Commerce v. Whiting*. While the remand was pending, the Supreme Court decided *Arizona v. United States*. About one year later, in July 2013, the Third Circuit issued another decision in *Lozano*.

Applying both Supreme Court decisions, the Third Circuit again found that federal law preempts the Hazelton employment and housing provisions. The court reasoned that even though federal law did not preempt the Arizona employment law, the Hazleton ordinance was different. Its provisions "apply to a much broader range of actors and activities than Congress intended under IRCA," especially independent contractors and other economic activities outside the scope of employer-employee relationships. *Lozano v. Hazleton*, 724 F.3d 297, 306 (3d Cir. 2013). Unlike the Arizona employment law, the Hazleton ordinance lacked an affirmative defense for employers who use the federal process for verifying work authorization. Moreover, its "lack of procedural protections presents yet another 'obstacle to the accomplishment and execution of the full purposes and objectives' of federal law." *Id.* at 312.

As for the Hazleton housing ordinance, the Third Circuit ruled:

> We previously found the housing provisions in the [Illegal Immigration Relief Act Ordinance] and the [Rental Registration Ordinance] pre-empted on three separate pre-emption grounds.

No part of *Whiting* or *Arizona* considered provisions of a state or local ordinance that, like the housing provisions here, prohibit, and define "harboring" to include, allowing unauthorized aliens to reside in rental housing. Moreover, nothing in *Whiting* or *Arizona* undermines our analysis of the contested housing provisions here. On the contrary, the Court's language reinforces our view that Hazleton's attempt to prohibit unauthorized aliens from renting dwelling units in the City are pre-empted.

Id. at 314.

The Third Circuit rejected Hazleton's argument that federal law does not preempt "concurrent enforcement" by states and localities:

> * * * [In *Arizona*] * * * , the Court reasoned that "[a]lthough § 5(C) attempts to achieve one of the same goals as federal law— the deterrence of unlawful employment—it involves a conflict in the method of enforcement." The Court went on to explain that it had previously "recognized that a '[c]onflict in technique can be fully as disruptive to the system Congress enacted as conflict in overt policy.'" (quoting *Motor Coach Employees [v. Lockridge,* 403 U.S. 274, 287, 91 S.Ct. 1909), 29 L.Ed.2d 473 (1971)]. Thus, the Court found § 5(C) pre-empted even though the provision imposed sanctions only on conduct already prohibited under federal law.

Id. at 320.

After this resolution, the federal district court ordered the City of Hazleton to pay $1.4 million in attorneys' fees to the plaintiffs' lawyers. *See Pennsylvania city must pay $1.4 mln legal fees in immigration fight,* Reuters, Oct. 7, 2015.

Two other federal appellate decisions in this period addressed similar local ordinances. The Fifth Circuit, sitting en banc, considered a city ordinance in Farmers Branch, Texas, that required adults living in local rental housing to obtain an occupancy license conditioned upon U.S. citizenship or lawful immigration status. The ordinance also established civil and criminal penalties for violations. The court invalidated these provisions as preempted by federal law. *See Villas at Parkside Partners v. City of Farmers Branch,* 726 F.3d 524 (5th Cir. 2013) (en banc), *cert. denied,* 134 S.Ct. 1491 (2014). After the Supreme Court denied certiorari, the City of Farmers Branch agreed in June 2014 to pay $1.4 million in attorneys' fees to the plaintiffs' lawyers. *See Farmers Branch settles last part of lawsuit over rental ordinance for $1.4 million,* Dallas News, June 3, 2014.

Another decision went the other way, upholding a local ordinance in Fremont, Nebraska, that limited access to employment and housing for unauthorized migrants. One section required employers to use federal E–Verify to check employees' work authorization. The district court applied *Chamber of Commerce v. Whiting* to hold that this requirement was not preempted, and the challengers did not appeal that holding. *See Keller v. City of Fremont*, 719 F.3d 931, 937–38 (8th Cir. 2013), *cert. denied*, 134 S.Ct. 2140 (2014).

The Fremont housing restrictions then became the main point of contention, and the Tenth Circuit held that federal law did not preempt them. Expressing its disagreement with the *Hazleton* and *Farmers Branch* preemption findings that the Third Circuit and Fifth Circuit would later reassert, the court reasoned that the preemption argument suffered from a major flaw—the restrictions did not interfere with "the broad discretion exercised by federal immigration officials to determine which noncitizens will be removed from the United States." *Id.* at 944. Instead: "As the rental provisions do not 'remove' any alien from the United States (or even from the City), federal immigration officials retain complete discretion to decide whether and when to pursue removal proceedings." *Id.* Noting the similarity with § 2(B) of SB 1070, the court continued:

> This case presents an analogous situation. Before the rental provisions have been construed and implemented by state and local officials, and before we know how federal authorities will respond to the City's inquiries under § 1373(c), we decline to speculate whether the rental provisions might, as applied, "stand[ ] as an obstacle to the accomplishment and execution of the full purposes and objectives of Congress" as reflected in the complex removal provisions of federal immigration law.

Id. at 945.

CONCLUDING NOTES AND QUESTIONS ON THE STATE AND LOCAL ROLE

1.   Assume that you are an elected city official or state legislator who would like to reduce the unauthorized population in your jurisdiction. You are considering (1) checks of federal immigration status and the enactment of state criminal penalties for immigration violations, and (2) state and local laws that target unauthorized migration more indirectly by addressing housing and employment. How would you assess and compare these two approaches in general? How would you assess and compare what your jurisdiction might do within each general approach? Consider practical effectiveness as well as constitutionality in light of *Chamber of Commerce v. Whiting* and *Arizona v. United States*.

2.   As noted in the discussion of Secure Communities and the Priority Enforcement Program earlier in this Section C, some states and localities

have laws or policies that directly offset or neutralize federal immigration enforcement, for example by limiting compliance with federal detainers. Another category of state and local laws and policies address federal immigration enforcement more indirectly, by operating to integrate unauthorized migrants in spite of their unlawful presence. *See generally* Peter L. Markowitz, *Undocumented No More: The Power of State Citizenship*, 67 Stan. L. Rev. 869 (2015); Julia Preston, *States Are Divided by the Lines They Draw on Immigration*, N.Y. Times, Mar. 30, 2015, at A10. *See generally* Cristina Rodríguez, *The Significance of the Local in Immigration Regulation*, 106 Mich. L. Rev. 567 (2008).

Such state integration laws and policies include eligibility, regardless of immigration law status, for state driver's licenses or other driving permits. The federal REAL ID Act of 2005 accelerated the trend to limit eligibility to U.S. citizens and lawfully present noncitizens, but it left room for state driving documents that would not require lawful immigration status—but which also cannot be used for commercial air travel once the Act goes into full effect. (Such driver's licenses must be marked prominently to indicate that they are not "REAL-ID compliant.") As we go to press in late spring 2016, around a dozen states—with California having the largest unauthorized population—issue some form of driving permit without proof of lawful immigration status. *See generally* National Immigration Law Center, Immigrant-inclusive State and Local Policies Move Ahead in 2014–15, at 2–4 (2015); Kate M. Manuel & Michael John Garcia, Unlawfully Present Aliens, Driver's Licenses, and Other State-Issued ID: Select Legal Issues (Cong. Res. Serv. 2014).

At the municipal level, a few cities, most prominently New York, San Francisco, and New Haven, Connecticut, issue identification cards for which unauthorized migrants are eligible. *See* Matt Flegenheimer, *New York City to Formally Start Its Municipal ID Card Program*, N.Y. Times, Jan. 12, 2015, at A11; Heather Knight, *Hundreds Wait for Hours to Buy ID Card*, San Francisco Chronicle, Jan. 16, 2009, at B1; Jennifer Medina, *New Haven Approves Program To Issue Illegal Immigrants IDs*, N.Y. Times, June 5, 2007, at B6. *See* Manuel & Garcia, *supra*, at 20–21.

Another significant area is access to public colleges and universities. About 20 states allow unauthorized migrants who have connections to the state and meet other requirements to pay tuition at some or all public universities and colleges at resident rates that are significantly lower than what nonresidents pay. For example, California's AB 540 offers resident rates regardless of immigration status to students with three years of attendance and graduation from a California high school. In addition to resident tuition rates, eight states offer state financial aid regardless of immigration status. *See Immigrant-inclusive State and Local Policies*, *supra*, at 6–7. Relatedly, a California statute that took effect in January 2014 makes persons who are unlawfully present in the United States eligible to be admitted to the practice of law. Another California statute, effective January 2016, allows any persons, regardless of immigration status, to obtain any professional license for which they are otherwise eligible.

3.   In considering the scope of federal preemption, one might consider an apparent irony. Many of those who argued strenuously for preemption of Arizona's SB 1070 and emphasized the need for uniform federal laws and the avoidance of a patchwork enforcement pattern later defended the emerging local resistance to Secure Communities and ICE detainers. They also strongly supported local measures to integrate unauthorized migrants, such as driver's licenses and in-state tuition and public colleges and universities. On the other end of the political spectrum, defenders of SB 1070 and similar laws in other states also criticized state and local decisionmaking when it took the form of sanctuary cities and the TRUST Act. They also opposed driver's licenses and in-state tuition. Is either set of positions self-contradictory?

Consider the possibility that federal preemption of state and local laws addressing immigration and immigrants should depend on how those state and local laws might operate, and in particular on whether those laws may lead to discrimination that will go undetected or unremedied. That possibility may be prominent in immigration law enforcement, when it is undertaken by street-level officers who exercise great discretion in deciding to arrest potentially removable individuals. In anticipation of such situations, can prophylactic preemption of state and law decisionmaking serve as a middle ground between recognizing or rejecting discrimination claims that may result from state and local activity?

* * * [D]iscrimination claims * * * require courts to identify specific victims of specific discriminatory practices, as well as blame specific culprits, perhaps as racists. These are high stakes, and judges may hesitate. Decisions will turn on a simple yes-or-no decision as to whether certain defendants have discriminated. * * *

* * *

* * * When equal protection violations based on discriminatory intent are a serious concern but are hard to define and prove, a preemption challenge can shift who bears the practical risk that the truth is hard to ascertain. Plaintiffs would no longer need to prove that state and local governments intend to discriminate, as an equal protection challenge would require to succeed. Instead, preemption analysis would require state and local governments to allay concerns about allowing them to enforce immigration law. A broad view of preemption manages doubt differently, essentially shifting the burden of proof. * * *

Hiroshi Motomura, Immigration Outside the Law 134–35 (2014).

According to this approach, preemption should be broader when state and local enforcement may lead to undetected or unremedied discrimination. Discrimination against specific individuals may be less of a concern when state and local measures resist federal immigration law enforcement or attempt to integrate unauthorized migrants in spite of their unlawful presence in the United States.

> When state and local activity supports immigration enforcement, the risk of exclusion increases. Some of the targets will be US citizens and lawfully present noncitizens. Others will be unauthorized migrants, but that is just as troubling if race or ethnicity drives decisions to choose them for selective enforcement, given the broad role of discretion. In contrast, measures at the state and local levels to integrate unauthorized migrants run some risk of diffuse harm to US citizens, but it is not the harm of racial or ethnic exclusion. When it comes to assessing state and local authority, immigration enforcement and immigrant integration are not the same.

Id. at 153–54. *See also* Kerry Abrams, *Plenary Power Preemption*, 99 Va. L. Rev. 601, 638 (2013); Lucas Guttentag, *Immigration Preemption and the Limits on State Power: Reflections on* Arizona v. United States, 9 Stan. J. Civ. Rts. & Civ. Lib. 1, 35–42 (2013)..

Does this approach to preemption amount to an end-run around the basic requirement of proving a violation of equal protection through evidence of discriminatory intent? Are there other problems with this approach, which one critic has called "Equal Pro-Emption"? *See* David S. Rubenstein, *Black-Box Immigration Federalism*, 114 Mich. L. Rev. 983, 1006–12 (2016). *See also* Clare Huntington, *The Constitutional Dimension of Immigration Federalism*, 61 Vand. L. Rev. 787 (2008); Peter H. Schuck, *Taking Immigration Federalism Seriously*, 2007 U. Chi. Legal F. 57.

Is this approach to preemption also a way of saying that the Supreme Court should have struck down § 2(B) of Arizona SB 1070 as preempted? *See* Jennifer M. Chacón, *The Transformation of Immigration Federalism*, 21 Wm. & Mary Bill Rts. J. 577, 617 (2012) ("It is only by de-emphasizing antidiscrimination norms that the Court is able to avoid a finding of obstacle preemption with respect to Section 2(B).").

Does conceptual and doctrinal consistency require that preemption operate the same way for enforcement of immigration law and integration of unauthorized migrants?

4.   Stepping back and looking broadly at state and local enforcement, how much authority should states and local governments have to address immigration and immigrants? Do they now have too much, or too little? Could and should Congress enact a federal statute that expressly preempts certain types of state and local laws, and expressly authorizes state and local laws of other types? How would you define how far preemption reaches? If it depends on the issue, how and why does it depend? Are states different from cities?

D. PROPOSALS TO REFORM THE LEGAL IMMIGRATION SYSTEM

Today, widespread agreement that the current U.S. immigration system is broken coexists with dramatically different notions about how to fix it—and a discouragingly polarized debate among the contending camps. For some the key feature of the breakdown is the ineffectiveness of enforcement. For others the central failure is manifested in hardships that the current system imposes on migrants, either through deportation that can divide families or the enforcement strategies that have diverted entry patterns through dangerous deserts. And for still others, particularly in influential sectors of the U.S. business community, the key is the mismatch of temporary and permanent immigration opportunities with the claimed needs of the U.S. economy or the desires of prospective immigrants and their sponsors.

Many of those in the first camp favor legislative and administrative changes that deal with enforcement only. Most in the latter camps either embrace or acquiesce in the argument that improved enforcement must be part of any new regime, and so have tried to develop legislative proposals that would include enhanced enforcement but also address the other concerns. They push for "comprehensive immigration reform," in contrast to an enforcement-only package. Comprehensive reform proposals include three major components: (1) enforcement—through enhanced resources for the enforcement agencies, new approaches at the border and in the interior, and improved employer screening; (2) reform of legal immigration categories, especially to satisfy perceived labor market needs—often including proposals for an expansive guest-worker program; and (3) legalization, with conditions, of most of the current population present without authorization (opponents call this element "amnesty"; proponents favor "earned legalization").

The immigration reform debate covers a very wide scope of issues and proposals. Coverage here is necessarily selective, but provides the raw material for discussion of several key issues, including an overview of reform attempts over the last two decades. The materials that follow the principal reading pick up on selected issues addressed therein, offering additional perspectives or proposals as grist for policy discussion.

EXERCISE ON IMMIGRATION REFORM

To frame and focus your reading of the following material, assume that you are a legislative aide to a newly elected member of Congress. She wants to devote much of her legislative effort to fixing the immigration system and she has asked you to outline preliminary ideas for her legislative initiatives in this field. Therefore, keep track of the policy issues you regard as the most important to be addressed in any new round of reform, and note which of the competing proposals on each of the elements seem most promising. Pay attention to the assumptions you make about the underlying goals that the system should serve and also about what the political climate will bear.

---

1.   A SURVEY AND INTRODUCTION

We begin with excerpts from a 2009 report of an independent and bipartisan task force chartered by the Council on Foreign Relations and chaired by former Republican Governor Jeb Bush of Florida and Thomas (Mac) McLarty, who served as Chief of Staff to Democratic President Bill Clinton. The report argues for a version of comprehensive immigration reform, but it also equips its readers to understand the primary elements that have sometimes been proposed for piecemeal enactment. It discusses briefly the salient history, including the previous attempt at comprehensive reforms in the 1986 Immigration Reform and Control Act (IRCA), which contained both legalization and new enforcement measures, and sustained legislative efforts in 2006–2007.

Though this report is seven years old as this casebook goes to press, the policy terrain and controversies remain largely the same. The further history of (unsuccessful) legislative reform efforts since 2009 is summarized in the materials following this report, as is President Obama's decision to move toward some of the reform goals through unilateral presidential action.

Context is important. The task force convened at the end of a decade when the unauthorized population was growing by 500,000 to 800,000 per year, reaching an estimated peak above 12 million in 2007. Thereafter, the Great Recession (which was in its early stages when this report appeared) plus enhanced border deployments and economic and demographic changes in Mexico brought a significant reduction in illegal migration. By 2016 estimates of the unauthorized population fell below 11 million.

JEB BUSH, THOMAS F. MCLARTY III &
EDWARD ALDEN, U.S. IMMIGRATION POLICY

Independent Task Force Report No. 63; Council on Foreign Relations, 2009.
Chapter on "The Need for Comprehensive Immigration Reform," pp. 44–69, 76–79.

* * *

It has been said many times before, but it is also the conclusion of this Task Force that the current immigration system is badly broken. It will take both changes to the law and changes to current practices to make the system function more effectively. * * *

Congress has tried repeatedly to address some of the problems in the immigration system, passing significant legislation in 1986, 1990, and 1996. Yet the conclusions of the congressionally established Jordan Commission in 1994 remain as true today as they were then. "Serious problems undermine present immigration policies, their implementation, and their credibility: people who should get in find a cumbersome process that often impedes their entry; people who should not get in find it all too easy to enter; and people who are here without permission remain with impunity."

The Bush administration and Congress made efforts to overhaul U.S. immigration laws in 2006 and 2007, but in the face of strong opposition from both sides of the debate, a compromise could not be found. * * * Although there was considerable support for the 2007 Senate bill, little of it was enthusiastic, with many backers considering it only marginally preferable to the status quo. In addition, opponents of the legislation were strong and vocal in their denunciations. And, though the principles of the congressional proposals were generally sound, by the time of its eventual defeat, the Senate bill had become so complex that effective implementation by the Department of Homeland Security and other agencies would likely have been impossible. * * *

Since 2007, the administration's primary response to the failure of comprehensive immigration reform has been to escalate enforcement at the border and to toughen measures to stop companies from employing unauthorized migrants. In an effort to keep out illegal immigrants, the United States has expanded the Border Patrol into the nation's largest law enforcement agency, spent billions on deploying high-tech virtual barriers, and is close to completing construction of nearly seven hundred miles of pedestrian and vehicle fences along its southern border with Mexico. * * *

Although many in the media, and some in Congress, continue to insist that U.S. borders are out of control and insecure, the Task Force believes that the border enforcement efforts of the past several years are impressive and not well enough understood by the public. * * * The United States has also used intelligence gathering and modern technologies to help target terrorists, criminals, and others it wants to exclude from the country.

The Task Force finds that these measures represent determined, expansive efforts to control America's borders and enforce U.S. immigration laws. But no amount of enforcement can eliminate the underlying problem, which is that aggressively enforcing a broken regime does not fix it. Unless the United States has a more sensible and efficient system for admitting legal migrants who come to take advantage of work opportunities, no reasonable level of enforcement is likely to be enough to resolve the illegal immigration problem.

* * *

There are improvements to the immigration system that can and should be undertaken without legislation, but a piecemeal effort at reform is unlikely to make anything other than modest progress, given the flaws in the current legal regime and the complexity of the competing interests and concerns. * * * [This] report will discuss the four central elements of any immigration reform effort: improvements in the legal immigration system, more effective enforcement to discourage illegal immigration, a plan for dealing with those already living illegally in this country, and, finally, a strategy for ensuring successful integration of the growing number of immigrants who are arriving and settling in the United States.[a]

ENCOURAGING LEGAL IMMIGRATION

Most immigrants come to the United States to work. * * *

As is being demonstrated by the current recession, the quickest way to discourage illegal migration is to stop creating jobs for migrants and everyone else. When the economy recovers, the demand for new immigrants, whether legal or illegal, will also recover. The current slowdown, therefore, should be seen as an opportunity to overhaul U.S. immigration policies to better serve U.S. economic needs as the economy regains its footing.

* * *

Three central principles should guide the reform of the legal immigration system: first, the United States should be admitting immigrants (and their close family members) in the number and range of skills that reflect the demands from its economy; second, it needs a much simpler and more transparent system for admitting both migrants and temporary workers; and finally, the government must invest in making the legal immigration system work more efficiently.

---

[a]   The immigrant integration discussion is omitted from this excerpt.—eds.

Immigrant numbers

The current immigration system does not respond well to supply and demand in the U.S. labor market. Economics should not be the only factor shaping American immigration policy decisions, but neither can the United States simply ignore the vast economic forces that drive international migration. The effort to gain control of illegal migration is certain to fail unless the supply of foreign workers and the demand for them in the United States are brought more closely into line. * * * Indeed, one of the reasons illegal immigration is so attractive not only to the migrants but also to U.S. employers is that it responds quickly to market pressures. The lengthy waits and substantial expense required for hiring most foreign workers through existing legal channels have discouraged many employers from using those channels, except for the most highly skilled workers.

Labor market needs currently get far too little attention in deciding who gets priority to immigrate. For the past half century, most new immigrants coming to the United States have been family members of legal migrants or U.S. citizens. In 2008, nearly 700,000 people acquired green cards on the basis of family ties. By contrast, only just over 166,000 did so on the basis of employment, 76,000 to the employees and the remaining 90,000 to their spouses and children. There has long been a debate over whether the strong preference for family reunification in U.S. immigration law serves American interests. There are clearly some good reasons for maintaining the policy—the family is a core unit of American society, and strong families are critical for the education, financial support, and social integration of newcomers to the country. Families can also serve as an information network, alerting relatives at home to job prospects in the United States, and providing them with support after they arrive. * * *

The current system for family-based immigration, however, is exceedingly slow, and does not work well even in bringing families together. As a result of quotas designed to limit immigrants from a handful of countries such as Mexico, India, and China, waits for sponsoring family members can stretch to a decade or more. * * * Even the waiting times for spouses and minor children of legal immigrants from anywhere in the world are often more than five years—a delay that is so long as to make a mockery of the concept of family reunification.

However, the system for admitting immigrants with needed skills but without family connections is even worse. Changes to the quotas as part of the 1990 Immigration Act raised the number of green cards for employment-based immigrants and their families from 56,000 to 140,000, but this remains a fraction of the numbers available for family members. In addition, most of the employment-based slots are claimed by individuals already living in the United States under some sort of temporary status. At the higher-skilled end, the main temporary visa available for bringing skilled workers to the United States and putting them on a path to permanent residence has been the H–1B visa program, though that same program has also been used heavily by Indian companies bringing over strictly temporary workers to support their business model of outsourcing back-office work for U.S. companies. * * * [The H–1B cap has been changed by Congress several times over the past decade,] but it is clear that the [current] quota [of 65,000] is inadequate in anything but a deep recession.

The logic of the current quotas is that hiring more foreign technology workers will mean fewer jobs for American technology workers. There is little evidence, however, that those restrictions end up creating more jobs for American workers. * * * A recent survey by the National Venture Capital Association found that one-third of privately held venture capital-backed U.S. companies—the most innovative firms in the United States—had been increasing hiring abroad due to restrictions that prevented them from hiring foreign workers in this country.

A number of other advanced industrialized nations have implemented policies that explicitly target immigrants whose skills the government believes are valuable to the economy, or are thought to be in short supply. Canada, Britain, Australia, and New Zealand all have what are known as points-based systems for selecting immigrants. They use factors such as education, occupation, work experience, age, and language skills to decide which immigrants to admit. The system is implemented by the government, in contrast to the U.S. scheme, which depends more on private companies identifying and hiring particular foreign workers.

* * * Despite the arguments in favor of a points system, the United States, under its current system, has been the most successful country in the world in attracting the most highly skilled immigrants—a record that calls for reforming the current system to make it more efficient, easier to use, and more responsive to market demand, rather than adopting a different system wholesale.

U.S. policies for attracting low-skilled workers have also been divorced from the realities of supply and demand. The current legal quota for green cards for unskilled laborers and their families, for example, is just ten thousand each year, a miniscule number that does not begin to reflect actual demand. The H–2A visa program for temporary agricultural workers tends to be underused by employers because of its cost and complexity, whereas the H–2B program for seasonal workers has a quota that is normally too low to meet demand. * * *

There has long been serious consideration given to expanding temporary worker programs, especially for low-skilled migrants from

Mexico who would otherwise be likely to enter the United States illegally. A temporary worker program was a central feature of the failed immigration reform efforts in both 2006 and 2007. Temporary and seasonal work programs have been the only mechanism that has allowed the cross-border flow of workers from Mexico to the United States to be funneled into a program that can be monitored by government authorities. The biggest dilemma has been how to enforce labor certification, minimum wage, and labor rights provisions in an effort to ensure that migrant workers are not being exploited, and are not used by employers to drive down wages and standards for American workers. * * *

Temporary worker programs have never been a panacea, and the U.S. experience with such schemes has been decidedly mixed. The biggest of these was the Bracero Program for Mexican agricultural workers[, which] * * * became notorious for widespread labor rights abuses and was shut down by Congress in 1965. * * *

The United States is not alone in its mixed experiences. Other countries have generally been unsuccessful in creating smoothly functioning guest worker programs for at least two reasons. First, except in certain industries, such as agriculture and tourism, which have large seasonal employment fluctuations, temporary work is something of a misnomer. Many temporary work permits are for full-time, year-round jobs, but with the assumption that at the end of a certain period, usually three years, the individual will return home. The assumption collides with too much of what is known about human nature and economic realities. Someone who leaves home for three years almost invariably puts down some roots in the new community, and is unlikely to leave voluntarily at the end of that period. The employee may have come to depend on the higher wage, much of which is often sent back home to families as remittances. An employer may also be reluctant to lose a good employee. * * * As a result, many temporary workers try to find legal channels to remain permanently in their adopted countries or, failing that, often remain illegally.

The second problem is that the conditions of employment for temporary workers tend to be substandard, with employers sometimes paying workers below the legal minimum wage and withholding normal employment benefits. In cases where an individual's legal status in the host country depends on a particular job, as is frequently the case, those workers have little or no ability to seek better wages or working conditions. Unions have found it particularly difficult, and usually impossible, to organize foreign workers enrolled in such programs. The United States has attempted to deal with these criticisms by requiring that employers attest that they have been unable to find enough workers domestically, and that they will offer foreign workers the same wages and working conditions as domestic employees. But in practice such labor certification requirements have been extremely difficult to enforce, particularly with the inadequate resources devoted to the task.

Complexity

The current legal immigration system is inordinately complex and cumbersome. Lengthy delays in processing routine requests make it difficult, if not impossible, to carry out an immigration policy that serves the nation's interests. According to the U.S. Citizenship and Immigration Services (USCIS) ombudsman, many of the "pervasive and serious problems" in the handling of legal immigration and visa claims "stem from the complexity and opaque nature of the immigration rules and the agency administering them." The basic law underlying U.S. immigration policy was written in 1952, and since that time most of the changes approved by Congress have simply layered additional burdens on an already inadequate law and an ineffective bureaucracy.

* * *

The current template for legal immigration to the United States also bears little resemblance to how most immigration actually takes place. The assumption on which the laws are written is that most aspiring immigrants will apply from their home countries for permission to immigrate to the United States, and then wait their turn in line. That may once have been an accurate reflection of the reality, but currently most who immigrate permanently to the United States spend many years living here first on some kind of temporary visa.

In theory, almost everyone who comes to the United States on a temporary visa—whether as a tourist, a student, or an employee—is expected to demonstrate the intent to return home after the visa expires. * * * Yet in practice, the distinction between temporary employees and permanent immigrants has utterly broken down. Because permanent visas are so difficult to obtain, temporary ones have become a substitute. Far more temporary work visas are therefore issued each year than employment-based green cards. In 2008, for instance, more than 166,000 employment-based green cards were issued to both employees and their family members; in comparison, more than 600,000 temporary work visas were issued, many to people living in the United States for years and waiting for a green card. More than 60 percent of those seeking green cards each year are already in the United States; that figure is nearly 90 percent for employment-based immigrants.

There are good arguments in favor of an immigration system that allows many people to come here first on some sort of temporary basis. The process permits a potential immigrant to experience living and working in the United States before making the more consequential decision to immigrate. The student visa program, for instance, has been an enormously important channel for attracting young, highly skilled individuals who often end up living permanently in the United States. On the demand side, temporary schemes are also easier for the government to adjust upward and downward as economic conditions in the United States change, a flexibility that does not exist with family-based permanent immigration.

* * * In simplifying the immigration system, the United States needs to move to a scheme that more closely resembles how migration actually occurs in the world today.

Government Investment

Even if the current system can be simplified, it will not work properly without a more effective funding system for facilitating legal immigration. * * *

Congress has mandated that USCIS be self-funded. Under the current system, the cost of immigration processing is paid for entirely by a series of fees levied on visa applicants, temporary immigrants, green-card applicants, and those seeking U.S. citizenship. Certain types of visa applications are particularly expensive.

* * *

The underlying message is that America as a country believes that immigration serves only the interests of immigrants, and therefore they should pay the entire cost themselves. Further, the refusal to use any taxpayer money to pay for immigration services indicates that the United States does not believe that facilitating legal immigration is a significant national priority. * * * *The Task Force believes that both facilitating legal immigration and preventing unlawful entry should be considered equally important priorities, and should receive the funding and oversight to ensure they perform at an optimal level.*

In particular, Congress should be prepared to appropriate funds to support the development of a modern infrastructure for processing immigrant and temporary visa applications.

* * *

DISCOURAGING ILLEGAL IMMIGRATION

The United States has the right, and the duty, to control and secure its borders. It is an affront to the rule of law that hundreds of thousands of people each year can enter the country unannounced or pose as visitors when their intention is to live here permanently. It is also true that, except for the small percentage who come here as drug smugglers or with the intention of committing other crimes, the vast majority of illegal immigrants have broken the law only in pursuit of a dream shared by many, to make better lives for themselves and for their families. But a central feature of the American dream is the idea that success comes from playing by the rules; that so many who wish to come here now try to succeed by violating the rules is a sad distortion of that ideal. *The Task Force believes that in any effort to reform immigration laws, the rule of law must be reasserted. No reform will be accepted by the American people, nor should it be, unless it restores respect for the law.* This means that alongside reform of its legal immigration system, the United States must assert greater control over its borders, assure compliance with terms of admission, and sharply reduce the number of jobs available to persons not authorized to work in this country.

Comprehensive immigration reform would substantially lower the flow of illegal migrants by providing alternative legal channels for migrants to live and work in the United States. * * * Reducing the flow would also allow for a much higher apprehension rate, which would in turn discourage others who might be thinking about trying to enter the United States illegally. There is a law enforcement tipping point at which the costs and difficulty of entering illegally would become a powerful disincentive, particularly given the existence of new legal options. The sharp reduction in illegal entry into the United States over the past two years as the economy has softened and enforcement has grown indicates that it is possible to reach this tipping point in a recession; the challenge is to do so when the economy recovers and the demand for new employees again rises.

The Task Force believes that an effective enforcement regime centers on three elements: first, a comprehensive and accurate system that discourages employers from hiring unauthorized migrants; second, tougher enforcement at the borders that stops those who should not be admitted at a U.S. land border or port of entry; and, third, closer cooperation among federal, state, and local law enforcement officials in enforcing immigration laws.[b]

Employment Enforcement

Since the 1986 Immigration Reform and Control Act, the biggest missing piece in the enforcement effort has been the absence of any serious attempt to discourage employers from hiring undocumented workers. The grand bargain of 1986 was supposed to offer legalization for those already here in exchange for much tougher enforcement measures to bar the employment of illegal workers in the future. In practice, for both political and technological reasons, the employer sanctions provisions have not been adequately enforced, particularly not in recent years. * * * The result was that rather than discouraging illegal

---

[b] The Task Force's discussion of cooperation with state and local law enforcement is omitted from this excerpt. That broad issue is considered in Section C above.—eds.

immigration, the 1986 act almost certainly accelerated it. * * * The failure was not conception; it was implementation.

Employment opportunities are the magnet that pulls most illegal migrants to the United States; if those opportunities can be diminished, illegal immigration will also diminish. *The Task Force believes employer sanctions need to be strengthened to discourage employers from hiring unauthorized workers; there should be clear guidelines to enable employers to comply with employer sanctions law, and these laws should be enforced to achieve optimal deterrence. Such measures are the most effective and humane way to discourage illegal migration to the United States.* * * *

Why should enforcement at the work site be any more effective than it was after 1986? In some ways, the problem is more difficult because the hiring of unauthorized migrants is so pervasive that many employers have a strong incentive to continue the practice. On the other hand, the U.S. government now has the capability to use information technologies that allow for quicker and more accurate verification that new employees are authorized to work in the United States. The E–Verify system, begun on a pilot basis in 1997, has gradually been expanded to encompass many more employers. * * *

Although still in its infancy, the E–Verify system shows considerable promise. * * *

* * *

Generally, employer sanctions have been almost an afterthought in the U.S. enforcement regime, even as all other aspects of enforcement have been ramped up significantly in recent years. * * *

* * * It will take strengthened employer sanctions, along with a robust electronic verification system that provides immunity from prosecution for employers who use it, to achieve compliance by the vast majority of U.S. employers. This, in turn, would permit focused and targeted investigations and prosecution of noncompliant employers, further increasing the deterrent effect of the strengthened law. There is a tipping point where violations become the exception, but getting to it will require tougher sanctions. Both the carrot and the stick are needed.

The Task Force believes that as more legal immigrant workers become available, and as the government increasingly puts in place tools to encourage and to make it easier for legitimate companies to comply with the law, tough enforcement against violations by employers needs to become routine.

Border Enforcement

The United States has made impressive strides in the past several years in strengthening its border enforcement measures. Border enforcement is vital to safeguarding the nation against those who would do it harm, particularly terrorists and serious criminals, and for keeping out those trying to enter the United States illegally. Along with a comprehensive reform of the immigration system that allows new legal paths for immigrants, border enforcement is needed for deterring and catching those who would still try to enter the United States illegally. As the experience of the 1986 legislation has shown, there cannot be meaningful and lasting reform of U.S. legal immigration policies without an effective system to secure the borders.

The fundamental goal of border enforcement is to permit the United States to know, to the fullest extent possible, who is entering the country, but to do so in a way that does not disrupt legitimate cross-border movement.

* * *

EARNED LEGALIZATION

The toughest issue is what to do with the millions already living illegally in the United States. This, more than any other issue, led to the failure of congressional efforts at immigration reform in 2006 and 2007. By the best estimates, slightly fewer than twelve million unauthorized immigrants are thought to be living currently in the United States, though that number is likely shrinking as a result of the weakening economy and tougher enforcement. Public opinion polls, perhaps surprisingly, show that about two-thirds of Americans support finding a way for those who live illegally in the United States to gain lawful status, providing they develop English-language skills, pass background checks, and pay some sort of restitution. But deep suspicion rightly remains that a mass legalization will simply repeat the 1986 experience and do nothing to stem the problem of illegal migration in the future.

Language matters a great deal in the debate over immigration, but it matters here particularly. The legalization provisions in many of the bills considered by Congress from 2004 to 2007 were denounced by some critics as amnesty. More than any other single argument, it was the amnesty claim that did the most to kill the legislation. By any reasonable definition, however, the use of the term *amnesty* to describe the proposed reforms was a gross misstatement. The *Merriam-Webster Dictionary* defines amnesty as the "the act of an authority (as a government) by which pardon is granted to a large group of individuals." In other words, amnesty means wiping a transgressor's record clean—it is a free ride. Moreover, amnesty implies a serious threat of criminal prosecution and conviction. Like it or not, for the millions of illegal immigrants in the United States, there has never been a serious threat of criminal prosecution. * * *

* * * [In contrast, even] the most generous bills [considered in Congress recently] would have required those living in the United States unlawfully to earn their legalization. Illegal migrants would have had to demonstrate a long, virtually uninterrupted period of gainful employment, pass criminal and national security background checks, pay substantial fines, and demonstrate basic mastery of English. In a number of versions of the legislation, those who qualified would only be eligible initially for a temporary work visa, and would need to live and work in the United States for another significant period before being permitted to seek permanent residence.

Other, more targeted bills such as the Development, Relief, and Education for Alien Minors (DREAM) Act were aimed at providing some path to legalization for children who were brought to the United States illegally by their parents and thus had no active part in the decision to violate U.S. immigration laws. Those who had been present in the United States for at least five years, had earned a high school diploma, had been admitted to a postsecondary program, and had demonstrated good moral character would be eligible to adjust to permanent residence. The Agricultural Job Opportunities, Benefits, and Security (AgJOBS) Act would similarly have offered temporary status to those already employed as farm workers. If they remained in good standing for the following three to six years, those individuals could seek permanent residence.

* * *

The strongest argument against some form of earned legalization is that it will simply set the United States up for further illegal immigration and another round of legalization one or two or three decades from now. The experience of 1986 serves as a stark warning, and there is indeed a degree of moral hazard in any legalization scheme. There is no question that earned legalization creates an incentive for others to try to enter the United States illegally in the hope that they too will be allowed to stay by a future act of legalization. *The Task Force believes it is critical that any legalization program be accompanied both by more realistic immigration and temporary worker quotas and by stringent enforcement.*

Weighed against those arguments are the stronger, practical, ethical, economic, and national security arguments in favor of earned legalization. Practically, the difficulties in deporting so many illegal immigrants are extraordinary. Although not impossible, by any measure the undertaking would be extremely costly. For all the resources already been dedicated to increasing the number of removals, and the weak economy that has encouraged some to leave on their own, there appears to have been only a small decline in the number of illegal migrants living in the United States. Given both the expense and the further damage mass deportation would do to America's economy and to its reputation as a nation of immigrants, such an effort would not be in the country's interest.

The United States has long been a country that believes in second chances. The alternative—to break up families and wrench people away from communities where they have lived for many years, and in some cases even decades—is morally unacceptable. In many cases, it would require breaking up families in which some of the members are undocumented, others are legal residents, and others, particularly children, were born in the United States and are therefore U.S. citizens. * * *

Economically, the existence of a kind of shadow workforce that comprises more than 5 percent of the U.S. workforce makes little sense. Given the danger of deportation, it is impossible for these workers to press for better wages or working conditions. The result is an unfair advantage to employers who hire undocumented immigrants rather than native-born workers or legal migrants. Normalizing the status of undocumented workers in the United States could help improve both wages and working conditions for all those in lower-skilled jobs, and create fairer competition for American workers.

* * *

As unsatisfactory as it is to many from a rule-of-law perspective, including members of this Task Force, we believe there is little choice but to find some way to bring illegal migrants already in the United States who wish to remain out of the shadows and to offer them an earned pathway to legal status. It is the right policy choice—for economic reasons, for security reasons, and for the simply pragmatic reason that the United States should not attempt to deport people who have lived here for a long time, raised their families here, worked hard, and otherwise obeyed the law.

2. REFORM ACTIVITY DURING THE OBAMA YEARS

a. Obama's First Term

President Obama had campaigned in 2008 on a platform that made comprehensive immigration reform a high priority. During 2009 and 2010, his administration worked behind the scenes to refine legislative proposals and to build support for comprehensive reform, primarily seeking cooperation with the chairman and ranking member of the Senate subcommittee having jurisdiction over immigration, Charles Schumer (D-NY) and Lindsey Graham (R-SC). The inability to find another Republican who would join Graham as a cosponsor and strong proponent of reform helped to stymie those efforts, as did the longer-than-expected battle over the Affordable Care Act. As frustration over the delays built in 2010, the two senators published an op-ed essay with the outlines of their own comprehensive reform plans. Charles E. Schumer & Lindsey O. Graham, *The Right Way to Mend Immigration,* Wash. Post, Mar. 19, 2010. Nonetheless, progress remained stalled as the 2010 elections neared. Proponents did make a last-ditch effort during the lame-duck session to pass the DREAM Act, a narrower reform bill providing a path to legalization for persons who had been brought to the United States as children. The bill gained majority support in the House, but a filibuster in the Senate prevented enactment. (The DREAM Act is considered more closely below at pp. 1295–1298.)

The 2010 elections brought a Republican majority to the House of Representatives, dimming the prospects for reform. Some members of Congress introduced their own proposals for accomplishing portions of the reform agenda in piecemeal fashion. Several focused exclusively on new or expanded enforcement measures, especially to make E–Verify into a national mandatory employee screening system. Others addressed the admissions or legalization side. Some looked to expand the admission opportunities for entrepreneurs or for high-skilled migrants (including a flashy proposal described as "stapling" a green card to the diploma of any student obtaining an advanced degree from a U.S. university in scientific and technical (STEM) fields). Still others sought to expand and streamline the system for admitting temporary agricultural workers. None of these changes were enacted.

In June 2012, the Obama administration announced its Deferred Action for Childhood Arrivals (DACA) program, covering roughly those who would have benefited from the DREAM Act. Persons who came as children and had been living without authorization in the United States for five years could obtain this formalized version of prosecutorial discretion. By the end of 2014, over 600,000 had received this status, most with work authorization. President Obama's reelection in 2012, winning heavy majorities from Latino and Asian-American voters (among the most rapidly growing population segments) brought renewed interest in comprehensive reform.

b.   The Senate Passes Comprehensive Reform

In 2013, a bipartisan group of eight senators worked together to craft a massive comprehensive reform bill, and the Senate passed it in June by a vote of 68–32, with significant Republican support. Border Security, Economic Opportunity, and Immigration Modernization Act, S.744, 113th Cong (passed Senate June 27, 2013). It included a broad earned legalization program covering persons unlawfully present in the country since December 31, 2011, with more favorable legalization opportunities for many noncitizens who arrived as children, including those who would have been covered by earlier versions of the DREAM Act. Currently employed unauthorized agricultural workers would also benefit from special measures for legalization.

The INA's legal migration provisions were set to be modified and generally expanded. Highlights included "merit visas" for immigrant admissions in two tracks, one based on a point system and another on backlog reduction; expansion of employment-based immigration, especially in STEM fields; treating beneficiaries of the current FS–2A category as immediate relatives exempt from quotas; similarly exempting from ceilings current EB–1 immigrants, as well as derivative family members of employment-based immigrants. These increases in immigrant admissions would have been partially offset by the phasing out of diversity visas, the fourth family-based preference for brothers and sisters, and third-preference eligibility for married children over age 30. (Nevertheless some estimated that annual LPR admissions under the new provisions, when fully implemented, might have been above two million a year, double current totals.)

The bill contained new temporary worker provisions, with separate branches for agricultural and nonagricultural workers, generally providing higher admission numbers, with specific formulas for later adjustments in the ceilings. H–1B ceilings would have been raised, with new measures meant to minimize displacement or wage reduction for U.S. workers. The bill would have eliminated the one-year filing deadline for asylum applications. Within four years, all employers would have to be using E–Verify for their new hires, with the requirement phased in by size of the employer's workforce (largest first). An amendment proposed during the latest stages of Senate consideration also mandated massive increases in border security measures, including a near-doubling of the Border Patrol by FY 2022.

Following Senate passage of S. 744, the House leadership for many months sent conflicting signals about its interest in taking up immigration reform. As the House delayed, opposition from Republican ranks mounted. In June 2014, the Republican leadership made it clear that there would be no movement on immigration reform in 2014—a stance attributed in part to calculations that Republican candidates would be in better shape for that year's congressional elections without acting on such a controversial measure. David Nakamura & Ed O'Keefe, *Immigration Reform Effectively Dead until after Obama Leaves Office, Both Sides Say*, Wash. Post, June 26, 2014. In that election, Republicans made significant gains in the House and took majority control of the Senate.

c. Unilateral Executive Actions

Two weeks later, in late November 2014, President Obama announced a series of executive actions to provide deferred action and work authorization for many of those who would have qualified for legalization or other benefits under the Senate bill. President Obama's executive package also included the use of parole and other executive measures to expand migration opportunities for certain categories favored by business and for family members of U.S. military personnel. *See* Fixing Our Broken Immigration System through Executive Action—Key Facts (DHS Information Page, Nov. 20, 2014), available on the DHS website, http://www.dhs.gov/immigration-action.

The President's initiative was welcomed in some circles, but touched off considerable controversy over whether it exceeded his statutory and constitutional powers—even among some who supported the objective of shielding long-time de facto residents from removal. Twenty-six states sued DHS to block the expansion of deferred action for childhood arrivals (DACA) and the new deferred action program Obama had announced for parents of U.S. citizens and lawful permanent residents (DAPA). A district court enjoined these new deferred action measures (the original DACA program was not affected, and its beneficiaries could still receive two-year renewals of deferred action). The Fifth Circuit affirmed, and the Supreme Court granted certiorari in January 2016. No decision has been issued as this book goes to press. Key elements of the President's executive actions package, particularly the deferred action programs, are discussed in Chapter Seven, pp. 774–786 *supra*. The President's actions were sharply attacked by most of the candidates in the 2016 Republican primaries, and the overall tone of the discussion turned exceptionally harsh.

3. SPECIFIC REFORM PROPOSALS: A SELECTIVE SURVEY

a. Reforms to Family-Sponsored Legal Immigration Categories

Family reunification has obviously been a key element of permanent immigration to the United States. But the lengthy backlogs that now characterize all family categories except immediate relatives of U.S. citizens, in the words of the Council on Foreign Relations task force, "make a mockery of the concept of family reunification." How could those categories be reformed to serve the goal more closely?

The congressionally chartered Commission on Immigration Reform, chaired by former Congresswoman Barbara Jordan, recommended in 1995 that several current categories (family-sponsored preferences 1, 2B, 3, and 4) be eliminated so as to focus on what it regarded as the highest priority, the nuclear family. It proposed that there should be just three family preference categories: (1) spouses and minor children of U.S. citizens; (2) parents of U.S. citizens; and (3) spouses and minor children, plus adult physically or mentally dependent offspring of lawful permanent residents. It also favored a true preference system: numbers would be available to a lower preference only if the preceding category did not make full use of that year's family numbers (which the Commission recommended be set at 550,000 for a transition period, with possible lowering later). U.S. Commission on Immigration Reform, Legal Immigration: Setting Priorities xi-xix (1995). The 2006 bill passed by the Senate, however, moved in the opposite direction. It would have maintained existing family categories and increased the ceilings in virtually all of them. Because the immediate relative category would remain uncapped, this would have produced nearly a million family-based admissions each year. S. 2611, 109th Cong., 2d Sess. (passed Senate on May 25, 2006).

After the 2006 reform bill failed to win passage in the House, a 2007 "grand bargain" reform bill tacked back in a restrictive direction, in the hopes of securing a majority in both chambers. S. 1639, 110th Cong., 1st Sess. (2007). It adopted the Commission's basic proposal to eliminate several family preferences, but went further to take parents of U.S. citizens out of the quota-free immediate relative category. Instead, parents of U.S. citizens would have their own capped preference category with 40,000 permanent admissions annually, plus a new nonimmigrant category for parental visits to the United States, but with restrictions to help assure departure at the end. The maximum admission period would be 30 days, and overstaying would result in a permanent bar for the parent.

As noted, the 2013 Senate bill would have retrieved some spaces by eliminating diversity visas, eliminating the sibling preference, and restricting the third preference to married sons and daughters under age 30. But the major thrust of the 2013 bill was to *expand* the openings for family members, by raising the effective FS preference cap from 226,000 to 480,000. Further, current FS–2A, for spouses and children of LPRs, would have been treated like the current immediate relative category, exempt from even this higher annual quota.

NOTES AND QUESTIONS ON
FAMILY-SPONSORED IMMIGRATION

1.   Obviously there are many ways in which family categories could be revised. What would be the primary goals that a revision should serve? Once you have pondered that question and identified your own priorities, what changes to family migration would you favor?

2.   What are the advantages and disadvantages of eliminating or restricting certain current admission categories, in order to open up additional spaces for family relationships deemed closer? Are there

employment-based categories that should be cut or eliminated to serve that end?

3.   Should some family categories be added? Should some brothers and sisters (such as unmarried siblings with only limited family in the country of nationality) still have an immigration avenue? Should parents of U.S. citizens continue to receive nonquota treatment as immediate relatives?

4.   What should be done about people who have already waited years in line for preference admission at the time when their category is eliminated? Whether family openings are increased or decreased, should there be a firm annual ceiling on all such admissions?

5.   For a comprehensive discussion of policy considerations relevant to family reunification, see Hiroshi Motomura, *The Family and Immigration: A Roadmap for the Ruritanian Lawmaker*, 43 Am. J. Comp. L. 511 (1995).

b.   Reforms to Employment-Based Immigration

Dissatisfaction with the employment-based portion of our immigration system comes from many directions and covers a wide range of issues, including selection criteria and procedures (including concerns about the labor certification and attestation processes), admission levels, the effectiveness of protections for both the imported workers and the wage levels and working conditions of U.S. workers in the same field, the need for flexibility to respond to changes in the labor market without having to wait for Congress to amend the levels and categories by statute, and claims for either more or less reliance on temporary worker programs. This book's primary treatment of temporary worker categories and programs, for both high-skilled and low-skilled workers, appears in Chapter Five Section B, supra, pp. 421–444. The readings in this subsection deal primarily with other questions in the reform debate over employment-related immigration.

(i)   High-Skilled Versus Low-Skilled Immigration

Many of those who favor reorienting immigration toward more high-skilled admissions rely on the findings of an extensive study carried out by the National Research Council (NRC). The New Americans: Economic, Demographic, and Fiscal Effects of Immigration (James P. Smith and Barry Edmonston, eds. 1997). Its findings about the overall long-term fiscal impacts of immigration have been summarized as follows:

> * * * [An] immigrant's fiscal balance—the taxes paid minus the cost of services consumed—depends primarily on the immigrant's earnings. A third of immigrants have not graduated from high school, and if they live in high-service states such as California, a combination of low taxes and extensive services

means that households headed by U.S.-born persons pay higher taxes to provide services to immigrant-headed households. * * *

Fiscal-balance studies are snapshots. However, immigrant earnings tend to rise with time in the United States, and so do immigrant tax contributions. The NRC attempted to construct a motion picture of immigrant integration, projecting future patterns of immigrant and native earnings, taxes paid and use of government services, and the earnings and taxes-benefit ratios for the children and grandchildren of immigrants and natives.

The lifetime contribution of an immigrant was estimated at $80,000 in 1996, reflecting a negative $3,000 for the immigrant, but a positive $83,000 for the immigrant's children. The NRC found that immigrants with more education earn more and thus have a more favorable fiscal balance. Immigrants with more than a high-school diploma make a lifetime contribution of $105,000, and if the benefits from their children are included, a benefit for the United States of $198,000. However, immigrants with less than a high-school diploma impose a lifetime cost of $89,000 and, even with the gain of $76,000 from their children, the net effect is a $13,000 loss. The NRC concluded: "If the policy goal were to maximize the positive contribution of immigration to public sector budgets, that could be achieved by policies favoring highly educated immigrants and not admitting immigrants over age 50."

Philip Martin & Elizabeth Midgley, Immigration: Shaping and Reshaping America 22–23 (Population Reference Bureau, revised and updated 2d ed. 2006).

The Commission on Immigration Reform pointed to the NRC study in the course of making its core recommendations in 1997, which strongly favored high-skilled admissions:

[The Commission recommends:] Skill-based admissions policies that enhance opportunities for the entry of highly-skilled immigrants, particularly those with advanced degrees, and eliminate the category for admission of unskilled workers. The Commission continues to recommend that immigrants be chosen on the basis of the skills they contribute to the U.S. economy. Only if there is a compelling national interest—such as nuclear family reunification or humanitarian admissions—should immigrants be admitted without regard to the economic contributions they can make. The reunification of adult children and siblings of adult citizens solely because of family relationship is not as compelling.

A number of the * * * findings [of the NRC report] argue for increasing the proportion of immigrants who are highly-skilled and educated so as to maximize fiscal contributions, minimize fiscal impacts, and protect the economic opportunities of unskilled U.S. workers. The NRC research shows that education plays a major role in determining the impacts of immigration. Immigration of unskilled immigrants comes at a cost to unskilled U.S. workers, particularly established immigrants for whom new immigrants are economic substitutes. Further, the difference in estimated fiscal effects of immigrants by education is striking: using the same methodology to estimate net costs and benefits, immigrants with a high school education or more are likely to be net contributors while those without a high school degree are likely to be net costs to taxpayers.

Shifting priorities to higher skilled employment-based immigrants will have a beneficial multiplier effect. The highly-skilled are, in effect, new seed immigrants who will petition for their family members. The educational level of the spouses and children of highly-educated persons tends to be in the same range. Hence, our society benefits not only from the entry of highly-skilled immigrants themselves, but also from the entry of their family.

The Commission's framework for legal skills-based admissions includes two broad categories. The first category would cover individuals who are exempt from labor market tests because their entry will generate economic growth and/or significantly enhance U.S. intellectual and cultural strength without undermining the employment prospects and remuneration of U.S. workers: aliens with extraordinary ability, multinational executives and managers, entrepreneurs, and ministers and religious workers. The second category covers individuals subject to labor market tests, including professionals with advanced degrees, professionals with baccalaureate degrees, and skilled workers with specialized work experience.

U.S. Commission on Immigration Reform, Becoming an American: Immigration and Immigrant Policy 67–68 (1997 Report to Congress).

By the time the reform debate was seriously rejoined in the middle of the following decade, however, one heard far more arguments for large numbers of unskilled or low-skilled workers (though proposals varied with regard to whether they should come on temporary visas or as permanent immigrants). The following passage by Tamar Jacoby, written in 2006, is representative:

Arguably the most important statistic for anyone seeking to understand the immigration issue is this: in 1960, half of all American men dropped out of high school to look for unskilled work, whereas less than ten percent do so now. [And half of the 56 million jobs expected to be created in 2002–2012 will require no more than a high school education, but U.S. workers are becoming more educated.]

The resulting shortfall of unskilled labor—estimated to run to hundreds of thousands of workers a year—is showing up in sector after sector. The construction industry creates some 185,000 jobs annually, and although construction workers now earn between $30,000 and $50,000 a year, employers in trades such as masonry and dry-walling report that they cannot find enough young Americans to do the work. The prospects for the restaurant business are even bleaker. With 12.5 million workers nationwide, restaurants are the nation's largest private-sector employer, and their demand for labor is expected to grow by 15 percent between 2005 and 2015. But the native-born work force will grow by only ten percent in that period, and the number of 16- to 24-year-old job seekers—the key demographic for the restaurant trade—will not expand at all. So unless the share of older Americans willing to bus tables and flip hamburgers increases—and in truth, it is decreasing—without immigrants, the restaurant sector will have trouble growing through the next decade.

Fortunately for the United States, economic changes south of the border are freeing up a supply of unskilled labor to meet these growing needs in a timely way. * * *

The market mechanisms that connect U.S. demand with foreign supply, particularly from Latin America, are surprisingly efficient. Immigrants already here communicate to their compatriots still at home that the job market in, say, Detroit is flat, while that in Las Vegas is booming—and this produces a just-in-time delivery of workers wherever they are most needed. * * *

This is the paradox at the heart of the comprehensive consensus. The best way to regain control is not to crack down but to liberalize—to expand quotas, with a guest-worker program or some other method, until they line up with labor needs. The analogy is Prohibition: an unrealistic ban on alcohol was all but impossible to enforce. Realistic limits, in contrast, are relatively easy to implement.

Tamar Jacoby, *Immigration Nation*, 85 Foreign Affairs 50, 52–54, 60 (2006).

If the nation really needs a larger supply of low-skilled workers, however, why not rely on family reunification categories to supply that need rather than starting up a new guest worker program? The passage from the Commission on Immigration Reform above (coupled with its recommendations for sharp cutbacks in family quotas) bespeaks resistance to family migration *precisely because* so much of it in recent years has been low skilled. But low-skilled family members with green cards would not be as easily subject to employer control or exploitation as are temporary workers, because their status would not be tied to a particular employer. Could that be why the calls for more unskilled workers often tend to focus on temporary categories?

Labor economist Vernon Briggs, in a book published in 2003, reached very different conclusions from Jacoby's about the need for and impact of low-skilled immigrant labor. Though he supported focused use of high-skilled admissions, managed by an administrative body that would have much greater flexibility in adjusting numbers and criteria, he argued that low-skilled immigration should be curtailed:

> * * * The employment trends associated with the transformation of the nation's labor market are patently clear. On the demand side, occupations that stress skill and educational achievement are expanding, and those that do not are contracting. * * * As for unskilled and poorly educated workers, their ranks continue to swell. * * * [T]he major domestic economic policy challenge confronting the nation is what to do with so many poorly skilled workers at a time when the demand for their services is contracting. Since 1990, immigration has increased the number of high school dropouts in the labor force by 21 percent while increasing the supply of all other workers by only 5 percent.* * *

> The nation is at an economic crossroad. It must choose between being a nation of high wages, made possible by a highly productive labor force, or becoming a nation of low wages, the consequence of a lowly productive labor force. * * *

> * * * While there is no prospect for a general labor shortage as the twenty-first century begins, there may be spot shortages. * * * These shortages will most likely be in occupations that require extensive training and educational preparation. * * *

> In this economic environment, an immigration policy designed to admit a flexible number of highly skilled and educated workers is what is required. The Immigration Act of 1990 was ostensibly intended to move public policy in this

direction. But, as has been shown, it actually expanded the nepotistic family reunification focus that had been the [predominant] feature of the law it replaced and only marginally increased employment-based immigration. * * * It is always possible for more highly skilled and educated persons to do unskilled work. * * * But the reverse is not possible. * * *

If the prevailing policy of mass and unguided immigration continues, it is unlikely that there will be sufficient pressure to enact the long-term human resource development policies needed to prepare and to incorporate these citizens from minority groups into the mainstream economy. Instead, by providing both competition and alternatives, the large and unplanned influx of immigrant labor will serve to maintain the social marginalization of many blacks and Hispanics who are citizens and permanent resident aliens. * * *

Vernon Briggs, Jr., Mass Immigration and the National Interest: Policy Directions for the New Century 274–80 (3d ed. 2003).

Briggs labels family admission "nepotistic" (a phrase also used by other critics who advocate deep cuts in those categories), as compared to his preferred emphasis on persons with high skills. (Is that a fair way to describe the family unification impulse that lies behind much of such immigration?) Consider Alan Hyde's contrasting perspective on the economic contributions of family-sponsored immigrants.

ALAN HYDE, THE LAW AND ECONOMICS OF FAMILY UNIFICATION

28 Georgetown Immigration Law Journal, 2014.
pp. 355, 362, 365–66, 369–78, 381–85, 389–90.

Beginning in the early 1980s, the preference for family unification became politically controversial among free-market economists associated with the Council of Economic Advisers and American Enterprise Institute, who argued that immigration, in general, could be positive for the United States, but had to be rebalanced away from family unification and toward skilled workers.

* * *

The thesis of this article is that * * * family unification visas should not be sacrificed in order to expand skilled labor visas. Family-based visas are actually a good economic bargain for the United States. * * * [T]he limited economic literature [available] * * * suggest[s] very small differences in economic performance in the year following admission [between persons admitted on family visas and those on employment-based visas]. * * * [T]he data [also] indicate that the skills and education of immigrants do not necessarily differ sharply by type of visa. Many skilled professionals have immigrated through family unification visas, particularly since these are numerically greater. * * *

* * *

Overall, the above literature reveals a paradoxical trend. Immigrants admitted because employers want them or because they are well-educated should do better economically than immigrants who gain admission simply because they are related to U.S. residents. Yet, the data instead suggest that the differences are not great * * * . What could explain this surprising fact? * * *

A [significant] part of the story is that immigrants sponsored by family arrive with networks and connections. That is why, irrespective of visa (or even whether their migration is authorized at all), migrants with family ties do better economically than similar migrants who lack them. In contrast, immigrants who arrive sponsored by employers have a connection with that employer, but not necessarily anywhere else in the economy. Moreover, immigrants who arrive in Canada or Australia under those countries' points systems have no necessary connection with anyone in the economy—and as a result such immigrants have dismal economic performance.

* * *

The human capital framework [which underlies the main critiques of family-based migration] focuses on the individual. In general, under this framework increasing individuals' accumulation of knowledge (human capital) raises their productivity in the economic sector as well as their utility in the household. Thus, in order to realize potential gains in economic productivity, the individual has an incentive to obtain formal education and on-the-job training. * * * [V]ariations in immigrant earnings would be explained entirely by the skills each immigrant has accumulated; their earnings are the return on their self-investments.

* * *

A human capital framework cannot explain migration. Normally, assets are worth more in markets in which their supply is scarce. * * * [Why, as happens with skilled migration,] would any asset move from a market in which it is scarce to one in which it is plentiful? * * *

* * *

The framework known as "family investment models" or the "New Economics of Migration" [explains many of the puzzles]. In this framework, the principal economic actors are families, sometimes communities, but not individuals. Individuals normally live in the world with familial and social ties and one must not hastily dismiss the economic role of such ties. * * * [H]ouseholds diversify investment and protect against risk by having family members work in different labor markets. By diversifying the source of income, the family avoids the risk of having all members suffer lost income when one labor market collapses.

While neither framework is without value, the New Economics model does a better job [than the human capital model] of explaining readily observable immigration frequently involving young people traveling long distances and sending remittances home. Such migrants are not trying to maximize their personal gains, but rather the family is trying to insulate itself from economic risk.

* * *

[A family economics model is also useful.] As used in this article, the term "family economics" simply means that women should also be counted and that unpaid labor should be valued. In particular, women's economic contributions often show up, not in her earnings, but in the earnings of another: her husband, children, or a family firm. Most of the attention in feminist economics has gone to "unpaid domestic labor." But women also perform "unpaid market labor," such as informal assistance to family businesses, for example, that ultimately results in economic gains for those businesses, which is conceptually distinct from "unpaid domestic labor." Immigrants * * * are particularly likely to do both. By taking such labor into account, we can gain a better understanding of the added economic benefits family members bring as a unit, as opposed to focusing only on the economic benefits of the skilled migrant.

* * *

The relatively similar economic performance of immigrants sponsored by relatives to those admitted for skills may now be explained. In almost every context, family migrants arrive networked, complement rather than substitute for domestic labor, take jobs that advance family investment rather than individual advancement, and may make economic contributions that are not paid as such but show up in increased earnings for family members or family businesses.

* * * [There are] three particularly common contexts for these observed economic results: immigrants who (A) care for children and other family members, (B) work in family businesses, or (C) support other family members who are in school or building family businesses. These are all "family investment" models. Immigrants who care for children, or build family businesses, function economically as part of a family, and seek to maximize family income or growth. They may be paid little or nothing, and thus their economic contributions are systematically

underestimated in snapshots limited to immigrants' earned income in their first year after migration.

* * *

Should Congress ever eliminate visas for parents, as it nearly did in 2007, the immediate impact would be a radical decrease in the availability of child care for immigrant and native families. * * * Working families in the United States are heavily dependent on relatives for child care; Latino families are even more dependent. Immigrant families seem to be particularly heavy users of relatives for child care. Moreover, immigrants also disproportionately perform paid child care and thus contribute to increased earnings for working mothers of all ethnicities and immigration status.

* * *

Children in immigrant families are significantly more likely to live with two parents: 84% of children in immigrant families compared to 76% of children in all-native families. Children in immigrant families are two to four times more likely than children in native European-American families to have a grandparent in the home. Among some immigrant groups, it is also common for aunts and uncles to live in the home. About 25–37% of children in families with at least one parent from Mexico, Central America, Caribbean, South America, Philippines, Indochina, Pakistan, Bangladesh, Afghanistan, Iraq, or Africa have aunts or uncles living in the home. Again, it is precisely these elderly parents and aunts and uncles, who were targeted for elimination of visa eligibility in earlier legislative proposals. Immigrants are also low users of formal child care programs and are concomitantly highly reliant on family members for child care. * * *

[Immigrants also dominate provision of paid child care. There is a close correlation] among: percentage of immigrants in the workforce from five sending countries in which low-education immigrants predominate; cost of paid child care; and labor force participation by college-educated women with at least one small child. * * * Obviously, understanding the economics of this relationship cannot be done simply by examining the earnings of the immigrant nanny. One must also consider the economic contribution now made by the female college graduate who can return to her career.[c]

In sum, the heavy reliance by immigrants on family members for child care evidences a major, although hidden, economic contribution on the part of family members. * * * Thus, the existence of visas for parents and adult siblings permits immigrant businesses to grow, and immigrant children to thrive in ways not fully understood. * * *

---

[c] Relocated paragraph—eds.

Immigrants sponsored by family members are [also] particularly likely to work in family businesses. They may or may not have reported income, unlike the unpaid child care family member. However, their reported individual earnings undervalue their economic contributions, which show up instead in the income of the business. [Ethnographies of immigrant families show that wives working in the family business may not be paid. They may not even consider themselves principals of the business. For example, many immigrant women from Korea did not report themselves to the Census as self-employed business owners, even though they worked for their family-owned stores.]

Immigrants are particularly likely to found businesses, especially small businesses; they are twice as likely to do so as similarly situated nonimmigrants. This ability to found businesses depends in part on relatives' availability. Family members support business formation by providing labor, pooling financial resources, sharing living arrangements, extending intra-family loans, and receiving highly-productive labor despite low wages, because "family labor can be trusted to handle sensitive transactions in which the risk of opportunism and malfeasance is high." While English-language proficiency is normally beneficial for immigrant business formation, this advantage disappears for immigrants whose compatriots are geographically concentrated; thus, the language barriers disappear and the immigrants may found businesses serving these concentrated communities.

* * *

The ability of U.S. citizens to petition for their parents, siblings, married sons and daughters, and for U.S. citizens and lawful permanent residents to petition for unmarried adult sons and daughters, is probably a very good economic bargain for the United States. Conclusions must be tentative, given the limited data that actually compares immigrant economic performance by visa type at admission. I have attempted to draw plausible inferences from [available] data sets.

Some things are clear. If visas for parents of U.S. citizens were eliminated or trimmed, many working families would scramble for child care. Mothers would trim or eliminate their work hours, whether inside or outside a family business. The bodega or greengrocer would not be able to stay open as late, eliminating its chief comparative advantage over the supermarket. * * * If current measures of immigrant economic success would expand beyond the first year after arrival, the data would likely reveal long-term economic gains and advantages.

Overall, it appears that the United States is well served by family unification. Our search for the skilled and talented should not blind us to the crucial kind of economic growth that comes when children are well cared-for and educated; their health needs observed and attended; when family businesses employ family members and obviate their demand for social services; when family members pool earned income while one member builds a small business. * * *

NOTES AND QUESTIONS ON THE SKILLS DEBATE

1.   Hyde's arguments could support expanding family-based permanent migration in order to address shortages in low-skilled labor, instead of relying on the far more cumbersome employment-based selection system, particularly if the latter is used to bring temporary guest workers tied to specific jobs or industries. For further exploration of those possibilities, see Stephen Lee, *Productivity and Affinity in The Age of Dignity*, 114 Mich. L. Rev. 1137, 1147–51 (2016) (in reviewing a book that suggests expanding employment-based immigration to fill growing U.S. demand for eldercare, Lee suggests instead efforts to facilitate family-based or affinity migrants, who could more reliably and flexibly provide such care); Kerry Abrams, *What Makes the Family Special?*, 80 U.Chi.L.Rev. 7, 19–22 (2013) (posing similar suggestions).

2.   The second decade of the 21st century, marked by a steady but less than robust recovery from the Great Recession of 2008–2010, presents a far different U.S. employment picture from the one that formed the backdrop to Jacoby's 2006 article. What conclusions do you draw from those changes?

3.   What reforms to the employment-based categories, both temporary and permanent, would you favor?

(ii) Different Ways to Select Employment-Based Immigrants

Discontent with the labor certification system has been manifest for many years. One complaint is that the system is highly artificial, asking employers to go through expensive maneuvers ostensibly seeking U.S. workers when the whole point and true motivation of their efforts is to hire the targeted noncitizen. As a result, labor certification (and perhaps even more so with any system relying on attestations) fails to provide realistic safeguards to protect the job prospects or wages and working conditions of U.S. workers. Moreover, there is no guarantee that workers who enter on a labor certification will remain with that employer for any significant period—or even in the same field of employment.

In 1996, two experienced observers offered these observations on the core shortcomings of the current approach:

> [T]he labor certification system focuses on only a short-term goal: the immediate needs of the labor market. Immigrants are *permanent* additions to the labor force. It makes little sense to admit them (using the labor certification or any similar system) *solely* on the basis of a specific job opening that may quickly become redundant or for a function that may offer few long-term

benefits for either the employer or the country. Instead, a key goal of the economic immigrant selection system should be to satisfy ourselves that those who are admitted into the United States as presumptive members of our society have a proper mix of skills and other attributes, such as experience, education, and language, that maximizes the probability of long-term success in the labor force. Even if it worked perfectly, the existing labor certification process would have no more than a haphazard relationship to that goal.

Demetrios Papademetriou & Stephen Yale-Loehr. Balancing Interests: Rethinking U.S. Selection of Skilled Immigrants 145 (1996). They went on to propose a points system for selection of employment-based immigrants, building on versions used in several other countries with advanced economies. The following reading assesses the advantages and disadvantages of shifting to a points system, highlighting some of the potential pitfalls.

DEMETRIOS G. PAPADEMETRIOU & MADELEINE SUMPTION, RETHINKING POINTS SYSTEMS AND EMPLOYER-SELECTED IMMIGRATION
Migration Policy Institute, 2011, pp. 1, 3–7.

Two competing models for selecting economic-stream immigrants are now widely used in advanced industrialized economies: points-based and employer-led selection. Points-based systems admit immigrants who have a sufficient number of qualifications and experiences from a list that typically includes language skills, work experience, education, and age. Points systems appeal to policymakers because they are transparent, flexible, and can be adjusted to meet evolving economic needs or respond to evidence on immigrants' integration outcomes. But since employers are not involved in selection, points systems often admit immigrants who are unable to find work at their skill level once they arrive.

* * *

POINTS SYSTEMS

* * * [Although policymakers are often attracted to points systems, evidence] of problems with points-based selection formulae * * * abounds. Perhaps the greatest single flaw of the traditional points-based model is that immigrants arrive without a job offer and there is no guarantee that they will find work easily at their skill level. Points systems can only assess quantifiable skills and credentials, and have difficulty distinguishing between qualifications of different quality or utility. They are also ill equipped to reward "soft" attributes that employers care about, such as interpersonal skills or informal on-the-job training.

Research from Canada and Australia points to substantial un- and underemployment among points-selected foreign workers—giving credence to the concern that points systems often lead to "brain waste" and do not identify workers with skills that local employers value. Integration suffers accordingly.

* * *

EMPLOYER-LED SYSTEMS

The demand-driven, employer-led system resolves many of these problems. As a direct policy vehicle for economic growth and firms' competitiveness, this selection system has no equal, responding directly to the needs of firms and allowing employers to find workers who meet their specific needs from within the enormous global talent pool.

Second, employer selection ensures a level of immigrant integration that points systems have struggled to achieve. * * * And even though employers select workers, governments can still require minimum levels of education, language proficiency, or earnings to ensure that workers qualify as highly skilled. Evidence from countries that admit economic-stream immigrants both with and without job offers is compelling: employer-selected immigrants fare better.

Concerns about employer-led immigration focus primarily on the risk that employers will manipulate the system to access cheaper labor. Unlike points systems, employer-driven systems tend to tie workers to specific jobs, making it difficult for them to stand up to exploitative employers or respond to changing labor demand by moving jobs. Crucially, this may allow employers to pay them below-market wages. Meanwhile, there is a risk that open access to a foreign labor pool will allow employers to pay lower wages or avoid responsibility for training domestic workers—or indeed the foreign workers that they hire—thus doing little to reduce the scarcity of skills that economic-stream immigration is in part designed to address. Finally, there is a gnawing fear that temporary employer-driven immigration may spill over into illegal immigration if workers lose their jobs.

Moreover, many of the regulations that governments create to shape employers' use of the system are viewed with suspicion by some advocates, who argue that they fail to prevent employers from discriminating against local workers or from paying immigrants lower wages. Ultimately, one of the most effective safeguards against these problems is visa "portability": that is, worker's ability to move between employers, perhaps after a probationary period. Freedom of movement between employers is one of the benefits of the points system and has also been incorporated into hybrid immigration systems, described next.

HYBRID SELECTION SYSTEMS:
ALTERNATIVES THAT COMBINE THE BEST OF BOTH SYSTEMS

* * * [P]olicymakers in several immigrant-receiving nations have experimented with ways of combining the best ideas from both. Led by Australia, countries dependent on points systems have come to appreciate and accommodate the unparalleled advantages that employer selection brings in terms of both immigrant integration and firms' competitiveness. Meanwhile, some governments with demand-driven systems have also seen the value of giving workers more independence from their employers and of raising the "quality" of employer-selected immigrants using a flexible set of criteria such as a points test.

* * *

* * *[One] way that points systems can accommodate employer demand is by *awarding points for job offers*. This approach, used in both Canada and New Zealand, helps to prioritize the admission of immigrants who have already found employment, without making a job offer compulsory. Canada also provides priority processing for applicants who have a job offer[.] * * *

[Second,] hybrid systems can be created by *developing temporary-to-permanent visa pathways*. Increasing proportions of skilled workers in both points and demand-driven systems now enter on temporary visas that can be converted into permanent ones if their holders meet certain conditions. In many cases, these workers are initially employer selected. In New Zealand, for example, employer-driven visas are explicitly designed as an initial entry route for workers who hope to qualify for permanent residence under the points system. In the United Kingdom, almost all economic-stream immigrants must now have an employer sponsor to enter the country, but those who pass a points test from within the country can apply to become independent of their sponsor. In Sweden, work-based immigration is employer selected but work authorization becomes fully portable after two years, and the temporary visa can be converted into permanent residence after four years. * * *

Several countries now emphasize *foreign students* as a pool from which temporary foreign workers are recruited. This policy has some obvious advantages. Foreign students' graduation, particularly in fields of study that the host economy values, is a direct measure of both language competence and qualifications. Many students are also preselected by universities that have high standards.[14] Graduating students can be

---

[14] Of course, not all educational institutions have high standards, as policymakers in Australia and the United Kingdom recently discovered. In both countries, a lack of quality control over sponsoring colleges led to the growth of "diploma mills" that attracted students whose real interest was in the labor market. This phenomenon has prompted policymakers to rethink the student-to-worker pathway and to make it more selective.

required to have an employer sponsor to stay on, making the credential-recognition and employability issue moot. And the fact that the initial period of work authorization is temporary creates a transitional period during which a real vetting of the worker can assuage most concerns about his or her employability and ability to integrate.

Finally, systems that rely on employers to select most or even all immigrants can *require that their workers pass a points test*. This approach allows governments to raise the skill profile of economic-stream immigrants by requiring them to meet a flexible set of criteria that may include language proficiency, education level, and prospective earnings.

---

c. Provisional Visas

Papademetriou and Sumption speak of the possibility of greater use of "temporary-to-permanent" visas, an idea that has gained increasing attention. A high-level task force gathered by the Migration Policy Institute in 2005, chaired by former Rep. Lee Hamilton (D-Indiana) and former Senator Spencer Abraham (R-Michigan), devoted considerable attention to this idea (using the terminology of "provisional visas") in its 2006 report on ways to fix the overall immigration system.

> The [proposed] provisional visa bridges the false divide that now exists between certain forms of temporary and permanent immigration, creating an integrated system that organizes immigration around the ways in which immigration and labor markets work in practice.

> Provisional visas would allow employers to recruit workers for permanent jobs who may eventually be interested in permanent immigration and applying for a "green" card. Such visas provide both employers and workers the flexibility to exercise choices before committing to permanent immigration. The visas would act as a tool to attract the best and brightest at all skill levels, many of whom are shopping for the best offer in a competitive international marketplace.

> Provisional visas would also be suitable for large numbers of workers who are not in temporary or seasonal jobs across the occupational spectrum. Such a program would meet employer needs for foreign-born workers in jobs that are more permanent than envisioned by the temporary immigration stream. In combination with temporary visas, the new provisional visa category ensures that sufficient opportunities would exist to meet the current and longer term needs of the economy in ways well-tailored to individuals and the labor market.

* * * This category provides for applicants of all skill levels who have employer sponsors. Provisional visa holders would be admitted for three-year periods, renewable once. Provisional visa holders would work in permanent or year-round jobs and transition into permanent residence after three years if they qualify and so choose. Provisional visas would be issued to workers with extraordinary ability, workers in jobs that require a BA or more, and workers in low- and semi-skilled jobs who currently have no real chance for legal immigration. Provisional visa holders would be able to bring dependent family members with them.

Employers of most provisional workers would be required to participate in an attestation process or become pre-certified as a licensed employer of foreign-born workers. * * * Those with provisional visas would be eligible to change employers after an initial period and would have the same labor protections as similarly employed US workers.

The number of provisional visas would initially be set to approximate current flows of such workers who enter both legally and illegally. The numbers would then be adjusted according to recommendations made by [an expert nonpartisan] Standing Commission [on Immigration and Labor Markets].

In addition to an employment offer, qualifications for adjusting to permanent status would include evidence of continued employment in the occupation or field for which the applicant's educational or professional credentials served as the basis for the provisional visa, ability to speak English, and renewed clearance of a security and background check.

Doris Meissner, Deborah W. Myers, Demetrios Papademetriou & Michael Fix, Immigration And America's Future: A New Chapter (Report of the Independent Task Force on Immigration and America's Future), Migration Policy Institute, 2006, at 38–39.

NOTES AND QUESTIONS ON PROVISIONAL VISAS

1.   Which of the following occupational fields are the most logical to bring within a provisional visa system? Why? What criteria guide your judgment? Consider these occupations: nannies, gardeners, high-tech engineers, law professors, high school teachers, managers or supervisors being transferred within a global company, chefs, waiters, and construction workers.

2.   The Task Force states that provisional visas "provide both employers and workers the flexibility to exercise choices before committing to permanent immigration." This sounds like a balanced benefit with

comparable advantages for both sides. But are provisional visas really superior from the standpoint of the worker? With a green card, wouldn't she have the same flexibility to change her mind about the permanency of the work after a few months or even years on the job? After all, no lawful permanent resident is required to remain in the United States, and historically a significant percentage of LPRs do return to their home countries rather than live their entire lives in the United States. Moreover, a worker with a green card rather than a provisional visa would almost always have a wider range of choices to exercise. How could the proposal be revised to minimize the classic difficulty with all temporary visas—that the employee remains vulnerable to unfair practices by managers or supervisors because the employer holds the key to any future permanent status?

3.   The Task Force suggests that the number of provisional visas should initially be set to approximate the flows of comparable workers who enter both legally and illegally. Is this politically realistic? Even with the seemingly strong support for guest worker programs in Congress in 2006 and 2007, the totals of such visas to be permitted were cut substantially before final consideration of the legislation, to 200,000 annual admissions—far below the estimated 500–800,000 flow of unauthorized workers at that time. Further, recall that the report of the Council of Foreign Relations task force above opined that "[c]omprehensive immigration reform would substantially lower the flow of illegal migrants by providing alternative legal channels for migrants to live and work in the United States." How high would admissions have to be in order to provide a sufficient alternative to dissuade future migrants from coming without authorization? *See generally* David A. Martin, *Eight Myths About Immigration Enforcement*, 10 N.Y.U.J. Legis. & Pub. Pol'y 525, 532–34 (2006–07) (expressing skepticism about any such channeling effect and suggesting that substantial enforcement efforts will still be needed after comprehensive reform).

The 2006 MPI task force report was written during flush economic times with low unemployment. By 2011, following the major economic slowdown and deployment of additional enforcement resources, the flow of undocumented migration has been considerably lower and the overall population of the unauthorized has at least plateaued. What then should be the benchmark for setting the level of provisional visas?

Ex Ante vs. Ex Post Immigration Screening

Legal scholars Adam Cox and Eric Posner offer a more theoretical approach to admission issues, but reach a conclusion that provides support for the MPI Task Force's idea of expanding the use of provisional visas—an ex post system that allows the ultimate governmental decision on permanent immigration to be made after gaining more knowledge of the immigrant. Adam B. Cox & Eric A. Posner, *The Second-Order Structure of Immigration Law*, 59 Stan. L. Rev. 809 (2007). Analogizing a nation's immigration decisions to the process whereby employers choose employees, they write:

* * * [I]mmigration screening presents an information problem[.] The main screening advantage of the ex post system is that it uses more information (both about the immigrants and about the country's current needs) than the ex ante system does, which minimizes errors. The main advantage of the ex ante system is that it reduces the risk faced by potential immigrants that they will be deported, so that risk-averse noncitizens are more likely to enter and invest in the country than they are under the ex post system. * * *

Our framework clarifies numerous positive and normative questions about immigration law. * * * [P]ort-of-entry exclusion systems (which are predominantly ex ante) result in poorer screening than post-entry deportation systems (which are predominantly ex post), but also encourage risk-averse immigrants to make country-specific investments of value to the host country, and may be cheaper to enforce. The choice between the two systems turns in part on tradeoffs among these variables. We also argue that although the U.S. de jure system is highly (although not entirely) ex ante, the U.S. de facto system is predominantly ex post—this is the "illegal immigration system" that results from deliberate underenforcement of immigration law plus periodic amnesties.

59 Stan. L. Rev. at 811–14.

In a commentary on the Cox & Posner article, Hiroshi Motomura finds much that is valuable in the basic analytical approach, but adds words of caution:

The real effects of ex post screening are part of the complex process of immigrant integration. All else being equal, immigrants who face ex post screening will feel less attached to and accepted by the host country, and immigrants will feel more attached and accepted where ex ante screening is the norm. * * * The probationary message that would be inherent in a decision by the United States to rely heavily on ex post screening is easily read as an enduring message of exclusion, especially in light of the long history of racial and ethnic exclusion in U.S. immigration law.

* * * The exclusionary message inherent in ex post screening applies more to lawful nonimmigrants. And most importantly, the exclusionary message applies even more directly and profoundly to permanent residents, for whom naturalization is the next point of ex post screening. Putting them on probation, even if the chances of failure are remote, makes them less likely to integrate and perhaps even less likely to naturalize. In short, immigrant integration depends on a wider variety of factors than [the Cox and Posner article] discusses. It is important not to read its reasoning to justify ex post screening in a broad range of settings. As potentially applied to lawfully present nonimmigrants through adjustment of status and to lawful permanent residents through naturalization, ex post screening deserves special caution.

* * * [The article, however,] is quite correct in observing that the "illegal immigration system . . . can be seen as a de facto ex post screening system operated under the guise of an ex ante system." * * * In this zone of underenforced law, government officials make many discretionary immigration law decisions that add up to ex post screening.

* * *

For [lawful migrants, especially permanent residents], the question with the most consequences is whether they progress toward citizenship, so for them it is important to adopt a citizenship frame.

Modern European experience provides a cautionary tale about adopting an immigration rather than a citizenship frame when dealing with noncitizens who come lawfully and whose natural concern is the transition to permanent residence and in turn to citizenship. The industrialized European countries recruited foreign workers in the 1960s and 1970s as if they were employers picking employees. The incomplete integration of these immigrant communities into their adopted countries has been a social problem of very troubling dimensions. As Swiss writer Max Frisch put it: "We asked for workers, but people came." In fortunate contrast, the principal legislative proposals in the United States for the legalization of undocumented immigrants include a "path to citizenship." This reflects an important understanding of the dangers of choosing immigrants without making citizens. Though it makes sense initially to approach undocumented immigration as a matter of choosing immigrants, it would be a mistake to adopt it as an overall frame of reference for immigration law.

Hiroshi Motomura, *Choosing Immigrants, Making Citizens*, 59 Stan. L. Rev. 857, 864–70 (2007). *See also* Cristina Rodríguez, *Guest Workers and Integration: Toward a Theory of What Immigrants and Americans Owe One Another*, 2007 U. Chi. Legal F. 219, and the full discussion of guest workers in Chapter Five Section B, pp. 421–444 supra.

4. LEGALIZATION

The most recent major round of what might be described as comprehensive immigration reform, in the Immigration Reform and Control Act of 1986, offered legalization to a significant portion of the undocumented population then living in the United States. Approximately 2.7 million persons were legalized, and later, after obtaining full LPR status or even citizenship, a great many of the legalized noncitizens petitioned for family members to join them. In bringing vulnerable individuals out of the shadows and recognizing the connections they had built with their communities during their years in the United States, IRCA's legalization program was a success.

But because the enforcement portions of IRCA proved ineffective, many view IRCA as a failure and voice skepticism of another round of legalization. It would only reward lawbreaking, they maintain, and would entice a new generation of unlawful migrants to come in the hopes of yet another legalization in the future. Proponents of legalization, as reflected in the Council on Foreign Relations Task Force report that opened this section, respond that the current enforcement capacity of the government is now much stronger, and that added enforcement innovations and resources in a comprehensive bill can help strengthen future enforcement.

Some also argue that the new enforcement measures themselves are likely to fail if they have to be applied not only to new arrivals but also to the 10 to 11 million persons already long-resident here. In addition to the sheer cost of such measures, enforcement cases involving persons with deep community ties often lead to bad publicity that can bring indiscriminate discredit on resolute enforcement and to case law that strains to find interpretive loopholes, potentially weakening the new enforcement push in a different fashion. *See* David A. Martin, *Resolute Enforcement is Not Just for Restrictionists: Building a Stable and Efficient Immigration Enforcement System*, 30 J.L. & Pol. 411, 426 (2015) (legalization has strong roots in humanitarian principles, "but it should also be seen as an important enforcement-empowering measure, facilitating wider public support for [broader enforcement] actions to be taken thereafter"). For further reflections on legalization, see Hiroshi Motomura, *What is "Comprehensive Immigration Reform"?: Taking the Long View*, 63 Ark. L. Rev. 225 (2010).

MARSHALL FITZ, GEBE MARTINEZ & MADURA WIJEWARDENA, THE COSTS OF MASS DEPORTATION: IMPRACTICAL, EXPENSIVE, AND INEFFECTIVE

Center for American Progress (March 2010), pp. 1–3.

* * * [The] legislative battle for immigration reform now looms again on the horizon. There are three options for restoring order to our immigration system:

- Live with the dysfunctional status quo, pouring billions of dollars into immigration enforcement programs at the worksite, in communities, and on the border without reducing the numbers of undocumented immigrants in the country

- Double down on this failed enforcement strategy in an attempt to apprehend and remove all current undocumented immigrants

- Combine a strict enforcement strategy with a program that would require undocumented workers to register, pass background checks, pay their full share of taxes, and earn the privilege of citizenship while creating legal channels for future migration flows

The first alternative would leave in place policies that have allowed 5 percent of our nation's workforce—approximately 8.3 million workers in March 2008—to remain undocumented in our country. This is clearly an unsustainable position in a democratic society—permitting a class of workers to operate in a shadow economy subject to exploitation and undermining all workers' rights and opportunities.

The second option, mass deportation of undocumented immigrants, is essentially the enforcement-only status quo on steroids. As this paper demonstrates, this option would be prohibitively expensive and trigger profound collateral consequences. Our analysis is comprised of a detailed review of all federal spending to prevent unauthorized immigration and deport undocumented immigrants in FY 2008, the last fiscal year (ending in October 2008) for which there is complete data. It shows that the total cost of mass deportation and continuing border interdiction and interior enforcement efforts would be $285 billion (in 2008 dollars) over five years.

Specifically, this report calculates a price tag of $200 billion to enforce a federal dragnet that would snare the estimated 10.8 million undocumented immigrants in the United States over five years [$158 billion for apprehension, $29 billion for detention, $7 billion for legal processing, and $6 billion for transportation]. That amount, however, does not include the annual recurring border and interior enforcement spending that will necessarily have to occur. It would cost taxpayers at least another $17 billion annually (in 2008 dollars) to maintain the status quo at the border and in the interior, or a total of nearly $85 billion over five years. That means the total five-year immigration enforcement cost under a mass deportation strategy would be approximately $285 billion.

* * * Spending $285 billion would require $922 in new taxes for every man, woman, and child in this country.

* * *

That leaves the third course, comprehensive immigration reform, as the only rational alternative. The solution to our broken immigration system must combine tough border and workplace enforcement with practical reforms that promote economic growth, protect all workers, and reunite immediate family members. Among other things, that means we must establish a realistic program to require undocumented immigrants to register with the government while creating legal immigration channels that are flexible, serve the national interest, and curtail future illegal immigration. * * *

_____

Mark Krikorian believes that legalization should not be enacted until after effective enforcement has been demonstrated for several years. *See, e.g.,* Mark Krikorian, *Enforcement, Then Amnesty, on Immigration,* National Review, Jan. 30, 2014. Here he challenges some of the arguments made in the previous reading in support of legalization.

MARK KRIKORIAN, ON IMMIGRATION, CONSERVATIVES ADVOCATE ATTRITION THROUGH ENFORCEMENT, NOT MASS DEPORTATION

Center for Immigration Studies (February 2009),
http://cis.org/node/1071.

* * * [M]ass deportation is not the only alternative to amnesty. Instead, the position that many conservatives (and others) actually favor is attrition through enforcement—a reduction over time in the illegal population through consistent, comprehensive application of the law, something we have never really attempted.

The principle behind an attrition policy is simple enough: dissuade more prospective illegals from coming and get more of those already here to leave—partly through increasing regular deportations but mostly through voluntary return. The result would not be a magical disappearance of the problem but a reversal of the trend, so that the total number of illegals starts decreasing with each year, instead of increasing.

This can be accomplished through a variety of means. Limiting the arrival of new illegals involves not only additional fencing and other border-control measures, but also tighter standards in permitting the admission of visitors (people who overstayed their visas account for a quarter to half of all illegals). The key to encouraging self-deportation is to make it as difficult as possible for illegals to live a normal life here—getting a job, opening a bank account, driving a car. None of these things require tanks or machine guns, just the consistent application of existing law and the spread of tools like E–Verify, an online system that enables employers to check the legal status of new hires.

This is not fanciful. My organization's analysis of Census Bureau surveys, confirmed by the Pew Hispanic Center, suggests that the illegal population peaked at 12.5 million in August of 2007, shortly after the collapse of the Bush-Kennedy-McCain amnesty bill in the Senate, and through May of 2008 had declined to 11.2 million. And, unlike in past recessions, which were not preceded by stepped-up enforcement, this decline in the illegal population started *before* the unemployment rate for illegals began to increase. In other words, attrition works.

It's also preferred by the public. During the 2006 amnesty debate, we commissioned a Zogby poll offering respondents not the false choice between mass deportation or amnesty (a word we did not use in the survey), but rather a three-way choice between mass deportation, earned legalization, and attrition—and attrition was preferred two-to-one over legalization.

The DREAM Act and Wider Perspectives on Legalization

When progress on comprehensive immigration reform stalled in 2009–2010, advocates focused considerable effort on passing the Development, Relief and Education for Alien Minors (DREAM) Act. It would provide legal status and eventual lawful permanent resident status for persons who had been brought to the United States as children. Proponents believe in the justice of such a measure and the importance of providing stable status (as well as improved access to higher education) for members of the U.S. community who have little or no acquaintance with life in another country. But they also have thought it would be easier to pass than a wider legalization measure, because it would benefit only those who should not be held responsible for their illegal presence.

A version of the DREAM Act was included in the legislation that passed the Senate in May 2006 but was never voted on in the House. That version covered students who (a) initially entered the United States before the age of 16; (b) were physically present in the United States for five years immediately preceding enactment; and (c) earned a high school diploma or the equivalent in the United States, or had been admitted to an institution of higher education in the United States. These persons would be eligible for cancellation of removal, which would lead first to conditional permanent resident status, then, after six years, to permanent residence upon the fulfillment of certain other conditions. The most important such condition was the earning of a college degree, the completion of at least two years of college, or two years of service in the U.S. armed forces.

The DREAM Act was reintroduced regularly in later Congresses, each version providing somewhat different criteria for who would be covered. The House finally passed a version during the lame-duck congressional session in December 2010. To gain passage, sponsors had to tighten up the provisions considerably, especially in light of concerns about the federal budgetary impact, given new estimates of the population eligible for DREAM Act-based legalization, which by then had climbed to 2.1 million persons. Covered individuals would have received only conditional *nonimmigrant* status for five years, subject to further extensions in five-year increments, provided they had by then completed the requisite two years of college study or military service. Only after 10 years could they seek LPR status. High fees were also imposed (in addition to processing costs): $525 for the initial application, and an additional $2,000 at the time of each extension. *See* Andorra Bruno, Unauthorized Alien Students: Issues and "DREAM Act" Legislation (Cong. Res. Serv. 2010). Even with these stringent limits and exactions, the bill failed on an unsuccessful procedural vote in the Senate. *See* 87 Interp. Rel. 2334, 2419 (2010).

In reflecting on the DREAM Act and related measures, Hiroshi Motomura summarizes various perspectives that have been brought to bear in making judgments about legalization. Consider what conclusions each such perspective suggests about the appropriate criteria and scope of legislated legalization (if it is justified at all).

> Arguments for the DREAM Act fall into two basic categories. Some arguments are policy-based appeals to fairness or justice. Other arguments are pragmatic—or consequentialist, some might say. The fairness arguments for the DREAM Act draw heavily on the meaning of unlawful presence within the highly discretionary U.S. immigration law system, and on arguments for integrating unauthorized migrants and treating them as Americans in waiting. Some arguments for integration rely on what I have called "immigration as contract," acknowledging a tacit invitation that unauthorized migrants accept when they come to work in the United States, often bringing their families with them. * * * Other arguments for integration rely on immigration as affiliation, which captures the view that unauthorized migrants' ties to individuals or communities in the United States deserve recognition. * * *

* * *

Pragmatic arguments for the DREAM Act overlap with fairness arguments * * *. For unlawful presence, these pragmatic arguments assume that the government has only limited control over the basic contours of unauthorized migration. Even with stiffer laws or more enforcement, unauthorized migration will be substantial, given ingrained tolerance of a large, flexible unauthorized workforce. * * * Because the vast majority of the young unauthorized migrants will stay in the United States, as will their children, it is pragmatic for immigration status to reflect this reality.

As for integration, pragmatic arguments emphasize that full integration is impossible without lawful immigration status. * * * [H]osting a large marginalized population would cause great harm to the national interest. In contrast, lawful status would nurture positive contributions to society by DREAM Act beneficiaries and their children and grandchildren. Requirements to attend college or serve in the military work specifically toward this goal. * * *

Arguments against the DREAM Act are also grounded in fairness, pragmatism, or a blend. Fairness objections start with the meaning of unlawful presence by stressing that unauthorized migrants, whether children or not, are by definition violating federal immigration law. Other fairness objections are anchored in rejecting integration, emphasizing that these noncitizens are not Americans in waiting and have no legitimate claims to integration based on either contract or affiliation. If there is an immigration contract, their parents broke it by breaking the law, and children have to live with their parents' choices. * * * As for immigration as affiliation, their ties are unworthy of recognition because they result from lawbreaking, especially because lawful status would give them access to scarce public resources. All of these fairness objections invoke the rule of law by insisting that unauthorized migrants must not cut in line ahead of immigrants who play by the rules. * * *

Pragmatic objections to the DREAM Act also connect the meaning of unlawful presence to the integration of unauthorized migrants. First, noncitizens who are unlawfully present pose a straightforward problem that the government can solve by apprehending and deporting them, or by making life so hard that they will leave. Such enforcement policies are needed, this argument continues, to uphold the system for lawful admission to the United States. Pragmatic objections emphasize that any need to integrate beneficiaries of the DREAM Act will diminish or disappear with effective immigration law enforcement, and that it is unsound and dangerously self-fulfilling to assume that any of them will stay indefinitely. Moreover, granting lawful status to individuals brought to the United States as children will create incentives for parents to come to the United States, in turn undermining enforcement. * * *

Hiroshi Motomura, Immigration Outside the Law 176–78 (2014).*

CHAPTER ELEVEN

CONSTITUTIONAL PROTECTION IN ALIENAGE LAW

■ ■ ■

Chapter Three noted how the Supreme Court, in the late nineteenth century, appeared to separate the questions of noncitizens entering and remaining in the United States from the questions of their constitutional protection on matters other than admission and expulsion itself. Thus arose a fundamental contrast: between the Court's severe rulings in *Fong Yue Ting* and the *Chinese Exclusion Case*, and other rulings that protected Chinese noncitizens in other ways while they were in the United States—particularly the landmark *Yick Wo* and *Wong Wing* decisions.

This chapter examines the treatment of noncitizens after admission to the United States. Our focus is principally on permanent residents: how does the law treat them differently from citizens? We also consider noncitizens who are lawfully present in the United States as nonimmigrants, especially if they remain for extended periods. This chapter generally does not address the treatment of unauthorized migrants, which is central to Chapter Ten's coverage of enforcement.

As we have seen in previous chapters, some differences between citizens and lawfully present noncitizens are matters of *immigration law*, which, as traditionally defined, concerns the admission of noncitizens to the United States and the terms under which they may remain. A citizen must be admitted to the United States, while a noncitizen may be refused admission. Permanent residents also have fewer opportunities than citizens to sponsor their relatives for admission as immigrants. A citizen may not be removed from the United States, unless she first loses her citizenship through renunciation or denaturalization. In contrast, noncitizens may be removed on various deportability grounds set forth in INA § 237.

Other differences between citizens and permanent residents are part of *alienage law*, which as traditionally defined is distinguished from immigration law and addresses other matters relating to the consequences of a noncitizen's immigration or citizenship status. In fact, noncitizens largely enjoy the same substantive rights as citizens. For instance, citizenship status does not matter for access to the civil courts, or for protection under a wide variety of regulatory schemes. And as Chapter Ten explained, laws governing the workplace protect not only permanent residents but sometimes cover the undocumented. But there are differences between the rights of citizens and noncitizens. For example, noncitizens generally may not vote in public elections, nor hold federal civil service jobs. Their access to some state and local public employment and their eligibility for federal welfare and other public benefits are limited. Such distinctions between citizens and noncitizens raise constitutional law and public policy issues, not only as to when treatment must be equal, but also whether it is a federal, state, or local government that may draw such distinctions. Chapter Two discussed who is a citizen of the United States; in this chapter, we ask: what does it mean to be (or not to be) a citizen of the United States?

A. PUBLIC BENEFITS

1. THE FOUNDATION CASES

From *Yick Wo* onward, a steady stream of U.S. Supreme Court decisions addressed constitutional protection of noncitizens in the United States. The next case, *Graham v. Richardson*, comments on several of the most important of these decisions. But first, some background.

One idea that figured prominently from *Yick Wo* to *Graham* was that under the U.S. federal system, a state could constitutionally treat citizens and noncitizens differently in order to protect a "special public interest" in its common property or resources. This idea drew support from *Truax v. Raich*, 239 U.S. 33, 36 S.Ct. 7, 60 L.Ed. 131 (1915), which struck down an Arizona employment statute as violating equal protection.

The statute challenged in *Truax* required any employer with more than five employees to employ at least 80 percent "qualified electors or native-born citizens of the United States or some sub-division thereof." Central to the Court's holding was that a state statute denying work would be tantamount to a denial of entry and abode, and therefore would be inconsistent with exclusive federal authority to "admit or exclude aliens." But the Court also left open the possibility that if alienage classifications were needed to protect a "special public interest," states could adopt them in contexts other than employment in the general labor market.

After *Truax*, the Supreme Court applied the special public interest doctrine or similar reasoning to uphold other state alienage classifications. One was a New York state law barring the employment of noncitizens on public works projects, where the state's "special public interest" was to devote public funds to employ its own citizens. *Crane v. New York*, 239 U.S. 195, 198, 36 S.Ct. 85, 85–86, 60 L.Ed. 218 (1915). In

Patsone v. Pennsylvania, 232 U.S. 138, 143–46, 34 S.Ct. 281, 282–83, 58 L.Ed. 539 (1914), the Court upheld a Pennsylvania law that barred noncitizens from hunting wild game and also "to that end" from owning shotguns or rifles. The Court explained that the ownership ban was intended to protect wildlife, "which the state may preserve for its own citizens if it pleases," and that the state legislature's choice of methods was entitled to great deference. Further Court decisions adopted other rationales in rejecting constitutional challenges to state and local alienage classifications. For example, *State ex rel. Clarke v. Deckebach*, 274 U.S. 392, 394, 396, 47 S.Ct. 630, 631, 71 L.Ed. 1115 (1927), upheld a Cincinnati city ordinance that required U.S. citizenship to operate a pool hall. The Court said it was not unreasonable for the city to conclude that noncitizens were not as well-qualified to run businesses that were "meeting places of idle and vicious persons," and that therefore required "strict police surveillance."

The Supreme Court declined to apply the special public interest doctrine in *Takahashi v. Fish & Game Comm'n*, 334 U.S. 410, 68 S.Ct. 1138, 92 L.Ed. 1478 (1948). In 1943, California barred the issuance of a commercial fishing license to any "alien Japanese." In 1945, this text was changed to bar any "person ineligible to citizenship," which the legislature intended to refer to Japanese noncitizens. The Court struck down the amended statute, rejecting the argument that California was the owner-trustee of all fish in its coastal waters. According to the Court, a nondiscrimination principle applies to residence in any state by "all persons lawfully in this country."

Takahashi differed from the earlier cases in one key respect. The Court clearly understood that the phrase "ineligible to citizenship" made the California statute a race-based law, not a law that discriminated against noncitizens generally. Justice Black explained for the majority:

> It does not follow, as California seems to argue, that because the United States regulates immigration and naturalization in part on the basis of race and color classifications, a state can adopt one or more of the same classifications to prevent lawfully admitted aliens within its borders from earning a living in the same way that other state inhabitants earn their living.

334 U.S. at 418–19, 68 S.Ct. at 1142.

Yet, *Takahashi* distinguished (without overruling) several decisions that had upheld state laws barring land ownership by aliens "ineligible to citizenship." *See Terrace v. Thompson*, 263 U.S. 197, 44 S.Ct. 15, 68 L.Ed. 255 (1923); *Porterfield v. Webb*, 263 U.S. 225, 44 S.Ct. 21, 68 L.Ed. 278 (1923); *Webb v. O'Brien*, 263 U.S. 313, 44 S.Ct. 112, 68 L.Ed. 318 (1923); *Frick v. Webb*, 263 U.S. 326, 44 S.Ct. 115, 68 L.Ed. 323 (1923).

Takahashi left important questions unanswered: How much was it a decision that turned on race? What did it say about alienage classifications in general? And what was left of the special public interest doctrine?

a. State Laws

In 1971, a few years before the Court rejected a constitutional challenge to the federal immigration statute in *Fiallo v. Bell*, in Chapter Five, p. 296, it issued a landmark decision that struck down state laws limiting permanent residents' access to welfare benefits.

GRAHAM V. RICHARDSON

Supreme Court of the United States, 1971.
403 U.S. 365, 91 S.Ct. 1848, 29 L.Ed.2d 534.

MR. JUSTICE BLACKMUN delivered the opinion of the Court.

* * * The issue here is whether the Equal Protection Clause of the Fourteenth Amendment prevents a State from conditioning welfare benefits either (a) upon the beneficiary's possession of United States citizenship, or (b) if the beneficiary is an alien, upon his having resided in this country for a specified number of years. The facts are not in dispute.

I

No. 609. This case, from Arizona, concerns the State's participation in federal categorical assistance programs. * * * Arizona Rev. Stat. Ann., Tit. 46, Art. 2, as amended, provides for assistance to persons permanently and totally disabled (APTD). Arizona Rev. Stat. Ann. § 46–233, as amended in 1962, reads:

> A. No person shall be entitled to general assistance who does not meet and maintain the following requirements:
>
> 1. Is a citizen of the United States, or has resided in the United States a total of fifteen years. . . .

A like eligibility provision conditioned upon citizenship or durational residence appears in § 46–252(2), providing old-age assistance, and in § 46–272(4), providing assistance to the needy blind.

Appellee Carmen Richardson, at the institution of this suit in July 1969, was 64 years of age. She is a lawfully admitted resident alien. She emigrated from Mexico in 1956 and since then has resided continuously in Arizona. She became permanently and totally disabled. She also met all other requirements for eligibility for APTD benefits except the 15-year residency specified for aliens by § 46–233(a)(1). * * *

No. 727. This case, from Pennsylvania, concerns that portion of a general assistance program that is not federally supported. The relevant statute is § 432(2) of the Pennsylvania Public Welfare Code, [which] * * * provides that those eligible for assistance shall be (1) needy persons who qualify under the federally supported categorical assistance programs and (2) those other needy persons who are citizens of the United States. * * *

Appellee Elsie Mary Jane Leger is a lawfully admitted resident alien. She was born in Scotland in 1937. She came to this country in 1965 at the age of 28 under contract for domestic service with a family in Havertown. She has resided continuously in Pennsylvania since then and has been a taxpaying resident of the Commonwealth. In 1967 she left her domestic employment to accept more remunerative work in Philadelphia. She entered into a common-law marriage with a United States citizen. In 1969 illness forced both Mrs. Leger and her husband to give up their employment. They applied for public assistance. Each was ineligible under the federal programs. Mr. Leger, however, qualified for aid under the state program. Aid to Mrs. Leger was denied because of her alienage. * * *

Appellee Beryl Jervis was added as a party plaintiff to the Leger action. She was born in Panama in 1912 and is a citizen of that country. In March 1968, at the age of 55, she came to the United States to undertake domestic work under contract in Philadelphia. She has resided continuously in Pennsylvania since then and has been a taxpaying resident of the Commonwealth. After working as a domestic for approximately one year, she obtained other, more remunerative, work in the city. In February 1970 illness forced her to give up her employment. She applied for aid. However, she was ineligible for benefits under the federally assisted programs and she was denied general assistance solely because of her alienage. * * *

It was stipulated that "the denial of General Assistance to aliens otherwise eligible for such assistance causes undue hardship to them by depriving them of the means to secure the necessities of life, including food, clothing and shelter," and that "the citizenship bar to the receipt of General Assistance in Pennsylvania discourages continued residence in Pennsylvania of indigent resident aliens and causes such needy persons to remove to other States which will meet their needs."

* * *

II

The appellants argue initially that the States, consistent with the Equal Protection Clause, may favor United States citizens over aliens in the distribution of welfare benefits. It is said that this distinction involves no "invidious discrimination" for the State is not discriminating with respect to race or nationality.

The Fourteenth Amendment provides, "[N]or shall any State deprive any person of life, liberty, or property, without due process of law; nor deny to any person within its jurisdiction the equal protection of the laws." It has long been settled, and it is not disputed here, that the term "person" in this context encompasses lawfully admitted resident aliens as well as citizens of the United States and entitles both citizens and aliens to the equal protection of the laws of the State in which they reside. *Yick Wo v. Hopkins*, 118 U.S. 356, 369, 6 S.Ct. 1064, 1070, 30 L.Ed. 220 (1886); *Truax v. Raich*, 239 U.S. 33, 39, 36 S.Ct. 7, 9, 60 L.Ed. 131 (1915); *Takahashi v. Fish & Game Comm'n*, [334 U.S. 410, 420, 68 S.Ct. 1138, 1143, 92 L.Ed. 1478 (1948)]. Nor is it disputed that the Arizona and Pennsylvania statutes in question create two classes of needy persons, indistinguishable except with respect to whether they are or are not citizens of this country. Otherwise qualified United States citizens living in Arizona are entitled to federally funded categorical assistance benefits without regard to length of national residency, but aliens must have lived in this country for 15 years in order to qualify for aid. United States citizens living in Pennsylvania, unable to meet the requirements for federally funded benefits, may be eligible for state-supported general assistance, but resident aliens as a class are precluded from that assistance.

Under traditional equal protection principles, a State retains broad discretion to classify as long as its classification has a reasonable basis. This is so in "the area of economics and social welfare." *Dandridge v. Williams*, 397 U.S. 471, 485, 90 S.Ct. 1153, 1161, 25 L.Ed.2d 491 (1970). But the Court's decisions have established that classifications based on alienage, like those based on nationality or race, are inherently suspect and subject to close judicial scrutiny. Aliens as a class are a prime example of a "discrete and insular" minority (*see United States v. Carolene Products Co.*, 304 U.S. 144, 152–153, n.4, 58 S.Ct. 778, 783–784, 82 L.Ed. 1234 (1938)) for whom such heightened judicial solicitude is appropriate. Accordingly, it was said in *Takahashi*, that "the power of a state to apply its laws exclusively to its alien inhabitants as a class is confined within narrow limits."

Arizona and Pennsylvania seek to justify their restrictions on the eligibility of aliens for public assistance solely on the basis of a State's "special public interest" in favoring its own citizens over aliens in the distribution of limited resources such as welfare benefits. It is true that this Court on occasion has upheld state statutes that treat citizens and noncitizens differently, the ground for distinction having been that such laws were necessary to protect special interests of the State or its citizens. Thus, in *Truax v. Raich*, 239 U.S. 33, 36 S.Ct. 7, 60 L.Ed. 131 (1915), the Court, in striking down an Arizona statute restricting the employment of aliens, emphasized that "[t]he discrimination defined by the act does not pertain to the regulation or distribution of the public domain, or of the common property or resources of the people of the state, the enjoyment of which may be limited to its citizens as against both aliens and the citizens of other states." 239 U.S., at 39–40, 36 S.Ct., at 10. And in *Crane v. New York*, 239 U.S. 195, 36 S.Ct. 85, 60 L.Ed. 218 (1915), the Court affirmed the judgment in *People v. Crane*, 214 N.Y. 154, 108 N.E. 427 (1915), upholding a New York statute prohibiting the employment of aliens on public works projects. * * * On the same theory, the Court has upheld statutes that, in the absence of overriding treaties, limit the right of noncitizens to engage in exploitation of a State's natural resources, restrict the devolution of real property to aliens, or deny to aliens the right to acquire and own land.

Takahashi, however, cast doubt on the continuing validity of the special public-interest doctrine in all contexts. There the Court held that California's purported ownership of fish in the ocean off its shores was not such a special public interest as would justify prohibiting aliens from making a living by fishing in those waters while permitting all others to do so. It was said:

> The Fourteenth Amendment and the laws adopted under its authority thus embody a general policy that all persons lawfully in this country shall abide 'in any state' on an equality of legal privileges with all citizens under nondiscriminatory laws.

334 U.S., at 420, 68 S.Ct., at 1143.

Whatever may be the contemporary vitality of the special public-interest doctrine in other contexts after *Takahashi*, we conclude that a State's desire to preserve limited welfare benefits for its own citizens is inadequate to justify Pennsylvania's making noncitizens ineligible for public assistance, and Arizona's restricting benefits to citizens and longtime resident aliens. First, the special public interest doctrine was heavily grounded on the notion that "[w]hatever is a privilege, rather than a right, may be made dependent upon citizenship." *People v. Crane*, 214 N.Y., at 164, 108 N.E., at 430. But this Court now has rejected the concept that constitutional rights turn upon whether a governmental benefit is characterized as a "right" or as a "privilege." Second, as the Court recognized in *Shapiro* [*v. Thompson*]:

> [A] State has a valid interest in preserving the fiscal integrity of its programs. It may legitimately attempt to limit its expenditures, whether for public assistance, public education, or any other program. But a State may not accomplish such a purpose by invidious distinctions between classes of its citizens.... The saving of welfare costs cannot justify an otherwise invidious classification.

394 U.S. 618, 633, 89 S.Ct. 1322, 1330, 22 L.Ed.2d 600 (1969).] Since an alien as well as a citizen is a "person" for equal protection purposes, a concern for fiscal integrity is no more compelling a justification for the questioned classification in these cases than it was in *Shapiro*.

* * * The classifications involved in the instant cases * * * are inherently suspect and are therefore subject to strict judicial scrutiny whether or not a fundamental right is impaired. * * *

We agree with the three-judge court in the Pennsylvania case that the "justification of limiting expenses is particularly inappropriate and unreasonable when the discriminated class consists of aliens. Aliens like citizens pay taxes and may be called into the armed forces. Unlike the short-term residents in *Shapiro*, aliens may live within a state for many years, work in the state and contribute to the economic growth of the state." There can be no "special public interest" in tax revenues to which aliens have contributed on an equal basis with the residents of the State.

Accordingly, we hold that a state statute that denies welfare benefits to resident aliens and one that denies them to aliens who have not resided in the United States for a specified number of years violate the Equal Protection Clause.

III

An additional reason why the state statutes at issue in these cases do not withstand constitutional scrutiny emerges from the area of federal-state relations. The National Government has "broad constitutional powers in determining what aliens shall be admitted to the United States, the period they may remain, regulation of their conduct before naturalization, and the terms and conditions of their naturalization." *Takahashi v. Fish & Game Comm'n*, 334 U.S., at 419, 68 S.Ct., at 1142. Pursuant to that power, Congress has provided, as part of a comprehensive plan for the regulation of immigration and naturalization, that "[a]liens who are paupers, professional beggars, or vagrants" or aliens who "are likely at any time to become public charges" shall be excluded from admission into the United States, and that any alien lawfully admitted shall be deported who "has within five years after entry become a public charge from causes not affirmatively shown to have arisen after entry. . . ." Admission of aliens likely to become public charges may be conditioned upon the posting of a bond or cash deposit. But Congress has not seen fit to impose any burden or restriction on aliens who become indigent after their entry into the United States. Rather, it has broadly declared: "All persons within the jurisdiction of the United States shall have the same right in every State and Territory . . . to the full and equal benefit of all laws and proceedings for the security of persons and property as is enjoyed by white citizens. . . ." 42 U.S.C. § 1981. The protection of this statute has been held to extend to aliens as well as to citizens. *Takahashi*, 334 U.S., at 419 n.7, 68 S.Ct., at 1142. Moreover, this Court has made it clear that, whatever may be the scope of the constitutional right of interstate travel, aliens lawfully within this country have a right to enter and abide in any State in the Union "on an equality of legal privileges with all citizens under nondiscriminatory laws." *Takahashi*, 334 U.S., at 420, 68 S.Ct., at 1143.

State laws that restrict the eligibility of aliens for welfare benefits merely because of their alienage conflict with these overriding national policies in an area constitutionally entrusted to the Federal Government. In *Hines v. Davidowitz*, 312 U.S., at 66–67, 61 S.Ct., at 403–404, where this Court struck down a Pennsylvania alien registration statute (enacted in 1939, as was the statute under challenge in No. 727) on grounds of federal pre-emption, it was observed that "where the federal government, in the exercise of its superior authority in this field, has enacted a complete scheme of regulation . . . states cannot, inconsistently with the purpose of Congress, conflict or interfere with, curtail or complement, the federal law, or enforce additional or auxiliary regulations." And in *Takahashi* it was said that the States

> can neither add to nor take from the conditions lawfully imposed by Congress upon admission, naturalization and residence of aliens in the United States or the several states. State laws which impose discriminatory burdens upon the entrance or residence of aliens lawfully within the United States conflict with this constitutionally derived federal power to regulate immigration, and have accordingly been held invalid.

334 U.S., at 419, 68 S.Ct., at 1142.

Congress has broadly declared as federal policy that lawfully admitted resident aliens who become public charges for causes arising after their entry are not subject to deportation, and that as long as they are here they are entitled to the full and equal benefit of all state laws for the security of persons and property. The state statutes at issue in the instant cases impose auxiliary burdens upon the entrance or residence of aliens who suffer the distress, after entry, of economic dependency on public assistance. Alien residency requirements for welfare benefits necessarily operate, as did the residency requirements in *Shapiro*, to discourage entry into or continued residency in the State. Indeed, in No. 727 the parties stipulated that this was so.

In *Truax* the Court considered the "reasonableness" of a state restriction on the employment of aliens in terms of its effect on the right of a lawfully admitted alien to live where he chooses:

> * * * The authority to control immigration—to admit or exclude aliens—is vested solely in the Federal Government. . . . The assertion of an authority to deny to aliens the opportunity of

earning a livelihood when lawfully admitted to the state would be tantamount to the assertion of the right to deny them entrance and abode, for in ordinary cases they cannot live where they cannot work. And, if such a policy were permissible, the practical result would be that those lawfully admitted to the country under the authority of the acts of Congress, instead of enjoying in a substantial sense and in their full scope the privileges conferred by the admission, would be segregated in such of the states as chose to offer hospitality.

239 U.S., at 42, 36 S.Ct., at 11. The same is true here, for in the ordinary case an alien, becoming indigent and unable to work, will be unable to live where, because of discriminatory denial of public assistance, he cannot "secure the necessities of life, including food, clothing and shelter." State alien residency requirements that either deny welfare benefits to noncitizens or condition them on longtime residency, equate with the assertion of a right, inconsistent with federal policy, to deny entrance and abode. Since such laws encroach upon exclusive federal power, they are constitutionally impermissible.

IV

Arizona suggests, finally, that its 15-year durational residency requirement for aliens is actually authorized by federal law. Reliance is placed on § 1402(b) of the Social Security Act of 1935. That section provides:

> The Secretary shall approve any plan which fulfills the conditions specified in subsection (a) of this section, except that he shall not approve any plan which imposes, as a condition of eligibility for aid to the permanently and totally disabled under the plan—

> . . .

> (2) Any citizenship requirement which excludes any citizen of the United States.

The meaning of this provision is not entirely clear. On its face, the statute does not affirmatively authorize, much less command, the States to adopt durational residency requirements or other eligibility restrictions applicable to aliens; it merely directs the Secretary not to approve state-submitted plans that exclude citizens of the United States from eligibility.

* * * [I]f § 1402(b), as well as the identical provisions for old-age assistance and aid to the blind, were to be read so as to authorize discriminatory treatment of aliens at the option of the States, *Takahashi* demonstrates that serious constitutional questions are presented. Although the Federal Government admittedly has broad constitutional power to determine what aliens shall be admitted to the United States,

the period they may remain, and the terms and conditions of their naturalization, Congress does not have the power to authorize the individual States to violate the Equal Protection Clause. Under Art. I, § 8, cl. 4, of the Constitution, Congress' power is to "establish an uniform Rule of Naturalization." A congressional enactment construed so as to permit state legislatures to adopt divergent laws on the subject of citizenship requirements for federally supported welfare programs would appear to contravene this explicit constitutional requirement of uniformity.[14] Since "statutes should be construed whenever possible so as to uphold their constitutionality," *United States v. Vuitch*, 402 U.S. 62, 70, 91 S.Ct. 1294, 1298, 28 L.Ed.2d 601 (1971), we conclude that § 1402(b) does not authorize the Arizona 15-year national residency requirement.

The judgments appealed from are affirmed.

* * *

MR. JUSTICE HARLAN joins in Parts III and IV of the Court's opinion, and in the judgment of the Court.

NOTES AND QUESTIONS ON GRAHAM V. RICHARDSON

1.   The famous footnote four in *Carolene Products*, from which *Graham* takes the "discrete and insular minority" idea, reads as follows:

> There may be narrower scope for operation of the presumption of constitutionality when legislation appears on its face to be within a specific prohibition of the Constitution, such as those of the first ten Amendments, which are deemed equally specific when held to be embraced within the Fourteenth.
>
> It is unnecessary to consider now whether legislation which restricts those political processes which can ordinarily be expected to bring about repeal of undesirable legislation, is to be subjected to more exacting judicial scrutiny under the general prohibitions of the Fourteenth Amendment than are most other types of legislation.
>
> Nor need we enquire whether similar considerations enter into the review of statutes directed at particular religious, or national, or racial minorities; whether prejudice against discrete and insular minorities may be a special condition, which tends seriously to curtail the operation of those political processes ordinarily to be relied upon to protect minorities, and which may call for a correspondingly more searching judicial inquiry.

United States v. Carolene Products Co., 304 U.S. 144, 152–153, n.4, 58 S.Ct. 778, 783–784 n.4, 82 L.Ed. 1234 (1938) (citations omitted).

---

[14] We have no occasion to decide whether Congress, in the exercise of the immigration and naturalization power, could itself enact a statute imposing on aliens a uniform nationwide residency requirement as a condition of federally funded welfare benefits.

2.   *Graham* involved permanent residents, not nonimmigrants or the undocumented. Even with his reasoning so cabined, is Justice Blackmun correct that "aliens as a class" are a discrete and insular minority? Are aliens as a class truly discrete? Are they insular? Are they politically powerless? Does the possibility of diplomatic intervention by their home governments undercut this argument? And why can't they overcome their relative lack of political power by naturalizing?

Arguing that aliens are a "relatively easy case" of a discrete and insular minority, John Hart Ely explained:

> Aliens cannot vote in any state, which means that any representation they receive will be exclusively "virtual." That fact should at the very least require an unusually strong showing of a favorable environment for empathy, something that is lacking here. Hostility toward "foreigners" is a time-honored American tradition. Moreover, our legislatures are composed almost entirely of citizens who have always been such. Neither, finally, is the exaggerated stereotyping to which that situation lends itself ameliorated by any substantial degree of social intercourse between recent immigrants and those who make the laws.

John Hart Ely, Democracy and Distrust: A Theory of Judicial Review 161–62 (1980). But consider this, from T. Alexander Aleinikoff, *Citizens, Aliens, Membership and the Constitution*, 7 Const. Comm. 9, 24 n.58 (1990): "To be sure, discrimination against aliens has a persistent and ugly history in this country; but generally such hatred has been based on racial or ethnic backgrounds, not the fact of 'alienage.' Aliens, as a class, are remarkably diverse and not particularly 'insular.' "

3.   A related question is whether certain groups of noncitizens are discrete and insular minorities, even if noncitizens in general are not. Kevin Johnson has argued that "restriction of benefits and services, besides affecting persons with a certain immigration status, has a disparate impact on people of color . . . , women . . . , and the poor." Kevin R. Johnson, *Public Benefits and Immigration: The Intersection of Immigration Status, Ethnicity, Gender, and Class*, 42 UCLA L. Rev. 1509, 1516 (1995).

4.   Is there any other explanation for *Graham* besides the basic idea that noncitizens are a discrete and insular minority? Suppose instead that noncitizens cannot be so described, and therefore are not a defenseless group needing judicial protection. Here is an alternative analysis:

> The statutes in *Graham* should be invalidated not because aliens are a defenseless group needing judicial protection, but rather because—at least from the state's perspective—they are indistinguishable from other residents of the state. State laws excluding aliens from opportunities should be seen as no more legitimate than laws excluding redheads. Both would be invalid, not

because such groups are downtrodden but because the state can offer no legitimate reason for singling them out.

Aleinikoff, *Citizens, Aliens, Membership and the Constitution, supra*, at 24. Is this approach to alienage classifications more persuasive than the discrete and insular minority approach?

b. Federal Laws

In footnote 14 of *Graham*, the Court noted that it was not addressing the validity of a citizenship requirement for *federal* benefits. For equal protection—assuming that was what the Court applied in *Graham*—why should it matter if it is a federal or state law? Recall from Chapter Two that in *Bolling v. Sharpe*, 347 U.S. 497, 74 S.Ct. 693, 98 L.Ed. 884 (1954), a companion case to *Brown v. Board of Education*, the Court held that segregated schools in the District of Columbia violated the Due Process Clause of the Fifth Amendment. It has been accepted since *Bolling* that as a general rule "[e]qual protection analysis in the Fifth Amendment area is the same as that under the Fourteenth Amendment." *Buckley v. Valeo*, 424 U.S. 1, 93, 96 S.Ct. 612, 670, 46 L.Ed.2d 659 (1976) (per curiam). Does *Graham* combine with *Bolling* to suggest that federal laws limiting noncitizen access to public benefits are unconstitutional? Read the next case.

MATHEWS V. DIAZ

Supreme Court of the United States, 1976.
426 U.S. 67, 96 S.Ct. 1883, 48 L.Ed.2d 478.

MR. JUSTICE STEVENS delivered the opinion of the Court.

* * *

Each of the appellees is a resident alien who was lawfully admitted to the United States less than five years ago. Appellees Diaz and Clara are Cuban refugees who remain in this country at the discretion of the Attorney General; appellee Espinosa has been admitted for permanent residence. All three are over 65 years old and have been denied enrollment in the Medicare Part B supplemental medical insurance program * * *. * * * [T]hey attack 42 U.S.C. § 1395o(2), which grants eligibility to resident citizens who are 65 or older but denies eligibility to comparable aliens unless they have been admitted for permanent residence and also have resided in the United States for at least five years. Appellees Diaz and Clara meet neither requirement; appellee Espinosa meets only the first.

* * *

II

There are literally millions of aliens within the jurisdiction of the United States. The Fifth Amendment, as well as the Fourteenth Amendment, protects every one of these persons from deprivation of life, liberty, or property without due process of law. Even one whose presence in this country is unlawful, involuntary, or transitory is entitled to that constitutional protection.

The fact that all persons, aliens and citizens alike, are protected by the Due Process Clause does not lead to the further conclusion that all aliens are entitled to enjoy all the advantages of citizenship or, indeed, to the conclusion that all aliens must be placed in a single homogeneous legal classification. For a host of constitutional and statutory provisions rest on the premise that a legitimate distinction between citizens and aliens may justify attributes and benefits for one class not accorded to the other;[12] and the class of aliens is itself a heterogeneous multitude of persons with a wide-ranging variety of ties to this country.

In the exercise of its broad power over naturalization and immigration, Congress regularly makes rules that would be unacceptable if applied to citizens. The exclusion of aliens and the reservation of the power to deport have no permissible counterpart in the Federal Government's power to regulate the conduct of its own citizenry. The fact that an Act of Congress treats aliens differently from citizens does not in itself imply that such disparate treatment is "invidious."

In particular, the fact that Congress has provided some welfare benefits for citizens does not require it to provide like benefits for all aliens. Neither the overnight visitor, the unfriendly agent of a hostile foreign power, the resident diplomat, nor the illegal entrant, can advance even a colorable constitutional claim to a share in the bounty that a conscientious sovereign makes available to its own citizens and some of its guests. The decision to share that bounty with our guests may take into account the character of the relationship between the alien and this

---

[12] The Constitution protects the privileges and immunities only of citizens, Amdt. 14, § 1; see Art. IV, § 2, cl. 1, and the right to vote only of citizens. Amdts. 15, 19, 24, 26. It requires that Representatives have been citizens for seven years, Art. I, § 2, cl. 2, and Senators citizens for nine, Art. I, § 3, cl. 3, and that the President be a "natural born Citizen." Art. II, § 1, cl. 5.

A multitude of federal statutes distinguish between citizens and aliens. The whole of Title 8 of the United States Code, regulating aliens and nationality, is founded on the legitimacy of distinguishing between citizens and aliens. A variety of other federal statutes provide for disparate treatment of aliens and citizens. These include prohibitions and restrictions upon Government employment of aliens, upon private employment of aliens, and upon investments and businesses of aliens, statutes excluding aliens from benefits available to citizens, and from protections extended to citizens; and statutes imposing added burdens upon aliens. Several statutes treat certain aliens more favorably than citizens. Other statutes, similar to the one at issue in this case, provide for equal treatment of citizens and aliens lawfully admitted for permanent residence. Still others equate citizens and aliens who have declared their intention to become citizens. Yet others condition equal treatment of an alien upon reciprocal treatment of United States citizens by the alien's own country.

country: Congress may decide that as the alien's tie grows stronger, so does the strength of his claim to an equal share of that munificence.

The real question presented by this case is not whether discrimination between citizens and aliens is permissible; rather, it is whether the statutory discrimination within the class of aliens—allowing benefits to some aliens but not to others—is permissible. We turn to that question.

III

For reasons long recognized as valid, the responsibility for regulating the relationship between the United States and our alien visitors has been committed to the political branches of the Federal Government.[17] Since decisions in these matters may implicate our relations with foreign powers, and since a wide variety of classifications must be defined in the light of changing political and economic circumstances, such decisions are frequently of a character more appropriate to either the Legislature or the Executive than to the Judiciary. This very case illustrates the need for flexibility in policy choices rather than the rigidity often characteristic of constitutional adjudication. Appellees Diaz and Clara are but two of over 440,000 Cuban refugees who arrived in the United States between 1961 and 1972. And the Cuban parolees are but one of several categories of aliens who have been admitted in order to make a humane response to a natural catastrophe or an international political situation. Any rule of constitutional law that would inhibit the flexibility of the political branches of government to respond to changing world conditions should be adopted only with the greatest caution. The reasons that preclude judicial review of political questions[21] also dictate a narrow standard of review of decisions made by the Congress or the President in the area of immigration and naturalization.

---

[17] "(A)ny policy toward aliens is vitally and intricately interwoven with contemporaneous policies in regard to the conduct of foreign relations, the war power, and the maintenance of a republican form of government. Such matters are so exclusively entrusted to the political branches of government as to be largely immune from judicial inquiry or interference." *Harisiades v. Shaughnessy*, supra, 342 U.S., at 588–589, 72 S.Ct. 512, 519, 96 L.Ed. 586, 598 (footnote omitted). *Accord, e.g. Kleindienst v. Mandel, supra,* 408 U.S., at 765–767, 92 S.Ct. 2576, 2582–2584, 33 L.Ed.2d 683, 693–695; *Fong Yue Ting v. United States,* 149 U.S. 698, 711–713, 13 S.Ct. 1016, 1021–1022, 37 L.Ed. 905, 912–913.

[21] "It is apparent that several formulations which vary slightly according to the settings in which the questions arise may describe a political question, although each has one or more elements which identify it as essentially a function of the separation of powers. Prominent on the surface of any case held to involve a political question is found a textually demonstrable constitutional commitment of the issue to a coordinate political department; or a lack of judicially discoverable and manageable standards for resolving it; or the impossibility of deciding without an initial policy determination of a kind clearly for nonjudicial discretion; or the impossibility of a court's undertaking independent resolution without expressing lack of the respect due coordinate branches of government; or an unusual need for unquestioning adherence to a political decision already made; or the potentiality of embarrassment from multifarious pronouncements by various departments on one question." *Baker v. Carr,* 369 U.S. 186, 217, 82 S.Ct. 691, 710, 7 L.Ed.2d 663, 685.

Since it is obvious that Congress has no constitutional duty to provide all aliens with the welfare benefits provided to citizens, the party challenging the constitutionality of the particular line Congress has drawn has the burden of advancing principled reasoning that will at once invalidate that line and yet tolerate a different line separating some aliens from others. In this case the appellees have challenged two requirements—first, that the alien be admitted as a permanent resident, and, second, that his residence be of a duration of at least five years. But if these requirements were eliminated, surely Congress would at least require that the alien's entry be lawful; even then, unless mere transients are to be held constitutionally entitled to benefits, some durational requirement would certainly be appropriate. In short, it is unquestionably reasonable for Congress to make an alien's eligibility depend on both the character and the duration of his residence. Since neither requirement is wholly irrational, this case essentially involves nothing more than a claim that it would have been more reasonable for Congress to select somewhat different requirements of the same kind.

We may assume that the five-year line drawn by Congress is longer than necessary to protect the fiscal integrity of the program. We may also assume that unnecessary hardship is incurred by persons just short of qualifying. But it remains true that some line is essential, that any line must produce some harsh and apparently arbitrary consequences, and, of greatest importance, that those who qualify under the test Congress has chosen may reasonably be presumed to have a greater affinity with the United States than those who do not. In short, citizens and those who are most like citizens qualify. Those who are less like citizens do not.

The task of classifying persons for medical benefits, like the task of drawing lines for federal tax purposes, inevitably requires that some persons who have an almost equally strong claim to favored treatment be placed on different sides of the line; the differences between the eligible and the ineligible are differences in degree rather than differences in the character of their respective claims. When this kind of policy choice must be made, we are especially reluctant to question the exercise of congressional judgment. In this case, since appellees have not identified a principled basis for prescribing a different standard than the one selected by Congress, they have, in effect, merely invited us to substitute our judgment for that of Congress in deciding which aliens shall be eligible to participate in the supplementary insurance program on the same conditions as citizens. We decline the invitation.

IV

The cases on which appellees rely are consistent with our conclusion that this statutory classification does not deprive them of liberty or property without due process of law.

Graham v. Richardson, 403 U.S. 365, 91 S.Ct. 1848, 29 L.Ed.2d 534, provides the strongest support for appellees' position. That case holds that state statutes that deny welfare benefits to resident aliens, or to aliens not meeting a requirement of durational residence within the United States, violate the Equal Protection Clause of the Fourteenth Amendment and encroach upon the exclusive federal power over the entrance and residence of aliens. Of course, the latter ground of decision actually supports our holding today that it is the business of the political branches of the Federal Government, rather than that of either the States or the Federal Judiciary, to regulate the conditions of entry and residence of aliens. The equal protection analysis also involves significantly different considerations because it concerns the relationship between aliens and the States rather than between aliens and the Federal Government.

Insofar as state welfare policy is concerned,[24] there is little, if any, basis for treating persons who are citizens of another State differently from persons who are citizens of another country. Both groups are noncitizens as far as the State's interests in administering its welfare programs are concerned. Thus, a division by a State of the category of persons who are not citizens of that State into subcategories of United States citizens and aliens has no apparent justification, whereas, a comparable classification by the Federal Government is a routine and normally legitimate part of its business. Furthermore, whereas the Constitution inhibits every State's power to restrict travel across its own borders, Congress is explicitly empowered to exercise that type of control over travel across the borders of the United States.

* * *

We hold that § 1395o(2)(B) has not deprived appellees of liberty or property without due process of law.

* * *

NOTES AND QUESTIONS ON MATHEWS V. DIAZ

1. How analytically helpful is it to say that the classification in *Mathews v. Diaz* was a classification among aliens rather than between aliens and citizens? That may be true, in that some noncitizens are eligible for Medicare, while others are not. But does this characterization mask the line that the Medicare eligibility rules draw between citizens and noncitizens?

---

[24] We have left open the question whether a State may prohibit aliens from holding elective or important nonelective positions or whether a State may, in some circumstances, consider the alien status of an applicant or employee in making an individualized employment decision. *See Sugarman v. Dougall*, 413 U.S. 634, 646–649, 93 S.Ct. 2842, 2849–2851, 37 L.Ed.2d 853, 862–864; *In re Griffiths*, 413 U.S. 717, 728–729 and n.21, 93 S.Ct. 2851, 2858–2859, 37 L.Ed.2d 910, 919–920.

2.   Does *Mathews v. Diaz* silently repudiate—even with regard to state alienage classifications—the idea in *Graham* that alienage classifications should prompt close judicial scrutiny because aliens are a discrete and insular minority? Even if some aspects of *Diaz* might be read that way, the Supreme Court applied *Graham* in later cases to strike down some state alienage classifications. These include the cases on citizenship requirements for state public employment in Section B of this chapter.

3.   One of the most quoted sentences from *Diaz* is: "In the exercise of its broad power over naturalization and immigration, Congress regularly makes rules that would be unacceptable if applied to citizens." But does this mean that the plenary power doctrine operates with as much force in alienage law as in immigration law? Compare the judicial deference in *Diaz* with *Fiallo v. Bell*, 430 U.S. 787, 97 S.Ct. 1473, 52 L.Ed.2d 50 (1977), in Chapter Five, p. 296. Would the *Diaz* Court have upheld a Medicare rule that limited noncitizen eligibility by gender or illegitimacy?

Diaz based Congress' power to classify by alienage on its "broad power over naturalization and immigration," citing the power to refuse admission and to remove noncitizens. Should the Constitution apply to alienage classifications and immigration rules in the similar way, and if so, why? Does it follow from the judicial deference to an immigration statute in *Fiallo* that courts should likewise defer to a statute—like the Medicare statute in *Diaz*—that disadvantages noncitizens after their admission?

4.   To understand the immigration-alienage line, consider the following comment on Proposition 187, approved by California voters in 1994, discussed in Chapter Ten, pp. 1201–1204.

> * * * "Alienage" rules may be surrogates for "immigration" rules. Often, the intended and/or actual effect of an alienage rule is to affect immigration patterns. * * * Proposition 187 is a good example. It does not purport to regulate admission to the United States directly; instead, its principal effect is to deny public education and non-emergency medical services to undocumented aliens. However, Proposition 187 is clearly meant to deter undocumented aliens from entering California and to encourage the voluntary exit of those already there. Governor Wilson has expressed his hope that undocumented aliens, once denied access to public benefits, will "self-deport."
>
> Similarly, "immigration" rules may be surrogates for "alienage" rules. For example, the law governing deportation traditionally belongs to "immigration law." This understanding makes sense in that deportation grounds allow the government to undo an alien's original admission (or surreptitious entry or parole) into the United States. Yet the intended and actual effect of deportation grounds is to regulate the everyday lives of aliens in the United States no less than do rules governing their access to public benefits.

Hiroshi Motomura, *Immigration and Alienage, Federalism and Proposition 187*, 35 Va. J. Int'l L. 201, 202–03 (1994).

5.   Linda Bosniak explains why it is not enough to distinguish immigration law from alienage law. She discusses the issues that persist even if we assume that an issue is a matter of alienage law:

> * * * [T]he law has constructed alienage as a hybrid legal status category that lies at the nexus of two legal—and moral—worlds. It lies, first of all, in the world of borders, sovereignty, and national community membership; this is the world of the government's immigration power, which regulates decisions about the admission and exclusion of outsiders and which places conditions on their entry and residence. * * * In the broader landscape of American public law, this power remains exceptionally unconstrained.
>
> Yet alienage as a legal category also lies in the world of social relationships among territorially present persons. In this world, government power to impose disabilities on people based on their status is substantially constrained. Formal commitments to norms of equal treatment and to the elimination of caste-like status have importantly shaped American public law, particularly during the past several decades. * * *
>
> Because alienage lies at the nexus of these two legal worlds—because it is a hybrid legal status that is the creature of both—the question of when and whether a person's status as an alien legitimately matters in determining the allocation of rights and benefits in our society tends to take the form of what can best be described as a "jurisdictional" dispute in case law. This dispute concerns the question of which of the two worlds (or regulatory domains) that define alienage—I will call them the domains of membership and equal personhood, respectively—properly controls in any given case.

Linda S. Bosniak, *Membership, Equality, and the Difference That Alienage Makes*, 69 N.Y.U. L. Rev. 1047, 1056–57 (1994).

c.   Preemption or Equal Protection?

In assessing the constitutionality of state alienage laws, compare the reliance on both equal protection and preemption in *Graham* with the exclusive reliance on preemption in the next case.

TOLL V. MORENO

Supreme Court of the United States, 1982.
458 U.S. 1, 102 S.Ct. 2977, 73 L.Ed.2d 563.

JUSTICE BRENNAN delivered the opinion of the Court.

* * *

In 1975, when this action was filed, respondents Juan Carlos Moreno, Juan Pablo Otero, and Clare B. Hogg were students at the University of Maryland. Each resided with, and was financially dependent on, a parent who was a nonimmigrant alien holding a "G–4" visa. Such visas are issued to nonimmigrant aliens who are officers or employees of certain international organizations, and to members of their immediate families. Despite respondents' residence in the State, the University denied them in-state status pursuant to its policy of excluding all nonimmigrant aliens. Seeking declaratory and injunctive relief, the three respondents filed a class action against the University of Maryland and its President. They contended that the University's policy violated various federal laws, the Due Process and Equal Protection Clauses of the Fourteenth Amendment, and the Supremacy Clause.

* * *

[T]he University adopted a "clarifying resolution" concerning its in-state policy. * * * The interests assertedly served by the policy were described in the following terms [in that resolution]:

(a) limiting the University's expenditures by granting a higher subsidy toward the expenses of providing educational services to that class of persons who, as a class, are more likely to have a close affinity to the State and to contribute more to its economic well-being;

(b) achieving equalization between the affected classes of the expenses of providing educational services;

(c) efficiently administering the University's in-state determination and appeals process; and

(d) preventing disparate treatment among categories of nonimmigrants with respect to admissions, tuition, and charge-differentials.

* * *

* * * [W]e hold that the University of Maryland's in-state policy, as applied to G–4 aliens and their dependents, violates the Supremacy Clause of the Constitution, and on that ground affirm the judgment of the Court of Appeals. We therefore have no occasion to consider whether the policy violates the Due Process or Equal Protection Clauses.

II

Our cases have long recognized the preeminent role of the Federal Government with respect to the regulation of aliens within our borders. Federal authority to regulate the status of aliens derives from various sources, including the Federal Government's power "[t]o establish [a] uniform Rule of Naturalization," U.S. Const. Art. I, § 8, cl. 4, its power "[t]o regulate Commerce with foreign Nations", *id.*, cl. 3, and its broad authority over foreign affairs.

Not surprisingly, therefore, our cases have also been at pains to note the substantial limitations upon the authority of the States in making classifications based upon alienage. In *Takahashi v. Fish & Game Comm'n,* [334 U.S. 410, 68 S.Ct. 1138, 1142–1143, 92 L.Ed. 1478 (1948)], we considered a California statute that precluded aliens who were "ineligible for citizenship under federal law" from obtaining commercial fishing licenses, even though they "met all other state requirements" and were lawful inhabitants of the State. In seeking to defend the statute, the State argued that it had "simply followed the Federal Government's lead" in classifying certain persons as "ineligible for citizenship." We rejected the argument, stressing the delicate nature of the federal-state relationship in regulating aliens * * *.[16]

The decision in *Graham v. Richardson,* [403 U.S. 365, 91 S.Ct. 1848, 29 L.Ed.2d 534 (1971)], followed directly from *Takahashi.* In *Graham* we held that a State may not withhold welfare benefits from resident aliens "merely because of their alienage." Such discrimination, the Court concluded, would not only violate the Equal Protection Clause, but would also encroach upon federal authority over lawfully admitted aliens. * * *

Read together, *Takahashi* and *Graham* stand for the broad principle[17] that "state regulation not congressionally sanctioned that discriminates against aliens lawfully admitted to the country is impermissible if it imposes additional burdens not contemplated by Congress." *De Canas v. Bica,* 424 U.S. 351, 358, n.6, 96 S.Ct. 933, 938, n.6, 47 L.Ed.2d 43 (1976).[18] To be sure, when Congress has done nothing

---

[16] * * * While pre-emption played a significant role in the Court's analysis in *Takahashi,* the actual basis for invalidation of the California statute was apparently the Equal Protection Clause of the Constitution. Commentators have noted, however, that many of the Court's decisions concerning alienage classifications, such as *Takahashi,* are better explained in pre-emption than in equal protection terms. See, *e.g.,* Perry, *Modern Equal Protection: A Conceptualization and Appraisal,* 79 Colum. L. Rev. 1023, 1060–1065 (1979); Note, *The Equal Treatment of Aliens: Preemption or Equal Protection?,* 31 Stan. L. Rev. 1069 (1979).

[17] Our cases do recognize, however, that a State, in the course of defining its political community, may, in appropriate circumstances, limit the participation of noncitizens in the States' political and governmental functions. See, *e.g., Cabell v. Chavez-Salido,* 454 U.S. 432, 102 S.Ct. 735, 70 L.Ed.2d 677 (1982).

[18] In *De Canas,* we considered whether a California statute making it unlawful in some circumstances to employ *illegal* aliens was invalid under the Supremacy Clause. We upheld the statute. Justice Rehnquist's dissent in the present case suggests that the pre-emption claim was rejected in *De Canas* because "the Court found no strong evidence that Congress intended to pre-

more than permit a class of aliens to enter the country temporarily, the proper application of the principle is likely to be a matter of some dispute. But the instant case does not present such a situation, and there can be little doubt regarding the invalidity of the challenged portion of the University's in-state policy.

For many * * * nonimmigrant categories, Congress has precluded the covered alien from establishing domicile in the United States. But significantly, Congress has allowed G–4 aliens—employees of various international organizations, and their immediate families—to enter the country on terms permitting the establishment of domicile in the United States. In light of Congress' explicit decision not to bar G–4 aliens from acquiring domicile, the State's decision to deny "in-state" status to G–4 aliens, *solely* on account of the G–4 alien's federal immigration status, surely amounts to an ancillary "burden not contemplated by Congress" in admitting these aliens to the United States. We need not rely, however, simply on Congress' decision to permit the G–4 alien to establish domicile in this country; the Federal Government has also taken the additional affirmative step of conferring special tax privileges on G–4 aliens.

As a result of an array of treaties, international agreements, and federal statutes, G–4 visaholders employed by the international organizations described in INA § 101(a)(15)(G)(iv) are relieved of federal and, in many instances, state and local taxes on the salaries paid by the organizations. * * *

In affording G–4 visaholders such tax exemption, the Federal Government has undoubtedly sought to benefit the employing international organizations by enabling them to pay salaries not encumbered by the full panoply of taxes, thereby lowering the organizations' costs. The tax benefits serve as an inducement for these organizations to locate significant operations in the United States. By imposing on those G–4 aliens who are domiciled in Maryland higher tuition and fees than are imposed on other domiciliaries of the State, the University's policy frustrates these federal policies. * * *

JUSTICE BLACKMUN, concurring.

I join the Court's opinion. Its action today provides an eloquent and sufficient answer to Justice Rehnquist's dissent: despite the vehemence with which his opinion is written, Justice Rehnquist has persuaded only one Justice to his position. But because the dissent attempts to plumb the

---

empt" the State's action. Justice Rehnquist has misread *De Canas.* We rejected the pre-emption claim not because of an absence of congressional intent to pre-empt, but because Congress *intended* that the States be allowed, "to the extent consistent with federal law, [to] regulate the employment of illegal aliens." 424 U.S., at 361, 96 S.Ct., at 939.

Court's psyche,[1] I feel compelled to add comments addressed to Justice Rehnquist's ruminations on equal protection. In particular, I cannot leave unchallenged his suggestion that the Court's decisions holding resident aliens to be a "suspect class" no longer are good law.

Justice Rehnquist's analysis on this point is based on a simple syllogism. Alienage classifications have been subjected to strict scrutiny, he suggests, because "aliens [are] barred from asserting their interests in the governmental body responsible for imposing burdens upon them." But "[m]ore recent decisions," he continues, have established that "the political powerlessness of aliens is itself the consequence of distinctions on the basis of alienage that are constitutionally permissible." This prompts Justice Rehnquist to pose what one supposes to be a rhetorical question: "whether political powerlessness is any longer a legitimate reason for treating aliens as a 'suspect class' deserving of 'heightened judicial solicitude.'" The reader would infer from this analysis that Justice Rehnquist would uphold state enactments disadvantaging aliens unless those enactments are wholly irrational.

With respect, in my view it is Justice Rehnquist's analysis that is wholly irrational; simply to state his proposition is to demonstrate its logical flaws. Most obviously, his exegesis of the Court's reasons for according aliens "suspect class" status is simplistic to the point of caricature. By labeling aliens a " 'discrete and insular' minority," *Graham v. Richardson*, 403 U.S. 365, 372, 91 S.Ct. 1848, 1852, 29 L.Ed.2d 534 (1971), the Court did something more than provide an historical description of their political standing. That label also reflected the Court's considered conclusion that for most legislative purposes there simply are no meaningful differences between resident aliens and citizens, so that aliens and citizens are "persons similarly circumstanced" who must "be treated alike." *F.S. Royster Guano Co. v. Virginia*, 253 U.S. 412, 415, 40 S.Ct. 560, 562, 64 L.Ed. 989 (1920). At the same time, both common experience and the unhappy history reflected in our cases demonstrate that aliens often have been the victims of irrational discrimination.

In combination, these factors—disparate treatment accorded a class of "similarly circumstanced" persons who historically have been disabled by the prejudice of the majority led the Court to conclude that alienage classifications "in themselves supply a reason to infer antipathy," *Personnel Administrator of Massachusetts v. Feeney*, 442 U.S. 256, 272, 99 S.Ct. 2282, 2292, 60 L.Ed.2d 870 (1979), and therefore demand close judicial scrutiny. * * *

* * *

---

[1] The Justice opines that "[i]f the Court has eschewed strict scrutiny in the 'political process' [alienage-equal protection] cases, it may be because the Court is becoming uncomfortable with the categorization of aliens as a suspect class."

Justice Rehnquist nevertheless suggests that the Court's original understanding somehow has been undercut by "more recent decisions" recognizing that aliens may be excluded from the governmental process. * * * Again, with all due respect, Justice Rehnquist is simply wrong. The idea that aliens may be denied political rights is not a recently discovered concept or a newly molded principle that can be said to have eroded the prior understanding. To the contrary, the Court always has recognized that aliens may be denied use of the mechanisms of self-government, and *all* of the alienage cases have been decided against the backdrop of that principle. * * *

Finally, even were I to accept Justice Rehnquist's view that powerlessness is the end-all of alienage-equal protection doctrine, I would find preposterous his further suggestion that, because States do not violate the Constitution when they exclude aliens from participation in the government of the community, the alien's powerlessness therefore is constitutionally irrelevant. From the moment the Court began constructing modern equal protection doctrine in *United States v. Carolene Products Co.*, 304 U.S. 144, 58 S.Ct. 778, 82 L.Ed. 1234 (1938), it never has been suggested that the *reason* for a discrete class' political powerlessness is significant; instead, the *fact* of powerlessness is crucial, for in combination with prejudice it is the minority group's inability to assert its political interests that "curtail[s] the operation of those political processes ordinarily to be relied upon to protect minorities." *Id.*, at 152–153, n.4, 58 S.Ct., at 783–784, n.4. * * *

* * *

JUSTICE O'CONNOR, concurring in part and dissenting in part.

I concur in the Court's opinion insofar as it holds that the State may not charge out-of-state tuition to nonimmigrant aliens who, under federal law, are exempt from both state and federal taxes, and who are domiciled in the State. Imposition of out-of-state tuition on such aliens conflicts with federal law exempting them from state taxes, since, after all, the University admits that it seeks to charge the higher tuition in order to recover costs that state income taxes normally would cover.

I cannot join the remainder of the Court's opinion, however, for it wholly fails to address the criticisms leveled in Justice Rehnquist's dissenting opinion. As Justice Rehnquist makes clear, the class of G–4 aliens is not homogenous: some G–4 aliens are exempt under federal law from state taxes, while other G–4 aliens are not. * * * Thus, I disagree with the Court when it states that the "State may not recoup indirectly from respondents' parents the taxes that the Federal Government has expressly barred the State from collecting," for in fact Congress has not barred the State from collecting state taxes from many G–4 aliens. Accordingly, I conclude that the Supremacy Clause does not prohibit the

University from charging out-of-state tuition to those G–4 aliens who are exempted by federal law from federal taxes only.

JUSTICE REHNQUIST, with whom THE CHIEF JUSTICE joins, dissenting.

* * *

[N]either Congress' unexercised constitutional power over immigration and naturalization, nor its exercise of that power in passing the INA, precludes the States from enforcing laws and regulations that prove burdensome to aliens. Under our precedents, therefore, state law is invalid only if there is "such actual conflict between the two schemes of regulation that both cannot stand in the same area," *Florida Lime & Avocado Growers, Inc. v. Paul,* [373 U.S. 132,] 141, 83 S.Ct., [1210,] 1217, 10 L.Ed.2d 248 (1963), or if Congress has in some other way unambiguously declared its intention to foreclose the state law in question. * * *

Notwithstanding these settled principles, the Court suggests in dicta that any state law which discriminates against lawfully admitted aliens is void, presumably without regard to the strength of the State's justification, if Congress did not contemplate such a law. This standard seems to me clearly to reverse the presumption that normally prevails when state laws are challenged under the Supremacy Clause. * * *

[In *Takahashi v. Fish & Game Comm'n*, 334 U.S. 410, 68 S.Ct. 1138, 92 L.Ed. 1478 (1948); *Truax v. Raich*, 239 U.S. 33, 36 S.Ct. 7, 60 L.Ed. 131 (1915); and *Hines v. Davidowitz*, 312 U.S. 52, 61 S.Ct. 399, 85 L.Ed. 581 (1941);] the Court found either a clear encroachment on exclusive federal power to admit aliens into the country or a clear conflict with a specific congressional purpose. It was with these cases in mind that the Court in *Takahashi* condemned "[s]tate laws which impose discriminatory burdens upon the entrance or residence of aliens lawfully within the United States." 334 U.S., at 419, 68 S.Ct., at 1142. * * *

The Court also relies on *Graham v. Richardson*, 403 U.S. 365, 91 S.Ct. 1848, 29 L.Ed.2d 534 (1971), which struck down as a denial of equal protection a California law that withheld welfare benefits from lawfully resident aliens. As an alternative ground, the Court also declared the law invalid as an encroachment on federal power. On the basis of specific federal statutes barring the admission of aliens likely to become public charges, and providing for the deportation of aliens who become public charges because of factors that existed prior to entry, the Court inferred a congressional purpose not "to impose any burden or restriction on aliens who become indigent after their entry into the United States." * * * The holding in *Graham*, therefore, offers no support for a presumption that *all* state laws burdening aliens conflict with amorphous federal power over immigration.

* * *

The Court relies on two features of federal law. First, it notes that Congress has permitted nonimmigrant aliens holding G–4 visas to establish domicile in the United States. It then reasons that denying these aliens in-state tuition conflicts with Congress' decision. The Court offers no evidence that Congress' intent in permitting respondents to establish "domicile in the United States" has any bearing at all on the tuition available to them at state universities. * * *

The second feature of federal law on which the Court relies consists of certain statutes and treaties that affect the tax liability of G–4 visaholders. The Court considers these statutes and treaties as an amorphous whole and concludes that the University's policy "frustrates" the policies embodied in them. "The State may not recoup indirectly from respondents' parents the taxes that the Federal Government has expressly barred the State from collecting." There are two serious flaws in this argument. First, the Federal Government has not barred the States from collecting taxes from many, if not most, G–4 visaholders. Second, as to those G–4 nonimmigrants who *are* immune from state income taxes by treaty, Maryland's tuition policy cannot fairly be said to conflict with those treaties in a manner requiring its pre-emption.

* * *

The lower courts' principal basis for invalidating Maryland's tuition policy was not the Supremacy Clause, but the Equal Protection Clause. Those courts interpreted the State's policy as a classification based on alienage, and therefore subjected it to "strict scrutiny" on the authority of *Graham v. Richardson*, 403 U.S. 365, 91 S.Ct. 1848, 29 L.Ed.2d 534 (1971), and later cases. In light of several recent decisions, however, it is clear that not every alienage classification is subject to strict scrutiny. In my view, the classification relied upon by the State in this case cannot fairly be called "suspect," and therefore I would ask only whether it rests upon a rational basis. Because I believe it does, I cannot agree with the lower courts that it denies the equal protection of the laws.

* * *

In the vast majority of cases our judicial function permits us to ask only whether the judgment of relevance made by the State is rational. In a very few other cases, we have required that the State pass a more demanding test because of the judgment that the classification drawn by the State is virtually never permissible from a constitutional perspective. Such classifications are deemed "suspect" and strictly scrutinized. Until 1971, only race and national origin had been so classified by the Court.

In *Graham v. Richardson,* the Court added alienage to this select list. Apart from the abbreviated conclusion that "[a]liens as a class are a prime example of a 'discrete and insular' minority," the Court did not elaborate on the justification for "heightened judicial solicitude." Subsequently, the Court observed that aliens, unlike other members of the community, were subject to the particular disadvantage of being unable to vote, and thus were barred from participating formally in the process of self-government. *Hampton v. Mow Sun Wong*, 426 U.S. 88, 102, 96 S.Ct. 1895, 1905, 48 L.Ed.2d 495 (1976). One could infer that rigorous judicial scrutiny normally was necessary because aliens were barred from asserting their interests in the governmental body responsible for imposing burdens upon them.

More recent decisions have established, however, that the political powerlessness of aliens is itself the consequence of distinctions on the basis of alienage that are constitutionally permissible. [Justice Rehnquist discussed cases—in Section B of this chapter—that upheld the exclusion of noncitizens from the states' political and governmental functions.]

If the exclusion of aliens from the political processes is legitimate, as it clearly is, there is reason to doubt whether political powerlessness is any longer a legitimate reason for treating aliens as a "suspect class" deserving of "heightened judicial solicitude." * * * In my view, these decisions merely reflect the judgment that alienage, or the other side of the coin, citizenship, is for certain important state purposes a constitutionally relevant characteristic and therefore cannot always be considered invidious in the same manner as race or national origin.

* * *

In each case in which the Court has tested state alienage classifications under the Equal Protection Clause, the question has been the extent to which the States could permissibly distinguish between citizens and permanent resident aliens. In this case, however, the question is whether the State can distinguish between two groups, each of which consists of citizens and aliens. For two reasons, the State's classification should not be deemed "suspect" and subjected to strict scrutiny.

First, unlike immigrant aliens, nonimmigrants such as G–4 visaholders are significantly different from citizens in certain important respects. Our previous decisions have emphasized that immigrant aliens have been lawfully admitted to this country for permanent residence and share many of the normal burdens of citizenship, such as the duty to pay taxes and to serve in the Armed Forces. * * *

Second, the State's tuition policy, as it applies to G–4 visaholders, simply cannot be broadly characterized as a classification that discriminates on the basis of alienage. It is more accurately described as a policy that classifies on the basis of financial contribution toward the costs of operating the University. In one class are citizens and permanent resident aliens, all of whom have lived in the State and have contributed to state revenues through the payment of income taxes. * * *

In the other class is an equally mixed group of citizens and aliens. Some of these citizens do not reside in the State and therefore do not pay state taxes. Others do reside in the State, but are financially dependent on parents or a spouse who is domiciled elsewhere and therefore do not help finance the operation of the University through income taxes. Nonimmigrant aliens holding G–4 visas also reside in the State but, like citizens in this class, do not pay state income taxes. To all members of this class the State charges a higher, so-called "out-of-state" tuition, although one that still does not fully cover the cost of education. * * *

Consequently, for either of these reasons, the "strict scrutiny" authorized by *Graham v. Richardson*, even if it is still applicable to discrimination against permanent resident aliens, has no proper application to the State's policy in this case. The only question, therefore, is whether "the State's classification rationally furthers the purpose identified by the State." *Massachusetts Board of Retirement v. Murgia*, 427 U.S. 307, 314, 96 S.Ct. 2562, 2567, 49 L.Ed.2d 520 (1976). The State has articulated several purposes for its policy of denying in-state tuition to nonimmigrant aliens. One purpose is roughly to equalize the cost of higher education borne by those students who do and those who do not financially contribute to the University through income tax payments. The purpose surely is a legitimate one, and I should think it evident that the State's classification rationally furthers that purpose.

* * *

NOTES AND QUESTIONS ON
EQUAL PROTECTION AND PREEMPTION

1.   Are the different outcomes in *Graham* and *Diaz* attributable to a distinction between state and federal alienage classifications? And if it matters whether a state or the federal government classifies by alienage, *why* does it matter? More generally, should we understand *Graham* and *Diaz* as preemption cases or equal protection cases? Is it that federal law preempts state law, or that states have fewer governmental interests that they may use to defend a state law against an equal protection challenge?

2.   Footnote 17 in the *Toll* majority opinion and footnote 24 in *Mathews v. Diaz* observe that states can constitutionally exclude lawfully present noncitizens from political and governmental functions, such as voting or public offices. (*See also* Section B of this chapter.) Does *Toll* say that outside this exception, every distinction between citizens and lawfully present

noncitizens is preempted if it "imposes additional burdens not contemplated by Congress"? When does a state law that treats lawfully present noncitizens differently *not* impose such an "additional burden"?

What if a state law creates benefits rather than burdens? May a state give cash grants to new immigrants to help them integrate into American society? May a state organize and underwrite classes to help permanent residents prepare for naturalization? Is a line between burdens and benefits able to support a constitutional distinction?

d. Nonimmigrants

What about state laws that treat U.S. citizens and lawful permanent resident alike, but disadvantage lawfully present nonimmigrants in some way? In *LeClerc v. Webb*, 419 F.3d 405 (5th Cir. 2005), *cert. denied*, 551 U.S. 1158, 127 S.Ct. 1158, 168 L.Ed.2d 751 (2007), the plaintiffs were noncitizens who were eligible to take the Louisiana bar exam, except that at that time Louisiana limited bar admission to U.S. citizens or lawful permanent residents. Plaintiffs were lawfully present nonimmigrants who challenged the state rule on the grounds, among others, that it violated their rights to equal protection of the laws, and that it was preempted by federal law.

The court rejected the equal protection argument that state laws affecting nonimmigrants are subject to strict scrutiny:

> Nonimmigrant aliens' status is far more constricted than that of resident aliens. Nonimmigrant aliens are admitted to the United States only for the duration of their status, and on the express condition they have "no intention of abandoning" their countries of origin and do not intend to seek permanent residence in the United States. They are admitted, remain, and must depart at the discretion of the Attorney General.co_footnote_B0424220007061772_1 Plaintiffs acknowledge that nonimmigrant aliens may not serve in the U.S. military, are subject to strict employment restrictions, incur differential tax treatment, and may be denied federal welfare benefits. Finally, the Supreme Court has yet expressly to bestow equal protection status on nonimmigrant aliens.

> Based on the aggregate factual and legal distinctions between resident aliens and nonimmigrant aliens, we conclude that although aliens are a suspect class in general, they are not homogeneous and precedent does not support the proposition that nonimmigrant aliens are a suspect class entitled to have state legislative classifications concerning them subjected to strict scrutiny. We decline to extend the Supreme Court's

decisions concerning resident aliens to different alien categories when the Court itself has shied away from such expansion.

Id. at 418–19. The court rejected plaintiffs' preemption argument, distinguishing *Toll v. Moreno*:

> * * * *Toll* specifically distinguished between G–4 nonimmigrant aliens—upon whom Congress expressly declined to impose domicile restrictions—and the F–1 student and H–1B temporary worker nonimmigrant aliens at issue in this case— upon whom Congress has clearly imposed domicile restrictions. [The bar admission restriction in] Section 3(B) affects only the latter group.

> * * *

> Section 3(B) is a state Bar rule designed to address local problems arising from the transitory status of nonimmigrant aliens who, by the terms and conditions of their federal status, possess fewer ties to the United States than any other group (besides illegal aliens). Section 3(B) attempts to protect Louisiana residents seeking legal representation and affects a class of persons whom Congress has expressly prohibited from living or working permanently in the United States. Rather than standing as an obstacle to federal law, Section 3(B) is consistent with the federal policy embodied in the INA.

Id. at 424–26. In *LULAC v. Bredesen*, 500 F.3d 523 (6th Cir. 2007), the Sixth Circuit applied the equal protection analysis in *LeClerc* to reject an equal protection challenge to a Tennessee statute that limited eligibility for driver's licenses to U.S. citizens and lawful permanent residents.

The Second Circuit reached a contrasting result in *Dandamudi v. Tisch*, 686 F.3d 66 (2d Cir. 2012), which involved a New York state statute limiting pharmacist's licenses to U.S. citizens and lawful permanent residents. The plaintiffs, all nonimmigrants in H–1B or TN (NAFTA) statuses, challenged the statute on equal protection and preemption grounds. The court first held that the statute violated equal protection:

> Nonimmigrants do pay taxes, often on the same terms as citizens and LPRs, and certainly on income earned in the United States. Further, any claimed distinction based on permanency of residence is equally disingenuous. Although it is certainly true that nonimmigrants must indicate an intent not to remain permanently in the United States, this ignores the dual intent doctrine—nonimmigrant aliens are lawfully permitted to express an intent to remain temporarily (to obtain and maintain their work visas) as well as an intent to remain permanently (when

they apply for LPR status). And the final distinction—limited work permission—is wholly irrelevant where, as here, the state seeks to prohibit aliens from engaging in the very occupation for which the federal government granted the alien permission to enter the United States.

* * *

The core of the state's argument (and the analytical pivot of *LeClerc* and *LULAC*) is "transience." The state argues that the nonimmigrant's transient immigration status distinguishes nonimmigrant aliens from LPRs and introduces legitimate state concerns that would allow for rational basis review of the statute. This focus on transience is overly formalistic and wholly unpersuasive. The aliens at issue here are "transient" in name only. Certainly the status under which they were admitted to the United States was of limited duration. But the reality is quite different. A great number of these professionals remain in the United States for much longer than six years and many ultimately apply for, and obtain, permanent residence. These practicalities are not irrelevant. They demonstrate that there is little or no distinction between LPRs and the lawfully admitted nonimmigrant plaintiffs here.

Id. at 77–78. The court then addressed federal preemption.

* * * Through the INA, Congress exercised its immigration power to permit non-LPRs and non-citizens to become lawful residents of the United States and to participate in certain occupations so long as they are *professionally qualified* to engage in the particular speciality occupation they seek to practice. By making immigration status a professional qualification, and thereby causing the group of non-citizens and non-LPRs Congress intended to allow to practice specialty occupations to be ineligible to do so, the New York statute has created an obstacle to the accomplishment and execution of the INA.

We are also unpersuaded by the state's other arguments: that the statute does not regulate who may be admitted to the country and that *Toll*'s prescription that states may not be prohibited from imposing additional burdens "when Congress has done nothing more than permit a class of aliens to enter the country temporarily" applies here. The state's reliance on *Toll* is misplaced. The Court there only questioned whether a state could impose additional burdens if Congress only permitted aliens to enter temporarily. It did not hold that states were definitively allowed to impose such burdens. In this case, Congress *has* done more than merely allow the nonimmigrants to enter temporarily. It has granted them permission to work in certain occupations. That alone takes this case out of *Toll*'s potential exception.

Id. at 80–81. Though the court addressed preemption, its decision was on equal protection grounds only, because the federal law implementing NAFTA allowed only the federal government to bring actions against state laws inconsistent with NAFTA.

Is *LeClerc* or *Dandamudi* the more persuasive application of the equal protection analysis in *Graham*? In *Toll*, what would the U.S. Supreme Court have done if it had reached the equal protection issue? Which decision, *LeClerc* or *Dandamudi*, is the more persuasive application of the preemption analysis in *Toll*?

2. PUBLIC BENEFITS, IMMIGRATION, AND CITIZENSHIP

What basic principles—constitutional law and policy considerations—should guide legislators as they decide when noncitizens are eligible for public benefits? To explore these questions, we turn now to the rules for federal eligibility.

a. The 1996 Welfare Reform Act

Before 1996, the major federally-funded public benefits programs were open to citizens, lawful permanent residents, and noncitizens who were "otherwise permanently residing in the United States under color of law" (PRUCOL). This eligibility group generally excluded unauthorized migrants, but even the unauthorized were considered PRUCOL for most programs if they were in the United States "with the knowledge and permission of the Immigration and Naturalization Service and the agency does not contemplate enforcing [their] departure." *See, e.g.,* 20 C.F.R. § 416.1618 (Supplemental Security Income [SSI]).

In 1996, Congress enacted major welfare reform legislation, the Personal Responsibility and Work Opportunity Reconciliation Act, Pub. L. 104–193, 110 Stat. 2105 ("the Welfare Act" or PRWORA). It generally limited all welfare recipients to five years of benefits and required them to work within two years of receiving aid. Abandoning the PRUCOL language, the Welfare Act barred undocumented noncitizens from nonemergency assistance programs. In contrast, some "qualified aliens," as defined in the Act, could receive assistance, but subject to significant restrictions, as explained in *City of Chicago v. Shalala,* 189 F.3d 598 (7th Cir. 1999), *cert. denied,* 529 U.S. 1036, 120 S.Ct. 1530, 146 L.Ed.2d 345 (2000):

> * * * subject to certain exceptions, "qualified alien[s]" are not eligible to receive SSI or Food Stamp benefits. * * * [Q]ualified

aliens include permanent resident aliens, asylees, refugees, aliens who are paroled into the United States, aliens whose deportation is being withheld, aliens who have been granted conditional entry, certain Cuban and Haitian entrants, and certain "battered" aliens.

Id. at 600–01. Besides SSI and food stamps, the Welfare Act also barred anyone who became a "qualified alien" on or after August 22, 1996, from Medicaid and any other "federal means-tested public benefits" for five years. *See* § 403, 8 U.S.C.A. § 1613.

These bars did not apply to permanent residents who had worked for 40 quarters, some recipients who were 65 or older, under 18, or blind and disabled, certain refugees, asylees, noncitizens granted withholding of removal, veterans and active duty military personnel and their families, and some other exempt groups. Nor did the bars apply to some programs, including emergency Medicaid, child nutrition programs, Head Start, and community programs that provide in-kind assistance (domestic violence protection services, homeless shelters, food banks, and the like). *See* § 403(c)(2), 8 U.S.C.A. § 1613(c)(2).

After the five-year bar expires, immigrants with financial sponsors generally stay ineligible for public assistance due to provisions that "deem"—that is, assume—a sponsor's income to be the immigrant's income for deciding eligibility. Deeming (also discussed in Chapter Seven, p. 577–579) generally continues until the noncitizen naturalizes or has worked 40 quarters without receiving federal means-tested benefits. *See* § 421, 8 U.S.C.A. § 1631.

The constitutionality of these benefits cutoffs was challenged in several cases. All upheld the statute. In *City of Chicago*, for example, the individual plaintiffs were lawful immigrants who were receiving or were eligible to receive federal SSI and food stamps in August 1996. Their co-plaintiff, the city of Chicago, claimed that the cutoffs imposed substantial financial burdens on it. Rejecting plaintiffs' argument that it was unconstitutional to take federal benefits away from lawful immigrants who had been eligible, the court first found that the controlling precedent was *Mathews v. Diaz*, not *Graham v. Richardson*:

> [I]n *Mathews v. Diaz*, the Court made clear that the standard of scrutiny applied to state legislation in *Richardson* does not govern judicial review of federal legislation involving alienage. * * * Although the Court did not adopt explicitly the "rational basis" standard of scrutiny, it in effect applied rational basis review, upholding the legislation because it was not "wholly irrational." The Court explicitly distinguished the *Richardson* case and explained that state and federal alienage classifications must be treated differently because of Congress'

plenary authority to regulate the conditions of entry and residence of aliens. In short, we believe that the *Diaz* case is directly on point on the issue of what level of scrutiny should be applied to Congressional regulation of aliens' welfare benefits.

Id. at 603–04. The court upheld the statute as having a rational basis:

* * * First, Congress stated that the Act's provisions are intended to foster the legitimate governmental purpose of encouraging aliens' self-sufficiency. * * *

* * * In Congress' view, such aliens ought to rely on their families, sponsors, or private organizations for support, rather than on the public welfare rolls. The statute is reasonably related to that goal. Indeed, even if some aliens have no access to support from these alternate sources, the citizenship requirement is still rationally related to the goal of encouraging aliens to rely on private, not public, resources to meet their needs.

Congress has stated its policy that "the availability of public benefits not constitute an incentive for immigration to the United States." 8 U.S.C. § 1601(2)(B). Although reasonable individuals certainly can disagree on the wisdom of controlling immigration through such a policy, we must conclude that the provisions of the Welfare Reform Act are rationally related to the legitimate governmental goal of discouraging immigration that is motivated by the availability of welfare benefits. * * *

Section 1612 also declares that Congress wanted to preserve the public fisc by reducing the rising costs of operating federal benefits programs. * * * [W]e cannot say that it was irrational for Congress to decide to achieve its budget objectives by eliminating aliens from these programs. * * *

The Executive Branch, defending the constitutionality of the statute before this court, offers a further justification not found in Congress' statement of policy. It submits that the Act's provisions are rationally related to the legitimate governmental purpose of encouraging naturalization. The Act gives resident aliens in need of welfare benefits a strong economic incentive to become naturalized citizens. * * * This court and other courts of appeals have recognized the legitimacy of this governmental interest in encouraging naturalization. The Supreme Court assumed in *Hampton v. Mow Sun Wong*, 426 U.S. 88, 96 S.Ct. 1895, 48 L.Ed.2d 495 (1976), that the "national interest in providing an incentive for aliens to become naturalized" would justify a citizenship requirement for federal civil service employment. *Id.* at 105. We cannot say, therefore, that it would be irrational for Congress to conclude that restricting the availability of welfare benefits to aliens would provide incentive for aliens to seek naturalization. As we have already mentioned, rational basis scrutiny does not require a perfect fit between this legitimate governmental purpose and the means chosen to achieve it.

The plaintiffs submit finally that the Act fails rational basis review because it was motivated by impermissible animus toward noncitizens. We disagree. As the Supreme Court made clear in *Diaz*, "it is obvious that Congress has no constitutional duty to provide all aliens with the welfare benefits provided to citizens." *Diaz*, 426 U.S. at 82, 96 S.Ct. 1883. * * *

Finally, we note that the Welfare Reform Act also contains a number of exceptions to its general exclusion of aliens from the welfare programs. Like the situation that confronted the Supreme Court in *Diaz*, therefore, we have a statutory scheme that, strictly speaking, distinguishes not between citizens and aliens but rather among subclasses within the alien population. * * *

Id. at 606–08. For similar reasoning, see *Aleman v. Glickman*, 217 F.3d 1191, 1197–1202 (9th Cir. 2000); *Rodriguez v. United States*, 169 F.3d 1342, 1346–53 (11th Cir. 1999).

Since 1996, Congress has modified the original bars several times. *See* Pub. L. 105–33, 111 Stat. 251 (1997); Pub. L. 105–185, 112 Stat. 523 (1998); Pub. L. 105–306, 112 Stat. 2926 (1998). In 2002, Congress restored food stamps to (1) new permanent residents, refugees, asylees, and certain battered spouses and children after they have resided in the United States for five years; (2) all "qualified alien" children regardless of arrival date; and (3) noncitizens lawfully residing in the United States and receiving benefits under specified disability-based programs. *See* § 4401, Pub. L. 107–171, 116 Stat. 134. These changes have combined to restore SSI to virtually all noncitizens receiving benefits on August 22, 1996, and restored food stamps to most noncitizens receiving benefits on that date and to future permanent residents after five years. Undocumented noncitizens remain ineligible for both SSI and food stamps.

b. Health Care Programs

Noncitizen eligibility rules for government health care programs resemble the rules for other public benefits, but a few key differences have emerged in two major federal programs. The first, the Children's Health Insurance Program (CHIP), covers children in families with incomes that are relatively low but too high to be eligible for Medicaid.

When Congress first established CHIP in 1997, eligibility for noncitizens lawfully in the United States required essentially the same five-year waiting period as Medicaid. In 2009, Congress changed the eligibility rules to allow states to eliminate the five-year waiting period. About half of the states did so. As a result, some noncitizen children who are ineligible for Medicaid are eligible for CHIP as long as they are "lawfully residing in the United States."

In 2010, the Patient Protection and Affordable Care Act (ACA), Pub. L. 111–148, 124 Stat. 119 (2010), also affected noncitizen eligibility for federally funded health care programs. One part of the ACA expanded Medicaid by allowing eligibility for persons with incomes up to 138% of the federal poverty line. The U.S. Supreme Court ruled in 2012 that state participation in Medicaid expansion, though drafted to be mandatory, must be optional. *See National Fed'n of Independent Business v. Sebelius*, 132 S.Ct. 2566, 2633–40, 183 L.Ed.3d 450 (2012). As of spring 2016, 32 states and the District of Columbia have expanded Medicaid in some way. The rest of the states apply their own lower, pre-ACA income limit for eligibility.

The ACA did not change the Medicaid eligibility rules based on immigration and citizenship. Now, as before, "qualified aliens" (lawful permanent residents and several categories of noncitizens, such as refugees, asylees, trafficking victims, and military veterans and their spouses and unmarried dependent children) are eligible for Medicaid only after a five-year waiting period. But the ACA had several major effects on noncitizen eligibility for Medicaid in states that have chosen to expand Medicaid. One was to extend coverage to noncitizens who have the required five years and qualify under the raised Medicaid income limit. In addition, the ACA expanded Medicaid eligibility to include adults, including noncitizens, who do not have dependent children.

The ACA also set up exchanges, now called "marketplaces," for the purchase of health insurance, with federal subsidies depending on income. With exceptions, a noncitizen, if expected to be "lawfully present" for the period of insurance enrollment, is subject to the ACA's "individual mandate" to have health insurance. Noncitizens qualify for subsidized insurance if they meet income guidelines, even if they do not satisfy the five-year waiting period for Medicaid eligibility. As a result, the ACA covers more noncitizens than Medicaid or the CHIP program do. One exception is that recipients of Deferred Action for Childhood Arrivals (DACA), see Chapter 7 at pp. 777–781, are excluded from ACA marketplaces, the insurance subsidies, and the individual mandate. The same exclusions apply to unauthorized migrants. In contrast, noncitizens with other forms of deferred action are covered by the ACA. *See generally* Maggie Morgan, *Healthy Regardless of Status: Expanding Access to Health Care for Noncitizens*, 15–02 Immigr. Briefings (2015).

c. The Significance of Citizenship

As a way of evaluating federal welfare eligibility, and more generally as a way of thinking about distinctions that lawmakers might draw between citizens and noncitizens, first consider this argument for including permanent residents within the circle of membership:

> [I]t is never explained why *citizenship* is the appropriate category for the development of a communitarian ethos. Why wouldn't we seek the formation of a sense of reciprocal obligations among all persons living and working within the territory of the United States? We know, as an empirical matter, that strong bonds between citizens and resident aliens exist. These ties, based on familial relationship, ethnicity, religion, race, or location may be far more powerful than those that can be fostered among citizens who share nothing but American nationality.

T. Alexander Aleinikoff, *Citizens, Aliens, Membership and the Constitution*, 7 Const. Comm. 9, 30–31 (1990). *See also* Stephen H. Legomsky, *Immigration, Federalism, and the Welfare State*, 42 UCLA L. Rev. 1453, 1462–68 (1995). *Cf.* Michael Scaperlanda, *Who is My Neighbor?: An Essay on Immigrants, Welfare Reform, and the Constitution*, 29 Conn. L. Rev. 1587, 1599 (1997) (arguing that discrimination against permanent residents "violates a Judeo-Christian and specifically Catholic Christian perspective of our constitutional heritage").

(i) A Comparative Side-Glance: The European Union

As an example of deemphasizing citizenship, the European Union adopted a Council Directive in 2003 that addressed "the status of third-country nationals who are long-term residents." ("Third-country" nationals means nationals of a country other than the host country or another EU country.) The Directive, which entered into force on February 12, 2004, provides:

Article 11: Equal treatment

1. Long-term residents shall enjoy equal treatment with nationals as regards:

(a) access to employment and self-employed activity, provided such activities do not entail even occasional involvement in the exercise of public authority, and conditions of employment and working conditions, including conditions regarding dismissal and remuneration;

(b) education and vocational training, including study grants in accordance with national law;

(c) recognition of professional diplomas, certificates and other qualifications, in accordance with the relevant national procedures;

(d) social security, social assistance and social protection as defined by national law;

(e) tax benefits;

(f) access to goods and services and the supply of goods and services made available to the public and to procedures for obtaining housing;

(g) freedom of association and affiliation and membership of an organisation representing workers or employers or of any organisation whose members are engaged in a specific occupation, including the benefits conferred by such organisations, without prejudice to the national provisions on public policy and public security;

(h) free access to the entire territory of the Member State concerned, within the limits provided for by the national legislation for reasons of security.

2.   With respect to the provisions of paragraph 1, points (b), (d), (e), (f) and (g), the Member State concerned may restrict equal treatment to cases where the registered or usual place of residence of the long-term resident, or that of family members for whom he/she claims benefits, lies within the territory of the Member State concerned.

3.   Member States may restrict equal treatment with nationals in the following cases:

(a) Member States may retain restrictions to access to employment or self-employed activities in cases where, in accordance with existing national or Community legislation, these activities are reserved to nationals, EU or EEA citizens;

(b) Member States may require proof of appropriate language proficiency for access to education and training. Access to university may be subject to the fulfilment of specific educational prerequisites.

4.   Member States may limit equal treatment in respect of social assistance and social protection to core benefits.

Member States may also decide to grant equal treatment with regard to areas not covered in paragraph 1.

Council Directive 2003/109/EC of 25 November 2003 concerning the status of third-country nationals who are long-term residents, Official Journal L 016, 23/01/2004 P. 0044–0053.

The official commentary to the Proposal that led to this Directive set out this basic rationale for equal treatment of long-term residents:

> [I]t is . . . essential to create a welcoming society and to recognise that integration is a two-way process involving adaptation on the part of both the immigrant and of the host society. The European Union is by its very nature a pluralistic society enriched by a variety of cultural and social traditions, which will in the future become even more diverse. There must, therefore be respect for cultural and social differences but also of our fundamental shared principles and values: respect for human rights and human dignity, appreciation of the value of pluralism and the recognition that membership of society is based on a series of rights but brings with it a number of responsibilities for all of its members be they nationals or migrants. The provision of equality with respect to conditions of work and access to services, together with the granting of civic and political rights to longer-term migrant residents brings with it such responsibilities and promotes integration.

¶ 5.1, Proposal for a Council Directive concerning the status of third-country nationals who are long-term residents, Brussels, 13.3.2001 COM(2001) 127 final 2001/0074 (CNS) (quoting Communication From the Commission to the Council and the European Parliament on a Community Integration Policy, Commission of the European Communities, Brussels, 22.11.2000 COM(2000)) 757 final.

On the provisions most analogous to those at issue in *Graham*, *Diaz*, and *Shalala*, the official commentary to the Proposal explained further:

> (d) Long-term residents must have the same social protection entitlements as nationals. This would include family allowances, retirement pensions, sickness insurance and unemployment benefits.

> (e) All forms of social assistance provided by the State for its nationals must be available to long-term residents. This would include the minimum income support or retirement pensions and free health-care.

> (f) The social benefits covered here are the economic or cultural benefits given in the Member States by public authorities or private bodies * * * . They include concessionary public transport fares, reduced admission charges for cultural and other events and subsidised meals for children of low-income

families. The tax reliefs are those given by the State: long-term residents must be eligible for them on the same terms as nationals.

Proposal for a Council Directive concerning the status of third-country nationals who are long-term residents, *supra*, at 18–19.

(ii) Distinguishing Citizens from Noncitizens

How might we think about drawing lines between citizens and noncitizens? The next excerpt identifies several answers to this question in U.S. law and policy by drawing on the framework, introduced in Chapter Seven, p. 658–660, that choices in immigration and immigrant policy may reflect immigration as contract, affiliation, or transition.

HIROSHI MOTOMURA, AMERICANS IN WAITING: THE LOST STORY OF IMMIGRATION AND CITIZENSHIP IN THE UNITED STATES*
52–53, 85–87, 154–55, 199–200 (2006).

The welfare law's preamble declared: "Self-sufficiency has been a basic principle of United States immigration law since this country's earliest immigration statutes." Along the same lines, President Bill Clinton explained, "when an immigrant comes to America, . . . they have to promise that they won't try to get on welfare and they won't take any public money." The Senate report had similar words: "immigrants make a promise to the American people that they will not become a financial burden," and "It was only on the basis of the assurance of the immigrant and the sponsor that the immigrant would not at any time become a public charge that the immigrant was allowed in this country." And in the debate over the immigration law changes in 1996, proponents of binding [sponsor] affidavits made a contract-based argument that they were needed to enforce each immigrant's promise of financial self-sufficiency.

But the debates about welfare eligibility and affidavits also made clear that contract-based arguments do not always disfavor noncitizens. It all depends on the terms of the contract. * * * [I]mmigration as contract can also be cited *against* the welfare bars and the affidavit requirement. * * * When supporters of the welfare bars and affidavit invoked contract-based arguments, opponents countered that *taking away* public benefits was the real breach of promise. Congress was changing the rules of the game, disappointing the settled expectations of lawful immigrants who had arrived when they were eligible for the safety net. * * *

Immigration as contract also played an important role in shaping litigation that challenged the constitutionality of the 1996 welfare bars. The plaintiffs were only the lawful immigrants with the strongest constitutional claims: those already in the United States and receiving welfare in August 1996. No lawsuit raised the constitutional claims of future lawful immigrants. The plaintiffs' acquiescence in the validity of a cutoff date reflected their acquiescence in casting the controversy in contract terms.

* * *

Supporters of [the post-1996] restorations also drew on immigration as contract and the rhetoric of broken promises. Thus Senator Frank Lautenberg: "Congress pulled the rug out from under these people and eliminated their disability benefits." One newspaper editorial argued for restorations: "More and more Republicans are starting to publicly agree that the welfare reform bill goes too far in punishing poor and elderly legal immigrants who had every right to believe American promises that they would not be left homeless and hungry." Opponents of the restorations countered with their own version of promises, as in one editorial: "Noncitizens who reap welfare benefits and their sponsors are breaking their pledge to the American people—the people who granted them the privilege of coming to the U.S. . . . The government did not promise to feed and care for the struggling immigrant; the sponsor did." This, too, shows the strong influence of immigration as contract in alienage law.

* * * But immigration as affiliation played just as large a role * * * . Affiliation shaped Congress's decision first to enact the 1996 bars, then the legal challenges, and later the laws restoring eligibility for some noncitizens. Like contract, affiliation was crucial to arguments on both sides. In the original legislation, for example, noncitizen eligibility depended partly on ties; the bars never applied to noncitizens who had worked ten years in the United States without receiving federal welfare.

Affiliation next became the conceptual basis for the many court decisions that sustained the bars as constitutional. Typical is the 1999 federal appeals court decision in *City of Chicago v. Shalala*. * * *

Like the Supreme Court in *Diaz*, the appeals court in *City of Chicago* saw the issue not as a line between citizens and noncitizens, but between two groups of noncitizens. Then, to explain the constitutionality of the line that Congress had drawn, *City of Chicago* relied heavily on ties and immigration as affiliation. Congress could rationally extend benefits to noncitizens who had made "special contributions to this country," either to "reward such service or to encourage other aliens to make similar contributions in the future." Other federal court decisions that rejected similar constitutional challenges also emphasized ties to distinguish some noncitizens from others. And in Congress, many of the critics of the 1996 cutbacks made affiliation-based arguments that Congress had not recognized ties adequately. These arguments led to the restoration of many of the benefits taken away in 1996.

* * * Immigration as affiliation * * * says that new arrivals have only minimal ties but should be treated more like citizens as they build a life in the United States. Affiliation-based equality is to be earned. Permanent residence gradually resembles citizenship but does not equal it, although a few advocates of immigration as affiliation urge what amounts to automatic naturalization of longtime permanent residents. Immigration as affiliation recognizes that a group of newly arrived lawful immigrants will always be treated unlike citizens, but addresses the problem of defining equality in immigration and citizenship by letting individual lawful immigrants gradually earn near-equality through an approximation of citizenship.

* * *

In contrast, immigration as transition means treating lawful immigrants as Americans in waiting from their first day in this country. This means weakening distinctions between them and citizens. Generally, taking transition seriously means that equality is presumed and that lawful immigrants should be treated like citizens until they have been here long enough to naturalize. As a corollary, immigration as transition also allows sharper distinctions between prenaturalization lawful immigrants and other noncitizens, whether lawfully or unlawfully present.

The real difference between affiliation and transition thus lies in their end points. Affiliation works gradually toward equal citizenship but does not get all the way there. In this sense, immigration as affiliation represents a way to treat lawful immigrants well without citizenship. Though immigration as transition gives new lawful immigrants immediate near-equality with citizens, that is not transition's conceptual essence. Rather, immigration as transition recognizes that even the best treatment of lawful immigrants is always something less than citizenship, and instead tries to give them the best chance to reach complete equality in the future through the acquisition of citizenship itself.

This basic difference between affiliation and transition flips the relevance of time. Affiliation gives a lawful immigrant nothing on arrival, but gradually confers a favored status that approaches but never equals citizenship. Transition protects them during an earlier period—when they are Americans in waiting—that starts with arrival and ends with eligibility to naturalize.

* * *

[A]ffiliation-based benefits and protections for longtime lawful immigrants reduce naturalization incentives. For example, a lawful immigrant currently gains Medicare and food stamp eligibility after five years, but at that point he has satisfied the naturalization residency requirement. A law that denies him Medicare and food stamp eligibility even after five years would give him a tangible incentive to naturalize. But if he can get the same benefits without naturalizing, he may decide not to. Immigration as transition produces a very different incentive pattern, because its logic confines near-equal treatment of citizens and lawful immigrants to the prenaturalization years. Once a lawful immigrant does not naturalize, he can no longer invoke transition-based rationales for treatment as an American in waiting. The prospect of losing near-equal treatment can create significant naturalization incentives.

If transition were the *only* rationale for protecting lawful immigrants, then those who do not naturalize would suffer a precipitous drop in protection. This threat might be enough to turn incentives into coercion. But transition is not the only rationale for protecting lawful immigrants, as long as immigration as affiliation and immigration as contract offer complementary protections for non-naturalizing permanent residents. * * *

NOTES AND QUESTIONS ON
THE SIGNIFICANCE OF CITIZENSHIP

1. Would the EU Directive make sense as a set of guidelines for treatment of permanent residents in the United States? Why or why not?

2. As a distinct alternative to what Motomura calls "immigration as affiliation," Linda Bosniak has analyzed what she calls "ethical territoriality": that regardless of acquired ties or stake, the mere fact of a person's territorial presence should serve as the basis for rights and recognition. This perspective would support significant claims by a broader group of unauthorized migrants. *See* Linda Bosniak, *Being Here: Ethical Territoriality and the Rights of Immigrants*, 8 Theoretical Inquiries L. 389 (2007).

3. Does the option to naturalize make the 1996 welfare bars more justifiable? What about those who cannot naturalize, because they cannot afford the application fees, or because they cannot pass the English-language and civics test? More fundamentally, does it trouble you that access to welfare benefits—not deeper attachments to the United States—is the primary motivation for many permanent residents to naturalize?

If this troubles you, then should you reject a greater role for immigration as transition—*i.e.*, for aiding integration by treating permanent residents like citizens until they can naturalize? After all, such policies would give them incentives to naturalize, but those incentives arguably dilute the meaning of citizenship. Or do such policies give meaning to citizenship by making it worthwhile to become a citizen?

3. LIMITS ON FEDERAL ALIENAGE LAWS

After *Mathews v. Diaz* and the 1996 Welfare Act cases, when (if ever) is a federal alienage classification unconstitutional? For one answer, see the next case. It was decided the same day as *Diaz*, with Justice Stevens writing for the Court in both cases.

HAMPTON V. MOW SUN WONG
Supreme Court of the United States, 1976.
426 U.S. 88, 96 S.Ct. 1895, 48 L.Ed.2d 495.

MR. JUSTICE STEVENS delivered the opinion of the Court.

Five aliens, lawfully and permanently residing in the United States, brought this litigation to challenge the validity of a policy, adopted and enforced by the Civil Service Commission and certain other federal agencies, which excludes all persons except American citizens and natives of American Samoa from employment in most positions subject to their respective jurisdictions. * * *

Each of the five plaintiffs was denied federal employment solely because of his or her alienage. They were all Chinese residents of San Francisco and each was qualified for an available job. * * *

* * * In their brief, the petitioners rephrased the question presented as "(w)hether the Civil Service Commission's regulation . . . is within the constitutional powers of Congress and the President and hence not a constitutionally forbidden discrimination against aliens."

This phrasing of the question assumes that the Commission regulation is one that was mandated by the Congress, the President, or both. On this assumption, the petitioners advance alternative arguments to justify the discrimination as an exercise of the plenary federal power over immigration and naturalization. First, the petitioners argue that the equal protection aspect of the Due Process Clause of the Fifth Amendment is wholly inapplicable to the exercise of federal power over aliens, and therefore no justification for the rule is necessary. Alternatively, the petitioners argue that the Fifth Amendment imposes only a slight burden of justification on the Federal Government, and that such a burden is easily met by several factors not considered by the District Court or the Court of Appeals. Before addressing these arguments, we first discuss certain limitations which the Due Process Clause places on the power of the Federal Government to classify persons subject to its jurisdiction.

The federal sovereign, like the States, must govern impartially. The concept of equal justice under law is served by the Fifth Amendment's guarantee of due process, as well as by the Equal Protection Clause of the Fourteenth Amendment. Although both Amendments require the same type of analysis, the Court of Appeals correctly stated that the two protections are not always coextensive. Not only does the language of the two Amendments differ, but more importantly, there may be overriding national interests which justify selective federal legislation that would be unacceptable for an individual State. On the other hand, when a federal rule is applicable to only a limited territory, such as the District of Columbia, or an insular possession, and when there is no special national interest involved, the Due Process Clause has been construed as having the same significance as the Equal Protection Clause.

* * *

We do not agree * * * with the petitioners' primary submission that the federal power over aliens is so plenary that any agent of the National Government may arbitrarily subject all resident aliens to different substantive rules from those applied to citizens. We recognize that the petitioners' argument draws support from both the federal and the political character of the power over immigration and naturalization. Nevertheless, countervailing considerations require rejection of the extreme position advanced by the petitioners.

The rule enforced by the Commission has its impact on an identifiable class of persons who, entirely apart from the rule itself, are already subject to disadvantages not shared by the remainder of the community.[22] Aliens are not entitled to vote and, as alleged in the complaint, are often handicapped by a lack of familiarity with our language and customs. The added disadvantage resulting from the enforcement of the rule—ineligibility for employment in a major sector of the economy—is of sufficient significance to be characterized as a deprivation of an interest in liberty. Indeed, we deal with a rule which deprives a discrete class of persons of an interest in liberty on a wholesale basis. By reason of the Fifth Amendment, such a deprivation must be accompanied by due process. It follows that some judicial scrutiny of the deprivation is mandated by the Constitution.

Respondents argue that this scrutiny requires invalidation of the Commission rule under traditional equal protection analysis. It is true that our cases establish that the Due Process Clause of the Fifth

---

[22] Some of these disadvantages stem directly from the Constitution itself, see *Sugarman v. Dougall*, 413 U.S., at 651–653, 93 S.Ct., at 2862–2863, 37 L.Ed.2d, at 865–866 (Rehnquist, J., dissenting). The legitimacy of the delineation of the affected class buttresses the conclusion that it is "a 'discrete and insular' minority," see *In re Griffiths*, 413 U.S., at 721, 93 S.Ct., at 2854, 37 L.Ed.2d, at 915 and, of course is consistent with the premise that the class is one whose members suffer special disabilities.

Amendment authorizes that type of analysis of federal rules and therefore that the Clause has a substantive as well as a procedural aspect. However, it is not necessary to resolve respondents' substantive claim, if a narrower inquiry discloses that essential procedures have not been followed.

When the Federal Government asserts an overriding national interest as justification for a discriminatory rule which would violate the Equal Protection Clause if adopted by a State, due process requires that there be a legitimate basis for presuming that the rule was actually intended to serve that interest. If the agency which promulgates the rule has direct responsibility for fostering or protecting that interest, it may reasonably be presumed that the asserted interest was the actual predicate for the rule. That presumption would, of course, be fortified by an appropriate statement of reasons identifying the relevant interest. Alternatively, if the rule were expressly mandated by the Congress or the President, we might presume that any interest which might rationally be served by the rule did in fact give rise to its adoption.

In this case the petitioners have identified several interests which the Congress or the President might deem sufficient to justify the exclusion of noncitizens from the federal service. They argue, for example, that the broad exclusion may facilitate the President's negotiation of treaties with foreign powers by enabling him to offer employment opportunities to citizens of a given foreign country in exchange for reciprocal concessions—an offer he could not make if those aliens were already eligible for federal jobs. Alternatively, the petitioners argue that reserving the federal service for citizens provides an appropriate incentive to aliens to qualify for naturalization and thereby to participate more effectively in our society. They also point out that the citizenship requirement has been imposed in the United States with substantial consistency for over 100 years and accords with international law and the practice of most foreign countries. Finally, they correctly state that the need for undivided loyalty in certain sensitive positions clearly justifies a citizenship requirement in at least some parts of the federal service, and that the broad exclusion serves the valid administrative purpose of avoiding the trouble and expense of classifying those positions which properly belong in executive or sensitive categories.

The difficulty with all of these arguments except the last is that they do not identify any interest which can reasonably be assumed to have influenced the Civil Service Commission, the Postal Service, the General Service Administration, or the Department of Health, Education, and Welfare in the administration of their respective responsibilities or, specifically, in the decision to deny employment to the respondents in this litigation. We may assume with the petitioners that if the Congress or the President had expressly imposed the citizenship requirement, it would be justified by the national interest in providing an incentive for aliens to become naturalized, or possibly even as providing the President with an expendable token for treaty negotiating purposes; but we are not willing to presume that the Chairman of the Civil Service Commission, or any of the other original defendants, was deliberately fostering an interest so far removed from his normal responsibilities. * * *

It is the business of the Civil Service Commission to adopt and enforce regulations which will best promote the efficiency of the federal civil service. That agency has no responsibility for foreign affairs, for treaty negotiations, for establishing immigration quotas or conditions of entry, or for naturalization policies. Indeed, it is not even within the responsibility of the Commission to be concerned with the economic consequences of permitting or prohibiting the participation by aliens in employment opportunities in different parts of the national market. On the contrary, the Commission performs a limited and specific function.

The only concern of the Civil Service Commission is the promotion of an efficient federal service. In general it is fair to assume that its goal would be best served by removing unnecessary restrictions on the eligibility of qualified applicants for employment. With only one exception, the interests which the petitioners have put forth as supporting the Commission regulation at issue in this case are not matters which are properly the business of the Commission. That one exception is the administrative desirability of having one simple rule excluding all noncitizens when it is manifest that citizenship is an appropriate and legitimate requirement for some important and sensitive positions. Arguably, therefore, administrative convenience may provide a rational basis for the general rule.

For several reasons that justification is unacceptable in this case. The Civil Service Commission, like other administrative agencies, has an obligation to perform its responsibilities with some degree of expertise, and to make known the reasons for its important decisions. There is nothing in the record before us, or in matter of which we may properly take judicial notice, to indicate that the Commission actually made any considered evaluation of the relative desirability of a simple exclusionary rule on the one hand, or the value to the service of enlarging the pool of eligible employees on the other. Nor can we reasonably infer that the administrative burden of establishing the job classifications for which citizenship is an appropriate requirement would be a particularly onerous task for an expert in personnel matters; indeed, the Postal Service apparently encountered no particular difficulty in making such a classification. Of greater significance, however, is the quality of the interest at stake. Any fair balancing of the public interest in avoiding the wholesale deprivation of employment opportunities caused by the Commission's indiscriminate policy, as opposed to what may be nothing more than a hypothetical justification, requires rejection of the argument of administrative convenience in this case.

In sum, assuming without deciding that the national interests identified by the petitioners would adequately support an explicit determination by Congress or the President to exclude all noncitizens from the federal service, we conclude that those interests cannot provide an acceptable rationalization for such a determination by the Civil Service Commission. * * * By broadly denying this class substantial opportunities for employment, the Civil Service Commission rule deprives its members of an aspect of liberty. Since these residents were admitted as a result of decisions made by the Congress and the President, implemented by the Immigration and Naturalization Service acting under the Attorney General of the United States, due process requires that the decision to impose that deprivation of an important liberty be made either at a comparable level of government or, if it is to be permitted to be made by the Civil Service Commission, that it be justified by reasons which are properly the concern of that agency. We hold that § 338.101(a) of the Civil Service Commission Regulations has deprived these respondents of liberty without due process of law and is therefore invalid.

* * *

MR. JUSTICE BRENNAN, with whom MR. JUSTICE MARSHALL joins, concurring.

I join the Court's opinion with the understanding that there are reserved the equal protection questions that would be raised by congressional or Presidential enactment of a bar on employment of aliens by the Federal Government.

MR. JUSTICE REHNQUIST, with whom THE CHIEF JUSTICE, MR. JUSTICE WHITE, and MR. JUSTICE BLACKMUN join, dissenting.

* * *

[The majority's] holding overlooks the basic principle that a decision to exclude aliens from the civil service is a political decision reserved to Congress, the wisdom of which may not be challenged in the courts. Once it is determined that the agency in question was properly delegated the power by Congress to make decisions regarding citizenship of prospective civil servants, then the reasons for which that power was exercised are as foreclosed from judicial scrutiny as if Congress had made the decision itself. The fact that Congress has delegated a power does not provide a back door through which to attack a policy which would otherwise have been immune from attack.

For this Court to hold that the agency chosen by Congress, through the President, to effectuate its policies, has "no responsibility" in that area is to interfere in an area in which the Court itself clearly has "no responsibility": the organization of the Executive Branch. Congress, through the President, obviously gave responsibility in this area to the Civil Service Commission. The wisdom of that delegation is not for us to evaluate. * * *

* * *

The Rest of the Story

Soon after the Supreme Court decided *Mow Sun Wong*, President Ford issued Executive Order No. 11935, which limited federal civil service positions to U.S. citizens and nationals. Lower courts upheld the Order. *See, e.g., Mow Sun Wong v. Campbell*, 626 F.2d 739, 744–45 (9th Cir. 1980), *cert. denied*, 450 U.S. 959, 101 S.Ct. 1419, 67 L.Ed.2d 384 (1981).

Documents in the Gerald R. Ford Library provide a fascinating glimpse into the process by which the Civil Service Commission's order, once invalidated by the Supreme Court, reemerged as an Executive Order. Of particular interest is a memorandum from the General Counsel of the Office of Management and Budget to the White House when the matter came before President Ford. This excerpt briefly discusses comments from various federal agencies:

[The Civil Service Commission (CSC)] suggested various reasons related to the national interest which might serve as justification for the issuance of [the] order. Agency comments, although generally favoring or having no objection to such an order, indicate that CSC's suggested justifications (*e.g.,* need for undivided loyalty; consistency with the practices of foreign states) are more apparent than real. Further, the Postal Service advises that its recent practice of employing aliens in nonsensitive and nonpolicy-making positions has not presented any policy difficulties. Nevertheless, there is a widespread visceral feeling that Government jobs should be reserved for citizens, at least where there are qualified citizen applicants.

The Department of Justice is of the opinion that the Congress, pursuant to its constitutional authority over immigration, has the authority to broadly prohibit aliens from employment in the competitive civil service. Although the Supreme Court left open the question whether the President could exclude aliens from the competitive service, there are Presidential concerns (*e.g.,* foreign policy) which would lend some support to [a] Presidential order barring aliens from government employment. The Department of Justice concludes, based on the *Wong* decision, that an Executive order barring aliens would probably be upheld by a divided Supreme Court.

Memorandum from William N. Nichols, General Counsel, Office of Management and Budget, to Robert D. Linden, White House Chief Executive Clerk, Aug. 30, 1976 (on file, Gerald R. Ford Library, Ann Arbor, Michigan).

What does this memorandum tell you about the value of the Court's apparent insistence that an institutionally competent unit of the federal government articulate any federal interests offered in support of an alienage classification?

EXERCISE: FARM LOANS

A federal statute reads as follows:

> The Secretary [of Agriculture] is authorized to make and insure loans under this subchapter to farmers and ranchers in the United States, and to farm cooperatives and private domestic corporations, partnerships, joint operations, trusts, and limited liability companies that are controlled by farmers and ranchers and engaged primarily and directly in farming or ranching in the United States, subject to the conditions specified in this section. To be eligible for such loans, applicants who are individuals, or, in the case of cooperatives, corporations, partnerships, joint operations, trusts, and limited liability companies, individuals holding a majority interest such entity, must be citizens of the United States.

Antonio Lopez has been a lawful permanent resident of the United States since 1968, but he has never applied for naturalization. His application for a farm operating loan under this statute has been denied because he is not a U.S. citizen. What policy arguments can you muster to persuade your Congressional delegation that this citizenship requirement is not sound policy? How might you argue that this statute is unconstitutional? What are the best counter-arguments at both policy and constitutional levels?

---

4. BLURRING THE FEDERAL-STATE LINE

For lawfully present noncitizens, the 1996 Welfare Act gave states new authority to decide eligibility for jointly funded federal-state programs (*e.g.*, TANF, non-emergency Medicaid), and for state-funded public benefits. *See* § 412, 8 U.S.C.A. § 1622. In fact, more than half of the states provide benefits to at least some noncitizens who are ineligible for federal services. *See* Tanya Broder & Jonathan Blazer, Overview of Immigrant Eligibility for Federal Programs, 1 (Nat'l Immigr. L. Ctr. 2011). The result has been a shift in costs from the federal government to the states and localities. (For unauthorized migrants, the Act allowed states and localities to grant certain public benefits, but this generally requires them to enact new state legislation to that effect. *See* § 411, 8 U.S.C.A. § 1621.)

The grant of authority by the federal government to the states to draw lines for benefits eligibility raises several questions. Assuming the federal government has much more power than the states to treat citizens and noncitizens differently, could it delegate all or part of this power to the states? Relatedly, what does this statement near the end of *Graham* mean: "Congress does not have the power to authorize the individual States to violate the Equal Protection Clause"? The next two decisions suggest that the answer may depend on how a state program is structured in relation to an analogous federal program.

ALIESSA V. NOVELLO

New York Court of Appeals, 2001.
96 N.Y.2d 418, 754 N.E.2d 1085, 730 N.Y.S.2d 1.

ROSENBLATT, J.

* * *

Plaintiffs are 12 aliens who lawfully reside in New York State. They immigrated to the United States from various countries, including Bangladesh, Belorussia, Ecuador, Greece, Guyana, Haiti, Italy, Malaysia, the Philippines, Syria and Turkey. As legal aliens, they fall into two groups. Some are lawfully admitted permanent residents of the United States under the Immigration and Nationality Act (i.e., green card holders) the rest are permanently residing in the United States under color of law (PRUCOLs). All suffer from potentially life-threatening illnesses and, but for the exclusion under Social Services Law § 122, would allegedly qualify for Medicaid benefits funded solely by the State.

* * *

The Legislature established New York's Medicaid system in 1966, the year after Congress created the federally funded Medicaid program. Under this complex scheme, the Federal government and States share the cost of providing Medicaid to certain categories of needy individuals. The shared program provides benefits to the disabled, the blind, the elderly, children, pregnant women, single-parent families and parents of children where there is a deprivation factor in the household. To remain eligible for Federal matching funds, New York must conform its Medicaid program to evolving Federal standards.

If a State wants to extend Medicaid benefits to others, it is free to proceed at its own expense. New York has done so. It has provided non-federally subsidized Medicaid benefits to certain categories of individuals, including residents between the ages of 21 and 65 whose income and resources fall below a statutory "standard of need" and who are not otherwise entitled to federally subsidized Medicaid. Thus, New York State's Medicaid system has two components: one that is federally subsidized and one that the State funds entirely on its own.

New York had long provided State Medicaid to needy recipients without distinguishing between legal aliens and citizens. It ceased to do so, however, after Congress enacted the Personal Responsibility and Work Opportunity Reconciliation Act of 1996 (PRWORA). Asserting that they have been unlawfully deprived of State Medicaid for which they would otherwise qualify, plaintiffs have brought this challenge.

* * *

In response to PRWORA, New York enacted Social Services Law § 122, terminating Medicaid for non-qualified aliens—including PRUCOL plaintiffs. New York did, however, maintain Medicaid for otherwise eligible PRUCOLs who, as of August 4, 1997, were receiving Medicaid and were diagnosed with AIDS or residing in certain licensed residential health care facilities.

As for qualified aliens, section 122 provides Medicaid to all otherwise eligible qualified aliens who entered the United States before August 22, 1996 and continuously resided in the United States until attaining qualified status. Those entering on or after August 22, 1996, however, are no longer immediately eligible for State Medicaid, but must now wait five years for coverage. This group includes the lawfully admitted permanent resident plaintiffs. Finally, all plaintiffs (both PRUCOLs and qualified aliens) may receive safety net assistance and emergency medical treatment.

* * *

The State does not attempt to justify section 122 under a strict scrutiny standard. Nor has it identified any "compelling governmental interest" that section 122 promotes. Instead, the State argues that strict scrutiny does not apply here. It contends that section 122 implements [the 1996 Welfare Act's] Federal immigration policy and should therefore be evaluated under the less stringent "rational basis" standard. * * *

* * *

When allocating Federal welfare benefits, the Constitution does not prohibit Congress from distinguishing between aliens and citizens. In *Mathews v. Diaz,* a group of aliens challenged a Federal statute that denied aliens Medicare eligibility unless they had been admitted for permanent residence and resided in the United States for at least five years. The Court held that the "decision to share [our] bounty with our guests may take into account the character of the relationship between the alien and this country: Congress may decide that as the alien's tie grows stronger, so does the strength of his claim to an equal share of that munificence" (*id.* at 80, 96 S.Ct. 1883). * * *

Graham v. Richardson is at the center of our analysis. There, the State of Arizona administered a Federal disability program under Federal guidelines much the same as New York administers Medicaid. Arizona argued that because its 15-year residency period for aliens was impliedly authorized by Federal law, it did not violate the Fourteenth Amendment. The Supreme Court rejected this contention, holding that a Federal statute authorizing "discriminatory treatment of aliens *at the option of States*" would present "serious constitutional questions." The Court recognized that although the Federal government has broad constitutional power to distinguish among aliens in setting the rules for their admission and naturalization, "Congress does not have the power to authorize the individual States to violate the Equal Protection Clause." Indeed, the Court went on to state that a "congressional enactment construed so as to permit state legislatures to adopt divergent laws on the subject of citizenship requirements for federally supported welfare programs would appear to contravene this explicit constitutional requirement of uniformity."

* * * [I]n *Mathews v. Diaz,* the Court recognized that when it comes to State welfare policy, "there is little, if any, basis for treating persons who are citizens of another State differently from persons who are citizens of another country." In distinguishing between Federal and State powers, the Court held that a "division by a State of the category of persons who are not citizens of that State into subcategories of United States citizens and aliens has no apparent justification, whereas, a comparable classification by the Federal Government is a routine and normally legitimate part of its business."

Finally, in *Hampton v. Mow Sun Wong,* the Supreme Court drew limits on the power of entities other than Congress or the President to make alienage classifications in furtherance of Federal immigration policy. In addressing whether Federal agencies could make such classifications for civil service eligibility, the Court concluded that if Congress or the President had created the classification, it could be justifiable as a valid exercise of immigration authority in the national interest. When, however, it came to Federal agencies that did not deal directly with immigration, the Court was not willing to presume they would deliberately foster national immigration interests, which are "so far removed from [their] normal responsibilities." Surely this is also true of the States.

Title IV [of the 1996 Welfare Act] does not impose a *uniform* immigration rule for States to follow. Indeed, it expressly authorizes States to enact laws extending "any State or local public benefit" even to those aliens not lawfully present within the United States. The converse is also true and exacerbates the lack of uniformity: Section 1622(a) provides that, subject to certain exceptions, States are authorized to withhold State Medicaid from even those qualified aliens who are eligible for Federal Medicaid * * * . Thus, in administering their own programs, the States are free to discriminate in either direction—producing not uniformity, but potentially wide variation based on localized or idiosyncratic concepts of largesse, economics and politics. * * *

In exercising its discretion under title IV, New York has chosen to continue Medicaid coverage for any PRUCOL who, as of August 4, 1997, was receiving Medicaid and was either diagnosed with AIDS or residing in certain licensed residential health care facilities. This demonstrates that New York—along with every other State—with Congressional permission is choosing its own policy with respect to health benefits for resident, indigent legal aliens. Thus, we address this case outside the context of a Congressional command for nationwide uniformity in the scope of Medicaid coverage for indigent aliens as a matter of federal immigration policy.

We conclude that section 122 is subject to—and cannot pass—strict scrutiny, notwithstanding title IV's authorization. Because title IV authorizes each State to extend the ineligibility period for Federal Medicaid beyond the mandatory five years and terminate Federal Medicaid eligibility for certain refugees and asylees after seven years, it is directly in the teeth of *Graham* insofar as it allows the States to "adopt divergent laws on the subject of citizenship requirements for *federally* supported welfare programs." Moreover, title IV goes significantly beyond what the *Graham* Court declared constitutionally questionable. In the name of national immigration policy, it impermissibly authorizes each State to decide whether to disqualify many otherwise eligible aliens from State Medicaid. Section 122 is a product of this authorization. In light of *Graham* and its progeny, title IV can give section 122 no special insulation from strict scrutiny review. Thus, section 122 must be evaluated as any other State statute that classifies based on alienage. * * *

BRUNS V. MAYHEW
United States Court of Appeals, First Circuit, 2014.
750 F.3d 61.

HOWARD, CIRCUIT JUDGE.

After Congress passed the Personal Responsibility and Work Opportunity Reconciliation Act of 1996 ("PRWORA"), narrowing the eligibility of non-citizens for Medicaid and other federal benefits, the state of Maine responded in 1997 by extending state-funded medical assistance benefits to certain legal aliens rendered ineligible for Medicaid. In 2011, the Maine Legislature terminated these benefits. The appellants allege that this termination of their benefits violated their rights under the Equal Protection Clause of the Fourteenth Amendment, and presently appeal from the district court's denial of their motion for a preliminary injunction. * * *

* * *

* * * A state's participation in the Medicaid program is voluntary, but once a state chooses to participate it must comply with federal statutory and regulatory requirements in order to receive federal matching funds. The eligibility requirements for Medicaid coverage are governed by federal law. Under the Medicaid Act, participating states must provide full Medicaid services under the approved state plan to certain groups of individuals who meet the eligibility criteria, including "categorically needy" groups. For years, federal Medicaid extended medical assistance to eligible individuals without regard to citizenship status or durational residency. By act of Congress, however, the alien eligibility requirements for publicly-funded benefits, including Medicaid, changed dramatically in 1996.

In enacting PRWORA, Congress restricted the ability of aliens to access federal public welfare benefits, including Medicaid. PRWORA divided non-citizens into categories of "qualified" and "non-qualified" aliens, and further restricted eligibility for federal welfare benefits by imposing a five-year United States residency requirement for most qualified aliens. Although PRWORA authorized states to expand the category of qualified aliens eligible for federal benefits, it prohibited the states from extending federal benefits to most aliens residing in the United States for less than five years.

PRWORA left the states more discretion in the dispensation of *state* public benefits, authorizing the states "to determine the eligibility for any State public benefits of an alien who is a qualified alien," including qualified aliens residing less than five years in the United States. The Maine Legislature accordingly responded to PRWORA by * * * empower[ing] the state Department of Health and Human Services ("DHHS") to provide medical assistance benefits to PRWORA-ineligible aliens residing in Maine. Although these benefits were purely state-funded, this program was jointly administered with the federal-state cooperative Medicaid program for eligible citizens and qualified aliens, and both the state-funded program and the state Medicaid program became known as "MaineCare." In June 2011, however, the Maine Legislature passed * * * a budgetary measure that terminated state-funded non-emergency medical assistance benefits for PRWORA-ineligible aliens residing less than five years in the United States, essentially repealing the 1997 State Legislation. * * *

* * *

The appellants argue that the termination of their state-funded medical benefits under the 2011 Legislation represented selective alienage-based treatment by the state of Maine. In the appellants' estimation, the state's action discriminated against a suspect class and therefore warrants strict scrutiny, requiring the state to demonstrate that the alienage classification advances a compelling state interest by the least restrictive means available.

* * *

Alienage, like race and nationality, constitutes a suspect classification under the Fourteenth Amendment. *See Graham v. Richardson,* 403 U.S. 365, 372, 91 S.Ct. 1848, 29 L.Ed.2d 534 (1971) (invalidating state-imposed alienage-based classifications). Because "[a]liens as a class are a prime example of a 'discrete and insular' minority," a state's alienage-based classifications inherently raise concerns of invidious discrimination and are therefore generally subject to strict judicial scrutiny. *Id.* (quoting *United States v. Carolene Prods. Co.,* 304 U.S. 144, 152–53 n. 4, 58 S.Ct. 778, 82 L.Ed. 1234 (1938)). * * *

The calculus is markedly different for *congressional* acts distinguishing on the basis of alienage, evaluated under the Due Process Clause of the Fifth Amendment. *See Mathews v. Díaz,* 426 U.S. 67, 80–85, 96 S.Ct. 1883, 48 L.Ed.2d 478 (1976) (holding that congressional alienage-based restrictions on federal Medicare benefits did not violate due process). Unlike other suspect classifications such as race and nationality, congressional disparate treatment of aliens is presumed to rest on national immigration policy rather than invidious discrimination. Because Congress acts with plenary authority when it legislates the rights and benefits to be afforded aliens present in this country, such congressional acts are appropriately afforded rational basis judicial review. States do not share in this plenary federal power, though they obviously are impacted by its exercise. The Supreme Court has, however, stated that "if the Federal Government has by uniform rule prescribed what it believes to be appropriate standards for the treatment of an alien subclass, the States may, of course, follow the federal direction." *Plyler [v. Doe,* 457 U.S. 202,] 219 n.19, 102 S.Ct. 2382 (1982).

Because Medicaid, unlike Medicare, is not solely funded and administered by the federal government, this case does not fall neatly within the holding of *Mathews.* On the other hand, the alienage-based distinction in this case does not originate purely from state legislation, unlike the restrictions struck down in *Graham.* Instead, this case presents a Gordian knot of federal and state legislation effecting an adverse impact on resident aliens: a federal-state cooperative program (Medicaid), the eligibility for which was subsequently limited on the basis of alienage by federal legislation (PRWORA), to which the state of Maine responded by first creating, and then terminating, supplemental state-funded medical assistance benefits for PRWORA-ineligible aliens only. * * *

* * *

* * * Despite the cooperative federal-state nature of Medicaid benefits, PRWORA classifies Medicaid as a "federal program" from which many subclasses of aliens are excluded, including legal residents who have not yet resided in this country for five years. Participating states are statutorily obligated to alter Medicaid benefits available to their residents in order to remain compliant with evolving federal law. Nevertheless, in enacting PRWORA Congress authorized the states to provide purely state-funded welfare benefits to legal aliens, and in 1997, the state of Maine enacted legislation to ameliorate the effects of PRWORA for legal aliens who would have remained eligible for Medicaid benefits but for PRWORA. * * *

* * *

* * * The veneer of a single MaineCare program merely obscured the legal reality that, from 1997 to 2011, MaineCare recipients received benefits from two distinct programs: one funded jointly by the federal and state governments, with the federal government retaining ultimate authority over, *inter alia,* eligibility criteria; and the other fully funded and controlled by the state government. It was the federal government that determined the appellants' ineligibility for Medicaid benefits by enacting PRWORA, to which the state responded by extending equivalent state-funded medical assistance benefits to the appellants for a time.

* * *

Contrary to the appellants' suggestion that Maine operated a single state medical assistance program for all state residents, we therefore agree with the district court's conclusion that MaineCare comprised two separate medical assistance programs: federal-state cooperative Medicaid and a state supplemental program for PRWORA-ineligible aliens only. When it repealed the supplemental aliens-only program, the state of Maine did not deprive the appellants of a benefit that it continued to provide to citizens—or to anyone else, for that matter. * * *[2]

---

[2]   In light of this distinction between federal and state action, we find the appellants' cases unpersuasive. *Aliessa v. Novello,* 96 N.Y.2d 418, 730 N.Y.S.2d 1, 754 N.E.2d 1085 (2001), addressed a *state's* discretionary imposition of alienage-based criteria for purely state-funded

* * *

* * * The fact that *Congress* discriminated on the basis of alienage in enacting PRWORA does not also establish alienage-based discrimination by Maine merely because of its continued Medicaid participation and required compliance with PRWORA. While the federal government determines certain baseline eligibility requirements and selects particular classes of categorically needy persons who are eligible to receive Medicaid benefits, a state, by choosing to participate in Medicaid, generally adopts the grouping of federal eligibility requirements as a whole. * * * [W]e therefore conclude that if Maine can be said to have "discriminated" at all, it only did so on the basis of federal Medicaid eligibility, a benign classification subject to mere rational basis review.

Like other courts facing similar post-PRWORA equal protection claims, we therefore conclude that the state was under no constitutional obligation to "fill the gap" created by PRWORA by extending equivalent state-funded benefits to federally-ineligible aliens. Because Maine was not obligated to extend equivalent state-funded benefits to the appellants in the first place, it follows that the termination of those benefits does not violate the Equal Protection Clause.

As a last stand, the appellants rely on *Graham's* proclamation that Congress "does not have the power to authorize the individual States to violate the Equal Protection Clause." 403 U.S. at 382, 91 S.Ct. 1848. More specifically, they contend that "[t]he Commissioner cannot seek shelter for her equal protection violation in Congress's enactment of PRWORA" because PRWORA did not "create a national uniform immigration policy with respect to access to medical care," and instead left "the decision of whether to provide medical assistance for medically indigent non-citizens who have been in the country less than five years to the individual states." However, as we have explained above, the appellants' argument rests on the assumption that a state's mere participation in Medicaid, subject to PRWORA's mandatory eligibility restrictions, represents alienage-based discrimination. Because we conclude that the state drew no distinctions on the basis of alienage, *Graham's* proscription does not apply here, and we therefore need not reach the question of whether Maine acted in accordance with uniform federal policy.[3]

---

benefits, rendering the plaintiff aliens similarly situated to citizens still receiving these benefits. * * *

[3] Even assuming *arguendo* that Maine discriminated on the basis of alienage in declining to extend state-funded benefits to PRWORA-ineligible aliens, we question whether the state's action would in fact run afoul of *Graham*. We need not decide the question today, but we note that both the Ninth and Tenth Circuits have held that PRWORA represents a uniform federal policy such that a state's exercise of its discretion under 8 U.S.C. §§ 1612(b) and 1622(a) garners only rational basis review under *Plyler. See Korab [v. Fink,* 797 F.3d 572, 580–82 (9th Cir. 2014)]; *Soskin [v. Reinertson,* 353 F.3d 1242, 1255 (10th Cir. 2004)].

* * * [T]he appellants are experiencing the impact of a congressional decision—PRWORA's mandatory five-year residency requirement—restricting their eligibility for public welfare benefits, including federal-state cooperative programs such as Medicaid. As a result, there is no class of similarly situated citizens with whom the appellants can be compared vis-à-vis the state of Maine. We therefore conclude that the appellants' equal protection claim fails on the merits and that the district court properly denied the appellants' request for a preliminary injunction.

* * *

NOTES AND QUESTIONS ON DELEGATION BY THE FEDERAL GOVERNMENT

1.   Several judicial decisions adopted reasoning similar to *Bruns* in rejecting equal protection challenges to the termination of state programs limited to noncitizens. *See, e.g., Pimentel v. Dreyfus,* 670 F.3d 1096 (9th Cir. 2012); *Hong Pham v. Starkowski,* 300 Conn. 412, 16 A.3d. 635 (2011); *Khrapunskiy v. Doar,* 12 N.Y.3d 478, 909 N.E.2d 70, 881 N.Y.S.2d 377 (2009); *Soskin v. Reinertson,* 353 F.3d 1242 (10th Cir. 2004).

2.   After PRWORA limited noncitizen eligibility for federal public benefits, some states adopted programs to replace that federal aid. The history of the state-funded part of MaineCare is typical of a trend in some states after the 2008 financial crisis to curtail or eliminate such state replacement assistance programs. *See, e.g.,* Angela Delli Santi, *NJ Budget Cuts Health Care for Immigrants, Poor,* Associated Press, Apr. 15, 2010; Abby Goodnough, *Massachusetts Cuts Back Immigrants' Health Care,* N.Y. Times, Aug. 31, 2009.

3.   The New York state public benefits program struck down as violating equal protection in *Aliessa* included citizens and only some noncitizens. *Bruns* involved two public benefits programs in Maine. One had joint federal and state funding, with the federal government setting eligibility criteria. The other was a state-funded and state-administered program for which only some noncitizens were eligible. Maine eliminated the second program—without violating equal protection, said the court. Should there be a constitutional difference between these two situations?

4.   Michael Wishnie has argued that the constitutional immigration power—which he views as including both immigration law and alienage law—is exclusively federal and not devolvable by statute to the states:

The plenary power doctrine of immigration law inevitably shields governmental action from the level of judicial scrutiny that ordinarily would be applied, distorting constitutional jurisprudence and countenancing what otherwise would be invalidated as arbitrary or discriminatory government behavior. Permitting devolution would amplify this distortion, privileging the plenary power doctrine over equal protection norms at the state and local level.

Michael J. Wishnie, *Laboratories of Bigotry?: Devolution of the Immigration Power, Equal Protection, and Federalism*, 76 N.Y.U. L. Rev. 493, 553 (2001).

5.   Compare   Howard   F.   Chang,   *Public   Benefits   and   Federal Authorization for Alienage Discrimination by the States*, 58 N.Y.U Surv. Am. L. 357, 363–64 (2002):

> Rather than creating "laboratories of bigotry against immigrants," to use Wishnie's phrase, we might just as plausibly view federal authorization of divergent state policies as creating laboratories of generosity toward immigrants. If we had bound Congress with a constitutional constraint of uniformity in the political atmosphere of 1996, then Congress might have excluded immigrants from Medicaid or welfare rather than leaving the question of immigrant access up to the states.

6.   Or is it true that even if states are less generous to noncitizens, "state-level authority will allow those states harboring intense anti-alien sentiment to act on those sentiments at the state level, thus diminishing any interest on their part to seek national legislation to similarly restrictionist ends"? Peter J. Spiro, *Learning to Live With Immigration Federalism*, 29 Conn. L. Rev. 1627, 1627 (1997).

7.   Compare the delegation in the 1996 Welfare Act with express federal authorization of state and local involvement in the enforcement of federal immigration laws, discussed in Chapter Nine, pp. 1215–1227. Clare Huntington has identified these as the only two instances of express federal delegation to states of federal authority in immigration law and alienage law. *See* Clare Huntington, *The Constitutional Dimension of Immigration Federalism*, 61 Vand. L. Rev. 787 (2008). Do the Wishnie's concerns about discrimination in the alienage law context apply equally—or less or more— when the federal government delegates authority to enforce immigration laws?

B. GOVERNMENT AND POLITICS

According   to   both   tradition   and   doctrine,   some   alienage classifications are permissible in matters of government and politics. The key modern court decision is *Sugarman v. Dougall*, 413 U.S. 634, 93 S.Ct. 2842, 37 L.Ed.2d 853 (1973). In that case, the U.S. Supreme Court relied on *Graham* in striking down a New York state law that limited state competitive civil service positions to U.S. citizens. Drawing on the concept of political community and discussing the right to vote, *Sugarman* suggested that a U.S. citizenship requirement for a narrower group of state positions would pass constitutional muster:

* * * [W]e do not hold that, on the basis of an individualized determination, an alien may not be refused, or discharged from, public employment, even on the basis of noncitizenship, if the refusal to hire, or the discharge, rests on legitimate state interests that relate to qualifications for a particular position or to the characteristics of the employee. We hold only that a flat ban on the employment of aliens in positions that have little, if any relation to a State's legitimate interest, cannot withstand scrutiny under the Fourteenth Amendment.

Neither do we hold that a State may not, in an appropriately defined class of positions, require citizenship as a qualification for office. Just as "the Framers of the Constitution intended the States to keep for themselves, as provided in the Tenth Amendment, the power to regulate elections," *Oregon v. Mitchell*, 400 U.S. 112, 124–125, 91 S.Ct. 260, 263, 27 L.Ed.2d 272 (1970) (opinion of Black, J.); "(e)ach State has the power to prescribe the qualifications of its officers and the manner in which they shall be chosen." *Boyd v. Thayer*, 143 U.S. 135, 161, 12 S.Ct. 375, 382, 36 L.Ed. 103 (1892). Such power inheres in the State by virtue of its obligation, already noted above, "to preserve the basic conception of a political community." *Dunn v. Blumstein*, 405 U.S., at 344, 92 S.Ct., at 1004. And this power and responsibility of the State applies, not only to the qualifications of voters, but also to persons holding state elective or important nonelective executive, legislative, and judicial positions, for officers who participate directly in the formulation, execution, or review of broad public policy perform functions that go to the heart of representative government. There, as Judge Lumbard phrased it in his separate concurrence, is "where citizenship bears some rational relationship to the special demands of the particular position." [*Dougall v. Sugarman*, 339 F. Supp. 906, 911 (S.D.N.Y. 1971) (Lumbard, J., concurring).]

We have held, of course, that such state action, particularly with respect to voter qualifications is not wholly immune from scrutiny under the Equal Protection Clause. But our scrutiny will not be so demanding where we deal with matters resting firmly within a State's constitutional prerogatives. This is no more than a recognition of a State's historical power to exclude aliens from participation in its democratic political institutions, and a recognition of a State's constitutional responsibility for the establishment and operation of its own government, as well as the qualifications of an appropriately designated class of public office holders. This Court has never held that aliens have a constitutional right to vote or to hold high public office under the

Equal Protection Clause. Indeed, implicit in many of this Court's voting rights decisions is the notion that citizenship is a permissible criterion for limiting such rights. A restriction on the employment of noncitizens, narrowly confined, could have particular relevance to this important state responsibility, for alienage itself is a factor that reasonably could be employed in defining "political community."

413 U.S. at 646–49, 93 S.Ct. at 2849–51.

Consider how the ideas in this excerpt from *Sugarman* bear on the two topics in this Section: public employment and political participation.

1. PUBLIC EMPLOYMENT

Is it constitutional—or sound policy—to limit public employment to citizens? After *Sugarman*, the Court began to carve out an area where states may require citizenship for some state positions. For example, it upheld citizenship requirements for state troopers, *see Foley v. Connelie*, 435 U.S. 291, 297–300, 98 S.Ct. 1067, 55 L.Ed.2d 287 (1978); and public school teachers, *see Ambach v. Norwick*, 441 U.S. 68, 69–72, 99 S.Ct. 1589, 60 L.Ed.2d 49 (1979). But it struck down—as equal protection violations—citizenship requirements that kept permanent residents from becoming lawyers, *see Matter of Griffiths*, 413 U.S. 717, 718, 93 S.Ct. 2851, 37 L.Ed.2d 910 (1973); and notaries public, *see Bernal v. Fainter*, 467 U.S. 216, 219–28, 104 S.Ct. 2312, 81 L.Ed.2d 175 (1984). In the next case, a divided Court explained and applied this "political community" exception.

CABELL V. CHAVEZ-SALIDO
Supreme Court of the United States, 1982.
454 U.S. 432, 102 S.Ct. 735, 70 L.Ed.2d 677.

JUSTICE WHITE delivered the opinion of the Court.

In this case we once again consider a citizenship requirement imposed by a State on those seeking to fill certain governmental offices. California Gov't Code Ann. § 1031(a) requires "public officers or employees declared by law to be peace officers" to be citizens of the United States. California Penal Code Ann. § 830.5 provides that probation officers and deputy probation officers are "peace officers." * * *

I

Appellees were, at the time the complaint was filed, lawfully admitted permanent resident aliens living in Los Angeles County, Cal. Each applied unsuccessfully for positions as Deputy Probation Officers with the Los Angeles County Probation Department. With respect to two of the three appellees, the parties stipulated that the failure to obtain the positions sought was the result of the statutory citizenship requirement.

* * *

II

Over the years, this Court has many times considered state classifications dealing with aliens. As we have noted before, those cases "have not formed an unwavering line over the years." *Ambach v. Norwick*, [441 U.S. 68, 72, 99 S.Ct. 1589, 1592, 60 L.Ed.2d 49 (1979)]. But to say that the decisions do not fall into a neat pattern is not to say that they fall into no pattern. In fact, they illustrate a not unusual characteristic of legal development; broad principles are articulated, narrowed when applied to new contexts, and finally replaced when the distinctions they rely upon are no longer tenable.

* * *

The cases through *Graham* dealt for the most part with attempts by the States to retain certain economic benefits exclusively for citizens. Since *Graham*, the Court has confronted claims distinguishing between the economic and sovereign functions of government. This distinction has been supported by the argument that although citizenship is not a relevant ground for the distribution of economic benefits, it is a relevant ground for determining membership in the political community. * * * While not retreating from the position that restrictions on lawfully resident aliens that primarily affect economic interests are subject to heightened judicial scrutiny, we have concluded that strict scrutiny is out of place when the restriction primarily serves a political function * * *. We have thus "not abandoned the general principle that some state functions are so bound up with the operation of the State as a governmental entity as to permit the exclusion from those functions of all persons who have not become part of the process of self-government." *Ambach v. Norwick*, 441 U.S., at 73–74, 99 S.Ct., at 1593. And in those areas the State's exclusion of aliens need not "clear the high hurdle of 'strict scrutiny,' because [that] would 'obliterate all the distinctions between citizens and aliens, and thus depreciate the historic value of citizenship.'" *Foley v. Connelie*, [435 U.S. 291, 295, 98 S.Ct. 1067, 1070, 55 L.Ed.2d 287 (1978).]

The exclusion of aliens from basic governmental processes is not a deficiency in the democratic system but a necessary consequence of the community's process of political self-definition. Self-government, whether direct or through representatives, begins by defining the scope of the community of the governed and thus of the governors as well: Aliens are by definition those outside of this community. Judicial incursions in this area may interfere with those aspects of democratic self-government that are most essential to it. This distinction between the economic and political functions of government has, therefore, replaced the old public/private distinction. Although this distinction rests on firmer foundations than the old public/private distinction, it may be difficult to apply in particular cases.

Sugarman advised that a claim that a particular restriction on legally resident aliens serves political and not economic goals is to be evaluated in a two-step process. First, the specificity of the classification will be examined: a classification that is substantially overinclusive or underinclusive tends to undercut the governmental claim that the classification serves legitimate political ends. The classification in *Sugarman* itself—all members of the competitive civil service—could not support the claim that it was an element in "the State's broad power to define its political community," 413 U.S., at 643, 93 S.Ct., at 2848, because it indiscriminately swept in menial occupations, while leaving out some of the State's most important political functions. Second, even if the classification is sufficiently tailored, it may be applied in the particular case only to "persons holding state elective or important nonelective executive, legislative, and judicial positions," those officers who "participate directly in the formulation, execution, or review of broad public policy" and hence "perform functions that go to the heart of representative government." *Id.*, at 647, 93 S.Ct., at 2850.[7] We must therefore inquire whether the "position in question . . . involves discretionary decisionmaking, or execution of policy, which substantially affects members of the political community." *Foley v. Connelie*, 435 U.S., at 296, 98 S.Ct., at 1070.

The restriction at issue in this case passes both of the *Sugarman* tests.

III

Appellees argue, and the District Court agreed, that Cal. Gov't Code Ann. § 1031(a), which requires all state "peace officers" to be citizens, is unconstitutionally overinclusive: "Section 1031(a) is void as a law requiring citizenship which 'sweeps too broadly.'" 490 F.Supp., at 986. The District Court failed to articulate any standard in reaching this conclusion. Rather, it relied wholly on its belief that of the more than 70 positions included within the statutory classification of "peace officer," some undefined number of them "cannot be considered members of the political community no matter how liberally that category is viewed." The

---

7   * * * [A]lmost every governmental official can be understood as participating in the execution of broad public policies. The limits on this category within which citizenship is relevant to the political community are not easily defined, but our cases since *Sugarman—Foley v. Connelie*, 435 U.S. 291, 98 S.Ct. 1067, 55 L.Ed.2d 287 (1978), and *Ambach v. Norwick, 441 U.S. 68, 99 S.Ct. 1589, 60 L.Ed.2d 49 (1979)*—suggest that this Court will not look to the breadth of policy judgments required of a particular employee. Rather, the Court will look to the importance of the function as a factor giving substance to the concept of democratic self-government.

District Court's entire argument on this point consisted of just one sentence: "There appears to be no justification whatever for excluding aliens, even those who have applied for citizenship, from holding public employment as cemetery sextons, furniture and bedding inspectors, livestock identification inspectors, and toll service employees." In believing this sufficient, the District Court applied a standard of review far stricter than that approved in *Sugarman* and later cases.

We need not hold that the District Court was wrong in concluding that citizenship may not be required of toll-service employees, cemetery sextons, and inspectors to hold that the District Court was wrong in striking down the statute on its face. The District Court assumed that if the statute was overinclusive at all, it could not stand. This is not the proper standard. Rather, the inquiry is whether the restriction reaches so far and is so broad and haphazard as to belie the State's claim that it is only attempting to ensure that an important function of government be in the hands of those having the "fundamental legal bond of citizenship." *Ambach v. Norwick*, 441 U.S., at 75, 99 S.Ct., at 1593. Under this standard, the classifications used need not be precise; there need only be a substantial fit. Our examination of the California scheme convinces us that it is sufficiently tailored to withstand a facial challenge.

The general requirements, including citizenship, for all California peace officers are found in Cal. Gov't Code Ann. § 1031. That section, however, does not designate any particular official as a peace officer; rather, Cal. Penal Code Ann. § 830 lists the specific occupations that fall within the general category of "peace officer." Even a casual reading of the Penal Code makes clear that the unifying character of all categories of peace officers is their law enforcement function. Specific categories are defined by either their geographical jurisdiction or the specific substantive laws they have the responsibility to enforce. Thus, not surprisingly, the first categories listed include police officers at the county, city, and district levels. This is followed by various categories of police power authorized by the State: *e.g.*, highway patrol officers, the state police, and members of the California National Guard when ordered into active service. After this, the statute includes a long list of particular officers with responsibility for enforcement of different substantive areas of the law: *e.g.*, individuals charged with enforcement of the alcoholic beverage laws, the food and drug laws, fire laws, and the horse racing laws. Finally, there are several catchall provisions that include some officers with narrow geographic responsibilities—*e.g.*, park rangers, San Francisco Bay Area Rapid Transit District police, harbor police, community college police, security officers of municipal utility districts, and security officers employed in government buildings—and some with narrow "clientele"—*e.g.*, welfare-fraud or child-support investigators, correctional officers, parole and probation officers.

Although some of these categories may have only a tenuous connection to traditional police functions of law enforcement, the questionable classifications are comparatively few in number. The general law enforcement character of all California "peace officers" is underscored by the fact that all have the power to make arrests, and all receive a course of training in the exercise of their respective arrest powers and in the use of firearms. *Foley* made clear that a State may limit the exercise of the sovereign's coercive police powers over the members of the community to citizens. The California statutes at issue here are an attempt to do just that. They are sufficiently tailored in light of that aim to pass the lower level of scrutiny we articulated as the appropriate equal protection standard for such an exercise of sovereign power in *Sugarman*.

IV

The District Court also held that the citizenship requirement was invalid as applied to the positions at issue here—deputy probation officers. In reaching this conclusion, it focused too narrowly on a comparison of the characteristics and functions of probation officers with those of the state troopers at issue in *Foley* and the teachers in *Ambach*. *Foley* and *Ambach* did not describe the outer limits of permissible citizenship requirements. For example, although both of those cases emphasized the communitywide responsibilities of teachers and police, there was no suggestion that judges, who deal only with a narrow subclass of the community, cannot be subject to a citizenship requirement. Similarly, although both *Foley* and *Ambach* emphasized the unsupervised discretion that must be exercised by the teacher and the police officer in the performance of their duties, neither case suggested that jurors, who act under a very specific set of instructions, could not be required to be citizens. Definition of the important sovereign functions of the political community is necessarily the primary responsibility of the representative branches of government, subject to limited judicial review.

Looking at the functions of California probation officers, we conclude that they, like the state troopers involved in *Foley*, sufficiently partake of the sovereign's power to exercise coercive force over the individual that they may be limited to citizens. Although the range of individuals over whom probation officers exercise supervisory authority is limited, the powers of the probation officer are broad with respect to those over whom they exercise that authority. The probation officer has the power both to arrest, and to release those over whom he has jurisdiction. He has the power and the responsibility to supervise probationers and insure that all the conditions of probation are met and that the probationer accomplishes a successful reintegration into the community. With respect to juveniles, the probation officer has the responsibility to determine whether to release or detain offenders, and whether to institute judicial proceedings or take other supervisory steps over the minor. In carrying out these responsibilities the probation officer necessarily has a great deal of discretion that, just like that of the police officer and the teacher, must be exercised, in the first instance, without direct supervision.

* * *

One need not take an overly idealistic view of the educational functions of the probation officer during this period to recognize that the probation officer acts as an extension of the judiciary's authority to set the conditions under which particular individuals will lead their lives and of the executive's authority to coerce obedience to those conditions. From the perspective of the probationer, his probation officer may personify the State's sovereign powers; from the perspective of the larger community, the probation officer may symbolize the political community's control over, and thus responsibility for, those who have been found to have violated the norms of social order. From both of these perspectives, a citizenship requirement may seem an appropriate limitation on those who would exercise and, therefore, symbolize this power of the political community over those who fall within its jurisdiction.

Therefore, the judgment of the District Court is reversed, and the case is remanded for further proceedings consistent with this opinion.

JUSTICE BLACKMUN, with whom JUSTICE BRENNAN, JUSTICE MARSHALL, and JUSTICE STEVENS join, dissenting.

Appellees Jose Chavez-Salido, Pedro Luis Ybarra, and Ricardo Bohorquez are American-educated Spanish-speaking lawful residents of Los Angeles County, California. Seven years ago, each had a modest aspiration—to become a Los Angeles County "Deputy Probation Officer, Spanish-speaking." Each was willing to swear loyalty to the State and Federal Governments; indeed, appellee Chavez-Salido declared his intent to become a citizen. By competitive examination, two of the appellees, and possibly the third, demonstrated their fitness for the jobs they desired. Appellants denied them those jobs solely because they were not citizens.

The Court today concludes that appellees' exclusion from their chosen profession is "a necessary consequence of the community's process of political self-definition." The Court reaches this conclusion by misstating the standard of review it has long applied to alienage classifications. It then asserts that a lawfully admitted permanent resident alien is disabled from serving as a deputy probation officer because that job "go[es] to the heart of representative government."

* * *

Under the *Sugarman* standard, a state statute that bars aliens from political positions lying squarely within the political community nevertheless violates the Equal Protection Clause if it excludes aliens from other public jobs in an unthinking or haphazard manner. The statutes at issue here represent just such an unthinking and haphazard exercise of state power. The District Court found, and the Court does not deny, that some of the more than 70 "peace officer" positions from which aliens have been barred "cannot be considered members of the political community no matter how liberally that category is viewed." 490 F.Supp., at 987. At the same time, California has long permitted aliens to teach in public schools, to be employed on public works, and to serve in most state, city, and county employment positions—all positions arguably within the political community.

Thus, exactly like the statute struck down in *Sugarman*, California's statutory exclusion of aliens is fatally overinclusive and underinclusive. It bars aliens from employment in numerous public positions where the State's proffered justification has little, if any, relevance. At the same time, it allows aliens to fill other positions that would seem naturally to fall within the State's asserted purpose. "Our standard of review of statutes that treat aliens differently from citizens requires a greater degree of precision." [*Sugarman*, 413 U.S., at 642, 93 S.Ct., at 2847.]

Nor can the Court reconcile its new notion of a "substantial fit" with the stringent standard of review the Court long has applied to alienage classifications. Every time the State requires citizenship for a single "peace officer" position, it excludes permanent resident aliens from hundreds or even thousands of public jobs. The Court's novel standard of review condones a legislative classification that excludes aliens from more than 70 public occupations although citizenship cannot be even rationally required for a substantial number of them. The fact that many of those positions may involve law enforcement cannot justify barring noncitizens from any of the positions that plainly do not. * * *

* * *

I read *Foley* and *Ambach* to require the State to show that it has historically reserved a particular executive position for its citizens as a matter of its "constitutional prerogativ[e]." *Sugarman*, 413 U.S., at 648, 93 S.Ct., at 2850. Furthermore, the State must demonstrate that the public employee in that position exercises plenary coercive authority and control over a substantial portion of the citizen population. The public employee must exercise this authority over his clientele without intervening judicial or executive supervision. Even then, the State must prove that citizenship "bears some rational relationship to the special demands of the particular position." *Id.*, at 647, 93 S.Ct., at 2850, quoting *Dougall v. Sugarman*, 339 F. Supp. 906, 911 (S.D.N.Y. 1971) (Lumbard, J., concurring).

Without such a rigorous test, *Sugarman*'s exception swallows *Sugarman*'s rule. Yet the Court does not apply such a rigorous test today.

Instead, it "look[s] to the importance of the [governmental] function as a factor giving substance to the concept of democratic self-government." Applying this nebulous standard, the Court then concludes that Los Angeles County probation officers perform three "important sovereign functions of the political community." Yet on inspection, not one of those functions justifies excluding all permanent resident aliens from the deputy probation officer position.

First, the Court declares that probation officers "partake of the sovereign's power to exercise coercive force over the individual." Yet the Court concedes that "the range of individuals over whom probation officers exercise supervisory authority is limited." Even over those individuals, a probation officer's coercive powers are carefully conditioned by statute. Probation officers cannot carry guns. They may arrest only those probationers under their jurisdiction, and even then only for the purpose of bringing them before the court for a determination whether they should be held or released. State statutes authorize probation officers to detain juveniles only in emergencies and, even then, for only brief periods.

The Court claims that § 1031(a) "limit[s] the exercise of the sovereign's coercive police powers over the members of the community to citizens." Yet other statutes belie that assertion. The State gives the power of arrest to a number of public employees who are not peace officers, but does not require that those employees be citizens. Moreover, California authorizes any "private person," including permanent resident aliens, to arrest others who have actually committed felonies or who have committed or attempted public offenses in their presence. The Court's hollow assertion that the legislature has reserved its sovereign coercive powers for its citizens ignores the reality that the State has already bestowed some of those powers on all private persons, including aliens.

Second, the Court asserts that probation officers necessarily have "discretion that . . . must be exercised, in the first instance, without direct supervision." Yet to say this is to say very little. Almost everyone who works in the government bureaucracy exercises some discretion that is unsupervised in the first instance. The Court itself observes that probation officers have discretion primarily to investigate, to supervise, to evaluate, and to recommend. Their primary duties are preparing presentence reports, supervising probationers, and recommending sentences and probationary terms.

While I do not denigrate these functions, neither can I equate them with the discretionary duties of policemen, judges, and jurors. Unlike policemen, probation officers are not "clothed with authority to exercise an almost infinite variety of discretionary powers." *Foley v. Connelie*, 435 U.S., at 297, 98 S.Ct., at 1071. Unlike jurors who deliver final verdicts and judges who impose final sentences, the decisions of probation officers are always advisory to and supervised by judicial officers. California probation officers cannot by themselves declare revocation of probation. Furthermore, the investigative and reporting duties of a probation officer are extensively regulated by statute. The fact that probation officers play an integral role in the criminal justice system does not separate them from prison guards, bailiffs, court clerks, and the myriad other functionaries who execute a State's judicial policy.

More significantly, California's inflexible exclusion of aliens from deputy probation officer positions is inconsistent with its tolerance of aliens in other roles integral to the criminal justice system. * * *

* * * [A] criminal defendant in California may be represented at trial and on appeal by an alien attorney, have his case tried before an alien judge and appealed to an alien justice, and then have his probation supervised by a county probation department headed by an alien. I find constitutionally absurd the Court's suggestion that the same defendant cannot be entrusted to the supervised discretion of a resident alien deputy probation officer. In the Court's own words, a statutory scheme that tolerates such a result is sufficiently "haphazard as to belie the State's claim that it is only attempting to ensure that an important function of government be in the hands of those having the 'fundamental legal bond of citizenship.'"

The Court's third and final claim is that a probation officer acts as an actual and symbolic "extension" of the judiciary's authority to set conditions of probation and the executive's authority to coerce obedience to those conditions. Yet, by so saying, the Court simply concedes that the ultimate authority for a probation officer's acts lies elsewhere. In *Griffiths*, we held that aliens are not constitutionally disabled from serving as "officers of the court." 413 U.S., at 722–727, 93 S.Ct., at 2855–2857. Given the size of the State's judicial and executive bureaucracy, little would be left of *Sugarman*'s holding if a State could invoke the *Sugarman* exception to exclude probation officers from any position which "extended" judicial or executive authority.

Nor am I convinced by the Court's claim that a probation officer personifies the State's sovereign powers in the eyes of probationers and the larger community. This justification knows no limit. Surely a taxpayer feels the State's sovereign power when the local tax collector comes to his door; the larger community recognizes the sovereign power of the government when local firefighters put out a fire. The State could not also demand citizenship for those jobs, however, without thoroughly eviscerating *Sugarman*. Nor does the Court deny that the sight of foreign-born individuals not merely following, but encouraging others to follow, our laws is an equally powerful symbol of respect for our society's social norms.

In the end, the State has identified no characteristic of permanent resident aliens as a class which disables them from performing the job of deputy probation officer. The State does not dispute that these appellees possess the qualifications and educational background to perform the duties that job entails. Indeed, the State advances no rational reason why these appellees, native Spanish-speakers with graduate academic degrees, are not superbly qualified to act as probation officers for Spanish-speaking probationers, some of whom themselves may not be citizens.

The State cannot challenge the appellees' lack of familiarity with local laws or rules. Such a consideration might disqualify nonresident citizens, but not permanent resident aliens who have lived in California for much of their lives. Nor can the State presume that aliens as a class would be less loyal to the State. * * * [O]ne need not be a citizen in order to swear in good conscience to support the Constitution. When these appellees applied for their jobs, they expressed their willingness to take such oaths. One later declared his intent to become, and then became, a citizen. Finally, the State cannot claim that by enacting § 1031(a), it seeks to encourage aliens to become citizens. That objective is an exclusively federal interest.

I only can conclude that California's exclusion of these appellees from the position of deputy probation officer stems solely from state parochialism and hostility toward foreigners who have come to this country lawfully. I find it ironic that the Court invokes the principle of democratic self-government to exclude from the law enforcement process individuals who have not only resided here lawfully, but who now desire merely to help the State enforce its laws. Section 1031(a) violates appellees' rights to equal treatment and an individualized determination of fitness.

I would affirm the District Court's ruling that § 1031(a) is unconstitutional on its face and as applied.

NOTES AND QUESTIONS ON CITIZENSHIP REQUIREMENTS FOR PUBLIC EMPLOYMENT

1.   Is *Cabell* faithful to *Sugarman*'s original articulation of cases in which a state may require U.S. citizenship? Is the dissent correct to say that the majority has construed *Sugarman*'s exception so broadly that it swallows *Sugarman*'s rule?

2.   Has *Cabell* adequately explained the distinction between the economic and the political? Why isn't public employment economic? The

majority seems to see the issue as *public* employment, while the dissent seems to see the issue as public *employment*.

3.   What is the relationship between *Cabell* and *Mathews v. Diaz*? Did each case uphold a citizenship requirement that was within each government's authority to define a community? Linda Bosniak has written:

> [T]he membership interest at stake in this context is unlike any we have seen so far because it is not embodied in the federal immigration power. The community's concern here is not to regulate admission to the national territory or to formal citizenship status, but rather to regulate political—and perhaps, one senses, spiritual—admission to the "community of the governed and thus of the governors as well." Having affirmed states' authority to regulate such admission, the Court effectively treated membership questions as extending beyond matters of national immigration control and policy to include states' rights to ensure a "fundamental . . . identity between a government and the members, or citizens, of the state."

Linda S. Bosniak, Membership, *Equality, and the Difference That Alienage Makes*, 69 N.Y.U. L. Rev. 1047, 1112 (1994) (quoting Cabell and Sugarman. *See also* Hiroshi Motomura, *Whose Immigration Law?: Citizens, Aliens, and the Constitution*, 97 Colum. L. Rev. 1567, 1599–1601 (1997).

EXERCISE: NONCITIZENS AS SCHOOL TEACHERS

Ling Chen is a permanent resident from China who has lived in Fredonia (a hypothetical state of the United States) for about ten years. Having met all of the educational requirements, Ling has applied for a certificate that would qualify her to teach Chinese in the public high schools. She is married to a U.S. citizen and is eligible to naturalize, but she isn't interested in doing so. Under Fredonian law, state authorities will issue a teaching certificate to a permanent resident who has filed a declaration of intent to become a citizen, see INA § 334(f), but will revoke the teaching certificate if the teacher does not naturalize when eligible, or if she becomes ineligible to naturalize. Applying the analysis in *Cabell v. Chavez-Salido*, what are the arguments for and against its constitutionality? Does the statute reflect sound policy?

---

2.   VOTING AND POLITICAL PARTICIPATION

Should permanent residents be allowed to vote in state or federal elections? Central to *Cabell* is the idea of membership in a *political community*—a group of human beings united by, and for, self-governance. If this view accurately captures the essence of citizenship, then it is understandable why we, as a society, seem to have a consensus that denies noncitizens the right or privilege of voting in state and federal elections. To guarantee noncitizens a right to vote, so the argument might run, would destroy one of the few remaining distinctions between noncitizens and citizens and would fatally undermine our understanding of a nation as a self-governing political community.

Counterarguments are possible. In *Minor v. Happersett*, 88 U.S. (21 Wall.) 162, 22 L.Ed. 627 (1875), the Supreme Court upheld a Missouri state law that denied women the right to vote. The Court's reasoning rested on the idea that not all citizens were voters:

> As has been seen, all the citizens of the States were not invested with the right of suffrage. In all, save perhaps New Jersey, this right was only bestowed upon men and not upon all of them. Under these circumstances it is certainly now too late to contend that a government is not republican, within the meaning of this guaranty in the Constitution, because women are not made voters.

Id. at 176. And, the Court explained, not all voters were citizens:

> Besides this, citizenship has not in all cases been made a condition precedent to the enjoyment of the right of suffrage. Thus, in Missouri, persons of foreign birth, who have declared their intention to become citizens of the United States, may under certain circumstances vote. The same provision is to be found in the constitutions of Alabama, Arkansas, Florida, Georgia, Indiana, Kansas, Minnesota, and Texas.

Id. at 177. Only in 1920 did the Nineteenth Amendment provide, in part: "The right of citizens of the United States to vote shall not be denied or abridged by the United States or by any State on account of sex." U.S. Const. amend. XIX, § 1.

a. Historical Background

The next excerpt discusses the rise and fall of noncitizen voting in the nineteenth and early twentieth century.

JAMIN B. RASKIN, LEGAL ALIENS, LOCAL CITIZENS: THE HISTORICAL, CONSTITUTIONAL AND THEORETICAL MEANINGS OF ALIEN SUFFRAGE
141 U. Pa. L. Rev. 1391, 1401–16 (1993).

It is crucial to see that the early spirit of political openness toward aliens was perfectly compatible with the exclusionary definition of "the American people as Christian white men of property." Indeed, when properly cabined within the existing rules of suffrage, alien voting subtly reinforced the multiple ballot exclusions of the time. To exclude aliens from voting would have given rise to the dangerous inference that U.S. citizenship was the decisive criterion for suffrage at a time when the majority of U.S. citizens, including almost all women and substantial percentages of men without property, were categorically excluded from the franchise. On the other hand, alien enfranchisement reflected the assumption that the propertied white male alien voter would be sufficiently similar to other electors so as not to threaten fundamental cultural and political norms.

If alien suffrage in the early years of the Republic reflected the states' power to define their own electorates and their elevation of race, gender, and property over citizenship, the United States Congress used alien suffrage in an instrumental way to produce immigration in the northwest territories. In 1789, the first Congress to convene under the Constitution reenacted the Northwest Ordinance of 1787 to provide for the governance of the territories northwest of the Ohio River. The Ordinance gave freehold aliens who had been residents for two years the right to vote for representatives to territorial legislatures, and gave wealthier resident aliens who had been residents for three years the right to serve in these bodies. This remarkable willingness to welcome aliens *qua* aliens into the nascent political enterprise of the new nation continued as Congress supervised the organization of the territories and oversaw their passage into statehood. In the various congressional acts authorizing the election of representatives to statewide constitutional conventions in Ohio, Indiana, Michigan and Illinois, Congress deliberately extended the right to vote to aliens. This policy placed its stamp on the political culture of the states that would emerge from the territories. In 1802, for example, the new State of Ohio enfranchised all "white male inhabitants" twenty-one years old who had lived there for one year.

* * *

[T]he War of 1812, which produced a militant nationalism and suspicion of foreigners, heralded the end of the Revolutionary period of liberal attitudes toward noncitizen voting. In 1812, beginning with Louisiana, most newly admitted states, including Indiana (1816), Mississippi (1817), Alabama (1819), Maine (1820), and Missouri (1821), confined the franchise to citizens. Meanwhile, a number of early states which had permitted alien suffrage, revoked the practice during this same period, changing the "constitutional definition of voters from 'inhabitants' to 'citizens.'" In addition to the effects of the "'rise of national consciousness' engendered by the War of 1812," Rosberg suggests that the turn away from alien suffrage may have been due to "the increasing public dismay at the arrival of large numbers of new immigrants who were not of English stock and who were thought incapable of ready assimilation." [Gerald M. Rosberg, *Aliens and Equal Protection: Why Not the Right to Vote?*, 75 Mich. L. Rev. 1092, 1096–98 (1977).]

Another factor may have played a role in the eroding commitment to noncitizen voting in this period. If early alien suffrage was ideologically consistent with the property qualification, the "agitation for the abolition of property qualifications . . . [, which] began shortly after the [War of 1812] ended [,]" [Judith N. Shklar, American Citizenship: The Quest for Inclusion 46 (1991)] may have undermined popular support for alien suffrage. The abolition of the property qualification would have meant that, in states with alien suffrage, all male aliens, not simply the property owners and the wealthy, would have the right to vote. Thus, for the first time, alien suffrage states would be extending political membership to a different, and obviously more threatening, class of aliens—those generally deemed unworthy of the ballot.

* * *

* * * Wisconsin's admission to the Union in 1848 revived and transformed the practice of alien suffrage. The framers of Wisconsin's Constitution adopted a modified form of alien suffrage, extending full voting rights only to so-called "declarant aliens"—"[those] White persons of foreign birth who shall have declared their intention to become citizens, conformably to the laws of the United States on the subject of naturalization." As Neuman notes, this provision took advantage of federal naturalization law, which since 1795 had required aliens seeking citizenship to "first declare under oath to a competent court their intention to apply subsequently for citizenship (known colloquially as 'taking out first papers'), and had postponed eligibility for actual naturalization ('second' or 'final papers') until three years after the declaration." [Gerald L. Neuman, *"We Are the People": Alien Suffrage in German and American Perspective*, 13 Mich. J. Int'l L. 259, 297 (1992).] Neuman observes that such declaration, under federal law, did not deprive the alien of his original nationality, did not legally obligate him to complete the process of becoming a citizen, and did not even require an oath of allegiance to the United States. The Wisconsin plan would later come under attack for these reasons.

Nonetheless, the declarant alien qualification succeeded in weakening the force of nationalist opposition to alien suffrage by recasting the practice of alien suffrage. It now became, much more clearly, a pathway to citizenship rather than a possible substitute for it: noncitizen voting became pre-citizen voting. Thus, declarant aliens in Wisconsin, those presumably on the "citizenship track," won the right to participate in local, state, and national elections.

The Wisconsin formula of enfranchising aliens, but only those who had declared their intention to become citizens, proved popular as the country continued to push westward in the nineteenth century. The desire for immigration carried noncitizen voting along. Less than three months after Wisconsin's admission, Congress passed an organic act for the Oregon Territory which embodied the same terms on alien voting. It was followed in 1849 by a parallel provision in the organic act for the Territory of Minnesota. Although Congress did not extend voting rights to aliens in the territories of Utah, New Mexico, and California (lands won during the Mexican War), it did include provisions for declarant alien suffrage in the enabling acts of the territories of Washington, Kansas, Nebraska, Nevada, Dakota, Wyoming, and Oklahoma. After achieving statehood, some of these territories preserved the practice of declarant alien suffrage in their state constitutions; others decided to abandon the practice entirely; and a few dropped it but made provisions for grandfathering in noncitizens who were already voting.

* * *

During the period of the 1850s and 1860s, alien suffrage played a growing role in the struggle between north and south, with southerners trying to reduce and northerners trying to expand the political influence of immigrants, who were overwhelmingly hostile to slavery (if not necessarily friendly to blacks). The issue of noncitizen voting became a bone of contention in congressional debate over the laws governing new territories and states. * * *

After the Civil War began, the Union's military manpower needs caused the armed forces to turn to aliens for help, and the "foreign-born" came to constitute "nearly 25 percent of the Union Army." [J.W. Chambers II, To Raise an Army: The Draft Comes to Modern America 49 (1987).] Not all alien soldiers were there voluntarily. In confronting the thorny question of aliens and conscription, the government gradually chose voting as the crucial dividing line between draftable and undraftable aliens. On July 17, 1862, Congress passed the Militia Act, which called for the nine-month enrollment of "all able-bodied male citizens between the ages of 18 and 45, to be apportioned among the States according to representative population." The Act empowered the President "to draft citizens into the state militia if that state failed to fill its quota through voluntarism." In August, Wisconsin Governor Edward Salomon wrote to Secretary of War Edwin M. Stanton, informing him that approximately half of his state's able-bodied men were aliens, but pointing out that they had already declared their intentions to become citizens and were eligible to vote. Governor Salomon urged that these men not be exempted from the draft. In his answer, Stanton took the position that the mere declaration of intent to become a citizen did not subject these men to the draft but that declarant aliens who had in fact voted would be draftable.

* * *

The inadequacies of the Militia Act eventually led Congress to pass the Enrolment Act of March 3, 1863. This Act, often described as the first precedent for the modern selective service system, included in the draft males between the ages of twenty and forty-five "of foreign birth who shall have declared on oath their intention to become citizens." Suddenly, many aliens who had declared their intentions to become citizens now wanted to renounce their plans. On May 8, 1863 President Lincoln issued a proclamation giving such persons sixty-five days to exit the country or, at the lapse of this period, face the draft. Significantly, however, all declarant aliens who had already voted were excluded from this offer and could not renounce their declarations of intent. Thus, any alien who had voted in the United States was subject to the draft immediately, along with U.S. citizens. Aliens trying to escape military service were required to appear before their draft enrollment boards and show "that they had never voted in this country."

While the North mobilized aliens to fight for the Union at the outset of the war, southern opposition to alien suffrage deepened. Delegates to the Confederate constitutional convention in Montgomery, Alabama in 1861 chose to do what the original American Founders had not: ban alien voting as a matter of constitutional law. * * *

* * *

After the Civil War, noncitizen voting recaptured its lost ground as an electoral practice. At least thirteen new states adopted declarant alien suffrage, "all of them in the South or West and all of them evidently anxious to lure new settlers." [Rosberg, *supra*, 75 Mich. L. Rev. at 1099.] A number of the former Confederate states formed part of this trend as the Reconstruction governments of Alabama, Florida, Georgia, South Carolina, and Texas included provisions for declarant alien suffrage in their Constitutions. There are a number of plausible explanations for this phenomenon which await treatment by a historian to determine their relative weight. Some of the southern states may have been motivated by the progressive attitudes of Reconstruction and a corresponding eagerness to inject new blood into the post-slavery South. This desire to encourage immigration would have constituted a fairly typical motivation for alien suffrage, although designed more for political than economic purposes.

A second and related possibility is that it was seen as only fair to grant the vote to white male aliens, many of whom had fought for, and indeed been drafted by, the North during the Civil War. Shklar explains that suffrage history is repeatedly marked by returning soldiers demanding and obtaining the right to vote as the just reward for their services and "the most basic and characteristic political act of the citizen-soldier." [Shklar, American Citizenship, *supra*, at 45.] Surely this logic, operating fiercely at the time with regard to blacks, did not escape the notice of alien veterans, who had fought for the blacks' freedom. Finally, a more sobering interpretation of the move to alien suffrage is that the South had a great need to attract a cheap immigrant labor force in the wake of slavery's abolition.

At any rate, the spread of noncitizen voting after the Civil War renewed the vitality of the practice. In 1894, a political scientist hostile to alien voting attributed recent statewide election results in Wisconsin and Illinois to "the weight of a foreign element" and also described foreign newcomers as the heart of the Tammany political machine which "names a president, and in some degree controls an administration." By the time the nineteenth century came to a close, according to Rosberg, "nearly one-half of the states and territories had some experience with voting by aliens, and for some the experience lasted more than half a century." [Rosberg, *supra*, 75 Mich. L. Rev. at 1099.]

The late nineteenth century revival of alien suffrage, launched by Wisconsin and accelerated by the defeat of the Confederacy, came to a halt at the turn of the twentieth century, when anti-immigration feeling ran very high. Alabama stopped allowing aliens to vote by way of a constitutional change in 1901, followed by Colorado in 1902, Wisconsin in 1908, and Oregon in 1914. "With the quickening tempo of war, the enlightened tactic of education for immigrants steadily gave way to the harsh technique of repression." [David M. Kennedy, Over Here: The First World War and American Society 66 (1890).] The demise of alien suffrage was hastened by the "frantic and overreactive days of the First World War when attitudes of parochialism and fear of the foreigner were the order of the day." [*Ambach v. Norwick*, 441 U.S. 68, 82 (Blackmun, J., dissenting).] Just as the nationalism unleashed by the War of 1812 helped to reverse the alien suffrage policies inherited from the late eighteenth century, the hysteria attending World War I caused a sweeping retreat from the progressive alien suffrage policies of the late nineteenth century.

In 1918, Kansas, Nebraska, and South Dakota all changed their constitutions to purge alien suffrage, and Texas ended the practice of noncitizen voting in primary elections by statute. These changes apparently came on the heels of great and, as one observer remarked wryly, quite belated agitation in the press about the horrors of aliens voting. The momentum for cleansing state law of alien suffrage provisions continued as Indiana and Texas joined the trend in 1921, followed by Mississippi in 1924 and, finally, Arkansas in 1926. * * *

––––––––––––

For further discussion of the history of noncitizen voting, see Ron Hayduk, Democracy for All: Restoring Immigrant Voting Rights in the United States 15–40 (2006).

b.   Noncitizen Voting and the Constitution

Does the Constitution *allow* noncitizen voting? Historical practice suggests that the answer must be "yes," but Gerald Neuman has grounded this answer in an analysis of the idea of "political community."

> The move toward universal citizen suffrage, in the sense of overturning restrictions of class, property, race, religion, and gender, has been a great achievement. It could, however, mislead us into concluding that questions of electoral qualification always have unique right answers. Modern legal doctrine on voting rights could have a similar tendency. In the United States, restrictive voting qualifications, with a few traditional exceptions, are now subject to "strict scrutiny" under the Equal Protection Clause. When the permissible qualifications are cumulated, they define a constitutionally privileged category of citizens (nonfelonious residents over the age of eighteen, and so on), which I will call the core electorate. The breadth of this core electorate is a measure of the success of the egalitarian reforms. Members of the core electorate have not infrequently succumbed to the temptation to identify the core electorate with the political community and to regard any enfranchisement of others as a dilution of their votes and a violation of their rights.

Gerald L. Neuman, Strangers to the Constitution: Immigrants, Borders, and Fundamental Law 141 (1996). Pointing to U.S. Supreme Court decisions upholding non-resident voting in certain elections, Neuman continued:

> [T]he Constitution does not provide a single "conception of a political community" that uniquely determines the electorate of each governmental unit, resulting in a neatly nested hierarchy of political communities, towns within counties within states within a nation. Rather, it affords government some discretion to supplement the core electorate with a variety of optional electorates, consisting of categories of persons who have interests implicated in the community's political process.

Id. at 143.

Does the Constitution *require* noncitizen voting? The next excerpt addresses this question.

GERALD M. ROSBERG, ALIENS AND EQUAL PROTECTION: WHY NOT THE RIGHT TO VOTE?
75 Mich. L. Rev. 1092, 1127–1135 (1977).

* * * Immigrants who have arrived recently in the United States may know little about this country's institutions of government or about the

issues on which election campaigns are fought. They can certainly learn about these matters, and it would not take very long for many of them to gain this knowledge. But in all likelihood many immigrants are also largely ignorant of this country's values and traditions and therefore cannot have developed an appreciation of or commitment to them. The naturalization requirement for voting could be seen as responsive to this concern in two different ways. First, the durational residence feature gives the immigrant an opportunity to develop a feel for American values and traditions. Second, the act of naturalization itself represents a formal and solemn commitment to the country, its values, and its institutions. The testing of a prospective citizen's loyalty, knowledge, and character is critical, under this view, not so much because it screens out the undeserving candidate but rather because it makes the attainment of naturalization difficult and meaningful. The judicial setting and the oath of renunciation and allegiance (with its grand language about foreign princes and potentates and bearing true faith and allegiance to the United States) drive home to the new citizen the significance of the occasion. It all adds up to a very deliberate and ritualized act of opting into the community and accepting its values and traditions as one's own.

In my view, this argument is the most substantial one that can be made in defense of the citizenship qualification for voting. And yet it is by no means free of difficulty. If everything is going to turn on a sense of commitment to the country's values and traditions, it would seem important to know exactly what values and traditions * * * we have in mind. * * *

The very fact that neither candidate in an election wins all the votes is in itself a good indication that the electorate is already divided on fundamental value questions. Political analysts typically assume that different segments of American society—Catholics, Chicanos, blue-collar workers, Polish-Americans—have their own values and traditions that influence their voting behavior. To which set of values and traditions are the aliens expected to commit themselves? Do we exclude them from the polls until they have narrowed the choice to two—the Democratic tradition and the Republican tradition—and then turn them loose to make a free choice between Alexander Hamilton and Thomas Jefferson? Or is it rather that the central value and tradition of this country is that there is no central value and tradition? Perhaps aliens are entitled to hold whatever views they want, but they cannot be allowed to vote until they have come to understand and cherish the fact that they may hold whatever views they want. One has an intuitive sense that an alien who has not been socialized in the United States will lack certain characteristics or attitudes that are fundamentally American. But given the diversity of socialization experiences available in the United States, this intuition would seem a rather treacherous foundation on which to build an argument of compelling state interest.

Instead of trying to determine the substantive content of the country's values and traditions, one might do better to focus on the act of commitment to the United States that naturalization apparently involves. In terms of values, culture, and language, resident aliens may be indistinguishable from at least some group of American citizens. And their loyalty may be beyond question, at least in the sense that they think well of the country and wish it no harm. But what may be lacking is a willingness on the part of resident aliens to identify themselves with the country and its people and to give up once and for all their attachment to the countries in which they were born. The unnaturalized alien is perhaps holding something back, refusing to join in. * * *

[But] it is simply not correct to say that unnaturalized aliens have made no commitment to the United States. In contrast to native-born citizens, whose commitment, if any, is tacit, resident aliens have committed themselves knowingly and voluntarily. They have all had to make considerable effort to qualify for an immigrant visa, which is ordinarily a good deal harder to obtain than a certificate of naturalization. Even after proving themselves qualified, they have had to wait months and even more often years for a visa to become available. And they have given up their homes in the countries of their birth and resettled in the United States. Moreover, most resident aliens had ties to the United States even before they arrived, for they have tended to follow their countrymen and kinsmen in chains of migration. * * *

* * *

* * * We have come to accept and even cherish the fact that many citizens will retain what Justice Frankfurter called "old cultural loyalty" to another country, and the line between cultural matters and political matters is known to be indistinct. The internment during the Second World War of persons of Japanese ancestry—citizen and alien alike—is a powerful reminder of how far we have been willing to go on the supposition that national origin may be much more accurately predictive of loyalty than is citizenship. In short, it is hard to see what it is about resident aliens that makes us insist on excluding them from the polls for want of the necessary commitment to the United States.

Yet it may be objected that the net effect of this kind of argument is to deny the existence of any distinction at all between the citizen and the alien. If the alien is indistinguishable from the citizen in terms of knowledge of affairs in the United States, loyalty, and commitment to the people and institutions of the United States, and if for that reason the alien has a constitutional right to vote, then it may appear that the concept of citizenship has been robbed of all its meaning. Plainly, nothing that I have said would jeopardize the distinction between the citizen and the nonresident alien. But one might insist that under the view presented here resident aliens would in effect be naturalized as of the moment they take up residence in the United States. Much of the difficulty arises, however, from the assumed equation of citizenship and voting. My argument is not that resident aliens look like citizens, so therefore they must be citizens. It is rather that in pertinent respects resident aliens are enough like citizens that it may be unconstitutional to distinguish between them in allocating the right to vote.

Citizens have historically enjoyed certain rights and undertaken certain obligations that resident aliens did not share. Every time one of those rights or obligations is passed on to aliens the gap between citizens and aliens narrows. If we are determined to maintain a gap, to preserve a sense of "we" and "they," we could disqualify aliens from owning land or deny them welfare benefits or make them all wear green hats. The imposition of these disabilities on aliens may seem intolerable. But why should it be any more tolerable to make the burden of preserving the distinction between citizens and aliens fall exclusively on the right to vote, the most precious right of all?

Moreover, extending the franchise to aliens would not, in fact, completely close the gap between citizens and aliens, since voting is not the only distinction between the two that survives the Supreme Court's recent decisions on the rights of aliens. By the terms of the Constitution itself aliens are ineligible to hold certain offices in the government of the United States. Aliens do not have the same right as citizens to gain admission to the United States. Citizens born abroad can take up residence in this country whenever they desire. Citizens can abandon their residence in the United States without fear of losing their right to return. Aliens, on the other hand, gain the right to reside in the United States only upon compliance with the stringent terms of the immigration laws. And resident aliens who abandon their domicile in this country will not necessarily be readmitted. When citizens travel outside the United States they carry American passports, and they expect and ordinarily receive the diplomatic protection of the United States when the need for it arises. Aliens, even resident aliens, have no right to call upon the United States for that protection and would not receive it in any case. Citizens are entitled to have the government represent their interests in international tribunals. Aliens have no such right, and under international law the government would be barred from representing them even if it had any interest in doing so. Citizens are generally free from any obligation to register with the government or to inform the government regularly of their whereabouts. Aliens are subject to rather elaborate reporting requirements. Citizens can be held to account in American courts for conduct overseas in some circumstances where aliens apparently cannot. Citizens can confer an immigration preference on their relatives overseas in a considerable number of situations where aliens cannot.

* * * [C]onsidering the primacy of the right to vote one could reasonably argue that it is distinctions like these that should bear the burden of differentiating citizens from aliens, and not the distinction between voting and not voting. We could, in other words, grant the right to vote to resident aliens and still leave them readily distinguishable from citizens. Yet that result would remain unacceptable to those who believe that allowing aliens to vote would eviscerate the concept of citizenship. Their assumption must be that political rights are inherently and properly rights of citizenship, whereas civil rights have no necessary connection with citizenship and properly belong to "persons." In the earliest part of the country's history, however, the assumption was precisely the reverse: citizenship "carried with it civil rights but no political privileges." [Start, *Naturalization in the English Colonies in North America*, in American Historical Assn., Annual Report for the Year 1893, at 319 (1894).] Citizenship, and in particular naturalization, was thought important because it determined whether or not a new settler would be able to own and convey land. Even today, * * * the Supreme Court insists that citizenship as such confers no right to vote. Indeed, it would seem anomalous to equate citizenship with voting so long as we separate the power to make persons citizens from the power to make persons voters. The former power inheres in the national government, the latter in the states.

Yet I cannot deny the existence of a widespread assumption that the right to vote is not only a right of citizenship, but the quintessential right of citizenship. And the conferral of the right to vote on aliens would undermine that assumption. But where does the assumption come from, and why should we insist on preserving it? Intuitively, it seems that there must be some explanation for the assumption. After all, the very fact that it is so widespread may be an indication that it responds to some important inner need of citizens to distinguish themselves from what are perceived to be outsiders, even where the outsiders are their neighbors. But I do not believe that it is possible to articulate an explanation for this assumption without moving the discussion to a level of extremely high abstraction and without putting a great deal of weight on symbolic values. To sustain the disenfranchisement of aliens on the strength of that kind of reasoning would be fundamentally inconsistent, it seems to me, with our ordinary approach in determining which state interests are compelling. I am reluctant to conclude that, because I have so much difficulty articulating the state's interest, it must be less than compelling. But I am confident at least that the validity of laws denying aliens the vote is by no means self-evident. It is surely not enough to tip one's hat at the state interest in having knowledgeable and loyal voters and let it go at that.

NOTES AND QUESTIONS ON NONCITIZEN VOTING

1.   The Colorado Supreme Court rejected an equal protection challenge to a state statute that required citizenship to vote in school elections. *See Skafte v. Rorex*, 191 Colo. 399, 553 P.2d 830 (Colo.1976), *appeal dismissed for want of a substantial federal question*, 430 U.S. 961, 97 S.Ct. 1638, 52 L.Ed.2d 352 (1977). The court, relying heavily on *Sugarman*, explained: "The state has a rational interest in limiting participation in government to those persons within the political community. Aliens are not a part of the political community." Voting in school elections, the court explained, "involves participation in the decision making process of the polity." 191 Colo. at 402–03, 553 P.2d at 832–33.

2.   Today, noncitizen voting in the United States exists but is rare. Noncitizen parents of schoolchildren may vote in school elections in Chicago, as they could in New York City school board elections from 1970 until the school boards were disbanded in 2002. Residents, including some noncitizens, may vote in local elections in several Maryland communities.

Proposals for local noncitizen voting continue to surface, but none have been adopted recently. In 2004 and again in 2010, San Francisco voters defeated ballot initiatives that would have allowed noncitizens regardless of immigration law status to vote in school board elections if they have children in the public schools. In 2010, voters in Portland, Maine, rejected a proposal to allow residents who are "legal immigrants" to vote in local elections. On proposals in various U.S. cities, including Los Angeles and Washington, D.C., see Hayduk, Democracy for All, *supra*, at 109. *See also* Pamela Constable, *D.C., other cities debate whether legal immigrants should have voting rights*, Wash. Post., Feb. 9, 2015.

A more recent state proposal is part of the New York Is Home Act, which would grant New York state citizenship to taxpaying residents, including unauthorized migrants, regardless of immigration or citizenship status. State citizenship would include the right to vote in state and local elections and jury service obligations. *See* Peter L. Markowitz, *Undocumented No More: The Power of State Citizenship*, 67 Stan. L. Rev. 869, 905–11 (2015); Lauren Gilbert, *Reconceiving Citizenship: Noncitizen Voting in New York City Municipal Elections as a Case Study in Immigrant Integration and Local Governance*, 2 J. Migr. & Human Sec. 223 (2014).

3.   Even assuming the Constitution allows noncitizen voting, is it a good idea? Does it matter if the elections in question are local elections? Does noncitizen voting at federal, state, or local levels devalue citizenship, or rob it of meaning? Among the differences between U.S. citizens and permanent residents, just how significant is it that citizens have the right to participate in political affairs through voting, and permanent residents do not?

To return to the three views of immigration suggested by Hiroshi Motomura, see Chapter Seven (pp. 658–660) and earlier in this chapter (pp. 1338–1341), most arguments in favor of noncitizen voting are based on viewing immigration as affiliation. The idea is that noncitizens, after a period of residence, should have the right to vote based on their ties with U.S. society. But most long-time resident noncitizens are eligible to naturalize, so why not expect them to acquire voting rights through naturalization? For permanent residents who have not been here long enough to naturalize, immigration as affiliation lends much less support.

4.   Some proponents of noncitizen voting point to Europe, where it is practiced in certain circumstances. *See, e.g.*, Raskin, *supra*, 141 U. Pa. L. Rev. at 1458–60. Perhaps most prominently, the Treaty on European Union provides: "Every citizen of the Union residing in a Member State of which he is not a national shall have the right to vote and to stand as a candidate at municipal elections in the Members State in which he resides, under the same conditions as nationals of that State." Treaty on European Union, art. 8b, Feb. 7, 1992, art. G(C) 86, 31 I.L.M. 247 (1992).

This provision does not guarantee voting rights for all resident noncitizens—only for those who are citizens of an EU member country who are now residing in another EU country. Seventeen European countries have laws potentially allowing some lawfully present noncitizen residents who are not citizens of EU member countries may vote in local elections, but some of these laws are very restrictive. *See* Kees Groenendijk, Local Voting Rights for Non-Nationals in Europe: What We Know and What We Need to Learn (2008).

How useful is it to compare Europe and the United States? Where, as in Europe, naturalization is generally more difficult, viewing immigration as affiliation may support noncitizen voting more persuasively than it does where, as in the United States, naturalization is more commonplace. Some policymakers in Europe may view naturalization as an alternative to noncitizen voting. Kees Groenendijk, commenting on studies of naturalization rates in countries with local voting rights, concluded: "Local voting rights . . . are not a barrier, but rather function as an incentive to be become naturalized. Therefore, policymakers should see local voting rights and naturalization as complementary measures." *Id.*

5.   Compare the following proposal, described by its authors as "a modified form of the current effort to make noncitizens eligible to vote":

> We would add two twists. First, we would allow noncitizens to vote for the five-year period during which they are statutorily ineligible to naturalize. Under this system, recently immigrated permanent residents would be able to obtain a five-year voter registration card (transferable across jurisdictions, but not extendable). After the five years, they would no longer be eligible for permanent resident voting privileges, but would be able to naturalize. Recognizing that [processing of applications for immigration benefits] suffers from

frequent backlogs, we would allow some provision for extending the
temporary privileges while the application is on file. Although the
authors of this discussion do not fully agree on whether voting
should be limited to local elections (de la Garza) or should include
all elections (DeSipio), we both advocate the extension of noncitizen
voting privileges to local elections at a minimum.

The second twist is that naturalization applicants who can
show that they voted in most primary and general elections during
the five-year period of noncitizen voter registration would be exempt
from the naturalization exam. The exam is designed to test good
citizenship through indirect measures such as knowledge of
American history and civics. We propose that voting is an equally
good measure of commitment to and understanding of the American
system.

Rodolfo de la Garza & Louis DeSipio, *Save the Baby, Change the Bathwater,
and Scrub the Tub: Latino Electoral Participation After Seventeen Years of
Voting Rights Act Coverage*, 71 Tex. L. Rev. 1479, 1522–23 (1993). *See also*
Motomura, Americans in Waiting, *supra*, at 193 (linking the de la Garza-
DeSipio proposal to the historical practice of voting by intending citizens).

c. Noncitizens, Political Participation, and Democracy

So far, this Section has addressed voting as a form of political
participation by noncitizens. May noncitizens participate in politics in
other ways? Does the absence of noncitizen voting suggest that it is
constitutional to require citizenship for other forms of participation?

(i) Campaign Contributions

Assuming that noncitizens are entitled under the First Amendment
to debate issues that are pivotal in the election context, and to seek to
persuade others, what about making campaign contributions? Section
§ 319 of the Federal Election Campaign Act, 2 U.S.C.A. § 441e, bars
foreign nationals, with the express exception of lawful permanent
residents, from contributing to political candidates' campaigns. Two
lawfully present nonimmigrants challenged the constitutionality of this
provision, arguing that it violates the First Amendment. They sued ten
months after *Citizens United v. FEC*, 558 U.S. 310, 130 S.Ct. 876, 175
L.Ed. 2d 753 (2010). In that decision, the U.S. Supreme Court held that
the First Amendment prohibits an outright ban on independent
expenditures by corporations in a federal or state candidate's election
campaign.

One commentator wrote that *Citizens United*, by striking down
restrictions on a type of nonvoting entity, implied that the Constitution
also bars restrictions on financial campaign contributions by foreign
nationals living in the United States. *See* Toni M. Massaro, *Foreign*

Nationals, Electoral Spending, and the First Amendment, 34 Harv. J.L. & Pub. Pol'y 663 (2011). A three-judge federal district court rejected this argument and upheld the § 319 ban, noting that *Citizens United* did not address foreign contributions and expenditures. The Supreme Court affirmed without opinion. *See Bluman v. Federal Election Commission*, 800 F. Supp. 2d 281 (D.D.C. 2011), *aff'd without opinion*, 132 S.Ct. 1087 (2012).

On the basic question of whether noncitizens—or some noncitizens— should be allowed to contribute to political campaigns, what do the meaning of citizenship and the idea of political community suggest?

(ii) Jury Service

In 2013, the California state legislature approved a bill to include lawful permanent residents in jury service eligibility and obligations, subject to meeting other criteria unrelated to immigration and citizenship status. Governor Jerry Brown vetoed the legislation with a brief veto message: "Jury service, like voting, is quintessentially a prerogative and responsibility of citizenship. This bill would permit lawful permanent residents who are not citizens to serve on a jury. I don't think that's right." Is it accurate to think of jury service as a form of political participation and thus similar to voting? Interestingly, Governor Brown signed legislation around the same time to extend driver's license eligibility to California residents regardless of immigration status. *See* Jennifer Medina, *Veto Halts Bill for Jury Duty by Noncitizens in California*, N.Y. Times, Oct. 8, 2013. For an analysis of noncitizen jury service, see Amy R. Motomura, *The American Jury: Can Noncitizens Still Be Excluded?*, 64 Stan. L. Rev. 1503 (2012).

(iii) Legislative Districts

The role of noncitizens in a representative democracy reached the U.S. Supreme Court in another setting in *Evenwel v. Abbott*, decided in 2016. The case presented the question whether the Constitution allows or requires states, in legislative districting, to use total population, voting population, or some other population measure.

For the U.S. House of Representatives, the U.S. Constitution answers this question. Section 2 of the Fourteenth Amendment provides in part: "Representatives shall be apportioned among the several States according to their respective numbers, counting the whole number of persons in each State, excluding Indians not taxed." Pursuant to this clause and Article I, § 2, cl. 3, which requires an "actual enumeration," congressional districts are apportioned to achieve equal population based on the census, which counts all inhabitants, regardless of immigration status or other factors that may affect voting eligibility.

In districting for state and local offices, courts have consistently rejected the argument that the U.S. Constitution requires districts to be based on counts that are limited to citizen population rather than including noncitizens. *See, e.g., Chen v. City of Houston*, 206 F.3d 502, 522 (5th Cir. 2000). As a consequence of including noncitizens, a citizen's vote in a district with many noncitizen residents has greater influence in an election than a citizen's vote in a district with fewer noncitizens. Sociologist Marta Tienda has described this situation as problematic and analyzed two possible solutions to "align democracy with demography," as she puts it. One is "to equalize the voting power across districts" by disregarding noncitizens in redistricting. Another is "to strive for truly equal representation by allowing noncitizens to vote." Marta Tienda, *Demography and the Social Contract*, 39 Demography 587, 600 (2002).

According to a Ninth Circuit case involving district lines for the Los Angeles County Board of Supervisors, drawing districts without considering noncitizen residents would mean that elected office-holders in districts with more noncitizens would serve larger constituencies. This "would dilute the access of voting age citizens in that district to their representative, and would similarly abridge the right of aliens and minors to petition that representative." *Garza v. City of Los Angeles*, 918 F.2d 763, 775 (9th Cir. 1990). The court cited *Yick Wo v. Hopkins*, 118 U.S. 356, 368, 6 S.Ct. 1064, 1070, 30 L.Ed. 220 (1886), for an "equal protection right . . . to allow political participation short of voting or holding a sensitive public office." This approach is often called "representation equality."

Consistent with nationwide practice among states, Texas legislative districts have roughly equal total population. The plaintiffs in *Evenwel* live in districts with more voters than other districts. The plaintiffs argued that districting based on total population—not population eligible to vote—dilutes their votes. As compared to voters in districts with fewer voters, the plaintiffs' votes count for less because they must compete with more voters for influence over elected representatives. A three-judge federal district court rejected this argument, and the case went to the U.S. Supreme Court under its mandatory jurisdiction to hear direct appeals from three-judge district courts.

In the Supreme Court, the plaintiffs argued that the "one-person, one-vote" principle of the Equal Protection Clause requires the use of voter-eligible population for state legislative districts. The state of Texas argued that a state is free to choose any reliable method that results in "substantial equality," and that the Constitution allows but does not require states to use total population rather than voting population.

The Supreme Court ruled for the state of Texas, holding unanimously that states may use total population for legislative districting. But it refrained from a broader decision: "we need not and do not resolve whether, as Texas now argues, States *may* draw districts to equalize voter-eligible population rather than total population." *Evenwel v. Abbott*, 136 S.Ct. 1120, 1133 (2016) (emphasis added). Separate concurrences by Justices Thomas and Alito expressed skepticism of parts of the Court's opinion that might suggest that the Constitution not only *allows* states to use total population for districting, but also *requires* states to do so.

EXERCISE:
NONCITIZENS, LEGISLATIVE DISTRICTING,
AND THE IDEA OF POLITICAL COMMUNITY

With the Supreme Court's *Evenwel* decision having left open what the U.S. Constitution requires, you have been asked to prepare members of a state legislative commission that will consider proposals to adopt voter-eligible population, not total population, as the basis for assessing equal representation in the state legislature, county boards of supervisors, and city councils.

In particular, the commission members are interested in your views on whether it is wise to count some or all noncitizen residents in drawing districts. Given that some form of inequality arises no matter how districts are apportioned, which approach to districting is better policy?

INDEX

References are to Pages